Core
Reference

Microsoft

PROGRAMMING MICROSOFT
ACCESS
VERSION 2002

Rick Dobson

PUBLISHED BY
Microsoft Press
A Division of Microsoft Corporation
One Microsoft Way
Redmond, Washington 98052-6399

Library of Congress Cataloging-in-Publication Data
Dobson, Rick, 1944-
    Programming Microsoft Access Version 2002 Core Reference / Rick Dobson.
       p. cm.
    Includes index.
    ISBN 0-7356-1405-9
    1. Microsoft Access.   2. Database Management.   I. Title.

    QA76.9.D3 D5865   2001
    005.369--dc21   2001030706

Printed and bound in the United States of America.

1 2 3 4 5 6 7 8 9   QWT   6 5 4 3 2 1

Distributed in Canada by Penguin Books Canada Limited.

A CIP catalogue record for this book is available from the British Library.

Microsoft Press books are available through booksellers and distributors worldwide. For further
information about international editions, contact your local Microsoft Corporation office or contact
Microsoft Press International directly at fax (425) 936-7329. Visit our Web site at
mspress.microsoft.com. Send comments to *mspinput@microsoft.com*.

Active Directory, ActiveMovie, ActiveX, FoxPro, FrontPage, IntelliSense, JScript, Microsoft, Microsoft
Press, MS-DOS, MSDN, Outlook, PhotoDraw, PivotChart, PivotTable, PowerPoint, Visual Basic,
Visual InterDev, Visual SourceSafe, Windows, and Windows NT are either registered trademarks or
trademarks of Microsoft Corporation in the United States and/or other countries. Other product and
company names mentioned herein may be the trademarks of their respective owners.

The example companies, organizations, products, domain names, e-mail addresses, logos, people, places,
and events depicted herein are fictitious. No association with any real company, organization, product,
domain name, e-mail address, logo, person, place, or event is intended or should be inferred.

Acquisitions Editor: David Clark
Project Editor: Devon Musgrave
Technical Editor: Kurt Meyer
Manuscript Editor: Michelle Goodman

Body Part No. X08-05016

Over the last several years, I've become a fan of professional prizefighting. Therefore, it might not come as a surprise that I find the writing process analogous to a boxing match. At the end of a fight, the television announcer thrusts a microphone in front of the weary champ and asks, "How'd you do it?" Since the author is invited to write the book's dedication, this is my chance to say how I did it.

My answer is similar to that of many winning prizefighters. They begin by saying, "Thank you, Lord." Then they move on to thanking everyone who ever helped them. It's easy for me to start this list with my Mom and Pop, who raised me to believe that I could write the most useful book you'll ever read. Next on my list is my wife, who is the kind of friend, colleague, and lover that sustains me on the lonely trek from the first to the final chapter. An army of folks at Microsoft Press and the Microsoft Office Developer team also contributed mightily to making this a valuable book. Finally, I want to thank the many readers of my other books and the visitors to my Web site who took the time to tell me how to create more valuable content for developers. Without the guidance of my Lord and the collective help of so many individuals, I believe this book would have much less value for the tens of thousands of developers worldwide who will read it.

Contents at a Glance

Table of Contents

Table of Contents

10 Microsoft Office Objects **543**

Part IV Multiuser Development for Jet, SQL Server, and the Web

Introduction

I cover three topics in this introduction. First I discuss you, the reader. Briefly, this book is written for experienced Microsoft Access developers with an intermediate or advanced proficiency. Of course, if you are an aspiring intermediate Access developer, this book may also help you on your way. Then I discuss the book's contents, summarizing its four parts and then summarizing each chapter in more detail, highlighting the new, nearly new, and traditional topics. I also discuss the book's companion CD and product support information. Finally I conclude with a description of system requirements necessary to run the code samples included in this book. The exact system requirements vary slightly from chapter to chapter; however, I successfully ran all the samples on a computer running Microsoft Windows 2000 and Microsoft Office XP Developer and one running Microsoft Windows NT and Office XP Developer.

Who Should Read This Book

The book is written for intermediate to advanced Access developers as well as SQL Server DBAs and developers. Within this large audience are smaller audiences with specific needs. The book contains specific content that targets the needs of these smaller audiences. Most of my readers are busy, practicing database developers looking for programming solutions to typical Access development tasks. The book will also help developers using Access 2002 to build Microsoft SQL Server solutions with SQL Server 2000 and related technology, such as the Microsoft Desktop Engine for SQL Server 2000 (called MSDE 2000 in this book). This book also addresses the needs of those developers who want to add database-based Web techniques to their toolkit of solution development strategies. The book does not include a general introduction to Web technologies. Instead, it focuses on ways to make Access database files, SQL Server databases, and other relational databases provide content for Web pages.

While this book is substantially longer than its predecessor, *Programming Microsoft Access 2000* (Microsoft Press, 1999), a main aim of the book is to present just the material essential to improve your skills as a professional Access developer. At more than 1100 pages, the book is still relatively compact compared to other advanced Access programming books. This is by design. The book is long enough to convey important content in a way that makes sense to busy professional developers. In addition, the book saves you money by including all the core professional content in a single book, instead of requiring you to buy two or three books, as at least one other publisher does.

Practicing Access developers build solutions for their clients. Therefore, they do not need extensive introductory material or discussions of general systems analysis issues. They also do not want the Access Help files or other readily available online content to be included in a book. Practicing developers need code samples, like those found throughout this book, that they can readily adapt to their own solutions. These professionals seek a grasp of what's new (from a developer's perspective) in Access 2002 so that they can help their clients take advantage of this new version's functionality. At the very least, practicing developers need to learn about the new features so that competing developers can't lure their clients away with innovation.

This book builds on *Programming Microsoft Access 2000* and moves you to the next level of developer productivity. For example, Access 2000 introduced ActiveX Data Objects (ADO), which became an important interface for developers to master. Access 2000 shipped ADO version 2.1. Access 2002 ships with two different versions of ADO—2.5 and 2.6. Both versions included with Access 2002 feature new objects for data access and an enhanced capability for working in Web environments. The 2.6 version particularly targets interoperability with SQL Server 2000. For that reason, I urge you to consider ADO 2.6 whenever you are designing any application that might require an upgrade from Jet to SQL Server 2000.

You are a prime candidate for this book if you are looking for programming solutions to Access development issues. Reader feedback from *Programming Microsoft Access 2000* requested more programming samples and more advanced content. Among the programming topics presented in this book are Microsoft Visual Basic for Applications (VBA), ADO, ADOX, Jet SQL, Transact-SQL, SQL-DMO, and Visual Basic Scripting Edition (VBScript) in solutions for Active Server Pages and data access pages. The coverage of ADO data access techniques spans two chapters and concludes with a working sample of how to program event procedures for ADO objects. The book also presents programmatic means of defining database objects that illustrate how to use Jet SQL and ADOX (ADO Extensions for DDL and Security with Jet database files). The coverage of forms and reports includes a particularly rich array of material that demonstrates how to programmatically process main/subforms and reports, demonstrates how to dynamically assign record sources, and enhances your grasp of techniques for programming event procedures. In addition, I included an introduction to several new programming topics, such as how to create PivotTables and PivotCharts.

I cover programming techniques in four chapters. These chapters reinforce your mastery of VBA and the Access object model as well as related object models. Chapter 10, "Microsoft Office Objects," presents techniques for custom menu programming, such as how to hide the standard menu or toolbar. Chapter 11,

"Integrating Access with Other Office Applications," demonstrates how to develop Access solutions that integrate with other Office applications, in particular with Microsoft Excel, Outlook, and Word. Chapter 12, "Working with Multiuser Databases," addresses select multiuser issues with a particular emphasis on programming Access database security. Chapter 13, "Replicating Databases," focuses on programming database replication. When you have a relatively simple replication requirement that still requires a custom interface, these techniques will serve you well. The appendix, "Microsoft Office XP Developer," briefly mentions Replication Manager, which is a robust graphical tool for building complex replication solutions graphically.

This book will also help those developers who want to become proficient at building solutions for SQL Server 2000 with Access 2002. The book devotes two chapters to this topic and serves two audiences. First, it equips Access developers with the fundamentals of SQL Server so they can build professional SQL Server solutions. Second, the SQL Server chapters demonstrate how SQL Server DBAs can improve the value of their databases by making them more available to clients using Access forms, reports, and Web pages. At a minimum, this second community of analysts should read the two SQL Server chapters, and they should also take a look at the other chapters that demonstrate techniques for building forms, reports, PivotTables, and PivotCharts that draw on data sources.

Another likely audience is developers who want to add Web techniques to their toolkit for building solutions. The chapters on Web topics dig into data access pages, Office XP Web Components, and Active Server Pages (ASP). I also show how to use Microsoft FrontPage 2002 to both manage a Web site and assist in the development of data-based solutions. The coverage of data access pages emphasizes the advantages of developing forms and interactive reports on Web pages graphically. The presentation for data access pages also includes an introduction to programmatic techniques for managing data access pages. You can also learn how to extend functionality of data access pages with Office XP Web Components. A separate chapter, Chapter 17, focuses on working with Active Server Pages. This chapter concludes with three sets of pages that illustrate how to program the creation of HTML forms on Web pages with VBScript and the ASP object model.

Organization of This Book

This book has four parts. Part I, "VBA Fundamentals" discusses Visual Basic for Applications, the programming language used to write most of the samples in the book. Just about anything that you can do with Access, you can program with VBA. VBA is a language used to work with collections of objects (sometimes called an object library). As an experienced Access developer, you probably recall using

VBA with Data Access Objects (DAO) to program data access. Most new Access applications you develop probably work with ADO instead of DAO. ADO and DAO are two object libraries for data access. If you program a custom command bar, you will need to reference the Microsoft Office 10 Object Library. If you program administrative tasks for SQL Server (sometimes called a SQL Service), you will use VBA to program the Microsoft SQLDMO Object Library.

Part II, "Data Access and Data Definition," contains Chapter 2 through Chapter 5. Chapters 2 and 3, "Data Access Models" (Parts I and II), deal with data access using ADO. In particular, you learn how to make connections to a data source and how to access the record sources within a data source. It is critical that you master these techniques because you will use record sources throughout the remainder of the book. You will also learn techniques for manipulating record sources, such as adding, deleting, and updating records. Later chapters show in more detail how to create tables and queries programmatically.

After covering basic programming issues and carefully exploring data access and definition in Part II, the focus shifts in Part III, "User and Programmatic Interfaces." You will probably want to carefully review Chapter 6, "Forms, Controls, and Data." Because forms are so critical to Access development, material on them appears throughout the book. For example, Chapters 1 and 3 include excellent samples that demonstrate how to program forms. Other user interface objects presented in Part III include reports, command bars, the Office Assistant, and the file system. Another important focus is the design and use of programmatic interfaces (instead of user interfaces). Chapter 9 "Class, Form, and Report Modules," drills down on class modules, and Chapter 11, "Integrating Access with Other Office Applications," demonstrates techniques for extending Access by programmatically manipulating the object models for other Office applications, such as Excel, Outlook, and Word. Both chapters demonstrate the design and use of programmatic interfaces.

Part IV, "Multiuser Development for Jet, SQL Server, and the Web," examines Access multiuser issues from multiple perspectives. Chapter 12, "Working with Multiuser Databases," discusses typical Access multiuser issues, such as how to share files, forms, and recordsets as well as how to manage security for multiple users of an application for an Access database file. Database replication facilitates the use of Access databases by multiple users who can be in the same room or halfway around the world. With database replication, applications can synchronize two or more copies of a database; these copies are called replicas. Another way to deal with larger databases and more users is to build applications for SQL Server. SQL Server has design features that accommodate more users than a Jet database. SQL Server uses a client/server design that minimizes network traffic relative to Jet's file-server architecture for processing databases. In addition, SQL Server can assign its tasks to multiple processors for concurrent processing while Jet does not know how to process tasks concurrently. Another way of accommodating multiple users with an Access application is to put the database on the Web. The last two chapters drill down on this capability from contrasting perspectives. Chapter 16, "Access Does the Web: Part I," demonstrates development techniques for data access pages and the related topic of Office XP Web Components. Chapter 17, "Access Does the Web: Part II," shifts the focus to Active Server Pages for publishing data sheets and creating HTML forms. Because the techniques in Chapter 17 do not require any particular browser and do not require clients to have Office XP Web Components on their workstations, some businesses may find them more suitable for Internet applications. However, keep in mind that data access pages offer a powerful graphical development environment that is not available with Active Server Pages.

The book concludes with a short appendix on Microsoft Office XP Developer edition. If you are a professional Access developer, there are several compelling reasons for getting Office XP Developer. For example, if you intend to create custom Access solutions for workstations that do not have a license for Access 2002, then the run-time version of Access and the license to redistribute solutions built with MSDE 2000 can prove essential. If you are going to perform substantial database administration as you develop your SQL Server solutions, the developer edition of SQL Server 2000 that ships with Office XP Developer can drastically simplify your administration chores. This is because the developer edition includes Enterprise Manager, a graphical tool for administering SQL Server that offers much more functionality than is available from the Access project interface. For example, Enterprise Manager supplies built-in graphical tools to manage SQL Server security, but the Access project user interface does not offer graphical tools for this kind of task.

About the Companion CD

The companion CD for this book contains the source code for the sample programs presented in the text, as well as all supplementary files and data needed to run the samples. Additional code not covered in the book is included in some sample files for you to explore as you wish.

The companion CD also contains an Autorun menu (StartCD.exe) for linking to the resources on the CD, a setup program (Setup.exe in the \Setup folder) to install the sample files, a fully searchable electronic version of the book, and Microsoft Internet Explorer 5.5. Complete instructions for using these components are included in the Readme.txt file in the CD's root folder. The Readme.txt file also provides chapter-specific notes for setting up and running certain samples.

Microsoft Press Support Information

Every effort has been made to ensure the accuracy of this book and the contents of the companion CD. Microsoft Press provides corrections for books through the World Wide Web at *mspress.microsoft.com/support*. To connect directly to the Microsoft Press Knowledge Base and enter a query regarding a question or issue that you may have, go to *mspress.microsoft.com/support/search.htm*. If you have comments, questions, or ideas regarding this book or the companion CD, or questions that are not answered by querying the Knowledge Base, please send them to Microsoft Press via e-mail to *mspinput@microsoft.com* or via postal mail to

> Microsoft Press
> Attn: Programming Microsoft Access Version 2002 Editor
> One Microsoft Way
> Redmond, WA 98052-6399

Please note that product support is not offered through the above addresses. For support information regarding Access or SQL Server, you can connect to Microsoft Technical Support on the Web at *support.microsoft.com/directory*, or for product-specific support, you can connect to *www.microsoft.com/access* or *www.microsoft.com/sql*.

System Requirements

This book requires Access 2002, part of Office XP Professional or Office XP Developer. Access 2002 alone is sufficient for many LAN samples, but selected samples that work with SQL Server data sources—especially the NorthwindCS database—require Office XP. This is because MSDE 2000 and the NorthwindCS database ship as part of Office XP. You can use Access projects without MSDE 2000 if you are connected to a standard version of SQL Server 7 or SQL Server 2000. However, this will still not make the NorthwindCS database available. Standalone versions of SQL Server ship with two sample databases. One of these is the Northwind database, which is similar, but not identical, to the NorthwindCS database. Office XP, and its components, such as Access 2002, run on Windows 98, Windows Millennium edition, Windows NT, and Windows 2000.

When you want to use FrontPage 2002 to perform tasks enabled by its Server Extensions, you will have to run on either Windows NT or Windows 2000 with the latest service packs. The capabilities enabled by the FrontPage 2002 Server Extensions include creating a new Web site and running the Database Wizard in FrontPage 2002. Obtaining and installing Office XP Developer automatically updates Windows NT or Windows 2000 with the appropriate service packs. Running Active Server Pages or the Database Wizard in FrontPage 2002 requires the installation of Microsoft Internet Information Services (IIS). IIS 5 installs automatically with Windows 2000 Server, or you can use the Windows Component CD to install the appropriate version of IIS for the server you are running.

Part I

VBA Fundamentals

1

Introduction to VBA

More than a decade ago, Bill Gates proposed a universal macro language for desktop applications. Microsoft Visual Basic for Applications (VBA) is the fulfillment of that dream and more. The VBA in Microsoft Access 2002 is common to all Microsoft Office components as well as scores of third-party packages. Its syntax is also consistent with the standalone Visual Basic programming language. VBA's ubiquity enables developers to use a single programming language in any of dozens of contexts simply by learning a new object model for a particular context. VBA is like glue for an Access application. It holds everything together and gives an application form.

Access 2002 retains the Visual Basic Editor (VBE) that Microsoft first gave to Access developers with Access 2000. This integrated development environment brings the Access programming interface in line with other Office components and the standalone version of Visual Basic. However, you'll probably find yourself inserting VBA code behind the familiar Access forms instead of behind the user forms employed in the rest of Office. You can also place VBA behind Access reports to make them dynamic. This marriage of VBA with Access forms and reports will feel very natural.

This chapter introduces VBA in Access 2002 and reviews VBA fundamentals with a special focus on Access 2002 applications. It showcases major VBA innovations and demonstrates techniques for using code behind forms. While such techniques are traditional Access development topics, you'll find some new twists in how to implement them with the VBE. The differences will be especially evident to developers upgrading to Access 2002 from Access 97 or earlier versions.

This chapter covers these five aspects of VBA in Access:

- Collections, objects, properties, methods, and events
- Use of the VBE
- Jet and Visual Basic data types
- Procedures, standard modules, and class modules
- Conditional logic and looping constructs

Collections, Objects, Properties, Methods, and Events

VBA facilitates object-oriented development. The following sections introduce object-oriented development in the context of VBA and Access 2002. The information targets power users migrating to programmatic application development and mid-level developers who want to reinforce their object-oriented programming skills with VBA. The balance of this chapter, and much of the rest of the book, builds on the basic techniques presented in this section.

Collections and Objects

Access 2002 is an object-oriented development environment. Its Database window facilitates user access to tables, queries, forms, reports, pages, modules, and macros. Pages denote the collection of standalone data access pages with hyperlinks in the Database window of an Access database or Access project. An Access database is contained in a traditional database file (namely, an .mdb file). An Access project is contained in a file type (an .adp file) that was introduced with Access 2000 to specifically address building solutions with SQL Server databases. Access 2002 updates the Database window for an Access project to make it appear more like the window for the traditional Access database, while enhancing your ability to work with Microsoft SQL Server 2000.

> **Note**   Chapter 16, "Access Does the Web: Part I," takes an in-depth look at data access pages, Web pages with an ActiveX control for managing data access. Chapters 14 and 15, "Using Access to Build SQL Server Solutions" (Parts I and II), examine Access projects.

VBA offers programmatic control over the objects in the Database window as well as a broad array of programmatic constructs, such as *Recordset* and *Connection* objects. To get the most from VBA in Access, you have to understand objects and a number of related concepts.

An object represents a thing. Things that an object represents can be as diverse as cars, phones, and videos. All objects have properties. You can characterize cars by such properties as color, number of doors, and engine size. Properties can define individual instances of generic objects. For example, a red car and a black car define two unique instances of the car object.

Object properties vary according to the object class to which they refer. Cars have a different set of properties than do phones. Both have a color property, but phones can also have a speaker property. Cars, on the other hand, have a property describing the size of engine.

Some objects are containers for other objects. Contained objects can also have properties. Engines come in various sizes and configurations, for example, while speakers come with fidelity ratings. Different types of contained objects have different sets of properties; for example, a speakerphone has a different set of properties than a standard phone.

In addition to properties, objects have methods. An object's methods are the behaviors that it can perform. A phone makes connections. A car moves. Many objects have multiple methods. Phones let you make local calls and long-distance calls, for example.

Access developers do not manipulate physical objects. We manipulate programming objects that represent such things as forms, tables, and queries and their behaviors. The Access 2002 Database window shows some of the types of its database objects on its Microsoft Outlook–style toolbar. Figure 1-1 depicts the Objects bar on the left edge of the Database window. Clicking the Forms button in the Objects bar opens a view of form objects and displays two options for creating new forms: Create Form In Design View and Create Form By Using Wizard. A form object can contain other objects, called controls, which define the form's look and behavior.

The form objects you see in Figure 1-1 comprise a collection of forms. Access applications typically have collections of different classes of objects, such as forms, tables, and queries. The Database window automatically sorts objects into classes. Clicking a button for a class on the Objects bar reveals the objects in the corresponding collection.

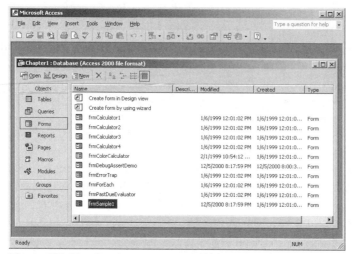

Figure 1-1 The Database window with a selection of form objects and two options for creating new forms.

> **Note**   The Access object model actually defines the *Forms* collection more precisely than the collection of forms that appears in the Database window. When you use VBA with the Access object model, the *Forms* collection is the set of all currently open forms in an Access database or Access project. The Database window shows all forms, open or not. The Access object model applies the name *AllForms* to the collection of all forms in an Access project or Access database. Membership in the *AllForms* collection does not depend on whether an individual form is open.

Each collection is itself an object with properties of its own. All Access collections have a *Count* property, which specifies the number of instances in the collection. Because a collection's members are individual objects, the items within a collection do not have a *Count* property. Collections can also have an *Item* property. You can use the read-only *Item* property to refer to an individual form in the *AllForms* collection. The member objects of a collection can facilitate different purposes. A convertible car can serve purposes different from a family sedan, but they can both belong to the car collection in a household.

Properties and Methods

Properties and methods characterize the appearance and behavior of objects. The syntax for referencing these is *<object>.<property>* or *<object>.<method>*. The term *<object>* can refer to either an individual object or a collection of objects. For example, *txtInput1.BackColor* specifies the background-color property of a text box on a form, and *AllForms.Item(0)* refers to the first form in the *AllForms* collection. If this form has the name *frmSample1*, you can also refer to the form as *AllForms.Item("frmSample")*.

You can see the properties of a database object by selecting it in Design view and clicking the Properties button on the toolbar. Figure 1-2 shows a form in Design view along with the form's property sheet. The property sheet shows a custom entry, My Default Caption, in the Caption property box. The figure shows the Close Button property selected. You can click the Close Button box and select No, which grays out the Close button when a form appears in Form view. Notice that the property sheet has multiple tabs. Figure 1-2 shows the Format tab selected. These tabs organize the properties into groups for fast retrieval.

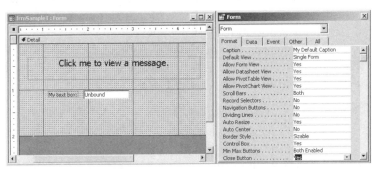

Figure 1-2 A simple form in Design view with its property sheet.

Note   Access 2002 continues the innovation Access 2000 introduced of making a form's property sheet available in both Design and Form view. Since you now can change a form's properties from either view, updating them is easier. In Design view, Access 2002 introduces a drop-down control at the top of the property sheet. You can use this drop-down control to rapidly navigate among the form and the objects within it. This drop-down control is available only in Design view.

The *DoCmd* object is a rich source of methods for all levels of Access developers, but beginners find it especially helpful for getting started with methods. This is because the *DoCmd* object has methods that correspond to Access macro actions. The *DoCmd* object has many methods, including *Close*, *OpenForm*, *GoToControl*, *FindRecord*, and *RunCommand*. Many methods require arguments that specify how the method performs. Some methods have optional as well as required arguments. If you do not specify values for an optional argument, the method uses a default setting. *RunCommand* is particularly attractive to power users who are upgrading to programmer status; you can use it to execute the commands that are available on the Access menus and toolbars.

You can close a form in Access using the *Close* method of the *DoCmd* object. This method has two required arguments and one optional argument. The first required argument specifies the type of object to close. To close a form, specify *acForm*. (This is a built-in Access constant whose value tells the *Close* method that you want to close a form. See the section titled "The Object Browser" for more information about built-in Access constants.) The second argument is the form's name. This value appears in the *Name* property of the form's property sheet. Enclose the name in quotes. The optional argument tells Access whether to save any changes to the form. The default setting is to prompt for whether to save. Specify either the built-in constant *acSaveYes* or *acSaveNo* to close the form with or without saving any changes. You invoke the *Close* method specifying these three arguments for a form using the following syntax:

```
DoCmd.Close acForm, "formname", acSaveNo
```

Many *DoCmd* methods apply directly to individual objects. For example, the *GoToControl* method assigns the focus to a specific control on a form. You can achieve the same result using the *SetFocus* method, which selects a control. Either method is convenient when your application needs to move the focus when prompting the user to enter new information or correct faulty information.

Events

Events are very important in VBA programming. You use events to make applications dynamic and interactive. As a user interacts with objects and collections, Access triggers events, which serve as launching points for a developer's custom code. When you work with forms, you can use events for such tasks as data validation, enabling or disabling controls, changing the control that has the focus, opening a form, and closing a form.

You must understand when each event fires as well as the order in which the events fire. When a form opens, it triggers a sequence of events: *Open*, *Load*, *Resize*, *Activate*, and *Current*. The *Open* event occurs when a form starts to open but before it displays any records. The *Load* event occurs after the *Open* event. When the *Load* event fires, a form shows its records. Any code that causes a form to change its size or location by means of the *MoveSize*, *Minimize*, *Maximize*, or *Restore DoCmd* methods fires the *Resize* event. The *Current* event is the last one that normally occurs as a form opens. It marks the moment at which a particular record becomes current or available. It also fires when a user navigates to a new record or requeries or refreshes a form.

> **Note**   Note Access 2002 substantially revises its events model for forms. Many (but not all) of the dozens of new events pertain to the new PivotTable and PivotChart views for forms. The *Record Exit* event is a new form event that roughly matches the *Current* event. Instead of firing just before a record gains focus, the *Record Exit* event fires just before the current record loses focus. Chapter 6, "Forms, Controls, and Data," takes a closer look at forms in Access 2002.

In Design view, you manually access the events for forms and their controls by selecting the form or control and then clicking on the Event tab of the property sheet. Clicking the Build button next to an event opens a dialog box that you can use to open the code module behind a form, which is a container for VBA behind a form. Choosing Code Builder opens an event procedure in the VBE. The event procedure is named *<Objectname>_<Eventname>*, where *<Objectname>* is the name of the object and *<Eventname>* is the name of the event. If you select a form and click the Build button for the *Close* event, for example, your event procedure will have the name *Form_Close*. If you create an event procedure for the *On Click* event of a label named *lblTitle*, VBA automatically names it *lblTitle_Click*. A procedure is a set of VBA statements that run as a unit.

The following are three event procedures for the form shown in Figure 1-2: *Form_Open*, *Form_Load*, and *lblTitle_Click*. When you first open the form in Form view, a message box opens that reads, "The form opened." When you click OK, you see a second message that says, "The form loaded." After the form completes its loading cycle, clicking the label opens a third message box that says, "Hello from the label."

```
Private Sub Form_Open(Cancel As Integer)
    MsgBox "The form opened.", vbInformation, _
        "Programming Microsoft Access Version 2002"
End Sub

Private Sub Form_Load()
'This is a simple statement not involving a property or method
    MsgBox "The form loaded.", vbInformation, _
        "Programming Microsoft Access Version 2002"
'This sets a property
    Me.Caption = "New Caption"
'Here are two methods for giving a control focus
'    DoCmd.GoToControl "txtMyTextBox"
    Me.txtMyTextBox.SetFocus
'Now that the method worked, set a property
    Me.txtMyTextBox.Text = "Hi, there!"
End Sub

Private Sub lblTitle_Click()
    MsgBox "Hello from the label.", vbInformation, _
        "Programming Microsoft Access Version 2002"
End Sub
```

The event procedures cause the message boxes to appear. Clicking the label invokes the *lblTitle_Click* event procedure. This procedure has a single statement that presents a message box. (The underscore at the end of a line is a continuation character.) The *Form_Open* event procedure also has a single statement. The *Form_Load* event procedure has several statements besides the one for its message box. This event procedure dynamically sets the *Caption* property for the form, which is particularly helpful when you have a form that has two or more roles in an application. It also sets the focus to the text box named *txtMyTextBox* and then assigns "Hi, there!" to the control's *Text* property. This event procedure demonstrates two different techniques for setting the focus. One relies on the *SetFocus* method, and the other uses the *GoToControl* method for the same purpose. An apostrophe at the beginning of a line of code marks that line as a comment. Notice that one of the two techniques is a comment line.

Using the VBE

The VBE in Access 2002 is the integrated development environment for programming objects. Access 2002 shares the VBE layout with other Office components, third-party packages using VBA, and the standalone version of Visual Basic. If you are an experienced Access or Visual Basic developer, you'll be familiar with the VBE components. However, you'll find some familiar programming tools in new places. If you're new to programming Access with VBA, consider your time spent learning this interface especially valuable since the interface is so broadly applicable.

Every Access database or Access project can have a VBA project. The VBA project is the container for the code that automates an application. You can use the VBE to enter, debug, and edit the VBA code in the VBA project associated with an Access database or Access project. Several important windows, which we'll discuss momentarily, help you manage the VBA code in a project. In addition, a collection of toolbars offers clusters of functionality to help you manage the code in a project.

There are at least four ways to open the VBE:

■ Select Modules in the Objects bar of a Database window and click New on the Database window control. This opens a new blank module in VBE.

■ Select the Modules control in the Objects bar of a Database window and highlight any existing module. Then click the Code control on the Database toolbar. This opens the VBE window with the code for the selected module having focus.

■ Open in Design view any form or report. Then click the Code control. This displays a module for the VBA code behind the form or report.

■ Select any form or report or any control within a form or report. Your selection must have code behind it. Next click in the Property window and on the Event tab of the resulting window. Then open the VBE window by clicking the Build button next to any existing event procedure.

> **Note**   You can discover the name for any toolbar control, such as the Code control on the Database toolbar, by hovering your cursor over the control. Access highlights the control and displays text describing or naming the tool.

VBE Windows

There are four VBE windows that you will definitely find useful: the Project Explorer, Code, and Immediate windows and the Object Browser. We'll discuss the first three windows now and examine the Object Browser on page 14.

The Project Explorer window offers a hierarchical view, in a Windows Explorer style, of all the objects containing code associated with the current VBA project (as well as any referenced projects). You can open the Project Explorer window by choosing View-Project Explorer from the VBE menu bar. The Project Explorer window organizes objects into categories, such as Access class objects, standard modules, and class modules. Double-clicking an entry for an object in the Project Explorer window shifts the focus to the Code window, displaying the code associated with that object.

> **Note**   All the items in the Project Explorer window contain code. Standard modules and class modules contain only code. (A standard module is one or more declarations followed by procedures. A class module contains the definition of a new object that uses declarations and procedures to implement its properties and methods.) Other objects, such as form and report modules, contain code and refer to objects. The Project Explorer window can group the latter two object types in a Microsoft Access Class Objects folder. When you select any item that belongs in this folder, you can click the View Object control on the Project Explorer window to expose the form or report object in Design view. You can return to VBE from the object's Design view by clicking the Code control on the Design view toolbar.

Three controls at the top of the Project Explorer window help you manage what has the current focus: the View Code, View Object, and Toggle Folders controls. These controls act like a toolbar in that placing your cursor over them describes them. Clicking the View Code control shifts the focus to the Code window and displays the code for the currently highlighted object. The outcome is the same one obtained by double-clicking the object. The View Object control operates only for objects in the Project Explorer window that have a noncode object associated with them, such as form and report modules. Highlighting a form or report module and clicking the View Object control moves the focus to the corresponding form or report in Design view. The Toggle Folders control toggles the organization of code containers into folders. If there aren't any folders, the code containers appear as an alphabetized list.

The Code window exposes the code in a module. The VBE permits you to open as many Code windows as there are modules. The Project Explorer window lets you open a Code window for any existing module. In addition, you can choose to insert a new module with the VBE standard toolbar, which opens a Code window for the new module. You can select code within one Code window and drag it to another Code window or to a different location in the same window.

Two drop-down boxes at the top of the Code window help you create templates for event procedures for forms and reports and the objects within them, as well as navigate to existing procedures within a module: the Object control and the Procedure control. When the Code window for a form or report has the focus, clicking the down arrow for the Object control reveals the names of the objects within a form or control as well as the form or report object itself. Making a selection from the Object drop-down list will cause the Procedure control to make available the names of event procedures for the selected object. In addition, the Code window opens the template for the default event procedure associated with the selected object. When you select a standard module in Project Explorer, the Procedures control shows the names of procedures within the module. Selecting a procedure navigates to that procedure.

The Immediate window serves as a scratchpad area for printing intermediate results from your procedures as well as testing the syntax of VBA statements before inserting them into a module's Code window. Figure 1-3 shows a pair of VBA statements in the Immediate window relevant to the Northwind Access database. The Immediate window appears directly below the Code window and to the right of the Project Explorer window. The first VBA statement in the Immediate window demonstrates the syntax for invoking a function procedure in the General area of the Form_Main Switchboard module. (A function procedure is a special type of procedure that returns a resulting value to the code that invokes it.) The statement prompts for a form name with an *InputBox* function and then uses the returned value as the argument for the *OpenForms* function in the module. The second statement shows the correct syntax for launching the *IsLoaded* function procedure in the Utility Functions module. The line checks whether the Orders form is open. Pressing the Enter key at the end of the line in the Immediate window invokes the *IsLoaded* function procedure and prints its return value (either True or False) on the next line. It is common in test code in an Immediate window to abbreviate the *Debug.Print* syntax with a question mark (?).

The Project Explorer in Figure 1-3 shows the selection of the module behind the Main Switchboard form. The Code window to the right presents the VBA for the *OpenForms* function procedure in the General area of the module. The Procedure control on the top right of the Code window displays the function procedure's name. The procedure uses the *OpenForm* method of the *DoCmd* object in the Access library to open a form designated by a string variable containing the form's name.

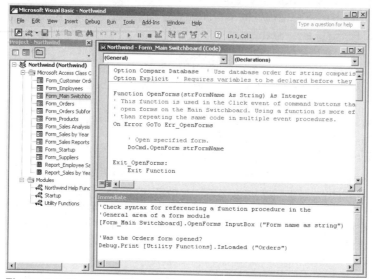

Figure 1-3 The Immediate window shows two sample VBA statements. You can use this window to test code syntax and print intermediate results from a VBA procedure.

The Object Browser

The Object Browser enables you to explore an object library referenced by your VBA project or a procedure in your VBA project. You can search for instances of keywords within the referenced libraries or procedures or browse through all the libraries and public procedures or any subset of them. An object library is a standard file type (.olb) that exposes COM interfaces for an application. Armed with these interfaces, you can program the application. As mentioned earlier, procedures are collections of VBA statements that run as a unit. VBA permits the assignment of subprocedure, function procedure, or property procedure names to these statements. You cannot nest one procedure within another, but one procedure can invoke another.

VBA projects in Access 2002 have three standard library references: Visual Basic for Applications Library, Microsoft Access 10 Object Library, and Microsoft ActiveX Data Objects (ADO) 2.5 Library. You can add other libraries or even replace the ADO library with the 2.6 version that installs with Microsoft Desktop Engine (MSDE), which ships with Office 2002. For example, if you want to programmatically manage security or create tables with ADO in an Access database file, you must add a reference to Microsoft ADO Ext. 2.5 for DDL and Security. To programmatically manage the same tasks for a SQL Server database with VBA, your VBA project must include a reference to the Microsoft SQLDMO Object Library. You can add a library reference to a VBA project by choosing Tools-References from the VBE menu. In the References dialog box, select the library name and then click OK to confirm your selection and close the dialog box.

> **Note**   Chapters 2 and 3, "Data Access Models" (Parts I and II), and Chapter 4, "The ADOX Library and Tables," focus on ADO data access and definition. The Microsoft ActiveX Data Objects 2.X Library is for data access, and the Microsoft ADO Ext. 2.5 for DDL and Security is for data definition and security with Jet databases. The Microsoft SQLDMO Object Library is for SQL Server database administration, including database definition and security. Chapter 15 explores programming the SQL-DMO object model.

Choose View-Object Browser from the VBE menu to open the Object Browser. Figure 1-4 shows a search of the ADODB library for the term *seek*. The ADODB in the top drop-down control is an abbreviation that designates the Microsoft ActiveX Data Objects 2.X Library. The Object Browser discovers nine instances of *seek* in the ADODB library. The Search Results box enumerates the instances by denoting their library name, class name, and member name within a class. A class in this context is a template that specifies the elements of objects, such as properties, methods, and events. The search results treat an enum name as a class.

> **Note**   An enum is a related set of intrinsic constant names that you can use with VBA in your applications. For example, the enum named *DataTypeEnum* specifies constant names for OLE DB data types that you can use for ADO statements to specify the data type of a field or a parameter. The constant names are the members of an enum. Using the enum member is more meaningful than its constant value. For instance, the specification for the Currency data type is easier to interpret when specified by *adCurrency* than by its numeric equivalent of 6.

Figure 1-4 The Object Browser with the search results for *seek* in the ADODB library. The screen depicts the selection of the *Seek* method of the *Recordset* class.

Figure 1-4 depicts the selection of the *Seek* method for the ADO *Recordset* object in the Search Results area of the Object Browser. The selection in the Search Results area sets the display of contents in the Classes and Members Of areas below it. Figure 1-4 shows that the *Seek* method has been found. Clicking the Help button (the question mark) opens a Help screen for the *Seek* method. This screen reveals the action performed by the method, the syntax for the statement, and additional background. By the way, you can designate one of the optional *Seek* method parameters with a member of an enum named *selenium*.

You do not have to search for instances of a term with the Object Browser. As its name implies, you can browse through the classes and enums within an object library. Instead of selecting ADODB (as shown in the top Project/Library control of Figure 1-4), you can designate <All Libraries> to browse all libraries and procedures.

Other VBE Windows

Several other windows add to the overall functionality from the VBE's integrated development environment. These include the Properties, Watch, and Locals windows. The Properties window lists the design-time properties along with their current settings for selected objects in the Project Explorer window. In order for this window to function, the object must already be open in Design view. You can open the Properties window from the View menu. This window also lets you drill down and expose the objects contained by a selected object. It enables you to both browse and edit the properties for the controls on a selected form or report.

The Watch and Locals windows can facilitate your ability to debug VBA code. Use the View menu to make either window visible. A Watch expression is a VBA variable, property value, function value, or other valid expression that shows its value in a Watch window when a program pauses, such as when encountering a breakpoint. (A breakpoint temporarily halts a program so that you can perform debugging functions.) You easily can add an expression by highlighting it in the Code window and then dragging it to the Watch window. The Locals window offers a snapshot of variables, constants, objects, and properties that are in scope whenever their values change. The Locals window provides information similar to the Watch window without you having to specify Watch expressions. However, you might find that it presents too much information for many debugging tasks.

VBE Toolbars

Three toolbars can simplify your management of the VBE: the Standard, Debug, and Edit toolbars. A fourth one, the UserForm toolbar, is available for Office XP. While this toolbar name shows on the list when you choose View-Toolbars from the menu, you cannot use it with Access 2002 because Access 2002 works with Access forms instead of the UserForm dialog boxes for other Office applications.

The VBE Standard Toolbar

Figure 1-5 shows the images, names, and shortcut keys for controls on the default Standard toolbar. To generate this display for any toolbar, click the Toolbar Options control, the drop-down control at the end of the toolbar with the down arrow. Then select Add Or Remove Buttons followed by the name of the toolbar for which you want to show the control images, names, and shortcut keys.

You can customize the Standard toolbar as you would any toolbar in an Office application. This toolbar contains several groups of controls that support different kinds of functions. The Microsoft Access control lets you toggle from the VBE window and to the current Access window. This is particularly convenient when you are fine-tuning an application by making changes to the design of form and report objects while creating and updating the code behind those objects. When you are ready to return from a form or report's Design view to VBE, click the Code control on the Form Design or Report Design toolbar.

Figure 1-5 Control images, names, and keyboard shortcuts on the VBE Standard toolbar.

The Insert Object control opens a menu. When no module has an open Code window, the menu exposes commands to insert either a standard or class module. As mentioned earlier in the chapter, a standard module is one or more declarations followed by procedures, and a class module contains the definition of a new object that can use declarations and procedures to implement the object's properties and methods. If a current Code window is open, the Insert Object control includes a third menu item. This item helps to launch the creation of a new procedure at the end of the active Code window.

> **Note**   You can add a new procedure at any point in a module by positioning your cursor there and typing the code for the procedure. The Code window helps in a variety of ways. For example, if you type *sub* followed by a procedure name and press the Enter key, the Code window capitalizes *Sub*, adds empty parentheses after the procedure name, and adds an *End Sub* line, which always ends a subprocedure.

The Save control stores the current VBA project. This commits your changes to the modules in a project. The text after Save is the name of the VBA project. If you try to close an Access database or Access project with unsaved changes to its modules, you will be prompted to abandon or commit those changes at that time. The Cut, Copy, and Paste controls work the same way they do in Microsoft Windows applications. Similarly, the Undo and Redo controls work as they do in Microsoft Word.

The Find control opens a dialog box that lets you search for text within any one of four ranges—the current procedure, the current module, the current VBA project, or a selected range. You can specify whether to search up or down for text, match only whole words, match the case, or use pattern matching characters, such as those for a Like statement. The Find control also enables you to specify replacement text for any matches that a search discovers.

The Run Sub/UserForm, Break, and Reset controls are especially helpful while debugging VBA code from the VBE. The UserForm portion of the Run Sub/UserForm tool name does not pertain to Access, but to other Office applications, such as Word, Excel, and PowerPoint. If the cursor rests within a procedure, clicking Run Sub launches that procedure. Use the Break control to halt the operation of a procedure if the procedure permits the use of the Standard toolbar. This control enters Break mode. The Ctrl+Break keyboard combination creates a higher priority interrupt for a program than the Break control. After a break in program execution, the Run Sub control changes its name to Continue to convey that it resumes running the execution stack at the last breakpoint. (An execution stack holds all the information about the current state of a running program.) The Reset control clears the VBA statement execution stack and resets the project. Since clicking Reset after a break clears the execution stack, if you try to continue after resetting, the procedure resumes from its first statement.

The Design Mode, Run Project, and Toolbox controls will not have much use in typical Access applications because they pertain to issues you are not likely to encounter in a VBA project associated with an Access database or Access project.

The Project Explorer, Properties Window, and Object Browser controls are one-button shortcuts for opening windows with the corresponding names. You can remove each of these windows with their Close buttons.

The Microsoft Visual Basic Help control works like the Help control in other Microsoft Windows applications.

The VBE Debug Toolbar

The default collection of controls on the Debug toolbar overlaps somewhat with those on the Standard toolbar, but it contains several distinct controls as well. The first five controls on the Debug toolbar also appear on the Standard toolbar. Figure 1-6 shows the Debug toolbar images, names, and keyboard shortcuts. The Toggle Breakpoint control sets or clears a breakpoint at whatever line the cursor rests on within a procedure. As you'll recall, a breakpoint temporarily halts a program so that you can perform debugging functions, such as examining the value of Watch expressions, and so that Watch expressions display values at breakpoints.

Figure 1-6 Control images, names, and keyboard shortcuts on the VBE Debug toolbar.

The Step Into, Step Over, and Step Out controls offer you a way to control when to execute code. Successively clicking the Step Into control runs the currently selected line of code. If you have one procedure that calls another, you might not care to individually step through the lines of the called procedure. To bypass this action, use the Step Over control instead. If you do decide to step into a called procedure, you might want to return to the calling routine without individually stepping through all the lines in the called procedure. Use the Step Out control for this effect.

The next three controls on the Debug toolbar open the Locals, Immediate, and Watch windows, which can tile or overlap one another. Use your mouse to position and size the windows according to your preferences. You can further fine-tune your ability to manipulate windows through the Docking tab on the Options dialog box. Open the tab by choosing Tools-Options from the menu and clicking Docking. You can select which windows you want to be dockable. The windows you designate as dockable automatically will snap to another window or the outside VBE application window when moved near one of these.

The Quick Watch control helps you enter a Watch expression. In the Code window, select an object, expression, or other candidate for tracking. Then click the Quick Watch control. Next click the Add control on the Quick Watch dialog box to add the expression to the Watch window. If the Watch window is not already open, adding the expression will open it.

The Call Stack control opens a dialog box showing the stack of procedures through which code reached the current line. You must close the Call Stack dialog box to resume executing a procedure.

The VBE Edit Toolbar

The default controls for the Edit toolbar facilitate editing VBA code within a module. Figure 1-7 displays the Edit toolbar images, names, and keyboard shortcuts.

Figure 1-7 Control images, names, and keyboard shortcuts on the VBE Edit toolbar.

The first four controls on the Edit toolbar help you explore the VBA coding options. For example, the List Properties/Methods control opens a scrollable list box with properties and methods for the term to the left of the period preceding the text insertion point. You can use this control to edit the contents of a Code window. Selecting an option from the shortcut menu overwrites the current property or method coded in your procedure. The List Constants, Quick Info, and Parameter Info controls also provide support for creating proper VBA statements. With these controls, you can start typing an expression and then click the Complete Word control to complete the expression for you.

The Indent and Outdent controls complement one another. Clicking the Indent control shifts all selected lines one tab to the right. You can reverse this operation with the Outdent control. Judicious use of these two controls make your code easier to read—particularly for lines that nest logically within others.

The Comment Block and Uncomment Block controls are useful for adding and removing comment designators (namely, a leading apostrophe) from multiple lines of code. Many developers find it convenient during development to retain coding lines from earlier versions of a procedure. Preceding these older lines with an apostrophe converts them into comment lines, or comments them out. This book sometimes shows alternate or optional ways of performing a task with code lines that are commented out. Use the Uncomment Block control to remove apostrophes easily from these lines.

The last four controls on the Edit toolbar help you manage the use of bookmarks within a module. A bookmark in a Code window is a marker for a line of code. You can add and remove bookmarks from lines of VBA code with the Toggle Bookmark control. Although the bookmarks you add will not have names, you can navigate among two or more of them with the Next Bookmark and Previous Bookmark controls. These two controls move you forward and backward through a collection of bookmarks in a round-robin fashion. Therefore, if you are at the last bookmark in a collection, clicking the Next Bookmark control takes you to the first bookmark. Use the Clear All Bookmarks control to remove all the bookmarks from a VBA project. Bookmarks, just like breakpoints, do not persist after you close an Access database or Access project associated with a VBA project.

Jet and Visual Basic Data Types

You must specify data types in many places within Access, including variables within procedures and tables of stored data on a storage device. The following two sections introduce issues pertaining to data types from Jet 4 and the use of variables in procedures.

Jet

Access 2002 natively supports two database engines. Historically, Access was tied to the Jet database engine. Access 2000 was tuned to take advantage of Jet 4, the latest release of the traditional Access database engine. Access 2002 works with the same version of Jet. This section deals with the effects of Jet 4 innovations on Access 2002 application design. These innovations can affect the size of database files and record locking, methods for working with selected field data types (including Memo, Hyperlink, and auto-incrementing key fields), and links to external data sources.

While Jet 4 remains the default database engine with Access 2002, it is now easier than ever to use SQL Server, too. Access 2000 introduced built-in data definition capabilities for SQL Server 7. Access 2002 upgraded this initial support by targeting SQL Server 2000. Chapters 14 and 15 examine techniques for building SQL Server solutions with Access 2002.

Access 2002 stores all text and memo data in Unicode format. This replaces the multi-byte character set (MBCS) format used in versions prior to Access 2000 for Japanese, Chinese, and other selected languages. Unicode is a subset of the ISO 10646 standard, which provides digital encoding for all written languages. This relatively new standard requires 2 bytes to represent each character, instead of the previous 1-byte requisite for most characters. This can nearly double the size of databases that rely heavily on character-based fields. To offset this increase, Jet automatically compresses and decompresses these data types whenever possible.

It compresses memo fields that are up to 4000 characters in length, which can result in compression for some but not all rows in a memo data field. Both Access and ADO automatically compress Unicode characters, but Data Access Objects (DAO) does not support compression for string data types. Developers who program in Jet SQL have a WITH COMPRESSION clause available for specifying tables.

Access 2002 Data File Format Vs. Access 2000 File Format

Access 2002 introduces a new file format, but this need not affect how you use data types with VBA. In fact, the Access 2000 file format is the default format for Access 2002. This makes it easy for environments with both Access 2000 and Access 2002 installations to share files and applications.

The major backwards-compatibility issue is that Access 2002 cannot create .mde and .ade files in the Access 2000 format. Access 2002 must use the new file format when creating these types of files. It is possible to use the new properties, methods, and events of Access when modifying a file created using Access 2000 in the old file format. However, a workstation running Access 2000 will not be able to compile or open the modified file. Also note that the new file format specifically aims to accommodate new objects that might appear in future Access versions.

You can manually set the default file format with a drop-down control on the Advanced tab of the Options dialog box. Use the *SetOption* and *GetOption* methods of the Access *Application* object to control the default file format programmatically. The following expression returns the value 10 for the new file format and 9 for the Access 2000 file format:

```
Application.GetOption("Default File Format")
```

You can change the Access 2002 default file format to the new one with this expression:

```
Application.SetOption "Default File Format", "10"
```

So, when do you use which file format? The Access 2000 file format is best for environments that require the use of Access applications by a mix of computers running both Access 2000 and Access 2002. The new Access file format is appropriate for at least two situations: when you need to create .mde or .ade files for your solution, and when all users of an application are running Access 2002 and you want to position the application for using new objects in future editions.

In addition to the new format for character data types, the page size has doubled to 4 KB. This can lead to reduced concurrency relative to Access versions prior to Access 2000 due to more page-lock conflicts. Jet addresses this by offering single-row locking. You can minimize the concurrency issue by locking individual records instead of whole pages. Access 2002 lets users concurrently update two records on the same page.

Note   The new page size increases the maximum database size from 1.07 GB to 2.14 GB.

While single-row locking is desirable for minimizing concurrency conflicts, it requires an overhead cost for setting and removing record locks. The impact of this overhead on the speed of your application depends on record size relative to page size as well as the number of locks necessary for a task.

The transition to Unicode also enables Windows NT–compatible sorting. This improves compatibility and performance because Access 2000 can deliver consistent sorting performance on Windows 95, Windows 98, and Windows NT systems. This is possible even though Windows 95 and Windows 98 support sorting on just the default system language, while Windows NT supports correct sorting on multiple languages. In addition, Visual Basic 7 and SQL Server 2000 support this same sorting standard, which provides cross-product standardization. Access 2002 sorting is 50 percent faster than Access 97 and earlier versions for most written languages, but the increase in sorting speed is even greater for certain languages, such as Thai.

Jet 4 supports indexing for the first 255 characters of Memo data types. Prior versions of Access and Jet did not support any indexing for Memo fields. While the limited length of the index is not appropriate for all Memo field applications, it has special significance for the Hyperlink data type, which is a derivative of the Memo data type. The new indexing enhances sorting and searching of Hyperlink fields.

Jet 4 also enables developers to specify a start value and a step value for auto-incrementing fields. In addition, a new ALTER TABLE statement enables Jet SQL developers to reset both the start and step values. You use another new statement, SELECT @@IDENTITY, to recover the last value for the auto-incrementing column. You pass the SQL statement value along as the SQL text for the *Open* method of the *Recordset* object in an ADO statement. DAO does not support the new statement.

Jet 4 has enhanced installable ISAM (indexed sequential access method) technology in several areas, which can affect Access development opportunities with external data sources. The Text/HTML ISAM lets you read Unicode-formatted Web documents. The Exchange ISAM offers enhancements in several areas. First, it reads indexes from Microsoft Exchange Server. This dramatically speeds up searches for records in Exchange data sources. Second, the new ISAM supports the Windows Address Book for the Microsoft Outlook Express client. In smaller business environments in which the mail focus is external rather than internal, this offers significant benefits (if only in personal productivity). Third, Jet can retrieve custom-defined Outlook clients as well as those for the Outlook Exchange client. Users of dBase and Paradox databases can continue to enjoy read/write access to these databases through the capabilities of Jet as of Jet 3.5. Those requiring support for more recent versions of these alternative databases must obtain a copy of the Borland Database Engine from a third-party source.

VBA Data Types

VBA regularly uses variables to save computed outcomes, set properties, designate arguments for methods, and pass values between procedures. To perform efficiently, VBA uses a set of data types for its memory variables. Several other Access tasks, such as defining column values, use data types. This section focuses on data types for VBA memory variables. When you code a solution that uses VBA memory variables, the solution uses VBA data types as opposed to Jet, SQL Server, or ADO data types, although the various sets of application data types are generally similar.

> **Note**   Access permits you to work with multiple data type sets that might not be fully compatible with VBA data types. For example, when using Access with .adp files and a SQL Server database, the Decimal data type can scale to 38 places. However, Access scales the Decimal data type within a Jet database to a limit of 28 places for a column in a table. VBA code does not directly recognize a Decimal data type. But you can declare a variable as a Variant data type and then use a *CDec* function to assign a Decimal subtype to the Variant data type. You will learn more about the uses of this Decimal subtype for VBA in the next section as well as in Chapter 4.

Table 1-1 lists the major types of variables and their storage requirements in VBA programs. Developers who need high levels of precision in their numerical computations can use the Decimal data type as a subtype of the Variant data type. VBA Decimal data types are unsigned 12-byte integers scaled by a variable power of 10. You cannot declare a Decimal data type with a *Dim* statement, but you can store a Decimal data type by transforming a Variant with the *CDec* function. It is generally a good idea to use the smallest possible data type to leave the maximum amount of memory for other variables and application logic. However, when you need the precision for numerical computations, the Decimal data type is available.

Table 1-1 VBA Data Types for Memory Variables

Name	Number of Bytes	Range
Byte	1	0 to 255
Boolean	2	True or False
Integer	2	−32,768 through 32,767
Long	4	−2,147,483,648 through 2,147,483,647
Single	4	−3.402823E38 through −1.401298E−45 for negative values
		1.40129E−45 through 3.402823E38 for positive values
Double	8	−1.79769313486232E308 through −4.94065645841247E−324 for negative values
		4.94065645841247E−324 through 1.79769313486232E308 for positive values
Currency	8	−922,337,203,685,477.5808 through 922,337,203,685,477.5807
Date	8	January 1, 100 through December 31, 9999
Object	4	A reference to an object (see *Set* statement in the online Help)
String (fixed)	String length	Up to approximately 64,000 characters
String (variable)	10 + String length	Up to approximately 2 billion characters
Variant (with numbers)	16	Same as Double
Variant (with characters)	22 + String length	Up to approximately 2 billion characters
User-defined	Number of bytes for elements	Sum of the constituent elements for the custom data type

When you fail to declare a variable as a specific type, VBA assigns it the Variant data type. This data type is flexible because Variants can assume both numeric and string values. The Variant data type can hold all the other data types except user-defined types (which are a superset of all the other data types). When VBA performs an operation on two Variants, it must first retrieve the contents of the second Variant and convert the result to the data subtype of the first Variant. This makes processing Variants slower than processing other data types. In addition, the data subtype returned by the operation might be incorrect for your application.

You can use the *VarType* function to determine the data subtype of a memory variable declared as a Variant. The *VarType* function takes a Variant data type and returns a VBA constant that indicates the subtype of the value in the Variant data type. For example, if *varMyVariable* contains "Hi, there!", *VarType(varMyVariable)* returns 8 for *vbString*, a member of the *VbVarType* enum. Similarly, if *varMyVariable* contains *#1/1/2002#*, *VarType(varMyVariable)* returns 7 for *vbDate*, another member of the *VbVarType* enum.

Figure 1-8 shows the complete list of *VbVarType* enum members, which includes special values, such as *vbNull*, as well as those for data types. The figure depicts the selection of the *vbDate* member. You can tell from the Object Browser's lowest pane that *vbDate* equals 7.

Figure 1-8 Object Browser display of the *VbVarType* enum members with the *vbDate* member highlighted.

VBA conversion functions let you convert a Variant data type to a specific data subtype. You can use this to specify the type of result that you expect when performing an operation on two Variants. For example, *CDbl(varMyVariable)* returns a Double data type from the contents of *varMyVariable*, which has a Variant data type.

Despite its potential for error and its need for extra processing, Variant is a popular data type. The data in table, query, report, and form fields is Variant by default. If you leave a field in a table unspecified, the field returns a Null value when queried (assuming it has not been assigned data), which is one of two special Variant data values. A Null indicates missing, unknown, or inapplicable data. You use the *IsNull* function in VBA to test for Null values, and you use the Is Null operator in query criterion statements to do the same for a field. Be careful how you process variables with Null values because Nulls propagate. This means that any combination of a variable that equals Null with any other variable always returns a Null.

> **Note**   Chapter 16 takes an in-depth look at data access pages, Web pages with an ActiveX control for managing data access. Chapters 14 and 15 examine Access projects.

Because only Variant data types can assume Null values, you must use this type when your application can benefit from Null values. Nulls avoid the need for arbitrary values to specify missing data from a field or variable.

The *Empty* keyword is used as a Variant subtype and represents an uninitialized variable value. You use the *IsEmpty* function in VBA to determine whether a variable has been initialized. Empty, Null, the value 0, and zero-length strings (" ") are different from each other. When VBA transforms a Variant variable that is equal to *Empty*, it transforms the variable to either 0 or " " depending on whether a number or string is most appropriate.

When you need to call Windows API functions through dynamic-link libraries (DLLs), you sometimes need a user-defined variable type. You must declare user-defined variable types between *Type* and *End Type* statements. The individual lines between these two statements should define the elements of a custom variable type. You can think of a book, for example, as a collection of elements, including an ISBN, a title, author, a publisher, and the page count. You can specify this custom data type as follows:

```
Type Book
    ISBN As Long
    Title As String
    Author As String
    Publisher As String
    PageCounts As Integer
End Type
```

```
Sub MyBook
Dim udvMyBook as Book
    udvMyBook.ISBN = 0-7356-1405-9
    udvMyBook.Title = "Programming Microsoft Access Version 2002"
    udvMyBook.Author = "Rick Dobson"
    udvMyBook.Publisher = "Microsoft Press"
    udvMyBook.PageCount = 700
End Sub
```

You insert the *Type...End Type* statement pair in the general declarations area of a module. The procedure *MyBook* creates an instance of the *Book* user-defined variable. We will dive deeper into procedures and modules in the next section.

Procedures, Standard Modules, and Class Modules

Any interesting Access application will have one or more modules to hold code for automating the application. For example, you can make your forms interactive by placing code behind them. Reports can also exhibit dynamic behavior if you place code behind them. In addition, you can have standard modules for holding procedures that have no tie to any particular form or report. Class modules are yet another container for code. The code in a class module differs from that of typical procedures because you invoke it through an object, such as a form or report object. The collection of modules associated with an Access database or Access project resides in a VBA project.

Let's start with an introduction to declarations for memory variables, an important building block for procedures.

Declarations

You can declare variables and constants. (A constant is a special value that cannot be changed during program execution. Its value is set using a *Constant* statement.) A declaration serves two purposes: it designates the variable's scope (the area within the application that can reference the variable), and it specifies a data type for the variable. Both are good reasons to declare variables before using them. You can require a variable declaration by using the *Option Explicit* statement at the top of a module before the first procedure. (If you don't use *Option Explicit*, a misspelled variable name can cause a bug that can be difficult to detect.)

You use the *Public* statement in a module's Declaration area to declare variables that your applications can use from any procedure within the application, including other modules. You can use the *Private* statement to explicitly define a variable as having local scope within a module. Specifying *Private* is not strictly required because the *Dim* and *Static* statements declare variables that are private to a module by default.

The *Dim* statement reserves memory for a variable only until the procedure in which the variable is declared ends. This means that variables declared using a *Dim* statement lose their value from one call of the procedure to the next. Variables declared using a *Static* statement are preserved throughout the life of the module or until an application resets or restarts the module. (You can use static variable declarations to keep track of running sums or to determine the number of times that a procedure is called.) You can use both the *Dim* and *Static* statements at the module level (in the General area, outside of a procedure). In addition, you can use *Static* as a keyword before a procedure declaration. This convention makes all variables declared with *Dim* within the procedure behave as though you used a *Static* statement to declare them.

> **Note** You can clear the values from the static variables in a procedure by choosing Reset from the Run menu in the VBE.

You can explicitly tag a variable as either *Private* or *Public*. The location at which you declare memory variables and whether you declare them as *Public* or *Private* determines their scope. There are four levels of scope for variables and objects in VBA: procedure, private module, public module, and private project. Variables declared within a procedure with a *Dim* statement have visibility only within that procedure. Variables declared within the General area of a module with a *Dim* statement have a module-level declaration. These variables have visibility only within that module. If you declare a variable in the General area of a module with a *Public* statement, any procedure in any module or project can read and assign the variable's value. Use an *Option Private Module* statement in a module's General area to restrict the scope of variables declared in a *Public* statement to the current project. This is the private project level.

You use the *As* keyword with either the *Dim*, *Static*, *Public*, or *Private* statements to specify a data type for a variable. For example, the statement *Dim intMyNumber As Integer* declares the *intMyNumber* variable to be an integer data type.

The following module listing illustrates some of the techniques described in this section. Copy the entire listing into a new module named Module1. Then copy the *OutsideAssignVariables* procedure to a second new module named Module2. Notice the listing includes two variable declarations. One, *intMyModNumber*, is at the module level, meaning any procedure in the module can read or write to the *intMyModNumber* variable. Since the *intMyModNumber* declaration initially uses a *Dim* statement, it is visible only in Module1. The variable has no scope in Module2 or any other module besides Module1.

```
'Run initially with Public declaration line commented
'in Module1.
'Then, switch comment marker from the Public to the
'Dim declaration line.

Dim intMyModNumber As Integer
'Public intMyModNumber As Integer

'First, assign values with this procedure
Sub AssignVariables()
    Dim intMyProcNumber As Integer
    intMyProcNumber = 10
    intMyModNumber = 10
    Debug.Print intMyProcNumber
End Sub

'Second, attempt to print variable values
'with this procedure; third, run same
'procedure from Module2
Sub OutsideAssignVariables()
    Debug.Print intMyProcNumber
    Debug.Print intMyModNumber
End Sub
```

After copying the listing, follow these instructions for running the procedures. Before running the code, open the Immediate window along with the Code window for Module1. Make sure Module1 does not include an *Option Explicit* statement. Click anywhere in the *AssignVariables* procedures. Then click the Run control on the Standard toolbar in the VBE. This procedure performs two tasks. First, it assigns values to variables, namely *intMyProcNumber* and *intMyModNumber*. Because the *Dim* statement in *AssignVariables* declares *intMyProcNumber*, this variable has scope in the procedure. The *intMyModNumber* is available for assignment in the procedure because of the *Dim* statement that appears before any procedure in Module1. Second, the *AssignVariables* procedure prints the current value of the *intMyProcNumber* variable to the Immediate window. As the procedure executes the *Debug.Print* statement, it prints 10 in the Immediate window, which is the current value for *intMyProcNumber*.

Next run the *OutsideAssignVariables* procedure in Module1. Click inside the procedure before clicking the Run button to execute the procedure. This procedure has two *Debug.Print* statements. One is an exact duplicate of the *Debug.Print* statement in the *AssignVariables* procedure. However, only the second statement returns a value. The first statement merely creates a blank line in the Immediate window. This is because the first statement attempts to print *intMyProcNumber*, which has scope in the *AssignVariables* procedure only. The second statement succeeds at printing the value of *intMyModNumber* because the variable has scope at a module level. Therefore, any procedure in Module1 can work with the variable, even though its assignment occurs in the *AssignVariables* procedure.

The third instruction in the preceding listing directs you to run the *OutsideAssignVariables* procedure in Module2. Make sure no *Option Explicit* statement appears at the top of Module2, to avoid a compile error that stops you from running the procedure. Running the procedure prints two blank lines to the Immediate window. Both lines are blank because neither variable in the *Debug.Print* statements has scope in Module2.

Return to Module 1 so that you can switch the statement used to declare *intMyModNumber*. Notice the instructions at the top of Module1 request that you move the comment marker from the *Dim* statement to the *Public* statement for the declaration of *intMyModNumber*. This action resets the assignment for *intMyModNumber*. More importantly, it makes the *intMyModNumber* variable available throughout the project. Run the *AssignVariables* procedure to give *intMyModNumber* a value of 10. Then return to Module2 and rerun the *OutsideAssignVariables* procedure. Notice that the procedure prints a blank line for *intMyProcNumber* but prints the value 10 for *intMyModNumber*. Since you changed the declaration statement for *intMyModNumber* from *Dim* to *Public*, Module2 can now see the *intMyModNumber* variable declared in Module1.

Arrays

An array is a variable, but an array does not have a one-to-one relationship with a value. Each normal (or scalar) memory variable holds just one value at a time. An array can hold multiple values of the same data type at a time. Arrays are particularly interesting for database developers since they can hold rowsets in memory. This makes working with rowsets faster than working with the same data on disk. Furthermore, the *GetRows* method for both ADO and DAO recordsets returns an array. This simplifies processing a recordset as an array. The section "Printing Recordset Rows" in Chapter 2 illustrates this approach for ADO.

In this section, you will discover the basics of working with arrays in VBA and learn how to populate and navigate the elements of an array. Later in this chapter, the "Conditional Logic and Looping Constructs" section returns to the subject of arrays.

Arrays have a data type specification, which is the same for all the elements in an array. Since arrays can contain many elements, you should use the data type with the smallest size. You can compute the memory requirements of an array by multiplying the number of elements by the size of each element and then adding a small overhead for the array itself and each dimension within the array. The maximum size of an array that will fit in memory depends on your operating system and how much physical memory (RAM) is available. Declaring arrays that are too large to fit in physical memory slows their performance because data must be read from and written to disk as you process the array elements.

You can declare an array with *Dim, Private, Public,* or *Static* statements at either the module level or the procedure level. VBA permits up to 60 dimensions for an array. The *ReDim* statement is an alternative statement for specifying the dimensional size of an array, but this statement operates only at the procedure level. Using the *ReDim* statement initially allows you to redimension an array later with a second *ReDim* statement. The option to redimension an array is available only when you initially declare the array with a *ReDim* statement. Arrays use zero-based indexing by default for the elements in each dimension. However, you can override this convention with either the *Option Base* statement or a *ReDim* statement. The *Option Base* statement allows you to designate either 0 or 1 as the base for indexing. With the *ReDim* statement, you can specify indexing over any range of numeric values.

After specifying the dimensions for an array, you can assign values to its elements. The *Array* function allows you to create an array and populate it with values in one step. It automatically returns a Variant array with element values equal to its comma-delimited list of arguments. This process always yields an array with zero-based indexing no matter what the *Option Base* statement specifies.

The following module listing illustrates several features of array declaration and use. The code resides in a module of its own. The initial *Dim* statement declares *str1* as a static array of three elements. Since there is no *Option Base* statement, you can access the array elements with index values of 0, 1, and 2. The *DeclaringArrays* procedure illustrates how to assign values to the *str1* array elements and then reference them in an expression as the arguments of a *MsgBox* function.

```
Dim str1(2) As String

Sub DeclaringArrays()

'Assign values to array elements
str1(0) = "Rick"
str1(1) = "Dobson"
str1(2) = "8629"

'Compute string expression with array elements
MsgBox str1(0) & " " & str1(1) & "'s extension is " & _
    str1(2) & ".", vbInformation, _
        "Programming Microsoft Access Version 2002"

End Sub
```

(continued)

```
Sub ReDeclaringArrays()
ReDim str2(1 To 3) As String

'Assign values to array elements
'scoped at the procedure level
str2(1) = "Rick"
str2(2) = "Dobson"
str2(3) = "8629"

'Compute string expression with array elements
MsgBox str2(1) & " " & str2(2) & "'s extension is " & _
    str2(3) & ".", vbInformation, _
        "Programming Microsoft Access Version 2002"

'Assign procedure-level array elements to
'module-level array elements
str1(0) = str2(1)
str1(1) = str2(2)
str1(2) = str2(3)

'Compute string expression with array elements
MsgBox str1(0) & " " & str1(1) & "'s extension is " & _
    str1(2) & ".", vbInformation, _
        "Programming Microsoft Access Version 2002"

'Preserve initial elements and add a new one
ReDim Preserve str2(1 To 4)
str2(4) = "rickd@cabinc.net"

'Compute string expression with array elements
MsgBox str2(1) & " " & str2(2) & "'s extension and " & _
    "email address are: " & str2(3) & " and " & _
    str2(4) & ".", vbInformation, _
        "Programming Microsoft Access Version 2002"

End Sub

Sub UsingArrayFunction()
Dim varArray As Variant

'Syntax for using Array function to create a Variant
'array; notice index starts at 0
varArray = Array("Virginia", "Dobson", "9294", "Virginia@cabinc.net")
MsgBox varArray(0) & " " & varArray(1) & "'s extension and " & _
    "email address are: " & varArray(2) & " and " & _
    varArray(3) & ".", vbInformation, _
        "Programming Microsoft Access Version 2002"

End Sub
```

The *ReDeclaringArrays* procedure contrasts a procedure-level array declared with the *ReDim* statement to the module-level array designated at the top of the module with the *Dim* statement. The *ReDim* statement at the top of the procedure specifies indexes of 1, 2, and 3 for *str2* instead of the index values of 0, 1, and 2 for *str1*. Aside from this minor distinction, you can use the elements in an expression identically. You can also assign the element values of the procedure-level array to the module-level array. The *ReDeclaringArrays* procedure also demonstrates the syntax for extending the dimension length of the procedure-level array. One major reason for using the *ReDim* statement is to gain the flexibility of adjusting the length and number of dimensions in an array. If your code adjusts the dimensionality of an array without the *Preserve* keyword, you lose any prior assignments to array elements.

The *UsingArrayFunction* procedure includes a sample demonstrating how to invoke the *Array* function. Notice the *Dim* statement for *varArray* does not assign a number of elements. The Variant memory variable can optionally contain an array. The *Array* function converts the *varArray* variable from a standard Variant memory variable to an array. The expression for the *MsgBox* function demonstrates that you refer to the Variant's elements using standard array indexing conventions, though the code initially declares the *varArray* variable using the syntax for scalar variables.

Sub Procedures

Sub procedures can perform actions, compute values, and update and revise built-in property settings. Access 2002 makes it possible for you to use sub procedures to program custom actions when events fire for forms, reports, and their controls. However, Access 2002 reserves a couple of special capabilities for other types of procedures. First, sub procedures never return values. Second, they do not define custom properties for form, report, or class modules.

> **Note**   Event procedures help make programming Access objects such as forms both easy and powerful. Access 2002 introduces roughly 30 new event procedures to further enhance your capability for controlling forms in custom solutions. We will explore forms and their events in Chapter 6.

A procedure consists of a series of VBA statements between *Sub* and *End Sub* statements. The *Sub* statement must declare a name for the procedure. While event procedures have very stylized names (such as *<object>_<event>*), procedure names generally follow standard variable naming conventions. They must begin with a letter, cannot exceed 255 characters, cannot include punctuation or spaces, and should not include a VBA keyword, such as *Sub* or an operator name. Procedures can take arguments, which you insert after the procedure name. If there is more than one argument, you separate them with commas.

One way to gain a basic familiarity with procedures is by using the Command Button wizard, which writes VBA code for more than 30 functions. All you have to do is make a few selections in dialog boxes. The procedures written by the wizard are generally simple, so they make good learning models. Even intermediate and advanced developers can benefit from the wizard because it generates a good skeleton for adding code with more specifics. Beginners can use the wizard to automate record navigation, database maintenance, general form and report operations, invocation of other applications, and miscellaneous tasks such as running a query or dialing a telephone number.

You invoke the Command Button wizard from the Toolbox in Form Design view. Select the Control Wizards button, and then drop a button on the form. This opens the dialog box shown in Figure 1-9. You can select from about a half-dozen actions in each category. After completing all the dialog boxes for the action you select, you can view the code in the Access 2002 VBE. Click the Code button on the Form Design toolbar to switch to the VBE. From there, you can fine-tune the wizard-generated code to accommodate your particular circumstances.

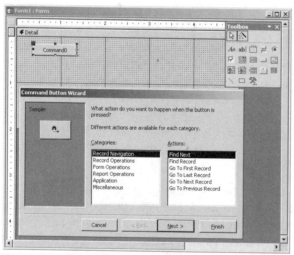

Figure 1-9 Using the Command Button wizard, you can create a whole event procedure by completing a few dialog boxes.

Many developers prefer to write their procedures from scratch. You can open a code window for an event procedure as just described, or you can create an ordinary procedure. There are two ways to start this kind of procedure, depending on where you put it. If the procedure will reside behind a form or report, click the Code button on the Design toolbar. If the code will exist in a standard module that is not behind any specific form or report, choose Tools -Macro -Visual Basic Editor from the menu or press Alt+F11. In either case, you end up in the VBE. Choose Insert-Procedure from the menu, and in the Add Procedure dialog box enter a name and confirm the selection of the Sub option button. This creates a shell for a procedure with a *Sub* and an *End Sub* statement. You can then add code to it.

Use your knowledge of the Access object model to code some actions. Recall that the *DoCmd* object has many methods. Type *DoCmd* and then press the period key. This opens a drop-down list box that displays all the legitimate entries after *DoCmd*. As you type an entry, Access converges on the subset of responses that match your entry. (See Figure 1-10.) If you are unsure what to type, you can scroll through the entries to find a method. This technique works for all objects, not just *DoCmd*. Microsoft calls this feature IntelliSense because it intelligently senses the subset of appropriate replies. IntelliSense actually does two things: it lists the properties and methods that are legitimate at any point in the construction of a VBA statement, and it provides syntax information about the content for the fields required for selected VBA statements. This dramatically reduces errors and helps you get started quickly. You can control the availability of these two IntelliSense features from the Edit tab of the Options dialog box in the VBE. The Auto List Members check box controls the listing of legitimate options after a period. The Auto Quick Info check box determines whether the VBE displays syntax information about functions and their parameters as you type them.

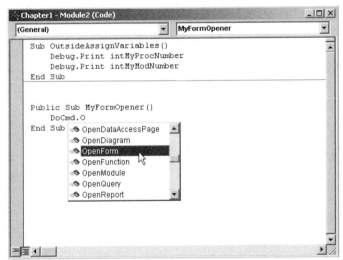

Figure 1-10 IntelliSense helps to complete a VBA statement for the *DoCmd* object. You type the beginning of a statement, and a list of legitimate ways to complete that portion of the statement appears.

The following is a simple procedure consisting of three lines. The first line reserves a memory location for a calculated result. The second adds two constants. The third prints the result in the Immediate window. This window is like a work pad for storing intermediate results as you check your code. You can open it from the VBE by choosing View-Immediate Window from the menu. You can run the procedure from the VBE by clicking anywhere in the procedure and then clicking the Run Sub/UserForm button on the Standard toolbar.

```
Sub MyFirstCalculator()
Dim Result
    Result = 1 + 2
    Debug.Print Result
End Sub
```

In a more typical situation, you can call a procedure in either of two ways. You can include its name on a line by itself; if the procedure has any arguments, you can include them after the name, separated by commas. Alternatively, you can precede the procedure name with *Call*. This is a VBA keyword for invoking a procedure. When you use *Call*, enclose arguments in parentheses after the procedure name.

The following is a slightly more flexible version of the initial calculator function. The calculator consists of a pair of procedures. The one named *MySecondCalculator* adds any two numbers and prints the result to the Immediate window. It determines what numbers to add from the two arguments that it receives. The other procedure calls the procedure that performs the sum. You can vary the numbers the second procedure adds by altering the value of the two arguments in the first procedure. In a more sophisticated application, you might tie these argument values to variables or form fields.

```
Sub CallSecondCalculator()
    MySecondCalculator 1, 3
End Sub

Sub MySecondCalculator(First, Second)
Dim Result
    Result = First + Second
    Debug.Print Result
End Sub
```

Here's another short sample that might clarify some points about data typing for memory variables. Recall from Table 1-1 (on page 26) that the upper limit of a Currency data type is 922,337,203,685,477.5807. If you want to represent a larger number, your choices are the Double data type or the Decimal data type. If you need a data type that is not susceptible to rounding error, you have only one choice—the Decimal data type. However, you cannot specify Decimal as a data type in a *Dim* statement. Instead, you must designate it as a subtype of the Variant data type.

Figure 1-11 shows the syntax for invoking the Decimal subtype of a Variant data type. Notice the *Dim* statement declares *num1* as a Variant. The *CDec* function returns a Decimal data type. By storing its return value in a memory variable with a Variant data type, you specify the Decimal subtype. This demonstration assigns 922,337,203,685,476 to *num1*. By the way, notice the pound sign (#) after the number in parentheses. This symbol appears for all integer values greater than the largest Long data type value until VBA converts the representation to a Double data type appearance. In any event, notice that adding 1.5807 creates the largest Currency value possible. Adding an additional value of .0001 exceeds the largest Currency data type value, but it is well within the limits of a Decimal data type. The Immediate window shows all three values that the *CDecSubType* procedure assigns or computes for *num1*. If you try the same assignment and calculations with a Currency subtype instead of the Decimal subtype of a Variant data type, your program will generate an Overflow error.

```
Sub CDecSubType()
Dim num1 As Variant

'num1 is 1.5807 less than
'maximum Currency value
num1 = CDec(922337203685476#)
Debug.Print num1

'Add a value to make sum equal
'the maximum Currency value
num1 = num1 + 1.5807
Debug.Print num1

'Add .0001 to exceed the
'maximum Currency value with a
'Decimal subtype of Variant data type
num1 = num1 + 0.0001
Debug.Print num1
```

```
922337203685476
922337203685477.5807
922337203685477.5808
```

Figure 1-11 A sub procedure that demonstrates the syntax for specifying the Decimal subtype of a memory variable declared with a Variant data type.

Just from the simple samples presented so far, you might be realizing that it would be nice to reuse sub procedures developed in another VBA project. Recall that each Access database file and Access project has its own VBA project. However, you can reference one VBA project from another. This enables one custom solution to reuse the procedures in the VBA project for another custom solution. The VBA project associated with the Northwind project has several procedures that you might want to reuse, such as one that tells whether a form is loaded.

The following pair of procedures demonstrates two techniques. First, the *AddNorthwindReference* procedure adds a reference to the VBA project in the Northwind Access database file. Just one line of code in a sub procedure can accomplish this. The line invokes the *AddFromFile* method for the *References* collection in the Access *Application* object. The argument is a string value that points to the location of the Access database file. The second sub procedure shows the syntax for invoking a file from another project. The *IsLoaded* function procedure in the Northwind database returns a Boolean value depending on whether a form, represented as a string argument for its name, is open. The function procedure resides in the Utility Functions module. Notice that both the *AddNorthwindReference* procedure and the *UseIsLoaded* procedure illustrate the proper syntax for using the underscore (_) as a continuation character for a line of VBA code.

```
Sub AddNorthwindReference()

    Application.References.AddFromFile _
        ("C:\Program Files\Microsoft Office\" & _
        "Office10\Samples\Northwind.mdb")

End Sub

Sub UseIsLoaded()

    Debug.Print Northwind.[Utility Functions]. _
        IsLoaded("frmSample1")

End Sub
```

Figure 1-12 shows the VBE with the two procedures from the previous listing. In the Project Explorer, you can see the reference to the Northwind database. The *AddNorthwindReference* procedure created this reference programmatically. You can also see the Modules folder of the Northwind VBA project open. It contains the Utility Functions module, which contains the *IsLoaded* function procedure. The Immediate window shows the outcome of running the *IsLoaded* function twice—once before opening frmSample1 and once after opening it.

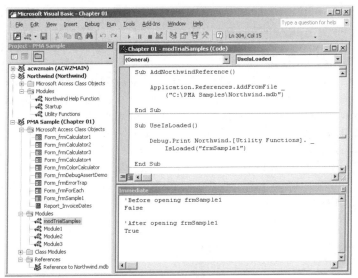

Figure 1-12 A VBE display in the Project Explorer showing the outcome of adding a reference programmatically to the VBA project in the Northwind Access database file.

Function Procedures

Function procedures differ from sub procedures in a couple of ways. First, they can return a value, so you can use them in expressions just as you use variables. Second, they do not serve as event procedures. Both sub procedures and function procedures can perform tasks. With the exceptions noted, function and sub procedures are generally interchangeable.

A function is a collection of VBA statements bounded by the *Function* and *End Function* statements. It can accept arguments in the same way that a procedure accepts arguments. A function can include one or more statements. Typically at least one of these statements sets the function's name equal to a value. You often terminate a function after setting its value by using an *Exit Function* statement. Any function can contain one or more *Exit Function* statements.

Although a function can return a value, it does not have to. A function can be a collection of statements that invoke methods and set properties without ever setting the function name equal to a value. This is one way in which functions and procedures are similar.

You create a function just like you do a procedure, but you select the Function option button instead of the Sub option button in the Add Procedure dialog box. You can invoke a function procedure by clicking the Run Sub/UserForm button on the Standard toolbar in the VBE. You can also invoke a function from the Immediate window: Type a question mark followed by the function name. If the function has arguments, place them in parentheses, separated by commas. You can run your own custom functions as well as built-in Access functions from the Immediate window.

Figure 1-13 shows a view of the VBE with a simple function that determines whether the date submitted as an argument is in the third millennium. To match popular conventions, we'll compute this millennium to start in the year 2000 rather than 2001. The function *Year2KTest* accepts a date and returns *3* if the date is in the third millennium, or returns *0* otherwise. The Immediate window below the code window shows the outcome for running the function with two different dates. The Immediate window in Figure 1-13 confirms this result by returning a *3* for the first day in 2000 and a *0* for the first day in 1999. Notice that you must enclose a date between pound signs.

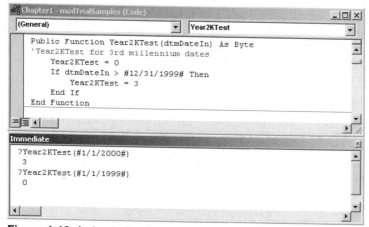

Figure 1-13 A simple function procedure invoked from the Immediate window.

The procedure that follows is a more sophisticated approach to millennium assessment. The function starts by declaring the range of dates for which it is accurate. Then it tests its argument against two millennium milestones. If the date does not fall within the first or second millennium, the function assumes that it belongs in the third millennium. The initial message box statement indicates the range of dates for which the function is accurate.

```
Public Function PopularMillennium(dtmDateIn) As Byte
    MsgBox "This works for dates after 12/31/0099" & _
        " and before 1/1/3000.", _
        vbInformation, _
        "Programming Microsoft Access Version 2002"
```

```
    If dtmDateIn <= #12/31/999# Then
        PopularMillennium = 1
    ElseIf dtmDateIn <= #12/31/1999# Then
        PopularMillennium = 2
    Else
        PopularMillennium = 3
    End If
End Function
```

VBA dates are valid from 1/1/100 through 12/31/9999. This range is sufficient for the vast majority of desktop applications. If you need a range beyond these dates, you should consider coding dates independently of the Access serial date system.

You often use both procedures and functions to develop a solution to a problem. Figure 1-14 shows a form that relies on both kinds of functions to develop answers. The form allows a user to type values in the text boxes labeled Number 1 and Number 2. Clicking a function button of /, *, -, or + computes a corresponding outcome in the Result text box.

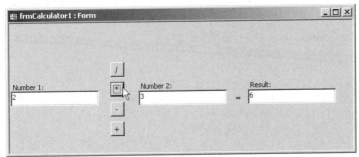

Figure 1-14 This form serves as a simple calculator. VBA functions enable the form's buttons and populate the Result text box based on entries in the other two text boxes.

The VBA code to implement the form in Figure 1-14 uses just four pairs of procedures and functions, as shown next. Four procedures act as the event handler for a click to the four function keys on the form. These event handlers simply call a function that pulls the values from the two text boxes, executes the computation indicated by the function button, and returns that value to the event procedure. The event procedure, in turn, assigns the return value from the function to the third text box on the form. Notice the optional use of the *Me* prefix before the text box names. Since the code is behind the form with the text box, specifying the form name is optional. The event procedures use *Me* instead of the form's longer, more formal class name (*Form_frmCalculator1*).

```
Option Compare Database
Option Explicit
Dim dblResult As Double

Private Sub cmdAddition_Click()
    Me.txtResult = MyAdder
End Sub

Private Function MyAdder()
    dblResult = CDbl(txtNumber1) + CDbl(txtNumber2)
    MyAdder = dblResult
End Function

Private Sub cmdSubtraction_Click()
    Me.txtResult = MySubtractor
End Sub

Private Function MySubtractor()
    dblResult = CDbl(txtNumber1) - CDbl(txtNumber2)
    MySubtractor = dblResult
End Function

Private Sub cmdMultiplication_Click()
    Me.txtResult = MyMultiplier
End Sub

Private Function MyMultiplier()
    dblResult = CDbl(txtNumber1) * CDbl(txtNumber2)
    MyMultiplier = dblResult
End Function

Private Sub cmdDivision_Click()
    Me.txtResult = MyDivider
End Sub

Private Function MyDivider()
    dblResult = CDbl(txtNumber1) / CDbl(txtNumber2)
    MyDivider = dblResult
End Function
```

The function and the procedures reside in the code module behind the form. The *Dim* statement at the top of the module declares a variable that all of the procedures in the module can use. Since users can click only one function key at a time, this sharing of *dblResult* works. The *Option Explicit* statement forces the declaration of variables before their use. This helps to guard against typographical errors, which are a common source of errors in programs. *Option Compare Database* is a module-level specification that designates string variables sorted in an order determined by the locale ID in the Control Panel. This is available through the Regional Settings icon in Windows 95, Windows 98, and Windows NT or through the Regional Options icon in Windows 2000.

The following pair of procedures illustrates much of what we have covered about procedures, functions, and methods. The form, frmCalculator2, has just two controls: a text box named *txtInput* and a command button named *cmdSquarer*. The form computes the square of the entry in the text box when the user clicks the button. The procedures display the result in a message box.

```
Option Compare Database
Option Explicit
Dim dblResult As Double

Private Sub cmdSquarer_Click()
    MySquarer Form_frmCalculator2.txtInput
End Sub

Public Sub MySquarer(MyOtherNumber As Double)
    dblResult = MyOtherNumber * MyOtherNumber
    MsgBox dblResult, vbInformation, _
        "Programming Microsoft Access Version 2002"
'Optional statements illustrating the use of methods
'    DoCmd.GoToControl "txtInput"
'    txtInput.SetFocus
'    DoCmd.Close acForm, "frmCalculator2", acSaveNo
End Sub
```

The *cmdSquarer_Click* event procedure invokes the *MySquarer* procedure and passes the contents of *txtInput* as an argument. *MySquarer* computes its result and then displays the result in a message box.

Three more comment lines suggest additional actions that you can perform. A line calling the *GoToControl* method shows how to move the focus from the button to the text box. The *SetFocus* example on the next line illustrates an alternative way to achieve the same result. The *Close* method shows how to close a form. Notice that this line uses yet another name, *frmCalculator2*, to refer to the form. Using the *acSaveNo* constant is important because it allows the form to close without a prompt asking whether to save the form.

Property Procedures

You use property procedures to implement custom properties for forms, reports, and class modules. The next section includes a brief introduction to class modules, and Chapter 9, "Class, Form, and Report Modules," digs deeper into class modules and offers more advanced samples.

There are three types of property statements: *Property Get, Property Let,* and *Property Set.* You use these statements to work with custom properties. The *Property Get* statement and its matching *End Property* statement can return a value, just like a function procedure. If you define a property with only a *Property Get* statement, that property is read-only. A read-only property is convenient when you want to grant the right to view a quantity but not to alter it—think of an application dealing with 401(k) balances or grades.

It is important to be able to change some properties without being able to read them. For example, database security administrators do not necessarily need to read the user passwords that they supervise. They only need to be able to write over them when users forget their password. Use the *Property Let* statement with its matching *End Property* statement to set a password.

The *Property Set* statement works similarly to the *Property Let* statement. Both create a setting for a property. The *Property Let* statement sets a property equal to a data type, such as a string or integer. The *Property Set* statement sets a property equal to an object reference. You use the *Property Set* statement with object references, such as references to a form or a report.

Since many properties are both read and write, you will frequently use both *Property Get* and either *Property Let* or *Property Set.* In this case, the pair of *Property* statements must have the same name so that they refer to the same property.

Modules

As you've learned, a module is a container for procedures and declarations, such as *Option Explicit* and *Dim.* There are two basic kinds of modules. First, there are standard modules. These appear under Modules in the Database window. The procedures in a standard module are independent of existing objects in an Access database file. This means you can't refer to *Me,* and you also can't reference a control name without using the appropriate prefixes for that control. However, your applications can reference procedures in standard modules readily from any object.

The second kind of module is a class module. There are three basic varieties of these modules: form class, report class, and custom class. The procedures within a module are generally accessible to other modules. You can take a procedure from this general scope by using the *Private* keyword when you initially specify the procedure. You can also explicitly declare procedures to have global scope by using the *Public* keyword.

A form module is the module for any form that has at least one declaration or procedure. Creating an event procedure for a form or a control on a form creates a form class module. Report class modules work about the same as form class modules, but the *Report* events are different from those for forms and you are unlikely to have the same mix of controls on a report as on a form. You can create custom class modules that comprise method functions and procedure functions for a custom object you define, such as an employee or an account. You can reference the methods and properties for custom class modules much as you do for built-in Access classes.

You use custom class modules like cookie cutters to make new instances of the custom class. Access offers two ways to accomplish this. First, you can use a single *Dim* statement to both declare the class and create a new instance of it. Here is the syntax for this type of statement:

```
Dim objInstance As New objClass
```

The second approach relies on a pair of statements. The first member of the pair declares the object instance. The second member sets a reference to the object. The second approach is the better practice since it defers the cost of using the object (execution time and memory space) until you actually require it. This is the syntax for these statements:

```
Dim <objInstance> as <objClass>
Set <objInstance> = New <objClass>
```

The <*objClass*> name refers to a class module populated with property procedures and public method functions. These method functions act as methods for the class just as the property procedures serve to define properties. Chapter 9 covers in detail how to create and use custom class modules.

Creating and Using a Class Module

You can start to create a class module by choosing Insert-Class Module from the menu. This creates an empty class module with a name such as Class1, Class2, or Class3. Access automatically assigns the next sequential number as the trailing number. You can replace the default name from the Database window. Class modules appear along with standard modules in the Database window when you highlight Modules on the Objects bar. Right-click any module, including a class module, and choose Rename to assign a new name to the module. Double-click the new name in the Database window to return to the VBE with the Code window open to the renamed module. In our example, we renamed our class module *modSquarer*.

In the module, you can enter code to define the properties and methods of the class. (See the next listing.) The *modSquarer* class provides properties and methods to support squaring a number. A Property Let statement creates a write-only property named *ValueToSquare*. This is a write-only property because there is no corresponding Property Get statement with the same name. The procedure saves the value in a private variable named *x*. Declaring the memory variable with the *Private* keyword is important since it makes the property defined by the

Property Let statement the only path to the value the class squares. While there is no way to read the precise value to be squared, there is a read-only property for the *modSquarer* class named *Is5*. This property returns a Boolean value of True if the value to be squared is 5. Otherwise, the property returns a value of False, which is the default value for a Boolean variable in VBA.

A subprocedure in the module defines a method named *ComputeIt*. This method works by passing the value of *x* to the *MySquarer* subprocedure in *Form_frmCalculator2*, the class module behind the *frmCalculator2* form. If you refer back to that module, you will discover a public declaration of the *MySquarer* subprocedure. The *MySquarer* procedure computes the square and displays the result with a message box. The syntax for these definitions follows:

```
Option Compare Database
Private x As Double

Property Let ValueToSquare(value As Double)
    x = value
End Property

Property Get Is5() As Boolean
    If x = 5 Then Is5 = True
End Property

Sub ComputeIt()
    Form_frmCalculator2.MySquarer (x)
End Sub
```

Your custom applications will not run the code in a class module directly. Instead, your code should instantiate an object based on the class in order to work with the properties and methods of the class. The following pair of procedures illustrates how to apply this principle for the *modSquarer* class. The *CallClassDemo* procedure performs two tasks. First, it uses an *InputBox* function to gather input from the user, and it saves the user input in the *dbl1* variable, which the procedures declares as a double. Then, it passes this value to the *ClassDemo* procedure, which accepts the user input as a Double data type.

```
Sub CallClassDemo()
Dim dbl1 As Double

'Request a number to square
dbl1 = InputBox("Number to square?")

'Call class module demo and pass value
'input by user
ClassDemo dbl1

End Sub
```

```
Sub ClassDemo(dbl1 As Double)
Dim MySquarer As modSquarer

'Instantiate MySquarer object reference
Set MySquarer = New modSquarer

'Assign value to get squared
'and compute the square
MySquarer.ValueToSquare = dbl1
MySquarer.ComputeIt

'Check current value to see whether
'current value to square equals 5
Debug.Print MySquarer.Is5

'Remove object reference from memory
Set MySquarer = Nothing

'The next line fails because the
'MySquarer object reference no longer exists;
'comment out the next line to avoid the failure
Debug.Print MySquarer.Is5

End Sub
```

The second procedure begins by declaring the *MySquarer* variable as an object reference for the *modSquarer* class. Next the procedure instantiates the reference by setting it equal to the *New* keyword followed by *modSquarer*, the name of the class to which the object reference refers. After the *Set* statement, the *MySquarer* variable is an object with the properties and methods defined by the *modSquarer* class module. The pair of lines uses the class's *ValueToSquare* property and its *ComputeIt* method. The procedure assigns *dbl1* as the setting for the *ValueToSquare* property. By invoking the *ComputeIt* method, the procedure runs code that opens a message box with the square of the *dbl1* value.

To help enhance your understanding of class modules, we'll examine three more statements in this example. After presenting the squared value, the procedure prints to the Immediate window the return value of the *Is5* property for the *MySquarer* object reference. Notice from the listing for the *modSquarer* class module that this property returns a Boolean value of True only if the value of *dbl1* is 5. For example, if a user typed *4* in response to the *InputBox* prompt, the *Is5* property returns a Boolean value of False. The procedure's next-to-last statement sets the *MySquarer* object reference to Nothing. This frees the memory resources used by the object, and it makes the object's properties and methods unavailable. Therefore, the procedure's final statement generates an error because it refers to one of the object's properties. You can comment out the line to eliminate the error.

Conditional Logic and Looping Constructs

Conditional code execution and looping are at the heart of many code-based solutions. VBA offers a rich choice of options for implementing this kind of logic. The following sections review the major statement types that enable conditional program execution and looping and provide practical examples.

If...Then

Many procedures cannot achieve their objective by progressing sequentially through lines of code. It is often desirable to execute code conditionally—to skip some lines and perform others. One flexible and robust way to achieve conditional execution in VBA procedures is with the *If...Then* statement. There are actually three major variations of this basic statement. The first variation conditionally performs a simple block of code. The syntax follows:

```
If <condition> Then
    'Statements
End If
```

One or more statements can reside within an *If...End If* block. The terminating *End If* marks the end of the block. VBA executes the statements within the block only when the condition evaluates to True. You can nest multiple *If...End If* blocks within one another.

A second variation of the *If...Then* statement enables your code to execute either of two blocks of code. It has this syntax:

```
If <condition> Then
    'Statements1
Else
    'Statements2
End If
```

This form of the statement executes one of two blocks of code. When the condition is true, the statements in the first group execute. Otherwise, the statements in the second block execute.

While this design is more flexible than the first format, it's still limiting because you have only two options. You can, in fact, nest *If...Then* statements to enable more options, but VBA offers a third design that simplifies execution of any one of three or more statement blocks. Here is the syntax:

```
If <condition1> Then
    'Statements
ElseIf <condition2> Then
    'Statements
Else
    'Statements
End If
```

This form of the *If...Then* statement incorporates multiple conditions and three or more groups of statements. You can easily add new statement groups and conditions by inserting new *ElseIf* clauses with their own conditions and statements. This design is more powerful than the second variation not only because it can accommodate more conditions, but also because it restricts the execution of each statement block (except the last) to the case in which there is a precise match to a condition test. The second variation of the *If...Then* statement executes its second statement block whenever the condition for the first statement block is not true. When failing a match to the first condition does not automatically serve as a basis for executing the second statement block, you need the third style of the *If...Then* statement.

Consider the form shown in Figure 1-15. It includes a text box, an option group, and a command button. The option group allows a user to designate either a square or a cube operation on the numerical value in the text box. To compute the square of a number, you type the number in the text box, select Square It in the Compute Type option group, and then click Compute.

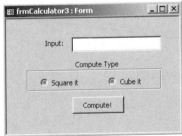

Figure 1-15 A form for calculating squares or cubes of numbers.

The following code shows the two procedures that make this squaring operation possible. The *cmdComputer_Click* event procedure responds to the click. If the option group *(opgComputeType)* equals 1, the user selected the Square It option button. The procedure calls *MySquarer* when the option group equals 1. Otherwise, it ends without performing any computations.

```
Sub cmdComputer_Click()
    If opgComputeType = 1 Then
        MySquarer txtInput.Value
    End If
End Sub


Sub MySquarer(MyOtherNumber As Double)
    dblResult = MyOtherNumber * MyOtherNumber
    MsgBox dblResult, vbInformation, _
        "Programming Microsoft Access Version 2002"
End Sub
```

This *cmdComputer_Click* procedure uses the first *If...Then* structure. It merely conditionally executes a single statement block. In this case, the block consists of just one line. If the user selects Square It, *MySquarer* multiplies the text box's value by itself and presents the result in a message box.

If the user selects Cube It before clicking the command button, the code does nothing. The option group returns a value of 2, but there is no condition to detect this. In fact, it is all or nothing when the option group equals 1. The following code shows a new version of the event procedure along with the code to handle the situation in which the user does not select Square It:

```
Sub cmdComputer_Click()
    If opgComputeType = 1 Then
        MySquarer txtInput.Value
    Else
        MyCuber txtInput.Value
    End If
End Sub

Sub MyCuber(MyOtherNumber As Double)
Dim dblResult As Double
    dblResult = MyOtherNumber ^ 3
    MsgBox dblResult, vbInformation, _
        "Programming Microsoft Access Version 2002"
End Sub
```

The *cmdComputer_Click* procedure uses the second form of the *If...Then* statement. It calls *MySquarer* if *opgComputeType* equals 1 but otherwise calls *MyCuber*. This works correctly if the user selects Cube It. However, at least one problem remains: The form opens with neither option button selected. If a user enters a number in the text box and then clicks the command button, the form returns the cubed value of the number despite the fact that the user selected neither option button. The fault lies in the design of the *If...Then* statement. We need the third variation with two separate conditions—one for squaring and the other for cubing. The following code shows this design:

```
Sub cmdComputer_Click()
    If opgComputeType = 1 Then
        MySquarer txtInput.Value
    ElseIf opgComputeType = 2 Then
        MyCuber txtInput.Value
    Else
        MsgBox "Click a computation type", _
            vbCritical, _
            "Programming Microsoft Access Version 2002"
    End If
End Sub
```

This sample includes two conditions. One tests whether the option group equals 1, and the other tests whether the option group equals 2. If the option group fails both tests, the procedure displays a message box reminding the user to click a computation type. If you add new option buttons to the option group for different computations, you can easily accommodate them. Just insert a new *ElseIf* clause with a special condition for each new button.

You can also use *If...Then...Else* statements to help compute quantities that require iteration to get to a valid result. The next sample demonstrates how to compute a cube root within a specified tolerance of error. While you probably will never want to perform this task (because VBA lets you do it automatically with a fractional exponent), businesses and scientific endeavors sometimes have to compute results for which no built-in function exists. The *Cuberoot* procedure has the tutorial benefit of being easy to understand. When situations call for iterative calculations to obtain a result, understanding the *If...Then* statement can improve your ability to code solutions quickly.

```
Sub Cuberoot()
Dim num1 As Double
Dim this_est As Double
Dim change As Double
Dim way_went As String

'Get number for which to compute the cube root
num1 = InputBox _
    ("Number for which to compute cube root?")

'Compute initial cube root estimate,
'amount by which to change estimate,
'and guess as to which way to change
this_est = num1 * 0.2
change = num1 * 0.2
way_went = "down"

'Perform 3 tasks
'1. If estimate is close enough, print cube root
'2. If not close enough, either add
'    or subtract a change quantity to
'    move in the right direction
'3. Reduce change quantity each time your application
'    changes the direction that the change quantity
'    alters
Test_Estimate:
If Abs(num1 - (this_est ^ 3)) < 0.0000001 Then
    Debug.Print "The cube root of " & num1 & _
        " is " & FormatNumber(this_est, 6) & "."
```

(continued)

```
ElseIf (num1 - (this_est ^ 3)) > 0 Then
    this_est = this_est + change
    If way_went = "down" Then
        change = change / 2
        way_went = "up"
    End If
    GoTo Test_Estimate
Else
    this_est = this_est - change
    If way_went = "up" Then
        change = change / 2
        way_went = "down"
    End If
    GoTo Test_Estimate

End If

End Sub
```

The procedure declares four memory variables to help compute the cube root of a number. The *num1* variable has a Double data type to accommodate a wide range of values. The *this_est* variable is a guess at the cube root that the procedure iteratively improves until the estimate is within an acceptable tolerance of error. The acceptable error tolerance is based on how close the cube of the current cube root estimate is to *num1*. The *change* variable is another quantity the procedure regularly adjusts. The procedure increments or decrements the current estimate by the value of the *change* variable. Every time the program flips from incrementing to decrementing an estimate (or vice versa), the program divides the *change* variable by half its previous value. The program uses the value of *change* to either increase or decrease the current estimate until the estimate reaches the tolerable error range (+/- 0.0000001). The fourth memory variable, *way_went*, has a String data type. This variable monitors the direction in which the program last changed the cube root estimate. It uses *"up"* to indicate that it increased the estimate and *"down"* to signal it reduced the estimate.

After the declarations, the procedure invokes the *InputBox* function to let users specify the number for which they seek the cube root. This function normally returns a string, but the declaration of *num1* as a Double data type stores the return value from the function as a Double data type. Next the program computes initial estimates for the cube root estimate and the size of the value by which it changes the estimate. It arbitrarily sets the *way_went* variable to *"down"*. It doesn't matter what the initial value of *way_went* is because the computational process automatically changes this variable if the direction is wrong.

These initial steps set up the computational part of the program, which ties to a label just before an *If...Then...ElseIf* statement. The *If, ElseIf,* and *Else* paths through the loop detect one of three conditions. The procedure follows the *If* path when the cube root estimate is close enough. In this situation, the code prints the estimate to the Immediate window formatted to show six places after the decimal by the *FormatNumber* function. The procedure takes the *ElseIf* path if the estimate is too small; it takes the *Else* path if the estimate is too large. When the program takes either of these last two paths, it revises *this_est* (and conditionally *way_went* with a nested *If...Then* statement). After making its changes, the procedure branches unconditionally with a *GoTo* statement to the beginning of the *If...Then...ElseIf* statement. The line to which the procedure branches has a label named *Test_Estimate*. VBA syntax conventions require you to terminate line labels with a colon. The jump to the beginning of the *If...Then...ElseIf* statement permits the procedure to iteratively calculate a more accurate answer.

As you can see, the *If...Then* statement is very flexible. You can use it to handle many possible options, but it handles one or two conditions most easily. Its syntax changes slightly depending on what you want to accomplish. The *If...Then* statement is especially appropriate when you need to evaluate criterion expressions of different formats for the various paths involved.

Select Case

The *Select Case* statement evaluates an expression and conditionally executes one block of statements. When you work with more than one or two conditional options, the *Select Case* statement can be simpler to set up and easier to maintain than the *If...Then* statement. The general syntax for *Select Case* follows:

```
Select Case <test expression>
    Case <expression list-1>
        'Statements
    Case <expression list-2>
        'Statements
    Case Else
        'Statements
End Select
```

Notice that *Select Case* evaluates an initial test expression. This can be as simple as a passed parameter or as complicated as a rocket science expression. The *<expression list-1>* and *<expression list-2>* terms represents ranges (or specific values) for the test expression. Some options for specifying expression lists include constants, delimited items in a series, or expressions that evaluate to a value that can be compared against the test expression. When an expression list is true because it matches the test expression, the corresponding block of statements executes. This syntax sample shows just two lists, but you can add more by inserting additional *Case* statements. The *Case Else* clause is optional, but it is good programming practice. This option captures any test expression values not trapped by the preceding *Case* clauses. You can nest *Select Case* statements within each other; each instance must start with *Select Case* and terminate with *End Select*.

Figure 1-16 shows a *Select Case* statement used in a function procedure. This procedure can perform one of four numerical operations on a pair of numbers passed to it. A string argument specifies the operation, and the Immediate window shows the result of the operation. As you can see from the Immediate window, the expression list tests are not case sensitive. The next to the last application of the *computer0* function procedure nests one call to the procedure inside another. A misspelled operation causes the *Case Else* clause to operate. In this situation, the function prints a message in the Immediate window announcing that the operation is not valid.

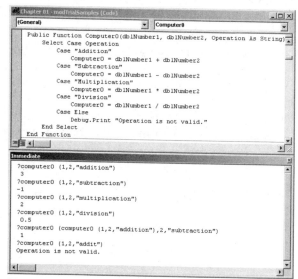

Figure 1-16 A function procedure and output illustrating the use of the *Select Case* statement.

For...Next

The *For...Next* statement is most commonly used for looping through a block of statements a known number of times. Because you can conditionally branch out of this kind of loop with an *Exit For* statement, you can also use the *For...Next* statement when you are not sure how many times to run before stopping. However, you must specify a maximum number of loops. Here is the general syntax for the statement:

```
For <counter> = <start> To <stop> Step <step>
    'Statements
    If <condition> Then
        Exit For
    End If
    'Statements
Next <counter>
```

The *For* loop extends from the *For counter* line to the *Next counter* line. The *For…Next* statement initializes *counter* to the value of *start* and then executes the statements between *For* and *Next*. The flow of execution then returns to the top of the *For* loop, where *counter* is incremented by the optional *step*. (If *step* is not specified, *counter* is incremented by 1.)

The statements in the *For* loop are executed repeatedly until the value of *counter* exceeds *stop* (or when *counter* is less than *stop* if *step* is a negative number). Control then passes to the statement immediately following the *Next counter* statement. The optional *Exit For* statement causes the *For* loop to terminate prior to *counter* exceeding *stop*.

You can nest *For…Next* statements within one another. An inner loop passes control to an outer one when *counter* exceeds *stop*. VBA can generate a run-time error if it encounters a *Next* statement without a matching *For* statement, as for example if you branch to a label inside of a *For…Next* statement. The *CountFor* procedure (see the next code listing) applies *For…Next* logic while reinforcing techniques for working with arrays and *Static* declarations. (The array *aryMyArray* has five elements. Recall that array indexing begins with 0 unless your code explicitly specifies otherwise.) Next the code declares an *Integer* variable to serve as a counter. The *For…Next* statement successively assigns the values *1* through *5* to the counter variable, *intIndex*.

```
Sub CountFor()
Static aryMyArray(4) As Integer
Dim intIndex As Integer
    For intIndex = 1 To 5
        aryMyArray(intIndex - 1) = _
            aryMyArray(intIndex - 1) + intIndex
        Debug.Print intIndex, aryMyArray(intIndex - 1)
    Next intIndex
    Debug.Print vbLf
End Sub
```

Two statements execute for each pass through the loop. First, the value of an element in *aryMyArray* adds the current value of *intIndex* to its current value. Since the code declares *aryMyArray* with a *Static* statement, the array elements retain their values on successive runs through the procedure. After the first pass through the procedure, each array element contains the same value as its index in the array. After the second pass through the procedure, each *aryMyArray* element contains twice the value of its index—and so on for each successive pass through the procedure. The second statement prints the current value of *intIndex* and the associated element of the array. Recall that you can reinitialize the value of the array elements to 0 by choosing Reset from the VBE Run menu.

> **Note**   The *vbLf* following the *Debug.Print* before the *End Sub* statement is a VBA constant that designates a line feed. You can discover the full array of VBA constants from the Object Browser. Search for Constants in the VBA library.

Figure 1-17 shows Immediate window output for three successive runs through the procedure. The column on the left shows the successive values of *intIndex*, and the column on the right shows the corresponding values of the array elements. On the first run through the procedure, the array elements exactly match *intIndex*. On the second and third passes, the array element values are two and three times the *intIndex* values. This accumulating outcome shows the impact of a *Static* variable declaration. If you change the *Static* keyword in the *aryMyArray* declaration to *Dim*, the values of *intIndex* and *aryMyArray* match each other on all passes through the procedure.

You can also use nested *For...Next* loops to pass through a multidimensional array. The *ComputeMultiplicationTable* procedure shown in the next code listing illustrates this approach. Back when I was a kid (during the era before calculators and the common availability of computers), it was common for students to memorize a multiplication table. This table typically had the numbers 1 through 13 in the outside row and column borders. The cells of the table contained the product of the row and column border values. For ease of showing the result in the Immediate window without any special formatting, the *ComputeMultiplicationTable* sample creates a 5-by-5 multiplication table with labels to the top and left.

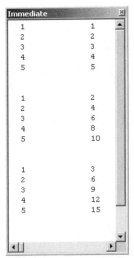

Figure 1-17 The Immediate window shows the result of running the *CountFor* procedure three successive times.

```
Sub ComputeMultiplicationTable()
ReDim aryMultable(0 To 5, 0 To 5) As Byte
Dim i As Byte
Dim j As Byte

'Write borders of the multiplication table
For i = 1 To 5
    aryMultable(i, 0) = i
    aryMultable(0, i) = i
Next i

'Compute body of the multiplication table
For i = 1 To 5
    For j = 1 To 5
        aryMultable(i, j) = i * j
    Next j
Next i

'Print multiplication table; blank top-left corner
For i = 0 To 5
    Debug.Print IIf(i = 0, "", aryMultable(i, 0)), _
        aryMultable(i, 1), aryMultable(i, 2), _
        aryMultable(i, 3), aryMultable(i, 4), _
        aryMultable(i, 5)
Next i

End Sub
```

The procedure starts with a *ReDim* statement for the *aryMultable* array. The declaration specifies a Byte data type for the array because all its elements fall in the range of 0 through 255. The first row and column are the numbers to be multiplied in the rest of the table. The array has zero-based indexes—one for each of its two dimensions that extend from 0 through 5. Next the procedure declares two additional variables with a Byte data type for pointing at the rows and columns of the array. The second through the sixth cells in the first row and the first column should have the values 1 through 5. The top-left cell should appear blank. The procedure handles this requirement as it prints the table. Until the time to print the table, the top-left cell (which prints with a default value of 0 for numeric quantities) is empty. The first *For...Next* loop populates the first row and first column cells with their required values.

The next block of code is actually a pair of nested loops. The outer loop moves successively through each of the five rows of the multiplication table. The inner loop computes the product for each cell within a row and deposits the value in the array.

Finally, one more loop concludes the task. This one prints the six elements on each of six rows. A value of *0*, which is the default Byte value, should appear as a blank in the table, but the procedure cannot assign an empty string (" ") to a variable with a Byte data type because that is not a permissible value. We use an Immediate If (*IIf*) function to check the element values in the first column in order to work around this problem. The *IIf* function takes three arguments. It returns the second argument if the first argument evaluates to true, otherwise it returns the third argument.

Figure 1-18 shows the Immediate window output from the *Compute-MultiplicationTable* procedure. Notice the blank in the top-left corner. Normally, you would deposit results like these to another receptacle besides the Immediate window, such as a table in your database.

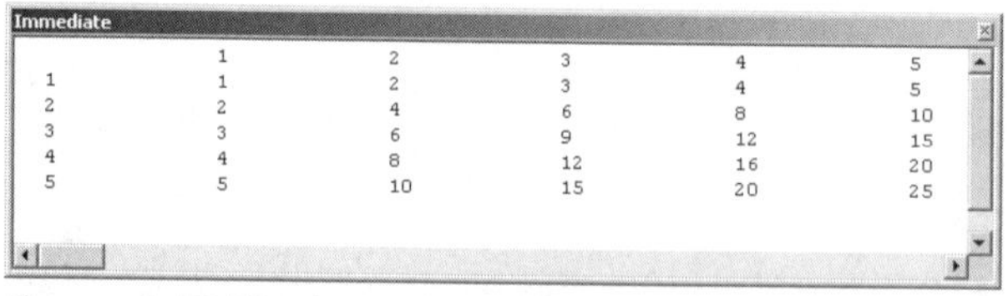

Immediate					
	1	2	3	4	5
1	1	2	3	4	5
2	2	4	6	8	10
3	3	6	9	12	15
4	4	8	12	16	20
5	5	10	15	20	25

Figure 1-18 The Immediate window showing the result of running the *Compute-MultiplicationTable* procedure.

For Each...Next and With...End With

The *For Each...Next* and *With...End With* statements can work together nicely for form data validation and classic enumeration tasks. *For Each...Next* iterates through any collection (such as the controls on a form) or array. It does not require that your application know the number of elements in the collection or array. The *With...End With* statement can complement *For Each...Next* by simplifying how you code multiple controls in a statement block.

The *For Each...Next* statement is both similar to and slightly less complicated than the *For...Next* statement. It is similar to *For...Next* in that its loop starts with a line that begins with *For* and ends with a line that begins with *Next*. However, the design of the *For* and *Next* lines are different for both versions of the *For* loop. The *For Each...Next* statement is less complicated than the *For...Next* statement because you do not have to track three separate parameters (*counter*, *start*, and *stop*) or worry about a positive or negative *step* value. The *For Each...Next* statement always starts at the beginning and loops forward until it reaches the end of a collection or the elements in an array. The general syntax for the statement follows:

```
For Each <element> In <group>
    'Statements
    If <condition> Then
        Exit For
    End If
    'Statements
Next <element>
```

The *<group>* term in the first line of the *For Each...Next* statement refers to the collection or the array name. The *<element>* in both the first and last lines designates individual objects in a collection or elements in an array.

The *For Each...Next* statement repetitively executes the statements in its body for each element in the specified collection or array. You will often want to have an *Exit For* or other conditionally executed statement somewhere in the body of the *For* loop. This enables your code to respond dynamically to a special outcome in its environment. The condition test identifies this special outcome, and the *Exit For* or other conditionally executed statements engage only when the outcome occurs.

As with the *For...Next* statement, *For Each...Next* statements can nest inside one another. At the conclusion of a *For Each...Next* loop, control passes to the first statement following the loop.

The *With...End With* statement simplifies the referencing of several different properties or methods of the same object. You specify the object whose properties or methods you want to reference in the beginning *With* line, and you close the reference to that object with the *End With* line at the end of the block. Between the *With* and the *End With* lines, you can access the object's properties or methods without specifying the object name. The code on the following page shows the general syntax of the *With...End With* statement.

```
With <object>
    .<propertyname1> = "new value 1"
    .<propertyname2> = "new value 2"
    .<method1>
    .<method2>
End With
```

The term *<object>* is the name of an object, a reference to an object, or an array name. The terms *<propertyname1>* and *<propertyname2>* are properties of the object, and *<method1>* and *<method2>* are methods of the object. As you can see, the *With...End With* statement make references to an object's properties and methods more concise.

Figures 1-19, 1-20, and 1-21 show a data validation form in action. Although the form has only a pair of text boxes that require validation, the form's code uses a *For Each...Next* loop that can be expanded to accommodate more text box controls. You can make a slight change to include other types of controls in the validation procedure. Figure 1-19 shows the layout of the basic Input form with a pair of text boxes and a command button.

Clicking the Do It! command button invokes an event procedure that checks the text boxes to make sure they do not contain Nulls. If either control contains a Null, the event procedure displays a message box reminding the user to enter information in both text boxes.

The event procedure also calls a procedure that changes the background of each text box that contains a Null from white to yellow. The procedure also moves the focus to the last text box that contains a Null. The background stays yellow until the user updates the data in the text box.

Figure 1-20 shows a text box that contained a Null but now contains 1. The background of the text box changes back to white as soon as the user enters some information and moves the focus off the text box. Figure 1-21 shows the form after the new value updates the text box's value.

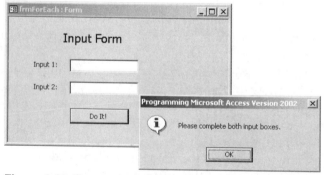

Figure 1-19 The result of clicking the Do It! command button when at least one text box contains a Null.

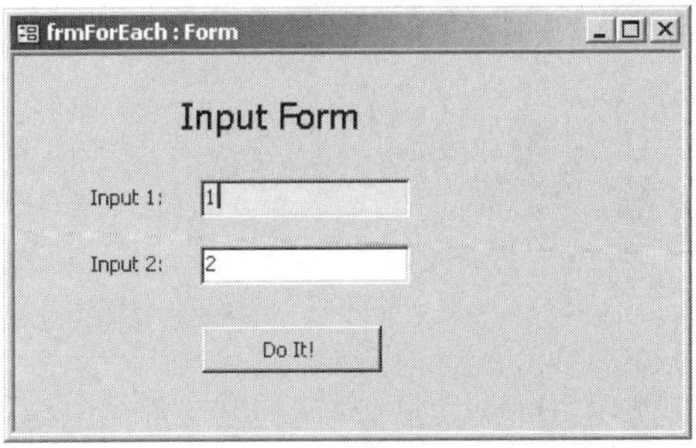

Figure 1-20 A yellow-highlighted text box that contained a Null but now contains 1.

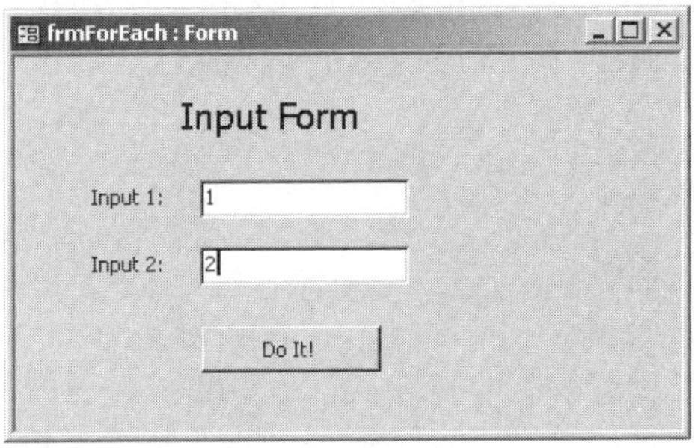

Figure 1-21 After the user enters information and moves the focus, the text box's background color is reset to white.

The following pair of procedures—named *cmdSubmit_Click* and *MarkFieldsToEdit*—examines the text boxes and yellow-highlights any text box that contains a Null. The *Click* event procedure for the command button loops through all the controls on the form. This includes text box as well as non–text box controls. The event procedure uses a *TypeOf* keyword to detect which control is a text box. Failure to take this measure can result in a run-time error because not all controls have a *Value* property. If the event procedure detects a text box control, it queries the control's *Value* property to determine whether it contains a Null. Any control with a Null triggers the code inside the *If…Then* statement. This code displays the message box and calls the procedure to highlight the control with the missing entry.

```
Private Sub cmdSubmit_Click()
'Check for valid entries.
    For Each ctl In Screen.ActiveForm.Controls
        If TypeOf ctl Is TextBox Then
            If IsNull(ctl.Value) Then
                MsgBox "Please enter information " _
                    & "in both input boxes.", _
                    vbInformation, _
                    "Programming Microsoft Access Version 2002"
```

(continued)

```
                    MarkFieldsToEdit
                    Exit For
                End If
            End If
        Next ctl
    End Sub

    Public Sub MarkFieldsToEdit()
        For Each ctl In Screen.ActiveForm.Controls
            If TypeOf ctl Is TextBox Then
                If IsNull(ctl.Value) Then
                    With ctl
                        .BackColor = RGB(255, 255, 0)
                        .SetFocus
                    End With
                End If
            End If
        Next ctl
    End Sub
```

The *MarkFieldsToEdit* procedure also uses the *TypeOf* keyword to identify text boxes. When it detects a text box that contains a Null, it uses a *With...End With* statement to change the control's background color and to move the focus to the control. This ensures that the last text box that contains Null has the focus at the end of the procedure.

Each of the event procedures in the following code fires on the *AfterUpdate* event. Each procedure uses a *With...End With* block to change the associated control's background color back to white if the background color is currently yellow. The *AfterUpdate* event occurs independently for both text boxes, but the code in each procedure is identical except for the name of the associated object (either *txtInput1* or *txtInput2*).

```
Private Sub txtInput1_AfterUpdate()
    With txtInput1
        If .BackColor = RGB(255, 255, 0) Then
            .BackColor = RGB(255, 255, 255)
        End If
    End With
End Sub

Private Sub txtInput2_AfterUpdate()
    With txtInput2
        If .BackColor = RGB(255, 255, 0) Then
            .BackColor = RGB(255, 255, 255)
        End If
    End With
End Sub
```

In addition to using the *For…Each* statements with members of a collection, such as controls on a form, you can use *For…Each* statements to iterate through the elements of an array. The *ForEachArrayElement* procedure and the *NullStr1* procedure demonstrate the syntax rules for doing this. In addition, the next code sample illustrates some other interesting techniques, including conditional compilation and the use of functions to return the lowest and highest index values for an array.

The code sample assumes the declaration of a *str1* array defined at the module level with index values of 0, 1, and 2. I remind you of this because the *str1* declaration does not show in the listing. The procedure undertakes several tasks with arrays:

1. It declares a local array, *str2*, and populates it with values in each of its three elements.

2. In between declaring and populating the local array, the procedure conditionally erases any values in the module-level array, *str1*, by invoking the *NullStr1* procedure. The conditional execution of *NullStr1*, which depends on the value of *DebugOn*, demonstrates how to use the VBA conditional compilation feature. Note the # prefixes. By the way, the *NullStr1* succinctly reveals how to use a *For…Each* statement with an array. It loops through each of the elements in the *str1* array without ever specifying the exact number of elements in the array or the number of any element in the array.

3. The procedure uses the *ReDim* statement to enlarge the number of elements declared for the *str2* array, and it assigns a value to the new array element. This new element results in the *str2* array having one more element than the *str1* array. The *Print* method of the *Debug* object confirms this by contrasting the index ranges of the two arrays in the Immediate window.

4. The procedure copies elements from the local *str2* array into elements of the module-level *str1* array. It performs this task until there are no remaining module-level elements into which to copy values. The built-in *LBound* and *UBound* functions capture the smallest and largest index values for the module-level array. A *For…Each* loop determines the progression through the elements of the local array. The *ind1* variable tracks the index for the module-level array element into which the procedure copies a value. If the value of *ind1* exceeds the largest index value of the module-level array, the code processes an *Exit For* statement and stops copying values to the module-level array.

5. Another *For...Each* loop for the elements of the *str1* array passes successively through each value and prints that value to the Immediate window.

```
Sub ForEachArrayElement()
ReDim str2(1 To 3) As String
Dim el1 As Variant
Dim ind1 As Long

'Conditional compilation constant;
'set to False after debugging
#Const DebugOn = True

'Set all elements in str1 to Null
'if DebugOn flag is true
#If DebugOn Then
    NullStr1
#End If

'Assign values to array elements
'scoped at the procedure level;
'str2 and str1 have the same number of elements
str2(1) = "Rick"
str2(2) = "Dobson"
str2(3) = "8629"

'Redimension and preserve initial values;
'this makes str2 have one more element than str1
ReDim Preserve str2(1 To 4)
str2(4) = "rickd@cabinc.net"

'Print contrasting extents of str1 and st2 arrays
Debug.Print "Elements of str1 array have indexes " & _
    LBound(str1) & " through " & UBound(str1) & "," & _
    vbCrLf & "but elements of str2 array have indexes " & _
    "from " & LBound(str2) & " through " _
    & UBound(str2) & "."

'Copy procedure-level array elements into
'module-level array elements until str1
'has no more elements for copying into;
'element pointer (el1) must be a Variant
ind1 = LBound(str1)
For Each el1 In str2
    If ind1 > UBound(str1) Then Exit For
    str1(ind1) = el1
    ind1 = ind1 + 1
Next
```

```
'Print the values in str1
For Each el1 In str1
    Debug.Print el1
Next

End Sub


Sub NullStr1()
Dim el1 As Variant

'Assign Null to each element
'in str1 module-level array
For Each el1 In str1
    el1 = Null
Next

End Sub
```

To help clarify the operation of the *ForEachArrayElement* procedure, I included its output in Figure 1-22. Recall that, to achieve these results, you must declare the *str1* array at the module level with a statement such as *Dim str1(2) As String*.

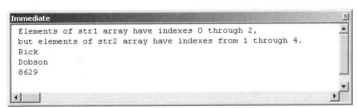

Figure 1-22 The output to the Immediate window from the *ForEachArrayElement* procedure.

Two points merit some extra commentary. First, conditional compilation is a relatively new VBA procedure introduced with Access 2000. You can use the feature to conditionally execute VBA code based on a conditional compiler constant that you declare and assign a value with the *#Const* directive. A new *#If...Then...#Else* directive allows your code to conditionally execute code. The *ForEachArrayElement* procedure uses a conditional compiler constant named *DebugOn*. The *#Const* directive sets this constant to True. An *#If...#End* block conditionally invokes the *NullStr1* procedure. I wanted to see the module-level element values in the process of developing the *ForEachArrayElement* procedure. Because the procedure writes over these values, it is not absolutely necessary to erase them. Therefore, you can bypass the calling of *NullStr1* by setting *DebugOn* to False in the *#Const* directive.

The second point that might not be obvious from reviewing the code is that you must declare the data type of the parameter that passes through the elements of the array in a *For…Each* statement as a Variant data type. This Variant data type argument has the name *el1* in the *ForEachArrayElement* and *NullStr1* procedures. The argument's data type is unrelated to the data type of the array elements. For example, notice that the *str1* and *str2* array elements both have String data types.

Do…Loop

The *Do…Loop* statement is yet another variety of looping statement available with VBA. The *Do…Loop* statement is a more flexible alternative to the *While…Wend* statement, which we won't cover. VBA retains *While…Wend* for backward compatibility.

You can use a *Do* loop to repeatedly execute a group of statements until a condition evaluates to either *True* or *False*. The *Do…Loop* statement syntax explicitly supports performing its test of a condition either before executing a block of statements or immediately after executing the block. As with the other looping statements, there is also a special statement for exiting a block in the midst of its execution. The two variations of syntax for the *Do…Loop* statement are as follows:

```
Do {While | Until} <condition>
    'Statements
    If <condition> Then
        Exit Do
    End If
    'Statements
Loop
```

And:

```
Do
    'Statements
    If <condition>Then
        Exit Do
    End If
    'Statements
Loop {While | Until} <condition>
```

The next two procedures illustrate the syntax for these two *Do* loop formulations. The *DaysToNextMonth* function procedure accepts a date and returns the number of days from that date to the first of the next month. If you enter 2/28/2002, the procedure counts the number days, including the one you input, to the first of next month, which is 3/1/2002 in our example. (See Figure 1-23 for the output to the Immediate window.) The procedure then sets the function's name, which serves as a counter variable, to 0. The third line launches a *Do* loop with a condition that tests for the inequality of the next month and of the input date plus the quantity stored in the function's name. As long as they are unequal, the loop executes its block, which consists of one statement that increments the function's value to 1.

```
Public Function DaysToNextMonth(dtmDateIn)
'Including input date
    dtmNextMonth = DateAdd("m", 1, dtmDateIn)
    DaysToNextMonth = 0
    Do While Month(dtmNextMonth) <> Month(dtmDateIn + DaysToNextMonth)
        DaysToNextMonth = DaysToNextMonth + 1
    Loop
End Function


Public Function DaysFromFirstOfLastMonth(dtmDateIn)
 'Not including input date
    dtmPreviousMonth = DateAdd("m", -1, dtmDateIn)
    dtm1stPreviousMonth = _
        DateValue(Month(dtmPreviousMonth) & "/1/" & _
            Year(dtmPreviousMonth))
    DaysFromFirstOfLastMonth = 0
    Do
        DaysFromFirstOfLastMonth = DaysFromFirstOfLastMonth + 1
    Loop While dtm1stPreviousMonth <> (dtmDateIn - _
        DaysFromFirstOfLastMonth)
End Function
```

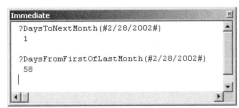

Figure 1-23 The output to the Immediate window from the *DaysToNextMonth* and *DaysFromFirstOfLastMonth* function procedures.

The *DaysFromFirstOfLastMonth* function procedure shows the effect of a condition test at the end of a *Do* loop. The output shows the number of days from 2/28/2002 to the first day of the previous month (1/1/2002), as shown in Figure 1-23. This equals 58 days, based on the 28 days in February and the last

30 days in January. This function begins by computing the previous month for the specified date. The function then passes that month to the *DateValue* function to determine the first day of that previous month. Just before starting the *Do* loop, the code sets *DaysFromFirstOfLastMonth* to 0. The code enters the loop without a condition test and increments *DaysFromFirstOfLastMonth* by 1. The condition test on the *Loop* line permits another pass through the loop as long as the input date minus *DaysFromFirstOfLastMonth* is less than the first of the previous month. In this way, the function counts 58 days from the input date to, but not including, the previous month's first day.

Part II

Data Access and Data Definition

2

Data Access Models: Part I

Microsoft Access 2000 supports two data access models: the traditional Data Access Objects (DAO) and ActiveX Data Objects (ADO). DAO targets just the Jet database engine. Access 2000 was the first Access version to support ADO for data access to Jet as well as other databases in a single programming language. With Access 2002, Microsoft improved on past functionality and added new capabilities to ADO programming. Instead of being based on a single database engine, ADO uses a common programming model to access data universally. It relies on OLE DB providers for low-level links to data sources. OLE DB technologies will eventually make their ODBC predecessors obsolete, much as ADO will replace DAO. Therefore, if you invest in learning ADO now, you will get on the fast track to adopting future improvements in data access with upcoming versions of Access. And you'll be able to programmatically manage more and different kinds of data sources.

DAO was the main data access model for Access developers from Access 1.0 through Access 97. Therefore, it is finely tuned to the Jet database engine. This feature is both a strength and a weakness. While DAO can still perform a few selected tasks for the Jet engine that are not possible or are very difficult to do with ADO, accessing data outside Jet using DAO is very awkward. ADO, however, was conceived as a universal data access language, and it is highly suitable for developing solutions based on the Web or on a LAN (local area network). DAO does not process data when used in a Web-based solution. For these reasons, DAO will not play a role in this book. For information on DAO code, see the Access online documentation and Microsoft's Support Online (support.microsoft.com/directory/). Click the Searchable Knowledge Base link for documents that discuss typical problems and their associated workarounds. Many of the articles include DAO code samples.

The subject of data access models is vast. To make this discussion more digestible, I've broken it into two chapters. This chapter and Chapter 3, "Data Access Models: Part II," focus primarily on data access for Jet with the ADO object model. The two chapters also include some coverage of ADO with other database engines—particularly Microsoft SQL Server. Numerous programming samples show you how to accomplish typical database chores.

This chapter begins with an overview of ActiveX Data Objects and then moves on to discuss the *Connection*, *Recordset*, and *Field* objects. In Chapter 3, you will learn about the *Command* and *Parameters* objects and the *Errors* collection. Chapter 3 also devotes considerable attention to techniques for managing access to the files on a Web server, as well as demonstrating the features of the new ADO *Record* and *Stream* objects. This topic also serves as a platform for exploring the new functionality of the *Recordset* object. Finally, Chapter 3 examines the subject of ADO event programming. Later chapters in this book will build on the information presented in Chapters 2 and 3 and will cover additional ADO topics, such as database replication, remote database access, and multiuser security.

ADO Overview

Access 2002 installs ADO version 2.5 by default. The Microsoft DAO 3.6 Object Library is still available for those who prefer to use it. As with ADO 2.1 from Access 2000, developers can still reference any of three ADO models: the ADODB library, the ADOX library, and the JRO library. New Microsoft Visual Basic for Applications (VBA) projects associated with Access database files and Access projects have a default reference to the ADODB library, but you must explicitly create a reference to the other two ADO models. Microsoft ships the sample Northwind database with a reference to the DAO 3.6 library. If you want to program with ADO, you must add a reference to one or more of the appropriate ADO libraries. Their shorthand names appear in the References dialog box, respectively, as:

- Microsoft ActiveX Data Objects 2.5 Library
- Microsoft ADO Ext. 2.5 for DDL and Security
- Microsoft Jet and Replication Objects 2.5 Library

Note   If you install the optional SQL Server 2000 Desktop Engine that ships with Access 2000, Access automatically upgrades ADO 2.5 to version 2.6. If you experience difficulty connecting to a commercial release of SQL Server 2000, you will need the 2.6 version of ADO. See Chapter 14, "Using Access to Build SQL Server Solutions: Part I," for a description of how to install the SQL Server 2000 Desktop Engine.

Recall that the ADODB library reference installs by default, but references for the other two libraries do not appear unless you specifically add them. By segmenting data access into three libraries, Access offers a smaller footprint for applications that do not require all three. Another major component of the Access 2002 data access strategy is reliance on OLE DB providers, which work with ADO to offer access to traditional data sources as well as new ones, such as e-mail and file directories. This vastly expands the power of database programming.

Although the ADODB library reference installs by default, users can remove the reference from their workstation settings. You should account for this in your custom applications by either issuing a warning about installing the ADODB library when you need it or automatically creating the reference programmatically. Chapter 9, "Class, Form, and Report Modules," provides a code sample that demonstrates how to add library references programmatically with the *References* collection in the Access library.

The ADODB library is a small, lightweight library that contains core objects and offers the basics for making connections, issuing commands, and retrieving recordsets; it also enables recordset navigation. You can use this library to perform basic database maintenance tasks, such as modifying, adding, and deleting records. The nonhierarchical design of this library makes it easy for beginning programmers to use.

The ADOX library supports data definition language and security issues. It offers objects that let you examine and control a database's schema. For example, it lets you create tables and relations. The model includes support for referential integrity and cascading updates and deletes. It also offers the *Procedures* and *Views* collections, as well as the *Users* and *Groups* collections for user-level database security. The elements of the *Procedures* and *Views* collections comprise what Access developers normally refer to as queries. The *Catalog* object is a container for the tables, groups, users, procedures, and views that compose a schema.

The JRO library enables Jet database replication. Access 2002 supports database replication with both Jet and SQL Server databases. Database replication is especially important for applications built with Access database files (.mdb files) because this capability vastly extends their availability. Chapter 13, "Replicating Databases," covers database replication in depth, showing you how to program it with the JRO library and how to manage replica collections with the Replication Manager in Microsoft Office Developer Edition.

Before you can use any of the ADO libraries, you must create a reference to at least one of them. You do this from the Visual Basic Editor (VBE) window by using the Tools-References command. Figure 2-1 shows the References dialog box with all three libraries selected. Notice that the screen shot uses the 2.6 versions of these libraries. If you do not load the SQL Server 2000 Desktop Engine shipping with Office XP, you will have the 2.5 versions available. Use them instead of the 2.6 versions.

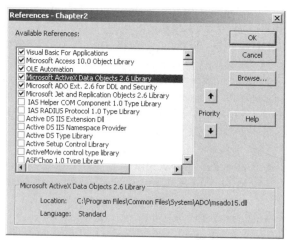

Figure 2-1 You can use the References dialog box to add ADO libraries to an application.

While it might be more convenient to select all three ADO libraries, you can conserve resources by selecting just the libraries that you need. Experiment with the selections for your applications and the machines on which they run to determine what's optimal for your environment. If you have a production application that runs on many types of machines, you should conserve resources for other application requirements. Keep in mind that you can load references at run time with the *References* collection from the Access *Application* object.

Note   Choosing a library version isn't always as simple as picking the reference with the highest version number. For example, if you need the same application to run on multiple machines, some of which have the 2.6 version of ADO and others that have the 2.5 version, you should use the 2.5 version to eliminate the possibility of a failure due to a MISSING reference on computers without the 2.6 version of the ADODB library. Alternatively, you can upgrade the ADO version on machines running the 2.5 version by installing the Microsoft Desktop Engine that ships with Office XP. This latter approach is especially appealing when some of your machines require ADO 2.6 for a specific purpose, such as interfacing with SQL Server 2000.

One major advantage that ADO offers is an event model. ODBCDirect, which is a part of the DAO 3.5 and DAO 3.6 libraries that targets programmatic access to SQL Server, permits asynchronous operations, but ADO provides events. This frees an application from polling an object and checking its *StillExecuting* property. Instead, you can create event handlers to respond to events whenever they occur. Unlike the simple event procedures that you invoke for forms and reports, ADO event programming is an advanced capability. You will typically use ADO events with unbound forms, and your application is likely to supply values for controls from an ADO recordset. Chapter 3 will discuss ADO event programming in more detail.

OLE DB data providers make ADO powerful by providing a consistent programming interface for different data sources. Data providers, as well as other types of providers, offer an easy way to extend the kinds of data sources that you can reach with ADO programs. Access 2002 ships with a variety of OLE DB data providers for traditional databases, including those for Jet, SQL Server, Oracle, and general ODBC data sources. In addition, Microsoft makes available other data providers that enable Access 2002 developers to process such nontraditional sources as pages and folders at a Web site, as well as Windows NT 4 and Windows 2000 directory services. Just as with ODBC drivers, you can obtain OLE DB data providers from Microsoft as well as third-party sources. Table 2-1 lists the OLE DB data providers available from Microsoft, along with brief descriptions of when to use them.

Table 2-1 Microsoft-Supplied OLE DB Data Providers

Provider Name	Description
Microsoft OLE DB Provider for ODBC	Use this provider to connect to any ODBC-compliant data source for which you do not have a more specific OLE DB provider, such as the SQLOLEDB provider for SQL Server.
Microsoft OLE DB Provider for Microsoft Indexing Service	Use this provider to gain read-only access to file system and Web data indexed by the Microsoft Indexing Service.
Microsoft OLE DB Provider for Microsoft Active Directory Service	Use this provider for read-only access to Microsoft Active Directory Service Interfaces (ADSI). Currently, this provider connects to Windows NT 4, Windows 2000, and Novell directory services, as well as any LDAP-compliant directory service.
OLE DB Provider for Microsoft Jet	Use this provider to connect to Jet 4 databases.
Microsoft OLE DB Provider for SQL Server	Use this provider to connect to databases on SQL Server.
Microsoft OLE DB Provider for Oracle	Use this provider to connect to Oracle databases.
Microsoft OLE DB Provider for Internet Publishing	Use this provider to access resources served by Microsoft FrontPage and Microsoft Internet Information Services (IIS). In other words, you can manipulate and open Web pages at a Web site programmatically from an Access application.

Enter the provider name from Table 2-1 into Access 2002's Help to obtain more information about it. Standard information includes the purpose of the provider, as well as the syntax for referencing it. Code samples presented in this chapter will demonstrate the use of these providers.

At least two remaining issues affect the use of providers with ADO. First, ADO makes service providers (as well as data providers) available. Service providers can consume data from a data provider and offer services not directly available from a data provider, such as query processing. At the time of this writing, Microsoft offers three ADO service providers, which I'll describe momentarily.

Second, the Microsoft Cursor Service for OLE DB enhances native cursor services available from data providers. Microsoft calls this a service component (as opposed to either a service provider or a data provider) because the Cursor

Service for OLE DB focuses on the cursor element of a data provider. Table 2-2 includes a short summary of the three Microsoft service providers and the service component.

Table 2-2 Microsoft-Supplied ADO Service Providers and Components

Provider/Component Name	Description
Microsoft Data Shaping Service for OLE DB	Use this service to construct hierarchical (or shaped) recordset objects. These shaped recordset objects expose data in the same style as main/sub forms.
Microsoft OLE DB Persistence Provider	Use this service to persist a recordset in a proprietary or an Extensible Markup Language (XML) file format. This capability is particularly valuable when computers must access data sources to which they are not always connected.
Microsoft OLE DB Remoting Provider	Use this service to invoke data providers on a computer with a database server from another computer. This provider offers Access developers the opportunity to build advanced three-tiered solutions by referring to a remote server.
Microsoft Cursor Service for OLE DB	Use this service to expand the functionality of native cursors for a service provider. For example, the Cursor Service for OLE DB can expand the range of cursor types available for a data source, dynamically construct an index to speed searches with the *Find* method for ADO recordsets, and allow the specification of sort criteria for recordsets.

The providers and component in Table 2-2 have many uses. This chapter specifically illustrates several of them. Because I emphasize other topics in the chapter, data shaping (and its provider) does not receive as much coverage. A hierarchically shaped recordset can more parsimoniously represent data in a one-to-many relationship than a standard SQL join can. If you find relational database representations unsatisfactorily expressing links between elements, you might find hierarchical-shaped recordsets useful. If you need to know more about this topic, enter the phrase *data shaping* into a Help prompt in the VBE to open this section in the Visual Basic Help file.

The ADODB object library has grown from seven objects in the release of Access 2000 to nine objects with Access 2002. The two new object classes are *Record* and *Stream* objects. While the number of collections stayed the same, you can now use the *Fields* and *Properties* collections with the new *Record* object.

See the latest version of the ADODB library objects, shown in Figure 2-2. The object model still remains a relatively flat one in comparison to DAO. This makes it fast, lightweight, and easy to learn. In addition, ADO has vastly superior extensibility than DAO. For traditional database development tasks, you are still likely to find yourself using the objects provided with Access 2000. However, for those of you working in emerging nontraditional areas, such as file services management and Web file management, the new *Record* and *Stream* objects will have special appeal.

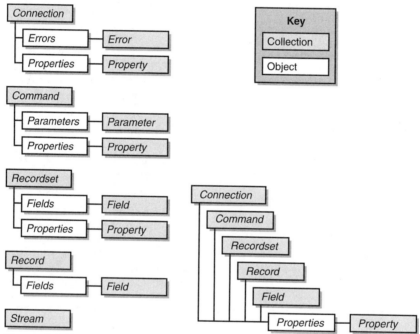

Figure 2-2 The ADODB object library.

The *Connection* Object

The *Connection* object establishes a link to a database. You always use a *Connection* object implicitly or explicitly when you work with a database. When you explicitly create this object, you can efficiently manage one or more connections and reassign the roles that these connections serve in an application. By implicitly creating a *Connection* object, you can shorten your code. Each new object that you create with an implicit connection consumes more resources. If your application has only one or two objects, each requiring its own connection, implicit connections might serve your needs best. ADO lets you choose how to create and manage connections as you see fit.

Unlike DAO, ADO is a general data access language, so not all of its properties, methods, or even data types are appropriate for the Jet engine. There is, however, a special OLE DB provider for Jet 4. Microsoft introduced this provider with Access 2000, and it remains in Access 2002. Since *Connection* objects critically depend on provider specifications, the ability to set a *Connection* parameter that references the Jet 4 provider is valuable. This custom provider allows ADO to reflect many of the special strengths that Jet offers. When you refer to a database in another file, you might want to include a *Data Source* parameter, which points to the physical location of a database that is not in the current project.

Connecting to Databases

The following simple code sample, *OpenMyDB*, opens the familiar Northwind database. Notice that a *Dim* statement declares and creates a reference to *cnn1* as a *Connection* object. The use of the *Open* method on *cnn1* makes the database available to the rest of the procedure. Notice that the *Provider* and *Data Source* parameters appear within a single pair of double quotes. The *Provider* parameter points to the Jet 4 OLE DB provider, and the *Data Source* parameter points to the physical location of the Northwind database.

```
Sub OpenMyDB()
Dim cnn1 As New Connection
Dim rst1 As Recordset

'Create the connection
cnn1.Open "Provider=Microsoft.Jet.OLEDB.4.0;" & _
    "Data Source=C:\PMA Samples\Northwind.mdb;"

'Create recordset reference, and set its properties
Set rst1 = New ADODB.Recordset
rst1.CursorType = adOpenKeyset
rst1.LockType = adLockOptimistic

'Open recordset, and print a test record
rst1.Open "Customers", cnn1
Debug.Print rst1.Fields(0).Value, rst1.Fields(1).Value

'Clean up objects
rst1.Close
cnn1.Close
Set rst1 = Nothing
Set cnn1 = Nothing

End Sub
```

After creating a reference to the connection, the code instantiates a *Recordset* object. Instantiating an object reference makes it available for use within the procedure. Next the procedure assigns values to a couple of properties for the recordset. The next-to-last block of code opens the recordset and prints a couple of fields from the current record when the recordset initially opens. The *Open* method for a *Recordset* object can reference a connection to a database and some source of records in the database. The previous code selects all of the records from the *Customers* table in the Northwind database. The *Open* method initially makes the first record available based on the order of records in a source, such as a table ordered by its primary key. Just before closing, the procedure closes the recordset and connection and sets their object references to *Nothing*.

> **Note**   You can specify the connection to the database for the current Access database file with the syntax *CurrentProject.Connection*. If you have a table or query named *Customers* in your current database file, you can reference it by replacing *cnn1* in the preceding sample with *CurrentProject.Connection*. This eliminates the need for an explicit connection object when referring to the current database.

Although object references declared within a procedure normally go out of scope when the procedure closes, it is good programming practice to close objects and set them to *Nothing* before exiting a procedure. By setting an object reference to *Nothing*, you formally release the object's memory. This practice can help avoid memory leaks, which can slow an application. If objects do not close successfully when your application exits a procedure, the memory remains reserved for the object. After repeatedly running a procedure, these memory reservations can slow down your application.

Closing an object and setting it to *Nothing* provides other benefits besides inoculating your applications from memory leaks. First, an object must be closed in order for you to reassign its property settings. Second, setting a *Connection* object to *Nothing* can guard against the impact of a silent error and recovery by ADO. If your application reuses a *Connection* object but you fail to set its properties correctly, the ADO provider automatically and silently reverts to the object's prior setting. Setting a *Connection* object to *Nothing* after you are through with it forces a trappable run-time error for a *Connection* object reference with an improper setting. Implicitly creating a connection for an object also guards against errors that are not trappable, because the object has use of the connection just for its lifetime.

The next code sample, *OpenMySQLDB*, demonstrates two additional points about the behavior of the *Connection* object. First, this sample shows how to perform an analogous task for a SQL Server database instead of a Jet one. In this case, the database is the NorthwindCS database, a SQL Server database shipping with generally the same tables, queries, forms, reports, and data access pages as those in the Northwind Access database file.

Second, this sample highlights the similar programming ADO employs for two entirely different databases. In both this sample and the preceding one, you declare, instantiate, and open a *Connection* object in similar ways. The major difference is the connection string, which is always unique for individual data providers. This sample then instantiates a recordset, assigns it property settings, and uses the connection as a parameter for the recordset's *Open* method. This code is identical in the two procedures—despite the fact that the earlier sample references a file-server database and this one references a client/server database.

> **Note**   The first time you open the NorthwindCS Access project, it automatically attempts to install the NorthwindCS database if you do not have a copy of the Northwind SQL Server database on your local server. You install the NorthwindCS Access project in the same manner that you would the Northwind Access database file—just make a different selection during the initial Access installation or when you update the installation.

```
Sub OpenMySQLDB()
Dim cnn1 As Connection
Dim rst1 As Recordset
Dim str1 As String

'Create a Connection object after instantiating it,
'this time to a SQL Server database
Set cnn1 = New ADODB.Connection
str1 = "Provider=SQLOLEDB;Data Source=cab2000;" & _
    "Initial Catalog=NorthwindCS;User Id=sa;Password=password;"
cnn1.Open str1

'Create recordset reference, and set its properties
Set rst1 = New ADODB.Recordset
rst1.CursorType = adOpenKeyset
rst1.LockType = adLockOptimistic
```

(continued)

```
'Open recordset, and print a test record
rst1.Open "Customers", cnn1
Debug.Print rst1.Fields(0).Value, rst1.Fields(1).Value

'Clean up objects
rst1.Close
cnn1.Close
Set rst1 = Nothing
Set cnn1 = Nothing

End Sub
```

Notice that the connection string syntax is different between the first and second code samples. The *Provider* parameter in the second sample points at the "SQLOLEDB" provider. This is the ADO data provider specifically designed for SQL Server databases. When connecting to a SQL Server database, you must designate the server name, which is "cab2000" in this case, and the database name. As mentioned, this sample connects to the NorthwindCS database. The designation of a user ID and password depends on the type of authentication your SQL server uses. If your application uses SQL Server authentication, you must specify the user ID and password. If the SQL server for an application uses Windows NT authentication, you do not need to specify a user ID and password in your connection string. If your application ever runs on a Windows 98 computer or a computer disconnected from an office, department, or enterprise server, SQL Server authentication is a necessity. This is because your application will not necessarily have Windows NT or Windows 2000 available to authenticate the identification of users when it runs. Finally, notice that the call to the *Open* method for the *Connection* object uses a string variable rather than a string constant as an argument. This makes it easy for your application to construct connection strings based on user information and the availability of a Windows NT or Windows 2000 server.

The following sub procedure, *OpenFast*, also opens a recordset based on the *Customers* table in the Northwind Access database file and prints the first record. However, it uses fewer lines of code, and the code is less complicated than the preceding two samples because it implicitly creates a connection and accepts more default settings.

```
Sub OpenFast()
Dim rst1 As Recordset

'Less code, but potentially greater resource consumption
Set rst1 = New ADODB.Recordset
rst1.Open "Customers", "Provider=Microsoft.Jet.OLEDB.4.0;" & _
    "Data Source=C:\PMA Samples\Northwind.mdb;"
Debug.Print rst1.Fields(0), rst1.Fields(1)
```

```
'Clean up objects
rst1.Close
Set rst1 = Nothing

End Sub
```

Since there is no explicit connection, the *OpenFast* procedure does not need to declare a *Connection* object (and therefore doesn't have to open or close such an object). As you can see, the *Open* method for a *Recordset* object can include the essential connection information of a provider and a data source. Calling the Open method on a *Recordset* object instead of a *Connection* object requires only one additional parameter—the source for the recordset, which is the *Customers* table. The *Open* method relies on the default *CursorType* and *LockType* settings, which are, respectively, forward-only and read-only. These settings provide for very fast operations, but they do not offer a lot of functionality. Nevertheless, if they suit your needs and let you divert your attention to other aspects of application development, they might be the best choice.

The *ReuseAConnection* sub procedure shown next illustrates a couple of ADO programming features not yet covered and reinforces several others. The best way to discover what this sample offers is to step through it (for example, with the Step Into control on the Debug toolbar). First, the sample demonstrates how to reuse a *Connection* object (or any other ADO object). You must close an object before you can reset its properties so that the object can serve another purpose, such as to connect to a different database. If you step through the sample, you'll see that the code generates and traps a 3705 run-time error. The code in the error trap closes the *cnn1* connection so that the procedure can reuse the object reference to connect to another database.

```
Sub ReuseAConnection()
Dim cnn1 As ADODB.Connection
On Error GoTo connTrap

'Assign the connection reference
Set cnn1 = New ADODB.Connection

'Use Jet provider to connect to Northwind
cnn1.Open "Provider=Microsoft.Jet.OLEDB.4.0;" & _
    "Data Source=C:\PMA Samples\Northwind.mdb;"
'Run initially with the next statement commented;
'then rerun with the next statement uncommented
'cnn1.Close
```

(continued)

```
'Incrementally builds connection string.
'Forces error when the Connection object is already open.
cnn1.ConnectionString = "Provider=Microsoft.Jet.OLEDB.4.0;"
cnn1.ConnectionString = cnn1.ConnectionString & _
    "Data Source=C:\PMA Samples\Northwind_backup.mdb;"
cnn1.Open

connExit:
'Close any connection still open before exiting
cnn1.Close
Set cnn1 = Nothing
Exit Sub

connTrap:
If err.Number = 3705 Then
'Close an open connection for its reuse
    Debug.Print "Closing cnn1"
    cnn1.Close
    Resume
Else
    Debug.Print err.Number; err.Description
    Debug.Print cnn1.Provider
    Debug.Print cnn1.Provider; cnn1.ConnectionString
End If

End Sub
```

The *ReuseAConnection* sub procedure demonstrates another other point worthy of your attention. Notice the *cnn1* declaration includes an ADODB prefix before *Connection*. While not necessary, this is good programming practice. This is especially true when a VBA project has references to both the DAO and ADODB libraries. Since both libraries contain classes with the same name, you might end up with an object based on the wrong class if you do not use the library prefix in your declaration. As you work with more and more references (an easy way to expand the capabilities of your applications), it becomes increasingly desirable to use library name prefixes. The chance of your libraries having identical names for different classes increases as you reference more libraries.

If you are not highly experienced with VBA programming, take note of the syntax for declaring an error trap. Just like events, errors happen. In many cases, these errors do not necessarily indicate a problem with the code in a solution (other than the need for more code for an error trap). Error traps give your solutions a way to dynamically adapt to run-time errors.

Adding an error trap to a procedure requires three steps. First, you need an *On Error* statement somewhere before the first place in a procedure that an error is possible (for example, immediately after a *Sub* or *Function* statement). This *On Error* statement should direct the program flow to a portion of the procedure that diagnoses the error and responds appropriately. Building this section is the second step. In the sample, the *connTrap* label marks an area of the procedure that fixes a 3705 error by closing the connection and resuming where the error occurred. If another type of error occurs, the trap prints the built-in error diagnostics along with the connection string associated with the error before concluding. The third step to a successful error trap is the insertion of code to exit the procedure before the error-trap logic and after the last line of code in the normal body of the program. Failing to complete this step can cause your application to wander into the error-trap area when no error exists.

> **Note**   It is often a good practice *not* to close and remove objects when you detect an error. This is because run-time errors can result from an unanticipated problem associated with the instantiation, closing, or opening of object references. If such an error occurs, looping to a code segment that attempts to close a noninstantiated object can generate an infinite loop.

One of the major strengths of ADO is its ability to connect to remote data sources. The *ThreeWaysToConnectRemotely* procedure highlights three different syntaxes for connecting to remote databases:

```
Sub ThreeWaysToConnectRemotely()
Dim cnn1 As ADODB.Connection
On Error GoTo connTrap

'Assign the connection reference
Set cnn1 = New ADODB.Connection

'A connection based on SQLOLEDB
With cnn1
    .Provider = "SQLOLEDB"
    .ConnectionString = "data source = cab2000;" & _
        "user id = sa; Password=password; initial catalog =Pubs"
    .Open
End With
cnn1.Close

'Use connection string parameters with MSDASQL provider.
'Notice syntax difference from MSDASQL and SQLOLEDB providers.
cnn1.Open "Provider=MSDASQL;Driver=SQL Server;" & _
    "Server=cab2000;Database=Pubs;uid=sa;pwd=password;"
cnn1.Close
```

(continued)

```
'Designation of the provider, or even the user ID and password,
'might not be necessary with a DSN
cnn1.Open "DSN=Pubs; User ID=sa; Password=password"
'The following close, in combination with the next one,
'raises a 3704 error number
cnn1.Close

connExit:
'Close any connection still open before exiting
cnn1.Close
Set cnn1 = Nothing
Exit Sub

connTrap:
If err.Number = 3704 Then
'The connection is already closed; skip close method
    Resume Next
Else
'Unanticipated run-time error
    Debug.Print err.Number; err.Description
    Debug.Print cnn1.Provider; cnn1.ConnectionString
End If

End Sub
```

All three examples in the *ThreeWaysToConnectRemotely* procedure connect to the *Pubs* database on a server named "cab2000". The first connection uses the SQLOLEDB provider. Consider using this provider whenever you are connecting to a SQL Server database. The second example in the code reveals the correct syntax for using the MSDASQL provider, the default provider. If you omit the provider name from a connection string, ADO automatically uses this provider. This provider is appropriate for databases that do not have a specific OLE DB data provider. The third example in the procedure uses a data source name (DSN) to designate the connection string. This technique is very popular when using ADO on a Web server and in some large organizations that push the DSN onto each computer on a network. Use the ODBC Data Source Administrator available through the Control Panel in Windows 98 and Windows NT or the Administration Tools menu on Windows 2000 to create a DSN. The sample explicitly specifies a user ID and password. This is necessary because the connection string specifies SQL Server authentication. With Windows NT authentication, you do not need to specify a user ID and password.

> Note   You can readily hide the user ID and password with either of two approaches. First, VBA offers you the opportunity to lock projects for viewing except by those users with a password. Second, you can convert your .mdb file to an .mde format. This process removes all editable code. Both approaches receive more coverage in Chapter 12, "Working with Multiuser Databases."

The *Mode* Property

By default, the *Connection* object's *Open* method creates a database for shared access. However, you can set the *Connection* object's *Mode* property to any of eight other settings that grant various degrees of restricted access to a database. These mode settings for *Connection* objects pertain generally to recordsets and commands that inherit *Connection* object settings through their *ActiveConnection* property. Additionally, when you open a *Recordset* object on a *Command* object, the *Recordset* object inherits the mode setting that applies to the command. *Record* and *Stream* objects, like *Connection* objects, have a *Mode* argument for their *Open* methods.

The following code shows the impact of the read-only mode setting on the ability to update a recordset. Depending on the value of a conditional compiler constant named *varPermitError*, the procedure opens the Northwind database in either the default shared mode or read-only mode. Since the procedure attempts to update the *Customers* table in the Northwind database, opening the database in read-only mode forces a run-time error. Setting the *varPermitError* constant to True causes the error by setting the *Mode* property for *cnn1* to read-only mode. The recordset inherits this setting through its *ActiveConnection* property. An error trap catches the error and shuts down the program gracefully with a custom error message.

```
Sub OpenLookOnly()
On Error GoTo LookOnlyTrap
Dim cnn1 As New ADODB.Connection
Dim rst1 As ADODB.Recordset
Dim varPermitError As Variant

'Set varPermitError to True to generate
'error from Mode property restriction
#Const varPermitError = True
```

(continued)

```
'Instantiate a Connection object, and
'conditionally set it to read-only data access
Set cnn1 = New ADODB.Connection
#If varPermitError = True Then
    cnn1.Mode = adModeRead
#End If

'Open the Connection object
cnn1.Open "Provider=Microsoft.Jet.OLEDB.4.0;" & _
    "Data Source=C:\PMA Samples\Northwind.mdb;"

'Use the next line to determine the default mode setting
Debug.Print cnn1.Mode
Set rst1 = New ADODB.Recordset
rst1.ActiveConnection = cnn1
rst1.Open "Customers", , adOpenKeyset, adLockOptimistic, adCmdTable

'An adModeRead setting for cnn1.Mode causes an error in this
'procedure when you execute the next two lines
rst1.Fields("CustomerID") = "xxxxx"
rst1.Update
Debug.Print rst1.Fields("CustomerID")

LookOnlyExit:
'Clean up objects
rst1.Close
cnn1.Close
Set rst1 = Nothing
Set cnn1 = Nothing
Exit Sub

LookOnlyTrap:
If err.Number = -2147217911 Then
'Error -2147217911 signals an attempt to edit a database open
'in read-only mode
    MsgBox "Forced error by attempt to update with a " & _
        "read-only connection.", vbInformation, _
        "Programming Microsoft Access Version 2002"
    Resume LookOnlyExit
Else
'Another unanticipated error occurred
    Debug.Print err.Number; err.Description
    MsgBox "View Immediate window for error diagnostics.", _
        vbInformation, "Programming Microsoft Access Version 2002"
End If

End Sub
```

Running the *OpenLookOnly* procedure with *varPermitError* equal to any value other than True opens the recordset in shared mode. This setting permits you to modify the value of table cells in the database. The first time you run the procedure it succeeds, unless you previously created a customer with a *CustomerID* field value of *"xxxxx"*. The procedure fails the second time you run it because it attempts to create a duplicate value for the primary key field. The *RestoreFirstCustomerID* procedure, found on the companion CD, replaces the *"xxxxx" CustomerID* value with the original value of *"ALFKI"*, which is the original *CustomerID* field value for the first customer in the table.

Besides demonstrating the impact of mode settings, the *OpenLookOnly* procedure is noteworthy for at least one other reason. The recordset *Open* method includes a parameter after the cursor-type setting of *adLockOptimistic*. This is the first sample to show this optional *Open* method parameter. In fact, the parameter has the name *Options*. You designate a value for the parameter with intrinsic constants that are members of either the *CommandTypeEnum* or the *ExecuteOptionEnum* enums. Recall from Chapter 1, "Introduction to VBA," that the Object Browser can help you with the member names and values of enums. The *Options* parameter can designate the type of source for a recordset and indicate how the recordset returns records (for example, synchronously or asynchronously). In the case of the *OpenLookOnly* procedure, the *Options* parameter of *adCmdTable* instructs the *Open* method to treat the first parameter designating *Customers* as a table accessed via an SQL query.

Table 2-3 describes the nine constants that you can use to set a connection's *Mode* property. These constants control the type of editing that one or more users can do through a connection to a database.

Table 2-3 *ConnectModeEnum* Members

Constant	Value	Behavior
adModeUnknown	0	Permissions not set or determined
adModeRead	1	Read-only permission
adModeWrite	2	Write-only permission
adModeReadWrite	3	Read/write permission
adModeShareDenyRead	4	Prevents others from opening record source with read permissions
adModeShareDenyWrite	8	Prevents others from opening record source with write permissions
adModeShareExclusive	12	Prevents others from opening the connection
adModeShareDenyNone	16	Shared access (default)
AdModeRecursive	4194304	Can propagate share-deny restrictions to children of the current record

The *OpenSchema* Method

The *Connection* object's *OpenSchema* method lets an application browse the objects in the collections available through a connection without the requirement of creating a reference to the ADOX library and enumerating the elements in a collection. The output from the *OpenSchema* method for an Access database file provides information about the design of a database, such as the names of user-defined tables, its queries, and even details such as column and table validation rules. The specific details depend on how a given OLE DB provider implements the general capabilities of the method. To discover additional details on the scope of this method, search Help in the VBE window for the term "SchemaEnum."

> Note   If you go to the SchemaEnum Help page in the ADO Help file, you will notice that the hyperlinks in the Description column do not work. The links only work from a Web page at the Microsoft Developer Network (MSDN) site. Open your browser to msdn.microsoft.com/library/psdk/dasdk/mdae0wfh.htm for a version of the page with working hyperlinks in the Description column. By the way, the information on the linked pages enumerates the field names, along with other useful information, for the recordset returned by the *OpenSchema* method.

The following code uses the *OpenSchema* method with the Jet 4 provider to list the user-defined tables available from a connection. These tables appear in the Database window when you select Tables from the Objects bar (and the default option of not showing system tables prevails). The procedure starts by declaring a connection and a recordset. The connection acts as the source for the output from the *OpenSchema* method. The recordset holds the output from the *OpenSchema* method. The argument for the *OpenSchema* method indicates that the method returns a rowset of all tables in the data source designated in the connection. By filtering the rows returned by the method, the procedure prints just the names of user-defined tables.

```
Sub OpenSchemaTableTables()
Dim cnn1 As ADODB.Connection
Dim rst1 As ADODB.Recordset

'Connect to the Northwind database
Set cnn1 = New ADODB.Connection
cnn1.Open "Provider=Microsoft.Jet.OLEDB.4.0;" & _
    "Data Source=C:\PMA Samples\Northwind.mdb;"
```

```
Set rst1 = cnn1.OpenSchema(adSchemaTables)

'Print just tables; other selection criteria include
'TABLE, ACCESS TABLE, and SYSTEM TABLE
Do Until rst1.EOF
    If rst1.Fields("TABLE_TYPE") = "TABLE" Then
        Debug.Print "Table name: " & _
            rst1.Fields("TABLE_NAME") & vbCr
    End If
    rst1.MoveNext
Loop

'Clean up objects
rst1.Close
cnn1.Close
Set rst1 = Nothing
Set cnn1 = Nothing

End Sub
```

New Access developers, and perhaps some experienced ones, might be surprised to learn that some types of queries can also be considered as tables. For example, you can use the *OpenSchema* method to discover the names of all stored queries that return rows and do not depend on parameters in an Access database file. Access database files typically refer to this type of query as a view. The following code sample is a simple adaptation of the preceding one; it enumerates all the views in a connection:

```
Sub OpenSchemaTableViews()
Dim cnn1 As ADODB.Connection
Dim rst1 As ADODB.Recordset

'Connect to the Northwind database
Set cnn1 = New ADODB.Connection
cnn1.Open "Provider=Microsoft.Jet.OLEDB.4.0;" & _
    "Data Source=C:\PMA Samples\Northwind.mdb;"

Set rst1 = cnn1.OpenSchema(adSchemaTables)

'Print just views; other selection criteria include
'TABLE, ACCESS TABLE, and SYSTEM TABLE
Do Until rst1.EOF
    If rst1.Fields("TABLE_TYPE") = "VIEW" Then
        Debug.Print "View name: " & _
            rst1.Fields("TABLE_NAME") & vbCr
    End If
    rst1.MoveNext
Loop
```

(continued)

```
'Clean up objects
rst1.Close
cnn1.Close
Set rst1 = Nothing
Set cnn1 = Nothing

End Sub
```

The information provided by the *OpenSchema* method can be substantially richer than just the names of tables within a database. Examine members of the *SchemaEnum* enum to discover the valid arguments for the *OpenSchema* method. You use an enum member to specify a domain about which to gather schema-based information and then examine the column names for the rowset returned by the method to retrieve the detailed information available for that category. These columns vary according to the enum member.

The *OpenSchemaConstraints* sub procedure that appears next uses the *adSchemaCheckConstraints* argument value to return the set of validation rules in an Access database file. Before listing information in individual rows from the rowset returned by the method, the procedure shows the syntax for enumerating the field column names. As you can see, the columns are zero-based. You can use this enumeration to help decide which detailed information you want to examine. The sample that follows lists the CONSTRAINT_NAME, CHECK_CLAUSE, and DESCRIPTION columns. Some additional code in the sample spaces the string data for columns evenly across the Immediate window. I will review the logic to achieve this result after we examine the procedure's output.

```
Sub OpenSchemaConstraints()
Dim cnn1 As ADODB.Connection
Dim rst1 As ADODB.Recordset
Dim int1 As Integer
Dim int2 As Integer
Dim i As Integer

'Connect to a backup of the Northwind database with a
'clean set of constraints
Set cnn1 = New ADODB.Connection
cnn1.Open "Provider=Microsoft.Jet.OLEDB.4.0;" & _
    "Data Source=C:\PMA Samples\Northwind_backup.mdb;"

'Open the constraints in the database
Set rst1 = cnn1.OpenSchema(adSchemaCheckConstraints)

'Demonstrate syntax for enumerating the column names
'in the recordset returned by the OpenSchema method;
'the columns vary depending on the method's parameter
```

```
For i = 0 To rst1.Fields.Count - 1
    Debug.Print rst1.Fields(i).Name
Next i

'Find the length of each of the first two columns
int1 = FindTheLongest(rst1, "CONSTRAINT_NAME") + 1
rst1.MoveFirst
int2 = FindTheLongest(rst1, "CHECK_CLAUSE") + 1
rst1.MoveFirst

'Print contraint names, expressions, and descriptions
Do Until rst1.EOF
    Debug.Print rst1(2) & String(int1 - Len(rst1(2)), " ") & _
        rst1(3) & String(int2 - Len(rst1(3)), " ") & " " & rst1(4)
    rst1.MoveNext
Loop

'Clean up objects
rst1.Close
cnn1.Close
Set rst1 = Nothing
Set cnn1 = Nothing

End Sub


Function FindTheLongest(rst1 As ADODB.Recordset, _
    FieldIndex As String) As Integer
Dim Length As Integer

'Loop to return longest string in a field
Do Until rst1.EOF
    Length = Len(rst1.Fields(FieldIndex))
    If Length > FindTheLongest Then
        FindTheLongest = Length
    End If
    rst1.MoveNext
Loop

End Function
```

The output from the *OpenSchemaConstraints* procedure appears in Figure 2-3. It begins by listing the names for the five columns from the *OpenSchema* method called with an *adSchemaCheckConstraints* argument. Next the output shows the constraints for the columns within the Access Northwind database file. The procedure succinctly provides that information by listing the table and column of each constraint along with the expression governing the input for a column.

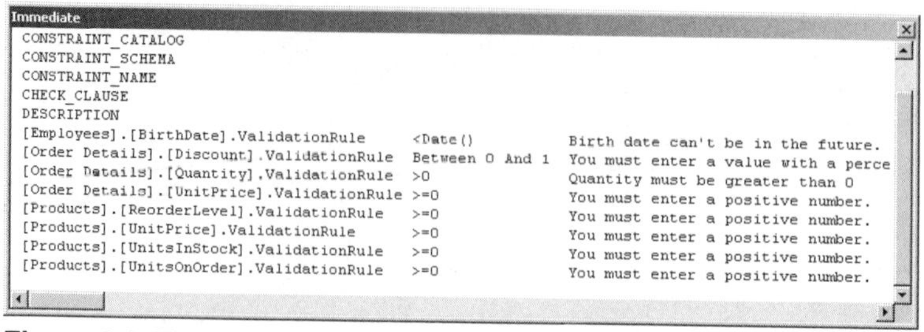

```
Immediate                                                                        ×
CONSTRAINT_CATALOG
CONSTRAINT_SCHEMA
CONSTRAINT_NAME
CHECK_CLAUSE
DESCRIPTION
[Employees].[BirthDate].ValidationRule    <Date()          Birth date can't be in the future.
[Order Details].[Discount].ValidationRule  Between 0 And 1  You must enter a value with a perce
[Order Details].[Quantity].ValidationRule  >0               Quantity must be greater than 0
[Order Details].[UnitPrice].ValidationRule >=0              You must enter a positive number.
[Products].[ReorderLevel].ValidationRule   >=0              You must enter a positive number.
[Products].[UnitPrice].ValidationRule      >=0              You must enter a positive number.
[Products].[UnitsInStock].ValidationRule   >=0              You must enter a positive number.
[Products].[UnitsOnOrder].ValidationRule   >=0              You must enter a positive number.
```

Figure 2-3 The Immediate window output from the *OpenSchemaConstraints* procedure.

Multicolumn string data of uneven lengths do not normally appear in neat columns within the Immediate window. The arrangement of columns is typically uneven because the length of a string in any column usually varies from row to row. This can make the results difficult to read. However, the preceding code sample circumvents this difficulty by padding each string after using a function procedure to determine the longest string in a field within a recordset. The main procedure spaces columns of string data evenly across the Immediate window, based on the longest strings in the CONSTRAINT_NAME and CHECK_CLAUSE columns.

The *Recordset* Object

As you've seen, a recordset is a programmatic construct for working with records. You can base your records on a table or a row-returning query stored in the current project or in another file, on an SQL statement, or on a command that returns rows. What you can do with a recordset depends on its OLE DB provider and on native data source attributes for the *Connection* object or connection string associated with the recordset's *ActiveConnection* property.

While you can extract recordsets using other objects, such as connections and commands, the *Recordset* object's rich mix of properties and methods make it a natural choice for doing much of your rowset processing. You can use recordsets to perform multiple actions against a set of rows: you can navigate between rows; print all or some of their contents; add, revise, and delete records; find records; and filter records to select one row or any subset of rows from a full recordset. There are two methods for finding records: *Find* and *Seek*. They offer related but not identical benefits, and they have contrasting requirements. Historically, recordsets are nonpersistent objects—they normally exist only while they are open in a program. Access 2000 and later versions of the program allow developers to persist recordsets to disk and then reopen them later.

Selected Recordset Properties

This section will introduce you to recordsets by describing some of their properties. I will briefly review a few properties of the *Recordset*. Use the Object Browser in the VBE to survey the full range of recordset properties and to further explore the properties that this section summarizes.

A recordset's *ActiveConnection* property lets your application tap an open connection to support a recordset. You can set this property after instantiating the object reference for the recordset. However, the reference must be closed. Using this property simplifies your *Open* method statement for the recordset. Setting the recordset's *ActiveConnection* property to a previously opened *Connection* object eliminates the need for including a connection string as part of the recordset's *Open* method statement. When you set the *ActiveConnection* property before the calling the *Open* method, you do not even need to reference an existing connection in the *Open* method statement. In that case, the *Connection* object is implicitly created for you.

The cursor type is among the most basic features of a recordset. Use the CursorType property to designate a cursor for a recordset. The property setting determines the ways you can navigate through the recordset, the visibility of changes by other users, and the types of locks that you can impose on its records. ADO supports four cursor types:

- **Dynamic**   This type of cursor lets users view changes to a data source made by other users. It enables recordset maintenance functions such as adding, changing, and deleting records, and it permits bidirectional navigation around a database. Users can see all changes to a database made by other users. Assign an intrinsic constant of *adOpenDynamic* to the *CursorType* property to specify this type of cursor.

- **Keyset**   This cursor has many of the properties of a dynamic cursor, except it does not offer immediate access to records added by other users. Records deleted by other users are inaccessible, but they appear in the recordset with a marker. Invoke a recordset's *Requery* method to view records added by other users and to clear the deleted markers for records removed by other users. Assign an intrinsic constant of *adOpenKeyset* to the *CursorType* property to designate this type of cursor.

- **Static**   This cursor is a snapshot of a recordset at a particular point in time. It allows bidirectional navigation. Changes to the database by other users are not visible. This type of cursor is suitable when you do not need information about updates by other users, such as reports from a specific moment in time. Use an intrinsic constant setting of *adOpenStatic* to create this type of cursor.

■ **Forward-only**   Sometimes called the fire-hydrant cursor, this type moves in one direction only and can speed up cursor performance. This is the default ADO cursor type. If you need another type of cursor, you must set the *CursorType* property before opening the recordset. If you are changing a recordset's cursor type back to the default setting, assign *adOpenForwardOnly* to its *CursorType* property.

> **Note**   Developers migrating from DAO will be surprised to learn that the keyset cursor is not the default ADO cursor type. You must explicitly designate *adOpenKeyset* as the *CursorType* property if your application requires a keyset cursor.

The *LockType* property partially interacts with the cursor type because it controls how users can manipulate a recordset. One lock-type setting (*adLockReadOnly*) specifically matches forward-only cursors. This is the default lock type. Table 2-4 describes the four possible settings for the *LockType* property. The *adLockBatchOptimistic* setting is used specifically for remote databases, such as SQL Server or Oracle, as opposed to a local Jet database.

Table 2-4 *LockTypeEnum* **Members**

Constant	Value	Behavior
adLockUnspecified	−1	Only for use with recordset clones. One of two possible clone lock-type settings; the other is *adLockReadOnly*.
adLockReadOnly	1	Read-only access (default).
adLockPessimistic	2	Locks a record as soon as a user chooses to start editing it.
adLockOptimistic	3	Locks a record only when a user chooses to commit edits back to the database.
adLockBatchOptimistic	4	Allows edits to a batch of records before an attempt to update a remote database from the local batch of records; use with the *UpdateBatch* method to propagate changes to a local cache back to a remote server.

Note   A recordset's cursor-type property setting interacts with its lock-type setting with lock type taking precedence over cursor type. If you designate a forward-only cursor type with a lock type other than read-only (*adLockReadOnly*), ADO overrides your cursor-type setting. Similarly, ADO automatically converts a forward-only cursor type to a keyset cursor type if you designate optimistic locking.

ADO supports two ways to update data in a data source. When you specify an *adLockOptimistic* or *adLockPessimistic* setting for the *LockType* property, your application immediately updates a record whenever it invokes the *Update* method for a recordset. By using the *adLockBatchOptimistic* intrinsic constant for the *LockType* property, your application can save up changes to one or more records until the application issues an *UpdateBatch* method for a recordset. The *UpdateBatch* method then transfers all changes from a local record cache to disk. If the update does not succeed because of conflicts with the underlying recordset, as in an attempt to revise a deleted record, ADO generates a run-time error. Use the *Errors* collection to view warnings and the *Filter* property with an *adFilterAffectedRecords* setting to locate records with conflicts.

Use the *CursorLocation* property to invoke the Cursor Service for OLE DB. Refer back to Table 2-2 for a short description of the capabilities that ADO makes available through this service. Set the *CursorLocation* property to the *adUseClient* intrinsic constant for a *Recordset* object or a *Connection* object. The *CursorLocation* property also enables the *Seek* method. You cannot use the *Seek* method to search a recordset unless its *CursorLocation* property equals the *adUseServer* intrinsic constant.

A recordset *Sort* property can affect the results of both the *Find* and *Move* methods. (See the next section for more on these methods.) This property designates one or more fields that can determine the order in which rows display. The *Sort* property setting allows the designation of an ascending or descending order for any field. The default is ascending order. The *Sort* property settings do not physically rearrange the underlying rows—they merely determine the order in which a recordset makes its rows available.

The *Filter* property for a recordset defines a subset of the rows from an existing recordset. While this property has specialized applications for database synchronization and batch updating of a remote data source, it can also be a simple alternative to defining a new recordset based on an SQL statement or other source. If you already have a recordset and you need only a subset for another purpose, this property can serve admirably. Filter rules can contain compound as well as simple criteria statements. Set a *Filter* property to *adFilterNone* to remove a filter setting from a recordset and restore the full set of original values.

Selected Recordset Methods

Recordset methods complement recordset properties as a means of manipulating the values in a recordset. This section offers a brief review of selected methods and will give you a general idea of the kinds of functions that methods enable you to perform with recordsets. Use the Object Browser to survey the total set of recordset methods. You can get detailed help for any method by clicking the Help control in the Object Browser window.

The recordset's *Open* method is one common route for making a recordset available in a procedure. The source argument is the most critical one for this method. It designates the data source on which the method patterns the object that it opens. Typical options for the source argument include a table, an SQL statement, a saved recordset file, a *Command* object, or a stored procedure. Access 2002 introduces the option of a URL or a *Stream* object as a potential source for a recordset. You use the *Open* method's *Options* argument to designate the source type when you open a recordset. When you designate a *Stream* object as the source for a recordset, you should not designate any other parameters.

Several methods enable recordset navigation. These navigation methods also allow you to specify the current record in a recordset, which is necessary or desirable for certain methods, such as the *Find* method. These four methods reflect functionality comparable to that of a standard built-in bound form:

- **MoveFirst**   This method changes the current record position to the first record in a recordset. The order of records depends on the current index or, if no index exists, on the order of entry. This method functions with all cursor types. Its use with forward-only cursors can force a reexecution of the command that generated the recordset.

- **MoveLast**   This method establishes the last record in a recordset as the current record position. It requires a cursor type that supports backward movement or at least movement based on bookmarks. Using this method with a forward-only cursor generates a run-time error.

- **MoveNext**   This method relocates the current record position one record forward (that is, in the direction of the recordset's final record). If the current record position is the last record, the recordset's *EOF* property is set to True. If this method is called when the recordset's *EOF* property is already True, a run-time error results.

■ *MovePrevious*   This method sends the current record position one record backward. If the current record position is the first record, the recordset's *BOF* property is set to True. If this method is called when the recordset's *BOF* property is already True, a run-time error results. This method also generates a run-time error if you use it with a forward-only cursor type.

The *Move* method works differently than the other four recordset navigation methods because it can move the current record position a variable number of records in either direction. You use a positive argument to indicate movement toward the last record and a negative argument to specify movement toward the first record. If a move will extend beyond the first or last record, the *Move* method sets the recordset's *BOF* or *EOF* property to True. If that property is already True, the *Move* method generates a run-time error. Movement is relative to the current record unless you specify a *Start* parameter, in which case you specify movement from the first or last record.

You can enhance the *Move* method's performance in a couple of ways by using it with a recordset's *CacheSize* property set to greater than the default value, which is 1. *CacheSize* settings cause ADO to store a fixed number of records in the local workstation's memory. Because it is much faster to retrieve records from local memory than from a provider's data store, you can speed record navigation by using a larger cache size. With a forward-only cursor and a larger cache size, you can actually enable backward scrolling as well as forward scrolling. If your cache setting is equal to the number of records in a recordset, you can scroll the full extent of the recordset in both directions. The *CacheSize* property does not enable backward scrolling within the cache with the *MovePrevious* method when using a forward-only cursor. However, you can use the *Move* method with a negative argument to achieve backward scrolling.

The recordset's *Find* method searches for the first record that matches a specified selection criterion. While this method bears a striking similarity to a collection of *Find* methods in Access 97 and earlier Access versions, the Access 2002 version of *Find* has a different syntax and behavior. Rather than attempt to map the similarities and differences, you should simply learn the syntax and behavior of the new version.

The new *Find* method takes as many as four arguments. The first argument is required and is the criterion for the search. Its syntax follows that of SQL statement WHERE clauses. If you do not specify any other arguments, the method searches from the current record through the last record to find a record that matches the criterion. Once the method finds a match, you must explicitly move off that record to find a subsequent match in the recordset. If there is no match, the method sets the recordset's *EOF* property to True. See the online help for a description of the remaining three optional arguments. The ADO event programming sample you will see in Chapter 3 also illustrates the use of these other *Find* arguments.

Several requirements govern the operation of the *Find* method. You must set the current record in a recordset before invoking the *Find* method. The only required argument for the *Find* method is a criterion indicating what to search for. You can only search for a value in a single field at a time. The default start location for a search in a recordset is the current row. You can also specify the starting row by using the method's arguments. This approach removes the need to reposition the current row. Otherwise, you must set the current record in a recordset before invoking the *Find* method. You can use one of the *Move* method variations to set the current record. If the *CursorLocation* property is *adUseClient*, the *Find* method can dynamically create indexes for fields that do not have an index specified in the recordset source. These are dynamic indexes that do not permanently update the source for a recordset.

Note   Although the *Find* method works only for one field at a time, ADO readily permits the development of subsets from a data source based on two or more fields. For example, you can open a recordset using a *Select* statement with compound criteria or filter an existing recordset with compound criteria.

The *AddNew* method inserts a new record into a recordset. After you invoke the method, you set the values for the fields in a new row that you want to add. Then you either move off the record using a *Move* method or you call the *Update* method while still on the row. (You can modify the values in a field using a similar pair of techniques. You update fields by assigning them new values, and then you move off the record. Alternatively, you can remain on an edited record as long as you call the *Update* method. You can delete a record by simply navigating to it and then invoking the *Delete* method. The deleted record remains current until you move away from it.)

The *GetRows* method copies a recordset's contents from disk to an array in memory. This can make retrieving recordset values much faster since an application can gather data from memory rather than reading it from a disk storage device. Optional parameters enable you to specify subsets of an original recordset for copying into memory. You can designate a starting row to indicate when to start copying records, and you can designate which columns to include in the memory-based version of a recordset.

The *GetString* method enables you to return rows from a recordset as a sequence of text lines. This method is especially convenient for displaying values from a recordset in the Immediate window. Use *GetString* so that you don't need a loop to pass a group of rows from a recordset to the Immediate window. Optional parameters let you restrict the number of returned rows as well as the row and column delimiters for the values from a recordset. You can also designate a special value to represent fields with Null values.

Printing Recordset Rows

Printing recordset values to the Immediate window is a good tutorial for processing recordsets. As you first start to work with ADO recordsets, you will frequently be interested in testing whether you populated them with the intended values. The following procedure, *EasyLoop*, successively prints all the rows of a recordset. A loop passes through all the records and prints the first two fields of each record, *CustomerID* and *CompanyName*.

```
Sub EasyLoop()
Dim rst1 As ADODB.Recordset

'Instantiate and open recordset
Set rst1 = New ADODB.Recordset
With rst1
    .ActiveConnection = "Provider=Microsoft.Jet.OLEDB.4.0;" & _
        "Data Source=C:\PMA Samples\Northwind.mdb;"
    .Open "Customers", , , , adCmdTable
End With

'Loop through recordset
Do Until rst1.EOF
    Debug.Print rst1.Fields(0), rst1.Fields(1)
    rst1.MoveNext
Loop

'Clean up objects
rst1.Close
Set rst1 = Nothing

End Sub
```

Notice that the procedure has three parts. First, it instantiates a recordset and opens the recordset based on the *Customers* table. This table is the source for the recordset. The *ActiveConnection* property setting points the recordset at the database containing this table. The *Open* method for the *Recordset* object makes the rows of the source available to the procedure. Notice there are three vacant parameter spaces between the recordset's source and the *Options* parameter, *adCmdTable*. Since the statement specifies an *Options* parameter, it must include placeholders for the intervening parameters of the *ActiveConnection*, *CursorType*, and *LockType* properties. The procedure uses an assignment statement for the recordset's connection property, which is then used as the default value for the *ActiveConnection* parameter in the *Open* method and the *Connection* object is implicitly created. By not including values for the *CursorType* and *LockType* settings, the procedure accepts the default values of *adOpenForwardOnly* and *adLockReadOnly*.

The second part of the procedure loops through all the rows in the recordset while printing the first and second field values in each row to the Immediate window. The sample uses a *Do* loop to navigate through the recordset until reaching an *EOF* flag after the last record. The *MoveNext* method advances the cursor one row with each pass through the loop. The code demonstrates how to reference fields by their index number. The reference to the *Fields* collection for a recordset is not strictly necessary. For example, you can replace *rst1.Fields(0)* with *rst1(0)*. If you know the field names and prefer to use them, you can replace the column index numbers with names, such as *rst1.Fields("CustomerID")* or *rst1("CustomerID")*.

The third part of the procedure merely closes the *Recordset* object and sets its reference to Nothing. There is no need to close a *Connection* object since the code sample assigns a connection string rather than a *Connection* object to the recordset's *ActiveConnection* property.

One weakness of the *EasyLoop* procedure is that it prints only the values of the fields you specifically request. The *EasyLoop2a* procedure that follows circumvents this difficulty. No matter how many fields the data source for a recordset has, the procedure automatically prints all of them. In addition, it labels each value with its field name. The main trick to iterating through all the fields is to include a *For...Each...Next* loop inside the *Do* loop. The *For...Each...Next* loop iterates through the *Fields* collection for each row in the recordset while constructing a string that includes the field name and value for each field in the row. After passing through all the fields in the row, the code sample uses the *Left* function to trim the trailing two characters, which are the field delimiters added inside the *For...Each...Next* loop.

```
Sub EasyLoop2a()
Dim rst1 As ADODB.Recordset
Dim fldMyField As ADODB.Field
Dim strForRow As String

'Instantiate and open recordset
Set rst1 = New ADODB.Recordset
```

```
rst1.Open "customers", "Provider=Microsoft.Jet.OLEDB.4.0;" & _
    "Data Source=C:\PMA Samples\Northwind.mdb;"

'Loop through recordset and fields within rows
Do Until rst1.EOF
    strForRow = ""
    For Each fldMyField In rst1.Fields
        strForRow = strForRow & _
            fldMyField.Name & " = " & fldMyField.Value & "; "
    Next fldMyField
    strForRow = Left(strForRow, Len(strForRow) - 2)
    Debug.Print strForRow & vbCrLf
    rst1.MoveNext
Loop

'Clean up objects
rst1.Close
Set rst1 = Nothing

End Sub
```

Figure 2-4 shows the last two rows of output. You can scroll right in the Immediate window to view the whole record, but it would be more convenient if you could see the whole record without having to scroll the window.

Figure 2-4 The Immediate window output from the *EasyLoop2a* procedure.

The following adaptation of the preceding code sample breaks the line for a row into lines of about 60 characters. An *If...ElseIf* statement inserts as many as four *vbCrLf* dividers into each line for a customer. We cannot use a *Select...Case* statement in this situation because the condition is a compound one based on independent numeric and Boolean values. The procedure resets the Boolean values to their default values of False at the end of each customer.

```
Sub EasyLoop2b()
Dim rst1 As ADODB.Recordset
Dim fldMyField As Field
Dim strForRow As String
Dim bolGT60 As Boolean
Dim bolGT120 As Boolean
Dim bolGT180 As Boolean
Dim bolGT240 As Boolean
```

```
'Instantiate and open recordset
Set rst1 = New ADODB.Recordset
rst1.Open "customers", "Provider=Microsoft.Jet.OLEDB.4.0;" & _
    "Data Source=C:\PMA Samples\Northwind.mdb;"

'Loop through recordset and fields with rows.
'Insert vbCrLf after exceeding each multiple of 60 characters.
Do Until rst1.EOF
    strForRow = ""
    bolGT60 = False
    bolGT120 = False
    bolGT180 = False
    bolGT240 = False
    For Each fldMyField In rst1.Fields
        strForRow = strForRow & _
            fldMyField.Name & " = " & fldMyField.Value & "; "
        If Len(strForRow) > 60 And bolGT60 = False Then
            strForRow = strForRow & vbCrLf
            bolGT60 = True
        ElseIf Len(strForRow) > 120 And bolGT120 = False Then
            strForRow = strForRow & vbCrLf
            bolGT120 = True
        ElseIf Len(strForRow) > 180 And bolGT180 = False Then
            strForRow = strForRow & vbCrLf
            bolGT180 = True
        ElseIf Len(strForRow) > 240 And bolGT240 = False Then
            strForRow = strForRow & vbCrLf
            bolGT240 = True
        End If
    Next fldMyField
    strForRow = Left(strForRow, Len(strForRow) - 2)
    Debug.Print strForRow & vbCrLf
    rst1.MoveNext
Loop

'Clean up objects
rst1.Close
Set rst1 = Nothing

End Sub
```

Figure 2-5 shows the improvement in the formatting of the output to the Immediate window.

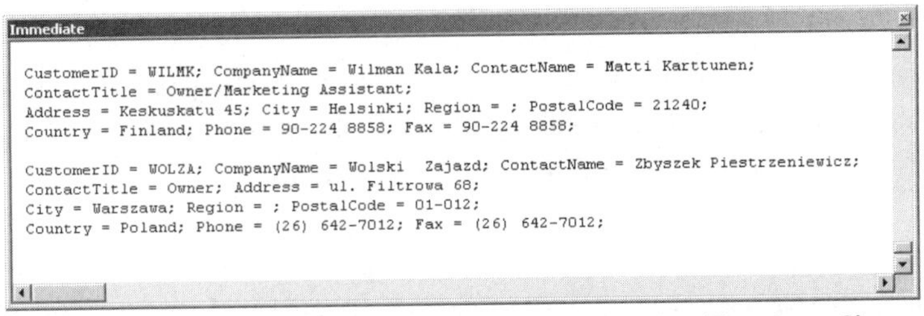

Figure 2-5 The Immediate window output from the *EasyLoop2b* procedure.

Looping is an easy way to perform an operation on the rows and columns within a recordset. However, it is not the most efficient way to retrieve field values from a recordset. The *NoEasyLoop* procedure that follows uses the *GetString* method to retrieve and print all the fields from the first five rows of a recordset in one step:

```
Sub NoEasyLoop()
Dim rst1 As ADODB.Recordset

'Instantiate and open recordset
Set rst1 = New ADODB.Recordset
rst1.Open "customers", _
    "Provider=Microsoft.Jet.OLEDB.4.0;" & _
    "Data Source=C:\PMA Samples\Northwind.mdb;"

'Print records without a loop
Debug.Print rst1.GetString(adClipString, 5, "; ")

'Clean up objects
rst1.Close
Set rst1 = Nothing

End Sub
```

The *GetString* method returns a recordset as a string. It can take up to five arguments; the code uses three of those arguments. According to the documentation, you must designate the *adClipString* constant as the first argument in order to assign values to the other optional arguments, which designate the column delimiters, row delimiters, and expressions for Null values. The second argument specifies the number of recordset rows to return. The preceding code sample requests the return of five rows. Leaving the second argument blank tells the method to return all the rows in the recordset. The third argument in the code sample designates a semicolon followed by a space as the column delimiter. The default column delimiter is a tab. The fourth and fifth arguments, neither of which appears in the code, specify a row delimiter and a representation for Null values. The default values for these arguments are a carriage return and a zero-length string.

> **Note**   In my experience, you can omit assigning a value of *adClipString* to the first argument and still specify values for row and column delimiters, as well as representations for Null values.

The *GetString* method replaces a pair of nested loops. If the defaults are acceptable, you can use the method without any arguments. This makes for a simple way to extract values from a recordset. Although nested loops are the intuitive way to retrieve values from a recordset, the *GetString* method can achieve a similar result in a single line of code.

Another method, *GetRows*, offers several benefits when retrieving recordset values. First, it captures the recordset values to memory in an array. This makes it possible to delete a *Recordset* object and still work with its values. At the very least, this reduces the resource load of an application. In Web applications where a server collects the data for many users, this advantage can be important. Second, you can achieve performance gains by working with an array in memory rather than on disk. These gains depend on the recordset being sufficiently small to fit in physical memory. Third, the ADO *GetRows* method syntax lets you specify a starting row and an array that denotes a subset of columns to retrieve from a recordset. Because you are storing the recordset values in memory, you should include just the minimum set of rows and fields necessary for your needs.

In using the *GetRows* method, you must literally reorient your way of thinking about the data in a recordset. This is because *GetRows* transposes the rows and columns from disk storage to a two-dimensional Variant array. When you declare the Variant array for the method's results set, you do not need to specify the number of rows or columns for the array. However, when retrieving data from the array, you must remember that recordset rows populate columns (instead of rows) in the Variant array.

The *GettingRows* procedure shown next demonstrates a couple of approaches to retrieving recordset contents with the *GetRows* method. The first application invokes the method with no arguments. This approach reveals just how simple it is to capture a recordset to memory with the *GetRows* method. The syntax for this approach copies all the rows and all their columns from disk to memory. The loop for printing values to the Immediate window shows the syntax for iterating through copied recordset rows as columns in the array. Review Chapter 1 for an introduction to processing arrays with VBA.

```
Sub GettingRows()
Dim rst1 As ADODB.Recordset
Dim varArray As Variant
Dim int1 As Integer

'Instantiate and open recordset
Set rst1 = New ADODB.Recordset
rst1.Open "customers", "Provider=Microsoft.Jet.OLEDB.4.0;" & _
    "Data Source=C:\PMA Samples\Northwind.mdb;"

'Copy all rows with all columns to varArray in memory
varArray = rst1.GetRows

'Loop through array based on recordset, printing first two fields
For int1 = 0 To UBound(varArray, 2)
    Debug.Print varArray(0, int1), varArray(1, int1)
Next int1

'Restore the pointer to the first record, and copy
'the first five rows with CustomerID and CompanyName
'fields into varArray in memory
rst1.MoveFirst
varArray = rst1.GetRows(5, , _
    Array("CustomerID", "CompanyName"))

'Loop through array based on recordset
For int1 = 0 To UBound(varArray, 2)
    Debug.Print varArray(0, int1), varArray(1, int1)
Next int1

'Clean up objects
rst1.Close
Set rst1 = Nothing

End Sub
```

The second application of the *GetRows* method in the *GettingRows* procedure demonstrates just how easy it is to specify a subset of the rows to copy to memory. The code instructs the ADO interpreter to copy only five rows from disk to memory. These rows are from the top of the recordset because the use of the *MoveFirst* method precedes the use of the second *GetRows* method. By default, the *GetRows* method copies records starting from the current row. However, you can designate a bookmark for another record as the second argument if you want the method to start from a location other than the current row. The second application of *GetRows* also illustrates how to use the built-in *Array* function to specify a subset of fields to copy from disk to memory. In particular, it copies just the *CustomerID* and *CompanyName* column values from the *Customers* table.

> **Note**   Often you will want to start copying with the *GetRows* method from
> the first row, even when the current row has a different position. In this
> situation, use the intrinsic constant *adBookmarkFirst* for the method's
> second parameter to point to the first row.

Adding, Editing, and Deleting Records

The preceding set of samples for printing recordsets all accepted the default
settings for the *CursorType* and *LockType* properties. Recall that the default settings are forward-only and read-only. In other words, you cannot change existing rows in a recordset or add new ones with these default settings. When all
you want to do is print recordset values, these property settings are fast and
efficient. However, by overriding these default settings to change the cursor type
to keyset with optimistic locking, you can readily modify the field values within
the rows of a recordset. Because the samples in this section all modify recordsets,
they all use these nondefault settings.

One way to modify a recordset is by adding a new row of field values. The
AddAShipper function procedure shown next demonstrates an approach to this
task using the *AddNew* method for an ADO recordset. The sample applies this
method to a recordset based on the *Shippers* table in the Northwind database.
This table has an AutoNumber field named *ShipperID* and two string fields named
CompanyName and *Phone*. Since Access automatically assigns AutoNumber field
values, the procedure only has to assign values to the *CompanyName* and *Phone*
fields. The procedure inserts these assignments between a statement that invokes
the *AddNew* method and another one that launches the *Update* method.

```
Function AddAShipper()
Dim rst1 As ADODB.Recordset

'Set your cursor so that it is not read-only
'in order to add a row
Set rst1 = New ADODB.Recordset
rst1.ActiveConnection = "Provider=Microsoft.Jet.OLEDB.4.0;" & _
    "Data Source=C:\PMA Samples\Northwind.mdb;"
rst1.Open "Shippers", , adOpenKeyset, adLockOptimistic, _
    adCmdTable

'Invoke the AddNew method
With rst1
    .AddNew
```

```
        .Fields("CompanyName") = "Access 2002 Delivers"
        .Fields("Phone") = "(555) 123-4567"
    .Update
End With

'Return ShipperID of new shipper
AddAShipper = rst1("ShipperID")

'Clean up objects
rst1.Close
Set rst1 = Nothing

End Function
```

Because the *AddAShipper* sample uses a function procedure, it can return a value, such as the *ShipperID* value that Access assigns automatically. This AutoNumber field is the primary key for the *Shippers* table. If your application inserts records into both a main table and a related table, such as *Orders* and *Order Details*, the AutoNumber primary key field value from the main table would be essential for setting the foreign key values in the related table.

Another task that you likely will want to perform with recordsets is deleting records. The following pair of procedures shows one approach to this task. While this approach might not be optimal in some respects, it has the benefit of not requiring any special SQL syntax or even advanced ADO functionality. Basically, you loop through a recordset until you find a match. Then you just delete the matching record.

The code sample in the *CallDeleteARecordsetRow* and *DeleteARecordsetRow* procedures lets a user specify any field as a criterion for the row to delete. If a recordset contains multiple rows with the same field value, it deletes just the first of these rows. The *CallDeleteARecordsetRow* procedure includes the code to delete a row based on *CompanyName*, *Phone*, or *ShipperID* field values. The sample leaves uncommented only the syntax for deleting a row based on *CompanyName*.

```
Sub CallDeleteARecordsetRow()
Dim rst1 As ADODB.Recordset
Dim int1 As Integer

'Set your cursor so that it is not read-only
'in order to delete
Set rst1 = New ADODB.Recordset
rst1.ActiveConnection = "Provider=Microsoft.Jet.OLEDB.4.0;" & _
    "Data Source=C:\PMA Samples\Northwind.mdb;"
rst1.Open "Shippers", , adOpenKeyset, adLockOptimistic, _
    adCmdTable
```

(continued)

```
'Delete a shipper indexed by CompanyName or Phone
DeleteARecordsetRow rst1, "CompanyName", "Access 2002 Delivers"
'DeleteARecordsetRow rst1, "Phone", "(555) 123-4567"

'Delete a shipper indexed by ShipperID
'just after adding it
'int1 = AddAShipper()
'DeleteARecordsetRow rst1, "ShipperID", int1

'Clean up objects
rst1.Close
Set rst1 = Nothing

End Sub


Sub DeleteARecordsetRow(rst1 As ADODB.Recordset, _
    FieldName As String, FieldValue As Variant)

'Designate rst1 as repeated value in
'With...End With statement
With rst1
'Loop through recordset to find target
'field value for selected field
    Do Until .EOF
        If .Fields(FieldName) = FieldValue Then
            .Delete
            Exit Do
        End If
        .MoveNext
    Loop
End With

End Sub
```

The calling procedure, *CallDeleteARecordsetRow*, passes a recordset, field name, and a field value. The called procedure, *DeleteARecordsetRow*, loops through the recordset. If the loop uncovers a row with a field value that matches the input parameters, it deletes the row and exits the loop.

The sample enables you to delete a recordset row based on the *ShipperID* field by adding a new row and saving the *ShipperID* value for that new row. It does this by saving the return value of the *AddAShipper* function procedure in a memory variable named *int1*. Then it uses the value of that memory variable as an argument when it calls *DeleteARecordsetRow*. This aspect of the sample demonstrates how to use the value of an automatically added primary key to control another action. In this case, the other action is to delete a row, but it could just as easily be to insert rows in a related table.

The third sample in this section demonstrates how to update an existing field value in a recordset row with a new field value. The calling procedure, *CallUpdateAFieldValue*, passes four arguments to the called procedure, *UpdateAFieldValue*. In this case, the passed parameters are the recordset, the name of the field to update, and the old and new field values. The *UpdateAFieldValue* procedure loops through the recordset's rows until it finds a match. Then it assigns the new field value and invokes the *Update* method for the recordset. This commits the changed value to disk. After performing the update, the sub procedure exits the loop and restores control to the calling routine. If multiple records have field values that match the *OldFieldValue* input parameter, the sub procedure updates just the first record. You can update all the rows with matching values by removing the *Exit Do* statement inside the loop.

```
Sub CallUpdateAFieldValue()
Dim rst1 As ADODB.Recordset

'Set your cursor so that it is not read-only
'in order to udpate a record
Set rst1 = New ADODB.Recordset
rst1.ActiveConnection = "Provider=Microsoft.Jet.OLEDB.4.0;" & _
    "Data Source=C:\PMA Samples\Northwind.mdb;"
rst1.Open "Shippers", , adOpenKeyset, adLockOptimistic, _
    adCmdTable

'Call updating routine, and pass it update info
UpdateAFieldValue rst1, "CompanyName", "Access 2002 Delivers", _
    "Access 2002 Delivers More"

'Clean up objects
rst1.Close
Set rst1 = Nothing

End Sub


Sub UpdateAFieldValue(rst1 As ADODB.Recordset, _
    FieldName As String, _
    OldFieldValue As Variant, _
    NewFieldValue As Variant)

'Designate rst1 as repeated value in
'With...End With statement
With rst1
'Loop through recordset to find target
'field value for selected field
    Do Until .EOF
```

(continued)

```
                    If .Fields(FieldName) = OldFieldValue Then
                        .Fields(FieldName) = NewFieldValue
                        .Update
                        Exit Do
                    End If
                    .MoveNext
            Loop
        End With

    End Sub
```

Finding Records

Another common task with a recordset is to find one or more records that meet specified criteria. Access offers several approaches to this task. With earlier versions of Access, many developers used one or more variations of the *Find* method. Access 2000 introduced a single *Find* method that consolidates the functionality of the earlier *Find* methods. If your applications used the earlier Find methods, you can achieve the same results with the consolidated method that Access 2000 introduced. Access 2002 adds a new capability to the Find method initially made available to Access developers with Access 2000.

The following code shows a simple application of the *Find* method that searches for a record with a customer ID that begins with the letter *D*. When it finds a record matching its criteria, the method relocates the current record to that location. The code prints the *CustomerID*, *ContactName*, and *Phone* fields to confirm exactly which record matches the criterion.

```
Sub FindAMatch()
Dim rst1 As Recordset

'Instantiate and open recordset
Set rst1 = New ADODB.Recordset
rst1.ActiveConnection = _
    "Provider=Microsoft.Jet.OLEDB.4.0;" & _
    "Data Source=C:\PMA Samples\Northwind.mdb;"
rst1.Open "Customers", , adOpenKeyset, adLockPessimistic, _
    adCmdTable

'Find the first row with a CustomerID beginning with D,
'and print the result
rst1.Find ("CustomerID Like 'D*'")
Debug.Print rst1("CustomerID"), rst1("ContactName"), rst1("Phone")

'Clean up objects
rst1.Close
Set rst1 = Nothing

End Sub
```

One drawback to the *FindAMatch* procedure is that it searches for a single match to the criteria and then stops immediately after finding it. The code that follows, which shows the *FindAMatch2* procedure, discovers all the records that match the criterion statement. This simple application reveals more of the flexibility of the *Find* method:

```
Sub FindAMatch2()
Dim rst1 As Recordset

'Instantiate and open recordset
Set rst1 = New ADODB.Recordset
rst1.ActiveConnection = _
    "Provider=Microsoft.Jet.OLEDB.4.0;" & _
    "Data Source=C:\PMA Samples\Northwind.mdb;"
rst1.Open "Customers", , adOpenKeyset, _
    adLockPessimistic, adCmdTable

'Open an infinite loop for all records matching
'the criterion
Do
    rst1.Find ("CustomerID Like 'D*'")
    If rst1.EOF Then
'Exit the procedure when no more matches exist
        Exit Do
    End If
    Debug.Print rst1.Fields("CustomerID"), rst1("ContactName"), _
        rst1("Phone")
    rst1.MoveNext
Loop

'Clean up objects
rst1.Close
Set rst1 = Nothing

End Sub
```

The trick to finding all the records that match the search criterion is to embed the *Find* method in an infinite *Do* loop. When the *Find* method sets the recordset's *EOF* property to True, there are no additional matching records. In this case, the code executes an *Exit Do* statement to exit the loop. As long as *Find* keeps discovering new matches, the procedure prints *CustomerID*, *ContactName*, and *Phone* fields in the Immediate window. After printing a matching record, the procedure advances the current record by one. Without this, the *Find* method would repeatedly return the same record.

One innovation available to those using Access 2002 is the dynamic index capability of the Cursor Service. Access 2002 ships natively with an ADO version that supports dynamic indexes. To speed the operation of the *Find* method, developers can create dynamic indexes on the fly for record sources that do not have an index on a search field. Creating a dynamic index is a two-step process. First, assign the *adUseClient* intrinsic constant to the recordset's *CursorLocation* property. Second, set the *Optimize* property to True in the *Properties* collection so that the field will gain the dynamic index. The index goes out of scope when you close the procedure, but you can force the index's removal by setting the field's *Optimize* property to False.

> **Note**   You can acquire the dynamic index feature in Access 2000 by installing a more recent ADO version than the one initially shipped with Access 2000.

The following pair of procedures demonstrates how to use a dynamic index to speed the search for all the customers from a particular country. The first procedure, *CallFindCustomersInACountry*, assigns a search string value and passes it to the second procedure, *FindCustomersInACountry*. Notice that the sample code uses a pound sign (#) to delimit the country string within the criterion string. With Access 2002, you can use either # or an apostrophe (') for this purpose.

Before opening a recordset on the *Customers* table, the second procedure turns on the Cursor Service by setting the *CursorLocation* property to *adUseClient*. Then after the recordset is open, the procedure sets the *Country* field's *Optimize* priority to True. This causes the creation of the index. Next the procedure performs a normal search to find all the customers from the country designated by *strCriterion*. In the cleanup process for the procedure, there is nothing special you need to do with the index. It goes out of scope automatically.

```
Sub CallFindCustomersInACountry()
Dim strCriterion As String

'Set string for country criterion, and pass it
'to the routine to do the search
strCriterion = "Country = #USA#"
FindCustomersInACountry strCriterion

End Sub
```

```
Sub FindCustomersInACountry(strCriterion As String)
Dim rst1 As ADODB.Recordset
Dim int1 As Integer

'Instantiate and open recordset; invoke the Cursor Service by
'setting the CursorLocation property to adUseClient
Set rst1 = New ADODB.Recordset
With rst1
    .ActiveConnection = _
        "Provider=Microsoft.Jet.OLEDB.4.0;" & _
        "Data Source=C:\PMA Samples\Northwind.mdb;"
    .CursorLocation = adUseClient
    .Open "customers", , adOpenKeyset, _
        adLockPessimistic, adCmdTable
End With

'Create a dynamic index on Country
rst1.Fields("Country").Properties("Optimize") = True

'Find the longest ContactName field, and add one to it
int1 = FindTheLongest(rst1, "ContactName") + 1

'Open an infinite loop for all records matching
'the criterion
rst1.MoveFirst
Do
    rst1.Find (strCriterion)
    If rst1.EOF Then
'Exit the procedure when no more matches exist
        Exit Sub
    End If
    Debug.Print rst1.Fields("CustomerID"), rst1("ContactName") & _
        String(int1 -
 Len(rst1("ContactName")), " ") & " " & rst1("Phone")
    rst1.MoveNext
Loop

'Clean up objects
rst1.Close
Set rst1 = Nothing

End Sub
```

Seeking Records

The *Seek* method is another recordset method that can facilitate finding records in a record source. This method is exclusively used for recordsets that specify a table as their source. In addition, you must set the *Options* parameter for the recordset *Open* method to *adCmdTableDirect*, instead of setting it to *adCmdTable* or leaving it blank. Furthermore, the table serving as a record source must have an index on the field or fields that your application searches to find matches for criterion values. ADO does not offer built-in support for creating dynamic indexes for the *Seek* method, but your application can programmatically create an index using the ADOX library for Jet and the SQL-DMO library for SQL Server. The *Seek* method also requires a server-side cursor. Using any value other than *adUseServer* for a recordset's *CursorLocation* property disables the method.

> **Note**   The *Seek* method is not a core ADO data access feature. ADO providers can optionally offer it. Use the recordset *Supports* method with *adSeek* as an argument to return a Boolean indicating whether a provider offers the *Seek* method. To seek on an index, apply the method to a recordset after opening it.

The *Seek* method searches for a key value or values, and it optionally takes a *SeekOption* parameter that can guide the operation of the method. If the index for the *Seek* method has just one column, you can specify only a single criterion value. If the index for a recordset relies on multiple columns, use an *Array* function to specify values for all the columns in the index. This capability to search concurrently on multiple columns is one feature distinguishing the *Seek* method from the *Find* method. The *Seek* method makes available the recordset in the order of the index and positions the current record at the first record matching the criteria.

You can refine the search behavior of the *Seek* method with some settings for its *SeekOptions* parameter using one of the *SeekEnum* enums. The *SeekOptions* setting appears immediately after the key value or values for a *Seek* method. The syntax for the *Seek* method with both key values and *SeekOptions* is *rst.Seek <Keyvalues>, <SeekOptions>*. Table 2-5 lists the *SeekEnum* members with their values and behavior.

Table 2-5 **Intrinsic Constants for the *SeekEnum***

Constant	Value	Behavior
adSeekFirstEQ	*1*	Seek the first record on the index or indexes matching the key value or values.
adSeekLastEQ	*2*	Seek the last record on the index or indexes matching the key value or values.
adSeekAfterEQ	*4*	Seek the first record (or the one after it when no match exists) on the index or indexes matching the key value or values.
adSeekAfter	*8*	Seek the first record after that potential match to the key value or values on the index or indexes.
adSeekBeforeEQ	*16*	Seek the first record (or the one before it when no match exists) on the index or indexes matching the key value or values.
adSeekBefore	*32*	Seek the first record before a potential match to the key value or values on the index or indexes.

The *SeekingUnShippedOrders* procedure that follows illustrates three ways to use the *Seek* method. Before actually invoking the *Seek* method, your application must properly prepare the recordset. First, assign the *Index* property so that it contains the values for which you want to search. Second, open the recordset with the *adCmdTableDirect* setting for the *Options* parameter. Third, ensure the *CursorLocation* property has a setting of *adUseServer*. This is the default setting, so you don't need to assign the property a setting unless your application has changed its default setting. The following procedure demonstrates the first two steps. The third step is not necessary in this sample.

```
Sub SeekingUnshippedOrders()
Dim rst1 As ADODB.Recordset

'Instantiate and open recordset; Seek method requires
'index assignment, adCmdTableDirection Open option, and
'adUserServer setting for CursorLoction (default)
Set rst1 = New ADODB.Recordset
rst1.ActiveConnection = _
    "Provider=Microsoft.Jet.OLEDB.4.0;" & _
    "Data Source=C:\PMA Samples\Northwind.mdb;"
rst1.CursorType = adOpenKeyset
rst1.LockType = adLockOptimistic
rst1.Index = "ShippedDate"
rst1.Open "Orders", , , , adCmdTableDirect
```

(continued)

```
'Print first order not shipped
rst1.Seek Null, adSeekFirstEQ
Debug.Print rst1("OrderID"), rst1("OrderDate")

'Print last order not shipped
rst1.Seek Null, adSeekLastEQ
Debug.Print rst1("OrderID"), rst1("OrderDate")

'Print all orders not shipped
rst1.Seek Null
Do
    Debug.Print rst1("OrderID"), rst1("OrderDate")
    rst1.MoveNext
Loop Until IsNull(rst1("ShippedDate")) = False

'Clean up objects
rst1.Close
Set rst1 = Nothing

End Sub
```

The first two instances of the *Seek* method in *SeekingUnShippedOrders* both demonstrate the syntax for the *Keyvalues* and *SeekOptions* parameters. The first instance of the *Seek* method sets the cursor at the first record in the *Orders* table that is unshipped. This record has the order ID 11008. The steps for opening the *rst1* recordset on the *Orders* table arrange the records in order on the *ShippedDate* index, so that the special ordering indicated by the *Seek* method's *Keyvalues* and *SeekOptions* parameters will work. The second instance of the *Seek* method in the *SeekingUnShippedOrders* procedure sets the cursor at the last *Orders* table record with a Null value for the *ShippedDate* field. This record has the order ID 11077. The third instance of the *Seek* method in the preceding procedure searches for all unshipped orders without specifying a *SeekOptions* setting. Its following *Do* loop iterates through the reordered recordset to print the *OrderID* field and *OrderDate* field for each record with a Null *ShippedDate* field value.

The *SeekWith2IndexValues* procedure demonstrates the syntax for designating a seek for two criterion values: the *OrderID* and *ProductID* fields of the primary key for the *Order Details* table. The procedure also demonstrates how to reuse a *Recordset* object. In the first use of the *rst1* recordset, the procedure searches for all line items matching an *OrderID* input by the user. The procedure uses an *InputBox* function nested inside a *CInt* function to permit a user to input an *OrderID* field value. It then returns the *OrderID* and *ProductID* for the line items associated with that record. This first seek relies on the *OrderID* index for the *Order Details* table.

```
Sub SeekWith2IndexValues()
Dim rst1 As ADODB.Recordset
Dim int1 As Integer
Dim int2 As Integer
Dim int3 As Integer

'Instantiate and open recordset; Seek method requires
'index assignment, adCmdTableDirection Open option, and
'adUserServer setting for CursorLocation (default)
Set rst1 = New ADODB.Recordset
rst1.ActiveConnection = _
    "Provider=Microsoft.Jet.OLEDB.4.0;" & _
    "Data Source=C:\PMA Samples\Northwind.mdb;"
rst1.CursorType = adOpenKeyset
rst1.LockType = adLockOptimistic
rst1.Index = "OrderID"
rst1.Open "Order Details", , , , adCmdTableDirect

'Search for a user-specified OrderID;
'save OrderID and ProductID of order's last line item
int1 = CInt(InputBox("Input OrderID: "))
rst1.Seek int1
Do Until rst1("OrderID") <> int1
    Debug.Print rst1("OrderID"), rst1("ProductID")
    rst1.MoveNext
    If rst1.EOF Then Exit Do
Loop
rst1.MovePrevious
int2 = rst1("OrderID")
int3 = rst1("ProductID")

'Close and reopen Order Details to seek
'last line item in the order
rst1.Close
rst1.Index = "PrimaryKey"
rst1.Open "Order Details", , , , adCmdTableDirect

rst1.Seek Array(int2, int3)
Debug.Print rst1("OrderID"), rst1("ProductID"), _
    FormatCurrency(rst1("UnitPrice")), _
    rst1("Quantity"), FormatPercent(rst1("Discount"), 0)

'Clean up objects
rst1.Close
Set rst1 = Nothing

End Sub
```

The second instance of the *Seek* method in the *SeekWith2IndexValues* procedure seeks the last item for the *OrderID* that a user input. At the conclusion of the first *Seek* instance, the procedure saves the *OrderID* and *ProductID* field values for the last line item in the order a user referenced. Then the procedure closes the recordset to assign a new index. The index is the primary key that relies on both *OrderID* and *ProductID*. Next the procedure reopens the recordset. The new index is critical for permitting the use of a compound criterion that includes values for both the *OrderID* and *ProductID* field values. Notice the use of the *Array* function for indicating more than one key value. The cursor points to the record in the recordset for the line item sought. The procedure prints it while formatting the *UnitPrice* and *Discount* columns.

Filtering Records

The *Find* method can go through a recordset sequentially and disclose matches one at a time. The method does not create another version of the recordset that contains all the records that match the criterion values. When you need a new or alternate recordset containing just the matches, your application needs a different approach. The *Seek* method offers a partial solution to this *Find* method deficiency, but the *Seek* method has special requirements that restrict its applicability, such as the need for an index. In addition, the *Seek* method does not truly exclude nonmatching records. It merely positions the current record at the first matching record.

The recordset *Filter* property offers a second solution to the *Find* method's inability to return a subset of a recordset based on one or more fields. This property lets you designate a simple criterion for a field, and it returns a filtered version of the original recordset with only those records that match the criterion value or values. By setting the *Filter* property to any of a series of constants instead of to a criterion string, you can achieve special effects for database replication or for updating a remote data source. One filter constant, *adFilterNone*, removes the filter setting from a recordset and restores the original rowset. The *Filter* property also resolves another shortcoming of the *Find* method: it can select records based on more than one field value. Furthermore, it does not require an index to accomplish this goal, as does the *Seek* method.

The following two procedures filter a recordset based on the *Customers* table in the Northwind database. The *FilterRecordset* procedure manages the overall use of the *Filter* property, prints the results set, clears the filter, and then prints the results set again. The *FilterRecordset* procedure relies on the *FilterLikeField* function. This custom function manages the setting of the *Filter* property based on parameters passed to it by the *FilterRecordset* procedure, and it returns the filtered recordset.

```
Sub FilterRecordset()
Dim rst1 As ADODB.Recordset

'Instantiate and open recordset
Set rst1 = New ADODB.Recordset
rst1.ActiveConnection = "Provider=Microsoft.Jet.OLEDB.4.0;" & _
    "Data Source=C:\PMA Samples\Northwind.mdb;"
rst1.Open "Customers", , , , adCmdTable

'Filter recordset, and print filtered result
Set rst1 = _
    FilterLikeField(rst1, "CustomerID", "D*")
Debug.Print rst1.GetString

'Restore recordset, and print restored result
rst1.Filter = adFilterNone
Debug.Print rst1.GetString

'Clean up objects
rst1.Close
Set rst1 = Nothing

End Sub


Function FilterLikeField(rst1 As ADODB.Recordset, _
strField As String, strFilter As String) As ADODB.Recordset

'Set a filter on the specified Recordset object, and then
'return the filtered recordset
rst1.Filter = strField & " LIKE '" & strFilter & "'"
Set FilterLikeField = rst1

End Function
```

The *FilterRecordset* procedure starts by creating and opening the *rst1* recordset. Next it applies a filter by calling the *FilterLikeField* function, which takes three arguments and returns a filtered recordset based on them. *FilterRecordset* assigns the filtered return set to *rst1* and prints the filtered recordset to confirm the result.

The arguments to *FilterLikeField* include *rst1*, a field name on which to filter records, and a filter criterion value, which can include any legitimate expression for the Like operator used by *FilterLikeField*. *FilterRecordset* passes *D** to find just the records that have a *CustomerID* beginning with the letter *D*. The *Filter* property does not restrict you to filtering with the LIKE operator. Other acceptable operators include <, >, <=, >=, <>, and =. You can also include AND and OR operators in your criteria expressions to combine two or more criteria expressions based on the other legitimate operators.

The *Filter* property restricts your criteria expressions to those of the form *<FieldName> <Operator> <Value>*. However, some *Filter* intrinsic constants that are members of the *FilterGroupEnum* enumenable special uses of the property. The *FilterRecordset* procedure uses the *adFilterNone* constant to restore a recordset by removing its filters. You can also use other *FilterGroupEnum* enum members to resolve conflicts associated with performing a batch update against a remote data source.

The following pair of procedures demonstrates just how easy it is to filter on multiple criterion fields. You can compound simple filter phrases, such as *"Country ='USA'"*, with AND and OR operators. This capability permits you to filter a recordset on more than one field. You can also group criteria expressions with parentheses and then link them with AND and OR operators for the construction of complex compound criteria. This next sample shows a compound criteria expression that does not require parentheses.

The sample demonstrating compound filters uses two procedures. The first procedure, *CallFilterOnCountryAndCity*, sets the criteria strings for both country and city, the two filter fields for the *Customers* table. Then the sample calls *FilterOnCountryAndCity*, the procedure that applies the filter, and it saves a reference to the filtered recordset. The main procedure concludes by printing selected fields. Before printing field values, however, it uses the *FindTheLongest* function procedure to determine the longest character for each of two fields.

```
Sub CallFilterOnCountryAndCity()
Dim rst1 As ADODB.Recordset
Dim strCountry As String
Dim strCity As String
Dim int1 As Integer
Dim int2 As Integer

'Set Country and City criteria
strCountry = "USA"
strCity = "Portland"

'Call Filter routine, and store reference to
'filtered return set
Set rst1 = FilterOnCountryAndCity(strCountry, strCity)

'Get the longest lengths for the
'ContactName and CompanyName fields
int1 = FindTheLongest(rst1, "ContactName") + 1
rst1.MoveFirst
int2 = FindTheLongest(rst1, "CompanyName") + 1
```

```
'Print selected fields from filtered recordset
rst1.MoveFirst
Do Until rst1.EOF
    Debug.Print rst1("ContactName") & _
        String(int1 - Len(rst1("ContactName")), " ") & _
        rst1("CompanyName") & _
        String(int2 - Len(rst1("CompanyName")), " ") & _
        rst1("City"), rst1("Country")
    rst1.MoveNext
Loop

'Clean up objects
rst1.Close
Set rst1 = Nothing

End Sub


Function FilterOnCountryAndCity(strCountry As String, _
    strCity As String) As ADODB.Recordset
Dim rst1 As ADODB.Recordset

'Instantiate and open recordset
Set rst1 = New ADODB.Recordset
rst1.ActiveConnection = "Provider=Microsoft.Jet.OLEDB.4.0;" & _
    "Data Source=C:\PMA Samples\Northwind.mdb;"
rst1.Open "Customers", , adOpenKeyset, adLockOptimistic, adCmdTable

'Set Filter property
rst1.Filter = "Country = '" & strCountry & _
    "' AND City = '" & strCity & "'"

'Return filtered recordset
Set FilterOnCountryAndCity = rst1

End Function
```

Persisting Recordsets

By using the *Save* method, you can persist a recordset. Later, with the *Open* method and the MSPersist provider, you can open a saved recordset. This capability serves a couple of purposes particularly well. First, this capability comes in handy when you need to take a snapshot of a record source for viewing later on a computer that is disconnected from the data source for the records. Second, when remote server access is either slow or unreliable, using a saved recordset based on a record source from a remote server gives an application fast, reliable data access. This is especially convenient for read-only record sources. In either context, you can modify a saved record source and later update the remote source with the *UpdateBatch* method.

You can persist a recordset's contents with either of two formats, a proprietary format or an XML format. Designate your preferred format with a member of the *PersistFormatEnum* enum in the statement using the *Save* method. Saving a file in XML format enables another application to open and view the recordset's data. The *Open* method, which inserts the file's contents into a recordset, works equally well with either format. For example, you can readily view the saved XML file in the Microsoft Internet Explorer browser shipping with Office XP. Internet Explorer allows you to view the XML tags and data. The proprietary format is not so easy to view natively. However, users can readily open a file in the proprietary format and then examine its contents in the recordset to which the *Open* method deposits the file's contents.

The following sample opens a recordset on the *Shippers* table from the Northwind database on the C share of a remote computer named cabarmada. It saves the recordset to a drive on the local computer. The *Save* method designates an XML file format by using the *adPersistXML* intrinsic constant. Specifying the *adPersistADTG* intrinsic constant saves the recordset in the proprietary format.

```
Sub SaveAccessDBRecordSource()
On Error GoTo SaveAccessDB_Trap
Dim cnn1 As ADODB.Connection
Dim rst1 As ADODB.Recordset
Dim varLocalAddress As Variant

'Create the connection
Set cnn1 = New ADODB.Connection
cnn1.Open "Provider=Microsoft.Jet.OLEDB.4.0;" & _
    "Data Source=\\cabarmada\c\Program Files\Microsoft Office\" & _
    "Office10\Samples\Northwind.mdb;"

'Open recordset on Shippers table in the copy of
'Northwind.mdb on a machine named cabarmada
Set rst1 = New ADODB.Recordset
rst1.Open "Shippers", cnn1, adOpenKeyset, adLockOptimistic, adCmdTable

'Specify a local address for the recordset based on Shippers table,
'and save the recordset in XML format to that address
varLocalAddress = "C:\PMA Samples\Chapter 02\ShippersFromCabarmada.xml"
rst1.Save varLocalAddress, adPersistXML
```

```
SaveAccessDB_Exit:
rst1.Close
Set rst1 = Nothing
cnn1.Close
Set cnn1 = Nothing
Exit Sub

SaveAccessDB_Trap:
If err.Number = 58 Then
'Kill the temporary file of table data because it already exists,
'and resume writing to the file
    Kill varLocalAddress
    Resume
Else
    MsgBox "Procedure failed with an error number = " _
        & err.Number & ", " & vbCrLf & "and an " & _
        "error description of """ & _
        err.Description & """" & ".", vbInformation, _
        "Programming Microsoft Access Version 2002"
End If

End Sub
```

The sample's error trap is slightly more robust than necessary, but you will typically need an error trap with a procedure that saves a recordset to a file. This is because you will generate a run-time error if you attempt to save a recordset over an existing file. Since the number for this specific error is 58, the sample kills the old version of the file and resumes executing the line of code with the *Save* method.

Figure 2-6 shows the saved file open in Internet Explorer. Notice that the XML tags show the schema information, such as data type and length for recordset fields, as well as the data for the file's contents.

The *OpenSavedRecordset* sample that appears next illustrates the syntax for opening and browsing the contents of the file saved in the previous code sample. After declaring and instantiating a recordset, the procedure invokes the recordset's *Open* method. The source for the *Open* method is the path and filename for the recordset saved previously. In order to use the *Open* method this way, you must designate MSPersist as the provider for the connection argument. Notice that the *Options* argument is *adCmdFile*. I include this just to remind you of the general usefulness of specifying an *Options* argument. In this particular case, the argument is not necessary since ADO assumes an *adCmdFile* argument when you designate MSPersist as the provider.

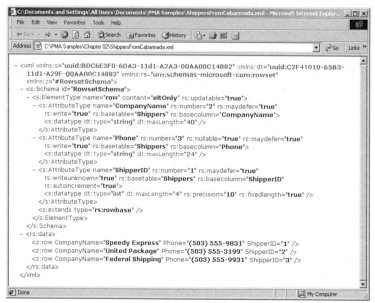

Figure 2-6 The XML contents as seen from Internet Explorer for the file saved by the *SaveAccessDBRecordSource* procedure.

After opening the file as a recordset, the code sample loops through the columns of each row as it prints the field name and value of each element in the recordset. With this simple code, you can open the local file and view its contents even when you are disconnected from the original version of the *Shippers* table on the cabarmada computer.

```
Sub OpenSavedRecordset()
Dim rst1 As ADODB.Recordset
Dim int1 As Integer

'Instantiate recordset, and open from file with Persistence provider
Set rst1 = New ADODB.Recordset
rst1.Open _
    "C:\PMA Samples\Chapter 02\ShippersFromCabarmada.xml", _
    "Provider=MSPersist;", _
    , , adCmdFile

'Loop through all rows; with each row loop through all columns
Do Until rst1.EOF
    For int1 = 0 To rst1.Fields.Count - 1
        Debug.Print rst1.Fields(int1).Name, rst1(int1)
    Next int1
    rst1.MoveNext
Loop
```

```
'Clean up objects
rst1.Close
Set rst1 = Nothing

End Sub
```

As developers, we can use this technology to empower employees that must travel, enter data on a disconnected recordset, and then update the connected recorded source when they return to the office. By using the recordset's *UpdateBatch* method along with the ability to persist recordsets, you can readily meet this need. The *SaveEditInsertShippersAtNorthwindCS* procedure demonstrates the syntax that can help you empower "road warrior" employees. The sample creates a local recordset based on the *Shippers* table in the NorthwindCS database on the cab2000 SQL server. (Recall that the NorthwindCS database ships with Office XP.) Then the procedure saves this recordset to a local drive.

```
Sub SaveEditInsertShippersAtNorthwindCS()
On Error GoTo EditInsertCS_Trap
Dim cnn1 As ADODB.Connection
Dim rst1 As ADODB.Recordset
Dim varLocalAddress As Variant

'Local address for saved recordset
varLocalAddress = "c:\PMA Samples\Chapter 02\ShippersFromCab2000.xml"

'Instantiate and open a recordset
Set rst1 = New ADODB.Recordset
rst1.Open "SELECT ShipperID, CompanyName, Phone FROM Shippers", _
        "Provider=SQLOLEDB;Data Source=cab2000;User Id=sa;" & _
        "Password=password;Initial Catalog=NorthwindCS;", _
        adOpenDynamic, adLockOptimistic, adCmdText

'Persist the recordset to disk as an XML file; this saves it
'based on the Shippers table in the NorthwindCS database on the
'cab2000 server
Kill varLocalAddress
rst1.Save varLocalAddress, adPersistXML

'Open the XML file locally
Set rst1 = New ADODB.Recordset
rst1.Open varLocalAddress, "Provider=MSPersist;", , , adCmdFile

'Find a record, and edit it in the local cache
rst1.Find "CompanyName = 'Federal Shipping'"
If rst1.EOF Then
    Debug.Print "Name not found."
    Exit Sub
End If
```
(continued)

```
rst1("CompanyName") = "Federal Shippers"
rst1.Update

'Add a record to the local cache
rst1.AddNew
    rst1("CompanyName") = "CAB Movers"
    rst1("Phone") = "(555) 234.5678"
rst1.Update

'After committing the edit locally, connect to the remote
'data source and update the remote source
Set cnn1 = New ADODB.Connection
cnn1.Open "Provider=SQLOLEDB;Data Source=cab2000;User Id=sa;" & _
        "Password=password;Initial Catalog=NorthwindCS;"
rst1.ActiveConnection = cnn1
rst1.UpdateBatch

EditInsertCS_Exit:
'Clean up objects
rst1.Close
Set rst1 = Nothing
cnn1.Close
Set cnn1 = Nothing
Exit Sub

EditInsertCS_Trap:
If err.Number = 53 Then
'Tried to kill a file that doesn't exist, so simply resume
    Resume  Next
ElseIf err.Number = 58 Then
'Kill the temporary file of table data if it already exists,
'and resume writing to the file
    Kill varLocalAddress
    Resume
Else
    MsgBox "Procedure failed with an error number = " _
        & err.Number & ", " & vbCrLf & "and an " & _
        "error description of """ & _
        err.Description & """" & ".", vbInformation, _
        "Programming Microsoft Access Version 2002"
End If

End Sub
```

A traveling employee can use this file-based version of a recordset to edit existing data and enter new data. The code sample simulates these tasks programmatically. The application of the *Update* method commits the changes to the recordset's local cache, but another *Save* method could transfer those updates from memory to the disk-based version of the local recordset.

After returning from the field, employees will want to update the database at headquarters with their entries from the road. They can accomplish this goal by running a program you prepare that opens the file-based version of the recordset, connects the recordset to the server at headquarters, and invokes the *UpdateBatch* method for the local recordset. The *UpdateBatch* method, along with the recordset *Filter* property, enables developers to reconcile conflicts when they occur. See the Access Help files for more detailed coverage of conflict resolution issues. Database replication, another Access feature, offers more elaborate support for this capability, but some developers might care to build custom solutions using this technology.

Note   If you run the same procedure as *SaveEditInsertShippersAt-NorthwindCS*, except for updating its connections so that it initially opens and later updates the Access Northwind database file, it will fail. The precise error description is "Cannot update 'ShipperID'; field not updateable." The solution to this problem for Access database files is to construct the initial file-based recordset without any primary keys that have an AutoNumber data type. Use an SQL statement as your source for the saved recordset to accomplish this. The companion CD includes a sample procedure, *SaveEditInsertShippersAtNorthwind*, with the detailed code to perform this task.

Sorting Recordsets

Many database applications benefit from a sorted recordset. Therefore, Microsoft added a *Sort* property to ADO recordsets. This is a very natural property for Access developers to use. Simply set the *Sort* property for a recordset to the list of field names on which you want the recordset sorted. Represent the field names as a comma-delimited string. The default sort order is ascending. However, you can explicitly set an ascending sort order for any field by trailing the field name with a blank followed by the *ASC* keyword. Replace the *ASC* keyword with *DESC* if you want a recordset sorted in descending order on the values within a field.

In order for *Sort* property assignments to operate, you must assign the *adUseClient* intrinsic constant to the recordset's *CursorLocation* property. ADO takes advantage of user-defined indexes for tables when sorting recordsets. When no user-defined indexes exist, ADO constructs a temporary index to help speed the sorting of recordset rows on a field. You can clear any special sort (and delete temporary indexes that are automatically constructed) by assigning an empty string to the *Sort* property. You can also dynamically rearrange the order of rows within a recordset by designating a modified string of field names for the recordset's *Sort* property.

The following code sample demonstrates how to set the *Sort* property, while revealing the syntax for most of its typical uses. The sample begins by creating a recordset based on the *Customers* table. Notice that the sample assigns the *adUseClient* intrinsic constant to the recordset's *CursorLocation* property. This is essential. (Without making the setting, the *Sort* property assignments fail at run time.)

The procedure prints an excerpt of columns for the first five records in the currently sorted version of the recordset four different times. The first set of five records shows the default order, which is the order of the primary key or the order of entry for rows if no primary key exists. You don't need to set the *Sort* property to return records in this order (unless you are clearing a prior sort setting). The second set of five records sorts in ascending order on the *City* field values. To impose this order, the procedure merely assigns the string *"City"* to the *Sort* property. The next set of five records also sorts records on *City* field values, but in descending order. The *Sort* property setting for this order merely trails the field name by a space and the *DESC* keyword. The final sort order is by *City* field values within *Country* field values. Place the outer sort key, *Country*, first in the string for the *Sort* property so that the *City* field values appear in ascending order within each country.

```
Sub SortCustomersDefaultCityUpDown()
Dim rst1 As ADODB.Recordset
Dim int1 As Integer
Dim int2 As Integer
Dim int3 As Integer
Dim int4 As Integer

'Instantiate and open recordset based on customers;
'set CursorLocation to adUseClient to support sorting
Set rst1 = New ADODB.Recordset
rst1.CursorLocation = adUseClient
rst1.Open "Customers", "Provider=Microsoft.Jet.OLEDB.4.0;" & _
    "Data Source=C:\PMA Samples\Northwind.mdb;"

'Find and save maximum length of CustomerID, CompanyName,
'and ContactName fields
int2 = FindTheLongest(rst1, "CustomerID") + 1
rst1.MoveFirst
```

```
int3 = FindTheLongest(rst1, "CompanyName") + 1
rst1.MoveFirst
int4 = FindTheLongest(rst1, "ContactName") + 1

'Print records in default order
rst1.MoveFirst
Debug.Print "Default Order" & vbCr
For int1 = 1 To 5
    Debug.Print rst1("CustomerID") & _
        String(int2 - Len(rst1("CustomerID")), " ") & _
        rst1("CompanyName") & _
        String(int3 - Len(rst1("CompanyName")), " ") & _
        rst1("ContactName") & _
        String(int4 - Len(rst1("ContactName")), " ") & _
        rst1("Phone"), rst1("City"), rst1("Country")
    rst1.MoveNext
Next int1

'Sort by City and print
rst1.Sort = "City"
rst1.MoveFirst
Debug.Print String(2, vbCr) & "Order by City Ascending" & vbCr
For int1 = 1 To 5
    Debug.Print rst1("CustomerID") & _
        String(int2 - Len(rst1("CustomerID")), " ") & _
        rst1("CompanyName") & _
        String(int3 - Len(rst1("CompanyName")), " ") & _
        rst1("ContactName") & _
        String(int4 - Len(rst1("ContactName")), " ") & _
        rst1("Phone"), rst1("City"), rst1("Country")
    rst1.MoveNext
Next int1

'Sort by descending City order and print
rst1.Sort = "City DESC"
rst1.MoveFirst
Debug.Print String(2, vbCr) & "Order by City Descending" & vbCr
For int1 = 1 To 5
    Debug.Print rst1("CustomerID") & _
        String(int2 - Len(rst1("CustomerID")), " ") & _
        rst1("CompanyName") & _
        String(int3 - Len(rst1("CompanyName")), " ") & _
        rst1("ContactName") & _
        String(int4 - Len(rst1("ContactName")), " ") & _
        rst1("Phone"), rst1("City"), rst1("Country")
    rst1.MoveNext
Next int1
```

(continued)

```
'Sort by City within Country and print
rst1.Sort = "Country, City"
rst1.MoveFirst
Debug.Print String(2, vbCr) & _
"Order by Country Ascending, City Ascending" & vbCr
For int1 = 1 To 5
    Debug.Print rst1("CustomerID") & _
        String(int2 - Len(rst1("CustomerID")), " ") & _
        rst1("CompanyName") & _
        String(int3 - Len(rst1("CompanyName")), " ") & _
        rst1("ContactName") & _
        String(int4 - Len(rst1("ContactName")), " ") & _
        rst1("Phone"), rst1("City"), rst1("Country")
    rst1.MoveNext
Next int1

'Clean up objects
rst1.Close
Set rst1 = Nothing

End Sub
```

You can combine the *Sort* property for recordsets with other Access programming features to achieve useful results that are difficult to obtain programmatically any other way. For example, it is easy to list all the tables in an Access database file with any number of properties sorted however you need. The *OpenSchema* method for the *Connection* object returns recordsets with fields describing classes of objects within a database. This chapter demonstrated how to use this method earlier, but it did not show you how to customize the order of the output. This section demonstrates how to use the *Save* and *Open* methods in combination with the *Sort* property to arrange *OpenSchema* output to suit your needs.

When used with a parameter set to *adSchemaTables*, the *OpenSchema* method outputs a recordset of table properties with information ordered by table name. However, this list mixes information about all types of tables in rows adjacent to one another. Therefore, it is difficult to find information about a particular user-defined table, view, or system table. Figure 2-7 shows the output to the Immediate window from a VBA program that sorts tables by table name, within table type. Along with the other two columns, this feature makes it easy to look up when a table was last modified or created.

```
Immediate
~TMPCLP74311             ACCESS TABLE 9/20/2000 6:13:19 PM    6/8/2000 11:48:59 AM
MSysAccessObjects        ACCESS TABLE 9/13/2000 3:42:01 PM    9/13/2000 3:42:00 PM
MSysAccessXML            ACCESS TABLE 12/26/2000 6:58:56 AM   12/26/2000 6:58:56 AM
MSysCmdbars              ACCESS TABLE 8/16/1996 10:39:41 AM   8/16/1996 10:39:41 AM
MSysIMEXColumns          ACCESS TABLE 11/24/1998 5:33:09 PM   9/13/1995 10:25:06 AM
MSysIMEXSpecs            ACCESS TABLE 9/13/1995 10:25:06 AM   9/13/1995 10:25:06 AM
MSysACEs                 SYSTEM TABLE 9/13/1995 10:25:04 AM   9/13/1995 10:25:04 AM
MSysObjects              SYSTEM TABLE 9/13/1995 10:25:04 AM   9/13/1995 10:25:04 AM
MSysQueries              SYSTEM TABLE 9/13/1995 10:25:04 AM   9/13/1995 10:25:04 AM
MSysRelationships        SYSTEM TABLE 9/13/1995 10:25:04 AM   9/13/1995 10:25:04 AM
Categories               TABLE        11/30/1998 4:53:01 PM   9/13/1995 10:51:30 AM
Customers                TABLE        11/30/1998 4:53:08 PM   9/13/1995 10:51:32 AM
Employees                TABLE        8/7/2000 5:35:10 PM     9/13/1995 10:51:33 AM
Order Details            TABLE        7/31/2000 9:46:55 AM    9/13/1995 10:51:38 AM
Orders                   TABLE        7/19/2000 9:39:08 AM    9/13/1995 10:51:41 AM
Products                 TABLE        7/19/2000 9:39:12 AM    9/13/1995 10:51:41 AM
Shippers                 TABLE        11/24/1998 5:59:22 PM   9/13/1995 10:51:42 AM
Suppliers                TABLE        7/31/2000 9:46:27 AM    9/13/1995 10:51:42 AM
Alphabetical List of Products VIEW    9/13/2000 3:38:30 PM    6/21/1996 6:18:31 PM
Category Sales for 1997  VIEW         11/30/1998 4:54:42 PM   9/13/1995 10:51:43 AM
Current Product List     VIEW         11/24/1998 6:02:51 PM   9/13/1995 10:51:44 AM
Invoices                 VIEW         9/13/2000 3:38:33 PM    9/13/1995 10:51:44 AM
Order Details Extended   VIEW         9/6/2000 8:55:05 AM     9/13/1995 10:51:45 AM
Order Subtotals          VIEW         9/13/2000 3:38:26 PM    9/13/1995 10:51:45 AM
Orders Qry               VIEW         9/13/2000 3:38:20 PM    6/21/1996 6:14:07 PM
Product Sales for 1997   VIEW         11/30/1998 4:57:15 PM   9/13/1995 10:51:45 AM
Products Above Average Price VIEW     11/24/1998 6:30:25 PM   9/13/1995 10:51:46 AM
Products by Category     VIEW         9/13/2000 3:38:33 PM    6/21/1996 6:22:44 PM
Quarterly Orders         VIEW         9/13/2000 3:38:17 PM    9/13/1995 10:51:46 AM
Sales by Category        VIEW         9/13/2000 3:38:34 PM    9/13/1995 10:51:47 AM
Ten Most Expensive Products VIEW      11/24/1998 6:31:22 PM   9/13/1995 10:51:47 AM
```

Figure 2-7 Program output from the *SortedTableTypes* procedure, showing a list of tables sorted by table name within table type from the Northwind Access database file.

The following pair of procedures generate the output shown in Figure 2-7. While this listing is long, you are already familiar with all the techniques that it integrates. The calling procedure, *CallSortedTableTypes*, designates a string that points at a database file and passes that string to the second procedure, *SortedTableTypes*. You can get a listing like the one in Figure 2-7 for any Access database file, just by changing the string.

The second procedure generates a recordset about the tables in a database file by invoking the *OpenSchema* method with the *adSchemaTables* intrinsic constant as an argument. You cannot sort the output from the *OpenSchema* method because it sets the *CursorLocation* property to *adUseServer*. Therefore, the procedure saves the recordset and opens it again. This two-step process creates a version of the recordset with a *CursorLocation* property equal to *adUseClient*. In addition, the process yields a local version of the recordset for future use (for example, when you are disconnected from the computer with the database file). After changing the *CursorLocation* property setting, the procedure just needs to set the *Sort* property and print the results to the Immediate window. By specifying TABLE_TYPE before TABLE_NAME, the procedure forces the output to show table names sorted alphabetically within the table type.

```
Sub CallSortedTableTypes()
Dim str1 As String

'Specify database for which to generate a sorted list of tables
str1 = "Provider=Microsoft.Jet.OLEDB.4.0;" & _
    "Data Source=C:\PMA Samples\Northwind.mdb;"

'Call sub procedure to create sorted list of tables
SortedTableTypes str1

End Sub


Sub SortedTableTypes(str1 As String)
On Error GoTo SortedTableTypes_Trap
Dim cnn1 As ADODB.Connection
Dim rst1 As ADODB.Recordset
Dim rst2 As ADODB.Recordset
Dim int1 As Integer
Dim int2 As Integer

'Instantiate and open connection
Set cnn1 = New ADODB.Connection
cnn1.Open str1

'Save tables report in rst1
Set rst1 = cnn1.OpenSchema(adSchemaTables)

'Since OpenSchema returns a server-based cursor, save original
'returned recordset and reopen saved data with a new recordset;
'the new recordset has a local cursor that you can sort
rst1.Save "C:\PMA Samples\Chapter 02\foo.adtg", adPersistADTG
Set rst2 = New ADODB.Recordset
rst2.Open "C:\PMA Samples\Chapter 02\foo.adtg", "Provider=MSPersist"

'Sort copied data by table name within table type
rst2.Sort = "TABLE_TYPE, TABLE_NAME"

'Compute maximum length of TABLE_NAME and TABLE_TYPE columns
int1 = FindTheLongest(rst2, "TABLE_NAME") + 1
rst2.MoveFirst
int2 = FindTheLongest(rst2, "TABLE_TYPE") + 1
rst2.MoveFirst

'Loop through sorted results set from OPENSCHEMA query,
'and print selected columns
Do Until rst2.EOF
```

```
        Debug.Print rst2.Fields("TABLE_NAME") & _
            String(int1 - Len(rst2("TABLE_NAME")), " ") & _
            rst2.Fields("TABLE_TYPE") & _
            String(int2 - Len(rst2("TABLE_TYPE")), " ") & _
            rst2.Fields("DATE_MODIFIED"), _
            rst2.Fields("DATE_CREATED")
        rst2.MoveNext
Loop

SortedTableTypes_Exit:
rst1.Close
rst2.Close
cnn1.Close
Set rst1 = Nothing
Set rst2 = Nothing
Set cnn1 = Nothing
Exit Sub


SortedTableTypes_Trap:
If err.Number = 58 Then
'Kill the temporary file of table data if it already exists,
'and resume writing to the file
    Kill "C:\PMA Samples\Chapter 02\foo.adtg"
    Resume
Else
    MsgBox "Procedure failed with an error number = " _
        & err.Number & ", " & vbCrLf & "and an " & _
        "error description of """ & _
        err.Description & """" & ".", vbInformation, _
        "Programming Microsoft Access Version 2002"
    Resume SortedTableTypes_Exit
End If

End Sub
```

The *Field* Object

A field is a column of data containing entries with the same data type. In the ADODB library, the *Fields* collection used to belong exclusively to recordsets, and its members are *Field* objects. *Field* objects have properties and methods for storing and retrieving data. With Access 2002, the *Fields* collection also became a member of the *Record* object. This expands the scope of a field beyond relational database models so that it can also embrace the parent-child model suitable for working with child files as members of parent folders.

Recordsets use a *Field* object's *Value* property to display the contents of a column in the current record. Many of the other *Field* properties contain metadata about the data in a record. The *Name* property is a handle by which your applications can reference a field. The *DefinedSize* property characterizes the maximum size of a field (in characters for *Text* fields). The *ActualSize* property is the actual length (in bytes) of the contents of a *Field* object's value. The *Attributes* property contains an array of information features about a field. It can indicate whether a field's value is updateable or whether it can contain Nulls.

> **Note**   The *DefinedSize* and *ActualSize* properties use different measurements for *Text* fields. *DefinedSize* is the maximum number of characters in the field, and *ActualSize* is the number of bytes in the field. Since a *Text* field with Jet 4 represents characters with 2 bytes each, its *ActualSize* value can be up to twice the *DefinedSize* value. For numeric fields, and *Text* fields in databases that represent characters using a single byte (for example, a Jet 3.51 database), this difference does not exist. If you are migrating from Access 97 to Access 2002, you are probably using Jet 3.51. Therefore, you should be especially sensitive to this distinction.

The *GetChunk* and *AppendChunk* methods of the *Field* object facilitate the processing of large text or binary data fields in smaller chunks that fit into memory more conveniently. You use the *GetChunk* method to bring a portion of a large field into memory. The *Size* argument specifies the number of bytes to retrieve in one invocation of the *GetChunk* method. Each uninterrupted, successive invocation of the method starts reading new data from where the previous one finished. The *AppendChunk* method lets you construct a large text or binary data field in chunks from memory. Like the *GetChunk* method, *AppendChunk* writes new data into a field from where the previous *AppendChunk* method finished. To use either method correctly, a *Field* object's *adFldLong* bit in the *Attributes* property must be set to True.

Name and *Value* Properties

The following pair of procedures demonstrates an application for the *Name* and *Value* properties of the *Field* object. The application enumerates the field names and values in any row of any table in any database. The first procedure, *CallFieldNameValue*, passes information that points at a row in a table of a database. The called procedure, *FieldNameValue*, constructs a single-record recordset based on the passed arguments. It then enumerates the field names and values for the row in the recordset.

Two alternate sets of passed arguments appear in first procedure. The set without comment markers is for a string criterion, such as the *CustomerID* field in the *Customers* table. The set with comments is for a numeric criterion, such as the *ShipperID* field in the *Shippers* table. Both sets rely on the Northwind database, but you can freely change all these arguments to specify the field names and values in any particular row of any table within any database. The value for *str3* should be the name of a field that has a unique value for each row in the table, such as a primary key. The *var1* variable should contain a string value or a number value for the field denoted by *str3*.

```
Sub CallFieldNameValue()
Dim str1 As String
Dim str2 As String
Dim str3 As String
Dim var1 As Variant

'Specify data source for field name
'and value data
str1 = "Provider=Microsoft.Jet.OLEDB.4.0;" & _
    "Data Source=C:\PMA Samples\Northwind.mdb;"

'Denote a specific record source
'within the data source
str2 = "Customers"
'str2 = "Shippers"

'Designate a criterion field (str3) and a criterion
'value (str4) for picking a particular row from
'the record source
str3 = "CustomerID"
var1 = "BONAP"
'str3 = "ShipperID"
'var1 = 2

'Call the procedure to enumerate field names
'and values
FieldNameValue str1, str2, str3, var1

End Sub
```

(continued)

```
Sub FieldNameValue(str1 As String, _
    str2 As String, str3 As String, _
    var1 As Variant)
Dim cnn1 As ADODB.Connection
Dim rst1 As ADODB.Recordset
Dim str5 As String
Dim fld1 As ADODB.Field

'Open connection and recordset
Set cnn1 = New ADODB.Connection
cnn1.Open str1
Set rst1 = New ADODB.Recordset
rst1.ActiveConnection = cnn1
If IsNumeric(var1) Then
    str5 = "SELECT * FROM " & str2 & _
        " WHERE " & str3 & "=" & var1
Else
    str5 = "SELECT * FROM " & str2 & _
        " WHERE " & str3 & "='" & var1 & "'"

End If
rst1.Open str5, , , , adCmdText

'Report field names and values for record
For Each fld1 In rst1.Fields
    Debug.Print fld1.Name, fld1.Value
Next fld1

End Sub
```

The second procedure uses an SQL string to designate the source for the single-row recordset. It selects all the rows from any table where the field value in *str3* equals *var1*. After constructing the recordset, a *Do* loop passes through each row. On each iteration, the loop prints the *Name* and *Value* properties for one field.

The *Type* Property

A *Field* object's *Type* property indicates the kind of data it can contain. This property returns one of the data type constants in the *DataTypeEnum* values range. You can view these options in the Object Browser for the ADODB library. Figure 2-8 shows these constants in the Object Browser screen. By selecting the type for a field, you can determine legitimate values for its *Value* property.

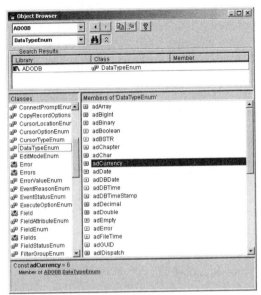

Figure 2-8 The Object Browser showing a selection of data type constants for defining fields.

Printing Field Data Types

The following two procedures work together to process data type constants with ADO. The *FieldNameType* procedure opens a recordset based on the *Orders* table in the Northwind database. This table has a reasonable variety of data types, so it makes a nice case study for examining data types. After opening a recordset, the procedure loops through the fields in the recordset and prints each *Field* object's name and type. The *FieldType* function translates the numeric constant's value to a string that represents the constant's name. The *adCurrency* constant has a value of 6, for example, as shown in Figure 2-8. The *FieldType* function decodes the value 6 to the string *"adCurrency"*. The *FieldNameType* procedure then prints each field's name and data type constant name.

```
Sub FieldNameType()
Dim cnn1 As ADODB.Connection
Dim rst1 As ADODB.Recordset
Dim fld1 As ADODB.Field
Dim str1 As String

'Open connection and recordset
    str1 = "Provider=Microsoft.Jet.OLEDB.4.0;" & _
        "Data Source=C:\PMA Samples\Northwind.mdb;"
    Set cnn1 = New ADODB.Connection
```

(continued)

```
        cnn1.Open str1
        Set rst1 = New ADODB.Recordset
        rst1.ActiveConnection = cnn1
        rst1.Open "orders", , , , adCmdTable

    'Report field names and types for record
        For Each fld1 In rst1.Fields
            Debug.Print "  Name: " & fld1.Name & vbCr & _
                " Type: " & FieldType(fld1.Type) & vbCr
        Next fld1
    End Sub


    Public Function FieldType(intType As Integer) As String
        Select Case intType
            Case adVarWChar
                FieldType = "adVarWChar"
            Case adCurrency
                FieldType = "adCurrency"
            Case adInteger
                FieldType = "adInteger"
            Case adDate
                FieldType = "adDate"
        End Select
    End Function
```

You can easily run *FieldNameType* and *FieldType* against recordsets based on other data sources than the *Orders* table, but the *FieldType* function checks only for the four data types in the *Orders* table. When you use a record source other than the *Orders* table, you might encounter a data type other than the four in the list. In this case, the *Type* field in the report will be blank. You can fix this problem by determining the value of the field. You can do this by putting a breakpoint on the *Debug.Print* statement inside the *Do* loop in the *FieldNameType* procedure. You examine the value of *fld1.Type* for a field whose type doesn't display and then match that constant value against the constant names in the Object Browser for *DataTypeEnum*. (See Figure 2-8.) Finally, you amend the *Select Case* statement in the *FieldType* procedure to decode the new constant.

> **Note**   Place your cursor over an expression or memory variable to determine its value at a breakpoint. You can also track the values of expressions and memory variables in the Watch window. See Chapter 1 for a discussion of how to use the Watch window.

Creating Fields for a Recordset

Using the *Fields* collection *Append* method, you can create fields for a recordset. In addition, your applications can assign values to those fields. Because it is possible to persist recordsets, you can save recordsets that your applications create on the fly to hold data originally stored as a disconnected recordset. You can leave the recordset on the workstation used to create it or transfer it later to a network-based database for sharing by many users.

The following procedure, *CreateRecordset*, demonstrates the key elements of this approach. First, the procedure instantiates an empty recordset. The procedure uses the *Append* method to populate the empty recordset with fields. As you can see, the procedure assigns the minimum number of *Append* arguments. These include the field name and data type. When you specify a string data type, such as *adVarWChar*, you must also designate its maximum length—ADO terminology calls this the *DefinedSize* argument. Use the third positional argument to specify a field's *DefinedSize*. After defining the schema for the recordset, the procedure moves on to populating its two fields with two rows of data. Then it echoes the data to the Immediate window to confirm the data entry operation. Finally, the procedure persists the recordset to a file using the proprietary Microsoft format. So long as the data is exclusively for reading by the recordset's *Open* method, there is no compelling factor that establishes a preference for either of the two formats available with the *Save* method.

```
Sub CreateRecordset()
On Error GoTo CreateRecordset_Trap
Dim rst1 As ADODB.Recordset
Dim strPath As String
Dim strFileName As String
Dim str1 As String

'Instantiate a recordset
Set rst1 = New ADODB.Recordset

'Specify recordset field name and data type.
'Append to recordset object.
rst1.Fields.Append "LastName", adVarWChar, 10
rst1.Fields.Append "ContactID", adInteger

'Add rows to the recordset
rst1.Open
With rst1
    rst1.AddNew
        rst1("LastName") = "Dobson"
        rst1("ContactID") = 9
```

(continued)

```
        rst1.Update
        rst1.AddNew
            rst1("LastName") = "Edelstein"
            rst1("ContactID") = 10
        rst1.Update
    End With

    'Echo new contact data to Immediate window
    rst1.MoveFirst
    Do While Not rst1.EOF
        Debug.Print rst1("LastName") & _
            " " & rst1("ContactID")
        rst1.MoveNext
    Loop

    'Specify path and file to hold persisted recordset,
    'and save recordset to it
    strPath = "C:\PMA Samples\Chapter 02\"
    strFileName = "NewContactData.adtg"
    str1 = strPath + strFileName
    rst1.Save str1, adPersistXML

CreateRecordset_Exit:
    rst1.Close
    Set rst1 = Nothing
    Exit Sub

CreateRecordset_Trap:
    'Kill previous version of file to hold
    'persisted recordset if it exists already
    'Otherwise, present error info in a message box.
    If err.Number = 58 Then
        Kill str1
        Resume
    Else
        MsgBox "Procedure failed with an error number = " _
            & err.Number & ", " & vbCrLf & "and an " & _
            "error description of """ & _
            err.Description & """" & ".", vbInformation, _
            "Programming Microsoft Access Version 2002"
        Resume CreateRecordset_Exit
    End If

End Sub
```

3

Data Access Models: Part II

This is the second of two chapters covering data access models. As I mentioned at the beginning of Chapter 2 ("Data Access Models: Part I"), the topic of data access models is extensive, which is why I've broken it into two chapters. Chapter 2 presented you with an overview of ActiveX Data Objects (ADO) and examined the *Connection, Recordset,* and *Field* objects. In this chapter, you'll learn about the *Command* and *Parameter* objects and the *Errors* collection. I'll also show you several techniques for managing access to the files on a Web server, demonstrate the features of the new *Record* and *Stream* ADO objects, and explore further the new functionality of the *Recordset* object. Furthermore, the end of this chapter presents a discussion of ADO event programming and provides code samples.

Command and *Parameter* Objects

The *Command* object within the ADODB library delivers three major benefits. First, it can be used to perform a select query to return a set of rows from a data source. Second, it can be used to execute a parameter query so that users can input run-time search criteria. And finally, it supports action queries against a data source to perform operations such as updating, deleting, and adding records.

You must designate a *Connection* object on which to run a command. You can either implicitly create a *Connection* object when you specify a command or explicitly assign an existing *Connection* object to a command. These are the same options as you have for recordsets.

The *CommandTimeout* property determines how long ADO waits for the execution of a command to conclude. This property takes a *Long* value that specifies the maximum wait time in seconds. The default value for this property is 30 seconds. If the timeout interval elapses before the *Command* object completes execution, ADO cancels the command and returns an error. The *Connection* object also supports a *CommandTimeout* property. Although this property has the same name as the *CommandTimeout* property of the *Command* object, it is independent of that property; the *Command* object's *CommandTimeout* property does not inherit the setting of the *Connection* object's *CommandTimeout* property.

> **Note** When a *Command* object's *CommandTimeout* setting is important to your application, make sure it's compatible with the *Connection* object's *CommandTimeout* setting. For example, the default *Command* object's timeout setting is 30 seconds, but the default *Connection* object's timeout setting is 15 seconds. Therefore, if a workstation using your application does not make a connection within 15 sections, it will never have an opportunity to use the *Command* object.

There are actually several types for the *Command* object. The *CommandType* property sets the type of the *Command* object and lets ADO know how to interpret the object's *CommandText* property. You can base your command on an SQL statement, a table, or a stored procedure by setting the *CommandType* property to one of the values shown in Table 3-1. When working with a database, a stored procedure is equivalent to either a stored action query or a stored select query with parameters. Basing your command on an SQL statement keeps your query out of the Database window, although performance isn't as good as basing the command on a stored query.

Table 3-1 Intrinsic Constants for the *CommandTypeEnum*

Constant	Value	Behavior
adCmdUnspecified	−1	Informs ADO that no *CommandText* property setting exists. Do not use this setting with the OLE DB provider for AS/400 and VSAM or the OLE DB provider for DB 2.
adCmdText	1	Lets you run a command based on an SQL statement, a stored procedure, or even a table. Usually, you reserve this setting for an SQL statement. This is the only legitimate setting for the OLE DB provider for AS/400 and VSAM or the OLE DB provider for DB 2.
adCmdTable	2	Bases the return set on a previously designed table. Returns all columns from a table based on an internally generated SQL statement.

Constant	Value	Behavior
adCmdStoredProc	*4*	Runs a command based on text for a stored procedure.
adCmdUnknown	*8*	Informs ADO that there is no specification of the type of command. This is the default, except when MSPersist serves as the provider.
adCmdFile	*256*	Evaluates a source argument for a recordset's *Open* method based on the filename for a persistent recordset. This is the default when MSPersist is the provider. This setting is not appropriate for *Command* objects.
adCmdTableDirect	*512*	Evaluates a command as a table name. Returns all columns in a table without any intermediate SQL code. Use with the *Seek* method for a recordset.

The default setting for the *CommandType* property is *adCmdUnknown*. Changing the *CommandType* property from its default setting can speed up the operation of a command by reducing the need for ADO to call your provider to properly interpret a command's *CommandText* setting.

> **Note**   You can further improve the performance of commands that do not return records (such as action queries) by adding *adExecuteNoRecords* to a command's *CommandType* specification. Be sure to always use *adExecuteNoRecords,* which has the value 128, with another setting, as shown here:
>
> ```
> cmd1.CommandType = adCmdText + adExecuteNoRecords
> ```

The *CommandText* setting lets you designate what the command should do. You can assign an SQL string to define an operation for the command to perform. Use SQL syntax compatible with the provider for your command's *ActiveConnection* setting. You can also set the *CommandText* property to the name of a stored query or the name of a table. You should update the *CommandType* property to synchronize it with the setting of the *CommandText* property. For example, if a *CommandText* property points at a stored action query, designate *adCmdStoredProc* for the *CommandType* property.

If an application stays open for extended periods of time during which it executes a command repeatedly, you can improve the command's performance by using the *Prepared* property with an SQL statement. If the *Prepared* property is set to True, the SQL statement is compiled and saved on the database server the first time the statement is used. This slows the first execution of the command but speeds up subsequent ones..

The *Execute* method for a *Command* object invokes the code behind the *Command* object (for example, a stored query or an SQL statement). You can specify up to three optional arguments for the *Execute* method. The first argument allows the *Command* object to tell the procedure invoking it how many records it has affected. This argument pertains exclusively to action queries with Jet data sources or stored procedures on other types of databases, such as Microsoft SQL Server. (Use the *RecordCount* property on the resulting recordset to determine the number of records returned by a row-returning select query.) The second argument is a *Variant* array containing parameters to drive the command. This approach to designating parameters is for input parameters only. The third argument tells ADO how to evaluate the source. This argument can be any appropriate *CommandTypeEnum* member listed in Table 3-1, possibly combined with the *adExecuteNoRecords* intrinsic constant.

The *Command* object's *CreateParameter* method creates a new parameter for a command. After creating the parameter, you can use the *Append* method to add the parameter to the *Parameters* collection of a command. Before running a parameter query, you must assign a value to the parameter. Using the *CreateParameter* method works for input parameters, output parameters, and return values from stored procedures. While it's somewhat more complicated to code, I generally prefer this approach for working with parameters because it is more robust than using the *Array* argument of the *Execute* method.

> **Note**   You can use either an array or the *CreateParameter* method for passing parameters. In this case, the *Array* argument for the *Execute* method overrides any prior settings for your parameter values.

Creating a Recordset with a Select Query

One of the most straightforward tasks you can perform with a *Command* object is to create a recordset based on a select query. The *Execute* method of the *Command* object runs the select query and returns the resulting recordset. The *SelectCommand* procedure that follows shows how to do this. This procedure has two parts: the first part creates the *Command* object and a connection for it to relate to a database, and the second part processes a recordset returned from the *Command* object.

> **Note**   Before running the following procedure, make sure that *MyTable* in the Chapter 03.mdb sample file contains some data. If the file is empty, run the *InsertRecords* procedure on the companion CD to populate *MyTable* with values automatically.

```
Sub SelectCommand()
Dim cmd1 As ADODB.Command
Dim rst1 As ADODB.Recordset
Dim str1 As String
Dim fld1 As ADODB.Field

'Define and execute command
Set cmd1 = New ADODB.Command
With cmd1
    .ActiveConnection = CurrentProject.Connection
    .CommandText = "SELECT MyTable.* FROM MyTable"
    .CommandType = adCmdText
End With

'Set rst1 to the recordset returned by the command's
'Execute method, and print the recordset
Set rst1 = cmd1.Execute
Do Until rst1.EOF
    str1 = ""
    For Each fld1 In rst1.Fields
        str1 = str1 & fld1.Value & vbTab
    Next fld1
    Debug.Print str1
    rst1.MoveNext
Loop

'Clean up objects
rst1.Close
Set fld1 = Nothing
Set rst1 = Nothing
Set cmd1 = Nothing

End Sub
```

The first part of the procedure declares *cmd1* as a *Command* object and then sets three critical properties. Every command must have an *ActiveConnection* property in order to run against a database. The *Command* object in this sample relies on an SQL statement to represent its select query. The third assignment in the *With...End With* block sets the *CommandType* property to *adCmdText*. You can substitute a saved query for the SQL statement, as shown in the following example:

```
.CommandText = "CustomerID"
.CommandType = adCmdStoredProc
```

The second part of the procedure saves a reference to the recordset returned by the *Execute* method. This is necessary if you want to view the rows returned by the SQL string in the *CommandText* property because commands offer no methods for navigating through a recordset. Notice that you don't need to instantiate the *Recordset* object before assigning the return from the command's *Execute* method to it. The assignment instantiates the *Recordset* object. After saving a reference to the result, the procedure prints each record in the recordset with tab delimiters (*vbTab*) between fields in the Immediate window. The procedure can handle any number of columns in any number of rows.

Creating a Recordset with a Parameter Query

The following code demonstrates the syntax for a parameter query. This procedure also has two major parts to its design. The parameter query in the first part has some extra lines of ADO code and a different SQL statement syntax from that of the previous select query. The second part of this procedure, which assigns the result of the command to a recordset and prints the recordset, is the same as that of the previous select query.

```
Sub ParameterQCommand()
Dim cmd1 As ADODB.Command
Dim rst1 As ADODB.Recordset
Dim str1 As String
Dim fld1 As ADODB.Field
Dim prm1 As ADODB.Parameter
Dim int1 As Integer

'Create and define command
Set cmd1 = New ADODB.Command
With cmd1
    .ActiveConnection = CurrentProject.Connection
    .CommandText = "Parameters [Lowest] Long;" & _
        "SELECT Column1, Column2, Column3 " & _
        "FROM MyTable " & _
        "WHERE Column1>=[Lowest]"
    .CommandType = adCmdText
End With
```

```
'Create and define parameter
Set prm1 = cmd1.CreateParameter("[Lowest]", _
    adInteger, adParamInput)
cmd1.Parameters.Append prm1
int1 = Trim(InputBox("Lowest value?", _
    "Programming Microsoft Access Version 2002"))
prm1.Value = int1

'Open recordset on return from cmd1 and print
'the recordset
Set rst1 = cmd1.Execute
Do Until rst1.EOF
    str1 = ""
    For Each fld1 In rst1.Fields
        str1 = str1 & fld1.Value & vbTab
    Next fld1
    Debug.Print str1
    rst1.MoveNext
Loop

'Clean up objects
rst1.Close
Set fld1 = Nothing
Set rst1 = Nothing
Set cmd1 = Nothing

End Sub
```

The SQL statement syntax uses a *Parameters* declaration line that specifies the parameter's name and data type. The WHERE clause should also reference one or more parameters so that the parameters can affect the results set. By themselves, these adjustments to the SQL syntax statement are not sufficient to make the parameter query work—you must create the parameter and append it to the command using ADO code.

To create the parameter, invoke the *CreateParameter* method. The previous code uses three arguments with the *CreateParameter* method. The first one names the parameter, the second designates a data type for the parameter, and the third declares the input/output direction for the parameter. The *adParamInput* intrinsic constant is actually the default that declares the parameter an input to the query. Other constants let you designate output, input/output, and return value parameters. These other parameter types are appropriate for databases other than Jet, such as SQL Server. After creating a parameter, you must append it to the *Parameters* collection of the command.

> **Note**   When creating a string parameter with the *CreateParameter* method, you must specify the number of characters after designating the data type. It is not necessary to designate the length of numeric data types.

After adding a parameter, you must assign a value to it to make the command's parameter query function properly. The previous code uses an *InputBox* function to gather input from a user. The procedure then invokes the *Command* object's *Execute* method in an assignment statement to save a reference to the resulting recordset so that it can be printed.

Deleting Records

As mentioned earlier, you can use the *Command* object to delete, update, and add records to a data source. *Command* objects offer a programmatic means to maintain a data source. The *DeleteARecord* and *DeleteAllRecords* procedures that follow prune records from a record source, such as the *MyTable* table in Chapter 03.mdb. The *DeleteARecord* procedure removes at most a single row from the table with the *Column1* value equal to 13. The *DeleteAllRecords* procedure removes all rows from the table no matter what values they have. These samples designate the record source and the criteria for selecting records using an SQL DELETE statement.

With the Microsoft Access Database window's query designer, you can graphically design a query and then copy the code from the query's SQL view to the *CommandText* property of a command. Normally, it is possible to improve the readability of the SQL code from the Access query designer by editing it slightly. For example, examine the SQL statement for extra parentheses that you can remove. If your query operates on a single table, you can remove the table prefix shown before field names. Compare for readability the following SQL statements with those that you generate automatically with the Access query designer.

```
Sub DeleteARecord()
Dim cmd1 As ADODB.Command

Set cmd1 = New ADODB.Command

With cmd1
    .ActiveConnection = CurrentProject.Connection
    .CommandText = "DELETE Column1 FROM " & _
        "MyTable WHERE Column1=13;"
    .CommandType = adCmdText
    .Execute
```

```
End With

End Sub


Sub DeleteAllRecords()
Dim cmd1 As ADODB.Command

Set cmd1 = New ADODB.Command

With cmd1
    .ActiveConnection = CurrentProject.Connection
    .CommandText = "DELETE * FROM MyTable"
    .CommandType = adCmdText
    .Execute
End With

End Sub
```

Inserting Records

When you develop an application, you might want to delete all the records from a table and then reset its contents. The *InsertRecords* procedure, shown next, uses the *Command* object to stock a table with values. You can use this procedure in conjunction with the *DeleteAllRecords* procedure to refresh a table with a small base set of records.

```
Sub InsertRecords()
Dim cmd1 As ADODB.Command

Set cmd1 = New ADODB.Command

With cmd1
    .ActiveConnection = CurrentProject.Connection
    .CommandText = "INSERT INTO MyTable(Column1, " & _
        "Column2, Column3) VALUES (1,2,'3')"
    .CommandType = adCmdText
    .Execute
    .CommandText = "INSERT INTO MyTable(Column1, " & _
        "Column2, Column3) VALUES (4,5,'6')"

    .Execute
    .CommandText = "INSERT INTO MyTable(Column1, " & _
        "Column2, Column3) VALUES (7,8,'9')"

    .Execute
    .CommandText = "INSERT INTO MyTable(Column1, " & _
        "Column2, Column3) VALUES (10,11,'12')"
```

(continued)

```
      .Execute
      .CommandText = "INSERT INTO MyTable(Column1, " & _
          "Column2, Column3) VALUES (13,14,'15')"

      .Execute
      .CommandText = "INSERT INTO MyTable(Column1, " & _
          "Column2, Column3) VALUES (16,17,'18')"

      .Execute
  End With

  End Sub
```

The general elements of the *InsertRecords* procedure are shared with other applications of the *Command* object and do not depend on the design of a particular table. You must create a reference to the *Command* object and set its *Connection* property. Three lines are required for each row that you add to a recordset: the *CommandText* property setting, which indicates what the command will do; the *CommandType* property setting, which designates the format of the instruction; and the *Execute* method, which launches the addition of the new record. You can repeat these three lines for each row added to the data source (though you don't need to reset *CommandType* unless you are changing the type). If you specify an updatable dynaset as the target, these steps can concurrently add records to two or more tables at the same time. When you add records to a table, you must consider the field data types. In the previous code, the *CommandText* settings are tailored specifically for the structure of the *MyTable* table. You can determine the data types for the columns in *MyTable* by running the *FieldNameType* subprocedure described at the end of Chapter 2. Just change the connection string so that it points to the Access database file holding *MyTable*, Chapter 03.mdb. If *MyTable* is in the current database, you can denote the connection with the expression *CurrentProject.Connection*. The first two columns in *MyTable* have Long Integer data types, and the third column has a Text data type.

The syntax of the *CommandText* SQL statement in this sample has three parts. (This syntax is not available from the SQL view of the Access query designer.) First, the statement uses the INSERT INTO keyword, which is followed by the name of the data source to which you want to add records. Second, it takes the optional step of listing the field names for which it submits values. If you do not list the field names, the values in the next step will be appended in sequential order, which could be a problem if the data source design changes over time. Third, the VALUES keyword appears before the field values for the new record.

You will frequently want to add a new row to a table with some values that you acquire from another source, such as a form. The following code shows two procedures. The first procedure assigns values to three string variables and invokes the second procedure, which actually inserts the values into the table. In actual practice, you can assign the strings in the first procedure's value from a form or even with an *InputBox* function. The second procedure splices the string values into the INSERT INTO SQL statement. While we could make this more complicated by using parameters, this simple design gets the job done. Invoking a parameter query lets users type input values for the parameters (for example, with an *InputBox* function). The simple design of the following procedure uses string data types for all fields on input and then splices them into the INSERT INTO statement so that strings for numeric fields become numbers and others remain strings.

```
Sub CallInsertARecord()
Dim str1 As String
Dim str2 As String
Dim str3 As String

str1 = "19"
str2 = "20"
str3 = "21"

InsertARecord str1, str2, str3

End Sub


Sub InsertARecord(str1 As String, _
    str2 As String, str3 As String)
Dim cmd1 As ADODB.Command

Set cmd1 = New Command

With cmd1
    .ActiveConnection = CurrentProject.Connection
    .CommandText = "INSERT INTO MyTable(Column1, " & _
        "Column2, Column3) VALUES (" & str1 & "," & _
        str2 & ",'" & str3 & "')"
    .CommandType = adCmdText
    .Execute
End With

End Sub
```

Updating Values

The *OddToEven* and *EvenToOdd* procedures that follow update the data source values of *Column1* using the *Command* object. Make sure that *MyTable* has row values before running the procedures in this section. If *MyTable* does not have row values, invoke both the *InsertRecords* procedure and the *CallInsertARecord* procedure.

Notice from the *InsertRecords* procedure that the *Column1* values alternate between odd and even numbers. The first row has the value 1 in *Column1*, and the second row has the value 4 in *Column1*. The rows of *Column1* continue to alternate between odd and even values throughout *MyTable*. The procedures in this next code sample use this information to manage the contents of the table.

```
Sub OddToEven()
Dim cmd1 As ADODB.Command
Dim intRowsChanged As Integer

Set cmd1 = New ADODB.Command

With cmd1
    .ActiveConnection = CurrentProject.Connection
    .CommandText = "UPDATE MyTable SET Column1 = " & _
        "Column1+1 WHERE ((-1*(Column1 Mod 2))=True)"
    .CommandType = adCmdText
    .Execute intRowsChanged
    MsgBox intRowsChanged & " rows were affected.", _
        vbInformation, "Programming Microsoft Access Version 2002"
End With

End Sub



Sub EvenToOdd()
Dim cmd1 As ADODB.Command
Dim intRowsChanged As Integer

Set cmd1 = New ADODB.Command

With cmd1
    .ActiveConnection = CurrentProject.Connection
    .CommandText = "UPDATE MyTable SET Column1 = " & _
        "Column1-1 WHERE ((-1*(Column2 Mod 2))=False)"
    .CommandType = adCmdText
    .Execute intRowsChanged
    MsgBox intRowsChanged & " rows were affected.", _
        vbInformation, "Programming Microsoft Access Version 2002"
End With

End Sub
```

The overall design of these procedures should be familiar to you by now. The most significant difference between these code samples and the ones you saw earlier in the chapter is in the syntax of the SQL statement for the *CommandText* property. In this case, you can easily derive that general syntax from the Access query designer. The WHERE clause in the *OddToEven* procedure selects records whose *Column1* value is odd. The UPDATE part of the syntax adds 1 to the value to convert it from an odd number to an even number. The statement invoking the *Execute* method takes advantage of the method's first argument to determine the number of rows that the command changes. A simple *MsgBox* function reports the result to the user.

The *EvenToOdd* procedure reverses the effect of running the *OddToEven* procedure. The latter procedure examines the entry in *Column2* to determine whether it should subtract 1 from the value in *Column1*. When the entry in *Column2* is not odd, the SQL statement operates on the value in *Column1*. This restores the entries in *Column1* to their initial values if *EvenToOdd* runs immediately after the *OddToEven* procedure.

The *Errors* Collection

The *Errors* collection lets you trap some but not all errors that occur in an ADO application. The members of this collection let you examine errors returned from an OLE data provider. A single error condition can return multiple errors, each of which causes a new *Error* object to be placed in the *Errors* collection. Some errors cause a program termination; others do not. A new failure automatically clears the *Errors* collection of all previous errors. ADO errors, as opposed to data provider errors, enter the Visual Basic for Applications (VBA) *Err* object rather than the *Errors* collection. The *Errors* collection is most appropriate for handling connection-based errors returned from a remote database through the database's OLE data provider. Because the *Errors* collection belongs to the *Connection* object, you need an explicit *Connection* object to examine errors returned by a data provider.

> **Note** The members of *ErrorValueEnum* represent a complete list of ADO errors. You can learn more about these errors from the Object Browser.

Error Object Properties

The *Error* objects in the *Errors* collection have six properties to help you gather more information so that you can respond to them with program logic. The *Number* and *Description* properties parallel those for the *Err* object that you've already seen in VBA error traps. The *Error* object's *Number* and *Description* properties complement one another. The *Number* property returns a unique number that identifies an error, and the *Description* property returns a brief string that describes the error. The *NativeError* property offers a provider-specific error code. If you often work with a particular provider, this property might provide useful information about how to resolve an error. The *Source* property names the object or application that originated the error. The *SQLState* property can contain error messages originating from the database server to which you submit your request concerning errors in your SQL statement syntax. Providers can also return *HelpFile* and *HelpContext* properties for error objects. Since these properties work together, I count them one property. Furthermore, *HelpFile* and *HelpContext* are not always available. A zero-length string for an error's *HelpFile* property signals that the two properties are not available.

Generating and Trapping *Error* and *Err* Objects

The *OpenLookOnlySQLErrors* procedure shown next is an adaptation of the *OpenLookOnly* procedure in Chapter 2 that reveals the impact of the *Connection* object's *Mode* property. This update uses a connection to a computer running SQL Server instead of a local Jet database, and it includes advice in comments on how to create various errors. Implementing these errors and stepping through the procedure will help you understand how the ADO *Errors* collection and the VBA *Err* object complement one another. A read-only setting for the procedure (as it appears here) generates an error when you attempt to update a database. Interestingly, this error does not become part of the *Errors* collection. You can confirm this by stepping through the *OpenLookOnlySQLErrors* procedure. The *Err* object traps the error instead.

> **Note** Database connection errors that generate *Error* objects propagate through to the VBA *Err* object. When the *Err* object does not provide sufficient context for you to fix an error, use the *Errors* collection for more detail on the cause of the error.

```
Sub OpenLookOnlySQLErrors()
Dim cnn1 As Connection
Dim rst1 As Recordset
Dim errLoop As Error, intInErrors As Integer
On Error GoTo LookOnlyTrap

Set cnn1 = New ADODB.Connection
cnn1.Mode = adModeRead
cnn1.Open "Provider=sqloledb;Data Source=cab2000;" & _
    "Initial Catalog=NorthwindCS;User Id=sa;Password=password;"

'Spell NorthwindCS incorrectly to force VBA error only
'cnn1.Open "Provider=sqloledb;Data Source=cab2000;" & _
    "Initial Catalog=NorthwindsCS;User Id=sa;Password=password;"

'Spell sqloledb incorrectly to force VBA and provider error
'cnn1.Open "Provider=sqloledbs;Data Source=cab2000;" & _
    "Initial Catalog=NorthwindCS;User Id=sa;Password=password;"

'Manually stop SQL Server to force VBA and provider error

'Spell user ID incorrectly to generate VBA and provider errors
'cnn1.Open "Provider=sqloledb;Data Source=cab2000;" & _
    "Initial Catalog=NorthwindCS;User Id=sas;Password=password;"


Set rst1 = New ADODB.Recordset
rst1.ActiveConnection = cnn1
'Spell rst1 incorrectly to force a 424 VBA error
'Spell cnn1 as cnn to force a 3001 VBA error
'rst.ActiveConnection = cnn1
'rst1.ActiveConnection = cnn

'Spell table name as "Customer" to force VBA and provider
'error that equals -2147217900
rst1.Open "Customers"
'rst1.Open "Customer"

'adModeRead setting for cnn1.Mode causes a VBA error
'of 3251 here; remove cnn1.Mode line to enable updates
rst1.Fields("CustomerID") = "xxxxx"
rst1.Update
Debug.Print rst1.Fields("CustomerID")
rst1.Close
```

(continued)

```
LookOnlyTrap:
'Loop through and print provider errors
For Each errLoop In cnn1.Errors
Debug.Print errLoop.Number, errLoop.Description
Next errLoop

'Print VBA Err object
Debug.Print err.Number, err.Description

End Sub
```

The last member of the *Errors* collection also appears in the *Err* object, illustrating that one or more provider errors propagate to both the *Errors* collection and the VBA *Err* object. Commenting the first *Open* method and removing the comment marker from the second use of the *Open* method generates an attempt to link to an invalid database. (The *Initial Catalog* parameter spells the database name incorrectly.) This flaw causes a provider error that populates the *Errors* collection and writes the same error number and message to the VBA *Err* object.

Review the comments throughout the program to see how to generate a selection of errors that creates ADO errors exclusively for the *Err* object or provides errors for both the *Err* object and the *Errors* collection. The companion CD contains a procedure named *OpenLookOnlyErrors* that parallels this one except that it connects to a Jet database instead of an SQL Server database.

Recordsets, Records, Streams, and the Web

The ADO *Record* and *Stream* objects are particularly well suited for working with nonrelational data, such as files in directories and content in electronic mail systems. In addition, the OLE DB Provider for Internet Publishing extends these capabilities for accessing and manipulating files and Web folders at a Microsoft FrontPage Web site. These innovations permit Access 2002 database developers to access and manipulate these nontraditional data sources with only minor extensions to the way they work with relational databases. This section examines how to use records, streams, and recordsets to navigate through the files in Web folders at URLs.

> **Note**   A Uniform Resource Locator (URL) designates the location of a resource, such as a text file or a binary file on a local or networked computer. Although the concept of URLs emerged from use of the Internet, it has evolved into a broader method for specifying the location of resources on networked computers. As time passes, your use of URLs is likely to increase beyond what was once narrowly considered "Web work."

A *Record* object can point directly at an absolute URL, a combination of a relative and an absolute URL, or the current row in a recordset. (I'll define absolute and relative URLs in a moment.) When a record points at the current row of a recordset, that row is a node in a hierarchical system, which can be the files and folders of a URL.

URLs can have as many as four parts: scheme, server, path, and resource. The scheme specifies a means of reaching a resource. When working on the Internet or an intranet, you will commonly use the http: scheme. The http designation stands for Hypertext Transfer Protocol. The server references the name of the computer hosting the resource; this will often be a Web server. The path is the sequence of directories on the server that leads to the target resource. You can optionally include the resource within the path or specify it separately as the resource component of a URL.

As I hinted at earlier, there are two kinds of URLs: absolute and relative. An absolute URL designates the full location for a resource, from the scheme to the target resource. A relative URL typically will not contain the URL scheme or server, and it divides the URL into two parts, the second of which can vary. The first part of a relative URL is its base part. If all the files your application uses as resources reside in a single folder on a server that you access via the http protocol, your base URL might appear as /pathtomyfolder/. This is considered a partial absolute URL. The filenames in the target resource can serve as the second, variable portion of the URL. You can isolate more than the resource targets in the variable portion of a URL. For example, if your application draws information from several folders in a Web server's root, you can include these folders in the variable portion of a URL. A system using relative URLs can locate resources by concatenating the base and variable portions of a URL with a standard scheme and server.

You can use URLs as inputs for the *Source* and *ActiveConnection* arguments for records and recordsets. For example, a recordset opened for a relative URL can designate the base portion of the URL for *ActiveConnection* and the variable portion for *Source*. When using absolute or relative URLs to specify what a recordset connects to, use *adCmdTableDirect* as the *Options* argument. Your statement using the recordset *Open* method can appear as follows:

```
rst1.Open <variableURL>, <baseURL>, , , adCmdTableDirect
```

The *Record* object also has an *Open* method, but this object features a tailored set of arguments that targets file access on the Web. In addition to the *Source* and *ActiveConnection* arguments, other specialized arguments facilitate the use of the *Record* object's *Open* method with Web files and folders. For example, the *Record* object's *Open* method includes arguments for creating Web folders when none exist for a URL specified by the *Source* and *ActiveConnection* arguments.

Alternatively, you can force a failure if a URL points to a path or resource that does not exist. In addition, other *Open* method arguments let you designate a username and password for gaining access to a secure URL. Furthermore, the *Record* object has a *ParentURL* property that can expose the next highest node in a file hierarchy and a *GetChildren* property that returns a recordset representing the files and subdirectories within the URL for the current record.

A stream is an ADO object that resides in memory. It can store the contents of a saved file read from a disk. You can use a stream to access and manipulate the contents of these saved files with ADO programming. Streams are very flexible. For example, they enable you to work with both text and binary files. You can open a stream on objects such as a record or a binary large object (BLOB) field in a recordset. *Stream* objects offer different methods for reading the contents of binary and text files. You can read text files in any number of bytes you specify, one line at a time, or a whole file at a time. You can also persist streams to files and load them from files. You use Uniform Naming Convention (UNC) format to specify file locations.

Printing Web Folder Contents

A relatively easy way to begin understanding how to process the contents of a URL with records and recordsets is to print the contents of a Web folder. The *PrintFolderContents* procedure shown here demonstrates a straightforward approach to printing the contents of two Web folders. The sample demonstrates how to use the *Record* object to point at a node in the directory for a Web site. It starts by referencing the root directory for the cab2000 Web server. After printing the contents of that folder, the code reorients its attention to the PMA10 Web site on the cab2000 server. Then it applies the same technique for printing the contents of the Web site's folder.

```
Sub PrintFolderContents()
Dim rec1 As ADODB.Record
Dim rst1 As ADODB.Recordset

'Instantiate record and recordset objects
Set rec1 = New Record
Set rst1 = New Recordset

'Specify the URL over which the record applies
'Open the record only if it exists
rec1.Open "", "URL=http://cab2000/", , _
    adOpenIfExists Or adCreateCollection

'Return the files and subdirectories
'in rec1 to rst1
Set rst1 = rec1.GetChildren
```

```
'Print the first field's values in the recordset; this
'value matches its representation at a node in the file
'directory tree
'These results are for the server's root directory
Debug.Print "Server root directory contents:"
Do Until rst1.EOF
    Debug.Print rst1(0).Value
    rst1.MoveNext
Loop

'Close recordset and record objects for reuse
'with the directory for the PMA10 site
rst1.Close
rec1.Close
rec1.Open "", "URL=http://cab2000/PMA10", , _
    adOpenIfExists Or adCreateCollection
Set rst1 = rec1.GetChildren

'Print the first field's values in the recordset; this
'value matches its representation at a node in the file
'directory tree
'These results are for the PMA10 site's root directory
Debug.Print vbCrLf & String(10, "_") & vbCrLf
Debug.Print "PMA10 site root directory contents:"
Do Until rst1.EOF
    Debug.Print rst1(0).Value
    rst1.MoveNext
Loop

'Clean up objects
rst1.Close
rec1.Close
Set rst1 = Nothing
Set rec1 = Nothing

End Sub
```

The procedure starts by declaring and instantiating both a record and a recordset. These two objects work together to allow the sample to enumerate the contents of a Web folder. After instantiating the *rec1* object, the procedure invokes the *Open* method for the *Recordset* object. This sample references the first four arguments for the *Open* method. (Refer to Access 2002 Help for the complete list of *Open* method arguments.) The leading *Source* argument is an empty string because the second argument, *ActiveConnection*, fully specifies the Web address for the cab2000 server. This server resides on the local intranet in my office. (You cannot access it from the Internet.) To run this sample in your office, replace the server name *cab2000* with the name of another Internet Information

Services (IIS) 5 server that is locally available. The third argument, *Mode*, grants read-only permission for the directory node. The fourth argument, *CreateOptions*, uses two intrinsic constants to indicate its objective. When used together, the *adOpenIfExists* constant and the *adCreateCollection* constant open the record to an existing directory node.

After the code opens the record to the directory node, the record will contain information about the node. The next sample you will see explores this information further. At this point, the current sample does not directly expose the files and folders of the current node. Invoke the *GetChildren* method against the *rec1* object to return a recordset with a row for each file and folder at the current node, which is the root directory of the cab2000 Web server in the sample.

The recordset created by the *GetChildren* method contains many fields of information about the individual files and folders at a directory node. You can discover the names and values of these fields as you would for any recordset. For example, the *PrintFolderContents* sample uses a *Do* loop to print the recordset row values for the first field. Each row's value for this field contains the name of one file or folder at the record's directory node.

After printing the names for files and folders at the server's root directory, the sample closes the *rec1* and *rst1* objects to prepare for their reuse with another directory. Then the code opens the *rec1* object to the PMA10 directory at the Web server. This is the folder for a FrontPage Web site with the same name (PMA10). The sample then repeats the code for printing the names of the files and folders at a Web site. Figure 3-1 shows the sample output from the procedure. The root directory listing contains files, such as iisstart.asp and localstart.asp, that are typical for any IIS root folder. The PMA10 directory listing contains files, such as Default.htm, that are common for Web sites.

Figure 3-1 Representative output from running the *PrintFolderContents* procedure.

Printing the Properties for Web Folder Contents

Opening either a record or a recordset with a URL designated for the *Source* or *ActiveConnection* argument creates a set of resources that provide metadata about the URL contents. For example, a recordset provides 20 fields of metadata about its URL resource. A record offers 30 fields of metadata about its URL. These fields act as properties for the URL contents. You can use these fields to gather valuable information programmatically about the files and folders within a URL. To enumerate the field names for records and recordsets based on URLs, you can adapt the code from the section "The *Field* Object" at the end of Chapter 2. Use the field properties discussed in that section of Chapter 2 to discover more information (such as data type and actual size) about the recordset and record resources available for URL file and folder contents.

The *OpenRecordWithRecordsetSource* procedure that follows illustrates how to use selected fields for recordsets and records based on URLs. The procedure has three parts. First, it begins by opening a recordset based on the root directory for the PMA10 Web site. As mentioned previously, this Web site is on my office intranet. In this part of the code, the procedure also prints selected information about the first row in the recordset. Second, the procedure opens a record based on the recordset's first row. Again, the procedure prints selected information about the row, but this time it prints from the record based on the current recordset row. Third, the procedure moves the current row in the recordset to the second row. Then it opens a record based on this new row, and it prints some information about the row again.

After the object and variable declarations, the *OpenRecordWithRecordsetSource* procedure instantiates both recordset and record object references (namely, *rst1* and *rec1*). The next two lines confirm the syntax for opening a recordset based on a URL. The URL points to a FrontPage Web site that initially contains a selection of files and folders after its creation. In addition, I added a couple of files and modified another one to help populate the site with Web content. The recordset contains a single row for each file and folder in the root directory of the PMA10 Web site.

The next block of code completes the first part of the procedure. This block prints selected data about the first row in the recordset using the *rst1* object reference. The first set of output lines, shown in Figure 3-2, presents the output from the procedure's first part. The recordset opens with the default forward-only cursor. While the code shows how to decipher a cursor type, be aware that you cannot override the default setting when working with a URL as an *ActiveConnection*. (I left in the deciphering code because I thought some readers might enjoy examining the approach.) Notice in Figure 3-2 that the recordset for the URL contains 20 fields. The screen shot shows the name of the first field as well as its value, which happens to be the file or folder name in the Web site's root folder.

```
Sub OpenRecordWithRecordsetSource()
Dim rec1 As ADODB.Record
Dim rst1 As ADODB.Recordset
Dim strURL As String
Dim enm1 As Integer
Dim strenm1 As String

'Instantiate recordset and record
Set rst1 = New ADODB.Recordset
Set rec1 = New ADODB.Record

'Open recordset based on folders and files in
'the PMA10 Web site on the cab2000 Web server
strURL = "URL=http://cab2000/PMA10"
rst1.Open "", strURL, , , adCmdTableDirect

'Print CursorTypeEnum for the recordset, number of
'fields in recordset, along with name and value of first field
'on the recordset's first row
enm1 = rst1.CursorType
strenm1 = Choose(enm1 + 1, "adOpenForwardOnly", _
    "adOpenKeyset", "adOpenDynamic", "adOpenStatic")
Debug.Print "Selected data for recordset and its first row"
Debug.Print "CursorTypeEnum name is: " & strenm1
Debug.Print "Number of fields in recordset is: " & _
    rst1.Fields.Count
Debug.Print "Name for first field is: " & _
    rst1.Fields(0).Name
Debug.Print "Value for first field is: " & _
    rst1(0).Value & vbCrLf

'Open record based on recordset's current row, and
'print the number of fields in record, along with the
'name and value of the first field in the record
rec1.Open rst1
Debug.Print "Selected data for record based on " & _
    "recordset's first row"
Debug.Print "Number of fields in records is: " & _
    rec1.Fields.Count
Debug.Print "Name for first field is: " & _
    rec1.Fields(0).Name
Debug.Print "Value for first field is: " & _
    rec1(0)
Debug.Print rec1(0) & _
    IIf(rec1("RESOURCE_ISCOLLECTION"), _
    " is a folder.", " is not a folder.")
```

```
'Move to the recordset's next row; then close the record
'based on the first row, and reopen it for the second row
rst1.MoveNext
rec1.Close
rec1.Open rst1
'Print the value and folder status of the first field in
'the second record
Debug.Print vbCrLf & "Selected data for record based on " & _
    "recordset's second row"
Debug.Print "The first field's value for"
Debug.Print "the recordset's second row: " & rst1(0)
Debug.Print rec1(0) & _
    IIf(rec1("RESOURCE_ISCOLLECTION"), _
    " is a folder.", " is not a folder.")

'Clean up objects
rst1.Close
rec1.Close
Set rst1 = Nothing
Set rec1 = Nothing

End Sub
```

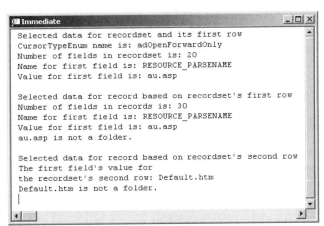

Figure 3-2 Representative output from running the *OpenRecordWithRecordsetSource*
procedure.

To open a record based on the current row of a recordset, just designate
the recordset object reference as the *Source* argument for the record. The first
line in the second section of code illustrates how simple this syntax is. You should
always move the recordset's current row to the row that you want to serve as
the source for the record. After opening a record based on the first record, the
procedure prints selected information for the row.

The second block of output shown in Figure 3-2 illustrates the output from the procedure's second part. Since the source for the first and second blocks of code is the same, it is not surprising that the field names and values are identical in both blocks. The output does confirm that there are more fields for the source of a record than for a recordset. In addition, the code for the second part of the procedure demonstrates how to detect whether a row item is a file or a folder. If the RESOURCE_ISCOLLECTION field is True, the source for the record or the recordset's current row is a folder. Otherwise, the source is a file.

The next block of code in the *OpenRecordWithRecordsetSource* procedure defines the third part of the procedure. This block starts by invoking the *MoveNext* method for *rst1*, which advances the recordset to its second row. You must always position a recordset's current row to the one that you want to serve as the source for a record. The sample then closes the record object, *rec1*, in order to reopen it based on the newly positioned row in the recordset. The third block of output lines seen in Figure 3-2 corresponds to the *Debug.Print* statements that detail information for the record based on the recordset's second row.

I included the preceding code sample as a tutorial on the syntax for extracting resources about the files and folders within a URL. In practice, this is not a procedure that you are likely to write. However, you might want to run a variation of the two procedures shown in the next code sample because they generate a standard report about the files and folders at a URL. The first procedure, *CallListSiteFilesAndFolders*, offers an easy way to print the report for either of two URLs using compiler directives. The *#Const* directive in this next code sample initially assigns *varPassRoot* a value of False, which directs the sample to report about the //cab2000/PMA10 URL. Changing the *#Const* directive to True generates a report for the //cab2000/ URL.

Figure 3-3 shows the reports for both URLs, one after the other. The first line of each report details the URL name and date of printing. The report prints this information from the first procedure in the code sample. The remaining lines in each report appear from the code sample's second procedure, *ListSiteFilesAndFolders*. For each of the two possible sources, the report prints four columns, which correspond to the fields RESOURCE_PARSENAME, RESOURCE_ABSOLUTEPARSENAME, RESOURCE_ISROOT, and RESOURCE_IS COLLECTION in the *rst1* recordset. The parse name and absolute parse name columns return relative and absolute URL information for each entry in a folder. The RESOURCE_ISROOT field returns a value of True whenever the folder on its row is the root directory of a Web site. For example, notice that the PMA10 row in the second report has a value of True. The pma folder is the root directory for the Web site. The RESOURCE_ISCOLLECTION column also returns a Boolean value that is True whenever the item for a row in the recordset is a folder.

```
Immediate                                                    _|□|×|

   -- Folders and files in pma10 Web site root at 12/31/2000 6:24:15 AM --
au.asp        http://cab2000/pma10/au.asp        False      False
Default.htm   http://cab2000/pma10/Default.htm   False      False
global.asa    http://cab2000/pma10/global.asa    False      False
_private      http://cab2000/pma10/_private      False      True
fpdb          http://cab2000/pma10/fpdb          False      True
images        http://cab2000/pma10/images        False      True

   -- Folders and files in cab2000 Web server root at 12/31/2000 6:24:36 AM --
desktop.ini   http://cab2000/desktop.ini         False      False
help.gif      http://cab2000/help.gif            False      False
iisstart.asp  http://cab2000/iisstart.asp        False      False
localstart.asp http://cab2000/localstart.asp     False      False
mmc.gif       http://cab2000/mmc.gif             False      False
pagerror.gif  http://cab2000/pagerror.gif        False      False
print.gif     http://cab2000/print.gif           False      False
warning.gif   http://cab2000/warning.gif         False      False
web.gif       http://cab2000/web.gif             False      False
win2000.gif   http://cab2000/win2000.gif         False      False
_private      http://cab2000/_private            False      True
images        http://cab2000/images              False      True
pma10         http://cab2000/pma10               True       True
temp          http://cab2000/temp                False      True
|
```

Figure 3-3 Representative output from running the *CallListSiteFilesAndFolders* and *ListSiteFilesAndFolders* procedures.

```
Sub CallListSiteFilesAndFolders()
Dim strURL As String
#Const varPassRoot = False

'Print folders and files in either a Web server's or
'a Web site's root directory
#If varPassRoot Then
    strURL = "URL=http://cab2000/"
    Debug.Print vbCrLf & "  -- Folders and Files in " & _
        "cab2000 web server root at " & Now() & " --"
    ListSiteFilesAndFolders (strURL)
#Else
    strURL = "URL=http://cab2000/PMA10"
    Debug.Print vbCrLf & "  -- Folders and files in " & _
        "PMA10 Web site root at " & Now() & " --"
    ListSiteFilesAndFolders (strURL)
#End If

End Sub

Sub ListSiteFilesAndFolders(strURL)
Dim rec1 As ADODB.Record
Dim rst1 As ADODB.Recordset
Dim int1 As Integer
Dim int2 As Integer

'Instantiate record and recordset objects
Set rec1 = New Record
Set rst1 = New Recordset
```

(continued)

169

```
'Specify the URL over which the record applies
'Open the record only if it exists
rec1.Open "", strURL, , _
    adOpenIfExists Or adCreateCollection

'Return the files and subdirectories
'in rec1 to rst1
Set rst1 = rec1.GetChildren

'Find length of longest RESOURCE_PARSENAME field value
int1 = FindTheLongest(rst1, "RESOURCE_PARSENAME") + 1
rst1.MoveFirst
int2 = FindTheLongest(rst1, "RESOURCE_ABSOLUTEPARSENAME") + 1

'Move to beginning of recordset, and print for each row in the
'recordset RESOURCE_PARSENAME and RESOURCE_ABSOLUTEPARSENAME
'fields, along with Boolean values indicating whether the row
'item is a root or a collection (folder)
rst1.MoveFirst
Do Until rst1.EOF
    Debug.Print rst1("RESOURCE_PARSENAME") & _
        String(int1 - Len(rst1("RESOURCE_PARSENAME")), " ") & _
        rst1("RESOURCE_ABSOLUTEPARSENAME") & _
        String(int2 - _
            Len(rst1("RESOURCE_ABSOLUTEPARSENAME")), " ") & _
        rst1("RESOURCE_ISROOT"), rst1("RESOURCE_ISCOLLECTION")
    rst1.MoveNext
Loop

'Clean up objects
rst1.Close
rec1.Close
Set rst1 = Nothing
Set rec1 = Nothing

End Sub
```

The second procedure opens by instantiating record and recordset objects. You do not strictly need both objects in the sample, but the sample uses them to reinforce your understanding of how the two can work together. The procedure initially opens a record for the target URL passed from the first procedure. Then it gets the items in the URL by applying the *GetChildren* method to the record. This populates the *rst1* recordset with a row for each file or folder in the target URL. After computing the length of the report's first two columns, the procedure prints the rows of the report with the help of a *Do* loop.

Reading Text Files with Streams

This section introduces you to techniques for working with *Stream* objects and text files at a URL. Hypertext Markup Language (HTML) files and files with Active Server Pages (ASP) scripting are text files. You therefore can print them programmatically with a *Stream* object. You can also selectively read the content of a text file with a *Stream* object. Because you can base streams on records, they are a natural tool to use for ADO programming. And because streams can process binary files, you can also use them to manipulate files with graphic formats into and out of databases.

The following procedure, *ShowStreamForRecord*, illustrates just how easy it is to print the contents of a file that you have in a record. After pointing a record at a file using a URL and instantiating a stream, the procedure sets a couple of stream properties before opening the stream on the record. The *Charset* property assignment is essential for this task. The *Type* property assignment is not strictly necessary here because it assigns the default value. Invoking the stream's *Open* method copies the text for the file to which the record points from disk to memory. The procedure concludes by copying the stream's content to a string variable that it prints.

```
Sub ShowStreamForRecord()
Dim rec1 As ADODB.Record
Dim stm1 As ADODB.Stream
Dim str1 As String

'Instantiate Record and Stream objects
Set rec1 = New ADODB.Record
Set stm1 = New ADODB.Stream

'Open a record for an HTML file
rec1.Open "postinfo.html", "URL=http://cab2000/"

'Set selected stream properties for printing with an
'ASCII character set, and open the stream on the file
'to which the record points
stm1.Type = adTypeText
stm1.Charset = "ascii"
stm1.Open rec1, adModeRead, adOpenStreamFromRecord


'Read all the lines from the stream to a string variable,
'and print the string variable
str1 = stm1.ReadText
Debug.Print str1

End Sub
```

The next sample uses two procedures to print the metatags of any text file at a Web folder. The first file, *CallPrintMetaTags*, assigns two strings. The first string points at the file for which you want print metatags. The second string indicates the Web folder's URL. This sample works for any text file in a Web folder.

The second file, *PrintMetaTags*, begins by instantiating a record that it opens to the designated file within the Web folder. While the preceding sample reads the whole file into a string variable, this sample reads the text file one line at a time while looking for metatags on each line. It's common practice to embed these metatags between the <head> and </head> tags; the code relies on this style convention to sharpen the focus of its search. If you are using files that follow a different convention, change the code accordingly. In any event, the procedure stops reading lines from the stream after encountering an *EOS* property value. *EOS* is similar to the *EOF* property in a recordset. By extending the logic of this procedure, you can start to devise your own procedures for parsing .xml files.

```
Sub CallPrintMetaTags()
Dim str1 As String
Dim str2 As String

'Use str1 and str2 as the names for the file
'and URL, respectively
str1 = "au.asp"
str2 = "URL=http://cab2000/PMA10/"

'Pass arguments to subprocedure
PrintMetaTags str1, str2

End Sub


Sub PrintMetaTags(str1 As String, str2 As String)
Dim rec1 As ADODB.Record
Dim str3 As String
Dim stm1 As Stream

'Open record based on current recordset row
Set rec1 = New ADODB.Record
rec1.Open str1, str2

'Instantiate stream, set properties for a reading text
'file, and open it on the file to which the
'record points
Set stm1 = New ADODB.Stream
stm1.Type = adTypeText
stm1.Charset = "ascii"
stm1.Open rec1, adModeRead, adOpenStreamFromRecord
```

```
'Print just metatag content
'Exit loop, even if there are no <head> tags
Do
    str3 = stm1.ReadText(adReadLine)
    If (InStr(str3, "</head>")) Then Exit Do
    If stm1.EOS = True Then Exit Do
    If (InStr(str3, "<meta")) Then
        Debug.Print str3
    End If
Loop

'Clean up objects
stm1.Close
rec1.Close
Set stm1 = Nothing
Set rec1 = Nothing

End Sub
```

Programming ADO Events

ADO events share several similarities with the classic *Form* events with which most Access developers are intimately familiar. Both classes of events typically are notifications about pending or completed actions. The ADO *ConnectComplete* event occurs after a connection starts, and the *WillChangeField* event occurs before a pending change. Other ADO events mark progress, such as the *FetchProgress* event. This event at the end of each record's fetch cycle gives the count of completed rows, along with an estimate of the total rows to collect.

Despite the above similarities, ADO events differ from the classic *Form* events in several important ways. For example, you have to build your own procedure shell. In addition, you have to know the arguments that each event requires and include those arguments in your handcrafted shell. Many events must appear in sets within your application, despite whether you need all members of an event set in the application. For example, you must include a *Disconnect* event whenever you include a *ConnectComplete* event. The same holds true for the *FetchProgress* and *FetchComplete* events. Your event procedures will fail unless you include all the members of a set.

Overview of ADO Event Programming

There are two families of ADO events—one for connections, and one for recordsets. These families determine which of the two object classes the events pertain to. Object classes other than connections and recordsets do not have ADO events that you can program. Table 3-2 lists the event names in each family.

Table 3-2 ADO Events

***Connection* Object Events**
BeginTransComplete
CommitTransComplete
RollbackTransComplete
WillConnect
ConnectComplete
Disconnect
WillExecute
ExecuteComplete
InfoMessage

***Recordset* Object Events**
FetchProgress
FetchComplete
WillChangeField
FieldChangeComplete
WillMove
MoveComplete
EndOfRecordset
WillChangeRecord (for the current row or the entire recordset)
RecordChangeComplete (for the current row or the entire recordset)

The ADO Help files that ship with Access 2002 include documentation for each of these events. VBA programmers are likely to find this documentation most useful for its description of the events, membership in sets of related events, and the arguments to specify for each type of event procedure. Many of the code samples apply to C++ programmers, but a couple of them will be of interest to VBA developers, including a general discussion of how to set up your application to use ADO events.

Two important considerations of ADO event programming relate to the type of module in which you program events and the way you declare an event's object. First, you must program ADO event procedures within class modules. Since forms automatically have class modules, these modules make a suitable environment for ADO event programs. In this section, I will use ADO events with unbound forms, that is, forms not bound to a table or query, to illustrate how to program ADO events. (Chapter 6, "Forms, Controls, and Data," will continue exploring how to use unbound Access forms with ADO.)

You must declare the objects that take events at the module level. This simply involves declaring either an ADO *Connection* or *Recordset* object at the top of a module outside the scope of any individual procedure. Your declaration must include the *WithEvents* keyword. This enables ADO to propagate its events to the class module. (Chapter 1, "Introduction to VBA," included a short introduction to class modules. Chapter 9, "Class, Form, and Report Modules," will revisit this topic and give more detailed coverage of the *WithEvents* keyword.) In this section, you will learn the syntax for using the *WithEvents* keyword for ADO event programming.

ADO Event Programming Sample

Figure 3-4 shows an unbound Access form, called Form1 in Chapter 03.mdb, that was created to demonstrate the basics of ADO event programming from an Access database file. The form permits a user to connect or refresh a connection to a recordset that serves as the source of records for the form. The Previous and Next buttons offer forward and backward navigation through the recordset. The Find button automatically navigates to the record for the customer whose customer ID appears in the text box next to the Find button. The three text boxes at the bottom of the form display information for the current record of the recordset that the code behind the form manages. Clicking the Close button closes the form.

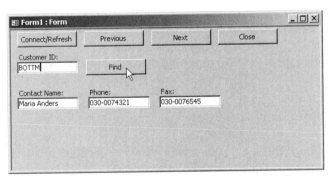

Figure 3-4 An unbound form that demonstrates ADO event programming.

The form has four ADO event procedures in the module behind it for the following events:

- **ConnectComplete**   This event normally gives the user some instructions on how to start the application. If there is a failure to connect, the procedure prints the ADO error number and description. (See "The *Errors* Collection" section earlier in the chapter if you need a refresher on errors.)

- **Disconnect**   This event gives a goodbye message when the user closes the form. This is because the Close button invokes the *Close* method for the *Connection* object.

- **FetchProgress**   This event of the *Recordset* object returns a count of the cumulative records fetched after it fetches each batch of records. This event also gives a crude estimate of the total number of records that must be fetched to complete the retrieval of all the records. The first pass through the procedure populates the text boxes for displaying data with the recordset's first record, and it clears the text box next to the Find button. Users can click the Connect/Refresh button any time after the form opens to return to the recordset's first record and gather any input by other users of the recordset. Clicking this button fires the *FetchProgress* event after the execution of the *Open* method in the event procedure for the button's click event.

- **FetchComplete**   This event of the *Recordset* object opens a message alerting the user that all records are loaded. This event fires after the last successful firing of the *FetchProgress* event.

For your easy reference, the following listing includes all the declarations and procedures behind the form in Figure 3-4. The General area at the top of the module includes two *Dim* statements for the *Connection* and *Recordset* objects used throughout the application. Notice that the declarations include the *WithEvents* keyword. Declaring the *Connection* and *Recordset* objects in the General area makes them available to all procedures within the module.

The *Form_Load* event fires when the form initially opens. Its sole purpose is to open a connection to the database for the form. The procedure references the *str1* string variable that includes a connection string for the Northwind database. Update this string to adapt the procedure to your custom databases. The conclusion of the *Form_Load* event fires the *cnn1_ConnectComplete* event. If the connection succeeds, this event procedure issues a message telling the user how to start using the form. Otherwise, the event prints an ADO error number and description. The event procedure checks the *adStatus* constant that ADO returns to determine whether the connection attempt succeeded.

The process of checking the *adStatus* constant returned by ADO is a typical way to tell whether an attempt to perform a task succeeded. You can also use the *adStatus* constant to inform ADO that you want to discontinue event notification. When you use the *adStatus* constant in combination with the *adReason* constant, you can elect to discontinue event notifications for some reasons while continuing to receive them for other reasons. For example, you can pass through notifications for attempts to delete records but discontinue notifications for updating records.

After the form loads and connects to a data source, a user must open a record source for the form so that it can display data. Clicking the Connect/Refresh button (named *cmdConnect* on the form) launches this process from a click event procedure. The procedure sets both *Initial Fetch Size* and *Background Fetch Size* properties for the recordset that provides a record source for the form. The event procedure also starts to open the recordset asynchronously. This makes the form able to show data before the last fetch completes.

The *rst1_FetchProgress* event fires as soon as each fetch completes. This event procedure monitors the fetching of records and is useful for processing very large recordsets. You can use *rst1_FetchProgress* to determine how long it takes to fetch successive batches of records, and it can help users by providing some feedback as the opening of a record source is in progress. In this particular instance, the procedure for the event populates the data display controls on its first pass. If this task completes successfully, the code populates the text boxes to reveal the first customer's data on the form before all the data loads. The code also inserts an empty string into the *txtCustomerID* text box, which sits next to the Find button. This action is useful when a user clicks the Connect/Refresh button after the start of a form session.

The other event procedures in the module are standard Access form events. These work more or less the same way for bound and unbound forms. I include the event listings here to help you to dissect the application without loading the form and testing it manually. The *cmdFind_Click* event procedure reveals more syntax for the ADO *Find* method than we discussed in Chapter 2. In particular, *cmdFind_Click* shows how to control the direction of the search and the starting point for the search, irrespective of the current row in a recordset. If I did not include the trailing *adBookmarkFirst* constant for the *Find* method, the procedure would fail to find any records before the recordset's current record. This constant forces the procedure to start its search from the recordset's first record.

The following code is in the Form_Form1 module in the sample file Chapter 03.mdb on the companion CD.

```
Option Explicit

'Update connection and SQL strings as appropriate
'for your environment
Const str1 = "Provider=Microsoft.Jet.OLEDB.4.0;" & _
    "Data Source=C:\PMA Samples\Northwind.mdb;"
Const strDefaultSQL = "SELECT * FROM customers"

'Must declare cnn1 and rst1 at module level
'and specify WithEvents to enable events
Dim WithEvents cnn1 As ADODB.Connection
Dim WithEvents rst1 As ADODB.Recordset
```

(continued)

```
Private Sub Form_Load()

'Connect to specification in str1
Set cnn1 = New ADODB.Connection
cnn1.Open str1

End Sub


Private Sub cmdConnect_Click()
Dim strSQL As String
strSQL = strDefaultSQL

'Instantiate recordset object
Set rst1 = New ADODB.Recordset

'Assign a local cursor property,
'set dynamic properties Initial Fetch Size
'and Background Fetch Size, and
'start printing progress report for records fetched;
'open recordset asynchronously during fetch
With rst1
    .CursorLocation = adUseClient

    .Properties("Initial Fetch Size") = 15
    .Properties("Background Fetch Size") = 15

    Debug.Print "Start"
    Debug.Print "Initial Fetch Size: " & _
            .Properties("Initial Fetch Size")
    Debug.Print "Background Fetch Size" & _
            .Properties("Background Fetch Size")

    .Open strSQL, cnn1, , , adAsyncFetch
End With

End Sub


'If you have either the ConnectComplete event procedure
'or the Disconnect event procedure, you must have
'the other
Private Sub cnn1_ConnectComplete _
    (ByVal pError As ADODB.Error, _
    adStatus As ADODB.EventStatusEnum, _
    ByVal pConnection As ADODB.Connection)
```

```
'If connection did not complete, say so
'and give error number and description
If adStatus <> adStatusOK Then
    Debug.Print "Failed"
    Debug.Print "Error: " & _
        pError.Number & _
        " - " & pError.Description
Else
'Otherwise, inform user and give instructions on how
'to use the application
    MsgBox "Connection Successful.  When form " & _
        "appears, click Connect/Refresh before " & _
        "entering a CustomerID and clicking Find.", _
        vbInformation, "Programming Microsoft Access 2002"
End If

End Sub


Private Sub cnn1_Disconnect _
    (adStatus As ADODB.EventStatusEnum, _
    ByVal pConnection As ADODB.Connection)

'If close did not succeed, say so
If adStatus <> adStatusOK Then
    Debug.Print "Cannot disconnect now."
Else
'Otherwise, set connection to Nothing,
'close the form, and say goodbye
    Set cnn1 = Nothing
    DoCmd.Close acForm, Me.Name
    MsgBox "Goodbye.", vbInformation, _
        "Programming Microsoft Access Version 2002"
End If
End Sub


'If you have either the FetchProgress event procedure
'or the FetchComplete event procedure, you must have
'the other
Private Sub rst1_FetchProgress(ByVal Progress As Long, _
    ByVal MaxProgress As Long, _
    adStatus As ADODB.EventStatusEnum, _
    ByVal pRecordset As ADODB.Recordset)
```

(continued)

```
                'Print progress report of records fetched
                Debug.Print "Fetch: " & Progress & _
                    " Max: " & MaxProgress

                End Sub


                Private Sub rst1_FetchComplete _
                    (ByVal pError As ADODB.Error, _
                    adStatus As ADODB.EventStatusEnum, _
                    ByVal pRecordset As ADODB.Recordset)

                'If recordset fetch did not finish, say so
                'and give error number and description
                If adStatus <> adStatusOK Then
                    Debug.Print "Failed"
                    Debug.Print "Error: " & _
                        pError.Number & " - " & _
                        pError.Description
                Else
                'Otherwise, display current record and
                'blank text box for CustomerID
                    PopulateBoxes
                    Me.txtCustomerID = ""
                End If

                End Sub


                Private Sub cmdClose_Click()

                'Closing the connection invokes the
                'cnn1_Disconnect event procedure
                cnn1.Close

                End Sub


                Sub PopulateBoxes()

                'Uses properties instead of events to
                'determine moves outside recordset
                If rst1.EOF Then
                    rst1.MoveLast
                ElseIf rst1.BOF Then
                    rst1.MoveFirst
                End If
```

```
Me.txtContactName = rst1("ContactName")
Me.txtPhone = rst1("Phone")
Me.txtFax = rst1("Fax")

End Sub


Private Sub cmdFind_Click()

'Move current record to the CustomerID in the form's
'txtCustomerID control
rst1.Find "" & "CustomerID = " & "'" & _
    txtCustomerID & "'" & "", , adSearchForward, adBookmarkFirst

'Display current record's data
PopulateBoxes

End Sub


Private Sub cmdNext_Click()

Me.txtCustomerID = ""
'Move current record forward one record
rst1.MoveNext

'Display current record's data
PopulateBoxes

End Sub


Private Sub cmdPrevious_Click()

Me.txtCustomerID = ""
'Move current record backward one record
rst1.MovePrevious

'Display current record's data
PopulateBoxes

End Sub
```

4

The ADOX Library and Tables

Much of Chapters 2 and 3 ("Data Access Models: Part I" and "Data Access Models: Part II") focused on a single model of ActiveX Data Objects (ADO): the ADODB model for data access. This chapter examines another of the three ADO models: the ADOX library. (We'll examine the third ADO model, the JRO library, in Chapter 13, "Replicating Databases.") This chapter delivers a quick overview of the ADOX library and then provides a diverse series of samples, many of which demonstrate how to program table components, such as columns, keys, and indexes. The samples will lay a firm foundation for your understanding of how to use the ADOX model for table design and table-related schema management, including the enumeration, deletion, and counting of tables in a database. In Chapter 5, "Jet SQL, the ADOX Library, and Queries," we'll explore using the ADOX model with query design and management, and in Chapter 12, "Working with Multiuser Databases," we'll look at the database security features of ADOX.

The main objective of this chapter is to equip you with the skills needed to start designing tables with the ADOX object model for Jet databases. This chapter assumes you have an intermediate to advanced knowledge of table design. However, the chapter also assumes you have a novice or intermediate level of experience with the ADOX library. This will be the case for all experienced Microsoft Access developers switching from Access 97 and earlier versions to Access 2002. Even if you have had moderate exposure to ADOX programmatic table design, such as that discussed in the preceding edition of this book, this chapter will reinforce your existing ADOX skills and prepare you for more advanced programmatic table design. The chapter concludes with a series of samples that illustrate how to populate tables with data after creating them with the ADOX model. The samples focus primarily on gathering data from sources outside the current Access project.

Overview of the ADOX Model

The ADOX library supports schema and security tasks. You can use this library to manage objects and thereby modify the architecture of your application's design. With the exception of the *Catalog* object, all objects in the ADOX library have matching collections. The catalog is the container of the elements within an Access database file. For example, within a Jet database there is a *Tables* collection of *Table* objects. You use these collections to add and organize new objects in a catalog. Selected objects—such as a table, an index, a key, and a column—have a *Properties* collections. You use these *Properties* collections to manage the behavior of the objects within an application. You manage the *Users* and *Groups* collections to control permissions for other ADOX objects, such as tables, views, and procedures. Figure 4-1 shows an overview of the ADOX library.

> **Note**   You must impose a logon requirement before your application can list the members of the *Users* and *Groups* collections. Any attempt to process the members of these collections without logging on can generate a run-time error. You can impose a logon requirement by setting a password for the Admin user.

The ADOX library is an extension of the ADODB library. The Jet ADO provider fully supports ADOX. You can use the two libraries together to build applications. For example, you can build *Command* objects with the ADODB library and then save them as procedures with the ADOX library. The ADOX library will equip you to build tables in ADOX programmatically and to search for tables and their elements in a database. For example, you can determine whether a table with a particular name exists in a database, and you can examine the table's columns to discover their names, data types, and membership in keys and indexes. If a table does not exist, you can add it to the database and populate it with values. Alternatively, you can rename or delete an existing table from a database and replace it with a new one. The ability of the ADOX library to define new data structures and modify existing ones makes it a viable alternative to the SQL Data Definition Language.

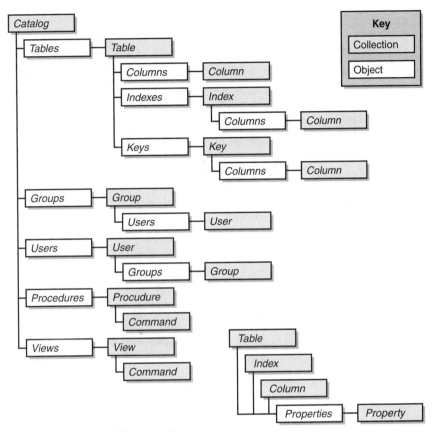

Figure 4-1 The ADOX object library.

The *Catalog* Object

The *Catalog* object is the highest-level container in the ADOX library. Its members define the schema and security model for a database. Its *ActiveConnection* property defines the connection to which the catalog belongs. The *Catalog* object is the database's container for tables, views, procedures, users, and groups within a connection or database. A *Catalog* object does not require a name, because there will be only one such object per database. Nevertheless, your application can have multiple catalogs open concurrently, with each pointing to a different database. Use the *Catalog* object's *Create* method to open a new database and access its catalog.

You need a *Connection* object for the catalog so that ADO knows which catalog to make available. You assign the *Connection* object to the catalog by setting its *ActiveConnection* property. Once ADO knows which database to reference with a catalog, you have programmatic access to the contents of the catalog. You control access using database and user-level security techniques. While you can reference a table's contents with an ADODB library reference, you must use an ADOX reference to loop through the *Columns* collection of a table. Only the ADOX library has *Tables* and *Columns* collections.

You can use the *Catalog* object to enumerate the members of any of the collections within it. This chapter will demonstrate techniques for enumerating the members of the *Tables* collection. In addition, you'll learn how to loop through the elements of tables, such as columns, keys, and indexes.

The *Table* Object

The *Table* object is a member of the *Tables* collection, which is a member of the *Catalog* object. Each *Table* object has a *Name* property and a *Type* property. A *Table* object can be a standard table within the current database or a linked table based on ODBC and non-ODBC data sources. A *Table* object can even be a view. The *Type* property values also include two system table types: Jet system tables and the Access system tables. Table 4-1 shows these property values.

Table 4-1 ADOX *Type* Values for the *Table* Object

Type Value	Description
ACCESS TABLE	An Access system table
LINK	A linked table from a non-ODBC data source
PASS-THROUGH	A linked table through an ODBC data source
SYSTEM TABLE	A Jet system table
TABLE	A table developed by or for your application
VIEW	A virtual table from a nonparameterized query that returns rows

You also are likely to find the *ParentCatalog* property particularly useful. This property must be set if you plan to invoke the *AutoIncrement* property for a column. You need the *AutoIncrement* property to create AutoNumber data types programmatically with ADOX, but you cannot set the *AutoIncrement* property to True unless you first set the *ParentCatalog* property to point at the catalog for a column's parent. (A column's parent is simply the table to which the *Column* object belongs.)

In addition to the *Columns* collection, a *Table* object has a *Keys* collection and an *Indexes* collection. You probably will use the primary key and foreign key property settings frequently. There is also a unique key property for tables that can benefit from a candidate key. Members of the *Indexes* collection can speed up some tasks (such as sorting) and enable others (such as using the *Seek* method to find a subset or records in a recordset).

The *Column* Object

A *Columns* collection can belong to tables, keys, and indexes. A *Column* object is roughly comparable to a *Field* object in the ADODB library. A column represents a set of data that refers to a specific characteristic of the entity represented by the table. The *Column* object has several properties:

- **Name**   This property is the name of the column.

- **Type**   This property indicates the data type of the column. All the data within a column is of the same type.

- **Attributes**   This property describes the two possible characteristics of a column: whether the column can contain Nulls and whether it has a fixed length.

- **DefinedSize**   This property designates the maximum size in number of characters for entries within the column.

- **Precision** and **NumericScale**   These properties are used exclusively for numeric fields, such as integers, currency, and floating-point numbers. *Precision* represents the maximum total number of digits used to convey a value in the column. *NumericScale* designates how many digits to the right of the decimal point are available to express a value.

When a *Column* object is an index or a key, other properties are available too, such as *SortOrder* and *RelatedColumn*.

> **Note**   The *NumericScale* property can yield confusing results. For example, *Currency* values utilize four places to the right of the decimal point, but their *NumericScale* property equals 0 because Access stores Currency data types as scaled integers. When you modify the Scale setting of a column that uses a Decimal data type in a table's Design view, the column's *NumericScale* property adjusts accordingly.

The *Index* Object

The *Index* object sets indexes for a table. It has five properties: *Name, IndexNulls, PrimaryKey, Unique,* and *Clustered*. With the exception of the *Name* property, all these properties will be read-only after you append the index. The *Name* property represents the name of the index. The *PrimaryKey*, *Unique*, and *Clustered* properties are Boolean and indicate, respectively, whether the index is a primary key, unique, or clustered. (An index is described as *clustered* when the physical order of rows matches the indexed order of rows.)

> **Note** Jet databases do not support the clustered property for an index. Therefore, the value of this property will always be False for any index in a Jet database.

The *IndexNulls* property can assume one of three different values. Setting this property to *adIndexNullsDisallow*, the default setting, causes the *Index* construction to fail if a Null exists in the column's index. Assigning the *adIndexNullsIgnore* constant to *IndexNulls* allows the construction of the index if a Null exists in the index but sets the Ignore Nulls property (on the Indexes window in the user interface) to *Yes*. Using *adIndexNullsIgnoreAny* also constructs the index even when the index contains a Null, but it sets the Ignore Nulls property in the user interface to *No*. Finally, assigning *adIndexNullsAllow* permits the entry of Null key column values without consequence.

The *Key* Object

The *Key* object embodies the behavior of foreign keys in its properties. Of course, the *Name* property is the name of the key. The *RelatedTable* property designates the table to which a foreign key points. The *DeleteRule* and *UpdateRule* properties determine what happens when a primary key is deleted or updated. The *Type* property of the *Key* object represents the type of key and has three options: *adKeyForeign* for foreign keys, *adKeyPrimary* for primary keys, and *adKeyUnique* for unique keys.

Creating a New Database

The *Catalog* object is at the top of the ADOX object model. You can use this object to iterate through the members of its collections or to create a new database whose collections you subsequently populate. The two procedures in the following listing demonstrate the syntax for programmatically creating a new Access database. If an existing file has the same name as the target file for the new database, a run-time error occurs. The second procedure recovers from this failure by deleting the existing file and resuming. You can use the *FileSystemObject* object in the Microsoft Scripting Runtime library to perform more sophisticated solution, such as renaming an existing file. We'll examine the *FileSystemObject* object along with its properties and methods in Chapter 10, "Microsoft Office Objects."

The first procedure performs just two functions. First, it specifies the path and filename for the new Access database file. Second, it passes these as a single variable to the second procedure. The second procedure instantiates a new *Catalog* object and then uses the *Create* method to generate a new Access database file. The *Create* method takes a simple ADO connection string as an argument. The connection string consists of the designation of a data provider (for a Jet 4 database in this sample) and the string variable passed to the procedure with the path and filename for the new database. Because the ADOX model is a special ADO extension for Jet, you should use the ADOX model to create Access database files only.

```
Sub CallMakeAJetDB()
Dim str1 As String

'Specify path and filename for the new database
str1 = "c:\PMA Samples\Chapter 04\MyNewDB.mdb"
MakeAJetDB str1

End Sub


Sub MakeAJetDB(str1 As String)
On Error GoTo MakeAJetDB_Trap
Dim cat1 As ADOX.Catalog

'Instantiate catalog, and create a new
'database file based on it
Set cat1 = New ADOX.Catalog
cat1.create "Provider=Microsoft.Jet.OLEDB.4.0;" & _
    "Data Source=" & str1

MakeAJetDB_Exit:
'Clean up objects
Set cat1 = Nothing
Exit Sub

MakeAJetDB_Trap:
If Err.Number = -2147217897 Then
'When the file already exists,
'kill the prior version
    Debug.Print str1
    Kill (str1)
```

(continued)

```
        Resume
    Else
        Debug.Print Err.Number, Err.Description
        MsgBox "View Immediate window for error diagnostics.", _
            vbInformation, "Programming Microsoft Access Version 2002"
    End If

End Sub
```

Enumerating Tables

The *Tables* collection in the ADOX object model is an obvious means for enumerating the tables in an Access database. As shown in Table 4-1 (on page 186), the *Tables* collection contains several types of tables. You might prefer to filter out one or more of these table types during a typical enumeration task. Besides the ADOX library, you can also use *AccessObject* objects to enumerate tables. Several types of *AccessObject* objects correspond to major elements within an Access database file. This chapter will concentrate on *AccessObject* objects for tables.

Listing All Table Types in a Catalog

The first sample for enumerating tables lists all the tables within a catalog's *ActiveConnection* property setting. This setting is just a connection string that points at a data source through an ADO data provider. The sample consists of two procedures. The first procedure designates a data source argument for the connection string. The listing that appears here sets the string variable *str1* to the path and filename for a backup of the Northwind database. In my office, I use this file when I need a clean, unaltered copy of the Northwind database. You can designate any Access database file that you prefer to use instead of the Northwind database. For example, this listing contains an alternate file named MyNewDB that is commented out. This file was generated in the preceding sample.

```
Sub CallListTablesRaw()
Dim str1 As String

'Run with either backup copy of Northwind or MyNewDB.mdb
str1 = "c:\PMA Samples\Northwind_backup.mdb"
'str1 = "c:\PMA Samples\Chapter 04\MyNewDB.mdb"
ListTablesRaw str1

End Sub
```

```
Sub ListTablesRaw(str1)
Dim cat1 As ADOX.Catalog
Dim tbl1 As ADOX.Table
Dim str2 As String
Dim str3 As String
Dim mwd As Integer

'Instantiate a catalog, and point it to the target database
Set cat1 = New ADOX.Catalog
cat1.ActiveConnection = "Provider=Microsoft.Jet.OLEDB.4.0;" & _
    "Data Source=" & str1

'Compute the length of the longest table name in the database.
'Assume minimum length of 5 characters.
mwd = 5
For Each tbl1 In cat1.Tables
    If Left(tbl1.Name, 4) <> "~TMP" And _
        Len(tbl1.Name) > mwd Then mwd = Len(tbl1.Name)
Next tbl1
mwd = mwd + 1

'Print a row to the Immediate window containing the name
'and type of member in the catalog's Tables collection
For Each tbl1 In cat1.Tables
    If Left(tbl1.Name, 4) <> "~TMP" Then
        str2 = tbl1.Name
        str3 = String(mwd - Len(str2), " ")
        Debug.Print str2 & str3 & tbl1.Type
    End If
Next tbl1

'Clean up objects
Set cat1 = Nothing

End Sub
```

After its declarations, the second procedure instantiates a *Catalog* object and sets its *ActiveConnection* property to the path and filename passed from the first procedure. Next the second procedure passes through the members of the *Tables* collection to compute the longest table name. This permits the next block of code to space content evenly across the Immediate window for any table name in the catalog. The block of code that does the printing filters out tables that begin with ~TMP. Access uses files beginning with ~TMP to manage a database.

Figure 4-2 shows the output to the Immediate window from the sample for the backup of the Northwind database. Notice the first column lists many more tables than you normally see in the Database window when you open the Northwind database. The second column shows each table type. This enumeration lists all the table types in the Northwind database but not all possible table types. Review Table 4-1 for a complete list of the possible table types along with a brief description of each. Those tables with a TABLE type specification appear in the Database window by default. Recall from Chapter 2 that views are virtual tables. The term *virtual table* correctly conveys the notion that a view is not actually a table. Instead, it is an SQL statement that returns a rowset, which it presents in a datasheet—just like the rowset contained in a real table.

Figure 4-2 Output from the *CallListTablesRaw* and *ListTablesRaw* procedures for a clean backup copy of the Northwind database.

The output of MyNewDB might surprise you. Running *CallListTablesRaw* on MyNewDB generates output even before we populate the database file with any user-defined tables, such as those with a type of TABLE, LINK, or PASS-THROUGH. The listing of tables for the empty MyNewDB database consists of the ACCESS TABLE and SYSTEM TABLE types. These two table categories depend on system-generated activity, as opposed to end-user activity or developer activity.

Filtering Table Types Before Enumerating

The preceding sample includes some of the resources that table enumeration can deliver to an application. However, instead of having a broad array of every table type, you can specify the return of a small subset of the total tables by designating the return of just one table type. By implementing this capability, you can gather precise information about the tables in any Access database file on a local area network (LAN) or wide area network (WAN). The reduced number of items associated with a filtered subset makes for a better record source for a combo box or list box. User interfaces work best when they show users only the information that they need to view.

The next pair of procedures implements filtering to return just one type of table. The first procedure has three variables for a user to set. The first is a string variable that designates the path and filename for an Access database file. You must also assign a value to a second string variable that specifies a table type to return from the search target. This next listing sets this second string variable to the TABLE type. Recall that this type of table includes just tables in the local database created by or for users. The third variable has a Boolean data type. Setting the Boolean variable to True in the first procedure causes the second procedure to return a list of tables in the current Access database file. A False Boolean value points the catalog at the database specified by the first string, *str1*.

```
Sub CallListTablesTypeFilter()
Dim str1 As String
Dim str2 As String
Dim bol1 As Boolean

str1 = "c:\PMA Samples\Northwind_backup.mdb"
str2 = "TABLE"
bol1 = False
ListTablesTypeFilter str1, str2, bol1

End Sub


Sub ListTablesTypeFilter(str1 As String, _
    str2 As String, bol1 As Boolean)
Dim cat1 As ADOX.Catalog
Dim tbl1 As ADOX.Table
Dim str3 As String
Dim str4 As String
Dim mwd As Integer


'Instantiate catalog, and connect to CurrentProject
'or another database
Set cat1 = New ADOX.Catalog
If bol1 = True Then
    Set cat1.ActiveConnection = _
        CurrentProject.Connection
```

(continued)

```
    Else
        cat1.ActiveConnection = _
            "Provider=Microsoft.Jet.OLEDB.4.0;" & _
            "Data Source=" & str1
    End If

    'Create reference to Tables collection for catalog,
    'and determine longest table name in the catalog
    mwd = 5
    For Each tbl1 In cat1.Tables
        If (tbl1.Type = str2 And Left(tbl1.Name, 4) <> "~TMP") Then _
            If Len(tbl1.Name) > mwd Then mwd = Len(tbl1.Name)
    Next tbl1
    mwd = mwd + 1

    'Print table names and their type
    For Each tbl1 In cat1.Tables
        If tbl1.Type = str2 And Left(tbl1.Name, 4) <> "~TMP" Then
            str3 = tbl1.Name
            str4 = String(mwd - Len(str3), " ")
            Debug.Print str3 & str4 & tbl1.Type
        End If
    Next tbl1

    'Clean up objects
    Set cat1 = Nothing

End Sub
```

The second procedure in this sample employs the design of the previous sample, with one major exception. This exception relates to how the sample develops a setting for the *Catalog* object's *ActiveConnection* property. An *If…Else* statement assigns one of two data sources for the catalog's *ActiveConnection* property. The second procedure chooses a path from the *If…Else* statement based on the Boolean value passed to it from the first procedure. By using a *Select…Case* statement, the second procedure could easily enable the selection of any of a wide set of prespecified sources for the catalog's *ActiveConnection* property.

Printing Data for the Table Details View

The Details view in the Access Database window returns more than just the name of a table and its type. It also returns two other particularly useful bits of information, the table's date of creation and its last modification date. Because the *Table* object exposes *DateCreated* and *DateModified* properties, generating a display like the one in the Database window's Details view is relatively straightforward.

To keep the design of the next code listing simple, the first procedure passes just one argument to the second procedure. This argument is a string parameter that designates the filename and path for the target database file. The second procedure has hard-coded filters that return only user-defined tables in the target database and exclude table names that begin with ~TMP. Because this sample generates four columns of output, it prints a row of headers that clarify what each column contains for the members of the tables collection.

```
Sub CallTablesDetail()
Dim str1 As String

str1 = "c:\PMA Samples\Northwind_backup.mdb"
TablesDetail str1

End Sub


Sub TablesDetail(str1 As String)
Dim cat1 As ADOX.Catalog
Dim tbl1 As Table
Dim mwd As Byte

'Instantiate a catalog, and point it at the target database
Set cat1 = New ADOX.Catalog
cat1.ActiveConnection = "Provider=Microsoft.Jet.OLEDB.4.0;" & _
    "Data Source=" & str1

'Compute the length of the longest table name in the database.
'Minimum width of 10 matches the column header.
mwd = 10
For Each tbl1 In cat1.Tables
    If tbl1.Type = "TABLE" And Left(tbl1.Name, 4) <> "~TMP" Then _
        If Len(tbl1.Name) > mwd Then mwd = Len(tbl1.Name)
Next tbl1
mwd = mwd + 1

'Print a row of column headers to the Immediate window before
'printing the name, date modified, date created, and type of members
'in the catalog's Tables collection
Debug.Print "Table Name" & String(mwd - Len("Table Name"), " ") & _
    "Date Modified" & String(22 - Len("Date Modified"), " ") & _
    "Date Created" & String(22 - Len("Date Created"), " ") & "Type"
For Each tbl1 In cat1.Tables
```

(continued)

```
        If tbl1.Type = "TABLE" And Left(tbl1.Name, 4) <> "~TMP" Then _
            Debug.Print tbl1.Name & String(mwd - Len(tbl1.Name), " ") & _
            tbl1.DateModified & _
            String(22 - Len(tbl1.DateModified), " ") & _
            tbl1.DateCreated & String(22 - Len(tbl1.DateCreated), " ") & _
            tbl1.Type
Next tbl1

'Clean up objects
Set cat1 = Nothing

End Sub
```

Figure 4-3 shows the Immediate window output from the preceding sample positioned above the Details view from the Database window for the Northwind_backup Access database file. Notice that the information about Modified and Created dates is the same in both windows. In addition, both listings of tables contain the same table names in the same order.

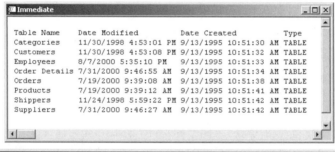

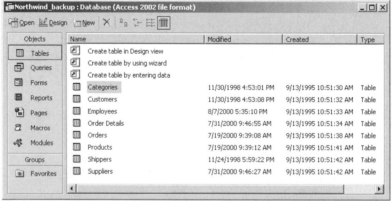

Figure 4-3 Output from the *CallTablesDetail* and *TablesDetail* procedures contrasted with the Details view from the Database window for the same target database.

Using the *AllTables* Collection

The *AllTables* collection can enumerate tables in a style similar to that of the *Tables* collection in the ADOX library. Unlike the *Tables* collection, the *AllTables* collection does not require the creation of a special reference to the ADOX library. This is because the *AllTables* collection is a part of the Microsoft Access 10 Object Library. Therefore, when you start Access, the *AllTables* collection is available automatically. Access refers to the members of the *AllTables* collection as *AccessObject* objects.

The Access library contains multiple *Allxxx* collections, including *AllTables*, *AllForms*, *AllQueries*, and *AllReports*. The AccessObject can refer to a member of any of these collections. You can use the *Type* property to distinguish among the members of these different collections. An *AccessObject* object has the same *Name* property setting as the database object to which it refers. For example, the *AccessObject* object named *Categories* corresponds to the *Categories* table in the Northwind database. You can use an *AccessObject* object to enumerate forms and reports even when they are closed. In addition, you can use an *AccessObject* object to determine whether the database object corresponding to that *AccessObject* object is open.

The similarities between the *Allxxx* collection members and the ADOX collection members should not obscure the fundamental distinctions among them. For example, the *Type* property for an ADOX *Tables* collection member denotes a type of table, such as local or linked. The *Type* property for an *AllTables* collection member identifies a type of *AccessObject* object, such as an object pointing at a table (rather than an object pointing at a form, for example). Therefore, the *AllTables* collection has no built-in feature for filtering tables by their type. In addition, the *AllTables* collection automatically excludes views, while the *Tables* collection includes them. (Recall that a view is a special type of stored query.) Even more critical is the fact that *Allxxx* collections exclusively apply to the current project or a project linked to the current project via a reference. However, the collections in the ADOX library can refer to any Access database file.

Printing Table Details with the *AllTables* Collection

The next sample enumerates the tables in the current project via the *AllTables* collection. Notice that the *AllTables* collection belongs to the *CurrentData* object in the Access *Application* object. The *atc1* variable points to this collection. The program requires an *AccessObject* object to enumerate the members of the collection. The sample references the *AccessObject* object with the *atb1* variable.

Since *AccessObject* objects have *DateModified* and *DateCreated* properties, you can create a report similar to the one made for the Details view of tables in an Access Database window. The following listing shows the code to print the name, date last modified, date created, and type of *AccessObject* object for the members of the *AllTables* collection in the *CurrentData* object:

```
Sub TablesDetailFromAllTables()
Dim atbl As Access.AccessObject
Dim atcl As Object
Dim mwd As Integer

'Create object reference to AllTables
'in CurrentProject
Set atcl = Application.CurrentData.AllTables

'Determine name of longest table
mwd = 10
For Each atbl In atcl
    If Len(atbl.Name) > mwd Then mwd = Len(atbl.Name)
Next atbl
mwd = mwd + 1

'Print hearder for table detail followed by
'a row for each table
Debug.Print "Table Name" & _
    String(mwd - Len("Table Name"), " ") & _
    "Date Modified" & String(24 - Len("Date Modified"), " ") & _
    "Date Created" & String(28 - Len("Date Created"), " ") & "Type"
For Each atbl In atcl
    Debug.Print atbl.Name & _
        String(mwd - Len(atbl.Name), " ") & _
        atbl.DateModified, atbl.DateCreated, _
        IIf(atbl.Type = acTable, "Table", "Error")
Next atbl

End Sub
```

The members of the *AllTables* collection include local tables as well as linked tables based on ISAM (indexed sequential access method) and ODBC data sources. In addition, the *AllTables* members include system tables. Because the *AllTables* collection has no *Type* property that distinguishes among these different types of tables, there is no easy way to enumerate the tables of just one type. The output from the preceding code sample appears in Figure 4-4. By comparing this output with the output in Figure 4-2 (on page 192), you can see that the tables in Figure 4-4 include the system, Access, and other kinds of tables.

```
Immediate                                                          _ □ ×
Table Name          Date Modified           Date Created            Type
CustomersNW         9/22/1998 6:45:43 PM     9/22/1998 6:39:55 PM    Table
DataTypes           9/23/1998 3:42:36 PM     9/23/1998 2:21:06 PM    Table
FamilyMembers       9/16/1998 8:04:12 AM     9/15/1998 3:39:28 PM    Table
ImportedOrders      1/8/2001 7:47:33 PM      1/8/2001 7:47:32 PM     Table
Invoice Details     9/22/1998 12:42:05 AM    9/22/1998 12:42:05 AM   Table
Invoices            9/22/1998 3:27:33 PM     9/21/1998 11:10:32 PM   Table
MSysAccessObjects   1/5/2001 6:18:12 AM      1/5/2001 6:18:11 AM     Table
MSysACEs            9/15/1998 3:33:05 PM     9/15/1998 3:33:05 PM    Table
MSysIMEXColumns     1/8/2001 9:56:18 AM      1/8/2001 9:56:18 AM     Table
MSysIMEXSpecs       1/8/2001 9:56:18 AM      1/8/2001 9:56:18 AM     Table
MSysObjects         9/15/1998 3:33:05 PM     9/15/1998 3:33:05 PM    Table
MSysQueries         9/15/1998 3:33:05 PM     9/15/1998 3:33:05 PM    Table
MSysRelationships   9/15/1998 3:33:05 PM     9/15/1998 3:33:05 PM    Table
Order DetailsNW     9/22/1998 6:45:24 PM     9/22/1998 6:41:24 PM    Table
OrdersNW            9/26/1998 11:23:50 PM    9/22/1998 6:40:46 PM    Table
Persons             10/31/1998 6:24:27 PM    9/15/1998 9:49:42 PM    Table
ProductsNW          9/22/1998 6:43:31 PM     9/22/1998 6:41:25 PM    Table
Shippers            1/9/2001 10:29:45 PM     1/9/2001 10:29:45 PM    Table
Table1              9/15/1998 10:12:02 PM    9/15/1998 10:12:02 PM   Table
Titles              9/15/1998 10:25:50 PM    9/15/1998 9:45:50 PM    Table
```

Figure 4-4 Output from the *TablesDetailFromAllTables* procedure. Contrast with the output in Figure 4-2 to appreciate the differences between the *AllTables* collection and the *Tables* collection.

Detecting When Tables Are Open

One of the main benefits of *AccessObject* objects is their ability to determine whether a matching database object with the same name is open or closed. The following sample uses the *atb1* variable that points to an *AccessObject* object to tell whether a table is open (or loaded). If the table is open, the procedure prints the table's name before closing it without saving any changes. The sample repeats this process for each member in the *AllTables* collection.

```
Sub PrintAndCloseOpenTables()
Dim atb1 As Access.AccessObject
Dim atc1 As Object

'Create object reference to AllTables
'in CurrentProject
Set atc1 = Application.CurrentData.AllTables

'Loop through the members of the AllTables collection
Debug.Print "The following tables are open. " & _
    "I will close them without saving changes for you."
For Each atb1 In atc1
    If atb1.IsLoaded = True Then
        Debug.Print atb1.Name
        DoCmd.Close acTable, atb1.Name, acSaveNo
    End If
Next atb1

End Sub
```

Creating Tables and Columns

Creating a table programmatically has several important advantages over creating one manually. First, the process yields a precise statement about the design of a table. Second, you can rerun the program or programs that define a table and duplicate its design in another database file or on another computer. Third, expressing a table's design programmatically makes it easy to experiment with different designs.

Creating a table in a database using code always involves at least four steps. First, you instantiate a new catalog, which allows you to specify the Access database file to which the new table will belong. Second, you create a new table and assign its *Name* property. The table's *Name* property provides a handle in the Database window to your new table. Third, you append one or more columns to the table. These columns are one of the main defining features of a table. You can further refine your table by declaring a primary key or a foreign key. Fourth, you append your table to the catalog. This step adds the table to an Access database file. You will not have a table in an Access database file until you invoke this step.

A Code Sample to Create a Table

The next code listing illustrates the application of the steps just discussed. The sample begins by opening a connection that refers to the database file created by the first sample in this chapter (on page 189). The procedure designates a location for the new table by assigning the connection to the *ActiveConnection* property of the catalog containing the new table. It is not absolutely necessary to designate the table location at this point since you do not reference the catalog again until after the table's design is complete. However, specifying the table's location might help you visualize the table as belonging in a particular database.

Next the procedure instantiates a new table. This provides a container for the table's columns. Before adding columns to the design, the code performs two functions. First, it assigns the *Name* property for the table. This will signify how you refer to the table after your code adds it to a database file. Second, the procedure assigns the table's *ParentCatalog* property. This is necessary when you want to assign an *AutoIncrement* property to a column within a table. Although this table does not assign the *AutoIncrement* property, assigning the *ParentCatalog* property is a good habit to adopt because it offers access to provider-specific properties. As Microsoft implements more of these properties, your designs will be ready to take advantage of them.

You add columns to a table through the *Append* method of the table's *Columns* collection. At a minimum, you specify a column name and a data type for each column. The name designates a handle for referring to the column, and the data type designates an ADO data type. The ADOX library refers to the data type of a column as its *Type* property.

I will review the correspondence between the Access table data types and the ADO data types in "Understanding ADOX Column Properties" later in this chapter, but you should understand that not all the features in one system align with features in the other system. You need to learn these correspondences because ADO has many more data types than Access tables, many of which are very similar but should not be interchanged. For example, the intrinsic constant *adInteger* is used to declare the data type for the *FamID* column in the preceding listing. This constant refers to a Long Integer data type instead of the Access table Integer data type. As another example, the intrinsic constant *adVarWChar* refers to a Text data type in an Access table. Selected ADO data type constants that look similar include *adWChar*, *adVarChar*, and *adLongVarWChar*. Do not use these constants when specifying a data type for a column holding text data. When specifying a column by designating *adVarWChar* as its *Type* property value, you will always want to set its *DefinedSize* property using the third argument for the *Append* method. The *DefinedSize* property sets the maximum length in characters for a column holding text values. The default value for the *DefinedSize* property is 0.

Once you have completed the design of the new table, one more step remains: to persist the table and make it available for holding data. Your code does this by appending the table to the *Tables* collection for a catalog. The following sample illustrates the syntax for the catalog's *Append* method.

```
Sub MakeFamilyMembersTableInMyNewDB()
Dim cat1 As ADOX.Catalog
Dim tbl1 As ADOX.Table
Dim cnn1 As ADODB.Connection

'Prepare to add table to MyNewDB database schema
Set cnn1 = New ADODB.Connection
cnn1.Open "Provider=Microsoft.Jet.OLEDB.4.0;" & _
    "Data Source=" & "c:\PMA Samples\Chapter 04\MyNewDB.mdb"
Set cat1 = New ADOX.Catalog
Set cat1.ActiveConnection = cnn1

'Instantiate table, name it, and append columns.
'Assignment of ParentCatalog property is optional
'for a table without an AutoIncrement field.
Set tbl1 = New ADOX.Table
With tbl1
    .Name = "FamilyMembers"
    Set .ParentCatalog = cat1
```

(continued)

```
        .Columns.Append "FamID", adInteger
        .Columns.Append "Fname", adVarWChar, 20
        .Columns.Append "Lname", adVarWChar, 25
        .Columns.Append "Relation", adVarWChar, 30
    End With

    'Append new table to Tables collection of MyNewDB
    cat1.Tables.Append tbl1

    'Clean up objects
    Set tbl1 = Nothing
    Set cat1 = Nothing
    cnn1.Close
    Set cnn1 = Nothing

End Sub
```

The preceding sample is easy to follow, but it fails to achieve one common design feature of many Access tables. It does not include an AutoNumber column. Incorporating this type of column within a table requires three steps. First, you have to set the *ParentCatalog* property for the table. Your code will not run successfully without this step. Second, you must designate the column's *Type* property as *adInteger*. Third, you have to assign the value of True to the column's *AutoIncrement* property.

The following excerpt from the *MakeFamilyMembers2TableInMyNewDB* procedure illustrates the syntax of these three steps. The excerpt gives the code to make the FamID column show the behavior of an AutoNumber column. The full procedure is available on the companion CD.

```
⋮
'Instantiate table, name it, and append columns.
'Assignment of ParentCatalog property is optional
'unless you are creating an AutoIncrement field.
Set tbl1 = New ADOX.Table
With tbl1
    .Name = "FamilyMembers2"
    Set .ParentCatalog = cat1
    With .Columns
        .Append "FamID", adInteger
        .Item("FamID").Properties("AutoIncrement") = True
        .Append "Fname", adVarWChar, 20
        .Append "Lname", adVarWChar, 25
        .Append "Relation", adVarWChar, 30
    End With
End With
⋮
```

Deleting and Replacing Tables

When developers begin a database project, they often need to tweak a project's design. Sometimes this means removing a table altogether. The following sample demonstrates the syntax for invoking the *Delete* method of the *Tables* collection to remove any table on a LAN. The first procedure designates the target database and the table to be removed and passes this information along to the second procedure. The second procedure instantiates a catalog with a connection to the database. Then it invokes the *Delete* method of the *Tables* collection of the target database for the particular table denoted by the second string argument.

```
Sub CallDeleteATable()
Dim str1 As String
Dim str2 As String

'Designate a database filename and table name
'before invoking the DeleteATable procedure
str1 = "c:\PMA Samples\Chapter 04\MyNewDB.mdb"
str2 = "FamilyMembers"
DeleteATable str1, str2

End Sub


Sub DeleteATable(str1 As String, str2)
Dim cat1 As ADOX.Catalog

'Instantiate a catalog with the target
'table that you want to delete
Set cat1 = New ADOX.Catalog
cat1.ActiveConnection = _
    "Provider=Microsoft.Jet.OLEDB.4.0;" & _
    "Data Source=" & str1

'Invoke the table's Delete method, specifying
'the name of the table to remove as a string
cat1.Tables.Delete str2

'Clean up objects
Set cat1 = Nothing

End Sub
```

You might think that the easiest approach for changing a table's design is to just create a new table with the same name. However, this approach fails because the *Append* method of the *Tables* collection will not create a new table with the same name as one that already exists. Instead, this method generates a run-time error. The following sample works around this difficulty by deleting the previous version of a table when it encounters a "table already exists" error. This approach is particularly useful when you need a dataset that can be installed automatically for testing purposes.

The sample either adds or replaces the *FamilyMembers2* table in the MyNewDB database. When the *FamilyMembers2* table already exists in the database, the procedure transfers control to its error trap. If the trap detects a "table already exists" error, the trap invokes the *Delete* method for the table. Next the trap transfers control back to the *Append* method for the new version of the table.

```
Sub AddOrReplaceFamilyMembers2TableInMyNewDB()
On Error GoTo TableErrCatcher
Dim cat1 As ADOX.Catalog
Dim tbl1 As ADOX.Table

'Reference objects for table
Set cat1 = New Catalog
cat1.ActiveConnection = "Provider=Microsoft.Jet.OLEDB.4.0;" & _
    "Data Source=" & "c:\PMA Samples\Chapter 04\MyNewDB.mdb"
Set tbl1 = New Table

'Name table and append columns
With tbl1
    .Name = "FamilyMembers2"
    .Columns.Append "FamID", adInteger
    .Columns.Append "Fname", adVarWChar, 20
    .Columns.Append "Lname", adVarWChar, 25
    .Columns.Append "Relation", adVarWChar, 30
End With


'Append new table to Tables collection,
'and free catalog resource
cat1.Tables.Append tbl1

'Exit the procedure
TableErrExit:
Set tbl1 = Nothing
Set cat1 = Nothing
Exit Sub
```

```
TableErrCatcher:
'Trap "table already exits" error.
'Delete table and resume.
If Err.Number = -2147217857 Then
    cat1.Tables.Delete "FamilyMembers2"
    Resume
End If
'Print details for other errors
Debug.Print Err.Number, Err.Description

End Sub
```

Understanding ADOX Column Properties

Column property settings differ between the Access user interface and the ADOX programmatic interface. This is most obvious when using the intrinsic constants that denote data types. For the following sample, I've created a table named *DataTypes* in the Chapter4.mdb file that contains all possible Access data types. Figure 4-5 shows the Design view for the *DataTypes* table. Running the sample code with this table generates a list of all the corresponding ADOX data types, which you can retain for easy reference. Alternatively, you can use this sample code to examine any existing table so that you can view its settings in ADOX nomenclature while viewing its design in the Access Table Design view interface.

Figure 4-5 The Design view for the *DataTypes* table contains a column for each Access table data type.

The data type translator that follows consists of a pair of procedures. The first procedure instantiates a catalog for the current database. Then it instantiates a *Table* object and points it at the *DataTypes* table. After printing some header information to label the output, the first procedure simply loops through each column in the *DataTypes* table. The procedure prints each column's name, its ADOX intrinsic constant value for the data type, and the corresponding intrinsic constant name. The *Name* property for each column is the Access table data type name for a column, which was set in the Access user interface. The second procedure consists primarily of a *Select...Case* statement. This procedure translates each ADOX column's *Type* property setting to a string that matches the ADOX name for the data type. If there is no match for an input data type number, the *CStr* function translates the number to a string so the function procedure can return it.

```
Sub AccessToADODataTypeTranslator()
Dim cat1 As ADOX.Catalog
Dim tbl1 As ADOX.Table
Dim col1 As ADOX.Column
Dim strType As String

'The DataTypes table contains one of each Access
'table data type
Set cat1 = New ADOX.Catalog
cat1.ActiveConnection = CurrentProject.Connection
Set tbl1 = cat1.Tables("DataTypes")

'Print DataType column names from Access, their intrinsic
'constant values, and names from ADO
Debug.Print "Access-to-ADO Data Type Translator"
Debug.Print "Access name", " ADO value", "ADO name"
For Each col1 In tbl1.Columns
    Debug.Print col1.Name, col1.Type, ColumnType(col1.Type)
Next col1

'Clean up objects
Set tbl1 = Nothing
Set cat1 = Nothing

End Sub


Function ColumnType(intType As Integer) As String
    Select Case intType
        Case adVarWChar
            ColumnType = "adVarWChar"
```

```
        Case adCurrency
            ColumnType = "adCurrency"
        Case adInteger
            ColumnType = "adInteger"
        Case adDate
            ColumnType = "adDate"
        Case adWChar
            ColumnType = "adWChar"
        Case adLongVarWChar
            ColumnType = "adLongVarWChar"
        Case adLongVarBinary
            ColumnType = "adLongVarBinary"
        Case adBoolean
            ColumnType = "adBoolean"
        Case adSmallInt
            ColumnType = "adSmallInt"
        Case adDouble
            ColumnType = "adDouble"
        Case adGUID
            ColumnType = "adGuid"
        Case adSingle
            ColumnType = "adSingle"
        Case adUnsignedTinyInt
            ColumnType = "adUnsignedTinyInt"
        Case adNumeric
            ColumnType = "adNumeric"
        Case Else
            ColumnType = CStr(intType)
    End Select
End Function
```

The next sample extends the logic of the data type translator in several ways. First it works with any Access database file—not just the Chapter 04.mdb file. Next the sample iterates through all the tables in an Access database file—not just one table. Finally it prints the *DefinedSize* property setting for each column. You can readily extend this application to add as many column properties as you need.

The sample assumes that no table name is longer than 30 characters and no column name is longer than 20 characters. These assumptions save you from having to compute the maximum length for table and column names. They also keep the sample code short so that it is easy to follow. If the names for one or more tables exceeds 30 characters, or the names for one or more columns exceeds 20 characters, simply adjust the expressions for padding *str3*.

```
Sub CallEnumerateDBTablesColumnsAndColumnProps()
Dim str1 As String

'Designate database path and filename from which
'you want to retrieve tables, columns, and their properties
str1 = "c:\PMA Samples\Northwind_backup.mdb"
EnumerateDBTablesColumnsAndColumnProps str1

End Sub


Sub EnumerateDBTablesColumnsAndColumnProps(str1 As String)
Dim cat1 As ADOX.Catalog
Dim tbl1 As ADOX.Table
Dim col1 As ADOX.Column
Dim str2 As String
Dim str3 As String

'Point catalog at target database file
Set cat1 = New ADOX.Catalog
cat1.ActiveConnection = _
    "Provider=Microsoft.Jet.OLEDB.4.0;" & _
    "Data Source=" & str1

'Loop through all user-defined nontemporary tables in the
'database file and every column within each table;
'add additional table and column properties, or even column
'collections, for analyzing the tables within a database
For Each tbl1 In cat1.Tables
    If tbl1.Type = "TABLE" And Left(tbl1.Name, 4) <> "~TMP" Then
        str2 = tbl1.Name
        str3 = String(30 - Len(tbl1.Name), " ")
        Debug.Print str2 & str3 & tbl1.Columns.Count
            For Each col1 In tbl1.Columns
                str3 = String(20 - Len(col1.Name), " ")
                Debug.Print String(5, " ") & col1.Name & _
                    str3 & ColumnType(col1.Type), col1.DefinedSize
            Next col1
    End If
Next tbl1

'Clean up objects

Set cat1 = Nothing

End Sub
```

Processing Primary and Foreign Keys

You can add and delete primary and foreign keys to an Access database design with the ADOX object model. The model also supports the use of unique keys that do not serve as primary keys for a table. Because this type of key is not widely used by Access developers, I will not dwell on it further.

Adding Primary Keys

To add a primary key to a table, you need an object reference to that table. You can obtain such a reference in the program that initially created a table, or you can return to a table that is otherwise complete, make a new reference to the table, and then add the primary key.

A primary key is a special index for a table. Each table has an *Indexes* collection. Adding a primary key to a table is a three-step process. First, you must define the index with property settings appropriate for a primary key. Second, you add one or more columns to the index. These columns together represent the values for the individual primary key. Third, you append the new index to the *Indexes* collection for the table.

In addition to setting a name for future use, the index for the primary key must have three special property assignments: *PrimaryKey*, *Unique*, and *IndexNulls*. The *PrimaryKey* and *Unique* properties take Boolean value assignments and must both be set to True. Since primary keys cannot contain Null values, you must set the *IndexNulls* property to *adIndexNullsDisallow* The following listing shows the basic syntax for adding a new primary key to a table. It begins by pointing a catalog at an Access database file through the catalog's *ActiveConnection* property. Then it instantiates a *Table* object and references the table, namely the *FamilyMembers2* table in the MyNewDB database, to which it will add a primary key. Next it instantiates an index using the *pk1* variable. This variable serves as an object reference that allows the procedure to build the primary key by assigning property values, appending columns to it, and appending the index to the object reference for the *FamilyMembers2* table, *tbl1*. When all the assignments and append methods complete, the procedure sets the object references for the index, table, and catalog to Nothing. This is the standard cleanup step for all object references at the end of procedures that terminate successfully.

```
Sub AddPK()
Dim cat1 As ADOX.Catalog
Dim tbl1 As ADOX.Table
Dim pk1 As ADOX.Index
```

(continued)

```
'Create a context for the new primary key
Set cat1 = New ADOX.Catalog
cat1.ActiveConnection = _
    "Provider=Microsoft.Jet.OLEDB.4.0;" & _
    "Data Source=" & "c:\PMA Samples\Chapter 04\MyNewDB.mdb"
Set tbl1 = cat1.Tables("FamilyMembers2")

'Set the primary key properties
Set pk1 = New ADOX.Index
With pk1
    .Name = "MyPrimaryKey"
    .PrimaryKey = True
    .Unique = True
    .IndexNulls = adIndexNullsDisallow
End With

'Append column to index and index to table
pk1.Columns.Append "FamID"
tbl1.Indexes.Append pk1

'Clean up objects
Set pk1 = Nothing

Set tbl1 = Nothing
Set cat1 = Nothing

End Sub
```

If you run the preceding program a second time it will fail because the primary key already exists and a table can have only one primary key. You can also encounter run-time errors for issues unrelated to the validity of your logic. For example, a user might have the table open, but Access does not permit you to add a primary key to a table unless it can lock the table's design. The following listing shows how to trap and respond to typical kinds of run-time errors that can occur as you attempt to add a primary key to a table that already exists. In particular, the code traps the two types of run-time errors discussed in the preceding paragraph. The best way to understand the program logic is to set the error condition and then step through the program. This will show you which line generates the error and how the program handles the error. For example, you might open the table and then step through the procedure to see what happens when Access can't lock the table in order to add the primary key.

The first part of the *AddPKErr* listing shown next is identical to the *AddPK* listing in the previous sample, except for the addition of a couple of lines. An *On Error* statement immediately following the sub procedure declaration permits control to flow to the error-trapping logic in the event of an error. Just before the error-trapping logic, the listing contains a label, *PKErr_Exit*, that precedes the normal object cleanup code. This is a useful point at which to resume for one type of error.

The procedure implements the error-trapping logic with an *If...ElseIf* statement. Each clause of the statement traps a different error condition. You can replace the *If...ElseIf* statement with a *Select...Case* statement if you prefer. If the table is already open when you invoke the *Append* method for the *Indexes* collection in the *Table* object, the program fails with an error number of –2147217856. In the event of this error, the procedure informs the user of the problem and then exits in a normal way. If the primary key already exists when the program invokes the *Append* method for the *Indexes* collection, the resulting error causes control to branch to the *ElseIf* clause in the error trap. This clause searches for the initial version of the primary key to remove it from the table's *Indexes* collection. Then the clause passes control back to a point in the procedure that attempts again to append the primary key to the *Indexes* collection.

```
Sub AddPKErr()
On Error GoTo PKErr_Trap
Dim cat1 As ADOX.Catalog
Dim tbl1 As ADOX.Table
Dim pk1 As ADOX.Index
Dim iNumber As Integer

Set cat1 = New ADOX.Catalog
Set tbl1 = New ADOX.Table
Set pk1 = New ADOX.Index

'Create a context for the new primary key
cat1.ActiveConnection = _
    "Provider=Microsoft.Jet.OLEDB.4.0;" & _
    "Data Source=" & "c:\PMA Samples\Chapter 04\MyNewDB.mdb"
Set tbl1 = cat1.Tables("FamilyMembers2")

'Set the primary key properties.
'The label (SetPKvariable) gives the procedure a
'recovery point from a previously existing primary key.
SetPKvariable:
With pk1
    .Name = "MyPrimaryKey"
    .PrimaryKey = True
    .Unique = True
    .IndexNulls = adIndexNullsDisallow
End With

'Append column to index and index to table
pk1.Columns.Append "FamID"
```

(continued)

```
    .tbl1.Indexes.Append pk1

'Exit procedure
PKErr_Exit:
Set pk1 = Nothing
Set tbl1 = Nothing
Set cat1 = Nothing
Exit Sub

PKErr_Trap:
'Checks for table already in use
If Err.Number = -2147217856 Then
    MsgBox "FamilyMembers2 currently in use.  This" & _
        " operation requires the table to be closed."
    Resume PKErr_Exit
'Checks whether primary key already exists
ElseIf Err.Number = -2147467259 Then
    For Each pk1 In tbl1.Indexes
        If pk1.PrimaryKey = True Then
            tbl1.Indexes.Delete (iNumber)
            Resume SetPKvariable
        End If
        iNumber = iNumber + 1
    Next pk1
'Trap for other errors
Else
    MsgBox "Open Immediate window for Bug report"
    Debug.Print Err.Number; Err.Description
End If

End Sub
```

In spite of the popularity of using *AutoNumber* or other system-assigned integer values as primary keys, sometimes it is helpful to use a combination of fields to denote the primary key. For example, rows in the *FamilyMembers2* table are made unique by their *FamID* column value as well as the combination of their *Lname*, *Fname*, and *Relation* field values. In a situation where you prefer (or an application requires) a primary key defined on multiple columns, you simply append these columns to the index before appending the index to the *Indexes* collection for a table. The following code excerpt from the *AddPK3* procedure on the companion CD illustrates the application of this approach. In other respects, you specify a primary key on multiple columns the same way you define it on a single column.

```
⋮
'Append multiple columns to index, and then
'append the index to table's Indexes collection
```

```
pk1.Columns.Append "Lname"
pk1.Columns.Append "Fname"
pk1.Columns.Append "Relation"
tbl1.Indexes.Append pk1
⋮
```

Adding Foreign Keys

Foreign keys are inherently more complex than primary keys because they relate to two tables instead of to a single table. In addition, foreign keys support referential integrity, and modern implementations of referential integrity must account for cascading updates and deletes. Therefore, you must account for these additional properties when working with foreign keys. Finally, primary keys are associated with an index, but foreign keys do not necessarily require an associated index. Therefore, you can add a primary key through the *Indexes* collection (or the *Keys* collection) of a table, but you must add a foreign key directly to the table's *Keys* collection.

The following listing creates a foreign key in the Northwind database. The key is for the *Orders* table and points back at the *Customers* table. The code sample accounts for those properties explicitly mentioned in the preceding paragraph as well as other properties implied by the preceding paragraph. *AddFK*, the primary procedure in the listing, has two main segments. First, it searches to see whether there already is a foreign key with the name that you want to use for your new key. If the procedure discovers such a key, it documents the old version to the Immediate window before deleting it. Second, the procedure constructs the foreign key and ultimately appends it to the *Keys* collection for the *Orders* table.

The code sample uses a *For...Each* loop to enumerate the members of the *Keys* collection for the *Orders* table. If the code finds a member with the name *CustomersOrders*, it writes the specs for the key to the Immediate window. These specs include the name, the type of key, the related table, the columns on which the key is defined, and two additional properties that indicate how the key enforces cascading updates and deletes.

Several specific programming techniques support the behavior of the sample as it documents the old foreign key before deleting it. For example, the *AddFK* procedure uses a nested *For...Each* loop to enumerate the column or columns in the *CustomersOrders* key. The outer loop contains calls to two function procedures for returning strings corresponding to the intrinsic constant settings for the key's *Type*, *UpdateRule*, and *DeleteRule* properties. The *KeyType* function procedure returns a label (*adForeignKey* in this case) for the key, declaring it a foreign key. The *RuleType* function returns any of several labels, depending on the cascading settings for the foreign key. The Northwind database originally ships with settings of *adRICascasde* and *adRINone* for cascading updates and deletes, respectively. The last line in the outer loop demonstrates the syntax for deleting an existing foreign key.

The second part of the *AddFK* procedure uses a simple *With...End With* statement to abbreviate the code for making foreign key property assignments. After completing the assignments, the procedure appends the fully specified foreign key to the *Keys* collection for the *Orders* table. When removing a key, you can merely specify its *Name* property. But when adding a key to a collection, your code must designate the object reference.

```
Sub AddFK()
Dim cat1 As ADOX.Catalog
Dim key1 As ADOX.key
Dim col1 As ADOX.Column

'Assign ActiveConnection property for catalog
Set cat1 = New ADOX.Catalog
cat1.ActiveConnection = "Provider=Microsoft.Jet.OLEDB.4.0;" & _
    "Data Source=C:\PMA Samples\Northwind.mdb;"

'If there is an existing CustomersOrders key for
'the Orders table, print its specs for manual restoration,
'if necessary, and then delete the key
For Each key1 In cat1.Tables("Orders").Keys
    With key1
        If .Name = "CustomersOrders" Then
            Debug.Print .Name
            Debug.Print String(5, " ") & "Key Type = " & _
                KeyType(.Type)
            Debug.Print String(5, " ") & "Related Table = " & _
                .RelatedTable
            For Each col1 In _
                cat1.Tables("Orders").Keys(.Name).Columns
                Debug.Print String(5, " ") & "Key column name = " _
                    & col1.Name
            Next col1
            Debug.Print String(5, " ") & "Cascading Updates = " & _
                RuleType(.UpdateRule)
            Debug.Print String(5, " ") & "Cascading Deletes = " & _
                RuleType(.DeleteRule)
            cat1.Tables("Orders").Keys.Delete .Name
        End If
    End With
Next key1

'Create a new version of CustomersOrders key, which is a
'foreign key that permits cascading updates; use CustomerID
'in the Orders table to point back at the Customers table
```

```
Set key1 = New ADOX.key
With key1
    .Name = "CustomersOrders"
    .Type = adKeyForeign
    .RelatedTable = "Customers"
    .Columns.Append "CustomerId"
    .Columns("CustomerId").RelatedColumn = "CustomerId"
    .UpdateRule = adRICascade
End With
cat1.Tables("Orders").Keys.Append key1

'Clean up objects
Set key1 = Nothing
Set cat1 = Nothing

End Sub


Function KeyType(intType As Integer) As String
    Select Case intType
        Case adKeyPrimary
            KeyType = "adKeyPrimary"
        Case adKeyForeign
            KeyType = "adKeyForeign"
        Case adKeyUnique
            KeyType = "adKeyUnique"
        Case Else
            KeyType = CStr(intType)
    End Select
End Function


Function RuleType(intType As Integer) As String
    Select Case intType
        Case adRINone
            RuleType = "adRINone"
        Case adRICascade
            RuleType = "adRICascade"
        Case adRISetNull
            RuleType = "adRISetNull"
        Case adRISetDefault
            RuleType = "adRISetDefault"
        Case Else
            RuleType = CStr(intType)
    End Select
End Function
```

Enumerating Keys

Sometimes you need an overview of all the keys in a database. The following listing satisfies this need. The listing has two procedures. The first one sets a string value that points at the Access database for which the application is to develop a list of keys. The first procedure passes this value along to the second procedure, which uses the string to set the *ActiveConnection* property for a catalog object. Then the second procedure iterates through the keys in all tables of the catalog to discover the length of the longest key name. This procedure stores the result in the integer variable *mwd*. Notice that it takes a nested loop to pass through the keys in a database. The outer loop selects each table in the catalog. The inner loop iterates through the members of the *Keys* collection for each table. Next the procedure prints the heading for the report.

The second procedure concludes by looping through the keys in the catalog a second time. On this second pass, the procedure prints the name of each table it encounters. Then it prints the key names and types. The expressions for controlling the layout of printed content take advantage of the maximum length for a key name to help align columns. Actually, the report indents the key names and types under the table to which they belong. Figure 4-6 shows the report for the keys in the Northwind database. By changing the string parameter in the listing's first procedure, you can generate a similar report for any other Access database file.

Figure 4-6 Output from the *CallListKeysAndTypes* and *ListKeysAndTypes* procedures for the Northwind database.

```
Sub CallListKeysAndTypes()
Dim str1 As String

'Database name and path
str1 = "c:\PMA Samples\Northwind.mdb;"

ListKeysAndTypes str1

End Sub


Sub ListKeysAndTypes(str1 As String)
Dim cat1 As ADOX.Catalog
Dim tbl1 As ADOX.Table
Dim key1 As ADOX.key
Dim str2 As String
Dim mwd As Integer

'Instantiate catalog, and point at target database file
Set cat1 = New ADOX.Catalog
cat1.ActiveConnection = "Provider=Microsoft.Jet.OLEDB.4.0;" & _
    "Data Source=" & str1

'Find width plus one of longest key name
mwd = 8
For Each tbl1 In cat1.Tables
    For Each key1 In cat1.Tables(tbl1.Name).Keys
        If mwd < Len(key1.Name) Then mwd = Len(key1.Name)
    Next key1
Next tbl1
mwd = mwd + 1'Print heading for key report
Debug.Print "Enumeration of Key Names and Types within Tables"
Debug.Print "Table Name"
Debug.Print String(5, " ") & "Key Name" & _
    String(mwd - 8, " ") & "Key Type"

'Loop through the tables within a catalog
For Each tbl1 In cat1.Tables
    If tbl1.Type = "table" And _
        Left(tbl1.Name, 4) <> "~TMP" Then
        Debug.Print tbl1.Name

'Print name and type of key
        For Each key1 In tbl1.Keys
            Debug.Print String(5, " ") & key1.Name & _
                String(mwd - Len(key1.Name), " ") & _
                KeyType(key1.Type)
```

(continued)

```
        Next key1

    End If
Next tbl1

'Clean up objects
Set cat1 = Nothing

End Sub
```

Processing Indexes

Indexes can speed up many processes in database applications, such as sorting records, joining tables, and looking up values. Although the ADO Cursor Service can dynamically add an index, you can enhance runtime performance by creating indexes that an application is likely to use ahead of time. In addition, you cannot use dynamic indexes with the *Seek* method because this method requires a *CursorLocation* property setting that is incompatible with the Cursor Service. You can build a report of all the indexes in a database by iterating through the *Indexes* collection for each table within a catalog.

> **Note** If you examine the ADOX properties for an *Index* object, you will note a *Clustered* property. This property takes a Boolean value. The *Clustered* property does not apply to Access database files. Therefore, you cannot successfully set the property, and it always returns a value of False.

Creating an Index

Four types of actions help you create indexes. First, you specify a catalog and a table within it for your index. Second, you assign three properties for an *Index* object: the *Name*, *Unique*, and *IndexNulls* properties. Each index column also has a *SortOrder* property, which is ascending by default. Third, you append one or more columns to the index. The values for these columns together represent the index value for each record. Fourth, you append the index to the *Indexes* collection for a table.

The following procedure, *AddIdx*, demonstrates the syntax for creating an index in a table. The procedure begins by designating the *FamilyMembers2* table in the MyNewDB database as the source for the index. Next it names the index, sets its *Unique* property to True, and specifies that the index does not allow Null values. It can safely assign the *Unique* property to True since the index is made up of the FamID column, which is the primary key for the table. The index distinguishes itself from the primary key by setting the sort order to *adSortDescending*. Both the *AddPK* and the *AddPKErr* procedures (shown in the previous section) accepted an ascending sort order as the default for the primary key. After setting all the properties for the index, the *AddIdx* procedure appends the index to the *Indexes* collection for the *FamilyMembers2* table.

```
Sub AddIdx()
Dim cat1 As New ADOX.Catalog
Dim tbl1 As ADOX.Table
Dim idx1 As New ADOX.Index

'Create a context for the new index
cat1.ActiveConnection = _
"Provider=Microsoft.Jet.OLEDB.4.0;" & _
    "Data Source=" & "c:\PMA Samples\Chapter 04\MyNewDB.mdb"
Set tbl1 = cat1.Tables("FamilyMembers2")

'Set the index properties
With idx1
    .Name = "LastIsFirst"
    .Unique = True
    .IndexNulls = adIndexNullsDisallow
End With

'Append column to index, and set its sort order.
'Append new index to table.
idx1.Columns.Append "FamID"
idx1.Columns(0).SortOrder = adSortDescending
tbl1.Indexes.Append idx1

'Clean up objects
Set cat1 = Nothing
Set tbl1 = Nothing
Set idx1 = Nothing

End Sub
```

Sorting Based on an Index

When your application displays content based on a single table, it can use the *Index* property instead of the recordset *Sort* property to designate the sort order for records. Using the *Index* property can save time and resources. The index already maintains an ordered list of the items in a record source. When you set the *Sort* property, ADO can optionally build a dynamic index. However, using a previously built index eliminates the time needed to construct the dynamic index during your application's execution.

The following listing demonstrates the syntax for creating an index to control a sort order. First it re-creates the table, adding a new index for a different sort order. Of course, in a normal application you would typically create the index only once, not each time you want to process the recordset. In order for the procedure to demonstrate the impact of a sort, it populates the *FamilyMembers2* table with some values. It does this with a series of INSERT INTO statements. Next it lists the *FamilyMembers2* table in two different orders. The procedure initially prints a report of the records in the default order of the primary keys. Then it prints a second report based on the *LastIsFirst* index created in the previous sample. Notice that in order to use an index to control the sort order of the records in a record source, you must open a recordset for a record source with the *Options* parameter set to *adCmdTableDirect*. Failing to use this parameter prevents the index from controlling the order of the records.

```
Sub SortByIndex()
Dim str1 As String
Dim str2 As String
Dim cmd1 As ADODB.Command
Dim rst1 As ADODB.Recordset

'Delete FamilyMembers2, and re-create it to make
'sure you start with a fresh table
str1 = "c:\PMA Samples\Chapter 04\MyNewDB.mdb"
str2 = "FamilyMembers2"
DeleteATable str1, str2
MakeFamilyMembers2TableInMyNewDB

'Add an index for the primary key on FamID
'and an index to allow designating an
'alternate sort order
AddPK
AddIdx

'Populate FamilyMembers2 table with rows
Set cmd1 = New ADODB.Command
With cmd1
    .ActiveConnection = "Provider=Microsoft.Jet.OLEDB.4.0;" & _
        "Data Source=" & str1

    .CommandText = "INSERT INTO FamilyMembers2" & _
        "(Fname, Lname, Relation) VALUES ('Rick','Dobson','me')"
    .CommandType = adCmdText
    .Execute
```

```
        .CommandText = "INSERT INTO FamilyMembers2" & _
            "(Fname, Lname, Relation) VALUES ('Virginia','Dobson','wife')"

        .Execute
        .CommandText = "INSERT INTO FamilyMembers2" & _
            "(Fname, Lname, Relation) VALUES ('Glen','Hill','son')"

        .Execute
        .CommandText = "INSERT INTO FamilyMembers2" & _
            "(Fname, Lname, Relation) VALUES ('Tony','Hill','son')"

        .Execute
        .CommandText = "INSERT INTO FamilyMembers2" & _
            "(Fname, Lname, Relation) VALUES " & _
            "('Shelly','Hill','daughter-in-law')"

        .Execute
    End With

    'Instantiate recordset, and print in default
    'primary key order
    Set rst1 = New ADODB.Recordset
    rst1.Open "FamilyMembers2", cmd1.ActiveConnection
    Debug.Print "In order of the primary key"
    Do Until rst1.EOF
        Debug.Print rst1(0), rst1(1), rst1(2), rst1(3)
        rst1.MoveNext
    Loop

    'Reinstantiate recordset, open recordset, and print in
    'order of the the LastIsFirst index; must use the
    'adCmdTableDirect constant to reflect index
    Set rst1 = New ADODB.Recordset
    rst1.Index = "LastIsFirst"
    rst1.Open "FamilyMembers2", cmd1.ActiveConnection, _
        , , adCmdTableDirect
    Debug.Print "In order of the LastIsFirst index"
    Do Until rst1.EOF
        Debug.Print rst1(0), rst1(1), rst1(2), rst1(3)
        rst1.MoveNext
    Loop

    'Clean up objects
    Set cmd1 = Nothing
    rst1.Close
    Set rst1 = Nothing
End Sub
```

Dynamically Creating an Index for the *Seek* Method

Creating an index on a table permits you to take advantage of the *Seek* method for finding records. Chapter 2 introduced you to using the *Seek* method with previously available indexes. Recall that the *Seek* method is generally faster than the *Find* method and that the *Seek* method makes available a subset of a recordset that's easy to use. However, using the *Seek* method requires a previously built index. Since ADO permits you to enumerate indexes, you can check whether the *Seek* method requires the construction of an index.

The listing in this section highlights two techniques for using indexes with the *Seek* method. First, the code creates an index to enable the use of the *Seek* method. Second, it removes the index after the *Seek* method no longer needs it. One main advantage of an index is that it persists automatically. However, you can remove an index if you rarely use it and prefer that your application not maintain the index while adding, deleting, and updating records.

The *Employees* table in the Northwind database contains a *Region* field, but it does not have an index built for that field. Therefore, applications cannot use the *Seek* method to develop a list of employees from a region without first building an index on the *Region* field. The following listing demonstrates an approach for accomplishing this task.

The *SeekEmployeesInRegionWA* procedure starts by opening a *Connection* object for the Northwind database. It then instantiates a *Catalog* object for the Northwind database by pointing the catalog's *ActiveConnection* property at the database. Next the procedure instantiates an *Index* object and makes the property assignments for its use before appending the object to the *Indexes* collection of the *Employees* table. This completes the construction of the index for the *Seek* method. The next two blocks of code demonstrate the use of the *Seek* method with a recordset. See Chapter 2 for an introduction to the *Seek* method that clarifies the code.

```
Sub SeekEmployeesInRegionWA()
Dim str1 As String
Dim cnn1 As ADODB.Connection
Dim rst1 As ADODB.Recordset
Dim cat1 As ADOX.Catalog
Dim idx1 As ADOX.Index

'Open connection
str1 = "Provider=Microsoft.Jet.OLEDB.4.0;" & _
    "Data Source=c:\PMA Samples\Northwind.mdb;"
Set cnn1 = New ADODB.Connection
cnn1.Open str1
```

```
'Set active connection for catalog
Set cat1 = New ADOX.Catalog
Set cat1.ActiveConnection = cnn1

'Define and append index (temporarily)
Set idx1 = New ADOX.Index
idx1.Name = "Region"
idx1.Columns.Append ("Region")
idx1.IndexNulls = adIndexNullsAllow
cat1.Tables("Employees").Indexes.Append idx1

'Open employee table with support for Seek method
'by referencing an index and using adCmdTableDirect
'option parameter
Set rst1 = New ADODB.Recordset
rst1.CursorType = adOpenKeyset
rst1.LockType = adLockOptimistic
rst1.Index = "Region"
rst1.Open "employees", cnn1, , , adCmdTableDirect

'Seek for set of records from WA region
rst1.Seek "WA"
Do Until rst1.EOF
    Debug.Print rst1("FirstName"), rst1("LastName")
    rst1.MoveNext
Loop


'Delete temporary Region index from Employees table
rst1.Close
cat1.Tables("Employees").Indexes.Delete idx1.Name

'Clean up objects
Set rst1 = Nothing
Set idx1 = Nothing
Set cat1 = Nothing
cnn1.Close
Set cnn1 = Nothing

End Sub
```

The block of code preceding the syntax for cleaning up objects removes the index from the *Employees* table based on the *Region* field. This block contains just two lines of code. First, it closes the *Recordset* object. This releases the hold of the recordset on the *cnn1 Connection* object. Second, it invokes the *Delete* method for the *idx1* object created toward the beginning of the procedure. While the *Delete* method is for the *Indexes* collection, this collection is dependent on the *Tables* collection of the *cat1 Catalog* object. The catalog requires the closing of the recordset so that the catalog can use the *cnn1 Connection* object to perform the *Delete* method.

Enumerating Indexes

Since the *Indexes* collection belongs to the *Tables* collection, you can enumerate them by walking the model path from catalog to table to index. The performance of a database will often depend on the proper use of indexes, but the Access Table Design view does not make it easy for developers to get an overall list of the indexes in a database. (Recall that the Table Design view shows the indexes for one table at a time.) This section demonstrates the syntax for techniques you should be highly familiar with by now. However, it applies those techniques in a new context—enumerating indexes.

The following listing includes two procedures. The first procedure specifies an Access database file for which you want to generate a list of indexes. The second procedure itemizes the indexes within each table of the database file. Additionally, the second procedure indicates whether the index also serves as a primary key by reporting its *PrimaryKey* property.

```
Sub CallListIndexes()
Dim str1 As String

'Database name and path
str1 = "c:\PMA Samples\Northwind.mdb;"

ListIndexes str1

End Sub


Sub ListIndexes(str1 As String)
Dim cat1 As ADOX.Catalog
Dim tbl1 As ADOX.Table
Dim idx1 As ADOX.Index
Dim str2 As String
Dim str3 As String
Dim mwd As Integer

'Instantiate catalog, and point it at target database file
Set cat1 = New ADOX.Catalog
cat1.ActiveConnection = "Provider=Microsoft.Jet.OLEDB.4.0;" & _
    "Data Source=" & str1
```

```
'Find width plus one of longest key name
mwd = 1
For Each tbl1 In cat1.Tables
    For Each idx1 In cat1.Tables(tbl1.Name).Indexes
        If mwd < Len(idx1.Name) Then mwd = Len(idx1.Name)
    Next idx1
Next tbl1
mwd = mwd + 1

'Loop through tables in a catalog
For Each tbl1 In cat1.Tables
    If tbl1.Type = "TABLE" And _
        Left(tbl1.Name, 4) <> "~TMP" Then
        Debug.Print tbl1.Name

'Print index name and status as a primary key
        For Each idx1 In tbl1.Indexes
            Debug.Print String(5, " ") & idx1.Name & _
            String(mwd - Len(idx1.Name), " ") & _
            idx1.PrimaryKey
        Next idx1


    End If
Next tbl1

'Clean up objects
Set cat1 = Nothing

End Sub
```

Populating Tables with Data

The major reason for creating tables is to populate them with data. One obvious way to satisfy this objective is to open a recordset on a table and then invoke the *AddNew* method for the recordset. Another approach for adding data to a table is to use SQL statements, such as INSERT INTO. There are other attractive techniques as well, but they rely on stored queries, which we will explore in Chapter 5.

This section provides an overview of the resources available for adding data to tables. The initial sample contrasts populating a table with data from an SQL statement and copying data from one table to another via recordset objects. Once you have data in a recordset, transferring it to another recordset is straightforward. Therefore, you can benefit from revisiting the discussion of recordsets in Chapter 2, particularly the review of the recordset *Open* method on page 125.

In this section, we'll examine creating read/write links with non-Access data sources, such as Microsoft Excel workbooks and Microsoft SQL Server databases. You can manage links programmatically either through an ADO *Connection* object or by creating a linked table in a Database window with the *DoCmd* object. With either approach, you generally can create read/write or read-only links. However, links to text files through an ISAM driver are always read-only.

Inserting vs. Copying

The first listing in this section contrasts two approaches to populating a table with data. The sample creates fresh copies of the *FamilyMembers* and *FamilyMembers2* tables in the MyNewDB database. Then it adds records to one table and copies those records to the other table. The code sample reinforces techniques covered earlier in the chapter by applying them to the chores for this application.

The sample consists of two procedures. The first procedure designates three parameters and passes them to the second procedure, which performs the main objectives of the sample. The three parameters designate the path and filename of an Access database file and the names of the two tables within the database that the application uses.

The second procedure hard-codes some data into the *FamilyMembers2* table with an INSERT INTO statement. You probably won't populate many databases this way, but the approach does work for small record sources, such as the one in this sample. Next the sample illustrates the syntax for copying records from one record source (namely, the *FamilyMembers2* table) to another record container (in this instance, the *FamilyMembers* table). This part of the application is both easy to understand and easy to apply. It is also very flexible because you can readily filter a recordset to contain a subset of the original recordset's rows and columns before copying it to a second record container.

> **Note** SQL statements are widely regarded as a fast way to process record sources because you work with the record source as a whole instead of just its individual records. On the other hand, looping techniques for records with ADO recordsets are easy to understand and grasp. As long as your record sources are not too large (thousands of records as opposed to hundreds of thousands of records or more), you can achieve acceptable performance with ADO looping methods.

The second procedure starts by calling the *DeleteATable* procedure to remove the *FamilyMembers2* table from the MyNewDB database. This can generate an error if the table is not already there, but the application ignores the error with an *On Error* statement that resumes with the next line of code. Next the procedure creates a fresh copy of the Family Members2 table. The procedure then repeats this entire process to create a fresh copy of the *FamilyMembers* table as well.

After creating the tables, the procedure moves on to populate them with data. First it runs a series of INSERT INTO statements to add records to the *FamilyMembers2* table. Then it creates two recordsets—one pointed at the *FamilyMembers2* table and the other pointed at the *FamilyMembers* table. With a *Do* loop, the procedure iterates through each of the rows in the *FamilyMembers2* table. For each row in the *FamilyMembers2* table it invokes the *AddNew* method to add a new row to the *FamilyMembers* table. Nested within the *Do* loop is a *For…Each* loop that passes through each field of the *FamilyMembers2* recordset, copying column values from one recordset to the other. After completing the *For…Each* loop, the procedure invokes the *Update* method to transfer the copied values to the *FamilyMembers* table.

```
Sub CallTwoWaysToPopulateTables()
Dim str1 As String
Dim str2 As String
Dim str3 As String

'Assign strings to pass arguments
str1 = "c:\PMA Samples\Chapter 04\MyNewDB.mdb"
str2 = "FamilyMembers2"
str3 = "FamilyMembers"

'Pass arguments
TwoWaysToPopulateTables str1, str2, str3

End Sub

Sub TwoWaysToPopulateTables(str1 As String, str2 As String, _
    str3 As String)
Dim cmd1 As ADODB.Command
Dim rst1 As ADODB.Recordset
Dim rst2 As ADODB.Recordset
Dim fld1 As ADODB.Field

'Delete source table (str2), and re-create it
'to make sure you start with a fresh table
On Error Resume Next
DeleteATable str1, str2
On Error GoTo 0
MakeFamilyMembers2TableInMyNewDB
```

(continued)

```
'Delete destination table (str3), and re-create it
'to make sure you start with a fresh table; placed
'early in the procedure on purpose to allow time
'for automatic refresh to work because Refresh method used
'later in the procedure is not fast enough
On Error Resume Next
DeleteATable str1, str3
On Error GoTo 0
MakeFamilyMembersTableInMyNewDB

'Add an index for the primary key on FamID

AddPK

'Populate FamilyMembers2 table with command
'object based on an SQL statement
Set cmd1 = New ADODB.Command
With cmd1
    .ActiveConnection = "Provider=Microsoft.Jet.OLEDB.4.0;" & _
        "Data Source=" & str1

    .CommandText = "INSERT INTO " & str2 & _
        "(Fname, Lname, Relation) VALUES ('Rick','Dobson','me')"
    .CommandType = adCmdText
    .Execute
    .CommandText = "INSERT INTO " & str2 & _
        "(Fname, Lname, Relation) VALUES ('Virginia','Dobson','wife')"

    .Execute
    .CommandText = "INSERT INTO " & str2 & _
        "(Fname, Lname, Relation) VALUES ('Glen','Hill','son')"

    .Execute
    .CommandText = "INSERT INTO " & str2 & _
        "(Fname, Lname, Relation) VALUES ('Tony','Hill','son')"

    .Execute
    .CommandText = "INSERT INTO " & str2 & _
        "(Fname, Lname, Relation) VALUES " & _
        "('Shelly','Hill','daughter-in-law')"

    .Execute
End With

'Open recordsets pointed at populated FamilyMembers2 table
'and unpopulated FamilyMembers table
Set rst1 = New ADODB.Recordset
Set rst2 = New ADODB.Recordset
```

```
rst1.Open "FamilyMembers2", cmd1.ActiveConnection
rst2.Open "FamilyMembers", cmd1.ActiveConnection, _
    adOpenKeyset, adLockOptimistic, adCmdTable

'Use ADO techniques to populate one table
'based on the values in another
With rst2
    Do Until rst1.EOF
        .AddNew
            For Each fld1 In rst1.Fields
                .Fields(fld1.Name) = fld1.Value
            Next fld1
        .Update
    rst1.MoveNext
    Loop

End With

'Clean up objects
Set cmd1 = Nothing
rst1.Close
rst2.Close
Set rst1 = Nothing
Set rst2 = Nothing

End Sub
```

Linking via the *Connection* Object

You can link a database through the ADO *Connection* object and then select a specific record source within the database to populate a table with data. One key advantage of using a *Connection* object as opposed to a classic Access linked table is that the object does not appear in the Database window. This helps to maintain the security and integrity of your database. By using the Connection object, you can expose a record source in any mode that your *Connection* object and *Recordset* object settings permit. For example, by using a keyset cursor with a connection to a remote database, you can enable reading and writing to a record source within a database.

The following listing shows how to apply these concepts to an Excel spreadsheet file. The key to specifying an appropriate connection string is to designate the correct ISAM driver. The inclusion of Excel 8.0 in the connection string accomplishes this for Excel 97, Excel 2000, and Excel 2002 workbook files. The source argument for the recordset *Open* method points to a range within the worksheet. Use the Insert-Name-Define command within Excel to create and update custom ranges that meet your application requirements.

Notice that the *Open* method in the following listing uses cursor settings that make the spreadsheet available for editing. In fact, the code sample appends *xxxx* to the first column in the first row. The procedure also prints to the Immediate window the first two columns of each row in the Customers range within the Customers.xls workbook file.

```
Sub OpenAndWriteToXLDataSource()
Dim cnn1 As New ADODB.Connection
Dim rst1 As Recordset
Dim bol1 As Boolean

'Open and set recordset
cnn1.Open "Provider=Microsoft.Jet.OLEDB.4.0;" & _
    "Data Source=C:\PMA Samples\Chapter 04\Customers.xls;" & _
    "Extended Properties=Excel 8.0;"
Set rst1 = New ADODB.Recordset
rst1.CursorType = adOpenKeyset
rst1.LockType = adLockOptimistic
rst1.Open "Customers", cnn1, , , adCmdTable

'Open recordset, and print a test record
Do Until rst1.EOF
    If bol1 = False Then
        rst1(0) = rst1(0) & "xxxx"
        bol1 = True
    End If
    Debug.Print rst1.Fields(0).Value, rst1.Fields(1).Value
    rst1.MoveNext
Loop

'Clean up objects
rst1.Close
Set rst1 = Nothing
cnn1.Close
Set cnn1 = Nothing

End Sub
```

The next listing shows the same technique, but this time the target data source is a table in a SQL Server database. Because the sample uses the MSDASQL provider, you can use the same basic code with any ODBC data source. The sample references the authors table in the pubs database. The sample uses a DSN (data source name) to abbreviate the connection string for the data source. Abbreviating the connection string using a DSN requires that you previously define a DSN on the workstation with the correct connection string details. One advantage of using a DSN for small and mid-sized organizations is that you can use the ODBC Administrator interface to define the connection string graphically. Some large businesses write custom procedures to automate the installation of DSNs on workstations throughout an organization.

Notice the similarity of the following listing's design with that of the preceding one. This similarity occurs despite the fact that one listing references a spreadsheet and the other references a SQL Server database. That's a big advantage of using the ADO approach. This similarity also positions Access as a development environment for analyzing data from heterogeneous data sources.

```
Sub OpenAndRestoreODBCDataSource()
Dim cnn1 As New ADODB.Connection
Dim rst1 As ADODB.Recordset
Dim bol1 As Boolean

'Open ODBC sources with MSDASQL and connection string info
    cnn1.Open "Provider=MSDASQL;DRIVER=SQL Server;" & _
        "SERVER=CAB2000;DATABASE=Pubs;uid=sa;pwd=password;"
    Set rst1 = New ADODB.Recordset
    rst1.CursorType = adOpenKeyset
    rst1.LockType = adLockOptimistic
    rst1.Open "authors", cnn1, , , adCmdTable

'Open recordset, and print a test record
    Do Until rst1.EOF
        If bol1 = False And Right(rst1(1), 4) = "xxxx" Then
            rst1(1) = Left(rst1(1), Len(rst1(1)) - 4)
            bol1 = True
        End If
        Debug.Print rst1.Fields(0).Value, _
            rst1.Fields(2), rst1.Fields(1).Value
        rst1.MoveNext
    Loop

'Clean up objects
rst1.Close
Set rst1 = Nothing
cnn1.Close
Set cnn1 = Nothing

E3nd Sub
```

Linking Using the *DoCmd* Method

You can link or import data sources with the *DoCmd* method. Since many developers and users are familiar with linked tables, this approach will appeal to those who prefer traditional techniques. The next listing includes three procedures. The first one links to a spreadsheet range. The second procedure links to an ODBC data source, and the third creates a linked table that points to a table in another Access database file. If you are an experienced Access developer, chances are you have applied these methods in the past. They appear here as a reminder that a venerable object, such as *DoCmd*, can still serve some important and valuable purposes. If you are just beginning to program Access, you might find extensions to these samples an especially easy way to link data from data sources outside the current Access database file. Access Help provides full explanations of all the arguments. The code presented here complements those explanations with easy-to-follow examples of the commands in action.

> **Note**   If you already have a linked table in your database by the name that the *TransferSpreadsheet* or *TransferDatabase* method specifies, the method will create a linked table with a new name. The new name consists of the table name specified by the method argument followed by a number. So, if your method attempts to create a linked table named *dboAuthors* when a linked table with that name already exists, the method creates a linked table with the name *dboAuthors1*.

```
Sub linkXLCustomers()
Dim rst1 As ADODB.Recordset
Dim bol1 As Boolean

'Use DoCmd to programmatically make the link
DoCmd.TransferSpreadsheet acLink, acSpreadsheetTypeExcel97, _
    "XLCustomers", "C:\PMA Samples\Chapter 04\Customers.xls", _
    True, "Customers"

'Open and set recordset
Set rst1 = New ADODB.Recordset
rst1.ActiveConnection = CurrentProject.Connection
rst1.CursorType = adOpenKeyset
rst1.LockType = adLockOptimistic
rst1.Open "XLCustomers", , , , adCmdTable

'Open recordset, and print a test record
Do Until rst1.EOF
    Debug.Print rst1.Fields(0).Value, rst1.Fields(2)
    rst1.MoveNext
Loop
'Clean up objects
rst1.Close
```

```
set rst1 = Nothing

End Sub


Sub linkODBCAuthors()
Dim rst1 As ADODB.Recordset

'Use DoCmd to programmatically make the link
DoCmd.TransferDatabase acLink, "ODBC Database", _
    "ODBC;DSN=Pubs;UID=sa;PWD=password;DATABASE=pubs", _
    acTable, "Authors", "dboAuthors"

'Open and set recordset
Set rst1 = New ADODB.Recordset
rst1.ActiveConnection = CurrentProject.Connection
rst1.CursorType = adOpenKeyset
rst1.LockType = adLockOptimistic
rst1.Open "dboAuthors", , , , adCmdTable

'Open recordset, and print a test record
Do Until rst1.EOF
    Debug.Print rst1.Fields(0).Value, rst1.Fields(2)
    rst1.MoveNext
Loop

'Clean up objects
rst1.Close
set rst1 = Nothing

End Sub


Sub linkNWCustomers()
Dim rst1 As ADODB.Recordset

'Use DAO to programmatically make the link
DoCmd.TransferDatabase acLink, "Microsoft Access", _
    "C:\PMA Samples\Northwind.mdb", _
    acTable, "Customers", "NWCustomers"

'Open and set recordset
Set rst1 = New ADODB.Recordset
rst1.ActiveConnection = CurrentProject.Connection
rst1.CursorType = adOpenKeyset
rst1.LockType = adLockOptimistic
rst1.Open "NWCustomers", , , , adCmdTable
```

(continued)

233

```
'Open recordset, and print a test record
Do Until rst1.EOF
    Debug.Print rst1.Fields(0).Value, rst1.Fields(2)
    rst1.MoveNext
Loop

'Clean up objects
rst1.Close
Set rst1 = Nothing

End Sub
```

If you plan to work with linked tables programmatically, you need a way to track and manage the linked tables. Before we examine how to do this, recall that Access can represent linked tables in two ways. Linked tables pointing at ISAM data sources, such as an Excel workbook file or another Access database file, have a table *Type* property of *LINK*. Linked tables pointing at ODBC data sources, such as a SQL Server database, have a table *Type* property of *PASS-THROUGH*. To denote the set of all linked tables, you must specify tables with both *Type* properties. In addition, Access maintains linked tables for its own use that begin with ~TMP. You should exclude these from your processing.

The following listing prints the names of all linked tables in the Immediate window for any Access database that you specify. You denote the Access database file in the first procedure. The application passes the database file path and filename to the second procedure, which creates a catalog that points at the database. Then the procedure loops through the catalog's *Tables* collection, filtering for linked tables that are user defined. When the procedure finds a user-defined linked table, it prints the table name and type to the Immediate window.

```
Sub CallListLinkedTables()
Dim str1 As String

str1 = "c:\PMA Samples\Chapter 04\Chapter 04.mdb"
ListLinkedTables str1

End Sub


Sub ListLinkedTables(str1 As String)
Dim cat1 As ADOX.Catalog
Dim tbl1 As ADOX.Table
Dim str2 As String
Dim mwd As Integer

'Point catalog at target database file
Set cat1 = New ADOX.Catalog
```

```
cat1.ActiveConnection = "Provider=Microsoft.Jet.OLEDB.4.0;" & _
    "Data Source=" & str1

'Find length of longest table name
mwd = 1
For Each tbl1 In cat1.Tables
    If (tbl1.Type = "LINK" Or tbl1.Type = "PASS-THROUGH") _
        And Left(tbl1.Name, 4) <> "~TMP" Then
        If mwd < Len(tbl1.Name) Then mwd = Len(tbl1.Name)
    End If
Next tbl1
mwd = mwd + 1

'Print linked table names
For Each tbl1 In cat1.Tables
    If (tbl1.Type = "LINK" Or tbl1.Type = "PASS-THROUGH") _
        And Left(tbl1.Name, 4) <> "~TMP" Then
        str2 = String(mwd - Len(tbl1.Name), " ")
        Debug.Print tbl1.Name & str2 & tbl1.Type
    End If
Next tbl1

'Clean up objects
Set cat1 = Nothing

End Sub
```

A variation of the procedure just shown deletes all linked tables from a designated database. This variation merits special attention because you cannot use a *For...Each* loop to pass through the members of the *Tables* collection if you are going to delete a table within the loop. This is because the *Delete* method forces a reindexing of the objects in a collection each time that you invoke it. This reindexing causes the *Delete* method to miss some items that you meant to delete.

The solution to this problem is to use a *For...Next* loop that steps from the last to the first item in a collection. This approach ensures that the *Delete* method operates on each qualified member of a collection. The following listing illustrates the syntax for this approach:

```
Sub CallDeleteLinkedTables()
Dim str1 As String

str1 = "c:\PMA Samples\Chapter 04\Chapter 04.mdb"
DeleteLinkedTables str1

End Sub
```

(continued)

```
Sub DeleteLinkedTables(str1 As String)
Dim cat1 As ADOX.Catalog
Dim tbl1 As ADOX.Table
Dim int1 As Integer

'Point catalog at target database file
Set cat1 = New ADOX.Catalog
cat1.ActiveConnection = "Provider=Microsoft.Jet.OLEDB.4.0;" & _
    "Data Source=" & str1

'Loop through ISAM and ODBC linked tables
'to delete all linked tables
For int1 = cat1.Tables.Count - 1 To 0 Step -1
    Set tbl1 = cat1.Tables(int1)
    If (tbl1.Type = "LINK" Or tbl1.Type = "PASS-THROUGH") _
        And Left(tbl1.Name, 4) <> "~TMP" Then
        cat1.Tables.Delete tbl1.Name
    End If
Next int1

'Refresh Database window to show deleted
'table links
Application.RefreshDatabaseWindow

'Clean up objects
Set cat1 = Nothing

End Sub
```

Importing Data from Text Files

One common need that arises when populating a database is to import delimited text data into an Access database. This need is especially common when you are working with legacy mainframe applications or UNIX applications. Developers can use the *TransferText* method of the *DoCmd* object to assist with this task. Because this is one of the method's most straightforward uses, you can designate just three arguments for it: the type of source (such as a delimited text file), the table name for the target within the Access database file, and the path and filename of the text file.

To demonstrate how this process works, you can export a table or two (such as the Northwind *Orders* table) from the Access database to create a suitable source for importing. Figure 4-7 shows the first several rows of the *Orders* table exported to a text file as Orders.txt, which is also provided for you on the companion CD. The lines wrap in Notepad view. The data is comma delimited with quotes around text fields.

Figure 4-7 The first several rows of the *Orders* table from the Northwind database exported as Orders.txt and viewed from Notepad.

You can readily process text files in alternative formats to the one shown in Figure 4-7. When using these alternate formats, you might find a specification helpful for importing the data from the text file. One especially easy way to develop a specification is to manually invoke the File-Get External Data-Link Tables command. Then select the Text Files file type. Select a file to link, then click the Link button. Click the Advanced control at the lower-left corner of the first Link Text Wizard dialog box. Then make selections, assign field names, and specify data types in the Link Specification dialog box. Click the Save As control to save your set of specifications with a name that lets you reuse it by designating this name as the second argument in the *TransferText* method. For a well-formed text file, the use of a specification is optional.

> **Note**   The *TransferText* method has arguments that appear to enable the linking and importing of text data. However, you should understand that the text ISAM driver does not permit you to update the text source for a linked file from Access.

The following listing shows the syntax for basic use of the *TransferText* method. Notice that this sample specifies just three arguments. You can designate input and output formats for data other than *acLinkDelim*. That intrinsic constant denotes the input of a delimited text file. The second argument, a specification name, is blank. If you use a specification name, you enclose its name in double quotes. The third argument is the name of the table that contains the text file data. The fourth argument is the path and filename for the text file. An excerpt from this file appears in Figure 4-7.

```
Sub ImportOrdersTxt()
Dim rst1 As ADODB.Recordset
Dim int1 As Integer
```

(continued)

```
'Import a delimited text file (Orders.txt) to the ImportedOrders table
DoCmd.TransferText _
    acLinkDelim, , _
    "ImportedOrders", _
    "c:\PMA Samples\Chapter 04\Orders.txt"

'Make a recordset based on imported data
Set rst1 = New ADODB.Recordset
rst1.Open "ImportedOrders", CurrentProject.Connection, , , adCmdTable

'Print first five rows from recordset
For int1 = 1 To 5
    Debug.Print rst1(0), rst1(1), rst1(2), rst1(3)
    rst1.MoveNext
Next int1

End Sub
```

The instructions and code sample can bring text files into Access as tables. If a table with the specified name already exists in the database, the method creates the table using the specified name followed by a number. If one or more other tables with a trailing number exist, the method adds 1 to the last number, giving you a series of table names—as in *tablename*, *tablename1*, and *tablename2*. You can manage the linked tables with any of the procedures demonstrated throughout this chapter.

5

Jet SQL, the ADOX Library, and Queries

Tables are the basic building blocks of databases, but queries are where much of the literal and figurative action occurs. Developers use queries to extract information from tables. These queries often serve as the record sources for forms, reports, and Web pages. Therefore, database users typically view database tables filtered through queries.

In addition to this support for forms, reports, and Web pages, queries and languages for expressing them (ADOX and Jet SQL) support three literal kinds of action. First, you can use parameter queries to enable run-time user interaction with an application. Second, you can use queries to insert, delete, and update the records in a record source. Third, you can use Jet SQL, the language for expressing queries for the Jet database engine, to create tables and other database objects. Using Jet SQL to create database objects is an alternative to performing data definition tasks with the ADOX library.

This chapter contains five major sections. The first section, "Jet SQL Syntax for Select Queries," will examine the most common Jet SQL formulations for returning records from tables. Learning Jet SQL liberates you from depending on the Microsoft Access Query Designer to develop queries. Mastering Jet SQL will also help you expand the roles that recordsets play in your applications.

The second section, "Enumerating ADOX Views and Procedures," demonstrates how to enumerate the members of the ADOX *Views* and *Procedures* collections and their most important properties, such as the SQL text behind them. These two collections contain what Access developers typically refer to as queries.

The third section, "Managing Row-Returning Queries with ADOX," will show you how to create new queries programmatically by adding members to the *Views* and *Procedures* collections. This section also demonstrates how to add or modify queries in a database even when you temporarily disconnect your workstation from the database.

"Creating and Running Action Queries with ADOX" drills down on the design and use of parameter queries. This section pays special attention to using parameters for inserting, deleting, and updating records from a record source.

This final section of this chapter, "Introduction to Jet SQL's DDL," discusses the use of Jet SQL for table definition tasks. By learning how to perform data definition with Jet SQL, you can take advantage of features not supported by the ADOX library, such as creating check constraints for columns.

Jet SQL Syntax for Select Queries

Both experienced and novice ActiveX Data Objects (ADO) developers have expressed their desire to become more proficient in programming SQL. When you are using ADO, you frequently will want to code an SQL statement when setting properties or calling methods for connections, recordsets, and commands. Therefore, to fully exploit the potential of these ADO and Access objects, you need some knowledge of SQL. This section details the use of Jet SQL for select queries. Because applications frequently rely on select queries to provide record sources for forms, reports, and Web pages, learning the syntax of these queries can be very helpful.

This section systematically examines nearly all the Jet SQL clauses that assist in returning rows from record sources. By mastering the samples in this section, you will gain two benefits. First, you'll learn to rapidly design the types of select queries that you're most likely to use. Second, you'll gain the confidence needed to easily understand select queries that are not explicitly covered in this section.

Basic Select Queries

Perhaps the best place to start learning SQL is with the most basic statement, which returns all the columns from all the rows of a record source. This record source can be a table, another query, or a combination of two or more tables and queries. In its most basic format, the source for a select query is a table. The statement's general form is:

```
SELECT * FROM <table-name>
```

Traditionally, SQL developers express keywords in uppercase, such as SELECT and FROM, but Jet SQL and many other SQL dialects do not require you to use uppercase for keywords. The asterisk (*) is a shortcut that denotes all the fields in a record source. The *<table-name>* placeholder appearing directly after the FROM keyword denotes the record source for the query.

While select queries have uses in several ADO contexts, one of their most typical uses is as the source argument for a recordset. This is because select queries return a virtual table that *Recordset* objects are especially equipped to process. For example, recordsets have navigation methods and collections for passing through the data values in the virtual table returned by a select query.

This chapter's first code sample demonstrates the most basic SQL select query. It returns all the columns from all the rows of the *Orders* table in the Northwind database. The first procedure, *SelectAllFields*, assigns values to two string variables before passing them on to the second procedure, *PreviewRecordsetSource*. The first string variable, *strSrc*, denotes the connection string for the Northwind database. The second string variable illustrates the application of the most basic SQL statement to the *Orders* table.

The basic design of this first sample will be the standard format I'll use to demonstrate all select query samples in this section of the chapter. In fact, all the subsequent code samples in this section reuse the *PreviewRecordsetSource* procedure, which enumerates all the columns for the first 10 rows of the result set returned by the SQL statement. It organizes and labels the results by record. As we move on to more complex select queries, this procedure will help you understand the effects of alternate SQL syntax formulations. In addition, you can use the second procedure to explore your own design changes to the samples in this chapter.

```
Sub SelectAllFields()
Dim strSrc As String
Dim strSQL As String

strSrc = "Provider=Microsoft.Jet.OLEDB.4.0;" & _
    "Data Source=C:\PMA Samples\Northwind.mdb"

'Query, selecting all fields from the Orders table
strSQL = "SELECT * FROM Orders"

'Pass arguments
PreviewRecordsetSource strSrc, strSQL

End Sub


Sub PreviewRecordsetSource(strSrc As String, _
    strSQL As String)
Dim rst1 As ADODB.Recordset
Dim fld1 As Field
Dim int1 As Integer
```

(continued)

```
'Open recordset on passed SQL string (strSQL)
'from the designated data source (strSrc)
Set rst1 = New ADODB.Recordset
rst1.ActiveConnection = strSrc
rst1.Open strSQL

'Loop through first 10 records,
'and print all non-OLE object fields to the
'Immediate window
int1 = 1
Do Until rst1.EOF
    Debug.Print "Output for record: " & int1
    For Each fld1 In rst1.Fields
        If Not (fld1.Type = adLongVarBinary) Then _
            Debug.Print String(5, " ") & _
            fld1.Name & " = " & fld1.Value
    Next fld1
    rst1.MoveNext
    If int1 >= 10 Then
        Exit Do
    Else
        int1 = int1 + 1
        Debug.Print
    End If
Loop


'Clean up objects
rst1.Close
Set rst1 = Nothing

End Sub
```

Figure 5-1 presents an excerpt from the output generated by running this code sample. This screen shot of the Immediate window shows the output from the last two records. The Northwind database contains 830 records in its *Orders* table, but the second procedure limits the rows processed to the first 10 rows. However, the procedure does print values for all the columns available on each row. Each row's output starts with a header label. Then the procedure shows each column's name and value separated by an equal sign (=).

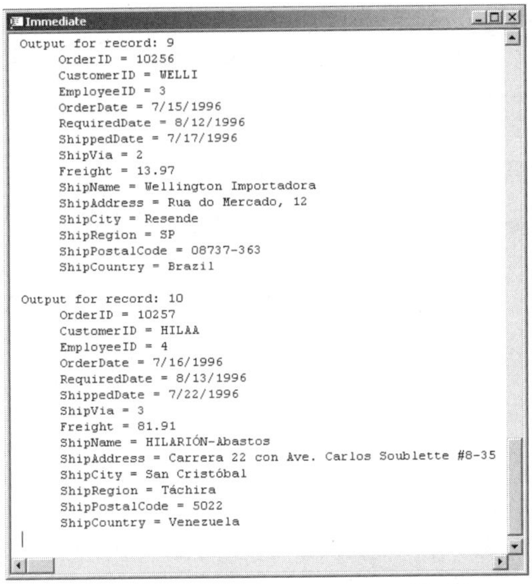

Figure 5-1 Output from the *SelectAllFields* procedure used with the *PreviewRecordsetSource* procedure.

Selecting Fields from Every Record

Instead of displaying all fields from a record source, a select query can return a subset of the columns. To achieve this, you list individual field names within the SELECT statement in the order that you want them to appear. The following sample prints values from just two columns in the *Products* table to the Immediate window:

```
Sub SelectSomeFields()
Dim strSrc As String
Dim strSQL As String

strSrc = "Provider=Microsoft.Jet.OLEDB.4.0;" & _
    "Data Source=C:\PMA Samples\Northwind.mdb"

'Query returning selected fields from the Products table
strSQL = "SELECT ProductName, Discontinued FROM Products"

PreviewRecordsetSource strSrc, strSQL

End Sub
```

In general, you should return only the subset of columns that your application needs. This improves performance. If your application needs all the columns in a record source, you can list them in the SELECT statement. However, using the asterisk wildcard symbol (*) to indicate that you want all the columns eliminates the need to update your code if a column is added, deleted, or renamed in the table.

Selecting Fields from Some Records

Many applications require a subset of both the columns and rows from an original record source. When you need to filter the rows, add a WHERE clause to your select query. This clause should have at least one character, such as a blank space or carriage return, between its start and the FROM keyword argument. The WHERE clause arguments correspond to the Criteria row of the Query Designer. The following code sample returns rows that represent all currently active inventory items in the *Products* table. The WHERE clause excludes discontinued items. Whenever the expression in the WHERE clause is true, the corresponding row from the original source appears in the result set. This code sample differs from the preceding one, which showed products regardless of whether they were still being sold.

```
Sub SelectSomeFieldsAndRows()
Dim strSrc As String
Dim strSQL As String
Dim boll as Boolean

strSrc = "Provider=Microsoft.Jet.OLEDB.4.0;" & _
    "Data Source=C:\PMA Samples\Northwind.mdb"

'Query demonstrates use of Boolean variable in WHERE clause
'to return a list of discontinued products
boll = False
strSQL = "SELECT ProductName, Discontinued FROM Products " & _
    "WHERE Discontinued = " & boll

PreviewRecordsetSource strSrc, strSQL

End Sub
```

WHERE clause arguments frequently have the form *<columnname> <operator> <expression>*, such as *Discontinued = False*. You can also write compound expressions by using the AND and OR operators. In addition, you can use parentheses to designate the order in which operators compute. Enclose terms and operators in parentheses when you want the operator between them to compute before adjacent operators.

Your expressions for WHERE clauses can draw on the full extent of SQL. For example, you can use the IN keyword as an operator. Using the IN keyword enables you to easily specify values for any column that qualify a record for inclusion in a select query's result set. The following sample shows only customers from the UK and USA:

```
Sub SelectWithInClause()
Dim strSrc As String
Dim strSQL As String

strSrc = "Provider=Microsoft.Jet.OLEDB.4.0;" & _
    "Data Source=C:\PMA Samples\Northwind.mdb"

'Query demonstrates use of IN keyword to return customers
'from UK and USA
strSQL = "SELECT CompanyName, ContactName, Country FROM Customers " & _
    "WHERE Country IN ('UK', 'USA')"

PreviewRecordsetSource strSrc, strSQL

End Sub
```

Writing Criteria Expressions with Wildcards

Wildcard symbols in expressions expand the flexibility with which you can designate rows for inclusion in a select query's result set. However, some traditional wildcard symbols from the Query Designer will need modification before you can use them in SQL WHERE clauses with ADO. This can be confusing because it means you cannot simply cut and paste code from the Query Designer's SQL windows into the source argument for a recordset's *Open* method; before the copied code can run, you must translate wildcard symbols for use with ADO. Table 5-1 compares traditional Access wildcard parameters with those suitable for use in SQL WHERE clauses with ADO.

Table 5-1   Correspondence of Access and ADO Wildcard Symbols

Access Wildcard Symbol	Wildcard Symbol for SQL Expressions in ADO	Meaning
*	%	Zero or more characters.
?	_	Any single character.
!	!	Not (used in conjunction with a list or range of characters in brackets); note that this is not compliant with SQL Server.

You can use the percent symbol (%) at either the beginning or the end of an expression for a *LIKE* argument. You can also use % in combination with the other symbols shown in Table 5-1. The pattern-matching code samples, which appear after the % and underscore (_) samples in this section, show how to use the exclamation point (!) and % symbols together. One of the most common uses of the % symbol is for extracting all records with a particular prefix. The following sample shows the syntax for extracting all customers from countries beginning with the letter *U.* In the Access Northwind database, this code would return only customers from the UK and the USA—the same results you just saw in the IN keyword sample. However, adding the % symbol might return more results, depending on the table's contents. If the source table included customers from Uruguay, the *LIKE 'U%'* expression would include these customers in its result set, but the *IN ('UK', 'USA')* expression would not.

```
Sub SelectWithMultiCharacterWildcard()
Dim strSrc As String
Dim strSQL As String

strSrc = "Provider=Microsoft.Jet.OLEDB.4.0;" & _
    "Data Source=C:\PMA Samples\Northwind.mdb"

'Use % instead of * with multicharacter wildcard searches.
'Query returns customers from any country beginning with U.
strSQL = "SELECT CompanyName, ContactName, Country FROM Customers " & _
    "WHERE Country LIKE 'U%'"

PreviewRecordsetSource strSrc, strSQL

End Sub
```

The next sample shows the use of the _ wildcard symbol. This symbol matches any single character in a string. You use the _ symbol to develop more restrictive criteria than the % symbol allows. In this sample, the *TRA_H* argument for the LIKE operator extracts records with *CustomerID* column values of *TRADH* and *TRAIH.* Any customer record will match the expression, as long as the first three characters for *CustomerID* are *TRA* and the fifth character is *H.*

```
Sub SelectWithSingleCharacterWildcard()
Dim strSrc As String
Dim strSQL As String

strSrc = "Provider=Microsoft.Jet.OLEDB.4.0;" & _
    "Data Source=C:\PMA Samples\Northwind.mdb"

'Use _ instead of ? with single-character wildcard searches.
'Query returns any customer starting with TRA and ending
```

```
'with H (CustomerID is always 5 characters long).
strSQL = "SELECT CustomerID, CompanyName, ContactName, " & _
    "Country FROM Customers " & _
    "WHERE CustomerID LIKE 'TRA_H'"

PreviewRecordsetSource strSrc, strSQL

End Sub
```

You can use the wildcard symbols with [ ] delimiters to denote lists and ranges of characters that satisfy a criterion. The expression *[ACEH-M]* indicates a match with the letters *A*, *C*, *E*, or any letter from *H* through *M*. The expression *A[A-M]%* in the following sample specifies a *CustomerID* field value with *A* as its first character and any letter from *A* through *M* as its second character, with no restrictions on the remaining *CustomerID* characters. For the *Customers* table, this criterion expression returns a single record whose *CustomerID* field value is *ALFKI*.

```
Sub SelectWithPatternMatch()
Dim strSrc As String
Dim strSQL As String

strSrc = "Provider=Microsoft.Jet.OLEDB.4.0;" & _
    "Data Source=C:\PMA Samples\Northwind.mdb"

'Use traditional [begin-end] syntax for pattern matches.
'Query returns customer IDs beginning with A and containing
'any of the first 13 letters of the alphabet in their
'second character.
strSQL = "SELECT CustomerID, CompanyName, ContactName, " & _
    "Country FROM Customers " & _
    "WHERE CustomerID LIKE 'A[A-M]%'"

PreviewRecordsetSource strSrc, strSQL

End Sub
```

The next two samples reinforce the use of [ ] delimiters in LIKE arguments while introducing the ! symbol. When used within brackets, the ! symbol serves as a NOT operator. The first of these two samples has an argument of *A[N-Z]%*. This argument specifies all records with a customer ID that begins with *A* and is followed by any letter from *N* through *Z*. The expression places no restrictions on the remaining customer ID characters. For the *Customers* table in the Northwind database, this criterion expression returns records with customer ID values of *ANATR*, *ANTON*, and *AROUT*.

The second sample places a ! symbol in front of the range *N* through *Z* for the second character. Here, the ! symbol specifies that this character cannot fall in the range of *N* through *Z*; in other words, the letters *A* through *M*—as well as numbers, punctuation characters, and so forth—satisfy the criterion. This second sample returns a record with a *CustomerID* value of *ALFKI*. Because of a constraint (or validation rule) for the *CustomerID* field in the *Customers* table, only letters are legitimate characters for *CustomerID* field values.

Using SQL Server–Compatible Syntax Switches

As noted in the previous discussion, traditional Access wildcard symbols differ from the wildcard symbols for SQL expressions in ADO. An alternate set of Access wildcard symbols is available. The traditional symbols are the default ones for use in the Query Designer. However, by choosing Tools-Options from the Access Database menu you can change the default setting from the wildcard symbols in the first column of Table 5-1 to those in the second column. Select the Tables/Queries tab from the Options dialog box. The first check box in the Microsoft SQL Server Compatible Syntax (ANSI 92) group on the Tables/Queries tab permits you to invoke the alternate set of wildcard symbols for the current database. An additional check box lets you select the alternate set of wildcard symbols as the default when creating a new database. However, you cannot affect the wildcard setting for other existing databases. Also, changing the wildcard setting can break existing query expressions that use the traditional wildcard symbols in the current database.

The Help display for these controls says that they ensure SQL Server compatibility. This is true for the * and ? wildcard symbols. However, when working with a Jet database, the traditional ! symbol applies rather than the caret symbol (∧) that SQL Server uses. For example, the following SQL statement returns one record with a *CustomerID* value of *ALFKI* when run from a Query Designer SQL window against the Access Northwind database. The same statement run from the SQL Server Query Analyzer against the SQL Server Northwind database returns three records with *CustomerID* field values of *ANATR*, *ANTON*, and *AROUT* because SQL Server interprets the ! character as a regular character in the character list instead of as a wildcard.

```
SELECT CustomerID, CompanyName, ContactName, Country
FROM Customers
WHERE CustomerID LIKE 'A[!N-Z]%'
```

(continued)

Using SQL Server–Compatible Syntax Switches *(continued)*

By changing the ! to a ^ in the SQL Server Query Analyzer (as shown in the following code), you can return a single record whose *CustomerID* is *ALFKI*. However, this same expression returns three rows with *CustomerID* values of *ANATR*, *ANTON*, and *AROUT* when run from the a Query Designer SQL window against the Access Northwind database. That's because Access interprets the ^ character as a regular character in the character list instead of as a wildcard.

```
SELECT CustomerID, CompanyName, ContactName, Country
FROM Customers
WHERE CustomerID LIKE 'A[^N-Z]%'
```

Selecting with the DISTINCT Keyword

When working with imported data from legacy systems, you will commonly encounter situations where values in fields are repeated. Many applications working with this kind of data will nevertheless require a list of unique column values in a result set. For example, when working with a combo box, you do not want the items in the drop-down box to be repeated, even if they are repeated in the original record source.

The *Order Details* table in the Northwind database repeats values in an important field named *OrderID*. This field occurs once for each line item within an order. The Northwind database contains a separate *Orders* table that has *OrderID* as its primary key; however, legacy databases do not always offer this convenience. Even if the legacy database you're using does have this feature, a copy of it might not be available when you need it.

The next two procedures provide a listing of *OrderID* field values from the *Order Details* table. The procedure named *SelectNotDistinctOrderDetails* defines a basic select query against the *Order Details* table with *OrderID* as the sole field returned. The first 10 rows from this query—see the list on the left in Figure 5-2—repeats *OrderID* whenever an order has more than one line item. For example, *OrderID 10248* appears in the first three rows. The *SelectDistinctOrderDetails* procedure adds the DISTINCT keyword to the basic select query syntax. The addition of the DISTINCT keyword eliminates duplicates in the result set from the query. The list on the right in Figure 5-2 shows each *OrderID* on just one row. In the following code, note the brackets around *Order Details*. These are necessary because the table name contains an internal blank character.

```
Sub SelectNotDistinctOrderDetails()
Dim strSrc As String
Dim strSQL As String

strSrc = "Provider=Microsoft.Jet.OLEDB.4.0;" & _
    "Data Source=C:\PMA Samples\Northwind.mdb"

'Query returns order IDs from line items even if they repeat
strSQL = "SELECT OrderID FROM [Order Details] "

PreviewRecordsetSource strSrc, strSQL

End Sub


Sub SelectDistinctOrderDetails()
Dim strSrc As String
Dim strSQL As String

strSrc = "Provider=Microsoft.Jet.OLEDB.4.0;" & _
    "Data Source=C:\PMA Samples\Northwind.mdb"

'Query returns unique order IDs from table of order line
'items (Order Details)
strSQL = "SELECT DISTINCT OrderID FROM [Order Details] "

PreviewRecordsetSource strSrc, strSQL

End Sub
```

The DISTINCT keyword is a predicate for a SELECT statement in SQL. As you can see, it modifies the behavior of the SELECT keyword. Jet SQL supports other predicates that you might find useful, including TOP, DISTINCTROW, and ALL. Access Help for Jet SQL contains discussions and samples of these predicate terms. Table 5-2 lists the SELECT keyword predicates and brief descriptions of their behavior.

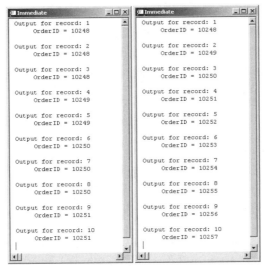

Figure 5-2 The output on the left comes from the *SelectNotDistinctOrderDetails* procedure. The output on the right without repeated values is produced by the *SelectDistinctOrderDetails* procedure.

Table 5-2 **Jet SQL SELECT Keyword Predicates**

Predicate	Behavior
ALL	Directs SELECT to return all the rows in a result set without any filtering. This is the default SELECT behavior.
DISTINCT	Corresponds to the Unique Values property of an Access query. DISTINCT filters out rows from the final result set that have duplicate field values. You cannot update its rows directly through the query.
DISTINCTROW	Corresponds to the Unique Records property of an Access query. In most cases, you'll find the DISTINCT predicate more suitable for removing duplicates. DISTINCTROW is most useful for joins between record sources where the SELECT field list does not include at least one column from each table. You can update its rows directly through the query. (Joins are discussed later in this chapter.)
TOP *n* [Percent]	Returns the top *n* records or *n* percent of records only, where *n* is an integer value.

Selecting and Ordering with Calculated Fields

A calculated field is a field that your SQL code computes for each row in a record source. The calculation can be for string, date, integer, currency, or floating-point values. A calculated field unites two or more independent column values into a new column within the virtual table that the select query statement defines.

Use the ORDER BY clause in a select query to override the default order of rows in a result set. The ORDER BY clause should be the last clause in a select query's SQL statement. The arguments within an ORDER BY clause specify on which fields to sort rows in the result set. When you have more than one field on which to sort records, separate them by commas. When you have multiple sort fields, records are sorted according to the order of the field names in the ORDER BY clause. The default sort order for individual fields in an ORDER BY clause is ascending. You can explicitly specify to sort records in an ascending order by following the column name with a space and the keyword ASC. If you want rows to appear in descending order, use the keyword DESC.

If you do not designate an ORDER BY clause, Jet arranges rows in the order of the primary key. When a select query joins two or more tables, Jet's default order is determined by the primary key of the table that participates on the one-side of a one-to-many relationship at the top-level join in the record source. If no primary key exists, Jet arranges the records in the order of entry.

SQL does not require any special correspondence between the ORDER BY clause and calculated fields. However, using calculated fields when ordering the rows of a virtual table can lead to several special issues, which I'll discuss here.

The next sample demonstrates the syntax for combining two columns with string values into a calculated column. The input columns are *FirstName* and *LastName*; they originate from the *Employees* table in the Northwind database. The expression for the calculated field creates a new column by combining the *FirstName* and *LastName* columns with a blank space between them.

```
Sub SelectWithCaculatedField()
Dim strSrc As String
Dim strSQL As String

strSrc = "Provider=Microsoft.Jet.OLEDB.4.0;" & _
    "Data Source=C:\PMA Samples\Northwind.mdb"

'A calculated field (Full name) based on text columns
strSQL = "SELECT FirstName & ' ' & LastName AS [Full name], " & _
    "City FROM Employees"

PreviewRecordsetSource strSrc, strSQL

End Sub
```

Although the *EmployeeID* field does not appear in the SQL statement in the *SelectWithCalculatedField* procedure, the records appear sorted according to the value of this field because *EmployeeID* is the primary key for the *Employees* table. You can override this default order by appending an ORDER BY clause to the SQL statement. You can force a sort on any original field or on a field calculated from within the SQL statement. The following sample sorts the result set. The result set from the next SQL statement shows the calculated *Full name* field sorted by the *LastName* column from the *Employees* table.

```
Sub SelectWithCalculatedFieldAndOrderLastNames()
Dim strSrc As String
Dim strSQL As String

strSrc = "Provider=Microsoft.Jet.OLEDB.4.0;" & _
    "Data Source=C:\PMA Samples\Northwind.mdb"

'A calculated field (Full name) based on text columns
'with a sort on an original text column (LastName)
strSQL = "SELECT FirstName & ' ' & LastName AS [Full name], " & _
    "City FROM Employees ORDER BY LastName"

PreviewRecordsetSource strSrc, strSQL

End Sub
```

The next sample includes an SQL statement that returns all rows from the *Orders* table with an *OrderDate* field value less than or equal to the last day in 1997. The ORDER BY clause sorts the rows, using the most recent date as the first record. This SQL statement shows the syntax for including a date as a criterion. Notice that the date appears within two pound signs (#). Recall that Access represents dates as floating numbers internally. The larger the number's value, the more recent the date. Therefore, you use DESC to sort records with the most recent date appearing first.

```
Sub SelectForDateCriterionAndDescendingOrder()
Dim strSrc As String
Dim strSQL As String
Dim strDate As String

strSrc = "Provider=Microsoft.Jet.OLEDB.4.0;" & _
    "Data Source=C:\PMA Samples\Northwind.mdb"
strDate = "#12/31/97#"

'Query returns orders through end of 1997 sorted
'with most recent dates first
strSQL = "SELECT OrderID, OrderDate FROM Orders " & _
```

(continued)

```
        "WHERE OrderDate <= " & strDate & _
        " ORDER BY OrderDate DESC"

    PreviewRecordsetSource strSrc, strSQL

End Sub
```

The two samples you just saw illustrate how to use the ORDER BY clause with columns that already exist in a record source. However, the syntax changes slightly if you use the ORDER BY clause with a calculated field. In such an instance, you cannot use the name of the calculated field; instead your SQL statement must restate the expression for the calculated field in the ORDER BY field list. The following sample sorts its rows by a calculated field named *Total Revenue*, which is the product of the *UnitPrice* and *Quantity* columns multiplied by 1 minus the value of the *Discount* column. Notice that the ORDER BY clause repeats the full expression for the calculated *Total Revenue* field rather than using just the field name, as in the two samples we just looked at. The SQL statement in the next sample uses the FORMATCURRENCY function to apply a currency format to a calculated field. Notice that you can designate the number of places that appear after the decimal point. The sample shows *Total Revenue* to the nearest penny for line items in the *Order Details* table.

> **Note** *Total Revenue* has a data type of Single because it relies on a product including *Discount*, which has a data type of Single. Multiplying any value by a data type of Single creates another value with a data type of Single unless Access must promote the data type to a data type of Double to represent the outcome correctly.

```
Sub SelectDescendingOnACalculatedField()
Dim strSrc As String
Dim strSQL As String

strSrc = "Provider=Microsoft.Jet.OLEDB.4.0;" & _
    "Data Source=C:\PMA Samples\Northwind.mdb"

'Query returns order line items with formatted, calculated
'field (Total Revenue) and sorts in descending order on the
'same field
strSQL = "SELECT OrderID, " & _
    "FORMATCURRENCY(UnitPrice*Quantity*(1-Discount),2) " & _
```

```
    "AS [Total Revenue] FROM [Order Details] " & _
    "ORDER BY UnitPrice*Quantity*(1-Discount) DESC"

PreviewRecordsetSource strSrc, strSQL

End Sub
```

Using Aggregates with **GROUP BY** and **HAVING** Clauses

An aggregated field is a calculated field that computes a result across multiple rows instead of within a single row. In addition, an aggregated field relies on SQL aggregate functions. The obvious SQL functions are SUM, AVG, and COUNT. The other SQL functions an aggregated field might use include those for computing standard deviation and variance, finding minimum or maximum values, and returning the first or last row in a result set.

You will frequently invoke an aggregate function in an SQL statement that includes a GROUP BY clause. The GROUP BY clause collapses multiple records with the same field values into a single record. If you specify an aggregate function for the new collapsed record, that function reflects the aggregated field value for the rows that were collapsed. If you use an aggregate function without a GROUP BY clause, the function computes its aggregated results across all the records in the recordset; that is, all the records denoted by the arguments of the FROM clause.

The following sample demonstrates the use of the SUM, AVG, and COUNT functions to compute aggregated results across all the records in the *Order Details* table. The SQL statement returns a single row with three fields labeled *Total Revenue*, *Total Order Line Items*, and *Avg Revenue/Item*. The SUM function aggregates the extended price, *UnitPrice*Quantity*(1-Discount)*, across all line items to generate *Total Revenue*. The *Total Order Line Items* column value reflects the number of line item rows in the *Order Details* table. The *Avg Revenue/Item* column value is the average amount of all line items' extended price—again across every row in the *Order Details* table.

```
Sub SelectWithAggregatedFunctions()
Dim strSrc As String
Dim strSQL As String

strSrc = "Provider=Microsoft.Jet.OLEDB.4.0;" & _
    "Data Source=C:\PMA Samples\Northwind.mdb"

'Selected aggregate function results
strSQL = "SELECT " & _
    "FORMATCURRENCY(SUM(UnitPrice*Quantity*(1-Discount)),2) " & _
    "AS [Total Revenue], " & _
```

(continued)

```
            "COUNT(OrderID) AS [Total Order Line Items], " & _
            "FORMATCURRENCY(AVG(UnitPrice*Quantity*(1-Discount)),2) " & _
            "AS [Avg Revenue/Item] " & _
            "FROM [Order Details]"

PreviewRecordsetSource strSrc, strSQL

End Sub
```

Many applications require aggregated results across subsets of the records in a record source instead of the whole recordset. Adding a GROUP BY clause to an SQL statement with an aggregate function satisfies this need. You can invoke the GROUP BY clause with one or more fields in its list, just as you can with the ORDER BY clause. If you have more than one field in the list for a GROUP BY clause, the records will group in a nested fashion (the second field nesting within the first field, the third field nesting within the second, and so forth).

The following sample computes the units in stock from the *Products* table of the Northwind database for product groupings defined by whether they have been discontinued and by their category. Figure 5-3 presents an excerpt from the sample's output. The first five records in the result set all represent discontinued products. All eight of the remaining records in the result set (of which the excerpt shows three) denote current products. This ordering of records occurs because the *Discontinued* column appears before *CategoryID* in the GROUP BY list. Notice also that the output does not contain output for discontinued items with *CategoryID* values of 3 and 4. This is because the *Products* table has no rows with discontinued products for these categories. Finally, observe that the second record's output has no units in stock. This record appears in the result set because there is a discontinued product with a value of *0* representing the units in stock. The alias for the *UnitsInStock* column provides for a nicer label in the output.

```
Sub SelectGroupBy()
Dim strSrc As String
Dim strSQL As String

strSrc = "Provider=Microsoft.Jet.OLEDB.4.0;" & _
    "Data Source=C:\PMA Samples\Northwind.mdb"

'Query returns sum of units in stock by category,
'regardless of whether the product is discontinued
strSQL = "SELECT Discontinued, CategoryID, SUM(UnitsInStock) " & _
    "AS [Units In Stock]" & _
    "FROM Products " & _
    "GROUP BY Discontinued, CategoryID"
```

```
PreviewRecordsetSource strSrc, strSQL

End Sub
```

Figure 5-3 Output of the *SelectGroupBy* procedure demonstrates the effect of a GROUP BY clause on the result set from a select query's SQL statement.

By adding a HAVING clause to an SQL statement with a GROUP BY clause, you can filter the result set from the SQL statement. The HAVING clause operates like a WHERE clause, except that the HAVING clause filters results from a GROUP BY clause. For example, the *SelectGroupByWithHaving* procedure shown next returns only four records. These four records denote products that are discontinued, because the expression in the HAVING clause filters for just these records from the GROUP BY clause. In addition, the result set excludes the row containing a value of *0* for units in stock. The second term in the HAVING clause filters such records from the result set.

```
Sub SelectGroupByWithHaving()
Dim strSrc As String
Dim strSQL As String
strSrc = "Provider=Microsoft.Jet.OLEDB.4.0;" & _
    "Data Source=C:\PMA Samples\Northwind.mdb"
```

(continued)

```
'Query returns sum of units in stock by category
'for discontinued products only
strSQL = "SELECT Discontinued, CategoryID, SUM(UnitsInStock) " & _
    "AS [Units In Stock]" & _
    "FROM Products " & _
    "GROUP BY Discontinued, CategoryID " & _
    "HAVING Discontinued=True and SUM(UnitsInStock)>0"

PreviewRecordsetSource strSrc, strSQL

End Sub
```

Selecting with Inner Joins

One of the most powerful features of select queries is their ability to combine two or more tables into one virtual table. An inner join offers one way to accomplish this. This technique permits only the merger of two tables. But you can join two merged tables with a third record source, and you can merge that result with yet another, and so on. These nested inner joins can occur in a single SELECT statement. The result set from the select query can include fields from any record sources that it merges.

You can join two record sources on any field or fields with the same data type (other than Memo or OLEObject data types). Designate the tables to join as arguments of the FROM keyword in a select query. Separate the table names with the INNER JOIN keywords. Follow the second record source with the ON keyword, which signals the subsequent identification of the fields on which to join the record sources. Typically, you merge record sources when the corresponding fields from each record source are equal (called an equijoin), but you can use any equality operator, including <, >, <=, >=, and <>.

The following code sample, the *SelectInnerJoin* procedure, demonstrates the syntax for an inner join between the *Categories* and *Products* tables in the Northwind database. The SQL statement merges the two record sources with an equijoin of the *CategoryID* field in each table. The SELECT statement has a field list that extracts the *CategoryName* column from the *Categories* table and the *ProductName* and *Discontinued* columns from the *Products* table. Notice that table names serve as prefixes to field names. Using table names as prefixes is optional, unless two or more tables in the SQL statement contain fields with the same name.

```
Sub SelectInnerJoin()
Dim strSrc As String
Dim strSQL As String
```

```
strSrc = "Provider=Microsoft.Jet.OLEDB.4.0;" & _
    "Data Source=C:\PMA Samples\Northwind.mdb"

'Query returns products with their category names
strSQL = "SELECT Categories.CategoryName, Products.ProductName, " & _
    "Products.Discontinued " & _
    "FROM Categories INNER JOIN Products " & _
    "ON Categories.CategoryID = Products.CategoryID"

PreviewRecordsetSource strSrc, strSQL

End Sub
```

The *SelectInnerJoinWithAliases* procedure performs an identical join to the sample you just saw. However, it uses aliases to designate record sources. The letter *c* represents the *Categories* table name, and the letter *p* denotes the *Products* table. The syntax shows how you define the table aliases as arguments for the FROM keyword. You can use the aliases in place of record source names both in the SELECT statement field list and as prefixes for the fields listed as ON keyword arguments for merging the two record sources. The following code sample illustrates this concept:

```
Sub SelectInnerJoinWithAliases()
Dim strSrc As String
Dim strSQL As String

strSrc = "Provider=Microsoft.Jet.OLEDB.4.0;" & _
    "Data Source=C:\PMA Samples\Northwind.mdb"

'Query returns products with their category names
strSQL = "SELECT c.CategoryName, p.ProductName, " & _
    "p.Discontinued " & _
    "FROM Categories c INNER JOIN Products p " & _
    "ON c.CategoryID = p.CategoryID"

PreviewRecordsetSource strSrc, strSQL

End Sub
```

The final inner join sample we'll look at demonstrates the integration of several design elements of select queries. This next sample shows the syntax for joining three tables in a single SELECT statement. The first join is between the *Customers* and *Orders* tables. The merge occurs on the *CustomerID* field in both tables. The result set from that merger joins with the *Order Details* table on the *OrderID* field. This field exists in the merger of the *Customers* and *Orders* tables as well as in the *Order Details* table.

The SQL statement for this final inner join sample groups records by the *CompanyName* field in the *Customers* table, and it computes the revenue for each customer. The code uses a SUM function to aggregate revenue. The GROUP BY clause causes SUM to aggregate revenue by customer, or more specifically, by the *CompanyName* field. Nesting the SUM function within a FORMATCURRENCY function makes the aggregated revenue easy to read. The SQL statement's closing ORDER BY clause arranges the records so that the company with the largest revenue appears first.

```
Sub SelectThreeTableJoin()
Dim strSrc As String
Dim strSQL As String

strSrc = "Provider=Microsoft.Jet.OLEDB.4.0;" & _
    "Data Source=C:\PMA Samples\Northwind.mdb"
'Compute revenue from each customer and return orders by revenue
strSQL = "SELECT c.CompanyName, " & _
    "FORMATCURRENCY(" & _
    "SUM(od.[UnitPrice]*od.[Quantity]*(1-od.[Discount])),2) " & _
    "AS Revenue " & _
    "FROM (Customers c " & _
    "INNER JOIN Orders o ON c.CustomerID = o.CustomerID) " & _
    "INNER JOIN [Order Details] od " & _
    "ON o.OrderID = od.OrderID " & _
    "GROUP BY c.CompanyName " & _
    "ORDER BY " & _
    "SUM(od.[UnitPrice]*od.[Quantity]*(1-od.[Discount])) DESC"

PreviewRecordsetSource strSrc, strSQL

End Sub
```

Selecting with Outer Joins and Self Joins

Inner joins merge records from two tables when the records satisfy join criteria, such as having equal values for a designated field. Access permits other kinds of joins as well. For example, you can force all the records from one table into a result set regardless of whether they satisfy a matching criterion. This is called an outer join. You can also merge the records of a table with themselves; SQL calls this a self join. This type of join can be useful when you have two fields in the same table that denote related concepts with the same data type.

Right Outer Joins

As we've discussed, a join takes place between two record sources. SQL designates these sources as left and right sources depending on their order in the FROM argument list. The first record source is the left source, and the second record source is the right. A right outer join forces all records from the second source into the result set even when no match for them exists in the left source. Entries from the left source can enter the result set only when they satisfy a matching criterion with a record from the right source.

Figure 5-4 contrasts three join types: equijoins, left outer joins, and right outer joins. All three joins in the table join the same left and right tables. The left and right tables have two records with matching join field values: *A* and *B*. The left table has a join field value, *C*, that does not match any join field value in the right table. Similarly, the right table has a join field value, *D*, that does not match any join field value in the left table. The equijoin generates a result set with just two records having join field values of *A* and *B*. The left outer join includes three records in result set whose join field values are *A*, *B*, and *C*. The right outer join also includes three records in its result set, but the join field values for this result are *A*, *B*, and *D*.

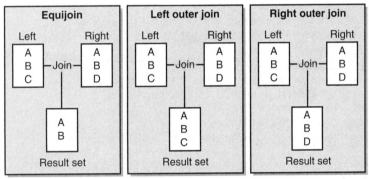

Figure 5-4 A schematic contrasting equijoins, left outer joins, and right outer joins.

In the *SelectRightOuterJoin* procedure below, the SQL statement for a right outer join appears as the assignment for the *strSQL* string. The keyword RIGHT OUTER JOIN denotes the type of join. Because the *Products* table appears to the right of the keyword, it is the right record source. Therefore, the join unconditionally selects each record from the *Products* table for inclusion in the query's result set. Rows from the *Categories* table enter the select query's result set only when they match join criteria specified by the ON keyword. In addition, a WHERE clause further filters the result set. The argument for the WHERE clause specifies that records must have a Null *CategoryID* value in the *Products* table.

To ensure that there is at least one record from the *Products* table that doesn't have a matching *CategoryID* value in the *Categories* table, the *SelectRightOuterJoin* procedure adds a record to the *Products* table by specifying just its *ProductName*. The procedure uses the recordset *AddNew* method to accomplish the task.

If you work with a freshly installed version of the Northwind database, *SelectRightOuterJoin* returns just the newly added record when it invokes the *PreviewRecordsetSource* procedure. After printing the newly added record to the Immediate window with the *PreviewRecordsetSource* procedure, the sample restores the *Products* table by deleting the newly added record.

```
Sub SelectRightOuterJoin()
Dim rst1 As ADODB.Recordset
Dim strSrc As String
Dim strSQL As String

'Create strings for connection (strSrc) and right outer join (strSQL).
'Inclusion of OUTER in RIGHT OUTER JOIN is optional.
'Query returns data on Products rows with a Null CategoryID.
strSrc = "Provider=Microsoft.Jet.OLEDB.4.0;" & _
    "Data Source=C:\PMA Samples\Northwind.mdb"

strSQL = "SELECT c.CategoryName, p.ProductName, " & _
    "p.Discontinued " & _
    "FROM Categories c RIGHT OUTER JOIN Products p " & _
    "ON c.CategoryID = p.CategoryID " & _
    "WHERE IsNull(p.CategoryID)"

'Open recordset on Products table in the connection
'that permits adding a record to the recordset
Set rst1 = New ADODB.Recordset
rst1.ActiveConnection = strSrc
rst1.Open "Products", , adOpenKeyset, adLockOptimistic, adCmdTable

'Add a record with a ProductName of foo, but no CategoryID value.
'Close recordset and set to Nothing to flush the change through.
rst1.AddNew
    rst1("ProductName") = "foo"
rst1.Update
rst1.Close
Set rst1 = Nothing

'Preview right outer join with newly added record
PreviewRecordsetSource strSrc, strSQL

'Reopen the rst1 recordset to find a record
'with a ProductName of foo and delete it
Set rst1 = New ADODB.Recordset
rst1.ActiveConnection = strSrc
rst1.Open "Products", , adOpenKeyset, adLockOptimistic, adCmdTable
rst1.Find "ProductName = 'foo'"
rst1.Delete
```

```
'Clean up objects
rst1.Close
Set rst1 = Nothing

End Sub
```

Self Joins

The classic self join sample from the Northwind database finds the managers from the *Employees* table. This table uses two separate columns to represents two related concepts. First, each employee has a unique *EmployeeID* value; this is the table's primary key. Second, all employees except one have a *ReportsTo* column value. This value denotes the *EmployeeID* for an employee's immediate manager. The top-level manager, Andrew Fuller, does not have a value in the *ReportsTo* column because he does not report to another employee in the table.

A handy SQL trick when joining a table with itself is to assign the table two different aliases. The *SelectSelfJoinForManagers* procedure shown next demonstrates the syntax for this. The two aliases for the *Employees* table are *eMgr* and *eInfo*. The procedure's logic uses *eMgr* to refer to managers found in any employee's *ReportsTo* column and *eInfo* to refer to the information for each manager. The arguments for the ON keyword specify the joining of these two tables. The sample seeks to generate a list of managers, so it prefixes the *EmployeeID*, *FirstName*, and *LastName* fields in the *Select* field list with *eInfo* because each manager's ID and name are contained in *eInfo*. (If the sample used the ID and name from *eMgr*, it would print the information for the employee who reports to that manager.) And because managers can have more than one direct report, we eliminate identical rows using the DISTINCT predicate.

```
Sub SelectSelfJoinForManagers()
Dim strSrc As String
Dim strSQL As String

strSrc = "Provider=Microsoft.Jet.OLEDB.4.0;" & _
    "Data Source=C:\PMA Samples\Northwind.mdb"

'Select employees whose EmployeeID is in the ReportsTo column
strSQL = "SELECT DISTINCT eInfo.EmployeeID, eInfo.FirstName, " & _
    "eInfo.LastName " & _
    "FROM Employees AS eMgr INNER JOIN Employees AS eInfo " & _
    "ON eMgr.ReportsTo = eInfo.EmployeeID"

PreviewRecordsetSource strSrc, strSQL

End Sub
```

The next sample lists orders placed during 1998 that shipped after the required date. The *Orders* table contains a *ShippedDate* and *RequiredDate* column, making it possible to perform the task with a self join. The *o1* alias refers to the columns associated with the *ShippedDate*; the *o2* alias designates columns associated with the *RequiredDate*.

The arguments for the ON keyword include two join criteria. First, the *OrderID* column value must match between the two aliases. Second, the *ShippedDate* column value must be greater than (temporally later than) the *RequiredDate* column value.

The SELECT field list in this instance can use either alias for its prefixes. In addition, you don't need a DISTINCT predicate because the *OrderID* requirement in the ON argument removes duplicates. Let's take a look at the code now:

```
Sub SelectSelfJoinForMissed1998Dates()
Dim strSrc As String
Dim strSQL As String

strSrc = "Provider=Microsoft.Jet.OLEDB.4.0;" & _
    "Data Source=C:\PMA Samples\Northwind.mdb"

'Select orders with matching OrderIDs where the ShippedDate
'is later than the RequiredDate in 1998
strSQL = "SELECT o1.OrderID, o1.ShippedDate, " & _
    "o2.RequiredDate " & _
    "FROM Orders AS o1 " & _
    "INNER JOIN Orders AS o2 " & _
    "ON (o1.OrderID = o2.OrderID) " & _
    "AND (o1.ShippedDate > o2.RequiredDate)" & _
    "WHERE Year(o1.OrderDate) = 1998"

PreviewRecordsetSource strSrc, strSQL

End Sub
```

Selecting with Subqueries

A subquery is a SELECT statement that is nested within another SELECT statement. The nested query is sometimes called an inner query, and the query that surrounds the inner query is sometimes called an outer query. There are two types of subqueries. First, you can express the subquery so that the inner query computes just once for the outer query. SQL terminology uses the term *subquery* for this scenario. Second, you can write a subquery that computes the inner query for each row in the outer query's result set. SQL terminology refers to this second scenario as a *correlated subquery*.

Often, you can also express a basic subquery either as an inner join or a self join. These alternative formulations can sometimes lead to faster performance. Explore them when you are working with a record source large enough that performance matters substantially.

Expressing a select query with a subquery can be a more natural approach than creating a join to obtain a result set. The following sample shows a query of the Northwind *Employees* table that returns all employees who are managers. The query returns the *EmployeeID*, *FirstName*, and *LastName* column values for any employee whose *EmployeeID* field value is in the *ReportsTo* column. The inner query computes just once for the outer query in this sample. If you are like me, the subquery formulation will be a more natural approach to finding managers in the table than the *SelectSelfJoinForManagers* sample query given earlier, which demonstrated a self join. Unless performance issues are substantial, deciding whether to use a subquery or a join might simply be a matter of personal preference.

```
Sub SelectSubQuery()
Dim strSrc As String
Dim strSQL As String

strSrc = "Provider=Microsoft.Jet.OLEDB.4.0;" & _
"Data Source=C:\PMA Samples\Northwind.mdb"

'Select employees with another employee reporting to them
strSQL = "SELECT DISTINCT EmployeeID, " & _
    "FirstName, LastName " & _
    "FROM Employees " & _
    "WHERE EmployeeID IN (SELECT ReportsTo FROM Employees)"

PreviewRecordsetSource strSrc, strSQL

End Sub
```

This next code sample demonstrates the use of a correlated subquery to find the *OrderID* with the largest extended price for each *ProductID*. The outer query specifies the return of *OrderID*, *ProductID*, and the following calculated field for computing extended price: *UnitPrice*Quantity*(1-Discount)*. For each row, the outer query looks in the inner query to see whether there is a match for its calculated field value. The inner query computes the maximum extended price for a *ProductID* in the *Order Details* table for rows in which the inner query's *ProductID* (*odsub.ProductID*) matches the outer query's *ProductID* (*od.ProductID*). The WHERE clause for the inner query causes the code to recompute for each row of the outer query.

```
Sub SelectCorrelatedSubQuery()
Dim strSrc As String
Dim strSQL As String

strSrc = "Provider=Microsoft.Jet.OLEDB.4.0;" & _
    "Data Source=C:\PMA Samples\Northwind.mdb"

'Find OrderIDs with the maximum price for a ProductID
strSQL = "SELECT od.OrderID, od.ProductID, " & _
    "od.UnitPrice*od.Quantity AS Price " & _
    "FROM [Order Details] od " & _
    "WHERE od.UnitPrice*od.Quantity*(1-od.Discount) IN " & _
    "(SELECT " & _
    "MAX(odsub.UnitPrice*odsub.Quantity*(1-odsub.Discount)) " & _
    "FROM [Order Details] odsub " & _
    "WHERE od.ProductID = odsub.ProductID)"

PreviewRecordsetSource strSrc, strSQL

End Sub
```

Selecting with Unions

All the ways to merge record sources we've discussed so far focused on joining two or more sources on one or more common fields. Think of this as a side-by-side linking of record sources. A union query, on the other hand, merges record sources in a very different way. It stacks one record source on top of another. Fields from different record sources participating in a union query must have matching data types for at least those fields involved in the query. If the data types or the data itself among record sources that you want to combine with a union query do not exactly correspond, you might be able to compute calculated fields that are compatible between record sources. For example, the *Customers* table has a *ContactName* column that contains first and last names. The *Employees* table has two separate columns for first and last names. By creating a calculated field to concatenate the *FirstName* and *LastName* columns in the *Employees* table within the union query, you can merge the *Employees* table with the *Customers* table.

The syntax for a union query reflects the design of the record sources that it merges. A union query merges multiple record sources, and it builds its syntax much like a multidecker sandwich. SELECT statements layer between UNION keywords. Each SELECT statement points at one of the record sources for the union query to merge. The field list for the SELECT statements must have matching data types.

The *SelectThreeTableUnion* procedure merges three record sources from the Northwind database: the *Customers*, *Suppliers*, and *Employees* tables. The field list for the SELECT statements of the *Customers* and *Suppliers* tables each include *CompanyName*, *ContactName*, and *Phone* from their record sources.

The SELECT statement for the *Employees* table differs from the *Customers* and *Suppliers* tables in several respects. First, it uses a string constant, *"Northwind"*, for the *CompanyName* field. Second, it creates a calculated field to match the other two tables, called *ContactName*, that is based on its *FirstName* and *LastName* column values. Third, it uses *HomePhone* as the field to match *Phone* in the preceding SELECT statements. Let's take a look at the syntax now:

```
Sub SelectThreeTableUnion()
Dim strSrc As String
Dim strSQL As String

strSrc = "Provider=Microsoft.Jet.OLEDB.4.0;" & _
    "Data Source=C:\PMA Samples\Northwind.mdb"

'Concatenate Supplier contact info after employees contact info.
'Sorts by default on first column.
strSQL = "SELECT CompanyName, ContactName, Phone " & _
    "FROM Customers " & _
    "UNION " & _
    "SELECT CompanyName, ContactName, Phone " & _
    "FROM Suppliers " & _
    "UNION " & _
    "SELECT 'Northwind', " & _
    "FirstName & ' ' & LastName AS ContactName, HomePhone " & _
    "FROM EMPLOYEES"

PreviewRecordsetSource strSrc, strSQL

End Sub
```

This procedure offers one considerable advantage over working with the three tables independently. It provides a common interface for all the contact information for customers, suppliers, and employees. But the procedure has at least two weaknesses. First, it does not specify the source for a contact. Second, it sorts records by default order according to the first column. However, your application might require a different sort (for example, sorting by *ContactName* values instead of *CompanyName* values). The *SelectSortedUnion* procedure shows how easy it is to adapt the union query to meet these requirements:

```
Sub SelectSortedUnion()
Dim strSrc As String
Dim strSQL As String
```

```
strSrc = "Provider=Microsoft.Jet.OLEDB.4.0;" & _
    "Data Source=C:\PMA Samples\Northwind.mdb"

'A single ORDER BY clause for the last SELECT can
'apply to all preceding SELECT statements in the UNION.
'You can add columns (like Source in this example) inside
'UNION queries.
strSQL = "SELECT CompanyName, ContactName, Phone, " & _
    "'Customers' AS Source " & _
    "FROM Customers " & _
    "UNION " & _
    "SELECT CompanyName, ContactName, Phone, " & _
    "'Suppliers' AS Source " & _
    "FROM Suppliers " & _
    "UNION " & _
    "SELECT 'Northwind' AS CompanyName, " & _
    "FirstName & ' ' & LastName AS ContactName, HomePhone, " & _
    "'Employees' AS Source " & _
    "FROM EMPLOYEES " & _
    "ORDER BY ContactName"

PreviewRecordsetSource strSrc, strSQL

End Sub
```

Figure 5-5 shows an excerpt from the *SelectSortedUnion* procedure's output. Notice that the output contains four fields for each record; one of these denotes the source for a record. The first five records come from the *Customers* table, but the sixth record comes from the *Employees* table. Also, the records sort according to *ContactName*—not *CompanyName*, which is the default. The sort order reflects the ORDER BY clause at the end of the *SelectSortedUnion* procedure.

Enumerating ADOX Views and Procedures

When you programmatically save, or store, a Jet SQL statement in an Access database file as a query, it adds a member to either the *Views* or *Procedures* ADOX collections. These collections reside in the catalog that contains the schema for a database file.

Views are stored Jet SQL statements that return a rowset without parameters and without multiple SELECT statements, such as union queries have. View objects have *Name*, *DateCreated*, *DateModified*, and *Command* properties. The

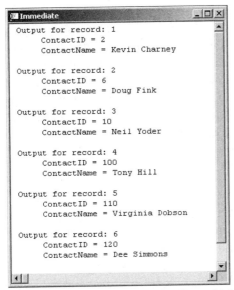

```
Immediate                                    _ □ ×
Output for record: 1
     ContactID = 2
     ContactName = Kevin Charney

Output for record: 2
     ContactID = 6
     ContactName = Doug Fink

Output for record: 3
     ContactID = 10
     ContactName = Neil Yoder

Output for record: 4
     ContactID = 100
     ContactName = Tony Hill

Output for record: 5
     ContactID = 110
     ContactName = Virginia Dobson

Output for record: 6
     ContactID = 120
     ContactName = Dee Simmons
```

Figure 5-5 Output of the *SelectSortedUnion* procedure.

Name property is the name for the query as displayed in the Database window. The *DateCreated* property reflects the date and time that you originally saved a Jet SQL statement. The *DateModified* property contains the date and time the view was most recently modified. The *Command* object contains the Jet SQL statement that defines what rows a view returns.

The ADOX *Procedures* collection contains all the Access queries that do not belong to the *Views* collection. These include parameter queries, action queries, and an assortment of other queries, such as union queries and cross-tab queries. Procedure objects also have *Name*, *DateCreated*, *DateModified*, and *Command* properties. Parameter queries can have a *Parameters* collection that exposes parameter names and data types. Your applications can enumerate the parameters for parameter queries that have *Parameters* collections.

> **Note** Do not confuse ADOX procedures with Visual Basic for Applications (VBA) procedures. VBA procedures contain VBA statements, but ADOX procedures contain Jet SQL statements. This section discusses how to use VBA procedures to enumerate ADOX procedures.

After appropriate filtering, the members of the *Views* and *Procedures* collections comprise the set of user-defined queries that appear in the Database window of an Access database file. Learning to enumerate the members of these two ADOX collections can empower you to programmatically discover the queries in an Access database and expose their Jet SQL code. In this chapter, I use the term *user-defined queries* for those queries that appear in the Database window when the *System* objects and *Hidden* objects on the View tab of the Options dialog box are not selected. You can open this dialog box by choosing Tools-Options from the Database window menu.

Enumerating Views

The Database window for an Access database file permits you to list queries by showing each query's name, date created, date last modified, and a couple of other properties not exposed through the ADOX library. The next sample demonstrates how you can enumerate the views within a database file in the same style that the Database window does. One advantage of using the *Views* collection is that the database file need not be open.

The design of this next code sample demonstrates the flexibility of listing queries from database files, regardless of whether those files are open. A calling procedure passes a single parameter to a called procedure that enumerates the *Views* collection members. The passed parameter contains the name of the database file and the path to it. The called procedure has three main sections. First, it opens a catalog with an *ActiveConnection* property that points at the specified filename. Second, the procedure iterates through the *Views* collection of the catalog to determine the length of the longest view name in the collection. Performing this step provides information that helps to align the data printed by the third step. Third, the procedure prints the *Name*, *DateModified*, and *DateCreated* properties for each member in the *Views* collection.

The procedure builds one long string for the data about a view. The view's name is padded to accommodate the longest view name. Next the procedure appends the *DateModified* property to the string. The date and time elements of this property can comprise up to 22 characters, but the actual length can be less, depending on the number of characters representing the month, hour, and other elements. Therefore, the procedure pads *DateModified*, allowing at least one blank column between the end of the *DateModified* property and the start of the *DateCreated* property.

```
Sub CallEnumerateViews()
Dim strSrc As String

'Specify path and filename to database with views
strSrc = "C:\PMA Samples\Northwind.mdb"
```

```
'Pass argument
EnumerateViews strSrc

End Sub


Sub EnumerateViews(strSrc As String)
Dim cat1 As ADOX.Catalog
Dim vew1 As ADOX.View
Dim mwd As Integer

'Instantiate catalog that points at database
'named in strSrc
Set cat1 = New ADOX.Catalog
cat1.ActiveConnection = _
    "Provider=Microsoft.Jet.OLEDB.4.0;" & _
    "Data Source=" & strSrc

'Determine longest view name in the catalog
mwd = 5
For Each vew1 In cat1.Views
    If Len(vew1.Name) > mwd Then mwd = Len(vew1.Name)
Next vew1
mwd = mwd + 1

'Enumerate the views in the catalog, showing
'date last modified and date created
For Each vew1 In cat1.Views
    Debug.Print vew1.Name & _
        String(mwd - Len(vew1.Name), " ") & _
        vew1.DateModified & _
        String(23 - Len(vew1.DateModified), " ") & _
        vew1.DateCreated
Next vew1

'Clean up objects
Set cat1 = Nothing

End Sub
```

Enumerating Procedures

Enumerating procedures is almost as easy as enumerating views. Access creates members of the *Procedures* collection to help Access manage the database. Therefore, you need to filter out these members when you want to generate a list of procedures that matches the list that appears in the Database window. You can do this by excluding procedures that begin with either *~sq_* or *~TMP*. The sample that follows implements this filter while it computes the length of the longest procedure name and repeats this process when it prints the *Name*, *DateModified*, and *DateCreated* properties for each procedure.

> **Note**   Because Access begins procedure names with either *~sq_* or *~TMP*, you should refrain from starting the names of your custom procedures with these characters.

Like the sample you saw for enumerating views, the following code will work for any Access database file. Just pass the path and filename from the first procedure to the second one. The process is automatic after that.

```
Sub CallEnumerateProcs()
Dim strSrc As String

'Specify path and filename to database with procedures
strSrc = "C:\PMA Samples\Northwind.mdb"

'Pass argument
EnumerateProcs strSrc

End Sub


Sub EnumerateProcs(strSrc As String)
Dim cat1 As ADOX.Catalog
Dim prc1 As ADOX.Procedure
Dim mwd As Integer

'Instantiate catalog that points at database
'named in strSrc
Set cat1 = New ADOX.Catalog
cat1.ActiveConnection = _
    "Provider=Microsoft.Jet.OLEDB.4.0;" & _
    "Data Source=" & strSrc

'Determine longest procedure name in the catalog
mwd = 5
For Each prc1 In cat1.Procedures
    If Left(prc1.Name, 4) <> "~sq_" And _
        Left(prc1.Name, 4) <> "~TMP" Then _
        If Len(prc1.Name) > mwd Then mwd = Len(prc1.Name)
Next prc1
mwd = mwd + 1
```

```
'Enumerate the procedures in the catalog, showing
'date last modified and date created
For Each prc1 In cat1.Procedures
    If Left(prc1.Name, 4) <> "~sq_" And _
        Left(prc1.Name, 4) <> "~TMP" Then
        Debug.Print prc1.Name & _
            String(mwd - Len(prc1.Name), " ") & _
            prc1.DateModified & _
            String(23 - Len(prc1.DateModified), " ") & _
            prc1.DateCreated
    End If
Next prc1

'Clean up objects
Set cat1 = Nothing

End Sub
```

Creating a Recordset for View and Procedure Properties

The next sample we'll look at takes advantage of ADOX's ability to enumerate views and procedures. First, the code creates an overall listing of all the queries in an Access database file. (The previous two samples shown in this section enumerated just a subset of all user-defined queries for an Access database file.) This procedure's output lists the same properties as shown in the Database window for the *Queries* collection of a database file. Second, this next sample persists properties for the views and procedures to a recordset. If you have a recurring need for such information about the contents of a data source, you might find it useful to avoid computing the information each time—particularly if you work with a relatively stable database design.

The first procedure of this application, *CallCreateViewsProcsRecordset*, passes three string arguments to the second procedure, *CreateViewsProcsRecordset*. The first argument contains the path and filename for the Access database file whose queries you want to inventory. The second and third arguments contain, respectively, the path and filename for the file that the application uses to store the information about the views and procedures in the database file's catalog.

```
Sub CallCreateViewsProcsRecordset()
Dim strSrc As String
Dim strXMLPath As String
Dim strXMLFile As String

'Specify path and filename to database with
'views and procedures
strSrc = "C:\PMA Samples\Northwind.mdb"
```

(continued)

```
'Designate path and filename for XML file that will
'store enumerated views and procedures from the data
'source named in strXMLPath
strXMLPath = "C:\PMA Samples\Chapter 05\"
strXMLFile = "NorthwindQueries.xml"

'Pass arguments
CreateViewsProcsRecordset strSrc, strXMLPath, strXMLFile

End Sub
```

The *CreateViewsProcsRecordset* procedure has six major steps. First, it instantiates a recordset, *rst1*, and appends fields to it for persisting the view and procedure properties. Second, it instantiates a catalog that points at the database file whose queries the procedure will inventory. The procedure's third step iterates through the *Views* collection of the catalog, saving the longest current view name and persisting the view's *Name, DateModified*, and *DateCreated* property settings to the *rst1* recordset. The fourth step performs comparable tasks for the *Procedures* collection. If appropriate, it updates *mwd*, the integer variable that tracks the name of the longest view or procedure.

The fifth step of *CreateViewsProcsRecordset* performs two tasks. Initially, it sorts the recordset by its *QueryName* field, which holds the names of views and procedures. Assigning the *Sort* property to the *QueryName* field at this point resets the current position to the start of the recordset. The procedure next loops through the recordset rows from its current position while printing the properties of the recordset's views and procedures. Finally, the procedure saves the recordset to the path and filename specified by the first procedure. If the file already exists, the procedure traps a run-time error. The error trap removes the prior version of the file and resumes saving the recordset to the file. Let's take a look at *CreateViewsProcsRecordset* now:

```
Sub CreateViewsProcsRecordset(strSrc As String, _
    strXMLPath As String, strFile As String)
On Error GoTo CreateRecordset_Trap
Dim cat1 As ADOX.Catalog
Dim vew1 As ADOX.View
Dim prc1 As ADOX.Procedure
Dim rst1 As ADODB.Recordset
Dim mwd As Integer

'Instantiate a recordset
Set rst1 = New ADODB.Recordset

'Specify recordset fieldname and data type.
'Append to recordset object.
With rst1
```

```
        .Fields.Append "QueryName", adVarWChar, 64
        .Fields.Append "DateModified", adDate
        .Fields.Append "DateCreated", adDate
        .Open
End With

'Instantiate catalog that points at database
'named in strSrc
Set cat1 = New ADOX.Catalog
cat1.ActiveConnection = _
    "Provider=Microsoft.Jet.OLEDB.4.0;" & _
    "Data Source=" & strSrc

'Enumerate the views in the catalog along
'with date last modified and date created for
'storage in rst1
For Each vew1 In cat1.Views
With vew1
    If mwd < Len(.Name) Then _
        mwd = Len(.Name)
        rst1.AddNew
            rst1("QueryName") = .Name
            rst1("DateModified") = .DateModified
            rst1("DateCreated") = .DateCreated
        rst1.Update
    End With
Next vew1

'Enumerate the procedures in the catalog along
'with date last modified and date created for
'storage in rst1
For Each prc1 In cat1.Procedures
    With prc1
        If Left(.Name, 4) <> "~sq_" And _
            Left(.Name, 4) <> "~TMP" Then
            If mwd < Len(.Name) Then _
                mwd = Len(.Name)
            rst1.AddNew
                rst1("QueryName") = .Name
                rst1("DateModified") = .DateModified
                rst1("DateCreated") = .DateCreated
            rst1.Update
        End If
    End With
Next prc1
mwd = mwd + 1

'Sort recordset by QueryName before printing names
```

(continued)

```
'along with date modified and date created
rst1.Sort = "QueryName"
Do While Not rst1.EOF
    Debug.Print rst1("QueryName") & _
        String(mwd - Len(rst1("QueryName")), " ") & _
        rst1("DateModified") & _
        String(23 - Len(rst1("DateModified")), " ") & _
        rst1("DateCreated")
    rst1.MoveNext
Loop

'Save recordset to specified path and file
rst1.Save strXMLPath + strXMLFile, adPersistXML

CreateRecordset_Exit:
rst1.Close
Set rst1 = Nothing
Set cat1 = Nothing
Exit Sub

CreateRecordset_Trap:
'Kill previous version of file to hold
'persisted recordset if it exists.
'Otherwise, present error info in a message box.
If Err.Number = 58 Then
    Kill strXMLPath + strXMLFile
    Resume
Else
    MsgBox "Procedure failed with an error number = " _
        & Err.Number & ", " & vbCrLf & "and an " & _
        "error description of """ & _
        Err.Description & """" & "." , vbInformation, _
        "Programming Microsoft Access Version 2002"
End If

End Sub
```

Listing the *CommandText* Property for Views

At the beginning of this chapter, I provided many of the Jet SQL statement formulations that you are likely to use. Another great way to learn SQL is to print the SQL code for the queries in some of your favorite applications. The Northwind_backup.mdb Access database file is used widely in this book. Recall that this file is the original version of the Northwind database. The following sample shows how to print the SQL code for all the views in this database. You can readily update the string specifying a target database's path and filename to examine the SQL code from views in other Access database files.

The sample procedure that prints the SQL code for the views has a very simple design. First, it instantiates a catalog and points its *ActiveConnection* property at the target database. Then it just loops through the members of the catalog's *Views* collection. For each pass through the loop, the sample prints the view's name. Then it creates a reference to the view's *Command* property. Next it prints the *CommandText* property for the command. The *CommandText* property contains the SQL code for the query in the view. A closing *Debug.Print* statement within the loop prints a blank line to separate the output for each view in the Immediate window. Here is the procedure:

```
Sub CallEnumerateCommandTextInViews()
Dim strSrc As String

'Assign string value for file with views
strSrc = "C:\PMA Samples\Northwind_backup.mdb"

'Pass argument
EnumerateCommandTextInViews strSrc

End Sub


Sub EnumerateCommandTextInViews(strSrc As String)
Dim cat1 As ADOX.Catalog
Dim vew1 As ADOX.View
Dim cmd1 As ADODB.Command
Dim mwd As Integer

'Instantiate catalog that points at database
'named in strSrc
Set cat1 = New ADOX.Catalog
cat1.ActiveConnection = _
    "Provider=Microsoft.Jet.OLEDB.4.0;" & _
    "Data Source=" & strSrc

'Print all view names and SQL strings
'in the database
For Each vew1 In cat1.Views
    Debug.Print vew1.Name
    Set cmd1 = vew1.Command
    Debug.Print cmd1.CommandText
    Debug.Print
Next vew1

'Clean up objects
Set cat1 = Nothing

End Sub
```

Listing the *CommandText* Property and *Parameters* Collection for Procedures

Processing procedures is inherently more complicated than processing views because you also typically enumerate each procedure's *Parameters* collection. You must also filter out those procedures that are not user defined. (Recall that these are procedures whose names begin with either ~*sq_* or ~*TMP.*)

In the following code, the outer *For...Each* loop enumerates the procedures within a catalog. Nested within this loop are *If* statements, *With...End With* statements, and other *For...Each* loops. These assorted structures facilitate a variety of tasks, such as extracting the *CommandText* property from the *Command* property for procedures.

If the procedure has a *Parameters* collection with a *Count* property greater than 0, the sample determines the length of the longest parameter name, then prints certain properties for each parameter. The application uses two lookup function procedures, *ParameterType* and *ParameterDirection*. These functions decode each property from its numeric value to the intrinsic constant name for the value. When working with a Jet database, the *Direction* property must always be *adParamInput*, because this is the only type of parameter Jet supports. At present, there are no data providers or service providers to offer enhanced functionality for the *Direction* property. The *Size* parameter setting appears only if the data type is *adVarWChar*. An Immediate If function (*IIf*) controls whether the *Size* property appears. If the *IIf* function detects a data type of *adVarWChar*, the function prints the *Size* property setting; otherwise, it prints an empty string. Here's the sample:

```
Sub CallEnumerateCommandTextAndParameters()
Dim strSrc As String

'Assign string value for file with procedures
strSrc = "C:\PMA Samples\Northwind_backup.mdb"

'Pass argument
EnumerateCommandTextAndParameters strSrc

End Sub


Sub EnumerateCommandTextAndParameters(strSrc As String)
Dim cat1 As ADOX.Catalog
Dim prc1 As ADOX.Procedure
Dim cmd1 As ADODB.Command
Dim prm1 As ADODB.Parameter
Dim mwd As Integer
```

```
'Instantiate catalog that points at database
'named in strSrc
Set cat1 = New ADOX.Catalog
cat1.ActiveConnection = _
    "Provider=Microsoft.Jet.OLEDB.4.0;" & _
    "Data Source=" & strSrc

'Print all procedure names and SQL strings in the
'catalog
For Each prc1 In cat1.Procedures
    With prc1
        If Left(.Name, 4) <> "~sq_" And _
            Left(.Name, 4) <> "~TMP" Then
            Debug.Print .Name
            Set cmd1 = .Command
            With cmd1
                Debug.Print .CommandText
                If .Parameters.Count > 0 Then
                    Debug.Print .Parameters.Count
                    mwd = 0
                    For Each prm1 In .Parameters
                        If mwd < Len(prm1.Name) Then _
                            mwd = Len(prm1.Name)
                    Next prm1
                    mwd = mwd + 1
                    For Each prm1 In .Parameters
                        With prm1
                            Debug.Print .Name & _
                                String(mwd - Len(.Name), " ") & _
                                ParameterType(.Type), _
                                ParameterDirection(.Direction), _
                                IIf(.Type = adVarWChar, .Size, "")
                        End With
                    Next prm1
                End If
            End With
            Debug.Print
        End If
    End With
Next prc1

'Clean up objects
Set cmd1 = Nothing
Set cat1 = Nothing

End Sub
```

(continued)

```
Function ParameterType(intType As Integer) As String
    Select Case intType
        Case adVarWChar
            ParameterType = "adVarWChar"
        Case adCurrency
            ParameterType = "adCurrency"
        Case adInteger
            ParameterType = "adInteger"
        Case adDate
            ParameterType = "adDate"
        Case adWChar
            ParameterType = "adWChar"
        Case adLongVarWChar
            ParameterType = "adLongVarWChar"
        Case adLongVarBinary
            ParameterType = "adLongVarBinary"
        Case adBoolean
            ParameterType = "adBoolean"
        Case adSmallInt
            ParameterType = "adSmallInt"
        Case adDouble
            ParameterType = "adDouble"
        Case adGUID
            ParameterType = "adGuid"
        Case adSingle
            ParameterType = "adSingle"
        Case adUnsignedTinyInt
            ParameterType = "adUnsignedTinyInt"
        Case adNumeric
            ParameterType = "adNumeric"
        Case Else
            ParameterType = CStr(intType)
    End Select
End Function


Function ParameterDirection(intType As Integer) As String
    Select Case intType
        Case adParamUnknown
            ParameterDirection = "adParamUnknown"
        Case adParamInput
            ParameterDirection = "adParamInput"
        Case adParamOutput
            ParameterDirection = "adParamOutput"
        Case adParamInputOutput
            ParameterDirection = "adParamInputOutput"
        Case adParamReturnValue
            ParameterDirection = "adParamReturnValue"
```

```
        Case Else
            ParameterDirection = CStr(intType)
    End Select
End Function
```

Managing Row-Returning Queries with ADOX

Saving, updating, and deleting queries that return rows are some of the most common programmatic database design changes you'll want to implement. Chapters 2 and 3, "Data Access Models: Part I" and "Data Access Models: Part II," examined techniques for running row-returning queries. And earlier in this chapter, the section "Jet SQL Syntax for Select Queries" presented Jet SQL rules for expressing row-returning queries. In this section of the chapter, we'll focus on techniques for programmatically building and managing query objects that return rows. In particular, you'll learn how to use an ADOX *View* object to add or remove a query from a database. Next we'll discuss designing and running a query that accepts parameters. Parameters are especially important because they permit run-time control over the rows that a query returns. The samples illustrating this topic will increase your understanding of how to use parameters with the ADOX and ADODB libraries. The closing samples in this section demonstrate techniques for adding queries to a database's schema even when you are disconnected from it. This code outlines a process for persisting a database design to disk, modifying the design while you are disconnected from the database, and then updating the original database with the queries you added or changed while disconnected.

Adding and Removing Queries

Adding a query to a database programmatically is a simple process. You start by defining a new view. This merely involves instantiating an ADOX *View* object and assigning its properties. *Command* is among the most important of these properties. To set the view's *Command* property, you can create a local command, assign its properties, and then assign the local command to the view's *Command* property. Creating a local *Command* object enables you to set its *CommandText* property, through which you specify the Jet SQL that defines the query. To finish adding the query to a database, you append the command to the *Views* collection of the catalog for the target database file.

> **Note**   After you append a view to the *Views* collection of a catalog to create a stored query for the current database, the view will not appear in the database file's Database window—although you can enumerate it programmatically. When you append a view (or a procedure) to another database file, the view will be visible in the Database window of the other file—after the window refreshes.

The next sample details the process of adding a view to a database as a stored query. In the first procedure, *CallAddAView*, the sample defines three string variables. The first variable is the path and filename for the Access database file to which you will add a query. The second variable, *strSQL*, is the Jet SQL statement for the query. The third variable, *strQry*, designates a name for the new query.

The *AddAView* procedure contains just three essential steps. First it instantiates a catalog and points it at the database filename passed to it from *CallAddAView*. Second it instantiates a command. The command does not require an *ActiveConnection* property setting because we're just using it as a container for a Jet SQL statement represented as a string. The command's *CommandText* property holds the Jet SQL expression for the query. The third step for adding a view to a database's schema as a query is to append the view to the catalog. To do so, you invoke the *Append* method for the catalog's *Views* collection. The *Append* method requires two arguments: a string to name the query and a *Command* object that defines the query.

If you repeatedly work with a catalog's schema, you might encounter a situation where you attempt to save a view using a name that already exists. This will generate a run-time error. The following sample deals with this by using an error trap that calls the *RemoveAView* procedure, which removes a targeted query from a database. I will discuss this procedure momentarily, after we examine the logic for adding a view. Once the error trap removes the prior version of the query, the *AddAView* procedure resumes the attempt to save the local *Command* object to the database as a query.

```
Sub CallAddAView()
Dim strSrc As String
Dim strSQL As String
Dim strQry As String

'Set strSrc to the path and filename of the database in which
'you want to create a view, strSQL to the SQL string, and strQry
'to the name of the view that you want to add
```

```
strSrc = "C:\PMA Samples\Northwind.mdb"
strSQL = "SELECT * FROM Orders"
strQry = "AllOrders"

'Pass arguments to AddAView
AddAView strSrc, strSQL, strQry

End Sub


Sub AddAView(strSrc As String, strSQL As String, _
    strQry As String)
On Error GoTo AddAView_Trap
Dim cat1 As ADOX.Catalog
Dim cmd1 As ADODB.Command

'Instantiate a catalog for the Access data
'source named in strSrc
Set cat1 = New ADOX.Catalog
cat1.ActiveConnection = _
    "Provider=Microsoft.Jet.OLEDB.4.0;" & _
    "Data Source=" & strSrc

'Instantiate a command with the SQL statement
'in strSQL
Set cmd1 = New ADODB.Command
cmd1.CommandText = strSQL

'Append the view with the name in strQry and the
'CommandText in cmd1
cat1.Views.Append strQry, cmd1

'Clean up objects
AddAView_Exit:
Set cmd1 = Nothing
Set cat1 = Nothing
Exit Sub

AddAView_Trap:
If Err.Number = -2147217816 Then
'If view already exists, remove old version and resume
    RemoveAView strSrc, strQry
    Resume
Else
'Otherwise, print error message and exit gracefully
    Debug.Print Err.Number, Err.Description
End If

End Sub
```

As you work with a database's design, you will encounter situations where you need to remove database objects. The preceding sample's error trap shows one scenario in which this need might arise. Normal database maintenance requires you to remove obsolete queries from a database file periodically. Databases load faster and are easier to manage when they contain just the objects that are necessary for an application. To remove a query from a database programmatically, you invoke the *Delete* method. The following sample demonstrates how to perform this process for a view, but the technique is the same for a procedure. You simply invoke the *Delete* method for the *Views* (or *Procedures*) collection of a catalog pointing at the appropriate database This next sample contains two procedures. The first assigns one string for the path and filename for the Access database file with the obsolete query and a second string for the name of the query to remove.

The second procedure starts by instantiating a catalog and pointing it at the database with the query to remove. If the specified query is not found in the database, a run-time error occurs when the procedure invokes the *Delete* method for the *Views* collection. Instead of implementing a labeled error trap to catch these mistakes, the sample implements an in-line error trap. The code first clears the *Err* object to make sure no entries from prior errors exist. Then it instructs the VBA processor to respond to an error by resuming at the line after the line that generated the error. When it invokes the *Delete* method for the *Views* collection, if all goes well, the method completes successfully, and the *Err* object retains its 0 value. The program then exits with a confirmation message and clears the catalog from memory. If the *Delete* method does not execute successfully, Access updates the *Err* object with the number for the error and the procedure issues a message that the deletion failed.

The *RemoveAView* design is convenient because it provides interactive user feedback through a message box. However, when you want a procedure to run automatically without user interaction, this feedback can actually stall a process You can handle this issue in any of a number of ways, including by making the feedback available only when a calling procedure explicitly requests it. Here's the syntax for the *CallRemoveAView* and *RemoveAView* procedures:

```
Sub CallRemoveAView()
Dim strSrc As String
Dim strQry As String


'Set strSrc to the path and filename of the database in which
'you want to delete a view and strQry to the name of the view
'that you want to remove
strSrc = "C:\PMA Samples\Northwind.mdb"
strQry = "AllOrders"
```

```
'Pass arguments to RemoveAView
RemoveAView strSrc, strQry

End Sub


Sub RemoveAView(strSrc As String, strQry As String)
Dim cat1 As ADOX.Catalog
Dim vew1 As ADOX.View
Dim cmd1 As ADODB.Command


'Instantiate a catalog for the Access data
'source named in strSrc
Set cat1 = New ADOX.Catalog
cat1.ActiveConnection = _
    "Provider=Microsoft.Jet.OLEDB.4.0;" & _
    "Data Source=" & strSrc

'Remove the view named in strQry, and report
'success or failure of attempt in a message box
Err.Clear
On Error Resume Next
cat1.Views.Delete cat1.Views(strQry).Name
If Err <> 0 Then
    MsgBox "Deletion of view failed.", vbCritical, _
    "Programming Microsoft Access Version 2002"
    Exit Sub
Else
    MsgBox "Deletion of view succeeded.", vbInformation, _
        "Programming Microsoft Access Version 2002"
End If
Set cat1 = Nothing

End Sub
```

Creating and Using Parameter Queries

With parameters, you can allow users to vary the result set of a query at run time.
You add parameter queries through the *Procedures* collection instead of through
the *Views* collection. ADOX lets you save a parameter query with or without a
PARAMETERS declaration. However, keep in mind that the parameter query state-
ment itself is a Jet SQL statement—not an ADOX statement. Omitting the PARAM-
ETERS declaration can prevent you from enumerating the members of a query's
Parameters collection. Omitting the PARAMETERS declaration does *not* stop your
application from running the query and supplying parameter values at run time.

The *SelectInClauseParameters* sample demonstrates how to add a parameter query named *TwoParametersIn* to the Northwind database file. The sample starts by defining two strings: *strSrc* for the connection string to the database file, and *strSQL* for the Jet SQL statement defining the parameter query. The procedure actually includes two versions of the Jet SQL statement for the parameter query; the uncommented version does not have a PARAMETERS declaration, but the commented version does. Either version will enable you to save the parameter query and run it successfully. If you want to, you can use the version that doesn't contain the PARAMETERS declaration and then use ADOX to add a *Parameters* collection to the *Command* object for the query before saving it. This achieves nearly the same result as including a PARAMETERS declaration in the Jet SQL statement for the command. The only difference between adding a *Parameters* collection before saving a parameter query and saving the query without the collection is the effect it has on your ability to enumerate the parameters. Refer back to the *EnumerateCommandTextAndParameters* procedure we examined in the earlier section "Listing the *CommandText* Property and *Parameters* Collection for Procedures" to see how to enumerate the *Parameters* collection members.

> **Note** Developers who are more familiar with Access data type names than they are with ADO names might find declaring parameter variables with the PARAMETERS keyword inside the query preferable to adding parameters outside the Jet SQL statement. Using the PARAMETERS keyword requires the use of Access data type designations.

After defining the strings for the database and the Jet SQL statement, the *SelectInClauseParameters* procedure instantiates a command and assigns properties to it. Just as with adding a command to the *Views* collection, you do not need to assign the *ActiveConnection* property for a command you append to the *Procedures* collection; this is because the Catalog object contains the connection information. Simply set the *Name* and *CommandText* properties for the command. Then instantiate a catalog that points at the database to which you want to add the procedure as a stored query. Conclude the task by invoking the *Append* method for the catalog's *Procedures* collection. A simple error trap recovers from cases in which a user attempts to append a procedure with the same name as a query that already exists in the database. The error trap in this routine works just like the one in the AddAView procedure. Here's the code:

```
Sub SelectInClauseParameters()
On Error GoTo InParameters_Trap
Dim strSrc As String
Dim strSQL As String
```

```
Dim cmd1 As ADODB.Command
Dim cat1 As ADOX.Catalog
Dim prm1 As ADODB.Parameter
Dim prm2 As ADODB.Parameter

'Assign strSrc value for connection string to database
'that will gain the new procedure
strSrc = "Provider=Microsoft.Jet.OLEDB.4.0;" & _
    "Data Source=C:\PMA Samples\Northwind.mdb"

'Query demonstrates use of IN keyword to return customers
'matching two parameters (Country1 and Country2).
'Use of a PARAMETERS declaration is optional (see commented strSQL).
strSQL = "SELECT CompanyName, ContactName, Country FROM Customers " & _
    "WHERE Country IN (Country1, Country2)"
'strSQL = "PARAMETERS " & _
'    Country1 Text ( 255 ), Country2 Text ( 255 ); " & _
'    "SELECT CompanyName, ContactName, Country FROM Customers " & _
'    "WHERE Country IN (Country1, Country2)"

'Instantiate a command based on the parameter query
Set cmd1 = New ADODB.Command
cmd1.Name = "TwoParametersIn"
cmd1.CommandText = strSQL

'Instantiate a catalog, and append command to the
'catalog as a procedure
Set cat1 = New ADOX.Catalog
cat1.ActiveConnection = strSrc
cat1.Procedures.Append cmd1.Name, cmd1

InParameters_Exit:
Set cmd1 = Nothing
Set cat1 = Nothing
Exit Sub


InParameters_Trap:
If Err.Number = -2147217816 Then
'If procedure exists, delete it
    cat1.Procedures.Delete cmd1.Name
    Resume
Else
    Debug.Print Err.Number, Err.Description
    MsgBox "Program aborted for unanticipated reasons.", _
        vbCritical, "Programming Microsoft Access Version 2002"
End If

End Sub
```

Once a parameter query has been added to a database, running it differs only slightly from running a *Command* object with parameters in the *CommandText* property's SQL string. (See the section "Creating a Recordset with a Parameter Query" in Chapter 3 for a sample that demonstrates how to run a *Command* object with parameters.) The following procedure, *RunTwoParametersIn*, illustrates how to run a parameter query that has been added to a database. It runs the parameter query added in the preceding code sample.

The *RunTwoParametersIn* procedure has three sections. First it instantiates a catalog and points it at the database with the stored parameter query. Second it assigns a reference to the *Command* property of the stored query, *TwoParametersIn*, to a local variable. Then it assigns parameter values for the *Country1* and *Country2* parameters. Before executing the command, the VBA procedure must append the parameters to the *Command* object. In the third part, the procedure executes the query and saves a reference to the resulting recordset, and then prints the first 10 records.

```
Sub RunTwoParametersIn()
Dim cat1 As ADOX.Catalog
Dim cmd1 As ADODB.Command
Dim rst1 As ADODB.Recordset
Dim prm1 As ADODB.Parameter
Dim prm2 As ADODB.Parameter
Dim int1 As Integer
Dim fld1 As ADODB.Field

'Instantiate catalog for Northwind database
Set cat1 = New ADOX.Catalog
cat1.ActiveConnection = "Provider=Microsoft.Jet.OLEDB.4.0;" & _
    "Data Source=C:\PMA Samples\Northwind.mdb"

'Assign a reference to TwoParametersIn Command property
Set cmd1 = cat1.Procedures("TwoParametersIn").Command

'Create parameters, and assign values for them.
'Append parameters to command.
Set prm1 = cmd1.CreateParameter("Country1", adVarWChar, _
    adParamInput, 255, "UK")
Set prm2 = cmd1.CreateParameter("Country2", adVarWChar, _
    adParamInput, 255, "USA")
cmd1.Parameters.Append prm1
cmd1.Parameters.Append prm2

'Execute and save reference to resulting recordset.
'Print first 10 records to Immediate window.
Set rst1 = cmd1.Execute
int1 = 1
```

```
Do Until rst1.EOF
    Debug.Print "Output for record: " & int1
    For Each fld1 In rst1.Fields
        If Not (fld1.Type = adLongVarBinary) Then _
            Debug.Print String(5, " ") & _
            fld1.Name & " = " & fld1.Value
    Next fld1
    rst1.MoveNext
    If int1 >= 10 Then
        Exit Do
    Else
        int1 = int1 + 1
        Debug.Print
    End If
Loop


'Clean up objects
Set cat1 = Nothing
rst1.Close
Set rst1 = Nothing
Set cmd1 = Nothing

End Sub
```

You have to invoke the stored query with a *Command* object because recordsets do not support parameters. Also note that the stored query includes parameters, but you have to set specific values for those parameters. You can use the *CreateParameter* method to do this. In addition, when you execute the command, you need to save a reference to the resulting recordset so that you can use the result set after running the stored query. *Command* objects do not offer the same properties and methods for working with result sets that recordsets do.

Case Study: Remotely Adding and Updating Queries

This case study presents and integrates design elements for remotely managing queries. Its general approach is suitable for technical people who have to create new queries or revise existing ones while they are disconnected from a database file. This solution uses three VBA procedures. The first procedure creates and saves to disk a recordset that documents the queries (including views and procedures) in an Access database file. The developer will create this file while still connected to the database file. The second procedure reveals how to add new or replacement queries to the recordset documenting the queries in the original database file. A developer can use this procedure while he or she is disconnected from the original database. The final procedure copies new or updated queries from the recordset back to the original database file.

Documenting a Database's Queries

The code sample that documents the queries in a database file does so in two formats. First, it saves a recordset in XML format. XML makes it easy to read the file back in again for updating. However, this format creates the file with a collection of tags and attribute labels that can be distracting to users trying to read the file's contents. Second, the sample creates a file that documents the queries within a database in an easy-to-read text format. This format allows for convenient viewing and manual markup.

> **Note**   If you plan to output in text format, using a text file has definite advantages over using the Immediate window. First, the Immediate window limits you to 200 lines of output—too few lines for our sample. Second, the text file persists the text beyond the current Access session.

The next sample contains two procedures: *CallCreateViewsProcsRecordset2* and *CreateViewsProcsRecordset2*. The first procedure sets three string variables. One of these variables represents the database file. The other two variables indicate the path and filename of the XML and text files that hold the data about the queries in the database file.

The second procedure in the code sample performs five major tasks. It begins by instantiating a recordset, *rst1*, and adding five fields to it. These fields enable the recordset to hold the documentation necessary to update the original database. The first field identifies the name of a query, the second represents the date a query was last modified, the third signifies the date a query was created, the fourth stores the Jet SQL statement for a query, and the fifth field, a Boolean data type that is initially set to False, indicates whether a query is unchanged.

For its second task, the procedure instantiates a catalog and points its *ActiveConnection* property at the database file containing the queries that you want to document. The procedure's third task copies the property settings for the views and procedures in the catalog to the fields of the *rst1* recordset. At the end of this step, the *rst1* recordset has a row for each query in the database file. The procedure's fourth task creates a string variable, *strText*, that stores the contents of the recordset. This string variable assists in the creation of the easy-to-read text file with the documentation on the queries. Therefore, the string is formatted with some blank lines to improve readability of the file.

The final task of the procedure uses a *FileSystemObject* object to create a text file that stores the contents of *strText*. The code sample uses a textstream object, tso1, to help accomplish this. The procedure then copies the contents of *strText* to the text file. The code assigns a name to the text file based on the name passed to the procedure for the XML file. The procedure also copies the *rst1* recordset to the path and file passed to the procedure for the XML file. If the file already exists, the procedure kills the old version and copies the new version to disk. (It's not necessary to check this for the text file because the *CreateTextFile* method overwrites any previous file of the same name.) The code for the *CallCreateViewsProcsRecordset2* and *CreateViewsProcsRecordset2* procedures follows.

> **Note**   Use of *FileSystemObject* in the *CreateViewsProcsRecordset2*
> procedure requires a reference to the Microsoft Scripting Runtime library.
> Make sure you have selected this reference from the References dialog box before attempting to run the procedure.

```
Sub CallCreateViewsProcsRecordset2()
Dim strSrc As String
Dim strXMLPath As String
Dim strXMLFile As String

'Specify path and filename to database with
'views and procedures
strSrc = "C:\PMA Samples\Northwind.mdb"

'Designate path and filename for XML and text files that
'will store enumerated views and procedures from the data
'source named in strSrc
strXMLPath = "C:\PMA Samples\Chapter 05\"
strXMLFile = "NorthwindQueries.xml"

'Pass arguments
CreateViewsProcsRecordset2 strSrc, strXMLPath, strXMLFile

End Sub
```

(continued)

```
Sub CreateViewsProcsRecordset2(strSrc As String, _
    strXMLPath As String, strXMLFile As String)
On Error GoTo CreateRecordset_Trap
Dim cat1 As ADOX.Catalog
Dim cmd1 As ADODB.Command
Dim vew1 As ADOX.View
Dim prc1 As ADOX.Procedure
Dim rst1 As ADODB.Recordset
Dim mwd As Integer
Dim strText As String
Dim fso1 As Scripting.FileSystemObject
Dim tso1 As Scripting.TextStream
Dim strTxtFile As String

'Instantiate a recordset
Set rst1 = New ADODB.Recordset

'Specify recordset field names and data types.
'Append to recordset object.
With rst1
    .Fields.Append "QueryName", adVarWChar, 64
    .Fields.Append "DateModified", adDate
    .Fields.Append "DateCreated", adDate
    .Fields.Append "CommandText", adLongVarWChar, 2000
    .Fields.Append "AddedUpdated", adBoolean
    .Open
End With

'Instantiate catalog that points at database
'named in strSrc
Set cat1 = New ADOX.Catalog
cat1.ActiveConnection = _
    "Provider=Microsoft.Jet.OLEDB.4.0;" & _
    "Data Source=" & strSrc

'Enumerate the views in the catalog along
'with date last modified and date created for
'storage in rst1
For Each vew1 In cat1.Views
    With rst1
        .AddNew
        With vew1
            If mwd < Len(.Name) Then _
                mwd = Len(.Name) + 1
            rst1("QueryName") = .Name
            rst1("DateModified") = .DateModified
```

```
                rst1("DateCreated") = .DateCreated
                Set cmd1 = .Command
                rst1("CommandText") = cmd1.CommandText
                rst1("AddedUpdated") = False
            End With
            Update
        End With
    Next vew1


    'Enumerate the procedures in the catalog along
    'with date last modified and date created for
    'storage in rst1
    For Each prc1 In cat1.Procedures
        With prc1
            If Left(.Name, 4) <> "~sq_" And _
                Left(.Name, 4) <> "~TMP" Then
                If mwd < Len(.Name) Then _
                    mwd = Len(.Name)
                rst1.AddNew
                    rst1("QueryName") = .Name
                    rst1("DateModified") = .DateModified
                    rst1("DateCreated") = .DateCreated
                    Set cmd1 = .Command
                    rst1("CommandText") = cmd1.CommandText
                    rst1("AddedUpdated") = False
                rst1.Update
            End If
        End With
    Next prc1
    mwd = mwd + 1


    'Sort recordset by QueryName before saving
    rst1.Sort = "QueryName"
    strText = ""
    Do While Not rst1.EOF
        strText = strText & vbCrLf & rst1("QueryName") & _
            String(mwd - Len(rst1("QueryName")), " ") & _
            rst1("DateModified") & _
            String(23 - Len(rst1("DateModified")), " ") & _
            rst1("DateCreated") & vbCrLf & vbCrLf & _
            "Text for query:" & vbCrLf & rst1("CommandText")
        rst1.MoveNext
    Loop


    'Save strText to text file based on name of XML file.
    'Remove the leading vbCrLf characters from strText
    'when writing the string to disk.
    Set fso1 = CreateObject("Scripting.FileSystemObject")
```

(continued)

```
strTxtFile = Left(strXMLFile, Len(strXMLFile) - 3) & "txt"
Set tso1 = fso1.CreateTextFile(strXMLPath + strTxtFile, True)
tso1.Write Right(strText, Len(strText) - 2)

'Save recordset in XML format
rst1.Save strXMLPath + strXMLFile, adPersistXML

CreateRecordset_Exit:
rst1.Close
Set rst1 = Nothing
Set cat1 = Nothing
Exit Sub

CreateRecordset_Trap:
'Kill previous version of file to hold
'persisted recordset if it exists.
'Otherwise, present error info in a message box.
If Err.Number = 58 Then
    Kill strXMLPath + strXMLFile
    Resume
Else
    MsgBox "Procedure failed with an error number = " _
        & Err.Number & ", " & vbCrLf & "and an " & _
        "error description of """ & _
        Err.Description & """" & ".", vbInformation, _
        "Programming Microsoft Access Version 2002"
End If

End Sub
```

Adding and Updating Queries on the Recordset

When the developer is disconnected from the original database, he or she can add and update queries in the XML documentation file. A simple programming template, such as the one you will see next, can assist with that task. Begin by opening the persisted recordset in the XML file. Next make recordset field assignments that correspond to the new or modified query. Then set the *AddedUpdated* field to True. Now add the record for the new or modified query to the recordset. You can readily add more than one record. Finally, resave the updated recordset to disk.

The following procedure, *AddTwoQueriesToARecordset*, demonstrates the syntax for adding two queries to the documentation recordset. You should find most of the syntax familiar by now, and it is fully commented. Notice that the procedure sets the recordset's *CursorLocation* property to *adUseClient*. This enables you to update the XML file's recordset. It also eliminates the need to kill the prior version of the recordset before saving the new one; the *adUseClient* setting permits the procedure to save over the recordset's prior version.

```
Sub AddTwoQueriesToARecordset()
Dim rst1 As ADODB.Recordset
Dim cmd1 As ADODB.Command
Dim strSrc As String

'Assign string that points at file to receive new query
strSrc = "C:\PMA Samples\Chapter 05\NorthwindQueries.xml"

'You must set CursorLocation to adUseClient to
'permit updating the recordset
Set rst1 = New ADODB.Recordset
'rst1.CursorLocation = adUseClient
rst1.Open strSrc, "Provider = MSPersist"

'Add AllOrders query
rst1.AddNew
    rst1("QueryName") = "AllOrders"
    rst1("DateModified") = Now()
    rst1("DateCreated") = Now()
    rst1("CommandText") = "SELECT * FROM Orders"
    rst1("AddedUpdated") = True
rst1.Update

'Add UKUSACustomers
rst1.AddNew
    rst1("QueryName") = "UKUSACustomers"
    rst1("DateModified") = Now()
    rst1("DateCreated") = Now()
    rst1("CommandText") = "SELECT CompanyName, " & _
        "ContactName, Country FROM Customers " & _
        "WHERE Country IN ('UK', 'USA')"
    rst1("AddedUpdated") = True
rst1.Update

'Save the newly updated recordset over its prior copy
Kill strSrc
rst1.Save strSrc, adPersistXML

'Clean up objects
rst1.Close
Set rst1 = Nothing

End Sub
```

Adding and Updating Database Queries from the Recordset

In essence, the XML file acts as a scratchpad for the developer who is away from the office. The persisted recordset enables the developer to write queries to the file persisting the recordset. When the developer is ready to update the original database, a simple procedure can scan the persisted recordset for records that have a value of True for their *AddedUpdated* field. Then the procedure can extract the recordset information from the record and use a procedure, such as *AddAView*, to copy the new or updated query from the persisted recordset to the database file.

The sample that follows demonstrates one approach to transferring queries from the XML file to the database. It starts by instantiating a recordset and opening it based on the XML file that stored changes to the *Queries* collection while the developer was disconnected from the database file. This task requires a setting of *adUseClient* for the *CursorLocation* property to enable the use of the *Find* method for the recordset. Next the procedure opens a loop to find records with an *AddedUpdated* field value of True. Within the loop, the sample calls the *AddAView* procedure, which we discussed earlier in this section. When the recordset contains no more records with a value of True for the *AddedUpdated* field, the procedure exits the *Do* loop.

```
Sub CallAddAViewFromRecordset()
Dim rst1 As ADODB.Recordset
Dim strSrc As String
Dim strSQL As String
Dim strQry As String

'Instantiate a recordset, and set the CursorLocation
'property to adUseClient to permit finding records
Set rst1 = New ADODB.Recordset
rst1.CursorLocation = adUseClient
rst1.Open "C:\PMA Samples\Chapter 05\NorthwindQueries.xml", _
    "Provider = MSPersist"

'Assign a string value to point at the destination file
'for the new queries
strSrc = "C:\PMA Samples\Northwind.mdb"

'Start a loop through the data in NorthwindQueries.xml
'file to search for added or updated queries
Do
    rst1.Find "AddedUpdated = True"
    If rst1.EOF Then
        Exit Do
    Else
        strSQL = rst1("CommandText")
        strQry = rst1("QueryName")
        rst1.MoveNext
        AddAView strSrc, strSQL, strQry
    End If
Loop
```

```
'Clean up objects
rst1.Close
Set rst1 = Nothing

End Sub
```

This case study offers a broad outline of an application that you can readily customize to fit your unique requirements. For example, the procedure in the previous code sample saves only views. However, you might want to amend it to save both views and procedures. In addition, you might want to augment the code so that it permits you to mark queries for deletion. How you customize this sample will depend on your special needs, but it offers you a framework for modifying the stored queries in a database file while you are disconnected from that file.

Creating and Running Action Queries with ADOX

Inserting, deleting, and updating records in a record source are classic database tasks. From its inception, Access offered special queries to facilitate these tasks; these queries are known as action queries. While you can specify these tasks with SQL text each time you perform them, the operations perform faster when you run them from a stored query. This is because Jet already has the SQL statement compiled when it runs a stored query; Jet doesn't have to compile the statement each time as it would if you passed it an SQL string.

Stored action queries are most versatile when you design them with parameters. The parameters allow users to reuse stored action queries in more circumstances. For example, you can re-use the same insert parameter query to add many different records to a database. This, in turn, reduces the number of queries in a database file, which can help your custom applications load faster.

This section discusses different ways to use parameters with stored action queries. It shows you the Jet SQL statements for adding, deleting, and updating records and demonstrates how to parameterize those statements. It covers how to save the action queries and how to assign parameters when you are ready to run those queries.

An Insert Parameter Query

The key to saving an insert action query with one or more parameters is to understand the structure of the INSERT INTO statement in SQL. After the INSERT INTO keyword, designate the name of the table to which you will add a record.

Follow the table name with a list in parentheses of field names. The field names denote those fields for which your statement specifies values. Although using the list is optional when you specify values for all fields in the order in which the fields exist in the record source, it is good practice to use the list in all instances. Follow the list of field names with the VALUES keyword. This keyword signals the beginning of a list in parentheses of values that matches the order of the field name list. When creating a parameter query to let users enter the values to insert at run time, specify parameter names instead of actual values. After designing the Jet SQL statement for an action query, save it by assigning the statement to a *Command* object and appending the command to the *Procedures* collection of a database's catalog.

> **Note**   Jet SQL supports copying a group of records from one table to another. This approach follows the format for a typical append query with the Query Designer. You can use the Query Designer's SQL View for any typical append query to review the Jet SQL syntax for that design.

The following procedure, *ParamQInsertsShippers*, demonstrates the syntax for saving an insert action query. The stored query inserts one new record into the *Shippers* table in the Northwind database. The procedure begins by assigning the connection string to a string variable, *strSrc*. Then it assigns the SQL statement with the parameters to a second string variable, *strSQL*. Next the procedure instantiates a command and assigns the *strSQL* string to its *CommandText* property. It names the command *InsertAShipper*. Then the sample instantiates a catalog and assigns the *strSrc* string to its *ActiveConnection* property.

Instead of using a labeled error trap to recover from an attempt to save over an existing procedure in the catalog, the sample uses an in-line trap design. (The *RemoveAView* procedure, which we examined earlier in the chapter, in the section titled "Managing Row-Returning Queries with ADOX," uses a similar approach to recover from an attempt to delete a view that's not in a catalog.)

```
Sub ParamQInsertsShippers()
Dim strSrc As String
Dim strSQL As String
Dim cmd1 As ADODB.Command
Dim cat1 As ADOX.Catalog

'Assign strSrc value for connection string to database
'that will gain the new procedure
strSrc = "Provider=Microsoft.Jet.OLEDB.4.0;" & _
```

```
"Data Source=C:\PMA Samples\Northwind.mdb"

'Instantiate a command based on a parameter query
strSQL = "INSERT INTO Shippers (CompanyName, Phone) " & _
            "VALUES (CNameIn, PhoneIn)"
Set cmd1 = New ADODB.Command
cmd1.Name = "InsertAShipper"
cmd1.CommandText = strSQL

'Instantiate a catalog, and point it at the command's
'database connection
Set cat1 = New ADOX.Catalog
cat1.ActiveConnection = strSrc

'Create a new procedure that appears in the
'Database window as a new query; embed process in
'an error trap that relies on the Err object
'to check for an already existing query
Err.Clear
On Error Resume Next
cat1.Procedures.Append cmd1.Name, cmd1
If Err.Number = -2147217816 Then
    cat1.Procedures.Delete cmd1.Name
    cat1.Procedures.Append cmd1.Name, cmd1
ElseIf Err.Number <> 0 Then
    Debug.Print Err.Number, Err.Description
    MsgBox "Error; see Immediate window diagnostics.", _
        vbCritical, "Programming Microsoft Access Version 2002"
    Exit Sub
End If

'Clean up objects
    Set cmd1 = Nothing
    Set cat1 = Nothing

End Sub
```

Although this sample saves a parameter query, it does not run the query. Therefore, you still need to invoke the parameter query to add a record to the *Shippers* table. To do so, you must run the Execute method using a local reference to the stored action query's command.

The following procedure illustrates how to run a stored parameter query for inserting new records into the *Shippers* table. The procedure starts by instantiating a catalog for the Northwind database. Next it creates a reference named *cmd1* to the *Command* property for the *InsertAShipper* query. Then the sample invokes the *CreateParameter* method a couple of times to create parameters for the *cmd1* object. The *CreateParameter* method adds a new parameter, but assigning a value to the parameter with this method is optional. This sample sets the parameter values directly using a couple of *InputBox* function statements. After a user responds to the InputBox dialog boxes, the procedure appends the parameters to the *Parameters* collection for the *cmd1* object. Finally, the procedure executes the *cmd1* object's command.

```
Sub RunParamQInsertsShippers()
Dim cat1 As ADOX.Catalog
Dim cmd1 As ADODB.Command
Dim prm1 As ADODB.Parameter
Dim prm2 As ADODB.Parameter

'Instantiate catalog for Northwind database
Set cat1 = New ADOX.Catalog
cat1.ActiveConnection = "Provider=Microsoft.Jet.OLEDB.4.0;" & _
    "Data Source=C:\PMA Samples\Northwind.mdb"

'Assign a reference to the InsertAShipper query's
'Command property
Set cmd1 = cat1.Procedures("InsertAShipper").Command

'Create parameters and assign values for them.
'Append parameters to command.
Set prm1 = cmd1.CreateParameter("CnameIn", adVarWChar, _
    adParamInput, 40)
Set prm2 = cmd1.CreateParameter("Phone", adVarWChar, _
    adParamInput, 24)

prm1.Value = Left(InputBox("Company Name: "), 40)
prm2.Value = Left(InputBox("Phone: "), 24)
cmd1.Parameters.Append prm1
cmd1.Parameters.Append prm2

'Run the insert action query
cmd1.Execute

'Clean up objects
Set cmd1 = Nothing
Set cat1 = Nothing

End Sub
```

You do not have to repeat all the setup steps to run a stored action query each time you add a new record. If an application adds more than one new record at a time, you can just change the parameter value assignments—don't append the parameters a second time—and re-execute the *cmd1* object.

A Delete Parameter Query

The sample for adding an insert action query that you just saw is easy to follow, but you might want a more general model for saving action queries or any type of query that can be a member of the *Procedures* collection in the ADOX object library. The next sample you'll see for saving a delete action query provides a more general design. While the upcoming sample is suitable for the delete action query that it presents, you can readily adapt the code for use with any action query, including the *InsertAShipper* action query you saw in the previous code sample. Of course, even if you have a general routine for saving an action query with parameters, you still need a specific VBA procedure to invoke the action query that passes the query the appropriate parameters.

Together, the next two procedures create a delete action query. The first procedure, *CallAddParamQuery*, assigns three string constants—one for the database in which to store the action query, another for the SQL statement defining the action query, and a third with the name of the action query. By changing the SQL string, this sample could create an insert or update action query just as easily as it creates a delete action query. The WHERE clause in the SQL statement for *strSQL* contains a parameter named *CNameOut*. When your application invokes the query, the Access will delete all records from the *Shippers* table for the shipper indicated by the *CNameOut* parameter. Here's the *CallAddParamQuery* procedure:

```
Sub CallAddParamQuery()
Dim strSrc As String
Dim strSQL As String
Dim strQry As String

'Assign strSrc for connection to database
'that will gain the new query
strSrc = "Provider=Microsoft.Jet.OLEDB.4.0;" & _
    "Data Source=C:\PMA Samples\Northwind.mdb"
'Assign the SQL statement
strSQL = "DELETE * FROM Shippers " & _
            "WHERE CompanyName = CNameOut"
strQry = "RemoveAShipper"

'Pass arguments
AddParamQuery strSrc, strSQL, strQry

End Sub
```

The actual process of adding the query to a database file takes place in the second procedure. The steps for performing this task should be familiar by now. Their presentation here illustrates two points: how to use the steps with an action query, and how to make the steps more general so that they are suitable for saving any query that belongs to the *Procedures* collection. Here's the *AddParamQuery* procedure:

```
Sub AddParamQuery(strSrc As String, _
    strSQL As String, strQry As String)
Dim cmd1 As ADODB.Command
Dim cat1 As ADOX.Catalog

'Instantiate a command based on the parameter query
Set cmd1 = New ADODB.Command
cmd1.Name = strQry
cmd1.CommandText = strSQL

'Instantiate a catalog, and point it at the command's
'database connection
Set cat1 = New ADOX.Catalog
cat1.ActiveConnection = strSrc

'Create a new procedure that appears in the
'Database window as a new query; embed process in
'an error trap that relies on the Err object
'to check for an already existing query

Err.Clear
On Error Resume Next
cat1.Procedures.Append cmd1.Name, cmd1
If Err.Number = -2147217816 Then
    cat1.Procedures.Delete cmd1.Name
    Err.Clear
    cat1.Procedures.Append cmd1.Name, cmd1
ElseIf Err.Number <> 0 Then
    Debug.Print Err.Number, Err.Description
    MsgBox "Error; see Immediate window diagnostics.", _
        vbCritical, "Programming Microsoft Access Version 2002"
    Exit Sub
End If

'Clean up objects
Set cmd1 = Nothing
Set cat1 = Nothing

End Sub
```

Once you save the action query to delete records, you still need a routine to set the parameters and invoke the query. The *RunRemoveShippers* procedure that appears next provides that model. The overall process is straightforward. First, create a catalog that points at the database file with the action query. Second, create a reference to the action query's *Command* property. Third, create a parameter for the query, assign it a value, and append the parameter to the *Parameters* collection for the *Command* object. Finally, execute the local reference to the command.

Designating the parameter value is the only part of the process for running the *RemoveAShipper* query that isn't generic. You should prompt for a value that is appropriate for the specific parameter query with which you are working. In this case, the sample uses an *InputBox* function to prompt for a company name to use as the *CNameOut* parameter:

```
Sub RunRemoveShippers()
Dim cat1 As ADOX.Catalog
Dim cmd1 As ADODB.Command
Dim prm1 As ADODB.Parameter

'Instantiate catalog for Northwind database
Set cat1 = New ADOX.Catalog
cat1.ActiveConnection = "Provider=Microsoft.Jet.OLEDB.4.0;" & _
    "Data Source=C:\PMA Samples\Northwind.mdb"

'Assign reference to the RemoveAShipper query's
'Command property
Set cmd1 = cat1.Procedures("RemoveAShipper").Command

'Create parameter, and assign value for it.
'Append parameter to command.
Set prm1 = cmd1.CreateParameter("CNameOut", adVarWChar, _
    adParamInput, 40)

prm1.Value = Left(InputBox("Company Name: "), 40)
cmd1.Parameters.Append prm1

'Run the delete action query
cmd1.Execute

'Clean up objects
Set cmd1 = Nothing
Set cat1 = Nothing

End Sub
```

An Update Parameter Query

The UPDATE statement in SQL lets you change an old fie ld value to a new one. By using parameters, you can let users designate the old and new values at run time. An UPDATE statement contains three clauses.

In the first clause, the UPDATE keyword designates a record source for updating. The SET keyword, the second clause in an UPDATE statement, assigns a new value for a field name. Without the optional third clause, the UPDATE statement transforms the field value for each row within a record source to the new value designated by the SET clause. If your update includes an optional WHERE clause, it can restrict which rows change to the new value. This WHERE clause can take any expressions appropriate for a WHERE clause in a normal SELECT statement.

The following sample creates an update action query in the Northwind database. Notice that the sample calls the *AddParamQuery* procedure from the previous section. This reuse of the AddParamQuery procedure demonstrates its versatility with another type of parameter action query.

The Jet SQL statement for the update action query is saved in the *strSQL* string variable. The statement has two parameters for the *CompanyName* field in the *Shippers* table of the Northwind database. The *CNameNew* parameter specifies the new name that you want to set in the *CompanyName* field. The *CNameOld* parameter signifies which records in the *Shippers* table to transform to the new value. Only rows with a *CompanyName* field equal to the value of the *CNameOld* parameter get their *CompanyName* field transformed to the value of the *CNameNew* parameter.

```
Sub CreateParamQForUpdating()
Dim strSrc As String
Dim strSQL As String
Dim strQry As String

'Assign strSrc value for connection to database
'that will gain the new query
strSrc = "Provider=Microsoft.Jet.OLEDB.4.0;" & _
    "Data Source=C:\PMA Samples\Northwind.mdb"
'Assign SQL statement
strSQL = "UPDATE Shippers SET CompanyName = CNameNew " & _
    "WHERE CompanyName = CNameOld"
strQry = "UpdateOldToNewShipper"

'Pass arguments
AddParamQuery strSrc, strSQL, strQry

End Sub
```

After running *CreateParamQForUpdating*, you will have an update action query in the Northwind database. The next pair of procedures allows you to see the behavior of the update action query. The *AddFooRecord* procedure adds a record to the *Shippers* table with a *CompanyName* of *foo*. You should run the procedure and then open the Northwind database to verify the addition of the new record before running the second procedure. The second procedure, *RunUpdateFooToBoo*, transforms any *CompanyName* with a value of *foo* to *boo*. After running the second procedure, you will see a new company named *boo* in the *Shippers* table.

The *RunUpdateFooToBoo* procedure applies standard techniques for running a parameter query. First, it creates a catalog that points at the database file containing the parameter query. Second, it creates a reference to the parameter query's *Command* property. Third, it creates parameters for the command that correspond to those for the stored parameter query. This involves assigning values to the parameters and appending them to the *Command* object. Finally, it executes the local *Command* object.

```
Sub AddFooRecord()
Dim cmd1 As ADODB.Command
Dim strSrc As String
Dim strSQL As String

strSrc = "Provider=Microsoft.Jet.OLEDB.4.0;" & _
    "Data Source=C:\PMA Samples\Northwind.mdb"
strSQL = "INSERT INTO Shippers (CompanyName) " & _
        "Values ('foo')"

Set cmd1 = New ADODB.Command
cmd1.ActiveConnection = strSrc
cmd1.CommandText = strSQL
cmd1.Execute

End Sub


Sub RunUpdateFooToBoo()
Dim strSrc As String
Dim strSQL As String
Dim cat1 As ADOX.Catalog
Dim cmd1 As ADODB.Command
Dim prm1 As ADODB.Parameter
Dim prm2 As ADODB.Parameter

'Assign strSrc value for connection string to database
'that contains the query you want to run
strSrc = "Provider=Microsoft.Jet.OLEDB.4.0;" & _
    "Data Source=C:\PMA Samples\Northwind.mdb"

'Instantiate catalog for Northwind database
Set cat1 = New ADOX.Catalog
cat1.ActiveConnection = strSrc
```

(continued)

```
'Assign reference to UpdateOldToNewShipper query's
'Command property
Set cmd1 = cat1.Procedures("UpdateOldToNewShipper").Command

'Create parameters, and assign values for them.
'Append parameters to command.
Set prm1 = cmd1.CreateParameter("CnameNew", adVarWChar, _
    adParamInput, 40, "boo")
Set prm2 = cmd1.CreateParameter("CnameOld", adVarWChar, _
    adParamInput, 40, "foo")
cmd1.Parameters.Append prm1
cmd1.Parameters.Append prm2
cmd1.Execute

End Sub
```

Introduction to Jet SQL's DDL

In addition to row-returning queries and action queries, Jet SQL also supports a data definition language (DDL). Developers can use this language to create database objects, such as tables and queries. Because DDL and ADOX both let you create database objects, you can use them interchangeably in many circumstances. DDL offers a series of statements for creating and modifying objects. For example, you use the CREATE TABLE statement to make a new table; you run an ALTER TABLE statement to modify an existing table; and you run a DROP TABLE statement to delete a table. Because DDL is not a hierarchical model and is not VBA-based, Access developers might prefer ADOX. Nevertheless, Jet SQL's DDL has a very intimate relationship with Jet databases, and you will find that learning its syntax yields many advantages.

Creating a Table with Custom AutoNumber Settings

One advantage of using Jet SQL to create tables is that your application does not require a reference to the ADOX library. This is because you can run Jet SQL statements from *Command* objects. Recall that *Command* objects are members of the ADODB library. Because applications require the ADODB library for basic data access functions and Access creates a default reference to the library, the ADODB library is likely to be available without you having to perform any special measures, such as creating a reference.

The syntax for creating a table requires the CREATE TABLE keyword, followed by a table name. For example, to create a table named *Contacts*, specify a *CommandText* property equal to *"CREATE TABLE Contacts"*. This statement creates an empty table with no columns. The table name will appear in the Database window, but there will be nothing for the Datasheet view to show—not even an empty row.

You need to add one or more columns in the CREATE TABLE statement. Column specifications appear in parentheses after the table name in this statement. Within parentheses after the table name, you separate column specifications with commas. As a minimum, you must designate a column name and data type for each column. You are likely to reference the INTEGER and the CHAR data types. An INTEGER data type can have an IDENTITY setting. This enables the column to behave as though it contained *AutoNumber* field values. However, you have more control over *AutoNumber* field values through the Jet SQL IDENTITY setting than through the Access user interface because you can specify start and step values. Column specifications can also include constraints that restrict the column values. For example, you can include the PRIMARY KEY keyword after the data type for a column to indicate that the column is a primary key for a table.

The following code sample illustrates a very basic task: creating a table named *Contacts*. The table has two columns, one named *ContactID* and the other named *ContactName*. The *ContactID* column has an INTEGER data type with an IDENTITY setting. Recall that these settings correspond to an AutoNumber data type setting. As is typical for columns with AutoNumber data types, the *ContactID* column is a primary key. The *ContactName* field has a CHAR data type with a maximum size of 50 characters.

This sample does considerably more than just create the *Contacts* table; it also adds data and prints the table. Creating the table requires just two steps. First, you need to specify a connection. You can accomplish this by instantiating a *Connection* object and then opening the object so that it points at a database file. Second, you need to instantiate a *Command* object, set its properties, and then execute the command. Because the *Command* object includes an *ActiveConnection* property, you can omit the first step if you set the command's *ActiveConnection* property directly. The *CommandText* property accepts the SQL statement. This statement implements the table design described in the preceding paragraph.

```
Sub SetStartAndStep()
On Error GoTo StartAndStep_Trap
Dim cnn1 As ADODB.Connection
Dim cmd1 As ADODB.Command
Dim strSrc As String
Dim strSQL As String
Dim strTemp As String

'Instantiate a connection, and point it at a database
Set cnn1 = New ADODB.Connection
```

(continued)

```
    strSrc = "Provider=Microsoft.Jet.OLEDB.4.0; " & _
        "Data Source=C:\PMA Samples\Northwind.mdb"

cnn1.Open strSrc

'Instantiate a command for adding a database object
'and adding data to the database
Set cmd1 = New ADODB.Command
With cmd1
    .ActiveConnection = cnn1
'First create a table with two columns.
'Assign IDENTITY setting to PRIMARY KEY column.
'Set its start value (2) and its step value (4).
    .CommandType = adCmdText
    .CommandText = "CREATE TABLE Contacts (ContactID INTEGER " & _
        "IDENTITY(2,4) PRIMARY KEY, ContactName CHAR(50))"
    .Execute
'After creating the table with the autoincrement/identity
'column, you should add data
    .CommandText = "INSERT INTO Contacts(ContactName) " & _
        "Values ('Kevin Charney')"
    .CommandType = adCmdText
    .Execute
    .CommandText = "INSERT INTO Contacts(ContactName) " & _
        "Values ('Doug Fink')"
    .CommandType = adCmdText
    .Execute
    .CommandText = "INSERT INTO Contacts(ContactName) " & _
        "Values ('Neil Yoder')"
    .CommandType = adCmdText
    .Execute
End With

'Close connection to flush changes through
cnn1.Close
Set cnn1 = Nothing

'Echo Contacts table to Immediate window using
'query selecting all fields from the Orders table
strSQL = "SELECT * FROM Contacts"
PreviewRecordsetSource strSrc, strSQL

StartAndStep_Exit:
Set cmd1 = Nothing
Exit Sub

StartAndStep_Trap:
If Err.Number = -2147217900 Then
```

```
'If table exists, drop it
'before resuming
    strTemp = cmd1.CommandText
    cmd1.CommandText = "DROP TABLE Contacts"
    cmd1.Execute
    cmd1.CommandText = strTemp
    Resume
Else
    Debug.Print Err.Number, Err.Description
    MsgBox "Error; see Immediate window diagnostics.", _
        vbCritical, "Programming Microsoft Access Version 2002"
End If

End Sub
```

This sample also implements an error trap for trying to create the *Contacts* table if it already exists in a database. In this case, the procedure saves the *CommandText* setting in a string variable, *strTemp*. Then it executes a command to drop the old version of the *Contacts* table from the database. Finally, the trap copies the *strTemp* string back to the *CommandText* property and resumes at the point that generated the error.

After the first *Execute* method creates the table, the procedure adds three contacts to the table using the INSERT INTO keyword so that we can observe the behavior of the AutoNumber data type in the *ContactID* column. Notice from the Jet SQL statement for the table that the AutoNumber values have a start value of *2* and a step value of *4*. Therefore, the *ContactID* column values should be *2*, *6*, and *10*. This behavior is not possible with the Access user interface, which always has start and step values of *1*. After populating the table with records, the procedure prints the records to the Immediate window to confirm the results.

Changing AutoNumber Settings

One especially cool feature of Jet SQL is its ability to reset AutoNumber columns, such as *ContactID*, on the fly. You can reset both the start and the step values. To perform this task, alter the column settings for the AutoNumber column. You can do this by embedding an ALTER COLUMN statement within an ALTER TABLE statement. After the ALTER COLUMN statement, designate the column name. Follow that with the IDENTITY keyword, adding the start and step values in parentheses. You can execute the ALTER TABLE statement with its nested ALTER COLUMN statement from either a *Command* or a *Connection* object.

The next sample demonstrates the syntax for altering an AutoNumber column on the fly. It starts by instantiating a connection and pointing it at the database with the AutoNumber column to update. Next it sets new start and step values for the AutoNumber column and passes these values, the database connection, and the AutoNumber column name to the *ResetCounter* procedure. *ResetCounter* constructs a string with the proper syntax for the ALTER TABLE statement and executes the statement using the *Execute* method for the connection. When *ResetCounter* returns control to the procedure that called it, the sample inserts three more records into the *Contacts* table. Then the code prints the contents of a recordset based on the *Contacts* table to the Immediate window. This output starts with three records that use the initial start and step values of *2* and *4*. Then the output shows three additional records with start and step values of *100* and *10*. See Figure 5-6 for the display of the records in the Immediate window. Note that the start and step values you specify should not cause duplicate indexes; otherwise, the new records you add will be rejected.

```
Sub CallAndDemoResetCounter()
Dim cnn1 As ADODB.Connection
Dim cmd1 As ADODB.Command
Dim int1 As Integer
Dim int2 As Integer
Dim str1 As String
Dim str2 As String

'Instantiate a connection and point it at a database
Set cnn1 = New ADODB.Connection
cnn1.Open "Provider=Microsoft.Jet.OLEDB.4.0; " & _
    "Data Source=C:\PMA Samples\Northwind.mdb"

'Reset AutoNumber start (int1) and step (int2) values; then
'pass these along with table name and database connection to
'the procedure to reset the counter for a table
int1 = 100
int2 = 10
str1 = "Contacts"
ResetCounter int1, int2, cnn1, str1

'Add data with new start and step settings
Set cmd1 = New ADODB.Command
With cmd1
    .ActiveConnection = cnn1

    .CommandText = "INSERT INTO Contacts(ContactName) " & _
        "Values ('Tony Hill')"
    .CommandType = adCmdText
    .Execute
    .CommandText = "INSERT INTO Contacts(ContactName) " & _
        "Values ('Virginia Dobson')"
    .CommandType = adCmdText
```

```
        .Execute
        .CommandText = "INSERT INTO Contacts(ContactName) " & _
            "Values ('Dee Simmons')"
        .CommandType = adCmdText
        .Execute
End With

'Close connection to flush changes through
cnn1.Close
Set cnn1 = Nothing

'Echo Contacts table to Immediate window
str1 = "Provider=Microsoft.Jet.OLEDB.4.0;" & _
    "Data Source=C:\PMA Samples\Northwind.mdb"
'Query selecting all fields from the Orders table
str2 = "SELECT * FROM Contacts"
PreviewRecordsetSource str1, str2

'Clean up objects
Set cmd1 = Nothing

End Sub


Sub ResetCounter(int1 As Integer, _
    int2 As Integer, cnn1 As ADODB.Connection, _
    str1 As String)
Dim str2 As String

'Revise start and step autoincrement values
'according to int1 and int2 settings
str2 = "ALTER TABLE " & str1 & vbCrLf & _
    "ALTER COLUMN ContactID IDENTITY (" & _
    int1 & ", " & int2 & ")"

cnn1.Execute str2

End Sub
```

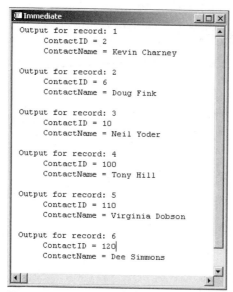

Figure 5-6 Output from the *CallAndDemoResetCounter* procedure that confirms programmatic changes to start and step AutoNumber values.

Creating Check Constraints for Columns

Column check constraints enable the designation of a set of legitimate values for a column. The Access user interface (and the Data Access Objects [DAO] model) allows you to set these constraints through the Validation Rule property. The ADOX library exposes a validation rule property as well, but this property is buried in the provider-specific properties for *Column* objects. ADO developers using Jet SQL's DDL can take advantage of the CHECK keyword when creating or altering a table. The CHECK keyword enables you to write an expression that restricts the range of legitimate values for a field. While the expression constrains the values in a column and acts like a normal validation rule, it does not appear within the Access user interface.

> **Note** In ADOX, the syntax for adding provider-specific properties has a somewhat different appearance than that of standard property settings. Here's how you might create a validity rule and its corresponding text in ADOX:
>
> ```
> col.Properties("Jet OLEDB:Column Validation Rule").Value = "> Date()"
> col.Properties("Jet OLEDB:Column Validation Text").Value = _
>     "Must be greater than today."
> ```

The next sample shows the syntax for creating a column check constraint with the CHECK keyword and demonstrates the constraint's behavior. In the first *CommandText* string, notice the CHECK keyword at the end of the table definition. A comma separates it from the last column definition, which denotes the *EAddress* column. This column contains e-mail addresses and therefore should include the at sign (@). The CHECK keyword and expression causes Access to use this rule to verify the value for the *EAddress* column before accepting a row into the table. A failure of the rule generates a run-time error with a number of −2147467259. An error trap toward the end of the procedure replaces the default error message with a more specific one that might be easier for users to understand. The attempt to enter the third record for Neil Yoder triggers the error, because his e-mail address contains a # rather than an @. In addition to printing the message, the table rejects the record for Neil Yoder.

```
Sub CheckEAddress()
On Error GoTo StartAndStep_Trap
Dim cnn1 As ADODB.Connection
Dim cmd1 As ADODB.Command
Dim strTemp As String
Dim strSQL As String

'Instantiate a connection, and point it at a database
Set cnn1 = New ADODB.Connection
cnn1.Open "Provider=Microsoft.Jet.OLEDB.4.0; " & _
    "Data Source=C:\PMA Samples\Northwind.mdb"

'Instantiate a command for adding a database object
'and adding data to the database
Set cmd1 = New ADODB.Command
With cmd1
    .ActiveConnection = cnn1
'Same table as in SetStartAndStep, except this table has an
'EAddress field with a check constraint for @ in the field value
    .CommandType = adCmdText
    .CommandText = "CREATE TABLE Contacts (ContactID " & _
        "IDENTITY(2,4) PRIMARY KEY, ContactName CHAR(50), " & _
        "EAddress CHAR, CHECK(Instr(EAddress, '@')))"
    .Execute
    .CommandText = "INSERT INTO Contacts(ContactName, EAddress) " & _
        "Values ('Kevin Charney', 'kcharney@cab.com')"
    .CommandType = adCmdText
    .Execute
    .CommandText = "INSERT INTO Contacts(ContactName, EAddress) " & _
        "Values ('Doug Fink','dfink@cab.com')"
    .CommandType = adCmdText
    .Execute
```

(continued)

```
'The e-mail address for Neil Yoder does not contain @.
'Therefore, its input forces an error from the CHECK clause.
    .CommandText = "INSERT INTO Contacts(ContactName, EAddress) " & _
        "Values ('Neil Yoder','nyoder#cab.com')"
    .CommandType = adCmdText
    .Execute
End With

StartAndStep_Exit:
Set cmd1 = Nothing
Exit Sub

StartAndStep_Trap:
Debug.Print Err.Number, Err.Description
If Err.Number = -2147217900 Then
'If table exists, drop it
'before resuming
    strTemp = cmd1.CommandText
    cmd1.CommandText = " DROP TABLE Contacts"
    cmd1.Execute
    cmd1.CommandText = strTemp
    Resume
ElseIf Err.Number = -2147467259 Then
    MsgBox "An e-mail address failed to contain @.", _
        vbCritical, "Programming Microsoft Access Version 2002"
Else
    Debug.Print Err.Number, Err.Description
    MsgBox "Unanticipated error.  See details in Immediate window.", _
        vbCritical, "Programming Microsoft Access Version 2002"
End If

End Sub
```

Part III

User and Programmatic Interfaces

6

Forms, Controls, and Data

Applications use forms, along with reports, to present data. Forms are also a means of accepting and responding to user input. Because database application users interact with an application almost entirely through forms, form design and behavior are very important.

This chapter discusses how to use Microsoft Access forms with data and offers a general introduction to working with forms and their controls. If you have not worked with forms programmatically, take a moment to review the form samples in Chapter 1, "Introduction to VBA," before diving into this chapter. The samples in Chapter 1 demonstrate techniques for programmatically managing forms with Microsoft Visual Basic for Applications (VBA). In this chapter, you'll see many more samples that explore forms from several different perspectives.

The chapter's early samples illustrate techniques for developing and presenting application splash screens and switchboard forms. In the process, you'll get an introduction to the form's timer event and ways of using hyperlinks to invoke VBA procedures.

Next, the focus shifts to using forms with data. A progression of examples and samples demonstrate techniques building simple bound forms and linking them to programmatically controlled record sources. Particular attention is paid to how to use ADO recordsets as record sources for forms. After an introduction to using forms with record sources, the chapter switches its focus to main/subform design and data management issues. The presentation of this topic focuses on the parent-child relationship between the data behind the form. You'll learn about the relationships between main/subforms and subdatasheets for tables. The code samples demonstrate how to reference and manipulate the controls in subforms and their sub-subforms. Two additional collections of samples round out the treatment of data via forms. One of these sample collections demonstrates conditionally formatting the display of data values on forms. The other collection dwells on techniques for looking up and displaying data via Access forms.

The chapter concludes with two sections that treat programmatic issues related to form development. The first demonstrates techniques for enumerating and managing the status of forms in applications, including working with the forms in another Access database file. The second section introduces form classes. The topic gets more in-depth coverage in Chapter 9, "Class, Form, and Report Modules."

Developing solutions with forms is integral to most Access solutions. Therefore, do not expect to find every possible technique for using forms with Access in this chapter. The presentation of reports in the next chapter includes additional information that can help you build Access solutions with forms. Chapter 15, "Using Access to Build SQL Server Solutions: Part II," includes many samples of using forms with Access projects, but some of those samples bear on the use of forms with Access database files—just as many of the samples in this chapter apply to Access projects.

Using the Form *Timer* Event

The *Timer* event lets you set an event to fire at the end of an interval. In your *Timer* event procedure, you can cause anything to happen that you can program using VBA. The samples in this section introduce you to forms with two applications for this exceedingly useful event. The first is a splash form that demonstrates an application that needs to run the *Timer* event just once. The second sample highlights how to use the *Timer* event to refresh a form automatically. This second application repeatedly runs the *Timer* event, and it reconnects a computer screen with a record source so that the screen always shows the most recent data in the source.

Splash Screen Forms

One easy way to get started with forms is by creating a splash screen. A splash screen is a form that appears before another, more interactive form appears. Splash screens often state what an application does or who created it. You can easily control how long this form stays visible using the *Timer* event. Figure 6-1 shows a sample splash screen from the companion CD, which you can adapt to your own purposes.

Figure 6-1 A sample splash screen.

Creating a Splash Screen

You can start by creating a tiled background. You do so by setting two form properties while the form is open in Design view. First, you set the form's Picture property (on the Format page of the property sheet) to the path and file-name for the image. You can use a bitmap in .bmp, .ico, .dib, .wmf, or .emf format, as well as other graphic file formats. Access can also use any graphic file formats for which you have filters installed. (Rerun the Office XP Setup program if you need to install additional filters.) Images that contain gray or other muted colors work best for backgrounds because they make your foreground images and text look more prominent. Second, you change the form's Picture Tiling property to Yes. (It is No by default.)

Next you can add a foreground image by choosing Picture from the Insert menu. You can also add an Image control to the form. Either method opens the Insert Picture dialog box, where you can select an image to add. Clicking OK automatically sets the image's Picture property. Access lets you programmatically set the Picture property with VBA so that you can construct the look of a form dynamically in response to user input (such as a text box entry) or environmental factors (such as a user's security ID). You can position and size the image and use the special effects created by various Size Mode property settings. The property accepts three values: Clip, Stretch, and Zoom.

You complete the splash screen by adding one or more Label controls. You can use VBA to set properties for the Label controls at run time. This lets you dynamically format a splash screen's text. You can set a splash screen to open automatically by choosing Startup from the Tools menu and selecting the splash screen's form name in the Display Form/Page drop-down list in the Startup dialog box. You can also hide the Database window when an application opens by deselecting the Display Database Window check box in the Startup dialog box. Click OK to save your choices.

Controlling Display Duration

The following pair of event procedures displays a splash screen for 10 seconds. (To get to the VBA behind a form, right-click on the form, choose Build Event from the shortcut menu, and then select Code Builder in the Choose Builder dialog box and click OK.) The *Form_Open* event procedure sets the form's *TimerInterval* property value to 10,000. (This value is equal to 10 seconds; the interval is in milliseconds.) Notice that the *Form_Open* event procedure uses the *Me* keyword to denote the form. You could replace the first instance of *"frmSplashTimer"* with *Me.Name* in the *Form_Timer* event procedure; the *Me* naming convention is more robust because it lets you change a form's name without revising the code. Replacing the second instance of *"frmSplashTimer"* is also possible, but you must use a slightly different technique because the form to which *Me* refers is closed when the procedure reaches the second instance.

Because of the settings made in the Startup dialog box, Access opens the form when the database is opened. As the form opens, Access fires the *Open* event, which causes the *Form_Open* procedure to run. The *Form_Open* procedure sets a timer interval that causes Access to fire the *Timer* event when the interval expires. When the *Timer* event fires, Access calls the *Form_Timer* event procedure.

```
Private Sub Form_Open(Cancel As Integer)

'When form opens, wait 10 seconds before
'firing the Timer event
Me.TimerInterval = 10000

End Sub



Private Sub Form_Timer()
#Const OpenDBWindow = True

'When the timer event happens, close the form and
'then expose the Database window or
'a switchboard form
DoCmd.Close acForm, "frmSplashTimer"

#If OpenDBWindow = True Then
    DoCmd.SelectObject acForm, "frmSplashTimer", _
        True
#Else
    DoCmd.OpenForm "frmHyperlinkSwitchboard"
#End If

End Sub
```

The *Form_Timer* event procedure closes the form and opens either the Database window or a sample switchboard form. A conditional compilation constant and a *#If...Then...#Else* statement control which option the procedure selects. Use the *OpenForm* method of the *DoCmd* object to open a form. This method can take several arguments. However, if you simply want to show a form, just name the form using a string variable or string constant. Exposing a hidden Database window is a less obvious process. To accomplish this, you can select an object from the Database window and elect to show that object in the Database window. The *DoCmd* object's *SelectObject* method can accomplish this. This method takes three arguments for this purpose, listed here with the values used in our sample:

- **ObjectType**   The intrinsic constant *acForm* denotes a form object.

- **ObjectName**   Using *frmSplashTime*, the name of the splash form, ensures that the object exists in the database.

- **InDatabaseWindow**   Using True causes Access to select the object in the Database window.

> Note   To have a *Timer* event procedure for a form, you must manually enter a value in the form's *Timer Interval* property setting box on the Event tab of the form's Property dialog box. Even if you override this setting (as the preceding sample does), you need to make a setting manually. The sample form on the book's companion CD uses a value of *0*.

Automatically Requerying Forms

While the splash screen application for the *Timer* event is interesting, it falls more in the category of look and feel than data delivery. However, automatically refreshing a form or report at intervals can ensure a timely display even with inexperienced operators. Because the timer event recurs at regular intervals—namely, the interval specified by the *TimerInterval* property—you can force a form or report to requery the data source at the end of each interval. The *TimerInterval* property can assume values from 0 milliseconds through 2,147,483,647 milliseconds. Because computers with sufficient power to run Access are very inexpensive, organizations can afford to deploy them in many situations that demand constantly fresh data—for example, manufacturing and health applications.

Figure 6-2 shows two forms based on the *Shippers* table from the Northwind database. The table in the bottom window shows the addition of a new record (highlighted). The two forms at the top are the same, except that one has a *Timer* event procedure that requeries the data behind the form every 10 seconds. Therefore, that form reflects the new record count of 4. Because the form on the left has no *Timer* event, it reflects the original record count of 3.

Figure 6-2 Two forms that reveal the ability of the *Timer* event to requery the record source behind a form to show the most recent data automatically.

The code behind the form on the right appears next. Again, the sample uses two procedures. The *Open* event procedure, shown first, sets the requery interval to 10 seconds. Neither of the two event procedures in this sample close or change the display. Therefore, the *Timer* event will continue to recur at 10-second intervals until a user closes the form.

The second procedure is a *Timer* event procedure. It controls the action that occurs when the timer goes off every 10 seconds, which in this case is to requery the form's record source. This requerying allows the form on the right to reflect without manual intervention data changed from other workstations. The procedure starts by saving the primary key for the current record in *int1*. Then it turns off screen refreshing by invoking the *DoCmd* object's *Echo* method with a setting of False. After that, the procedure requeries the data source. The requery captures new additions or updates and clears away deletions from other workstations, and it moves the current record position back to the first record in the source behind the form. Using the *FindRecord* method with the saved primary key value from before the requery allows the application to restore the initial position. (If the record being viewed was deleted, the current position reverts to the top of the data source.) Setting the focus to the *ShipperID* field before invoking the *FindRecord* method allows the method to run without a special argument setting that tells the method to search only the current column.

When using the *Echo* method, be sure to restore screen updates if you turn them off. (To turn screen updates off, use a value of False with the *Echo* method.) You can restore screen updates by running the *Echo* method with a value of True.

If you fail to restore screen updates, your application's users will not be able to view any changes to the screen.

```
Private Sub Form_Open(Cancel As Integer)

'When form opens, wait 10 seconds before
'firing the Timer event
Me.TimerInterval = 10000

End Sub


Private Sub Form_Timer()
Dim int1 As Long

'Save value of primary key before requerying
int1 = Me.ShipperID

'Turn off echo and requery
DoCmd.Echo False
Me.Requery

'Move focus to primary key field and move to
'record in field that was current before requerying;
'turn echo back on
Me.ShipperID.SetFocus
DoCmd.FindRecord int1
DoCmd.Echo True

End Sub
```

Switchboard Forms

Switchboard forms are a common way to facilitate navigation among other forms in an application. Switchboard forms typically contain several command buttons that users can click to open another form. This section offers three approaches for implementing switchboard forms: using hyperlinks without any associated code, invoking function procedures in a standalone code module from hyperlinks on a form, and using VBA procedures in a module behind a form.

Navigating with Hyperlinks

Hyperlink navigation is particularly easy to construct because you do not have to write any code (although you can manage hyperlinks with VBA). Hyperlinks can act as shortcuts to database objects in an application, documents on your hard drive, files on a network, or Web pages on the Internet or an intranet. Access lets you assign hyperlinks to labels, buttons, and images.

You can set and edit hyperlink properties from a form's Design view or programmatically using VBA. Using the manual procedures for setting and editing hyperlinks is not only easier but can yield faster-loading forms because forms with hyperlinks created in Design view do not require that a module contain VBA code. To deliver this benefit, a form must have its Has Module property set to No.

> **Note**   The Hyperlink data type lets an Access application launch hyperlinks from table or query fields. While hyperlink fields are in many ways like the hyperlink properties, you use them differently. See Chapter 16, "Access Does the Web: Part I ," for coverage of using hyperlinks for Web development.

Figure 6-3 shows four forms that use a simple navigation system. The main switchboard form on the left transfers focus to one of the other three forms when the user clicks a hyperlink. Once another form has the focus, the user can return the focus to the switchboard form by clicking the hyperlink to it.

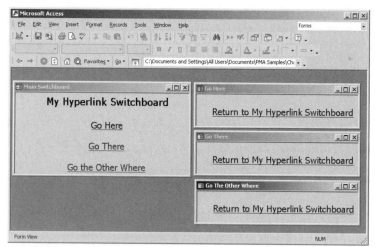

Figure 6-3 A simple hyperlink form navigation system.

You can easily introduce more than two tiers into a navigation system. Typically, each child form can return focus to its parent form. Main forms often include a way to exit the application or exit Access.

To create a hyperlink using the Label control, follow these steps:

1. Click the Build button next to the Hyperlink Address property or the Hyperlink SubAddress property on the label's property sheet.

2. In the Insert Hyperlink dialog box, select the type of object to link to from the Link To list on the left edge of the dialog box.

3. Enter the appropriate information for the type of object you selected.

4. Click OK.

> **Note**   By default, unfollowed hyperlinks in an Access session are blue and followed hyperlinks are violet. You can change these colors by choosing Options from the Tools menu, clicking on the General tab, and then clicking Web Options. Use the two list boxes in the Web Options dialog box to set the colors. The Web Options dialog box also offers a check box that lets you set whether hyperlinks are underlined. Any settings that you make in the Web Options dialog box affect new hyperlinks that you create, but they won't affect previously created hyperlinks.

Figure 6-4 shows the Insert Hyperlink dialog box for the label on the *frmGoHere* form in this chapter's sample database. The hyperlink simply transfers focus back to the switchboard form.

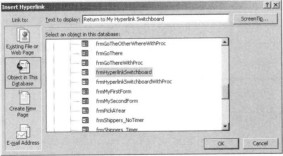

Figure 6-4 The Insert Hyperlink dialog box for the label on the *frmGoHere* form.

Running Procedures from Hyperlinks

One drawback of the navigation system we just examined is that the form stays open after the hyperlink transfers the focus from the current form to another location. Recall that one key advantage of a hyperlink navigation system is that your forms do not require modules behind them. This absence robs your application of the traditional place where code resides to close forms automatically.

You can still automatically remove forms from the screen when using hyperlink navigation. The trick is to use a function procedure in a stand-alone module or a macro. (You cannot use a sub procedure.) Many different hyperlinks can call the same function procedure. The argument that the link passes to the function procedure tells the procedure which form to close. You can invoke the function procedure from the *On Click* event setting of a hyperlink's label control. The event procedure fires before the hyperlink action transfers the focus.

Figure 6-5 shows a label control selected with a hyperlink setting. The Property dialog box below the form shows the expression for invoking the *CloseNamedForm* function procedure from the *On Click* event of the hyperlink. Notice that the name of a form appears as an argument in the function procedure call. This design lets multiple hyperlinks from different forms use the same function procedure. The following code demonstrates that it takes just one function procedure to close all the forms in a hyperlink navigation system, such as the system shown in Figure 6-3:

```
Function CloseNamedForm(frmName)

'Closes the form whose name is passed
'to it
DoCmd.Close acForm, frmName

End Function
```

Navigating with Code Behind Form

Another common way to manage switchboard navigation is with VBA code from *Click* events for command buttons. This approach offers richer exposure to Access functionality than hyperlink-based navigation without calls to function procedures

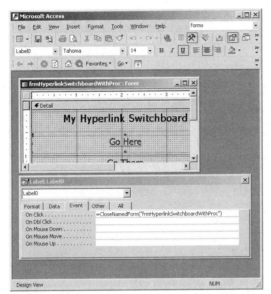

Figure 6-5 A sample *On Click* event setting that lets a hyperlink execute a function procedure (in this case, to close a form) even though the form on which the hyperlink resides has no module behind it.

because you can mix navigation functions with other events, such as the closing of a form. An event procedure also gives you greater control over multiple database objects. Hyperlink-based navigation merely transfers focus to another object, such as a form.

Figure 6-6 shows a pair of forms that use the VBA approach to navigation. This sample relies on command button *Click* events. When the user clicks one of the switchboard buttons, the code for the button's *Click* event opens the target form and closes the main switchboard. Clicking the Return To Main button on the target form closes the form and opens the main switchboard form. (The sample uses command buttons, but you can use any other type of control that lets a user generate events.)

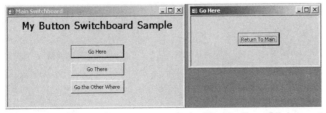

Figure 6-6 These forms use code behind button *Click* events to perform navigation.

The following pair of event procedures shows the code for the *Click* events of the two buttons in Figure 6-6. The first procedure switches control from the main switchboard form to the second form. It also closes the main form. The second procedure transfers control back to the main switchboard and then closes the second form. I used the Command Button wizard to create a first draft of each procedure; I then added a line of code to each procedure to close the appropriate form.

```
Private Sub cmdGoHere_Click()
On Error GoTo Err_cmdGoHere_Click

Dim strDocName As String

strDocName = "frmButtonGoHere"
DoCmd.OpenForm strDocName
DoCmd.Close acForm, "frmButtonSwitchboard"

Exit_cmdGoHere_Click:
Exit Sub

Err_cmdGoHere_Click:
MsgBox Err.Description
Resume Exit_cmdGoHere_Click

End Sub


Private Sub cmdReturnToMain_Click()
On Error GoTo Err_cmdReturnToMain_Click

Dim strDocName As String
Dim strLinkCriteria As String

strDocName = "frmButtonSwitchboard"
DoCmd.OpenForm strDocName
strDocName = "frmButtonGoHere"
DoCmd.Close acForm, strDocName, acSaveNo

Exit_cmdReturnToMain_Click:
Exit Sub

Err_cmdReturnToMain_Click:
MsgBox Err.Description
Resume Exit_cmdReturnToMain_Click

End Sub
```

Linking Forms to a Single Record Source

Access has always let you bind forms to data simply and easily. This is one major reason why it is a rapid application development environment. In this section, we'll look at several ways to bind forms to data. I'll start with creating a simple bound form and then move on to dynamically assigning ADO recordsets and SQL statements as form sources. Next I'll show you how to use an ADO recordset assignment to update form data. And finally, I'll cover using an ADO recordset to insert data into a form.

Creating a Simple Bound Form

To bind a form to data, you can use the AutoForm wizard. Select a table or query in the database window and click the New Object: AutoForm button on the Database toolbar. The wizard opens a new form that binds directly to the selected data source. Figure 6-7 shows a sample form based on the *Order Details* table, which is a linked table in this chapter's sample database that points to the table of the same name in the Northwind database. You can use this form for browsing, editing, adding, and deleting records in the *Order Details* table.

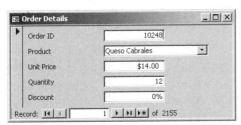

Figure 6-7 A form based on a single record source (the *Order Details* table) created by the AutoForm wizard.

Because the data source for the form's *Product* field is a lookup field in the underlying *Order Details* table, the *Product* field automatically appears as a combo box that displays product names instead of the underlying *ProductID* values. All of this functionality was provided automatically by the wizard.

If the table or query that you select as the record source for a form has a one-to-many relationship with another record source, Access 2002 automatically creates a main/subform. If your application truly calls for a table bound to a single form, you can open the form in Design view and remove the subform control. The section "Processing Main/Subforms" in this chapter takes a closer look at subforms.

Dynamically Assigning Record Sources to Forms

The ease of applying the AutoForm wizard and the flexibility of its forms are two of the reasons Access is such a popular database development package. Another reason for Access's popularity is that you can readily adapt forms created by the AutoForm wizard to any custom data source created on the fly.

Access offers two complementary techniques for adapting a wizard-generated form for use with a dynamically assigned source. First, you can set the form's Recordset property. (Access 2000 was the first version to enable developers to assign the Recordset property of its forms.) Because this book emphasizes ActiveX Data Objects (ADO), I will explain how to use an ADO recordset to create a record source behind a form. However, you can also use a traditional Data Access Objects (DAO) recordset to do this. Second, you can also use an SQL statement, which is a traditional way to dynamically specify a form's record source.

Assigning an ADO Recordset as the Source

After creating a bound form with the AutoForm wizard, you can use the form for dynamic record source assignment. Dynamically assigning record sources to forms greatly increases their flexibility. Taking advantage of this capability can reduce the size of a database and improve its load time.

There are two techniques for converting a form created by the AutoForm wizard to one that is suitable for dynamic record source assignment. First, you can clear the Record Source property setting from the form's Property dialog box. (When you view such a form without first dynamically assigning a record source to it, its text boxes contain the text "#Name?".) Second, you can leave the Record Source setting created by the AutoForm wizard. This approach uses the AutoForm Record Source property setting as a default record source. When your application programmatically assigns a record source, it overrides the default setting.

Each of the two approaches has its advantages. Leaving the form's settings undisturbed avoids a form opening with #Name? in its text boxes when no dynamic record source assignment exists. If your application does not logically have a default record source for a form, clearing the Record Source property ensures that the form will never display data unless the application specifically assigns it to the form. The samples in this section use a wizard-generated form that has its Record Source property cleared. The form is otherwise identical to the one shown in Figure 6-7.

When you dynamically assign a record source to a form, the source lasts as long as the form is open. If a user opens the form without using the application, the form will not have a dynamic record source assignment, even if it was previously opened through the application.

By dynamically assigning a record source to a form, you can use the same form for different needs within a single application. For example, a single form can show sales for different employees, date ranges, departments, products, and so on. Your application simply needs to create a recordset with the proper SQL statement for the *Open* method of an ADO recordset. Then just assign the ADO recordset to the form's *Recordset* property, and your application can display that data in the form. This assignment is only possible programmatically.

When you assign an ADO recordset with the default *CursorLocation* property setting, you create a read-only form. The form supports browsing, but users cannot add, update, or delete records through it. To enable read/write access, you must explicitly assign the *adUseClient* intrinsic constant to the *CursorLocation* property setting of a recordset for a form. The next sample we'll examine shows the syntax and behavior of a form based on the default *CursorLocation* property.

> **Note**   If you assign an ADO recordset based on a single table to a form in an Access project (as opposed to an Access database file), your form will be read/write by default. Chapter 15 extends this chapter's coverage of forms and explores topics that pertain particularly to the use of forms in Access projects.

The following code sample demonstrates the syntax for dynamically assigning a recordset to a form. After assigning the form's *Recordset* property, the code browses the form and attempts to update a field value through the form. Because the form uses the default *CursorLocation* property, the attempt to revise a field value generates a run-time error that the procedure traps.

The procedure begins by instantiating a *Connection* object, *cnn1*, and pointing it at the Northwind database. Next the procedure instantiates a recordset, *rst1*. The form's *CursorType* and *LockType* properties permit updating. (But the sample demonstrates that these settings are not sufficient to enable updating.) Then the procedure uses *cnn1* to open the *rst1* recordset based on an inner join of the *Orders* and *Order Details* tables. The recordset returns the five fields from the *Order Details* tables for all records whose *OrderDate* field value is in 1998.

After creating the recordset for the form, the focus shifts to the form. The code uses the *DoCmd* object's *OpenForm* method to open a form named *frmSimpleUnboundForm*. This form has the same layout as the one in Figure 6-7. In addition, this form has no Record Source property setting. The line after the *OpenForm* method dynamically assigns the *rst1* recordset to the form's *Recordset* property.

After executing the line that makes the *Recordset* property assignment, you have a form with a recordset that is open in Access. If you place a breakpoint at the next line, you can click the View Microsoft Access control in the Visual Basic Editor (VBE) window and see the open form.

The procedure goes on to use the form programmatically. First it invokes the *DoCmd* object's *GoToRecord* method with an argument of *acNext* to move from the first to the second record. Then the procedure returns to the initial record behind the form. This confirms the ability to browse using the form. Next the procedure modifies the value in the Quantity text box control on the form and attempts to revise the database through the form's *Refresh* method. Because the form is read-only, invoking the *Refresh* method generates a run-time error that the program traps. After presenting a message box about the form's read-only status, the code exits the procedure by passing control to *BindRst_Exit*. Let's take a look at the syntax now:

```
Sub BindRstToSimpleUnboundFormRO()
On Error GoTo BindRst_Trap
Dim cnn1 As ADODB.Connection
Dim rst1 As Recordset

'Create the connection
Set cnn1 = New ADODB.Connection
cnn1.Open "Provider=Microsoft.Jet.OLEDB.4.0;" & _
    "Data Source=C:\PMA Samples\Northwind.mdb;"

'Create recordset reference and set its properties
Set rst1 = New ADODB.Recordset
rst1.CursorType = adOpenKeyset
rst1.LockType = adLockOptimistic

'Open recordset based on orders in 1998 for
'frmSimpleUnboundForm
rst1.Open "SELECT od.OrderID, od.ProductID, od.UnitPrice, " & _
    "od.Quantity, od.Discount " & _
    "FROM [Order Details] AS od " & _
    "INNER JOIN Orders AS o " & _
    "ON od.OrderID = o.OrderID " & _
    "WHERE Year(o.OrderDate) = 1998", cnn1

'Assign ADO recordset to Recordset property of
'Forms("frmSimpleUnboundForm")
DoCmd.OpenForm "frmSimpleUnboundForm"
Set Application.Forms("frmSimpleUnboundForm").Recordset = rst1
```

```
'Browse the form by moving to the next record
'and then back again
DoCmd.GoToRecord , , acNext
DoCmd.GoToRecord , , acPrevious

'Attempt to modify a field in the form
Forms("frmSimpleUnboundForm").Quantity = 2000
Forms("frmSimpleUnboundForm").Refresh

BindRst_Exit:
rst1.Close
cnn1.Close
Set rst1 = Nothing
Set cnn1 = Nothing
Exit Sub

BindRst_Trap:
If Err.Number = -2147352567 Then
    MsgBox "The form is open in read-only mode. " & _
        "Change how you assign the source to " & _
        "the form.", vbCritical, _
        "Programming Microsoft Access Version 2002"
    Resume BindRst_Exit
Else
    Debug.Print Err.Number, Err.Description
    MsgBox "Program aborted for unanticipated reasons.", _
        vbCritical, "Programming Microsoft Access Version 2002"
End If

End Sub
```

Assigning an SQL Statement as the Source

You can use VBA to assign an SQL string as a record source for a form through its *RecordSource* property. The form's *RecordSource* property corresponds to the Record Source property on the form's Properties sheet. Therefore, you can set the *RecordSource* property programmatically or manually. When you set the property programmatically, it overrides any manual setting. When you make the assignment via VBA as described, the setting lasts only until you close the form.

> **Note**   VBA allows you to set a form's *RecordSource* property in Design view. When you do this, the assignment persists beyond the current form session. You cannot assign an ADO recordset to a form in Design view. Any setting to a form's *Recordset* property will always be transient.

Using an SQL string requires that you get the SQL syntax right for the database server that you are using. This approach does not allow you to take advantage of saved queries in other Access database files or of stored procedures in Microsoft SQL Server and other client/server databases. However, using the *Recordset* property to assign the record source for a form does. When you use an SQL string to designate a record source for a form, the database server must always compile the SQL string. When you set a form's *Recordset* property to an ADO recordset, you automatically invoke a previously compiled SQL string.

The following sample demonstrates the syntax for assigning an SQL string to a form. It uses the same SQL string from the preceding sample. After assigning an SQL string to the form's *RecordSource* property, the sample reopens the form in Form view and browses the record source through the form. In addition, it updates the record source via the form, and closes the form without saving the assignment of the SQL string to the form. The remainder of the sample confirms the modification of the record source using an ADO recordset. Then it restores the updated field value to its original value.

This sample starts by immediately opening the form with the *DoCmd* object's *OpenForm* method. This method opens a form in Normal view unless you use an intrinsic constant to specify a different view. For example, to open a form in Design view, you use this syntax:

```
DoCmd.OpenForm "frmSimpleUnboundForm", acDesign
```

Recall that using Design view enables an application to persist changes to the *RecordSource* property beyond the current form session.

The sample's next statement shows the syntax for assigning an SQL string to a form's *RecordSource* property. Notice this approach uses just two lines of code to open a form with a dynamically assigned record source.

After assigning the record source using an SQL string, you can browse records and add, update, and delete them through the form. The next two lines of code demonstrate browsing by moving forward and backward one record. Next the sample revises the value in the Quantity control to 2000 for the form's first record and invokes the form's *Refresh* method. This does not generate an error because the form's record source is set to an SQL string. Before updating the value in the Quantity text box, the sample saves the original Quantity value as well as the values in the OrderID and ProductID text boxes. These values are necessary for restoring the first record to its original state.

The remainder of the sample demonstrates how to use ADO to confirm that an updated Quantity value exists and to restore that value. First, the sample instantiates a connection and points it at the Northwind database. Next it instantiates *rst1*, a recordset that is suitable for seeking the updated record. The recordset explicitly sets its *Index* property to the index named *PrimaryKey* for the *Order*

Details table. This index has two fields: *OrderID* and *ProductID*. The code does not alter the default setting for *CursorLocation*, which is *adUseServer*. In addition, the recordset's *Open* method specifies *adCmdTableDirection* for its *Options* argument. After taking these steps, the procedure invokes the *Seek* method for *rst1* with the *OrderID* and *ProductID* values previously saved in the *int2* and *int3* variables.

Once the procedure finds the altered record, it prints the current record to the Immediate window. The fourth recordset field will be 2000. This is the record's *Quantity* field. Next the procedure updates the altered *Quantity* field by assigning to it the saved original value (*int1*). This restores the field to the value it had before the sample updated the field through the form. After restoring the value, the procedure again prints the record to the Immediate window. The fourth field now shows its initial value of *20*.

```
Sub BindSQLToSimpleUnboundForm()
Dim int1 As Integer
Dim int2 As Long
Dim int3 As Long
Dim cnn1 As ADODB.Connection
Dim rst1 As Recordset

'Assign SQL to Recordsource property of
'Forms("frmSimpleUnboundForm")
DoCmd.OpenForm "frmSimpleUnboundForm"
Forms("frmSimpleUnboundForm").RecordSource = _
    "SELECT od.OrderID, od.ProductID, " & _
    "od.UnitPrice, od.Quantity, od.Discount " & _
    "FROM [Order Details] AS od " & _
    "INNER JOIN Orders AS o " & _
    "ON od.OrderID = o.OrderID " & _
    "WHERE Year(o.OrderDate) = 1998"

'Browse the form by moving to the next record
'and then back again
DoCmd.OpenForm "frmSimpleUnboundForm", acNormal
DoCmd.GoToRecord , , acNext
DoCmd.GoToRecord , , acPrevious

'Save original Quantity field value along with primary
'key values (OrderID and ProductID) before updating
'the Quantity field through the form.
'Close form when done.
int1 = Forms("frmSimpleUnboundForm").Quantity
int2 = Forms("frmSimpleUnboundForm").OrderID
int3 = Forms("frmSimpleUnboundForm").ProductID
```

(continued)

```
Forms("frmSimpleUnboundForm").Quantity = 2000
Forms("frmSimpleUnboundForm").Refresh
DoCmd.Close acForm, "frmSimpleUnboundForm"
DoCmd.Close acForm, "frmSimpleUnboundForm", acSaveNo

'Create the connection
Set cnn1 = New ADODB.Connection
cnn1.Open "Provider=Microsoft.Jet.OLEDB.4.0;" & _
    "Data Source=C:\PMA Samples\Northwind.mdb;"

'Create recordset reference and set its properties
Set rst1 = New ADODB.Recordset
With rst1
    .Index = "PrimaryKey"
    .CursorType = adOpenKeyset
    .LockType = adLockOptimistic
    .Open "Order Details", cnn1, , , adCmdTableDirect
    .Seek Array(int2, int3)
End With

'Print record with revised Quantity field
Debug.Print rst1(0), rst1(1), rst1(2), rst1(3), rst1(4)

'Restore Quantity field value and print again
rst1(3) = int1
rst1.Update
Debug.Print rst1(0), rst1(1), rst1(2), rst1(3), rst1(4)

'Clean up objects
rst1.Close
cnn1.Close
Set rst1 = Nothing
Set cnn1 = Nothing

End Sub
```

Updating Form Data with an ADO Recordset Assignment

As I just demonstrated, you can routinely update form data when you use an SQL string to designate the form's record source. When you assign an ADO recordset to a form's *Recordset* property with the default *CursorLocation* setting, users cannot update the data with the form. For some applications, the easy availability of read-only forms is an advantage. You can make forms read-only when you assign their record source with an SQL string, but this requires additional property settings. (For example, see the form's *AllowEdits*, *AllowDeletions*, *AllowAdditions*, and *DataEntry* property descriptions in Access Help.)

If you want to use ADO to create forms that permit users to edit data, you simply need to set the source recordset's *CursorLocation* property to *adUseClient*. Making this simple adjustment before assigning a recordset to a form will allow users to update the data in a form based on a single table. The next sample demonstrates this feature.

The sample begins by creating a connection to the Northwind database. Then it instantiates a recordset that uses the connection. However, before opening the recordset for the SQL string (the same one used in the preceding two samples), the code sets the *CursorLocation* property to *adUseClient*. This simple step makes the form's control values updateable.

The remainder of the sample assigns the recordset to a form's *Recordset* property and updates the Quantity text box value for the first record to 2000. After closing the form, the sample prints the updated record to the Immediate window before restoring the *Quantity* field in the recordset to its original value. Then the code prints the record again after restoring the field's value.

```
Sub BindRstToSimpleUnboundFormRWUpdate()
Dim cnn1 As ADODB.Connection
Dim rst1 As Recordset
Dim int1 As Integer

'Create the connection
Set cnn1 = New ADODB.Connection
cnn1.Open "Provider=Microsoft.Jet.OLEDB.4.0;" & _
    "Data Source=C:\PMA Samples\Northwind.mdb;"

'Create recordset reference and set its properties
'to permit read/write access to recordset
Set rst1 = New ADODB.Recordset
rst1.CursorType = adOpenKeyset
rst1.LockType = adLockOptimistic
rst1.CursorLocation = adUseClient

'Open recordset based on orders in 1998 for
'frmSimpleUnboundForm
rst1.Open "SELECT od.OrderID, od.ProductID, od.UnitPrice, " & _
    "od.Quantity, od.Discount " & _
    "FROM [Order Details] AS od " & _
    "INNER JOIN Orders AS o " & _
    "ON od.OrderID = o.OrderID " & _
    "WHERE Year(o.OrderDate) = 1998", cnn1

'Assign ADO recordset to Recordset property of
'Forms("frmSimpleUnboundForm")
DoCmd.OpenForm "frmSimpleUnboundForm"
Set Application.Forms("frmSimpleUnboundForm").Recordset = rst1
```

(continued)

```
'Modify Quantity field through the form, but
'save the original value first
int1 = Forms("frmSimpleUnboundForm").Quantity
Forms("frmSimpleUnboundForm").Quantity = 2000
Forms("frmSimpleUnboundForm").Refresh
DoCmd.Close acForm, "frmSimpleUnboundForm"

'Print record with revised Quantity field
Debug.Print rst1(0), rst1(1), rst1(2), rst1(3), rst1(4)

'Restore Quantity field value and print again
rst1(3) = int1
rst1.Update
Debug.Print rst1(0), rst1(1), rst1(2), rst1(3), rst1(4)

'Clean up objects
rst1.Close
cnn1.Close
Set rst1 = Nothing
Set cnn1 = Nothing

End Sub
```

Inserting Data Using a Form Based on an ADO Recordset

The *CursorLocation* setting that you assign to a form's *Recordset* property can determine whether the form is read-only or updateable. The same setting also determines whether users can insert new records with a form. The process of setting up a form so that users can read from it and write to it is the same whether you update existing values or add new ones programmatically. However, the process of actually inserting or deleting a record is different than that of updating a record.

The next sample sets up a form for read/write access and demonstrates how to insert and delete a record through the form. Even though users might manually perform some of these steps, it's important to know how to add a record programmatically through a form.

After creating the *rst1* recordset for the form, the sample opens the form the same way the preceding sample opened a form. However, the code next assigns the open form, *frmSimpleUnboundForm*, to the *frm1* object reference. The code uses this reference as a pointer to the open form. For example, the line after the form reference assignment sets the *rst1* recordset to the *Recordset* property of *frm1*. Then the procedure saves the *OrderID* field value for the first record to the *int1* variable.

The procedure launches the process of adding a new record by invoking the *DoCmd* object's *GoToRecord* command with an *acNewRec* argument. This displays a blank form and prepares Access to insert a new record. Inserting a new record is a two-step process. First the code assigns values to the form fields. The sample adds a new line item for the order using the first *OrderID* in the *rst1* recordset, which is the value in *int1*. As the procedure adds a new record, it saves the *ProductID* for the new record. (The sample will use these saved values to remove the new records later.) Then the sample invokes the form's *Requery* method to insert the form's control values into the recordset behind the form. After inserting the record, the procedure closes the form.

> **Note**   After invoking the *GoToRecord* method with the *acNewRec* argument, you do not have to use the *Requery* method to enter a new record. Closing the record without invoking the *Requery* method, or invoking the *Refresh* method instead of the *Requery* method, will also add a new record.

The remainder of the sample finds the newly added record and removes it from the recordset. The code uses the *Seek* method to search for all records matching the *OrderID* to which the form added a record. Then the code loops through the line items for the *OrderID* until it discovers the one with a *ProductID* equal to the *ProductID* on the new line item. When the sample discovers the line item with a *ProductID* that matches the newly added record, it deletes the record and exits the loop.

```
Sub BindRstToSimpleUnboundFormRWInsert()
Dim cnn1 As ADODB.Connection
Dim rst1 As Recordset
Dim frm1 As Form
Dim int1 As Long
Dim int2 As Long

'Create the connection
Set cnn1 = New ADODB.Connection
cnn1.Open "Provider=Microsoft.Jet.OLEDB.4.0;" & _
    "Data Source=C:\PMA Samples\Northwind.mdb;"
```

(continued)

```
'Create recordset reference and set its properties
'to permit read/write access to recordset
Set rst1 = New ADODB.Recordset
rst1.CursorType = adOpenKeyset
rst1.LockType = adLockOptimistic
rst1.CursorLocation = adUseClient

'Open recordset based on orders in 1998 for
'frmSimpleUnboundForm
rst1.Open "SELECT od.OrderID, od.ProductID, od.UnitPrice, " & _
    "od.Quantity, od.Discount " & _
    "FROM [Order Details] AS od " & _
    "INNER JOIN Orders AS o " & _
    "ON od.OrderID = o.OrderID " & _
    "WHERE Year(o.OrderDate) = 1998", cnn1

'Assign ADO recordset to Recordset property of
'Forms("frmSimpleUnboundForm")
DoCmd.OpenForm "frmSimpleUnboundForm"
Set frm1 = Forms("frmSimpleUnboundForm")
Set frm1.Recordset = rst1

'Add a new record through the form for the current OrderID
int1 = frm1.OrderID
DoCmd.GoToRecord , , acNewRec
With frm1
    .OrderID = int1
    .ProductID = 1
    int2 = .ProductID
    .Quantity = 1
    .UnitPrice = 1
    .Discount = 0
    .Requery
End With
DoCmd.Close acForm, frm1.Name

'Create recordset reference and set its properties so
'you can seek the records for the OrderID to which you
'added a record
Set rst1 = New ADODB.Recordset
With rst1
    .Index = "OrderID"
    .CursorType = adOpenKeyset
    .LockType = adLockOptimistic
    .Open "Order Details", cnn1, , , adCmdTableDirect
    .Seek int1
End With
```

```
'Loop through line items for OrderID to which you
'previously added a record; delete the record
'when you find it
Do Until rst1(0) <> int1
    If rst1(1) = int2 Then
'Delete the record because we do not want to change
'the Northwind database, but only show that we can
        rst1.Delete
        Exit Do
    End If
    rst1.MoveNext
Loop

'Clean up objects
rst1.Close
cnn1.Close
Set rst1 = Nothing
Set cnn1 = Nothing

End Sub
```

Processing Main/Subforms

A main/subform allows you to display a parent-child relationship between two record sources on a single form. The feature that makes the main/subform especially powerful is the way it links its two parts: the main form and the subform. The main/subform restricts the entries on the subform to just those records that match the record on the main form. Therefore, the main/subform shows just the child records on the subform of the main form's current parent record.

Any pair of tables in a one-to-many relationship is a candidate for display via a main/subform. In relational database terms, the table on the one side of the relationship is the parent, and the table on the many side is the child. Access relies on the matching field values between the parent and child record sources to display just the child records that correspond to the current parent record.

The Access user interface offers at least two ways to create main/subforms. First, the AutoForm wizard can automatically create a main/subform for any table that has a one-to-many relationship with another table. With this approach, you do not need a standalone form for the child record source. Access displays the Datasheet view of the child record source within the main form for the parent record source. Second, you can create separate forms for the child and parent record sources. Then you can drag the form for the child record source from the Database window into the Design view of the form for the parent record source.

As long as the parent and child record sources have a relationship defined in the Relationship window (or a subdatasheet relationship, which we'll discuss in a moment), Access will automatically match the child records to the parent records with related tables or tables with subdatasheet specifications. Otherwise, Access pops up a dialog box that prompts you for the matching fields in the parent and child record sources.

Subdatasheets

Subdatasheets provide a way to display parent-child relationships from a table's Datasheet view, regardless of whether a one-to-many relationship exists between record sources. Main/subforms interact with and build on Access subdatasheet technology. Figure 6-8 shows subdatasheets for the *Order Details* table within the *Orders* table. The screen shot expands the subdatasheets for orders 10248 and 10249. The other orders have their subdatasheet collapsed. Clicking the plus sign (+) next to an *OrderID* field with a collapsed subdatasheet expands the sub-datasheet. To close an expanded subdatasheet, just click the minus sign (−) next to an *OrderID* field value.

> **Note**   You can use the Format-Subdatasheet menu from the Datasheet view of a parent record source to manage the default display of sub-datasheets. By default, Access collapses all subdatasheets. You can ex-pand all subdatasheets by choosing Format-Subdatasheet-Expand All. You can restore the default display rule for subdatasheets by choosing Format-Subdatasheet-Collapse All.

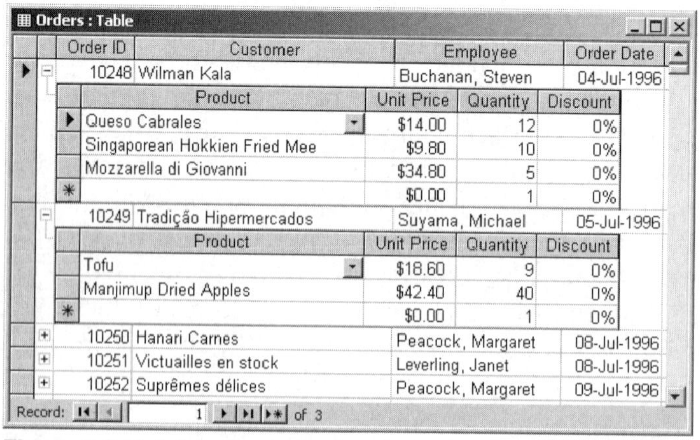

Figure 6-8 Subdatasheets for the *Order Details* table within the *Orders* table.

Access automatically builds subdatasheets for tables that share relationships in the Relationships window. If no prespecified relationship exists between two record sources, you can still create a subdatasheet for a child record source within its parent. Simply open the parent record source in Datasheet view and choose Insert-Subdatasheet from the menu. Then choose the table or query from the current database that you want as a child record source. If the child record source has one or more fields with names that match those in the parent source, Access automatically suggests matching the two record sources on these fields. If no fields in the parent and child record sources have the same names, you can use the combo boxes at the bottom of the Insert Subdatasheet dialog box to specify the fields for matching child records to parent records. Use a semicolon delimiter to separate fields when the record sources contain more than one matching field.

> **Note** You can delete a subdatasheet by choosing the Format-Subdatasheet-Remove command from the Datasheet view menu for the parent record source. This does not delete the child resource—just its subdatasheet relationship to the parent record source. Although Access inherits subdatasheets for linked tables, you cannot remove a subdata-sheet from a linked table. Instead, open the Access database file with the local table and remove the subdatasheet from there.

Creating Main/Subforms

When specifying record sources for main/subforms, you will often want to designate queries as record sources. This makes it easy to select columns and join tables to provide main or subform fields. After deciding on your sources for the forms, you can build the query graphically or programmatically. (See Chapter 5, "Jet SQL, the ADOX Library, and Queries," for code samples that illustrate how to programmatically add queries to a database.)

My subform sample has two levels of subforms. The main form has a subform that, in turn, has a subform of its own. The sample relies on three SQL statements. The outer query has the name *MyOrders*; this query is the record source for the main form. The query nested within *MyOrders* has the name *MyOrderDetails*; this query is the record source for the subform on the main form. The lowest-level query is *MyProducts*; this is the record source for the subform of the subform on the main form. The SQL statement for the main form (*frmMyOrders*) is on the following page.

```
SELECT Orders.OrderID, Orders.CustomerID, Orders.EmployeeID,
    Orders.OrderDate, Orders.RequiredDate, Orders.ShippedDate,
    Orders.ShipVia, Orders.Freight, Orders.ShipName,
    Orders.ShipAddress, Orders.ShipCity, Orders.ShipRegion,
    Orders.ShipPostalCode, Orders.ShipCountry
FROM Orders
```

The SQL statement for the subform (*frmMyOrderDetails*) of the main form follows:

```
SELECT [Order Details].OrderID, [Order Details].ProductID,
    [Order Details].UnitPrice, [Order Details].Quantity,
    [Order Details].Discount
FROM [Order Details]
```

The following is the SQL statement for the subform to the subform (*frmMyProducts*):

```
SELECT Products.ProductID, Products.UnitsInStock,
    Suppliers.CompanyName, Suppliers.ContactName,
    Suppliers.Phone
FROM Suppliers INNER JOIN Products
ON Suppliers.SupplierID = Products.SupplierID
```

These queries inherit the relationships between data sources in the Northwind database. Therefore, as you create the forms with the AutoForm wizard, the wizard automatically builds in the subforms. Because these automatically generated subforms do not depend on any custom record source specifications in custom queries, you delete the subform controls within forms so that you can add subforms with custom records source specifications.

After preparing the individual main and subforms, I start combining them. First, I open *frmMyOrderDetails* in Design view and drag *frmMyProducts* from the Database window. After saving and closing the new *frmOrderDetails* form, I open the *frmMyOrders* form in Design view. Then I drag the modified *frmOrderDetails* form from the Database window.

After completing the nesting layout issues, you still have a couple more issues to resolve. First, you change the Default View property for the *frmMyProducts* and *frmMyOrderDetails* forms to Datasheet view. This Default View adjustment enables the subforms to appear automatically as datasheets. Second, you assign appropriate Link Child Fields and Link Master Fields property settings for the subform control in the main form and the subform control in the subform of the main form. You can do this by opening the subform control's Properties dialog box to the appropriate tab. Select the Data tab of the subform control's Properties dialog box to display boxes for setting the Link Child Fields and Link Master Fields properties. Clicking the Build button to the right of either property displays a dialog box that helps you select fields from the record sources for the main and subforms.

In our example, you would click the *MyProducts* subform control in the *MyOrderDetails* subform. Then you would designate the *ProductID* for the Link Child Fields and Link Master Fields settings. Next you would click the *MyOrderDetails* subform control on the *frmMyOrders* form and specify *OrderID* for matching the subform records with its main form.

Figure 6-9 shows the sample form containing a subform within a subform. The main form provides details from the *MyOrders* record source. Its subform shows details from the *MyOrderDetails* record source. Notice that all the records on the subform have an *OrderID* value that matches the one on the main form. Finally, the subdatasheet within the subform displays data from the *MyProducts* record source. Again, the *ProductID* value on the subdatasheet corresponds to the subform *Product* field. However, recall that the *ProductID* field in the original Northwind *Order Details* table is a lookup field that shows the *Product* name instead of the *ProductID* value, and the *ProductID* field has a caption that shows *Product* instead of *ProductID* for a control based on the field.

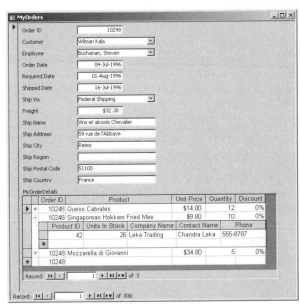

Figure 6-9 A main/subform that has a subform within a subform that appears as a subdatasheet.

Programmatically Referencing Main and SubForm Controls

When programmatically referencing subform controls, you need to keep a couple of things in mind. First, the subform is a control on the main form. This means you cannot refer to the subform controls directly. Instead, you must reference the *Form* property of the subform control. Then you can reference the subform controls in the standard way. See Chapter 1 for an introduction to using VBA to work with controls on forms. Second, when dealing with subforms with multiple levels of nesting, you can selectively choose to deal with only the levels your application requires. Therefore, if you have a set of forms with three levels (main, subform within main, and subform within subform within main), you can deal with just the top two levels if that's all your application requires.

The following sample demonstrates the syntax for processing the main/subform shown in Figure 6-9. Although the form includes two levels of subforms, this sample processes just the main form and its subform. (The code sample beginning on page 349 deals with the three levels of forms simultaneously.) The sample you're about to see begins by demonstrating a couple of syntax conventions for referencing subform control values. Next it contrasts conventions that expose the record sources of the main form and the subform. Then the code illustrates how to count the total number of controls on the main and subforms. The sample concludes by enumerating the first 10 records on the main form and printing the subform records for each.

The procedure in this code sample starts by opening the *frmMyOrders* form, the main form in the example. After opening this form so that it becomes a member of the *Forms* collection, the sample sets a form object reference, *frm1*, to the *frmMyOrders* form. Then it sets a control reference, *ctl1*, to the main form's subform control. This control has the name MyOrderDetails—the same name as the record source behind the subform. The next two lines of code demonstrate two different programming styles for referencing the OrderID text box control on the subform. The style that explicitly invokes the *Form* property of the subform control is very robust; you will often need to reference subform objects and properties with this syntax. In addition, the syntax makes it clear that the subform is a control on the main form that has a *Form* property.

The next two blocks of code demonstrate the similarity between referencing properties and collections for the main and subforms. The *RecordSource* property represents an SQL string or an object name representing the data behind the form. Because queries exist for both the main and subforms, the references to their record sources return the query names. Notice that *ctl1.Form* represents a form (the subform) in the same way that *frm1* represents the main form. A form's *Controls* collection contains all the controls on a form. In addition to text boxes and combo boxes, controls can include labels, lines, and subform controls. The *Count* property of the *Controls* collections of the main and subforms returns the count of all the controls—not just those that display data.

Perhaps the most interesting segment of the sample is the portion that contains three nested loops. The outer loop passes through the first 10 records on the main form. The middle loop iterates through the subform records for the current main form record. The inner loop searches the subform controls for either text box or combo box controls. When the inner loop finds either type of control, the sample prints a short message stating the name of the control and its current value.

The syntax in these three loops reinforces some familiar concepts and introduces some new ones. Notice that the *Form* property of the subform control exhibits a *Recordset* object. The procedure uses the *RecordCount* property of this object to loop as many times as there are subform records for a main form record. The procedure also invokes the *MoveNext* method of the subform's *Recordset* object to navigate from the first subform record through the last. Within a subform record, the procedure iterates through the *Controls* collection of the subform. The *TypeOf* function ascertains whether the current control is either a text box or a combo box. Let's take a look at the syntax now:

```
Sub SyntaxForSubForms()
Dim frm1 As Form
Dim ctl1 As Control
Dim ctl2 As Control
Dim int1 As Integer
Dim int2 As Integer

'Open a main/subform
DoCmd.OpenForm "frmMyOrders"

'Assign pointers for main form and subform
'control; MyOrderDetails is the name of the
'subform control on the frmMyOrders main form
Set frm1 = Forms("frmMyOrders")
Set ctl1 = frm1.MyOrderDetails

'Two different ways to print the OrderID control value
'on the subform
Debug.Print ctl1!OrderID
Debug.Print ctl1.Form.Controls("OrderID")
Debug.Print

'Print the record source settings for the main form
'and the subform
Debug.Print frm1.RecordSource
Debug.Print ctl1.Form.RecordSource
Debug.Print

'Print the number of controls on the main and subforms
Debug.Print frm1.Controls.Count & _
    " controls are on the main form."
Debug.Print ctl1.Form.Controls.Count & _
    " controls are on the subform."
Debug.Print
```

(continued)

```
'Move to the form's first record, and loop through the
'next 10 main form records and the subform records
'corresponding to each main record; within each subform
'record, loop through the controls on the subform
DoCmd.GoToRecord , , acFirst
For int1 = 1 To 10
    Debug.Print vbCrLf & "Data for record " & int1 & "."
    For int2 = 0 To ctl1.Form.Recordset.RecordCount - 1
        For Each ctl2 In ctl1.Form.Controls
            If TypeOf ctl2 Is TextBox Then
                Debug.Print String(5, " ") & ctl2.Name & _
                " is a text box that equals " & ctl2 & "."
            ElseIf TypeOf ctl2 Is ComboBox Then
                Debug.Print String(5, " ") & ctl2.Name & _
                " is a combo box that equals " & ctl2 & "."
            End If
        Next ctl2
        ctl1.Form.Recordset.MoveNext
        Debug.Print String(5, "-")
    Next int2
    DoCmd.GoToRecord , , acNext
Next int1
DoCmd.Close acForm, "frmMyOrders"

'Clean up objects
Set ctl1 = Nothing
Set frm1 = Nothing

End Sub
```

Programming a Subform's Subdatasheet Controls

This next sample builds on the previous one by adding another form level. Happily, adding another level of subform does not substantially change how you programmatically access controls. This section demonstrates how to access the subdatasheet of a subform on a main form. You still have to refer to the *Form* property of the subform control on the main form. In addition, you need to use this same referencing scheme for the subform control on the subform. This second reference provides a path to subdatasheet values.

There is another critical trick for accessing the control values in a subdatasheet for a subform: the subdatasheet must be open. You do this by setting the main form's subform *SubdatasheetExpanded* property to True. Without this step, references to subdatasheet control values can generate a run-time error. Although this won't always happen, keep in mind that it's good practice to set the *SubdatasheetExpanded* property to True whenever your code needs access to the controls on the subdatasheet of a subform.

In this sample, at the subdatasheet level the code merely prints the values of the subdatasheet row. The subdatasheet row specifies the additional detail, such as on-hand inventory or supplier name and contact information for the product in an individual line item of an order. See Figure 6-9 for a sample of the data that is available in the subdatasheet.

The code sample begins by opening the *frmMyOrders* form and creating three object references, which simplify the expressions throughout the procedure. The first object reference, *frm1*, points at the main form. The second reference, *ctl1*, points at the subform control on the main form, and the third reference, *ctl3*, points at the subdatasheet on the subform.

The next two blocks of code print the *RecordSource* property settings for the main form, its subform, and the subdatasheet on the subform. Notice that the code sets the *SubdatasheetExpanded* property to True before attempting to reference the subdatasheet. Next the procedure illustrates the syntax for counting the controls on the main form and the two subforms nested successively below it.

The next block repeats the code for enumerating the subform control values for each record on the main form. In addition, this sample accesses the control values on the subdatasheet. This provides the additional product detail described a moment ago.

The loop for the subform nested within a subform is less complicated than the loop for a subform on the main form. There are several reasons for this. Only one subdatasheet row exists per subform record. All the controls with data on the nested subform are text boxes. The program follows:

```
Sub SyntaxForSubDatasheetOnSubForm()
Dim frm1 As Form
Dim ctl1 As Control
Dim ctl2 As Control
Dim ctl3 As Control
Dim ctl4 As Control
Dim int1 As Integer
Dim int2 As Integer

'Open a main/subform
DoCmd.OpenForm "frmMyOrders"

'Assign pointers for main form and subform
'control
Set frm1 = Forms("frmMyOrders")
Set ctl1 = frm1.MyOrderDetails
Set ctl3 = ctl1.Form.MyProducts
```

(continued)

```
'Print the record source settings for
'the main form, the subform, and the
'expanded subdatasheet of the subform
Debug.Print frm1.RecordSource
Debug.Print ctl1.Form.RecordSource
ctl1.Form.SubdatasheetExpanded = True
Debug.Print ctl3.Form.RecordSource

Debug.Print

'Print the number of controls on the main and subforms
Debug.Print frm1.Controls.Count  & _
    " controls are on the main form."
Debug.Print ctl1.Form.Controls.Count & _
    " controls are on the subform."
Debug.Print ctl3.Form.Controls.Count & _
    " controls are on the subdatasheet."

'Move to the form's first record, and loop through the
'next 5 main form records and the subform records
'corresponding to each main record; within each subform
'record, loop through the controls on the subform
DoCmd.GoToRecord , , acFirst
For int1 = 1 To 5
    Debug.Print vbCrLf & "Data for record " & int1 & "."
    For int2 = 0 To ctl1.Form.Recordset.RecordCount - 1
        For Each ctl2 In ctl1.Form.Controls
            If TypeOf ctl2 Is TextBox Then
                Debug.Print String(5, " ") & ctl2.Name & _
                    " is a text box that equals " & ctl2 & "."
            ElseIf TypeOf ctl2 Is ComboBox Then
                Debug.Print String(5, " ") & ctl2.Name & _
                    " is a combo box that equals " & ctl2 & "."
            End If
        Next ctl2
'Loop through the controls on the subdatasheet
'returning just text boxes and their values
        For Each ctl4 In ctl3.Form.Controls
            If TypeOf ctl4 Is TextBox Then
                Debug.Print String(10, " ") & ctl4.Name & _
                    " is a text box that equals " & ctl4 & "."
            End If
        Next ctl4
        ctl1.Form.Recordset.MoveNext
        Debug.Print String(5, "-")
    Next int2
    DoCmd.GoToRecord , , acNext
Next int1
DoCmd.Close acForm, "MyOrdersMainSub"
```

```
'Clean up objects
Set ctl1 = Nothing
Set ctl3 = Nothing
Set frm1 = Nothing

End Sub
```

Figure 6-10 shows an excerpt from the output of this program. Notice that the output starts by listing the query names for the forms. Next it reports a count of the controls on each form. The last information from the Immediate window displays the subform record values along with the subdatasheet values for that subform record indented to the right. The sample shows the data for two order line items that correspond to the first record in the *Orders* table.

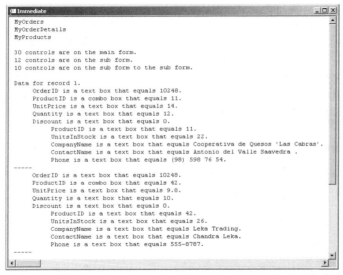

Figure 6-10 An excerpt of output from the *SyntaxForSubDataSheetOnSubForm* procedure.

Programmatically Inserting Data into a Subform Record

With a good grasp of the syntax for working with controls on subforms and inserting records into forms, you can readily insert records into subforms based on ADO recordsets. The code sample in this section demonstrates one way to do this.

The sample's first task is to create a recordset for the main form. The SQL string for the *rst1* recordset extracts records from the *Orders* table if their *Order-Date* field value is in 1998.

I continue using the *frmMyOrders* main/subform. The sample opens this form and assigns the *rst1* recordset to the form's *Recordset* property. This restricts the entries for the subform to OrderIDs with an *OrderDate* that occurs in 1998. The block of code opening the sample also includes an object reference assignment for *ctl1*, which represents the subform control on *frmMyOrders*, namely the *frmMyOrderDetails* subform.

Before creating a new record, the sample saves the *OrderID* value for the main form. This *OrderID* value is the first order in 1998. (The *OrderID* value happens to be 10808.) The sample saves this value in *int1*. Then the procedure invokes the *DoCmd* object's *GoToRecord* method with an *acNewRec* argument. This creates a blank form for data entry. Next the sample populates the controls in the subform inside a loop. Notice that we save the *ProductID* field value in *int2*. After passing through all the subform controls, the procedure closes the form. This action commits the new record to the form's record source.

The remainder of the sample removes the newly added record. This sample merely serves to demonstrate adding a record through the form—we do not actually want to change the standard Northwind table. The procedure invokes the *Seek* method to find those records from the *Order Details* table that match the value in *int1* (10808). Then it loops through these records to locate the one with the *ProductID* value for the newly added record. When the code finds the newly added record, it invokes the *Delete* method to remove the record.

```
Sub BindRstToSimpleMainSubFormRWInsert()
Dim cnn1 As ADODB.Connection
Dim rst1 As ADODB.Recordset
Dim frm1 As Form
Dim ctl1 As Control
Dim ctl2 As Control
Dim int1 As Long
Dim int2 As Long

'Create the connection
Set cnn1 = New ADODB.Connection
cnn1.Open "Provider=Microsoft.Jet.OLEDB.4.0;" & _
    "Data Source=C:\PMA Samples\Northwind.mdb;"

'Create recordset reference and set its properties
'to permit read/write access to recordset
Set rst1 = New ADODB.Recordset
rst1.CursorType = adOpenKeyset
rst1.LockType = adLockOptimistic
rst1.CursorLocation = adUseClient
```

```
'Open recordset based on orders in 1998 for
'frmSimpleUnboundForm
rst1.Open "SELECT * FROM Orders o " & _
    "WHERE Year(o.OrderDate) = 1998", cnn1

'Open a main/subform, assign pointers for main
'form and subform control, and assign recordset
'to the main form's Recordset property
DoCmd.OpenForm "frmMyOrders"
Set frm1 = Forms("frmMyOrders")
Set ctl1 = frm1.MyOrderDetails
Set frm1.Recordset = rst1

'Add a new record through the subform to the current OrderID
'value on the main form
int1 = frm1.OrderID
DoCmd.GoToRecord , , acNewRec
For Each ctl2 In ctl1.Form.Controls
    If TypeOf ctl2 Is TextBox Or TypeOf ctl2 Is ComboBox Then
        Select Case ctl2.Name
            Case "OrderID"
                ctl2.Value = int1
            Case "ProductID"
                ctl2.Value = 1
                int2 = ctl2.Value
            Case "Quantity"
                ctl2.Value = 1
            Case "UnitPrice"
                ctl2.Value = 1
            Case "Discount"
                ctl2.Value = 0
            Case Else
                MsgBox "Error on Insert."
                Exit Sub
        End Select
    End If
Next ctl2
DoCmd.Close acForm, frm1.Name

'Create recordset reference and set its properties so that
'you can seek the records for the OrderID to which you
'added a record
Set rst1 = New ADODB.Recordset
rst1.Index = "OrderID"
rst1.CursorType = adOpenKeyset
rst1.LockType = adLockOptimistic
rst1.Open "Order Details", cnn1, , , adCmdTableDirect
rst1.Seek int1
```

(continued)

```
'Loop through line items for OrderID to which you
'previously added a record; delete the record
'when you find it
Do Until rst1(0) <> int1
    If rst1(1) = int2 Then
'Delete the record because we do not want to change
'the Northwind database, but only show that we can
        rst1.Delete
        Exit Do
    End If
    rst1.MoveNext
Loop

'Clean up objects
rst1.Close
cnn1.Close
Set frm1 = Nothing
Set rst1 = Nothing
Set cnn1 = Nothing

End Sub
```

Formatting Controls on Main and Subforms

Formatting form controls—especially dynamically—is always an interesting topic. Often you will want to contrast some control values with other values. This section details three approaches to this. The first approach relies on manually creating conditional formats, which you can use to format controls dynamically without writing programs. Even experienced coders might find it desirable to try a formatting look without writing any programs. Second, you can programmatically set conditional formats using the *FormatConditions* collection and *FormatCondition* objects. The third approach—using event procedures and control properties—was the only way to achieve conditional formatting for controls before conditional formats were introduced in Access 2000. This approach might be more code intensive than working with conditional formats manually or programmatically, but it offers more flexibility.

Conditional Formatting

Access 2000 lets you conditionally format the data displayed by a text box or combo box control without programming. You can selectively apply formatting to form controls for both bound and calculated fields.

Figure 6-11 shows three instances of the same form. I used conditional formatting to control the appearance of the *Discount* and *Extended Price* fields. The

Discount field in the top form is disabled. The middle form highlights the value in the *Extended Price* field using bold and italic formatting. The bottom form enables the *Discount* field and highlights the value in the *Extended Price* field.

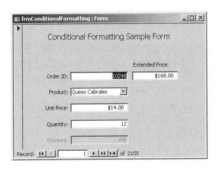

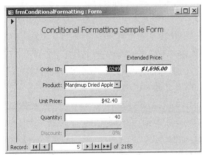

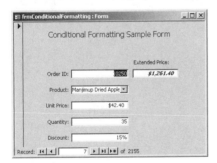

Figure 6-11 Conditional formatting controls the appearance of the *Extended Price* and *Discount* fields on this form.

The *Extended Price* field is calculated; it does not derive its value directly from an underlying table. The expression *[UnitPrice]*[Quantity]*(1-[Discount])* in the text box's Control Source property setting computes the value when the user moves to a new record or updates the *UnitPrice*, *Quantity*, or *Discount* field of the current record. (The terms in brackets reference controls, not field names for the underlying data source.)

> **Note**   Beginners sometimes give fields and controls the same name. This practice can be confusing and can lead to errors. (The AutoForm wizard and the Northwind sample are also guilty of this practice.) Consider adding prefixes to control names to distinguish them from their underlying field names. For example, a good name for a text box control that is bound to a field named *UnitPrice* would be txtUnitPrice.

To apply conditional formatting to a control, select the control and choose Conditional Formatting from the Format menu to open the Conditional Formatting dialog box, shown in Figure 6-12. Every control with conditional formatting has at least two formats—a default format and one special format when a specified condition is True. The Conditional Formatting dialog box permits up to three conditional formats for a control. The dialog box offers six formatting controls to help you specify each conditional format. These permit you to manage the application of boldface, italics, underlining, background color, and foreground color, as well as whether a control is enabled.

You can format based on a control's field value, its expression value, or whether it has the focus. When you work with the field value for a control, you can select from a list of equality operators, such as equal to (=), greater than (>), and less than (<). The condition for the *Discount* field in Figure 6-12 is that the *Field* value is equal to 0. The formatting option for this condition disables the control when the discount is 0.

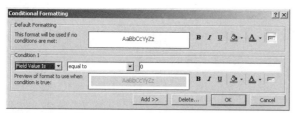

Figure 6-12 The Conditional Formatting dialog box.

If you apply conditional formatting to a calculated field, such as *Extended Price*, you must write an expression using standard VBA operators. The condition for the *Extended Price* field is that the expression is txtExtendedPrice.value>500. (The name of the control that displays the calculated value is txtExtendedPrice.) When the field is greater than 500, bold and italic formatting highlight the text box contents.

You can easily apply another condition and special format to a control by clicking the Add button in the Conditional Formatting dialog box and specifying the new condition and its formatting information.

Programming Conditional Formats

As desirable as conditional formats are for eliminating or minimizing the programming of special formats for form controls, there are legitimate reasons for programming conditional formats. The Conditional Formatting dialog box restricts you to three formats (plus a default one) per control. If your application requires more diversity, you can dynamically manage conditional formats through their programmatic interface. In addition, if you want to apply a set of formats to several forms in the same or different applications, having the conditional formats programmatically defined simplifies applying the identical set of formats to different forms.

Each text box and combo box on a form has a *FormatConditions* collection containing *FormatCondition* objects. Even with the programmatic interface, each control is limited to three special conditions at any one time. However, you can program these conditions to have different values under different circumstances, thus multiplying the number of formats that you can manage programmatically. Because *FormatCondition* objects do not have name properties, you must reference them by their index numbers or property settings. For example, the *Type* property indicates that you apply the *FormatCondition* object via an expression or field value, or depending on whether a control has focus. Other properties let you set the expression values that determine whether to impose a format and its features, such as boldface, italics, and color. These property settings both define and identify the *FormatCondition* object.

The conditional format programming sample that follows demonstrates several features of programmatically managing forms. The code begins by reinforcing your understanding of the process for dynamically assigning a recordset to the main form of a main/subform. After opening the form with an assigned recordset, the code prompts the user for the type of bolding on the form. Users can choose to bold all values for the OrderID control on the main form or any Discount control value greater than 14 percent on the subform, or they can select no boldface option at all. An *If...ElseIf* statement processes the user's reply to a message box to determine which path to pursue.

If a user chooses to bold all OrderID control values, the procedure uses the *DoCmd* object's *GoToRecord* method to navigate to the last record. Then it saves the *OrderID* value for that record. After moving back to the first record, the code creates an expression with the *Add* method for a *FormatCondition* object that is True for any *OrderID* value less than or equal to that of the last record.

If the user chooses to apply a bold font to any *Discount* control value greater than 14, the procedure creates an object reference pointing to the *Discount* control on the subform. Then the procedure invokes the *Add* method for the *Format-Conditions* collection of the object reference. The syntax creates an expression that is True for any *Discount* control with a value greater than 14 percent.

If the user chooses either Yes or No at the message box prompt, the code assigns a bold font to the *FormatCondition* object, *frc1*. The expression and the control for the *FormatCondition* object determine when to apply a bold font and which control to apply it to. If the user chooses Cancel in reply to the message box prompt, the program bypasses the creation of a *FormatCondition* object and the assignment of a format property for it.

```
Sub CreateConditionalFormat()
Dim cnn1 As ADODB.Connection
Dim rst1 As ADODB.Recordset
Dim frm1 As Form
Dim ctl1 As Control
Dim ctl2 As Control
Dim frc1 As FormatCondition
Dim int1 As Integer
Dim int2 As Integer

'Create the connection
Set cnn1 = New ADODB.Connection
cnn1.Open "Provider=Microsoft.Jet.OLEDB.4.0;" & _
    "Data Source=C:\PMA Samples\Northwind.mdb;"

'Create recordset reference and set its properties
'to permit read/write access to recordset
Set rst1 = New ADODB.Recordset
rst1.CursorType = adOpenKeyset
rst1.LockType = adLockOptimistic
rst1.CursorLocation = adUseClient

'Open recordset based on orders in 1998 for
'frmSimpleUnboundForm
rst1.Open "SELECT * FROM Orders o " & _
    "WHERE Year(o.OrderDate) = 1998", cnn1

'Open a main/subform, assign pointers for main
'form and subform control, and assign recordset
'to the main form's Recordset property
DoCmd.OpenForm "frmMyOrders"
Set frm1 = Forms("frmMyOrders")
Set ctl1 = frm1.[MyOrderDetails]
ctl1.Form.SubdatasheetExpanded = False
Set frm1.Recordset = rst1
```

```
'Depending on user input, add a format condition
'to a main form control or a subform control
int1 = MsgBox("Do you want to bold OrderID " & _
    "values on the Main form? (choosing 'No' bolds Discounts " & _
    "on the subform greater than 14%.)", vbYesNoCancel, _
    "Programming Microsoft Access Version 2002")
If int1 = vbYes Then
    DoCmd.GoToRecord , , acLast
    int2 = frm1.Controls("OrderID")
    DoCmd.GoToRecord , , acFirst
    Set frc1 = frm1.Controls("OrderID"). _
        FormatConditions.Add(acFieldValue, _
            acLessThanOrEqual, int2)
ElseIf int1 = vbNo Then
    Set ctl2 = ctl1.Form.Controls("Discount")
    Set frc1 = ctl2.FormatConditions. _
        Add(acFieldValue, acGreaterThan, 0.14)
Else
    GoTo ConditionalFormatSample_Exit
End If

'Set a format condition to bold a control value
With frc1
    .FontBold = True
End With

'Clean up objects
ConditionalFormatSample_Exit:
Set ctl2 = Nothing
Set ctl1 = Nothing
Set frm1 = Nothing
rst1.Close
Set rst1 = Nothing
Set cnn1 = Nothing

End Sub
```

This sample offers an attractive template for dynamically applying conditional formats to controls on main forms and subforms. The sample does not persist conditional formats to a *Form* object. Therefore, if a user opens a form outside the application code for dynamically assigning the conditional formats, the form controls will not appear with the formats. You can programmatically persist conditional formats to a form object, however. The next sample demonstrates the syntax for doing this to both main and subforms.

There are two tricks for persisting conditional formats. The first one requires you to use the *Save* method of the *DoCmd* object to save the form after creating the conditional format. The *acSaveYes* argument for the *DoCmd* object's *Close* method does not persist conditional formats to *Form* objects when it closes them. The second trick is to not persist conditional formats for subform controls through the *Form* property of a subform control on a main form. Instead, you must close the main form and open the subform so that you can apply conditional formats to it as a standalone form. Then you can close the subform and restore the main form. This convention is a departure from many of the subform samples discussed so far. In fact, the preceding sample demonstrates that you can create a conditional format for a control on a subform through the *Form* property of a subform control. However, you cannot save a conditional format created this way.

The next sample shows how to save conditional formats for controls on main forms and subforms. Because the subforms in this code sample operate differently than in many of the preceding examples, this sample includes a conditional compilation with an original value of True for the *SubFormFix* compilation constant. This setting causes the code to save successfully conditional formats for subform controls. Setting the constant to False follows the traditional route for processing subform controls, and it does not persist a conditional format created for a subform control.

The sample you're about to see starts by opening the *frmMyOrders* form and setting references to the main form and subform control on the main form. The code also saves the *SubdatasheetExpanded* property setting so that it can restore the setting later, if necessary. Next the sample presents a message box prompt as in the preceding sample. If the user chooses to set a conditional format for the *OrderID* control on the main form, the program logic proceeds as in the preceding sample until it reaches the code block with the label *Save conditional formats*. The code block contains two lines. One invokes the *DoCmd* object's *Save* method with the form name as an argument. This action persists the conditional format created for the *OrderID* control. If you set the *SubFormFix* compilation constant to a value of False, the sample attempts to save a conditional format for a subform control after creating it the same way as in the preceding sample. However, the action fails silently for the subform control.

When the *SubFormFix* compilation is True, the sample adopts special measures to create and save the conditional format for the subform control. Examine the *#Else* path to see the code for creating and saving a conditional format for a subform. This code segment starts by closing the main form, *frmMyOrders*. Then it opens the subform, *frmMyOrderDetails*, as a standalone form. Next it creates a *FormatCondition* object for the Discount control on the form and assigns a bold formatting property setting to the *FormatCondition* object. The task of persisting the conditional form requires you to save and close the form. For your convenience, this sample restores the main form before exiting the procedure. It even reinstates the status of the *SubdatasheetExpanded* property.

```
Sub PersistAConditionalFormat()
Dim cnn1 As ADODB.Connection
Dim rst1 As ADODB.Recordset
Dim frm1 As Form
Dim ctl1 As Control
Dim ctl2 As Control
Dim frc1 As FormatCondition
Dim int1 As Integer
Dim bol1 As Boolean
#Const SubFormFix = True

'Open a main/subform, assign pointers for main
'form and subform control, and save
'SubdatasheetExpanded setting
DoCmd.OpenForm "frmMyOrders"
Set frm1 = Forms("frmMyOrders")
Set ctl1 = frm1.MyOrderDetails
bol1 = ctl1.Form.SubdatasheetExpanded

'Depending on user input, add a format condition
'to a main form control or a subform control
int1 = MsgBox("Do you want to bold OrderID " & _
    "10248 on the Main form? (choosing 'No' bolds Discounts " & _
    "on the subform greater than 14%.)", vbYesNoCancel, _
    "Programming Microsoft Access Version 2002")
If int1 = vbYes Then
    Set frc1 = frm1.Controls("OrderID"). _
        FormatConditions.Add(acFieldValue, acEqual, 10248)
ElseIf int1 = vbNo Then
    #If SubFormFix = False Then
        Set ctl2 = ctl1.Form.Controls("Discount")
        Set frc1 = ctl2.FormatConditions. _
            Add(acFieldValue, acGreaterThan, 0.14)
    #Else
'Close the main/subform so that you can open the
'subform as a standalone form
        DoCmd.Close acForm, "frmMyOrders"
'Open subform, apply conditional format, and save it
        DoCmd.OpenForm "frmMyOrderDetails"
        Set frc1 = Forms("frmMyOrderDetails"). _
            Controls("Discount").FormatConditions. _
            Add(acFieldValue, acGreaterThan, 0.14)
        With frc1
            .FontBold = True
        End With
        DoCmd.Save acForm, "frmMyOrderDetails"
        DoCmd.Close acForm, "frmMyOrderDetails"
```

(continued)

```
'Reopen main/subform
        DoCmd.OpenForm "frmMyOrders"
        Set frml = Forms("frmMyOrders")
        Set ctll = frml.MyOrderDetails
        ctll.Form.SubdatasheetExpanded = boll
        Exit Sub
    #End If
Else
    GoTo ConditionalFormatSample_Exit
End If

'Set a format condition to bold a control value
With frcl
    .FontBold = True
End With

'Save conditional formats
DoCmd.Save acForm, "frmMyOrders"
DoCmd.Close acForm, "frmMyOrders"

'Clean up objects
ConditionalFormatSample_Exit:
Set ctl2 = Nothing
Set ctll = Nothing
Set frml = Nothing

End Sub
```

Formatting with Conditional Formats and Event Procedures

Before the introduction of conditional formats, the most popular way to assign formats to form controls was with event procedures for form events. Event procedures can test conditions for imposing a format on a control. The next example of formatting form controls mixes both conditional formats and event procedures to control the display of content on a main/subform.

The sample form we'll discuss appears in Figure 6-13. It shows a main/subform for the *Orders* and *Order Details* tables. These two tables are linked in the Chapter 06.mdb sample file that points back to the Northwind database. The main form's name is *frmConditionalMainSub*, and the subform's name is *frmConditionalOD*. The figure shows that the OrderID control is disabled on the main form. In addition, the OrderID and ProductID controls on the subform are disabled. Recall that the ProductID control appears with a caption of Product. Event procedures disable the main form and subform controls. In addition, the Discount control on the subform has three conditional formats. Values less than 5 percent appear in a green font, and values greater than 15 percent appear in red. Discount control values ranging from 5 to 15 percent appear in a shade of orange on my monitor with a True Color setting.

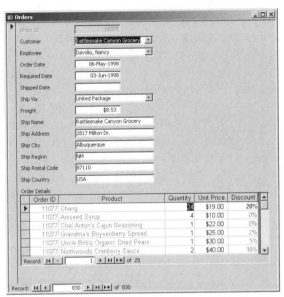

Figure 6-13 Conditional formatting controls the appearance of the Discount control values on this form, and event procedures conditionally disable the OrderID control on the main form and the OrderID and ProductID controls on the subform.

Figure 6-14 presents the Conditional Formatting dialog box for the Discount control in the subform. Its top, middle, and bottom expressions set green, orange, and red fonts, respectively. I opened the dialog box by selecting the Discount control on the subform in Design view and choosing Format-Conditional Formatting.

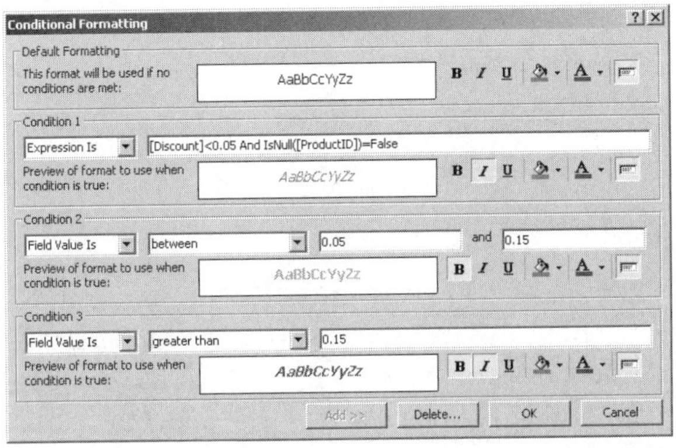

Figure 6-14 The expressions for the Discount control values in Figure 6-13.

The event procedures for the main and subforms rely on the *Current* event. This form event occurs when the focus moves to a record, making it the current one, or when a user requeries or refreshes a form so that the values of the form's controls might change. The *Current* event actually occurs before the record gains focus or the refresh or requery operation takes place. This event allows your program to test the control values before they are displayed. The sample's event procedures set the *Enabled* property of the controls. A compilation constant at the beginning of both event procedures simplifies turning off the effects of the procedures.

In the sample's main form, the *Form_Current* event procedure sets the OrderID control's *Enabled* property to a Boolean value. Setting a control's *Enabled* property to False protects its value from change. The *OrderID* field is the primary key for the record source behind the main form. While you might want to protect the value in this field for existing records, you will definitely want the control enabled if you have to enter values into it to complete a new record. When the control is Null (for example, when a user creates a new record), the *Form_Current* event procedure sets the control's *Enabled* property to True. This enabled setting is necessary so that Access can assign a new AutoNumber to the control. (A user can't edit the AutoNumber field, even if it is enabled.) The procedure moves the focus to the CustomerID control so that the user can start entering data with that control.

```
Private Sub Form_Current()
#Const EnableOnOff = True

#If EnableOnOff = True Then
'If cell is not Null, protect the
'primary key of the previously entered record;
'otherwise, enable the OrderID text box
    If IsNull(Me.OrderID) = False Then
        Me.OrderID.Enabled = False
    Else
        Me.OrderID.Enabled = True
        Me.OrderID.SetFocus
    End If
#End If

End Sub
```

The next *Form_Current* event procedure is for the subform. Notice that in the event procedures for both the main and subform, you can use the simple *Me* notation to reference controls on a form. You can create or edit the *Current* event procedure or a subform in the usual way. First, select the subform. Do this by clicking the top-left box of the subform control on the main form. Then open its Properties dialog box in Design view and click the Build button next to the *On Current* event. This will open the shell for a new or an existing *Form_Current* event procedure.

The *Form_Current* event procedure for the subform disables the OrderID and ProductID controls by setting their *Enabled* property to False if the OrderID control and the ProductID control are both populated. In this case, the event procedure sets the focus to Quantity, the first control after ProductID on the subform. When you move to a blank main form record to enter a new order and select a customer, Access automatically enters a value into the OrderID controls on the main form and current row of the subform. However, ProductID for the current row on the subform contains a Null, and the procedure enables the ProductID controls. In addition, it sets the focus to the ProductID control. This is perfectly reasonable here because the user needs to input values to the ProductID control to complete the record so that Access will enter it into the record source for the subform. Here's the subform's event procedure:

```
Private Sub Form_Current()
#Const EnableOnOff = True

#If EnableOnOff = True Then
'If primary key is not Null, protect the
'primary key of the previously entered record;
'otherwise, enable the ProductID text box
    If IsNull(Me.OrderID) = False And _
        IsNull(Me.ProductID) = False Then
        Me.Quantity.SetFocus
        Me.OrderID.Enabled = False
        Me.ProductID.Enabled = False
    Else
        Me.ProductID.Enabled = True
        Me.ProductID.SetFocus
    End If
#End If

End Sub
```

Looking Up and Displaying Data

A lookup form is similar to a parameter query with a custom front end; the form simply collects input that drives a query. When you use forms and VBA, you can be flexible in how you gather input as well as in the type of information that you can return to users.

Creating a Lookup Form

The easiest way to implement a form that looks up information is to have the user type the lookup information in a text box and click a button to start the search. The text box should be unbound because it doesn't enter information into the database; it simply gathers search information from the user. A query uses the value specified in the text box to find the matching information.

Figure 6-15 shows a form that opens the *qprHistoryfromTextBox* query when the user types a customer ID in the text box and clicks Look It Up. The query finds the total quantity ordered of each product bought by that customer.

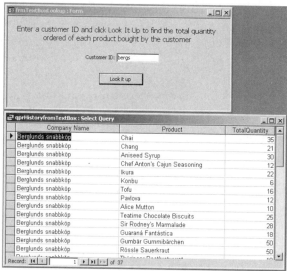

Figure 6-15 A form that performs a simple lookup operation.

The SQL statement for the *qprHistoryfromTextBox* query follows. Notice that the syntax specifies a parameter query. The parameter value is provided by the text box, *txtCustomerID*, on the *frmTextBoxLookup* form. This form appears at the top of Figure 6-15. If the *frmTextBoxLookup* form is closed when a user attempts to open the query, Access automatically prompts for a parameter to denote the value that the text box normally supplies. The query joins three tables to compute the quantity of each product ordered by the customer whose customer ID is in the *txtCustomerID* text box.

```
SELECT Customers.CompanyName, [Order Details].ProductID,
Sum([Order Details].Quantity) AS TotalQuantity
FROM (Customers INNER JOIN Orders
ON Customers.CustomerID = Orders.CustomerID)
INNER JOIN [Order Details]
```

```
ON Orders.OrderID = [Order Details].OrderID
WHERE Customers.CustomerID=Forms.frmTextBoxLookup.txtCustomerID
GROUP BY Customers.CompanyName, [Order Details].ProductID
```

The final element is a short VBA event procedure that fires when the user clicks the form's command button. The procedure has a single line that opens the query *qprHistoryfromTextBox*:

```
Private Sub cmdLookup_Click()
    DoCmd.OpenQuery "qprHistoryfromTextBox"
End Sub
```

Using a Combo Box for User Input

The form, *frmComboLookupSQL*, shown in Figure 6-16 has a better design than the one in Figure 6-15, provided that your list of customers isn't too long. Instead of forcing the user to enter a correct *CustomerID* field value, this form lets the user select the customer's name from a combo box. A procedure for the combo box's *AfterUpdate* event opens the *qprHistoryfromComboBox* query that uses the customer selected by the user, so the command button is unnecessary.

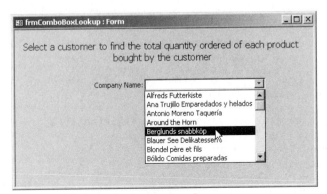

Figure 6-16 A combo box lookup form.

> **Note** Combo box lookup forms can become prohibitively slow as the number of lookup items becomes large. In this situation, you have at least two choices. First, you can revert to the text box lookup form. (See Figure 6-15.) Second, you can create a tiered system in which users make choices that restrict the range of items that a combo box makes available.

To populate the combo box with the values for the application, follow these simple steps:

1. Set the control's Row Source Type property to Table/Query (the default).

2. Set the control's Row Source property to an SQL string that returns the fields you want. (The SQL string for the sample is SELECT CustomerID, CompanyName FROM Customers.)

3. Set the control's Column Count property to *2*.

4. Specify the column widths, separated by a semicolon. (The first value should always be *0*.)

If you prefer, the Combo Box wizard can create the control for you. Simply select the Control Wizards button on the Toolbox, and then add the combo box to the form.

Your goal is to populate the combo box with two columns. The first column contains the customer IDs, and its width is 0. The second column contains customer names, and its width is appropriate for displaying these names. When the user opens the combo box, he or she sees the customer names. However, when the user makes a selection, the combo box assumes the value of the *CustomerID* corresponding to the selected customer. You need to understand this distinction because the query must use the *CustomerID* value and not the customer name as a criterion value. The following SQL statement for the *qprHistoryFromComboBox* query reinforces this point. Notice that the WHERE clause sets the cboLookup control on the *frmComboBoxLookup* form to *CustomerID—*not *CompanyName*.

```
SELECT Customers.CompanyName, [Order Details].ProductID,
Sum([Order Details].Quantity) AS TotalQuantity
FROM (Customers INNER JOIN Orders
ON Customers.CustomerID = Orders.CustomerID)
INNER JOIN [Order Details]
ON Orders.OrderID = [Order Details].OrderID
WHERE Customers.CustomerID=Forms.frmComboBoxLookup.cboLookup
GROUP BY Customers.CompanyName, [Order Details].ProductID
```

Displaying Results in a Message Box

The preceding samples in this section suffer from two weaknesses. First, they pass values to and expose values from queries in Datasheet view. This means that users can inadvertently damage the query's design. Second, a user can modify the data underlying a query.

The sample lookup form at the top of Figure 6-17 remedies both of these deficiencies by using VBA and ADO. The input form has the same look and feel as the form in Figure 6-16. While the result sets of the queries opened by both forms are identical, they are displayed in different ways. The sample in Figure 6-17 displays its result set in message boxes rather than in a query window in Datasheet view. (The sample uses as many message boxes as necessary to display its result set.) This protects the underlying data from inadvertent damage by a user.

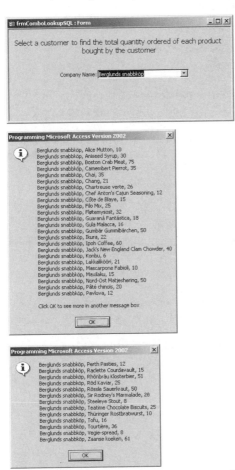

Figure 6-17 The form at the top displays its result set in message boxes so that users can view the result set but not alter its underlying data.

The following procedure fires on the *AfterUpdate* event of the combo box in Figure 6-17. It executes a command based on a query to develop a result set. It then assigns the result set from the command to a recordset and displays the recordset using one or more message boxes.

```
Private Sub cboLookup_AfterUpdate()
Dim ctl1 As Control
Dim cmd1 As Command
Dim rst1 As Recordset
Dim str1 As String

'Set reference to combo box control
Set ctl1 = Me.Controls("cboLookup")
'Create and define command.
'Use combo box value in SQL string for command.
    Set cmd1 = New ADODB.Command
    With cmd1
        .ActiveConnection = CurrentProject.Connection
        .CommandText = "SELECT Customers.CompanyName, " & _
            "Products.ProductName, " & _
            "SUM([Order Details].Quantity) AS TotalQuantity " & _
            "FROM Products INNER JOIN ((Customers INNER JOIN Orders " & _
            "ON Customers.CustomerID = Orders.CustomerID) " & _
            "INNER JOIN [Order Details] ON " & _
            "Orders.OrderID = [Order Details].OrderID) " & _
            "ON Products.ProductID = [Order Details].ProductID " & _
            "WHERE Customers.CustomerID = '" & ctl1.Value & "'" & _
            "GROUP BY Customers.CompanyName, Products.ProductName;"
        .CommandType = adCmdText
        .Execute
    End With

'Create recordset based on result set from SQL string
    Set rst1 = New ADODB.Recordset
    rst1.Open cmd1, , adOpenKeyset, adLockOptimistic

'Loop through result set to display in message box(es)
'in blocks of 925 characters or less
    Do Until rst1.EOF
        str1 = str1 & rst1.Fields(0) & ", " & _
            rst1.Fields(1) & ", " & rst1.Fields(2)
        str1 = str1 & vbCrLf
        If Len(str1) > 925 Then
            str1 = str1 & vbCrLf & "Click OK to see more " & _
                "in another message box"
            MsgBox str1, vbInformation, _
                "Programming Microsoft Access Version 2002"
            str1 = ""
        End If
        rst1.MoveNext
    Loop
    MsgBox str1, vbInformation, _
        "Programming Microsoft Access Version 2002"

End Sub
```

I could not use the SQL code from a query window in Design view in this procedure because the SQL string for *Command* objects does not support lookup fields. Therefore, I added the *Products* table to the query design so that I could report each product's name in the result set instead of just a product ID from the *Order Details* table. Adding this extra table further complicated the join logic for the query. (See Chapter 5 for an introduction to the SQL statement syntax.)

A *Do* loop steps through the recordset sequentially and writes its contents to a string. At the end of each record, the loop inserts a carriage return and a linefeed. If the string length exceeds 925 characters, the procedure inserts a blank line and an instruction to view the continuation of the sales history for the customer in the next message box. A message box can hold just over 1000 characters. (The *testmsgbox* procedure in this chapter's sample database helps you determine the maximum number of characters that a message box can hold; note that each of the top 19 lines in this test routine's output contains two nonprinting characters.) Limiting additions to the current message box to 925 characters allows the message box to be filled without truncating any characters.

Dynamically Displaying Information

You can display data, such as a record, in a form, and you can even design a form so that users can view the record but not edit it. Figure 6-18 shows a pair of forms that work together to let the user view a customer's record. The user selects a customer in the *frmCustomerLookup* form and clicks the Show Customer In Form button to open the Customers form, which displays the customer's record. (The Allow Edits, Allow Deletions, and Allow Additions properties of the Customers form are set to No, which prevents the user from changing the data.) The user can then click the Return To Customer Lookup Form button to transfer control back to the initial lookup form. The user can also launch another lookup or exit the application from this form.

The following elegant and simple event procedure is the code behind the command button with the Show Customer In Form caption:

```
Private Sub cmdShowCustomer_Click()
On Error GoTo ShowCustomerTrap
Dim str1 As String
Dim str2 As String

str1 = Me.cboCompanyName.Value
DoCmd.OpenForm "frmCustomers", acNormal, , _
    "CustomerID = '" & str1 & "'"

ShowCustomerTrapExit:
Exit Sub
```

(continued)

```
ShowCustomerTrap:
If Err.Number = 94 Then
    MsgBox "Select a customer in the combo box " & _
        "before attempting to open the Customer form.", _
        vbExclamation, "Programming Microsoft Access 2000"
Else
    str2 = "Error number: " & Err.Number & "caused " & _
        "failure.  Its description is:" & vbCrLf & _
        Err.Description
    MsgBox str2, vbExclamation, _
        "Programming Microsoft Access Version 2002"
End If
Resume ShowCustomerTrapExit

End Sub
```

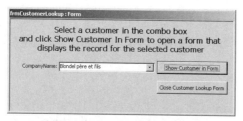

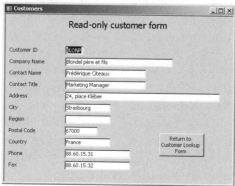

Figure 6-18 These forms let the user select and view a customer's record.

Charting a Subset of Data

The Microsoft Graph 2000 Chart object makes it easy to create professional-looking charts. (The Chart object is a mature Access development feature available since the first version of Access.) The object, which sits in an unbound object control on a form, can be bound to Access tables and queries, and you can choose from a wide selection of graph types and formatting options. (Double-click the object on a form in Design view to expose the custom menu for the object. When you finish using the Chart object's custom menu, click on the form outside the object to restore the normal Access form Design menu.)

You can add a Chart object manually, but using the Chart wizard is easier. Simply follow these steps:

1. Click the Forms object in the Database window and then click New.

2. Select Chart wizard and the table or query on which your chart will be based, and then click OK.

3. Select the fields that will be on your chart datasheet and then click Next.

4. Select the chart type and click Next.

5. Drag and drop the desired field buttons to the chart and click Next.

6. Select Modify The Design Of The Form Or The Chart and click Finish.

You can add aggregation and formatting functions by modifying the SQL statement in the Row Source property for the unbound object control containing the Chart object. (The wizard creates this SQL statement for you.)

Figure 6-19 shows two forms that let the user chart sales for a selected month. The top form lets the user select any year in the *Orders* table. The combo box's *AfterUpdate* event opens the bottom form, which uses the Microsoft Graph 2000 Chart object to display total sales quantity by month for the specified year.

In Figure 6-19, the chart is based on a query that retrieves all orders from the specified year. The query translates each order date to the first of its month. (The underlying data remains unchanged.) This makes it simple to aggregate sales quantity by month, which in turn makes it easy to chart sales quantity by month. (The Chart wizard automatically sums sales quantity by month for a record source such as this.)

The following three event procedures control the interaction between the two forms. The *cboPickAYear_AfterUpdate* procedure loads the charting form and minimizes the form in which the user selects a year. (You must minimize instead of close this form because the query for the chart determines what year the user selected using the combo box on the first form.)

```
Private Sub cboPickAYear_AfterUpdate()
    DoCmd.Minimize
    DoCmd.OpenForm "frmChart"
End Sub


Private Sub cmdClose_Click()
    DoCmd.Close acForm, "frmPickAYear"
    DoCmd.Close
End Sub
```

(continued)

```
Private Sub cmdPickAYear_Click()
    DoCmd.OpenForm "frmPickAYear"
    DoCmd.Close acForm, "frmChart"
End Sub
```

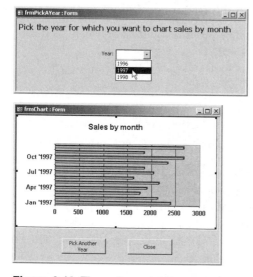

Figure 6-19 These forms let the user see monthly sales data for a selected year.

Manipulating Forms with VBA

This section describes some techniques for automating the use of forms. In particular, it illustrates how to enumerate forms and controls, techniques for programmatically hiding and showing forms, and methods for listing the forms in another project.

Enumerating Forms and Controls

The *AllForms* collection, which belongs to the *CurrentProject* object, contains an item for each form in a project. An application can enumerate the *AccessObject* objects in the *AllForms* collection to find all the forms in a project. The *AccessObject* object's *Name* and *IsLoaded* properties are particularly convenient: the *Name* property represents the name of each form in a project, and the *IsLoaded* property indicates whether the form is open.

The following procedure uses the *Count* property of the *AllForms* collection to determine how many forms are in the current project. Then it prints the name and loaded status of each form in the project. (The *AllForms* collection is indexed beginning with 0; therefore, the *For* loop runs from 0 to one less than the total number of forms in the project.)

```
Sub ListAllForms()
Dim int1 As Integer

'Print the number of forms in the project
Debug.Print CurrentProject.AllForms.Count
Debug.Print

'Enumerate each form in the project
For int1 = 0 To CurrentProject.AllForms.Count - 1
    Debug.Print CurrentProject.AllForms.Item(int1).Name
    Debug.Print CurrentProject.AllForms.Item(int1).IsLoaded
    Debug.Print
Next int1

End Sub
```

The *Forms* collection contains the set of all open forms in a project, and the *Controls* collection of the *Form* object contains the set of controls on a form. Your applications can use these collections to find a specific form and an individual control on that form.

The following procedure enumerates all open forms in a project. For each open form, the procedure lists the form's controls by name and type. The *Control* object's *ControlType* property indicates the type of control. You can use the *TypeOf* keyword in a similar way.

```
Sub ListControlsOnOpenForms()
Dim frm1 As Form, ctl1 As Control

'Enumerate all open forms
For Each frm1 In Forms
    Debug.Print frm1.Name

'Enumerate each control on a specific open form
    For Each ctl1 In frm1.Controls
        Debug.Print "      " & ctl1.Name & ", " & _
            IIf(ctl1.ControlType = acLabel, "label", "not label")
    Next ctl1
Next frm1

End Sub
```

Notice that the procedure decodes the value of the *ControlType* property. When this value is the intrinsic constant acLabel, the control is a label. In a practical decoding exercise, you are more likely to use a *Select Case* statement than the

Immediate If (*IIf*) function in the preceding sample. The *Immediate If* function, however, works adequately for decoding a single value. You can view the complete list of *ControlType* intrinsic constants in the Object Browser, as shown in Figure 6-20. From this window, you can get additional help about any form's control type.

Figure 6-20 The complete list of Access form control types from the Object Browser.

Hiding and Showing Forms

You can use VBA and the *AllForms* collection along with some other objects to make forms invisible in the Database window. If you also make the form invisible in your application, the user might think that you removed the form. Hidden forms can still expose values for use by the other objects in an application.

The following pair of procedures hide and unhide an Access form:

```
Sub HideAForm(frmName As String)

'Close form if it is open so that it can be hidden
If CurrentProject.AllForms(frmName).IsLoaded = True Then
    DoCmd.Close acForm, frmName
End If

'Set form's Hidden property and do not show hidden
'objects in Database window
Application.SetHiddenAttribute acForm, frmName, True
Application.SetOption "Show Hidden Objects", False
End Sub
```

```
Sub UnhideAForm(frmName As String)

'If form is hidden, set form's hidden property to False
'and open form
If Application.GetHiddenAttribute(acForm, frmName) = True Then
    Application.SetHiddenAttribute acForm, frmName, False
    DoCmd.OpenForm frmName
End If

End Sub
```

The *SetHiddenAttribute* method sets or clears the *Hidden* attribute from the Database window for database objects, such as forms, reports, and queries. This method takes two arguments, an *AccessObject* object and a Boolean argument that indicates whether the object is to be hidden. Calling this method with an object and the value True is the same as setting the object's Hidden property in the Database window.

By itself, *SetHiddenAttribute* just grays the object; users can still select and use it. To make hidden objects invisible to the user, choose Options from the Tools menu, click Hidden Objects, and then click OK.

Before invoking *SetHiddenAttribute*, you should check the *AccessObject* object's *IsLoaded* property. If the object is loaded, you should close it before attempting to invoke *SetHiddenAttribute*; calling the method with an open object generates an error.

Enumerating Forms in Another Project

VBA does not restrict you to working with database objects in the current project. For example, you can test for the existence of forms in another instance of an Access application. One essential step in this process is to compare the *Name* property of *AllForms* members to the name of the target form. There is also a new trick to learn: You open a new instance of an Access Application with the target database in it, and then you use the current project of that instance as the source for your *AllForms* collection. This subtle refinement lets you process database objects in another database file.

The following two procedures implement this with VBA. *FormToLookFor* sets the database path to the other database file and gathers the name of the target form. The second procedure, *FormExistsInDB*, searches for a target form. You call the second procedure from the first one.

```
Sub FormToLookFor()
Dim str1 As String
Dim str2 As String
```

(continued)

377

```
'Search for forms in the Northwind database
str1 = "C:\PMA Samples\Northwind.mdb"
'Get the name of the form to search for from the user.
str2 = InputBox("Enter name of form to search for: ", _
    "Programming Microsoft Access Version 2002")

'Call FormExistsInDB to check whether the form exists
FormExistsInDB str1, str2
End Sub


Sub FormExistsInDB(str1 As String, str2 As String)
Dim appAccess As Access.Application, int1 As Integer

'Return reference to Microsoft Access application
Set appAccess = New Access.Application

'Open a database in the other application
appAccess.OpenCurrentDatabase str1

'Check whether the form exists
For int1 = 0 To (appAccess.CurrentProject.AllForms.Count - 1)
    If (appAccess.CurrentProject.AllForms.Item(int1).Name = _
        str2) Then
        MsgBox "Form " & str2 & " exists in the " _
            & str1 & " database.", _
            vbInformation, "Programming Microsoft Access Version 2002"
        GoTo FormExistsExit
    End If
Next int1

'Report that form does not exist
MsgBox "Form " & str2 & " does not exist in the " _
    & str1 & " database."

'Close other Access application
FormExistsExit:
appAccess.CloseCurrentDatabase
Set appAccess = Nothing

End Sub
```

The first procedure sets *str1* equal to the path for the Northwind database. An *InputBox* function prompts the user to input the name of the form to search for, and then the first procedure calls the second procedure.

The second procedure sets and opens a reference for the new instance of the Access application, and then enters a loop that checks whether any of the forms in the new database match the target form name. The procedure reports whether it found the target form and frees its resources before returning.

Using Form Classes

Any Access 2002 form with a module behind it is a form class; you can create new instances of the class with the *New* keyword just as you do with any generic Access class. One advantage of form classes is that they have all the standard form properties and methods as well as your custom additions.

We'll take a cursory look at form classes in this section; Chapter 9 will provide more in-depth coverage of the topic.

Viewing Form Class Properties and Methods

You can view the properties and methods of form classes using the Object Browser. You select the project's name in the Project/Library drop-down list box and select a form class name to see its properties and methods.

The Object Browser in Figure 6-21 displays a subset of the members in the *Form_frmButtonSwitchboard* class. Recall that this form navigates to any of three other forms via event procedures. The event procedures are class methods, such as *cmdGoHere_click*. The buttons, such as *cmdGoHere*, are class properties.

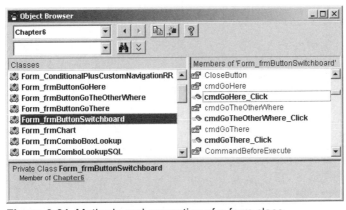

Figure 6-21 Methods and properties of a form class.

Manipulating Form Classes

The following procedure references class modules in Access 2002. It has several code segments that manipulate the basic form class in progressively more sophisticated ways. Working with form classes and their instances resembles working with a cookie cutter and cookies. The cutter is the form class, and the cookies are instances of it. Changes to a cookie do not impact the cutter. On the other hand, changes to the cutter impact all cookies after the change.

```
Sub testformclass()
Dim frm1 As Form

'First code segment:
'Saves reference to instance of a form class in frm1.
'Can reference with either class or reference name.
Set frm1 = Form_frmCustomers
frm1.Caption = "foo"
MsgBox Form_frmCustomers.Caption
MsgBox frm1.Caption
DoCmd.Close acForm, frm1.Name

'Second code segment:
'Programmatically alters and opens default form instance.
'Does not set reference to instance.
'Clears instance by setting Visible to False.
Form_frmCustomers.Caption = "foo"
Form_frmCustomers.Visible = True
MsgBox Form_frmCustomers.Caption
If MsgBox("Do you want to close form instance?", vbYesNo, _
    "Programming Microsoft Access 2000") = vbYes Then
    Form_frmCustomers.Visible = False
End If

'Third code segment:
'Open form in Design view to modify class properties.
'Open in Form view to see impact of Design view change.
DoCmd.OpenForm "frmCustomers", acDesign
Forms("frmCustomers").Caption = "foo"
MsgBox Form_frmCustomers.Caption
DoCmd.Close acForm, "frmCustomers", acSaveYes
Form_frmCustomers.Visible = True
MsgBox Form_frmCustomers.Caption

'Fourth code segment:
'Restore class caption property.
DoCmd.OpenForm "frmCustomers", acDesign
Set frm1 = Form_frmCustomers
frm1.Caption = "Customers"
DoCmd.Close acForm, frm1.Name, acSaveYes
Form_frmCustomers.Visible = True
MsgBox Form_frmCustomers.Caption

End Sub
```

The first code segment sets a reference to an instance of a form class. It creates an instance of the *Form_frmCustomers* class and assigns it to *frm1*. You can manipulate the instance using either the class designation or the reference name; the identical results from the two message boxes confirm this. Changing the instance of a form class does not alter the class itself.

You do not need references to designate or modify the properties of form class instances. The second segment accomplishes the same task as the initial one without creating a reference to the form class. This segment also includes a prompt to ask the user whether he or she wants to close the form instance. (An instance survives for the life of the procedure that creates it unless your code terminates it sooner.)

The third code segment opens a form in Design view and manipulates its properties. Unlike when you programmatically modify the properties of a form in Form view, changes to properties in Design view generally persist after you save the form. I noted one of the rare exceptions to this rule earlier in this chapter when describing how to persist *FormatCondition* objects for subform controls. The last two lines of the third segment open an instance of the form class in Form view. For the first time in the procedure, the form opens with the caption *foo*.

The fourth code segment restores the form class's caption to its original value of *Customers*.

References to Form Class Instances

The form class sample that follows further examines form classes. You can easily test the behavior of this procedure by using the *frmFirstWithControls* form, which includes a button that launches the *testformclass2* procedure. This procedure processes multiple instances of a form class.

```
Sub testformclass2()
On Error GoTo testclass2Trap
Dim frm1 As Form
Dim frm2 As New Form_frmCustomers
Dim int1 As Integer

'Show caption of frm2 before editing the property
MsgBox " Default caption of frm2 is " & frm2.Caption, _
    vbInformation, "Programming Microsoft Access 2000"

'Set frm1 as a reference to new instance of frmCustomers class
Set frm1 = Form_frmCustomers
frm1.Caption = "Caption of frm1 instance"

'Reset caption for frm2 instance
frm2.Caption = "Caption of frm2 instance"
```

(continued)

```
'Show the captions of the class instances referenced by
'frm1 and frm2
frm1.SetFocus
frm2.SetFocus
MsgBox frm1.Caption, vbInformation, _
    "Programming Microsoft Access Version 2002"
MsgBox frm2.Caption, vbInformation, _
    "Programming Microsoft Access Version 2002"

'Close form instances by their references
frm1.SetFocus
DoCmd.Close
frm2.SetFocus
DoCmd.Close

testclass2Exit:
Exit Sub

testclass2Trap:
If Err.Number = 2467 Then
'Trap attempt to print caption for closed form
    MsgBox "Cannot print caption of closed form", _
        vbInformation, "Programming Microsoft Access Version 2002"
    Resume Next
Else
    Debug.Print Err.Number, Err.Description
    Resume testclass2Exit
End If

End Sub
```

It is convenient to use references to form class instances when you deal with more than one instance. The previous sample uses the references *frm1* and *frm2*. After declaring *frm1* as a general form class, the code assigns a reference to an instance of the *Form_frmCustomers* class to *frm1*. The *frm2* declaration statement points *frm2* at an instance of the same form class using a different syntax. Therefore, *frm1* and *frm2* are two separate instances of the identical form class.

The second *Dim* statement creates an instance based on a form class using the *New* keyword. (You must refer to a form class with the *Form_* prefix when using the *New* keyword to create an instance.) After creating the references, you can invoke standard form properties and methods for the objects to which the variables refer. For example, the procedure resets the *Caption* property of *frm2* and then assigns the focus first to *frm1* and then to *frm2*. This opens both forms with one behind the other on the Access screen.

You can close a form instance by giving it the focus and then invoking the *DoCmd* object's *Close* method.

7

Reports, Controls, and Data

Your understanding of forms from the previous chapter will serve you well as you consider how to use reports in your applications. Although reports do not support interactive controls, you can populate reports with controls that display data, such as text boxes and check boxes. Reports can also contain bound and unbound graphic images and ActiveX controls for special displays, such as charts. The report-charting capability in Microsoft Access 2002 behaves much like the one for forms.

Access reports are sometimes the only contact a user has with a database. As a developer, you will likely encounter well-defined opinions from clients about what reports should convey and how they should arrange and summarize data. This chapter will equip you to respond creatively and rapidly to user-generated report specifications.

The chapter begins with an introduction to manual techniques for building reports, but it also includes a demonstration of their value for creating reports programmatically. Using one of the many Access report wizards will often be a great first step to developing a custom report. Instead of building a default layout, you can spend your time customizing a wizard-generated report. This can include customizing the record source as well as making the report's content or formatting responsive to run-time specifications. If you're going to programmatically create new reports or edit existing ones, you'll also require a solid understanding of the Access report architecture and its Design view environment. The summary of manually created reports covers these topics as well.

The second collection of topics in this chapter deals mostly with programmatic issues. It starts out by covering approaches for creating and deploying snapshots of Access reports. Next, the chapter drills down into a variety of ways for making existing reports dynamic through programming. Finally, the chapter ends with a case study that demonstrates how to work with a Microsoft FrontPage–generated guestbook. This case study starts out with cleaning and editing data and carries through to report generation.

Report Architecture and Creation Strategies

Access has always been a popular reporting engine because Access reports are easy to create and update. You can also deploy them easily to non-Access users by using the Snapshot format. (We'll cover this feature later in the chapter in the section, "Distributing Reports Using Snapshots.") Because it's so easy to link Access to record sources from other databases, Access development commonly features report generation for ODBC and other legacy data sources as well as traditional Access databases.

Report Sections

One of the main features that makes Access such a popular database reporting engine is its banded report sections. The standard default report design includes three sections: the Detail, Page Header, and Page Footer sections. The Detail section is bordered above and below, respectively, by the Page Header and Page Footer sections. The Page Header and Page Footer sections each appear once per page within a report. The Detail section repeats once for each record in a report's record source. In a simple tabular report, the Detail section is likely to repeat multiple times per page.

When you create a new report, Access relies on the current report template to determine the types of sections in the report as well as the dimensions. When first installed, Access will use its own standard Normal report template. However, you can use any other report in the current or another Access database file or Access project as the default template. Recall that an Access project is the front end of a Microsoft Access and SQL Server client/server solution. We'll examine this concept in more detail in Chapter 14, "Using Access to Build SQL Server Solutions: Part I." Choose Tools-Options from the Database window menu and select the Forms/Reports tab to expose the text box to specify a report template other than Normal. Changes to the Report Template text box on the Options dialog box will affect all future reports. Previously created reports retain the design specified in the Report Template text box when they were created unless you explicitly alter their design.

> **Note**   The Tools-Options command on the Database window menu displays the controls for setting the form template and the report template. You can use the Form Template text box just as you would use the Report Template text box to control the default design of a form.

The View menu on the Report Design menu offers two commands for adding and removing sections within the report when it is open in Design view. These menu items let you add or remove a pair of header/footer sections for the page or for the entire report. The menu items have toggle controls, but they do not simply toggle the visibility of a section; once you remove a section, you cannot use the menu to restore the section's content. Even if you do restore a section, its former content will be lost. The Page Header/Footer command on the View menu adds or removes the Page Header and Page Footer sections. The Report Header/Footer command adds or removes the Report Header and Report Footer sections. The Report Header and Report Footer sections appear once in each report—at the beginning and at the end, respectively. You can manually resize any section in a report by dragging its bottom edge up or down or dragging its right edge away from or toward its left edge. When you drag a section's right edge, you modify the size of all the report's sections—not just the one you are manipulating.

You can create custom header and footer report sections for groups that you create with the Sorting And Grouping command on the View menu in Report Design view. The custom header sections are often convenient for providing information at the beginning of a group, while custom footer sections make a good location for unbound report controls that display subtotals for the records in a group.

Creating Reports

You can create reports both manually and programmatically. The AutoReport Wizard on the Database window menu works the same way as the AutoForm Wizard. Select any row-returning record source in the Database window. Then, just click the New Object: AutoReport button on the Access toolbar. Although the AutoReport Wizard functions identically to the AutoForm Wizard, you might find the resulting layout unappealing as a starting point for programmatic customization. The default columnar layout without a delimiter between records makes it hard to discern where one record ends and another begins.

The AutoReport: Tabular Wizard provides a more typical layout for database reports. This wizard displays each record as a separate row in the Detail section. The wizard utilizes the Page Header section to display labels for the columns that appear on each page. If there are too many columns to fit on one page, the wizard automatically positions the columns for a single record across two or more pages.

The Report Wizard provides a richer graphical interface for designing single-column and multicolumn reports. It is especially convenient for designing reports that generate grand totals and subtotals for numeric fields. You can also use this wizard to create groups and specify sort orders for the rows of a report. A report's sort settings override any SQL instructions that specify the sort order for the report's record source.

There are other specialized wizards you can use to create reports, including the Label Wizard and the Chart Wizard. You can open the New Report dialog box to launch any of the report wizards by selecting Reports in the Database window's Objects bar and then clicking New on the toolbar. The New Report dialog box also lets you enter Design view to create a new report. This affords more flexibility than the wizards do, but it requires a more advanced understanding of Access report design as well as a mastery of the Design view menu for reports. If you plan to program reports, you should familiarize yourself with this view. You can also enter Design view for an existing report, such as a report created with a wizard or one that was previously created manually and requires editing. To open an existing report in Design view, select its name in the Database window. Then click the Design control on the Database window.

Finally, you can programmatically create reports, which provides substantial flexibility and permits you to make report design responsive and interactive. You can also programmatically manipulate existing reports to edit them permanently or to dynamically update them in response to user input or data values.

Creating Reports Programmatically

Because Access has such a powerful user interface for designing and manipulating reports, you probably will not find it convenient to create reports programmatically. However, if your application requires you to create a wizard that allows users to design custom reports, this section will show you how to get started. In addition, if you ever need to modify the controls on a large number of existing reports, this section will provide you with useful background on the subject. Later sections in the chapter will provide additional sample code that demonstrates how to manipulate existing reports programmatically.

Laying out a basic tabular report is a relatively simple task that requires just two methods: *CreateReport* and *CreateReportControl*. The Access *Application* object's *CreateReport* method creates a *Report* object. After you create a report, you need to assign a record source to it and populate the report with controls that display the contents of the record source. The Access *Application* object's *CreateReportControl* method adds controls to a report. We'll explore the use of both of these methods throughout this section.

Creating and Saving an Unnamed Empty Report

Invoking the *CreateReport* method by itself creates an empty report. Unless you change the Report template setting, the *CreateReport* method generates an empty report with three sections: the Page Header, a Detail section, and a Page Footer. When you create a report with this method, that report will not exist in any Access database file or Access project. Access automatically assigns the report a name, such as *Report1*. If the application's file already has a report named *Report1*, Access names the report *Report2*, and so on.

The first programming sample we'll look at in this section illustrates the syntax for creating an empty report with the default name. If you execute this procedure twice in a file that has no existing reports named *Reportx* (where *x* is a number), the procedure creates two reports: *Report1* and *Report2*. You can open either report in Design view and verify its empty status.

```
Sub CreateDefaultNamedReport()
Dim rpt1 As Report

'Create and save an empty report
'with a default name
Set rpt1 = CreateReport
DoCmd.Close , , acSaveYes

End Sub
```

Creating and Saving a Report with a Custom Name

One reason the preceding sample generates reports named *Report1*, *Report2*, and so on with the *CreateReport* method is that the method does not provide a means to name a report. Furthermore, the *DoCmd* object's *Close* method does not let you close a report and give it a custom name if the report does not already exist. The *acSaveYes* argument for the *DoCmd* object's *Close* method applies only to existing objects. In essence, this method lets you save over an existing object rather than save an object for the first time.

The *DoCmd* object's *Save* method can save a new object with a custom name. However, this method does not replace an existing object with a new object. Therefore, the trick to saving reports with a custom name is to use a two-step process. First, if the report already exists, you need to delete it. Once you have removed any prior versions of a report that have the custom name you want to use, you can perform the second step: using the *DoCmd* object's *Save* method to save the report. As long as you delete any prior versions of the report before invoking this method, it will always work correctly.

The following sample illustrates saving an empty report with a custom name. It relies on three procedures. The first, *CallCreateCustomNamedReport*, performs two tasks. First, it assigns a value to a string variable. This value is the custom name for the report. Second, it passes the string argument to the *CreateCustomNamedReport* procedure.

After creating a new report, the second procedure conditionally deletes any existing report that has the custom name passed to it. The code calls the *DoesReportExist* function procedure to assess this. If a report with the custom name already exists, the *DoesReportExist* procedure returns a Boolean value of True. When the function returns a value of True, the *CreateCustomNamedReport* procedure invokes the *DeleteObject* method of the *DoCmd* object for the prior version of the report. After ensuring the deletion of the report's prior version, the procedure can invoke the *DoCmd* object's *Save* method without the risk of generating a run-time error by saving over an object that already exists.

The *DoesReportExist* function procedure passes through all the members of the *AllReports* collection for the *CurrentProject* object. Recall from Chapter 4, "The ADOX Library and Tables," that members of the Access *Allxxx* collections are *AccessObject* objects. (Later in this chapter, the section "Manipulating Reports and Report Controls" will deal more fully with the *AllReports* collection.) The syntax in the *DoesReportExist* function procedure is appropriate for either an Access database file or an Access project.

> **Note**   The *AllReports* collection contains the names of all reports, regardless of whether they are open or closed. The *Reports* collection is not useful for detecting whether a report already exists because this collection contains only open reports.

```
Sub CallCreateCustomNamedReport()
Dim str1 As String

str1 = "rpt1"
CreateCustomNamedReport str1

End Sub

Sub CreateCustomNamedReport(str1 As String)
Dim rpt1 As Access.Report

'Create a report
Set rpt1 = CreateReport

'If the name for your new report already exists,
'delete the old version before saving the new version
If DoesReportExist(str1) Then
    DoCmd.DeleteObject acReport, str1
End If
DoCmd.Save , str1
DoCmd.Close

End Sub


Function DoesReportExist(str1 As String) As Boolean
Dim aro As AccessObject

'Search the members of the AllReports collection
'for a report with the name in str1; return True
'if report exists and False otherwise
For Each aro In CurrentProject.AllReports
    If aro.Name = str1 Then
        DoesReportExist = True
        Exit Function
    End If
Next aro

End Function
```

Programmatically Creating a Report with Controls

As you can see, adding a custom report is not very complicated; the syntax for calling the *CreateReport* method can be quite straightforward. Access Help documents two arguments for this method, but you do not need either of them unless you are using a nonstandard report template.

To add controls to a report created with the *CreateReport* method, you need to invoke the *Application* object's *CreateControlReport* method. The *CreateControlReport* method can take as many as nine arguments, but Access requires only two. You will usually need to specify a handful of arguments. Just like the *CreateReport* method, the *CreateControlReport* method returns an object—in this case, a control for a report.

The required arguments for the *CreateReportControl* method include the report name that will contain the control and the type of control to be added. You can specify the control type with an intrinsic constant—for example, specify *acTextBox* for a text box control. The complete list of intrinsic constants for control types appears in Figure 6-20 on page 376 in Chapter 6, "Forms, Controls, and Data"; both reports and forms share the same control types. While specifying a report section for the control is not mandatory (the Detail section is the default), you will normally specify the destination section for the report control. Any bound control, such as a text box, will require a *ColumnName* argument. This argument is equivalent to the *ControlSource* property for the control. Your *ColumnName* argument indicates the name of a column from the report's *RecordSource* property setting.

You often have to designate the position and size of controls. Parameters for these control properties can be set either in the *CreateReportControl* argument list or with separate property assignments. Both the method arguments and object properties use the same names to refer to these control settings. The *Top* and *Left* arguments indicate the offset of the control from the top-left corner of the report section in which the control resides. The *Width* and *Height* arguments denote a control's size. When designating the *Top*, *Left*, *Width*, or *Height* arguments in Microsoft Visual Basic for Applications (VBA), you should specify units in twips. (1440 twips equals 1 inch.)

When working with label controls that serve as column headings in tabular report layouts, you will need a *Height* setting. You can make this setting with an argument when you call the *CreateReportControl* method or by using a separate assignment statement.

The following code sample creates a report based on the *Customers* table in the Northwind database. The report shows four columns in a format that provides a basic telephone directory of customer contacts. Figure 7-1 shows an excerpt from the report's layout. Notice that the report's design distinguishes the column headers from the data rows by assigning them a bold font.

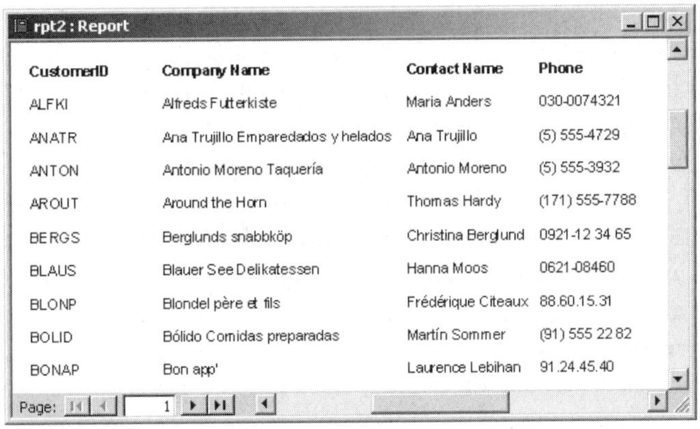

rpt2 : Report

CustomerID	Company Name	Contact Name	Phone
ALFKI	Alfreds Futterkiste	Maria Anders	030-0074321
ANATR	Ana Trujillo Emparedados y helados	Ana Trujillo	(5) 555-4729
ANTON	Antonio Moreno Taquería	Antonio Moreno	(5) 555-3932
AROUT	Around the Horn	Thomas Hardy	(171) 555-7788
BERGS	Berglunds snabbköp	Christina Berglund	0921-12 34 65
BLAUS	Blauer See Delikatessen	Hanna Moos	0621-08460
BLONP	Blondel père et fils	Frédérique Citeaux	88.60.15.31
BOLID	Bólido Comidas preparadas	Martín Sommer	(91) 555 22 82
BONAP	Bon app'	Laurence Lebihan	91.24.45.40

Page: 1

Figure 7-1 A report created programmatically based on the *CreateReport* and the *CreateReportControl* methods.

The code for the report in Figure 7-1 has several sections. It begins by creating a report with the *CreateReport* method. Then it assigns an SQL string to the *RecordSource* property of the report. Without this assignment, you would have to specify the record source for a report at run time before the report opens. Immediately after the record source assignment, the procedure specifies the height of the Details section as about a quarter of an inch. This height is needed to control the spacing between rows in the table. As with other size assignments for controls through VBA, the units are twips. Next the procedure adds the controls for the four columns. After adding controls to display and label data, the procedure saves the report with a custom name (*rpt2*). This name appears in Figure 7-1 in the title bar. The closing segment of the procedure invokes the *DoesReportExist* function described earlier in the section.

Four blocks of code successively add each column to the report. A comment that mentions the data for the column precedes each block. Within each block, the *CreateReportControl* adds two controls—a text box and a label.

The *CreateReportControl* method for the text box in the first column has four arguments. These specify the report name, the type of control, the report section for the control, and the column name from the report's record source. This last argument sets the *ControlSource* property for the text box. The *CreateReportControl* method does not have an argument for naming the control, so the procedure assigns a string to the control's *Name* property immediately after the invocation of the *CreateReportControl* method. The second invocation of the *CreateReportControl* method for the *CustomerID* column creates the column header. The arguments for this control designate a label control type that resides in the report's Page Header section. In addition to assigning a name to the control, the property assignments for the label control specify *Caption*, *Width*, and *Height* properties. You must always set these label control properties. The code block closes by assigning a bold font setting to the label.

The blocks of code that create controls for the report's second through fourth columns follow the example of the first column—but with one exception. The first block positions its label and text box controls flush with the report's left edge (which is the current printer's left margin setting). The second through fourth columns offset the left edge of their controls by the left edge of the text box for the preceding column plus the width of that text box plus 50 twips. The *wid1* memory variable is used to calculate the this spacing by adding the prior column's *Width* setting to the prior *Left* setting. The sixth argument for the *CreateReportControl* method adds 50 as an additional offset to *wid1* when specifying the left edge of controls in the second through the fourth columns.

> **Note**   Access 2002 introduces a new Printer object, which is a member of the new Printers collection. Use this object when you have multiple printers to which an application can connect, and you want to designate one in particular. With the Printer object, you can control such settings as the left margin, number of copies, and paper bin. See Access Help for Printer Object for more detailed information, including code samples.

There is one additional setting you can use when adding the controls for the columns. By default, the control width for text boxes is 1 inch (or, as mentioned earlier, 1440 twips). This setting is appropriate for all columns in the report, except for the second column, which needs a width of 2700 twips to accommodate longer customer names.

```
Sub CreateAReportWithASource()
On Error GoTo ReportSource_Trap
Dim rpt As Report
Dim txt1 As Access.TextBox
Dim lbl1 As Access.Label
Dim str1 As String
Dim wid1 As Integer

'Create a report with a RecordSource assignment
Set rpt1 = CreateReport
rpt1.RecordSource = "SELECT * FROM Customers"
rpt1.Section("Detail").Height = 365
```

```
'Add page column label and text box for CustomerID
Set txt1 = CreateReportControl(rpt1.Name, acTextBox, _
    acDetail, , "CustomerID")
txt1.Name = "txtCustomerID"
Set lbl1 = CreateReportControl(rpt1.Name, acLabel, _
    acPageHeader)
lbl1.Name = "lblCustomerID"
lbl1.Caption = "CustomerID"
lbl1.Width = txt1.Width
lbl1.Height = txt1.Height
lbl1.FontBold = True

'Add page column label and text box for CompanyName.
'Set the width of this column at 2700 twips, which is
'different than the default setting of 1440 twips.
wid1 = txt1.Width
Set txt1 = CreateReportControl(rpt1.Name, acTextBox, _
    acDetail, , "CompanyName", wid1 + 50)
txt1.Name = "txtCompany"
txt1.Width = 2700
Set lbl1 = CreateReportControl(rpt1.Name, acLabel, _
    acPageHeader, , , wid1 + 50)
lbl1.Name = "lblCompanyName"
lbl1.Caption = "Company Name"
lbl1.Width = 2700
lbl1.Height = txt1.Height
lbl1.FontBold = True

'Add page column label and text box for ContactName
wid1 = txt1.Left + txt1.Width
Set txt1 = CreateReportControl(rpt1.Name, acTextBox, _
    acDetail, , "ContactName", wid1 + 50)
txt1.Name = "txtContactName"
Set lbl1 = CreateReportControl(rpt1.Name, acLabel, _
    acPageHeader, , , wid1 + 50)
lbl1.Name = "lblContactName"
lbl1.Caption = "Contact Name"
lbl1.Width = txt1.Width
lbl1.Height = txt1.Height
lbl1.FontBold = True

'Add page column label and text box for Phone
wid1 = txt1.Left + txt1.Width
Set txt1 = CreateReportControl(rpt1.Name, acTextBox, _
    acDetail, , "Phone", wid1 + 50)
txt1.Name = "txtPhone"
Set lbl1 = CreateReportControl(rpt1.Name, acLabel, _
    acPageHeader, , , wid1 + 50)
```

(continued)

```
lbl1.Name = "lblPhone"
lbl1.Caption = "Phone"
lbl1.Width = txt1.Width
lbl1.Height = txt1.Height
lbl1.FontBold = True

'If the name for your new report already exists,
'delete the old version before saving the new version
str1 = "rpt2"
If DoesReportExist(str1) Then
    DoCmd.DeleteObject acReport, str1
End If
DoCmd.Save , str1
DoCmd.Close

ReportSource_Exit:
'Clean up objects
Set rpt = Nothing
Exit Sub

ReportSource_Trap:
If Err.Number = 2008 Then
'If the str1 report is already open,
'close it so that the procedure can delete it
    DoCmd.Close acReport, str1
    Resume
Else
    Debug.Print Err.Number, Err.Description
    MsgBox "Program aborted for unanticipated reasons.", _
    vbCritical, "Programming Microsoft Access Version 2002"
End If

End Sub
```

Creating Reports with Wizards

Since this is a programming book, you might be wondering why there is any mention of report wizards. However, wizards are an integral part of Access. If you build solutions and fail to take advantage of wizards that can address your problems meaningfully, you might as well use another development environment instead. In addition, wizards can create report shells that are well-suited for customization via programming. The best way to learn about the various features and capabilities of Access wizards is to experiment with them.

Report wizards are great for performing tasks that are awkward to execute programmatically. The first example in this section builds a Customer Phone List report like the one discussed in the preceding section. However, the Report Wizard automatically performs a lot of formatting, even with the most basic choices. In addition, the Report Wizard makes it easy to choose many formatting options and build many other kinds of reports. The second and third examples we'll look at in this section illustrate the capabilities of more specialized report wizards.

The Chart Wizard creates charts in Access reports. This wizard's charting capabilities resemble those available in Microsoft Excel, except that you can tap the wizard's charting capabilities more easily than you can by programmatically automating Excel. The charting examples presented in this section highlight how you can readily manipulate a chart both manually and programmatically with Access.

The Label Wizard integrates a highly functional label generator with a full-featured database manager. Later in this section, you'll see how to build a mailing label application.

Creating a Customer Phone List with the Report Wizard

The Access UI makes it easy to create a report like the one shown in Figure 7-1. Because that report requires a subset of the columns in the *Customers* table, you can either invoke the AutoReport Wizard with a custom query that selects just the columns for the report or you can invoke the Report Wizard and select just the four report columns from the *Customers* table. Recall that the AutoReport Wizard creates a columnar report instead of a tabular one, such as the report shown in Figure 7-1. However, you can generate the columnar report with a single click. An AutoReport Wizard exists for tabular reports, but you must start it through the New Reports dialog box. After selecting the wizard in the New Reports dialog box, you must designate a record source in the drop-down box below the box listing the report wizards. You create the report by clicking OK.

The Report Wizard can produce many kinds of reports, including one similar to the customer phone list. You launch the Report Wizard from the New Report dialog box by double-clicking on its name. On the dialog box's first screen, use the Tables/Queries drop-down box to select a table or query as a record source for the report. Figure 7-2 shows the Report Wizard with three columns selected and one more column about to be selected for inclusion in the report. After adding the *Phone* column to the Selected Fields box, you can accept the defaults through the wizard's last dialog box. The default naming convention for the report is to use the name of the record source. If a report with that name already exists, the wizard adds a number to the end of the report name to differentiate it from the names of other existing reports. You can override the default report name on the wizard's last screen. I assigned the name *rptWizCustomers* to the report created with the help of the Report Wizard.

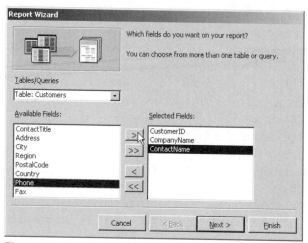

Figure 7-2 The first Report Wizard dialog box for creating the report in shown Figure 7-3.

Figure 7-3 shows an excerpt from the report generated by the Report Wizard. If you compare Figure 7-3 with Figure 7-1, you will see the contrast between programmatically and manually prepared reports. The wizard-generated report clearly looks better. For example, the wizard adds a report title, *rptWizCustomers*. The wizard inserts the label displaying the title in the Report Header section so that it appears only on the report's first page. The column headers appear above a horizontal line that separates them from the data rows. You can't see it in this excerpt, but the wizard-generated report also includes a Page Footer section that marks each report page with the date the report prints, the current page number, and the total number of pages in the report. In addition, the Report Wizard offers many formatting and data layout options that this basic sample does not exploit.

rptWizCustomers			
Customer ID	**Company Name**	**Contact Name**	**Phone**
ALFKI	Alfreds Futterkiste	Maria Anders	030-0074321
ANATR	Ana Trujillo Emparedados y helados	Ana Trujillo	(5) 555-4729
ANTON	Antonio Moreno Taquería	Antonio Moreno	(5) 555-3932
AROUT	Around the Horn	Thomas Hardy	(171) 555-7788
BERGS	Berglunds snabbköp	Christina Berglund	0921-12 34 65
BLAUS	Blauer See Delikatessen	Hanna Moos	0621-08460
BLONP	Blondel père et fils	Frédérique Citeaux	88.60.15.31
BOLID	Bólido Comidas preparadas	Martín Sommer	(91) 555 22 82
BONAP	Bon app'	Laurence Lebihan	91.24.45.40

Figure 7-3 A sample report generated by the Report Wizard in the style of the programmatically created report that appears in Figure 7-1.

The preceding example demonstrates the power of the Report Wizard in relation to a programmatic solution for creating a similar report. Although we could create the same report programmatically, doing so would substantially lengthen the code, which already exceeds several score of lines. When you simply need to crank out an ad hoc report or create a prototype for a system of reports, using the Report Wizard can be an excellent choice.

Using the Chart Wizard

Using the Chart Wizard is a little more complicated than using the Report Wizard. There are two reasons for this. First, the Chart Wizard adds an OLE object to the report. This OLE object actually charts the data. The Chart Wizard often will aggregate data before charting it. Second, you frequently will find it useful to prepare a query for your charts so that you can merge data from two record sources or restrict the result set with a criterion.

To prepare a chart that shows sales (quantity) by month, you must prepare a query that contains both the *OrderDate* and *Quantity* fields. The following SQL statement does this. The statement joins the *Orders* and *Order Details* tables by their *OrderID* fields so that it can include the *OrderDate* and *Quantity* fields in a result set. Additionally, a WHERE clause restricts the output to orders made in 1997.

```
SELECT OrderDate, Quantity AS Sales
FROM Orders INNER JOIN [Order Details]
ON Orders.OrderID = [Order Details].OrderID
WHERE Year(OrderDate)=1997
```

After saving the query statement with a name such as *qryForChart*, you can launch the Chart Wizard from the New Report dialog box. To proceed to the first Chart Wizard screen, you must designate the source of data for the chart. For example, select *qryForChart* from the drop-down box below the Wizard list. After clicking OK, move the *OrderDate* and *Sales* fields to the Fields For Chart box and click Next. Select a chart type, such as a 3-D Bar Chart. The wizard uses graphic images to denote the appearance of the various chart type options. (See Figure 7-4.) Click Next. To change the layout of your chart, you can move the fields around on the next wizard screen. Simply click Next to bypass this in the current sample.

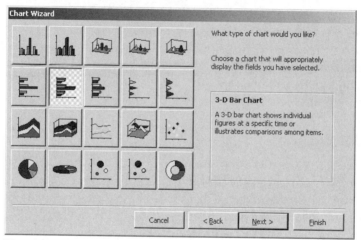

Figure 7-4 The Chart Wizard chart type screen with a 3-D Bar Chart selected.

In the final Chart Wizard screen, you can assign your chart a title, specify whether it will have a legend, and decide whether to view the chart or open it in Design view. The chart title is not the report name—it is merely a label that appears at the top of the chart. Choose the No Don't Display A Legend option because we have just one field to plot against another. Choose to open the report with the chart displayed on it (instead of choosing to modify the report).

> **Note**   The appearance of the chart can depend on your Microsoft Data Access Component (MDAC) references. These references need to be present and valid in the database file with which you're working. Access 2002 automatically installs MDAC 2.5 unless you install the Microsoft Desktop Engine (MSDE), which upgrades Access to MDAC 2.6. If you attempt to generate a chart from an Access database file with missing MDAC references, the chart described in our example will not appear. This can be confusing since a database's MDAC references can be valid on one computer but invalid on another computer. However, no matter what computer you're using, you can always fix the problem by choosing valid MDAC references from the Microsoft Visual Basic Editor (VBE) window.

Clicking Finish on the final Chart Wizard screen generates our example's initial chart. After the chart appears, you can revert to Design view to edit its layout on the report. You can right-click on the chart in Design view and choose Chart Options to modify the chart itself.

When Access opens the chart in Design view, it presents you with three nested containers. The outer container is the report. The middle container is the Detail section of the report. This container holds an unbound OLE object, which is your interface to the Microsoft Graph 2000 Chart object. Actually, the Class property for the unbound OLE object indicates that it's a holdover from Access 97. The Class property setting is *MSGraph.Chart.8*. The Row Source property is an especially important property of the unbound OLE object. The setting for this property is an SQL statement that determines the record source for the chart. You can programmatically update this property to dynamically assign different record sources to a single chart. In addition, if the Chart Wizard fails to perform the aggregation that your application requires, you can enter a revised SQL string as the Row Source setting on the Properties dialog box for the unbound OLE object.

The kind of editing you are likely to perform includes removing unused report sections, resizing the chart so that it's bigger and easier to examine, and changing the page orientation if you're printing just one chart per page. Double-click the unbound OLE object to expose the Access menu's Chart menu item. For example, you can add a title for the horizontal axis by choosing Chart-Chart Options. Then type the title you want for the horizontal axis into the Value (Z) Axis text box on the Titles tab in the Chart Options dialog box.

Figure 7-5 shows a completed chart for the SQL statement shown at the beginning of this section. The Chart Wizard has automatically aggregated the underlying data by month. You can verify or modify the chart's aggregation scheme by examining the unbound OLE object's Row Source property setting on its Properties dialog box. I added Unit Sales as the title for the horizontal axis using the technique described in the preceding paragraph. The chart's overall title, Sales Chart, came from a setting made on the last Chart Wizard screen. After selecting the OLE object, you can double-click the chart's title to open a dialog box to modify the title's formatting. In fact, you can double-click on any chart element to update its formatting. The chart in Figure 7-5 is available in the *rptChart* report for this chapter's sample file. Use it as a basis to experiment with your own custom formatting.

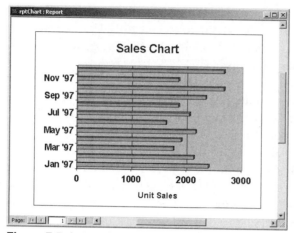

Figure 7-5 A sample chart created with the Chart Wizard for a query that selects the *OrderDate* and *Quantity* fields from the join of the *Orders* and *Order Details* tables in the Northwind database.

Using the Label Wizard

The Label Wizard is a great tool for creating reports that print batches of labels. The variety of label formats available is overwhelming. Standard label formats are available from 40 label manufacturers, and you can choose sheet or continuous-feed labels in either English or metric measurements. (The fact that one of the most difficult aspects of using the Label Wizard is selecting the right label format is a testimony to how easy this wizard is to use.)

> **Note**   One of the most common types of labels users print is the mailing label. If you use labels from Avery or a competitor with the same label format, choose product number 5260 for three-across laser labels. The Label Wizard example we'll examine here demonstrates how to automatically format a report for three-across laser mailing labels.

In addition, the Label Wizard offers tools to help you build and save your own label printing formats. This can be convenient if your application calls for printing to custom-sized labels or you want to develop a custom format for printing on a standard-sized label.

As with the Chart Wizard, you must specify a record source to start the Label Wizard from the New Report dialog box. For this example, you can choose the

Suppliers table from the Northwind database; the sample database for this chapter links all the Northwind tables.

In the first wizard screen, select 5260 from the Product Number list and click Next. The next wizard screen offers controls for altering the font and color of labels. For this example, click Next to bypasses this screen.

The next screen is more critical since it allows you to pick and format fields from the record source for inclusion on the label. Figure 7-6 displays the design of a label just before adding the final field, *PostalCode*, to the label. You can insert carriage returns, punctuation marks, and blank spaces between the fields on a label.

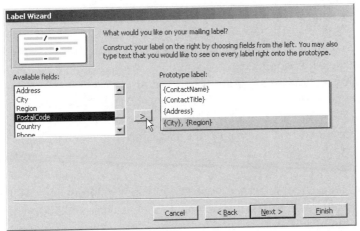

Figure 7-6 A screen depicting the layout of a mailing label just before adding the *PostalCode* field.

After you pick the fields to include on your label, the wizard offers you the opportunity to sort the order in which records appear as labels in the printed report. Sorting and bundling by ZIP code, or even subsets of a ZIP code, can sometimes help reduce mailing costs.

Finally, you can assign a name to the report. The default name is the word *Labels* followed by a space and the report's record source name. This name is how you will refer to the report in the Database window and programmatically in the *AllReports* and *Reports* collections.

Figure 7-7 displays an excerpt from the Labels Suppliers report. Notice that it automatically expands when a field, such as *Address*, extends beyond two lines. This feature is available because the wizard automatically selects Can Grow for each text box control on the report. The Design view of the report shows just four text boxes. These controls also have their Can Shrink property set to Yes, which prevents blank rows from being printed on the labels when a field is empty. For example, if a record has a missing *Address* field value, Access prints the text box with the city, region, and postal code immediately after the text box with the company name.

Figure 7-7 A sample report created by the Label Wizard for the *Suppliers* table.

After creating a report with the Label Wizard, you can reuse the report with new subsets of the original record source or with entirely new record sources. Alter the *RecordSource* property for the report programmatically or manually update the Record Source property on the report's Properties dialog box. Additionally, you can modify the contents of any text box by altering the *ControlSource* property for a text box control on the label report.

> **Note**   The Label Wizard in Access 2002 uses different label width, column width, and spacing assignments than in Access 2000. When you view the label report created in this example, Access 2002 displays a message stating that there isn't enough horizontal space on the page to display all the data in the report. To fix this, in Report Design view change all the label control Width settings to 2.1375 inches. Change the report's Width to 2.3375 inches. On the Margins tab of the Page Setup dialog box, change the Left margin to 0.3 inches. On the Columns tab of the Page Setup dialog box, change the Column Spacing to 0.4125 inches. These changes can restore the Label Wizard settings that worked with Access 2000 and print the labels without giving a warning about the horizontal space. Depending on your printer setup, you may need to specify slightly different values.

Creating Reports in Design View

Although this is a book about programming Access, let's review manual report design techniques for the same reasons we discussed report wizards. Access has an immensely powerful set of manual design techniques for reports. If you're a consultant building solutions for clients, many of your clients will expect you to deliver solutions that they can easily maintain and modify after your consulting engagement expires. Even if you manually design reports, there are many programmatic ways to make them dynamic after you create them. However, you will discover that getting the basic layout of controls on a report can be accomplished best graphically.

This section explores three aspects of report functionality. First it examines techniques for expediting the manual layout of reports and their controls. Next it moves on to discuss sorting and grouping techniques for the rows in a report's record source. Within this discussion, I'll cover the sorting and grouping of string data separately from the sorting and grouping of other kinds of data. The section concludes with a review of building reports that involve parent-child relationships. When I present this final topic, I'll drill down further into custom grouping and subreports. Here you'll learn how to use a chart just as you would a subreport.

Manually Laying Out a Customer Phone List Report

While using the report wizards can expedite the preparation of specialized reports, you might find that they do not provide the flexibility you need for some custom reports. Even if you start with a wizard, it's probable that you will enter Design view to customize a report. Depending on your requirements, you might decide to build a report from scratch in Design view.

This section describes building the Customer Phone List report in Design view. The Design view for the finished report appears in Figure 7-8. You'll find the sample report, which is named *rptManCustomers*, in the sample database for this chapter on the companion CD. Notice that the report contains a Detail section sandwiched by the Page Header and Page Footer sections. The report populates all these sections with text box and label controls. A Report Header section contains a label control that displays the report's name. Since the Report Footer section has no controls, I dragged its bottom edge to make it flush with its top edge—meaning this section won't occupy any space on the report.

You can start to create a report similar to the one depicted in Figure 7-8 by using a blank report based on the default Report template. Unless you changed the Normal report template, the blank report will have a Detail section sandwiched between the Page Header and Page Footer sections. You create the blank report by double-clicking Design View in the New Report dialog box.

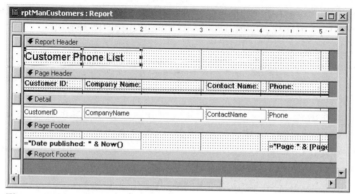

Figure 7-8 A Customer Phone List report prepared manually in Design view.

Immediately after opening the blank report, you should assign it a record source. Do this by opening the report's Properties dialog box. When you first open the report, it has the focus by default. However, if you've changed the focus to a particular section of the report, use the drop-down box at the top of the Properties dialog box to reselect the report. Then select the Data tab on the Properties dialog box and click the drop-down arrow in the Record Source box. This opens a list of existing tables and queries in the current database. For this example, choose the *Customers* table as the report's record source. You can also enter a custom SQL string as the Record Source setting, or you can click the Build button to the right of the Record Source box. The Build button opens a graphical Query Designer that lets you create a custom record source for a report.

The next step is to add text box and label controls to the Detail and Page Header sections, respectively. If the Field List box isn't already open, open it by clicking the Field List button on the Report Design toolbar. When you initially drag a field from the list to the report's Detail section, that field appears with a label and a text box. Drag the *CustomerID* field from the Field List box to the report's Detail section. The label caption is the field name followed by a semicolon. To conform to our design goals, the caption needs to reside in the Page Header section. Therefore, you must select the label control, cut it from the Detail section, and paste it into the Page Header section. (To select a particular section, click the bar at the top of the section.) After you paste in the label control, it remains selected in the top-left corner of the Page Header section.

Next align the left edges of the label and text box controls. You can do this by holding down the Shift key and clicking the text box to select both the label and text box controls. Then choose Format-Align-Left to align the left edges of the two controls. If you do not regularly design forms and reports manually, spend a moment exploring the Format menu, which offers items in its Align and Size submenus for managing the arrangement and size of report controls. Click any-where in the Detail section (except on the text box control) to remove the fo-cus from both controls. Then click the text box again. Hold down the Ctrl key and click the up arrow until the text box is nearly flush with the top of the Detail section. (See Figure 7-8 for the layout position.)

When you initially drag a control to a report, Access binds together its la-bel and text box. By cutting and pasting the label from the Detail section to the Page Header section, you unbind them. With the text box still selected, choose Format-Set Control Defaults. This step enables you to drag subsequent fields from the Field List box without an accompanying label control.

Next drag CompanyName from the Field List box to the Detail section. Properly arrange its text box next to the CustomerID text box. From the Properties dialog box for the CompanyName, select the Format tab. Then enter *2* to specify the Width property of the control (in inches). Recall that the CompanyName text box must exceed the default length. You can drag the *ContactName* and *Phone* fields to the report without making any size adjustments. After adding all four fields to the Detail section and arranging their text boxes, drag the lower boundary of the Detail sec-tion so that it rests just below the lower edge of the text boxes.

You can now shift your attention to the Page Header section. We need four label controls in this section to act as column headers in the report. Select the label with the caption Customer ID and choose Edit-Duplicate. Arrange the new label so that its top edge aligns with that of the original label control and its left edge aligns with the left edge of the CompanyName text box. Then select both labels and duplicate them. Arrange the new labels so that their top edges align with those of the other labels and their left edges match the corresponding text box controls in the Detail section. While it is not necessary to size label controls to match their corresponding text boxes, you might find it convenient. The Format-Size menu can help you accomplish this. Change the Caption properties for the label controls so that they properly describe the text box controls for which they serve as column headers. Complete your work on the label controls by selecting all of them and choosing a Font Weight property of Semi-bold from the Format tab of their Properties dialog box.

After completing the labels in the Page Header section, add and format a line that extends below the labels. To do so, click the Toolbox control on the Report Design toolbar if the Toolbox is not already open. Then select the Line control and drag it below the bottom edge of the label controls. With the line still having the focus, select the Format tab of its Properties dialog box and choose 2 Pt as the line's Border Width setting. Finally, complete your work on the Page Header section by dragging its lower edge until it's close to the line.

Shift the focus to the Page Footer section, and add a two-inch-wide text box that's flush with the section's left edge. In the Control Source setting for the text box, enter the expression *="Date published: " & Now()*. This expression documents the date and time when a report prints. Then add a second text box to the Page Footer section, and align its right edge with that of the Phone text box. In the Control Source setting for the second text box, enter the expression *="Page " & [Page] & " of " & [Pages]*. This expression shows the current page number and the total number of pages in a report. Select both text boxes in the Page Footer section. Make sure both text boxes align at their bottom edges by choosing Format-Align-Bottom from the menu. Assign a Semi-bold Font Weight property setting to the controls. Conclude your work with the Page Footer section by dragging the right edge of the report so that it's flush with the page number's text box.

Finish the report by adding a label that contains the report title. To do so, choose View-Report Header/Footer. Then drag the bottom edge of the Report Footer section until it's flush with the top edge. Select the Report Header section and insert a label control from the Toolbox. Type *Customer Phone List* inside the label control. Click outside the label control, and then click the control again to give it the focus. Assign a Font Size property of 12 points and a Font Weight property of Bold. Make the label flush with the left edge of the report, and assign it a Width property of 2 inches and a Height property of 0.25 inches. Conclude setting the report's layout by making the bottom edge of Report Header section slightly lower than the bottom edge of the label. (See Figure 7-8 for a reference.)

Figure 7-9 on page 408 displays two excerpts from this report. The top panel shows the report's title above the column headers on the first page. It also shows the first several rows of customer phone numbers. The bottom panel shows the Page Footer contents along with the last several rows of data on the first page. If you change the height of the Detail section from that displayed in the example, different rows will appear at the bottom of the page.

Sorting and Grouping String Data

The report in Figure 7-9 sorts the customer phone list by the *CustomerID* field for the report's underlying record source. This is because *CustomerID* is the primary key for the *Customers* table. However, some uses for a customer phone list might be better served with rows sorted by the *ContactName* field. Using the View-Sorting And Grouping command on the Report Design menu, you can create custom sort orders that organize rows differently than a primary key for a table or an ORDER BY clause in a query statement does.

The View-Sorting And Grouping command opens the Sorting And Grouping dialog box for a report. You can also open this dialog box by choosing the Sorting And Grouping control on the Report Design toolbar. The Field/Expression column in the dialog box allows you to select columns in the report's record source on which to sort rows. You can sort on multiple fields or expressions in the underlying record source. Access sorts at the highest level by the field or expression at the top of the column, and then it sorts by successive column entries in the dialog box. The dialog box's Sort Order column lets you choose to sort in ascending or descending order. The default order is ascending.

Figure 7-10 shows the Sorting And Grouping dialog box for the report design presented initially in Figure 7-8. The figure shows *ContactName* being selected as the sort column. For the moment, you can ignore the Group Properties settings in the lower portion of the dialog box.

Figure 7-11 on page 409 shows the top of the first page from the sorted report. Not surprisingly, the records appear in ascending order based on the *ContactName* field. As you can see by comparing this figure with Figure 7-9, in which the rows are ordered by customer ID, the sort settings in a report override any order settings in the underlying record source.

As convenient as the preceding report is, it would be better if you could easily tell when a transition occurs from contacts whose first name begins with *A* to contacts whose first name begins with *B*, and so on. Access reports offer two related features to accommodate this need. First, they allow you to group records on any field within the report's record source. When you group records on a field, Access automatically sorts them. However, your grouping and sorting criteria will often be different. Therefore, you'll need to set the sort criteria within the group criterion. Second, Access does not automatically separate or mark grouped records. However, you can specify places on a report that denote the beginning, the ending, or both the beginning and ending of a group.

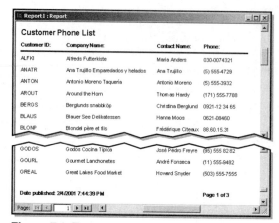

Figure 7-9 Two excerpts from a Customer Phone List report generated in Design view. The top panel shows the layout for the top of the first page; the bottom panel presents the layout for the bottom of the page.

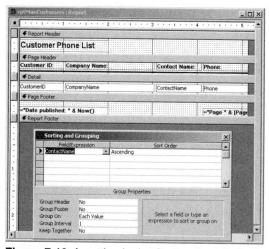

Figure 7-10 A setting in the Sorting And Grouping dialog box that alters the default order of the report.

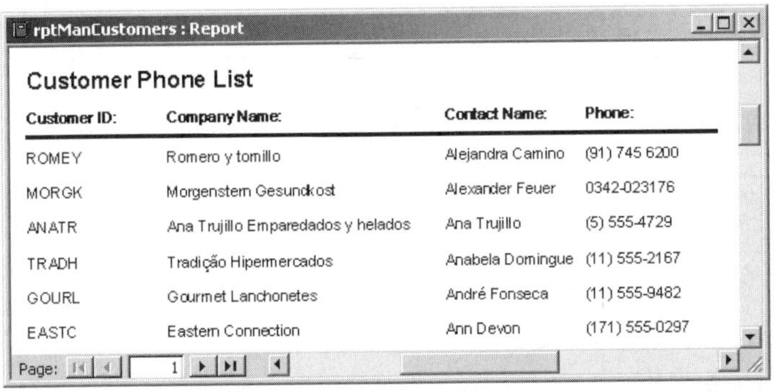

Figure 7-11 An excerpt from a report showing the customers phone list sorted in ascending order on the *ContactName* field for its record source.

Access calls the beginning and ending markers for groups Group Headers and Group Footers, respectively. These dividers introduce new sections within a report. Unlike the built-in report sections, you can elect to show just a Group Header or a Group Footer; you don't have to specify both.

Figure 7-12 shows a Sorting And Grouping dialog box for a modified Customer Phone List report that groups and sorts its records. The figure depicts the setting for grouping the records in the Group Properties area. The report groups records based on the first character in the *ContactName* field. By itself, this grouping criterion would not arrange a group's records in alphabetical order by *ContactName* field values. Instead, it would order the records within a group by their primary key value (*CustomerID*). However, because the Sorting And Grouping dialog box designates *ContactName* field values as a sort column in ascending order, the report shows the records in alphabetical order within each group. Since the Group Header setting is Yes, the report prints a divider at the start of each group. The report layout shown above the dialog box in Figure 7-12 shows an expression in the ContactName Header section. The expression retrieves the first letter of the *ContactName* field for the current record. Because this break occurs just once for each group, the expression causes the report to print the group's initial letter at the beginning of each group.

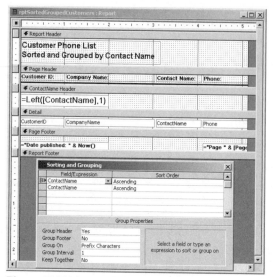

Figure 7-12 A report's Design view with its Sorting And Grouping dialog box that demonstrates how to group on the first letter of the *ContactName* field in the *Customers* table and sort the records within each group on the *ContactName* field values.

Figure 7-13 presents an excerpt from the report specified by the settings shown in Figure 7-12. Notice how easy it is to tell where a new group of contacts begins. Also, notice that the cost of improving the report was adding a single

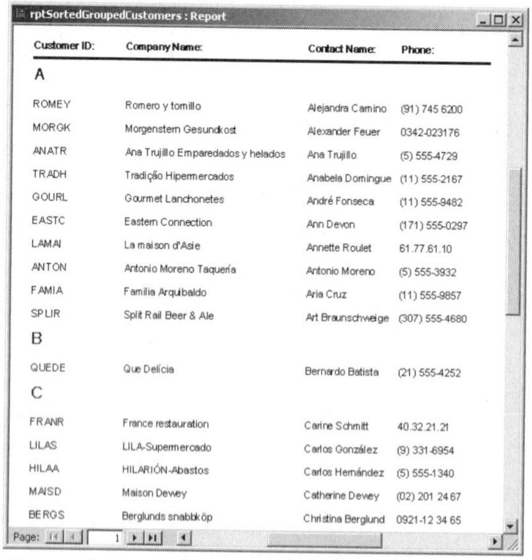

Figure 7-13 An excerpt from the report specified by the settings in Figure 7-12.

row in the Sorting And Grouping dialog box and an expression in the ContactName Header section. This is why Access is such a popular report generator for so many business applications.

Sorting and Grouping by Date

Although sorting and grouping techniques share some similarities, they require slightly different settings depending on the data types you use. While the previous sample used the first character in a string, the three samples we'll discuss next illustrate the use of date/time data types for sorting and grouping. I will not provide step-by-step descriptions of how to lay out these sample reports because I already described these steps earlier in the section and these reports are available in this chapter's sample database file.

The following SQL statement is a query saved as *qryOrdersByMonth*. This query serves as the data source for the three sample reports that follow. The SQL statement counts the number of order IDs by month. Notice that the statement nests the *Year* and *Month* functions and the value 1 as the day within a *DateSerial* function. By specifying the first day of the month regardless of the actual date contained in the underlying record, the *DateSerial* function generates a valid date that can be used to group records by month rather than by day.

```
SELECT DateSerial(Year([OrderDate]),Month([OrderDate]),1)
AS [Date], Count(OrderID) AS Orders
FROM Orders
GROUP BY DateSerial(Year([OrderDate]),Month([OrderDate]),1)
```

The left window in Figure 7-14 presents an excerpt from the first report that demonstrates the sorting of dates. This sample report mostly echoes the values from its *qryOrdersByMonth* report. By presenting the query results in a report, you make it harder for users to accidentally manipulate the query's design. You can also apply formatting options that are not available in a query's Datasheet view. The right window in Figure 7-14 highlights some of these formatting options. Both the Report Header and Page Footer sections use a gray background. This sample accentuates the report's title by using large, white letters against the gray background. You can control color properties by clicking the Build button next to the appropriate property name on the control's or section's Properties dialog box. The Build button opens a Color dialog box that lets you pick from a set of predetermined colors as well as create your own colors.

> **Note**   Not all date/time group functions work identically. Grouping by quarter aggregates all dates through the end of a quarter. This true for all date/time serial values, right down to the days. However, grouping date/time serial values by hour lumps together all times extending through the middle of the hour. When the report's grouping feature does not aggregate the way you prefer, construct a new field that will lead to a more acceptable result for your application. For example, if you need times grouped through the end of the hour, add a new column to a report's record source that applies the *Hour* function to the date/time serial number values and groups on the results from that function.

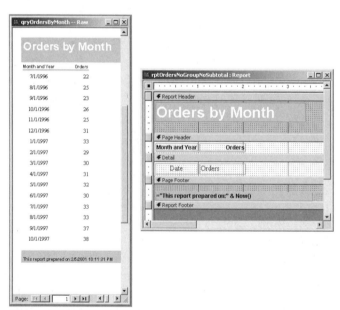

Figure 7-14 An excerpt from a report that displays the result set from the *qryOrdersByMonth* query.

The two text boxes in the report refer to the field names from the *qryOrdersByMonth* result set. No special processing of the result set occurs for this sample's report. Since the *Orders* field has numeric values, its column is right-justified automatically without any special formatting. The *Orders* column heading has its Text Align property set to Right so that its caption is flush with the right edge of the control. The *Date* column and the label control for its column heading each have the Text Align property set to Center so that the dates are displayed in the middle of the column.

One thing you cannot easily do with just a query is show data grouped in multiple ways. For example, it is difficult to show monthly data in a query while also presenting the data grouped by quarter. If you display a query using a report, the built-in Sorting And Grouping command on the Report Design menu radically simplifies this task: it features an option for grouping by quarter. Other date/time grouping options include the year, month, week, day, hour, and minute.

Figure 7-15 shows a sample report that groups the monthly data from the *qryOrdersByMonth* query by quarter. In the figure, the window on the left shows the layout of the report's data, and the window on the right displays the Report Design view along with its Sorting And Grouping dialog box. Notice the gap in the left window between the data for months within each quarter. Choosing *Qtr* for Group On and *Yes* for Group Footer in the Sorting And Grouping dialog box causes these gaps. You can see the Date Footer section in the report layout above the Sorting And Grouping dialog box. When you group data by a time period such as a quarter, the detailed data within a group does not automatically sort in ascending or descending order. The report in the left window illustrates this. To remedy the situation, add Date as a sort field below the Date as a grouping field. Leave the Group On setting at its default value of Each Value. If you want to sort in descending order, change the default Sort Order setting in the second column from Ascending to Descending.

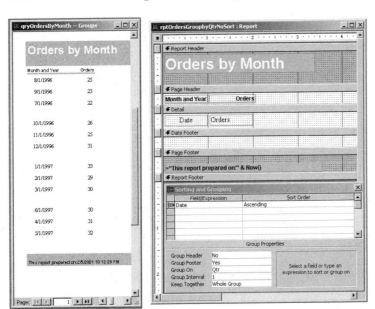

Figure 7-15 An excerpt from a report that groups by quarter the result set from the *qryOrdersByMonth* query.

Notice that the Keep Together property setting at the bottom of the Sorting And Grouping dialog box is Whole Group. This setting causes Access to keep together the three months of a quarter. If the group of months in a quarter would normally be split on the page, Access reformats the page so that the group of months in the quarter starts at the top of the next page.

Figure 7-16 presents the final example of a date-grouping report. This report does sort by month within a quarter. In addition, it calculates a subtotal of the monthly orders within a quarter. The expression in the Date Footer section shows that you can compute this result with a familiar aggregate function—namely, the *Sum* function. To help make the quarterly aggregate values stand out from the monthly order totals, the report applies a Bold Font Weight setting to the text box for the quarterly sum of orders. This text box differs from the two text boxes in the Detail section in that it's not bound to any particular columns in the report's record source. Instead, this text box depends on the expression within it.

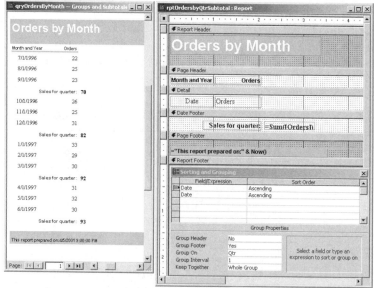

Figure 7-16 An excerpt from a report that groups and subtotals by quarter the result set from the *qryOrdersByMonth* query. Unlike the report shown in Figure 7-14, this report sorts the monthly totals by date within a quarter.

Hierarchical Reports with Groups, Subreports, and Charts

As a rule, subreports are less important to report design than subforms are to form design. This is because reports do not accommodate the input or updating of data—they merely reflect the contents of a record source in a format suitable for a printer. Nevertheless, subreports do play a role in report design. One major reason for using subreports and subforms is so that you can easily display data with hierarchical relationships, such as products within a category. This need is particularly evident when you want to include a graph that updates for each group within a report. In this kind of application, the chart serves a role similar to that of a subreport within the group.

Representing Parent-Child Relationships with Groups

Whenever possible, you should look for ways to design reports that show hierarchical data relationships with groups created via the Sorting And Grouping dialog box. This style of representing hierarchical relationships with reports is simpler than developing a main/subreport combination because you do not have to maintain the relationship between the two reports. To make this approach work, you may need to create a specific query to support the report's grouping requirements.

Figure 7-17 displays an excerpt from a report with a hierarchical relationship between customers and product sales. The report contains a group for each customer. The Group Header section indicates the parent data (customer) to which the following set of child data (product sales) belongs. The report's design presents the child data, in this case the number of orders and total extended price for each product, in the report's Detail section. The report's Group Footer section presents the parent data, in this case the total orders and extended price for an individual customer. This section even compares the data about the current customer with the data for all customers in the report by displaying the current customer's percent of the total orders and extended price in the entire report.

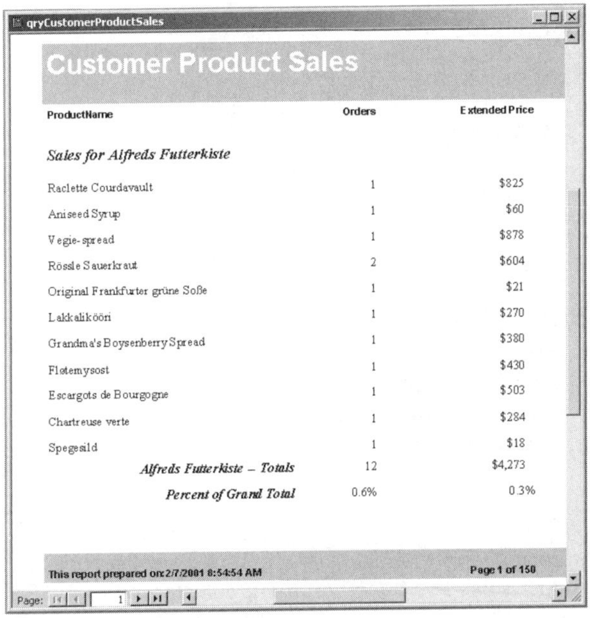

Figure 7-17 An excerpt from a single report that represents a hierarchical relationship between customers and product sales.

The main trick for representing parent-child relationships in a report is to specify the record source properly. The following SQL statement is the record source for the report just described. This statement appears in the sample database file for this chapter as *qryCustomerProductSales*. The three fields in the SELECT list are report fields. When you use an alias (such as *Orders* or *ExtPrice*) in a query for a calculated or an aggregated field, your Access report should refer to the result via the alias name.

```
SELECT cus.CompanyName, prd.ProductName,
Count(o.OrderID) AS Orders,
Sum(od.UnitPrice*[Quantity]*(1-[Discount])) AS ExtPrice
FROM Products AS prd INNER JOIN ((Customers AS cus
INNER JOIN Orders AS o ON cus.CustomerID = o.CustomerID)
INNER JOIN [Order Details] AS od ON o.OrderID = od.OrderID)
ON prd.ProductID = od.ProductID
GROUP BY cus.CustomerID, cus.CompanyName, prd.ProductName
```

Figure 7-18 shows the report in Design view. Notice that the Detail section uses aliases to refer back to the order count for a product (*Orders*) and the sum of the extended price (*ExtPrice*). When a field name appears within a function, you must delimit it with square brackets, such as *Sum([ExtPrice])*. Also, you must begin all expressions for the Control Source property of text boxes within a report with an equal sign (=). The CompanyName Header section contains a text box with a string expression for labeling the sales of a customer.

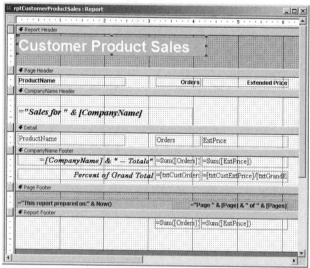

Figure 7-18 A report's Design view that displays a parent-child relationship between customers and their product sale rows based on *the qryCustomerProductSales* query.

The *Sum* function operates within the context of the section in which it resides. The CompanyName Footer section includes two *Sum* functions. These functions develop aggregates of product orders and the total extended price for that customer. The identical *Sum* functions in the Report Footer section generate the overall sum for all customers. The report names the two text boxes in the Report Footer section *txtGrandOrders* and *txtGrandExtPrice*. The corresponding two text boxes in the CompanyName Footer section are named *txtCustOrders* and *txtCustExtPrice*. The report uses these names to compute a customer's percentage of the grand total orders and extended price. Here are the Control Source expressions for the calculated percentages in the CompanyName Footer sections:

```
=[txtCustOrders]/[txtGrandOrders]
=[txtCustExtPrice]/[txtGrandExtPrice]
```

Representing Parent-Child Relationships with Main/Subreports

The next sample report deals with a parent-child relationship between categories in the Northwind *Categories* table and the total extended price for the category's products. The aggregated sales for individual products within a category represent the category's children. I used an SQL statement (shown next) that accumulates sales by product for shipments during 1997. This same statement serves as the record source for both the main report and subreport. The query includes *CategoryID*. This field is the primary key for the parent *Categories* table. When working with main/subreports, include the primary key for the parent table in the SELECT list. This example uses the primary key, *CategoryID*, to link the subreport to the main report. When you do this, you don't need to include a text box with the primary key on either the main report or the subreport. The following SQL statement is available as *qryProductSalesWithinCategory* in this chapter's database on the companion CD:

```
SELECT cat.CategoryID, cat.CategoryName, prd.ProductName,
FormatCurrency(Sum(od.UnitPrice*[Quantity]*(1-[Discount])),2)
AS ProductSales
FROM (Categories AS cat INNER JOIN Products AS prd
ON cat.CategoryID = prd.CategoryID)
INNER JOIN (Orders AS o INNER JOIN [Order Details] AS od
ON o.OrderID = od.OrderID)
ON prd.ProductID = od.ProductID
WHERE o.ShippedDate Between #1/1/1997# And #12/31/1997#
GROUP BY cat.CategoryID, cat.CategoryName, prd.ProductName
```

Figure 7-19 displays an excerpt from the report for the first category, Beverages. The gray box below the statement about total sales within a category is the subreport. Everything else on the report is part of the main report. The individual rows within the subreport represent individual products within a category. As the main report enumerates different categories, it uses the subreport to show sales for just the products within that category. For example, all the products in the subreport shown in Figure 7-19 are beverages. In addition, the heading above the subreport includes the sum of sales for a category. This calculation changes for each category.

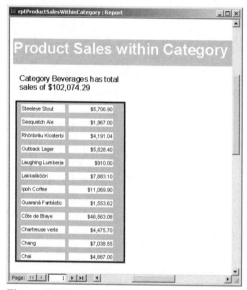

Figure 7-19 An excerpt from a main/subreport that represents a hierarchical relationship between categories and product sales.

Figure 7-20 shows the Design view for the main report (*rptProductSalesWithinCategory*) of the report we just discussed. Recall that the record source for the main report and subreport is *qryProductSalesWithinCategory*. The main report includes a CategoryName Header section. In fact, both of the main report's data-bound controls—the text box and the subreport—reside in the CategoryName Header section.

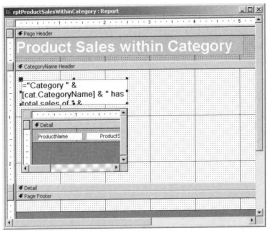

Figure 7-20 A report's Design view that displays a parent-child relationship between categories and their product sale rows based on the *qryProductSalesWithinCategory* query.

The subreport, *rptSubTableProductSales*, exists as a standalone report with just two fields in its Detail section. To construct the main/subreport, drag the subreport from the Database window into the Design view of the main report. Locate the control in the CategoryName Header section. You have the option to remove the label that the process assigns to the subreport control on the main report. If Access does not automatically prompt you to link fields between the main report and subreport, select the Data tab on the Properties dialog box for subreport control on the main report. Then click the Build button to the right of either the Link Child Fields or Link Master Fields property setting box. This opens a Subreport Field Linker that lets you link fields from the record sources for the main report and subreport. The sample report uses the *CategoryID* field.

The control immediately above the subreport control on the main form is a text box. This text box contains an expression for its Control Source property setting. This expression references two fields from the report's record source:

```
="Category " & [cat.CategoryName] & "has total sales of " &
   FormatCurrency(Sum([ProductSales]),2)
```

Notice that the expression references the *CategoryName* field with the same prefix that appears in the SQL string for the report's form. You must use this prefix. In addition, the expression taps the *FormatCurrency* function for displaying the sum of the *ProductSales* field in currency format with two places after the decimal.

Graphing Child Data in a Main/Subreport Design

When you add a graph to a report, you can make it function like a subreport. In order to synchronize a chart's contents with a main report, make assignments to the Link Child Fields and Link Master Fields settings for the control containing the chart. You will need to add a new chart to a report rather than drag an existing chart report from the Database window. Use the Insert-Chart command in a report's Design view to launch the Chart Wizard. This adds a new chart to the report. The Chart Wizard includes screens for specifying the chart's record source and chart type as well as the fields for linking the chart to the main report. Despite your selections, the wizard might construct a record source that differs from your needs. If the chart does not display the data the way you want, respecify the Record Source property setting for the Chart control. In this example, I needed to respecify the Record Source property as the following:

```
SELECT ProductName, ProductSales FROM qryProductSalesWithinCategory
```

Figure 7-21 shows an excerpt from the report created by following the steps for adding a chart to the report shown in Figure 7-19. I had to edit the layout of the chart as well; in particular, I changed the font size for the horizontal and vertical axes to 7 point. In addition, I created more space for the chart on the report's pages by reducing the right margin setting in the File-Page Setup command to 0.25 inches. The other margins remained at their default setting of 1 inch.

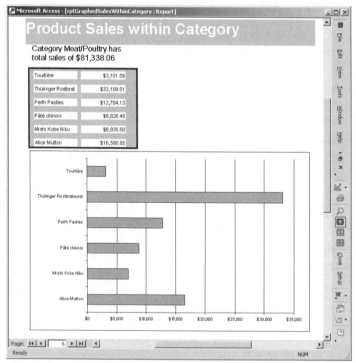

Figure 7-21 An excerpt from a main/subreport with a chart that depicts a hierarchical relationship between categories and product sales by plotting the product sales for each category immediately below the table showing product sales within a category.

Distributing Reports Using Snapshots

You can make Access reports available to others via the World Wide Web or e-mail by using snapshot files. The workstation viewing a snapshot of an Access report requires the Snapshot viewer, which is available free as a standalone application. The viewer application includes an ActiveX control for use in Web browsers that support it, such as Internet Explorer 4 or later. (The Snapshot viewer ships with Access 2002 and Access 2000.) Snapshots allow a much wider audience to use your reports, including users without Access or those not connected to your local area network (LAN). While the Netscape browser does not support ActiveX controls, it can download snapshot files over an http connection. Netscape users can then use the standalone version of the Snapshot viewer with the saved file on their local hard drive.

Note   The Web site www.ProgrammingMSAccess.com maintains an online tutorial on using and deploying Access snapshot solutions. The tutorial includes an overview of snapshots, step-by-step instructions for their use, and several samples that illustrate the performance of the Snapshot viewer in different contexts. If you use an older version of Access, or if you don't even use Access or Internet Explorer, you can still use Access snapshots. The tutorial explains how. The URL for downloading the free viewer is www.microsoft.com/accessdev/prodinfo/snapshot.htm.

Creating a Snapshot

You can create a snapshot for a report by selecting the report in the Database window and choosing File-Export. From the Save As Type drop-down list box, select Snapshot Format (*.snp). This enters the selected report name as the name of the snapshot file in the Export Report dialog box. (See Figure 7-22.) In the Save In drop-down list box, designate a location for your snapshot file. Figure 7-22 shows the report you saw in Figure 7-5 being saved to a folder named pma10 that contains the intranet site for this book on my local computer. You will, of course, need to change this folder name for your computing environment. Clicking Export in the dialog box in Figure 7-22 opens a progress dialog box and, after the file has been saved, opens it in the Snapshot viewer. The file resides on the server and has an .snp extension.

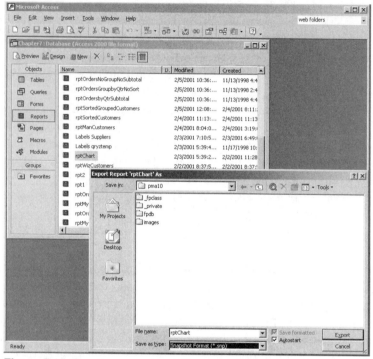

Figure 7-22 Creating a snapshot file manually.

Viewing a Snapshot

A workstation running Internet Explorer 3 or later that has the Snapshot viewer installed can open the snapshot file. Figure 7-23 shows the report in Internet Explorer 5. The viewer appears to be inside the browser, but it actually takes control of the browser. Special navigator controls on a bar at the bottom of the ActiveX control enable navigation through the pages of a report. The same navigator bar also includes a button for printing. (This is because the control disables the native browser printing functionality.)

Notice the close correspondence between the browser image in Figure 7-23 and the original report shown in Figure 7-5. This level of correspondence does not occur when you export to the HTML Documents format. In fact, the HTML Documents format cannot handle Access charts in reports. However, the Snapshot format accommodates both text and graphic content. In addition, exporting to HTML does not provide the built-in navigation functionality that the Snapshot viewer control offers.

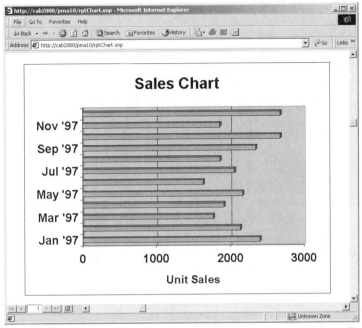

Figure 7-23 An Access chart-based report viewed from Internet Explorer 5.

The Snapshot viewer control lets you embed an Access report on a Web page along with other content. The following HTML excerpt shows the body of a Web page containing <h3> and <h4> tags before the object reference to the Snapshot viewer control. The full file is available on the book's companion CD. The text blocks preceding the control explain how to download the viewer if the report does not appear, and they offer a hyperlink to a site from which you can download the viewer. The instructions also explain how to view the report in Netscape Navigator. Of course you need to update the *SnapshotPath* parameter to the URL for the snapshot file that you want to show.

```
<body>
<H3>Snapshot Sample page</H3>
<H4>If you have an Internet Explorer 3 or later browser but
 cannot see the report below, download and install the
 <a href="http://www.microsoft.com/accessdev/prodinfo/snapdl.htm">
 Microsoft Access Snapshot viewer</a>.
 Then refresh the page. Netscape Navigator users will not even see
 the report container in their browsers, but they can open the report
 outside their browser using the same Snapshot viewer just mentioned.
 Netscape users can download the snapshot file from
 a Web server through http protocol to their workstation.</H4>
<OBJECT ID="SnapshotViewer" WIDTH=640 HEIGHT=480
CLASSID="CLSID:F0E42D60-368C-11D0-AD81-00A0C90DC8D9">
```

(continued)

```
    <PARAM NAME="_ExtentX" VALUE="16722">
    <PARAM NAME="_ExtentY" VALUE="11774">
    <PARAM NAME="_Version" VALUE="65536">
    <PARAM NAME="SnapshotPath"
    VALUE="http://cab2000/pma10/rptChart.snp">
    <PARAM NAME="Zoom" VALUE="0">
    <PARAM NAME="AllowContextMenu" VALUE="-1">
    <PARAM NAME="ShowNavigationButtons" VALUE="-1">
</OBJECT>
</body>
```

Other Uses for Snapshots

Snapshot files based on Access reports have many other uses. For example, you can electronically mail a report as an attached snapshot file by right-clicking on the report in the Database window and choosing Send To and then Mail Recipient from the shortcut menu. Remember to include a link in your message to the download site for the Snapshot viewer. This will enable recipients who do not have the viewer to install it.

You can also use the *DoCmd* object's *OutputTo* and *SendObject* methods to automate the conversion and copying of snapshot files to an intranet site or to e-mail recipients. The section "Mailing Snapshots" later in this chapter includes a code sample that programmatically e-mails multiple files to one or more recipients. The following statement publishes a report we developed earlier in this chapter to a local site on my intranet. The *SaveSnapShot* procedure in this chapter's sample file on the book's CD executes the statement shown below. Update the destination path from \\cab2000\c\inetpub\wwwroot\pma10 to an appropriate destination for your workstation. This type of solution works well when your clients know the location of one or more snapshot files.

```
DoCmd.OutputTo acOutputReport, "rptSortedGroupedCustomers", _
    "Snapshot Format", _
    "\\cab2000\c\inetpub\wwwroot\pma10\mysnapshot.snp", True
```

Making Reports Dynamic

Three report section events—*Format, Retreat,* and *Print*—can help you create dynamic formatting and content in a report. Other report events that can help you build smart reports include *Open, Close, No Data,* and *Page*. These events can also help you manage the application's behavior before, during, and after the opening of a report. You can use combinations of report events to create report formatting and special effects.

Use the *Open* event to programmatically set properties for reports and their controls. This is the first event that fires when a report is opened. When creating conditional formats for a specific instance of a report, use an *Open* event procedure to instantiate your *FormatCondition* objects and assign properties to them. If your application can have more than one report open at the same time, you can use the *Activate* and *Deactivate* events to monitor the flow of focus to and away from a report. Use the *Close* event to perform special actions just before a report closes, such as opening a form or presenting a message box.

You use the *NoData* event to detect a report that has no data in its record source. This event occurs after Access formats a report for printing. Your application can use this event to cancel a report that is about to print without any data. You can also program event procedures that prompt a user to enter data in the underlying record source or to select a different record source for the report.

Formatting Reports with the *Print* Event

The following sample formats a report using the *Print* event for various report sections. The *Print* event occurs after formatting for each section or line of detail is complete but before the report actually prints. Each report section can have its own *Print* event procedure, and the event occurs each time Access works with that section to prepare the report. For example, the Report Header *Print* event occurs just once, unless a *Retreat* event forces Access to return to the Report Header section. The *Retreat* event enables Access to manage special report requirements, such as keeping a group together.

Figure 7-24 shows a report that uses the *Print* event for three sections to add red rectangles around the Report Header section and the Page Footer section. Note the different thicknesses of the rectangular borders. The Detail section displays an oval around all monthly order totals greater than or equal to 30.

While the Report Header *Print* event occurs once per report and the Page Footer *Print* event occurs just once per page, the Detail section *Print* event occurs once for each row on a page. This means that for the page shown in Figure 7-24 the Detail section fires the *Print* event 16 times. With each event, your application can examine control values for the current record. Therefore, you can selectively display ovals around monthly order totals.

The code for the report in Figure 7-24 comprises the following three event procedures. Your applications can apply the *Line* method (as in the Report Header and Page Footer event procedures) to draw a rectangle around the report section. The first four arguments of the *Line* method have a data type of Single and are used to indicate two pairs of coordinates for the line. These four values specify the top, left, width, and height values for a rectangle in twips, which is the default metric for the *Line* method. The *ReportHeader_Print* procedure sets these parameters to the appropriate measurements for the Report Header section.

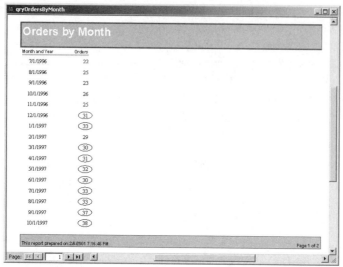

Figure 7-24 One *Print* event procedure for this report draws rectangles around the Report Header and Page Footer sections. Another *Print* event procedure selectively draws ovals around the monthly order totals.

Another argument of the *Line* method has a Long data type and designates the color of the rectangle's border. The sample uses the *RGB* function to designate a number that represents the color red in the *lngColor* variable. Just before invoking the *Line* method to draw the rectangle, the *ReportHeader_Print* procedure assigns a value to the report's *DrawWidth* property. This property always uses pixels. Therefore, the border around the Report Header section is 25 pixels. The *Line* method's closing argument, *B*, instructs the method to draw a rectangle or box using the two coordinates mentioned earlier as diagonally opposite endpoints.

```
Private Sub PageFooterSection_Print(Cancel As Integer, _
    PrintCount As Integer)
Dim sngTop As Single, sngLeft As Single
Dim sngWidth As Single, sngHeight As Single
Dim lngColor As Long
Const conPrinterFudge = 25

'Set top, left, width, and height
'conPrinterFudge accounts for printer-specific
'variation of content placement near page edges
    sngTop = Me.ScaleTop
    sngLeft = Me.ScaleLeft
```

```
    sngWidth = Me.ScaleWidth - conPrinterFudge
    sngHeight = Me.ScaleHeight - conPrinterFudge
    'Set color
    lngColor = RGB(255, 0, 0)

'Draw line as a box
    Me.Line (sngTop, sngLeft)-(sngWidth, sngHeight), lngColor, B

End Sub


Private Sub ReportHeader_Print(Cancel As Integer, PrintCount As Integer)
Dim sngTop As Single, sngLeft As Single
Dim sngWidth As Single, sngHeight As Single
Dim lngColor As Long

'Set top, left, width, and height
    sngTop = Me.ScaleTop
    sngLeft = Me.ScaleLeft
    sngWidth = Me.ScaleWidth
    sngHeight = Me.ScaleHeight

'Set color
    lngColor = RGB(255, 0, 0)

'Draw line as a box
    Me.DrawWidth = 25
    Me.Line (sngTop, sngLeft)-(sngWidth, sngHeight), lngColor, B

End Sub

Private Sub Detail_Print(Cancel As Integer, PrintCount As Integer)
Dim sngHCtr As Single, sngVCtr As Single
Dim sngRadius As Single

'Position and size circle
    sngHCtr = (Me.ScaleWidth / 2) - 3670
    sngVCtr = (Me.ScaleHeight / 2) - 20
    sngRadius = Me.ScaleHeight / 1.5

'Conditionally draw circle; last argument sets aspect ratio
    If Me.CountOfOrderID.Value >= 30 Then
        Me.Circle (sngHCtr, sngVCtr), sngRadius, , , , 0.5
    End If

End Sub
```

The only differences between the *ReportHeader_Print* and *PageFooter_Print* procedures are the line setting the width of the rectangle's border and the off-set factor to position the rectangle on a page. The Report Header section uses a width of 25 pixels, but the Page Footer section draws a rectangle with the default width of 1 pixel. This is the default value for the *DrawWidth* property. Both procedures draw a rectangle on a layer in front of the standard report layer. You can see that the red border from the *Line* method appears above the background shading for the report title. The *conPrinterFudge* constant is a printer-specific value in twips. Sometimes when you get near the edge of a page in an Access report, placement can depend on the printer. For the printer I used when testing the samples for this book, I needed an offset of 25 twips. A value of 0 caused the right and bottom lines of the rectangle for the Page Footer section to print off the page. You can determine the appropriate *conPrinterFudge* value for a specific printer through trial runs.

The Detail section's event procedure relies on the *Circle* method to draw an oval around the order totals for each row in that section. You must empirically determine horizontal and vertical centers as well as the radius of your circle. Use an aspect ratio argument in the *Circle* method to transform a circle to a long or narrow oval. Like the *Line* method, the *Circle* method draws its output on a layer in front of the standard report layer. Embedding the *Circle* method in an *If...Then* statement allows the procedure to draw the oval conditionally around some—but not all—*Orders* field values. The previous sample draws ovals around any count of order IDs that's greater than or equal to 30 in a month.

Formatting Report Controls with *FormatCondition* Objects

The application of the *Circle* method in the preceding sample illustrates a traditional technique for distinguishing values on a report. However, *FormatCondition* objects offer a newer approach that synchronizes with the Access user interface. Your clients are likely to request conditional formatting because Access users can readily implement such formats from the user interface.

The excerpt of a sample report shown in Figure 7-25 illustrates the use of *ConditionalFormat* objects with one other feature. Basically, the report prints monthly order totals in either of two colors. Each color corresponds to a *FormatCondition* object. The second feature makes the application of these contrasting colors dynamic. Just before the report opens, the application prompts the user for a cut-off value. Values below the cut-off criterion appear in red, otherwise they are green. By rerunning the report with different criterion values, users can change which values appear in red and which appear in green. As a reminder, the report documents the criterion a user entered in its Report Header section.

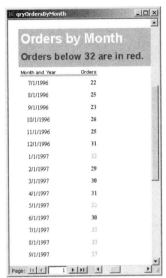

Figure 7-25 An excerpt from a report that uses *FormatCondition* objects to control the color of row values.

If you instantiate *FormatCondition* objects in a report's *Open* event, you need instantiate them only once. The *FormatCondition* objects remain in effect until the report closes. If a report already has conditional formats set through the Access user interface, the *FormatCondition* objects add to the existing objects. Because you can have only three *FormatCondition* objects at any time, you might need to manage the number of active *FormatCondition* objects. The *FormatConditions* collection offers a *Count* property that tells you the number of active conditional formats, and the *FormatCondition* object has a *Delete* method that enables you to remove a conditional format. See "Formatting Controls on Main and Subforms" in Chapter 6 for more code samples containing *FormatCondition* objects.

The *Open* event procedure for the report excerpted in Figure 7-25 follows. An *InputBox* function prompts for a minimum sales target. Monthly order totals less than the minimum criterion that a user enters appear in red. The procedure assigns a caption value to document the criterion in effect for any printing or viewing of the report. Next the procedure adds the first *FormatCondition* object, which applies to values greater than or equal to the criterion. Then the focus shifts to the addition of the second *FormatCondition* object for values less than the criterion. Notice that the *RGB* function assigns the number for the color red to this *FormatCondition* object's *ForeColor* property.

After adding the *FormatCondition* objects through the *frc1* and *frc2* object references, the procedure can safely remove the object references from memory. Their purpose was to set the conditional formats for the CountOfOrderID control. The conditional formats will remain in effect until the report closes.

```
Private Sub Report_Open(Cancel As Integer)
Dim frc1 As FormatCondition
Dim frc2 As FormatCondition
Dim int1 As Integer
Dim str1 As String

'Prompt for criterion value for color assignments, and
'update the lblTarget control caption
int1 = CInt(InputBox("What's the minimum sales target?", _
    "Programming Microsoft Access Version 2002", 30))
str1 = "Orders below " & int1 & " are in red."
Me.lblTarget.Caption = str1

'Condition for values greater than or equal to criterion;
'format is green
Set frc1 = Me.Controls("CountOfOrderID"). _
    FormatConditions. _
    Add(acFieldValue, acGreaterThanOrEqual, int1)
frc1.ForeColor = RGB(0, 255, 0)

'Condition for values less than criterion;
'format is bold, red
Set frc2 = Me.Controls("CountOfOrderID"). _
    FormatConditions. _
    Add(acFieldValue, acLessThan, int1)
frc2.FontBold = True
frc2.ForeColor = RGB(255, 0, 0)

'Clean up objects
Set frc1 = Nothing
Set frc2 = Nothing

End Sub
```

Summing Page Values

If your report requires totaling the entries on a report page, you must program these page sums using event procedures because Access offers no built-in way to do this. The sample we'll examine uses a text box with its Running Sum property set to Over All. This causes the text box to total its Control Source field over the whole report. Figure 7-26 shows the first and second pages of a report that contains an extra column for computing the running sum. The far-right column appears for tutorial purposes, but in practice, you'll set the Visible property for the control with the running sum to False. This sample gives you a way to show or hide this column through compiler constants and the report's *Open* event procedure. The second page of the report, which is shown in Figure 7-26, appears without the running sum column.

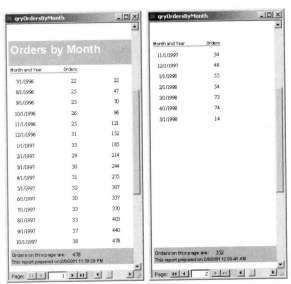

Figure 7-26 This report uses two event procedures and a text box to compute a page sum in its Page Footer section. A third event procedure lets the developer hide the text box that assists in computing the running sum.

You can compute page sums with as few as two event procedures (shown next). Public declarations make the variables conveniently available in either of the event procedures. The *PageFooterSection_Format* event procedure requires only two lines. First, it copies, the value for the pagesum control with the running sum to *lngCurrentRSum*, a memory variable. Then it sets another text box in the Page Footer section (txtpagesum) to the difference between *lngCurrentRSum* and *lngLastRSum*. The value of *lngLastRSum* is initially 0. After every page finishes formatting, a procedure firing with the report's *Page* event copies the current value of *lngCurrentRSum* into *lngLastRSum*. Therefore, the difference between *lngLastRSum* and *lngCurrentRSum* in the *Report_Page* event procedure is the page sum for the current page.

```
Public lngLastRSum As Long,
Public lngCurrentRSum As Long
Public lngPageRSum As Long


Private Sub PageFooterSection_Format _
    (Cancel As Integer, FormatCount As Integer)
    lngCurrentRSum = Me.pagesum
    Me.txtpagesum = lngCurrentRSum - lngLastRSum
End Sub
```

(continued)

```
Private Sub Report_Page()
    lngLastRSum = lngCurrentRSum
End Sub


Private Sub Report_Open(Cancel As Integer)
#Const ShowRunningSum = False

#If ShowRunningSum = True Then
    Me.pagesum.Visible = True
#Else
    Me.pagesum.Visible = False
#End If

End Sub
```

Notice that the *PageFooterSection_Format* event procedure in the sample computes and displays page sums by writing a value into a text box within the Page Footer section. *Print* event procedures do not allow this kind of manipulation because the *Print* event fires after the report is already formatted. The *Format* event fires as your application formats the report.

The *Open* event procedure lets you manage the visibility of the text box that assists with the computation of the running sum. The value of the *#ShowRunningSum*, a compiler constant, is set to False in the sample. Change this value setting to True to hide the pagesum text box. Regardless of whether the text box is visible, it will participate in the computation of the page sums.

Dynamically Updating Reports

In addition to revising the format of a report dynamically, you can devise solutions that let users dynamically specify the contents of a report. Use the *RecordSource* property of a report to set its records dynamically. Unlike Access forms, Access reports do not expose a *Recordset* property for Access database files. Therefore, you cannot dynamically assign an ADO recordset as the source for a report in these files. However, this section describes a workaround you can use.

> **Note**   In contrast to Access database files, Access projects—which are used for SQL Server and MSDE (Microsoft Desktop Engine) databases—do expose a *Recordset* property for their reports. Chapter 15, "Using Access to Build SQL Server Solutions: Part II," covers the use of reports in Access projects.

Programming the *RecordSource* Property

The *RecordSource* property takes a string value as a setting. Therefore, you can design an SQL string that specifies a record source for the report based on user input. This string can reference any local tables and queries, as well as any linked record sources from other databases. Your code can update the report's title to reflect the new content.

Figure 7-27 shows a form and a report. Users can manipulate the form to change the content for the report. The form includes a text box, an option group of five check boxes, and a command button. After entering a number in the text box and selecting a Price Comparison Operator, the user can click the command button to open the report shown on the right in Design view. This view is necessary to add a new record source property and to reset the *Caption* property for the label that displays the report's title. After programmatically updating the two report properties, the application opens the results in Preview mode to display the results of the new record source. Instructions below the report's title explain how to close the form.

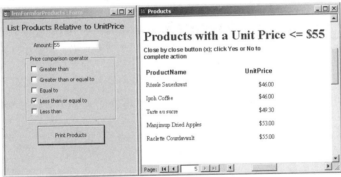

Figure 7-27 In the form on the left, users can designate a record source and a corresponding title for the report on the right.

The *cmdPrintThem_Click* event procedure (shown in the next code listing) for the command button in the form that appears in Figure 7-27 performs three tasks. First, it constructs an SQL string based on selections made in the form. Some default values are generated if the user doesn't set the controls before clicking the button. The procedure successively adds clauses to a starter statement that lists product name and unit price from the *Products* table. The procedure initially appends a WHERE clause to the core statement based on the selected check box and the quantity entered in the text box. After adding the WHERE clause, the procedure appends an ORDER BY clause that sorts the return set from the SQL string by unit price. If a user selects the greater than operator (>) or the greater than or equal to operator (>=), the procedure specifies a descending sort order. Otherwise, the return set sorts by unit price in the default ascending order.

The second component of the *cmdPrintThem_Click* procedure programmatically revises the record source setting and caption for a label on the report. After opening the report in Design view, the code executes a *With...End With* statement based on the report. To eliminate screen clutter, the second component invokes the *Echo* method with an argument of False. This suppresses screen updates until a subsequent statement invokes the *Echo* method with an argument of True. Inside the *With...End With* block, the procedure sets the report's *RecordSource* property to the SQL string computed from the first part of the procedure. Then the procedure changes the caption for the label that displays the report's title. A string expression that draws on the option group value and the amount in the text box facilitates this task.

> **Note**   After making the changes in the second component, the procedure closes the report and saves the revisions. In the earlier versions of Access, it wasn't necessary to commit the changes in order to preview them. However, Access 2002 requires that you explicitly save the changes in Design view before you can view them in Preview mode.

The third component performs two functions. It opens the report in Preview mode so that users can see it. Then the final command restores the *Echo* function, which displays the report. This technique of turning off and then restoring the *Echo* effect leads to crisp screen transitions. Let's take a look at the procedure now:

```
Private Sub cmdPrintThem_Click()
Dim str1 As String, strOperator As String
Dim strWhere As String

'Set up SQL statement for report record source
    str1 = "Select ProductName, UnitPrice " & _
        "from Products"
    If IsNull(optRule) Then optRule = 1
    If IsNull(txtAmount) Then txtAmount = 0
    strOperator = Choose(optRule, ">", ">=", "=", "<=", "<")
    strWhere = "Where UnitPrice" & strOperator & txtAmount
    str1 = str1 & " " & strWhere & " Order By UnitPrice"
    If optRule <= 2 Then
        str1 = str1 & " Desc"
    End If
```

```
'The commented Debug.Print statement is convenient for debugging
'your SQL statement; remove the comment when you change the
'SQL statement construction
'    Debug.Print str1

'Open report in Design view to set the report's record source
'and its label's caption
    DoCmd.Echo False
    DoCmd.OpenReport "rptProductsfromForm", acViewDesign
    With Reports("rptProductsfromForm")
        .RecordSource = str1
        .Controls("lblTitle").Caption = _
            "Products with a Unit Price " & strOperator & _
            " $" & txtAmount
    End With
    DoCmd.Close , , acSaveYes

'Now show the form to the user
    DoCmd.OpenReport "rptProductsfromForm", acViewPreview
    DoCmd.Echo True

End Sub
```

Using an ADO Recordset as the Report's Record Source

Unlike forms, reports do not expose a *Recordset* property within Access database files. Therefore, if you have an ADO recordset you're using for some other purpose, you cannot simply assign it to the *Recordset* property of a report. However, you can link the data source for a recordset in an Access database file. Then you can assign the SQL statement that serves as the source for the ADO recordset to the *RecordSource* property. The connection from the report to the records does not actually pass through the recordset. However, an Access report can emulate the recordset connection with a link from the database file to the recordset data source and the SQL statement that serves as the recordset's *Source* property.

The next sample demonstrates how to use the records in an ADO recordset as the source for a report in an Access database file. By using an *InputBox* function, the sample lets a user dynamically set the source for a recordset. The sample loops through the members of the *AllTables* collection to determine whether the Access database file contains a link to the data source for the recordset. If the database file already contains a link, the report can use the SQL statement that serves as the *Source* property for the recordset. If no link to the remote data source for the recordset exists, the procedure creates a link to the data source for the recordset's connection.

The sample procedure starts by instantiating and opening a connection to the Northwind database. Any database source will work, but you might have to change the method for linking the database. This sample demonstrates linking to an Access database file. Chapter 2, "Data Access Models: Part I," includes a code sample for linking to any ODBC-compliant data source. Next the procedure prompts for the first letter of a customer ID. The *rst1* recordset uses this criterion value to select only those customer IDs with the specified first letter.

After opening the recordset, the procedure prepares to start using the excerpt from the *Customers* table as the source for a report of mailing labels. This chapter's database file on the companion CD contains the layout for the report saved in *rptMailingLabels*.

Before transferring the *Source* property from the recordset to the *RecordSource* property for the *rptMailingLabels* report, the procedure takes a couple of preliminary steps. First, the procedure lets the user know that it might take a while to compile the data for the report, and it temporarily turns off screen updating. Second, the procedure relies on the *IsLinked* function to search for a table named *Customers* in the current database. If the linked table does not exist, the procedure links to the *Customers* table in the Northwind database. Otherwise, the procedure uses the existing linked table. In any event, the procedure uses a Boolean memory variable (*bol1*) to note whether the linked table existed previously.

> **Note** This sample assumes no conflicts exist between the names in the current database and those in the database to which you're connecting. You will typically control the names of the tables in the local database and sometimes even in the linked database.

At this point in the procedure, a link to the *Customers* table definitely exists in the Northwind database. Therefore, the sample assigns the recordset's *Source* property to the report's *RecordSource* property. After saving the change made in Design view to the report, the procedure opens the report in Preview mode and restores screen updating. This last step is necessary to view the report. As the procedure closes, it performs the usual object cleanup and checks whether it can remove the link to the *Customers* table in the Northwind database. If the link was added exclusively for the report, the procedure can delete the link; otherwise, it will not remove the link.

```
Sub ReportBasedOnADORecordset()
Dim cnn1 As ADODB.Connection
Dim rst1 As ADODB.Recordset
```

```
Dim str2 As String
Dim rpt1 As Access.Report
Dim bol1 As Boolean

'Open the Connection object
Set cnn1 = New ADODB.Connection
cnn1.Open "Provider=Microsoft.Jet.OLEDB.4.0;" & _
    "Data Source=C:\PMA Samples\Northwind.mdb;"

'Obtain a criterion for rst1 WHERE clause, and
'construct Select statement
str1 = InputBox("Enter the first letter for a CustomerID", _
    "Programming Microsoft Access Version 2002", "A")
str1 = "SELECT * FROM Customers WHERE Left(CustomerID,1) " & _
    "= '" & str1 & "'"

'Open the ADO Recordset object
Set rst1 = New ADODB.Recordset
rst1.ActiveConnection = cnn1
rst1.Open str1, , adOpenKeyset, adLockOptimistic, _
    adCmdText

'Link Customers if not in AllTables
MsgBox "Click OK to start compiling data for report.  " & _
    "Please be patient.", vbInformation, _
    "Programming Microsoft Access Version 2002"
DoCmd.Echo False
bol1 = IsLinked("Customers")
If bol1 = False Then
    DoCmd.TransferDatabase acLink, "Microsoft Access", _
        "C:\PMA Samples\Northwind.mdb", _
        acTable, "Customers", "Customers", False
End If

'Assign Source property of ADO recordset to RecordSource
'property for the report, and save the report
str2 = "rptMailingLabels"
DoCmd.OpenReport str2, acViewDesign
Set rpt1 = Reports(str2)
rpt1.RecordSource = rst1.Source
DoCmd.Close , , acSaveYes

'Open report for viewing
DoCmd.OpenReport str2, acViewPreview
DoCmd.Echo True

'Clean up objects and links
rst1.Close
```

(continued)

```
        cnn1.Close
        Set rst1 = Nothing
        Set cnn1 = Nothing
        If bol1 = False Then DoCmd.DeleteObject acTable, "Customers"

        End Sub


        Function IsLinked(str1 As String) As Boolean
        Dim obj1 As Access.AccessObject

        'Returns True if filename is in AllTables
        For Each obj1 In CurrentData.AllTables
            If obj1.Name = str1 Then
                IsLinked = True
                Exit Function
            End If
        Next obj1

        End Function
```

> **Note**   While it is not entirely relevant to the sample, I stuck the following
> *NoData* event procedure into the code for the *rptMailingLabels* report:
>
> ```
> Private Sub Report_NoData(Cancel As Integer)
>     MsgBox "No data for report. Report canceled."
>     Cancel = True
> End Sub
> ```
>
> This event procedure shows you the syntax to cancel a report when no
> data exists in the report's record source.

Manipulating Reports and Report Controls

In Chapter 6, you learned about the *AllForms* collection. Access also provides an
AllReports collection as well as the *AllTables*, *AllQueries*, *AllMacros*, *AllViews*,
AllModules, *AllStoredProcedures*, *AllDataAccessPages*, and *AllDataDiagrams* collections. A member of any of these collections is an *AccessObject* object. Microsoft
first introduced *AccessObject* objects with Access 2000. You can refer to an *AllReports*
member by one of three conventions:

```
AllReports (0)
AllReports ("name")
AllReports![name]
```

Enumerating Reports

Your code can enumerate *AccessObject* objects in any of the *Allxxx* collections to determine whether objects exist in a database connection. It does not matter whether the object is open or closed. When an *AccessObject* object is loaded or open, your application can work with corresponding collections. that encompass all the open reports, forms, and other important objects in an Access database. For example, members of the *Reports* collection are individual reports that are open in an application. These open *Report* objects contain a richer set of properties than the more restricted set of objects in the *AllReports* collection. In addition, members of the *Reports* collection employ methods that the *AllReports* collection members do not make available. You can use the *Name* property in *AllReports* and *Reports* to identify a particular object in either collection. By using the *IsLoaded* property in the *AllReports* collection, you can verify whether you need to open a report before attempting to manipulate its properties and methods using the *Reports* collection.

The *ListAllReports* procedure that follows enumerates the members of the *AllReports* collection listing each report's name and loaded status. The *AllReports* collection belongs to either the *CurrentProject* or the *CodeProject*. *CurrentProject* and *CodeProject* are members of the *Application* object. You must reference one of these two members to expose the *AllReports* members. Therefore, the *ListAllReports* procedure starts by setting a reference to the *CurrentProject* member of the *Application* object. You need this reference to reach the members of the *AllReports* collection. Notice that the *For...Each* loop passes through each *AccessObject* object (*obj1*) in *AllReports*, but the path to *AllReports* starts with the reference to *Application.CurrentProject*.

```
Sub ListAllReports()
Dim obj1 As AccessObject, app1 As Object

'Create a reference to the current project instance
Set app1 = Application.CurrentProject

'List each report in the application, and
'describe as loaded or not
For Each obj1 In app1.AllReports
    If obj1.IsLoaded = True Then
        Debug.Print obj1.Name & " is loaded."
```

(continued)

```
      Else
          Debug.Print obj1.Name & " is not loaded."
      End If
Next obj1

End Sub
```

The *AllReports* and *AllForms* collections are directly analogous to one another. You are not restricted to examining *AccessObject* members in the active project. The *ListAllFormsElsewhere* and *ListAllReportsElsewhere* procedures, which you'll see in a moment, show how to program both collections when they point at another project. Notice the similarity between the code that manipulates the two collections as well as between the procedure shown above which works with the current project and the two procedures shown below which work with another project.

The *ListAllFormsElsewhere* procedure shown next prints the total number and the names of individual members in the *AllForms* collection for Chapter 06.mdb. This procedure demonstrates how to enumerate *AccessObject* objects in another database file. You'll find this file on the book's companion CD.

```
Sub ListAllFormsElsewhere()
Dim appAccess1 As Access.Application
Dim obj1 As AccessObject

'Create a reference to another database file
Set appAccess1 = New Access.Application
appAccess1.OpenCurrentDatabase _
    "C:\PMA Samples\Chapter 06\Chapter 06.mdb"

'Print the total number of forms in the database
Debug.Print appAccess1.CurrentProject.AllForms.Count
For Each obj1 In appAccess1.CurrentProject.AllForms
    Debug.Print obj1.Name
Next obj1

'Close objects
appAccess1.CloseCurrentDatabase

End Sub
```

The *ListAllReportsElsewhere* procedure shown next follows the same general design as the preceding one, although it deals with the *AllReports* collection instead of the *AllForms* collection and it uses the Northwind.mdb database instead of Chapter 06.mdb. The layout is nearly identical except for the use of string variables to define the database name. This change is strictly for convenience and to make the code more generally applicable—nothing in Access or VBA mandates the use of a string variable instead of a string constant in the call to the *OpenCurrentDatabase* method.

```
Sub ListAllReportsElsewhere()
Dim obj1 As AccessObject
Dim srtPath As String, strFile As String, strDBName As String

'Create a reference to another database file
Set appAccess1 = New Access.Application
strPath = "C:\PMA Samples\"
strFile = "Northwind.mdb"
strDBName = strPath & strFile
appAccess1.OpenCurrentDatabase strDBName

'Print the total number of reports in the database
Debug.Print appAccess1.CurrentProject.AllReports.Count
For Each obj1 In appAccess1.CurrentProject.AllReports
    Debug.Print obj1.Name
Next obj1

'Close objects
appAccess1.CloseCurrentDatabase

End Sub
```

Modifying Report Control Properties

Your application code can use the *AllReports* collection as a pathway to individual reports that are open and their controls. Using this pathway, your application can read and modify the properties of these open reports and their controls. The *ControlsInReports* procedure (shown next) drills down from the *AllReports* collection members to the text box and label properties on individual reports that are open.

The *ControlsInReports* procedure starts with a *For...Each* loop that iterates through the members of the *AllReports* collection. If a member is open, as indicated by a value of True for its *IsLoaded* property, the code enters a nested *For...Each* loop to enumerate the controls on that report. You can use the *ControlType* property to determine a control's type. You need to know the control type because this determines the properties that the control exposes. For example, a label control displays its *Caption* property, but a text box displays its *Value* property. You can use the Object Browser in the VBE to view the intrinsic constants of other control types that you want to edit or examine. Forms and reports share the same set of control types. For the full set of control types from the Object Browser, see Figure 6-20 on page 376 in Chapter 6.

This program contains an error trap in case the procedure loops to a report that's open in Design view. A report open in Design view has an *IsLoaded* property value of True. However, the display value of a text box control is not available in Design view. Attempting to print or otherwise access this report generates an *Err* object with a *Number* property of 2186. The solution is to open the report in Preview mode. Then when the procedure completes printing the text box values, the code restores the Design view for the report.

```
Sub ControlsInReports()
On Error GoTo ControlsInReports_Trap
Dim obj1 As AccessObject
Dim ctl1 As Control
Dim bol1 As Boolean


'Loop through the reports in the Access database file
'or Access project
For Each obj1 In CurrentProject.AllReports
    If obj1.IsLoaded = True Then
Start_Printing:
'If the report is open, loop through the report's
'controls and print property values for label and
'text box controls
        For Each ctl1 In Reports(obj1.Name).Controls
            If ctl1.ControlType = acLabel Then
                Debug.Print ctl1.Name, ctl1.Caption
            ElseIf ctl1.ControlType = acTextBox Then
                Debug.Print ctl1.Name, ctl1.Value
            Else
                Debug.Print ctl1.Name & " is not a" & _
                    " label or a text box."
            End If
        Next ctl1
'Restore Design view if the procedure changed the view

        If bol1 = True Then
            DoCmd.OpenReport obj1.Name, acViewDesign
            bol1 = False
        End If
    End If
Next obj1

ControlsInReports_Exit:
Exit Sub

ControlsInReports_Trap:
If Err.Number = 2186 Then
'Open in Preview mode if Design view generates error
```

```
        DoCmd.OpenReport obj1.Name, acViewPreview
        bol1 = True
        Resume Start_Printing
    Else
        Debug.Print Err.Number, Err.Description
    End If

    End Sub
```

Mailing Snapshots

The next sample enumerates reports to determine whether they are marked for mailing as snapshot files. The sample relies on two procedures: *SendSnapshots* and *CheckMailItTag*. First, the *SendSnapshots* procedure enumerates the members of the *AllReports* collection. In order to check whether the report's *Tag* property is *"mail it"*, the report must be open. The *Tag* property is not available through the *AllReports* collection—it is available only through the *Reports* collection. The *SendSnapshots* procedure checks the *IsLoaded* status of each *AllReports* member. If the report is loaded, the procedure calls the *CheckMailItTag* procedure. If *IsLoaded* has a value of False, the procedure opens the report before calling the second procedure.

The sample does not call the *Echo* method with a *False* parameter, so a user can easily obtain feedback as the second procedure runs. This is particularly appropriate in cases where it takes a while to create and mail the snapshot file. By the way, in the collection of reports in the CD's database file for this chapter, only one report (*rptOrdersByMonth*) has a setting of *"mail it"* for its *Tag* property.

The *CheckMailItTag* procedure accepts the report name passed to it by *SendSnapshots*. *CheckMailItTag* uses this report name to create a reference to the *Reports* collection member with the same name. Then *CheckMailItTag* checks the *Tag* property of the report to determine whether it equals *"mail it"*. If it does, the procedure invokes the *DoCmd* object's *SendObject* method to create a snapshot file and send it to an e-mail address (in this case, virginia@cabinc.net). You can replace the string constant for the address with any single address or series of addresses that your application requires. Be sure that the argument after the message body (*"Here is the report."*) remains False. If you use the default value of True, your procedure will halt with the message open and wait for the user to edit the message. Setting the value to False enables the procedure to loop through all the reports without any user intervention.

> **Note**   Make sure that Microsoft Outlook is open before invoking the
> *DoCmd.SendObject* command in the *CheckMailItTag* procedure. Oth-
> erwise, the *SendObject* method will try to launch Outlook and link to the
> Internet as if being launched for the first time. See Chapter 11, "Integrat-
> ing Access with Other Office Applications," for samples that open Outlook
> automatically.

```
Sub SendSnapshots()
Dim obj1 As AccessObject
Dim app1 As Object

'Create a reference to the current project instance
    Set app1 = Application.CurrentProject

'Enumerate each member in AllReports to verify if loaded.
'If not loaded, open before calling CheckMailItTag.
    For Each obj1 In app1.AllReports
        If obj1.IsLoaded = True Then
            CheckMailItTag obj1.Name
        Else
            DoCmd.OpenReport obj1.Name, acViewPreview
            CheckMailItTag obj1.Name
            DoCmd.Close acReport, obj1.Name, acSaveNo
        End If
    Next obj1

End Sub


'Open Outlook before invoking this procedure
Sub CheckMailItTag(obj1name)
Dim rep1 As Report

'Set reference to Reports member corresponding
'to AllReports member
    Set rep1 = Reports(obj1name)

'If Tag property says "mail it",
'create a snapshot file and mail it
    If rep1.Tag = "mail it" Then
        DoCmd.SendObject acOutputReport, obj1name, _
        acFormatSNP, "virginia@cabinc.net", , , _
```

```
        "Snapshot Report", "Here is the report.", False
    End If

End Sub
```

Case Study: A FrontPage Guestbook

Using FrontPage, you can easily create and view a guestbook that collects visitor information (such as names and e-mail addresses) in an HTML-formatted Web page. Visitors to the Web site will see a professional-looking form in which they can enter their contact information. Building a guestbook requires no knowledge of databases or ODBC connections. In fact, because a FrontPage wizard can create the guestbook file, this technique requires very little knowledge of FrontPage either. This approach to creating a guestbook works well as long as the site does not attract a high volume of guestbook registrants.

If visitor volume swells, you can transfer the complete set of contact information to a database file. Even if a site switches to depositing the data directly into a database, you still have the problem of recovering the initial HTML-formatted information. This case study illustrates one approach to recovering legacy text data and demonstrates how to generate mailing labels and form letters with the converted information.

This section provides some sample code for converting the content from a FrontPage guestbook for use with Access. As with most of the code in this book, the emphasis is on starting to tackle the problem. A production system or even a commercial conversion will likely have much more code for importing and cleaning the data. However, the sample code here illustrates the kinds of tasks that you're almost certain to include in your programs. This sample also illustrates general techniques for converting text data for use in Access. As you read the case study, remember that it's not only about processing HTML data; these techniques are applicable to any text-processing requirements, and such requirements arise regularly for developers.

Importing Data

One of the most straightforward ways to capture content from a guestbook file in FrontPage is to copy and paste an excerpt from the file's HTML tab into Notepad. Microsoft Windows will automatically upgrade to WordPad if the amount of content exceeds Notepad's limits. In any event, save the content as a text file. Then you can use the Access Text Import Wizard to convert the data to a table. Recall that you launch the wizard by choosing File-Get External Data-Import. Your guestbook data will be imported into Access as one column, and by default, the wizard will add an *AutoNumber* column to distinguish the rows.

Figure 7-28 shows excerpts from the raw HTML-formatted file that display two records (for Karl Doe1 and Boban Doe2). Notice the huge number of HTML tags. The internal FrontPage browser uses these tags to format the guestbook display, but the tags make it impossible to directly import the data into an Access table for the preparation of mailing labels. All the contact information appears in one wide column. Some rows contain contact data, but other rows hold descriptive labels or serve general formatting purposes. Relational database processing conventions dictate a separate row for each guestbook registrant. This requires spreading the information that appears for one registrant in a single column across several columns.

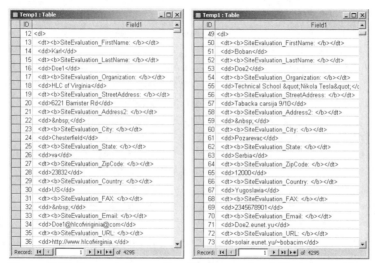

Figure 7-28 Excerpts from a FrontPage guestbook file imported into an Access table.

Regardless of whether you encounter this precise data conversion requirement, Access development typically requires the processing of a text stream. Large businesses often must convert legacy departmental data to a relational database format using a similar process. The rich array of string processing functions and VBA in Access help you customize and automate this kind of task in a more robust manner than by using the Text Import Wizard alone.

Converting the Data Structure

The goal of this string processing effort is to transform the data in a table similar to the *Temp1* table in Figure 7-28 into a more traditional contact table layout, such as that of the table shown in Figure 7-29. The conversion strategy relies on two recordsets—one for the source table and one for the destination table. The procedure moves down the rows of the source table to extract the contact information and store the parsed data in variables. After parsing all the essential data for a contact, the procedure adds the parsed data as a new row to the destination table. Because different contact fields have unique requirements, the parsing rules sometimes vary between fields. Rules can also vary because the raw data for a field represents unique problems not present for other fields.

The following excerpt from the procedure transforms the data from the format shown in the table in Figure 7-28 to the format shown in the table in Figure 7-29. This sample presents the conversion code for typical contact fields containing items such as the user's first name, last name, company name, and e-mail address. While the listing is lengthy, converting data is a critical first step for Access database projects. If you don't successfully address this issue, your Access project and any special reports that you develop might not start!

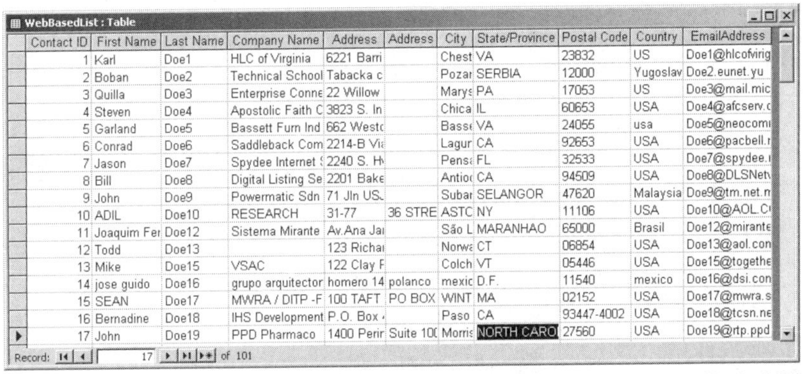

WebBasedList : Table

Contact ID	First Name	Last Name	Company Name	Address	Address	City	State/Province	Postal Code	Country	EmailAddress
1	Karl	Doe1	HLC of Virginia	6221 Barri		Chest	VA	23832	US	Doe1@hlcofvirig
2	Boban	Doe2	Technical School	Tabacka c		Pozar	SERBIA	12000	Yugoslav	Doe2.eunet.yu
3	Quilla	Doe3	Enterprise Conne	22 Willow		Marys	PA	17053	US	Doe3@mail.mic
4	Steven	Doe4	Apostolic Faith C	3823 S. In		Chica	IL	60653	USA	Doe4@afcserv.c
5	Garland	Doe5	Bassett Furn Ind	662 Westc		Bass	VA	24055	usa	Doe5@neocom
6	Conrad	Doe6	Saddleback Com	2214-B Vi		Lagur	CA	92653	USA	Doe6@pacbell.r
7	Jason	Doe7	Spydee Internet	2240 S. H		Pens	FL	32533	USA	Doe7@spydee.
8	Bill	Doe8	Digital Listing Se	2201 Bake		Antio	CA	94509	USA	Doe8@DLSNet
9	John	Doe9	Powermatic Sdn	71 Jln US.		Subar	SELANGOR	47620	Malaysia	Doe9@tm.net.m
10	ADIL	Doe10	RESEARCH	31-77	36 STRE	ASTC	NY	11106	USA	Doe10@AOL.C
11	Joaquim Fer	Doe12	Sistema Mirante	Av.Ana Jai		São L	MARANHAO	65000	Brasil	Doe12@mirante
12	Todd	Doe13		123 Richa		Norwa	CT	06854	USA	Doe13@aol.con
13	Mike	Doe15	VSAC	122 Clay F		Colch	VT	05446	USA	Doe15@togethe
14	jose guido	Doe16	grupo arquitector	homero 14	polanco	mexic	D.F.	11540	mexico	Doe16@dsi.con
15	SEAN	Doe17	MWRA / DITP -F	100 TAFT	PO BOX	WINT	MA	02152	USA	Doe17@mwra.s
16	Bernadine	Doe18	IHS Development	P.O. Box		Paso	CA	93447-4002	USA	Doe18@tcsn.ne
17	John	Doe19	PPD Pharmaco	1400 Perir	Suite 10	Morris	NORTH CARO	27560	USA	Doe19@rtp.ppd

Record: 17 of 101

Figure 7-29 Converted contact data from a FrontPage guestbook file in HTML format. The conversion removes HTML tags and places each contact record on a separate row.

The code sample uses two recordsets. One points at the *temp1* table. (Excerpts from this table appear in Figure 7-28.) This table contains the raw guestbook data with HTML tags. The second recordset points at the *WebBasedList* table. (An excerpt from this table appears in Figure 7-29.) The sample code copies fields from the first recordset and to the second one by looping through each of the rows in the first recordset. After the procedure compiles the data for a single contact record in a set of memory variables, it uses the variables to set new field values for the second recordset.

The code for the first three contact fields illustrates typical techniques used for other fields throughout the procedure. Each of the three converted fields relies on slightly different parsing logic. You can read the comments and study the code to gain insights about VBA functions useful for string processing. After conversion, the code checks to make sure that any field conversion did not set the skip flag (*blSkip*) to True. A False value for the skip flag enables the procedure to add a new record to the relational contact table in the format shown in Figure 7-29. The procedure then moves on to a new record in the source table (the copy of the FrontPage guestbook). When the original source table returns its end of file (EOF) as True, the outer *Do* loop ends and the procedure halts.

```
Sub getfp()
Dim rst1 As ADODB.Recordset
Dim strFname As String
Dim strLname As String
Dim strCname As String
Dim strSt1 As String
Dim strSt2 As String
Dim strCity As String
Dim strSt As String
Dim strPostal As String
Dim strCountry As String
Dim blSkip As Boolean
Dim strEmail As String
Dim rst2 As ADODB.Recordset

'Open two recordsets, and set references to them
Set rst1 = New ADODB.Recordset
Set rst2 = New ADODB.Recordset
With rst1
    .ActiveConnection = CurrentProject.Connection
    .CursorType = adOpenKeyset
    .LockType = adLockOptimistic
'Raw contact info is in table temp1
    .Open "temp1"
End With
With rst2
    .ActiveConnection = CurrentProject.Connection
    .CursorType = adOpenKeyset
    .LockType = adLockOptimistic
'The application stores parsed contact info in the WebBasedList table
    .Open "WebBasedList"
End With

'Start a loop through the recordset of raw contact information
Do Until rst1.EOF
    blSkip = False
```

```
'Start a new contact record when you find
'a label named "SiteEvaluation_FirstName:"
    If InStr(1, rst1.Fields(1), "SiteEvaluation_FirstName:") <> 0 Then
        rst1.MoveNext
        If rst1.Fields(1) <> "  <dd> </dd>" Then
'The length of the first name field is the number of
'characters between ">" and "<" delimiters
            intFirst = InStr(1, rst1.Fields(1), ">") + 1
            intLen = InStr(6, rst1.Fields(1), "<") - intFirst
            strFname = Mid(rst1.Fields(1), intFirst, intLen)
'Move two records to process last name field
            rst1.Move 2
        Else
'If the first name is blank, set a Boolean flag
'to skip the whole record
            blSkip = True
        End If
'Process last name field
        intFirst = InStr(1, rst1.Fields(1), ">") + 1
        intLen = InStr(6, rst1.Fields(1), "<") - intFirst
        strLname = Mid(rst1.Fields(1), intFirst, intLen)
'Process company name field
        rst1.Move 2
        If rst1.Fields(1) <> "  <dd> </dd>" Then
            intFirst = InStr(1, rst1.Fields(1), ">") + 1
            intLen = InStr(6, rst1.Fields(1), "<") - intFirst
'If there is a leading blank in the company name field,
'see if you can find the name after the blank
            If InStr(2, rst1.Fields(1), " ") <> 0 Then
                intLen = _
                    InStr(6, rst1.Fields(1), " ") - intFirst
            End If
'The parsing rule for the company name field converts with the
'VBA Replace function HTML's &quot; into a single apostrophe
            strCname = _
                Replace(Mid(rst1.Fields(1), intFirst, intLen), _
                "&quot;", "'")
        Else
'Set company name to zero-length string if there is no
'entry for the field
            strCname = ""
        End If
'Move to first street field
        rst1.Move 2
        If rst1.Fields(1) <> "  <dd> </dd>" Then
            intFirst = InStr(1, rst1.Fields(1), ">") + 1
            intLen = InStr(6, rst1.Fields(1), "<") - intFirst
            If InStr(2, rst1.Fields(1), " ") <> 0 Then
```

(continued)

```
                        intLen = InStr(6, rst1.Fields(1), " ") - intFirst
                    End If
                    strSt1 = Mid(rst1.Fields(1), intFirst, intLen)
                Else
                    blSkip = True
                End If
    'Move to second street field
            rst1.Move 2
            intFirst = InStr(1, rst1.Fields(1), ">") + 1
            intLen = InStr(6, rst1.Fields(1), "<") - intFirst
                If InStr(2, rst1.Fields(1), " ") <> 0 Then
                    intLen = _
                        InStr(6, rst1.Fields(1), " ") - intFirst
                End If
            strSt2 = Mid(rst1.Fields(1), intFirst, intLen)
    'Move to city field
            rst1.Move 2
            intFirst = InStr(1, rst1.Fields(1), ">") + 1
            intLen = InStr(6, rst1.Fields(1), "<") - intFirst
                If InStr(2, rst1.Fields(1), " ") <> 0 Then
                    intLen = _
                        InStr(6, rst1.Fields(1), " ") - intFirst
                End If
            strCity = Mid(rst1.Fields(1), intFirst, intLen)
    'Move to state field
            rst1.Move 2
            intFirst = InStr(1, rst1.Fields(1), ">") + 1
            intLen = InStr(6, rst1.Fields(1), "<") - intFirst
                If InStr(2, rst1.Fields(1), " ") <> 0 Then
                    intLen = _
                        InStr(6, rst1.Fields(1), " ") - intFirst
                End If
    'Use the VBA StrConv function to make state field UPPERCASE
            strSt = StrConv(Mid(rst1.Fields(1), intFirst, intLen), _
            vbUpperCase)
            If strCity = "" Or strSt = "" Then
                blSkip = True
            End If
    'Move to postal code field
            rst1.Move 2
            intFirst = InStr(1, rst1.Fields(1), ">") + 1
            intLen = InStr(6, rst1.Fields(1), "<") - intFirst
                If InStr(2, rst1.Fields(1), " ") <> 0 Then
                    intLen = _
                        InStr(6, rst1.Fields(1), " ") - intFirst
                End If
            strPostal = Mid(rst1.Fields(1), intFirst, intLen)
    'Move to country field
```

```
        rst1.Move 2
        If rst1.Fields(1) <> "  <dd> </dd>" Then
            intFirst = InStr(1, rst1.Fields(1), ">") + 1
            intLen = InStr(6, rst1.Fields(1), "<") - intFirst
            strCountry = Mid(rst1.Fields(1), intFirst, intLen)
        Else
            strCountry = ""
        End If
'Move to EmailAddress field
        rst1.Move 4
        If rst1.Fields(1) <> "  <dd> </dd>" Then
            intFirst = InStr(1, rst1.Fields(1), ">") + 1
            intLen = InStr(6, rst1.Fields(1), "<") - intFirst
            strEmailAddress = Mid(rst1.Fields(1), intFirst, intLen)
        Else
            strEmailAddress = ""
        End If
'If Boolean skip flag is False, copy converted contact info
'to rst2, which is reference for WebBasedList table
        If blSkip = False Then
            With rst2
                .AddNew
                    .Fields("FirstName") = strFname
                    .Fields("LastName") = strLname
                    .Fields("CompanyName") = strCname
                    .Fields("Address1") = strSt1
                    .Fields("Address2") = strSt2
                    .Fields("City") = strCity
                    .Fields("StateOrProvince") = strSt
                    .Fields("PostalCode") = strPostal
                    .Fields("Country") = strCountry
                    .Fields("EmailAddress") = strEmailAddress
                .Update
            End With
        End If
    End If
'Move to next record in temp1 table, and start search
'for a record including label for first name
    rst1.MoveNext
Loop

'Clean up objects
rst1.Close
rst2.Close
Set rst1 = Nothing
Set rst2 = Nothing

End Sub
```

Cleaning Converted Data

Whenever you work with data, it's prudent to plan for inconsistent or downright erroneous input. A casual glance at Figure 7-29 confirms that the case study's data illustrates this problem. The *EmailAddress* field for the record with a *ContactID* value of 2 has an invalid e-mail address because the e-mail address doesn't contain an at (@) sign. In addition, most rows use two-letter abbreviations to represent state names, but the entry with a *ContactID* of 17 lists the full name of a state. Inconsistent and erroneous data can make queries and programs fail. Therefore, you should devise cleaning procedures for your data. The next two samples illustrate approaches to this. The first code sample cleans the state and country designations. The second sample excludes records with erroneous or missing e-mail addresses.

The program to clean the country designations relies on a table of state abbreviations (*tblStateAbbreviations*). This table, which is contained in the chapter's sample file on the companion CD, includes two columns and 55 rows for each of the 50 states as well as other U.S. geographic locations, such as Washington, D.C.; Guam; and Puerto Rico. The first column, *StateName*, contains the long name for the geographic units. The second column contains the abbreviations for the geographic units.

The next procedure uses the *tblStateAbbreviations* table twice with the *WebBasedList* table. First, the procedure compares the *StateOrProvince* field values in the *WebBasedList* table to see whether there's a match in the *Abbreviation* column of *tblStateAbbreviations*. When it finds a match, the procedure changes the *Country* column value to *USA*. Second, the sample procedure checks whether a user entered the full name for a geographic unit, such as *North Carolina*. When the code finds an instance of this, the program replaces the geographic unit's full name with its abbreviation and revises the *Country* column value to *USA*.

```
Sub CleanUSStatesAndCountry()
Dim rst1 As ADODB.Recordset
Dim rst2 As ADODB.Recordset
Dim str1 As String

'Point rst1 at WebBasedList table
Set rst1 = New ADODB.Recordset
rst1.Open "WebBasedList", _
    CurrentProject.Connection, _
    adOpenKeyset, adLockOptimistic

'Instantiate rst2 for SELECT statement
Set rst2 = New ADODB.Recordset

'Loop through WebBasedList rows
```

```
Do Until rst1.EOF
'Open recordset to check for valid U.S. state abbreviation
    str1 = "SELECT Abbreviation " & _
        "FROM tblStateAbbreviations " & _
        "WHERE Abbreviation = '" & _
        rst1("StateOrProvince") & "'"
    rst2.Open str1, CurrentProject.Connection, adOpenKeyset, _
        adLockOptimistic
'If abbreviation is valid, revise Country field to standard for USA
    If rst2.RecordCount <> 0 Then
        rst1("Country") = "USA"
    End If
    rst2.Close
'Open recordset to check for valid U.S. state name
    str1 = "SELECT Abbreviation " & _
        "FROM tblStateAbbreviations " & _
        "WHERE StateName = '" & _
        rst1("StateOrProvince") & "'"
    rst2.Open str1, CurrentProject.Connection, adOpenKeyset, _
        adLockOptimistic
'If state name is valid, replace with state abreviation and
'revise Country field to standard for USA
    If rst2.RecordCount <> 0 Then
        rst1("StateOrProvince") = rst2("Abbreviation")
        rst1("Country") = "USA"
    End If
    rst2.Close
    rst1.MoveNext
Loop

'Clean up objects
rst1.Close
Set rst1 = Nothing
Set rst2 = Nothing

End Sub
```

The second cleaning program takes a different approach. This sample procedure removes records that have invalid e-mail addresses from the *WebBasedList* table. The code saves these records in the *WebBasedListBadData* table for recovery by manually fixing the bad e-mail addresses. The procedure uses two criteria to assess whether an e-mail address is bad. First, if the address does not contain an @, the address is considered bad. An *int1* value of *0* reflects this condition. Records with missing e-mail addresses also fail this test. Second, if an address contains two @ signs, it is also considered invalid. A value of *int2* other than *0* reflects this second condition for bad data. When a record passes either of these bad data tests, the procedure copies its field values to the

WebBasedListBadData table and removes the record from the *WebBasedList* table.

```
Sub BadEmailAddresses()
Dim rst1 As ADODB.Recordset
Dim rst2 As ADODB.Recordset
Dim int1 As Integer
Dim int2 As Integer
Dim fld1 As ADODB.Field

'Point rst1 at WebBasedList table and
'rst2 at WebBasedListBadData table
Set rst1 = New ADODB.Recordset
Set rst2 = New ADODB.Recordset
rst1.Open "WebBasedList", _
    CurrentProject.Connection, _
    adOpenKeyset, adLockOptimistic, adCmdTable
rst2.Open "WebBasedListBadData", _
    CurrentProject.Connection, _
    adOpenKeyset, adLockOptimistic, adCmdTable

'Remove records with missing @ or more than one
'@ in their EmailAddress field
Do Until rst1.EOF
    int1 = InStr(1, rst1("EmailAddress"), "@")
    int2 = InStr(int1 + 1, rst1("EmailAddress"), "@")
    If int1 = 0 Or int2 <> 0 Then
        rst2.AddNew
            For Each fld1 In rst2.Fields
                rst2(fld1.Name) = rst1(fld1.Name)
            Next fld1
            rst1.Delete
        rst2.Update
    End If
    rst1.MoveNext
Loop

'Clean up objects
rst1.Close
rst2.Close
Set rst1 = Nothing
Set rst2 = Nothing

End Sub
```

Figure 7-30 includes excerpts from two tables. The top panel shows the cleaned version of the *WebBasedList* table. Notice that the *StateOrProvince* field for the record with a *ContactID* value of 17 contains an abbreviation, although the initial version of this field (shown in Figure 7-29) contains a state name. The second panel shows the four records transferred from the *WebBasedList* table to the *WebBasedListBadData* table. The first record in the *WebBasedListBadData* table has two @ signs in its *EmailAddress* field. One of these @ signs is clipped by the shortened column width. The remaining three records obviously do not contain valid e-mail addresses.

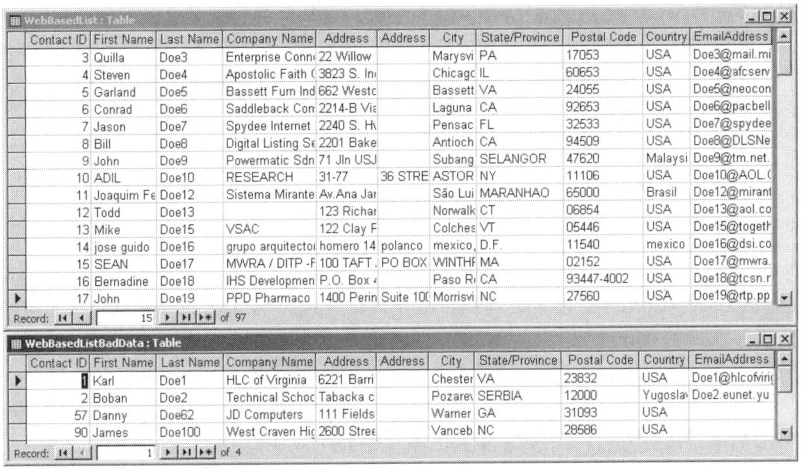

WebBasedList : Table

Contact ID	First Name	Last Name	Company Name	Address	Address	City	State/Province	Postal Code	Country	EmailAddress
3	Quilla	Doe3	Enterprise Conn	22 Willow		Marysvi	PA	17053	USA	Doe3@mail.mi
4	Steven	Doe4	Apostolic Faith (	3823 S. In		Chicagc	IL	60653	USA	Doe4@afcserv
5	Garland	Doe5	Bassett Furn Ind	662 Westc		Bassett	VA	24055	USA	Doe5@neocon
6	Conrad	Doe6	Saddleback Con	2214-B Via		Laguna	CA	92653	USA	Doe6@pacbell
7	Jason	Doe7	Spydee Internet	2240 S. H\		Pensac	FL	32533	USA	Doe7@spydee
8	Bill	Doe8	Digital Listing Se	2201 Bake		Antioch	CA	94509	USA	Doe8@DLSNe
9	John	Doe9	Powermatic Sdn	71 Jln USJ		Subang	SELANGOR	47620	Malaysi	Doe9@tm.net.
10	ADIL	Doe10	RESEARCH	31-77	36 STRE	ASTOR	NY	11106	USA	Doe10@AOL.(
11	Joaquim Fe	Doe12	Sistema Mirante	Av.Ana Jar		São Lui	MARANHAO	65000	Brasil	Doe12@mirant
12	Todd	Doe13		123 Richar		Norwalk	CT	06854	USA	Doe13@aol.co
13	Mike	Doe15	VSAC	122 Clay F		Colches	VT	05446	USA	Doe15@togeth
14	jose guido	Doe16	grupo arquitectoi	homero 14	polanco	mexico,	D.F.	11540	mexico	Doe16@dsi.co
15	SEAN	Doe17	MWRA / DITP -F	100 TAFT .	PO BOX	WINTHF	MA	02152	USA	Doe17@mwra.
16	Bernadine	Doe18	IHS Developmen	P.O. Box 4		Paso R	CA	93447-4002	USA	Doe18@tcsn.r
17	John	Doe19	PPD Pharmaco	1400 Perin	Suite 10(	Morrisvi	NC	27560	USA	Doe19@rtp.pp

Record: 15 of 97

WebBasedListBadData : Table

Contact ID	First Name	Last Name	Company Name	Address	Address	City	State/Province	Postal Code	Country	EmailAddress
1	Karl	Doe1	HLC of Virginia	6221 Barri		Chester	VA	23832	USA	Doe1@hlcofviri(
2	Boban	Doe2	Technical Schoc	Tabacka c		Pozare\	SERBIA	12000	Yugosla\	Doe2.eunet.yu
57	Danny	Doe62	JD Computers	111 Fields		Warner	GA	31093	USA	
90	James	Doe100	West Craven Hi(	2600 Stree		Vanceb	NC	28586	USA	

Record: 1 of 4

Figure 7-30 An excerpt from the cleaned *WebBasedList* table, and all the records transferred to the *WebBasedListBadData* table.

Creating Mailing Labels with Guestbook Data

One major reason for reorganizing and cleaning the guestbook data is to use it for reports. The following procedure illustrates how to reuse guestbook data with a report that prints mailing labels that we developed earlier in "Creating Reports with Wizards."

The sample code for this example uses the *WebBasedTableList*. The code starts by opening the *rptMailingLabels* report in Design view. Then the procedure assigns an SQL string to the *RecordSource* property of the report. The SQL string regroups fields and uses aliases to change the *WebBasedList* record source to one that matches the field names the report uses. After assigning the *RecordSource* property, the procedure saves the change and opens the report in Normal view to print it. You could save and later restore the original SQL string after printing, if this was important for other uses of the report.

```
Sub LabelsForWebBasedList()

'Open rptMailingLabels in Design view, and assign it a
'record source based on the WebBasedList
DoCmd.OpenReport "rptMailingLabels", acViewDesign
Reports("rptMailingLabels").RecordSource = _
    "SELECT [FirstName] & ' ' & [LastName] " & _
    "AS ContactName, " & _
    "CompanyName, " & _
    "[Address1] & IIf(IsNull([Address2]) Or " & _
    "[Address2]='','',', ' & [Address2]) AS Address, " & _
    "City, StateOrProvince AS Region, PostalCode " & _
    "FROM WebBasedList"

'Save the report with the new record source
DoCmd.Close , , acSaveYes

'Open the record source in Normal mode
DoCmd.OpenReport "rptMailingLabels", acViewNormal

End Sub
```

Creating a Form Letter with Guestbook Data

Another typical use for a table of contacts is to apply them to a form letter. Using a mix of controls, string constants and variables, and custom VBA functions, you can create a form letter such as the one depicted in Figure 7-31, which features several noteworthy Access report features:

- A logo heads the letter.
- The return address information appears in a different font than the body of the letter.
- The letter's date spells out the name of the month.
- The outgoing address and salutation change for each record.
- The letter's final paragraph also changes for each record.
- The letter's closing appears with a signature.

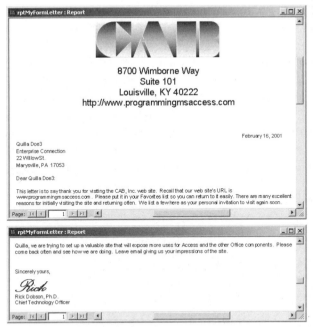

Figure 7-31 Excerpts from a form letter.

While it was never a programmatic challenge to convert a month number to a month name (such as converting 1 to January), VBA in Access 2002 contains built-in functionality that makes this task especially easy. The text box showing the date reveals the technique and one way to use it. It contains the following string expression:

```
=ThisMonthName() & " " & Day(Date()) & ", " & Year(Date())
```

The expression contains a pair of nested built-in functions for the day and the year, but a custom function (*ThisMonthName*) returns the month's name. This custom function calls a built-in VBA function, *MonthName*, that converts a month's number to its matching name. Calling the *MonthName* function relieves you from having to code a *Select Case* statement in a function procedure or invoke a *Choose* function to make a month name appear in a report.

```
Public Function ThisMonthName()
    ThisMonthName = MonthName(Month(Date))
End Function
```

Figure 7-32 presents the Design view of the form letter report showing a mix of label and text box controls. If the body of the letter includes no customization for each record, a simple label can display all the text. However, because the last paragraph starts with the contact's first name, the report needs a way to recover the *FirstName* field value. A string expression inside a text box is an easy way to accomplish this. The bottom portion mixes the field value with the string constant. You can tell that you have to experiment with the placement of the text box in relation to the preceding label control. To have the text flow nicely in Preview mode, you must overlap the controls in Design view. Proper alignment can require some trial and error and may depend on your printer driver.

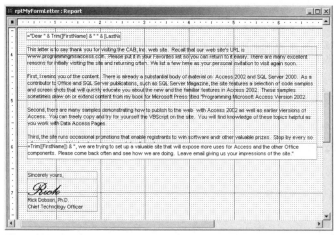

Figure 7-32 The bottom portion of the letter in Figure 7-31 in Design view.

Note the use of a script font with a label control to simulate a signature. This is a viable option when you don't need an actual signature—for example, for large mailings such as form letters.

Using Access for your form letters can simplify and speed the performance of your applications over using both Microsoft Word and Access together. When you have a set of routine communications that go to defined subsets of a mailing list in your database, using Access alone rather that merging the subset into Word and automating Word might be a better solution. For developers who prefer to work with the object model for just one application, using Access might be a satisfying approach.

8

Designing and Using PivotTables and PivotCharts

This chapter explores the capabilities of PivotTables and PivotCharts in Microsoft Access 2002. PivotTables and PivotCharts initially gained popularity in Microsoft Excel, where they're used by financial and operational analysts to probe data to support strategic and tactical decision making. PivotCharts appear for the first time in Access in the 2002 version. Moreover, Access 2002 substantially improves upon the PivotTable capabilities of prior versions of Access. Access 95 was the first version of the program to offer PivotTables. Since then, the capabilities and analytical speed of this feature have grown steadily.

The fact that tables, queries, forms, reports, views, and stored procedures in Access projects now utilize PivotTable and PivotChart views is a testament to how integral PivotTables and PivotCharts are in Access 2002. In addition, a new object model available through the Microsoft Office XP Web Components (OWC) library simplifies constructing PivotTables and PivotCharts programmatically.

Both PivotTables and PivotCharts enable you to display data in an interactive manner. End users are likely to find PivotTables and PivotCharts appealing because of their easy-to-use, interactive interface. And programmers can readily compute the data depicted in PivotTables and PivotCharts based on their clients' record sources. The usefulness of programmatically constructed PivotTables and PivotCharts might render obsolete some traditional data analysis tools, such as crosstab queries and charts based on older technology. As the popularity of PivotTables and PivotCharts grows among end users, the demand for programmers who can readily create and edit these display devices will increase as well.

Overview of PivotTables

A PivotTable summarizes and analyzes data in a datasheet. The datasheet for a PivotTable contains several sections known as drop areas into which you can deposit fields. A field can correspond to a column in a relational table from an Access database file or from a Microsoft SQL Server database. The PivotTable user interface (UI) and programmatic interface simplify computing statistics for the data in the detail drop area based on other fieldsets in the row and column drop areas. (A fieldset is a collection of related fields.) PivotTables offer a generalized way to perform cross-tabulations of relational data. In addition, you can readily filter the data that appears in a PivotTable's datasheet.

The great thing about the widespread availability of PivotTables in Access is that programmers no longer have to transfer their output to Excel for their clients to view it in this format. PivotTables enable more end users to perform analyses with the data provided by programmers. Furthermore, the ease with which end users can manipulate data with a PivotTable increases the demand for the services of database programmers who understand how to create and manage PivotTables programmatically.

Just as you can with PivotTables, you can move PivotChart fields from one drop area to another. A PivotChart will automatically update as you move fields to and from its drop areas. You can also readily update the graph type of a PivotChart. Access 2002 offers 12 major graph types from which you can choose, including column, line, pie, and area charts. Each category of graph offers several subtypes of chart you can select from. Unlike the Microsoft Graph 2000 Chart object, an Access PivotChart does not force you to work with an OLE DB object outside of Access.

Sample PivotTable

Figure 8-1 presents an excerpt from a sample PivotTable based on the *Orders* table from the Northwind database. The .mdb file for this chapter on the companion CD includes this table along with several others copied from the Northwind database. The PivotTable displays the freight and order ID information according to the ship country and shipper. As you can see, the *Ship Country* and *Shipper* fieldsets organize the two detail fieldsets, *Freight* and *Order ID*. The entries at each intersection of a country and a shipper are the freight charges and order ID values for orders transported to a country by a shipper.

Figure 8-1 A sample PivotTable based on a copy of the *Orders* table from the Northwind database.

Ship Country ▼	Federal Shipping Freight ▼	Order ID ▼	Speedy Express Freight ▼	Order ID ▼	United Package Freight ▼	Order ID ▼	Grand Total Freight Average	Order ID Count
Argentina	$1.10	10782	$29.83	10409	$38.82	10448	$37.41	16
	$19.76	10819	$8.12	10531	$17.22	10521		
	$31.51	10937	$90.85	10828	$22.57	10716		
	$3.17	11019	$2.84	10881	$1.27	10898		
			$0.33	11054	$63.77	10916		
					$49.56	10958		
					$217.86	10986		
	$13.89	4	$26.39	5	$58.72	7		
Austria	$146.06	10263	$140.51	10258	$101.95	10368	$184.79	40
	$360.63	10353	$162.33	10351	$67.88	10402		
	$122.46	10392	$94.77	10382	$31.29	10427		
	$73.79	10403	$126.38	10390	$47.94	10442		
	$26.06	10571	$458.78	10430	$5.29	10489		
	$35.12	10597	$96.78	10595	$789.95	10514		
	$477.90	10633	$78.09	10667	$339.22	10530		
	$145.45	10764	$96.50	10686	$11.19	10771		
	$96.43	10773	$272.47	10698	$126.66	10795		
	$351.53	10776	$117.33	10747	$25.22	10844		
	$74.60	10968	$411.88	10836	$100.22	10854		
	$117.61	10990	$162.75	10895	$353.07	10979		
	$79.46	11008			$754.26	11017		
					$53.05	11053		
					$258.64	11072		
	$162.08	13	$184.88	12	$204.39	15		
Belgium								

Designing and Using PivotTables and PivotCharts   Chapter 8

Note   You can open a PivotTable view with the same toolbar control used to expose the more familiar Datasheet view and Design view. This control has a View tooltip. Click the control in Access 2002 to expose the view types, and notice that there are two new selections: one for a PivotTable view and one for a PivotChart view.

In addition to listing raw values, the PivotTable also presents the average freight charge and the count of order IDs. These average and count values appear within the cell at the intersection of each country and shipper as well as in the Grand Total columns at the right edge of the PivotTable. The values in the pair of Grand Total columns for each row represent the data for all shippers for a particular country. The final row in the PivotTable, which also has the label Grand Total, displays the average freight charges and order counts for each shipper for all countries. By default, both the Grand Total row and column hide the detail freight charges and order IDs. A user can show and hide these detail values with the Show/Hide Details controls that appear as a plus sign (+) and a minus sign (−) within each row or column of a fieldset, including the Grand Total fields. In addition, the toolbar controls in the PivotTable view enable you to expand and contract detail for the entire table. Move the cursor over the toolbar controls to see the tooltips that indicate which controls support these actions.

A Field List control on the toolbar in the PivotTable view determines the visibility of the PivotTable Field List control. (See Figure 8-2.) This dialog box displays the list of all items available for inclusion in the PivotTable. Items that the PivotTable currently contains appear in a bold font; items not contained in the PivotTable appear in a normal font. The *Order ID, Freight,* and *Ship Country* fields are boldface because the PivotTable currently contains them. In addition, the *Freight Average* and *Order ID Count* fields appear in boldface within the *Totalss* fieldset at the top of the dialog box.

Figure 8-2 The PivotTable Field List dialog box for the PivotTable shown in Figure 8-1.

As you've no doubt gathered, PivotTables work with fieldsets. (We'll examine this topic in more detail in the section "Programmatically Creating PivotTables.") When working with relational tables as data sources, your fieldsets almost always will contain just one field. However, Access automatically breaks date/time field values into hierarchically dependent fieldsets. Expand the *Order Data By Month* fieldset to see the nested fields that Access automatically makes available to you. Of course, you do not have to work with these hierarchical collections of fields. The PivotTable Field List control offers a fieldset item named *Order Date* that has a single item below it as its sole field—also named *Order Date.*

Notice that there is no *Shipper* fieldset in Figure 8-2. Instead, *Shipper* appears below a *Calculated (2)* fieldset heading. While shipper names appear in the PivotTable, the *Orders* table actually contains numeric values that represent the shippers in its *ShipVia* column. (The *ShipVia* column is actually a Lookup data type in the *Orders* table.) These shipper names appear in the PivotTable's column drop area. The formula for converting the *ShipVia* numeric values to shipper names follows:

```
IIf(Shipvia=1, "Speedy Express", _
    IIf(Shipvia=2, "United Package", "Federal Shipping"))
```

You can open a dialog box that displays the formula for calculating the *Shipper* field display value. First, select the Shipper tab in the PivotTable. Next click the Properties control on the PivotTable toolbar. Finally, select the Calculation tab in the Properties dialog box.

The PivotTable Template

As we've discussed, a PivotTable is a view for standard database objects in Access 2002. Therefore, you use the View control on a toolbar to expose the template for constructing and editing a PivotTable. If a database object has no previously saved PivotTable view, you will see a blank template. This template contains four drop areas into which you can place fieldsets. Click the Field List control on the toolbar in a PivotTable view to open the PivotTable Field List dialog box. The Field List control in a PivotTable view looks identical to the Field List control in a Form Design view. This control exposes all the built-in fieldsets for a database object along with any calculated fields or *Totals* fields. You can add items to a PivotTable by dragging them from the dialog box to a drop area. To remove items from a PivotTable, drag them from the drop area right off the table.

> **Note**   For analysts, one of the major benefits of PivotTables is that you can drag items from one drop area to another. A PivotTable automatically recomputes after an item assumes its new position.

Figure 8-3 shows an empty PivotTable along with a PivotTable Field List dialog box for the *Products* table. The four PivotTable drop areas are named Totals Or Detail Fields, Row Fields, Column Fields, and Filter Fields. A message in each drop area instructs you to drop items in it. Figure 8-3 shows how the screen looks before I drop the *Product Name* field into the Row Fields drop area.

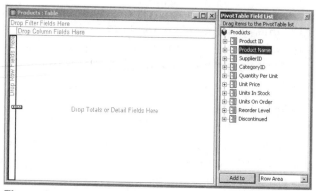

Figure 8-3 You can drag fields from the PivotTable Field List dialog box to drop areas on the PivotTable, as this example for the *Products* table shows.

> **Note**   The Filter Fields drop area name is somewhat misleading since you can filter a PivotTable from the Row Fields and Column Fields drop areas as well. Think of the Filter Fields drop area as a third dimension for a PivotTable, with its Row Fields area and Column Fields area comprising the first two dimensions.

You can drag multiple fields to any of the drop areas. For a query based on both the *Categories* and *Products* tables, you can drag both the *CategoryName* and *ProductName* fields to the Row Fields drop area. The PivotTable Field List dialog box automatically picks up the caption and field name in the table. Therefore, the dialog box shows the *CategoryName* field by its caption, Category Name, but it correctly refers to the field by its name, *CategoryName*.

When you click the Close button to exit a PivotTable view, Access prompts you to save your changes. Choosing to save the changes causes the PivotTable view to open to the current settings the next time a user selects the PivotTable view for that database object. Not choosing to save the changes causes the PivotTable to open the next time with the settings that were in effect when you initially opened the view. For example, if the view was blank and contained no fields in its drop areas, it will appear that way the next time you open it.

Overview of PivotCharts

A PivotChart is a chart you can build with the same general approach with which you construct PivotTables. A PivotChart can provide a view to the data in a database object, such as a table or a query.

A PivotChart can graphically represent the data depicted in a PivotTable. As you create a PivotTable with aggregated data, the aggregated values automatically become the data points for a corresponding PivotChart. You can also construct a PivotChart immediately, without first creating a PivotTable. As stated earlier, the Office XP Web Components library offers a programmatic interface for managing PivotTable and PivotChart capabilities. PivotCharts offer newer technology than former graphing options. In addition, your PivotChart development skills will directly transfer to Web applications that use PivotCharts on Data Access Pages.

Figure 8-4 shows the PivotChart that corresponds to the PivotTable shown in Figure 8-1. Except for clicking a control on the Formatting (PivotTable/PivotChart) toolbar to display the legend, this chart was prepared automatically as a result of constructing the PivotTable. Notice that the chart contains the average freight charges and the order count by country for each of the three shippers.

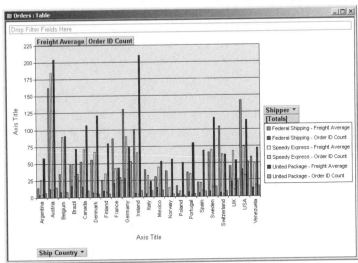

Figure 8-4 A PivotChart automatically generated by the construction of the PivotTable shown in Figure 8-1.

You can modify this chart in a variety of ways. For example, you can filter the data by country to obtain a simpler chart that shows just one or several countries. Click the Ship Country control at the bottom of the chart, clear the All control, and then select the countries that you want to show in the new view. Click OK in the popup Ship Country dialog box to close it, which displays the chart with the selected countries. You can perform the same kind of filtering for the Shipper dialog box as well. To do so, click the Shipper control to the right of the chart. Then select just those shippers for which you want the chart to display data. Clicking OK constructs the new view according to your selections.

The PivotChart in Figure 8-4 includes default labels for the horizontal and vertical axes. These labels are place markers to help you easily customize the chart. In a finished chart, you can readily edit the horizontal and vertical axis title labels. To do so, simply click on a label to select it. Then open the Properties dialog box with a control on the toolbar. Next select the Format tab. Change the entry in the Caption text box on the Format tab. While you have the Format tab selected, you can also modify the boldface, italic, underlining, and font color formatting of the axis title, as well as the font style and size.

Programmatically Creating PivotTables

One easy way to start creating PivotTables programmatically is by assigning a record source to a form. That way, you can program the PivotTable view for the form. If you specify PivotTable as the form's default view, users will see your PivotTable immediately upon opening the form. Alternatively, you can work with a normal Access form. You programmatically create a PivotTable for the form and save it, but you don't make the PivotTable view the form's default view. This approach allows users to open the form and view the data in Form view. Then when they're ready, users can change the view and examine a PivotTable based on the form's record source. A form can have only one PivotTable at a time. However, since PivotTables are programmable, you can create them dynamically, so that one form can organize data in several standard PivotTable views.

All the samples in this section process the *Invoices* query. This query ties together most of the Northwind tables that have anything to do with orders. The .mdb file for this chapter contains the tables and the *Invoices* SQL string that ties them together. While examining the query's SQL statement, it can be helpful to see a diagram of the relationships between tables that the query specifies. Figure 8-5 shows such a diagram. You can view the SQL code by opening the SQL window for the query.

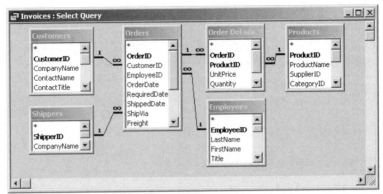

Figure 8-5 A diagram depicting the relationships between tables specified by the *Invoices* query.

Constructing a PivotTable for a Query

To create a form as the basis for a PivotTable, you just need to assign a record source to it. This form's record source then becomes the record source for the PivotTable view. You can programmatically create a form and assign it a record source with just a handful of code lines.

The following sample actually goes beyond the requirements for creating a form as the basis for a PivotTable; the code creates a text box control on the form for each field in the record source behind the form. Though not absolutely necessary, having the text boxes makes it possible to examine the field values for individual records in Form view. This sample is very elementary—it just adds text box controls without adding label controls for each text box. For samples that demonstrate how to add label controls that correspond to text box controls, see the programmatic samples for creating forms in Chapter 7, "Reports, Controls, and Data." The following sample demonstrates the use of the *CreateControl* method, which follows the same general syntax and conventions as the *CreateReportControl* method used in Chapter 7. However, the *CreateControl* method is used with forms instead of reports.

The initial sample to build a PivotTable that we'll examine relies on three procedures. The first procedure, *CreateAFormWithPivotTableOnInvoices*, which serves as a main routine, merely calls two other procedures, and it passes a return value from the first called procedure to the second one. The procedure starts by invoking the *FormName* procedure and passing it the name of a query: *Invoices*. The *FormName* procedure is a function procedure, so it returns a value that the *CreateAFormWithPivotTableOnInvoices* procedure stores in *strFormName*. This return value is the name of the custom form, automatically generated by Access, that uses the *Invoices* query as a record source. Next the main routine invokes the *CreatePivotTableForInvoices* procedure and passes the called procedure the value in *strFormName*. That second called procedure builds a PivotTable view for the record source behind the form whose name is in *strFormName*.

```
Sub CreateAFormWithPivotTableOnInvoices()
Dim strFormName As String

'Create a form with controls for all the fields in
'the Invoices query
strFormName = FormName("Invoices")

'Create a PivotTable view for the new form
'with the selected row, column, and detail fieldset members
CreatePivotTableForInvoices strFormName

End Sub
```

The *FormName* function procedure takes a single argument as a string variable indicating the record source and returns a string value that's the name of the form it creates. The first three lines after the declarations and two lines for saving the form toward the end of the procedure are absolutely necessary here. The first line after the declarations starts by invoking the *Application* object's *CreateForm* method. Because the method belongs to the top-level object in Access, you do not need to precede it with the object's name. The first line establishes *frm1* as a pointer to the form created by the method. The second line assigns the query named in the argument passed to the procedure as the form's *RecordSource* property. The third line designates the PivotTable view as the default view for the form. When users open the form from the Database window, they will automatically see the PivotTable view instead of the Form view.

After constructing the form, the procedure creates an ActiveX Data Objects (ADO) recordset based on the same record source as the form. The procedure loops through the *Fields* collection of the *Recordset* object to add a text box to the form for each field in the recordset. The most important line of code within the *For* loop for the recordset's *Fields* collection invokes the *CreateControl* method. This is another method of the Access *Application* object; its purpose is to add a control to a form. The two arguments for the method designate the form name to add a control to and the type of control to add. Another important line within the loop assigns the current field name value to the *ControlSource* property for the text box control. The remaining lines within the loop and the four lines before the loop assist in spacing the text box controls evenly along the length of the form.

The first two lines after the loop perform two critical functions. The first of these lines saves the name of the form created by the procedure as the return value from the function procedure. The second line after the loop closes the form and saves the changes. This commits the *RecordSource* and *ControlSource* property assignments. Let's take a look at the procedure now:

```
Function FormName(strSourceName As String) As String
Dim frm1 As Access.Form
Dim txt1 As Access.TextBox
Dim rst1 As ADODB.Recordset
Dim fld1 As ADODB.Field
Dim intLeft As Integer
Dim intLastTop As Integer
Dim intOffset As Integer
Dim intWidth As Integer
Dim intHeight As Integer

'Create a form with the specified record source
Set frm1 = CreateForm
frm1.RecordSource = strSourceName
frm1.DefaultView = acFormPivotTable

'Create a recordset using the specified source
Set rst1 = New ADODB.Recordset
rst1.Open strSourceName, CurrentProject.Connection

'Assign control size and position parameters
intLeft = 144
intOffset = 72
intWidth = 4320
intHeight = 288

'Iterate through recordset fields and create
'corresponding text box controls on the form
For Each fld1 In rst1.Fields
    Set txt1 = CreateControl(frm1.Name, acTextBox)
    With txt1
        .ControlSource = fld1.Name
        .Left = intLeft
        .Top = intLastTop + intHeight + intOffset
        intLastTop = .Top
        .Width = intWidth
        .Height = intHeight
        .Name = "txt" & fld1.Name
    End With
Next fld1

'Close the form, save changes, and pass its name back
FormName = frm1.Name
DoCmd.Close acForm, frm1.Name, acSaveYes
```

(continued)

```
'Clean up objects
rst1.Close
Set rst1 = Nothing
Set frm1 = Nothing
Set txt1 = Nothing

End Function
```

After you have a form with a *RecordSource* setting, you can create a PivotTable view for the data behind the form. The *CreatePivotTableForInvoices* procedure creates a PivotTable view for the form generated by the *FormName* procedure. The procedure begins by opening the form in Design view. This view is necessary to make an assignment for a form's *DefaultView* property. The sample assigns a value of 3 to the property. This property value causes a form to open automatically with a PivotTable view instead of the default Form view from the Access UI. After saving this change to the form, the procedure reopens the form. This time the procedure opens the form in PivotTable view so that it can make changes to the design of the PivotTable.

A PivotTable view organizes selected fields in the record source for a form with a crosstab. The format arranges detail data field values according to their column and row field values. When you programmatically refer to the fields in a record source, your code refers to them as *PivotFieldset* objects.

After referencing a field in the form's record source, use the *InsertFieldset* method to assign the fieldset object to a drop area in the PivotTable. The code sample in *CreatePivotTableForInvoices* invokes the *InsertFieldset* method four times. First, it assigns the *Shippers_CompanyName* field to the column drop area. Visual Basic for Applications (VBA) refers to this area as the *ColumnAxis* property of the *Fieldsets* collection for a PivotTable. Next the code sample assigns the *ProductName* field to the row drop area (*RowAxis*). Then the last two assignments assign the *Quantity* and *ExtendedPrice* fields to the detail drop areas (*DataAxis*). The PivotTable organizes the field values in the detail drop areas according to the row and column drop area field values. After making all the fieldset assignments, the procedure commits the changes to the form by closing the form and saving the changes.

```
Sub CreatePivotTableForInvoices(strFormName As String)
Dim frm1 As Access.Form
Dim fset1 As PivotFieldSet

'Create reference to form on which to base PivotTable,
'but first set PivotTable as the default view
```

```
DoCmd.OpenForm strFormName, acDesign
Set frml = Forms(strFormName)
frml.DefaultView = 3
DoCmd.Close acForm, strFormName, acSaveYes
DoCmd.OpenForm strFormName, acFormPivotTable
Set frml = Forms(strFormName)

With frml.PivotTable.ActiveView
    'Assign fieldset members to the column, row, and detail sections of
    'the PivotTable
    Set fsetl = .FieldSets("Shippers_CompanyName")
    .ColumnAxis.InsertFieldSet fsetl
    Set fsetl = .FieldSets("ProductName")
    .RowAxis.InsertFieldSet fsetl
    Set fsetl = .FieldSets("Quantity")
    .DataAxis.InsertFieldSet fsetl
    Set fsetl = .FieldSets("ExtendedPrice")
    .DataAxis.InsertFieldSet fsetl
End With
'Close form with its PivotTable view
DoCmd.Close acForm, strFormName, acSaveYes

End Sub
```

Figure 8-6 presents an excerpt from the PivotTable view created by the preceding sample. Notice from the window's title bar that the form has the name *Form1*. If *Form1* already exists in the database, the sample creates *Form2*, and so on. Observe that the row, column, and detail field names appear with the control names for the corresponding record source fields. These control names are derived from the record source's field name and have a *txt* prefix. The *FormName* procedure assigns this prefix when it assigns the *Name* property of each text box on a form. You can modify this convention and use any naming rule that meets the requirements of your application.

> Note   The sample in this section uses default naming conventions for the forms. Code samples in the section "Programmatically Creating PivotCharts" demonstrate how to assign custom form names programmatically. These techniques apply equally to PivotCharts and PivotTables.

Form1 : Form

Drop Filter Fields Here

txtProductName ▾	txtShippers.CompanyName ▾						Grand Total
	Federal Shipping		Speedy Express		United Package		
	txtQuantity ▾	txtExtendedPrice ▾	txtQuantity ▾	txtExtendedPrice ▾	txtQuantity ▾	txtExtendedPrice ▾	No Totals
Alice Mutton	6	$234.00	15	$585.00	40	$1,248.00	
	8	$249.60	12	$468.00	15	$468.00	
	20	$624.00	45	$1,123.20	15	$351.00	
	36	$1,010.88	6	$234.00	70	$2,074.80	
	18	$702.00	8	$296.40	50	$1,170.00	
	8	$280.80	30	$936.00	25	$877.50	
	16	$592.80	20	$741.00	40	$1,560.00	
	33	$1,287.00	100	$3,900.00	35	$1,023.75	
	20	$780.00	2	$62.40	42	$1,638.00	
	27	$789.75	30	$936.00	40	$1,170.00	
	10	$312.00	77	$2,702.70	10	$390.00	
	15	$585.00			6	$234.00	
					16	$592.80	
					12	$468.00	
Aniseed Syrup	30	$240.00	6	$60.00	4	$40.00	
	20	$180.00	14	$140.00	20	$144.00	
	20	$200.00	50	$400.00	49	$490.00	
	60	$600.00			30	$300.00	
					25	$250.00	
Boston Crab Meat							

Figure 8-6 An excerpt from the PivotTable created by the *CreateAFormWithPivotTableOnInvoices* sample.

In Figure 8-6, the No Totals cells in the *Grand Total* column are empty by default. By clicking the + Show/Hide Details control, you can display all the values in the preceding columns for each row. If there are more values than can fit in a PivotTable cell, click inside the cell. The PivotTable will display a scroll bar that lets you scroll up and down the list of values for that PivotTable cell. The *ProductName* row values also have + Show/Hide Details controls. Clicking the – control hides all the detail values in any row. However, if any totals were computed in the PivotTable, they would still appear in the row.

Sometimes you might not know the name of a fieldset, which means that you won't be able to use it as an index for *Fieldsets* collection members. Such a fieldset name usually will match the record source field name, but there are exceptions. For example, the *ControlSource* setting for the text box named *txtShippers.CompanyName* is *Shippers.CompanyName*. However, the corresponding fieldset name is *Shippers_CompanyName*. If you forget the naming convention for a fieldset, or if you just want to verify the fieldset names on a PivotTable, use the following code sample. The first procedure assigns a form name with a PivotTable view and calls the second procedure, which is a utility that enumerates the fieldset names. This second procedure reports to the Immediate window the total number of members in the *Fieldsets* collection for a PivotTable view and the names of each of those fieldset members.

```
Sub CallUtilityToNameFieldSetMembersForm1()
Dim strFName As String

strFName = "Form1"
```

```
UtilityToNameFieldSetMembers strFName

End Sub


Sub UtilityToNameFieldSetMembers(strFName As String)
Dim frm1 As Access.Form
Dim fset1

'Open a form named strFName
DoCmd.OpenForm strFName, acFormPivotTable
Set frm1 = Forms(strFName)

'Enumerate names of elements in the Fieldsets collection.
'This is useful for compound names, such as Shippers_CompanyName.
Debug.Print frm1.PivotTable.ActiveView.FieldSets.Count
For Each fset1 In frm1.PivotTable.ActiveView.FieldSets
    Debug.Print fset1.Name
Next fset1

'Clean up objects
Set frm1 = Nothing

End Sub
```

Adding and Removing PivotTable Totals

The preceding sample application organized the *Quantity* and *ExtendedPrice* fields from the *Invoices* query in a PivotTable. However, it did not develop any summary statistics for the *Quantity* and *ExtendedPrice* field values. One typical reason for composing a PivotTable is to compute summary statistics for the values in the detail drop area. The main vehicle for adding summary statistics to a PivotTable view is the *AddTotal* method. The samples that follow illustrate how to apply this method to the PivotTable returned by the *ActiveView* property of the PivotTable for a form.

The *AddTotal* method creates a new *Totals* field, which contains summary statistics for another field in a PivotTable. The *Totals* fields that the method creates appear both in the PivotTable and in the PivotTable Field List through the Access UI for PivotTable views. The *AddTotal* method takes three arguments. First, you name the new *Totals* field. Use a string for this. Next you reference a field, such as one of the fields in the detail drop area. Then you specify a function for computing the summary statistic on the field. These functions are the standard aggregate functions available in many contexts throughout Access. They compute the average, count, maximum value, minimum value, sum, the standard deviation and variance, and the population for a sample.

When you attempt to add a new *Total* field to a PivotTable, the field cannot already exist. Attempting to add a new *Total* field that has the same name as an existing one generates a run-time error. Because the insertion of a *Total* field adds it to the PivotTable's detail drop area and the PivotTable Field List, you need to remove it from both locations before attempting to add a new field with the same name.

Adding *Total* Fields

The following pair of procedures demonstrates the syntax for adding two *Totals* fields to the PivotTable created by the preceding sample. The *Totals* fields compute the sum of the *Quantity* and the *ExtendedPrice* field values. The corresponding cells in the PivotTable will reflect the total business handled by a shipper for a product. The first procedure names the form to process and passes that name to the second procedure, which actually creates the two *Totals* fields. For this sample to work, you have to verify the name of the form created by the preceding sample. In my sample, the name of this form is *Form1*. However, it could be *Form2*, *Form3*, or *Formx*, depending on how many times you run the sample without deleting the previously created sample forms. In the section "Adding a PivotChart View to a Custom Form," I will show you how to assign a specific name to the form with a PivotTable view that you create. However, you will always have to specify the name of a form when processing its PivotTable view.

The second procedure includes two important variable declarations. First it specifies *fld1* as a PivotField, which is a field in a PivotTable. Next the procedure specifies *tot1* as a PivotTotal. A PivotTotal represents a total in a PivotTable, such as one created by the *AddTotal* method. The sample reuses the *fld1* and *tot1* variables. First the code adds the sum of *ExtendedPrice* to the PivotTable, and then it adds the sum of *Quantity* to the PivotTable.

After the declarations, the procedure opens the form corresponding to the name passed to it. Then the code assigns the form to the *frm1* object reference. This simplifies subsequent code in the sample.

Next the procedure open a *With...End With* block of code that operates on the form reference. The block contains two groups of lines. The first group adds the sum of *ExtendedPrice* to the PivotTable, and the second group applies the same function to compute the sum of *Quantity*. Adding a *Totals* field involves three steps. First, you reference the field that the *Totals* field summarizes. Second, you invoke the *AddTotal* method to create the *Totals* field. Third, you assign the new *Totals* field to the PivotTable. The procedure executes this third step in two lines. The first line assigns the *Totals* field to an object reference, *tot1*. The second line inserts that object into the detail section of the PivotTable by using the *InsertTotal* method.

One reason to add *Totals* fields to a PivotTable is to summarize detail data. Often, presenting detail data and summary data in the same PivotTable can be distracting. Therefore, the sample invokes two methods that highlight the display of summary statistics in the resulting PivotTable. First the code invokes the *HideDetails* method. This forces the suppression of all detail data. With this one step, a user could restore the visibility of the detail data if he so desired. However, as the creator of the PivotTable view, you can disable this capability by assigning a value of False to the *AllowDetails* property for the PivotTable. The sample illustrates this optional step.

Whenever you make changes to a PivotTable, you must save them if you want them to persist the next time a user views the PivotTable. Therefore, the procedure concludes by closing the form and saving the changes as it closes. Let's examine the procedure now:

```
Sub CallTotalExtendedPriceAndQuantity()
Dim strFName As String

'Set strFName so that it points at the form with the
'PivotTable view that you want to revise
strFName = "Form1"


TotalExtendedPriceAndQuantity strFName

End Sub


Sub TotalExtendedPriceAndQuantity(strFName As String)
Dim frm1 As Access.Form
Dim fld1 As PivotField
Dim tot1 As PivotTotal

'Open a form named strFName
DoCmd.OpenForm strFName, acFormPivotTable
Set frm1 = Forms(strFName)

With frm1
    'Add total for sum of ExtendedPrice field
    Set fld1 = .PivotTable.ActiveView.FieldSets("ExtendedPrice"). _
        Fields("ExtendedPrice")
    .PivotTable.ActiveView.AddTotal "Sum of Price", fld1, plFunctionSum
    Set tot1 = .PivotTable.ActiveView.Totals("Sum of Price")
    .PivotTable.ActiveView.DataAxis.InsertTotal tot1
```

(continued)

```
'Add total for sum of Quantity field
Set fld1 = .PivotTable.ActiveView.FieldSets("Quantity").Fields("Quantity")
.PivotTable.ActiveView.AddTotal "Sum of Quantity", fld1, plFunctionSum
Set tot1 = .PivotTable.ActiveView.Totals("Sum of Quantity")
.PivotTable.ActiveView.DataAxis.InsertTotal tot1
End With


'Hide detail rows
Screen.ActiveDatasheet.PivotTable.ActiveData.HideDetails
frm1.PivotTable.AllowDetails = False


'Save changes as you close the form's PivotTable view
DoCmd.Close acForm, frm1.Name, acSaveYes


End Sub
```

Figure 8-7 shows an excerpt of how *Form1* looks when you open it after running the *CallTotalExtendedPriceAndQuantity* procedure. Recall that the PivotTable is the default view for the form, so this is what a user sees when she initially opens the form. Compare the appearance of the PivotTable in this screen shot with the one shown in Figure 8-6. The new version of the PivotTable suppresses all detail data and presents only summary data. Therefore, it's much easier to identify the differences between cells in the PivotTable shown in Figure 8-7. Invoking the *HideDetails* method in the procedure suppresses the detail data.

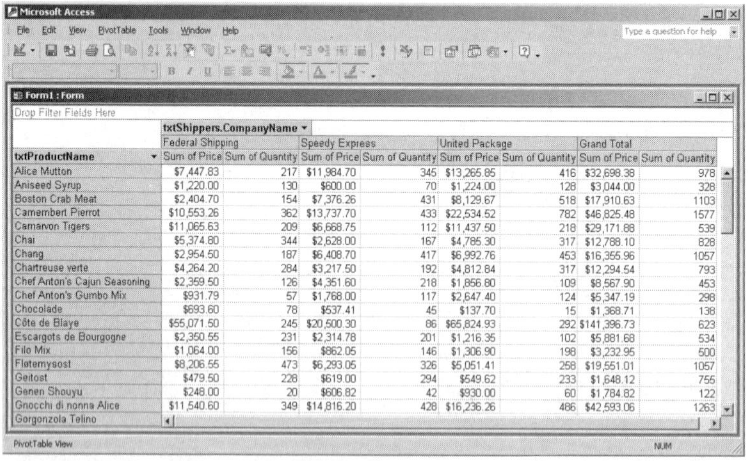

Figure 8-7 An updated excerpt from our sample PivotTable that shows summary data for the *Quantity* and *ExtendedPrice* fields.

I purposely included the outer Access window in Figure 8-7 so that you could see how many toolbar controls are disabled. The PivotTable does not allow the operation of any controls that expand and collapse rows and columns or that show and hide fields in the detail drop areas. The controls for showing and hiding details on the PivotTable are not visible in this figure. The inoperability of these features is the direct result of setting the *AllowDetails* property to False.

Removing *Total* Fields

When working with PivotTables, you might want to redefine the formula you use for a *Total* field. To do this, you must first remove the old *Total* field from the detail drop area as well as from the collection of *Total* fields for the PivotTable.

Use the *RemoveTotal* method to eliminate the appearance of a *Total* field in the detail section of a PivotTable. This method applies to the *DataAxis* property of the PivotTable returned by the *ActiveView* property of a form's PivotTable. *RemoveTotal* takes a single argument, a string variable that names the *Total* field you want to eliminate from the PivotTable's detail drop area.

A *Total* field is not completely removed from a PivotTable until you also remove it from the *Total* fields collection. To do so, invoke the *DeleteTotal* method. This method applies directly to the PivotTable returned by the *ActiveView* property. Like the *RemoveTotal* method, the *DeleteTotal* method takes a single string variable as an argument that names the *Total* field to strike from the *Total* fields collection of the PivotTable.

The following pair of procedures demonstrates the correct syntax for the *RemoveTotal* and *DeleteTotal* methods. The first procedure passes a form name to the second procedure. The form has the PivotTable from which the second procedure eliminates the *Total* fields. The second procedure starts by opening the form and setting an object reference, *frm1*, to it. Next the procedure removes the two summary fields from the PivotTable detail drop area and from the *Total* fields collection. This occurs inside a *With…End With* block.

Before closing, the second procedure restores the visibility of detail field values and enables users to show and hide fields as well as expand and collapse rows and columns. The procedure's final line closes the form and saves these changes. After running the *CallRemovePriceAndQuantityTotals* procedure, the PivotTable view for *Form1* returns to its initial condition (the way it appeared after running the sample that created it). Here are the two procedures:

```
Sub CallRemovePriceAndQuantityTotals()
Dim strFName As String

'Set strFName so it points at the form with the
'PivotTable view that you want to revise
strFName = "Form1"
RemovePriceAndQuantityTotals strFName

End Sub
```

(continued)

```
Sub RemovePriceAndQuantityTotals(strFName As String)
Dim frm1 As Access.Form

'Open a form named strFName
DoCmd.OpenForm strFName, acFormPivotTable
Set frm1 = Forms(strFName)

'Remove totals from datasheet and Totals field list setting
With frm1.PivotTable.ActiveView
    .DataAxis.RemoveTotal "Sum of Price"
    .DataAxis.RemoveTotal "Sum of Quantity"
    .DeleteTotal "Sum of Price"
    .DeleteTotal "Sum of Quantity"
End With

'Show Detail Rows
Screen.ActiveDatasheet.PivotTable.ActiveData.ShowDetails
frm1.PivotTable.AllowDetails = True

'Save changes as you close form's PivotTable view
DoCmd.Close acForm, frm1.Name, acSaveYes

End Sub
```

Filtering PivotTables

One of the most valuable features of PivotTables is the ease with which you can include and exclude records for processing. Use the *IncludedMembers* property to specify members that you want to include in a PivotTable. Assign values to the *ExcludedMembers* property to designate fields you want excluded. You can assign an individual field name to these properties, or if you want to filter on more than field value, you can assign an array of field names. Since the array technique works for individual field names as well as sets of field names, you can use it for all your assignments to the *IncludedMembers* and *ExcludedMembers* properties.

The *IncludedMembers* and *ExcludedMembers* properties apply to PivotTable *Fields* collections. Recall that these *Fields* collections belong to a *Fieldsets* collection. When working with hierarchical data—such as cities, which reside within states, which reside within countries, which reside within continents—the *Fieldsets* collection represents the parent data, and the *Fields* collection denotes the child data. When working with a normal relational table (as in the current sample), the *Fieldsets* and *Fields* collection members are identical. Regardless of whether the *Fieldsets* and *Fields* collection members match, you need to designate them separately.

The sample we'll look at next demonstrates the syntax for filtering on a single column field value for the data in the PivotTable for *Form1*. The syntax shows a reference to the *ColumnAxis* property of the PivotTable. Then the *Fieldsets* and *Fields* collections specifically point at the *Shippers_CompanyName* field in the record source behind the PivotTable. The *IncludedMembers* property next opens a filter for the values the procedure assigns to it. In this sample, the filter designates rows in the *Invoices* query with a shipper value of United Package. You can add another field value by following United Package with a comma and a second field value. For example, the following excerpt from a procedure on the companion CD filters to include rows with a shipper value of either Federal Shipping or Speedy Express:

```
With frm1.PivotTable
    .ActiveView.ColumnAxis.FieldSets("Shippers_CompanyName"). _
        Fields("Shippers_CompanyName").IncludedMembers = _
        Array("Federal Shipping", "Speedy Express")
    .AllowFiltering = False
End With
```

By setting the *AllowFiltering* property for the form's PivotTable to False, you remove users' ability to change your filtering setting. You do not need to make this assignment to open a PivotTable with a custom filter. *AllowFiltering* and *AllowDetails* are two independent properties. For example, setting *AllowDetails* to False still enables a user to manually filter a PivotTable. Here's the syntax:

```
Sub FilterFor1ShipperAfterPriorFilter()
Dim frm1 As Access.Form
Dim strFormName As String

'Open a form name strFormName
strFormName = "Form1"
DoCmd.OpenForm strFormName, acFormPivotTable
Set frm1 = Forms(strFormName)

'Assign single-shipper filter
```

(continued)

```
With frm1.PivotTable
    .ActiveView.ColumnAxis.FieldSets("Shippers_CompanyName"). _
        Fields("Shippers_CompanyName").IncludedMembers = _
        Array("United Package")
    .AllowFiltering = False
End With

End Sub
```

When you assign fields to the *IncludedMembers* property, you must specify all the items to be included. Therefore, a design such as the preceding sample is awkward because you have to manually edit the procedure by updating the number of members of the *Array* function used to assign values to the *IncludedMembers* property. As a workaround, you could instead designate the *IncludedMembers* values with a parameter array. Then your code would be able to use the *UBound* function to determine the number of parameters passed, and it would automatically branch to an assignment statement for *IncludedMembers* with the correct number of arguments.

The two procedures in the following sample demonstrate this approach. The first procedure, *CallFilterForShippers*, designates the shipper names to filter for. The second procedure, *FilterForShippers*, opens *Form1* and counts the number of values passed in the parameter array. The procedure then uses a *Select Case* statement to branch to the correct assignment statement for the *IncludedMembers* properties. If a user does not enter any filter values for the parameter array or enters more than three values, the procedure resets the PivotTable to show data for all shippers and reenables manual filtering. In addition, the procedure presents a message box to remind the user that the submitted number of filter values is invalid.

```
Sub CallFilterForShippers()

'Run this to include just two shippers
FilterForShippers" "Federal Shipping"," "Speedy Express"

'Run this to restore all shippers
'FilterForShippers "Federal Shipping", "Federal Shipping", _
'    "Federal Shipping", "Federal Shipping"

End Sub


Sub FilterForShippers(ParamArray ShipperArray() As Variant)
'Sub FilterForShippers(strFilter As String)
Dim frm1 As Access.Form
Dim strFormName As String
```

```
'Dim ShipperArray As Variant

'Open a form named strFormName
strFormName = "Form1"
DoCmd.OpenForm strFormName, acFormPivotTable
Set frm1 = Forms(strFormName)

'Include one, two, or three shippers
With frm1.PivotTable
    Select Case UBound(ShipperArray())
        Case 0
            .ActiveView.ColumnAxis.FieldSets("Shippers_CompanyName"). _
                Fields("Shippers_CompanyName").IncludedMembers = _
                Array(ShipperArray(0))
        Case 1
            .ActiveView.ColumnAxis.FieldSets("Shippers_CompanyName"). _
                Fields("Shippers_CompanyName").IncludedMembers = _
                Array(ShipperArray(0), ShipperArray(1))
        Case 2
            .ActiveView.ColumnAxis.FieldSets("Shippers_CompanyName"). _
                Fields("Shippers_CompanyName").IncludedMembers = _
                Array(ShipperArray(0), ShipperArray(1), ShipperArray(2))
        Case Else
            .ActiveView.ColumnAxis.FieldSets("Shippers_CompanyName"). _
                Fields("Shippers_CompanyName").IncludedMembers = _
                Array("Federal Shipping", "Speedy Express", _
                    "United Package")
            .AllowFiltering = True
            MsgBox "Not a valid filter.", vbInformation, _
                "Programming Microsoft Access Version 2002"


            Exit Sub
    End Select
    .AllowFiltering = False
End With

End Sub
```

Programmatically Creating PivotCharts

Creating PivotCharts involves processing a form's *ChartSpace* object, which is returned by the form's *ChartSpace* property. Once you have a reference to the *ChartSpace* object, you can set parameters for that object and its hierarchically dependent objects to format a PivotChart for the data behind the form. As with PivotTables, you can make the PivotChart view the default view for a form so that when a user opens the form, the chart immediately displays. Alternatively, you can leave the Form view as the default view and let users select the PivotChart view for the form when they need it.

Adding a PivotChart View to a Custom Form

The first PivotChart sample we'll examine builds on the PivotTable samples from the previous section and explores the basics of creating a simple bar chart in a form's PivotChart view. This sample involves a main procedure that calls three other procedures. These three procedures create a custom query in an Access database file, base a new form on the custom query, and design a PivotChart view for the new form.

The main procedure, *CreateAPivotChartBasedOnACustomQuery*, starts by assigning names to two string variables. One of these variables represents the custom query's name, *qryExtPriceByShipper*. The second string denotes the name of the form based on the query *frmqryExtPriceByShipper*. Next the procedure defines the SQL string for a custom query. This query statement uses the *Invoices* query as a record source. It totals *ExtendedPrice* by date, shipper, and product name. In addition, the custom query filters out all records containing orders placed on or after May 1, 1998. This is because the data ends in May of 1998, and is incomplete for that month. The field labels for shipper and product name directly originate from corresponding fields in the *Invoices* query. The date field has the name *YearMonth*. This field uses the built-in *DateSerial*, *DatePart*, and *Month* functions to transform the *OrderDate* field in the *Invoices* query so that all dates assume a value of the first day of the month in which they occur. This kind of transformation is useful when you want to plot data by month, as you'll see in the code sample on page 491.

After defining the SQL string for the custom query, the procedure calls three other sub procedures that perform most of the work in the sample. Let's take a look at the main procedure first:

```
Sub CreateAPivotChartBasedOnACustomQuery()
Dim strSQL As String
Dim strQName As String
Dim strFName As String

'Assign names for new query and form
strQName = "qryExtPriceByShipper"
strFName = "frmqryExtPriceByShipper"
```

```
'Assign SQL for custom query and create query
strSQL =" "SELECT DateSerial(DatePart(" & """" & "yyyy" & """" & _
    ",[OrderDate]), Month([OrderDate]),1) AS YearMonth, " & _
    "Invoices.Shippers.CompanyName, Invoices.ProductName, " & _
    "Sum(Invoices.ExtendedPrice) AS ExtPrice FROM Invoices " & _
    "GROUP BY DateSerial(DatePart(" & """" & "yyyy" & """" & _
    ",[OrderDate]),Month([OrderDate]),1), " & _
    "Invoices.Shippers.CompanyName, Invoices.ProductName " & _
    "HAVING (((DateSerial(DatePart(" & """" & "yyyy" & """" & _
    ", [OrderDate]), Month([OrderDate]), 1)) < #5/1/1998#))"


CreateCustomQuery strSQL, strQName

'Use query as record source for form with value of strFName
CreateFormBasedOnQuery strFName, strQName

'Create PivotChart for data behind form
CreateChart strFName


End Sub
```

The procedure for creating a custom view accepts the SQL string and query name as arguments. This procedure requires a reference to the Microsoft ADO Ext. 2.x for DDL and Security library. This is because the sample uses the ADOX *Catalog* and *View* objects. The procedure begins by instantiating a catalog and assigning its *ActiveConnection* property to the current project. Then the project attempts to delete any prior query that has the name of the view that it plans to create. If there is no prior view with the same name, the procedure ignores the resulting error. The *On Error GoTo 0* statement restores normal error behavior by Access. The procedure's last block of code starts by instantiating a new ADO *Command* object. Next it assigns the SQL string passed to the procedure to the *CommandText* property for the command. Finally, the procedure uses the *Catalog* object to append a new view with the name of the query passed to the procedure and the SQL statement associated with the *Command* object. For a more thorough review of the techniques for creating custom queries, see Chapter 5, "Jet SQL, the ADOX Library, and Queries."

```
Sub CreateCustomQuery(strSQL As String, _
    strQName As String)
Dim cat1 As ADOX.Catalog
Dim cmd1 As ADODB.Command
Dim vew1 As ADOX.View
```

```
'Create a reference to the catalog for the current project
Set cat1 = New ADOX.Catalog
cat1.ActiveConnection = CurrentProject.Connection

'Remove a query before creating a new copy of it
On Error Resume Next
cat1.Views.Delete strQName
On Error GoTo 0

'Append a select query as a view to the current project
Set cmd1 = New ADODB.Command
cmd1.CommandText = strSQL
cat1.Views.Append strQName, cmd1

'Clean up objects
Set cmd1 = Nothing
Set cat1 = Nothing

End Sub
```

The procedure for basing a form on the custom query also illustrates an approach for assigning a custom name to a form. This sample illustrates one way to avoid accepting the default name for a form as all the preceding samples in this chapter do. The *CreateFormBasedOnQuery* procedure accepts two string arguments. One designates the name of the new form, *strFName*, and the other denotes the name of the query to serve as a record source for the form, *strQName*. This procedure uses the function procedure, *FormName*, for creating a custom form that we discussed earlier in the chapter.

The sample starts by iterating through the members of the *AllForms* collection. This iteration searches for an existing form with the same name as the new form the procedure will create. If such a form exists, the code deletes the old form. (Chapter 6 discusses the *AllForms* collection and describes several samples that demonstrate how to use it.) If the iteration discovers a form with the same name as the new form, the sample uses the *SelectObject* method of the *DoCmd* object to select the form. Then the procedure invokes the *DoCmd* object's *DeleteObject* method to remove the form from the current project.

After eliminating a prior version of the form (if one exists), the sample calls the *FormName* function procedure and passes it the name of the custom query. This creates a new form with an arbitrary name, such as *Form2*. The procedure saves the name of the new form returned by the function procedure. Then the sample uses *DoCmd* object methods to select the form and give it a new custom named as specified by the argument to the procedure. Before saving the form to commit the changes, the procedure assigns a value of *4* to the form's

DefaultView property. This causes the form to open automatically with its PivotChart view. Here's the procedure:

```
Sub CreateFormBasedOnQuery(strFName As String, strQName As String)
Dim obj1 As AccessObject
Dim strDefaultName As String
Dim frm1 As Access.Form

'Delete any prior form with the name of the new one (if one exists)
For Each obj1 In CurrentProject.AllForms
    If obj1.Name = strFName Then
        DoCmd.SelectObject acForm, obj1.Name, True
        DoCmd.DeleteObject acForm, obj1.Name
        Exit For
    End If
Next obj1

'Create a form with controls for all the fields in
'the custom query
strDefaultName  = FormName(strQName)

'Rename form from default name and assign a
'default view of a PivotChart for manual opening
DoCmd.SelectObject acForm, strDefaultName , True
DoCmd.Rename strFName, acForm, strDefaultName
DoCmd.OpenForm strFName, acDesign
Set frm1 = Forms(strFName)
frm1.DefaultView = 4
DoCmd.Close acForm, frm1.Name, acSaveYes

End Sub
```

Finally, you're ready to create the PivotChart view for the custom form. The *CreateChart* procedure that accomplishes this starts by opening the custom form and assigning a reference to it, *frm1*. Next the procedure invokes the *SetData* method twice. The first application of the method sets the *CompanyName* field of the record source to be represented by the bars in a chart that plots a series. The second application specifies the *ExtPrice* field as the series that gets plotted across the *CompanyName* field values represented by the bars. Recall that *CompanyName* refers to the three shippers that transport goods in the Northwind sample. After setting the fields for the chart to plot, the procedure turns off the *DisplayFieldButtons* property. The display field buttons serve as drop areas for adding fields to a chart. This essentially prevents users from easily changing the chart by adding new fields.

> **Note**   Users can reverse a setting of False for the *DisplayFieldButtons* property by resetting the Field Buttons/Drop Zones check box on the Show/Hide tab of the PivotChart's Properties dialog box. A developer can use the techniques for creating a custom startup and programming custom command bars illustrated in Chapter 10, "Microsoft Office Objects," to prevent access to the Properties dialog box.

The *SetData* method enables you to designate the data for a chart, including a form's *ChartSpace* object. This object represents a chart workspace where you can programmatically define a form. The *SetData* method takes three arguments. The first argument designates the chart object to which the method will assign the data. The sample that follows illustrates the setting for a bar chart and the series it plots. See the *SetData* method description in Access Help for a complete list of the 15 possible settings for this argument. The appropriate setting varies according to the type of chart and the chart axis you use. The second argument specifies how the chart object connects with the data source. The third argument can name the data source. When working with a database as a data source, this argument will typically be a field name, such as *CompanyName* or *ExtPrice*.

After assigning data to the chart, the procedure moves on to format the chart. This formatting assigns values to the chart that the PivotChart view displays. For example, the procedure assigns string values to the title captions for the vertical and horizontal axes—*Axis(0)* and *Axis(1)*, respectively. To assign a caption to the chart's overall title, you must specify that the chart has a title. Do this by setting the chart's *HasTitle* property to True. The default value is False. Next assign a string to the *Caption* property for the chart's title. The *Font* property is another especially useful chart title property. This property returns a *Font* object that you can use to set the chart title's font style, size, and name. The sample that follows illustrates the syntax for designating a 14-point font.

The last step the procedure takes is to close the form and save the changes to the PivotChart view. This action is essential for preserving the settings so that they're available the next time a user opens the form.

```
Sub CreateChart(strFName As String)
Dim frm1 As Access.Form

'Open form to contain PivotChart
DoCmd.OpenForm strFName, acFormPivotChart
Set frm1 = Forms(strFName)

With frm1.ChartSpace
'Open PivotChart without drop areas, and set its categories and values
    .SetData chDimCategories, chDataBound, "CompanyName"
    .SetData chDimValues, chDataBound, "ExtPrice"
    .DisplayFieldButtons = False

'Assign and format titles to axes and overall chart
    With .Charts(0)
        .Axes(1).Title.Caption = "Sales ($)"
        .Axes(0).Title.Caption = "Shippers"
        .HasTitle = True
        .Title.Caption = "Sales By Shipper"
        .Title.Font.Size = 14
    End With
End With

'Close form and save PivotChart view
DoCmd.Close acForm, strFName, acSaveYes

End Sub
```

Figure 8-8 shows the PivotChart view created by the *CreateChart* procedure. Notice that this view has just three bars—one for each of the shippers. A bar chart automatically aggregates the series into its bars. In addition, the bar chart specification automatically gives the bars names that correspond to the *CompanyName* field values. As you've seen, explicit programming actions create the titles for the chart's two axes and the chart as a whole.

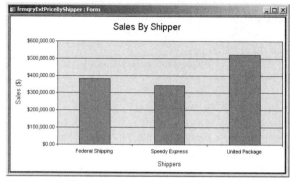

Figure 8-8 The PivotChart view created by the *CreateChart* procedure.

Updating a Bar Chart to a 3-D Bar Chart

The bar chart shown in Figure 8-8 effectively conveys the differences among the values of goods transported by various shippers. Yet charts can be even more powerful when given a dramatic presentation. Your clients won't always seek drama, however; sometimes they'll just want a bit of variety. In any event, by learning to implement all the style variations that PivotCharts offer, you'll be equipped to accommodate all your clients' needs.

You can determine the style of a chart by assigning a *ChartChartTypeEnum* value to its *Type* property. The *Type* property has more than 65 enum settings. The full list is available in the Object Browser. A setting of *chChartTypeBar3D* can transform the two-dimensional bar chart shown in Figure 8-8 into a 3-D bar chart, as shown in Figure 8-9. The syntax for this transformation is very straightforward. Just assign the enum constant to the chart's *Type* property.

The following sample demonstrates this syntax. The sample also allows a user to conditionally save the change if they like the appearance of the altered view. The procedure starts by opening the *frmqryExtPriceByShipper* form. Next the sample assigns the 3-D bar chart constant to the *Type* property. Then the sample opens a message box that asks the user whether he wants to save the new format. Clicking Yes updates the form's PivotChart view with the new 3-D format, but clicking No preserves the original format.

```
Sub Format3DBarChart()
Dim frm1 As Access.Form

'Open a form in its PivotChart view
DoCmd.OpenForm "frmqryExtPriceByShipper", acFormPivotChart
Set frm1 = Forms("frmqryExtPriceByShipper")
```

```
'Assign 3D Bar Chart Format and blank Series axis
frm1.ChartSpace.Charts(0).Type = chChartTypeBar3D

'Prompt for whether to save with the new format
If MsgBox("Do you want to save the format?", vbYesNo, _
    "Programming Microsoft Access Version 2002") = vbYes Then
    DoCmd.Close acForm, "frmqryExtPriceByShipper", acSaveYes
Else
    DoCmd.Close acForm, "frmqryExtPriceByShipper", acSaveNo
End If

End Sub
```

Figure 8-9 shows the reformatted PivotChart view. Notice the message box in the lower left corner. With this message box, a user can preserve the new format or revert to the original two-dimensional format that appears in Figure 8-8.

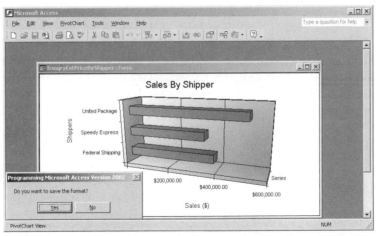

Figure 8-9 The display that results from running the *Format3DBarChart* procedure.

Creating a Time-Based Line Chart

A line chart is similar to a bar chart in two important respects. Therefore, your understanding of the preceding chart sample can help you develop a line chart in a form's PivotChart view. The first similarity is that a line chart contains categories. These categories are the values for grouping a series. When you create a line chart, the categories normally possess some natural order, as is the case with dates. Note that you will often have more categories in a line chart than in a bar chart. The second similarity is that a line chart aggregates a series into its individual categories—just like a bar chart aggregates a series into its bars. Each point along a line chart represents the total of the series for that point. Therefore, if your series is *ExtPrice*, each date (or point) represents the total of *ExtPrice* values for that point.

The main differences between line and bar charts stem from the way each chart type represents aggregated category values. A bar chart uses a bar to signify a category value, while a line chart represents its categories by using points, which it subsequently connects with a line.

Because of their similarities, you can create a line chart almost the same way that you create a bar chart. Be aware that your category values must have a natural progression and you must group them prior to referencing them with the *SetData* method. For example, the *qryExtPriceByShipper* query created by the preceding sample transforms *OrderDate* field values to create a new *YearMonth* field that reflects just the year and month of the *OrderDate* field value. If you were to use the ungrouped *OrderDate* field values from the *Invoices* query, a line chart would group its series in a PivotChart by day, instead of by month. After you correctly transform the categories, which you can do with a query, you reference the grouped values with a *SetData* method and set the chart's *Type* property to one of the variations of line charts.

The following sample shows the syntax for creating a line chart that displays aggregated *ExtPrice* values by month from the *qryExtPriceByShipper* query. The code starts by naming the source query for the chart and the source form. The PivotChart accesses the data in the query through the form. Next it creates a form based on the query. The sample uses the same *CreateFormBasedOnQuery* procedure shown in the initial sample for creating a bar chart, on page 485. In this case, the name of the form differs from that of the preceding sample, but the query name remains the same.

After creating the form, the procedure opens it and hides the field buttons for manually adding fields to a PivotChart. Then the procedure invokes the *SetData* method twice. The first time this sample invokes the *SetData* method, it references the *YearMonth* field as the chart's categories axis. The *YearMonth* field is the transformed field for the *OrderDate* field from the *Invoices* query. The *YearMonth* field value is always the first day of a month. The month and year for the *YearMonth* field correspond to the *OrderDate* field on which it is based. The second time the sample invokes the *SetData* method, the procedure adds the *ExtPrice* field to the line chart the same way it did for the bar chart.

Aside from the first invocation of the *SetData* method, there is one more critical distinction between the processes used to create the bar chart and the line chart. The initial bar chart sample did not specify a chart type. That's because the default type for a chart that assigns values to *chDimCategories* is a bar chart. When you want to create a line chart, you must therefore explicitly assign a value to the chart's *Type* property. The appropriate setting for a line chart with markers for the points is *chChartTypeLineMarkers*.

The formatting for the line chart follows the same pattern as for the bar chart. The only distinction is that different strings define the chart title and the axis title for the categories dimension. Here's the procedure:

```
Sub CreateTimeBasedLineChart()
Dim frml As Access.Form
Dim strQName As String
Dim strFName As String

'Assign names for query and form
strQName = "qryExtPriceByShipper"
strFName = "frmqryExtPriceByShipper1"

'Create a form based on query
CreateFormBasedOnQuery strFName, strQName

'Open a form in its PivotChart view
DoCmd.OpenForm strFName, acFormPivotChart
Set frml = Forms(strFName)
frml.ChartSpace.DisplayFieldButtons = False

With frml.ChartSpace
'Open PiovtChart without drop areas, and set its categories and values
    .SetData chDimCategories, chDataBound, "[YearMonth]"
    .SetData chDimValues, chDataBound, "ExtPrice"
    .Charts(0).Type = chChartTypeLineMarkers

'Assign and format titles to axes and overall chart
    With .Charts(0)
        .Axes(1).Title.Caption = "Sales ($)"
        .Axes(0).Title.Caption = "Dates"
        .HasTitle = True
        .Title.Caption = "Sales By Month"
        .Title.Font.Size = 14
    End With
End With

'Close form and save PivotChart view
DoCmd.Close acForm, strFName, acSaveYes

End Sub
```

Figure 8-10 shows the line chart created by the *CreateTimeBasedLineChart* procedure. Notice that it has a single point for each month. Those points represent the total sales during each month. The single line in the chart represents the sales made by all three shippers.

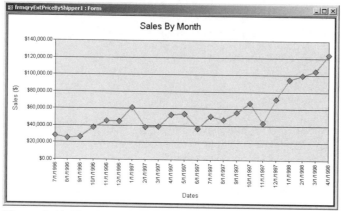

Figure 8-10 The PivotChart that results from running the *CreateTimeBasedLineChart* procedure.

Creating a 3-D Line Chart

This chapter's concluding sample modifies the basic line chart shown in Figure 8-9 in two ways. First, it adds a new series dimension to the chart. The new dimension represents the shippers—namely, the *CompanyName* field in the *qryExtPriceByShipper* query. This new dimension does not replace either of the dimension assignments from the preceding sample. Instead, it refines those dimension assignments. The modified chart contains three lines instead of just one. Each line denotes the sales over time for a different shipper. As a result of the new three-line format, the new chart includes a legend so that viewers can easily identify the shippers. Second, the chart uses a 3-D format for drawing lines. Some users might find that the 3-D lines make it easier to distinguish among the shippers than the two-dimensional line in the preceding sample.

Since this sample modifies an existing chart instead of creating a new one, the code begins by referencing a form and opening it in its PivotChart view. As with the preceding sample, the code hides the Field buttons. Next the code invokes the *SetData* method to add a new dimension, which represents the *CompanyName* field. This new dimension enables the chart to use a separate line to display the sales transported by each shipper. The line of code after the one invoking the *SetData* method assigns a value of True to the chart's *HasLegend* property. Then the code sets the chart's *Type* property to *chChartTypeLine3D*. This draws a 3-D line for each shipper. The final portion of the sample permits the user to accept the new format or reject it in favor of the original line chart format.

```
Sub UpdateTimeBasedLineChart()
Dim frm1 As Access.Form
Dim strFName As String

'Form to update
strFName = "frmqryExtPriceByShipper1"

'Open a form in its PivotChart view
DoCmd.OpenForm strFName, acFormPivotChart
Set frm1 = Forms(strFName)
frm1.ChartSpace.DisplayFieldButtons = False

With frm1.ChartSpace
'Add CompanyName series to the chart, draw 3-D lines, and
'add a legend
    .SetData chDimSeriesNames, chDataBound, "CompanyName"
    .Charts(0).HasLegend = True
    .Charts(0).Type = chChartTypeLine3D
End With


'Prompt for whether to save with the new format
If MsgBox("Do you want to save the format?", vbYesNo, _
    "Programming Microsoft Access Version 2002") = vbYes Then
    DoCmd.Close acForm, strFName, acSaveYes
Else
    DoCmd.Close acForm, strFName, acSaveNo
End If

End Sub
```

Figure 8-11 shows the final chart sample. Take a look at the 3-D line formatting. Do you like being able to easily tell the difference between shippers? Regardless of whether these aesthetic choices appeal to you personally, it's helpful to know how to implement them for your clients.

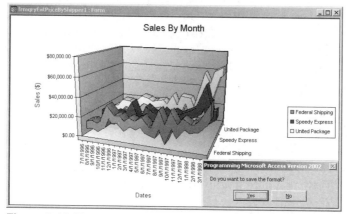

Figure 8-11 The display that results from running the *UpdateTimeBasedLineChart* procedure.

9

Class, Form, and Report Modules

To program Microsoft Access efficiently, you must manage your programmatic resources so that they are easy to use and reuse. The value of your code grows in proportion to how much use you can get from it. Class modules package code for easy reuse. The class module acts as a container that exposes the code and selected variables inside it in a way that's familiar to Microsoft Visual Basic for Applications (VBA) developers. Basically, you invoke class procedures and assign values to variables and objects with the same syntax used for the properties and methods of built-in Access objects and ActiveX Data Objects (ADO) objects. To use the code in a class module, you do not have to know anything about the internals of how it works. Since class modules expose properties, methods, and events as other objects do, even beginning VBA developers can use them.

This chapter first introduces standalone class modules and form and report class modules. Then it demonstrates simple ways to build classes into your Access applications and to develop custom properties and methods. Next comes a case study that uses three forms, a few custom *Property Get* and *Property Let* functions, and a couple of techniques based on ADO to build a custom password security application. The section after the case study shows the syntax for programming events into your custom classes and introduces the *WithEvents* keyword.

The focus then shifts to the containers for class, form, and report modules as we look at the *All* collections that were introduced in Access 2000. Just as there are *AllForms* and *AllReports* collections, there is an *AllModules* collection. (In fact, there are a total of 10 *All* collections.) The chapter wraps up by explaining how to combine the *AllModules* collection with the *Modules* collection to manage code in an application.

There are three basic kinds of modules:

■ **Standard modules**   These hold sub procedures and function procedures that you want to make available throughout a database file. Standard modules can also contain variables defined with a *Public* declaration that you want to make available to procedures in other modules.

■ **Standalone class modules**   These let you create custom objects. You can define properties, methods, and events for these objects, and you can use the *New* keyword to create instances of the form objects.

■ **Class modules for forms and reports**   These modules are often called form and report modules. By default, all forms and reports have modules behind them. (Their *HasModule* property is set to True by default.) You can use the *Me* keyword when referring to the modules behind forms and reports.

Class Modules

Standalone class modules differ from form and report class modules in several ways. First, standalone class modules do not have a built-in user interface, as form and report class modules do. This makes standalone class modules more suited to tasks that do not require an interface, such as performing calculations, looking up data, or modifying a database. When form or report modules require computationally intensive tasks, they can call a standalone class module.

Second, standalone class modules offer *Initialize* and *Terminate* events that provide for operations that need to take place at the opening and closing of a class instance. Report and form modules do not have these events, but you can perform similar functionality with the *Load* and *Close* events.

Third, you must use the *New* keyword to create instances of the class defined in a standalone class module. Report and form class modules also let you create instances with the *DoCmd* object's *OpenForm* and *OpenReport* methods as well as by referencing the report or form class module's properties or methods. For example, *Form_MyForm.SetFocus* opens the MyForm form.

You can create a standalone class module from the Insert menu in the Visual Basic Editor (VBE). (The same menu offers commands for building a standard module or a procedure.) After creating a class module shell, you can populate it with procedures and declarations, which equip it with custom properties and methods.

Custom Property Functions and Custom Methods

Special property functions make it easier to develop any combination of read-only, write-only, and read/write properties for your classes. If your application permits, you can define properties by simply declaring a public variable. When a class module defines a property with a public variable, it's always a read/write property. The ability to declare custom properties lets you extend the basic Access functionality for forms and reports. In addition, these property functions allow you to create powerful standalone classes.

Your applications can also build custom methods into a class. You can use sub procedures or function procedures to accomplish this. By selectively exposing variables and procedures with the *Public* keyword, you can narrowly define what methods and properties the class exposes. This lets your applications define interfaces to your class object that perform in very specific ways.

Instantiating Classes

The public methods and procedures support programmatic access by procedures outside the class. You must first instantiate the class in a host procedure within another module, using the *New* keyword. (You use the same keyword to instantiate objects from built-in classes, such as ADO *Connection* and *Recordset* objects. In fact, your applications can instantiate multiple copies of a custom class at the same time—just like the ADO classes.) After instantiating a class, the code in your host procedure manipulates the instance of the class, not the class itself. You can change a property in one instance of a form, but when you instantiate a second instance of the form, it appears with the default property setting.

Custom Classes and Events

VBA in Access lets you build custom classes with their own properties and methods. You can process custom events raised within standalone class modules. Furthermore, you can design a class that hooks onto a built-in class or type library. For example, you can build a class module that launches VBA code in response to the *ItemAdded* and *ItemRemoved* events of the *References* collection. This collection tracks links to external type libraries and ActiveX controls.

After referencing a library, such as the Microsoft ActiveX Data Objects 2.5 or 2.6 Library, you can build custom events around the ADO events for the *Connection* and *Recordset* objects. These events can enable asynchronous data access that lets your application respond to users even while it remains ready to respond to a completed connection or the availability of a fetched set of records. We examined this topic in Chapter 3, "Data Access Models: Part II." The ADO samples in this chapter shift the emphasis from ADO to design principles for class modules.

You use the *WithEvents* keyword within a *Public* declaration to create an object reference that monitors and reports events within an ActiveX control. This keyword is valid only in class modules. You can define multiple variables within a module with the *WithEvents* keyword, but you cannot create arrays with it. Also, a declaration cannot contain both the *WithEvents* and *New* keywords.

Built-In Class Events

Class modules have two built-in events: *Initialize* and *Terminate*. The *Initialize* event occurs when you create a new instance of a class module. You create a shell for the *Initialize* event procedure by selecting Class from the class's Object control and Initialize from the Procedure control. The Object control is on the upper left side of the Code window, and the Procedure control is on the upper right side. You can do anything necessary in an *Initialize* event procedure to prepare your class instance for use.

The *Terminate* event procedure is where you should clean up after your current application. This can be as simple as closing an object reference and setting it to Nothing. The *Initialize* and *Terminate* events occur just once, at the beginning and end (respectively) of a class instance's life. Therefore, they are not particularly handy for generating interactive or dynamic behavior outside the birth and death of a class instance.

Custom Properties and Methods

When you use class modules, you inevitably work with two separate modules. The class module exposes properties and methods and propagates events. A second module references the class module; it assigns and reads property values as well as invokes methods. This module can initiate actions that fire events, and these, in turn, can invoke any associated event procedures in the class module.

The syntax for invoking a custom method and printing a property value is identical in the two samples that follow, although the properties are declared differently. The properties work the same way whether you define them with a *Public* declaration for a variable or with one or more property functions. Public variables might be a simpler way to implement properties in class modules, but property functions offer a more flexible way to expose them. You use a *Property Get* function by itself for a read-only property, and you use a *Property Let* function by itself for a write-only property. You use both types of property functions for a read/write property. If your property references an object instead of a normal, or scalar, variable, you can use a *Property Set* function instead of a *Property Let* function. You use the *Property Get* function to return a property value whether you're working with a scalar variable or an object.

Exposing a Property with a Public Variable

The following sample shows two listings. The first is from the MyTestClass module. This class module starts with a couple of variable declarations—one for this sample and one for the next sample. The procedure named *EP* computes the extended price from three arguments passed to it: *units*, *price*, and *discount*. The procedure saves the result of its expression in the *ExtendedPrice* variable. A declaration in the module's general area defines *ExtendedPrice* as a public variable. This enables a host procedure in another module that works with an instance of the *MyTestClass* object to read or update the variable's value.

```
'FROM MyTestClass module (a class module)
Public ExtendedPrice As Currency
Private MyComputedPrice As Currency

Public Sub EP(units As Long, price As Currency, _
    discount As Single)

'Compute with result in public variable
ExtendedPrice = units * price * (1 - discount)

End Sub


'FROM Module1 (a standard module)
Sub ComputeExtendedPrice()
'Create new instance of class module
Dim MyPriceComputer As New MyTestClass

'Invoke EP method for class, and
'print Extended Price property
MyPriceComputer.EP 5, 5, 0.02
Debug.Print MyPriceComputer.ExtendedPrice

End Sub
```

The host procedure, *ComputeExtendedPrice*, resides in a standard module named Module1. This procedure instantiates an object based on the class defined by MyTestClass. Next it invokes the *EP* method for the object. Finally, it prints the *ExtendedPrice* property for the object.

This sample is basic, but it demonstrates several important points about using class modules:

- Class modules are a good choice for computing critical business expressions. You will generally use class modules for encapsulating a more sophisticated computation than the one for extended price.

- The second procedure, which is in the standard module, starts by referencing the class module, MyTestClass. The *New* keyword instantiates an object based on the class. In the sample, the variable named *MyPriceComputer* references the instance of the class.

- You can use the object reference for the instance of the class to invoke methods and set or read property values. You reference the class's *EP* method with the standard dot notation. You list arguments after the method's name, and you reference properties with the same basic notation.

- Creating a property for a class can be as simple as declaring a *Public* variable in the class module.

Exposing a Property with a Property Function

The following listing shows a different approach to the same task. It relies on a property defined with a *Property Get* function. The *ep2* method is nearly identical to the *EP* method shown in the preceding sample. The only difference is that *ep2* deposits the result of its expression into a private variable, *MyComputedPrice*. (See the private variable declaration in the preceding sample.) By itself, this means that instances of the class cannot expose the expression's result. You must use a *Property Get* function to expose a private variable. Since no other property function is defined for *ComputedPrice*, the property is read-only. If there were a *Property Let* function with the same name, the property would be read/write. Using read-only properties can help to secure the values of your properties—or at least the ways to set them.

```
'FROM MyTestClass module (a class module)
Public Sub ep2(units As Long, price As Currency, _
    discount As Single)

'Compute with result in private variable; expose
'result through Property Get function
MyComputedPrice = units * price * (1 - discount)

End Sub

Property Get ComputedPrice()
```

```
'This is how to return a private variable,
'in this case a read-only property
ComputedPrice = MyComputedPrice

End Property


'FROM Module1 (a standard module)
Sub GetComputedPrice()
Dim MyPriceComputer As New MyTestClass

'Using a value defined as a property looks the same
'as using one defined with a public variable
MyPriceComputer.ep2 5, 5, 0.02
Debug.Print MyPriceComputer.ComputedPrice

End Sub
```

Class Modules and Data Sources

Class modules are good for encapsulating any kind of code. They have special value when you want to make a data source available for updating or viewing, but you need to secure the data source from accidental or inadvertent damage by users.

Updating Inventory Data with an SQL String

The following sample uses a class module to update the *UnitsInStock* field for the *Products* table given a product ID and the quantity ordered. A procedure with two lines passes two arguments to a sub procedure in a class module. This sample uses a different class module from the samples for calculating extended price (MyTestClass2 instead of MyTestClass). In practice, you divide your functions and declarations into homogeneous collections of method procedures and properties representing distinct object classes. The *OrderIt* variable represents an instance of the class defined in the MyTestClass2 module. Within the module is a function named *PO1*. This function takes two arguments, one for the product ID and one for the units ordered.

```
Sub MyOrder()
Dim OrderIt As New MyTestClass

    OrderIt.PO1 1, 10

End Sub
```

The *PO1* procedure, shown next, updates the *Products* table. Specifically, it decreases *UnitsInStock* by the number of units ordered. This procedure resides in the class module (MyTestClass2). Note the procedure's design: it uses a *Command* object with an SQL string that defines the update query. Although the procedure accepts two arguments, it does not apply a parameter query. Instead, it uses the passed arguments as variables in the string expression defining the SQL string. This design leads to a compact procedure that is relatively easy to read.

```
'A method for updating a table
Public Sub PO1(ProductID, units)
Dim cmd1 As Command
Dim strSQL As String

'Assign the command reference and connection
Set cmd1 = New ADODB.Command
cmd1.ActiveConnection = CurrentProject.Connection

'Define the SQL string; notice
'the insertion of passed arguments
strSQL = "UPDATE Products " & _
    "SET UnitsInStock = " & _
    "UnitsInStock-" & units & " " & _
    "WHERE ProductID=" & ProductID

'Assign the SQL string to the command, and run it
With cmd1
    .CommandText = strSQL
    .CommandType = adCmdText
    .Execute
End With

End Sub
```

Updating Inventory Data with a Parameter Query

Many developers prefer a more traditional approach that relies on a parameter query. The *PO2* procedure that follows uses a parameter query to perform the same task accomplished by *PO1*. A parameter query lets you declare data types with traditional VBA conventions. Notice that the ADO constant *adInteger* represents a Long data type, and the constant *adSmallInt* designates an Integer data type. You must create the parameters with the *CreateParameter* method in the same order in which you declare them in the *Parameters* clause of the query statement. Failing to do so will generate a run-time error. (If you need to review ADO data types, refer to Chapter 2, "Data Access Models: Part I.")

```
Public Sub PO2(ProductID As Long, units As Integer)
Dim cmd1 As Command
Dim strSQL As String
Dim prm1 As ADODB.Parameter, prm2 As ADODB.Parameter

'Assign the command reference and connection
Set cmd1 = New ADODB.Command
cmd1.ActiveConnection = CurrentProject.Connection

'Write out SQL statement with parameters and assign to cmd1
strSQL = "Parameters PID Long,Quantity Integer;" & _
    "UPDATE Products " & _
    "SET UnitsInStock = " & _
    "UnitsInStock-Quantity " & _
    "WHERE ProductID=PID;"
cmd1.CommandText = strSQL
cmd1.CommandType = adCmdText

'Declare parameters; must have same order as declaration
Set prm1 = cmd1.CreateParameter("PID", adSmallInt, _
    adParamInput)
prm1.Value = ProductID
cmd1.Parameters.Append prm1
Set prm2 = cmd1.CreateParameter("Quantity", adSmallInt, _
    adParamInput)
prm2.Value = units
cmd1.Parameters.Append prm2

'Run update query
cmd1.Execute

End Sub
```

There are four main components to the parameter query design of the update task:

■ The procedure makes variable declarations and assigns references.

■ It specifies the SQL string for the update query and assigns that string to a command property.

■ It creates and assigns values to the parameters declared in the second step.

■ It runs the command to update the database.

Opening a Recordset in a Class Module

Any code that's even moderately complex is a candidate for a class module. You can bundle the code in a module and then make it easy to invoke by choosing a simple method to launch a procedure within the module. Incidentally, you can use just the properties that are appropriate for your needs. This section shows how to open a recordset in a class module and provides two techniques for making the recordset available.

The first code sample we'll look at references the MyRecordset class module. This class module contains a private object declaration for a *Recordset* object as well as four procedures to help manipulate the recordset and make it available to a host procedure invoking the class. The first procedure, *MyRecordsetOpen*, opens a recordset on a subset of records identified in an SQL string (*str1*). The string serves as the source argument for a statement that invokes the recordset *Open* method. After executing the *Open* method inside the class, VBA doesn't make the recordset available to the host application that invokes the class. This is because the method opens a private *Recordset* object (*p_rst1*), which isn't visible outside the class module. For the host application to gain access to the recordset, it must use the class's *MyRst* property.

When the host application finishes working with the recordset, it performs the normal cleanup operations. Since the recordset inside the *MyRecordset* class isn't directly available to the host application, the class module automatically closes the recordset and removes it from memory when the host application terminates the class instance. A host application can terminate an object based on a class by setting its object reference to Nothing.

I'll discuss the *Property Set* procedure in the MyRecordset class module in a subsequent sample.

```
'FROM the MyRecordset Class module
Private p_rst1 As ADODB.recordset

Public Sub MyRecordsetOpen(str1 As String)

'Instantiate p_rst1 as a new Recordset object
Set p_rst1 = New ADODB.recordset

'Open a new p_rst1 as a new recordset according
'to the SQL source statement in str1
p_rst1.Open str1, CurrentProject.Connection, _
    adOpenKeyset, adLockOptimistic, adCmdText

End Sub
```

```
Property Get MyRst() As recordset

'Return the current value of p_rst1
'as MyRst
Set MyRst = p_rst1

End Property


Property Set MyRst(p_rst2 As ADODB.recordset)

'Instantiate p_rst1 as a new Recordset object
Set p_rst1 = New ADODB.recordset

'Assign an input recordset to the p_rst1
Set p_rst1 = p_rst2

End Property


Private Sub Class_Terminate()

'Close local recordset, p_rst1; bypass error for
'closing object more than once
On Error Resume Next
p_rst1.Close
Set p_rst1 = Nothing

End Sub
```

A class module such as MyRecordset can have multiple host applications. The first procedure serving as a host for the *MyRecordset* class is the *OpenARecordset* procedure, shown next. This procedure exists in a standard module (named Module2) of this chapter's sample Access database file on the companion CD. Instead of declaring and instantiating a class-based object in one step, this procedure uses one statement to declare an object based on the *MyRecordset* class and another statement to instantiate it. Using a two-step process is generally preferable in order to more efficiently manage memory usage—especially as your procedures get longer. In very short host procedures, there's no particular advantage to using one statement for an object declaration and another one for object instantiation.

After instantiating an object based on the MyRecordset class module, the host procedure constructs an SQL string with the help of user responses to an *InputBox* statement. The SQL string in *str1* specifies all records from the local *Employees* table that have an employee ID greater than the reply to the *InputBox* prompt. The *InputBox* statement specifies a default value of *1* in case the user clicks OK without typing a value. If you have not changed the table, the host application prepares an SQL string that returns eight records when you specify the default employee ID of 1.

After developing the *str1* SQL string, the procedure passes the string to the *MyRecordset* class represented by the *MyEmployees* object reference. Then the host procedure assigns the *MyRst* property to its local recordset object reference, *rst1*. Recall that a *Property Get* function implements this property. Referencing the MyRst property makes the recordset available to the host application. Without using this property, you could not do anything with the recordset specified by the SQL string. After creating this reference to the *p_rst1* recordset from the *MyRecordset* class instance, the host application prints the number of records in the recordset.

The first of the final two lines in the host application launches the *Terminate* event procedure for the MyRecordset class module. In the class module listing, notice that the event procedure performs two tasks. First it closes the *p_rst1* recordset. Second it sets the recordset object to Nothing. Since *rst1* in the host application points at the *p_rst1* recordset inside the MyRecordset class module, attempting to close the *rst1* recordset after closing the *p_rst1* recordset generates a run-time error. Therefore, the host application skips this step in its cleanup and just sets *rst1* to Nothing.

```
Sub OpenARecordset()
Dim MyEmployees As MyRecordset
Dim rst1 As ADODB.recordset
Dim str1 As String
Dim str2 As String

'Instantiate a new instance of the MyRecordset
'class as the MyEmployees object
Set MyEmployees = New MyRecordset

'Gather user input for string to define rows
'in the MyEmployees object
str1 = "Select * From Employees WHERE EmployeeID > "


str2 = InputBox("Enter an EmployeeID to define " & _
    "recordset members", _
    "Programming Microsoft Access Version 2002", 1)
str1 = str1 & str2
MyEmployees.MyRecordsetOpen (str1)

'Assign MyEmployees object to a local recordset
'and print the local recordset's RecordCount property
Set rst1 = MyEmployees.MyRst
Debug.Print rst1.RecordCount
```

```
'Clean up objects
Set MyEmployees = Nothing
Set rst1 = Nothing

End Sub
```

The *MyRecordset* class makes its internal recordset, *p_rst1*, available to a host application through its *Property Get* procedure. Sometimes your application might not call for displaying the internal recordset in this way. You might prefer to just display a limited set of information about the procedure. You can do this by removing the *Property Get* procedure and replacing it with properties that return whatever information you want to show. The *MyRecordsetReadOnly* class module that appears next drops the *Property Get* procedure for the whole recordset and replaces it with *MyRecordCount*, another *Property Get* procedure that returns just the count of records generated by the SQL string:

```
'FROM MyRecordsetReadOnly Class module
Private p_rst1 As ADODB.recordset

Public Sub MyRecordsetOpen(str1 As String)

'Instantiate p_rst1 as a new Recordset object
Set p_rst1 = New ADODB.recordset

'Open a new p_rst1 as a new recordset according
'to the SQL source statement in str1
p_rst1.Open str1, CurrentProject.Connection, _
    adOpenKeyset, adLockOptimistic, adCmdText

End Sub


Property Get MyRecordCount() As Long

MyRecordCount = p_rst1.RecordCount

End Property


Private Sub Class_Terminate()

'Close and set recordset to Nothing
p_rst1.Close
Set p_rst1 = Nothing

End Sub
```

The *OpenARecordsetReadOnly* procedure in Module2 serves as the host for the *MyRecordsetReadOnly* class. This host procedure generally follows the format of the preceding host procedure until just after passing the string to the class to generate the recordset. Instead of instantiating an object based on the *MyRecordset* class, the host procedure bases its version of the *MyEmployees* object on the *MyRecordsetReadOnly* class. When the *MyRecordsetReadOnly* class generates its recordset, that recordset never becomes available to the host application. However, the host can print the *MyRecordCount* property of the *MyEmployees* object, which is based on the *MyRecordsetReadOnly* class. This property returns the number of records generated by the SQL string compiled in the *OpenARecordsetReadOnly* procedure. Notice also that the cleanup in this host application just sets the *MyEmployees* object to Nothing. This is because there's no local recordset to clean up in this sample.

```
Sub OpenARecordsetReadOnly()
Dim MyEmployees As MyRecordsetReadOnly
Dim str1 As String
Dim str2 As String

'Instantiate a new instance of the MyRecordsetReadOnly
'class as the MyEmployees object
Set MyEmployees = New MyRecordsetReadOnly

'Gather user input for string to define rows
'in the MyEmployees object
str1 = "Select * From Employees WHERE EmployeeID > "
str2 = InputBox("Enter an EmployeeID to define " & _
    "recordset members", _
    "Programming Microsoft Access Version 2002", 1)
str1 = str1 & str2
MyEmployees.MyRecordsetOpen (str1)

'Invoke Property Get function to return record count
'for recordset in the class
Debug.Print MyEmployees.MyRecordCount

'Clean up objects
Set MyEmployees = Nothing

End Sub
```

Assigning Multiple Objects to a Single Class

The preceding pair of samples highlights the role of the *Property Get* procedure. The *Property Get* procedure exposes an object from within the class so that a host application can retrieve the object. A *Property Set* procedure enables a host application to assign a value to an object within a class. While you can create an object within a class by invoking a class method, a *Property Set* procedure enables a host application to create an object and then pass the object reference to the class.

The following excerpt from the *MyRecordset* class module displays for a second time the *Property Set* procedure named *MyRst*. Note that all *Property Set* procedures must have at least one argument. In this case, the passed argument has the name *p_rst2* and an *ADODB.recordset* type. The required argument is the object reference that the host application passes to the class. The *MyRst Property Set* procedure has two lines. First, it instantiates a fresh recordset and saves a reference to it in the *p_rst1* object reference. Second, it assigns the *p_rst2* object reference to the *p_rst1* reference. Be aware that while the host application and the class module each have distinct object references, they both point to the same object. In this case, that object is the source object for *p_rst2* in the host application.

```
Property Set MyRst(p_rst2 As ADODB.recordset)

'Instantiate p_rst1 as a new Recordset object
Set p_rst1 = New ADODB.recordset

'Assign an input recordset to the p_rst1
Set p_rst1 = p_rst2

End Property
```

The following host application procedure, *AssigningMultipleObjects*, illustrates how to use a *Property Set* procedure from a host application. The host procedure sequentially creates two recordsets for different tables in a backup copy of the Northwind database. (Recall that this is our clean copy of the database.) After creating a recordset locally, the host procedure passes the object reference to the class module and then uses the *Property Get* procedure within the class to return another reference to the same object. The host application confirms the validity of the newly created object reference from the class by printing its record count and first field name.

After the declarations in *AssigningMultipleObjects*, the procedure first creates a recordset (*rst1*) based on the *Products* table in the Northwind backup database. Notice that the *Open* method uses the default settings for the cursor type. Recall that this type of cursor does not support the *RecordCount* property.

Next the procedure instantiates a copy of the *MyRecordset* class and saves its reference in the *MyProducts* object reference. Then the procedure assigns the *rst1* recordset to the *MyProducts* object's *MyRst* property. A *Property Set* procedure in the class by the same name as the property enables updating this property. After assigning the recordset to the class, the host application gets the recordset from the class, again through its *MyRst* property. As mentioned previously, a *Property Get* procedure enables reading this property. This completes the first assignment to a class and retrieval from a class of a recordset object.

The test of the host procedure's first use of the *Property Set* and *Property Get* procedures prints the *RecordCount* property and the first field name for the *rst2* object reference. The *RecordCount* property returns the value −1 since its recordset does not support the *RecordCount* property, but the field name returns *ProductID*, the name for the first column in the *Products* table.

After printing results from a reference to the *Products* table in the Northwind backup database, the host procedure creates a new recordset for the *rst1* object reference and opens it for a new table. (The *MyProducts* object continues to point to the old recordset, so we don't close *rst1* before setting it to a new recordset.) The new *rst1* object reference points to the *Employees* table. Moreover, the new object reference uses a keyset cursor instead of the default cursor. The keyset cursor supports the *RecordCount* property, but the default cursor does not. After creating the new object reference for *rst1*, the host procedure instantiates a new instance of the *MyRecordset* class as *MyEmployees*. Next the procedure assigns *rst1* to the *MyRst* property of the *MyEmployees* object. Then it recovers the recordset from the object by assigning its *MyRst* property to *rst3*. When the procedure attempts to print the *RecordCount* property for *rst3*, it successfully prints the number of records in the *Employees* table since the original object in *rst1* has a keyset cursor. In addition, the first field name appears as *EmployeeID* rather than *ProductID*, as it did with the previous recovery of a recordset from an object based on the *MyRecordset* class.

Finally, the *AssigningMultipleObjects* procedure performs its object cleanup. This code merits more commentary than most object cleanups. When the host application sets a *MyRecordset* object to Nothing, it launches the *Terminate* procedure and closes the recordset for the *MyRecordset* object reference. If the host procedure closes the recordset using its local reference before setting the *MyRecordset* object to Nothing, the *Terminate* procedure will fail because it cannot close a recordset that is already closed. To safeguard against this, the *Terminate* event procedure includes an *On Error Resume Next* statement. The statement bypasses the error that stems from trying to close an object that's already closed. Unlike setting *rst1* to Nothing, setting *MyEmployees* to Nothing both closes the recordset if necessary and assures the removal of the corresponding object references from memory.

```
Sub AssigningMultipleObjects()
Dim rst1 As ADODB.recordset
Dim MyProducts As MyRecordset
Dim rst2 As ADODB.recordset
Dim MyEmployees As MyRecordset
Dim rst3 As ADODB.recordset

'Open a local recordset object on the Products table
'in the backup version of the Northwind database
'with the default ADO cursor settings
Set rst1 = New ADODB.recordset
rst1.Open "Products", "Provider=Microsoft.Jet.OLEDB.4.0;" & _
    "Data Source=C:\PMA Samples\Northwind_backup.mdb;"

'Instantiate MyProducts as a MyRecordset class
Set MyProducts = New MyRecordset

'Assign rst1 to the MyProducts object, get the
'assigned object in rst2, and attempt to print
'RecordCount property for rst2 and the first field name
Set MyProducts.MyRst = rst1
Set rst2 = MyProducts.MyRst
Debug.Print rst2.RecordCount
Debug.Print rst2.Fields(0).Name

'Open a local recordset object in the Employees table
'with a keyset cursor
Set rst1 = New ADODB.recordset
rst1.Open "Employees", "Provider=Microsoft.Jet.OLEDB.4.0;" & _
    "Data Source=C:\PMA Samples\Northwind_backup.mdb;", adOpenKeyset, _
    adLockOptimistic, adCmdTable

'Instantiate MyEmployees as a MyRecordset class
Set MyEmployees = New MyRecordset

'Assign rst1 to the MyEmployees object, get the
'assigned object in rst3, and attempt to print
'RecordCount property for rst3 and the first field
'name; notice RecordCount property works this time
Set MyEmployees.MyRst = rst1
Set rst3 = MyEmployees.MyRst
Debug.Print rst3.RecordCount
Debug.Print rst3.Fields(0).Name
```

(continued)

```
'Clean up objects
Set MyProducts = Nothing
Set MyEmployees = Nothing
Set rst1 = Nothing
End Sub
```

Case Study: Coding a Login Interface

This case study shows one approach to coding a login interface with Access. It uses both standalone class modules and form class modules. The login process and the class module contents use coding techniques that are applicable to any task requiring the use of data with unbound forms.

To highlight the role of class modules and to keep the process transparent, the sample does not use built-in Access security. Instead, it relies on a pair of tables and three forms. The *Passwords* table has just two fields: *EmployeeID* and *Password*. The *Employees* table, which is imported directly from the Northwind database, contains *EmployeeID* as a primary key along with other business, personal, and contact information about employees. The three forms refer to the contents of these tables to manage the login process.

> **Note**   The case study excludes error trapping, which any operational system should have. Error trapping is especially important if the system is dependent on user input. After this case study reinforces your understanding of the basics of class modules, you might want to incorporate some of the error-trapping techniques demonstrated elsewhere in this chapter and in samples throughout the book.

The First Login Form

Figure 9-1 shows the first form, along with two message boxes that it can generate. A user enters values into both text boxes on the form and clicks Let Me In. If the password matches the saved one for the *EmployeeID* field, the application presents a welcome message box. If the password does not match the stored one for an employee ID, the user can try again or change the password.

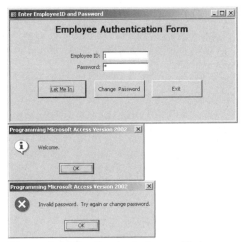

Figure 9-1 The first login form with two possible reply messages.

The Password Mask

In addition to the code behind the form and the class module invoked by the form, you should closely examine the Password text box. It has a password mask that displays an asterisk for each character entered in the box. You assign this mask to a text box from the Data tab of its Properties dialog box. Click the Build button next to the Input Mask property to open a dialog box that lets you select a mask.

The Code Behind the Form

The module behind the form, shown next, contains three event procedures—one for each button. The Exit button merely closes the form. The Change Password button opens a second form and copies the value of a field from the current form into it. The procedure that opens the *frmWhoAmI* form also moves the focus to an empty text box. Then it closes the current form.

The Let Me In button invokes a standalone class module (MyTestClass3). Notice that the procedure passes the contents of its two text boxes to the *cpw* method procedure in the class module. This module looks up the password for the employee ID and determines whether it matches the password on the form. The class replies with one of the two possible messages. (See Figure 9-1.) The class module simplifies the code in the event procedure. This points to another benefit of class modules—they facilitate team development. Advanced developers can write more involved procedures in class modules, and beginning developers can perform basic development tasks and simply reference class modules to incorporate advanced ones.

```
Private Sub cmdExit_Click()
```

```
DoCmd.Close

End Sub


Private Sub cmdNewPassword_Click()

DoCmd.openform "frmWhoAmI"
Forms("frmWhoAmI").txtEmpID = Me.txtEmpID
Forms("frmWhoAmI").txtHireDate.SetFocus
DoCmd.Close acForm, "frmInputPassword"

End Sub


Private Sub cmdLetMeIn_Click()
Dim PWT As New MyTestClass3

PWT.cpw Me.txtEmpID, Me.txtPassword

End Sub
```

Invoking the Class Module

The *cpw* procedure in *MyTestClass3*, shown next, uses a parameter query to look up the password for an employee ID in the *Passwords* table. One of the two arguments passed to the procedure is the employee ID. The procedure sets its parameter equal to the value of this argument. After executing the *Command* object with a select query, the procedure assigns the return set to a *Recordset* object. Since the *EmployeeID* field in the *Passwords* table is a primary key, the select query always returns a single record.

The *cpw* procedure closes by comparing the password returned by the query with the password typed on the form as the condition of an *If...Then* statement. If there is a match, the procedure welcomes the user into the application. In practice, you open another form or some other database object to which you are restricting access with password security. If there is no match, the procedure asks the user to resubmit the password or change the password.

```
Sub cpw(empid As Long, pw As String)
Dim cmd1 As Command
Dim strSQL As String
Dim prm1 As ADODB.Parameter
Dim rst1 As ADODB.recordset
```

```
'Assign the command reference and connection
Set cmd1 = New ADODB.Command
cmd1.ActiveConnection = CurrentProject.Connection

'Write out SQL statement with parameters and assign to cmd1
strSQL = "Parameters Secret Long;" & _
    "Select EmployeeID, Password from Passwords " & _
    "Where EmployeeID=Secret"
cmd1.CommandText = strSQL
cmd1.CommandType = adCmdText
Set prm1 = cmd1.CreateParameter("Secret", adInteger, adParamInput)
prm1.Value = empid
cmd1.Parameters.Append prm1

'A handy line for catching SQL syntax errors
'   Debug.Print cmd1.CommandText

cmd1.Execute

Set rst1 = New ADODB.recordset
rst1.Open cmd1
If rst1.Fields("Password") = pw Then
    MsgBox "Welcome.", vbInformation, _
        "Programming Microsoft Access Version 2002"
Else
    MsgBox "Invalid password.  Try again or " & _
        "change password.", vbCritical, _
        "Programming Microsoft Access Version 2002"
End If

End Sub
```

The Second Login Form

Figure 9-2 shows the form that appears when a user opts to change the password for the employee ID. This form merely asks users to confirm their identity. The system requires this confirmation before it permits users to change a password. The form has two text boxes. Under normal circumstances, the first text box is always filled by the form that loads it. (See the *cmdNewPassword_Click* procedure shown earlier.) All users do is enter their hire date and click Submit. The main point here is to use a field whose value is known only by the employee. Use one or more other fields if you have better alternatives available.

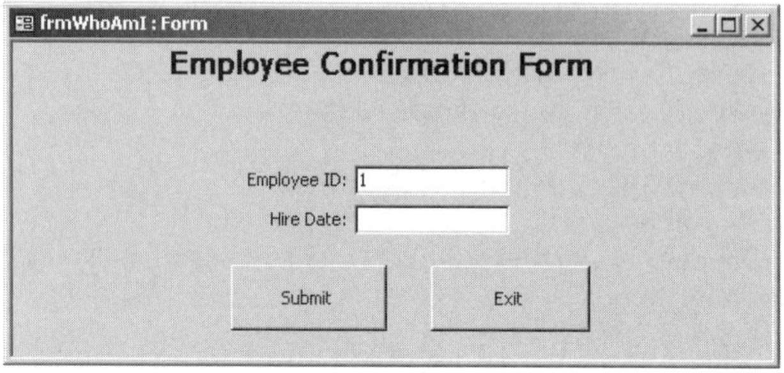

Figure 9-2 The second login form, which asks users to confirm their identity.

The Code Behind the Form

The form launches a query when a user clicks the Submit button. A form class module processes the query and matches the return set result to the user input. The event procedure behind the Submit button has a *Dim* statement that instantiates a copy of the *MyTestClass3* module with a reference to *ProcessMe*. A second line invokes the *WhoAmI* method for the class, as shown here:

```
Private Sub cmdSubmit_Click()
Dim ProcessMe As New MyTestClass3

ProcessMe.WhoAmI CLng(txtEmpID), _
    CDate(txtHireDate)

End Sub
```

Invoking the Form Class Module

The lookup procedure for the second form appears next. It uses a parameter query to perform the lookup of a hire date for an employee ID. By strongly typing the variables (notice the *CLng* and *CDate* functions in *cmdSubmit_Click*) before going into the class module, you can take advantage of the data typing option in a *Parameters* declaration as well as the data typing in the table. Without this data typing, Access must perform internal transformations to the Variant data type. The basic design for the lookup and return messages follows the design for the password lookup. If the hire date on the form matches the one in the *Employees* table, the procedure opens the third form.

```
Sub WhoAmI(empid As Long, hd As Date)
Dim cmd1 As Command
Dim strSQL As String
```

```
Dim prm1 As ADODB.Parameter
Dim rst1 As ADODB.recordset

'Assign the command reference and connection
Set cmd1 = New ADODB.Command
cmd1.ActiveConnection = CurrentProject.Connection

'Write out SQL statement with parameters and assign to cmd1
strSQL = "Parameters InEID Long;" & _
    "Select EmployeeID, HireDate From Employees " & _
    "Where EmployeeID=InEID"
cmd1.CommandText = strSQL
cmd1.CommandType = adCmdText
Set prm1 = cmd1.CreateParameter("InEID", adInteger, adParamInput)
prm1.Value = empid
cmd1.Parameters.Append prm1

'A handy line for catching SQL syntax errors
Debug.Print cmd1.CommandText

'Execute command
cmd1.Execute

'Check input vs. table HireDate
Set rst1 = New ADODB.recordset
rst1.Open cmd1
If rst1("HireDate") = hd Then
    DoCmd.openform "frmChangePassword"
    Forms("frmChangePassword").txtEmpID = Forms("frmWhoAmI").txtEmpID
    DoCmd.Close acForm, "frmWhoAmI"
Else
    MsgBox "HireDate not valid for EmployeeID.  Try " & _
        "again or Quit.", vbCritical, _
        "Programming Microsoft Access Version 2002"
End If

End Sub
```

The Third Login Form

Figure 9-3 shows the final form, which appears when a user clicks the Submit button on the second form after entering the correct hire date. The form has three text boxes. One is for the employee ID. (This box fills in automatically under normal circumstances.) The second text box is for a new password, and a third text box is for confirming the password. If those text boxes do not match, the system alerts the user. If the user clicks the Submit button without entries in all three boxes, another reminder message appears. Finally, if the form satisfies these two requirements, the class module referenced by the form updates the password for an employee ID in the *Passwords* table.

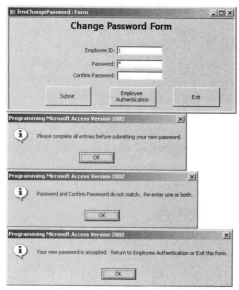

Figure 9-3 The third form, which lets users update their password.

The Code Behind the Form

The module behind this form is the most interesting one in the case study. The module performs data validation instead of passing off the data to a class module. The procedure still invokes a class module for the SQL statement that updates the password for an employee.

This split of data validation from database updates shows another way to apply class modules—by performing sensitive tasks using a class module. This standardizes the tasks and ensures proper performance. Other application elements that do not require standardization are candidates for customization by end-user departments.

This particular data validation logic relies on a pair of *Property Let* and *Property Get* functions. The *AfterUpdate* event for each of the three text boxes invokes the *Property Let* function, which updates the value of the *AllFilled* variable to True or False. (It's True if all the boxes are filled with legitimate values; it's False otherwise.)

A *Property Get* function reflects the status of all three text boxes with the form's *filledCheck* property. The *cmdSubmit_Click* procedure checks this single value to determine whether all three boxes are checked. If the value is False, the procedure displays a message reminding the user to complete all boxes. Otherwise, the click event procedure tests whether the password and confirm password text boxes match. If they do not, another message reminds the user to make them match. Finally, when a user clears these two obstacles, the procedure invokes the *NewPS* method of the local instance of the MyTestClass3 module. Let's take a look at the code for this now:

```
Private AllFilled As Boolean


Private Sub txtConfirm_AfterUpdate()

Me.filledCheck = txtConfirm

End Sub


Private Sub txtEmpID_AfterUpdate()

Me.filledCheck = txtEmpID

End Sub


Private Sub txtPassword_AfterUpdate()

Me.filledCheck = txtPassword

End Sub


Public Property Let filledCheck(vntNewValu)

If (IsNull(txtEmpID) Or txtEmpID = "") Or _
    (IsNull(txtPassword) Or txtPassword = "") Or _
    (IsNull(txtConfirm) Or txtConfirm = "") Then
    AllFilled = False
Else
```

(continued)

```
        AllFilled = True
End If

End Property


Public Property Get filledCheck()

filledCheck = AllFilled

End Property


Private Sub cmdSubmit_Click()
Dim UpdatePW As New MyTestClass3

If Me.filledCheck = False Then
    MsgBox "Please complete all entries before " & _
        "submitting your new password.", vbInformation, _
        "Programming Microsoft Access Version 2002"
ElseIf txtPassword <> txtConfirm Then
    MsgBox "Password and Confirm Password do not " & _
        "match.  Re-enter one or both.", vbInformation, _
        "Programming Microsoft Access Version 2002"
Else
    UpdatePW.NewPW txtEmpID, txtPassword
End If

End Sub


Private Sub cmdLogin_Click()

DoCmd.openform "frmInputPassword"
Forms("frmInputPassword").txtEmpID = txtEmpID
Forms("frmInputPassword").txtPassword = txtPassword
DoCmd.Close acForm, "frmChangePassword"

End Sub
```

```
Private Sub cmdExit_Click()

DoCmd.Close

End Sub
```

Transferring Values to Another Form

Two remaining procedures complete the functionality of the module behind the third form. A click event procedure behind the Employee Authentication button takes a user back to the first form and fills in the employee ID and password text boxes with their values from the third form. This feature relieves the user from having to reenter this data just after confirming it, but returning to the first form offers a single point of entry into the application. This simplifies maintenance in the long run. The form's Exit button simply closes the form.

Invoking the Class Module

The class module invoked by the module behind the third form uses a string expression to compute the SQL statement that a *Command* object uses to update an employee's password. This is one way to represent a string (such as the password value) inside another string (the overall SQL statement). Notice the multiple quotation marks (") both before and after the new password value. These are escape codes for representing a quotation mark inside another pair of quotation marks. Aside from this VBA requirement for nesting one string inside another, the code is easy to read. A message block statement at the procedure's close confirms the password change and advises the user how to proceed.

```
Sub NewPW(eid As Long, NuPassword As String)
Dim cmd1 As Command
Dim strSQL As String

'Assign the command reference and connection
Set cmd1 = New ADODB.Command
cmd1.ActiveConnection = CurrentProject.Connection

'Define the SQL string; notice
'the insertion of passed arguments
strSQL = "UPDATE Passwords " & _
    "SET Passwords.Password = """ & NuPassword & """ "   & _
    "WHERE EmployeeID=" & eid & ";"
Debug.Print strSQL
```

(continued)

```
'Assign the SQL string to the command and run it
cmd1.CommandText = strSQL
cmd1.CommandType = adCmdText
cmd1.Execute

'Confirmation message
MsgBox "Your new password is accepted.  " & _
    "Return to Employee Authentication or " & _
    "Exit this form.", vbInformation, _
    "Programming Microsoft Access Version 2002"

End Sub
```

Programming Events into Custom Classes

You can use VBA in Access to create classes for instantiating objects. This permits you to process properties and methods of the instantiated objects. The samples you've seen so far in this chapter demonstrate this functionality.

You can also build classes around type libraries and ActiveX controls that propagate their events to a host environment. For objects that propagate events, your VBA application can wrap code around events that occur within the class. When a host procedure launches a class method that causes the firing of an event from inside the class, the event works its way to the host for the class module. (See Figure 9-4.) Use the *WithEvents* keyword when declaring an object within a class module for which you want to propagate events to a host procedure. In addition, Access developers can raise custom events in their class modules and then process those events with event procedures from form or report class modules. Standard modules, unlike form and report class modules, cannot process custom events raised in class modules.

Chapter 2 explains how to add references manually to the three ADO libraries. This section explains how to add references programmatically to any library or ActiveX control. You can issue a confirmation message when your application finishes adding or removing a reference. The initial sample in this section demonstrates using the *WithEvents* keyword to process events raised by the Access *References* collection. This section also illustrates how to process custom events raised by your own class modules.

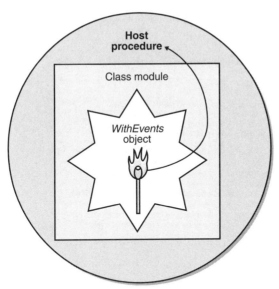

Figure 9-4 The *WithEvents* keyword propagates an object's event procedures to the object's host when an event fires.

Using the *WithEvents* Keyword to Trap Propagated Events

The *References* collection relates hierarchically to the Access *Application* object. You invoke the *AddFromFile* and *Remove* methods to enable an application to add and delete references to type libraries programmatically. These library files contain standard descriptions of exposed objects, methods, properties, and events. Recall that the ADODB object model is dependent on a library. You can add references to it and other libraries manually or programmatically.

The following class module uses the *WithEvents* keyword to trap events propagated by the *References* collection. The *References* collection has a separate item for each checked entry in the References dialog box. The *ItemAdded* and *ItemRemoved* events occur only when your code adds or removes references. If a user manually modifies the *References* collection, these events do not fire.

```
'Declare object variable to represent References collection
Public WithEvents evtReferences As References


'When instance of class is created, initialize evtReferences
'variable
Private Sub Class_Initialize()

    Set evtReferences = Application.References

End Sub
```

(continued)

```
'When instance is removed, set evtReferences to Nothing
Private Sub Class_Terminate()

    Set evtReferences = Nothing

End Sub


'Display message when reference is added
Private Sub evtReferences_ItemAdded(ByVal Reference As _
    Access.Reference)

    MsgBox "Reference to " & Reference.Name & " added.", _
        vbInformation, _
        "Programming Microsoft Access Version 2002"

End Sub


'Display message when reference is removed
Private Sub evtReferences_ItemRemoved(ByVal Reference As _
    Access.Reference)

    MsgBox "Reference to " & Reference.Name & " removed.", _
        vbInformation, _
        "Programming Microsoft Access Version 2002"

End Sub
```

Starting and Ending a *WithEvents* Reference

You use the *WithEvents* keyword in combination with a class that propagates events. The *Public* statement in the class module shown a moment ago declares a reference (*evtReferences*) to the *References* collection in the Access *Application* object. The *WithEvents* keyword within the statement enables the class module to trap events propagated by the *References* collection. The *Class_Initialize* event procedure sets a reference. Recall that you cannot use the *New* keyword for a reference that you declare with *WithEvents*.

Wrapping Code Around Captured Events

Two event procedures in the class module, *ItemAdded* and *ItemRemoved*, invoke message block statements. These show messages naming the reference that a method adds or removes. The event procedures show the syntax for wrapping custom code around objects that propagate events. In this case, the object is the *References* collection. The event procedures merely write out the name of the library being added to or removed from the *References* collection.

Initiating Events with Standard Modules

As with any class module, you need one or more procedures in a standard module to instantiate the class (see the following sample) and to invoke methods, assign property values, or read property values. In the declarations area of the module hosting the class, you include a *Dim* or *Public* statement with the *New* keyword and the class name. This instantiates the class and sets an object reference (*objRefEvents* in the sample).

Standard Module Syntax for Events

If the instance of the class propagates events from an embedded object, you should use a *Public* statement with the *WithEvents* keyword. This statement exposes the events to other modules referencing the class. When you invoke the methods from the underlying class, you must traverse the local object reference (*objRefEvents*), the reference within the class module exposing the events (*evtReferences*), and then a specific method name, such as *AddFromFile* or *Remove*. Unlike a normal reference to a class module, this one points to a method for the source object in the *WithEvents* declaration.

```
'Create new instance of RefEvents class
Dim objRefEvents As New RefEvents


Sub InvokeAddReference()

'Pass filename and path of type library to AddReference procedure
AddReference _
    "C:\Program Files\Common Files\System\ado\msjro.dll"


End Sub


Sub InvokeRemoveReference()
```

```
'Pass name of existing reference. (Use internal name from File
'Properties list; same name appears when adding reference.)
RemoveReference "JRO"

End Sub


Sub AddReference(strFileName As String)
On Error GoTo AddReference_Trap

    objRefEvents.evtReferences.AddFromFile (strFileName)

AddReference_Exit:
Exit Sub

AddReference_Trap:
If Err.Number = 32813 Then
    MsgBox "Library is already a member of the " & _
        "References collection.", vbCritical, _
        "Programming Microsoft Access Version 2002"


Else
    Debug.Print Err.Number, Err.Description
    MsgBox "Failure for unanticipated reasons; " & _
        "see Immediate window for more detail.", _
        vbCritical, _
        "Programming Microsoft Access Version 2002"
End If

End Sub


Sub RemoveReference(strRefName As String)
On Error GoTo RemoveReference_Trap

objRefEvents.evtReferences.Remove _
    objRefEvents.evtReferences(strRefName)

RemoveReference_Exit:
Exit Sub
```

```
RemoveReference_Trap:
If Err.Number = 9 Then
    MsgBox "Library is not a member of the " & _
        "References collection.", vbCritical, _
        "Programming Microsoft Access Version 2002"


Else
    Debug.Print Err.Number, Err.Description
    MsgBox "Failure for unanticipated reasons; " & _
        "see Immediate window for more detail.", _
        vbCritical, _
        "Programming Microsoft Access Version 2002"


End If

End Sub
```

This sample adds a reference to the library holding the JRO model. (This model enables Jet replication via ADO.) You run the *InvokeAddReference* procedure to create the reference. The procedure calls a procedure, *AddReference*, with the syntax for adding an item to the *References* collection via the *RefEvents* class module. The library holding the JRO model is a dynamic-link library (DLL) that typically resides in the ADO folder of the System folder in the Common Files directory of the Program Files directory. If the JRO library has already been added, Access generates a run-time error. The sample code traps this error with an *err.number* value of 32813 and prints an error message explaining that the library is already attached.

Launching the *InvokeRemoveReference* procedure eliminates the JRO item from the *References* collection. The JRO designation is the *Name* property for the item in the *References* collection. Again, you might generate a run-time error (this time, an *err.number* value of 9) if you try to remove a library that's not a member of the *References* collection. Another error trap catches an attempt to remove the JRO library event when it isn't referenced.

> **Note**   To discover the arguments for the *AddFromFile* and *Remove* methods, first add the references manually. Then you can enumerate the items in the *References* collection with a *For...Each* statement, listing their *Name* and *FullPath* properties. You can use these property values to uniquely identify arguments for the *AddFromFile* and *Remove* methods.

Extending the Application

You can easily adapt the *RefEvents* class by using the *AddReference* and *RemoveReference* procedures to accommodate a broader and more flexible selection process. For example, your application can derive the input to the *AddReference* procedure from a collection of type libraries, executables, ActiveX controls, and even database files. A combo box can offer users a list of references to add or remove.

Another simple extension of the application just described can toggle the Microsoft Data Access Component (MDAC) library between version 2.5 and 2.6. These libraries underlie slightly different versions of the ADODB object model. Access 2002 installs MDAC 2.5 by default. However, you automatically upgrade to MDAC 2.6 when you install the Microsoft Desktop Engine (MSDE) that ships with Microsoft Office XP. Referencing MDAC 2.6 on a computer without the appropriate library file can generate misleading errors. Using the class modules and the other logic of the preceding code sample, it's easy to develop a short set of procedures that toggle between MDAC 2.5 and MDAC 2.6. This feature will allow your application to rapidly switch to the library that's most appropriate for a given computer.

Processing Custom Events Raised by a Class Module

My demonstration for processing custom events from a class module uses a form with two command buttons and a text box. (See Figure 9-5.) The buttons have the captions Return True and Return False. The form's text box reflects the last button clicked by showing either True or False. What makes this form special is the way that it populates the text box. The text receives its value from a custom event raised in a class module. The sample form is available as *Form1* in this chapter's Access database file on the companion CD.

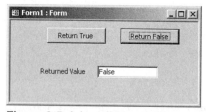

Figure 9-5 A form that populates a text box using an event procedure that processes a custom event raised in a class module.

Setting Up Custom Events in a Class Module

Since the form depends on an event raised in a class module, the best place to start understanding the form's operation is with the class module. The module has the name MyCustomEventTester. Its code follows. Notice that the first line declares an event with the *Public* keyword. The event returns a Boolean value.

The MyCustomEventTester class module also contains a sub procedure named *foo* that implements a method for the class. This method raises the event and assigns the value *True* or *False* to the event declared in the class module's *Public* statement. The *RaiseEvent* statement fires the *MyCustomEvent* event and assigns a return value to the event. The module-level *Public* declaration allows the event to propagate outside the class module. An *If...Else* statement within *foo* determines the return value for the event. The outcome from the statement depends on the value passed to *foo*.

```
Public Event MyCustomEvent(ByVal TrueOrFalse As Boolean)


Public Sub foo(SetMyCustomEvent As Boolean)

'Raise the MyCustomEvent event with a
'value of True or False, depending on
'the value of SetMyCustomEvent
If SetMyCustomEvent = True Then
    RaiseEvent MyCustomEvent(True)
Else
    RaiseEvent MyCustomEvent(False)
End If

End Sub
```

Processing Custom Events in a Form Module

The code for the form in Figure 9-5 calls the class module and uses the event's return value from *MyCustomEventTester* to populate its text box. The module for *Form1* appears next. The *Public* declaration at the top of the module references the *MyCustomEventTester* class with an object named *Testing*. The *WithEvents* keyword prepares *Testing* to pass along events from its class to the form module. Next a *Form_Load* event procedure clears the text box from any prior assignments and sets miscellaneous properties for the form's use in an unbound data application.

A pair of click event procedures for the command buttons instantiate *Testing* as an instance of the *MyCustomEventTester* class. Then the procedures invoke the *foo* method for the class and pass it the value *True* or *False*, depending on the button.

The *MyCustomEvent* event procedure for the *Testing* object has just one line. It assigns the return value from the event to the form's text box.

```
Public WithEvents Testing As MyCustomEventTester


Private Sub Form_Load()

'Clear text box of any former values from
'previous button clicks
Me.txtReturnedValue = ""



'Format form in ways that are typical for
'a form not used for data entry or display
Me.RecordSelectors = False
Me.NavigationButtons = False
Me.DividingLines = False

End Sub


Private Sub cmdTrue_Click()

'Instantiate Testing as a
'MyCustomEventTester object
Set Testing = New MyCustomEventTester

'Invoke the foo method of the Testing
'object, and pass it a value of False
Testing.foo (True)

End Sub


Private Sub cmdFalse_Click()

'Instantiate Testing as a
'MyCustomEventTester object
Set Testing = New MyCustomEventTester

'Invoke the foo method of the Testing
'object, and pass it a value of False
Testing.foo (False)

End Sub


'Process MyCustomEvent for the Testing object
Private Sub Testing_MyCustomEvent _
    (ByVal ReturnValue As Boolean)
```

```
'Assign the return value from the MyCustomEvent
'event procedure to the form's text box
Me.txtReturnedValue = ReturnValue

End Sub
```

Extending the Application

This kind of design is flexible and adaptable. For example, you can compute scientific and financial results in the class method and return the results through the event procedure. Alternatively, a class module can iterate through subform field values and compute the total extended price for an order's line items. Users can initiate these or other calculations on demand by clicking a button that invokes a class method with a return value through an event procedure.

Using the *All*xxx Collections

If you are the type of developer who likes to track your objects in a database project (most of us find this essential), you'll be happy to know that there is an *AllModules* collection, which is a counterpart of the *AllForms* and *AllReports* collections you learned about in Chapters 6 and 7, "Forms, Controls, and Data" and "Reports, Controls, and Data." The members of the *All*xxx collections are not database objects, such as forms, reports, and modules, but *AccessObject* objects that contain a minimal amount of detail about most types of saved objects in a database.

AccessObject Properties

You can quickly enumerate the *AccessObject* objects in any *All*xxx collection. Since *AccessObject* objects point at saved objects, you cannot add or delete members. You perform these tasks through the open collections they point to.

When you encounter an *AccessObject* object that your application needs more detail about, you can use the *IsLoaded* and *Name* properties to examine the properties of the object the *AccessObject* object points to. These open object collections have a fuller set of properties and methods that are not available with the *All*xxx collections.

AccessObject objects have a *Type* property that describes the type of *AccessObject* rather than the type of database object. The *Type* property value of any *AllModules* member is 5. This distinguishes an *AccessObject* member in the *AllModules* collection from one in the *AllForms* collection, for example, with a *Type* property value of 2. In either case, you cannot determine whether you are dealing with a class module or a form class module by simply examining the *AccessObject* member of the *Allxxx* collection. You must examine the *Type* property of a *Module* object and the *HasModule* property of a *Form* object.

The Set of *Allxxx* Collections

There are seven *Allxxx* collections besides *AllModules*, *AllForms*, and *AllReports*. This set of ten collections (shown in Figure 9-6) divides naturally into two sets of five. The *AllForms*, *AllReports*, *AllMacros*, *AllModules*, and *AllDataAccessPages* collections are members of the *CurrentProject* and *CodeProject* objects in the Access *Application* object. The *AllTables*, *AllQueries*, *AllViews*, *AllStoredProcedures*, and *AllDatabaseDiagrams* collections are members of the *CurrentData* and *CodeData* objects in the Access *Application* object. When you designate *AccessObject* objects in any of the ten *Allxxx* collections, you must set a reference that points to the appropriate antecedent object. Failing to do so will generate an error.

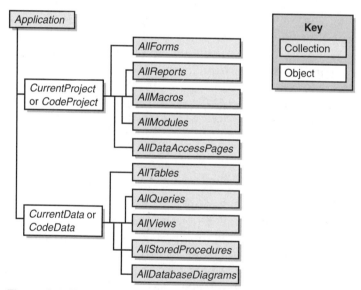

Figure 9-6 The 10 *Allxxx* collections and their hierarchical relationship to *Project* and *Data* objects.

The *AllQueries*, *AllViews*, *AllStoredProcedures*, and *AllDatabaseDiagrams* collections have restricted availability by Access file type. Recall that Access applications can reside in a traditional .mdb file or in the new Access project file (.adp). Chapters 14 and 15, "Using Access to Build SQL Server Solutions" (Parts I and II), will discuss Access projects in .adp files. The *AllQueries* collection is available in .mdb files but not .adp files. In contrast, you can tap the *AllViews*,

AllStoredProcedures, and *AllDatabaseDiagrams* collections from .adp files but not from .mdb files. Your applications can still reference views and stored procedures in .mdb files by using the ADOX object library.

Enumerating the *Allxxx* Collection Members

The following three procedures show the high degree of similarity in programming different *Allxxx* collections. The first procedure performs a simple enumeration of all the modules in the current project. Notice that it initially declares *obj1* as an *AccessObject* type because it accepts the identity of elements in the *AllModules* collection, which contains *AccessObject* objects. Also note that the enumeration loop passes through the *AllModules* collection but the code reaches this collection through the *Application* and *CurrentProject* objects.

```
Sub EnumerateAllModules()
Dim obj1 As AccessObject
For Each obj1 In Application.CurrentProject.AllModules
    Debug.Print obj1.Name & vbTab & obj1.Type & _
        vbTab & obj1.IsLoaded
Next obj1
End Sub
```

```
Sub EnumerateAllForms()
Dim obj1 As AccessObject
For Each obj1 In Application.CurrentProject.AllForms
    Debug.Print obj1.Name & vbTab & obj1.Type & _
        vbTab & obj1.IsLoaded
Next obj1
End Sub
```

```
Sub EnumerateAllTables()
Dim obj1 As AccessObject
For Each obj1 In Application.CurrentData.AllTables
    Debug.Print obj1.Name & vbTab & obj1.Type & _
        vbTab & obj1.IsLoaded
Next obj1
End Sub
```

The *EnumerateAllForms* and *EnumerateAllTables* procedures have the same structure as the *EnumerateAllModules* procedure. You should note some significant differences in content, however. First, the specific *AccessObject* collection changes from *AllModules* to *AllForms* in one procedure and *AllTables* in the other procedure. Second, the path to the *AllTables* collection passes through the *CurrentData* object rather than through the *CurrentProject* object.

If we were to switch the *AllTables* collection to either an *AllViews* collection or an *AllStoredProcedures* collection, the code would work in an .adp file but not in an .mdb file.

Adapting to .mdb and .adp File Types

Using the *ProjectType* property of the *CurrentProject* object, you can detect whether you are working with an .adp or an .mdb file. This lets you write single procedures that adapt to their environment. The following sample prints the names of all the views and stored procedures in an .adp file, but it switches to printing all the queries in an .mdb file. As you can see, the only trick required is to test for the value of the *ProjectType* property. The *Type* property of the *AccessObject* object adds values by distinctly differentiating objects for views, with the type value 7, from objects pointing at stored procedures, whose type value is 9.

```
Sub EnumerateAllViews2()
Dim obj1 As AccessObject, dbs1 As Object
Set dbs1 = Application.CurrentData
If Application.CurrentProject.ProjectType = acADP Then
    For Each obj1 In dbs1.AllViews
        Debug.Print obj1.Name & vbTab & obj1.Type & _
            vbTab & obj1.IsLoaded
    Next obj1
    For Each obj1 In dbs1.AllStoredProcedures
        Debug.Print obj1.Name & vbTab & obj1.Type & _
            vbTab & obj1.IsLoaded
    Next obj1
Else
    For Each obj1 In dbs1.AllQueries
        Debug.Print obj1.Name & vbTab & obj1.Type & _
            vbTab & obj1.IsLoaded
    Next obj1
End If
End Sub
```

Using *AllForms* and *AllModules*

The next sample uses the *Allxxx* collections and the corresponding collections of open modules and forms to develop a list of all the modules (by type) and the class modules for forms in a project. Since the property for denoting standard class modules is different from the one for class modules for forms, the code requires different expressions to test for standard class modules vs. class modules for forms.

Recall that modules have a *Type* property but forms have a *HasModule* property. The code must iterate through the members of the *AllModules* and

AllForms collections because some, or even all, modules and forms can be closed. You check the *IsLoaded* status of the *AccessObject* objects in *AllModules* and *AllForms* to determine whether you need to open a module or form before assessing its module type, or to determine whether a form has a class module. The procedure recloses forms and modules after it examines them.

```
Sub ListAllModulesByTypeAndClassForms()
Dim obj1 As AccessObject, dbs1 As Object
Dim mod1 As Module, frm1 As Form

Set dbs1 = Application.CurrentProject

'Search for open AccessObject objects in AllModules collection.
'Open and reclose those that are not open.

For Each obj1 In dbs1.AllModules
    If obj1.IsLoaded = True Then
        ListTypeOfModule obj1.Name
    Else
        DoCmd.OpenModule obj1.Name
        ListTypeOfModule obj1.Name
        DoCmd.Close acModule, obj1.Name
    End If
Next obj1

'Search for open AccessObject objects in AllForms collection.
'Open and reclose those that are not open.

For Each obj1 In dbs1.AllForms
    If obj1.IsLoaded Then
        DoesFormHaveModule obj1.Name
    Else
        DoCmd.openform obj1.Name
        DoesFormHaveModule obj1.Name
        DoCmd.Close acForm, obj1.Name
    End If
Next obj1

End Sub
Sub ListTypeOfModule(modname)
Dim strType As String

'Decode module type value
If Modules(modname).Type = 0 Then
    strType = "Standard Module"
```

```
    Else
        strType = "Class Module"
    End If

    'Print module name and type
    Debug.Print Modules(modname).Name & vbTab & strType

    End Sub


Sub DoesFormHaveModule(frmname)

    'Print form name only if it has a module
    If Forms(frmname).HasModule = True Then
        Debug.Print frmname & vbTab & "Form Class Module"
    End If

    End Sub
```

Programmatically Editing Modules

Since you can perform so many different tasks with standard modules, standalone class modules, and class modules for forms, your applications are likely to have many of these modules. This will eventually create a need for maintenance. One common maintenance requirement is the insertion or deletion of one or more lines of code in a set of modules. This section shows how to add a line to and remove a line from all the standard and standalone class modules, and then it shows how to do so for form class modules. Because the code for standard and standalone class modules is stored differently from the code for class modules for forms, the steps differ slightly.

Editing Approaches

The *Module* object offers an array of methods and properties that can help you programmatically edit modules. The samples in this section use the *InsertLines*, *Find*, and *DeleteLines* methods. These methods process both standard and class modules, including standalone class modules and report and form class modules. These are a subset of the methods and properties that support programmatically managing module content.

You use the *InsertLines* method with a *Module* object to insert one or more lines into the module. Module line numbers start with the value *1* and extend through the *CountOfLines* property value for the module. The method takes a line number and a string argument. If you need to insert multiple lines into a module, add *vbCrLf* constants into the string expression representing the method's string argument. When you insert lines with this method, it moves down the remaining lines in the module.

The *Find* method searches for a text string in a module. It returns the value True if it finds the search text; otherwise, it returns False. If you know precisely where some text is, you can specify a starting line and column and an ending line and column. If you do not know where some search text resides in a module, leave the text position arguments blank, and the function will return the values of the search text in the module. You can also designate pattern searches and case-restrictive searches.

The *DeleteLines* method removes one or more lines of text from a module. The method takes two arguments: a start line and the total number of lines to remove from a module. You can use the *DeleteLines* method in combination with the *Find* method. You use the *Find* method to search for text in a module. You can then base the invocation of the *DeleteLines* method on the return value from the *Find* method.

Inserting Text into Modules

The procedures that follow combine the *AllModules* and *Modules* collections to edit the text in a collection of modules. Specifically, they insert a comment line at the beginning of each module, proclaiming it a standard module or a class module. The *EnumerateAllModulestoInsert* procedure loops through the members of the *AllModules* collection and calls the other procedure, which actually updates the target modules. Since the *InsertIntoModules* procedure requires an open module, the first procedure opens the module if it is not already open. Then, when the second procedure returns control to the first one, it closes the module again to restore its initial state.

```
Sub EnumerateAllModulestoInsert()
Dim obj1 As AccessObject

'Loop through AllModules members.
'If module is open, call sub procedure to insert lines.
'Else open module first; then close afterwards.
For Each obj1 In Application.CurrentProject.AllModules
    If obj1.IsLoaded = True Then
        InsertIntoModules obj1.Name
    Else
        DoCmd.OpenModule obj1.Name
        InsertIntoModules obj1.Name
```

```
            DoCmd.Close acModule, obj1.Name, acSaveYes
        End If
    Next obj1

    End Sub


    Sub InsertIntoModules(modname)
    Dim strType As String, mod1 As Module

    Set mod1 = Modules(modname)

    'Detect module type to determine which
    'string to insert
    If mod1.Type = 0 Then
        strType = "'Standard Module"
    Else
        strType = "'Class Module"
    End If
    mod1.InsertLines 1, strType
    Set mod1 = Nothing

    End Sub
```

The *InsertIntoModules* procedure accepts a single argument—the name of the module to edit. It performs no iteration because the first procedure calls it once for each member in the *AllModules* collection. The procedure begins by setting a reference to the module named in the passed argument. Then it determines the type of module to which the reference points and sets a string variable to a comment naming the module type. After determining the text to insert, the procedure invokes the *InsertLines* method for the referenced module.

Deleting Text from Modules

The following two procedures delete a line from a procedure. In fact, they remove the line added by the preceding pair of procedures. The design of these next two procedures is flexible enough so that you can easily extend them to accommodate the deletion of multiple selected lines from any set of modules.

The procedures follow the same general logic as the preceding pair, with one major difference: this pair uses the *Find* and *DeleteLines* methods to remove text instead of the *InsertLines* method. The *Find* method is often critical when you prepare to use the *DeleteLines* method because the *Find* method lets your code determine whether some text is present before it deletes any content. In this instance, the *Find* method looks for the word *Module* in the first 40 characters of the first line. The *DeletefromModules* procedure invokes the *DeleteLines* method to delete one line starting with the first line in the module. The *DeleteLines* method removes lines unconditionally. However, you can manually invoke the *Undo Delete* function to restore removed text.

```
Sub EnumerateAllModulestoDelete()
Dim obj1 As AccessObject, dbs As Object
Dim mod1 As Module, frm1 As Form

'Loop through AllModules members.
'If module is open, call sub procedure to delete line.
'Else open module first; then close afterwards.
For Each obj1 In Application.CurrentProject.AllModules
    If obj1.IsLoaded = True Then
        DeletefromModules obj1.Name
    Else
        DoCmd.OpenModule obj1.Name
        DeletefromModules obj1.Name
        DoCmd.Close acModule, obj1.Name
    End If
Next obj1

End Sub


Sub DeletefromModules(modname)
Dim mod1 As Module

Set mod1 = Modules(modname)

'Delete first line if first 40 characters
'contain "Module"
If mod1.Find("Module", 1, 1, 1, 40) = True Then
    mod1.DeleteLines 1, 1
End If
Set mod1 = Nothing

End Sub
```

Inserting Text into Form Class Modules

The following two procedures insert a line at the beginning of each form class module with a comment stating that it's a class module. Instead of looping through the *AllModules* collection, the first procedure loops through the *AllForms* collection. For each member of the *AllForms* collection, the code calls the *InsertIntoForms* procedure.

This second procedure assesses whether the passed form name is a class module. If it is, the procedure sets a reference to the module behind the form. This step displays that module. The procedure closes by inserting the comment line into the module and setting the reference to Nothing to free its resources.

```
Sub EnumerateAllFormsToInsert()
Dim obj1 As AccessObject

'Loop through AllForms members.
'If form is loaded, invoke module to insert line.
'Else open form first and then close afterwards.
For Each obj1 In Application.CurrentProject.AllForms
    If obj1.IsLoaded Then
        InsertIntoForms obj1.Name
    Else
        DoCmd.openform obj1.Name
        InsertIntoForms obj1.Name
        DoCmd.Close acForm, obj1.Name, acSaveYes
    End If
Next obj1

End Sub


Sub InsertIntoForms(frmname)
Dim mod1 As Module, strType As String

'If form has module, set reference to it
'and insert line into the module.
'Free reference resource when done.
If Forms(frmname).HasModule = True Then
    Set mod1 = Forms(frmname).Module
    strType =" "'Form Class Module"
    mod1.InsertLines 1, strType
    Set mod1 = Nothing
End If

End Sub
```

Deleting Text from Form Class Modules

The next two procedures remove the *Class Module* comment line on the first line of all modules behind forms. As you can see, this pair's design mimics critical elements from the preceding pairs of procedures for inserting and deleting lines. This pair iterates through the *AllForms* collection, like the pair that added a comment line to the beginning of all form class modules in a project.

However, the second procedure in this pair uses the *Find* and *DeleteLines* methods to remove the first line in a module if it contains the word *Module* in the first 40 characters of its first line. This resembles the procedure for deleting lines from the *Modules* collection.

```
Sub EnumerateAllFormstoDelete()
Dim obj1 As AccessObject

'Loop through AllForms members.
'If form is loaded, invoke module to remove line.
'Else open form first and then close afterwards.
For Each obj1 In Application.CurrentProject.AllForms
    If obj1.IsLoaded Then
        DeletefromForms obj1.Name
    Else
        DoCmd.openform obj1.Name
        DeletefromForms obj1.Name
        DoCmd.Close acForm, obj1.Name, acSaveYes
    End If
Next obj1

End Sub



Sub DeletefromForms(frmname)
Dim mod1 As Module, strType As String

'If form has module, check contents of first line
'for "Module" and delete the first line if it is present.
'Free module reference resource when done.
    If Forms(frmname).HasModule = True Then
        Set mod1 = Forms(frmname).Module
        If mod1.Find("Module", 1, 1, 1, 40) = True Then
            mod1.DeleteLines 1, 1
        End If
        Set mod1 = Nothing
    End If

End Sub
```

10

Microsoft Office Objects

As part of Microsoft Office XP, Microsoft Access 2002 shares a select group of objects with the other Office applications. These objects let you carry out such tasks as searching for files, manipulating the Office Assistant help feature, modifying standard menus and toolbars, and developing custom menus and toolbars. In addition, your knowledge of how to program these objects in Access will transfer to the other Office applications—Microsoft Excel, Microsoft Word, and even Microsoft FrontPage. Most of the objects work in all of the Office applications.

This chapter starts with an overview of Office objects. After the overview, we'll examine the *DocumentProperty* object and related Access objects from Access database and Access project files. Within this discussion, I'll drill down on techniques for replacing the Database window with a custom startup form. Next we'll explore three specific objects: *FileSearch*, which you use to programmatically manage file searches; *Assistant*, which provides a programmatic interface to the Office Assistant; and *CommandBars*, which you use to create custom menus and toolbars.

Using the Shared Office Objects

The shared Office objects, listed in Table 10-1, provide support in several important areas of functionality. Some of these object models are not available in all Office components (including Access). The table describes the models, mentions when they have restricted availability across Office components, and highlights where you can find further information about them in this book. To get online help and work with any of these objects, you must reference the Microsoft Office 10.0 Object Library. You can do this through the Tools menu in the Microsoft Visual Basic Editor (VBE) or programmatically (as this chapter will show later in "Automatically Referencing the Office Object Library").

Table 10-1   Shared Office Objects

Object	Description	Comment
CommandBar	You can use this object and its collections to create and modify toolbars, the menu bar, and shortcut menus. You can make design-time changes manually and with Visual Basic for Applications (VBA) code. You can make run-time changes exclusively with VBA code.	See further discussion and samples in this chapter.
Assistant	You use this object to support custom help requirements for the Office Assistant and Office Assistant balloon. Various properties and methods let you control the type and animation of the Assistant as well as the content and behavior of the balloon.	See further discussion and samples in this chapter.
FileSearch	You use this object to represent the functionality of the Open dialog box.	When processing files, you can complement the functionality of this object model with the *FileDialog* object and the *FileSystemObject* object. See further discussion and samples in this chapter.
DocumentProperty	This object represents a built-in or custom property of an Office document. There are up to 28 built-in properties, which include such document attributes as title, author, comments, last print date, last save time, and total editing time. This object also supports custom document properties.	For Word documents, Excel workbooks, and Microsoft PowerPoint presentations only.

Object	Description	Comment
NewFile	This object allows you to add and remove entries on the Office Task Pane toolbar.	This object is available with Access, Excel, FrontPage, PowerPoint, and Word applications, but the route for opening the object changes for each application. See further discussion and samples in the chapter.
FileDialog	This object provides a programmatic interface for presenting dialog boxes similar to the File Open and Save As dialog boxes in Microsoft Office.	Full functionality is available with Word, Excel, and PowerPoint applications. Partial functionality is available with Access.
COMAddin	This is a representation of a COM add-in in Access and other Office host applications.	
LanguageSettings	This object lets you programmatically return information about language installation, user interface, and help settings.	Tracks locale identifier information when deploying Office internationally.
AnswerWizard	You use this object to programmatically manipulate the Answer wizard.	Includes properties and methods for manipulating files returned by the Answer wizard. This wizard is available exclusively through Microsoft Office XP Developer Edition.
MsoEnvelope	This object lets you send documents as e-mail messages.	For Word documents, Excel charts, and Excel worksheets.
OfficeData-SourceObject	This object represents the data source for a mail merge operation. It offers simplified properties and methods for manipulating a data source for a mail merge.	This object is exclusively for use with Microsoft Publisher, but the Office XP documentation refers to it as part of the Office library.
HTMLProject	This object is a top-level project in the Microsoft Script Editor. You use the *HTMLProjectItem* collection to track HTML documents within a project.	For Word documents, Excel workbooks, and PowerPoint presentations only.

(continued)

Table 10-1 *(continued)*

Object	Description	Comment
Script	This object represents a block of script in the Script Editor.	For Word documents, Excel workbooks, and PowerPoint presentations only.
WebPageFont	This object represents the default font when a document is saved as a Web page.	For Word documents, Excel workbooks, and PowerPoint presentations only.

The *DocumentProperty* Object and the *CurrentDB* Object

Although the Microsoft Office *DocumentProperties* collection and the *Properties* collection for the *CurrentDB* object in Data Access Objects (DAO) have similar names, they serve different purposes. The members of the *DocumentProperties* collection are *DocumentProperty* objects. You declare these objects with a *DocumentProperty* variable type. Word, Excel, and PowerPoint store information about documents as *DocumentProperty* objects. Typical *DocumentProperties* collection members point to the author, location, and date created. Developers can use built-in *DocumentProperty* objects as well as add their own custom *DocumentProperty* objects.

A *Property* object in DAO represents a built-in or user-defined characteristic of a DAO object, such as the *CurrentDB* object. The collection of these *Property* objects is the set of built-in and custom properties for the Jet database serving as the current database. You declare a *Property* object for the *CurrentDB* object with a *DAO.Property* variable.

Unlike Access database files, Access project files do not have a *Properties* collection for the *CurrentDB* object. In fact, Access projects do not have a *CurrentDB* object. This is because Access projects do not use DAO. Nevertheless, Access projects store similar information to the members of the *Properties* collections for the *CurrentProject* object. You declare a variable of type *AccessObjectProperty* when designating a pointer for a *Property* object of the *CurrentProject* object. The *Property* object collections for the *CurrentDB* and the *CurrentProject* objects can serve similar roles in helping to manage how an Access application starts.

Counting and Enumerating *DocumentProperty* Objects in Word

It's extremely easy to process *DocumentProperty* objects. The following listing, from Table1.doc on the companion CD, counts the built-in and custom *DocumentProperty* objects for the active document in a Word application. Then it loops through the members of the *BuiltinDocumentProperties* collection. The *On Error* statement allows the loop to easily bypass *DocumentProperty* objects that do not have a printable value. Make sure you run the procedure from a VBA project with a reference to the Microsoft Office 10.0 Object Library.

```
Sub PrintDocumentProperties()
Dim dpr1 As DocumentProperty

'Print total number of built-in and custom
'DocumentProperty objects
Debug.Print ActiveDocument.BuiltInDocumentProperties.Count
Debug.Print ActiveDocument.CustomDocumentProperties.Count

'Loop through built-in DocumentProperty objects and
'print name and value; bypass errors for properties
'without a value that prints
For Each dpr1 In ActiveDocument.BuiltInDocumentProperties
    On Error Resume Next
    Debug.Print dpr1.Name, dpr1.Value
Next dpr1

End Sub
```

You can demonstrate the behavior of this macro by opening Word. Before loading the file Table1.doc, change the Macro Security setting. Choose Tools-Macro-Security. Then select the Medium option button control on the Security Level tab of the Security dialog and click OK. Next open the Table1.doc file. Before Word finishes opening the file, it presents a prompt about viruses and macros. Click Enable Macros. Choose Tools-Macro-Visual Basic Editor. In the Project Explorer of the VBE, double-click This Document if the *PrintDocumentProperties* procedure does not appear in the Code window. Open the Immediate window so that you see the output from the procedure. Then run the procedure as you would any VBA procedure in Access. Its output appears in the Immediate window.

Printing Access *DocumentProperty* Object Information

Access does not have a shared *DocumentProperty* object as Word, Excel, and PowerPoint do, but it makes much of the same information available using three *Documents* objects: *UserDefined*, *SummaryInfo*, and *MSysDB*. These objects are available exclusively through the DAO Database Container. You can't use these three objects with Microsoft ActiveX Data Objects (ADO). The *UserDefined* object contains all properties on the Custom tab of the Database Properties dialog box. The *SummaryInfo* object contains all properties on the Summary tab of that dialog box. The *MSysDB* object contains all the properties defined under the Tools-Startup menu in a database.

The following sample enumerates the properties collections of each DAO Database Container object:

```
Sub enumDBProps()

Dim db As Database, p As DAO.Property

'Set reference to current database
    Set db = CurrentDb

'Print heading for results
    Debug.Print "User defined properties"
    Debug.Print "======================="

'Iterate through UserDefined database properties
    For Each p In db.Containers!Databases. _
        Documents!UserDefined.Properties
        Debug.Print p.Name, p.Value
    Next

'Print heading for results
    Debug.Print
    Debug.Print "Summary Properties"
    Debug.Print "=================="

'Iterate through SummaryInfo database properties
    For Each p In db.Containers!Databases. _
        Documents!SummaryInfo.Properties
        Debug.Print p.Name, p.Value
    Next

'Print heading for results
    Debug.Print
    Debug.Print "MSysDB Properties"
    Debug.Print "=================="
```

```
'Iterate through MSysDB database properties
    For Each p In db.Containers!Databases. _
        Documents!MSysDB.Properties
        Debug.Print p.Name, p.Value
    Next

End Sub
```

Printing the *CurrentDB* and *CurrentProject* Properties

Many of the *CurrentDB* and *CurrentProject* properties designate items you can use to control how an Access application starts. For example, these properties permit you to control whether the Database window appears at startup and which form replaces it. You can even use a special property (*AllowBypassKey)* to suppress a user's ability to bypass your startup settings by holding down the Shift key while the user opens your file. I call this a special property because it's available exclusively through a VBA programmatic interface.

When using the *CurrentDB* property, you'll find it convenient to list the *Properties* collection's members. The following code sample illustrates this technique. As with the sample in the sidebar on *DocumentProperty* objects on page 547, this procedure bypasses error statements in a loop because some properties are not printable.

```
Sub EnumerateCurrentDBProperties()
Dim db As Database
Dim prp1 As DAO.Property

'Set reference to current database
Set db = CurrentDb

Debug.Print CurrentDb.Properties.Count
'Print name and value properties of all
'CurrentDB property objects
For Each prp1 In CurrentDb.Properties
    On Error Resume Next
    Debug.Print prp1.Name, prp1.Value
Next prp1

End Sub
```

Use an *AccessObjectProperty* variable declaration to reference a *Property* object for an Access project's *CurrentProject* object. This same kind of declaration applies when referencing *Property* objects of the *AccessObject* object. The code for referencing the *CurrentProject* and *CurrentDB* properties has slight differences besides the variable used to reference these properties. For example, you use the *Delete* method to remove an item from the *Properties* collection of the *CurrentDB* object, but you use a *Remove* method when working with the properties of a *CurrentProject* object. The following code segment shows how to loop through the elements of the *Properties* collection of the *CurrentProject* object:

```
Sub EnumerateCurrentProjectProperties()
Dim prp1 As AccessObjectProperty

'Print number of properties defined
'for CurrentProject
Debug.Print CurrentProject.Properties.Count

'Loop through CurrentProject properties
'and print their name and value
For Each prp1 In CurrentProject.Properties
    Debug.Print prp1.Name, prp1.Value
Next prp1

End Sub
```

Building a Custom Startup in an .mdb File

A custom startup permits your custom form to appear instead of the Database window when a user opens your Access database (.mdb) file. A custom startup typically involves three elements. The first element is an Autoexec macro, which fires automatically when a user opens an Access database file or Access project file. Only one Autoexec macro can exist in either type of file. The second element a custom startup requires is a function procedure to set the appropriate *CurrentDB* properties. The discussion of the function procedure code that follows highlights four of these properties. The third element a custom startup needs is a form that serves as the initial user interface (UI) for the custom application. This form replaces the Database window. End users can make selections from this initial form to access all the other features of your application.

Your Autoexec macro should contain just one macro action: the RunCode action. The RunCode action will run a function procedure only. Specify the function procedure name that assigns the *CurrentDB* properties for your custom startup. Figure 10-1 shows an Autoexec macro in Design view that invokes the *HideDBWindowAtStartupInMDB* function procedure. The Build button next to the Function Name argument box indicates that you can use the Expression Builder to select the function name (thus reducing the possibility of typos).

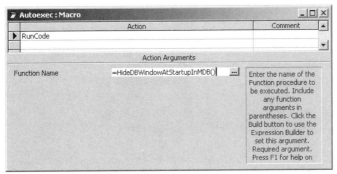

Figure 10-1 Design view of an Autoexec macro for a custom startup.

> **Note**   If you need to invoke a sub procedure or an event procedure from a macro, you must call a function procedure with the RunCode action. In turn, the function procedure can invoke any other types of procedures. This requirement exists because macros can invoke only function procedures.

When setting up a function procedure for a custom startup, you'll typically need to set four of the *CurrentDB* object's properties. First set the *Startup-ShowDBWindow* property to False so that the Database window doesn't show when a user opens the database file. Second assign False to the *AllowBypassKey* property. This prevents an end user from bypassing your custom startup by holding down the Shift key as the Access database file opens. Third set the *AllowSpecialKeys* property to False. This prohibits an end user from opening the Database window over your custom startup form by pressing the F11 function key. Fourth set the *StartupForm* property to a string that specifies the name of your custom startup form.

The function procedure for setting the *CurrentDB* properties for a custom startup appears next. Its error trap is an integral part of the procedure. This is because the first time you run the procedure the *CurrentDB* object might not have all the properties necessary to create a custom startup. The error trap detects when a property does not exist, and it adds the new property as it assigns a value. The startup form for the code sample has the name *frmNotDBWindow*. This form appears instead of the Database window when your application initially appears. Assign the name of your startup form as a string to the *StartupForm* property of the *CurrentDB* object.

```
Function HideDBWindowAtStartupInMDB()
On Error GoTo DAOStartup_Trap
```

(continued)

```
Dim db As Database
Dim prp1 As DAO.Property
Dim str1 As String

'Set reference to current database
Set db = CurrentDb

'Hide Database window the
'next time the database is opened
str1 = "StartupShowDBWindow"
db.Properties(str1) = False
str1 = "AllowBypassKey"
db.Properties(str1) = False
str1 = "AllowSpecialKeys"
db.Properties(str1) = False
str1 = "StartupForm"
db.Properties(str1) = "frmNotDBWindow"


DAOStartup_Exit:
Exit Function

DAOStartup_Trap:

If Err.Number = 3270 And str1 = "StartupShowDBWindow" Then
    Set prp1 = db.CreateProperty("StartupShowDBWindow", dbBoolean, _
        False)
    db.Properties.Append prp1
ElseIf Err.Number = 3270 And str1 = "AllowBypassKey" Then
    Set prp1 = db.CreateProperty("AllowBypassKey", dbBoolean, False)
    db.Properties.Append prp1
ElseIf Err.Number = 3270 And str1 = "AllowSpecialKeys" Then
    Set prp1 = db.CreateProperty("AllowSpecialKeys", dbBoolean, False)
    db.Properties.Append prp1
ElseIf Err.Number = 3270 And str1 = "StartupForm" Then
    Set prp1 = db.CreateProperty("StartupForm", dbText, _
        "frmNotDBWindow")
    db.Properties.Append prp1
Else
    Debug.Print Err.Number, Err.Description
    Exit Function
End If
Resume Next

End Function
```

The startup form for this demonstration contains a lone command button for opening the Database window. In practice, your startup form will include a menu that exposes the functionality of an application through its custom UI. This initial form will typically be unbound, just like the one in my demonstration. Therefore, you'll need to remove any bound data features (such as Navigator buttons) that Access automatically adds to a new form. The *Form_Load* event code handles this. The command button's click event code selects the startup form in the Database window before closing the form. Recall that there is no command for opening the Database window, but you can display the window by selecting an item to show in it. Here's the syntax for the two event procedures:

```
Private Sub Form_Load()

'Set unbound data form properties
Me.RecordSelectors = False
Me.DividingLines = False
Me.NavigationButtons = False

End Sub


Private Sub cmdOpenDBWindow_Click()

'Open Database window by selecting an object in it,
'and close current form
DoCmd.SelectObject acForm, "frmNotDBWindow", True
DoCmd.Close acForm, Me.Name, acSaveNo

End Sub
```

Once you install all three elements described a moment ago, you're ready to launch your custom startup process. Run the *HideDBWindowAtStartupInMDB* procedure once before saving the database file. This installs the settings for your custom startup in the Startup dialog box. Then the next time the database file opens, the *frmNotDBWindow* form appears instead of the Database window. The Autoexec macro fires to refresh your settings for the next time the file opens.

After installing a custom startup, you lose the ability to step through code within the VBE. One way to recover this ability is to remove the special settings on the Startup dialog box and rename the Autoexec macro (for example, by changing it to Autoexec1). By recovering from an error by executing the next line, you guard against an abort caused by the user manually modifying the Startup dialog box settings. Another strategy is to simply lock end users out of the Startup dialog box. "Securing an Application by Programming Command Bars" at the end of this chapter presents techniques for accomplishing this. After you no longer need step mode, you can resume using the custom startup by restoring the name of your Autoexec macro and the Startup dialog box settings. The following two procedures recover step mode and resume using the startup settings:

```
Sub RestoreStepMode()
Dim db As Database, p As DAO.Property

'Set reference to current database
Set db = CurrentDb

'Restore default startup property settings
On Error Resume Next
db.Properties.Delete "StartupShowDBWindow"
db.Properties.Delete "AllowBypassKey"
db.Properties.Delete "AllowSpecialKeys"
db.Properties.Delete "StartupForm"

'Rename Autoexec macro
DoCmd.Rename "Autoexec1", acMacro, "Autoexec"

End Sub


Sub RestoreAutoMode()

'Rename macro and reset startup properties
DoCmd.Rename "Autoexec", acMacro, "Autoexec1"
HideDBWindowAtStartupInMDB

End Sub
```

Building a Custom Startup in an .adp File

The general process for creating a custom startup in an Access project is similar to the one for creating a custom startup in an Access database file. However, the details for setting the startup properties are different. In addition, the process for recovering step mode and resuming the custom startup is similar, but the details vary because your code must deal with the *CurrentProject* object instead of the *CurrentDB* object. In particular, you do not need the DAO library when working with an Access project (.adp) file. However, the Autoexec macro and your custom startup form work identically in .mdb and .adp files.

> **Note** When you open the sample file Chapter 10.adp, Access will fail to reestablish the connection to CAB2000. Use the File-Connection menu command to replace CAB2000 with the name of an appropriate SQL server on your network. Chapter 14, "Using Access to Build SQL Server Solutions: Part I," discusses .adp files and SQL Server connections in depth.

The following three procedures demonstrate the specific changes that you must make when creating a custom startup in an .adp file. Notice that the syntax for adding and deleting properties is different.

```
Function HideStartupWindowInADP()
On Error GoTo ADPStartup_Trap
Dim str1 As String

'Set CurrentProject properties to hide Database
'window, suppress use of F11 to show it, and
'disallow bypass of startup settings with
'Shift key at startup
str1 = "StartUpShowDBWindow"
CurrentProject.Properties(str1) = False
str1 = "AllowBypassKey"
CurrentProject.Properties("str1") = False
str1 = "AllowSpecialKeys"
CurrentProject.Properties("str1") = False
str1 = "StartupForm"
CurrentProject.Properties("str1") = "frmNotDBWindow"

ADPStartup_Exit:
Exit Function

'If any of three CurrentProject properties do not exist,
'add them and set their values
ADPStartup_Trap:
If Err.Number = 2455 And str1 = "StartUpShowDBWindow" Then
    CurrentProject.Properties.Add "StartUpShowDBWindow", False
ElseIf Err.Number = 2455 And str1 = "AllowBypassKey" Then
    CurrentProject.Properties.Add "AllowBypasskey", False
ElseIf Err.Number = 2455 And str1 = "AllowSpecialKeys" Then
    CurrentProject.Properties.Add "AllowSpecialKeys", False
ElseIf Err.Number = 2455 And str1 = "StartupForm" Then
    CurrentProject.Properties.Add "StartupForm", "frmNotDBWindow"
```

(continued)

```
    Else
        Debug.Print Err.Number, Err.Description
        Exit Function
    End If
    Resume Next

    End Function


    Sub RestoreStepMode()

    'Remove three startup properties for Database
    'window control
    On Error Resume Next
    CurrentProject.Properties.Remove  "StartUpShowDBWindow"
    CurrentProject.Properties.Remove  "AllowSpecialKeys"
    CurrentProject.Properties.Remove  "AllowBypassKey"
    CurrentProject.Properties.Remove  "StartupForm"

    'Rename Autoexec macro
    DoCmd.Rename "Autoexec1", acMacro, "Autoexec"

    End Sub


    Sub RestoreAutoMode()

    'Rename macro and reset startup properties
    DoCmd.Rename "Autoexec", acMacro, "Autoexec1"
    HideStartupWindowInADP

    End Sub
```

The *FileSearch* Object

You can use the *FileSearch* object model (shown in Figure 10-2) and other selected technologies to integrate file searches into your applications. In Access 2002, the model has been improved to offer easy access to search scopes that include Web files, your computer's hard drives, and the publicly shared resources on the local area network (LAN) that a computer connects to. This object exposes the functionality of the Open and the Find dialog boxes. As Figure 10-2 shows, five collections are dependent on the *FileSearch* object. In addition to the *FoundFiles* and the *PropertyTests* collections from Access 2000, Access 2002 adds the *FileTypes*, *SearchFolders*, and *SearchScopes* collections for the *FileSearch* object.

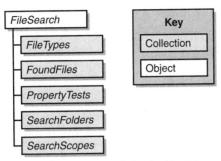

Figure 10-2 The *FileSearch* object is one of the shared Office objects.

> **Note**   Access Help contains code samples that illustrate how to loop
> through *SearchScopes* to find *SearchFolders* and, ultimately, paths
> within those folders in which you want to search for files. One major
> benefit of *SearchScopes* is its ability to search for files that are not on
> your computer or LAN, such as those located in Web folders. See the
> "Printing Web Folder Contents" section in Chapter 3, "Data Access
> Models: Part II," for code samples that itemize the files on a Web folder.

There are two basic ways to specify a file search, and each approach corresponds to options in the Open dialog box:

- You can designate a single criterion (a filename or pattern, a file type, or a path).

- You can designate multiple search criteria programmatically by using the *PropertyTests* collection.

With the second approach, you specify arguments that serve as input to the Open dialog box. You can use this dialog box to specify multiple search criteria and rules for concatenating them, such as And and Or operators. Use *FoundFiles* to enumerate the return set from either approach.

The *FileSearch* object has two methods: *NewSearch* and *Execute*. The *NewSearch* method resets all *FileSearch* properties to their default values. You can then edit the properties that require special values for a particular file search. If you do not invoke *NewSearch* at the beginning of a search specification, your new search inherits its property settings from the previous search.

You invoke the *Execute* method to launch a file search after you specify the search parameters. This method can take several arguments that control the arrangement of filenames in the *FoundFiles* object and that control whether to update the file index before conducting a new search. The return value from this method is the number of filenames that match the search specification.

Conducting a Basic File Search

Many *FileSearch* properties permit flexible search specifications. The simple code sample that follows specifies a search and retrieves its return set. It creates an instance of the *FileSearch* object by using the *FileSearch* property of the *Application* object. Then it restores all *FileSearch* property settings to their default values by invoking the *NewSearch* method. Next it assigns the *LookIn* and *FileName* properties, which specify where to look and what to look for. The test machine for this search includes a series of .mdb files with names such as Chapter 01 and Chapter 02.

The *SearchSubFolders* property accepts a Boolean value that indicates whether to restrict the search to the current folder or extend it to subfolders of the *LookIn* property setting. In this instance, the setting does not matter because it has no subfolders. However, when dealing with folders that can contain many subfolders (such as c:\), you should be careful about how you set the *SearchSubFolders* property because it can lead to some lengthy searches.

```
Sub FileSearch1XP()

'Search in PMA Samples path and its subfolders
'for Chapter*.mdb
With Application.FileSearch
'Start a new search
    .NewSearch
'Set search criteria
    .LookIn = "\\cab2000\c\PMA Samples\"
    .FileName = "Chapter*.mdb"
    .SearchSubFolders = True
End With

With Application.FileSearch
'Execute the search
    If .Execute() > 0 Then
        MsgBox "There were " & .FoundFiles.Count & _
            " file(s) found."
'Display names of all found files
        For i = 1 To .FoundFiles.Count
            MsgBox .FoundFiles(i)
        Next i
    Else
'If no files found, say so
        MsgBox "There were no files found."
```

```
        End If
End With

End Sub
```

After creating the specification for the search, the procedure invokes the *Execute* method for the *FileSearch* object. This method has a return value that indicates the number of files that meet the search criteria. If the value is 0, the criteria yield no matching filenames and the procedure issues a message indicating that no files were found. If the criteria yield one or more matching files, the procedure displays the *Count* property of the *FoundFiles* object before presenting each name in *FoundFiles*.

The preceding sample enumerates all the database files from the target folder specified by the *LookIn* setting that have an .mdb extension and start with "Chapter". You can easily broaden the scope of the search to include all database files no matter how their filename starts and regardless of whether they have an .mdb extension. For example, the next piece of code searches for database files in the same folder as the preceding sample. But this code snippet will retrieve database files with other extensions, such as .adp, .mde, and .ade. Also, the this sample places no restrictions on the filename. Therefore, it can find a database filename even if it does not begin with "Chapter".

```
Sub FileSearch1aXP()

'Search in PMA Samples path and its subfolders
'for database files
With Application.FileSearch
'Start a new search
    .NewSearch
'Set search criteria
    .LookIn = "\\cab2000\c\PMA Samples\"
    .FileType = msoFileTypeDatabases
    .SearchSubFolders = True
End With

With Application.FileSearch
'Execute the search
    If .Execute() > 0 Then
        MsgBox "There were " & .FoundFiles.Count & _
            " file(s) found."
'Display names of all found files
        For i = 1 To .FoundFiles.Count
            MsgBox .FoundFiles(i)
        Next i
    Else
'If no files found, say so
```

(continued)

```
            MsgBox "There were no files found."
        End If
    End With

End Sub
```

Generalizing a Search and Sorting Its Return Set

The following sample sorts by file size the return set from a search. The sample uses two procedures. The first procedure specifies a computer name, a share name, and a pathname. These three parameters can jointly designate the *LookIn* setting for a search. By specifying the parameters in a procedure that passes them to another, we make the procedure that invokes the *Execute* method for the *FileSearch* object more general.

The second procedure accepts the arguments passed to it by the first procedure, and it concatenates them to compute a value for the *LookIn* property of the *FileSearch* object. In addition, the second procedure uses two more parameters when it invokes the *Execute* method. These parameters designate the sort criterion and order, respectively, for arranging the return set from the search. The constant names for the *Execute* method's first parameter indicate the variable on which to sort the returned filenames. These constants are *msoSortByFileName*, *msoSortByFileType*, *msoSortByLastModified*, and *msoSortBySize*. The *Execute* method's second parameter specifies either ascending or descending order. The sample designates a search sorted by file size in descending order. This differs from the previous sample, which returned results in the default ascending order based on filename.

```
Sub CallFileSearch2XP()
Dim str1 As String
Dim str2 As String
Dim str3 As String
'Dim ftp1 As fil

str1 = "\\cab2000\"
str2 = "c\"
str3 = "Program Files"

FileSearch2XP str1, str2, str3

End Sub


Sub FileSearch2XP(ComputerName As String, _
    ShareName As String, PathName As String, _
    Optional FileType)
```

```
Dim sngMB As Single

'Search in folder specified by arguments and its
'subfolders for *.mdb
With Application.FileSearch
'Start a new search
    .NewSearch
'Set search criteria
    .LookIn = ComputerName & ShareName & PathName
    .FileName = "*.mdb"
    .SearchSubFolders = True
End With

With Application.FileSearch
'Return found files in descending order by file size
    If .Execute(msoSortBySize, msoSortOrderDescending) > 0 Then
        Debug.Print "There were " & .FoundFiles.Count & _
            " file(s) found."
        For i = 1 To .FoundFiles.Count
'Compute file size in MB and display with filename
            sngMB = FileLen(.FoundFiles(i)) / (1024 ^ 2)
            Debug.Print .FoundFiles(i) & vbCrLf & vbTab & _
                "Filesize (MB): " & Round(CDec(sngMB), 3)
        Next i
    Else
'If no files found, say so
        MsgBox "There were no files found."
    End If
End With

End Sub
```

The message box that displays the return set shows the file sizes and filenames. You pass the *FoundFiles* object to the *FileLen* function to determine the size of a file. The file sizes are rounded to the nearest 1/1000 of a MB.

Note The VBA *Round* function was introduced with VBA 6. To derive consistent results with this function, you should first pass its argument to the *CDec* function. The sample just shown uses this syntax. (See Chapter 1, "Introduction to VBA," for information on the *CDec* function.)

Searching Based on File Contents

Even with a simple search, as shown in the three previous samples, you can selectively search for specific text in the document or its *DocumentProperty* object. The sample that follows does this. You use the *FileSearch* object's *TextOrProperty* property to target a text string in the file's body or its *Properties* collection. Notice that you can specify folders on remote computers using the Uniform Naming Convention (UNC). This sample uses a different name and path than the preceding samples. (The path \\cab233\d\cab points to the cab folder in the share named d of a computer named cab233.) As with other samples in this book, you'll need to change these settings so that they point to the computers, shares, and paths that are relevant to your computing environment.

```vba
Sub FileSearch3XP()
Dim sngStart As Double
Dim sngEnd As Double
Dim int1 As Integer
Dim str1 As String
#Const AllFiles = False

'Search in cab folder on linked computer
'for files containing CAB
With Application.FileSearch
'Start a new search
    .NewSearch
'Set search criteria
    .LookIn = "\\cab233\d\cab\"
    .SearchSubFolders = False
'When searching for text, consider
'restricting the files you search
'*.* takes 145 seconds, but
'msoFileTypeWordDocuments takes 16 seconds
#If AllFiles = True Then
    .FileName = "*.*"
#Else
    .FileType = msoFileTypeWordDocuments
#End If
    .TextOrProperty = "CAB"
End With

With Application.FileSearch
'Execute the search
    sngStart = Now
    If .Execute() > 0 Then
        sngEnd = Now
        Debug.Print "The file search took " & _
            DateDiff("s", sngStart, sngEnd) & " seconds."
```

```
         str1 = "There were " & .FoundFiles.Count & _
             " file(s) found.  Do you want to see " & _
             "them in a series of messages boxes?"
         If MsgBox(str1, vbYesNo, _
             "Programming Microsoft Access Version 2002") = vbYes Then
'Display names of all found files
             For int1 = 1 To .FoundFiles.Count
                 MsgBox .FoundFiles(int1)
             Next int1
         End If
     Else
'If no files found, say so
         MsgBox "There were no files found."
     End If
 End With

 End Sub
```

Some file searches can be lengthy. By specifying a restrictive *FileSearch* property, you can dramatically improve the performance of the *Execute* method. For example, the sample just shown finds all Word documents in a folder that contain a specific string. By using the *msoFileTypeWordDocuments* constant for the *FileType* property, the sample restricts the search to just Word document files. You might be tempted to specify *.* for the *FileName* property and then filter the returned results, but this would seriously impair performance. For the sample files in the cab folder on the cab233 computer, the difference is 16 seconds for the *msoFileType* constant vs. 145 seconds for the *.* *FileName* specification. (Notice that it takes just three lines to time the operation—one line before the *Execute* method and two more immediately after it.)

This sample makes it easy for you to evaluate the performance improvement in your own computing environment. First, update the *LookIn* and *TextOrProperty* settings so that they're relevant to your computing environment. Second, run the sample as is to develop a baseline time with the *msoFileTypeWordDocuments* setting for the *FileType* property setting. Third, simply change the *AllFiles* compiler constant from False to True to see how much slower things can go with *.* as the *FileName* setting vs. using *msoFileTypeWordDocuments* as the *FileType* setting.

Controlling *FileType* with a Custom Form and Procedure

In general, your applications will offer file search capabilities through a form. The next sample demonstrates one technique for this while showing how to condition a search on one or more members of the *FileTypes* collection for the *FileSearch* object. The sample's form, which appears in Figure 10-3, allows a user to perform one of three tasks. First, users can specify a new search by designating a single file type for it. Second, users can add a new member to the *FileTypes* collection for the current *FileSearch* object. Third, they can execute the search with the *FileTypes* collection members showing in the form's list box. This last capability depends, in part, on a procedure named *FileSearch1a3aXP* in a standard module. A module behind the form supports all the form's capabilities, including the call to the procedure in the standard module.

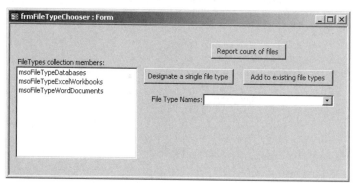

Figure 10-3 A form for adding members to the *FileTypes* collection of a *FileSearch* object. The form also enables executing the search.

The following procedure includes all the event procedures and sub procedures behind the form. These procedures provide two classes of services. The first class manages the form by performing tasks such as managing the entries that appear in the list box and responding to command button clicks. The second class of services manages the search. This involves tasks such as managing the members of the *FileTypes* collection for the open *FileSearch* object and launching the search with whatever members are in the list.

The module starts by declaring three public variables. These variables simplify sharing information across procedures (namely, the settings for the *FileSearch* object). These initial declarations also reduce the need to repetitively declare variables used in standard ways across procedures.

The first procedure is the *Form_Open* event procedure. This procedure handles the formatting and content settings for the form. It also sets a reference to the *FileSearch* object and uses that reference to populate the form's list box with members of the object's *FileTypes* collection. Furthermore, the procedure uses the *AddItem* and *RemoveItem* methods to control the content of the list box. These methods require a list box control to have a *Value List* setting for its *RowSourceType* property.

> **Note**   The *AddItem* and *RemoveItem* methods for list boxes and combo boxes were introduced in Access 2002. The code behind the form in Figure 10-3 illustrates how to use them. Refer to Access Help for online programmer reference materials.

The *Form_Open* event procedure has two loops. A backward-iterating loop that successively invokes the *RemoveItem* method erases any previously existing content from the list box. A forward-iterating loop passes through the members of the *FileTypes* collection. This loop uses the *AddItem* method to add the names of the members to the list box. Office stores members of the *FileTypes* collection as intrinsic constant values (numbers). A lookup table in the Chapter 10 .mdb file on the companion CD maps the numbers to their intrinsic constant names. A *DLookup* function within the loop operates on the table to extract the intrinsic constant name corresponding to the number for a *FileType* collection member. Notice in the code that *FileTypes* collection members belong to a 1-based collection, but the rows in a list box belong to a 0-based collection.

> **Note**   The form's combo box shows the names of all the intrinsic constants for *FileType* designations but stores a constant's number when a user makes a selection. The combo box uses the same lookup table as the *DLookup* function that decodes an intrinsic constant value to the name for the constant. However, the combo box works the table in reverse from the *DLookup* function in the final loop of the *Form_Open* event procedure.

The *cmdDesignateSingle_Click* and *cmdAddTo_Click* event procedures work in concert with the *RefreshWithNewFileTypeinFileSearch* procedure to keep the list box control rows in synchronicity with the members of the *FileTypes* collection. The two event procedures also populate the *FileTypes* collection with members. The event procedure for clicking the *cmdDesignateSingle* button starts by assigning the combo box's value to the *FileTypes* collection for the *FileSearch* object referenced in the *Form_Open* event procedure. The assignment statement clears any prior members of the *FileTypes* collection as it adds the combo box's value to the collection. Next it removes all row values from the list box in a backward-iterating loop. The call to the *RefreshWithNewFileTypeinFileSearch* procedure passes the last member from the *FileTypes* collection to the list box.

The *cmdAddTo_Click* event procedure has the same general design as the *cmdDesignateSingle_* event procedure, but *cmdAddTo_Click* merely adds an item from the combo box to the *FileTypes* collection and the list box rows. Instead of using an assignment statement to transfer the combo box value to the *FileTypes* collection, the *cmdAddTo_Click* procedure uses the collection's *Add* method. This method inserts the combo box's value as the last member of the collection without affecting any other members of the collection. Let's take a look at the syntax now:

```
Public fls1 As FileSearch
Public int1 As Integer
Public str1 As String

Private Sub Form_Open(Cancel As Integer)

'Set RowSourceType to Value List so that you can use
'AddItem and RemoveItem methods
Me.lstExistingFileTypes.RowSourceType = "Value List"

'Set form for unbound data use
Me.RecordSelectors = False
Me.NavigationButtons = False
Me.DividingLines = False

'Remove all existing items from the list box
'showing selected file types
For int1 = Me.lstExistingFileTypes.ListCount - 1 To 0 Step -1
    Me.lstExistingFileTypes.RemoveItem int1
Next int1

'Set FileSearch variable
Set fls1 = Application.FileSearch

'Loop through FileTypes in FileSearch object and
'add them to the list box.
'FileTypes collection is 1-based, and list box items
'are 0-based.
'Item:= and Index:= shows syntax for assigning values
'to named parameters (as opposed to positional parameters).
For int1 = 1 To fls1.FileTypes.Count
    str1 = "[msoFileTypeNumber] = " & _
        CStr(fls1.FileTypes.Item(int1))
    Me.lstExistingFileTypes.AddItem _
        Item:=DLookup("[msoFileTypeName]", _
        "msoFileTypeEnum", str1), _
        Index:=Me.lstExistingFileTypes.ListCount
Next int1

End Sub
```

```
Private Sub cmdDesignateSingle_Click()

'Refresh the FileTypes collection of the FileSearch
'object with the combo box selection
fls1.FileType = Combo0

'Remove all existing items from the list box
'showing selected file types
For int1 = Me.lstExistingFileTypes.ListCount - 1 To 0 Step -1
    Me.lstExistingFileTypes.RemoveItem int1
Next int1

'Refresh the list box with the newly selected item
RefreshWithNewFileTypeinFileSearch

'Blank combo after processing selection
Combo0 = ""

End Sub


Private Sub cmdAddTo_Click()

'Add the combo box selection to the existing list
'of members in the FileTypes collection of the
'FileSearch object
fls1.FileTypes.Add Combo0

'Refresh the list box with the newly selected item
RefreshWithNewFileTypeinFileSearch

'Blank combo after processing selection
Combo0 = ""

End Sub


Sub RefreshWithNewFileTypeinFileSearch()
'Dim int1 As Integer
'Dim str1 As String

'Find the index for the last item in the FilesTypes collection
int1 = fls1.FileTypes.Count
str1 = "[msoFileTypeNumber] = " & CStr(fls1.FileTypes.Item(int1))
```

(continued)

567

```
'Add name corresponding to the FileType number to the bottom
'of the list box
Me.lstExistingFileTypes.AddItem _
    Item:=DLookup("[msoFileTypeName]", "msoFileTypeEnum", str1), _
    Index:=Me.lstExistingFileTypes.ListCount

End Sub


Private Sub cmdSearch_Click()

'Launch search with setting from form
Module1.FileSearch1a3aXP

End Sub
```

The last event procedure in the code behind the form consists of a single line. This line invokes the *FileSearch1a3aXP* procedure in Module1, which is a standard module. The *FileSearch1a3aXP* procedure contains elements of the two preceding search procedures in the module whose names end with *1aXP* and *3aXP*. The actual code appears next. One distinction between this procedure and the ones we examined earlier in the section is that it doesn't invoke the *New* method for the *FileSearch* object. This is because the procedure needs to retain the *FileTypes* collection members set by the form.

Clicking the *cmdSearch* button on the form launches the search and displays a message box containing the results of the search. Some searches launched by users can take quite a while to run. If this search is against a remote computer, the user might not get any feedback that the computer is working. In situations like this, it helps to provide some visual cue that the program is working. You'll see how to do this later in the chapter in "The *Assistant* Object."

```
Sub FileSearch1a3aXP()

'Search in Program Files folder and its subfolders
With Application.FileSearch
'Start a new search.
'Set search criteria.
    .LookIn = "C:\PMA Samples"
    .SearchSubFolders = True
End With

With Application.FileSearch
'Execute the search
    If .Execute() > 0 Then
        str1 = "There were " & .FoundFiles.Count & _
            " file(s) found."
```

```
        MsgBox str1, vbInformation, _
            "Programming Microsoft Access Version 2002"
    Else
'If no files found, say so
        MsgBox "There were no files found.", vbInformation, _
            "Programming Microsoft Access Version 2002"
    End If
End With

End Sub
```

Specifying Multiple Search Criteria

The advanced search format lets you specify multiple search criteria for your return set in the *FoundFiles* collection. You use the *Add* method two or more times to specify multiple criteria for the *PropertyTests* collection. Your individual criterion specifications must include *Name* and *Condition* settings.

The *Add* method can specify a *Connector* setting as well as one or two *Value* settings. The *Add* method's *Condition* setting determines whether a criterion requires *Value* settings. You view the members of the *MsoCondition* class in the Object Browser to see all the available options. (Figure 10-4 shows an excerpt.) Your *Connector* settings can take one of two values to specify how to combine a criterion with other criteria. This setting enables And or Or operators for merging a criterion with other search criteria. You use Or to treat the criterion separately, and you use And to combine the designated criterion with others. The And operator is the default setting. Together, the *Condition*, *Value*, and *Connector* settings offer the same functionality as the Find dialog box.

You can enumerate *PropertyTests* members using a *For...Each* loop. Each member constitutes a unique search criterion. The *Name* property identifies the criterion as you enumerate them.

The file search sample that follows has three segments. The first segment specifies the criteria after setting a reference to a *FileSearch* object. The sample targets all database files between two dates. It shows the correct syntax for invoking the *Add* method for the *PropertyTests* collection. The first criterion designates a Web page file type. The second criterion denotes files last modified between October 30, 2000 and October 31, 2000. The *msoConnectorOr* setting indicates that files must meet both criteria separately to be in the return set. You need not specify a *Connector* property for the second criterion because it adopts the default *msoConnectorAnd* value. Before displaying the return set, the procedure enumerates the *PropertyTests* members in its second segment. The final segment displays the return set.

Figure 10-4 You use the members of the *MsoCondition* enumeration group to specify conditions for advanced criteria in the *PropertyTests* collection of the *FileSearch* object.

```
Sub FileSearch4XP()
Dim fls1 As FileSearch
Dim str1 As String
Dim int1 As Integer

Set fls1 = Application.FileSearch

'Set LookIn and SearchSubFolder properties
With fls1
    .NewSearch
    .LookIn = "\\cab2000\c\Program Files\" & _
    "Microsoft Office\Office10\Samples"
    .SearchSubFolders = False
End With

'Remove default PropertyTest for Office files
fls1.PropertyTests.Remove (1)

'Set a pair of PropertyTests to find all Web pages
'last modified on either 10/30/2000 or 10/31/2000
With fls1.PropertyTests
    .Add Name:="Files of Type", _
        Condition:=msoConditionFileTypeWebPages, _
        Connector:=msoConnectorOr
```

```
                .Add Name:="Last Modified", _
                    Condition:=msoConditionAnytimeBetween, _
                    Value:="10/30/2000", SecondValue:="10/31/2000"
        End With

        'Display PropertyTests
        For int1 = 1 To fls1.PropertyTests.Count
            With Application.FileSearch.PropertyTests(int1)
            str1 = "This is the search criteria: " & vbCrLf & _
                "The name is: " & .Name & ". " & vbCrLf & _
                "The condition is: " & .Condition
            If .Value <> "" Then
                str1 = str1 & "." & vbCrLf & "The value is: " & .Value
                If .SecondValue <> "" Then
                    str1 = str1 _
                        & ". " & vbCrLf & "The second value is: " _
                        & .SecondValue & ", and the connector is " _
                        & .Connector
                End If
            End If
            MsgBox str1

            End With
        Next int1

        'Display return set from property tests
        With fls1
        'Execute the search
            If .Execute() > 0 Then
                MsgBox "There were " & .FoundFiles.Count & _
                    " file(s) found."
        'Display names of all found files
                For int1 = 1 To .FoundFiles.Count
                    MsgBox .FoundFiles(int1)
                Next int1
            Else
        'If no files found, say so
                MsgBox "There were no files found."
            End If
        End With

        End Sub
```

A CopyFile Utility Based on *FileSystemObject*

One reason for finding files is to copy them to another destination or save them with a new name. The *FileSearch* object does not facilitate either task, but the

FileSystemObject object does. This object provides a general model for process-ing text and binary files. The *CopyFileUtility* sample described in this section il-lustrates a simple application of the *FileSystemObject* object that I hope will entice you to explore it more fully when your applications require file processing. You can learn more about this tool by searching for *FileSystemObject* in Access Help. The *FileSystemObject* object is an exceedingly robust tool for many Office applications.

The following code sample uses two procedures to demonstrate the CopyFile utility. The first procedure sets the computer and share names, the pathname, and the filename for the original file and the copy that the utility attempts to generate. This procedure also sets a Boolean variable to determine whether the utility will copy over a file that already exists. The second procedure instanti-ates a reference to the FileSystemObject with the *CreateObject* function. This book explores the *CreateObject* function in more depth in Chapter 11, "Integrating Access with Other Office Applications."   After instantiating the object, the procedure compiles the source and destination arguments for the object's *CopyFile* method.

By clearing the *Err* object and designating that Access recover from errors by processing the next line, the procedure displays one of three messages after completing the attempt to copy the file. If the *Err* object is still clear, the code announces that the copy attempt succeeded. If the procedure attempts to copy over an existing file without designating that it's OK to do so, the copy attempt fails and the procedure warns the user. Finally, if some unanticipated error oc-curs, the procedure returns the *Err* object's *Number* and *Description* properties in a message box. Here's the code for the utility:

```
Sub CallCopyFileUtility()
Dim strOrigShare As String
Dim strOrigPath As String
Dim strOrigFlNm As String
Dim strDestShare As String
Dim strDestPath As String
Dim strDestFlNm As String
Dim bolOver As Boolean
#Const ForcePathNotFound = False

'Specify inputs for file copy
strOrigShare = "\\cab2000\c\"
strOrigPath = "PMA Samples\"
strOrigFlNm = "Northwind_backup.mdb"
#If ForcePathNotFound = False Then
    strDestShare = "\\cab2000\c\"
#Else
    strDestShare = "\\xyz\c\"
```

```
#End If
strDestPath = "PMA Samples\"
strDestFlNm = "Northwind_backup2.mdb"

'Setting to False can generate a "File already
'exists" message if the file is already there
bolOver = True

'Pass arguments to CopyFileUtility
CopyFileUtility strOrigShare, strDestShare, _
    strOrigPath, strDestPath, _
    strOrigFlNm, strDestFlNm, _
    bolOver

End Sub


Sub CopyFileUtility(strOrigShare As String, _
    strDestShare As String, _
    strOrigPath As String, _
    strDestPath As String, _
    strOrigFlNm As String, _
    strDestFlNm As String, _
    Optional bolOver As Boolean = False)
Dim str1 As String
Dim str2 As String
Dim str3 As String
Dim int1 As Integer
Const msgTitle = "Programming Microsoft Access Version 2002"

'Reference FileSystemObject
Set fs = CreateObject("Scripting.FileSystemObject")

'Form origin and destination arguments for CopyFile method
str1 = strOrigShare & strOrigPath & strOrigFlNm
str2 = strDestShare & strDestPath & strDestFlNm

'Clear error and resume from error outcome at the next line
'from the CopyFile method
Err.Clear
On Error Resume Next
fs.CopyFile str1, str2, bolOver

'Print message describing CopyFile outcome
Select Case Err.Number
    Case 0
        str3 = "Copy succeeded."
        int1 = vbInformation
```

(continued)

```
        Case 58
            str3 = "File exists at destination already. Choose new name."
            int1 = vbCritical
        Case Else
            str3 = "Unanticipated error." & vbCr & _
            "Err.number = " & Err.Number & vbCr & _
            "Err.description = " & Err.Description
            int1 = vbCritical
    End Select
    MsgBox str3, int1, msgTitle

End Sub
```

You can test the error paths of the CopyFile utility by altering the settings for the first procedure in the utility. For example, to generate a message saying that the file already exists, change the assignment for *bolOver* from True to False and attempt to copy over a file you know exists. One typical unanticipated error occurs when a user attempts to copy to a destination path that does not exist. For example, the user might make a typo when specifying the path. Because it's unlikely that you already have a \\cab2000\c\computer name and share name in your computing environment, specifying these settings will probably generate a "Path not found" message with an error number of 76. However, even after you update the computer name and share name for your computing environment, you can still generate a "Path not found" message by setting the compiler constant *ForcePathNotFound* to True.

Empowering Users to Create Files with the Task Pane

Access 2002 introduces the Task Pane as part of its UI. The New File view of this toolbar includes five sections. End users can click on shortcuts in these sections to launch various actions, such as creating a file from a template or creating a new file based on an existing one. Developers can programmatically add and remove shortcuts on the Task Pane to enable users to add (or prevent them from adding) files from shortcuts on the Task Pane.

> **Note**   End users can open the Task Pane toolbar by choosing New from the File menu. A check box in the Task Pane's bottom section enables a user to specify that the Task Pane appear automatically at startup. Developers can program the Task Pane by using the *NewFileTaskPane* and *NewFile* objects, which represent the Task Pane and the items on the Task Pane, respectively.

The following pair of procedures shows how to add and remove a Copy Northwind link from the New From Existing File section of the Task Pane. When a user clicks the link, it creates a new file named Northwind1.mdb, which is a copy of the Northwind.mdb file. The new file appears in the same folder as the original one.

Adding a shortcut to the Task Pane requires managing the Task Pane and the proper shortcut specification. Notice that the *AddCopyNorthwindLink* procedure begins by declaring a *NewFile* object in the Office library. The declared object requires a reference to the Office 10.0 library in the References dialog box of the VBE window. Next the procedure sets a reference to a *NewFileTaskPane* object. The Task Pane has three views—one for searching, another for managing the Windows Clipboard, and a third for managing the creation of new files. The *NewFileTaskPane* object references the view of the Task Pane for managing the creation of new files. In between two command bar property assignments, the procedure invokes the *Add* method for the *nftpTemp* instance. Showing and hiding the Task Pane command bar refreshes the Task Pane to show the outcome of the *Add* method.

The *Add* method takes four arguments. Two of these rely on intrinsic constants in enum groups. The action argument specifies what a shortcut does. Its enum group, *MsoFileNewAction*, has three members. These members signify adding, editing, and opening a file. The sample that follows uses the constant for adding a file. The second enum group, *MsoFileNewSection*, denotes the section of the Task Pane. This group contains a separate intrinsic constant for each of the five Task Pane sections. This sample specifies the New From Existing File section. The *FileName* argument designates the source file for the action, and the *DisplayName* setting determines how the shortcut appears on the Task Pane.

```
Sub AddCopyNorthwindLink()
Dim nftpTemp As Office.NewFile

'Instantiate NewFile object for Task Pane
Set nftpTemp = Application.NewFileTaskPane

'Add link to Copy Northwind.mdb database to the New
'From Existing File section of the Task Pane
CommandBars("Task Pane").Visible = False
nftpTemp.Add _
    FileName:="C:\Program Files\Microsoft Office\Office10\" & _
    "Samples\Northwind.mdb", _
    Section:=msoNewfromExistingFile, _
    DisplayName:="Copy Northwind.mdb", _
    Action:=msoCreateNewFile
CommandBars("Task Pane").Visible = True
```

(continued)

```
End Sub


Sub RemoveCopyNorthwindLink2()
Dim nftpTemp As Office.NewFile

'Instantiate NewFile object for Task Pane
Set nftpTemp = Application.NewFileTaskPane

'Remove link to Copy Northwind.mdb database from the New
'From Existing File section of the Task Pane
CommandBars("Task Pane").Visible = False
nftpTemp.Remove _
    FileName:="C:\Program Files\Microsoft Office\Office10\" & _
    "Samples\Northwind.mdb", _
    Section:=msoNewfromExistingFile, _
    DisplayName:="Copy Northwind.mdb"
CommandBars("Task Pane").Visible = True

End Sub
```

Removing a shortcut from the Task Pane is especially easy. Just take the procedure for adding the shortcut and replace the *Add* method with the *Remove* method. That's all it takes!

There are four other sections to and from which you can add and remove shortcuts on the Task Pane. When you add the preceding shortcut to the Open A File section of the Task Pane by assigning the *msoOpenDocument* constant to the *Section* argument of the *Add* method, the shortcut appears below the More Files icon. Although this is slightly deviant behavior, the shortcut works. There is a problem because the *Remove* method does not work for a shortcut added to the Open A File section in this fashion. One way to solve this problem is to remove the shortcut via the registry. Start to open the registry by typing *regedit* into the Open text box of the Run dialog box from the Windows Start button. Then click OK. Next choose Find from the Edit menu. Search for the shortcut name (Copy Northwind.mdb, in this example). With the Microsoft Windows 2000 operating system, the editor discovers a reference to the shortcut under HKEY_CURRENT_USER, Software, Microsoft, Office, 10.0, Access, New File. In the test computer I used while writing this book, the shortcut was in the Custom1 folder at the end of the path. Delete the custom folder containing the shortcut specification. After removing the registry entry for the shortcut, you might need to close and open the Task Pane. This refreshes the Task Pane to reflect your changed registry settings.

> **Note**   Whenever you make changes to a registry, you should have a backup copy for restoring it. Detailed commentary on editing, backing up, and restoring registries is beyond the scope of this book.

The *Assistant* Object

The Office Assistant is a friendly help feature in Office. Although developers and power users might not like the Assistant, it's appealing to typical users. The Assistant is relatively simple to program, so you can easily give your custom Office applications the same look and feel as the standard Office applications. If it's important for your custom applications to have the look and feel of Office without requiring a lot of work on your part, the Assistant might be a worthwhile topic for you to master.

The *Assistant* object model is shown in Figure 10-5. The top-level *Assistant* object can appear on the screen with or without its hierarchically dependent *Balloon* object. Because the Assistant can use a wide range of characters and animations, it can be entertaining and informative without explanatory text. If you want to include explanatory text, you can program *Balloon* objects to appear with the Assistant. Balloons can include explanatory text or even serve as a simple data entry device. You use the *BalloonCheckBox* and the *BalloonLabel* collections with button controls to make your assistants interactive.

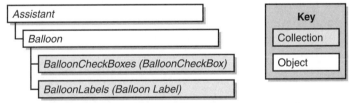

Figure 10-5 You use the *Assistant* object to present an assistant, animate it, and display a balloon.

Showing and Animating an Assistant

Assistants can add value to an application by visually conveying the various actions that your application is performing. You can further distinguish your custom application by consistently using a specific assistant or by regularly using different assistants but in highly differentiated circumstances. For example, use the Merlin assistant for help pertaining to computations, but use the F1 robot when offering help about computer system topics. Your development team can adopt a rule to always invoke the working animation for any task that takes more than a couple of seconds.

You can easily control the display and animation of an assistant by using the three short procedures shown here: *AssistantIdleOn*, *AssistantNotVisible*, and *AssistantSearchOn*. The *AssistantIdleOn* procedure contains a single line that sets the *Assistant* object's *Visible* property to True. Because *msoAnimationIdle* is the default animation type (the animation character is idle), the line that sets the *Animation* property is not needed and is commented out. In addition, this basic animation is part of the core Access library, so you can invoke it without referencing the Microsoft Office 10.0 Object Library. You can also run the *AssistantNotVisible* procedure without referencing the Office Object Library.

```
Sub AssistantIdleOn()

'Setting animation for idle is optional
'Assistant.Animation = msoAnimationIdle

Assistant.Visible = True

End Sub


Sub AssistantNotVisible()

Assistant.Visible = False

End Sub


Sub AssistantSearchOn()

If Assistant.Visible = False Then Assistant.Visible = True
Assistant.Animation = msoAnimationSearching

End Sub
```

To change the animation character's behavior to something other than idle, your procedure must set the object's *Animation* property as well as its *Visible* property. The *AssistantSearchOn* procedure causes an *Assistant* object to display its searching animation. Unlike many of the other animations, the searching animation repeats until you assign a new animation setting. In addition, your project must have a reference to the Office Object Library for the searching animation to appear. (You can set this manually using the Tools menu in the VBE.)

Automatically Referencing the Office Object Library

One disadvantage of the *AssistantSearchOn* procedure is that it assumes a reference to the Office Object Library. If there is no such reference, the procedure fails silently. The assistant appears, but it shows an idle, instead of a searching, animation. One way to handle this problem is to verify whether a reference to the Office Object Library exists and to add one automatically if necessary. Your application can then confidently invoke any animation, or indeed any other property of another shared Office object. The *AssistantSearchOn2* and *ReferenceOffice* procedures that follow show this solution.

```
Sub AssistantSearchOn2()

ReferenceOffice
AssistantSearchOn

End Sub


Sub ReferenceOffice()
Dim ref1 As Reference
Dim blnOfficeXPIn As Boolean
Dim mso10Library As String

'Enumerate members of References collection to determine
'whether Office Object Libary is already referenced
blnOfficeXPIn = False
For Each ref1 In References
    If ref1.Name = "Office" Then
        blnOfficeXPIn = True
    End If
Next ref1

'If Office Object Library reference is missing, reference it
If blnOfficeXPIn = False Then
    mso10Library = _
        "C:\Program Files\Common Files\Microsoft Shared\"& _
        "Office10\MSO.DLL"
    Application.References.AddFromFile mso10Library
End If

End Sub
```

AssistantSearchOn2 is nearly identical to the original procedure for invoking a searching animation. It actually calls *AssistantSearchOn*, but it calls *ReferenceOffice* first. *ReferenceOffice* ensures that the current project has a reference to the Office Object Library. It starts by enumerating all the members of the *References* collection to determine whether any of them have a *Name* property of *Office*. If yes, the procedure sets a Boolean variable to True. Otherwise, *blnOfficeXPIn* retains its default setting of False. The second segment of *ReferenceOffice* creates a reference to the Office Object Library if the Boolean variable is False. Having ensured that the Office Object Library is referenced, *AssistantSearchOn2* can invoke the *AssistantSearchOn* procedure to finish activating the animation.

> **Note**   Recall from Chapter 9, "Class, Form, and Report Modules," that you can derive the reference name, file, and path for any object library by manually including it and then enumerating the references. Print the *Name* and *FullPath* properties of each reference. The *AddFromFile* method requires an argument that designates the *FullPath* property value for a library. The Chapter 10.mdb file on the companion CD includes a short procedure to demonstrate the syntax for enumerating the *References* collection. I ran this procedure to discover the name, file, and path for the Office Object Library in Office XP.

Displaying a Searching Animation

You can use the Assistant object to complement the *FileSearch* object. I already noted that some searches can take a while. In these situations, it's useful to present some kind of cue on the screen to show that your application is at work. The Assistant's searching animation serves this purpose well.

The following procedure searches the entire C drive for .mdb files and returns a count of the files. By displaying the searching animation just before launching the search and restoring the idle animation just after the search, the Assistant informs the user that the search is in progress and then informs the user that it's completed. The procedure manages animation for the Assistant two times—once just before invoking the *Execute* method, and again just after the *End With* statement. Because the *FileSearch* and Assistant objects depend on the Office Object Library, the procedure calls *ReferenceOffice* as its first step. If a reference to the Office Object Library does not exist, the procedure creates one. Without this precaution, the procedure would fail if a user inadvertently canceled a reference to the Office Object Library.

```
Sub FileSearchAct()

'Reference the Office Object Library before using
'either the FileSearch or the Assistant objects
ReferenceOffice

'Search on C drive and its subfolders
'for *.mdb
With Application.FileSearch
'Start a new search
    .NewSearch
'Set search criteria conditions
    .LookIn = "C:\"
    .SearchSubFolders = True
    .FileName = "*.mdb"
End With

With Application.FileSearch
'Execute the search.
'Turn searching assistant on first.
    AssistantSearchOn
    If .Execute() > 0 Then
        MsgBox "There were " & .FoundFiles.Count & _
            " file(s) found."
    Else
'If no files found, say so
        MsgBox "There were no files found."
    End If
End With

'Show idle animation with Assistant
AssistantNotVisible
AssistantIdleOn

End Sub
```

Selecting Animation Types

The Office Object Library contains more than 30 animation types. Figure 10-6 shows an Object Browser view that enumerates a subset of the animation types. Most animations, such as *msoAnimationSendingMail* and *msoAnimationPrinting*, run through a single cycle and return to idle. Other animations, such as *msoAnimationSearching* and *msoAnimationThinking*, repeat until you invoke an alternative animation. Because of IntelliSense, you do not have to recall the constant names for referring to animations. You can often simply select one from a list.

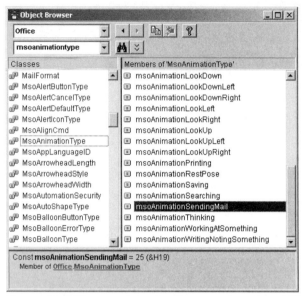

Figure 10-6 The *msoAnimationType* member of the Office Object Library contains more than 30 animation constants.

Selecting and Previewing Assistant Characters

Eight Assistant characters ship with Office XP, but Microsoft might add more in the future. (It has in the past.) You present an Assistant character by setting its *FileName* property to the name of that file. The following list shows the Assistant character names and their corresponding files.

Assistant Character	Filename
Clippit	Clippit.acs
Links	OffCat.acs
Rocky	Rocky.acs
Office Logo	Logo.acs
The Dot	Dot.acs
Mother Nature	MNature.acs
Merlin	Merlin.acs
F1	F1.acs

Note   If you carefully compare the preceding table with the corresponding one from *Programming Microsoft Access 2000*, you'll notice that Microsoft replaced the Genius with Merlin in Office XP. Including Merlin in the newer Windows releases helps make them compatible with Office XP. With the Office XP release, developers can use any Windows Agent character as an Assistant, including those from third parties. Microsoft does not support these agents, nor does it make promises about how they will work with Office. Visit *www.msagentring.org* to learn more about the range of agents available. In addition, you must load the character set file for an Assistant before you can use it.

Figure 10-7 shows a form in which the assistants act out their animations. The same animation can appear differently from one occurrence to the next. For example, there are at least three different versions of the goodbye animation for the F1 robot. The form offers seven animation types for each of three assistants. You can use the form to preview animations by making a selection from the Animation option group and then clicking an assistant command button. Analyzing the form's code will show you how to incorporate animations and change assistants in your applications.

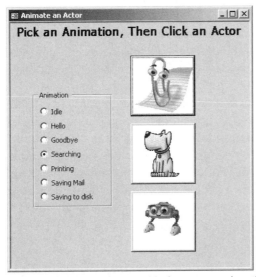

Figure 10-7 You can use this form to preview the assistant animations.

Figure 10-8 shows a selection of Assistant types and animations that you can preview using the form in Figure 10-7. At the top left, F1, the robot, executes the goodbye animation by burning to oblivion. Clippit rolls up a piece of paper and uses it as a telescope to portray its searching animation. When Rocky performs the saving to disk animation, it holds up the disk before moving it to a collar pocket for safekeeping. F1 turns into a printer for the printing animation.

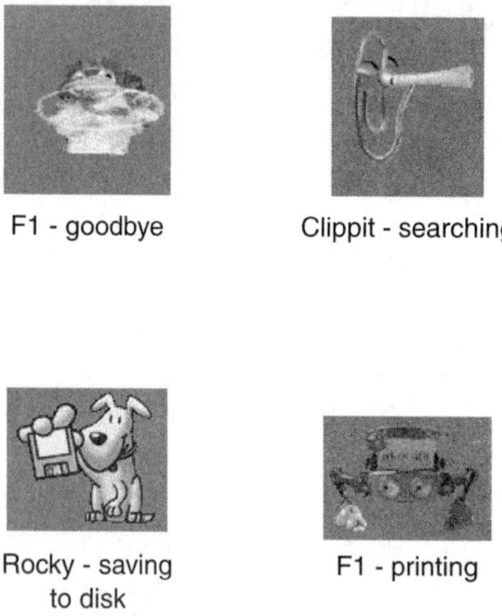

F1 - goodbye   Clippit - searching

Rocky - saving   F1 - printing
    to disk

Figure 10-8 A selection of animations performed by three different assistants. These were generated with the form shown in Figure 10-7.

The following listing shows the code behind the form in Figure 10-7. The declaration area at the top of the module contains the design-time settings for the command buttons showing the Assistant types as well as the buttons for different animation types in the option group. Notice that the buttons store the filename corresponding to the assistant on their face in their *Tag* property. Each button also has a simple event procedure for its click event. The buttons in the option group each have a value denoting an *msoAnimationType* constant. You use the Object Browser, shown in Figure 10-6 (on page 582), to determine the numerical value that matches a constant name. (For example, *msoAnimationSendingMail* equals 25.) As the form loads, it sets a series of properties to ensure that the assistant is ready when the user selects a button in the option group and clicks a command button.

```
Option Compare Database
'
'Design time Command button settings
'   Name: cmdClippit , cmdRocky, cmdF1
'   Picture: c:\My Documents\My Pictures\clippit.bmp,
'       or rocky.bmp, or F1.bmp
```

```
'    Picture Type: Embedded
'    Tag: clippit.acs, or rocky.acs, or F1.acs
'    On Click: [Event Procedure]
'
'Design time Option button settings
'    Idle button's Option Value = 1
'    Hello button's Option Value = 2
'    Goodbye button's Option Value = 3
'    Searching button's Option Value = 13
'    Printing button's Option Value = 18
'    Saving Mail button's Option Value = 25
'    Saving to disk button's Option Value = 112


Sub AnimateActor(Fname As String)
With Assistant
    .FileName = Fname
    .Visible = True
    .Animation = _
        Me.Controls("optAnimation")
End With

End Sub


Private Sub cmdClippit_Click()

AnimateActor Me.Controls("cmdClippit").Tag

End Sub


Private Sub cmdF1_Click()

AnimateActor Me.Controls("cmdF1").Tag

End Sub


Private Sub cmdRocky_Click()

AnimateActor Me.Controls("cmdRocky").Tag

End Sub
```

(continued)

```
Private Sub Form_Load()

With Assistant
    .On = True
    .Sounds = True
    .Visible = True
End With

End Sub
```

The command buttons are central to the process. When you click a command button, the event procedure passes its tag value to the *AnimateActor* procedure. This procedure uses its passed argument to set the assistant's *FileName* property. Next it sets the assistant's *Visible* property to True and sets its *Animation* property to the option group's value. The option group's value is, in turn, a function of the button that you clicked. The control has a default value of 1, in case the user does not make a selection.

Overview of Balloons and Balloon Graphics

You can use balloons to present text or graphics as well as gather feedback from users. You can present balloons as modal, modeless, or autodown dialog boxes. The balloon's *Mode* property controls the type of balloon. The *msoModeAutoDown* setting closes the balloon if the user clicks anywhere on the screen. The modeless (*msoModeModeless*) and modal (*msoModeModal*) settings are more common. The modeless setting keeps a balloon open while users work outside it. The modal setting forces a response that closes the balloon before allowing any other behavior to occur. The default value for the *Mode* property is *msoModeModal*.

You use the *NewBalloon* property for the Assistant object to create a *Balloon* object. Balloons have heading, text, label, check box, and button areas. You can populate these areas using corresponding property settings or hierarchical objects such as *BalloonCheckBoxes* and *BalloonLabels*. You assign text to the check boxes and labels using their *Text* property. You can further customize the content of a balloon using its *Icon* property. Six icons convey various types of message features, such as alerts, questions, information, and tips.

The following procedure presents a balloon with a heading, text, and icon. It also uses the default button (OK). The first three lines construct a string that concatenates the path to an image with the filename for an image. Escape formatting strings in the *Heading* property's text mark the beginning (*{ul 1}*) and end (*{ul 0}*) of underlined text in the heading area. (The escape formatting strings can also be used to designate underlined text in the text area.) The *Text* property setting includes a bitmap (.bmp) image in the text area. Notice that you can wrap text around an image. When embedding an image in a *Text* property setting, use braces as delimiters. Within the braces, specify the file type for the image, followed by its concatenated path and filename. The *Icon* property setting marks the balloon's content as information. Finally, the *Show* method opens the Assistant and its associated balloon. Figure 10-9 shows the Assistant and balloon that appear after you run the *balloonTextImageIcon* procedure.

> **Note**   The Chapter 10.mdb file on the companion CD includes several additional code samples that let you easily preview alternative icon settings. These samples also show the precise designation for selected *Icon* property settings.

```
Sub BalloonTextImageIcon()
Dim str1 As String
Dim str2 As String
Dim str3 As String

'Concatenate path to image and image of Assistant
str1 = "C:\PMA Samples\Chapter 10\"
str2 = "F1.bmp"
str3 = str1 & str2

'Assign Balloon Heading, Text, and Icon properties
'before showing the balloon
With Assistant.NewBalloon
    .Heading = "This is what {ul 1}F1{ul 0} looks like" & _
        " in a balloon text area"
    .Text = " Some text before it " & _
        "{bmp """ & str3 & """}" & _
        "and more after it."
    .Icon = msoIconAlertInfo
    .Show
End With

End Sub
```

Figure 10-9 You can include graphics in your balloons, and you can define the content using *Icon* property settings (such as the *AlertInfo* icon setting used for this balloon).

Using Balloon Labels

The two procedures prepare a balloon with labels and no buttons. The *SetLabelCount* procedure passes an argument to the *BalloonHeadTextLabel* routine. For valid arguments from 1 through 5, the called procedure presents an assistant with a balloon that contains as many labels as the value passed to it. Each label appears with a simple text string declaring the label number. Buttons in the balloon are not necessary with this design because clicking a label closes the balloon. The *Show* method opens the balloon and passes the value of the clicked label to the integer variable, *i*. A message box displays the number of the label the user clicked to close the balloon. Let's take a look at the code now:

```
Sub SetLabelCount()

BalloonHeadTextLabel 5

End Sub


Sub BalloonHeadTextLabel(LabelCount As Integer)
On Error GoTo LabelTrap
Dim b1 As balloon
Dim int1 As Integer

'Check for 0 or negative label count
If LabelCount <= 0 Then
    Err.Raise 9
End If
```

```
Set bl = Assistant.NewBalloon

'Create balloon with specified number of labels
With bl
    .Heading = "This is my heading"
    .Text = "Select one of these things:"
    For int1 = 1 To LabelCount
        .Labels(int1).Text = "Label " & int1
    Next int1
    .Button = msoButtonSetNone
    int1 = .Show
End With

'Confirm label that user clicked
MsgBox int1, vbInformation, _
    "Programming Microsoft Access Version 2002"

LabelExit:
Exit Sub

LabelTrap:
If Err.Number = 9 Then
    MsgBox "Number of labels more than 5 or less than " & _
        "1.  Retry with another number.", vbInformation, _
        "Programming Microsoft Access Version 2002"
Else
    Debug.Print Err.Number
    MsgBox "Unanticipated error.  Error number = " & _
        Err.Number & vbCrLf & "Error Description: " & _
        Err.Description, vbInformation, _
        "Programming Microsoft Access Version 2002"
End If
Resume LabelExit

End Sub
```

Built-in and custom error-trapping logic detects illegitimate arguments for the number of labels. If the passed argument is greater than 5, the *For...Next* loop that assigns label values fails on the attempt to assign text to the sixth label. This error (error number 9) results because balloons can show up to five labels only. Zero and negative arguments to the procedure do not generate the same error, but they also do not populate the balloon with labels. Therefore, the *BalloonHeadTextLabel* procedure traps these values with an *If...Then* statement and raises a custom error with a value of *9*. The procedure's trap for the error instructs the user to enter only values from *1* through *5*.

Collecting User Input with Balloons

The *BalloonCheckBoxes* collection lets you present a suite of options and collect user responses. You are again limited to five controls—in this case, the controls are check boxes. Unlike label controls, check box controls do not close a balloon after they are selected. Therefore, if you specify a balloon with check boxes, you must assign a button set that can close the balloon.

The two procedures that follow offer a general framework for displaying check box controls in a balloon. They do not include error trapping, but in practice, you should include error logic like that of the preceding sample. The *SetCheckCount* procedure passes an argument in the range of 1 through 5 to indicate how many check boxes to include. The second procedure starts by setting a reference, *b1*, to a new balloon. It assigns the *Balloon* object's *Button* property to *msoButtonSetOkCancel* to include OK and Cancel buttons. This offers two routes to closing the balloon. After setting values for the heading and text in the balloon, the procedure assigns text to each text box. The return value from the *Show* method in this case indicates which button the user clicked.

```
Sub SetCheckCount()

BalloonHeadTextCheck 5

End Sub


Sub BalloonHeadTextCheck(CheckCount As Integer)
Dim b1 As balloon
Dim int1 As Integer
Dim strChecks As String
Dim iChecks As Integer

'Set reference to the balloon
Set b1 = Assistant.NewBalloon

'Assign text to check box controls
With b1
    .Button = msoButtonSetOkCancel
    .Heading = "Here's the Heading"
    .Text = "This is some text in the balloon."
    For int1 = 1 To CheckCount
        .Checkboxes(int1).Text = "Check box # " & int1
    Next
    int1 = .Show
End With

'Did user click Cancel button?
```

```
If int1 = msoBalloonButtonCancel Then
    MsgBox "You cancelled the balloon.", vbInformation, _
        "Programming Microsoft Access Version 2002"
    Exit Sub
End If

'Record individual boxes checked and count of
'all checked boxes
For int1 = 1 To CheckCount
    If b1.Checkboxes(int1).Checked = True Then
        If strCheck = "" Then
            strCheck = CStr(int1)
        Else
            strCheck = strCheck & ", " & CStr(int1)
        End If
        iChecks = iChecks + 1
    End If
Next int1

'Present a message box with the results
If iChecks = 0 Then
    MsgBox "No boxes checked.", vbInformation, _
        "Programming Microsoft Access 2000"
ElseIf iChecks = 1 Then
    MsgBox "You checked box " & strCheck & ".", _
        vbInformation, "Programming Microsoft Access Version 2002"
Else
    MsgBox "You checked " & iChecks & " boxes.  " & _
        "These were boxes: " & strCheck & ".", _
        vbInformation, "Programming Microsoft Access Version 2002"
End If

End Sub
```

The remainder of the *BalloonHeadTextCheck* procedure processes the re-ply to the balloon. First the procedure checks the return value from the *Show* method. If this value equals the *msoBalloonButtonCancel* constant, it means the user clicked the Cancel button. After displaying a message announcing this, the procedure simply exits.

Because the only way to close the balloon is by clicking OK or Cancel, we can assume the user clicked OK if he or she did not click Cancel. The next block of code performs two tasks: it develops a text string indicating boxes with a check, and then it counts the number of boxes with checks. The last block of code in the procedure uses the string and count to prepare a message box statement that no boxes were checked, only one box was checked, or several boxes were checked.

Programming Modeless Balloons

The next sample processes modeless balloons, which stay open while the user performs a task in another part of the application. All the samples we've examined in this section so far have dealt with modal balloons. One feature tailored for working with modeless balloons is the *Callback* property. You set this property to the name of another procedure that will use the response to the balloon. The *Callback* procedure for a modeless balloon must contain three parameters in a set sequence. The first parameter includes a variable that represents the balloon reference. The second one includes a variable to pass along the control a user clicked. The third one uses a long variable that identifies the *Private* property of the balloon invoking the callback procedure. It's especially important with a modeless balloon that you designate a control for closing it. If you do not offer the user such a control, the balloon might stay open indefinitely.

The following procedure presents a balloon with four labels. Notice that the balloon's *Mode* property is *msoModeModeless*. This setting requires a *Callback* property setting. Without one, the procedure will generate an error. Notice that one of the labels explicitly denotes a close option. You can also represent a close option using a *Button* property setting. Clicking a label does not automatically close the balloon; it invokes the *Callback* procedure named *answerHelp*. This procedure appears in Figure 10-10.

```
Sub ModalCallbackDemo()
Dim b1 As balloon

Set b1 = Assistant.NewBalloon

With b1
    .Heading = "Balloon to Call for Help with a Process"
    .Text = "Give me more info about:"
    .Labels(1).Text = "Printing"
    .Labels(2).Text = "Saving as mail"
    .Labels(3).Text = "Saving to disk"
    .Labels(4).Text = "Close"
    .Button = msoButtonSetNone
    .Mode = msoModeModeless
    .Callback = "answerHelp"
    .Show
End With

End Sub


Sub AnswerHelp(b1 As balloon, ibtn As Long, iPriv As Long)
```

```
Select Case ibtn
    Case 1
        MsgBox "This is the Help screen on printing."
    Case 2
        MsgBox "This is the Help screen on mail."
    Case 3
        MsgBox "This is the Help screen on saving to disk."
    Case 4
        b1.Close
    Case Else
        MsgBox "To catch creative user input."
End Select

End Sub
```

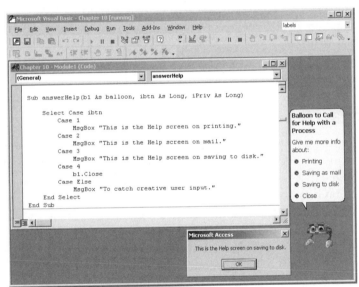

Figure 10-10 A modeless balloon and its callback routine.

The *AnswerHelp* procedure presents a message box whose content is determined by the label that was clicked in the balloon. The *Select Case* statement that processes the reply reads the label clicked from the second parameter passed to the callback procedure. After the user closes the message box, the balloon remains open. Generally, users can navigate around a form while a modeless balloon presents help on how to respond to a field on the form. If the user clicks the fourth button, the procedure uses the reference to the balloon, *b1*, to invoke the *Close* method.

The *CommandBar* Object

The *CommandBar* object model (shown in Figure 10-11) is very rich—it includes both built-in and custom command bars. Command bar is a generic term that refers to a menu bar, a toolbar, or a popup menu bar. CommandBar controls enable users to interface with command bars and interact with an application. The three broad classes of CommandBar controls are the *CommandBarButton*, *CommandBarComboBox*, and *CommandBarPopup* objects.

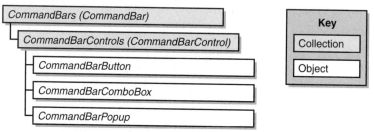

Figure 10-11 You use the *CommandBar* object model to customize built-in command bars and create custom command bars.

Enumerating Command Bar Elements

Enumerating command bar elements is critical to working with command bars. Enumeration is a vehicle for learning the hierarchy of the *CommandBar* object. The knowledge that you gain through the following samples will help you when you modify built-in command bars and develop custom ones.

The following short procedure gives a count of command bars in an application. If no custom command bars exist, the procedure reports a count of the built-in command bars, 173. The number would be higher if an application had custom command bars. There were only 140 command bars in Access 2000; obviously Access 2002 has enjoyed a substantial upgrade. Many of the new *CommandBars* in Access 2002 target pivot tables and pivot charts.

```
Sub CountCommandBars()

MsgBox "There are " & CommandBars.Count & _
    " bars in the CommandBars collection."

End Sub
```

> **Note**   Access 2002 solutions that draw on the newly added command
> bars will obviously not be compatible with those from Access 2000, de-
> spite the fact that the default file format is the same in both versions. Note
> also that the *CommandBars* object model is a part of the Office Object
> Library. This library was revised between Access 2000 and Access 2002.
> Therefore, to use programmatically specified custom command bars or
> customized versions of built-in command bars, plan to move all users to
> a single version of Access—preferably Access 2002 because it has en-
> hanced functionality.

There are three types of command bars. The Office Object Library includes the
msoBarType constants to reference these as *msoBarTypeNormal*, *msoBarType-
MenuBar*, and *msoBarTypePopup*. You can also distinguish between built-in and
custom command bars. The following procedure gives the count by type of command bar for each built-in toolbar. For a complete installation without any custom
command bars, the count is 1 menu bar, 49 toolbars, and 123 popup bars.

```
Sub BuiltinCommandBarCount()
Dim cbr1 As CommandBar
Dim iMbars As Integer
Dim iTbars As Integer
Dim iPbars As Integer
Dim iBuiltin As Integer

For Each cbr1 In CommandBars
    If cbr1.BuiltIn Then
        iBuiltin = iBuiltin + 1
        If cbr1.Type = msoBarTypeMenuBar Then
            iMbars = iMbars + 1
        ElseIf cbr1.Type = msoBarTypeNormal Then
            iTbars = iTbars + 1
        Else
            iPbars = iPbars + 1
        End If
    End If
Next
MsgBox "There are " & iBuiltin & " command bars. " & _
    iMbars & " is a menu bar, " & iTbars & " are toolbars, and " & _
    iPbars & " are popup bars."

End Sub
```

Listing Visible Command Bars

There are 173 built-in command bars—you probably won't want to enumerate all of them very often. However, subsets of them can be important to an application. For example, your application might want to know which command bars are visible. The following *enumerateVisibleCommandBars* procedure writes a line to the Immediate window for each visible command bar. The lines display three properties for each command bar—the command bar name, type, and count of controls. A pair of nested *Immediate If* functions decode the *Type* property. Rather than enumerate the controls on command bars to develop a count, the procedure simply reports the command bar's *Count* property.

```
Sub EnumerateVisibleCommandBars()
Dim cbr1 As CommandBar

For Each cbr1 In CommandBars
    If cbr1.Visible = True Then
        Debug.Print cbr1.Name, _
            (IIf(cbr1.Type = msoBarTypeNormal, _
            "toolbar", _
            IIf(cbr1.Type = msoBarTypeMenuBar, _
            "menu bar", "popup bar"))), _
            cbr1.Controls.Count
    End If
Next cbr1

End Sub
```

It's relatively easy to extend the previous code to enumerate the individual controls on each visible command bar. Command bars have a *Controls* collection, and the elements of this collection are *CommandBarControl* objects. The following procedure applies a *CommandBar* object and a *CommandBarControl* object while listing the captions for the controls on all visible command bars:

```
Sub EnumerateControlCaptions()
Dim cbr1 As CommandBar
Dim ctl1 As CommandBarControl

For Each cbr1 In CommandBars
    If cbr1.Visible = True Then
        Debug.Print "Command bar name: " & cbr1.Name & _
            " and control count: "; cbr1.Controls.Count
            For Each ctl1 In cbr1.Controls
                Debug.Print cbr1.Name, ctl1.Caption
            Next ctl1
    End If
Next cbr1

End Sub
```

Listing Menu Commands

Finally, you might need to list the individual commands on a menu. This involves treating the menu as a command bar so that the commands expose themselves as controls. You can determine the name for a command bar representing a menu using the *EnumerateControlCaptions* procedure (or a variation of it). Ignore the ampersands (&) in a caption when specifying the command bar's name for a menu. The following pair of procedures loop through the controls on a menu. The first procedure passes a command bar name to the second procedure, which loops through the controls for that command bar. Note that the command bar's name is Help, although its caption is *&Help*.

```
Sub ListCommands()

EnumerateCommandsOnMenu ("Help")

End Sub


Sub EnumerateCommandsOnMenu(menuName)
Dim cbr1 As CommandBar
Dim ctl1 As CommandBarControl

'Set a reference to a command bar
Set cbr1 = CommandBars(menuName)

'Loop through the controls for that command bar
For Each ctl1 In cbr1.Controls
    Debug.Print ctl1.Caption
Next ctl1

End Sub
```

Disabling and Reenabling Command Bars and Their Controls

You can disable and restore entire command bars. The following two procedures disable the built-in menu bar (called Menu Bar) and then reenable it. To make this command bar inoperable on a form, you simply set its *Enable* property to False within a form event procedure. Your applications can condition the disabling of a command bar on various factors, such as a user ID.

```
Sub DisableMenuBar()
Dim cbr1 As CommandBar
```

(continued)

```
For Each cbr1 In CommandBars
    If cbr1.Name = "Menu Bar" Then
        cbr1.Enabled = False
    End If
Next cbr1

End Sub


Sub EnableMenuBar()
Dim cbr1 As CommandBar

For Each cbr1 In CommandBars
    If cbr1.Name = "Menu Bar" Then
        cbr1.Enabled = True
    End If
Next cbr1

End Sub
```

You can also disable individual commands on a menu bar or toolbar. The first procedure in the following pair disables the View command on the Menu Bar menu bar and the Form View toolbar. This helps to secure a form's design by removing two familiar routes for switching from Form view to Design view. In addition to disabling the View control, the first procedure protects the change by setting the command bar's *Protection* property to *msoBarNoCustomize*. This setting grays the Reset button in the Customize dialog box for the Menu Bar and Form View command bars. The second procedure reenables the commands on both command bars and clears protection by setting the command bar *Protection* property to 0.

```
Sub DisableViewMenuAndControl()
Dim ctl1 As CommandBarControl

'Disable and protect View menu
Set ctl1 = CommandBars("Menu Bar").Controls("View")
ctl1.Enabled = False
CommandBars("Menu Bar").Protection = msoBarNoCustomize

'Disable and protect View control
Set ctl1 = CommandBars("Form View").Controls("View")
ctl1.Enabled = False
CommandBars("Form View").Protection = msoBarNoCustomize

End Sub
```

```
Sub EnableViewMenuAndControl()
Dim ctl1 As CommandBarControl

'Enable View menu
Set ctl1 = CommandBars("Menu Bar").Controls("View")
ctl1.Enabled = True
CommandBars("Menu Bar").Protection = 0

'Enable View control
Set ctl1 = CommandBars("Form View").Controls("View")
ctl1.Enabled = True
CommandBars("Form View").Protection = 0

End Sub
```

Making Invisible Command Bars Visible

Another simple but powerful manipulation you can perform is to expose a built-in menu that does not normally appear. The following procedure displays the name, type, and number of controls on each visible command bar. If the Web toolbar is not visible, the procedure resets its *Visible* property and leaves a record of it in the Immediate window by printing its name, type, and control count. You can make the Web toolbar disappear by resetting its *Visible* property to False.

```
Sub ShowWebBar()
Dim cbr1 As CommandBar

    For Each cbr1 In CommandBars
        If cbr1.Visible = True Then
            Debug.Print cbr1.Name, cbr1.Type, cbr1.Controls.Count
        ElseIf cbr1.Name = "Web" Then
            cbr1.Visible = True
            Debug.Print cbr1.Name, cbr1.Type, cbr1.Controls.Count
        End If
    Next cbr1

End Sub
```

> **Note**   The Chapter 10.mdb file on the companion CD includes a procedure named *HideWebBar*. This procedure makes the Web toolbar invisible again. With a collection of simple procedures like those discussed earlier throughout the "The *CommandBar* Object" section, you can build your own interface for managing built-in and custom command bars. This allows for tighter limits on user capabilities than the built-in toolbar management tools allow. If you want to secure changes to the *CommandBars* collection, you will almost surely enable manipulation of the toolbars through your own interface, which issues a subset of the built-in commands available from it.

Securing an Application by Programming Command Bars

Earlier in this chapter, in "The *DocumentProperty* Object and the *CurrentDB* Object," I presented an example containing a custom startup form. This approach suppresses the appearance of the Database window. However, a user can easily show the Database window by using the Unhide command on the Window menu. This next sample demonstrates the code for making the Unhide command unavailable as a menu selection and preventing a user from reversing the process.

The *NoHideUnhideToolbars* procedure that follows has two parts. First, it iterates through the controls on the Window menu of the menu bar. The procedure assigns False to the *Enabled* and *Visible* properties of controls with the captions *"&Hide"* or *"&Unhide..."*. This essentially makes the controls unavailable. If we were to stop here, the user could simply choose View-Toolbars-Customize and expose the command again through the Customize dialog box. While it's possible to lock the changes to a command bar by setting its *Protection* property, you might want to remove the ability of end users to invoke the Customize dialog box from the View-Toolbars menu or any shortcut menu. The *DisableCustomize* property of the *CommandBars* collection enables you to do this. Simply set the property to True to prevent end users from opening the Customize dialog box from any menu. By calling the *NoHideUnhide* procedure from a custom startup form, you make the Hide and Unhide commands on the Windows menu unavailable and you block end users from changing your settings. This can effectively lock users out of the Database window when you use it in combination with a custom startup technique.

```
Sub NoHideUnhide()
Dim cbr1 As CommandBar
Dim ctl1 As CommandBarControl

'Disable and make invisible Hide and Unhide
'commands on the Window menu
Set cbr1 = CommandBars("Window")
For Each ctl1 In cbr1.Controls
    If ctl1.Caption = "&Hide" Or _
        ctl1.Caption = "&Unhide..." Then
        ctl1.Enabled = False
        ctl1.Visible = False
    End If
Next ctl1

'Disable ability to open Customize dialog box
Application.CommandBars.DisableCustomize = True

End Sub
```

> **Note**   The .mdb file for this chapter includes a utility procedure for making the Hide and Unhide commands available again on the Window menu as well as for restoring the ability to open the Customize dialog box.

Adding Commands to Built-In Command Bars

Besides manipulating built-in members of the *CommandBars* collection, you can add custom commands to any built-in toolbar. One simple way to do this is to add a *CommandBarButton* object. You must know the precise name of a command bar to add a new button to it with the *Add* method. (Recall that you can run the *EnumerateControlCaptions* procedure to list the command bar names.) After adding the button, you set properties for the new *CommandBarButton* object so that it points at a custom procedure or function.

The *NewMenuItem* procedure and three related procedures shown next add new menu items. The *NewMenuItem* procedure adds *CommandBarButton* objects to the end of a Tools command bar. The three related procedures let users specify whether the Assistant appears as Clippit, Rocky, or F1. The new *CommandBarButton* objects lets users invoke the procedures that control which assistant to display.

```
Sub NewMenuItem()
Dim newItem As CommandBarButton

'Set reference to new control on the Tools command bar
Set newItem = CommandBars("Tools").Controls. _
    Add(Type:=msoControlButton)
'Start new group with command to invoke showClippit
With newItem
    .BeginGroup = True
    .Caption = "Show Clippit"
    .OnAction = "showClippit"
End With

'Set reference to new control on the Tools command bar
Set newItem = CommandBars("Tools").Controls. _
    Add(Type:=msoControlButton)
'Assign command to invoke showRocky
With newItem
    .Caption = "Show Rocky"
    .OnAction = "showRocky"
End With

'Set reference to new control on the Tools command bar
Set newItem = CommandBars("Tools").Controls. _
    Add(Type:=msoControlButton)
'Assign command to invoke showRocky
With newItem
    .Caption = "Show F1"
    .OnAction = "showF1"
End With

End Sub


Sub ShowRocky()

With Assistant
    .Visible = True
    .FileName = "Rocky.acs"
    .On = True
End With

End Sub


Sub ShowClippit()

With Assistant
```

```
        .Visible = True
        .FileName = "Clippit.acs"
        .On = True
    End With

    End Sub


    Sub ShowF1()

    With Assistant
        .Visible = True
        .FileName = "F1.acs"
        .On = True
    End With

    End Sub
```

You use the *Add* method for the *Controls* collection of a command bar to insert a new control on a built-in menu. This method takes several arguments, including a *Type* parameter. In addition to the button control (*msoControlButton*) in the sample, you can specify a simple text box (*msoConrolEdit*), a combo box (*msoControlComboBox*), and more. By default, the *Add* method inserts your new control at the end of a command bar, but you can override this feature so that the control appears elsewhere on the command bar. Another parameter, *ID*, facilitates the addition of built-in commands from other menus to your custom command bar.

After adding a control to a built-in command bar, you can tie it to a custom function using the *OnAction* property. You set the property's value equal to the name of a procedure you want your new control to invoke. The control's *Caption* property offers an easy way to label the new control. You can use the *CopyFace* and *PasteFace* methods to mark your custom controls. When the *BeginGroup* property is set to True, a control appears on a command bar with a divider line before it. The sample sets this property to True for the first of the three custom controls, but it leaves it at the default value of False for the remaining two controls.

As you refine custom applications, you'll sometimes want to remove custom controls on built-in menus. You can do this using the *Reset* method. The following procedure clears any custom controls on the Tools command bar:

```
Sub removeMenuItem()

CommandBars("Tools").Reset

End Sub
```

Creating Custom Command Bars

Creating a custom command bar involves at least three steps:

1. Adding a new command bar to your application. It will be blank when your code initially inserts it.

2. Positioning controls on the command bar. This is similar to placing controls on a built-in command bar.

3. Setting the *Visible* property of the command bar to True when you want to show it. You can also let users expose your custom command bar using standard features (such as the Customize dialog box).

The following two procedures add a custom command bar with a single button control to make Rocky appear. The *NewCommandBarAndButton* procedure passes off the first two steps of creating command bars to the procedure *AddShowAssistantsAndRocky*. Placing these steps in a separate procedure has advantages for a subsequent sample. The *AddShowAssistantsAndRocky* procedure names the new custom command bar Show Assistants. Next the procedure adds a custom control. When you specify controls for custom command bars, you must assign a value to the *Style* property as well as to the other properties that you set with built-in command bars. Failing to do so in the procedure *AddShowAssistantsAndRocky* can cause the button on the command bar to appear blank.

```
Sub NewCommandBarAndButton()
On Error GoTo CBarBtnTrap
Dim cbr1 As CommandBar
Dim cbr1btn1 As CommandBarButton
Dim cbr1Name As String

'Add command bar to show Rocky
AddShowAssistantsAndRocky

'Make command bar visible
Set cbr1 = CommandBars("Show Assistants")
cbr1.Visible = True

CBarBtnExit:
Exit Sub

CBarBtnTrap:
Debug.Print Err.Number; Err.Description
Resume CBarBtnExit

End Sub
```

```
Sub AddShowAssistantsAndRocky()
Dim cbr1 As CommandBar
Dim cbr1btn1 As CommandBarButton

'Add a command bar named Show Assistants
Set cbr1 = CommandBars.Add("Show Assistants", _
    msoBarTop, , True)

'Add a button control to the command bar
Set cbr1btn1 = cbr1.Controls _
    .Add(msoControlButton, , , , True)
'Set button properties
With cbr1btn1
    .Caption = "Show Rocky"
    .BeginGroup = True
    .OnAction = "showRocky"
    .Style = msoButtonCaption
End With

End Sub
```

After the *NewCommandBarAndButton* procedure regains control, it sets the control's *Visible* property to True. Without this step, the only way a user can view the new custom command bar is by explicitly showing it (for instance, by right-clicking a command bar and selecting the name of the command bar you want to show). The error-trapping logic in the *NewCommandBarAndButton* procedure allows the application to invoke the procedure even when the command bar is already present. Without the error-trapping logic, the *addShowAssistantsAndRocky* procedure generates a fatal error when it tries to add a command bar that already exists. Because this error is not critical—after all, the command bar is there already—it's reasonable to ignore it.

Modifying Custom Command Bars

The following three procedures add new controls to an existing custom command bar. They also reveal another approach to handling the problem of an existing command bar. The *AddCbrBtns* procedure inserts another pair of buttons on the Show Assistants command bar created in the previous sample. If that command bar does not already exist, this procedure is smart enough to run the *AddShowAssistantsAndRocky* procedure. *AddCbrBtns* conditionally calls the procedure that creates the Show Assistants command bar based on the return value of the *DoesCbrExist* function procedure. This function procedure checks for the existence of a command bar. Whether or not the Show Assistants command bar exists, the initial *If...Then...Else* statement sets a reference to it. The rest of the procedure adds two more buttons to the command bar. *AddCbrBtns* closes by making the command bar visible if it isn't already.

```
Sub MoreButtons()

AddCbrBtns "Show Assistants"

End Sub


Sub AddCbrBtns(cbrName As String)
Dim cbr1 As CommandBar
Dim cbr1btn1 As CommandBarButton

'Optionally create Show Assistants command bar.
'Reference it with a variable.
If Not doesCbrExist(cbrName) Then
    AddShowAssistantsAndRocky
    Set cbr1 = CommandBars(cbrName)
Else
    Set cbr1 = CommandBars(cbrName)
End If

'Add a new button to Show Assistants command bar
Set cbr1btn1 = cbr1.Controls _
    .Add(msoControlButton, , , , True)
'Set properties for button to show Clippit
With cbr1btn1
    .Caption = "Show Clippit"
    .OnAction = "showClippit"
    .Style = msoButtonCaption
End With

'Add a new button to Show Assistants command bar
Set cbr1btn1 = cbr1.Controls _
    .Add(msoControlButton, , , , True)
'Set properties for button to show F1
With cbr1btn1
    .Caption = "Show F1"
    .OnAction = "showF1"
    .Style = msoButtonCaption
End With

'Make the Show Assistants command bar visible
If Not cbr1.Visible = True Then cbr1.Visible = True

End Sub

Function doesCbrExist(cbrName As String) As Boolean
```

```
Dim cbr1 As CommandBar

doesCbrExist = False
For Each cbr1 In CommandBars
    If cbr1.Name = cbrName Then
        doesCbrExist = True
    End If
Next cbr1

End Function
```

Creating Popup Command Bars

The first sample procedure that follows enables a combo box control on a custom command bar and makes the command bar a popup menu bar. Figure 10-12 shows the behavior of the popup menu bar on a form. You click anywhere on the form to bring up a custom command bar with a single control. This control is a combo box with entries for selecting the Clippit, Rocky, or F1 assistant. The process starts with a click event for the form's Detail section. The next three procedures code the sample depicted in Figure 10-12.

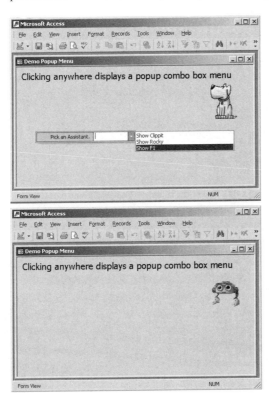

Figure 10-12 A custom popup menu bar with a combo box control. You click anywhere on the form to open the custom menu bar.

```
'From module behind form with popup toolbar
Private Sub Detail_Click()

ShowAndProcessComboBox

End Sub

'From standard module in Access database file
'with form containing popup toolbar
Sub ShowAndProcessComboBox()
Dim cbr1 As CommandBar

'Call from click event in form

    If doesCbrExist("Custom1") Then
        CommandBars("Custom1").ShowPopup
    Else
        CreateAndShowPopUpMenu
    End If

End Sub

Sub CreateAndShowPopUpMenu()
Dim cbr1 As CommandBar

'Add command bar named Custom1
    Set cbr1 = CommandBars _
        .Add(Name:="Custom1", Position:=msoBarPopup, Temporary:=True)

    With cbr1
        .Controls.Add Type:=msoControlComboBox
        With .Controls(1)
            .Style = msoComboLabel
            .Caption = "Pick an Assistant."
            .AddItem "Show Clippit"
            .AddItem "Show Rocky"
            .AddItem "Show F1"
            .OnAction = "processComboBoxChoice"
        End With
    End With

    cbr1.ShowPopup

End Sub
```

```
Sub ProcessComboBoxChoice()

'Decode selected item and implement corresponding method
    Select Case _
        CommandBars("custom1").Controls(1).ListIndex
        Case 1
            ShowClippit
        Case 2
            ShowRocky
        Case 3
            ShowF1
    End Select

End Sub
```

The first procedure is the event procedure behind the form. It calls *ShowAndProcessComboBox*, a procedure that resides in a standard module. This procedure determines whether the Custom1 command bar already exists. If the command bar exists, the procedure invokes the *ShowPopup* method to display the command bar as a popup menu bar. Otherwise, it creates the Custom1 command bar with a call to *CreateAndShowPopUpMenu*. As the name of this third procedure implies, it creates the custom command bar just before displaying it as a popup menu bar.

The *CreateAndShowPopUpMenu* procedure is compact, but it uses interesting techniques. First, it uses nested *With...End With* statements. The outer statement adds a new member to the *CommandBars* collection, and the inner one adds a control to that member. The property assignments within the inner *With...End With* statement specify a combo box style for the control, define the elements in the combo box list, and denote a procedure, *ProcessComboBoxChoice*, that fires after a selection from the combo box. This final procedure uses a *Select Case* statement based on the selected element from the combo box list to invoke one of three custom procedures that display an assistant.

Deleting Custom Command Bars

If you build custom command bars, you'll eventually need to remove one or more of them within an application. The following sample does this by looping through all the command bars to find the custom ones—those with a *BuiltIn* property of False. When the procedure finds a custom command bar, it asks the user whether it should delete the command bar. If the user replies Yes, the procedure deletes that command bar and adds one to the count of deleted command bars. In any event, the procedure increments a variable that tallies custom command bars.

```
Sub DeleteCustomCbr()
Dim cbr1 As CommandBar, delFlag As Boolean
Dim delBars As Integer, cusBars As Integer
```

(continued)

```
          'Not necessay to initialize delFlag, delBars, or
          'cusBars because their default values (False and 0)
          'are OK

          'Conditionally delete custom menu bars
              For Each cbr1 In CommandBars
                  If (cbr1.BuiltIn = False) Then
                      If MsgBox("Are you sure that you want to " & _
                          "delete the " & cbr1.Name & " command bar?", _
                          vbYesNo, _
                          "Programming Microsoft Access Version 2002") = _
                              vbYes Then
                              cbr1.Delete
                              delFlag = True
                              delBars = delBars + 1
                      End If
                      cusBars = cusBars + 1
                  End If
              Next cbr1

          'Report outcome of command bar enumeration
              If Not delFlag Then
                  If cusBars > 0 Then
                      MsgBox "No custom command bars deleted " & _
                          "out of a total of " & cusBars & ".", _
                          vbInformation, _
                          "Programming Microsoft Access Version 2002"
                  Else
                      MsgBox "No custom command bars.", vbInformation, _
                          "Programming Microsoft Access Version 2002"
                  End If
              Else
                  MsgBox delBars & " custom command bar(s) deleted.", _
                      vbInformation, _
                      "Programming Microsoft Access Version 2002"
              End If

End Sub
```

The *DeleteCustomCbr* procedure closes by presenting one of three possible statements based on the number of deletions and the number of custom command bars. A pair of nested *If...Then...Else* statements handles the routing to the correct message box statement. If there are no deletions but at least one custom command bar, the statement displays a message reporting that no custom command bars were deleted and showing the total number of custom command bars. If there are no deletions and no custom command bars, the procedure presents a message to that effect. Finally, if the procedure deleted any command bars, the message box reports that number.

11

Integrating Access with Other Office Applications

Microsoft Access initially gained immense popularity as a component of the Microsoft Office suite. The Access user interface shares many elements with the user interfaces of the other Office applications, and it's relatively easy to transfer data between Access and the rest of Office. In addition, you can integrate Access with the other Office components in custom applications, allowing you to provide the strengths of a database package in the familiar and friendly environment of word processors and spreadsheets.

This chapter explains how to programmatically integrate Access 2002 with the other Office applications using built-in Access features. For instance, your applications can tap installable indexed sequential access method (ISAM) drivers through the *Connection* object to work with the data in a Microsoft Excel spreadsheet. A *Connection* object based on an ISAM driver can serve as a two-way data-sharing channel between Access and Excel. An ISAM driver also enables Access developers to build solutions that retrieve data from Microsoft Outlook.

Furthermore, you can tap Access data sources programmatically with the Microsoft Word mail merge capability to facilitate creation of mailing labels, form letters, and product catalogs. Developers familiar with programming conventions for Word's rich formatting options can employ Word as a reporting vehicle for data otherwise managed by Access.

Using Automation, your applications can simultaneously exploit the object models from two or more Office applications. For example, an application can export names and addresses from an Access data store to an Outlook Contacts folder. Similarly, you can populate values to tables in a Word document from an Access data source.

The samples in this chapter focus on Access, Outlook, and Word, but the general principles extend to other Office applications as well as third-party packages that expose their object models through Automation and that enable manipulation using Microsoft Visual Basic for Applications (VBA).

Linking Access to Other Office Applications

This section introduces three techniques for making Access work with other Office applications: using installable ISAM drivers, employing the *OpenDataSource* method of the *MailMerge* object, and Automation. Subsequent sections will apply these techniques in practical contexts.

Installable ISAM Drivers

You use the familiar Microsoft ActiveX Data Objects (ADO) *Connection* object to link to other data sources through installable ISAM drivers. These data sources can include non-Jet, non-ODBC data sources such as Excel, dBASE, and Paradox. This section will demonstrate how Access developers can use the Excel ISAM driver for linking to Excel workbooks and the Outlook ISAM driver for linking to Outlook folders. Similar techniques apply to ISAM drivers for dBASE, Paradox, Lotus 1-2-3, text, and HTML files, but each driver has its unique features and restrictions.

> **Note**   Installable ISAM support continues to change with user requirements and technology developments. ISAM support for Microsoft FoxPro databases was discontinued with Access 2000 in favor of the Microsoft ODBC FoxPro driver. The traditional ISAM drivers still provide import/export/read access for dBASE and Paradox data in version 5 and earlier. If you need read/write access to these versions of dBASE and Paradox files, you must independently acquire the Borland Database Engine through Inprise or install Jet 4.0 SP5 separately (because Access 2002 ships with Jet 4.0 SP3). See Microsoft Knowledge Base article Q230125 for additional details.

Using ISAM Drivers with Excel

When you use an ISAM driver, your connection string has three arguments, each of which must terminate with a semicolon. First you designate a provider. When you use an installable ISAM driver, start your connection string with a reference to the Jet 4.0 provider. Follow this reference with a specification that points at the file for the data source. In the case of Excel, this specification includes the drive, path, and filename. In certain other cases, you can designate just the drive and the path. You designate this final parameter by setting the extended properties parameter equal to the name of the ISAM driver. There are specific drivers for different versions of Excel and for the other types of data sources you can link to. You reference an Excel 2000 workbook using the string *"Excel 8.0"* followed by a semicolon.

The following simple sample uses an ISAM driver to link to an Excel 2002 workbook in an Access 2002 application. The *Dim* statement declares and creates a new *Connection* object. The next statement opens the connection by pointing it at an Excel workbook through the Excel 8.0 ISAM driver. After creating the connection to the data source, your application must specify a range of cells in the workbook. This sample assigns the customers range within the file to a recordset named *rst1*. Access uses this link to work with the data in the workbook. The sample concludes by printing the first two columns of the first row from the range in the Excel workbook to the Immediate window in Access.

```
Sub Connect2XLPrintFromFirst()
Dim cnn1 As New ADODB.Connection, rst1 As ADODB.Recordset

'Make connection to Excel source
cnn1.Open "Provider=Microsoft.Jet.OLEDB.4.0;" & _
    "Data Source=C:\PMA Samples\Chapter 11\Customers.xls;" & _
    "Extended Properties=Excel 8.0;"

'Open read-only recordset based on Excel source
Set rst1 = New ADODB.Recordset
rst1.CursorType = adOpenForwardOnly
rst1.LockType = adLockReadOnly
rst1.Open "customers", cnn1, , , adCmdTable

'Print selected fields from first record
Debug.Print rst1.Fields(0).Value, rst1.Fields(1).Value

'Close connection to source
cnn1.Close

End Sub
```

When you work with an ISAM driver, the Excel data source (or even Excel itself) need not be open. Your application also doesn't require a reference to the Excel object model. Despite the Excel ISAM driver's minimal requirements, you can use it to both read and update Excel data sources.

Using ISAM Drivers with Outlook

You can use ISAM drivers to examine the contents of Outlook folders on the current machine from within Access. With this approach, you can read but not update the contents of Outlook folders through an ADO object, such as a recordset. An SQL SELECT statement can serve as the source for the *Recordset* object, and the recordset can reference the *CurrentProject* object's connection. No matter which cursor settings you assign the recordset, it will not let you update Outlook folder items.

The SQL string that serves as the source for the recordset requires three elements. First, you must designate a collection of columns to extract from the folder record source. Precede the string specifying the columns you want with the SELECT keyword. You can use an asterisk (*), but performance will be faster if you designate a specific subset of columns. Second, you must designate a folder name and a path to Outlook. Preface the folder name with the FROM keyword. For example, if you want incoming messages, reference the Inbox folder. Third, you need to specify a pathname and an Outlook ISAM driver name. A typical path is the one the Access Link Table wizard references when it links an Access table to an Outlook folder. (I'll discuss this wizard later in this chapter in "Working with Outlook from Access.") Designate the name for the top-level Outlook folder. (Unless you change the default, this will be Personal Folders.) Identify the start of the third element with the IN keyword.

The following sample prints the first record in the Contacts folder of Outlook's Personal Folders collection. Use the Outlook 9.0 ISAM driver for either Outlook 2000 or Outlook 2002. The sample extracts the First, Last, and E-mail Address fields from the Contacts folder. Although you cannot update Outlook through the Outlook ISAM driver, you can view changes (such as updated values) to the underlying recordset.

You will get the same results if you use either of the two paths that you can reference by setting your compiler constant to True or False. On the system that I am running, the D:\ folder points at a CD drive. Demonstrating this capability confirms that it doesn't matter what path you specify, so long as you designate some path.

```
Sub Connect2OutlookPrintFromFirst()
Dim rst1 As ADODB.Recordset
#Const AnyPath = False

'Instantiate recordset
Set rst1 = New ADODB.Recordset

'Open recordset on Contacts folder with either of
'two path designations
#If RootFolder = False Then
```

```
        rst1.Open "SELECT First, Last, [Email Address] " & _
            "FROM Contacts IN 'C:\Windows\Temp\;'" & _
            "[Outlook 9.0;MAPILEVEL=Personal Folders|;];", _
            CurrentProject.Connection
#Else
        rst1.Open "SELECT First, Last, [Email Address] " & _
            "FROM Contacts IN 'D:\;'" & _
            "[Outlook 9.0;MAPILEVEL=Personal Folders|;];", _
            CurrentProject.Connection
#End If

    'Print first row of Contacts folder
    Debug.Print rst1(0), rst1(1), rst1(2)

    'Clean up objects
    rst1.Close
    Set rst1 = Nothing

End Sub
```

The *OpenDataSource* Method

You can use the *OpenDataSource* method of the *MailMerge* object to link to an Access data source from within a Word application. You use Access—or more specifically, Jet—as a data store for mail merge applications that create mailing labels, form letters, product catalogs, and so on. While Access can do some of this through its *Report* object, Word is a more natural environment for composing content. It also has excellent text-formatting tools and WYSIWYG features that the Access *Report* object does not have. (For more information on the *Report* object, see Chapter 7, "Reports, Controls, and Data.") You can tap these resources with Word-based VBA procedures as well as through Automation from within Access.

> **Note**   The most appropriate development environment for database reports and mail merge documents might be a matter of developer preference. Although Word is a more natural environment for developing text documents, using Word from Access requires Automation. This means that a developer has to program two object models and that a computer needs to manage two Office applications. You might be able to achieve greater efficiency for sets of standard messages sent regularly in large volumes by building solutions entirely within Access. Refer to Chapter 7 for sample reports that illustrate the options available from Access.

When you reference an Access data source using the *OpenDataSource* method, you must first reference a Word document file and the Word *MailMerge* object. You specify two parameters for the method with Access: the *Name* parameter, which indicates the drive, path, and filename for the Access data source; and the *Connection* parameter, which designates either a Table or Query data source type and the name of the Access database object. Your Word document must have either bookmarks or mail merge fields that point to the fields in the Jet database. You invoke the *Execute* method for the *MailMerge* object to launch a merge that pulls data from a designated data source, such as an Access table, into a Word document.

You can filter values that appear in a Word mail merge document in several ways. For example, you can use the *OpenDataSource* method's *SQLStatement* parameter to specify which records to extract from a data source. When you do this with a Jet data source, you reference Access through an ODBC driver and specify *constr* as the *Connection* setting. You use SQL statement syntax to filter records from an Access table or query.

A second approach to filtering is with a special query within Access. The *OpenDataSource* method's *Connect* parameter merely references that query. You use the *FirstRecord* and *LastRecord* properties of the *DataSource* object to specify the first and last records to appear in a merged Word document. The *DataSource* object points to a target specified by the *OpenDataSource* method.

Automation

Using Automation, you can enable one application to control another. COM defines the protocol for this capability. The controlling application interacts with the controlled application by manipulating its exposed properties and methods and responding to its events. To do this, the controlling application must have a reference to the other application's object library and must create an instance of that application. (See "Automatically Referencing the Office Object Library" in Chapter 10, "Microsoft Office Objects," for information on how to create and manage references programmatically.) The controlling application invokes methods and assigns property values through that instance of the controlled application.

Figure 11-1 shows a References dialog box from an Access application with references to Excel, Outlook, and Word as well as the Office library with the shared object models. In a sense, Automation makes all the Office component object models shared. Access can expose its object model as an Automation server, and it can tap the object models of other applications by acting as an Automation client.

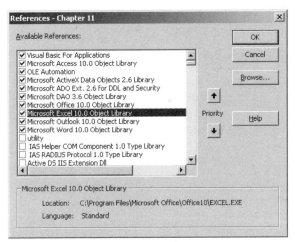

Figure 11-1 A References dialog box in Access showing references to Excel, Outlook, and Word.

CreateObject vs. GetObject

You use the *CreateObject* and *GetObject* functions to generate instances of other applications. You use *GetObject* to determine whether an instance of an application is already open. If it is, you can create a reference to it. If a user is not actively working with the instance, using an open instance might be acceptable. If the Automation server application is not already open or if you prefer not to use an open instance, you can use the *CreateObject* function to create a new instance of an application. You can also use *GetObject* to open an instance of an application with a particular file open in it.

The following two procedures create an instance of Excel from an Access application. The second procedure, *IsAppThere*, uses late binding to test for an instance of any Office application. An *objApp* variable with a generic object specification can represent any Office application (or even another COM object). The first procedure, *XLThere*, uses early binding. The *xlApp* variable can represent only an Excel *Application* object. You cannot replace *Excel.Application* in either the *CreateObject* or *GetObject* functions with another Office *Application* object, such as *Word.Application*. However, you can create another procedure altogether—for example, one named *WordThere*—that includes a variable declared as a *Word.Application* object type. This new procedure can reference the generic *IsAppThere* procedure in the same way that *XLThere* does.

```
Sub XLThere()
Dim xlApp As Excel.Application

If IsAppThere("Excel.Application") = False Then
'If not, create a new instance
    Set xlApp = CreateObject("Excel.Application")
    xlApp.Visible = True
Else
'Otherwise, reference the existing instance
    Set xlApp = GetObject(, "Excel.Application")
End If

'If user wants instance closed, close application
'and set reference to Nothing
If MsgBox("Close XL ?", vbYesNo, _
    "Programming Microsoft Access Version 2002") = vbYes Then
    xlApp.Quit
    Set xlApp = Nothing
End If

End Sub


Function IsAppThere(appName) As Boolean
On Error Resume Next
Dim objApp As Object

IsAppThere = True

Set objApp = GetObject(, appName)
If Err.Number <> 0 Then IsAppThere = False

End Function
```

Automation does not normally make an Office application visible when opening it. If you want an application to display, you must normally set its *Visible* property to True. Different applications expose different objects for you to automate. Excel causes objects such as *Application*, *Workbook*, and *Worksheet* to display. The latter two, of course, are not available with other Office applications.

Closing an Automation Reference

The *XLThere* procedure conditionally disposes of a reference to another Office application. First, you close or quit the application. (Excel supports a *Quit* method.) Then you set the reference to Nothing. Both steps are required to release the resources consumed by the Automation reference. As with many object references, *XLThere* closes the reference, but the application doesn't free the resource for the object reference until setting the reference to Nothing.

Working with Excel from Access

The first two samples in this section demonstrate some capabilities that the Excel installable ISAM can add to an application. The third sample shows a simple but powerful way to use Automation. Instead of directly manipulating detailed elements of the object model of an Automation server, the procedure launches a procedure within the Automation server. The second procedure, in turn, updates the spreadsheet file, but at the time and in the manner that an Access application determines.

Working with Values from Excel Worksheets

All three samples work with the Excel workbook depicted in Figure 11-2. The file is MyGas.xls. The first four columns of Sheet1 contain manually entered data, and the next four columns contain expressions based on the first four. The formula bar shows the expression for entries in the MPG (miles per gallon) column. The data resides in a range named gas. The Define Name dialog box shows the extent of the range in Sheet1.

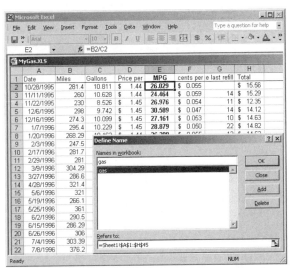

Figure 11-2 An Excel spreadsheet with a named range, gas, extending over cells A1 through H45.

The first sample reads the entries from Excel, performs some calculations in Access, and prints the results to the Immediate window. After establishing a connection to the Excel data source, your application can programmatically treat the data source just like an internal Access table. For example, you can enumerate records in the table or compute values based on the entries in the record source. The sample prints to the Immediate window the existing entries in the Excel worksheet alongside the results of expressions computed in Excel. This, incidentally, confirms that Access computations can generate results identical to those in Excel. This capability can reduce the amount of data that your application must read from a computationally intensive spreadsheet.

```
Sub OpenXLComputePrint()
Dim cnn1 As New ADODB.Connection
Dim rst1 As ADODB.Recordset
Dim computedMPG As Double
Dim computedTotal As Currency

'Make connection to Excel source
cnn1.Open "Provider=Microsoft.Jet.OLEDB.4.0;" & _
    "Data Source=C:\PMA Samples\Chapter 11\Mygas.xls;" & _
    "Extended Properties=Excel 8.0;"

'Open read-only recordset based on Excel source.
'Recall default is read-only.
Set rst1 = New ADODB.Recordset
rst1.Open "gas", cnn1, , , adCmdTable

'Enumerate records and compute with field values
Do Until rst1.EOF
computedMPG = rst1.Fields("Miles") / _
    rst1.Fields("Gallons")
computedTotal = rst1.Fields("Gallons") * _
    rst1.Fields("Price per Gallon")
Debug.Print rst1.Fields("Date"), _
    rst1.Fields("Miles"), _
    rst1.Fields("Gallons"), _
    rst1.Fields("Price per Gallon"), _
    rst1.Fields("MPG"), computedMPG, _
    rst1.Fields("days since last refill"), _
    rst1.Fields("Total"), computedTotal
rst1.MoveNext
Loop
```

```
'Clean up objects
rst1.Close
Set rst1 = Nothing
cnn1.Close
Set cnn1 = Nothing

End Sub
```

The sub procedure declares and creates a new *Connection* object, and then it opens the *Connection* object. This is critical when you work with most ISAM drivers because this is how you manage your link to the data source outside of Access. The connection string points the object at the Excel file MyGas.xls. (Figure 11-2 displays an excerpt of the data from the workbook file.) You must conclude the connection string with an Extended Properties specification that points at the ISAM driver that your application uses. The sample uses one (Excel 8.0) that works with Excel 2002, Excel 2000, and Excel 97 workbook files.

The *Recordset* reference that follows is another critical and relatively standard component of ISAM applications. By defining a recordset on the connection, your application can gain the ability to read from and write to the remote data source. The ability to update data depends on the functionality available through the ISAM driver. If your Access application links to the Excel data source, you can use the *Recordset* object's *AddNew* and *Update* methods to add new rows to a worksheet from Access. The recordset specification must also designate which portion of the workbook to link. If you reference the gas range, the recordset can use the built-in range for the worksheet. The syntax for referencing an external Excel table is identical to that for referencing an internal Access table.

> **Note**   If your application must write to or revise an Excel data source from Access, be sure to define a cursor that supports this functionality. (For example, pass the *adOpenKeyset* constant for the cursor type and the *adLockOptimistic* constant for the lock type.) Unlike Data Access Objects (DAO), the default ADO cursor does not support updating.

The next major element of the procedure is a *Do* loop that enumerates all the records in the gas range. The first two lines in the loop evaluate expressions for two computed values. The *computedMPG* and *computedTotal* variables compare Access to Excel arithmetic as they confirm your ability to manipulate data read from an Excel data source. The next seven lines within the *Do* loop print to the Immediate window Excel table field values along with the two computed variables for each row. You navigate through an Excel table exactly as you do through an internal table. Of course, you must invoke a *MoveNext* method within the loop to progress through the spreadsheet rows.

Figure 11-3 shows the five rightmost columns of the output from the preceding sample. The first two columns show identical results for MPG from Excel (the first column) and Access (the second column). The same is true for the total gas bill for each gas fill-up. This confirms that the double and currency data types from Access can duplicate results from Excel.

26.0290444917214	26.0290444917214	Null	15.557	15.557
24.4636808430561	24.4636808430561	14	15.2937	15.2937
26.9763077644851	26.9763077644851	11	12.3542	12.3542
30.5892013960172	30.5892013960172	14	14.1162	14.1162
27.1611050599069	27.1611050599069	10	14.6335	14.6335
28.8786782676703	28.8786782676703	22	14.8218	14.8218
26.3987011709141	26.3987011709141	13	14.6246	14.6246
23.0790749720254	23.0790749720254	14	13.287	13.287
26.3123482159537	26.3123482159537	14	13.0506	13.0506
26.7237280076082	26.7237280076082	12	12.8178	12.8178
30.6682120540214	30.6682120540214	9	12.2934	12.2934
25.8874537078855	25.8874537078855	18	13.6063	13.6063
30.6357830521399	30.6357830521399	32	14.6769	14.6769
30.2174526969783	30.2174526969783	8	15.2865	15.2865
25.7350096711799	25.7350096711799	13	15.1895	15.1895
34.9129593810445	34.9129593810445	6	15.0861	15.0861
32.2347980470484	32.2347980470484	8	13.1485	13.1485
28.8366236905721	28.8366236905721	13	14.3857	14.3857
31.3974964087831	31.3974964087831	11	14.122	14.122
31.8385979641096	31.8385979641096	8	13.7122	13.7122

Figure 11-3 An excerpt from the output of the *OpenXLComputePrint* procedure. Notice the identical computational results from Access and Excel.

Dynamically Creating Access Tables Based on Excel Worksheets

The preceding sample exposes the values in a spreadsheet through a recordset. If your application must regularly work with the data in a spreadsheet, you can improve performance by copying the spreadsheet values to a local table within Access. In addition, an application can reduce its demand for connection resources by copying spreadsheet values to local tables when it requires simultaneous access to several different spreadsheet ranges. The following sample programmatically creates a table that has an index for a spreadsheet range and then populates the table with values from the range. Incidentally, the sample uses the Identity data type to specify the start and step values for the table's index field (*MyID*).

```
Sub CreateTableFromXL()
On Error GoTo createTableTrap
Dim cnn1 As ADODB.Connection
Dim cnn2 As New ADODB.Connection
Dim rst1 As ADODB.Recordset
Dim rst2 As ADODB.Recordset
Dim cat1 As ADOX.Catalog
Dim tbl1 As ADOX.Table
```

```
Dim pk1 As ADOX.Index
Dim strSQL As String

'Set Connection, Catalog, and Table objects
Set cnn1 = CurrentProject.Connection
Set cat1 = New ADOX.Catalog
cat1.ActiveConnection = cnn1
Set tbl1 = New ADOX.Table

'Define table named "gas" and append it
'to the Tables collection
With tbl1
    .Name = "gas"
    .Columns.Append "Date", adDate
    .Columns.Append "Miles", adDouble
    .Columns.Append "Gallons", adDouble
    .Columns.Append "PricePerGallon", adCurrency
End With
cat1.Tables.Append tbl1

strSQL = "ALTER TABLE Gas ADD COLUMN MyID Identity(2,2)"
cnn1.Execute strSQL

Set pk1 = New ADOX.Index
With pk1
    .Name = "MyPrimaryKey"
    .PrimaryKey = True
    .Unique = True
    .IndexNulls = adIndexNullsDisallow
End With
pk1.Columns.Append "MyID"
tbl1.Indexes.Append pk1

'Make connection to Excel source
cnn2.Open "Provider=Microsoft.Jet.OLEDB.4.0;" & _
    "Data Source=C:\PMA Samples\Chapter 11\MyGas.xls;" & _
    "Extended Properties=Excel 8.0;"

'Open read-only recordset based on Excel source.
'Recall default is read-only.
Set rst1 = New ADODB.Recordset
rst1.Open "gas", cnn2, , , adCmdTable

'Open read-write recordset based on local table
'named "gas"
Set rst2 = New ADODB.Recordset
rst2.ActiveConnection = cnn1
```

(continued)

```
        rst2.CursorType = adOpenKeyset
        rst2.LockType = adLockOptimistic
        rst2.Open "gas", cnn1, , , adCmdTable

    Do Until rst1.EOF
        With rst2
            .AddNew
            .Fields("Date") = rst1.Fields("Date")
            .Fields("Miles") = rst1.Fields("Miles")
            .Fields("Gallons") = rst1.Fields("Gallons")
            .Fields("PricePerGallon") = _
                rst1.Fields("Price Per Gallon")
            .Update
        End With
        rst1.MoveNext
    Loop

createTableExit:
    Set pk1 = Nothing
    Set tbl1 = Nothing
    Set cat1 = Nothing
    rst1.Close
    rst2.Close
    Set rst1 = Nothing
    Set rst2 = Nothing
    cnn1.Close
    cnn2.Close
    Set cnn1 = Nothing
    Set cnn2 = Nothing
    Exit Sub

createTableTrap:
    If Err.Number = -2147217857 Then
    'If the gas table already exists, delete it
        cat1.Tables.Delete "gas"
        Resume
    Else
    'Else print the Err object Number
    'and Description properties
        Debug.Print Err.Number; Err.Description
    End If

End Sub
```

The previous procedure is lengthy because it performs several discrete but related functions. To create a local table with Excel spreadsheet values, the sample needs a pair of *Connection* and *Recordset* objects. These objects provide simultaneous connectivity to the spreadsheet and the local table so that the procedure can copy a row from one data source to the other. To define a local table program-matically within Access, the code declares *Catalog*, *Table*, and *Index* objects.

Before copying the data from Excel, the procedure prepares a local table to accept them. It starts by assigning the connection for the current project to the *cnn1* reference. Because *cnn1* refers to the native project connection, there is no need to include the *New* keyword in its declaration. On the other hand, the procedure does create new instances of the *Catalog* and *Table* objects (and their declarations reflect this by the inclusion of *New*). The procedure then uses ADO code to define and append fields for holding spreadsheet values. However, it reverts to SQL code for specifying the start and step values for the index. This capability depends completely on built-in Jet engine functionality. Therefore, the SQL code is specific to the Jet database engine. After completing the definition of the index and appending it to the table, the procedure opens a connection to the spreadsheet. (This sample uses the same spreadsheet as the preceding one.)

Any attempt to redefine an existing table generates error number −2147217857. The procedure deletes the old table and resumes adding the new table. In a full-scale application, you might want to archive the old table.

The procedure prepares for copying values by creating two *Recordset* objects—one for the spreadsheet and one for the local table. The code uses the default cursor for the spreadsheet because it just reads values sequentially from it, but it uses a keyset cursor type for the link to the local table so that it can add records. Because Access can exactly duplicate the computations of Excel, there is no need to copy computed fields. This keeps your table's field values independent of one another so that your table is normalized.

Running Excel Procedures from an Access Procedure

In the following procedure, *runXL*, Access uses the *GetObject* function to create an instance of the Excel *Application* object that contains the MyGas workbook shown in Figure 11-2 (on page 619). It sets the *Visible* property of the *Application* and *Window* objects to True. Then it invokes the *Application* object's *Run* method for the *ComputeOnGas* procedure in the ThisWorkbook folder of the MyGas.xls file.

You can set the security level for running Excel macros by choosing Tools-Macro-Security. Then choose High, Medium, or Low, depending on your needs and the policies of your organization. If you select the Medium security level, you will see a prompt. Choose Enable Macros to run the *ComputeOnGas* procedure. If you select the Low security level, the macros behind the worksheet will run without a prompt. Do not run the procedure with the High security level selected because that will disable the code in the unsigned module behind the worksheet.

After the *ComputeOnGas* procedure from the Excel file returns control to Access, the *runXL* procedure invokes the *Save* method for the *ActiveWorkbook* object in Excel. This commits the changes to storage and avoids a prompt asking whether to do so when the next line invokes the *Quit* method. If you want to close Excel without saving the changes and without a prompt that asks whether to save them, you set the workbook's *Saved* property to True before invoking the *Quit* method. (See the commented line for the correct syntax.) You retrieve the Automation resources by setting the Automation object reference to Nothing.

> **Note**   For your convenience when rerunning this sample, the .mdb file for this chapter includes a procedure called *RunRestoreXLSheet*. This procedure restores the MyGas.xls workbook to the state it was in prior to invoking *RunXL*.

```
Sub RunXL()
Dim myXLWrkBk As Excel.Workbook

'Open connection to XL workbook and make it visible
Set myXLWrkBk = GetObject("C:\PMA Samples\Chapter 11\MyGas.xls")
myXLWrkBk.Application.Visible = True
myXLWrkBk.Application.Windows("MyGas.xls").Visible = True

'Run procedure in ThisWorkBook folder
myXLWrkBk.Application.Run  "ThisWorkBook.computeOnGas"

'Close Automation object.
'Either invoke the Save method or set the Saved
'property to True to avoid a prompt about saving changes.
myXLWrkBk.Application.ActiveWorkbook.Save
'myXLWrkBk.Application.ActiveWorkbook.Saved = True
myXLWrkBk.Application.Quit
Set myXLWrkBk = Nothing

End Sub
```

Figure 11-4 shows the worksheet after *ComputeOnGas* runs. Notice that the worksheet computes summary information two rows below the table's last row, and it adds a new column that displays the miles traveled per day between refills. The procedure also resizes the columns so that they can contain their widest entry.

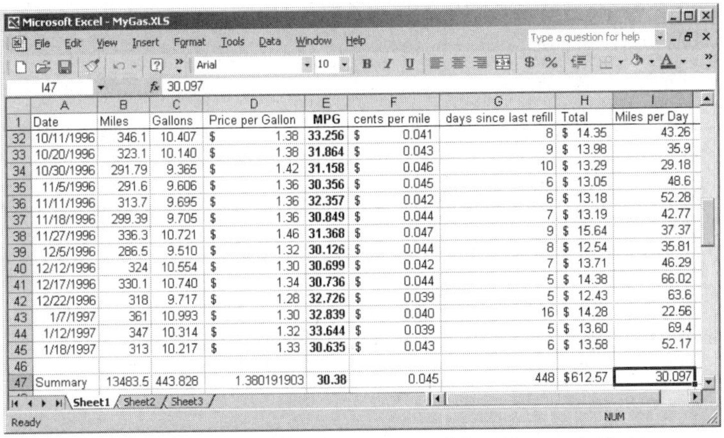

Figure 11-4 An excerpt from the output of the *ComputeOnGas* procedure. Notice the new column of data and the resized columns.

The *ComputeOnGas* procedure involves nothing more than standard VBA, but it uses objects, properties, and methods that are unique to Excel. When you perform Automation, you inevitably require some knowledge of at least one other object model—namely, the object model for the Office application that you're automating. One advantage of using the *Run* method, as in the *RunXL* procedure, is that it lets individual developers specialize in particular object models. When a developer wants to use a standard function in an unfamiliar application, he or she can copy a procedure designed by another developer. Even without detailed knowledge of an application, a developer can invoke the *Run* method for the copied procedure.

```
Sub ComputeOnGas()
Dim mySheet As Worksheet
Dim iRow As Integer, lastRow As Integer
Dim sumDays As Long

'Set reference to first worksheet
Set mySheet = Worksheets(1)
With mySheet
    lastRow = Range("gas").Rows.Count

'Assign column heading
    .Cells(1, 9) = "Miles per Day"

'Compute miles per day
    For iRow = 3 To lastRow
        .Cells(iRow, 9) = _
            Format(Range("gas").Cells(iRow, 2) / _
            Range("gas").Cells(iRow, 7), _
```

(continued)

```
                    "0.##")
            sumDays = sumDays + .Cells(iRow, 7)
        Next iRow

    'Compute summary statistics
        .Cells(Range("gas").Rows.Count + 2, 1).Select
        ActiveCell.Formula = "Summary"
    'Compute total miles
        ActiveCell.Offset(0, 1).Activate
        ActiveCell.Formula = "=Sum(b2:b" & lastRow & ")" & ""
    'Compute total gallons
        ActiveCell.Offset(0, 1).Activate
        ActiveCell.Formula = "=Sum(c2:c" & lastRow & ")" & ""
    'Compute total gas dollars
        ActiveCell.Offset(0, 5).Activate
        ActiveCell.Formula = "=Sum(h2:h" & lastRow & ")" & ""
    'Compute days since last refill
        ActiveCell.Offset(0, -1).Activate
        ActiveCell.Formula = "=Sum(g3:g" & lastRow & ")" & ""
    'Compute price per gallon and format cell like column D
        .Cells(Range("gas").Rows.Count + 2, 4).Select
        ActiveCell.Formula = "=H" & (lastRow + 2) & "/C" & (lastRow + 2)
    'Compute miles per gallon
        ActiveCell.Offset(0, 1).Activate
        ActiveCell = Format(.Cells(lastRow + 2, 2) / _
            .Cells(lastRow + 2, 3), "0.###")
        ActiveCell.Font.Bold = True
    'Compute cents per mile
        ActiveCell.Offset(0, 1).Activate
        ActiveCell = Format(.Cells(lastRow + 2, 8) / _
            .Cells(lastRow + 2, 2), "0.###")
    'Compute miles per day
        ActiveCell.Offset(0, 3).Activate
        temp = .Cells(lastRow + 2, 2)
        temp2 = sumDays
        ActiveCell = Format(.Cells(lastRow + 2, 2) / sumDays, "0.###")
End With
'Resize columns to show values
Worksheets("Sheet1").Columns("a:I").AutoFit

End Sub
```

Working with Outlook from Access

Outlook comes with a standard set of folders, including folders for its calendar, contacts, deleted items, drafts, e-mail Inbox, journal, notes, e-mail Outbox, sent e-mail, and tasks. Users can also add custom folders and can nest folders within one another. Users work with items within their folders—adding, deleting, viewing, and performing other functions.

The initial version of Outlook shipped with programmatic support only through Microsoft Visual Basic Scripting Edition (VBScript). Outlook 2000 added programmatic control with VBA. Outlook supports scripting with either VBA or VBScript. For compatibility with the rest of the book, this section focuses on scripting Outlook from Access using VBA. In addition, most of the samples use the Contacts folder to provide a familiar context.

This section starts with two samples that build on the Outlook ISAM driver sample you saw in the earlier section, "Linking Access to Other Office Applications." Using the ISAM driver offers a quick, convenient way to look at data in different Outlook folders. The two ISAM driver samples we'll examine momentarily manipulate the Inbox and Contacts folders. The sample that processes the Contacts folder demonstrates how easy it is to consolidate Outlook contents across multiple computers. However, this technique might not be obvious at first because the Outlook ISAM driver returns information for the local computer only.

You can establish an object reference to an instance of Outlook in Access with the *CreateObject* function. Before you can reference a particular folder, you typically must apply the *GetNameSpace* method to the *Application* object. The *NameSpace* object is an abstract root object that exists between the *Application* object and individual folders. The method takes a single argument, which must be *MAPI* (which stands for Mail Application Programming Interface) for the current release. You apply the *GetDefaultFolder* method to the *NameSpace* object to get the default folder of a certain type. You use a constant to designate which default folder your application will manipulate. The Contacts folder constant is *olFolderContacts*. Our Outlook Automation samples focus on the Contacts and Outbox folders as well as techniques for creating custom folders and populating them with items.

Viewing Outlook Inbox Items in an Access Form

Outlook has its own explorers for examining items in its folders. Nevertheless, you might find it useful to use an Access-based explorer for Outlook items. First of all, this is easy to do. Second, it offers an application better control over functionality and allows users to work in your application while using Outlook data. (The built-in Outlook explorers require users to exit your application while using Outlook data.) Third, when you build your own custom forms for exploring Outlook items, you can readily filter Outlook data and even merge it with data from other sources.

The form depicted in Figure 11-5 shows a custom explorer built in Access for Outlook Inbox items with *Welcome* in the Subject field. When I ran this form, my Inbox had five items, but only two of them contained *Welcome* in the Subject field. Notice the form's navigator buttons show that it's displaying the first of two records.

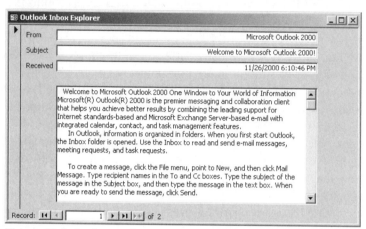

Figure 11-5 An Access form used to browse filtered Outlook Inbox items.

The form's Record Source property is Null, but the fields have Control Source settings that correspond to Inbox fields. The top three text boxes refer to the From, Subject, and Received fields, and the bottom text box with a vertical scroll bar references the Contents field. To simplify the presentation, I made these design settings manually. However, you can program them. (See Chapter 6, Forms, Controls, and Data," and Chapter 7 for more on programming controls and forms.) When the controls point at fields but the form itself does not reference a particular record source, it's easy to use a single form to explore Inbox items with different filter specifications. At the very least, you must explicitly designate a record source for the form in order for it to show any data at all. The sample code we'll examine in a moment assigns an ADO recordset to the form's *Recordset* property.

The code sets the form's recordset and opens the form. Because the code sets the form's *Recordset* property and no default setting exists, you cannot use the form to browse data without first running the code. The code sample performs two functions. First, it defines a recordset, which will become the record source for the form. Second, it opens the form and assigns the recordset to the form's *Recordset* property. The code for defining the recordset has three distinctive features. First, the recordset must have its *CursorLocation* property set to *adUseClient* if you plan to use it as input to a form. This is not necessary if you just want to print results to the Immediate window. Second, the fields after the SELECT keyword in the recordset's source statement delimit FROM with square brackets ([ ]). This is because FROM is both an SQL keyword and an Outlook Inbox item field name. To specify the field name, you need the brackets. Third, the SQL string for the recordset includes a WHERE clause. The form filters out all records that don't have *Welcome* in the Subject field through this WHERE clause. Notice that the WHERE clause appears after the IN keyword, which is an element of the FROM clause for the SQL statement.

After defining the recordset, the procedure opens the form. Next the procedure assigns the recordset to the form's *Recordset* property. In a typical application environment, the form appears automatically (for example, as you close another form). This simple demonstration resides in a standard module, so you need to click the View Microsoft Access control on the Standard toolbar of the Visual Basic Editor (VBE) to view the form.

```
'Click the View Microsoft Access control on the
'VBE Standard toolbar immediately after running this to
'see the form
Sub ShowWelcomeMessages()
Dim rst1 As ADODB.Recordset

'Instantiate recordset and open it on a subset
'of the columns and rows in the Outlook Inbox
'on the current computer
Set rst1 = New ADODB.Recordset
rst1.CursorLocation = adUseClient
rst1.Open "SELECT [From], Subject, Received, Contents " & _
    "FROM Inbox IN'C:\Windows\Temp\;'" & _
    "[Outlook 9.0;MAPILEVEL=Personal Folders|;]" & _
    "WHERE INSTR(Subject,'Welcome')>0;", _
    CurrentProject.Connection, , , adCmdText

'Open frmInboxExplorer and assign rst1 to it
DoCmd.OpenForm "frmInboxExplorer"
Set Application.Forms("frmInboxExplorer").Recordset = rst1

'Clean up objects
rst1.Close
Set rst1 = Nothing

End Sub
```

Consolidating Outlook Folders Across Different Computers

Small businesses—as well as some departments in mid-sized and large organizations—might find it convenient to consolidate the contents of their Outlook folders across multiple computers. This is likely to be the case for organizations that use Outlook in Internet Mail Only mode (as opposed to using a Microsoft Exchange Server client).

Because ISAM drivers always return results for the local computer, you cannot directly use these drivers to consolidate Outlook folder contents across multiple computers. You cannot even directly reference a query built on an ISAM driver for another computer because that query returns results for the local computer. However, you can link a table on another computer containing copied values from the return set for an ISAM driver. Linking a table of copied values enables a remote computer to consolidate Outlook items across multiple computers. The consolidating computer will always have the most recent results up to the moment when the last copy of the ISAM driver returned results to a local table.

You can easily create a table of copied values from an Outlook folder by performing two steps. First, create a linked (or imported) table based on the ISAM driver for the Outlook folder you want. Invoke the File-Get External Data command to open a wizard. Use the wizard to specify an Outlook folder. It doesn't matter whether you specify Import or Link Tables for the Get External Data command. For both options, the wizard creates a table that links to Outlook on the current computer. Changes to the folder contents update the table, but changes to the table do not update the folder contents. The second step is to run a make-table query to transfer the values from the linked table created in the first step to an Access table. If a remote computer links this second table, the linked table on the remote computer reflects the Outlook items of this second table on the local computer. Creating a linked table in a remote computer based on the table from the first step shows the Outlook items on the remote computer—not the local one.

After choosing File-Get External Data, you can select Outlook from the Files Of Type drop-down box on the Link dialog box. This launches the Link Exchange/Outlook wizard. Click the expander control (+) next to Personal Folders, and highlight the folder you want your linked table to represent. Figure 11-6 illustrates the selection of the Contacts folder. Click Next, and then click Finish to create your linked table for the folder.

> **Note** The table created with the Link Exchange/Outlook wizard is in a one-way link with Outlook. Changes in Outlook propagate to the linked table in Access. Access permits users to change values in its tables. However, these changes do not propagate to Outlook. Instead, they only cause the linked table values to become unsynchronized with the underlying Outlook folder.

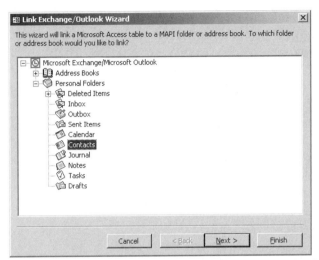

Figure 11-6 The Link Exchange/Outlook wizard with the Outlook Contacts folder selected for the linked table.

You will need to create these tables for linking in an Access database on each local computer participating in a consolidation. The computer that performs the consolidation can directly use the return set from its ISAM driver. The sample application consolidates the Outlook Contacts folders from one local computer and a remote computer, but the process can easily accommodate additional computers.

After creating a linked table in the local computer, you must copy its values to an Access table. A make-table query based on a SELECT...INTO SQL statement can accomplish this. Because the Link Exchange/Outlook wizard copies all the field values from an Outlook folder, you can use this make-table query to select just the subset of the fields necessary for your application. The procedure running the make-table query must also be able to erase a previous version of the table it attempts to create, because Access does not copy over existing tables by default.

Because the file formats and ISAM drivers are consistent from Outlook 2000 to Outlook 2002, you can run this consolidation process across computers supporting mixed versions of Outlook. I tested this application with a local computer running Outlook 2000 and a remote computer running Outlook 2002. The remote computer performed the consolidation. The database file for the local computer has the name ForRemoteContacts.mdb. The module with the procedure for creating the table uses both the ADOX and ADODB libraries in version 2.5. If you do not have that version available on your computer, revise the references so that they point to an available version.

The following procedure shows the code for executing the SELECT…INTO statement. The ADODB library reference facilitates the execution of the SELECT…INTO statement within a *Connection* object. The select list has just three items. The *Email Address* field appears in brackets because of the internal blank space in its field name. The ADOX library manages the removal of the prior version of the table from the database file.

```
Sub CopyLinkedTableToAccessTable()
Dim cnn1 As ADODB.Connection
Dim cat1 As ADOX.Catalog
On Error GoTo Table_Trap

'Run the make-table query from a Connection object
Set cnn1 = CurrentProject.Connection
cnn1.Execute ("SELECT First, Last, " & _
    "[Email Address] INTO ContactsRemote FROM Contacts;")

Table_Exit:
cnn1.Close
Set cnn1 = Nothing
Exit Sub

Table_Trap:
If Err.Number = -2147217900 Then
'Trap an existing version of the ContactsRemote table
'and remove it; then resume creating the Access table
'based on the linked table
    Set cat1 = New ADOX.Catalog
    Set cat1.ActiveConnection = CurrentProject.Connection
    cat1.Tables.Delete "ContactsRemote"
    Set cat1 = Nothing
    Resume
Else
'Code for any other errors
Debug.Print Err.Number, Err.Description
End If

End Sub
```

The remote computer uses a union query to consolidate the local computer's Outlook folder contents with its own. (See the *CreateConsolidateContactFoldersQuery* procedure that follows.) There are two inputs to the union query. The first is the linked table in the remote computer that points at the Contacts folder of Outlook.

This table is named *Contacts*. The second input to the union query is a linked table that points at the *ContactsRemote* table from the other computer. After expressing the SQL statement as the *CommandText* property of a *Command* object, the procedure uses the *Append* method of the *Views* collection to save the query. Opening this query and paging through its rows can confirm that it contains contact items from both folders, because the query assigns labels to the row for a contact item depending on its source. This union query automatically updates whenever the local Contacts folder items change or whenever the *CopyLinkedTableToAccessTable* procedure runs. Let's take a look at this procedure now:

```
Sub CreateConsolidateContactFoldersQuery()
Dim cat1 As ADOX.Catalog
Dim cmd1 As ADODB.Command
Dim vew1 As ADOX.View

'Create a Catalog object that points at the
'current project's connection
Set cat1 = New ADOX.Catalog
cat1.ActiveConnection = CurrentProject.Connection

'Make the Command settings for the union query
Set cmd1 = New ADODB.Command
cmd1.CommandText = "SELECT First, Last, [Email Address], " & _
    "'Contacts' AS FolderName " & _
    "FROM Contacts " & _
    "UNION " & _
    "SELECT First, Last, [Email Address], " & _
    "'ContactsRemote' AS FolderName " & _
    "FROM ContactsRemote"

'Add the union query to the Queries collection
cat1.Views.Append "ConsolidateContactFolders", cmd1

End Sub
```

Enumerating Items in the Contacts Folder

The following procedure uses Automation to manipulate the Outlook Contacts folder to enumerate all its items. You can set up a sample Contacts folder with a few entries to evaluate this and subsequent samples. The book's companion CD also includes some sample contact information for populating a Contacts folder.

> **Note**   Several Outlook Automation samples in this chapter directly manipulate the contents of your contact items in Outlook. Because such manipulation might be the result of a virus attack, Outlook prompts you through a popup dialog box when a user attempts to manipulate a contact item. The prompt lets you designate a use for a single item or for several intervals, each up to 10 minutes long. I'll discuss Outlook security features and their implications for VBA applications more comprehensively later in this section.

```
Sub ListContacts()
Dim myOlApp As Outlook.Application
Dim myNameSpace As NameSpace
Dim myContacts As Items
Dim myItem As ContactItem

'Create an instance of Outlook.
'Reference its MAPI NameSpace.
'Reference MAPI's Contact folder.
Set myOlApp = CreateObject("Outlook.Application")
Set myNameSpace = myOlApp.GetNamespace("MAPI")
Set myContacts = _
    myNameSpace.GetDefaultFolder(olFolderContacts).Items

'Enumerate items in Contact folder and
'print selected fields
For Each myItem In myContacts
    Debug.Print myItem.FirstName, myItem.LastName, _
        myItem.EmaillAddress
Next

'Clean up objects
Set myOlApp = Nothing

End Sub
```

The procedure starts by declaring four variables: one for the Outlook application, one for its *NameSpace* object, one for the collection of items in the Contacts folder, and one for enumerating those items. It takes three *Set* statements to display the items in the Contacts folder. The last of these statements uses the *GetDefaultFolder* method to return the Contacts folder, and it uses the *Items* property to access the individual items. The enumeration takes place with a *For...Each* loop. The items in the Contact folder have a series of properties that identify information about contacts. The sample uses three of these properties to print the first name, last name, and first e-mail address for each entry in the Contacts folder. These property names differ from the field names for the return sets from the Outlook ISAM driver, even when both types of name refer to the same data element.

Adding an Item to the Contacts Folder

You can also build Access-based solutions that manipulate the contents of the Contacts folder. The first of the next three procedures, *AddOneContact*, inserts a new contact into the folder. It uses string constants to define the first name, last name, and e-mail address for a contact, but you can easily modify the procedure to pass these as arguments. The next two procedures, *RemoveOneEmail* and *DeleteAContact*, do just that. The *RemoveOneEmail* procedure passes an e-mail address to the *DeleteAContact* procedure, finds a contact item with a matching e-mail address, and then deletes it.

```
Sub AddOneContact()
Dim myOlApp As Outlook.Application
Dim myItem As ContactItem

'Create an instance of Outlook
Set myOlApp = CreateObject("Outlook.Application")

'Create an item for the Contacts folder.
'Populate the item with values.
'Save the item.
Set myItem = myOlApp.CreateItem(olContactItem)
With myItem
    .FirstName = "foo"
    .LastName = "bar"
    .Email1Address = "foobar@yourcompany.com"
    .Save
End With

'Clean up objects
Set myItem = Nothing
Set myOlApp = Nothing

End Sub


Sub RemoveOneEmail()

DeleteAContact ("foobar@yourcompany.com")

End Sub
```

(continued)

```
Sub DeleteAContact(strEmail)
Dim myOlApp As Outlook.Application
Dim myNameSpace As NameSpace
Dim myContacts As Items
Dim myItem As ContactItem

'Create an instance of Outlook.
'Reference its MAPI Namespace.
'Reference MAPI's Contact folder.
Set myOlApp = CreateObject("Outlook.Application")
Set myNameSpace = myOlApp.GetNamespace("MAPI")
Set myContacts = _
    myNameSpace.GetDefaultFolder(olFolderContacts).Items

'Enumerate to search for item to delete
For Each myItem In myContacts
    If myItem.Email1Address = strEmail Then
        myItem.Delete
        Exit Sub
    End If
Next

'No entry found
MsgBox "No entry found with email of " & strEmail, vbCritical, _
    "Programming Microsoft Access Version 2002"

'Clean up objects
Set myOlApp = Nothing

End Sub
```

The procedure requires just two objects—the Outlook *Application* object and a *ContactItem* object to represent an item in the Contacts folder. The procedure creates a reference to the *Application* object with the *CreateObject* function. This reference supports the *CreateItem* method, which creates an empty instance of an item for any specified folder. You designate the type of folder for the item by using a constant that you pass to the *CreateItem* method. You can choose from more than 140 properties to specify the characteristics of a contact. The sample assigns string constants for the *FirstName*, *LastName*, and *Email1Address* properties. (Yes, each contact can have more than one e-mail address.) Then the sample invokes the *Save* method to store the new entry in the Contacts folder.

Deleting an Item from the Contacts Folder

The *DeleteAContact* procedure accepts a string argument that is the value of the *Email1Address* property of the contact item to delete. The procedure enumerates members of the Contacts folder until it finds one with an *Email1Address* property that matches the passed argument. When the procedure finds a match, it removes the item by invoking the *Delete* method and exits to eliminate further searching. If the procedure enumerates the entire contents of the Contacts folder without discovering a match, control passes to a message box statement, which reports that no entries match the e-mail address passed to it.

Adding Multiple Items to the Contacts Folder

One common task performed with a database manager such as Access is adding multiple contact items to the Contacts folder. These contacts can come from any source, such as the Contacts folder on another computer, addresses entered over the Internet, or even an old Access contact file. The *AddContacts* procedure that follows uses one approach to updating an Outlook Contacts folder with the contact information in an Access table:

```
Sub AddContacts()
Dim myOlApp As Outlook.Application
Dim myItem As ContactItem
Dim rst1 As New Recordset

'Open the Contacts folder in Outlook
Set myOlApp = CreateObject("Outlook.Application")

'Open the table with the new contacts
With rst1
    .ActiveConnection = CurrentProject.Connection
    .Open "oe4pab"
End With

'Create a contact item for adding contacts and
'loop through the table records to add them to the folder
AssistantWorkingOn
Do Until rst1.EOF
    Set myItem = myOlApp.CreateItem(olContactItem)
    With myItem
        .FirstName = IIf(IsNull(rst1.Fields(0)), _
            "", rst1.Fields(0))
        .LastName = rst1.Fields(1)
        .Email1Address = rst1.Fields(2)
        .Save
```

(continued)

```
        End With
        rst1.MoveNext
Loop
AssistantIdleOn

'Clean up objects
Set myItem = Nothing
Set myOlApp = Nothing

End Sub
```

The procedure sets a reference to the Outlook application and then opens a recordset based on the *oe4pab* table. This is the local table in the Access Tables folder. The table contains just 34 entries, but the procedure can accommodate a much longer list of addresses. For this reason, the procedure calls another procedure that turns on the Assistant with a working animation and leaves it on until Access and Outlook finish updating the Outlook Contacts folder with the entries in the *oe4pab* table. (Chapter 10 describes how to design procedures to control Assistant animation.) In between the two calls to turn Assistant animation on and off, a *Do* loop iterates through all the records in the *oe4pab* table. The loop creates a new *ContactItem* object on each pass, and then it assigns the records for that pass to the item and saves the item.

Deleting Multiple Items from the Contacts Folder

The following procedure, *RemoveEmails*, is an adaptation of the *DeleteAContact* procedure shown earlier in the section. *RemoveEmails* deletes multiple records from a Contacts folder. It removes one item at a time by successively calling *DeleteAContact* with different e-mail addresses. The sample uses the addresses in the *oe4pab* table as the source for the arguments. This procedure offers two advantages: it is easy to write, and it reuses the *DeleteAContact* procedure.

```
Sub RemoveEmails()
Dim rst1 As New Recordset

'Open the table with the new contacts
    With rst1
        .ActiveConnection = CurrentProject.Connection
        .Open "oe4pab"
    End With

'Loop through the table records to move them to the folder
    AssistantWorkingOn
    Do Until rst1.EOF
        DeleteAContact (rst1.Fields(2))
        rst1.MoveNext
```

```
        Loop
        AssistantIdleOn

'Clean up objects
rst1.Close
Set rst1 = Nothing

End Sub
```

While this procedure can get the job done, it has at least two deficiencies. First, it searches through the Contacts folder for each item that it wants to remove. This gets increasingly costly as the number of items to delete grows, the number of items in the Contacts folder grows, or both. Second, if there is no match for an item, the procedure pauses with a message box that requires the user to click a button to continue. If numerous entries in the list of items to delete are already missing from the Contacts folder, having to click a button for each item not present in the folder can become tedious. One solution to these weaknesses is to replace the call to *DeleteAContact* with a call to *DeleteAContact2*, shown here:

```
Sub DeleteAContact2(strEmail)
On Error GoTo delete2Trap
Dim myOlApp As Outlook.Application
Dim myNameSpace As NameSpace
Dim myContacts As Items
Dim myItem As ContactItem
Dim strFilter As String

'Create an instance of Outlook.
'Reference its MAPI NameSpace.
'Reference MAPI's Contact folder.
    Set myOlApp = CreateObject("Outlook.Application")
    Set myNameSpace = myOlApp.GetNamespace("MAPI")
    Set myContacts = _
        myNameSpace.GetDefaultFolder(olFolderContacts).Items

'Find target item and remove it
    strFilter = "[EmailAddress] = """ & strEmail & """"
    Set myItem = myContacts.Find(strFilter)
    myItem.Delete

delete2Exit:
    Exit Sub

delete2Trap:
    If Err.Number = 91 Then
'If item is not there, keep on going
```

(continued)

```
        Resume Next
    Else
'Otherwise, pause with a message box
        MsgBox Err.Number & ": " & vbCrLf & _
            Err.Description, vbCritical, _
            "Programming Microsoft Access Version 2002"
        Resume Next
    End If

'Clean up objects
Set myOlApp = Nothing

End Sub
```

This procedure expedites the search for an item to delete by using the *Find* method. It constructs a criterion for the *Find* method based on the e-mail address passed to it. After finding an item with a matching e-mail address, the procedure applies the *Delete* method to that item. Using *Find* saves a noticeable amount of time even with a short list of items such as those in the *oe4pab* table, but its speed advantage grows with longer lists of e-mail addresses or with Contact folders that have many items. The procedure also traps failures of the *Find* method to return an item. This happens when there is no matching item in the Contacts folder for an e-mail address. In this situation, *DeleteAContact2* silently returns control to the calling routine so that it can search again for a new e-mail address. There is no need for operator intervention.

Enumerating and Creating Outlook Folders from Access

All the Outlook Automation samples shown so far in the chapter have used the default folder for an Outlook item type (for example, using the Contacts folder for a *ContactItem*). However, you can create your own custom Outlook folders within an Access application, and you can enumerate the set of folders to serve as repositories for Outlook items. Another feature of the chapter samples you've seen so far is that they work with first-level folders within the Personal Folders collection. However, Outlook permits you to nest one or more additional folders within another folder. You can accomplish this both programmatically and manually.

Before beginning a programmatic demonstration of how to manage Outlook folders from Access, you might benefit from a highly stylized overview of the Outlook object model. (See Figure 11-7.) You already know that items belong to folders. In addition, folders belong to the MAPI *NameSpace* object, and this object relates to the Outlook *Application* object. If you plan to work with folders and their items, the Outlook object model requires that you pass through the MAPI *NameSpace* object.

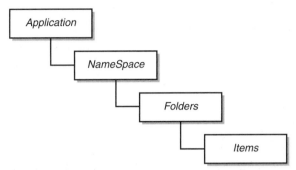

Figure 11-7 A stylized overview of the Outlook object model highlighting the dependency of folders and items on the *NameSpace* object.

The following code samples illustrate several important skills for working with Outlook folders and their items. First, it shows how to enumerate the first-level folders, the folders immediately below the top folder collection in Outlook. This is typically the Personal Folders collection. If you enumerate the first-level folders, you won't see any subfolders or item collections within them. Second, the sample depicts how to create your own custom first-level and second-level folders. The third and final achievement of the sample is to illustrate the syntax for counting first-level folders, second-level folders, and items within a folder.

The sample commences by setting an object reference, *myOlApp*, to the Outlook *Application* object. Only one instance of Outlook can exist at a time. Whenever your application needs to work with folders other than the default folders for item types, you must reference the MAPI *NameSpace* object. Use the *GetNamespace* method to return the object from the Outlook *Application* object. Once the procedure references the *NameSpace* object, it can create a pointer for the entire collection of first-level folders. With a reference to the folder collection, the sample can iterate through the collection members and print the name and item count within each folder. The sample can even remove obsolete folders. To accomplish this, use the *Delete* method for an instance of a folder.

Individual folders relate hierarchically to their parents. The next segment of the sample invokes the *Add* method for the first-level folders collection, *myFolders*. The name of the new first-level folder is PMADemo. This folder is used for holding other folders. Therefore, the procedure creates a reference to this folder before invoking the *Add* method twice for the *Folders* collection of PMADemo. The two folders created below PMADemo have the names PMAContacts (with a *DefaultItemType* property appropriate for contact items) and PMAMail (with a *DefaultItem Type* property for Inbox items).

The sample procedure concludes with the syntax for reporting counts of the items in selected folders as well as folders within folders. As you can see, the *Count* method develops the result in each case. The trick is defining the set of elements to count. The expression *myFolders.Count* returns the total number of first-level folders. This is because the *myFolders* object was initially set to the *Folders* collection of the top folder. Next the procedure shows how to count the second-level folders in the PMADemo folders collection. The final count represents the items within the first-level Contacts folder collection.

```
Sub EnumerateAndCreateFolders()
Dim myOlApp As Outlook.Application
Dim myNameSpace As Outlook.NameSpace
Dim myFolders As Outlook.Folders
Dim myFolder As Outlook.MAPIFolder

'Set reference to Outlook, NameSpace object,
'and the first-level folders collection
Set myOlApp = CreateObject("Outlook.Application")
Set myNameSpace = myOlApp.GetNamespace("MAPI")
Set myFolders = myNameSpace.Folders.Item(1).Folders

'Enumerate the first-level folders while
'printing parent name, folder name,
'and item count.
'Delete PMADemo folder if it exists.
For Each myFolder In myFolders
    Debug.Print myFolder.Parent, myFolder.Name, _
        myFolder.Items.Count
    If myFolder.Name = "PMADemo" Then
        myFolder.Delete
    End If
Next

'Create a new first-level folder and
'two second-level folders within it
myFolders.Add "PMADemo"
Set myFolder = myFolders.Item("PMADemo")
myFolder.Folders.Add "PMAContacts", olFolderContacts
myFolder.Folders.Add "PMAMail", olFolderInbox

'Print number of first-level folders in root folder,
'number of second-level folders in PMADemo,
'and number of items in the Contacts folder
Debug.Print myFolders.Count
Debug.Print myFolders.Item("PMADemo").Folders.Count
Debug.Print myFolders.Item("Contacts").Items.Count

'Clean up objects
Set myOlApp = Nothing

End Sub
```

Adding Items to a Custom Outlook Folder with Access

After creating custom folders, it's natural to explore populating them with items. For example, the PMAContacts folder can accept names and e-mail addresses along with other data elements. Data for populating Outlook folders can originate from many sources. For example, the case study in Chapter 7 shows how to create a table of addresses based on guestbook entries on a Web site. The table data consists of the names and e-mail addresses of visitors who sign the site's guestbook. The *oe4pab* table in the sample.mdb file for this chapter includes a small collection of records to demonstrate how you can transport names and e-mail addresses from an Access table to an Outlook folder.

You should feel comfortable with the techniques this sample uses. First, the following procedure sets a reference to the PMAContacts folder. This is the Outlook folder into which the sample will deposit the names and e-mail addresses. If you haven't run the previous sample to create the PMAContacts folder, do it now before proceeding with this one. Next the sample creates a *Recordset* object that points at the *oe4pab* table in the Access database file for this chapter. The table includes 35 rows with three columns of contact data. The columns represent the first name, last name, and e-mail address of each visitor who signs the guestbook. After creating separate references for an Outlook folder and a source of items to populate the folder, the procedure loops through the recordset rows to deposit them as items in the Outlook folder. The syntax adds a new contact item for each row of data in the table. After assigning the recordset values for the current row to the item fields, the procedure saves the item in the folder and advances to the next row in the table. Here's the routine:

```
Sub AddItemsToPMAContacts()
Dim myOlApp As Outlook.Application
Dim myNameSpace As Outlook.NameSpace
Dim myFolders As Outlook.Folders
Dim myFolder As Outlook.MAPIFolder
Dim myItems As Outlook.Items
Dim myContactItem As Outlook.ContactItem
Dim rst1 As New ADODB.Recordset

'Open the PMAContacts folder and show its Item collection
Set myOlApp = CreateObject("Outlook.Application")
Set myNameSpace = myOlApp.GetNamespace("MAPI")
Set myFolders = myNameSpace.Folders.Item(1).Folders
Set myFolder = myFolders.Item("PMADemo").Folders.Item("PMAContacts")
Set myItems = myFolder.Items

'Open the table with the new contacts
With rst1
    .ActiveConnection = CurrentProject.Connection
```

(continued)

```
            .Open "oe4pab"
    End With

    'Create a contact item for adding contacts and
    'loop through the table records to add them to the folder
    AssistantWorkingOn
    Do Until rst1.EOF
        Set myContactItem = myItems.Add(olContactItem)
        With myContactItem
            .FirstName = IIf(IsNull(rst1.Fields(0)), _
                "", rst1.Fields(0))
            .LastName = rst1.Fields(1)
            .EmailAddress = rst1.Fields(2)
            .Save
        End With
        rst1.MoveNext
    Loop
    AssistantIdleOn

    'Clean up objects
    rst1.Close
    Set rst1 = Nothing
    Set myOlApp = Nothing

End Sub
```

Merging Access Contacts with an Outlook Message

The Outlook mail item is the primary device for holding a message. Individual mail items have the properties *Subject*, *Body*, and *Recipients*. The *Body* property is a string representing the body of a message. If you prefer, you can designate the body of a message through its *HTMLBody* property, which represents the HTML content for a message. Mail items have numerous other properties that allow you to control the content of individual e-mail messages. Furthermore, a mail item has a variety of methods that correspond to what folks do with messages. The next sample demonstrates the invocation of the *Send* method. However, mail items include many additional methods, such as *Reply*, *ReplyAll*, *Copy*, and *Delete*.

The e-mail merge sample combines a subset of records from an Access table with a standard message for all members of the subset. An ADO recordset makes the table's contents available for inclusion in individual messages. A WHERE clause in the SQL string for the recordset allows the selection of a subset of records from a much lengthier record source. The mail item's body is a string, so you can vary its content based on the values in the Access table. For example, the sample shows how to personalize a message by addressing individuals by their first name. This name comes from the Access table. After setting a message's properties, the procedure sends the message and advances to the next row in the recordset.

```
Sub MergeEmail()
Dim myOlApp As Outlook.Application
Dim myNameSpace As Outlook.NameSpace
Dim myFolders As Outlook.Folders
Dim myFolder As Outlook.MAPIFolder
Dim myMailItem As Outlook.MailItem
Dim str1 As String
Dim rst1 As Recordset

'Set reference to Outlook, NameSpace object,
'and the first-level folders collection
Set myOlApp = CreateObject("Outlook.Application")
Set myNameSpace = myOlApp.GetNamespace("MAPI")
Set myFolders = myNameSpace.Folders.Item(1).Folders

'Set a reference to the PMAMail folder and
'select a subset from a table containing contacts
Set myFolder = _
    myFolders.Item("PMADemo").Folders.Item("PMAMail")
Set rst1 = New ADODB.Recordset
rst1.Open _
    "SELECT * FROM WebBasedList WHERE " & _
    "StateOrProvince='NY' OR " & _
    "StateOrProvince='NJ' OR " & _
    "StateOrProvince='CT'", _
    CurrentProject.Connection

'Loop through rst1 and assign the FirstName
'field to the body of the message
AssistantWorkingOn
Do Until rst1.EOF
    Set myMailItem = myFolder.Items.Add(olMailItem)
    str1 = "Dear " & rst1.Fields("FirstName")
    str1 = str1 & "," & vbCrLf & vbCrLf
    str1 = str1 & "On October 1, 2002, CAB, Inc. "
    str1 = str1 & "will be holding a seminar at the "
    str1 = str1 & "Hilton just this side of heaven.  "
    str1 = str1 & "You are cordially invited to attend "
    str1 = str1 & "the complimentary continental "
    str1 = str1 & "breakfast, with healthy servings of "
    str1 = str1 & "manna and water from 7:30 to 8:30 AM.  "
    str1 = str1 & "An enlightening multimedia "
    str1 = str1 & "presentation and demo follows "
    str1 = str1 & "from 8:30 to 11:30 AM." & vbCrLf
    str1 = str1 & vbCrLf & "Rick Dobson" & vbCrLf
```

(continued)

```
                  str1 = str1 & "President" & vbCrLf & "CAB, Inc."
                  str1 = str1 & vbCrLf & vbCrLf & "PS: Please "
                  str1 = str1 & "RSVP via a reply to this "
                  str1 = str1 & "message.  Thanks."
                  myMailItem.Body = str1
                  myMailItem.Subject = "Seminar Invitation"
                  myMailItem.Recipients.Add rst1.Fields("EmailAddress")
                  myMailItem.Send
                  rst1.MoveNext
Loop
AssistantIdleOn

'Clean up objects
rst1.Close
Set rst1 = Nothing
Set myOlApp = Nothing


End Sub
```

Outlook 2002 ships with enhanced security over the initial version of Outlook 2000. These same features are available for Outlook 2000 in a security update that was issued on June 7, 2000. (I described one aspect of these features when discussing the sample for listing items in the Contacts folder on page 636. See Microsoft Knowledge Base article Q263297 for more detail on this topic.) In the e-mail merge sample just shown, the enhanced security means that Outlook 2002 users must respond to an initial prompt to start manipulating address fields and an additional prompt for each message that Outlook places in its Outbox folder. If all the messages are not compiled during the 10-minute suspension of security (the maximum allowable suspension), the initial prompts repeats at 10-minute intervals until the mass e-mailing completes.

There are at least two workarounds to these security restrictions. First, if you're using Outlook with Exchange Server, you can update the security settings. For example, Exchange Server administrators can configure client workstations so that they do not contain the full complement of security limitations. The fix, available by downloading ADMPACK.EXE from www.microsoft.com/office/ork/ 2000/appndx/toolbox.htm#secupd, allows an Exchange Server administrator to eliminate the appearance of both security prompts.

If you're running Outlook without Exchange Server (for example, in Internet Mail Only mode), you can use an initial version of Outlook 2000 without the June 7, 2000 security update. While this update for Outlook 2000 adds the same security as is used in Outlook 2002, the initial Outlook version does not contain the security features. Therefore, you can run the sample we just discussed without getting any prompts. Of course, you will need to revise library references for

Office 2000. These revisions are likely to include a reference to a different Outlook object library (one for Outlook 2000 instead of Outlook 2002) and a different ADODB library (such as the 2.1 or 2.5 version).

> **Note**   One Outlook expert suggests another route for circumventing the features of the June 7, 2000 Outlook security update. The route still allows you to enjoy the other advanced features of Office XP. She recommends performing a custom install of Office XP without Outlook 2002 on a machine that already has Outlook 2000 installed (without the security update). If you seek selective implementation of security features and the previously mentioned remedies are not practical, this solution might merit investigation.

Working with Word from Access

The first sample in this section demonstrates how to build, design, and populate a table in Word based on data in an Access table. It uses Automation to control Word from Access, and it even includes a simple Access form for invoking the Automation procedure. The second and third samples tackle two mail merge tasks programmatically: generating mailing labels and generating a form letter.

The form letter sample in this chapter accomplishes the same thing as the form letter sample in Chapter 7. You can compare the two approaches to see which best fits your needs. In general, the philosophy behind having multiple components is that you should use each to do what it does best. The sample in this chapter enables Access to store data and Word to generate form letters for printing. If you find it easy to work with the Word object model and the *MailMerge* object, this approach might work best for you. If you prefer to concentrate on becoming expert in Access by itself, the approach in Chapter 7 might be preferable.

Automating Word from Access

The following Automation sample transfers contents from a recordset based on a table in Access to a table in Word. When you have references to multiple object models with similar terms, you should include a prefix before the object data type designation in its declaration—you should use *Word.Table* instead of *Table*, for example. This tells the VBA interpreter which kind of *Table* object you want. Recall that Access can also declare a *Table* object from the ADOX library. Also, note that the *Range* object in Word behaves differently than the one in Excel. VBA and IntelliSense let you build cross-application solutions, but they do not relieve you from learning the object models for individual applications.

```
Sub fromAccessToWordTable()
Dim myWDApp As Word.Application
Dim myRange As Word.Range, myTable As Word.Table
Dim acell As Word.Cell, emailCol As Integer
Dim rst1 As New Recordset, irow As Integer

'Open the table with the new contacts
With rst1
    .ActiveConnection = CurrentProject.Connection
    .Open "oe4pab", , adOpenKeyset, adLockOptimistic, adCmdTable
End With

'Create a Word application instance and turn on
'the Assistant's working animation
AssistantWorkingOn
Set myWDApp = CreateObject("Word.Application")

'Add a document to the application and a table to the document.
'Specify rows to equal one more than number of rows in e-mail
'address table in Access.
myWDApp.Documents.Add
Set myRange = myWDApp.ActiveDocument.Range(0, 0)
myWDApp.ActiveDocument.Tables.Add Range:=myRange, _
    NumRows:=rst1.RecordCount + 1, NumColumns:=3

'Insert column headings for table
With myWDApp.ActiveDocument.Tables(1).Rows(1)
    .Cells(1).Range.Text = rst1.Fields(0).Name
    .Cells(2).Range.Text = rst1.Fields(1).Name
    .Cells(3).Range.Text = rst1.Fields(2).Name
End With

'Insert first name, last name, and e-mail from Access table.
'Insert contact information in the second through the last row.
For irow = 2 To myWDApp.ActiveDocument.Tables(1).Rows.Count
emailCol = 0
    For Each acell In _
        myWDApp.ActiveDocument.Tables(1).Rows(irow).Cells
        acell.Range.Text = IIf(IsNull(rst1.Fields(emailCol)), _
            "", rst1.Fields(emailCol))
        emailCol = emailCol + 1
    Next acell
rst1.MoveNext
Next irow
```

```
'Format table to fit content, turn on idle animation, and
'make Word visible so that user can see table in Word
myWDApp.ActiveDocument.Tables(1).AutoFitBehavior  wdAutoFitContent
AssistantIdleOn
myWDApp.Visible = True

End Sub
```

The procedure starts by opening a *Recordset* object based on a table in Access—the familiar *oe4pab* table that you saw earlier in the Outlook samples in "Working with Outlook from Access." Because the application uses the *RecordCount* property, you should avoid using a forward-only cursor. The sample uses the *adOpenKeyset* constant for the cursor type specification. After opening the recordset, the application turns on the working animation for the Assistant and runs the *CreateObject* function to create a fresh instance of Word.

The procedure then constructs the table in Word. It adds a new document and then adds a table to the document's top left corner. The parameters of the *Add* method for the *Table* object specify that the table will have one more row than there are rows in the Access table. This allows one row of column headers plus all the data in the *oe4pab* table. Before starting to work with the recordset values, the procedure writes the column headers in the first row. These are the field names for the table in Access.

A pair of nested *For* loops navigate through the cells in the table. The outer loop progresses sequentially through the rows. The inner one marches across the columns within a row. Notice that Word has a *Cells* collection for the columns within the row of a table. The inner loop navigates to individual cells within the Word table. The reference to a cell starts with the Automation object, *myWDApp*, and then hierarchically moves to the *ActiveDocument* object, the first table on the document, and the row in the table. After identifying a cell within a row to process, an Immediate If (*IIf*) function based on the recordset values computes a value for the *Text* property of the cell.

After iterating through all of the table's cells, the procedure closes by performing three steps. First it reformats the columns' widths so that they're wide enough to display column values without wrapping. Then it assigns an idle animation to the Assistant. This essentially turns off the working animation that starts just before the Word *Application* object launches. Finally the procedure sets the *Application* object's *Visible* property to True. This changes the focus from Access to Word.

Figure 11-8 shows a form in Access that lets users start the procedure by clicking a button. The figure depicts the form just after a user clicks the button. You can see a still shot of the Assistant with its working animation. When the Assistant comes to rest, the focus shifts from the Access form to the Word document with the table created by the *fromAccessToWordTable* procedure.

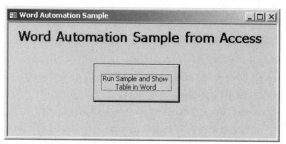

Figure 11-8 This form invokes the *fromAccessToWordTable* procedure. When the Assistant stops its working animation, the focus shifts to the table in Word.

Producing Mailing Labels

The built-in Word mail merge feature can draw on an Access database table or query as a record source for generating mailing labels. While you can programmatically lay out the mail merge fields or bookmarks to support the placement of Access data on Word documents, it's often much simpler to lay them out manually where you want data inserted on a document. In addition, you can use built-in wizards to help with the layout of controls for forms with multiple labels per page. For example, choose Tools-Letters And Mailings-Mail Merge Wizard to launch the Mail Merge wizard in Word 2002.

Figure 11-9 shows an excerpt from the mlabels.doc file. The mail merge fields were positioned with the built-in Mail Merge wizard that you can invoke from the Tools menu. After laying out the controls, you can programmatically control the printing of labels based on Access tables or queries through the *MailMerge* object.

The following Word procedure is designed to run from the ThisDocument folder of the Normal template. It starts by opening the mlabels.doc file that contains the mail merge fields depicted in Figure 11-9. Then it sets a reference, *myDoc*, to a document based on the file. The mlabels.doc file actually contains no code of its own.

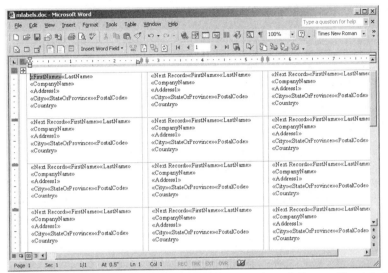

Figure 11-9 An excerpt from a Word document for printing mailing labels on Avery 5260 laser forms.

Note   To run the mailing sample and the form letter sample shown later in the section, you must update your Normal template in Word 2002 with two VBA scripts. The scripts appear on the book's companion CD. The advantage of putting VBA procedures in the Normal template is that you can run them from any document. A Readme.txt file on the book's CD provides step-by-step instructions on how to update your Normal template with sample VBA scripts for mailing labels and form letters. You will also need the mlabels.doc and formletter.doc files, which are also contained on the book's CD.

```
Sub PrintPreviewLabels()
Dim myDoc As Document

'Set reference to the document
Documents.Open FileName:="C:\PMA Samples\Chapter 11\mlabels.doc"
Set myDoc = Documents("mlabels.doc")
```

(continued)

```
'Reference the data source in Access
myDoc.MailMerge.OpenDataSource _
    Name:="C:\PMA Samples\Chapter 11\Chapter 11.mdb", _
    Connection:="TABLE WebBasedList"
'Send the labels to a new document
With myDoc.MailMerge
    .Destination = wdSendToNewDocument
    .Execute Pause:=True
End With

'Either preview or print labels
If MsgBox("Do you want to preview before printing?", _
    vbYesNo, _
    "Programming Microsoft Access Version 2002") = vbYes Then
    ActiveDocument.PrintPreview
Else
    ActiveDocument.PrintOut
End If

End Sub
```

The key to performing any mail merge with data from Access is to invoke the *OpenDataSource* method for the *MailMerge* object within a document, such as the document that the *myDoc* reference points to. You often must assign two arguments, *Name* and *Connection*. You point the *Name* argument at the Access source file containing the data for the mail merge. The *PrintPreviewLabels* procedure references Chapter 11.mdb, the file for this chapter on the companion CD. You use the *Connection* argument to designate a type of database object and its name. Your code can designate either a *Table* or a *Query*. The sample points to a table named *WebBasedList*.

You can use the Word *MailMerge* object to write over the template with the mail merge fields or create a new document with the merged data. You use the *MailMerge* object's *Destination* property to designate your choice. The sample uses the constant to create a new document for the merged data. After setting all the *MailMerge* properties that you want, you apply the *Execute* method to the *MailMerge* object. This merges the Access data into a Word document that creates your mailing labels. The sample presents a message box asking whether to print or preview the labels. After you no longer need the document with the merged fields and the one controlling the layout of the fields in a document, you can close both of them manually or with another program.

Note   A bug in the shipping version of Word 2002 prompts the user to select a table from the data source even though the code denotes one in its *Connection* parameter for the *OpenDataSource* method. This prompt appears before the message box mentioned in the preceding paragraph. For this sample, select *WebBasedList*. In general, users should choose whatever record source is appropriate for the current merge task. Look on the Office Update site (office.microsoft.com) for patches and service release updates to fix this problem and others noted in this book.

You can easily invoke a procedure such as *PrintPreviewLabels* from within Access. The next procedure does this in just three lines. This sample runs from a standard module in an Access file:

```
Sub RunMLabels()
Dim myWDApp As Word.Application

'Open connection to Word and make Word visible
Set myWDApp = CreateObject("Word.Application")
myWDApp.Application.Visible = True

'Run mailing label procedure
myWDApp.Application.Run "PrintPreviewLabels"

End Sub
```

Producing Form Letters

The procedure for producing form letters is essentially the same as the one for producing mailing labels except that the layout of mail merge fields is more straightforward. This is because you typically have just one occurrence of a record per page instead of multiple records on a page. Figure 11-10 shows the layout of a form letter in Word that is identical to the one discussed in Chapter 7. It is easy to include a mail merge field within the body of a letter. The figure shows this in its bottom panel.

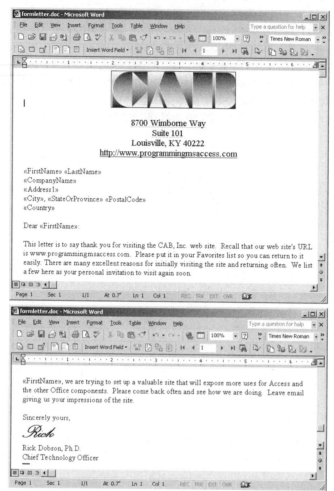

Figure 11-10 Excerpts from a Word document for printing form letters.

Do not use the full Mail Merge wizard if you plan to programmatically control the printing of labels. The code that the wizard generates has many extra parameters and is designed explicitly for use with the wizard, not necessarily with custom applications. The sample that follows and the one in the previous section are designed for use from the ThisDocument folder of the Normal template. Both are good starting points for your own custom form letter or mailing label applications. However, you should start the Mail Merge wizard to add the Mail Merge toolbar to the window of a document. Once you have the toolbar displayed, you can freely insert mail merge fields anywhere in a document. In fact, the new Mail Merge wizard that ships with Word 2002 includes tools for simplifying and speeding up the layout and formatting of address and greeting blocks within a form letter. However, you can still lay out the fields individually as the sample shows.

The following procedure works with the document depicted in Figure 11-10, which shows excerpts from the top and bottom of the formletter.doc file. The procedure opens this file. The use of the *OpenDataSource* method is the same for both a form letter and mailing labels. This sample, however, designates values for the *FirstRecord* and *LastRecord* properties of the *DataSource* object. The *OpenDataSource* method specifies parameters pointing at the data source that the *DataSource* object represents. Setting the *FirstRecord* and *LastRecord* properties establishes a range of records for which to print form letters. This sample works with the default sort order for the records in the data source.

```
Sub PrintPreviewLetters()
Dim myDoc As Document

'Load file and set a reference to it
Documents.Open FileName:="C:\PMA Samples\Chapter 11\formletter.doc"
Set myDoc = Documents("formletter.doc")

'Reference the data source in Access
myDoc.MailMerge.OpenDataSource _
    Name:="C:\PMA Samples\Chapter 11\Chapter 11.mdb", _
    Connection:="TABLE WebBasedList"

'Send the labels to a new document
With myDoc.MailMerge
    .Destination = wdSendToNewDocument
    With .DataSource
        .FirstRecord = 5
        .LastRecord = 9
    End With
    .Execute Pause:=True
End With

'Either preview or print labels
If MsgBox("Do you want to preview before printing?", _
    vbYesNo, _
    "Programming Microsoft Access Version 2002") = vbYes Then
    ActiveDocument.PrintPreview
Else
    ActiveDocument.PrintOut
End If

End Sub
```

You can invoke the procedure from within Access by invoking the *Run* method for the Word *Application* object, as shown in the following procedure. This takes just three lines. While the *RunFormLetters* and *RunLabels* procedures apply to a standard module in Access, you can place either or both of them behind an Access form and invoke them from command buttons. If your code designates a query in the *OpenDataSource Connection* parameter, you can modify the query before invoking the Word mail merge operation to further enhance your control of the mail merge.

> **Note**   The same Word 2002 bug that afflicts the mailing label sample affects this one. Basically, Word prompts you to select a table to serve as a record source even though the code already denotes one. The remedies are also the same. You manually designate the proper table to serve as a record source. In addition, you can visit the Office Update site (office.microsoft.com) for patches and service releases that remedy the problem.

```
Sub RunFormLetters()
Dim myWDApp As Word.Application

'Open connection to Word and make Word visible
Set myWDApp = CreateObject("Word.Application")
myWDApp.Application.Visible = True

'Run form letter procedure
myWDApp.Application.Run "PrintPreviewLetters"

End Sub
```

Part IV

Multiuser Development for Jet, SQL Server, and the Web

12

Working with Multiuser Databases

Much of the rest of this book covers building Microsoft Access applications for groups of users. This chapter discusses some core multiuser issues: sharing content and controlling security. In reviewing sharing, this chapter explicitly examines techniques and issues for sharing files, forms, and recordsets. Subsequent chapters explore technologies for sharing Access databases, such as database replication, using Microsoft SQL Server, and using Access databases over the World Wide Web.

   This chapter assumes you have a working knowledge of basic multiuser and security issues so that it can focus on the programmatic issues. For example, the chapter includes samples that compare row-level locking with the more traditional page-level locking for recordset manipulation, as well as samples that show how to control security programmatically with the ADOX library (as opposed to using Jet SQL and the ADODB library). The chapter closes with a sample demonstrating transactions in a multiuser environment.

Sharing Files

The first step in sharing an Access application is to make the default open mode shared. You can accomplish this using the Advanced tab of the Options dialog box. This tab also offers other options that facilitate sharing. The *SetOption* and *GetOption* methods of the Access *Application* object enable your applications to set and read these settings. Use *"Default Open Mode for Databases"* as the string parameter to set or read the default open mode. For example, *GetOption("Default*

Open Mode for Databases") returns the default open mode setting on the Advanced tab of the Options dialog box.

There are several issues to keep in mind as you toggle the open mode for an Access database file between shared and exclusive. First, setting the open mode option does not take effect until the next time the file opens. Second, opening a file from the MRU (most recently used) list on the File menu or the New File panel of the Task Pane ignores a prior setting of the open mode option. If you want the open mode option from the prior session to affect the way the current session opens a file, you must use the File-Open command and select a file from the Open dialog box interface.

> **Note**   In my experience, using the *Connection* object's *Mode* property and the *Recordset* object's cursor settings offers more reliable, granular control over how a user accesses a database than the open mode setting. For example, you cannot stop a user from selecting a file from the MRU list on the File menu, but this selection will ignore your setting from the prior session. When you use the *Connection* and *Recordset* objects, you will need to program your own custom interface to the data. (See Chapter 2, "Data Access Models: Part I," for in-depth coverage of these objects.) Because this book targets developers who frequently build custom solutions for others, using connections and recordsets to control the type of database access is a reasonable approach.

Make sure to locate Access multiuser files in shared file directory folders. Because Access with the Jet engine is a file server as opposed to a client/server database, you should minimize the file size that travels over the physical network connection. One way to do this is to split an application into two files. You save the data tables in an Access file on the shared directory folder and distribute another Access file to individual users for use on their local workstations. The distributed file links back to the data tables in the shared folders. This design speeds performance and reduces network traffic. You can generally improve performance by including more content in the distributed file, such as data that changes infrequently. You can use automated procedures to update locally stored data at specific times, such as when an application opens or a user clicks a button.

> **Note**   You can use the Database Splitter wizard to divide one Access
> file into two. (Choose Database Utilities from the Tools menu.) One file
> contains tables, and the other file holds queries, forms, reports, mac-
> ros, modules, and shortcuts to data access pages. (Data access pages
> are new with Access 2000 and substantially improved with Access
> 2002.) You place the first file in a shared folder on the network and link
> the other file to it. You distribute the second file to individual users for
> use on their workstations.

You can set user-level security settings that let a user open a file exclusively (so that others cannot use it). A user needs exclusive use of a database to make database modifications, such as adding new modules or revising existing ones. The *Connection Control* property and the User List feature help to obtain exclusive access to a database in a multiuser environment.

The *Connection Control* Property

The *Connection Control* property, which was introduced in Access 2000, facilitates programmatic control of database accessibility. You can set the *Connection Control* property for an ActiveX Data Objects (ADO) *Connection* object to make it impossible for new users to open a database and to prohibit existing users from reconnecting to it after they close the file. The *Connection Control* property allows you to obtain exclusive access to the database to store new modules and make other application design changes once the last current user disconnects from the database.

The following two procedures change the setting of the *Connection Control* property. You use the *Properties* collection of the *Connection* object to set the property. A property setting of *1* sets the feature so that it closes down passively when users disconnect from the application file. A value of *2* enables other users to resume connecting to the database file. This feature is handy for developers who need to evaluate their changes after saving them in the file.

```
Sub CloseDBConnection()
Dim cnn1 As ADODB.Connection

Set cnn1 = CurrentProject.Connection
cnn1.Properties("Jet OLEDB:Connection Control") = 1

End Sub
```

(continued)

```
Sub OpenDBConnection()
Dim cnn1 As ADODB.Connection

    Set cnn1 = CurrentProject.Connection
    cnn1.Properties("Jet OLEDB:Connection Control") = 2

End Sub
```

The User List

The User List, introduced with Jet 4 in Access 2000, is a set of user data stored in the lock file for an .mdb file. This information is available exclusively through the Jet provider, but you can gain access to the information only through ADO. (If your database resides on a read-only file share, this feature is not available because Jet does not create lock files for read-only shares.) You invoke the *OpenSchema* method for a *Connection* object to return a recordset with four fields of information for each recent user. The method extracts data from the lock file for an .mbd file. These are the four fields in the recordset:

- *computer_name*   The name of the computer the user connects from.

- *login_name*   The login user-level security name.

- *connected*   Indicates that a user is currently connected. (User IDs sometimes remain in the lock database after a user disconnects from a Jet database.)

- *suspected_state*   Indicates that a connection to the database has terminated abnormally.

The following procedure invokes the User List. You reference the User List using a globally unique identifier (GUID) that points at the control for returning the recordset of active users. The sample returns *computer_name* and *login_name* for all active users. When this list has a count of *1*, a developer can save changes to modules in a database. In addition, a developer can use the list to determine who to contact to gain exclusive control of a database. If an application has a list of machine or user names with corresponding e-mail addresses, it can send messages to users urging them to close the database for crucial maintenance work. (See Chapter 11, "Integrating Access with Other Office Applications," for samples demonstrating how to automate the sending of messages.)

```
Sub ListActiveUsers()
Dim cnn1 As ADODB.Connection
Dim rst1 As New ADODB.Recordset

'Set the connection for the current project and invoke the
```

```
'OpenSchema method to return the current list of users
Set cnn1 = CurrentProject.Connection
Set rst1 = cnn1.OpenSchema(adSchemaProviderSpecific, , _
    "{947bb102-5d43-11d1-bdbf-00c04fb92675}")

'Print a heading for the User List recordset set
'and enumerate list member
With rst1
    Debug.Print "Machine Name      " & "User Name"
    Debug.Print "============" & "      ========="
    Do Until .EOF
        Debug.Print .Fields("computer_name") & _
            .Fields("login_name")
        .MoveNext
    Loop
End With

End Sub
```

Sharing Forms

Even without any code, Access forms allow multiple users to edit, add, and delete records in a database. However, you can enhance this capability in a multiuser environment using modules behind forms.

A simple AutoForm based on a table or other recordset source can work in a multiuser environment. Two or more users can open such a form and then browse records. They can also modify the form's bound recordset in all the ways that Access permits. You can program Access to change the defaults for how and when one user can view the changes made by another. The database file for this chapter includes five forms that reflect varying types of programmatic control. These forms are WebBasedList, WebBasedList1, WebBasedList2, WebBasedList3, and WebBasedList4.

Locking Records Manually

You'll find form-sharing controls on the Advanced tab of the Options dialog box. The Edited Record option button imposes pessimistic page-level locking. With pessimistic page-level locking, Access locks the page (or pages) containing a record as soon as a form opens the record for editing. Any other records on the same page (or pages) also lock. The Open Databases With Record-Level Locking check box applies optimistic locking to just the current record. Other records on the same page remain unlocked. This new record-level locking feature was requested by many developers to reduce the chance of concurrency conflicts in a multiuser environment. Microsoft added this feature to counteract the impact of expanding its page size from 2 KB to 4 KB (which was necessary to accommodate Unicode format for character-based fields).

Refreshing Field Values

The default refresh interval on the Advanced tab specifies the maximum number of seconds before an updated field value on one form appears to other users. Users can manually refresh a field by choosing the Refresh command from the Records menu or by simply moving the cursor over the field. If the cursor is inactive on a form, a relatively long time might elapse before another user looking at the same record can see the change.

The WebBasedList form shows the behavior of the current lock and refresh settings for an Access form in a multiuser environment. If you open two different copies of the form and change the same record from two different computers (or two different Access sessions on the same computer), you can see the locking behavior and update refresh intervals.

The WebBasedList1 form improves on the no-module WebBasedList form using two short event procedures, shown next. The *Form_Open* event procedure sets the refresh interval option setting to 2 seconds. The *Form_Close* event procedure restores the default interval to 60 seconds. Note that the procedures use the *SetOption* method for the Access *Application* object.

```
Private Sub Form_Close()

Application.SetOption "Refresh Interval (Sec)", 60

End Sub



Private Sub Form_Open(Cancel As Integer)

Application.SetOption "Refresh Interval (Sec)", 2

End Sub
```

When two sessions open the WebBasedList1 form, simple data updates appear to propagate from one session to the next much more quickly than with the WebBasedList form. The shorter refresh interval does not reflect any reordering, adding, or deleting of records between sessions, but it reflects updates very quickly with a light resource consumption requirement.

The simple update that the *Form_Open* procedure achieves can dramatically affect the apparent responsiveness of a multiuser Access application. In fact, this setting has no impact in single-user operation. Its sole purpose is to influence when changes by other users are reflected on forms (and on datasheets).

Custom Refresh and Requery Controls

The WebBasedList2 form includes a Refresh button that invokes the *Refresh* method for the form. The code behind the button's click event is simply *Me.Refresh*. The *Refresh* method functions just like the timeout for a refresh interval. Again, users do not see revised sorts, added records, or deleted records, but they instantly see changes to records made by other users. While users can achieve similar results by moving the cursor over a field, the button is named Refresh so that users immediately know what it does.

The *Refresh* method is fast, but it does not update a form to reflect a new record, and it shows a deleted record with a deleted marker. You invoke a form's *Requery* method to reflect the look of a recordset after one or more users adds and deletes records. In the default mode, the *Refresh* method leaves the current record active, but the *Requery* method selects the first record after its operation. If you want to return to your previous position (which will likely not be the first record), you must add logic to navigate back to it. If any users alter sort criteria, such as primary key or sort key values, the *Requery* method reflects these changes but the *Refresh* method does not update the record order. The *Requery* method works in both single-user and multiuser environments. (The *Refresh* method has no effect in single-user applications.)

The following two procedures add a Requery button to the Refresh button in the WebBasedList2 form. The *cmdRequery_Click* procedure has three parts. First it saves the current primary key value to help relocate the record after the *Requery* method repositions the recordset point to the form's first record. Second it applies the *Requery* method. Third it sets the focus to the primary key field (*ContactID*) and invokes the *DoCmd FindRecord* command. This repositions the form from the first record to the record that was current before the application of the *Requery* method. If another user deleted that record, the form repositions the display to the first record in the rowset behind the form. You can use more elaborate logic to position the current record elsewhere.

```
Private Sub cmdRefresh_Click()

Me.Refresh

End Sub


Private Sub cmdRequery_Click()
Dim pkBefore As Long

'Save primary key value before requery
pkBefore = Me.ContactID.Value
```

(continued)

```
'Apply requery method
Me.Requery

'Attempt to find primary key value before requery
Me.ContactID.SetFocus
DoCmd.FindRecord pkBefore

End Sub
```

Locking Records Programmatically

Record locking means locking record values so that other users cannot edit them. Access 2002 continues to offer record locking features that were first introduced with Access 2000. Prior to Access 2000, Access supported only page locking. You control when to apply locks using the locking options on the Advanced tab of the Options dialog box. You can also programmatically assign values to the *RecordLocks* property for a form to determine whether it locks records optimistically or pessimistically at the page level or table level. The *RecordLocks* property can assume one of three values. The default value of *0* specifies optimistic page locking. The value of *2* specifies pessimistic page locking. The value of *1* exclusively locks the whole table.

The Advanced tab also offers a check box for record-level locking instead of page-level locking. It is selected by default. This setting lets two users simultaneously update two different records on the same page, using forms. Row-level locking is not available for memo data types or on index pages. Access does not generally support naming users with conflict locks. You can programmatically set row-level locking with the *SetOption* method for the Access *Application* object. The *GetOption* method offers a mechanism for returning row-vs.-page lock settings.

The *Form_Open* and *Form_Close* procedures that follow manipulate different styles of page locking and record-vs.-page locking. The *Form_Open* event offers form users the option of locking pages optimistically or pessimistically. If a user chooses either option, the procedure assigns a value of *False* to the row-level locking setting. If a user does not choose either page-locking option, the procedure assigns a value of *True* to the row-level locking setting. These *True/False* values correspond to a selected or deselected check box on the Advanced tab for record-level locking.

```
Private Sub Form_Open(Cancel As Integer)

'Present a series of message boxes to let a user set the
'page-locking style and record-level locking for a form
```

```
If MsgBox("Optimistic page locking?", vbYesNo, _
    "Programming Microsoft Access Version 2002") = vbYes Then
    Me.RecordLocks = 0
    Application.SetOption "Use Row Level Locking", False
ElseIf MsgBox("Pessimistic Page locking?", vbYesNo, _
    "Programming Microsoft Access Version 2002") = vbYes Then
    Me.RecordLocks = 2
    Application.SetOption "Use Row Level Locking", False
Else
    MsgBox "Setting new row level locking.", _
        vbInformation, "Programming Microsoft Access Version 2002"
    Application.SetOption "Use Row Level Locking", True
End If

'Handy for confirming selected states
Debug.Print Me.RecordLocks
Debug.Print Application.GetOption("Use Row Level Locking")

End Sub


Private Sub Form_Close()

'Restore default locking
'Me.RecordLocks = 2
Application.SetOption "Use Row Level Locking", True

End Sub
```

> **Note**   The first user to set locking options in a multiuser session con-
> trols locking for all other users in that session. When testing procedures
> assign values to different locking options, you should exit and restart
> Access between tests to initialize new locking options.

Not all of the *RecordLocks* settings have corresponding options on the Advanced tab. The two print statements at the bottom of the *Form_Open* event procedure reflect the current settings for the style and type of page locking as well
whether your system is using row-level instead of page-level locking.

Access 2002 has an optional feature for changing multiple page-level locks
to a single lock for the whole table. As the number of locks per table increases,
Access can automatically replace the individual record locks with a single lock
per table. This automatic lock promotion can dramatically lower the cost of lock

management while offering the flexibility of record locks when locks are sparse. You can select this feature by turning off default row-level locking and using the *SetOption* method for the *Application* object. You must also assign a value to the new *PagesLockedToTableLock* registry entry. A default value of *0* disables automatic lock promotion. Values greater than *0* indicate the minimum number of locks per table before Jet attempts to replace individual record locks with a single table lock. A value of *100* means that Jet will attempt to replace page locks with a single table lock on the application of the 101st lock per table, 201st lock per table, and so on. The attempts succeed only if Jet can get exclusive access to the table (because placing a lock on a table locks out all users except the one with the lock). Jet performs data manipulation much more rapidly when it has exclusive access to the table. This feature also removes the need for the developer to determine in advance when to apply exclusive table locks.

Sharing Recordsets

For recordsets and commands based on SQL statements, Jet uses smart defaults to determine which page and record locking settings to use. With ADO code that relies on cursors, Jet defaults to record-level locking. With SQL statements that can easily affect thousands of rows, Jet switches to page-level locking as the default. This, in turn, lets your application benefit from lock promotion (if lock promotion is enabled).

When you use row-level locking with recordsets, you achieve concurrency and performance enhancements only if you explicitly wrap recordset maintenance tasks in transactions. You use the *BeginTrans*, *CommitTrans*, and *Rollback* methods (discussed later in this chapter in the section "Transactions") to wrap each record operation. Without this precaution, locks accumulate until they reach the value of the *FlushTransactionTimeout* registry setting.

When you use record-level locking, you should carefully consider the data types for fields and record lengths to control the growth of database file size. Record-level locking writes rows rather than pages; rows that extend across a page boundary must be moved to a new page. Using fixed-length data types, you can determine the precise length of records; you cannot do this with the variable-length character fields for Access tables. (However, Jet SQL's data definition language includes a CHAR data type that lets you determine the length of string data type fields. This, in turn, can help to control record size bloat caused by records that do not fit entirely within one page.)

Row-Level Locking

The following procedure illustrates row locking in a multiuser application. It simulates a two-user application by running two connections against the same data file. The application also requires a second file named TestRowLocking.mdb. Run the procedure in step mode to see how the row locking succeeds and fails under different circumstances.

> **Note**   After copying TestRowLocking.mdb from the book's companion CD, be sure to remove the read-only property setting. Otherwise, you will not be able to update the recordsets based on the table in the file.

```
Sub RowLockingPessimistic()

'Use TestRowLocking.mdb to run this demo of
'row locking
'DO NOT HAVE TESTROWLOCKING.MDB OPEN WHEN RUNNING
'THE DEMO

Dim cnn1 As New ADODB.Connection
Dim cnn2 As New ADODB.Connection
Dim rs As New ADODB.Recordset
Dim rs2 As New ADODB.Recordset
Dim j As Integer

On Error GoTo ErrHandler

'Open two connections against the same database,
'both using row locking mode
'Jet OLEDB:Database Locking Mode info -
'0 is "page mode"
'1 is "row mode"

'Open first connection to TestRowLocking.mdb
cnn1.Open "Provider=Microsoft.Jet.OLEDB.4.0;Data " & _
    "Source=C:\PMA Samples\Chapter 12\TestRowLocking.mdb;" & _
    "Jet OLEDB:Database Locking Mode=1;"

'Open second connection to TestRowLocking.mdb
cnn2.Open "Provider=Microsoft.Jet.OLEDB.4.0;" & _
    "Data Source=C:\PMA Samples\Chapter 12\TestRowLocking.mdb;" & _
    "Jet OLEDB:Database Locking Mode=1;"
```

(continued)

```
'Open a recordset in the first connection and
'begin editing the first row
rs.Open "TestRowLocking", cnn1, adOpenKeyset, _
    adLockPessimistic, adCmdTableDirect

'Edit first row field value
Debug.Print rs.Fields("col1")
rs.Fields("col1") = 2
'rs2.Update; putting an update here would
'close the record lock
Debug.Print rs.Fields("col1")

'Open a recordset in the second connection
rs2.Open "TestRowLocking", cnn2, adOpenKeyset, _
    adLockPessimistic, adCmdTableDirect

'Attempt to edit the first row; even in row locking,
'because we are in the pessimistic
'locking mode, this will fail
Debug.Print rs2.Fields("col1")
rs2.Fields("col1") = 3
Debug.Print rs2.Fields("col1")

'Move to another row in the same page
rs2.MoveNext

'Attempt to edit the next row; this works under
'the row locking mode because the lock applies only
'to a single row, not the whole page
Debug.Print rs2.Fields("col1")
'Should not fail (row locking)
rs2.Fields("col1") = 4
Debug.Print rs2.Fields("col1")


'Update recordsets
rs.Update
rs2.Update
'Close connections and exit
cnn1.Close
cnn2.Close
Set cnn1 = Nothing
Set cnn2 = Nothing
Exit Sub

ErrHandler:
For j = 0 To cnn1.Errors.Count - 1
```

```
        Debug.Print "Errors from cnn1 connection"
        Debug.Print "Conn Err Num : "; cnn1.Errors(j).Number
        Debug.Print "Conn Err Desc: "; cnn1.Errors(j).Description
Next j

For j = 0 To cnn2.Errors.Count - 1
        Debug.Print "Errors from cnn2 connection"
        Debug.Print "Conn Err Num : "; cnn2.Errors(j).Number
        Debug.Print "Conn Err Desc: "; cnn2.Errors(j).Description
Next j

Resume Next

End Sub
```

Notice that the second connection's attempt to write to the first record in TestRowLocking.mdb fails because the first connection still has the first record open. This attempt can succeed if the first connection unlocks the record (for instance, by running a *rs.Update* statement). The second connection's attempt to write to the second record succeeds immediately because there are no locks on that record. The error-handling logic displays the entries from the Jet connection's *Errors* collection.

Note   The companion CD includes a locking sample not shown in the book: *RowLockingOptimistic.* This sample illustrates the use of optimistic locking for a cursor with row-level locking. You will achieve better concurrency with optimistic locking than with pessimistic locking at the expense of some exposure to updating errors. However, if these errors occur, you can trap them. In the trap, you can either try the updates again after a short wait or advise the user that the update attempt failed. For example, the Access default settings for bound forms schedule two retries spaced 250 milliseconds apart.

Page-Level Locking

The following is an excerpt from a similarly designed procedure that uses page locking instead of record locking. Notice that the Database Locking Mode value, which was *1* in the preceding sample, is *0* in this one. These values denote, respectively, row-level and page-level tracking. Both attempts by the second connection to update records fail because the first connection has a lock open and all the records for this short table fit on a single page.

```
'Open first connection to TestRowLocking.mdb
cnn1.Open "Provider=Microsoft.Jet.OLEDB.4.0;Data " & _
    "Source=C:\PMA Samples\Chapter 12\TestRowLocking.mdb;" & _
    "Jet OLEDB:Database Locking Mode=0;"

'Open second connection to TestRowLocking.mdb
cnn2.Open "Provider=Microsoft.Jet.OLEDB.4.0;" & _
    "Data Source=C:\PMA Samples\Chapter 12\TestRowLocking.mdb;" & _
    "Jet OLEDB:Database Locking Mode=0;"

'Open a recordset in the first connection and
'begin editing the first row
rs.Open "TestRowLocking", cnn1, adOpenKeyset, _
    adLockPessimistic, adCmdTableDirect

'Edit first row field value
Debug.Print rs.Fields("col1")
rs.Fields("col1") = 2
Debug.Print rs.Fields("col1")

'Open a recordset in the second connection
rs2.Open "TestRowLocking", cnn2, adOpenKeyset, _
    adLockPessimistic, adCmdTableDirect

'Attempt to edit the first row; because of
'pessimistic page locking mode setting, this fails
Debug.Print rs2.Fields("col1")
rs2.Fields("col1") = 3
Debug.Print rs2.Fields("col1")
'Move to another row in the same page
rs2.MoveNext

'Attempt to edit the next row; this fails also because
'the next row is on the same page
Debug.Print rs2.Fields("col1")
rs2.Fields("col1") = 4
Debug.Print rs2.Fields("col1")


'Update recordsets
rs.Update
rs2.Update
```

Securing Files Without User-Level Security

Access offers a rich array of security features to support the needs of different types of Access applications. Most multiuser Access applications can benefit from user-level security, which lets developers designate groups of users. But some applications have more specialized needs. This section offers a brief overview of security techniques other than user-level security. It also covers programmatic approaches to managing user-level security using ADO.

One of the strengths of Access is its ability to serve different audiences. Some applications are code intensive, so you need to secure your investment in source code. Other applications serve small workgroups with limited technical capabilities but still require minimum levels of security to restrict access to data. Still other applications benefit from a custom user interface (UI) that restricts functionality simply by exposing a restricted set of commands.

Using a Custom Interface

Sometimes you can adequately secure an application by simply replacing the standard Access interface with a custom one. Choose Startup from the Tools menu to open a dialog box that lets you specify a custom application title and icon, a custom startup form, and custom menus to replace the standard Access ones. This dialog box also lets you suppress the Database window and the status bar. You can also manipulate the features of the Startup dialog box programmatically. If this type of manipulation is suitable for your security needs, consider augmenting it with the *Show* and *Hide* methods, the *Visible* property, and the *Hidden* property for objects in the Database window.

> **Note**   See earlier chapters for creating custom features: Chapter 6, "Forms, Controls, and Data," introduces building a custom startup form, and Chapter 10, "Microsoft Office Objects," demonstrates how to eliminate access to the Database window with a custom startup form. Chapter 10 also illustrates programming techniques for building your own custom menus and adapting them with the *CommandBars* object model.

Setting a Database Password Manually

You can require users to enter a password to gain unrestricted access to all Access data and database objects. Passwords are easy to administer compared to user-level security. Password security is appropriate if you have a group whose members need equal access to all elements of a database file but not everyone in the office is a member of that group.

You cannot use a password-protected file as a member in a replica set because Jet database replication cannot synchronize with a password-protected file. (See Chapter 13, "Replicating Databases," for details.) You should also be careful about linking to database files with password protection because anyone who can access the file that links to the protected file has unrestricted access to the protected file. Furthermore, Access stores an encrypted version of the password along with other information about the linked file. Finally, if a user changes the password for a linked file, Access prompts for the new password the next time another database file links to it.

To assign and remove a database password, you need exclusive access to the file. You obtain exclusive access when you open a file by choosing Open Exclusive from the Open button's drop-down list in the Open dialog box.

To assign a database password perform the following steps:

1. Choose Security-Set Database Password from the Tools menu.

2. In the Set Database Password dialog box, enter your password of choice in the Password and Verify text boxes and then click OK. The application will ask for the password the next time a user opens the file.

To remove a database password, do the following:

1. Choose Tools-Security-Unset Database Password.

2. Type the password in the Unset Database Password dialog box. This removes the initial prompt for a password before a database is made available.

Setting a Database Password Programmatically

You can also programmatically initialize, change, and remove a database password. The next three samples draw on Jet SQL, offering a simple approach to managing the security for Jet databases. Use the ALTER DATABASE PASSWORD keyword to set and remove database passwords. The first argument signifies the new password, and the second argument denotes the old password. You represent the passwords as strings delimited by square brackets ([ ]), except in two cases. As with all SQL terms and expressions, you should leave a blank space between SQL statement arguments, such as the delimited old and new passwords. When initializing a database password, use NULL to signify the old password. When removing a database password, designate NULL as the new password. The keyword NULL should not appear within square brackets.

The *CreateDBPassword* procedure shown next initializes a database password for a database by performing three main steps. First the code constructs the string based on Jet SQL to assign a password to a database for the first time. The password is the word *password* and is the first argument after the ALTER DATABASE PASSWORD keyword. Notice that NULL appears as the second argument. This is because there is no password to replace. The next block of code creates a connection to the database for which the procedure assigns a password. Notice that the procedure opens the database file exclusively. This is imperative when you manipulate the password for a database. The sample assigns a password to the TestRowLocking.mdb file, which the preceding sample used. If you haven't copied the file from the book's companion CD, you can do it now to run this sample. When you do so, remember to remove the read-only file property setting. You can, of course, use any other file you choose, but you must revise the listing accordingly. The third step executes the SQL string with the ADO *Connection* object created in the second step. This takes just one line. Here's the syntax:

```
Sub CreateDBPassword()
Dim cnn1 As ADODB.Connection
Dim str1 As String

'SQL string to initialize the database password
'to password
str1 = "ALTER DATABASE PASSWORD [password] NULL;"

'Open unsecured database
Set cnn1 = New ADODB.Connection
With cnn1
    .Mode = adModeShareExclusive
    .Open "Provider=Microsoft.Jet.OLEDB.4.0;Data " & _
        "Source=C:\PMA Samples\Chapter 12\TestRowLocking.mdb;"

'Execute SQL in str1 to secure database with a password
    .Execute (str1)
End With

'Clean up objects
cnn1.Close
Set cnn1 = Nothing

End Sub
```

When your application changes the password for a database, you have to log in with the old password. (See the next code sample.) To do this, you assign the old password to the *Database Password* property of the *Connection* object for the database whose password will change. This is one of the extended properties for the *Connection* object, so you need to use a special syntax, as the sample demonstrates. The sample also confirms the Jet SQL syntax for replacing one password with another. In this instance, *foo* replaces the password. Aside from these two modifications, the code sample has the same structure as the preceding one; both initialize a database password for an Access database file.

```
Sub ChangeDBPassword()
Dim cnn1 As ADODB.Connection
Dim str1 As String

'SQL string to change the database password
'from password to foo
str1 = "ALTER DATABASE PASSWORD [foo] [password]"

'Open secured database with password for its
'database password
Set cnn1 = New ADODB.Connection
With cnn1
    .Mode = adModeShareExclusive
    .Provider = "Microsoft.Jet.OLEDB.4.0"
    .Properties("Jet OLEDB:Database Password") = "password"
    .Open "Data Source=C:\PMA Samples\Chapter 12\TestRowLocking.mdb;"

'Execute SQL in str1 to change database password from
'password to foo
    .Execute (str1)
End With

'Clean up objects
cnn1.Close
Set cnn1 = Nothing

End Sub
```

The next code sample demonstrates how to remove a database password from an Access database file. This sample borrows heavily from both of the preceding ones. In fact, the only way that this sample differs from the preceding two is in its definition of the SQL string. When you remove a password from a database, make the first argument for the ALTER DATABASE PASSWORD keyword NULL. The second argument password should be the current password for the database. This is the same password that you use to connect to the database.

If you've been following the progression of these code samples, you already know that this password will be *foo*.

```
Sub RemoveDBPassword()
Dim cnn1 As ADODB.Connection
Dim str1 As String

'SQL string to clear the database password
'from a database file
str1 = "ALTER DATABASE PASSWORD NULL [foo]"

'Open secured database with foo for its
'database password
Set cnn1 = New ADODB.Connection
With cnn1
    .Mode = adModeShareExclusive
    .Provider = "Microsoft.Jet.OLEDB.4.0"
    .Properties("Jet OLEDB:Database Password") = "foo"
    .Open "Data Source=C:\PMA Samples\Chapter 12\TestRowLocking.mdb;"

'Execute SQL in str1 to clear database password
'from a database file
    .Execute (str1)
End With

'Clean up objects
cnn1.Close
Set cnn1 = Nothing

End Sub
```

Setting a Module Password

Since its 2000 version, the Access UI has enabled password security for modules instead of offering user-level security. This new approach makes Access consistent with the other Office 2000 components. It applies to all standard and standalone class modules as well as the modules behind forms and reports.

> Note   In the "User-Level Security via Jet SQL and ADO" section that appears later in this chapter, you will read about user-level security for module containers. This feature is available through Jet SQL and the Jet Engine rather than the Access UI.

You set password security once for all the modules in a Visual Basic for Applications (VBA) project from the Visual Basic Editor (VBE). Choose the Properties command for the project from the Tools menu to open the Project Properties dialog box. The Protection tab (shown in Figure 12-1) offers the Lock Project For Viewing check box and text boxes for entering and confirming a password for the module. Assigning a password for viewing modules in a project does not prevent your code from running as though it were not protected. If you assign a password but do not select the Lock Project For Viewing check box, anyone can edit the code but the Project Properties dialog box will be protected. You remove password security from the modules in a project by clearing all entries on the Protection tab.

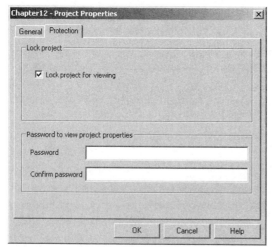

Figure 12-1 You use the Protection tab of the Project Properties dialog box to set password security for the modules in a project.

After securing your modules with a password, you must enter the password once per session before you can view, edit, or add new code. You can secure forms and reports with both user-level security and module password security. User-level security applies to designing and using forms and reports. You can require a user to have Modify Design permission to add controls to forms. That user will also need the password for modules in a project to write event procedures for the control. Conversely, knowing the password for the modules in a project does not enable a user to add controls to or remove controls from a form. Also, Modify Design permission does not allow a user to change the *HasModule* property of forms and reports to *No*; the user must first enter the password for the modules in a project.

Using .mde Files

An .mde file totally secures the code for an Access database file. When you convert an .mdb file to an .mde file, Access compiles all your modules, removes editable code, and compacts the destination database while preserving the original .mdb file. The size of your database will shrink because of the removal of editable code. Also, because the conversion optimizes memory usage, your code will run faster.

To convert an .mdb file to an .mde file, you must have exclusive access to the file. (See "Setting a Database Password Manually" on page 676.) Choose Database Utilities from the Tools menu and then choose Make MDE File. After saving the converted file, be sure to save your original file. The only way to edit or add to the code in a database file is to modify the original file and then convert it to an .mde file.

An .mde file has some restrictions:

- You cannot modify or add forms, reports, or modules.

- You cannot import or export forms, reports, or modules to a standard .mdb file. You can, however, freely import and export tables, queries, macros, and shortcuts for data access pages with other database files.

- You cannot add, delete, or change references to other object libraries or databases.

- You cannot dynamically change code because .mde files contain no editable code.

- You cannot convert any existing member of a replica set to an .mde file, but an .mde file can participate in a replica set.

- An .mde file can reference another database file only if that file is also an .mde file. You must start converting .mdb files (or .mda add-in files) that are referenced before you convert the .mdb file that references them. The new reference must point at the new .mde file.

User-Level Security via ADOX

With user-level security, you define a workgroup composed of user accounts and group accounts. This section demonstrates how to create user and group accounts as well as assign permissions to those accounts programmatically. The new ADOX model supports this functionality through its *Catalog* object as well as its *Users* and *Groups* collection objects. Figure 12-2 shows the hierarchy: groups can belong to users, and users can belong to groups; users and groups both belong to the *Catalog* object.

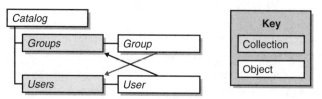

Figure 12-2 The relationship of the *User* and *Group* objects to the *Catalog* object and the *Users* and *Groups* collections.

You can assign permissions to users, groups, or both. It is generally most efficient to assign permissions to groups. You clear all default permissions from existing individual user accounts and then assign users to all appropriate groups. With this type of user-level design, you can administer permissions by assigning users to groups and assigning permissions to groups because users inherit all permissions from the groups to which they belong. By restricting permission assignments to groups, this design provides a single focal point for managing permissions.

The upcoming samples show how to code typical user-level administration tasks. Because they are meant to highlight basic security management procedures, only a couple of the samples demonstrate error-trapping logic. The samples assume you have a working knowledge of Access security concepts. To learn more about the basics of Access user-level security, search Access Help for the topics "Manage user and group accounts" and "Types of permissions."

> **Note**   The samples in this chapter use the Admin account to highlight the basic syntax for some of the most common security tasks. In an operational system, you will typically strip the Admin account of any database object ownership and permissions and create your own custom security administration account or accounts.

Connecting to a Secure Database

The following procedure connects to a secure database file. The connection string includes four phrases. The first phrase designates the *Provider* property for the procedure's *Connection* object. It specifies the Jet 4.0 OLE DB provider. The second phrase assigns the system database property for the connection. This is the name and path to the workgroup information file. (This file is Systemdemo.mdw in the Office10 folder; you must manually copy the file to the Office10 folder.) The third phrase specifies the data source, which in this case is the secure database file, UserLevel.mdb. The fourth phrase denotes user ID and password values for logging into the secure database. In this sample, the procedure logs on as the Admin user. Unless you change the default settings, this user has special administrative permissions.

> **Note**   Before attempting to run the following sample or any others in this section, you must copy the Systemdemo.mdw file from the book's companion CD to your hard drive and join the workgroup it defines. As with any file copied from the CD, clear the read-only property setting. To join the workgroup, choose the Tools-Security-Workgroup Administrator menu item, then click the Join button and select the Systemdemo.mdw file in the Office10 folder. In addition, turn on the Access logon feature (if it's not already on).

```
'Turn logon procedure on before running this procedure
'by assigning password of "password" to Admin user account

Sub OpenUserLevel()
Dim cnn1 As New ADODB.Connection
Dim rst1 As New ADODB.Recordset

'Open connection to target user-level secured data
'source; specify path for workgroup information
'file; designate logon ID and password
cnn1.Provider = "Microsoft.Jet.OLEDB.4.0"
cnn1.Properties("Jet OLEDB:System database") = _
    "C:\Program Files\Microsoft Office\" & _
    "Office10\Systemdemo.mdw"
cnn1.Open "Data Source=C:\PMA Samples\Chapter 12\UserLevel.mdb;" & _
    "User ID=Admin;Password=password;"

'cnn1.Open "Data Source=C:\PMA Samples\Chapter 12\" & _
'    "UserLevel.mdb,Admin,[password]"

'Print first field from first record to confirm connection
rst1.Open "WebBasedList", cnn1, , , adCmdTable
Debug.Print rst1.Fields(0)

'Clean up objects
cnn1.Close
Set cnn1 = Nothing

End Sub
```

The two lines following the comment open a recordset based on the connection and print the first field's value from the first record. This simply confirms the operation of the sample. The table, *WebBasedList*, is the same one used in the earlier multiuser sample.

For the *OpenUserLevel* procedure to work, you must invoke the logon procedure. This involves giving the Admin user a password. The procedure also requires a workgroup information file. In this case, its name must be Systemdemo.mdw, and you must save it in the path indicated by the procedure. The companion CD includes both the secure database file and the workgroup information file for easy testing of the procedure.

Adding and Deleting Users

When you develop and manage a custom application with user-level security, you are likely to add and delete users. Before you can add users, you must log on as a member of the Admins group, such as Admin. You can use the *Append* method of the *Users* collection to add users to a catalog or group. You must specify a name for the new user, and you can designate a password. ADO lets you assign a password later using the *ChangePassword* method for the *User* object. Unfortunately, you cannot assign a personal ID (PID) with this approach. Instead, ADO picks one randomly.

> **Note**   In the section "User-Level Security via Jet SQL and ADO," I'll show you another approach based on Jet SQL and ADO that enables you to set the PID. The discussion of that approach mentions why the ability to set the PID is important (as does the Access Help file).

The following two procedures show one approach to invoking the *Append* method to add a new user to an application. The *CallMakeUser* procedure launches the *MakeUser* procedure as it passes along two arguments. The first argument designates a new user's name. The second argument sends a password. In the sample, the string *"password"* is the value of the password argument.

```
'Make sure NewUser account does not exist prior to running
'this procedure; for example, run callDeleteUser first

Sub CallMakeUser()

MakeUser "NewUser", "password"

End Sub
```

```
Sub MakeUser(usrName As String, secureWord As String)
Dim cat1 As ADOX.Catalog

'Instantiate catalog
Set cat1 = New ADOX.Catalog

'Set ActiveConnection property for catalog for
'use in adding a new user
cat1.ActiveConnection = _
    "Provider=Microsoft.Jet.OLEDB.4.0;" & _
    "Data Source=C:\PMA Samples\Chapter 12\UserLevel.mdb;" & _
    "Jet OLEDB:System database=C:\Program Files\Microsoft Office\" & _
    "Office10\Systemdemo.mdw;" & _
    "User Id=Admin;Password=password;"

'Append user passed from calling routine
cat1.Users.Append usrName, secureWord

'Clean up objects
Set cat1 = Nothing

End Sub
```

The *MakeUser* procedure specifies a target for the new group using the *Catalog* object's *ActiveConnection* setting. Note that it designates a user ID with the authority to make a new user, and it points to a workgroup information file. The *Append* method in *MakeUser* adds a new member to the *Catalog* object. Therefore, this new user is not yet a member of any groups. You can also add a member to a *Group* object so that the user has immediate membership in that group. One of the following samples uses this technique.

The next two procedures remove a user from the catalog for a database. The *Delete* method for the *Users* collection has the same syntax as the *Delete* method for the *Tables, Procedures*, and *Views* collection objects. The first procedure, *CallDeleteUser*, passes a single argument—the user name—to the second procedure, *DeleteUser*. The second procedure removes the user from the catalog and concurrently removes the user from any groups as well.

```
'Make sure NewUser account exists prior to running this
'procedure; for example, run callMakeUser

Sub CallDeleteUser()

DeleteUser "NewUser"

End Sub
```

(continued)

```
Sub DeleteUser(usrName As String)
Dim cat1 As ADOX.Catalog

'Instantiate catalog
Set cat1 = New ADOX.Catalog

'Set ActiveConnection property for catalog for
'use in dropping a user
cat1.ActiveConnection = _
    "Provider=Microsoft.Jet.OLEDB.4.0;" & _
    "Data Source=C:\PMA Samples\Chapter 12\UserLevel.mdb;" & _
    "Jet OLEDB:System database=C:\Program Files\Microsoft Office\" & _
    "Office10\systemdemo.mdw;" & _
    "User Id=Admin;Password=password;"

'Remove user from workgroup
cat1.Users.Delete usrName

'Clean up objects
Set cat1 = Nothing

End Sub
```

You must log on to a database as a member of the Admins group to delete a user. The *Delete* method does not require a password. All that the second procedure needs is a string argument naming the user to delete.

Assigning Groups to Users

One common technique for administering permissions is to assign groups to users and manage permissions for groups. Users derive all their permissions implicitly through their group memberships. The samples in this discussion add and remove group memberships from a user account. Both samples use the built-in Users group, but the same techniques work for custom groups.

The following two procedures add a group to a user account called NewUser. Make sure the user account exists before running the procedure. The first procedure, *CallAddGroupToUser*, passes a user name and a group name to the second procedure, *AddGroupToUser*, which uses the *Append* method to add the *Group* object to the *Groups* collection for the user. The sample passes arguments to the second procedure that tell it to add the new group to the *Groups* collection for a particular *User* object.

```
Sub CallAddGroupToUser()

AddGroupToUser "NewUser", "Users"
```

```
'AddGroupToUser "Admin", "MySecretGroup1"

End Sub


Sub AddGroupToUser(usrName As String, grpName As String)
On Error GoTo AddTrap
Dim cat1 As New ADOX.Catalog
Const acctNameAlreadyExist = -2147467259

'Instantiate catalog
Set cat1 = New ADOX.Catalog

'Set ActiveConnection property for catalog for
'use in adding a new group to an existing user
cat1.ActiveConnection = _
    "Provider=Microsoft.Jet.OLEDB.4.0;" & _
    "Data Source=C:\PMA Samples\Chapter 12\UserLevel.mdb;" & _
    "Jet OLEDB:System database=C:\Program Files\Microsoft Office\" & _
    "Office10\systemdemo.mdw;" & _
    "User Id=Admin;Password=password;"

'Append new group to Groups collection for the
'workgroup, and then add group to the Groups
'collection for a user account passed in as an argument
cat1.Groups.Append grpName
cat1.Users(usrName).Groups.Append grpName

AddExit:
Set cat1 = Nothing
Exit Sub

AddTrap:
If Err.Number = acctNameAlreadyExist Then
'If account already exist, ignore the run-time error
    Resume Next
Else
    Debug.Print Err.Number; Err.Description
End If

End Sub
```

The second procedure invokes the *Append* method in an attempt to create a group with the name of the second argument passed to it. This procedure works for groups whether or not they already exist. Because Users is a built-in group account, it will always exist. If a group with the name of the second argument does not already exist, the *Append* method succeeds; otherwise, the procedure falls into an error trap with error number −2147467259 and moves on to the next statement. Then the procedure appends the group to the *Groups* collection for the *NewUser* object. Again, if the group is already in the *Groups* collection for the user, the procedure progresses to the next statement.

The next two procedures remove a group from a user's *Groups* collection. The first procedure, *CallRemoveUserFromGroup*, passes user and group name parameters to the second procedure, *RemoveUserFromGroup*, which does the work. There is no error checking in this sample, so make sure the group belongs to the user. You can do this by running the preceding sample.

```
'Make sure the group account exists for the user
'prior to running this procedure
'For example, run CallAddGroupToUser

Sub CallRemoveUserFromGroup()

RemoveUserFromGroup "NewUser", "Users"

End Sub

Sub RemoveUserFromGroup(usrName As String, grpName As String)
Dim cat1 As ADOX.Catalog

'Instantiate catalog
Set cat1 = New ADOX.Catalog

'Set ActiveConnection property for catalog for
'use in dropping a group from the Groups collection for
'an existing user
cat1.ActiveConnection = _
    "Provider=Microsoft.Jet.OLEDB.4.0;" & _
    "Data Source=C:\PMA Samples\Chapter 12\UserLevel.mdb;" & _
    "Jet OLEDB:System database=C:\Program Files\Microsoft Office\" & _
    "Office10\systemdemo.mdw;" & _
    "User Id=Admin;Password=password;"

'Drop the group from the Groups collection for a user
cat1.Users(usrName).Groups.Delete grpName

'Clean up objects
Set cat1 = Nothing

End Sub
```

You invoke the *Delete* method to remove a group from the *Groups* collection for a *User* object. Notice the hierarchical specification for an individual user. After identifying a user, the syntax requires the designation of the *Groups* collection and, finally, the *Delete* method. The syntax designates the group name as a parameter for the *Delete* method.

Creating, Deleting, and Tracking Groups in a Catalog

When you develop custom user-level solutions, you'll probably want to create custom groups with names that are meaningful to your clients and whose permissions fit the special requirements of your custom application. The four upcoming samples do the following:

- Create a custom group

- Delete a custom group

- Prepare a report itemizing all the groups in a catalog and the groups associated with each user account

- Toggle the membership of a user in the Admins group

The next two procedures add a group named *MySecretGroup1*. After referencing a database file with a user ID sufficient to make the addition, the procedure invokes the *Append* method of the *Groups* collection. You must specify a container for the *Groups* collection. When you add a new group to the project's *Users* collection, the container is a *Catalog* object. When you assign a group to the *Groups* collection of a *User* object, you must specify the user as the root object for the *Groups* collection.

```
'Make sure MySecretGroup1 does not exist before running
'this procedure; for example, run callDeleteGroup

Sub CallMakeGroup()

MakeGroup "MySecretGroup1"

End Sub


Sub MakeGroup(grpName As String)
Dim cat1 As ADOX.Catalog

'Instantiate catalog
Set cat1 = New ADOX.Catalog

'Set ActiveConnection property for catalog for
'creating a custom group
cat1.ActiveConnection = _
    "Provider=Microsoft.Jet.OLEDB.4.0;" & _
    "Data Source=C:\PMA Samples\Chapter 12\UserLevel.mdb;" & _
    "Jet OLEDB:System database=C:\Program Files\Microsoft Office\" & _
    "Office10\systemdemo.mdw;" & _
    "User Id=Admin;Password=password;"
```

(continued)

```
'Add custom group to the catalog's Groups collection
cat1.Groups.Append grpName

'Clean up objects
Set cat1 = Nothing

End Sub
```

The following two procedures remove a group from a catalog. You must make sure that the group already exists in the catalog before running the procedures. You can do this by running the preceding sample. In fact, the next sample removes the group added in the preceding one.

```
'Make sure MySecretGroup1 exists prior to running this
'procedure; for example, run callMakeGroup

Sub CallDeleteGroup()

DeleteGroup "MySecretGroup1"

End Sub


Sub DeleteGroup(grpName As String)
Dim cat1 As ADOX.Catalog

'Instantiate catalog
Set cat1 = New ADOX.Catalog

'Set ActiveConnection property for catalog for
'dropping a custom group
cat1.ActiveConnection = _
    "Provider=Microsoft.Jet.OLEDB.4.0;" & _
    "Data Source=C:\PMA Samples\Chapter 12\UserLevel.mdb;" & _
    "Jet OLEDB:System database=C:\Program Files\Microsoft Office\" & _
    "Office10\systemdemo.mdw;" & _
    "User Id=Admin;Password=password;"

'Drop a group from the catalog's Groups collection
cat1.Groups.Delete grpName

'Clean up objects
Set cat1 = Nothing

End Sub
```

The syntax for deleting a group closely parallels that for adding a group. The code invokes the *Delete* method of the catalog's *Groups* collection. You pass the method a single parameter—the name of the group to delete.

As you add and delete groups and users and reassign groups to users, you can easily create a custom report that tracks the group memberships for the *Catalog* and individual *User* objects. The following procedure itemizes the groups in a *Catalog* object that points at a specific database. Then it itemizes the *Groups* collection members for each user in the catalog's *Users* collection.

The report generated from this procedure appears in Figure 12-3. The report displays the total number of groups in the workgroup information file, and it lists the names of those groups. Then the procedure reports the number of groups to which each user belongs. If a user does belong to any groups, the procedure prints their names. The Admin user belongs to the built-in Admins and Users groups. The NewUser user does not belong to any group. You can use the samples just discussed to create and delete users, groups, and user membership in groups.

Figure 12-3 A group membership report from the *ListGroupsInCat* procedure.

The following procedure shows one possible application of the *ListGroupsIn-Cat* procedure shown a moment ago. The *ToggleNewUserInAdminsGroup* procedure does what its name implies. It toggles the membership of the *NewUser* object in the Admins group. It also documents the current status of the *NewUser* object in the Admins group by calling the *ListGroupsInCat* procedure.

```
Sub ToggleNewUserInAdminsGroup()
On Error GoTo ToggleTrap
Dim cat1 As ADOX.Catalog
Const notInAdmins = 3265

'Instantiate catalog
Set cat1 = New ADOX.Catalog
```

(continued)

```
'Set ActiveConnection property for catalog
cat1.ActiveConnection = _
    "Provider=Microsoft.Jet.OLEDB.4.0;" & _
    "Data Source=C:\PMA Samples\Chapter 12\UserLevel.mdb;" & _
    "Jet OLEDB:System database=C:\Program Files\Microsoft Office\" & _
    "Office10\systemdemo.mdw;" & _
    "User Id=Admin;Password=password;"

'Attempt to delete membership of user in the Admins group
cat1.Users("NewUser").Groups.Delete ("Admins")

ToggleExit:
Set cat1 = Nothing
ListGroupsInCat
Exit Sub

ToggleTrap:
If Err.Number = notInAdmins Then
'If user not in Admins group, add it to the group
    cat1.Users("NewUser").Groups.Append "Admins"
Else
    Debug.Print Err.Number; Err.Description
End If
Resume Next

End Sub
```

Notice that the toggling procedure relies on error trapping. After connecting to the target database and the workgroup information file through the *cat1* object reference, the procedure attempts to delete *Admins* from the *Groups* collection of *NewUser*. If it is successful, the procedure closes by calling *ListGroupsInCat* and exiting. Otherwise, an error occurs. If the error occurs because the group is not in the user's *Groups* collection, the procedure adds *Admins* to the *NewUser Groups* collection. Then it closes by resuming as though no error had occurred.

Setting Permissions

You can use the *SetPermissions* method for *Group* and *User* objects to manage the permissions available to a security account. You invoke the *GetPermissions* method for these objects to return a Long value that specifies the types of permissions assigned to a group or to a user. Both methods offer a wide array of outcomes; they can assign and report various permissions for a number of database object types. In addition, you can use the *SetPermissions* method to assign, revoke, and deny permissions as well as audit their use.

The two procedures that follow grant a group full permissions for any new table. Setting the permission for new tables has no impact for existing tables. Therefore, a group can have full permissions for all new tables and no permissions for existing tables.

```
'Make sure MySecretGroup1 exists before running procedure

Sub CallSetAllTablePermissionsForGroup()

SetAllTablePermissionsForGroup "MySecretGroup1"

End Sub


Sub SetAllTablePermissionsForGroup(grpName As String)
Dim cat1 As ADOX.Catalog

'Instantiate catalog, group, and user
Set cat1 = New ADOX.Catalog

'Set ActiveConnection property for catalog
cat1.ActiveConnection = _
    "Provider=Microsoft.Jet.OLEDB.4.0;" & _
    "Data Source=C:\PMA Samples\Chapter 12\UserLevel.mdb;" & _
    "Jet OLEDB:System database=C:\Program Files\Microsoft Office\" & _
    "Office10\systemdemo.mdw;" & _
    "User Id=Admin;Password=password;"

'Assign full rights to new tables to grpName group
cat1.Groups(grpName).SetPermissions Null, adPermObjTable, _
    adAccessSet, adRightFull

'Clean up objects
Set cat1 = Nothing

End Sub
```

The first procedure passes a group name, *MySecretGroup1*, to the second procedure. The second procedure invokes the *SetPermissions* method for the group member with that name. Therefore, you must make sure that the group exists before you run the procedure or add error-trapping logic. The method's first parameter has an explicit Null value. This parameter normally specifies the name of a database object, such as a table. A Null value indicates that you want to set permissions for any new database objects. The second parameter designates a *Table* object type. The third parameter serves as a verb; it indicates that the command will set a permission. Other constants indicate different actions that the method can launch, such as revoking permissions. The fourth parameter grants the user full rights. The method and its parameters grant *MySecretGroup1* full rights for all new tables in the UserLevel.mdb database file with the Systemdemo.mdw workgroup information file.

This basic design is flexible and can serve in many different situations. For example, to revoke all rights for new tables, you change the third parameter for the *SetPermissions* method from *adAccessSet* to *adAccessRevoke*. To set rights for an existing database object, you replace the Null for the first parameter with the database object's name.

> **Note** The book's companion CD contains more VBA samples illustrating how to revoke permissions for new objects and how to set and revoke permissions for existing objects.

Putting It All Together

The following two procedures tap a cross-section of prior samples and show a new twist to the *SetPermissions* method. The first procedure calls the *MakeGroup* procedure to create a new group in the Systemdemo.mdw workgroup information file. Then it invokes the second procedure and passes along the new group's name as well as the name of a database object for which it wants to assign permissions. The last two lines in the first procedure create a new user named *NewUser2* and add *MySecretGroup2* to its *Groups* collection. In this way, *NewUser2* inherits the permissions assigned to *MySecretGroup2* by the second procedure.

```
Sub CallSetRIDTablePermissionsForGroupTable()

'This procedure makes a group called MySecretGroup2
'Assigns Read/Insert/Delete permissions for
'WebBasedList table to MySecretGroup2
'Next, it creates NewUser2 and assigns
'MySecretGroup2 to NewUser2

'Before running this, delete MySecretGroup2 and
'NewUser2 from UserLevel.mdb if they exist

MakeGroup "MySecretGroup2"
SetRIDTablePermissionsForGroupTable "MySecretGroup2", "WebBasedList"
MakeUser "NewUser2"
AddGroupToUser "NewUser2", "MySecretGroup2"

End Sub
```

```
Sub SetRIDTablePermissionsForGroupTable(grpName As String, tblName)
Dim cat1 As New ADOX.Catalog
Dim grp1 As New ADOX.Group, usr1 As New ADOX.User

'Instantiate catalog
Set cat1 = New ADOX.Catalog

'Set ActiveConnection property for catalog
cat1.ActiveConnection = _
    "Provider=Microsoft.Jet.OLEDB.4.0;" & _
    "Data Source=C:\PMA Samples\Chapter 12\UserLevel.mdb;" & _
    "Jet OLEDB:System database=C:\Program Files\Microsoft Office\" & _
    "Office10\systemdemo.mdw;" & _
    "User Id=Admin;Password=password;"

'Assign read, insert, and delete rights to an existing table
'for grpName group
cat1.Groups(grpName).SetPermissions tblName, adPermObjTable, & _
    adAccessSet, adRightRead Or adRightInsert Or adRightDelete

'Clean up objects
Set cat1 = Nothing

End Sub
```

The second procedure assigns Read, Insert, and Delete permissions for the *WebBasedList* table in UserLevel.mdb to *MySecretGroup2*. This procedure is similar to the earlier sample that applied for rights to a specific database object, but this one illustrates how to concatenate three separate rights to get a combined set of permissions. Notice that the syntax uses an Or operator for concatenating rights.

User-Level Security via Jet SQL and ADO

Jet SQL is the language of the Jet database engine. With the release of Jet 4.0, selected language enhancements target user-level security issues. This section commences with an overview of Jet SQL statements and keywords for managing security and then moves on to present two samples. The first sample illustrates how to add and drop users. The second sample shows how to manage permissions for a user.

Jet SQL Statements and Keywords for User-Level Security

Four Jet SQL statements enable the management of user and group accounts: CREATE, ADD, ALTER, and DROP. Use these statements with the USER and GROUP keywords to create and drop user and group accounts. You can assign both a password and a PID when you initially create either type of user-level security account. Invoke ALTER statements to modify initial settings for user and group accounts. You add and remove users from groups with ADD and DROP statements. DROP statements also permit you to remove individual group accounts and user accounts from the currently active workgroup.

You can execute these statements from a VBA procedure via ADO *Connection* or *Command* objects. The USER and GROUP keywords fail in the Access SQL View window. Additionally, Data Access Objects (DAO) does not enable the use of the USER and GROUP keywords.

Use the GRANT and REVOKE statements to manage assigning and removing permissions for objects to user and group accounts. Typical objects include tables and stored queries (either views or procedures). However, you also have the capability to assign permissions to a whole database file; to its forms, reports, and macros; and to its containers, which behave similarly to *AccessObject* objects. The range of permissions that you can grant and revoke includes those available through the Access security permissions interface (by selecting Tools-Security-User And Group Permissions). The complete list of permissions available for Jet 4.0, which ships with Access 2002, is available on MSDN in a white paper titled "Advanced Microsoft Jet SQL for Access 2000."

Adding a New User

One advantage of adding a new user with Jet SQL and the ADO *Connection* object (rather than using ADOX) is that you can set the PID. When you create a new user with ADOX, Access randomly assigns the PID. Because Jet uses the PID and user name to compute a security identifier (SID) for tracking users, the ability to specify a PID is critical to recovering user accounts when the workgroup information file is destroyed, corrupted, or otherwise unavailable. Without the ability to recover user SIDs, you will have to re-create all the security settings for each user and group account.

The following pair of procedures adds and drops a new user, *NewUser2*, to the UserLevel.mdb database file. The first procedure, *AddNewUser2*, adds and drops the new user and calls the second procedure. The second procedure, *CountAndListUsers*, generates a user report. The procedures generate three reports that give the count of users and their names. The first report documents the baseline number of users and their names. The second report confirms the addition of the new user. The last report confirms the return to the baseline number of users.

Notice the syntax for creating a new user. The PID appears after the password. Like a database password, the password for a user appears in square brackets. However, unlike a database password, the password for a user doesn't contain blank spaces or other special characters. All SQL strings execute from the *cnn1 Connection* object. Let's take a look at the syntax now:

```
'Make sure that the workgroup information file does
'not contain a user named NewUser2

Sub AddNewUser2()
Dim cnn1 As ADODB.Connection
Dim str1 As String

'Make secure connection to target database
Set cnn1 = New ADODB.Connection
With cnn1
    .Provider = "Microsoft.Jet.OLEDB.4.0"
    .Properties("Jet OLEDB:System database") = _
        "C:\Program Files\Microsoft Office\" & _
        "Office10\systemdemo.mdw"
    .Open "Data Source=C:\PMA Samples\Chapter 12\UserLevel.mdb;" & _
        "User ID=Admin;Password=password;"

'Count and enumerate users before adding a user
    CountAndListUsers cnn1

'Set SQL string to add a new user and execute it.
'Notice the specification of a PID after the password.
    str1 = "CREATE USER NewUser2 [password] pidcode"
    .Execute (str1)

'Count and enumerate users again to confirm addition
'of the new user
    CountAndListUsers cnn1

'Set SQL string to drop a user and execute it
    str1 = "DROP USER NewUser2"
    .Execute (str1)

End With

'Count and enumerate users again to confirm dropping
'of previously added new user
CountAndListUsers cnn1
```

(continued)

```
'Clean up objects
cnn1.Close
Set cnn1 = Nothing

End Sub


Sub CountAndListUsers(cnn1 As ADODB.Connection)
Dim cat1 As ADOX.Catalog
Dim usr1 As ADOX.User

'Instantiate catalog and set its ActiveConnection property
'to the passed Connection object
Set cat1 = New ADOX.Catalog
cat1.ActiveConnection = cnn1

'Print count of users (less Creator and Engine)
'and enumerate their names
Debug.Print "Total number of users is = " & _
    cat1.Users.Count - 2
For Each usr1 In cat1.Users
    If usr1.Name <> "Creator" And usr1.Name <> "Engine" Then _
        Debug.Print usr1.Name
Next usr1

'Clean up objects
Set cat1 = Nothing

End Sub
```

Granting and Revoking Permissions

The next sample we'll look at contrasts permissions for a new user. Like the previous sample, this one uses two procedures. The first procedure, *AssignUpdatePermissionsToNewUser2*, creates a new user account and grants and revokes user permissions. The second procedure, *SelectAndUpdateWithNewUser2*, selects and prints the *FirstName* field value for the first record, updates and prints this value again, and restores this value to its initial setting. An error trap responds when the user does not have permission to update a value from the *WebBasedList* table in the UserLevel.mdb database file.

The *AssignUpdatePermissionsToNewUser2* procedure starts by making a connection to the UserlLevel.mdb file. Then it defines the SQL string for adding a new user and executes the string through the connection. Next the procedure grants the new user Select permission for the *MSysAccessObjects* table. This step is not absolutely necessary in the sample application. However, if a user manually attempts to open the database with the new user account, he or she won't be able to view the Database window without receiving Select permission for the table.

The critical part of the *AssignUpdatePermissionsToNewUser2* procedure is the execution of the next two SQL strings. The first of these SQL strings grants the new user Select and Update permissions to the *WebBasedList* table in the UserLevel.mdb file. After granting these two permissions, the procedure invokes the *SelectAndUpdateWithNewUser2* procedure. This prints the original and updated values of the *FirstName* field for the first record in the *WebBasedList* table. Next the *AssignUpdatePermissionsToNewUser2* procedure revokes the UPDATE permission of NewUser2 to the *WebBasedList* table. The procedure follows this action with a call to the *SelectAndUpdateWithNewUser2* procedure. This second call prints the initial value of the *FirstName* field for the first record. However, the procedure generates an error when it attempts to update the field value because the user had his or her UPDATE permission for the table revoked. The error trap prints a message explaining the problem instead of printing the updated value. Figure 12-4 shows the results printed to the Immediate window.

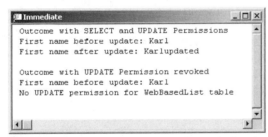

Figure 12-4 Output to the Immediate window from the *AssignUpdatePermissionsToNewUser2* procedure.

```
'Make sure that the workgroup information file does
'not contain a user named NewUser2

Sub AssignUpdatePermissionsToNewUser2()
Dim cnn1 As ADODB.Connection
Dim str1 As String

'Make secure connection to target database
Set cnn1 = New ADODB.Connection
With cnn1
    .Provider = "Microsoft.Jet.OLEDB.4.0"
    .Properties("Jet OLEDB:System database") = _
        "C:\Program Files\Microsoft Office\" & _
        "Office10\systemdemo.mdw"
```

(continued)

```
            .Open "Data Source=C:\PMA Samples\Chapter 12\UserLevel.mdb;" & _
                "User ID=Admin;Password=password;"

    'Set SQL string to add a new user and execute it
            str1 = "CREATE USER NewUser2 [password] pidcode"
            .Execute (str1)


    'Needed for viewing with manual opening of database
            str1 = "GRANT SELECT ON TABLE MSysAccessObjects TO NewUser2"
            .Execute (str1)

    'Grant SELECT and UPDATE permissions for WebBasedList table
    'and attempt to select and update from the table
            str1 = "GRANT SELECT, UPDATE ON TABLE WebBasedList TO NewUser2"
            .Execute (str1)
            Debug.Print "Outcome with SELECT and UPATE Permissions"
            SelectAndUpdateWithNewUser2

    'Revoke UPDATE permission for WebBasedList table
    'and attempt to select and update from the table
            str1 = "REVOKE UPDATE ON TABLE WebBasedList FROM NewUser2"
            .Execute (str1)
            Debug.Print vbLf & "Outcome with UPDATE Permission revoked"
            SelectAndUpdateWithNewUser2

    End With

    End Sub


    Sub SelectAndUpdateWithNewUser2()
    Dim cnn1 As New ADODB.Connection
    Dim rst1 As New ADODB.Recordset
    Dim str1 As String


    'Open connection to target user-level secured data
    'source; specify path for workgroup information
    'file; designate logon ID and password
    cnn1.Provider = "Microsoft.Jet.OLEDB.4.0"
    cnn1.Mode = adModeShareDenyNone
    cnn1.Properties("Jet OLEDB:System database") = _
        "C:\Program Files\Microsoft Office\" & _
        "Office10\systemdemo.mdw"
    cnn1.Open "Data Source=C:\PMA Samples\Chapter 12\UserLevel.mdb;" & _
        "User ID=NewUser2;Password=password;"
```

```
'Select and print FirstName field from first record
rst1.Open "WebBasedList", cnn1, adOpenKeyset, adLockOptimistic, _
    adCmdTable
Debug.Print "First name before update: " & rst1("FirstName")

'Clear Err object and trap for error with attempt to update
Err.Clear
On Error Resume Next

'Save FirstName field before attempting to update its value
str1 = rst1("FirstName")
rst1("FirstName") = rst1("FirstName") & "updated"

'Check results in Err object and respond appropriately
If Err.Number = -2147217911 Then
'Print no permission message
    Debug.Print "No UPDATE permission for WebBasedList table"
ElseIf Err.Number <> 0 Then
'Print alternate message for another error
    Debug.Print Err.Number, Err.Description
    Exit Sub
Else
'For FirstName field update table, print updated value
'and restore original FirstName field value
    rst1.Update
    Debug.Print "First name after update: " & _
        rst1("FirstName")
    rst1("FirstName") = str1
    rst1.Update
End If

'Clean up objects
cnn1.Close
Set cnn1 = Nothing

End Sub
```

Transactions

You can use transactions to bundle two or more database operations so that either they all occur or none of them occur. Transactions are useful in two types of situations: when your application must perform a set of operations as a unit (such as a funds transfer between a savings account and a checking account), and when you have to speed up a set of database operations by wrapping them in a transaction (because writing to a temporary cache in memory is faster than writing to a disk for each element within the transaction group).

Three *Connection* object methods in ADO support transactions: *BeginTrans*, *CommitTrans*, and *Rollback*. *BeginTrans* opens a transaction level. Jet supports up to five nested transactions. Once you start a transaction, you can end it with either the *CommitTrans* method or the *Rollback* method. You use *CommitTrans* to complete the database operations. You invoke the *Rollback* method to end a transaction without performing the database operations launched since the last *BeginTrans* method.

The procedure that follows uses three transaction methods for the *Connection* object. It loops through the records in a database while looking for one of three criteria matches. Once it finds a match, the procedure writes *US* in a field that Access stores in a data cache rather than to the database file. The procedure invokes the *BeginTrans* method just before starting the *Do* loop. At the end of the loop, the procedure asks whether the user wants to commit the changes. If the user replies *yes*, the sample invokes the *CommitTrans* method to commit the changes to the database. If the user replies *no*, the procedure discards the changes by invoking the *Rollback* method.

```
Sub ChangeInTrans()
On Error GoTo changeTrap
Dim cnn1 As ADODB.Connection
Dim rst1 As New ADODB.Recordset
Dim iChanges As Long
Const conLockedByAnotherUser = -2147217887

'Open recordset based on WebBasedList in current project
Set cnn1 = CurrentProject.Connection
rst1.Open "WebBasedList", cnn1, adOpenKeyset, _
    adLockPessimistic, adCmdTable

'Loop through all records to find those to update to US
cnn1.BeginTrans
Do Until rst1.EOF
    If rst1.Fields("Country") = "" _
        Or IsNull(rst1.Fields("Country")) = True _
        Or rst1.Fields("Country") = "USA" Then
        rst1.Fields("Country") = "US"
        iChanges = iChanges + 1
    End If
rst1.MoveNext
Loop
```

```
'Commit all changes if user says so.
'Roll changes back otherwise.
If MsgBox("Are you sure that you want to update" & _
    " these " & iChanges & " records?", vbYesNo, _
    "Programming Microsoft Access Version 2002") = vbYes Then
    cnn1.CommitTrans
Else
    cnn1.RollbackTrans
End If
Exit Sub

changeExit:
Exit Sub

changeTrap:
If Err.Number = conLockedByAnotherUser Then
    MsgBox "Recordset not available for update.  " & _
        "Try again later.", vbCritical, _
        "Programming Microsoft Access Version 2002"
Else
    Debug.Print Err.Number; Err.Description
End If
cnn1.RollbackTrans
Resume changeExit

End Sub
```

The *ChangeInTrans* procedure also invokes the *RollbackTrans* method if a run-time error occurs—such as when the database is locked by another user. In this situation, it is impossible to edit any records. With some databases, performing an operation on a subset of records can corrupt the whole database. If the procedure encounters an error for any reason, it rolls back any pending operations before exiting the procedure. Invoking the *RollbackTrans* method maintains the integrity of the database file.

13

Replicating Databases

A Microsoft Access application can present separate copies, or replicas, of databases to different groups of users while managing the replicas as a single database. This capability is particularly important for high-end Access applications with many users or with a few users who need exclusive database access while others read or update the database. Database replication also adds value to projects in which branch offices or mobile workers need to share parts of a database with a complete version at headquarters. Data can be shared without the need for a constantly open connection between two points. As the availability of inexpensive broadband telecommunications grows, Access database replication will increasingly become a viable solution for problems now addressed by proprietary, hardware-based solutions.

Access 2002 is the fourth version of Access to offer database replication, so this feature is mature and highly integrated. Database replication changed significantly with Access 2000, and Microsoft left those changes intact in Access 2002 without introducing any new ones. Therefore, this chapter presents an overview of replication, as well as the new replication features introduced with Access 2000 for those migrating to Access 2002 from Access 97 or an earlier version. The chapter also explains how to manage replication using the JRO 2.5 (or 2.6) library. (*JRO* stands for Jet and Replication Objects.) Microsoft introduced the JRO library with Access 2000 and then updated it in Access 2002 for compatibility with the other ActiveX Data Objects (ADO) components. The code samples in this chapter will benefit those who are just starting to program replication solutions. They also will help those who already know how to program replication with Data Access Objects (DAO) to make the transition to ADO. The JRO discussion in this chapter also includes advanced topics, such as processing system and hidden tables, as well as areas that do not explicitly relate to replication.

How Replication Works

Access lets you replicate multiple copies of a database over a local area network (LAN), wide area network (WAN), intranet, extranet, or the Internet. Users can modify their individual copies as their needs dictate. The connection between copies can be inoperable for long periods. You can also require that changes to any copy be replicated in all other copies.

Access calls the collective set of copies a *replica set*. (You are not restricted to working with a single replica set.) Each copy in the set is a replica. One copy within a replica set must function as a *Design Master*. The Design Master differs from the other replicas in that it can transfer structural changes (such as new forms and reports) and data changes to other members of the replica set. (Other products that offer database replication support data exchange between replicas, but they do not offer the ability to propagate structural changes across a replica set.)

Database replication occurs between pairs of replicas. Changes propagate throughout a replica set as replicas synchronize with each other. Each replica in a pair can send its changes to the other. If these changes do not conflict, the replicas update themselves with the package of changes they receive from each other. If some changes conflict because both replicas alter the same content, one change wins and the other loses. Access saves the losing change in a conflict table. You can use this table to manually resolve conflicts, or your application can apply automatic rules for processing the conflicts. Access has a built-in Conflict Resolution wizard; you can also build your own wizard to replace or supplement it.

Replication errors can occur when a change is valid in a local replica but is invalid in one or more other replicas within a set—for example, if you enter a record with the same primary key in two separate copies in a replica set. When you synchronize the two copies, the Jet database engine rejects the record with the duplicate primary key from the other replica. Other conditions can generate replication errors. For example, the introduction of a field or table-level validation rule in one replica can create invalid data in other replicas when users enter data without the validation rule.

There are workarounds to prevent both of these errors. However, you must design your database and administer it to reduce the likelihood of replication errors. Using a solution that relies on database replication introduces another level of complexity to your task as a developer. You can guard against identical primary key values in different replicas by using either globally unique identifiers (GUIDs) or a two-field primary key that uniquely identifies the replica ID in one field and uniquely identifies a record within the table in the second field. A solution based on a two-field primary key is easier to administer than one based on a GUID. You can guard against data validation rules in one replica that cause replication errors in other replicas by propagating the validation rule across the replica set before entering any new data that tests the rule.

> **Note**   Jet replication and other Microsoft applications generate GUIDs for tracking items known to be unique in space and time. A GUID's only representation is a 128-bit value. For this reason, GUIDs can be awkward to work with. For more detail on the uses of GUIDs in Access database replication, see the white paper at msdn.microsoft.com/library/techart/dbrepjet.htm.

Replicas can diverge from each another in one of two ways. First, they might need to complete a synchronization cycle in which all the replicas exchange data with one another. You can remedy this by completing the synchronizations among replica set members. Replicas can also diverge from one another because of replication conflicts and errors—even if they are completely synchronized.

You can replicate databases in five ways:

- Using the Microsoft Briefcase icon

- Using the Replication command

- Using JRO (or DAO) programming

- Using the Replication Manager

- Using Internet synchronization

Using the Briefcase Icon

Using the Briefcase icon, end users can take a copy of a database off site and make updates to it. When they return it, they can synchronize the replica on a laptop with the one on their desktop computer or department computer. Developers can use Briefcase replication to place a Design Master on their laptop and build custom forms and reports. Later they can synchronize the new database objects with the production version.

The Briefcase icon is available on the desktop in Microsoft Windows 95, Windows 98, Windows NT 4, and Windows 2000. Dragging an .mdb file from Windows Explorer to the Briefcase icon converts a database from a standard format to one equipped with special tables and fields that support replication. (With other Microsoft Office applications, the Briefcase merely makes copies of whole files without any synchronization between copies.) The Briefcase reconciler leaves the updated original as a Design Master at the source and places a replica in the Briefcase. You can alter this if you need a Design Master in the Briefcase.

Briefcase might not be installed on your computer. To install Briefcase on a computer running Windows 95 or Windows 98, double-click the Add/Remove Programs option in the Control Panel. Click the Windows Setup tab of the Add/Remove Programs Properties dialog box, select Accessories, and click the Details button. Then in the Accessories dialog box, select Briefcase, click OK, and follow the prompts. On a computer running Windows NT or Windows 2000, right-click the desktop and select New-Briefcase from the shortcut menu.

> **Note** When the Briefcase reconciler creates a replica set, it asks whether you want a backup version of the original database. Unless you are sure that you won't need to return to the original, you should accept this option because the conversion adds many new tables and fields. There is no simple, automatic way to remove these with built-in Access tools.

Using the Replication Command

You choose Tools-Replication to access the commands that make a database replicable, create more replicas, synchronize replicas, reconcile conflicts, and prototype test versions of a replication application. You can create a Prevent Deletes replica (a new feature) only through the Tools menu (although you can control it programmatically after you create it).

To reconcile replication conflicts and errors, you probably have to manually review individual exceptions that appear in the conflict tables. Even if you ultimately program custom reconciliation rules, you probably have to evaluate the rules manually before adopting them for production use.

Using JRO Programming

JRO programming is fundamentally an ADO approach because it relies on ADO connection objects. While ADO is a universal data access technology, the JRO extension functions exclusively with the Jet database engine. If you programmed custom replication solutions in Access 95 or Access 97, now is the time to transition from DAO to JRO programming.

The JRO model supports three general tasks:

- Creating and managing replica sets
- Compacting and encrypting databases
- Refreshing the memory cache to improve apparent performance

The three main objects in the JRO model are shown in Figure 13-1. The first is the *JetEngine* object, which supports features specific to the Jet database engine, including compacting and encrypting databases and refreshing the memory cache.

Figure 13-1 The main portion of the JRO model.

The second main object is the *Replica* object, which represents a copy of a database. *Replica* objects are the basic building block of a replica set. You can manage a replica set by manipulating the properties and methods of the *Replica* objects. The functions that you can administer include the following:

- Making a database replicable

- Creating replicas from the Design Master and other replicas

- Synchronizing replicas

- Reading the replicability of individual objects

- Assigning a new design master

- Managing the retention period for replication history

The JRO model also includes properties for managing many new and revised features, such as visibility, replica type, and priority-based conflict resolution. The third main object is the *Filter* object. You use this with partial replicas to restrict the contents of a database copy. You can base a filter on a table or a relationship. JRO has a *Filters* collection for all the filters in a replica. These collectively limit the data that can enter into a partial replica.

Using the Replication Manager

The Replication Manager, which ships with Microsoft Office XP Developer, helps you administer a replica set over a network, which can include LAN and WAN connections. In its initial release with Access 97, the Replication Manager supported Internet synchronization via FTP. The new Internet synchronization introduced with Access 2000 rendered this feature obsolete. However, you must still use the Replication Manager with the version of Internet synchronization first available with Access 2000. You use the Replication Manager to make occasional connections to a network or for indirect synchronization, in which changes from one replica to another can go to a drop box or shared Windows folder if the receiving replica is not open. Later, when the receiving database opens, the Synchronizer agent that the Replication Manager controls passes along the updates. The Replication Manager also offers a graphical user interface for scheduling periodic updates. You must configure the Replication Manager for your server.

You can also use the Replication Manager to coordinate replicas across a WAN. It offers a graphical depiction of your replica set's topology. One common design is a star topology in which a hub replica exchanges data with a related set of spoke replicas that each connect with just the central replica. A fully connected topology links each replica directly with all other replicas. This allows for much faster transfer of data updates throughout the replica set, but at the expense of increased network traffic. Other typologies offer different design/performance trade-offs.

This book's appendix, "Microsoft Office XP Developer," includes additional coverage on Replication Manager and other replication capabilities available from Office XP Developer.

Using Internet Synchronization

Using Internet synchronization, you can replicate databases across a World Wide Web (FTP or HTTP 1.1) connection. The connection can be across the Internet, an intranet, or an extranet, and the computers need not be connected all the time. Unlike the indirect synchronization supported by the Replication Manager, Internet synchronization does not require a Synchronizer agent running on the client computer. Furthermore, Internet synchronization can work with anonymous replicas. This is one of the replica *Visibility* property settings introduced with Access 2000. (See the white paper titled "Internet Synchronization with the Microsoft Jet Database Engine: A Technical Overview" at msdn.microsoft.com/library/backgrnd/html/intrjet4.htm for details on setting up, administering, and testing an Internet synchronization system.)

Programming Internet synchronization is straightforward, but configuring Internet Information Services (IIS) 4 or 5 to accommodate Internet synchronization can be challenging for Access developers who do not regularly administer IIS. If you are in this category, you might benefit from enlisting a sophisticated Web administrator to assist with configuring IIS for Internet synchronization.

As mentioned earlier, Internet synchronization with Access 2000 has made the Access 97 version obsolete. Four main enhancements differentiate Internet synchronization with Access 2000 from its predecessor:

■   Support for replication over an HTTP 1.1 protocol connection (Support for Netscape servers is available via this protocol.)

■   Performance enhancements relating to encryption

- Support for a new lightweight replica tailored for Web-based replication

- New registry keys to fine-tune synchronizer timeouts

When you select a Web server with which to synchronize, Access can automatically determine whether to use HTTP or FTP. Besides permitting operation on Netscape servers, the HTTP protocol lets a replica synchronize from behind a properly configured proxy server to a synchronizer on the Internet. Access 2000 does not explicitly support the reverse configuration. If your originating replica is not encrypted, Internet synchronization does not automatically encrypt the updates that it sends to the synchronizing target replica. The initial version of Internet replication automatically encrypted all updates for transfer over the Web. The new, lightweight anonymous replicas can replicate only with their parent replica on a Web server. You must manage that parent replica on the Web server using the Replication Manager.

Replication Design Changes

When you make a database replicable by any of the means discussed earlier, you typically add a collection of system tables as well as a set of fields to each table. Access uses these tables and fields to help manage the replication project. These tables and fields can also add substantially to the size of a database. Beyond that, the special replication tables and fields consume resources that slightly lower the maximum number of custom fields per table and the number of bytes per record available for custom uses in your database application. Therefore, understanding these design changes will help you manage Access replication projects.

> Note   To view most of the special replication fields and tables, choose Options from the Tools menu. Select the System Objects check box, and then click OK.

Replication System Fields

Tables in a replication application typically gain four new fields: *s_GUID*, *s_Generation*, *s_Lineage*, and *s_Collineage*. The *s_GUID* field uniquely identifies each row in each table in the replica set. The same row in the same table in two different replicas will have different GUID values.

When you design tables for a replication application, you can use an autogenerated GUID as the primary key for a database. If a GUID serves as the primary key field for a table, Access does not create the *s_GUID* field when you make a table replicable. Instead, it uses the primary key to serve the same purpose. To use a GUID as a primary key, select *Replication ID* as the *FieldSize* property for a field with Number or AutoNumber as the data type. As indicated previously, it's generally not preferable to use GUID values for a table's primary key values.

The *s_Generation* field tracks the generation of a change to a table. This field has a Long Integer data type. A value of *0* represents a new change that unconditionally requires replication. After initially propagating a change to another replica, Access updates the field value so that it represents the highest generation of change. The replication process keeps track of the last generation sent to each replica from each replica. When a new exchange commences, Access resumes with the next highest generation of change from the last synchronization with a replica.

The *s_Lineage* field tracks the history of changes to each row in a table. The field has an OLE Object data type. The field specifies when a row is sent to another replica. It eliminates the possibility of repetitively sending the same changes to another replica.

The *s_Collineage* field, which has an OLE Object data type, supports column-level replication. This feature was new with Access 2000. Prior versions of Access used row-level replication. (The upcoming section, "What's New in Access Replication," explores this further.) The *s_Collineage* field tracks information that enables the detection of changes at the column level during synchronization.

Each field with the Memo or OLE Object data type also receives a separate generation field. Because such fields can be especially large, they do not necessarily propagate from one replica to another when a field in a row changes value. These fields propagate between replicas only when they actually change value. Their individual generation fields track this for the replication process. A replicable version of the Northwind *Category* table has one special generation field for the category pictures, but the *Employees* table has two special generation fields—one each for the *Note* and *Photo* fields.

Replication System Tables

A number of system tables support the behavior of a replica set, as shown in Table 13-1. Some of these tables, such as *MSysTableGuids*, can be sparse and basic. *MSysTableGuids* stores GUIDs for each table name in a replica (excluding the replication system tables and the special hidden conflict tables). Some tables use the GUIDs denoted in *MSysTableGuids* to identify specific tables in a replica set. Other tables store information about historical or pending operations. The *MSysTombstone* table stores information on deleted records. The built-in replication logic uses this table to delete records in receiving replicas during synchronization.

Table 13-1 **Replication System Tables**

Provider Name	Description
MSysConflicts	Tracks all conflicts. Replicated to all members of the replica set.
MSysExchangeLog	Tracks synchronization information between a replica and all other members in the replica set.
MSysGenHistory	Stores information about each generation of synchronization. Avoids resending old generations to active replica members and updating replicas restored from backup copies.
MSysOthersHistory	Stores information about generations of updates from other replica members.
MSysRepInfo	Contains a single record with details relevant to the whole replica set. Replicated across the members of the replica set.
MSysReplicas	Stores information about all replicas in a replica set.
MSysSchChange	Stores information about changes to the design master replica for dissemination to other replica set members.
MSysSchemaProb	Stores information about conflicts between replica set members. If there are no unresolved conflicts, this table does not appear.
MSysSchedule	Used by the Local Synchronizer agent to manage timing of synchronizations with other replicas.
MSysSideTable	Contains detailed conflict information.
MSysTableGuids	Relates table names to GUIDs. Other replication system tables use these GUIDs.
MSysTombstone	Stores history of deleted records and supports delete updates throughout the replica set.
MSysTranspAddress	Stores information about synchronizers that manage replicas in a replica set.
MSysContents	Stores information about rows for partial replicas. Appears only in partial replicas.
MSysFilters	Stores information about filters for partial replicas. Appears only in partial replicas.

The *MSysConflicts* table references a set of nonsystem but hidden tables that store details about individual conflicts and errors for each table. The naming convention for these hidden tables is *UserTableName_Conflict*. For example, if there are one or more conflicts with the information between two replicas for the *Employees* tables, the replica that loses a conflict has a hidden table named *Employees_Conflict*. The rows of the tables document the losing record and contain a recommendation about how to proceed. When users resolve conflicts through the built-in logic, Access depends on and manages these tables. If you build custom conflict resolution logic, your custom solutions must also manage these tables. For example, after all the conflicts for a table are resolved, your application should remove the rows representing those conflicts from the *UserTableName_Conflict* table.

The replication fields and tables place additional constraints on the design of your Access applications. For example, Access permits an upper limit of 255 fields per table. However, replications typically add four fields (*s_GUID*, *s_Generation*, *s_Lineage*, and *s_Collineage*) plus one additional field for each Memo and OLE Object field in a table. As you plan the fields for a table, you must leave room for the special replication fields. The same type of considerations applies to the maximum byte count per record. See the white paper titled "Database Replication in Microsoft Jet 4.0" at msdn.microsoft.com/library for guidance on these and other advanced replication design matters.

Backing Up and Restoring the Original Database

You must carefully consider whether you want to make a file replicable because there is no built-in feature for restoring your original database. For this reason, you might want to back up the database file before making it replicable.

If you know the names of the replication tables and fields, you can reconstruct a new nonreplicable database file with the current information from any replica within a replica set. You must append tables from the selected replica to the new database copy. You append only the user fields, not any of the special replication fields. You can import all the tables instead (except, of course, the special replication tables) and then run delete queries to remove the special replication fields. You add the relationships between tables and then import the other database objects.

What's New in Access Replication

As mentioned earlier, Access 2002 retains all the replication innovations introduced with Access 2000. Among the most significant of these is the introduction of the JRO model for programmatically controlling replication. Some new features, such as the *Visibility* property, are not available with the traditional DAO programmatic interface—even in its latest upgrade (version 3.6)—so you should definitely learn the new way of programming replication.

Jet–SQL Server Bidirectional Replication

Access 2002 offers bidirectional merge replication between Jet and Microsoft SQL Server replicas. This kind of transfer requires you to use Jet 4 and SQL Server 7 or SQL Server 2000. Bidirectional transfer means that SQL Server can act as a central repository for a disconnected set of Access applications. Mobile workers with Access applications can transfer updates to a central database and download the latest changes from a headquarters database. You need to start with a SQL Server replica or upsize an Access replica to SQL Server.

Because replicating with SQL Server from a Jet replica relies on SQL Server replication, you will need to familiarize yourself with SQL Server replication concepts and techniques. One place to start is with the "Replication Overview" section in SQL Server Books Online (installed with SQL Server 2000; you can also download it from www.microsoft.com/sql/techinfo/productdoc/2000/books.asp). In addition, you should definitely review the "Implementing Merge Replication to Access Subscribers" section in SQL Server Books Online for specific details on the behavior of Jet–SQL Server replica sets.

When you set up a Jet–SQL Server replica set, a SQL Server replica must be at the hub and Jet replicas can function at the spokes. The Jet replicas can exchange content bidirectionally with the SQL Server hub replica. However, Jet replicas cannot exchange content bidirectionally with other Jet replicas at other spokes. The SQL Server hub replica must always serve as an intermediary between Jet replicas at the spokes. SQL Server is just a database engine and not a full application development environment like Access, so you cannot replicate Access-specific application objects, such as forms and reports, to the SQL Server hub. Nevertheless, this kind of design compensates by offering the other special advantages of SQL Server systems, such as client/server processing and multiprocessor scalability.

Column-Level Updates

One important way to improve the productivity of workers using a replicable database is to reduce the number of conflicts. Access 2000 introduced column-level updates to minimize collisions between two replicas. With prior Access versions, updates from two replicas collided if they changed the same record—even if they changed two different fields on the same record—because the lowest level of update tracking for replicas was the row. With Access 2000 and Access 2002, you can create replicas that detect changes down to the level of individual fields. Therefore, one user can change a customer's fax number in one replica while another user changes the street address of the contact person for the same customer in another replica. When the two replicas synchronize, no conflicts result.

Column-level tracking is the default setting for all new replicas. If you prefer, you can choose the traditional row-level tracking. When you update a replicable database from an earlier version of Access, it retains row-level tracking. Because there is a performance and size penalty for column-level tracking, you should not use it if conflicts are highly unlikely. The column-level tracking feature works in conjunction with SQL Server replicas as well.

Replica Visibility Levels

Access 2000 introduced three degrees of visibility for replicas: global, local, and anonymous. You can control the visibility of a replica as a property in JRO. You cannot change the visibility of a replica after you create it.

Replicas with global visibility function like traditional Access replicas. They can replicate with any other replica, and they are visible throughout a replica set. Local and anonymous replicas have special roles that allow a reduction in their size relative to the traditional global replicas. Replicas created from local and anonymous replicas share their parent's visibility property setting, except that they have a unique *ReplicaId* property. You cannot create a Design Master replica from either a local or an anonymous replica.

Local replicas are visible only to their parent, and they exchange content exclusively with their parent. Either the parent or the local replica can initiate an exchange. In addition, the hub parent for a local replica can schedule recurring synchronizations with a local replica. Local replicas cannot exchange information directly with other replicas in a replica set. However, changes to a local replica can propagate throughout a replica set by passing through the parent. Any conflicts between a local replica and its hub parent always result in the parent winning.

Anonymous replicas are for distribution across a Web-based (FTP or HTTP 1.1) connection. For successful synchronization of an anonymous client replica with a Web-based hub replica, the original anonymous replica must have as its source a global replica managed by the Replication Manager on the Web server. You can distribute copies using any appropriate means (for example, over the Web or using a CD). Like the local replica, the anonymous replica can synchronize only with its parent, but the parent cannot schedule replications with its anonymous children replicas. Exchanges must always be initiated by the anonymous replica to its parent. If any conflicts occur during synchronization, the parent replica always wins.

Note   The synchronization of anonymous replicas over the Internet has a known bug. If you've properly configured IIS 4 or 5, the solution could be to install Jet 4.0 Service Pack 5. Both Access 2000 and Access 2002 users can implement this solution by installing the Jet 5.0 Service Pack 5 upgrade. Neither version of Access ships with this upgrade. For detailed Service Pack 5 installation instructions, see support.microsoft.com/support/kb/articles/Q239/1/14.asp.

Priority-Based Conflict Resolution

Access 2000 introduced a new default conflict resolution rule that many replication users will find more intuitive than its predecessor. The earlier releases of Access resolved conflicts between two replicas by favoring the replica that changed a record the most. If two replicas changed a record an equal number of times, the replica with the lowest *ReplicaId* property won. The new default conflict resolution scheme employs a variation of the 800-pound gorilla rule: The replica with the highest priority wins. Priority property settings for replicas can range from *0* through *100*. Again, if two replicas have an equal priority, the one with the lowest *ReplicaId* property wins. This new rule has the advantage of being consistent with the one in SQL Server 7 replication.

A replica's *Priority* property setting is read-only after you create it. By default, the initial replica for a database has a setting of *90*. Any global replica based on another replica has a priority that is 90 percent of the initial one. Anonymous and local replicas have their *Priority* property forced to *0*. Replicas copied via MS-DOS or the *CompactDatabase* method have a priority that matches the original. Replicas converted from Access 97 have a priority of *90*. Otherwise, you can assign a *Priority* property anywhere in the legitimate range when you initially make a database replicable. All subsequent global replicas must have a *Priority* value that is less than or equal to their parent (unless the person creating the replica is a member of the Admins group or is an owner of the database).

> Note   To use individual Access 97 replicas with Access 2000 or Access 2002, convert the databases normally. If you want to upgrade a whole Access 97 replica set, the process is more involved. First you synchronize all Access 97 replicas twice in Access 97 to ensure that they are fully synchronized. Second you convert each replica as a normal database. Third you synchronize all replicas with Design Master in Access 2000 or Access 2002.

> Note   Converting partial replicas from Access 97 to Access 2000 or Access 2002 has a known bug. This bug deletes all database objects other than tables and queries in the partial replica after synchronization in Access 2000 or Access 2002. At the time of this writing, the only solution is to reconstruct the partial replica in Access 2000 or Access 2002.

Miscellaneous Refinements

A set of miscellaneous adjustments rounds out the new replication functionality introduced with Access 2000. A couple of them simplify such common tasks as restricting the behavior of a replica or reconciling synchronization errors. In another case, a design change can affect the optimal method of distributing application design changes.

The new Prevent Deletes replica (described earlier in "How Replication Works") prohibits users from deleting records. This feature offers an easy way to ensure that inexperienced users cannot inadvertently delete important content. The replica can still have deletions propagated to it from another replica, such as one managed by a database administrator.

As mentioned previously, you can now process synchronization conflicts and errors with the same interface. The Conflict Resolution wizard presents both conflicts and errors. (See Figure 13-2.) This removes the need for separate processing using different interfaces. In addition, the wizard works with both Jet 4.0 and SQL Server 7 replication.

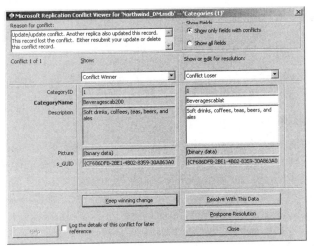

Figure 13-2 The Conflict Resolution wizard's Replication Conflict Viewer, which displays both conflicts and errors.

Deletions always have a higher priority than any change associated with a record in synchronization. This is true for all versions of Access, but with Access 2000, records losing to a delete add an entry to the conflict table for a user table. Prior versions simply ignored updates that lost to a delete.

Access 2000 introduced support for cascading through conflicting records. If the primary keys in two replicas conflict, one wins and the other loses. Records in other related tables also lose. When you fix the primary key in the losing replica, your fix in Access 2000 cascades through to the related records in other tables so that they do not require individual adjustment. Earlier Access versions required independent fixes to the primary table and its related tables.

Access 2000 introduced a new storage format that can affect how you decide to distribute software changes for a replicated project. With prior releases, you could synchronize changes to individual Access objects, such as forms and reports. With Access 2000, Access objects such as forms, reports, modules, and pages are contained either in a single binary large object or in the separate project.adp file. This storage design forces the replication of all objects if it is necessary to update any object. If this solution is not attractive, you can make prevent the Access project in the Design Master from being replicated. Then you are free to distribute design changes by other means (for example, by using a CD).

JRO Development Techniques

This section presents JRO development techniques for working with replication, including making a database replicable, creating full and partial replicas, compacting databases, synchronizing databases, and documenting replica properties.

Making a Database Replicable

You use the *MakeReplicable* method of a *Replica* object to make a database replicable. This process results in the new replica becoming a Design Master with a global *Visibility* property setting. Converting a standard Access database to a replicable database adds the special fields and tables discussed in the previous section. These additional fields and tables can increase the size of a database substantially, so you might want to make a backup copy of your database before making it replicable.

This is the syntax for the *MakeReplicable* method:

```
Replica.MakeReplicable ConnectionString, ColumnTracking
```

The connection string points at the database that you want to convert to a replicable format. You can set the *Replica* object's *ActiveConnection* property before invoking the *MakeReplicable* method. However, the connection string argument for the method overrides the *ActiveConnection* property for a replica. The *ColumnTracking* argument for the method is a Boolean variable. Its default value is True. Recall that this can potentially help to reduce synchronization conflicts. If conflicts are unlikely (for example, because all the editing will take place with one replica), you should consider setting the value to False. Synchronization conflict tracking then falls back to the traditional row-level tracking. This eliminates a performance hit associated with column-level tracking.

The following two routines apply the *MakeReplicable* method to the Northwind_DM database as the database performs backup and error-trapping functions. The *CallMakeDesignMaster* procedure assigns values to its *path* and *replicaName* arguments before calling the *MakeDesignMaster* procedure. The sample concatenates *path* and *replicaName* variables as it calls the second procedure. The second procedure invokes the *MakeReplicable* method for the values passed to it.

> **Note**   Northwind_DM is a copy of the Northwind database. The
> Northwind_DM database provides you with a version of the classic
> Northwind sample database to make replicable; that way you also main-
> tain an untransformed version of the database for your work that does
> not involve replication.

```
Sub CallMakeDesignMaster()
Dim path As String
Dim replicaName As String

path = "C:\PMA Samples\"
replicaName = "Northwind_DM.mdb"

'Set the second parameter to True to invoke
'column-level tracking of resolution conflicts
MakeDesignMaster path & replicaName

End Sub

Sub MakeDesignMaster(newReplica As String, _
    Optional ColumnTracking As Boolean)
On Error GoTo DMTrap
Dim repMaster As New JRO.Replica
Dim fs As Object

'Offer to copy database for restoring it after
'making the database replicable
If MsgBox("Do you want to make a backup copy", _
    vbYesNo, "Programming Microsoft Access Version 2002") = vbYes Then
    Set fs = _
        CreateObject("Scripting.FileSystemObject")
    fs.Copyfile newReplica, "C:\PMA Samples\DMBackup.mdb"
End If

'Optionally make the newReplica database replicable
If ColumnTracking = True Then
    repMaster.MakeReplicable newReplica
Else
    repMaster.MakeReplicable newReplica, False
End If
```

(continued)

```
'Clear reference to Design Master
Set repMaster = Nothing

DMExit:
Exit Sub

DMTrap:
If Err.Number = -2147467259 And _
    Left(Err.Description, 5) = "Could" Then
    MsgBox "Can not create replica because file does " & _
        "not exist. Fix path/file name and try again.", _
        vbCritical, _
        "Programming Microsoft Access Version 2002"
    Resume DMExit
ElseIf Err.Number = -2147467259 And _
    Left(Err.Description, 8) = "Database" Then
    MsgBox "Database is already replicable. Use the " & _
    "CreateReplica method to base a new replica " & _
    "on it.", vbCritical, _
    "Programming Microsoft Access Version 2002"
    Resume DMExit
ElseIf Err.Number = 53 Then
    MsgBox "Original file not found for backup copy.  " & _
        "Correct file name and try again.", vbCritical, _
        "Programming Microsoft Access Version 2002"
    Resume DMExit
Else
    Debug.Print Err.Number; Err.Description
End If

End Sub
```

Before invoking the *MakeReplicable* method, the *MakeDesignMaster* procedure asks whether the user wants to make a backup copy. If the user responds Yes, the procedure creates an instance of the *FileSystemObject*. Then it invokes the *Copyfile* method to back up the file. This makes it easy to return to a version of the database without the special replication fields and tables.

The *MakeDesignMaster* procedure accepts up to two arguments. The first argument is the concatenation of *path* and *replicaName*. The Design Master for the new replica set is a file named by the value for *replicaName*. The second procedure optionally accepts a second argument. If present, this Boolean variable specifies whether to invoke column-level tracking of synchronization conflicts. The sample passes a value of True. The sample's design requires the user to specify True for the second argument to obtain column-level tracking. Failure to specify the second argument causes the Boolean variable to assume its default value of False. The *MakeReplicable* method creates replicas with column-level tracking by default, so the procedure does not actually have to specify True to create a replica with this feature.

> **Note**   There is no column-level tracking property. Therefore, you must manually track the status of this variable for all your replicas.

The procedure explicitly traps three distinct errors. One is for the operation of the *FileSystemObject*, and the other two are from Jet. Notice that the replication component in Jet passes back the same *Err* number (−2147467259) for two distinctly different errors. Happily, these errors have different descriptions. The sample uses this feature to distinguish between the two. (A production system would use a longer description segment to identify the error type definitively or use a more advanced technique for parsing errors.)

> **Note**   You can differentiate native errors from Jet or SQL Server errors without relying on the *Err Description* property. However, using this property is potentially meaningful to more developers than the alternative, which involves enumerating the *Errors* collection of the *Connection* object and deciphering the native error codes. This alternative approach returns distinct error numbers from the native database engine. See the *DemonstrateNativeErrors* procedure in the Chapter 13.mdb file on the book's companion CD for one solution to this problem for a SQL Server database.

Creating Additional Full Replicas

You apply the *CreateReplica* method to a new instance of a *Replica* object to transform the instance into a new member of a replica set. Before invoking the method, you assign the *ActiveConnection* property for the new instance so that it points at the Design Master or another replica from the target replica set. This method fails if the *ActiveConnection* setting inadvertently denotes a database with a *ReplicaType* property of *jrRepTypeNotReplicable*. In general, this method returns a new replica of the same type and visibility as the model. However, because there should be only one Design Master, modeling a new replica on a Design

Master returns another global replica subject to the parameters for the method. The general syntax for the application of the method follows:

```
Replica.CreateReplica ReplicaName, Description, ReplicaType, _
    Visibility, Priority, Updatability
```

The *ReplicaName* parameter specifies the path and filename of the new replica. It can be up to 255 characters long. *Description* is an optional field that helps identify members in a replica set. The default *ReplicaType* value is *jrRepTypeFull* for a full replica. You can specify *jrRepTypePartial* instead. The *Visibility* parameter can have a value of *jrRepVisibilityGlobal* (the default), *jrRepVisibilityLocal*, or *jrRepVisibilityAnon*. If you do not specify a value for *Priority*, it uses its default rules; the range is *0* through *100*. A full replica has 90 percent of its parent's *Priority* value by default. The *Updatability* parameter can designate either a read-only replica (*jrRepUpdReadOnly*) or a read-write replica (*jrRepUpdFull*).

The following sample creates a replica based on the Northwind_DM Design Master from the preceding sample. The *ActiveConnection* setting establishes this replica. The new replica is a full one with global visibility. The name and path to the replica is c:\\cab2000\c\PMA Samples\foo.mdb. In accordance with the parameter settings for the new replica, its description is foo full replica.

```
Sub MakeFullReplica()
Dim repMaster As JRO.Replica

'Instantiate a replica
Set repMaster = New JRO.Replica

'Point repMaster at a Design Master .mdb file
repMaster.ActiveConnection = _
    "C:\PMA Samples\Northwind_DM.mdb"

'Make sure foo.mdb is deleted before running the next line
repMaster.CreateReplica "\\cab2000\c\PMA Samples\foo.mdb", _
    "foo full replica", jrRepTypeFull, _
    jrRepVisibilityGlobal, , jrRepUpdFull

End Sub
```

You need not create a backup in this case because the command creates a new replica that must be based on an existing one. However, the procedure can fail if the replica already exists or if the model for the replica does not exist (that is, if the file is missing). These are simple error-trapping issues. The initial sample took one approach to this kind of task while creating a replica. You might want to assume that the new version makes any existing version with the same name obsolete. The next sample we'll look at implements this logic by deleting the old replica, which eliminates the source of one error before it arises.

Creating Partial Replicas and Filters

A partial replica is a replica that doesn't have all the data a full replica does. Recall that this type of replica is useful for branch offices and mobile workers who need access to a subset of the data maintained at headquarters. Using partial replicas limits the amount of data that the users of a replica can view, and it reduces the amount of updating necessary to synchronize a replica.

After you make a blank partial replica with the *CreateReplica* method, you must populate the partial replica with data. Each partial replica has a *Filters* collection. Each *Filter* object within the *Filters* collection specifies a different slice of data that the partial replica contains. For a partial replica to contain data initially, you must specify one or more filters for it, append these to the replica's *Filters* collection, and then invoke the *PopulatePartial* method.

You can base a filter on the WHERE clause of an SQL statement (without the WHERE keyword) or on a relationship. You add and specify filters to a partial replica with the *Filters* collection's *Append* method. This method takes three arguments: The *TableName* property designates the table for which the filter specifies the content, the *FilterType* property denotes with a constant whether an SQL criteria statement (*jrFilterTypeTable*) or a relationship (*jrFilterTypeRelationship*) filters entries for the table, and the *FilterCriteria* property includes the relationship name or the WHERE phrase from an SQL statement that delimits the records for a table.

The *PopulatePartial* method for a replica clears all records in a partial replica and repopulates the replica based on its current filters. It does this by synchronizing the partial replica with a full replica. The method takes two arguments. The first one is an object variable that points to the partial replica to repopulate. The second is a string variable that designates the path and filename for the full replica with which the partial replica synchronizes. You should generally use the *PopulatePartial* method for a partial replica when you initialize the replica or change its filters. To use the *PopulatePartial* method with a partial replica, you must first open the replica with exclusive access because the method removes all records from the replica as the first step to repopulating the replica with records.

The following four procedures illustrate one approach to defining two partial replicas by using *Filter* collections and the *PopulatePartial* method. The *CallMakePartialFilter* procedure calls *MakePartialFilter* twice with two different sets of arguments. First, it launches the process to create a partial replica named Partial of Northwind.mdb. Then it repeats the process for another replica named Partial of foo.mdb.

```
Sub CallMakePartialFilter()

MakePartialFilter "Partial of Northwind_DM.mdb", _
    "Northwind_DM.mdb", "C:\PMA Samples\"
```

(continued)

```
    MakePartialFilter "Partial of foo.mdb", _
        "foo.mdb", "\\cab2000\c\PMA Samples\"

End Sub


Sub MakePartialFilter(replicaName As String, _
    sourceName As String, path As String)
Dim rep As New JRO.Replica
Dim flt1 As JRO.Filter
Dim strfile As String

'Delete old partial
strfile = path & replicaName
DeleteFile (strfile)

'Make partial
MakePartial path, replicaName, sourceName

'Open connection to partial and append filter
rep.ActiveConnection = _
    "Provider=Microsoft.Jet.OLEDB.4.0;Data Source=" & _
    path & replicaName & ";Mode=Share Exclusive"
rep.Filters.Append "Employees", jrFilterTypeTable, _
    "Title='Sales Representative'"
rep.Filters.Append "Customers", jrFilterTypeTable, _
    "Country='Spain' AND City='Madrid'"

'Populate partial from source
rep.PopulatePartial path & sourceName

End Sub


Sub DeleteFile(strfile)
On Error GoTo deleteTrap
Dim cnn1 As New ADODB.Connection
Dim fs As Object

'Prepare to delete file
Set fs = _
    CreateObject("Scripting.FileSystemObject")
fs.DeleteFile strfile

deleteExit:
Exit Sub
```

```
deleteTrap:
If Err.Number = 70 Or Err.Number = 75 Then
    MsgBox "Partial is unavailable to system.   " & _
        "Close it so that the system can create a " & _
        "new one.", vbCritical, _
        "Programming Microsoft Access Version 2002"
ElseIf Err.Number = 53 Then
    Resume Next
Else
    Debug.Print Err.Number; Err.Description
End If
Resume deleteExit

End Sub


Sub MakePartial(path As String, replicaName As String, _
    sourceName As String)
Dim rep As New JRO.Replica

rep.ActiveConnection = path & sourceName
rep.CreateReplica path & replicaName, _
    replicaName, jrRepTypePartial, _
    jrRepVisibilityGlobal, , jrRepUpdFull

End Sub
```

The *MakePartialFilter* procedure accepts arguments from the procedure *CallMakePartialFilter* that specify the name of the partial replica to create and the full replica data source for the partial replica. The *MakePartialFilter* procedure also defines and appends the *Filter* objects for a partial replica, and it invokes the *PopulatePartial* method to apply the filters.

The procedure first deletes the name of any existing partial replica with the same name and location as the one it wants to create. It does this by defining a string variable based on the *path* and *replicaName* variables it receives from the calling routine. Then it passes that new string variable to the *DeleteFile* procedure. Barring an unanticipated error, *DeleteFile* performs one of three tasks: it deletes the old file for the replica, it reminds a user to close a replica so that the application can delete it, or it ignores an error caused by the fact that the file does not exist (error number 53).

After attempting to delete the existing file, the procedure creates a new partial replica by calling the *MakePartial* procedure. The call passes three arguments: *path*, *replicaName*, and *sourceName*. The *MakePartial* procedure is nearly identical in design to the *MakeFullReplica* procedure. Both invoke the *CreateReplica* method for a new instance of a *Replica* object. Aside from using variables to denote the path and filename, the key difference is that the *MakePartial* procedure specifies *jrRepTypePartial* as the *ReplicaType* property while *makeFullReplica* uses *jrRepTypeFull* as its *ReplicaType* argument. Notice that *MakePartial* specifies the new replica's name as the concatenation of the *path* and *replicaName* variables. The *ActiveConnection* property for the new replica instance specifies the full replica source for the partial replica. The procedure specifies this source as the concatenation of the *path* and *sourceName* variables. It requires that the full and new partial replica both reside in the same path. It is easy to remove this constraint; the chapter's final sample (beginning on page 742) shows how to do this.

After the *MakePartial* procedure returns control to the procedure *MakePartialFilter*, the new partial replica exists but has no data, so *MakePartialFilter* populates it with data. First, it sets the *ActiveConnection* of a replica instance to the new partial replica and opens the replica in exclusive mode. Recall that this is necessary for the application of the *PopulatePartial* method. Next *MakePartialFilter* defines and appends a couple of *Filter* objects to the replica. The first filter extracts sales representatives from the *Employees* tables. The second filter extracts customers from Madrid, Spain. Finally, the *PopulatePartial* method synchronizes the full replica denoted by the concatenation of *path* and *sourceName* with the new partial replica. Only two tables receive records. (You can add filters to populate more tables in the partial replica.)

Synchronizing Replicas

The following two procedures synchronize replicas in typical replication scenarios. Both use basic ADO procedures. The *SynchNorthwindFooToAdd* procedure adds a new record to the *Employees* table in the Northwind.mdb replica. This is the Design Master for a replica set that includes foo.mdb. The procedure then synchronizes Northwind with foo to propagate the new record to foo.mdb. The second procedure, *SynchFooNorthwindToDelete*, deletes the new employee record from foo and then synchronizes foo with Northwind to remove the record from the Northwind replica as well.

```
Sub SynchNorthwindFooToAdd()
Dim rep1 As JRO.Replica
Dim cnn1 As New ADODB.Connection
Dim rst1 As ADODB.Recordset

'Open connection to Northwind and
'set reference for Northwind as a replica
cnn1.Open "Provider=Microsoft.Jet.OLEDB.4.0;" & _
    "Data Source=c:\PMA Samples\Northwind_DM.mdb"
Set rep1 = New JRO.Replica
rep1.ActiveConnection = cnn1
```

```
'Add a new employee to Northwind
Set rst1 = New ADODB.Recordset
rst1.Open "Employees", cnn1, adOpenKeyset, adLockOptimistic, _
    adCmdTable
rst1.AddNew
    rst1.Fields("FirstName") = "Rick"
    rst1.Fields("LastName") = "Dobson"
    rst1.Fields("BirthDate") = Date - 1
rst1.Update

'Synchronize Northwind with its full replica (foo.mdb)
rep1.Synchronize "\\cab2000\c\PMA Samples\foo.mdb", _
    jrSyncTypeImpExp, jrSyncModeDirect

End Sub


Sub SynchFooNorthwindToDelete()
Dim rep1 As JRO.Replica
Dim cnn1 As New ADODB.Connection, cmd1 As ADODB.Command

'Open connection to foo and
'set a reference to foo as a replica
cnn1.Open "Provider=Microsoft.Jet.OLEDB.4.0;" & _
    "Data Source=\\cab2000\c\PMA Samples\foo.mdb"
Set rep1 = New JRO.Replica
rep1.ActiveConnection = cnn1

'Execute command to remove an employee from foo.mdb
Set cmd1 = New ADODB.Command
With cmd1
    .ActiveConnection = cnn1
    .CommandText = "DELETE Employees.* FROM Employees" & _
        " WHERE LastName='Dobson'"
    .CommandType = adCmdText
    .Execute
End With

'Synchronize foo with its Design Master (Northwind.mdb)
rep1.Synchronize "c:\PMA Samples\Northwind_DM.mdb", jrSyncTypeImpExp, _
    jrSyncModeDirect

End Sub
```

The *SynchNorthwindFooToAdd* procedure uses ADO to add a record to a table in one replica and then propagate that record to a corresponding table in another replica. It starts by declaring *Replica*, *Connection*, and *Recordset* objects.

Then it opens a connection to the Northwind database and sets the *Active-Connection* property of the replica with the connection. It creates an instance of a *Recordset* object on the same connection as the replica. Then it adds an employee named Rick Dobson. The procedure closes by applying the *Synchronize* method to the Northwind replica and naming foo as the replica with which to exchange updates. This final step passes the new employee record from Northwind to foo.

The *SynchFooNorthwindToDelete* procedure removes the new record from foo. It also restores Northwind by synchronizing with it. This procedure uses a *Command* object to drop an employee with a last name of Dobson from the *Employees* table in foo. After executing the command, it applies the *Synchronize* method to the foo replica to propagate the delete to Northwind.

Working with Prevent Deletes Replicas

A Prevent Deletes replica is easy to create, but you must create it from the user interface. Choose Tools-Replication-Create Replica, and select the Prevent Deletes check box in the dialog box that opens. This type of replica allows an application to distribute a replica that does not support direct deletes to its contents. While you can achieve this result using Access security settings, it is much easier to just select the check box. While the user of a Prevent Deletes replica cannot directly delete records, the replica can accept delete updates from other replicas. One use for this type of replica is to enable an administrator to make sure that records are not deleted until they are properly archived.

The following three procedures manipulate Prevent Deletes replicas with ADO. *SynchAddToFoo2* adds a new employee to the foo2.mdb replica from the foo.mdb replica. The employee's name is Rick Dobson. The second procedure, *TryToDeleteFromFoo2*, attempts to delete the same record directly from the foo2.mdb replica. The error message in Figure 13-3 shows how Access responds to the *Execute* command in the procedure. If you need to restrict additions as well as deletions, you can set the *Updatability* argument in the *CreateReplica* method to *jrRepUpdReadOnly*. You do not need the user interface to do this. The third procedure, *synchFooFoo2ToDelete*, removes Rick Dobson from the foo.mdb replica and then propagates that deletion to the foo2.mdb replica. Although users cannot delete a record directly from a Prevent Deletes replica, an administrator can propagate a deletion using synchronization.

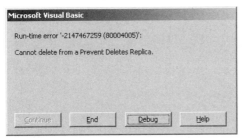

Figure 13-3 A Prevent Deletes replica returns an error message like this one when you try to delete one of its records.

```
Sub SynchAddToFoo2()
Dim rep1 As JRO.Replica
Dim cnn1 As New ADODB.Connection
Dim rst1 As ADODB.Recordset

'Open connection to foo and
'set a reference to foo as a replica
cnn1.Open "Provider=Microsoft.Jet.OLEDB.4.0;" & _
    "Data Source=\\cab2000\c\PMA Samples\foo.mdb"
Set rep1 = New JRO.Replica
rep1.ActiveConnection = cnn1

'Add a new employee to foo
Set rst1 = New ADODB.Recordset
rst1.Open "Employees", cnn1, adOpenKeyset, adLockOptimistic, _
    adCmdTable
rst1.AddNew
    rst1.Fields("FirstName") = "Rick"
    rst1.Fields("LastName") = "Dobson"
    rst1.Fields("BirthDate") = Date - 1
rst1.Update

'Synchronize foo with foo2.mdb
rep1.Synchronize "\\cab2000\c\PMA Samples\foo2.mdb", _
    jrSyncTypeImpExp, jrSyncModeDirect

End Sub


Sub TryToDeleteFromFoo2()
Dim rep1 As JRO.Replica
Dim cnn1 As New ADODB.Connection, cmd1 As ADODB.Command
```

(continued)

```
    'Open connection to foo2 and
    'set a reference to it as a replica
    cnn1.Open "Provider=Microsoft.Jet.OLEDB.4.0;" & _
        "Data Source=\\cab2000\c\PMA Samples\foo2.mdb"
    Set rep1 = New JRO.Replica
    rep1.ActiveConnection = cnn1

    'Execute command to remove employee from foo2.mdb;
    'it fails because foo2 is a Prevent Deletes replica
    Set cmd1 = New ADODB.Command
    With cmd1
        .ActiveConnection = cnn1
        .CommandText = "DELETE Employees.* FROM Employees" & _
            " WHERE LastName='Dobson'"
        .CommandType = adCmdText
        .Execute
    End With

End Sub


    Sub SynchFooFoo2ToDelete()
    Dim rep1 As JRO.Replica
    Dim cnn1 As New ADODB.Connection
    Dim cmd1 As ADODB.Command

    'Open connection to foo and
    'set a reference to foo as a replica
    cnn1.Open "Provider=Microsoft.Jet.OLEDB.4.0;" & _
        "Data Source=\\cab2000\c\PMA Samples\foo.mdb"
    Set rep1 = New JRO.Replica
    rep1.ActiveConnection = cnn1

    'Execute command to remove an employee from foo.mdb
    Set cmd1 = New ADODB.Command
    With cmd1
        .ActiveConnection = cnn1
        .CommandText = "DELETE Employees.* FROM Employees" & _
            " WHERE LastName='Dobson'"
        .CommandType = adCmdText
        .Execute
    End With

    'Synchronize foo with its Design Master (Northwind.mdb)
    rep1.Synchronize "\\cab2000\c\PMA Samples\foo2.mdb", _
        jrSyncTypeImpExp, jrSyncModeDirect

End Sub
```

Working with Replica Properties

By examining replica properties, you can understand the behavior of a replica set. For example, if you know a replica's type, you know whether it will share schema changes with other replicas. A replica's *Priority* property indicates which replica wins when two replicas conflict with one another. In general, the replica with the higher priority value wins. The three procedures that follow print replica properties and expose property values in the process.

Because there is no *Replicas* collection, you are likely to sequentially list a number of replicas when you want to process them—especially if the replicas belong to different replica sets. The *CallPrintTypePriority* procedure sets *path* and *replicaName* variables for each replica it wants to examine, and then it calls two subroutines. One subroutine (*PrintReplicaType*) returns information about the type of replica, and the other (*PrintPriority*) returns the *Priority* property value for a replica. In addition to *path* and *replicaName*, the set of procedures exchanges values with an argument named *Exist*. This Boolean variable tracks whether a file exists in a path. If a file does not exist, it obviously has no priority value.

```
Sub CallPrintTypePriority()
On Error GoTo TypeTrap
Dim repMaster As JRO.Replica
Dim path As String
Dim replicaName As String
Dim Exist As Boolean

'Instantiate replica
Set repMaster = New JRO.Replica

'Assign Boolean for file existing
Exist = True

'Assign path and replica names, and then
'call procedures for printing type and priority.
'PrintReplicaType procedure catches invalid file specifications.
path = "C:\PMA Samples\"
replicaName = "Northwind_DM.mdb"
repMaster.ActiveConnection = path & replicaName
PrintReplicaType replicaName, repMaster.ReplicaType, Exist
PrintPriority replicaName, path, Exist

'Change path if replica path is different from preceding one
path = "\\cab2000\c\PMA Samples\"
replicaName = "foo.mdb"
repMaster.ActiveConnection = path & replicaName
PrintReplicaType replicaName, repMaster.ReplicaType, Exist
PrintPriority replicaName, path, Exist
```

(continued)

```
'Leave path if replica has same path as preceding one
replicaName = "Partial of foo.mdb"
repMaster.ActiveConnection = path & replicaName
PrintReplicaType replicaName, repMaster.ReplicaType, Exist
PrintPriority replicaName, path, Exist

path = "C:\PMA Samples\"
replicaName = "Partial of Northwind_DM.mdb"
repMaster.ActiveConnection = path & replicaName
PrintReplicaType replicaName, repMaster.ReplicaType, Exist
PrintPriority replicaName, path, Exist

'This sample demonstrates detection of a nonreplicable database
replicaName = "DMBackup.mdb"
repMaster.ActiveConnection = path & replicaName
PrintReplicaType replicaName, repMaster.ReplicaType, Exist
PrintPriority replicaName, path, Exist

'This sample demonstrates detection of a wrong path/file specification
path = "\\badpath\c\PMA Samples\"
replicaName = "DMBackup.mdb"
repMaster.ActiveConnection = path & replicaName
PrintReplicaType replicaName, repMaster.ReplicaType, Exist
PrintPriority replicaName, path, Exist

TypeExit:
Set repMaster = Nothing
Exit Sub

TypeTrap:
If Err.Number = -2147467259 And _
    Left(Err.Description, 19) = _
    "Could not find file" Then
    Exist = False
    Resume Next
Else
    Debug.Print Err.Number, Err.Description
    Resume TypeExit
End If

End Sub


Sub PrintReplicaType(repName As String, _
    typeNumber As Integer, Exist As Boolean)

If Exist Then
'Decode replica type enumeration constants
```

```
        Select Case typeNumber
            Case jrRepTypeNotReplicable
                Debug.Print repName & " is not replicable."
            Case jrRepTypeDesignMaster
                Debug.Print repName & " is a Design Master."
            Case jrRepTypeFull
                Debug.Print repName & " is a Full Replica."
            Case jrRepTypePartial
                Debug.Print repName & " is a Partial Replica."
        End Select
Else
'If file does not exist, report it
    Debug.Print "Incorrect filename or path.  " & _
        repName & " does not exist.  "

End If

End Sub


Sub PrintPriority(replicaName As String, path As String, _
    Exist As Boolean)
Dim repMasterP As New JRO.Replica

'Print priorty and reset Exist
If Exist = True Then
'Assign connection for replica
    repMasterP.ActiveConnection = path & replicaName

    If repMasterP.ReplicaType <> jrRepTypeNotReplicable Then
'Print priority for replicas
        Debug.Print "Its priority is " & repMasterP.Priority & "."
    Else
'Print message for no replica
        Debug.Print "Therefore, it has no priority."
    End If
Else
'Print message for file does not exist
    Debug.Print "Therefore, it has no priority."
End If
Debug.Print

Exist = True

End Sub
```

The *CallPrintTypePriority* procedure uses error trapping to determine whether a file exists and to respond appropriately if it does not. When it tries to set the *ActiveConnection* property of a replica instance to a file that does not exist, the Jet replication component returns its standard *Err* number (−2147467259) with a descriptive phrase. The error trap checks for the phrase with the Jet replication *Err* number. If the error-trap logic determines that the file does not exist, the trap sets *Exist* to False and resumes. The two subroutines, *PrintReplicaType* and *PrintPriority*, interpret the False value for *Exist* and respond appropriately.

The *CallPrintTypePriority* procedure sends the *ReplicaType* property value for a replica when it calls the *PrintReplicaType* procedure. The *PrintReplicaType* procedure checks the value of *Exist* before trying to decipher the value of the *ReplicaType* property. If *Exist* is False, the procedure simply prints a message to the Immediate window that the file does not exist. If *Exist* is True, a *Select Case* statement decodes the *ReplicaType* property.

Note   The *PrintReplicaType* procedure represents *ReplicaType* values with the JRO *ReplicaTypeEnum* constant names. You can view these with the Object Browser. Type *ReplicaType* in the Search text box, and click the Search button. Select from the return set the *ReplicaTypeEnum* class for the JRO library. (Be careful: The DAO library has a different *ReplicaTypeEnum* class.) This selection lists the constant names and their *ReplicaType* values.

The design of the *PrintPriority* procedure is slightly different from that of the *PrintReplicaType* procedure. The *PrintPriority* procedure creates a replica instance within it. Then it derives a property value for the replica. In addition to checking the value of the *Exist* function, it checks the *ReplicaType* property of the replica instance. If the property shows that the file is not replicable by returning a value of *jrRepTypeNotReplicable*, the procedure prints that is the file has no priority. Otherwise, the procedure prints the value returned by the *Priority* property of its replica instance. Before returning control to the *CallPrintTypePriority* procedure, *PrintPriority* resets the value of *Exist* to True for processing the next replica.

Figure 13-4 presents the Immediate window output from running the *CallPrintTypePriority* procedure. Notice that the window contains six entries. These correspond to the six references to replicas in the *CallPrintTypePriority* procedure. The first four entries shown in the Immediate window are for the Northwind_DM.mdb, foo.mdb, Partial of foo.mdb, and Partial of Northwind_DM.mdb replicas. Notice that the output gives the replica name, replica type, and priority. The last two entries in the Immediate window show how the sample handles references to database files that are not replicas or have either an invalid filename or path.

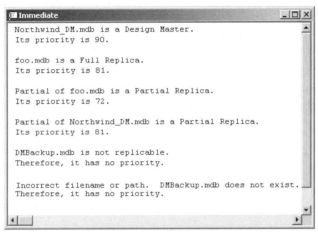

```
Immediate                                              _ □ ×
Northwind_DM.mdb is a Design Master.
Its priority is 90.

foo.mdb is a Full Replica.
Its priority is 81.

Partial of foo.mdb is a Partial Replica.
Its priority is 72.

Partial of Northwind_DM.mdb is a Partial Replica.
Its priority is 81.

DMBackup.mdb is not replicable.
Therefore, it has no priority.

Incorrect filename or path.  DMBackup.mdb does not exist.
Therefore, it has no priority.
```

Figure 13-4 Immediate window output from the *CallPrintTypePriority* procedure.

Processing Replication System Tables and Hidden Tables

Replication system tables, such as *MSysReplicas*, and hidden tables that contain information about conflicts in a replica are for internal use by Access. They are not intended for use by the typical developer. One reason is that the information contained in these tables can readily change between versions. Therefore, if you decide to use the contents of these tables, you should expect some instability between versions. Furthermore, these tables have no detailed published specifications on the meaning of their field values. Still, these tables contain very useful information, and you might want to peruse them for your custom replication applications.

Replication System Tables

The following sample enumerates the contents of all the fields for each record in the *MSysReplicas* table of the Northwind_DM.mdb replica. *MSysReplicas* has a row for each replica that is or was visible from Northwind_DM.mdb. This table can contain currently active replicas as well as deleted ones. Although you cannot open this table directly from the Database window, you can open it as the source for an ADO recordset. The following sample illustrates the syntax for this:

```
Sub LoopThroughReplicas()
Dim rst1 As ADODB.Recordset
Dim fld1 As ADODB.Field
Dim strType As String
```

(continued)

```
'Instantiate recordset pointing at a replica
Set rst1 = New ADODB.Recordset
rst1.Open "MSysReplicas", "Provider=Microsoft.Jet.OLEDB.4.0;" & _
    "Data Source=C:\PMA Samples\Northwind_DM.mdb;", _
    adOpenKeyset, adLockOptimistic, adCmdTable

'Print count of replicas in the replica set
Debug.Print rst1.RecordCount

'Print all field values for each replica in replica set
'from MSysReplicas table
Do Until rst1.EOF
    For Each fld1 In rst1.Fields
        Debug.Print fld1.Name, fld1.Value
    Next fld1
    Debug.Print
    rst1.MoveNext
Loop

End Sub
```

Figure 13-5 presents an excerpt from the Immediate window for the output from the sample listing the field values for the records in the *MSysReplicas* table. The first row of output indicates the number of replicas tracked by the *MSysReplicas* table. Because there are only four active replicas developed in this chapter and the value is 7, the rows include some replicas that I added and subsequently deleted.

Figure 13-5 An excerpt from the contents of the *MSysReplicas* table as generated by the *LoopThroughReplicas* procedure.

After listing the number of rows in the *MSysReplicas* table, the output enumerates field values for each row in the table. Notice that Pathname and UNCPathname denote the path and filename for the replica in two different formats. The *LastExchange* field presents the last time Access worked with the replica. For example, if the last task you performed on a replica was to create it, *LastExchange* will be the replica creation date. On the other hand, if your last use of a replica was for synchronization, the *LastExchange* field denotes the date and time of that synchronization. By contrasting the *Priority* field values for two different rows in the *MSysReplicas* record source, you can determine which replica will win in a conflict—unless both replicas have the same *Priority* value. In that case, you can examine the *ReplicaID* value to determine the winner; the one with the lower value wins. This *ReplicaID* value appears as a GUID with 32 hexadecimal characters. In my experience, the *ReplicaType* field value does not correspond to the *ReplicaType* property value for a replica.

Hidden Replication Tables

Hidden replication tables are another interesting collection of tables. Access generates these tables whenever a conflict arises. For example, if the Northwind_DM.mdb and foo.mdb replicas update an employee's first name differently, each replica will have an *Employees_Conflict* table after you synchronize the replicas. This *Employees_Conflict* table will have a separate row for each conflict. After a user reconciles the conflict, Access clears the corresponding row from the table. If you decide to custom-build a conflict resolver based on a rule other than replication priority values, linking the *Employees_Conflict* table and the *Employees* table by *EmployeeID* will permit you to view the winning and losing field values in the event of a conflict.

The following code sample synchronizes the Northwind_DM.mdb and foo.mdb replicas twice. The first synchronization occurs after the code adds a new employee named Rick Dobson to the *Employees* table in the foo.mdb replica. The synchronization copies the newly added employee from foo.mdb to Northwind_DM.mdb. Next the code modifies the first name of the new employee differently in each of the two replicas. The second synchronization exchanges the updates between the two replicas. Just before the second synchronization, the code sample refreshes the link to the foo.mdb replica. It does this by closing and reopening the connection to the foo.mdb database and setting that refreshed connection to the *ActiveConnection* property for the *rep1* replica instance. This refreshing is absolutely necessary only when foo.mdb is open. After the second synchronization, the code sample prints all the field values for all the rows in the *Employees_Conflict* table of the Northwind_DM.mdb database.

```
Sub SynchAddToFoo2X()
Dim rep1 As JRO.Replica
Dim cnn1 As New ADODB.Connection
Dim rst1 As ADODB.Recordset
Dim fld1 as Field

'Open connection to foo and
'set reference to foo as a replica
cnn1.Open "Provider=Microsoft.Jet.OLEDB.4.0;" & _
    "Data Source=\\cab2000\c\PMA Samples\foo.mdb"
Set rep1 = New JRO.Replica
rep1.ActiveConnection = cnn1

'Add a new employee to foo
Set rst1 = New ADODB.Recordset
rst1.Open "Employees", cnn1, adOpenKeyset, adLockOptimistic, _
    adCmdTable
rst1.AddNew
    rst1.Fields("FirstName") = "Rick"
    rst1.Fields("LastName") = "Dobson"
    rst1.Fields("BirthDate") = Date - 1
rst1.Update

'Synchronize foo with Northwind_DM.mdb
rep1.Synchronize "C:\PMA Samples\Northwind_DM.mdb", _
    jrSyncTypeImpExp, jrSyncModeDirect

'Change Northwind_DM.mdb for conflict with foo.mdb
rst1.Close
rst1.Open "Employees", "Provider=Microsoft.Jet.OLEDB.4.0;" & _
    "Data Source=C:\PMA Samples\Northwind_DM.mdb", _
    adOpenKeyset, adLockOptimistic, adCmdTable
rst1.Find ("LastName = 'Dobson'")
rst1("FirstName") = "Rickie"
rst1.Update

'Change foo.mdb for conflict with Northwind_DM.mdb
rst1.Close
rst1.Open "Employees", "Provider=Microsoft.Jet.OLEDB.4.0;" & _
    "Data Source=\\cab2000\c\PMA Samples\foo.mdb", _
    adOpenKeyset, adLockOptimistic, adCmdTable
rst1.Find ("LastName = 'Dobson'")
rst1("FirstName") = "Ricardo"
rst1.Update
rst1.Close
```

```
'Refresh replica before resynchronizing to detect conflict;
'only necessary if foo.mdb is open
cnn1.Close
cnn1.Open "Provider=Microsoft.Jet.OLEDB.4.0;" & _
    "Data Source=\\cab2000\c\PMA Samples\foo.mdb"
Set rep1 = New JRO.Replica
rep1.ActiveConnection = cnn1

'Synchronize foo.mdb with Northwind_DM.mdb to create conflict
rep1.Synchronize "C:\PMA Samples\Northwind_DM.mdb", _
    jrSyncTypeImpExp, jrSyncModeDirect

'Open Employees_Conflict table in Northwind_DM.mdb
'rst1.Close
rst1.Open "Employees_Conflict", "Provider=Microsoft.Jet.OLEDB.4.0;" & _
    "Data Source=C:\PMA Samples\Northwind_DM.mdb;", _
    adOpenKeyset, adLockOptimistic, adCmdTable

'Print count of conflicts for the Employees table in the replica
Debug.Print "Conflicts in Employees = " & rst1.RecordCount

'Print all field values for each conflict from Employees_Conflict table
Do Until rst1.EOF
    For Each fld1 In rst1.Fields
        Debug.Print fld1.Name, fld1.Value
    Next fld1
    Debug.Print
    rst1.MoveNext
Loop

'Clean up objects
rst1.Close
Set rst1 = Nothing
cnn1.Close
Set cnn1 = Nothing
Set rep1 = Nothing

End Sub
```

Because foo.mdb has a lower priority than does Northwind_DM.mdb, the *FirstName* field value from the Northwind_DM.mdb replica wins its conflict with the *FirstName* value from foo.mdb. This means that the *Employees_Conflict* tables in both the Northwind_DM.mdb and foo.mdb replicas contain the losing value from the foo.mdb table. The code sample prints the losing value, Ricardo Dobson, from foo.mdb. (See Figure 13-6.)

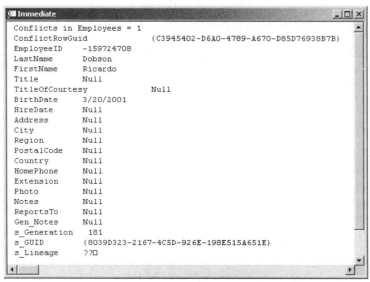

Figure 13-6 The field values from the *Employees_Conflict* table in the Northwind_DM.mdb replica after the second synchronization.

Figure 13-6 illustrates another replication feature. Notice that *EmployeeID* is a large negative number. As you will recall, the *EmployeeID* field in the *Employees* table has an Autonumber data type. The field value that appears in the figure is a random number—not a standard sequential Autonumber value. When you convert a database to a replica, Access converts the Autonumber fields in replicable tables to new values that are randomly chosen. Access does this to avoid duplicating primary key values in two replicas within a replica set.

Compacting and Encrypting Replicas

The JRO library supports more than just replication. For example, you can compact and encrypt files, and you can refresh the memory cache. The following two procedures make a backup of a replica by compacting it and encrypting the compacted copy. This approach is particularly appropriate when you send a file with sensitive information over the Internet. The sample compacts the Northwind.mdb file to Northwind2.mdb. You can optionally specify separate paths for Northwind and Northwind2.

```
Sub CallCompactADB()

CompactADB "Northwind.mdb", "Northwind2.mdb", _
    "C:\PMA Samples\"

End Sub
```

```
Sub CompactADB(oName As String, cName As String, _
    opath As String, Optional cpath As String)
Dim je As JRO.JetEngine
Dim strIn As String
Dim strOut As String

'Instantiate Jet Engine object
Set je = New JRO.JetEngine

'Is optional path specified?
If cpath = "" Then
    cpath = opath
End If

strIn = opath & oName
strOut = cpath & cName

DeleteFile strOut

je.CompactDatabase _
    "Provider=Microsoft.Jet.OLEDB.4.0;" & _
        "Data Source=" & strIn, _
    "Provider=Microsoft.Jet.OLEDB.4.0;" & _
        "Data Source=" & strOut & ";" & _
    "Jet OLEDB:Encrypt Database=True"

End Sub
```

14

Using Access to Build SQL Server Solutions: Part I

One of the most exciting advances Microsoft Access 2002 and Access 2000 have made over earlier versions of Access is to vastly improve upon the program's ability to build and manage Microsoft SQL Server solutions. If your organization or its clients are building or planning to build SQL Server solutions with Access, you should immediately upgrade Access.

These advances in administering SQL Server solutions deliver a number of substantial benefits. For starters, Access's friendly user interface (UI) and many powerful wizards dramatically drive down the cost of deploying SQL Server solutions by providing the solutions more quickly and easily. Second, Access enables tens of thousands of intermediate and advanced developers to start building more powerful solutions than they could with Jet databases. Third, Access gives SQL Server database administrators (DBAs) a rapid application development environment for creating forms, reports, and Web pages for their database clients. And finally, Access gives current SQL Server programmers a powerful, flexible development alternative that avoids the complexity of n-tier architectures.

Access 2002 offers tight integration with SQL Server 2000, and Access 2000 has a feature set tailored for SQL Server 7. You can obtain upgrades and patches to make Access 2000 compatible with SQL Server 2000. This chapter focuses almost exclusively on using Access 2002 with either SQL Server 2000 or the Microsoft SQL Server 2000 Desktop Engine.

The SQL Server 2000 Desktop Engine ships with any version of Microsoft Office XP that includes Access 2002. This engine version—abbreviated as MSDE 2000 throughout the chapter—is an upgrade to the Microsoft Date Engine (MSDE) that shipped with Office 2000. MSDE 2000 is compatible with SQL Server 2000, while its predecessor—MSDE—is compatible with SQL Server 7.

Besides its upgraded version of MSDE, Access 2002 ships with other enhancements that make it better suited than Access 2000 for developing SQL Server 2000 solutions. This chapter highlights these enhancements while explaining the basics of developing SQL Server solutions with Access. Building on this foundation, Chapter 15, "Using Access to Build SQL Server Solutions: Part II," will explore application development issues, database administration, and migrating Access database files to SQL Server.

See Chapter 12, "Building Solutions with MSDE and Access Projects," in *Programming Microsoft Access 2000* (Microsoft Press, 1999) for coverage of how to build SQL Server 7 solutions with Access 2000. Furthermore, another of my books, *Professional SQL Server Development with Access 2000* (Wrox Press, 2000), provides in-depth coverage of SQL Server development techniques—especially those applying to SQL Server 7.

Access Projects and SQL Server Versions

To understand how Access 2002 interoperates with SQL Server, you need to learn about Access projects. Access projects dramatically enhance the ability of developers to use Access to create, manage, and deploy SQL Server solutions. This section describes what an Access project is and presents the basic architecture of an Access project. It also examines the versions of SQL Server with which Access projects interoperate.

Understanding Access Projects

An Access project is a new Access file type that offers an alternative to the traditional Access database file. The new file type has an .adp extension, which differentiates it from the traditional .mdb file. Both file types feature a Database window for opening and designing database objects, such as tables, and application objects, such as forms and reports. The .mdb file is optimized for processing Jet databases in a file/server environment. The .adp file is optimized for working with SQL Server in a client/server environment.

> **Note**   Prior to Access 2000, Access developers typically worked with SQL Server databases by using linked tables from Access database files. The introduction of Access projects with Access 2000 did not eliminate this linked table capability, but its functionality is dwarfed by the vastly superior capabilities of Access projects.

What I find most exciting about Access projects is their ability to easily create SQL Server objects. Access 2002 provides visual designers for creating databases, tables, views, stored procedures, and user-defined functions, which appeared initially with SQL Server 2000. In addition, through database diagrams, you can create primary keys, indexes, constraints, and relationships between tables. A database diagram is similar to the Access database file Relationship window, but you can do more with a database diagram and you can have more than one diagram per database. Access 2002 makes basing forms and reports on SQL Server objects straightforward. By using server-side filters, you can improve the performance of your forms because less data will move over a network.

Because this book is about programming, you probably will be happy to learn that it's much easier now to program SQL Server from Access because of text-based design environments for creating and editing stored procedures and user-defined functions. This chapter will demonstrate the use of these environments.

The SQL Distributed Management Objects (SQLDMO) Object Library, which Access developers can readily program from Access project modules, helps you administer SQL Server. This hierarchical object model is great for enumerating, exploring, and creating server-side database objects, such as tables, views, stored procedures, and user-defined functions. A redesign to the UI for Access 2002 requires that you programmatically administer typical SQL Server security tasks, such as adding users and assigning permissions. You can easily program these tasks using SQL-DMO in an Access module or Transact-SQL (T-SQL) in a stored procedure. Chapter 15 discusses SQL Server security programming with SQL-DMO.

> **Note**   Transact-SQL is an extension of the SQL standards authorized by the American National Standards Institute (ANSI) and the International Organization for Standards (ISO). This extension conforms with all SQL Server versions, enabling you to optimize and simplify your code for any SQL Server version you use. The T-SQL extension for SQL Server is analogous to Jet SQL for Jet databases.

Access Project Architecture

The Access project represents the client side of a client/server application. The SQL Server database to which the Access project connects represents the server side of the client/server application. An OLE DB connection links the client and server sides of this application. Notice that there isn't a database file as in a traditional Access application. Instead, the connection to the database, the OLE DB connection, serves as a conduit through which an Access project provides data access.

Figure 14-1 depicts the Database window for an Access project connected to the NorthwindCS SQL Server database that ships with Office XP. This database is a client/server version of the classic Northwind sample database. The left panel in the figure displays the Data Link Properties dialog box for the connection. You can open this dialog box by choosing File-Connection for an Access project connected to the NorthwindCS database. The panel on the right shows the Database window for the Access project. From the title bar of the Database window, you can see that the Access project file name is adp3.adp and that the project connects to the NorthwindCS database.

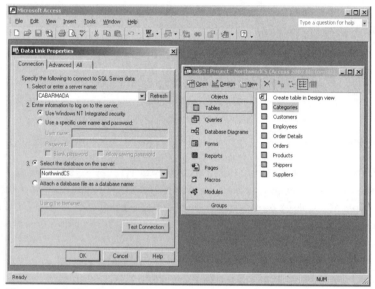

Figure 14-1 The Data Link Properties dialog box and the Database window for an Access project.

The Data Link Properties dialog box represents the OLE DB connection element of the Access project architecture. It shows that the NorthwindCS database for the Access project resides on a SQL server named CABARMADA. You can have other versions of the NorthwindCS database on different servers, but the database names on any one server must be unique. The CABARMADA SQL server in my office network happens to be running MSDE 2000 on a computer running Microsoft Windows NT 4. The Access project authenticates itself to the SQL server through Windows NT integrated security. Authentication is the process by which a SQL server verifies that a user has permission to access the server. This is MSDE 2000's default mode of authentication on Windows NT and Windows 2000 computers. On Windows 98 and Windows Millennium Edition, MSDE 2000 installs exclusively with SQL Server authentication. In Chapter 15, you will explore the different types of authentication and see how to control them programmatically.

The Database window in the right panel of Figure 14-1 shows the table names in the database connection for the Access project. Access 2002 has undergone a redesign of the Database window from the Access 2000 version. The Database window for the new version more closely aligns with the Database window in traditional Access database files. In particular, there are no Objects bar entries for views and stored procedures. These object classes, which used to appear with their own entries in the Access 2000 Objects bar, are now grouped in the *Queries* object class. This class appears in the Database window for traditional object classes. The Access 2002 version also provides access to user-defined functions through the *Queries* class in the Objects bar. User-defined functions enable you to use T-SQL to code custom functions that perform like built-in functions in many ways. I'll describe these functions more fully later in the chapter in "User-Defined Functions."

The first three object classes on the Objects bar are *Tables*, *Queries*, and *Database Diagrams*. These are server-side elements of the client/server architecture for an Access project. In other words, the objects in these classes do not reside within the Access project file, which is adp3.adp in this example. These objects reside within the NorthwindCS database on the CABARMADA server. You can use the Database window to open collections of the *Forms*, *Reports*, *Pages*, *Macros*, and *Modules* classes. The objects in these classes reside within the Access project file. They are client-side objects. If I had another Access project file (for example, adp4.adp) connected to the NorthwindCS database on the CABARMADA server, it could have a different collection of forms than the one in adp3.adp.

Table 14-1 provides a summary of the object classes available from the Database window of an Access project, along with their location on the server or client side of the client/server application. If you have experience designing SQL Server tables with Access 2000, you'll be familiar with the SQL Server data types. In any event, SQL Server 2000 introduces several new data types that you'll want to learn about. Developers migrating to Access 2002 from Access 97 or an earlier version will need to learn the new data types from scratch. The *Database Diagrams* object class is not available with traditional Access database files. If you find programming SQL Server databases more of a challenge than you prefer (or if you just want a break from programming), learn to use these diagrams. They offer a graphical approach to designing tables and the relationships between them. The *Tables*, *Queries*, and *Database Diagrams* collections contain all the server-side objects in an Access project.

The *Forms*, *Reports*, *Pages*, *Macros*, and *Modules* collection members for Access projects comprise the set of client-side objects in an Access project. These client-side objects work almost identically in Access projects to the way Access database files do. This is one of the main reasons Access projects are such an attractive model for developing SQL Server solutions. Whether you're an old hand at Access or a SQL Server DBA with limited Access experience, you can easily and quickly start generating custom forms and reports.

Table 14-1   Object Bar Classes in the Database Window of an Access Project

Class Name	Comment	Location
Tables	Tables for SQL Server databases work similarly to the way they do in traditional Access database files. However, you will have to learn some new designations for data types in order to specify columns. In addition, you will have to learn a new way to specify a column with the AutoNumbers data type.	Server
Queries	Although Access 2002 removes views and stored procedures from the Objects bar, it retains these objects. They are available from the Queries item in the Objects bar. You can also view user-defined functions from the *Queries* object class.	Server
Database Diagrams	SQL Server databases permit more than one database diagram per database. This is particularly handy when you want to break a large database application into parts. You can also use database diagrams to create other objects, such as tables.	Server
Forms	Works generally the same way as it does in a traditional Access database file.	Client
Reports	Works generally the same way as it does in a traditional Access database file.	Client
Pages	Works generally the same way as it does in a traditional Access database file.	Client
Macros	Works generally the same way as it does in a traditional Access database file.	Client
Modules	Works generally the same way as it does in a traditional Access database file.	Client

Supported SQL Server Databases

Microsoft upgraded Access 2002 to work especially well with SQL Server 2000 and MSDE 2000 on Windows 2000. However, Access 2000 supports a wide range of SQL Server versions on a variety on operating systems. Table 14-2 summarizes the three groups of SQL Server installations with which Access projects are compatible. Notice that if you use SQL Server 2000 or MSDE 2000, you cannot use Windows 95. However, Access projects do support working with SQL Server 7 and MSDE on Windows 95. In addition, you need to install a variety of service packs for earlier operating systems or SQL Server versions to obtain support by Access projects.

Table 14-2   SQL Server and Windows Versions Supported by Access Projects

SQL Server Version	Operating System Version
SQL Server 2000 or MSDE 2000	Works on Windows 2000, Windows NT (Service Pack 6 or later), or Windows 98
SQL Server 7 or MSDE	Works on Windows 2000, Windows NT (Service Pack 4 or later), and Windows 95 (or later)
SQL Server 6.5 (Service Pack 5 or later)	Works on Windows 2000, Windows NT (Service Pack 4 or later), and Windows 95 (or later)

Using MSDE 2000 is a great way to start learning SQL Server development techniques. MSDE 2000 is free with any version of Office XP. Its T-SQL and SQL-DMO programming syntax is compatible with SQL Server 2000. Its file format is compatible with SQL Server 2000, meaning you can reattach the MSDE 2000 database files to a SQL Server 2000 database for greater processing power and access to better graphical client management tools. These graphical tools can dramatically simplify the administration and use of a SQL Server database.

Like its predecessor, MSDE, MSDE 2000 has a built-in performance degrader after five users connect, but there is no hard limit on the number of users. Nevertheless, if you have many more than five users, you can boost performance by switching to the standard or enterprise edition of SQL Server 2000. By switching to either version of SQL Server 2000, you also gain the client management tools, Enterprise Manager and Query Analyzer. These easy-to-use yet powerful tools enable you to administer one or more SQL servers (Enterprise Manager) as well as an integrated development environment for debugging and running T-SQL (Query Analyzer). The full version of SQL Server 2000 delivers other SQL Server components that are unavailable with MSDE 2000. These include the Full-Text Search and Indexing tools as well as Online Analytical Services for data-warehousing applications. In addition, you cannot use MSDE 2000 as a transactional replication server. However, the standard edition of SQL Server 2000 (as well as the developer edition that ships with Microsoft Office XP Developer edition, MOD) can support this function.

Installing and Using MSDE 2000

MSDE 2000 ships with any version of Office XP that includes Access 2002, but it does not install with the standard Office XP setup.exe program. The Access Help file for MSDE advises you to remove MSDE if you have it installed before installing MSDE 2000. Then you run setup.exe in the \MSDE2000 folder on your Office XP installation CD. If you have a network installation of Office XP, you can run the MSDE 2000 setup.exe application from the network installation. Complete the installation by restarting the computer. This launches MSDE 2000 as a service on Windows NT and Windows 2000 computers.

If MSDE does not start automatically, run the Service Manager from the Startup folder of the Windows Start button. On Windows 98 computers, you might need to select the Auto-Start check box if you want MSDE 2000 to launch automatically when the computer boots. This check box appears at the bottom of the SQL Server Service Manager dialog box, shown in Figure 14-2. You can use this same dialog box to pause and stop the SQL Server service.

Figure 14-2 The SQL Server Service Manager dialog box.

After following the instructions for a standard MSDE 2000 installation, your old MSDE database files will still be available. However, they won't be attached to your new server. This is because you removed the old version of MSDE without attaching the old files to the new server. SQL Server databases typically have two files. (Very large and sophisticated database applications can have even more files.) The first is a data file with an .mdf extension. The second is a log file with an .ldf extension. Unless you changed the default location for your MSDE data files, you'll find them at c:\Mssql7\Data.

You can use the *sp_attachd_db* system stored procedure to reattach an old database file from MSDE to your new MSDE 2000 installation. This stored procedure takes three arguments. The *@dbname* parameter represents the name of the database and takes a string value. Microsoft recommends using Unicode format for string values—especially when dealing with the character set of more than one country. Enclose the string value in single quotes (') and precede it with an *N* to denote Unicode format. The *@filename1* and *@filename2* parameters are for the .mdf and .ldf files. You specify these files with both the path and filename.

The following code sample shows the syntax for invoking the *sp_attach_db* stored procedure. The code attaches a pair files for the adp1sql database to the SQL server for the current project. The SQL string for invoking the *sp_attach_db* stored procedure begins with the EXEC keyword. A *Connection* object invokes the SQL string with its *Execute* method. The *Connection* objection points at the database for the current project and indirectly to the SQL server for the project's *Connection* property. If you want to attach the files to another server, you'll have to use a *Connection* object for that server. In addition, your user ID must have permission to attach a database to the server.

```
Sub AttachAnOldDB()
Dim cnn1 As ADODB.Connection
Dim str1 As String

'Set up the SQL string to attach the database files
'from the default location for database files maintained
'by MSDE
str1 = "EXEC sp_attach_db @dbname = N'adp1sql', " & _
    "@filename1 = N'c:\Mssql7\Data\adp1sql.mdf', " & _
    "@filename2 = N'c:\Mssql7\Data\adp1sql.ldf'"

'Point a Connection object at the current project,
'and execute the SQL string
Set cnn1 = CurrentProject.Connection
cnn1.Execute (str1)

'Clean up objects
cnn1.Close
Set cnn1 = Nothing

End Sub
```

In Chapter 15, I will present a utility for automatically attaching all database files from a folder to a server. I will also examine SQL Server security and show you the permissions needed to attach a database to a server. When you initially install MSDE 2000, you have that permission by default.

> **Note**   You can customize the installation of MSDE 2000 by assigning values for named switches when you invoke setup.exe. Search Access Help for "Install and Configure SQL Server 2000 Desktop Engine" for details on a subset of the switches and their settings. Additional settings not documented in Access Help appear in the readme.txt file within the \MSDE2000 folder on your Office XP installation disc. Look under headings 3.1.4 and 3.1.23 for setup parameters that enable you to customize MSDE 2000 authentication at startup and database file recovery from a prior MSDE version.

Creating and Opening Access Projects

There are three ways to open Access projects. First, you can open an existing Access project with a link to a SQL Server database. This is typically the way users work with Access projects. Second, you can create a new Access project to connect to an existing SQL Server database. Third, you can create a new Access project and concurrently create a new SQL Server database for it.

> **Note**   This book often uses the term *SQL Server database* to refer generically to a database maintained by one of the versions of SQL Server 2000 or MSDE 2000. See the preceding paragraph for an example of this usage.

Opening an Existing Access Project

An existing Access project is stored in an .adp file just like an Access database file is stored in an .mdb file. You can find an existing Access project to open through the File-Open command. This command presents the Open dialog box, which you can use to search for an .adp file. This is one of the files in the default collection of Access file types. Other members include .mdb, .mda, .mde, and .ade.

If you opened an Access project recently, you can click on its name in the Open A File section of the New File view of the Task Pane. This is a new toolbar introduced in Office XP. The Open A File section depicts the most recently used files as links along with another link, named More Files, which presents the Open dialog box. See Chapter 10, "Microsoft Office Objects," for more programming samples that manage the Task Pane.

You might be able to open an existing Access project from a Windows desktop link to the file. To create such a link, right-click any object, such as a table, in the Database window for the Access project. Choose Create Shortcut, and then click OK on the Create Shortcut dialog box. Once you have the link on a desktop, a user can click the link and open the Access project to the short-cut. If you create a shortcut to the initial form in an application, the shortcut will open that form within the file.

Figure 14-3 shows the Database window for the NorthwindCS Access project. This project is a sample file that you can load with the Office XP setup installation program. You should have MSDE 2000 or SQL Server 2000 on your workstation before loading the NorthwindCS sample. This is because the sample Access project installs the NorthwindCS database the first time that you open it if no other version of the Northwind database exists on the local SQL Server machine. In any event, you must have a version of either the NorthwindCS or Northwind database installed on the local SQL Server machine for the NorthwindCS Access project file to open successfully the first time. After the Access project file connects to a database on a server, you can open it from another computer or you can make a copy of the Access project file and then open that copy from another computer.

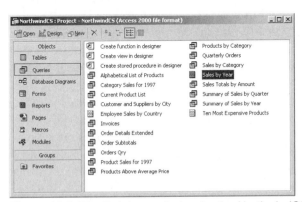

Figure 14-3 The Database window for the NorthwindCS Access project.

> **Note**   If the NorthwindCS project file does not successfully open the first time because you do not have SQL Server installed on the current computer, you can manually specify the project's connection to a SQL Server database on another computer. Use the File-Connection command to open the Data Link Properties dialog box. Then complete the dialog box by typing the remote server's name, your authentication information, and the name of the database to which you want to connect the project.

Do not confuse the reference to the Northwind database in the preceding paragraph with a reference to the Access Northwind database file. When you install either SQL Server 7 or SQL Server 2000, the setup program automatically installs a Northwind database. This SQL Server database has the same data tables as the Access Northwind database file. However, it does not have all the same queries. The SQL Server Northwind database contains no forms, reports, or Web pages because these are not SQL Server database objects. The Database window shown in Figure 14-3 has its *Queries* class highlighted in the Objects bar. Notice that the list of objects shows two types of icons next to the object names. The icon comprised of two datasheets represents views. The icon depicting text on a page represents stored procedures. In T-SQL, views return the output from a single SELECT statement that has no parameters or ORDER BY clause, unless the SELECT statement includes a TOP clause. While stored procedures enable this function, they also permit parameters and an ORDER BY clause without a TOP clause, as well as some additional capabilities. If the NorthwindCS database contains any user-defined functions, they will appear in the Database window shown in Figure 14-3. Just before the listing of objects, you'll notice three controls for launching wizards that permit you to graphically design views and some types of stored procedures and user-defined functions. We'll take a closer look at these components later in the chapter, in the sections, "SQL Server Views," "Creating and Using Stored Procedures," and "User-Defined Functions."

When you use Access projects in a multiuser application, every user should have his or her own copy of the Access project file. This is because Access opens these files exclusively. If two users open the same Access project, the second user to open the file gains read-only access. Recall that the Access project file is the client component of a client/server application. Every user needs his or her own copy of the client component. The sharing takes place for the server component.

Opening an Access Project for an Existing Database

To open a new Access project for an existing database, click the Project (Existing Data) link on the New File view of the Task Pane. The Task Pane opens by default when you start Access 2002 (unless you clear the Show At Startup check box at the bottom of the Task Pane's New File view). Clicking the Project (Existing Data) link opens the File New Database dialog box. (See Figure 14-4.) Access assigns a default name to the Access project file in the style of adp*x*.adp. You can override adpx with a custom name of your choice, and you can change the destination folder for the file by changing the selection in the Save In drop-down control. The display in Figure 14-4 will create an Access project with a filename of adp4.adp in the My Documents folder when the user clicks Create.

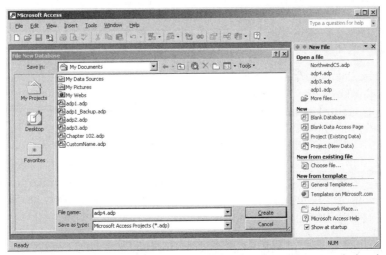

Figure 14-4 The File New Database dialog box in an Access window immediately after a click on the Project (Existing Data) link on the New File view of the Task Pane.

At this point, the project has no connection to a database. Therefore, Access automatically opens the Data Link Properties dialog box. Fill in the server name, authentication information, and database name to link the project to a database. Figure 14-5 shows a completed Data Link Properties dialog box that connects an Access project to the NorthwindCS database on the CABARMADA server with Windows NT integrated security.

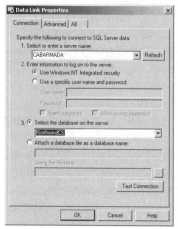

Figure 14-5 The Data Link Properties dialog box for connecting a new Access project to the NorthwindCS database on the CABARMADA server.

The database for the new Access project is the NorthwindCS database on the CABARMADA server. This is the same database used by the NorthwindCS project that appears in Figure 14-3. Therefore, both the NorthwindCS project file and the adp4.adp file show the same set of objects for their *Tables*, *Queries*, and *Database Diagrams* classes. This is because both Access projects connect to the same database and the object classes reside with the database. However, all the remaining objects differ because they reside with the Access project file rather than the database. The NorthwindCS project includes a couple of modules, but the *Modules* collection for the adp4 project is empty because the project has just been created.

If you fail to specify the Data Link Properties dialog box entries correctly or you don't complete the dialog box, the new Access project will be disconnected from a data source when it opens. An Access project can be disconnected from a data source upon opening because your server is stopped. Once you get the Access project to connect to a server, you can open the Data Link Properties dialog box with the File-Connection command and respecify its settings.

Manually Opening an Access Project for a New Database

Perhaps the most powerful way to open a new project is to open one that creates a new SQL Server database at the same time. To do this, click the Project (New Data) link on the New File view in the Task Pane. This opens the File New Database dialog box. Use the dialog box to designate the destination folder and the filename for the new Access project. For this example, I named the file Chapter 14.adp and clicked Create.

Except for clicking Project (New Data), this process is identical to the one for creating a new Access project to connect to an existing database. After you click Project (New Data), Access presents the initial dialog box for the Microsoft SQL Server Database Wizard. This dialog box enables you to specify the parameters for a new SQL Server database. These parameters include the name of the server on which you will store your new database, the type of authentication you will use for the SQL Server user ID that creates the new database, and the name of the new database.

Figure 14-6 shows an example of a completed dialog box for creating a new database. This dialog box specifies the local server. This example assumes you have SQL Server or MSDE 2000 running on the local server. The drop-down control that initially displays "(local)" enables you to select the name of any other SQL server to which you are connected. To connect to an instance of MSDE 2000 running on a Windows 98 computer, you must type the name of the server into the control. Notice that you can use either a trusted connection or an account with CREATE DATABASE privileges on a server. This example uses the sa user ID, which has unlimited authority on SQL Server machines. In order to reference this user ID, your server must use SQL Server security. The database creation wizard automatically names the database after the Access project by appending a suffix of SQL to the Access project name. In this case, the resulting name for the new database is Chapter 14SQL. You can override this default name with any other you prefer.

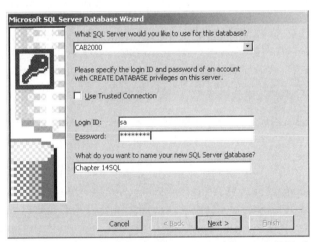

Figure 14-6 The initial dialog box of the Microsoft SQL Server Database Wizard.

After completing the entries referenced in the preceding paragraph, click Next on the initial wizard dialog box. Then click Finish on the second wizard dialog box. This creates the new database for the new Access project. When the process completes, your new Access project opens with a connection to the newly created SQL Server database on the server indicated in the initial dialog box for the database creation wizard.

Programming an Access Project for a New Database

You can also program the creation of a new SQL Server database and link it to an Access project without using the Microsoft SQL Server Database Wizard. Managing this process programmatically allows you to automatically create Access projects with attached databases. In addition, enabling the task programmatically allows you to show the functionality to end users by meeting the precise requirements of your custom applications.

Creating a SQL Server database for an Access project requires two distinct steps. First you need to create a new database. Then you need to assign that database to an Access project. This second step entails entering the database settings into the Data Link Properties dialog box, and it creates the OLE DB connection between an Access project and the SQL Server database.

The following three procedures comprise an application for creating a new SQL Server database and assigning it to the current project. The first procedure is the main routine. It designates the database name and a path for the database files—namely, its .mdf and .ldf files. The second procedure uses the information the first routine passes to it to create the database files. The third procedure assigns the new database to the current project.

As you can see, the first procedure assigns the name foo2 to the new database. This name must conform to SQL Server conventions for identifiers as well as to a special restriction for database names in the CREATE DATABASE T-SQL statement. Your database name must be no more than 123 characters. The path can follow standard Windows path requirements. After assigning the database name and path to the database files, the main routine passes both parameters to the procedure for creating a new database but passes only the database name to the procedure.

The second procedure in the following code invokes the CREATE DATABASE T-SQL statement with an ActiveX Data Objects (ADO) *Connection* object. The procedure accepts the database name and path for the creation of the .mdf and .ldf files. You aren't required to store database files in the default directory, but it's a good practice that makes finding your database files easy. The CREATE DATABASE statement creates a database based on the SQL Server model database. The model database is one of the ones that SQL Server sets up upon installation. If you have special requirements for your databases, you can modify the model database's design. For example, you can create a special table design or even a special table that is populated with preset values. The sample procedure accepts the default model database settings for the initial database size, its maximum size, and the amount that the database grows when nearing its current size limit.

The third procedure uses the *BaseConnectionString* property for the current project as a basis for specifying the connection string for a project connected to a new database—namely, the one created by the second procedure. A significant advantage of this approach is that it doesn't need to specify a valid connection string from scratch for an Access project. The *"Initial Catalog"* setting in the connection string points at the database name. Therefore, the procedure excises *"Initial Catalog"* and its setting and replaces the connection string with a setting that points at the new database. After composing the new connection string in *str1*, the procedure invokes the *OpenConnection* method for the

What's a SQL Server Identifier?

Every object in SQL Server, including a database and its elements, can have an identifier. The identifier is the name by which you reference the object. Identifiers have four general rules, and individual objects and special settings can further impact the valid names for SQL Server objects.

The first rule states that an identifier must begin with a letter from the Unicode Standard 2.0. These include but are not limited to the uppercase and lowercase letters of the English alphabet and those of other languages. It's good practice to avoid starting identifiers with characters that SQL Server uses for special purposes—such as the underscore (_), at sign (@), pound sign (#), double at sign (@@), and double pound sign (##)—unless you explicitly mean to reference the special purpose. For example, @ is a prefix for denoting a local variable in a stored procedure. A local variable in a stored procedure functions similarly to a memory variable that's local to a single procedure in Microsoft Visual Basic for Applications (VBA). In some contexts, starting a table name with @ invites SQL Server to treat the table as a local variable instead of a table.

The second rule for identifiers is that all characters after the first one can be letters, decimal numbers, or any of the following symbols: @, $, #, or _. Again, the letters and numbers are specified by the Unicode Standard 2.0. Third, you cannot specify object identifiers that are SQL Server reserved words. This page on the Microsoft Web site lists the SQL Server 2000 reserved words: msdn.microsoft.com/library/psdk/sql/ts_ra-rz_9oj7.htm. And finally, identifiers cannot contain embedded spaces or other special characters.

You can circumvent some of these rules by using double quotes or brackets, but, you will create more universally acceptable identifiers by following all four rules.

CurrentProject object. The method takes three arguments: the name of the new database for the Access project connection and the user ID and password that authorize the change.

> **Note**   You are not restricted to assigning a connection string to an existing project. Use the *CreateAccessProject* method in a VBA procedure to create a new Access project to which you can assign a connection string. Look up *CreateAccessProject* in Access Help to get the detailed syntax instructions for this method.

```
Sub CreateDBForCurrentProject()
Dim DBName As String
Dim DBFilename As String
Dim LogFilename As String
Dim DBFilePath As String

'Set string constants
DBName = "foo2"
DBFilePath = "c:\program files\microsoft sql server\mssql\data\"

'Create a database
CreateDBOnCurrentProjectServer DBName, DBFilePath

'Open the current project to the database
ChangeDBConnectionForCurrentProject DBName

End Sub


Sub CreateDBOnCurrentProjectServer(DBName As String, _
    DBFilePath As String)
Dim cnn1 As ADODB.Connection
Dim str1 As String

'Accept model database defaults for initial size,
'maximum size, and growth steps
str1 = "CREATE DATABASE " & DBName & " " & _
    "ON " & _
    "( NAME = " & DBName & "_dat, " & _
    "FILENAME = '" & DBFilePath & DBName & "dat.mdf') " & _
    "LOG ON " & _
```

```
                "( NAME = '" & DBName & "_log', " & _
                "FILENAME = '" & DBFilePath & DBName & "log.ldf')"

'Point Connection object at current project and
'execute SQL string in str1
Set cnn1 = CurrentProject.Connection
cnn1.Execute (str1)

End Sub


Sub ChangeDBConnectionForCurrentProject(DBName As String)
Dim str1 As String
Dim Beginpos As Integer
Dim Endpos As Integer

'Save BaseConnectionString for editing
str1 = CurrentProject.BaseConnectionString

'Optional printout to see the line being edited;
'remove comment prefix to see line in the Immediate window
Debug.Print str1

'Extract starting and ending positions for database assignment
'in the BaseConnectionString
Beginpos = InStr(1, str1, "Initial Catalog", 1)
Endpos = InStr(Beginpos, str1, ";")

'Replace the old database assignment with a new one
str1 = Left(str1, Beginpos - 1) & "Initial Catalog=" & _
    DBName & Right(str1, Len(str1) - Endpos + 1)

'Open the current project with the new BaseConnectionString
CurrentProject.OpenConnection str1, "sa", "password"

End Sub
```

By the end of this code sample, you've accomplished two tasks. First, you've added a new database to SQL Server. Second, you've changed the OLE DB connection for the current project. As you start developing a new database solution, it's typical to want to restore things to an earlier state. The first of the following two procedures restores the current project so that it designates Chapter 14SQL instead of foo2 as the database for the Access project. The next pair of procedures removes the foo2 database from the server to which the current project connects.

```
'Restores the Chapter 14SQL setting for the Chapter 14
'Access project
Sub RestoreDBSettingforChapter_14Project()
Dim str1 As String
Dim Beginpos As Integer
Dim Endpos As Integer

'Save BaseConnectionString for editing
str1 = CurrentProject.BaseConnectionString

'Extract starting and ending positions for database assignment
'in the BaseConnectionString
Beginpos = InStr(1, str1, "Initial Catalog", 1)
Endpos = InStr(Beginpos, str1, ";")

'Replace the old database assignment with a new one
str1 = Left(str1, Beginpos - 1) & "Initial Catalog=" & _
    "Chapter 14SQL" & Right(str1, Len(str1) - Endpos + 1)

'Open the current project with the new BaseConnectionString
CurrentProject.OpenConnection str1, "sa", "password"

End Sub


'This procedure and the next one are utilities to
'remove a database from the server for the
'current project
Sub CallDropDatabaseFromCurrentProjectServer()
Dim DBName As String

DBName = "foo2"
DropDatabaseFromCurrentProjectServer DBName

End Sub


Sub DropDatabaseFromCurrentProjectServer(DBName As String)
Dim cnn1 As ADODB.Connection
Dim str1 As String

'Create SQL string for dropping a database
str1 = "Drop Database " & DBName

'Execute the string
Set cnn1 = CurrentProject.Connection
cnn1.Execute (str1)

End Sub
```

Books Online and Other SQL Server Learning Resources

After you open an Access project and create a new SQL Server database, you need to learn how to use them. This chapter and Chapter 15 will get you started by providing fundamental instruction and helpful code samples. Because the topic is monumental in scope, the aim of these two chapters is to complement existing developer resources. One of the premiere resources is Books Online, the definitive Microsoft-supplied SQL Server reference. Another great resource is the collection of sample database applications that Microsoft makes available. One of the most readily available and familiar samples is the NorthwindCS project and its matching database. Another database sample that might not be as widely available to Access developers is the pubs database. This sample database relates to SQL Server much like the Northwind database relates to Access.

Getting Books Online

Books Online is a valuable source that discusses SQL Server administrative issues and T-SQL code samples. Because you're reading this book to learn about *programming* Access 2002, you probably care most about the code samples. You need to understand that the T-SQL code samples in Books Online primarily target Query Analyzer, one of the SQL Server client management tools. This tool does not ship with MSDE or MSDE 2000. In addition, Books Online does not ship with Office 2000 or most versions of Office XP—MOD is the exception. Of course, Query Analyzer ships with any version of SQL Server. For these reasons, you might want to obtain MOD because it ships with Books Online and Query Analyzer as part the SQL Server 2000 Developer Edition.

If you do not have MOD, you can still use Books Online. Be aware that there are two versions of Books Online you'll likely find useful. The SQL Server 7 version of Books Online synchronizes optimally with MSDE, and nearly all its samples apply to MSDE 2000 and SQL Server 2000. Furthermore, it's available as a free download from the Microsoft site, at www.microsoft.com/SQL/productinfo/70books.htm. The SQL Server 2000 version of Books Online is available for download from the Microsoft site (www.microsoft.com/SQL/techinfo/productdoc/2000/books.asp). In addition, a Web-based version of it is available on Microsoft's MSDN site, at msdn.microsoft.com/library/psdk/sql/portal_7ap1.htm.

Adapting Books Online Code for the SQL Pane

The following excerpt is the first T-SQL code sample (titled example A) for the CREATE VIEW statement in the SQL Server 2000 version of Books Online. The sample works perfectly from Query Analyzer, but it fails when you copy the code into the SQL pane of a view member in the *Views* collection of an Access project.

(Later in the chapter, in "SQL Server Views," I will explain how to work with the SQL pane in an Access project.) When you click the Run button after copying the code into the SQL pane and accept the prompt to save T-SQL, Access reports two errors. (See Figure 14-7.) These errors are caused by the USE and GO keywords, statements that Access projects do not process. Therefore, the Access compilation of T-SQL for creating the view fails.

> **Note**   This same sample is available from the SQL Server 7 version of Books Online. This will often be the case. However, all the samples in this section are from the SQL Server 2000 version of Books Online so that you can see the latest version of this resource.

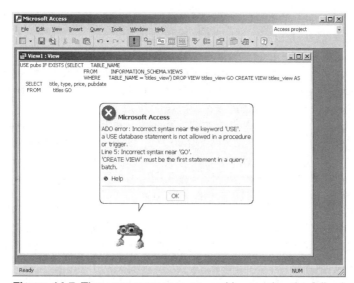

Figure 14-7 The error messages caused by running the following Books Online code sample in an Access project SQL window.

```
USE pubs
IF EXISTS (SELECT TABLE_NAME FROM INFORMATION_SCHEMA.VIEWS
    WHERE TABLE_NAME = 'titles_view')
    DROP VIEW titles_view
GO
CREATE VIEW titles_view
AS
SELECT title, type, price, pubdate
FROM titles
GO
```

Actually, the error messages shown in Figure 14-7 do not detect all the problems this code sample has when used in an Access project. The sample performs two tasks that can cause errors. First, the code deletes any existing view in the database with the identifier "*titles_view*". Second, it invokes the CREATE VIEW statement, which Access views do not support. There's no need to conditionally execute a DROP VIEW statement or unconditionally execute a CREATE VIEW statement from an Access project because the File-Save As and File-Save commands handle these tasks automatically.

To make the preceding sample work from a view in an Access project, simply copy two lines from the sample into the view's SQL pane: the SELECT statement after the AS keyword, and the SELECT statement before the trailing GO keyword. If you're running this sample from an Access project that doesn't link to the pubs database, such as Chapter 14.adp, you can still reference the *titles* table as the source for the query. When the pubs database resides on the server, you can specify the source for the query as *pubs..titles*. The first name represents the database. This database name qualifier replaces the need for the USE statement. The last name represents the table within the database. The complete syntax for the view follows:

```
SELECT title, type, price, pubdate
FROM pubs..titles
```

The syntax for specifying the source omits an intervening name for the database owner, which is implicitly dbo. As long as the user didn't create a table named *titles* in the pubs database, it's acceptable to omit the owner when specifying a database source owned by the dbo. If the user did create a table named *titles*, he or she needs to explicitly include an intervening owner name (such as dbo) to reference the table with the same name by a different owner (also dbo).

> **Note**   The database owner, or dbo, can be any member of the sysadmin group. This special security group of logins has broad authority in any database on a server, including the ability to create objects, such as tables. As long as a user connects to a database with one of the special logins in the sysadmin group, any objects he or she creates during a session will have dbo as their owner. If a user logs on with a login that's not in the sysadmin group, that object will always require an explicit owner name that refers to the login whenever anyone other than the object's owner refers to it. Database owners are a security topic that we'll cover in more detail in Chapter 15.

If the pubs database is not on the server for the current project, you can still reference the table. However, you'll have to reference the server name explicitly. SQL Server offers a couple of different approaches to this, which I'll cover later in this chapter in "SQL Server Views."

Adapting Books Online Code for the SQL Window

You can run the previous Books Online sample code in a VBA code window pretty much as is. The following sample shows an adaptation of the preceding one that works from the VBA code window. As you can see, this sample uses a lot more of the original Books Online sample. But it still has some changes. For example, the GO keyword after the DROP VIEW statement is commented out. Leaving it in would generate an error. The USE statement is removed so that the new view enters the database for the current project instead of the pubs database. Although the sample excludes the GO keywords, it follows their batching conventions for lines of T-SQL code. This is essential for the CREATE VIEW statement to succeed.

```
Sub CreateTitleViewInCurrentProject()
Dim cnn1 As ADODB.Connection
Dim str1 As String

'Point the Connection object at the current project
Set cnn1 = CurrentProject.Connection

'The code purposely leaves out the USE statement to create the
'view in the database for the current project, and it comments
'out the GO statement
str1 = "" & _
    "IF EXISTS (SELECT TABLE_NAME FROM INFORMATION_SCHEMA.VIEWS " & _
    "WHERE TABLE_NAME = 'titles_view') " & _
    "DROP VIEW titles_view " & _
    "--GO "
cnn1.Execute str1

'The code breaks here so that the CREATE VIEW statement is the first
'statement in its batch; comment prefix removes GO statement
str1 = "CREATE VIEW titles_view " & _
    "AS " & _
    "SELECT title, type, price, pubdate " & _
    "FROM pubs..titles " & _
    "--GO "
cnn1.Execute str1

End Sub
```

By the conclusion of the sample, your current project has a new view with an identifier of titles_view. This new object might not appear immediately in the Database window. In this case, select Queries from the Object bar in the Database window, and choose View-Refresh. Alternatively, you can write a pair of short VBA procedures that loop through the members of the *Views* collection and print their names to the Immediate window. (See the next code sample.) These members will include one of the newly created *title_view* objects. The procedure uses SQL-DMO objects, so your VBA project needs a reference to the Microsoft SQLDMO Object Library. The VBA project for the Chapter 14.adp file has this reference already. The following pair of procedures demonstrates the syntax for looping through the members of the *Views* collection:

```
Sub CallPrintViewsInADBOnLocalServer()
Dim DBName As String

DBName = "Chapter 14SQL"
PrintViewsInADBOnLocalServer DBName

End Sub


'A utility routine for printing views in a database
'on the local server
Sub PrintViewsInADBOnLocalServer(DBName)
Dim srv1 As New SQLDMO.SQLServer

srv1.Connect "(local)", "sa", "password"

For Each vew1 In srv1.Databases(DBName).Views
    Debug.Print vew1.Name
Next vew1

End Sub
```

Sample Databases

The NorthwindCS and pubs databases are the two most readily available databases that you can use as models for your custom application development. The NorthwindCS database ships as part of Office XP. Office XP also includes a NorthwindCS Access project that links to the NorthwindCS database. As mentioned earlier in this chapter, the NorthwindCS Access project includes a script for automatically loading the NorthwindCS database to a local server if the Northwind database isn't already installed. Otherwise, the script connects to the SQL Server Northwind database if it's available locally. The script for managing the first-time startup of the NorthwindCS project resides in its Startup module.

Working with the NorthwindCS Database

The NorthwindCS database is so attractive as a resource because nearly all Access developers have some familiarity with the Northwind database. The NorthwindCS Access project offers the same functionality as the Northwind Access database file. Therefore, you can use the NorthwindCS Access project as a model for performing any task in SQL Server that the Northwind Access database file performs for Jet databases. For example, the *Ten Most Expensive Products* stored procedure selects just the top 10 products in terms of unit price and lists them in descending order. The T-SQL script for this stored procedure follows:

```
ALTER PROCEDURE [Ten Most Expensive Products]
AS
SET ROWCOUNT 10
SELECT Products.ProductName AS TenMostExpensiveProducts,
Products.UnitPrice
FROM Products
ORDER BY Products.UnitPrice DESC
```

> **Note**   The preceding script is edited slightly (for ease of reading) from the version that appears when you open the stored procedure by highlighting it in the Database window and clicking Design. The script initially appears as one long line because Microsoft does not ship the script with built-in carriage returns. As you add the carriage returns to improve readability, remember to leave a blank space after all keywords. Then save and reopen the stored procedure with the revised format.

The syntax for this stored procedure is different than the corresponding query in the Access Northwind database file. That sample uses the TOP clause to moderate the behavior of the SELECT statement. However, this sample achieves the same result with a SET ROWCOUNT statement. This statement causes SQL Server to halt the processing of a SELECT statement after it returns a specified number of records—10, in the case of the sample script. The ORDER BY clause arranges those rows in descending order on UnitPrice.

If you're a SQL Server DBA or developer, you might be confused about why the script begins with an ALTER PROCEDURE statement instead of a CREATE PROCEDURE statement (as is common in the Books Online samples). When you design a stored procedure within an Access project's stored procedure template, you use CREATE PROCEDURE the very first time that you input and save the stored procedure. Thereafter, Access automatically changes the CREATE PROCEDURE statement to an ALTER PROCEDURE statement. This prevents you from having to drop the old stored procedure before re-creating a new one with the changes you make in Design view. In fact, Access projects do not permit you to drop and then re-create stored procedures from their stored procedure templates.

When you work with a stored procedure based on a single SELECT statement, Access permits you to create the query statement in its graphical Design view. This relieves you of some syntax requirements otherwise associated with specifying stored procedures. The following code comes from the SQL pane of the Design view for a stored procedure. The stored procedure's T-SQL representation appears without ALTER PROCEDURE, AS, or parameter declarations. To me, the most exciting aspect of the script is that it demonstrates the use of parameters without the bother of explicitly declaring them. The *@Beginning_Date* and *@Ending_Date* parameters control the range of orders about which the stored procedure returns records. Notice also that the syntax uses a three-part naming convention for the identifying fields. The field identifiers start with a reference to the owner (dbo), move on to specifying the source table, and conclude with the column name.

```
SELECT dbo.Orders.ShippedDate, dbo.Orders.OrderID,
    dbo.[Order Subtotals].Subtotal,
    DATENAME(yy, dbo.Orders.ShippedDate)
    AS Year
FROM dbo.Orders INNER JOIN dbo.[Order Subtotals]
    ON dbo.Orders.OrderID = dbo.[Order Subtotals].OrderID
WHERE (dbo.Orders.ShippedDate IS NOT NULL)
    AND (dbo.Orders.ShippedDate BETWEEN @Beginning_Date AND @Ending_Date)
```

The Access 2002 innovations for stored procedures based on a single SELECT statement are even better. Now you can design them with a graphical query designer—even when they contain parameters. Figure 14-8 depicts the graphical view of the *Sales by Year* stored procedure, represented in the preceding code sample from the NorthwindCS database. Notice that the code enables a join and the specification of parameters.

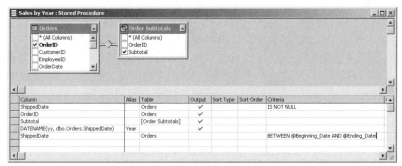

Figure 14-8 A graphical view of the *Sales by Year* stored procedure in the NorthwindCS database.

The graphical view in Figure 14-8 is the default for stored procedures based on a single SELECT statement. You can open an SQL pane in the query designer or open the stored procedure in SQL View. Using SQL View shows the syntax of the ALTER PROCEDURE statement, including its AS keyword. This view is necessary when a stored procedure relies on more than a single SELECT statement. In Access 2000, SQL View was the only view possible for stored procedures.

Working with the pubs Database

Many Access developers will be less familiar with the pubs database than with the NorthwindCS database, a look-alike of the Northwind Access database file. Nevertheless, the pubs database is the source for many samples in Books Online. For this reason, Access developers can boost their learning of SQL Server by getting comfortable with the pubs database. SQL Server DBAs and developers will likely have firsthand experience working with the pubs database.

No matter what your background, you need a version of SQL Server other than MSDE or MSDE 2000 to work with the pubs database. This is because the database does not ship with MSDE or MSDE 2000. Office developers planning to do extensive SQL Server work should consider getting MOD because this version ships with a developer version of SQL Server 2000. For this reason, MOD offers an opportunity to readily gain experience with pubs database samples.

One way to get started with pubs is to open an Access project for an existing database and then point that project at the pubs database on a server. After opening the Access project, you can examine the members of its *Tables* and *Queries* classes. Figure 14-9 displays the Database window and the Data Link Properties dialog box for an Access project connected to the pubs database on the CAB2000 server. The Access project file has the name Forpubs.adp. The Database window shows the names of the view and four stored procedures that ship as part of the pubs sample. By clicking Tables in the Objects bar for the Database window, you can display the names of all the tables in the pubs database. All the other object classes for the Access project will be empty because the pubs database does not ship with a database diagram, and the project has no client-side objects such as forms and reports.

One of the best ways to learn about a database is through a database diagram that indicates all the tables in the database and their relationships with other tables. You can create such a diagram for the pubs database by selecting Database Diagrams in the Objects bar and then clicking New on the Database window. This opens the Add Table dialog box. Successively click the Add control on the dialog box until all the tables appear in the diagram, and then close the Add Table dialog box. As an option, you can drag and rearrange the icons representing tables to improve the ease of viewing all tables in one database diagram display.

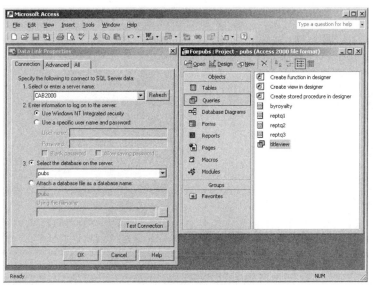

Figure 14-9 The Data Link Properties dialog box and Database window for an Access project connected to the pubs database.

Figure 14-10 shows a diagram for the pubs database after it's been saved with the name CustomizedDiagram. Notice that it includes the database's tables as well as the columns within them. In addition, the diagram also shows the relationships between tables. The line connecting the *stores* and *sales* tables indicates that any one store can have many sales. The *authors* and *titles* tables have a many-to-many relationship. The *titleauthor* table serves as the junction between these two tables. The *publishers* and *pub_info* tables have a one-to-one relationship. As you gain familiarity with the database diagram UI, you can probe relationships and table definitions. We'll discuss database diagrams in more detail in the next section, "Tables and Database Diagrams." These diagrams provide a way to graphically perform data definition for tables. Database diagrams offer a means of circumventing programming tasks that do not require highly customized code development. This frees the programming resources available to an assignment, saving them for the most valuable development tasks.

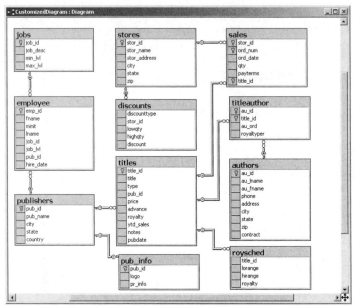

Figure 14-10 A database diagram for the pubs database.

The following code sample comes from example B for the AVG function in Books Online. The Books Online example, which is for the pubs database, demonstrates the behavior of the AVG and SUM aggregate functions with a GROUP BY clause. The code computes the average advance and the total advance by type of book.

```
USE pubs

SELECT type, AVG(advance), SUM(ytd_sales)
FROM titles
GROUP BY type
ORDER BY type
```

Copying the sample to the SQL Server database can result in a change or two. First I copied the T-SQL script to a new stored procedure template. Next I edited the code so that it would reference the pubs database even while running from a stored procedure in another database, such as Chapter 14SQL. I could have copied the sample directly into the Forpubs Access project, in which case it would run exactly as is, except for removing the USE statement. In this instance, I wanted to provide as much code as possible in the chapter's Access project.

Figure 14-11 shows the edited T-SQL script in a stored procedure template. In addition to the modification to the FROM clause argument, the sample starts with an ALTER PROCEDURE keyword followed by the procedure's name and the AS keyword to signal the start of the procedure's T-SQL. The result set from the stored procedure's SELECT statement appears in the figure on the right. You can flip to this view by selecting Datasheet View for the stored procedure.

Figure 14-11 An adapted T-SQL sample (along with its return values) from Books Online for the pubs database in an Access project.

Tables and Database Diagrams

This section orients you to some of the table design issues you will confront as you move from Access database files to SQL Server files. The presentation pays particular attention to the SQL Server data types. It also introduces you to the CREATE TABLE statement so that you can design your own custom tables programmatically. A pair of code samples demonstrates how to use one or more INSERT statements after a CREATE TABLE statement to populate a new table with values. These samples demonstrate techniques for working with contact data and graphic images in SQL Server databases. The section concludes with a brief introduction to database diagrams. The examples you'll see convey the simplicity and power of this graphical data definition tool.

SQL Server Column Data Types

Because the basics of designing a database are similar in Access and SQL Server, experienced Access developers will easily grasp the basics of designing SQL Server solutions. However, the data type names for table columns vary substantially in these two applications. In some cases, the same names point to different data types. In other cases, data types available in SQL Server are missing in Access. There's even one Access data type that's missing in SQL Server.

As Access developers migrate to SQL Server, specifying the right data type grows in importance. This is because SQL Server tables often have many more rows than Access tables. In fact, expanding tables are a big motivation for moving from an Access database solution to one based on SQL Server. Therefore, as you design your SQL database, specifying the column data type so that it is the smallest size possible can dramatically improve performance. Make your data types just large enough to hold the largest value possible for a column. If your numbers do not have fractional values, use one of the data types for whole numbers. Look for opportunities to take advantage of the Smalldatetime and

Smallmoney data types if a column's values fall within their ranges. These data types require 2 bytes less per column value than their siblings, Datetime and Money. When working with character data, use a fixed-length data type if all column values are the same length. This saves SQL Server from having to look for the end of the string.

Table 14-3 summarizes the SQL Server data types along with the closest matching Access data types. When a SQL Server data type is missing from Access, the corresponding Access data type column reads "Not applicable."

Table 14-3   SQL Server Column Data Types

SQL Server Data Type	Closest Matching Access Data Type	Bytes	SQL Server Data Type Description
Bit	Yes/No	1	If you have multiple Bit data type fields per record, SQL Server will group them into units of 8 so that an individual column value can take less than 1 byte. SQL Server represents Yes as *1* and No as *0*. In contrast, Access represents Yes and No as *−1* and *0*.
Tinyint	Number (byte)	1	This data type is the same in both databases; integers from 0 through $(2^8) - 1$.
Smallint	Integer	2	Integers in the range of -2^{15} through $(2^{15}) - 1$.
Integer	Long integer	4	Integers in the range of -2^{31} through $(2^{31}) - 1$.
Bigint	Not applicable	8	Integers in the range of -2^{63} through $(2^{63}) - 1$.
Real	Number (single)	4	Positive and negative numbers with whole and fractional parts, including 0. Positive numbers in the range from $1.18E - 38$ through $3.40E + 38$. Negative numbers in the range from $-1.18E - 38$ through $-3.40E + 38$.
Float	Number (double)	8	Positive and negative numbers with whole and fractional parts, including 0. Positive numbers in the range from $2.23E - 308$ through $1.79E + 308$. Negative numbers in the range from $-2.23E - 308$ through $-1.79E + 308$.

SQL Server Data Type	Closest Matching Access Data Type	Bytes	SQL Server Data Type Description
Money	Number (currency)	8	Values in the range from −922,337,203,685,477.5707 through 922,337,203,685,477.5807. Arithmetic with this data type is accurate to the nearest ten-thousandth of a unit within the specified range.
Smallmoney	Number (currency)	4	Values in the range from −214,748.3648 through 214,748.3647. Arithmetic with this data type is accurate to the nearest ten-thousandth of a unit within the specified range.
Decimal	Number (decimal)	Varies based on digits for scale and precision	Exactly represents values from −10^38 through (10^38) − 1. You can use the range to independently specify the total number of digits and the number of digits after the decimal. Numeric is a SQL Server synonym for the Decimal data type.
Datetime	Date/Time	8	A value capable of representing dates from January 1, 1753 through December 31, 9999 to an accuracy of 3.33 milliseconds.
Smalldatetime	Date/Time	4	A value capable of representing dates from January 1, 1900 through June 6, 2079 to an accuracy of within 1 minute.
Varchar	Text	Varies based on number of characters	A variable-length text string of up to 8000 non-Unicode characters.
Nvarchar	Text	Varies based on number of characters	A variable-length text string of up to 4000 Unicode characters.
Text	Memo	Varies depending on content	Can hold up to (2^31) − 1 non-Unicode characters. This data type is not valid for variables or parameters.
Ntext	Memo	Varies depending on content	Can hold up to (2^30) − 1 Unicode characters. This data type is not valid for variables or parameters.

(continued)

Table 14-3 *(continued)*

SQL Server Data Type	Closest Matching Access Data Type	Bytes	SQL Server Data Type Description
Image	OLE Object	Varies depending on content	Can hold up to (2^31) − 1 bytes of binary data. Use it for binary data that exceeds the limits of the Varbinary data type.
Unique-identifier	Number (replication ID)	16	A globally unique identifier (GUID). Carefully evaluate whether you truly need this data type because it's very long (16 bytes) and has a format that isn't easy to read or manipulate.
Char	Not	Varies applicable on content	A fixed-length text string of up to 8000 dependingnon-Unicode characters.
Nchar	Not applicable	Varies depending on content	A fixed-length text string of up to 4000 Unicode characters.
Varbinary	Not applicable	Varies depending on content	Can hold up to 8000 bytes of binary data in a variable-length format.
Timestamp	Not applicable	8	A binary value that increments by 1 whenever any table with a column of the Timestamp data type has an insertion or an update. This data type *does not* store Datetime values.
Sql_variant	Not applicable	Varies depending on content	A data type that accommodates multiple data types within a single column in a table. Can contain all other data types, except Text, Ntext, Image, and Timestamp.

The Access data type for table columns that's missing from SQL Server is the Hyperlink data type. Recall that this data type permits you to link to different parts of the same or a different Office document as well as Web pages. The Hyperlink data type is a text string comprised of up to four separate components: the link's display, main URL address, subaddress, and appearance when a mouse moves over it. Access projects enable the functions for this data type through form fields.

The new visual Table Designer in Access 2002 offers a Lookup tab in Table Design view. Although Access project files do not offer an explicit Lookup data type like Access database files do, Access projects provide a Lookup tab. You can use this tab to set the parameters for a lookup field. This graphical process mirrors the settings you make for a combo box but causes the table to display the lookup value. Any forms you base on the table will show the lookup value and can offer a drop-down list for changing existing values as well as inputting new ones.

Note   The sample files for this chapter include the *Orders_with_lookup* table, which demonstrates one way to make the lookup column settings. See "Create a Lookup Column" in Access Help for step-by-step instructions.

Setting and Looking Up Column Data Types

When you first working with SQL Server, the easiest way to start creating table columns is with the visual Table Designer. Even experienced developers frequently use a designer to create tables. You can invoke the Access 2002 Table Designer from the Database window. Just select the *Tables* class from the Objects bar and then click New. Figure 14-12 shows a table in the designer with a column named after each of the SQL Server column data types. I constructed this table by typing data type names into the *Column Name* column. You can populate the *Data Type* column by making a selection from its drop-down control. I chose the data type corresponding to the entry to the *Column Name* column. The only SQL Server column data type the table fails to include is the Numeric data type, which as you'll recall, is synonymous with the Decimal data type.

The specification for the *data_types* table shown in Figure 14-12 accepts the defaults for Length and Allow Nulls settings, with two exceptions. The first exception is the *pk* column. This column does not allow Nulls. You can make a column the primary key (like the *pk* column is) by clicking the Primary Key control with the cursor resting on the row containing the column specification. The second exception is the column named *int_with_identity*. This column also does not accept Nulls. Figure 14-12 shows the cursor resting on the row containing the specification for this column. As a result, the Columns tab offers additional column properties. In this case, you see the Identity selection and a default value of *1* for both the Identity Seed and Identity Increment settings. You can override these defaults by entering new values for the settings.

Figure 14-12 A view of the *data_types* table in the new Access 2002 Table Designer.

Mapping SQL Server to Access and ADO Data Types

Mapping between data types for different data stores can help you understand when to use which data type in which context. This kind of information is critical when migrating data from one database to another. The following code sample takes each of the columns in the *data_types* table shown in Figure 14-12 and prints their SQL Server, Access, and ADO data type names, as well as their defined size. The Access and ADO data type names and the *DefinedSize* property uniquely distinguish most SQL Server data types. However, the SQL Server Money, Smallmoney, Datetime, and Smalldatetime data types require you to provide more information to distinguish them. Although the SQL Server Datetime and Smalldatetime data types have identical ADO and *DefinedSize* settings, their *Precision* properties are different. This is because Datetime column values have more precision that Smalldatetime column values.

The following three procedures map the SQL Server data types in the *data_types* table to their Access data type names and ADO enum names. The report also prints the *DefinedSize* property for each column in the table. In the case of the Money, Smallmoney, Datetime, and Smalldatetime data types, the report also includes the precision of the columns. This helps to differentiate between data types that are otherwise identical in the report's other columns.

The main routine, *ReportDataTypes*, starts by printing a heading and setting it off with a line of equal signs below the report's column headings. Next it opens a recordset for the *data_types* table. Then it loops through all the fields in the recordset. Within the loop, an *If...Then...Else* statement directs the reporting to one of two *Debug.Print* statements. The *Then* clause prints results for the two sets of fields that require *Precision* to distinguish between them. The *Else* clause processes all the remaining data types. The two other procedures are function procedures that return the name of the Access data type and the enum name for the ADO data type value corresponding to the SQL Server data type. ADO automatically maps the SQL Server data types into its own data types to create a field *Type* property value.

```
Sub ReportDataTypes()
Dim rst1 As ADODB.Recordset
Dim fld1 As ADODB.Field

'Print and separate column headings from the rest
'of the report
Debug.Print "SQL Server name" & String(3, " ") & _
    "Access name" & String(12, " ") & _
    "ADO Enum name" & String(5, " ") & _
    "DefinedSize" & " " & "Precision"
Debug.Print String(17, "=") & " " & String(22, "=") & " " & _
    String(17, "=") & " " & String(11, "=") & " " & _
    String(9, "=")

'Base a recordset on the data_types table
Set rst1 = New ADODB.Recordset
rst1.Open "data_types", CurrentProject.Connection

'Loop through the columns in the data_types table and
'report their name, Access data type, ADO data type,
'DefinedSize, and Precision, if appropriate
For Each fld1 In rst1.Fields
    If (fld1.Type = adCurrency Or _
        fld1.Type = adDBTimeStamp) Then
        Debug.Print fld1.Name & _
            String(18 - Len(fld1.Name), " ") & _
            AccessDataTypeName(fld1.Type) & _
            String(23 - Len(AccessDataTypeName(fld1.Type)), " ") & _
            ADODataTypeName(fld1.Type) & _
            String(18 - Len(ADODataTypeName(fld1.Type)), " ") & _
            fld1.DefinedSize, fld1.Precision
    Else
```

(continued)

```
            Debug.Print fld1.Name & _
                String(18 - Len(fld1.Name), " ") & _
                AccessDataTypeName(fld1.Type) & _
                String(23 - Len(AccessDataTypeName(fld1.Type)), " ") & _
                ADODataTypeName(fld1.Type) & _
                String(18 - Len(ADODataTypeName(fld1.Type)), " ") & _
                fld1.DefinedSize


        End If
Next fld1

'Clean up objects
rst1.Close
Set rst1 = Nothing

End Sub


Function AccessDataTypeName(DataTypeEnum As Integer) As String

'Decodes SQL Server data type to Access data type
'based on the ADO enum value for the data type
Select Case DataTypeEnum
    Case 2
        AccessDataTypeName = "Number(Integer)"
    Case 3
        AccessDataTypeName = "Number(Long Integer)"
    Case 4
        AccessDataTypeName = "Number(Single)"
    Case 5
        AccessDataTypeName = "Number(Double)"
    Case 6
        AccessDataTypeName = "Number(Currency)"
    Case 11
        AccessDataTypeName = "Yes/No"
    Case 12
        AccessDataTypeName = "Not applicable"
    Case 17
        AccessDataTypeName = "Number(Byte)"
    Case 20
        AccessDataTypeName = "Not applicable"
    Case 72
        AccessDataTypeName = "Number(Replication ID)"
    Case 128
        AccessDataTypeName = "Not applicable"
    Case 129
        AccessDataTypeName = "Not applicable"
```

```
    Case 130
        AccessDataTypeName = "Not applicable"
    Case 131
        AccessDataTypeName = "Number(Decimal)"
    Case 135
        AccessDataTypeName = "Date/Time"
    Case 200
        AccessDataTypeName = "Text"
    Case 201
        AccessDataTypeName = "Memo"
    Case 202
        AccessDataTypeName = "Text"
    Case 203
        AccessDataTypeName = "Memo"
    Case 204
        AccessDataTypeName = "Not applicable"
    Case 205
        AccessDataTypeName = "OLE Object"
    Case Else
        AccessDataTypeName = "Data Type Not Decoded"
End Select

End Function


Function ADODataTypeName(DataTypeEnum As Integer) As String

'Decodes SQL Server data type to ADO data type
'based on the ADO enum value for the data type
Select Case DataTypeEnum
    Case 2
        ADODataTypeName = "adSmallInt"
    Case 3
        ADODataTypeName = "adInteger"
    Case 4
        ADODataTypeName = "adSingle"
    Case 5
        ADODataTypeName = "adDouble"
    Case 6
        ADODataTypeName = "adCurrency"
    Case 11
        ADODataTypeName = "adBoolean"
    Case 12
        ADODataTypeName = "adVariant"
    Case 17
        ADODataTypeName = "adUnsignedTinyInt"
```

(continued)

```
        Case 20
            ADODataTypeName = "adBigInt"
        Case 72
            ADODataTypeName = "adGUID"
        Case 128
            ADODataTypeName = "adBinary"
        Case 129
            ADODataTypeName = "adChar"
        Case 130
            ADODataTypeName = "adWChar"
        Case 131
            ADODataTypeName = "adNumeric"
        Case 135
            ADODataTypeName = "adDBTimeStamp"
        Case 200
            ADODataTypeName = "adVarChar"
        Case 201
            ADODataTypeName = "adLongVarChar"
        Case 202
            ADODataTypeName = "adVarWChar"
        Case 203
            ADODataTypeName = "adLongVarWChar"
        Case 204
            ADODataTypeName = "adVarBinary"
        Case 205
            ADODataTypeName = "adLongVarBinary"
        Case Else
            ADODataTypeName = "Data Type Not Decoded"
    End Select

End Function
```

Figure 14-13 shows the output from the *ReportDataTypes* procedure. It includes a row for each column in the *data_types* table. You can use this printout as a convenient mapping tool for naming data types. The *DefinedSize* property values are the default settings for the data types when the number of bytes used to store an entry varies according to each entry's content, as it does for Nvarchar and Nchar. As you can see, the Money and Smallmoney SQL Server data types have the same ADO enum name, *adCurrency*. They differ only in their *Precision* property. The same pattern holds for Datetime and Smalldatetime. In addition, the SQL Server Datetime and Smalldatetime data types translate into the same ADO enum name, *adDBTimeStamp*. However, neither data type is related to the SQL Server Timestamp data type, which is a binary value.

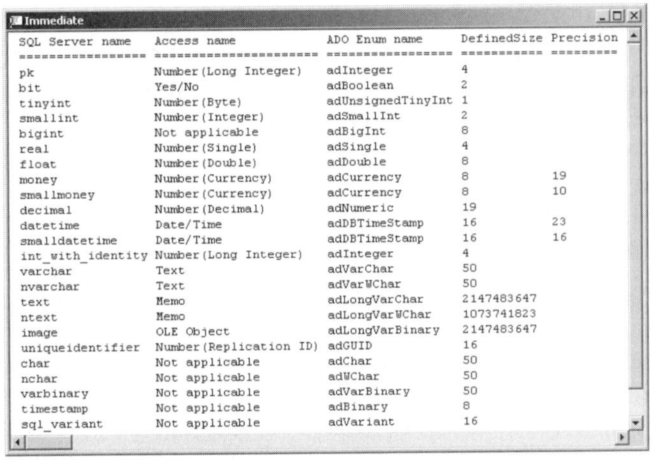

SQL Server name	Access name	ADO Enum name	DefinedSize	Precision
pk	Number(Long Integer)	adInteger	4	
bit	Yes/No	adBoolean	2	
tinyint	Number(Byte)	adUnsignedTinyInt	1	
smallint	Number(Integer)	adSmallInt	2	
bigint	Not applicable	adBigInt	8	
real	Number(Single)	adSingle	4	
float	Number(Double)	adDouble	8	
money	Number(Currency)	adCurrency	8	19
smallmoney	Number(Currency)	adCurrency	8	10
decimal	Number(Decimal)	adNumeric	19	
datetime	Date/Time	adDBTimeStamp	16	23
smalldatetime	Date/Time	adDBTimeStamp	16	16
int_with_identity	Number(Long Integer)	adInteger	4	
varchar	Text	adVarChar	50	
nvarchar	Text	adVarWChar	50	
text	Memo	adLongVarChar	2147483647	
ntext	Memo	adLongVarWChar	1073741823	
image	OLE Object	adLongVarBinary	2147483647	
uniqueidentifier	Number(Replication ID)	adGUID	16	
char	Not applicable	adChar	50	
nchar	Not applicable	adWChar	50	
varbinary	Not applicable	adVarBinary	50	
timestamp	Not applicable	adBinary	8	
sql_variant	Not applicable	adVariant	16	

Figure 14-13 The output generated by the *ReportDataTypes* procedure.

Defining Tables and Inserting Rows

One typical application for column data types is to create the columns in a table. To create a table, use the T-SQL CREATE TABLE statement. This statement lets you specify the table name and then declare each of the columns within the table. You must specify a data type for each table column. You can optionally specify various constraints, such as one for a table's primary key. Although SQL Server doesn't require a primary key, you should always declare one when migrating to SQL Server from Access because SQL Server doesn't allow manual input to tables without a primary key. Another special feature of primary keys in SQL Server is that they can be clustered. A clustered primary key orders the records on a storage device according to the primary key values. Primary keys are unclustered unless you explicitly declare them as clustered.

After you create a table, you probably will want to populate it with values. You can do this programmatically with the INSERT statement. This statement lets you populate all or a subset of the fields in a target table. You can specify the column values for each new row with a new INSERT statement. The source of the records can be individual values, another SQL Server table in the same or a different database, or data based on a legacy Access database file.

The next sample demonstrates the correct syntax for the CREATE TABLE and INSERT statements. Before using these statements, the sample removes any table, if one exists, that has the same name as the table it's about to create in a database. The sample demonstrates the use of an InformationSchema view to determine whether a prior version of a table exists. You can use the system-defined *sysobjects* table to determine whether a table or other database object exists already, but Microsoft recommends using InformationSchema views instead. Using

InformationSchema views enables your applications to work properly, even if Microsoft changes the design of system-defined tables such as *sysobjects*.

The sample hardcodes the *MyExtensions* table name and the *EmployeeID*, *FirstName*, *LastName*, and *Extension* column names. Hardcoding might be more typical when working with a table's design than with other coding tasks. This is because your application is likely to have custom requirements. However, if you plan to use one procedure to create many tables with the same basic design, it's trivial to generalize the procedure. Again, what to leave fixed and what to make variable will depend on the requirements of your custom applications.

After setting a *Connection* object for the current project, the *CreateMyExtensions* procedure features three main sections. Each of these sections demonstrates the use of T-SQL code to perform an independent task for creating and populating the *MyExtensions* table. The procedure repeatedly invokes the *Execute* method of the *Connection* object to run each of the sample's T-SQL code segments.

The first T-SQL segment uses an IF statement with an EXISTS keyword. This keyword permits the IF statement to conditionally execute a DROP TABLE statement if a prior version of the table exists. The sample uses an InformationSchema view to detect whether a table already exists in the database. If the table exists, the application simply drops the old version of it. In a production environment with critical operations or financial data, you might want to archive the table's data before dropping it. I'll illustrate a data archiving strategy later in the chapter in the "Triggers" section.

The second code segment invokes the CREATE TABLE statement to create the *MyExtensions* table. Because the column serves as the primary key, its declaration explicitly excludes Nulls. In addition, the *EmployeeID* declaration includes an IDENTITY setting with a default value of *1* for its seed and *1* for its increment. The other three table columns permit Nulls.

The third code segment invokes the INSERT statement three times. The first two instances of the statement populate all three nonidentity columns. SQL Server automatically populates the identity column value based on the last identity column value and the incremental value for the IDENTITY setting. Because the first two invocations of the INSERT statement specify values for all three nonidentity columns, the INSERT statements do not require a field list before the VALUES keyword. (This list indicates the fields for which the VALUES keyword designates values.) However, the third instance of the INSERT statement specifies only the *LastName* and *Extension* column values. Therefore, this instance of INSERT requires a field list before the VALUES keyword.

The procedure closes by invoking the *RefreshDatabaseWindow* method. This method refreshes the Database window so that the user can immediately see the newly added table. If the procedure did not include this method, the user might not see the new table in the Database window.

```
Sub CreateMyExtensions()
Dim str1 As String
Dim cnn1 As ADODB.Connection

'Point a Connection object at the current project
Set cnn1 = CurrentProject.Connection

'Delete the MyExtensions table if it exists already
str1 = "IF EXISTS(SELECT TABLE_NAME " & _
    "FROM INFORMATION_SCHEMA.TABLES " & _
    "WHERE TABLE_NAME = 'MyExtensions') " & _
    "DROP TABLE MyExtensions"
cnn1.Execute str1

'Create the MyExtensions table with an unclustered primary key
str1 = "CREATE TABLE MyExtensions " & _
    "( " & _
    "EmployeeID int IDENTITY(1,1) NOT NULL PRIMARY KEY, " & _
    "FirstName nvarchar(10) NULL, " & _
    "LastName nvarchar(20) NULL, " & _
    "Extension nvarchar(4) NULL " & _
    ")"
cnn1.Execute str1

'Populate the MyExtensions table with data; populate one record
'with a subset of the input fields
str1 = "INSERT INTO MyExtensions Values('Rick', 'Dobson', '8629')" & _
    "INSERT INTO MyExtensions Values('Virginia', 'Dobson', '9294')" & _
    "INSERT INTO MyExtensions (LastName, Extension) Values('Hill','3743')"
cnn1.Execute str1

'Refresh Database window to show new table
RefreshDatabaseWindow

End Sub
```

The next sample uses a nearly identical approach to create and populate a table of picture descriptions and file addresses for picture images. You can use this kind of table to display photographs, diagrams, or any graphically formatted file. By storing the file address instead of the image, you speed up the image retrieval time and shorten the image processing time. In Chapter 15, you'll see a sample that illustrates how to use this kind of table to populate controls on a form that contain photos.

The sample table in this next application is structurally unique from the one in the preceding sample because it uses a clustered primary key. Access database files do not support this kind of primary key. Recall that when an application specifies this type of primary key, SQL Server orders the records on the storage medium according to their primary key values. Each table can have just one clustered index, and it doesn't have to be the primary key. You should reserve the clustered index setting for the key that users are most likely to work with. A clustered index substantially expedites record retrieval.

The following code sample contains the same three main phases as the preceding sample, but the column names are different. In addition, this sample conditionally drops any prior version of the table by calling a sub procedure. While table designs and data tend to be unique from one table to the next, the process of dropping a table doesn't vary much. Therefore, the main procedure calls the *Drop_a_table* procedure by passing a connection argument and a string representing the table name.

When working with image files, it's common to store them with the operating system and store only their locations in the database. You can maintain the security of your image files by placing them on a read-only file share. This will allow users to query the table, but it will prevent them from adding, updating, and deleting image files. Some images are included with the chapter's sample materials on the companion CD so that you can experiment with displaying them. See Chapter 15 for a code sample that demonstrates this.

```
Sub CreatPic_Addresses()
Dim str1 As String
Dim cnn1 As ADODB.Connection
Dim TableName As String

'Point a Connection object at the current project
Set cnn1 = CurrentProject.Connection

'Delete the Pic_Addresses table if it exists already
TableName = "Pic_Addresses"
Drop_a_table cnn1, TableName

'Create the Pic_Addresses table with a clustered primary key
str1 = "CREATE TABLE Pic_Addresses " & _
    "( " & _
    "PictureID int IDENTITY NOT NULL PRIMARY KEY CLUSTERED, " & _
    "Pic_description nvarchar(50), " & _
    "Pic_address nvarchar(256) " & _
    ") "
cnn1.Execute str1

'Insert descriptions and addresses for four pictures
str1 = "INSERT INTO Pic_Addresses " & _
    "Values('Rick munches glasses', " & _
        "'C:\Documents and Settings\All Users\Documents\" & _
    "PMA Samples\Picture1.jpg')"
```

```
        "INSERT INTO Pic_Addresses " & _
            "Values('Rick not working at computer', " & _
            "'C:\Documents and Settings\All Users\Documents\" & _
            "PMA Samples\Picture2.jpg')"
        "INSERT INTO Pic_Addresses " & _
            "Values('Rick finally working at computer', " & _
            "'C:\Documents and Settings\All Users\Documents\" & _
            "PMA Samples\Picture3.jpg')"
        "INSERT INTO Pic_Addresses " & _
            "Values('Rick gets reward for working', " & _
            "'C:\Documents and Settings\All Users\Documents\" & _
            "PMA Samples\Picture4.jpg')"
cnn1.Execute str1

'Refresh Database window to show new table
RefreshDatabaseWindow

End Sub


Sub Drop_a_table(cnn1 As ADODB.Connection, TableName As String)

'Delete the table if it exists already
str1 = "IF EXISTS (SELECT TABLE_NAME " & _
    "FROM INFORMATION_SCHEMA.TABLES " & _
    "WHERE TABLE_NAME = '" & TableName & "') " & _
    "DROP TABLE " & TableName
cnn1.Execute str1

End Sub
```

Adding a Table from a Database Diagram

When you first migrate to SQL Server, you might want to use graphical approaches with the programmatic ones to help expedite your solution development. Database diagrams are a graphical development aid that resemble the Relationship window in Access. However, you can have multiple database diagrams for the same database. In addition, database diagrams have a much richer set of data definition capabilities than the Relationship window does. Think of database diagrams as the Relationship window on steroids!

This section introduces these data definition capabilities by building a new table. Database diagrams are graphical, so I'll present the example with step-by-step instructions. The sample table, *Orders_linked_to_MyExtensions*, will have three columns, *OrderID*, *OrderDate*, and *EmployeeID*. The *OrderID* column will be the table's primary key, with an IDENTITY property setting of *10* for its seed and *2* for its increment.

To create a new table with a database diagram, you have to open either a new or an existing diagram. To open a new diagram for a new table, follow these steps:

1. Open a diagram by selecting Database Diagrams in the Database window and clicking New.

2. Click Close on the Add Table dialog box, because you won't need an existing table to create a new one.

3. Right-click anywhere in the empty diagram, and click New Table from the shortcut menu.

4. Type the name *Orders_linked_to_MyExtensions* in the Choose Name dialog box, and click OK.

These steps open a blank table grid that you can use to help design your new table. The grid has a title with the name you assigned to the table, but otherwise it's empty. You can add columns to the table with these steps:

1. Type *OrderID* in the first Column Name row of the grid. Then select an Int data type and clear the Allow Nulls check box because this field will serve as the primary key.

2. Type *OrderDate* in the second Column Name row. Choose a Smalldate data type for this column because this application will be outdated well before 2079 and you don't need to track orders that are less than a minute apart. Leave Allow Nulls checked.

3. Finish entering columns by typing *EmployeeID* in the third row of the *EmployeeID* column. Because this column will eventually serve as a foreign key for linking this table to the *MyExtensions* table, choose Int as the data type so that it matches the data type for *EmployeeID* in the *MyExtensions* table.

You're almost finished defining your new table. However, you need to make OrderID the primary key. In addition, if you want the column to automatically populate itself with values, you need to give it an IDENTITY setting. After making these refinements, you can add the new table to the database. Follow these steps to finish creating the table:

1. Right-click anywhere on the OrderID row. Choose Primary Key from the shortcut menu.

2. Click the record selector for OrderID. Right-click a second time in the OrderID row, and choose Properties from the shortcut menu.

3. Select the Columns tab for the Properties dialog box, and confirm that the Column Name setting is OrderID. If not, use the drop-down control for the setting to select OrderID.

4. Next change the Identity setting to Yes. Then assign the Identity Seed a value of *10* and the Identity Increment a value of *2*. (See Figure 14-14.) This will cause OrderID to start at 10 and grow by increments of 2 for each new record. After making these settings, close the Properties dialog box by clicking the Close control in the top right corner.

5. Then click the Close control for the diagram. Click Yes when prompted about saving changes. Then assign a name to the diagram, such as *Adding_Orders_linked_to_MyExtensions*.

Figure 14-14 The Properties dialog box for the *OrderID* column that shows the setting for the Identity, Identity Seed, and Identity Increment.

Linking Two Tables in a Database Diagram

Now let's create a new database diagram that links the *Orders_linked_to_MyExtensions* table to the *MyExtensions* table. You can use the diagram to set up referential integrity and cascading updates and deletes. In this example, you don't want to throw away orders based on the status of an employee, but you do want to be able to switch accounts from one employee to the next. Therefore, you enable cascading updates but not cascading deletes.

Let's start the process of linking the tables by creating a new database diagram. (We could use the old diagram, but it is more instructive to start from scratch.) Use the steps on the following page.

1. Open a diagram by selecting Database Diagrams in the Database window and clicking New.

2. From the Add Table dialog box, select MyExtensions. Then click Add.

3. Repeat this process for the *Orders_linked_to_MyExtensions* table.

4. Click Close to remove the Add Table dialog box.

After rearranging the boxes representing the tables so that they're easy to use, you're ready to start linking the two tables. Follow these steps:

1. Click the record selector for *EmployeeID* in the *MyExtensions* table.

2. Drag the *EmployeeID* field from the *MyExtensions* table to the *EmployeeID* field in the *Orders_linked_to_MyExtensions* table. (See Figure 14-15.)

3. In the Create Relationship dialog box that appears, verify that the primary key table is *MyExtensions* and that its linking field is *EmployeeID*. In addition, verify that the foreign key table is *Orders_linked_to_MyExtensions* and that its linking field is also *EmployeeID*.

4. Verify that the Enforce Relationship For INSERTs And UPDATEs check box is checked.

5. Click the Cascade Update Related Fields check box.

6. Click OK to assign the settings in the dialog box.

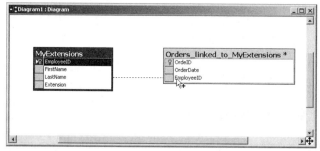

Figure 14-15 This database diagram shows the dragging of the *EmployeeID* field from the *MyExtensions* table to the *EmployeeID* field in the *Orders_linked_to_MyExtensions* table.

In the last sequence, you specified a foreign key for the *Orders_linked_to_MyExtensions* table that points at the *MyExtensions* table. However, Access hasn't yet saved the relationship to the database. You can facilitate this by closing the diagram and saving it. Before you close the diagram, Access will ask whether you want to save your changes. Follow these steps to save the relationship:

1. Click the Close button on your database diagram to close it.

2. Click Yes when prompted about saving your changes.

3. Assign the diagram a name, such as *Adding_A_Relationship*.

4. Access again asks whether you want to save changes. Click Yes. This prompt also allows you to write the changes to a text file.

There's a lot more to database diagrams, but these two examples can acquaint you with some of the basics and allow you to determine whether using database diagrams fits your personal style of developing. Some Access developers love to code, but others prefer graphical design techniques. If you're in the latter camp, database diagrams might be a good topic for you to explore further.

The following code sample resets the database to remove the objects created with the two database diagram examples you've seen. This permits you to review the steps from scratch, without having to work around previously defined objects, relationships, and diagrams. It also gives you some insight into programmatically managing database diagrams.

This sample has two components. First it conditionally drops the *Orders_linked_to_MyExtensions* table. Dropping the table also eliminates its relationship to the *MyExtensions* table. Then the procedure removes all the diagrams in the database. SQL Server stores information describing its database diagram collection members in the *dtproperties* table. Although SQL Server defines this as a user-defined table, it's typically managed by SQL Server. In addition, SQL Server provides no explicit means for programmatically referencing database diagrams. However, you can delete the rows in the *dtproperties* table. Doing so removes the diagrams associated with those rows. This procedure removes the diagrams created in this chapter.

```
Sub Drop_Orders_linked_table_and_Diagrams()
Dim str1 As String
Dim cnn1 As ADODB.Connection
Dim TableName As String

'Point a Connection object at the current project
Set cnn1 = CurrentProject.Connection

'Delete the Order_linked_to_MyExtensions table if it exists already
TableName = "Orders_linked_to_MyExtensions"
Drop_a_table cnn1, TableName

'Drop all database diagrams
str1 = "DELETE FROM dtProperties"
cnn1.Execute str1

End Sub
```

SQL Server Views

SQL Server views are a subset of the traditional Access queries that you know from Access database files and the T-SQL samples that you find in Books Online. A view is an object in a SQL Server database. However, SQL Server does not save the view as a table of data values. Instead, SQL Server stores a T-SQL SELECT statement and related properties that define the view. The purpose of a view is to act as a virtual table. Once you understand the purpose of a view in a database, some of its apparent limitations (when compared to other database objects and T-SQL statements) generally seem reasonable.

At its core, a SQL Server view is a single SELECT statement. The result set returned by this statement is the view's virtual table. The SELECT statement can include all the standard clauses of a typical SELECT statement except the ORDER BY clause. (The ORDER BY clause is permissible, but you must also include the TOP clause in the SELECT statement so that SQL Server can interpret the view and return a result set.) While a view does permit a WHERE clause, its arguments cannot be parameters. In addition, you cannot include multiple SELECT statements in a view, and a view cannot process INSERT, UPDATE, and DELETE statements.

These limitations of views stem from their basic purpose—to represent a single, virtual table in T-SQL code. When you need to accomplish this, the view is an able tool. In addition, Access projects offer a Query Designer for constructing and editing views that resembles the Query Designer available in Access database files for stored queries. The Access project Query Designer can make designing views fast. Furthermore, you can use this tool to teach yourself T-SQL syntax by graphically designing views and then examining the T-SQL underlying them in the Query Designer's SQL pane.

Creating Sample Tables

This section uses the *Orders* table and the *Shippers* table, which are based on the corresponding tables in the NorthwindCS database. As mentioned earlier in the chapter, if you don't have the NorthwindCS database on your server, you probably have the Northwind database. Recall that the NorthwindCS sample Access project automatically installs the NorthwindCS database on the local server the first time you open the project if a copy of the Northwind database doesn't already exist on the local server.

The following two procedures show the code for creating the tables and populating them with values. Each procedure handles the creation and data population of one table. The procedures start by conditionally removing a prior version of the table (if one exists). Next the procedures invoke a CREATE TABLE statement to define the table structure. After executing the CREATE TABLE statement, the database for the current project will have a new empty table. Then the procedures run a stored procedure that copies data from the NorthwindCS *Orders* table or the *Shippers* table to the local table of the same name. I'll discuss these stored procedures later in this chapter (in "Creating and Using Stored Procedures") so that you can modify them as needed.

```
Sub CreateAndPopulateOrdersTable()
Dim str1 As String
Dim cnn1 As ADODB.Connection
Dim TableName As String

'Point a Connection object at the current project
Set cnn1 = CurrentProject.Connection

'Delete the table if it exists already
TableName = "Orders"
Drop_a_table cnn1, TableName

'Create the table
str1 = "CREATE TABLE Orders " & _
    "( " & _
    "OrderID int IDENTITY (1, 1) NOT NULL PRIMARY KEY CLUSTERED, " & _
    "OrderDate datetime NULL , " & _
    "ShipVia int NULL , " & _
    "Freight money NULL " & _
    ")"
cnn1.Execute str1

'Run custom stored procedure to populate table based
'on NorthwindCS database
str1 = "EXEC Copy_from_NorthwindCS_Orders"
cnn1.Execute str1

'Refresh Database window to show new table
RefreshDatabaseWindow

End Sub


Sub CreateAndPopulateShippersTable()
Dim str1 As String
Dim cnn1 As ADODB.Connection
Dim TableName As String

'Point a Connection object at the current project
Set cnn1 = CurrentProject.Connection
```

(continued)

```
'Delete the table if it exists already
TableName = "Shippers"
Drop_a_table cnn1, TableName

'Create the table
str1 = "CREATE TABLE Shippers " & _
    "( " & _
    "ShipperID int IDENTITY (1, 1) NOT NULL PRIMARY KEY CLUSTERED, " & _
    "CompanyName varchar(40) NOT NULL , " & _
    "Phone varchar(24) NULL " & _
    ")"
cnn1.Execute str1

'Run custom stored procedure to populate table based
'on NorthwindCS database
str1 = "EXEC Copy_from_NorthwindCS_Shippers"
cnn1.Execute str1

'Refresh Database window to show new table
RefreshDatabaseWindow

End Sub
```

Using the Access Project Query Designer

You can launch the Query Designer by selecting Queries in the Objects bar and clicking New. This opens the New Query dialog box. Select Design View, and click OK. Next you will see the Add Table dialog box. You can choose from previously defined tables, views, and user-defined functions. The dialog box contains a tab for each of these objects. You can select objects from these tabs and click Add to include them as record sources for your view. When you are done, select Close to remove the Add Table dialog box. Alternatively, you can just click Close. This frees you to write T-SQL code directly into the SQL pane without having to use the graphical UI.

Figure 14-16 shows the graphical UI and code specifications for a view. I added the *Orders* table to this view, which, as you can see, offers three panes. The toolbar controls let you independently show or hide each of these panes in Design View. The top pane, which has an *Orders* table icon, is the Diagram pane. This pane can depict any joins between tables that serve as the record source for a view. In this case, just one table serves as the record source. You can add table columns to a view by selecting the check box next to the column you want in the Diagram pane.

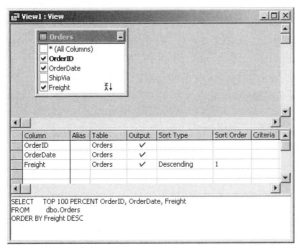

Figure 14-16 The three panes for the Access project Query Designer with a view that sorts orders by *Freight* column values in descending order.

The Query Designer automatically adds the column name for a checked box to the middle panel, called the Grid pane. The Grid pane contains a row for each column in the view's virtual table. Note that you can designate the order in which the view sorts its records. Figure 14-16 shows the *Freight* column being sorted in descending order. Because the view has only one sort key, its *Sort Order* column has a value of 1 and the *Sort Order* values for the other columns are blank.

The bottom pane is the SQL pane. This pane does not open by default, but you can manually open it with the SQL control on the Design view toolbar. The Query Designer automatically populates this pane with code when you commit changes to either of the other two panes. In addition, you can type T-SQL code into the SQL pane, and the Query Designer will revise the other two panes accordingly. Type your T-SQL syntax directly into this pane to avoid having to work with the graphical UI for the Query Designer.

When you're ready to examine the result set from a view, you must save the view before looking at the rows that it returns. The view depicted in Figure 14-16 appears in the sample database for this chapter as *Orders_sorted_by_Freight*. Whenever you edit a view's design, you must resave the view before you can see its result set. Click the Run control or the Datasheet View control to examine the result set. If you haven't saved the view since the last change, Access automatically prompts you to save it. If you're examining a view's result set for the first time, you must assign it a name. Access prompts with a name such as *View1*, but you can override this default name with one that is meaningful for your application.

Filtering by Date

SQL Server stores *datetime* and *smalldatetime* data type values internally in a format similar to that used for Access database files. However, SQL Server normally displays dates in a string format, such as *varchar* or *char*. Indeed, you can filter SQL Server fields with dates by using a string. Alternatively, you can also use various functions to help specify filtering criteria. The DATEPART function is particularly useful for this purpose.

The following T-SQL statement shows the syntax for using a string filter employed in the *Orders_in_1996_1* view. The statement specifies the return of rows that are less than or equal to the last day in 1996. The statement is from the SQL pane of the Query Designer. You do not necessarily need the dbo qualifier for the *Orders* table in the FROM clause, but the Query Designer forces its inclusion. Notice that we specify the string for the date using single quotes. Access developers migrating to SQL Server will have to get used to delimiting text strings with single rather than double quote marks.

```
SELECT    OrderID, OrderDate, ShipVia, Freight
FROM      dbo.Orders
WHERE     (OrderDate <= '1996-12-31')
```

Figure 14-17 shows an excerpt from the result set for the view. Notice that it contains just 152 rows, instead of the 830 rows in the original *Orders* table. This reduced number of rows stems directly from the filter in the WHERE clause's argument. Of the full set of 830 records in the *Orders* table, only 152 are from 1996. (This is the first year of data for the NorthwindCS database.)

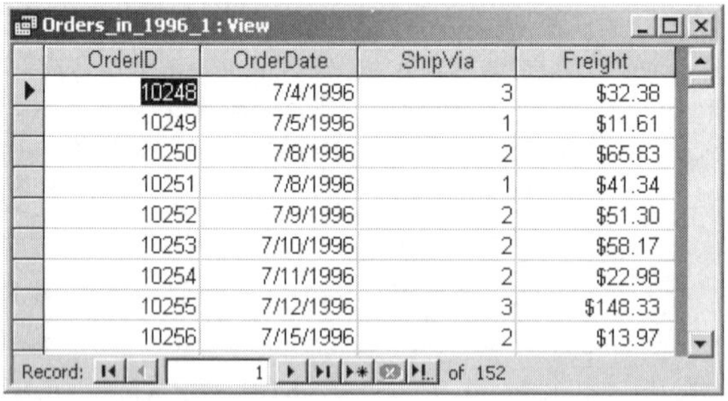

OrderID	OrderDate	ShipVia	Freight
10248	7/4/1996	3	$32.38
10249	7/5/1996	1	$11.61
10250	7/8/1996	2	$65.83
10251	7/8/1996	1	$41.34
10252	7/9/1996	2	$51.30
10253	7/10/1996	2	$58.17
10254	7/11/1996	2	$22.98
10255	7/12/1996	3	$148.33
10256	7/15/1996	2	$13.97

Figure 14-17 An excerpt from the result set for *Orders_in_1996_1*.

The following syntax for the *Orders_in_1996_2* view shows another piece of T-SQL syntax that generates the same result set as the one shown in Figure 14-7. Instead of filtering on a string value, the T-SQL code for this view applies the DATEPART function to the *OrderDate* column values. Those rows that return a value of 1996 pass through the filter into the result set for the *Orders_in_1996_2* view.

```
SELECT    OrderID, OrderDate, ShipVia, Freight
FROM      dbo.Orders
WHERE     (DATEPART(yyyy, OrderDate) = '1996')
```

If your work requires you to filter on different dates or units of time, you should get to know the DATEPART function. It works similarly though not identically to its counterpart for Access database files. The SQL Server DATEPART function lets you extract from columns of *datetime* values any of 11 different time parts, from the year down to the millisecond. Table 14-4 shows the DATEPART arguments that permit you to extract different time units from a *datetime* or *smalldatetime* value. The day of year and day of month numbering starts at 1 for the first respective day of the year or the month. The day of week runs from 1 (for Sunday) to 7 (for Saturday). This is the default setting for U.S. English. Use the SET DATEFIRST statement to alter the default day for the start of a week. (See Books Online for the syntax.)

Table 14-4   DATEPART Arguments for Extracting Time Units

Time Unit	DATEPART Argument
Year	*yy* or *yyyy*
Quarter	*qq* or *q*
Month	*mm* or *m*
Day of year	*dy* or *y*
Day of month	*dd* or *d*
Week of year	*wk* or *ww*
Day of week	*dw*
Hour	*hh*
Minute	*mi* or *n*
Second	*ss* or *s*
Millisecond	*ms*

Joining Tables for a Lookup

While Access offers a Query Designer for inputting the T-SQL code for a view, you don't have to script this way. You can use the ADO *Connection* object to execute T-SQL statements to create a view. This approach offers several advantages. First, it automatically creates an archive of the script for a view in a location that typical users aren't likely to access. If users inadvertently corrupt a view's T-SQL by opening and modifying it in the Database window, you can restore the view by rerunning the procedure to create the view. The second advantage is that your code more closely follows the samples in Books Online. For example, you must use a CREATE VIEW statement to create a view with the *Connection* object's *Execute* method. However, you cannot use a CREATE VIEW statement in the Query Designer. Third, the T-SQL code for a view will be easier to maintain when you prepare it to run with the *Connection* object, because you write the code according to your preferred styles. Recall that the Query Designer forces a dbo qualifier whether or not you want to use it.

The next sample demonstrates the syntax for creating a SQL Server view without the use of the Query Designer. This particular view joins the *Shippers* table to the *Orders* table so that a listing of orders shows a shipper's name instead of a shipper's ShipperID code. The code for this simulates the behavior of the Lookup tab settings for a table. Because you control the view through code, you have substantial flexibility regarding which shipper names you show and how you show them. For example, you could use a WHERE clause to decode only some names but hide others that require special permission for examination. This particular sample performs a simple equijoin that shows a shipper's name for every row in the *Orders* table with a *ShipperID* value.

The sample uses a main procedure and a sub procedure to create a new version of the *Orders_with_lookup_from_view* view. The main procedure starts by dropping any prior version of the view. A call to the *Drop_a_view* procedure does this. The call passes an ADO *Connection* object that points at a database and a string denoting the name of the view to remove from the database. Next the main procedure defines an SQL string that includes a CREATE VIEW statement. The SELECT statement element of the CREATE VIEW statement performs an inner join of the *Orders* table with the *Shippers* table by the *ShipperID* column values. This join permits the view to show the *CompanyName* field from the *Shippers* table—which contains the shipper's name—in place of the *ShipperID* field from the *Orders* table. This is the lookup behavior that we want.

Notice that the SELECT statement for the view includes an ORDER BY clause. This is only possible because the SELECT statement also includes a TOP clause immediately after the SELECT keyword. The sort by OrderID is necessary because the inner join sorts the result set based on the *ShipperID* field from the *Shippers* table. The ORDER BY clause reorders the returned rows based on *OrderID* values.

```
Sub CreateOrders_with_lookup_from_view()
Dim str1 As String
Dim cnn1 As ADODB.Connection
Dim ViewName As String

'Point a Connection object at the current project
Set cnn1 = CurrentProject.Connection
```

```
'Delete the view if it exists already
ViewName = "Orders_with_lookup_from_view"
Drop_a_view cnn1, ViewName

'Use TOP 100 PERCENT to permit use of ORDER BY clause in T-SQL for
'a view
str1 = "CREATE VIEW Orders_with_lookup_from_view " & _
    "AS " & _
    "SELECT TOP 100 PERCENT Orders.OrderID, Orders.OrderDate, " & _
    "Shippers.CompanyName as Shipvia, Orders.Freight " & _
    "FROM  Orders INNER JOIN " & _
    "Shippers ON Orders.ShipVia = Shippers.ShipperID " & _
    "ORDER BY Orders.OrderID "
cnn1.Execute str1

'Refresh Database window to show new table
RefreshDatabaseWindow

End Sub


Sub Drop_a_view(cnn1 As ADODB.Connection, ViewName As String)

'Delete the view if it exists already
str1 = "IF EXISTS (SELECT TABLE_NAME " & _
    "FROM INFORMATION_SCHEMA.VIEWS " & _
    "WHERE TABLE_NAME = '" & ViewName & "') " & _
    "DROP VIEW " & ViewName
cnn1.Execute str1

End Sub
```

After creating a view, it's natural to want to examine all or a subset of the its records. The following sample demonstrates one approach to this. The sample's first procedure specifies a *Connection* object that points at a database, the view's name from which to print rows, and the maximum number of rows to print. The *Connection* object needs to point at the database with the view. The first procedure passes these parameters to the second one, making the specified subset of the view's records available.

The second procedure opens a recordset on the view in the database specified. Next this procedure determines whether the recordset has the maximum number of records requested. If this number is less than the maximum, the procedure computes a new limit based on the number of records in the view. Because the numeric index for records in a recordset starts at 0, the procedure loops from 0 to one less than the maximum number of records to print. Inside the loop for the records, a nested loop passes through all the fields for the current record.

```
Sub CallOpenSubsetOfView()
Dim cnn1 As ADODB.Connection
Dim VName As String
Dim LimitToPrint As Byte

Set cnn1 = CurrentProject.Connection
VName = "Orders_with_lookup_from_view"
LimitToPrint = 10

OpenSubsetOfView cnn1, VName, LimitToPrint

End Sub


Sub OpenSubsetOfView(cnn1 As ADODB.Connection, VName As String, _
    LimitToPrint As Byte)
Dim rst1 As ADODB.Recordset
Dim byt1 As Byte
Dim byt2 As Byte

'Instantiate recordset, and open it on view
Set rst1 = New ADODB.Recordset
rst1.Open VName, CurrentProject.Connection, _
    adOpenKeyset, adLockOptimistic, adCmdTable

'Loop through all fields for the desired subset of records
byt1 = IIf(rst1.RecordCount < LimitToPrint, _
    rst1.RecordCount - 1, LimitToPrint - 1)
For byt2 = 0 To byt1
    Debug.Print "Results for record " & (byt2 + 1)
    For Each fld1 In rst1.Fields
        Debug.Print "    " & fld1.Name & " = " & rst1.Fields(fld1.Name)
    Next fld1
    rst1.MoveNext
    Debug.Print
Next byt2

End Sub
```

When working with SQL Server databases by using Access, it's common for the tables in a database to have a large number of rows. This can result in degraded performance for applications that attempt to open all the records without taking any special steps. One step you can take is to limit the number of records that a recordset retrieves. The built-in default for Access projects is 10,000 records. This setting applies to the whole database. You can manually update this setting from the Advanced tab of the Options dialog box. You can programmatically read and write this setting for any recordset by using the *MaxRecords* property. The

following adaptation of the *OpenSubsetOfView* procedure retrieves only the maximum number of records to print. When the recordset has many rows and the
sample is small, this approach provides a simple way to improve performance.

```
Sub OpenSubsetOfView1(cnn1 As ADODB.Connection, VName As String, _
    LimitToPrint As Byte)
Dim rst1 As ADODB.Recordset
Dim byt1 As Byte

'Instantiate recordset, and open it on view for just
'a subset of records
Set rst1 = New ADODB.Recordset
rst1.MaxRecords = LimitToPrint
rst1.Open VName, cnn1, adOpenKeyset, adLockOptimistic, adCmdTable

'Loop through all fields for the desired subset of records
byt1 = 0
Do Until rst1.EOF
    Debug.Print "Results for record " & (byt1 + 1)
    For Each fld1 In rst1.Fields
        Debug.Print "    " & fld1.Name & " = " & rst1.Fields(fld1.Name)
    Next fld1
    rst1.MoveNext
    byt1 = byt1 + 1
    Debug.Print
Loop

End Sub
```

Aggregating Records in a View

If you have a basic understanding of SQL, aggregating inside a view is very
straightforward. Chapter 5, "Jet SQL, the ADOX Library, and Queries," drills down
on Jet SQL syntax. This syntax is broadly applicable to SQL Server for select
queries—especially for simple aggregations. The following sample reuses code
from the preceding sample, which set the *MaxRecords* property for a recordset
before opening it. Because this sample generates a view that has just three records,
the Byte data type specification for the *MaxRecords* property, which has an upper
limit of 10 records, won't prevent you from retrieving all the view's records.

This sample aggregates the *Freight* column values in the *Orders* table by
year. The T-SQL syntax for the view generates just three rows because the *Orders*
table contains data for 1996 through 1998 only. The SELECT statement's column
list reveals a couple of interesting T-SQL features. First, it uses the DATEPART
function to transform the *OrderDate* field to a year. This same function specification
appears in the GROUP BY clause, aggregating the data by year. Second, the SUM

function has an alias with internal spaces. The default T-SQL delimiters for such identifiers are square brackets. After creating the view by executing the SQL string as the argument of a *Connection* object, the procedure opens the view and prints its contents to the Immediate window with a call to the *OpenSubsetof View1* procedure.

```
Sub CreateSum_of_Freight_by_year()
Dim str1 As String
Dim cnn1 As ADODB.Connection
Dim ViewName As String
Dim LimitToPrint As Byte

'Point a Connection object at the current project
Set cnn1 = CurrentProject.Connection

'Delete the view if it exists already
ViewName = "Sum_of_Freight_by_year"
Drop_a_view cnn1, ViewName

'Use TOP 100 PERCENT to permit use of ORDER BY clause in T-SQL for
'a view
str1 = "CREATE VIEW " & ViewName & " " & _
    "AS " & _
    "SELECT DATEPART(yyyy, OrderDate) AS Year, " & _
    "SUM(Freight) AS [Sum of Freight] " & _
    "FROM Orders " & _
    "GROUP BY DATEPART(yyyy, OrderDate) "
cnn1.Execute str1

'Print result set
LimitToPrint = 10
OpenSubsetOfView1 cnn1, ViewName, LimitToPrint

End Sub
```

Converting Dates and Times to Different Formats

CAST and CONVERT are two SQL Server system-defined functions that let you convert between data types. The CAST function is consistent with the ANSI SQL specification, but the CONVERT function is optimized more for use with SQL Server. If you don't plan to generate applications designed to run across multiple database servers from different vendors, CONVERT will deliver more simplicity and power to your data conversion tasks.

One of the nice things about the CONVERT function is its ability to represent *datetime* and *smalldatetime* column values in a variety of formats. For example,

CONVERT can represent times in the U.S., British/French, German, Italian, or Japanese date formats. This can be very useful for applications that need to display dates in the formats of several different countries. The CONVERT function takes three arguments for this kind of transformation. First, it takes the data type to which you are converting the *datetime* value. This value will typically be varchar or char. Second, it takes an expression that evaluates to a *datetime* value. This can be a column value with a Datetime data type, a function that returns a *datetime* value, or an expression based on either or both of these. Third, the function takes a style parameter that designates the format for the output. (See the CAST and CONVERT topic in Books Online for a list of style parameter values and the results that they return.)

The next sample shows how to return the results from the system-defined GETDATE function in five distinct formats, depending on country. The sample relies on two procedures. The first procedure calls the second procedure five times. Each time the first procedure calls the second procedure, it passes a different style parameter for the CONVERT function. The second procedure is a function procedure that returns its value as a string for use in a *Debug.print* statement in the first procedure. The second procedure invokes the CONVERT function with the style parameter passed to it by the first procedure.

```
Sub CallReturnDateStyle()
Dim str1 As String

'U.S. date style
str1 = "101"
Debug.Print "Date in the U.S. is: " & ReturnDateStyle(str1)

'British/French date style
str1 = "103"
Debug.Print "Date in Britain/France is: " & ReturnDateStyle(str1)

'German date style
str1 = "104"
Debug.Print "Date in Germany is: " & ReturnDateStyle(str1)

'Italian date style
str1 = "105"
Debug.Print "Date in Italy is: " & ReturnDateStyle(str1)

'Japanese date style
str1 = "111"
Debug.Print "Date in Japan is: " & ReturnDateStyle(str1)

End Sub
```

(continued)

```
Function ReturnDateStyle(StyleNumber As String) As String
Dim str1 As String
Dim cnn1 As ADODB.Connection
Dim rst1 As ADODB.Recordset

'Point a Connection object at the current project, and create
'a recordset based on the connection
Set cnn1 = CurrentProject.Connection
Set rst1 = New ADODB.Recordset
rst1.ActiveConnection = cnn1

'Create SQL string with CONVERT function and date style
'parameter for a country
str1 = "SELECT Convert(varchar,GETDATE()," & _
    StyleNumber & ")"
rst1.Open str1, cnn1

'Pass back value
ReturnDateStyle = rst1(0)

'Clean up objects
rst1.Close
Set rst1 = Nothing

End Function
```

One of the easiest ways to understand this sample is to examine its output to the Immediate window. Figure 14-18 shows this output. Notice that it includes five lines—one for each country-specific date representation. A remarkable feature of the CONVERT function is that the syntax for these distinct date formats is identical for all five of them. All the CONVERT function needs to switch from one format to another is a different style parameter. As you can see, this is a string value that the first procedure passes to the second one.

Figure 14-18 The output from the date conversion sample.

The CONVERT function can also use the time portion of a *datetime* value to represent time values in different formats. For example, you can express the time portion of the GETDATE function either in hours and minutes (as well as specifying AM or PM, referred to as *day parts* in the following code), or in hours, minutes, seconds, and milliseconds (again specifying AM or PM). Again, using one format over the other is as simple as passing a different style parameter to the CONVERT function. The next sample shows a pair of procedures that demonstrates this, along with the specific style parameters for each time format.

In this sample, the second procedure needs to do a little more processing than it did in the preceding sample. This is because the CONVERT function returns a full *datetime* value, with both a date and a time concatenated together. The second procedure extracts all the characters to the right of the date. These characters represent a time value. Then the procedure trims the result to remove any leading blanks. As with the previous sample, examining the output of the CONVERT function and its style parameters can help you understand how they work. Figure 14-19 shows the result of applying the two different time formats to the GETDATE function.

```
Sub CallReturnTimeStyle()
Dim str1 As String

'Hours, minutes, day part style
str1 = "100"
Debug.Print "Time to hours:minutes day part is: " & _
    ReturnTimeStyle(str1)

'Hours, minutes, seconds, milliseconds, day part style
str1 = "109"
Debug.Print "Time to hours:minutes:seconds:milliseconds " & _
    "day part is: " & ReturnTimeStyle(str1)

End Sub


Function ReturnTimeStyle(StyleNumber As String) As String
Dim str1 As String
Dim cnn1 As ADODB.Connection
Dim rst1 As ADODB.Recordset

'Point a Connection object at the current project, and create
'a recordset based on the connection
Set cnn1 = CurrentProject.Connection
Set rst1 = New ADODB.Recordset
rst1.ActiveConnection = cnn1

str1 = "SELECT LTRIM(RIGHT (CONVERT " & _
    "(varchar, GETDATE(), " & StyleNumber & "), " & _
    "LEN(CONVERT (varchar, GETDATE(), " & StyleNumber & _
    ")) - 11))"
rst1.Open str1, cnn1
```

(continued)

```
'Pass back value
ReturnTimeStyle = rst1(0)

'Clean up objects
rst1.Close
Set rst1 = Nothing

End Function
```

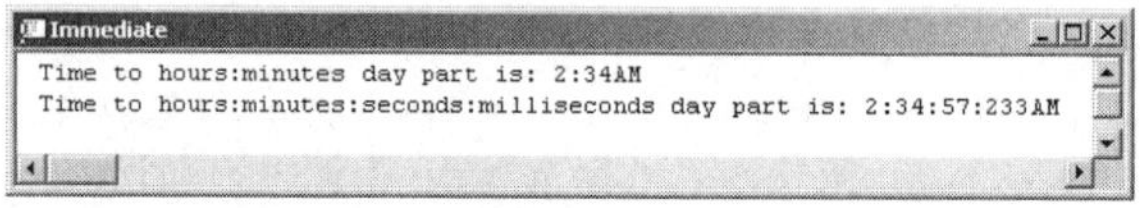

Figure 14-19 The output from the time conversion sample.

Creating and Using Stored Procedures

A stored procedure is a set of compiled T-SQL statements. Although these statements can return a result set just like a view, stored procedures offer many more capabilities. At the most basic level, you can use an ORDER BY clause in a stored procedure without also having to specify a TOP clause for a SELECT statement. Stored procedures enable basic programming capabilities, such as allowing IF...ELSE statements and parameters to facilitate the reuse of code. Parameters are particularly useful for stored procedures that maintain databases; parameters can enable the inserting, updating, and deleting of table records. You can also perform data definition with stored procedures. For example, you can create tables.

Because stored procedures are compiled T-SQL statements, they are ideal for increasing the performance of your database administration tasks. Instead of having to compile T-SQL statements to perform a task, SQL Server can immediately process the compiled code. Because you can specify the code with parameters, it's possible to modify the behavior of stored procedures through the values that you assign to their parameters at run time.

Stored procedures offer a variety of ways to accept input and return values. The input parameters for stored procedures work much like the parameters for stored queries for traditional database files. However, SQL Server parameters readily permit the return of values from a stored procedure. Of course, a stored procedure can return a result set. In fact, it can return multiple result sets. You also can pass back values from a stored procedure by using output parameters. These parameters can handle the return of scalar values instead of result sets. Additionally, you can use the RETURN statement in a stored procedure to pass back an integer value to the procedure that invokes it. The syntax rules for RETURN enable the use of a constant or an expression. Output parameters can return all kinds of data types—not just integer values. You will typically use an expression to specify an output parameter's value, but your T-SQL code can also designate a constant.

The Access UI for Stored Procedures

Access 2002 offers a couple of user interfaces for specifying stored procedures. You can view the different options by highlighting Queries in the Objects bar on the Database window and clicking New. The New Query dialog box shows two options for creating a stored procedure. (See Figure 14-20.) One has the name Create Text Stored Procedure. This is the original Access stored procedure template introduced with Access 2000. You can type T-SQL code into it. The template's layout and operation facilitate the creation and maintenance of stored procedures. Design Stored Procedure is the other option for creating a stored procedure. This option presents a visual designer that is similar to the one you use for views. This designer is appropriate when you want to develop a result set from a single SELECT statement without any other T-SQL statements. This graphical designer is also available for stored procedures that insert, update, and delete records. However, it is not appropriate for stored procedures that perform data definition tasks, such as creating a new table or altering an existing one.

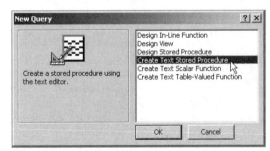

Figure 14-20 The New Query dialog box with the Create Text Stored Procedure option selected.

The two options for creating stored procedures are also available for maintaining them. To view the graphical or text-based version of an existing stored procedure, highlight the stored procedure in the Database window. Then click Design. If you open a stored procedure that returns a result set based on a single SELECT statement, you will see the visual designer for the stored procedure. If you open a procedure based on another kind of stored procedure (for example, one with more than a single SELECT statement), the text-based stored procedure template appears. Even if Access opens the visual designer view for a stored procedure, you can navigate to the text-based stored procedure template with the

View control on the toolbar. Although stored procedures with a single SELECT statement let you navigate freely between the two views, other kinds of stored procedures that open initially in the text-based template cannot be represented by the visual designer.

> **Note**   You can run a stored procedure by selecting it in the Database window and clicking Open. The Open control used to have the label Run In Access 2000. However, because Access 2002 offers a single mode for displaying views, stored procedures, and user-defined functions, you now click Open to run a stored procedure.

You can also manipulate stored procedures programmatically. This is more flexible and compatible with Books Online. For example, when you choose Create Text Stored Procedure, Access opens the stored procedure template with the CREATE PROCEDURE keyword phrase. After you initially save the stored procedure, it always opens with an ALTER PROCEDURE keyword phrase. This change in the keyword phrase makes it easy to modify a stored procedure, but the approach is at odds with most samples in Books Online. These samples typically drop the previously existing procedure and then execute a new CREATE PROCEDURE statement. When you create a stored procedure from a VBA module (as I will show you in subsequent samples in this section), you can follow the design guidelines in Books Online. In addition, creating the SQL Server stored procedure in a VBA procedure gives you more flexibility in using the stored procedure. For example, you can fire the stored procedure immediately after creating it. Whether you create the stored procedure with VBA or from the Access stored procedure template, you can invoke it from an event, such as the user clicking a button.

Using the LIKE Operator with *datetime* Column Values

Figure 14-21 shows the Design view for a stored procedure named *Orders_in_like_1996*. It uses the LIKE operator to specify a criterion for *OrderDate* column values. The rows with *OrderDate* column values that include 1996 pass through the filter for membership in the stored procedure's result set. Recall that SQL Server represents *datetime* values internally as numbers, but it displays and filters them as string values. This feature makes it possible to use the LIKE operator to filter rows based on their column values.

Orders_in_like_1996 : Stored Procedure
Orders
* (All Columns)
OrderID
OrderDate
ShipVia
Freight
Column
Alias
Table
Output
Sort Type
Sort Order
Criteria
OrderID
Orders
OrderDate
Orders
LIKE '%1996%'
ShipVia
Orders
Freight
Orders
SELECT OrderID, OrderDate, ShipVia, Freight
FROM dbo.Orders
WHERE (OrderDate LIKE '%1996%')

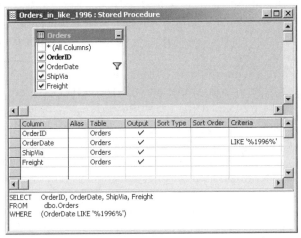

Figure 14-21 The Access 2002 visual designer for stored procedures.

As you can see, the visual designer for stored procedures has the same look and feel as the visual designer for views. Both designers enable the specification of a result set based on a single SELECT statement. However, one designer creates and maintains a stored procedure object, and the other manages a view. The visual designer for stored procedures offers special features, such as the ability to represent INSERT, UPDATE, and DELETE statements. While this chapter describes and illustrates how to program these statements, you can examine the programming samples with the visual designer to see how the designer handles INSERT, UPDATE, and DELETE.

Although all stored procedures like the one shown in Figure 14-21 open to the visual designer by default, you can switch to the text-based template. This lets you begin designing a stored procedure in the visual designer and then refine it in the text-based designer. Figure 14-22 presents a second stored procedure that filters the *Orders* table for rows with an order date occurring in 1997.

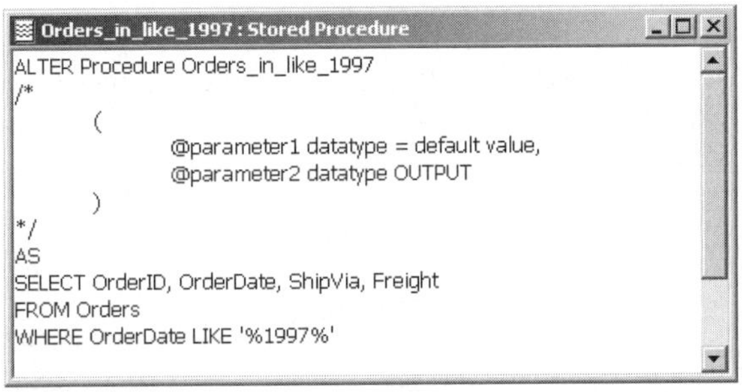

Orders_in_like_1997 : Stored Procedure
ALTER Procedure Orders_in_like_1997
/*
(
@parameter1 datatype = default value,
@parameter2 datatype OUTPUT
)
*/
AS
SELECT OrderID, OrderDate, ShipVia, Freight
FROM Orders
WHERE OrderDate LIKE '%1997%'

Figure 14-22 The Access 2002 text-based designer for stored procedures.

The text-based designer has a look and feel that Access developers who aren't familiar with SQL Server might find foreign. If you are familiar with SQL Server, you might notice that this designer is somewhat similar to the Query Analyzer. The sample in Figure 14-22 starts with ALTER PROCEDURE, followed by the stored procedure's name, because the sample is based on a previously created stored procedure. On your initial attempt to create a stored procedure, the first line reads CREATE PROCEDURE "StoredProcedure*x*", where *x* is a number such as 1, 2, or whatever. You can overwrite this default name with one that is more meaningful for your application.

The next group of lines before the AS keyword occurs within block comment markers (/* and */). The template includes these lines in comments to remind you of the format and location for parameters. The parentheses for parameters within the comment markers are optional. Subsequent samples in this section discuss and demonstrate the syntax for specifying parameters.

The T-SQL syntax after the AS keyword specifies the operation and the result set from a stored procedure. The text-based stored procedure template gives you more precise control over the layout and formatting of a stored procedure's T-SQL code than the visual designer's SQL pane. For example, in the text-based stored procedure template, you can drop the dbo qualifier for Orders in the FROM clause if it's not necessary. You can also insert comment lines. Use two contiguous hyphens (--) at the start of a line to mark it as a comment.

Specifying Parameters in the Text-Based Designer

The preceding two samples show how to extract all rows from the *Orders* table for a particular year. Without parameters, you're forced to create a separate stored procedure for each year for which you want to filter. The code sample that follows shows how to filter the rows for any year at run time. Instead of using the LIKE operator, this *Orders_in_@year* stored procedure relies on the DATEPART function to extract just the year from the *OrderDate* column value. Specifying the function extracts a four-digit field. Again, because SQL Server displays *datetime* values as strings, you must use a string instead of a numeric format to specify the parameter. Notice that the *@year* parameter has a Char format that's four characters in length. (This means that instead of using, say, *96*, you must use *1996*.)

```
ALTER PROCEDURE Orders_in_@year
@year char(4)
AS
SELECT OrderID, OrderDate, ShipVia, Freight
FROM Orders
WHERE DATEPART(yyyy, OrderDate) = @year
```

When you select the *Orders_in_@year* stored procedure in the Database window and click Open, Access displays a dialog box for you to type a parameter value into. (See Figure 14-23.) You are prompted for the parameter name that follows the @ sign in the stored procedure. Therefore, the prompt for the parameter in *Orders_in_@year* is for the year. This is how a typical parameter query from an Access database file would work.

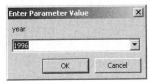

Figure 14-23 A prompt for a stored procedure parameter value.

The preceding sample requires you to input a value each time that you run the stored procedure. However, sometimes it's useful to have a default value for a parameter so that users don't have to specify one. By specifying a default value for a parameter, users can either accept the default value or override it with another one that they input.

The following code sample shows the syntax for designating a default value for a parameter. The *Orders_in_@year_96default* stored procedure shows how to assign a value in the parameter's declaration. Because *@year* takes a string value, it has single-quote delimiters ('). You can use double-quote delimiters (") if SET QUOTED_IDENTIFIER is OFF, which is the default setting. However, you do not have to enclose the value in quotes because the Char(4) data type specification for the parameter causes SQL Server to automatically interpret the value as a four-character field.

```
ALTER PROCEDURE Orders_in_@year_96default
@year char(4) = '1996'
AS
SELECT OrderID, OrderDate, ShipVia, Freight
FROM Orders
WHERE DATEPART(yyyy, OrderDate) = @year
```

If you run this stored procedure from the Database window by selecting *Orders_in_@year_96default* and clicking Open, the result set always contains rows for 1996. No prompt appears for a parameter with a default value. To override the default setting, you must invoke the stored procedure from another procedure that explicitly passes an alternative parameter value to the stored procedure's default setting. The following sample demonstrates this approach by passing a parameter of *1997* to override the default value of *1996*:

```
ALTER PROCEDURE Exec_96default_with_1997
AS
EXEC Orders_in_@year_96default '1997'
```

Sorting Result Sets

While you can sort the result set from a view, it's probably more natural to sort result sets from stored procedures. There are a couple of reasons for this. First, the syntax is more straightforward in stored procedures. Recall that you do not need to include a TOP clause in a SELECT statement. Second, you can make the sort order dynamic by assigning it at run time through a parameter. This capability is unavailable with a view.

Figure 14-24 presents two Design views. The top window shows a view, and the other shows a stored procedure. Both the view and the stored procedure sort the *Orders* table rows by freight in descending order. The top window, for the view, shows the TOP clause. That's because I used the visual designers to generate both the view and the stored procedure, but when you code manually, it's always nice to be able to leave out a clause. In addition, the stored procedure formulation (shown in the next sample) lends itself to an extension that isn't possible with a view.

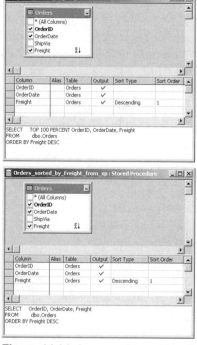

Figure 14-24 A comparison of two Design views that sort records: one for a view, and one for a stored procedure.

The following stored procedure illustrates an extension of the sample shown in the bottom window of Figure 14-24. This extension lets a user control the sort order at run time. The default calls for an ascending sort on *Freight*. However, if a user assigns a value of *1* to the parameters for the stored procedure, the code sorts on *Freight* in descending order. As you can see, the design of the *Orders_ sorted_by_Freight_Up_Or_Down* stored procedure uses an IF...ELSE statement to branch to one of two blocks of code. BEGIN and END keywords mark the start and conclusion of each block. You need to repeat the code once for a descending order sort and a second time for an ascending order sort because of the T-SQL syntax. You can't to specify the sort order (DESC or ASC) with a parameter.

```
ALTER PROCEDURE Orders_sorted_by_Freight_Up_Or_Down
@za bit = 0
AS

IF @za = 1
    BEGIN
        SELECT    OrderID, OrderDate, Freight
        FROM      dbo.Orders
        ORDER BY Freight DESC
    END
ELSE
    BEGIN
        SELECT    OrderID, OrderDate, Freight
        FROM      dbo.Orders
        ORDER BY Freight ASC
    END
```

You can use an Access application to invoke this SQL Server stored procedure and to return the values in its result set. The trick is to assign a value to the *@za* parameter. There are three basic steps to this process. First, you point an ADO *Command* object at the stored procedure. You need a *Command* object instead of a *Connection* object, because the approach requires you to set parameter values and a *Connection* object does not have a *Parameters* collection. Second, you need to create the parameter for *@za*, assign it a value, and append it to the *Command* object that points at the stored procedure. Third, you need to execute the stored procedure referenced by the *Command* object and print a subset of its records to confirm the order of the sort.

> **Note**   The section on user-defined functions at the end of the chapter illustrates how to run T-SQL statements that require parameters without using *Command* objects. While this alternative syntax is generally simpler, it forfeits the ability to specify the data type for an input parameter. Once you know how to execute both approaches, you can make an informed decision about which is appropriate for you.

The following pair of VBA procedures illustrates the syntax to run the *Orders_sorted_by_Freight_Up_Or_Down* stored procedure. The first procedure points a *Command* object at the stored procedure and assigns a parameter to the command. This parameter sets a value for the *@za* parameter and passes it to the stored procedure when the code executes the command. Notice that the command's *CommandType* property is *adCmdStoredProc*. This is necessary when running a stored procedure from a command. The *CommandText* property designates the name of the stored procedure. The first procedure calls the second procedure and passes it the *Command* object, signifying the number of records to print. The second procedure executes the command, passes a subset of the records in the result set to a *Recordset* object, and prints the values to the Immediate window.

```
Sub AssignFreightSortOrder()
Dim cmd1 As ADODB.Command
Dim prm1 As ADODB.Parameter

'Instantiate command and set up for use with stored procedure
Set cmd1 = New ADODB.Command
cmd1.ActiveConnection = CurrentProject.Connection
cmd1.CommandType = adCmdStoredProc
cmd1.CommandText = "Orders_sorted_by_Freight_Up_Or_Down"

'Create parameter, assign value, and append to command
Set prm1 = cmd1.CreateParameter("@za", adBoolean, adParamInput)
prm1.Value = InputBox("Enter 1 for Descending or 0 for " & _
    "Ascending.", "Programming Microsoft Access Version 2002", 0)
cmd1.Parameters.Append prm1

'Print subset of result set from the command
OpenSubsetOfCmd cmd1, 10

'Clean up objects
Set cmd1 = Nothing

End Sub
```

```
Sub OpenSubsetOfCmd(cmd1 As ADODB.Command, LimitToPrint As Byte)
'cmd1 As ADODB.Comand, LimitToPrint As Byte)
Dim rst1 As ADODB.Recordset
Dim byt1 As Byte

'Assign cmd1 result set to rst1
Set rst1 = New ADODB.Recordset
Set rst1 = cmd1.Execute

'Limit result set record count
rst1.Close
rst1.MaxRecords = LimitToPrint
rst1.Open

'Loop through all fields for the desired subset of records
byt1 = 0
Do Until rst1.EOF
    Debug.Print "Results for record " & (byt1 + 1)
    For Each fld1 In rst1.Fields
        Debug.Print "    " & fld1.Name & " = " & rst1.Fields(fld1.Name)
    Next fld1
    rst1.MoveNext
    byt1 = byt1 + 1
    Debug.Print
Loop

'Clean up objects
rst1.Close
Set rst1 = Nothing

End Sub
```

Managing Input Parameters, Output Parameters, and Return Values

One of the ways that stored procedures differ from stored queries in Access database files is in their ability to pass back scalar values as output parameters and return values. The next sample illustrates the syntax for concurrently handling an input parameter, an output parameter, and a return value. You have already seen samples demonstrating the use of input parameters, but they becomes more complicated when combined with output parameters and return values.

Recall that an output parameter is just a scalar value passed back from a stored procedure. It could be a datetime, string, number, or binary value, such as an image. A return value is the value passed back from a stored procedure that is the argument of a RETURN statement in the stored procedure. This argument can be a constant or an expression, but it must be an integer.

VBA parameters treat input parameters, output parameters, and return values as parameters. However, a few distinctions between these three entities might not be so obvious at first glance. First, whenever you use a return value along with either an input parameter or an output parameter, you must reserve the first ADO parameter for the return value. Second, the order in which you declare parameters in the stored procedure must match the order in which you create the parameters within a VBA procedure that invokes a command based on the stored procedure. It does not matter if you declare an input parameter before an output parameter. However, it does matter that you use the same order in both the stored procedure and the VBA procedure.

The following T-SQL script shows a SQL Server stored procedure from the text-based Access template for the sample that demonstrates the concurrent use of input and output parameters along with a return value. This stored procedure builds on one presented earlier that extracts the rows from the *Orders* table for a year that the user specifies at run time. The parameter that designates the year is an input parameter. The *@sum_of_freight* parameter is an output parameter. Notice that its declaration includes the keyword OUTPUT. T-SQL lets you compute scalar values, such as the one for the *@sum_of_freight* output parameter with a SELECT statement. In this instance, the statement computes the sum of *Freight* column values across the year the user specifies in the *@year* input parameter.

The RETURN statement is always the last one that a stored procedure processes. This is because RETURN transfers control back to the entity that called the current stored procedure. You can insert one or more RETURN statements in an IF...ELSE statement or any other branching logic statement to reflect which path a stored procedure took. If a VBA procedure initiated the stored procedure, the stored procedure passes back to the VBA procedure an argument for the RETURN statement. In the following stored procedure, the return value denotes the number of orders for the year in the *@year* input parameter:

```
ALTER PROCEDURE Orders_in_@year_in_out_return

--Input and output parameter declarations
@sum_of_freight money OUTPUT,
@year char(4)

AS

--Develop result set
SELECT OrderID, OrderDate, ShipVia, Freight
FROM Orders
WHERE DATEPART(yyyy,OrderDate) = @year

--Develop output parameter
```

```
SELECT @sum_of_freight =
SUM(Freight) FROM Orders
WHERE DATEPART(yyyy,OrderDate) = @year

--Develop return value
RETURN (SELECT COUNT(OrderID) FROM Orders
WHERE DATEPART(yyyy,OrderDate) = @year)
```

The following VBA procedure illustrates the syntax for invoking the preceding SQL Server stored procedure. Use the sample as a model for setting ADO parameters that denote a return value, an output parameter, and an input parameter. The VBA code assigns a value to the input parameter, executes the command pointing at the procedure, and captures the output parameter and return value. The sample also returns a subset of the result set from the SELECT statement for the stored procedure.

The sample begins by pointing a *Command* object at the preceding SQL Server stored procedure. Next it creates three parameters and appends each one to the parameter collection of the *Command* object. As indicated previously, the order of parameter declarations is important. The return value goes first. This value recovers the number of order IDs in the result set for the stored procedure. The second parameter points to the *@sum_of_freight* output parameter. This parameter must go before the input parameter because the stored procedure declares it first. Also notice that the data types match those inside the stored procedure. It's not always necessary that a parameter in a VBA procedure and a stored procedure coincide precisely, but it's a good practice.

After declaring and appending the parameters, the VBA procedure executes the command and assigns its result set to a *Recordset* object. These two steps make the output parameter and return value available to the VBA procedure. The sample uses these values to display the total freight, total orders, and average freight per order for whichever year the VBA procedure specifies as the input for the stored procedure. Then the sample reexecutes the command to recover the first three records in the result set for the stored procedure's result set. The sample takes this approach to reuse the *OpenSubsetOfCmd* procedure from the preceding VBA sample. In a production environment with a large result set, you might just reprocess the *rst1* procedure that's already available and save your time for reexecuting the stored procedure's SELECT statement.

```
Sub InOutReturnDemo()
Dim cmd1 As ADODB.Command
Dim prm1 As ADODB.Parameter
Dim prm2 As ADODB.Parameter
Dim prm3 As ADODB.Parameter
Dim rst1 As New ADODB.Recordset
```

(continued)

```
'Instantiate command and set up for use with stored procedure
Set cmd1 = New ADODB.Command
cmd1.ActiveConnection = CurrentProject.Connection
cmd1.CommandType = adCmdStoredProc
cmd1.CommandText = "Orders_in_@year_in_out_return"

'Set up a return parameter
Set prm1 = cmd1.CreateParameter("RETURN", adInteger, _
    adParamReturnValue)
cmd1.Parameters.Append prm1

'Set up an output parameter
Set prm2 = cmd1.CreateParameter("@sum_of_freight", _
    adCurrency, adParamOutput)
cmd1.Parameters.Append prm2

'Create parameter, assign value, and append to command
Set prm3 = cmd1.CreateParameter("@year", adChar, _
    adParamInput, 4)
prm3.Value = "1996"
cmd1.Parameters.Append prm3

'Execute the command to recover the return value (cmd1(0))
'and the output parameter (cmd1(1))
Set rst1 = New ADODB.Recordset
Set rst1 = cmd1.Execute

Debug.Print "Results for " & prm3.Value
Debug.Print "Total Freight = " & FormatCurrency(cmd1(1))
Debug.Print "Total Orders = " & cmd1(0)
Debug.Print "Average Freight/Order = " & _
    FormatCurrency(cmd1(1) / cmd1(0))

'Print subset of result set from the command
Debug.Print vbCr & "Partial list of Orders for " & prm3.Value
OpenSubsetOfCmd cmd1, 3

'Clean up objects
rst1.Close
Set rst1 = Nothing

End Sub
```

Figure 14-25 shows the output for the preceding VBA sample. Its header dynamically portrays the year for which it returns results. The year in the header title comes from the value for *prm3*. The next three lines signify the output parameter, the stored procedure's return value, and the ratio of the two. Next the listing shows the first three records in the result set from running the stored procedure to which the *Command* object in the preceding sample points.

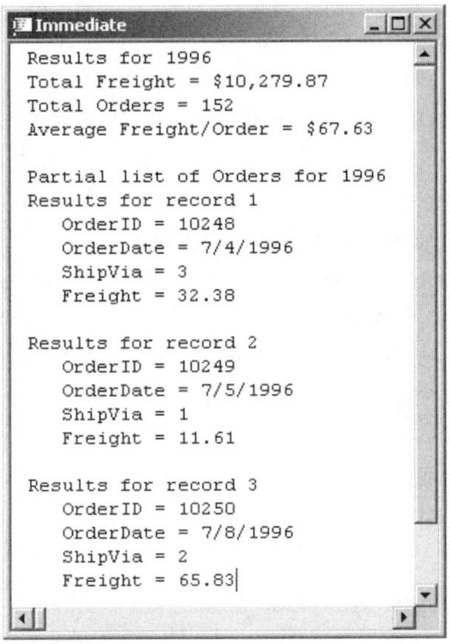

```
Immediate                              _ □ ×
Results for 1996
Total Freight = $10,279.87
Total Orders = 152
Average Freight/Order = $67.63

Partial list of Orders for 1996
Results for record 1
    OrderID = 10248
    OrderDate = 7/4/1996
    ShipVia = 3
    Freight = 32.38

Results for record 2
    OrderID = 10249
    OrderDate = 7/5/1996
    ShipVia = 1
    Freight = 11.61

Results for record 3
    OrderID = 10250
    OrderDate = 7/8/1996
    ShipVia = 2
    Freight = 65.83
```

Figure 14-25 The output to the Immediate window for the *InOutReturnDemo* VBA procedure.

Inserting, Updating, and Deleting Records

Inserting, updating, and deleting records are the three classic database maintenance tasks. There are at least two ways to use stored procedures when inserting records into a table. One method takes advantage of T-SQL to populate one table from all or a subset of another table's records. The source can reside in the same database, a different database, or even a database on a different server. Another way to facilitate inserting records into a table with a stored procedure is to use parameters. This permits you to reuse the stored procedure to input different records into the same table. This reuse model also enables you to update and delete records from a database. Again, one stored procedure can support an indefinite number of updates or deletions.

Inserting Records from a Source Table

Earlier in the section "Creating Sample Tables," we covered the stored procedures *CreateAndPopulateShippersTable* and *CreateAndPopulateOrdersTable*. These procedures execute a T-SQL statement to create a table. Then they invoke another stored procedure that copies data from one table to another. When the procedures were initially discussed, it was premature to examine the code for populating the tables. So let's take a look at the syntax now.

The stored procedures for populating the *Orders* and *Shippers* tables have the same basic design, except that they refer to different source and destination tables. In the case of the *Orders* table, the source is the *Orders* table from the

NorthwindCS database and the destination is the *Orders* table in the Chapter 14SQL database—the sample database for this chapter. In the case of the *Shippers* table, the source is the *Shippers* table from NorthwindCS and the destination is the *Shippers* table in Chapter 14SQL. Aside from different field designations, the two stored procedures are identical. One has the name *Copy_from_ NorthwindCS_Orders*, and the other is named *Copy_from_NorthwindCS_Shippers*.

The sample stored procedure for the *Orders* table follows. It starts by checking whether the *Orders* table in the current database has any records. If the number of records is greater than zero, the stored procedure deletes all records from the *Orders* table. Next the procedure executes the SET IDENTITY_INSERT statement and sets it to ON. This permits a stored procedure or other collection of T-SQL statements to add records that populate the column in a table with an IDENTITY value. Without this setting, you wouldn't be able to specify that the original IDENTITY values serving as primary key values in the source table populate the primary key in the destination table.

The most important statement in the *Copy_from_NorthwindCS_Orders* stored procedure is the INSERT statement. This statement has three arguments. Its first argument is the name of the source table, *Orders*. Its second is a set of column names for the destination table into which to deposit data. And its third argument is a set of source table column names from which to collect data for the destination table. The statement can transfer multiple rows from the source table to the destination table. The syntax for the SELECT statement in the INSERT statement determines which rows transfer from the source to the destination table.

After performing the INSERT statement, the stored procedure restores the SET IDENTITY_INSERT to OFF, its default value. This is critical because only one table in a procedure can have a setting of ON for SET IDENTITY_INSERT. The second table to attempt the assignment of ON generates a run-time error.

```
ALTER PROCEDURE ALTER PROCEDURE Copy_from_NorthwindCS_Orders
AS

--Remove any records already present in local Orders table
IF (SELECT COUNT(*) FROM Orders) > 0
    DELETE FROM Orders

--Allow writing to IDENTITY column
SET IDENTITY_INSERT [Chapter 14SQL]..Orders ON

--Specify target and source columns for INSERT
INSERT INTO Orders (OrderID, OrderDate, Shipvia, Freight)
SELECT OrderID, OrderDate, Shipvia, Freight
    FROM NorthwindCS..Orders
```

```
--Reset IDENTITY column
SET IDENTITY_INSERT [Chapter 14SQL]..Orders OFF

AS

--Remove any records already present in local Orders table
IF (SELECT COUNT(*) FROM Orders) > 0
    DELETE FROM Orders

--Allow writing to IDENTITY column
SET IDENTITY_INSERT [Chapter 14SQL]..Orders ON

--Specify target and source columns for INSERT
INSERT INTO Orders (OrderID, OrderDate, Shipvia, Freight)
SELECT OrderID, OrderDate, Shipvia, Freight
    FROM NorthwindCS..Orders

--Reset IDENTITY column
SET IDENTITY_INSERT [Chapter 14SQL]..Orders OFF
```

Inserting Records from Parameter Values

The next three VBA procedures (shown in the following code) create a SQL Server stored procedure for inserting new records and then use that stored procedure to add a new record. The sample isolates each of these actions in its own batch of T-SQL statements. If the stored procedure for inserting new records exists already, the sample removes the prior version with a third stored procedure. After creating a new stored procedure named *Insert_a_new_shipper*, you can invoke it by running the VBA procedure named *InsertANewShipper*. This VBA procedure passes parameter values to and starts the *Insert_a_new_shipper* stored procedure.

The first procedure, *CreateInsert_a_new_shipperProcedure*, illustrates how to use VBA to create a SQL Server stored procedure. SQL Server uses the CREATE PROCEDURE statement to create new stored procedures. Then SQL Server syntax calls for additional statements with parameter declarations and T-SQL code that comprise the body of the stored procedure. You can designate these statements with strings in VBA. Next executing the CREATE PROCEDURE statement with its embedded T-SQL statements saves the batch of embedded T-SQL statements as a stored procedure. The sample uses a *Connection* object to execute the CREATE PROCEDURE statement. The first procedure concludes with the invocation of the *RefreshDatabaseWindow* method. The method attempts to update the Database window to show the newly created stored procedure. If the procedure still does not appear, you can manually invoke the View-Refresh command from the Database window.

Before actually attempting to create a new stored procedure, the first procedure calls the *Drop_a_procedure* VBA procedure. *Drop_a_procedure* is the last of the three procedures shown in the following sample. The first procedure passes two parameters to *Drop_a_procedure*. The initial parameter designates the *Connection* object that points at a database to remove a stored procedure from (if it exists already). The second parameter is the name of the procedure. In the following sample, this is *Insert_a_new_shipper*. The *Drop_a_procedure* procedure invokes the DROP PROCEDURE statement only if it detects a stored procedure with the target name in the INFORMATION_SCHEMA.ROUTINES view. This view contains information about the stored procedure and user-defined functions in a database.

InsertANewShipper, the second procedure in the following sample, uses the stored procedure created by the first VBA procedure to add a new record to the *Shippers* table. *InsertANewShipper* commences by instantiating a new *Command* object and pointing it at the stored procedure for inserting new records. Next the *InsertANewShipper* procedure specifies and adds parameters to the *Command* object. Notice that both the *@CompanyName* and *@Phone* parameters have a Varchar data type. This kind of data type requires that you specify the maximum number of characters for the parameter. Other parameter data types, such as Numeric, Datetime, and Currency, do not require a length specification. The procedure for inserting a new record concludes by running the *Command* object. This executes the stored procedure for adding a new record with the values specified for the parameters.

```
Sub CreateInsert_a_new_shipperProcedure()
Dim str1 As String
Dim cnn1 As ADODB.Connection
Dim ProcedureName As String

'Point a Connection object at the current project
Set cnn1 = CurrentProject.Connection

'Delete the procedure if it exists already
ProcedureName = "Insert_a_new_shipper"
Drop_a_procedure cnn1, ProcedureName

'Create the procedure
str1 = "CREATE PROCEDURE " & ProcedureName & " " & vbLf & _
    " " & vbLf & _
    "@CompanyName varchar(40), " & vbLf & _
    "@phone varchar(24) " & vbLf & _
    " " & vbLf & _
    "AS " & vbLf & _
    "INSERT Shippers VALUES(@CompanyName, @Phone) "
cnn1.Execute str1
```

```
'Refresh Database window to show new procedure
RefreshDatabaseWindow

End Sub


Sub InsertANewShipper()
Dim cmd1 As ADODB.Command
Dim prm1 As ADODB.Parameter
Dim prm2 As ADODB.Parameter

'Point a Connection object at the stored procedure
Set cmd1 = New ADODB.Command
cmd1.ActiveConnection = CurrentProject.Connection
cmd1.CommandType = adCmdStoredProc
cmd1.CommandText = "Insert_a_new_shipper"

'Create and append parameters
Set prm1 = cmd1.CreateParameter("@CompanyName", adVarChar, _
    adParamInput, 40)
prm1.Value = "CAB Delivers"
cmd1.Parameters.Append prm1

Set prm2 = cmd1.CreateParameter("@Phone", adVarChar, _
    adParamInput, 24)
prm2.Value = "(123) 456-7890"
cmd1.Parameters.Append prm2

'Invoke a stored procedure by executing a command
cmd1.Execute

End Sub


Sub Drop_a_procedure(cnn1 As ADODB.Connection, _
    ProcedureName As String)
Dim str1 As String

'If the procedure name exists in the
'INFORMATION_SCHEMA.ROUTINES view, drop it
str1 = "IF EXISTS (SELECT ROUTINE_NAME " & _
    "FROM INFORMATION_SCHEMA.ROUTINES " & _
    "WHERE ROUTINE_NAME = '" & ProcedureName & "') " & _
    "DROP PROCEDURE " & ProcedureName
cnn1.Execute str1

End Sub
```

Updating and Deleting Records from Parameter Values

The following VBA procedure illustrates one approach to creating a stored procedure that revises a shipper's name in the *Shippers* table. To perform the revision, the update needs two pieces of information. The *Update_a_shipper* stored procedure represents these two pieces of information with parameters. One parameter is the *ShipperID* value for the shipper that will receive the new value. The second parameter represents the new shipper's name. The VBA procedure shows the syntax using these two parameters with the UPDATE statement in T-SQL within a stored procedure.

The *Create_Update_a_shipperProcedure* procedure that appears next shows the correct syntax for using a trusted connection to connect to a server. The Server and Database terms in the *str1* string should reflect the name of the server and the database in which you want to create the stored procedure. When running this sample on your computer, you will probably need to revise the server name. If you adapt this sample for your custom projects, you'll also need to update the database name. This general approach is very flexible because it works with any server and database for which the current user has permission to create new database objects.

```
Sub CreateUpdate_a_shipperProcedure()
Dim str1 As String
Dim cnn1 As ADODB.Connection
Dim ProcedureName As String

'Point a Connection object at the Chapter 14SQL
'database on the Cab2000 server with a trusted connection
Set cnn1 = New ADODB.Connection
cnn1.Provider = "sqloledb"
str1 = "Server=Cab2000;Database=Chapter 14SQL;" & _
    "Trusted_Connection=yes"
cnn1.Open str1

'Delete the table if it exists already
ProcedureName = "Update_a_shipper"
Drop_a_procedure cnn1, ProcedureName

'Create the procedure
str1 = "CREATE PROCEDURE " & ProcedureName & " " & vbLf & _
    " " & vbLf & _
    "@id_for_update int, " & vbLf & _
    "@new_name varchar(40) " & vbLf & _
    " " & vbLf & _
    "AS " & vbLf & _
    "UPDATE Shippers " & vbLf & _
    "SET CompanyName = @new_name " & vbLf & _
```

```
    "WHERE ShipperID = @id_for_update "
cnn1.Execute str1

'Refresh Database window to show new procedure
RefreshDatabaseWindow

End Sub
```

The next sample applies the *Update_a_shipper* stored procedure created by the preceding VBA sample. The *UpdateAShipper* VBA procedure reverts to referring to the current project's connection. This syntax for specifying a connection is less general than the preceding one, which used a trusted connection. However, designating the current project's connection is more straightforward. The sample procedure revises the name of the shipper that has a shipper ID of *4*. If you ran the *InsertANewShipper* VBA procedure from the preceding sample, the *Shippers* table likely has a record with a *ShipperID* value of *4*. If not, update the *prm1.Value* assignment so that it points to a row that you want to revise in the *Shippers* table.

```
Sub UpdateAShipper()
Dim cmd1 As ADODB.Command
Dim prm1 As ADODB.Parameter
Dim prm2 As ADODB.Parameter

'Point a Connection object at the stored procedure
Set cmd1 = New ADODB.Command
cmd1.ActiveConnection = CurrentProject.Connection
cmd1.CommandType = adCmdStoredProc
cmd1.CommandText = "Update_a_shipper"

'Create and append parameters
Set prm1 = cmd1.CreateParameter("@id_for_update", _
    adInteger, adParamInput)
prm1.Value = 4
cmd1.Parameters.Append prm1

Set prm2 = cmd1.CreateParameter("@new_name", adVarChar, _
    adParamInput, 40)
prm2.Value = "CAB Shipping Co."
cmd1.Parameters.Append prm2

'Invoke a stored procedure by executing a command
cmd1.Execute

End Sub
```

The next pair of procedures illustrates the VBA syntax for creating a stored procedure that deletes a record from the *Shippers* table and then invoking that stored procedure. This stored procedure follows the same basic design as the samples for inserting and updating records with parameters. In this case, the procedure for creating the *Delete_a_shipper* stored procedure reveals the T-SQL syntax to remove a single record from a table based on its *ShipperID* column value. The *@id_to_delete* parameter points to this column value.

```
Sub CreateDelete_a_shipperProcedure()
Dim str1 As String
Dim cnn1 As ADODB.Connection
Dim ProcedureName As String

'Point a Connection object at the current project
Set cnn1 = CurrentProject.Connection

'Delete the procedure if it exists already
ProcedureName = "Delete_a_shipper"
Drop_a_procedure cnn1, ProcedureName

'Create the procedure
str1 = "CREATE PROCEDURE " & ProcedureName & " " & vbLf & _
    " " & vbLf & _
    "@id_to_delete int " & vbLf & _
    " " & vbLf & _
    "AS " & vbLf & _
    "DELETE FROM Shippers " & vbLf & _
    "WHERE ShipperID = @id_to_delete "
cnn1.Execute str1

'Refresh Database window to show new procedure
RefreshDatabaseWindow

End Sub


Sub DeleteAShipper()
Dim cmd1 As ADODB.Command
Dim prm1 As ADODB.Parameter
Dim prm2 As ADODB.Parameter

'Point a Connection object at the stored procedure
Set cmd1 = New ADODB.Command
cmd1.ActiveConnection = CurrentProject.Connection
cmd1.CommandType = adCmdStoredProc
cmd1.CommandText = "Delete_a_shipper"

'Create and append parameter
Set prm1 = cmd1.CreateParameter("@id_to_delete", _
    adInteger, adParamInput)
```

```
prm1.Value = 4
cmd1.Parameters.Append prm1

'Invoke a stored procedure by executing a command
cmd1.Execute

End Sub
```

Triggers

A trigger is a special kind of stored procedure attached to a table. Triggers work for tables much like event procedures work for forms. You can place T-SQL code in a trigger that fires when a user attempts to modify a table.

Access 2002 offers support for SQL Server triggers through its UI as well as in VBA procedures. With SQL Server 2000, Microsoft introduced a new kind of trigger called an INSTEAD OF trigger and renamed traditional triggers AFTER triggers. INSTEAD OF triggers operate instead of AFTER triggers. The Access UI has a special interface for working with AFTER triggers. Due to this special interface and the fact that you need to understand AFTER triggers before you can appreciate INSTEAD OF triggers, this discussion focuses exclusively on AFTER triggers (which the UI calls triggers). See Books Online for more in-depth coverage of INSTEAD OF triggers.

When you create a trigger for a table, all database maintenance operations for the table occur within a transaction. You can specify triggers for insert, update, and delete actions. You can even specify multiple triggers for the same kind of action. For example, you can have two or more delete triggers for the same table. SQL Server 2000 introduces the capability to specify which trigger fires first and which fires last. However, any triggers that fire between the first and last ones will occur in an indeterminate order.

Within the transaction for a trigger, revisions to the table are available from two special temporary tables named *deleted* and *inserted*. All deleted records are in the *deleted* table, and all inserted records are in the *inserted* table. Updated records move the old version of the record to the *deleted* table and add the new version the *inserted* table. Changes are not committed to a table until the trigger transaction concludes. Within the trigger transaction, your T-SQL code can change the operation so that it performs none, some, or more of the action that initiated the trigger. For example, you can roll back a delete, copy a deleted record to another table in the same database, or maintain referential integrity with a table in another database. SQL Server declarative referential integrity does not support referential integrity across two different databases.

Creating and Using Triggers from the Access UI

The next set of instructions will guide you through creating and testing the operation of a trigger for the *Shippers* table. Start by creating a fresh version of the table. The easiest and most reliable way to do this is to run the *CreateAndPopulateShippersTable* VBA procedure. This procedure is available from Module1 of the Chapter 14SQL.adp file.

After creating a new version of the *Shippers* table, highlight Tables in the Database window and right-click Shippers. Choose Triggers from the menu, and then click New on the Trigger For Table: Shippers dialog box. This creates a template like the one that follows this paragraph. You can use this template as a guide for creating your own custom trigger. For example, suppose you wanted to roll back all attempts to modify the *Shippers* table. To do so, you could invoke a T-SQL statement and print a message to inform the user of what was happening.

```
CREATE TRIGGER Shippers_Trigger1
ON dbo.Shippers
FOR /* INSERT, UPDATE, DELETE */
AS
    /* IF UPDATE (column_name) ...*/
```

The next T-SQL script shows the text of a trigger for the *Shippers* table that blocks all changes to the table. Users can still open the table and examine its contents. However, if they try to change the table by inserting a new record, updating an existing record, or deleting a record, the trigger rolls back the action and prints a message that says, "I am untouchable!" The ROLLBACK TRAN statement rolls back any attempt to modify the table, and the RAISERROR statement presents a message to Access from SQL Server.

As with a stored procedure, Access opens the template with a CREATE statement for a trigger. However, any attempt to view the trigger after saving it changes the CREATE keyword to ALTER. The default name for the trigger is *Shippers_Trigger1*. You can override this default and use a name that's more meaningful for your application.

```
CREATE TRIGGER Shippers_Trigger1
ON Shippers
FOR INSERT, UPDATE, DELETE
AS
ROLLBACK TRAN
RAISERROR 50000 'I am untouchable!'
```

Figure 14-26 shows the error message generated by the *Shippers_Trigger1* trigger. Notice that the *Shippers* table shows an attempt to update the *CompanyName* field from *Speedy Express* to *Speedy Expressx*. This attempt generates the error message box. This action rollback is a cool, powerful feature:

With just a couple of lines of T-SQL code, you can protect a table from being changed. The protection applies even if users try to make a change directly in the table without using one of your Access forms.

Figure 14-26 An error message generated by the *Shippers_Trigger1* trigger.

You can clear the attempted change to the table by clicking Escape twice. Then close the table.

Programmatically Changing a Table with a Trigger

Recall that we have three VBA procedures for making changes to the *Shippers* table. These are the procedures that use parameters for inserting, updating, and deleting records in a table. Run the *InsertANewShipper* procedure from Module1 of the Chapter 14SQL.adp file. Notice that it fails with a run-time error. The message that accompanies the error message reads, "I am untouchable!" This message confirms that the *Shippers_Trigger1* trigger is preventing the *InsertANewShipper* procedure from adding a new record to the *Shippers* table. As you'll recall, this procedure ran successfully earlier in the chapter.

> **Note**   A sample in the "User-Defined Functions" section at the end of this chapter shows how to trap an error and retrieve its message without relinquishing control to the error.

You might need to temporarily disable a trigger to make some changes to a table that it's blocking. One way to do this is with an ALTER TABLE statement that includes a DISABLE TRIGGER statement. Recall that a trigger applies to a table. Therefore, you need to modify a table when you want to disable a trigger that applies to it. Follow the DISABLE TRIGGER keyword phrase with the name of the trigger that you want to disable. After making your changes to the table, you should reenable the trigger. To do so, embed an ENABLE TRIGGER statement inside another ALTER TABLE statement.

The following VBA procedure shows an updated version of the VBA procedure for inserting a record into the *Shippers* table. This procedure uses the DISABLE TRIGGER and ENABLE TRIGGER statements to determine when the trigger operates and to make a change to the table when the trigger is disabled. The sample runs the ALTER TABLE statements with a *Command* object because it's already available, thanks to the approach that inserts a new record by using the parameters.

```
Sub InsertANewShipper2()
Dim cmd1 As ADODB.Command
Dim prm1 As ADODB.Parameter
Dim prm2 As ADODB.Parameter

'Disable Shippers_Trigger1
Set cmd1 = New ADODB.Command
cmd1.ActiveConnection = CurrentProject.Connection
cmd1.CommandText = _
    "ALTER TABLE Shippers DISABLE TRIGGER Shippers_Trigger1"
cmd1.CommandType = adCmdText
cmd1.Execute

'Point a Connection object at the stored procedure
cmd1.CommandType = adCmdStoredProc
cmd1.CommandText = "Insert_a_new_shipper"

'Create and append parameters
Set prm1 = cmd1.CreateParameter("@CompanyName", adVarChar, _
    adParamInput, 40)
prm1.Value = "CAB Delivers"
cmd1.Parameters.Append prm1

Set prm2 = cmd1.CreateParameter("@Phone", adVarChar, _
    adParamInput, 24)
prm2.Value = "(123) 456-7890"
cmd1.Parameters.Append prm2

'Invoke a stored procedure by executing a command
cmd1.Execute

'Reenable Shippers_Trigger1
cmd1.CommandText = _
"ALTER TABLE Shippers ENABLE TRIGGER Shippers_Trigger1"
cmd1.CommandType = adCmdText
cmd1.Execute

End Sub
```

Problem and Fix for Manual Trigger Creation

If you create even a moderately sized collection of triggers manually, your code will be in jeopardy. There are a couple of reasons for this. First, users can readily update the triggers through the Access UI. If you have no backup for the triggers, diagnosing the problem and developing a solution can be time consuming. Second, if you need to drop a table, your application loses all triggers associated with that table. When you manually enter triggers using the Access UI, you make your code vulnerable to both problems. In addition, you have no way to automate a recovery from the problem after it occurs.

An alternative is to create your triggers in VBA programmatically. This still does not stop either problem from occurring. However, recovering a lost or corrupted trigger is as simple as dropping an existing version of the trigger and then running the code to create a new version of it. The next pair of VBA procedures modifies the *CreateAndPopulateShippersTable* procedure discussed earlier in this chapter so that it automatically creates the *Shippers_Trigger1* sample just presented. Before actually creating the new trigger, the procedure deletes a prior version if one is available. A call to the *Drop_a_trigger* procedure performs this. The *Drop_a_trigger* procedure demonstrates how to use the *Exists* keyword to test for such a condition—for example, the existence of a trigger in a database's *sysobjects* table. This system-defined table maintains one row for each object within a database. The *Type* column of this table denotes the type of object for each row, and the *Name* column represents an object's name.

```
Sub CreateAndPopulateShippersTable2()
Dim str1 As String
Dim cnn1 As ADODB.Connection
Dim TableName As String
Dim TriggerName As String

'Point a Connection object at the current project
Set cnn1 = CurrentProject.Connection

'Delete the table if it exists already
TableName = "Shippers"
Drop_a_table cnn1, TableName

'Create the table
str1 = "CREATE TABLE " & TableName & " " & _
    "( " & _
    "ShipperID int IDENTITY (1, 1) NOT NULL PRIMARY KEY CLUSTERED, " & _
    "CompanyName varchar(40) NOT NULL , " & _
    "Phone varchar(24) NULL " & _
    ")"
cnn1.Execute str1
```

(continued)

833

```
'Run custom stored procedure to populate table based
'on NorthwindCS database
str1 = "EXEC Copy_from_NorthwindCS_Shippers"
cnn1.Execute str1

'Delete the table if it exists already
TriggerName = "Shippers_Trigger1"
Drop_a_trigger cnn1, TriggerName

'Add the trigger after populating the table
str1 = "CREATE TRIGGER " & TriggerName & " " & vbLf & _
    "ON Shippers " & vbLf & _
    "FOR INSERT, UPDATE, DELETE " & vbLf & _
    "AS " & vbLf & _
    "ROLLBACK TRAN " & vbLf & _
    "RAISERROR 50000 'I am untouchable!'"
cnn1.Execute str1

'Refresh Database window to show new table
RefreshDatabaseWindow

End Sub


Sub Drop_a_trigger(cnn1 As ADODB.Connection, _
    TriggerName As String)
Dim str1 As String

'Point a Connection object at the current project
Set cnn1 = CurrentProject.Connection

'Search sysobjects for TriggerName, and drop
'the trigger if it exists
str1 = "IF EXISTS (SELECT name FROM sysobjects " & _
    "WHERE name = '" & TriggerName & "' AND type = 'TR') " & _
    "DROP TRIGGER " & TriggerName
cnn1.Execute str1

End Sub
```

Archiving Updated and Deleted Records

Instead of blocking changes, we can use triggers to archive them. The table of archived records provides a source of changes to a table that's easy to examine. To perform this kind of task, we need a table to hold the archived changes as well as a trigger to write the changes to that table.

The following procedure illustrates one approach to creating a table of archived records for the *Shippers* table. The *ArchivedShippers* table will store the *ShipperID*, *CompanyName*, and *Phone* column values for any updated or deleted records in the *Shippers* table. The *ArchivedShippers* table also includes a primary key with an IDENTITY property setting. This column provides a convenient way of tracking the order of changes to the *Shippers* table.

```
Sub CreateArchivedShippersTable()
Dim str1 As String
Dim cnn1 As ADODB.Connection
Dim TableName As String

'Point a Connection object at the current project
Set cnn1 = CurrentProject.Connection

'Delete the table if it exists already
TableName = "ArchivedShippers"
Drop_a_table cnn1, TableName

'Create the table
str1 = "CREATE TABLE " & TableName & " " & _
    "( " & _
    "ArchiveID int IDENTITY (1, 1) NOT NULL PRIMARY KEY CLUSTERED, " & _
    "ShipperID int NOT NULL, " & _
    "CompanyName varchar(40) NOT NULL , " & _
    "Phone varchar(24) NULL " & _
    ")"
cnn1.Execute str1

End Sub
```

The next code sample shows the VBA procedure to create the new trigger that does the archiving. This new version of the *Shippers_Trigger1* trigger fires whenever an attempt to update or delete a record in the *Shippers* table occurs. The INSERT INTO statement in the trigger copies the values from the deleted table to the *ArchivedShippers* table. This action preserves the records before the delete or update action takes effect.

```
Sub CreateArchivingTrigger()
Dim str1 As String
Dim cnn1 As ADODB.Connection
Dim TriggerName As String

'Point a Connection object at the current project
Set cnn1 = CurrentProject.Connection
```

(continued)

```
'Delete the table if it exists already
TriggerName = "Shippers_Trigger1"
Drop_a_trigger cnn1, TriggerName

'Add a trigger to archive deleted or updated records
str1 = "CREATE TRIGGER Shippers_Trigger1 " & vbLf & _
    "ON Shippers " & vbLf & _
    "FOR UPDATE, DELETE " & vbLf & _
    "AS " & _
    "INSERT INTO ArchivedShippers " & _
        "(ShipperID, CompanyName, Phone) " & vbLf & _
    "SELECT ShipperID, CompanyName, Phone FROM deleted "
cnn1.Execute str1

End Sub
```

Our example concludes with a procedure that demonstrates the operation of the *Shippers_Trigger1* trigger and the *ArchivedShippers* table. The next procedure merely calls procedures we've already discussed in this chapter. However, these procedures now preserve the unchanged values of records updated or deleted from the *Shippers* table.

The sample begins by creating a fresh copy of the *Shippers* table with a call to the *CreateAndPopulateShippersTable* procedure. Next it invokes the two procedures just discussed to create a fresh copy of the *Archived Shippers* table and the *Shippers_Trigger1* trigger. Then the procedure successively invokes the *InsertANewShipper*, *UpdateAShipper*, and *DeleteAShipper* procedures. We discussed the operation of these procedures earlier in the chapter. In this demonstration, these three procedures add a new record to the original *Shippers* table and then modify and delete that record. This creates two records in the *ArchivedShippers* table. The first record represents the newly added record just before it gets modified. The second record in the *ArchivedShippers* table represents the changed record just before it's deleted from the *Shippers* table. The sample procedure concludes by opening the *ArchivedShippers* table so that you can change the view to Access from the VBA code window and confirm the availability of the two records in the table.

```
Sub DemoArchivingWithTrigger()

'Generate a fresh copy of the Shippers table
CreateAndPopulateShippersTable

'Create the table for archiving deleted and
'updated records, and the trigger to populate
'the table
CreateArchivedShippersTable
CreateArchivingTrigger
```

```
'Add a record, then update to generate an archived record.
'Next, delete the updated record to generate a second
'archived record.
InsertANewShipper
UpdateAShipper
DeleteAShipper

'Open the archived table for viewing.
'Click View Microsoft Access toolbar control to see table.
DoCmd.OpenTable "ArchivedShippers"

End Sub
```

User-Defined Functions

User-defined functions are a SQL Server 2000 innovation, and Access 2002 interoperates well with this new capability on several different levels. With user-defined functions, you can define your own custom functions and use them similarly to the way you use the built-in SQL Server functions. User-defined functions contain collections of T-SQL statements that determine their behavior.

User-defined functions come in three different varieties. The first type of user-defined function returns a scalar value. This type of function can optionally take one or more arguments. While the output from a scalar function is always a single item value, its input can be comprised of scalar values or one or more tables. The second type of user-defined function is an in-line table-valued function. This type allows you to return a table from a function based on a single SELECT statement. SQL Server introduced a new data type that specifically accommodates the return values from this kind of user-defined function as well as the third kind. The third type of user-defined function relies on multiple statements and returns a table. You can explicitly declare this function's column data type. You also can conditionally define its result set by using an IF...ELSE statement based on a record source defined in the function or by using parameters passed to the function.

User-defined functions have a variety of features that affect how you use them. First, you can nest functions within one another, and you can use them in other database objects, such as views and stored procedures. In addition, you can invoke a function from a T-SQL statement, such as the source for a *Recordset* object within a VBA procedure. Second, you must always include at least a dbo qualifier in a function's identifier, as in *dbo.myfunction()*. As the last code sample in the previous section demonstrates, you must follow a function name with parentheses even if it takes no arguments. If the function does take arguments, you can position them within the parentheses. Comma-delimit the arguments when a function has more than one. Third, use the CREATE FUNCTION, ALTER

FUNCTION, and DROP FUNCTION statements to define, revise, and remove user-defined functions from a database, respectively. This feature allows you to manipulate functions such as those in the earlier samples for tables, views, and stored procedures.

Scalar User-Defined Functions

Scalar user-defined functions will often return a value based on one or more arguments passed to them. For example, you can develop scalar functions to convert from unit of measurement to another, such as degrees Fahrenheit to degrees centigrade, degrees to radians, feet to meters, and dollars to pounds. Another type of applications for user-defined functions is the computation of complicated formulas. This type application is appropriate in situations where all the units within an organization must identically perform a mission-critical calculation.

You can launch the creation of a user-defined function by highlighting Queries in the Objects bar of the Database window and clicking New. From the New Query dialog box, you can choose Create Text Scalar Function, Design In-Line Function, or Create Text Table-Valued Function. These correspond to the first, second, and third types of user-defined functions.

If you choose Create Text Scalar Function, Access responds by presenting a template such as the one that follows for constructing a scalar user-defined function. Notice that this template has a space for inserting arguments in parentheses after the function name. In addition, the template includes a mandatory RETURNS statement. Use this statement to specify the data type of the scalar value returned the function. An AS keyword marks the beginning of the user-defined code. All T-SQL statements for the function must reside between BEGIN and END statements. The T-SQL code within these statements must include at least one RETURN statement. The argument for this statement determines the return value of the function.

```
CREATE FUNCTION "Function1"
    (
    /*
    @parameter1 datatype = default value,
    @parameter2 datatype
    */
    )
RETURNS /* datatype */
AS
    BEGIN
        /* sql statement ... */
    RETURN /* value */
    END
```

The next T-SQL script is a very simple scalar function. Notice that the function starts with an ALTER FUNCTION statement. Access automatically converts a CREATE FUNCTION statement into an ALTER FUNCTION statement after you initially save the function from one of the Access user-defined function templates. The following function returns a single value. This value derives from the built-in AVG function applied to the *Freight* column values of the *Orders* table. Although the source for the function is a table, it returns a scalar value—the average *Freight* value from the *Orders* table. This value returns with a Money data type.

```
ALTER FUNCTION dbo.AVG_Freight_overall()
RETURNS money
AS
BEGIN
    RETURN (SELECT AVG(Freight) FROM Orders)
END
```

As long as the values in the *Freight* column do not change, this function will always return the identical value. Users cannot directly alter the function's return value based on arguments they submit to the function. However, functions often incorporate additional functions that determine what their output will be. For example, you can define a function that returns the average freight for just one year—instead of all the years combined as the preceding sample does. The following function illustrates the syntax for this kind of user-defined function. Notice the specification of the parameter to accept an argument in the parentheses after the function name. An argument declaration must always include a name and a data type specification. The SELECT statement for this function includes a WHERE clause that uses the argument to restrict the range of values over which the AVG function computes the average freight.

```
ALTER FUNCTION dbo.Avg_Freight_in_@year (@year char(4))
RETURNS money
AS
BEGIN
    RETURN (
        SELECT AVG(Freight)
        FROM Orders
        WHERE DATEPART(yyyy,OrderDate) = @year
        )
END
```

You can also base scalar user-defined functions exclusively on scalar inputs—without relying on a tabular row source. The next sample computes the percentage of change between two positive numbers. Both input values have a Float data type. The return value is a Decimal data type with a scale of *6* and a precision of *3*. This function illustrates the use of a local variable named *@change* with a Float data type. SQL Server local variables in functions and stored procedures have scope (or visibility) only within the function or procedure in which you define them. The local variable saves the difference between the two arguments for use in the percent change expression, which is the argument for the RETURN statement. This expression returns a percent with a value of *0.1* as 10 percent because it multiplies the percent change by 100.

```
ALTER FUNCTION dbo.Percent_change (@firstnumber float,
    @secondnumber float)
RETURNS decimal(6,3)
AS
BEGIN
DECLARE @change float
    SET @change = @secondnumber-@firstnumber
    RETURN @change/@firstnumber*100
END
```

You can invoke user-defined functions from other SQL Server database objects, such as stored procedures, or from VBA procedures. The following stored procedure invokes the preceding two user-defined functions to compute the average freight in each of two different years as well as the percent change between those two years. Because the functions return numeric data types, it's necessary to convert them for use as the argument of the RAISERROR statement. This statement, which concludes the stored procedure, presents a message box when you run the stored procedure from the Database window. If you run the stored procedure from a VBA procedure, it passes back its computed string as an error message to the VBA procedure.

```
ALTER PROCEDURE ComputePercentChangeBetweenYears
    @year1 char(4),
    @year2 char(4)
AS
DECLARE @str1 as varchar(100)

--Compute a string expression based on the Avg_Freight_in_@year
--and Percent_change functions
SET @str1 =
    'Freight in ' + @year1 + ' = $'
        + CONVERT(varchar(7),dbo.Avg_Freight_in_@year(@year1))
        + CHAR(10) +
    'Freight in ' + @year2 + ' = $'
        + CONVERT(varchar(7),dbo.Avg_Freight_in_@year(@year2))
        + CHAR(10) +
    'Percent change = '
        + CONVERT(varchar(7),
```

```
        dbo.Percent_change(dbo.Avg_Freight_in_@year(@year1),
        dbo.Avg_Freight_in_@year(@year2))) + '%'

--Return the string from the stored procedure
RAISERROR 50000 @str1
```

If you invoke this stored procedure from the Database window, it sequentially presents a pair of prompts for its two arguments. Insert *1996*, *1997*, or *1998*, because those are the only years for which the *Orders* table has data. Figure 14-27 shows the format of the message box that the procedure generates when it concludes. This message box shows the average freight in 1996 and 1997, along with the percent change from 1996 to 1997.

Figure 14-27 A message box generated by the *ComputePercentChangeBetweenYears* stored procedure when it's run from the database window.

When you run the same procedure from a VBA procedure, no message box appears. In fact, the procedure returns a run-time error. The *Description* property of the *Err* object for the error contains the same content shown in Figure 14-27. Therefore, you can print the *Err* object's *Description* property to the Immediate window to display this content. The following pair of procedures shows one approach to accomplishing this. The first procedure specifies the year parameters that serve as arguments for the stored procedure. It passes these values to the second procedure, which constructs an SQL string (*str1*) for a *Connection* object to execute. Before invoking the *Connection* object's *Execute* method, the procedure opens an error trap that passes control the next line of code. Because the stored procedure in the SQL string passes back its content through an error message, this error trap—which prints the *Err* object's *Description* property—retrieves the message. Without the error trap, an error box would still appear with the content but the procedure would lose control of the session.

```
Sub CallVBAPercentChange()
Dim str1 As String
Dim str2 As String

'Assign string values of 1996, 1997, or 1998
'to str1 and str2
str1 = "1996"
str2 = "1998"
```

(continued)

```
'Call procedure to invoke stored procedure
'that returns values from user-defined functions
VBAPercentChange str1, str2

End Sub


Sub VBAPercentChange(year1 As String, year2 As String)
Dim str1 As String
Dim cnn1 As ADODB.Connection

'Point cnn1 at current project's database connection
Set cnn1 = CurrentProject.Connection

'Invoke stored procedure, pass arguments, and print return
str1 = "Exec ComputePercentChangeBetweenYears " & year1 & _
    ", " & year2
On Error Resume Next
cnn1.Execute str1
Debug.Print Err.Description

End Sub
```

In-Line User-Defined Functions

In-line functions return a table of values in the result set for a single SELECT statement. In addition, in-line functions have a simplified syntax. They do not require BEGIN and END statements, and they must have only one RETURN statement for their single SELECT statement.

In-line functions can behave like views. In addition, you can assign parameters to their WHERE clauses—a feature that views lack. Stored procedures do possess this functionality, but you cannot use a stored procedure as a FROM clause argument like you can with an in-line function procedure.

Because an in-line function depends on a single SELECT statement, Access 2002 offers a graphical design tool that is very similar to the visual designer for views. You can create an in-line function by highlighting Queries in the Objects bar on the Database window and clicking New. Then you double-click Design In-Line Function. This opens the visual designer for in-line functions that appears in Figure 14-28. Notice that you can use tables, views, and other table-returning functions as sources for in-line functions. You can build the query similarly to the way you build a view, but you can specify criteria with parameters (as with stored procedures). In addition, the View control on the toolbar offers an SQL View option as well as an SQL pane. With the SQL pane, you can see the T-SQL syntax for the SELECT statement underlying an in-line function's graphical view. With the SQL View window, you can see the full ALTER FUNCTION statement defining the in-line function.

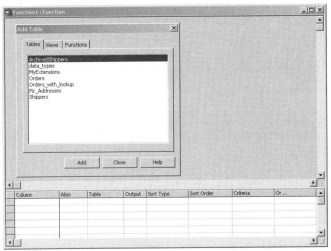

Figure 14-28 The visual designer for in-line functions lets you base a function on tables, views, or other table-returning functions.

Figure 14-29 shows the visual designer for an in-line function that returns all rows from the *Orders* table with a *Freight* column value greater than the average of the *Freight* values for all rows in that table. The function also sorts its result set in ascending order. The T-SQL code appears in the bottom SQL pane. Notice that it follows the view syntax for defining a sort—in other words, the SELECT statement must include a TOP clause. This syntax also shows the code for nesting one user-defined function within another. This is because the average *Freight* column value across all rows in the *Orders* table is based on the *AVG_Freight_overall* function. Notice that this function's identifier includes a user qualifier. This qualifier points to the dbo user, a topic discussed earlier in this chapter on page 767. Function identifiers must be unique within their respective owners. A pair of parentheses follows the function name even though the function takes no arguments. As mentioned previously, these parentheses are mandatory.

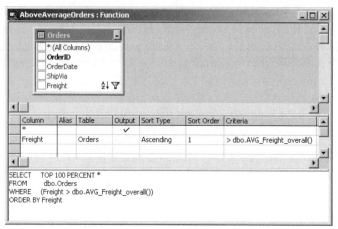

Figure 14-29 A visual designer view of an in-line function that has another user-defined function nested within it.

The following code listing shows the SQL View window of the in-line function whose design appears in Figure 14-29. The SQL View window exposes the ALTER FUNCTION, RETURNS, and RETURN statements. These statements serve as a shell and a conduit for returning the table defined by the function's SELECT statement. The ALTER FUNCTION is the outside wrapper for the T-SQL code. The RETURNS statement specifies that the function returns a TABLE. The RETURN statement is a wrapper for the SELECT statement that specifies the result set for the function.

```
ALTER FUNCTION dbo.AboveAverageOrders
( )
RETURNS TABLE
AS
RETURN ( SELECT TOP 100 PERCENT *
FROM    dbo.Orders
WHERE   (Freight > dbo.AVG_Freight_overall())
ORDER BY Freight )
```

The following VBA procedure offers one approach to extracting values from the result set for an in-line function. The trick here is to use a T-SQL statement that returns all columns from the result set for the function. This statement becomes the source for the *Open* method of a *Recordset* object. By setting the recordset's *MaxRecord* property to 5, we return a small subset of the entire result set to loop through and list in the Immediate window. If you want to retrieve the full result set, omit the *MaxRecord* property setting. Be aware that if you do so, you might need to change the data type setting for *byt1* to a data type that can accommodate a larger limit.

```
Sub ReturnResultsSetFromInlineFunction()
Dim rst1 As ADODB.Recordset
Dim byt1 As Byte

'Get a subset of the results set from an in-line function
Set rst1 = New ADODB.Recordset
rst1.MaxRecords = 5
rst1.Open "SELECT * FROM dbo.AboveAverageOrders()", _
    CurrentProject.Connection

'Print a subset of results set record from the in-line function
Do Until rst1.EOF
    Debug.Print "Results for record " & (byt1 + 1)
    For Each fld1 In rst1.Fields
        Debug.Print "   " & fld1.Name & " = " & rst1.Fields(fld1.Name)
    Next fld1
    rst1.MoveNext
    byt1 = byt1 + 1
    Debug.Print
Loop

End Sub
```

Multistatement User-Defined Functions

User-defined functions returning tables can also contain multiple statements—instead of just the single SELECT statement in a typical user-defined function. Books Online calls this type of user-defined function a multistatement table-valued function. This long way description accurately reflects the structure of this kind of user-defined function. This kind of function lets you use many different types of T-SQL statements to define its result set. At a minimum, using this function will require you to specify the data types for columns and the record sources for the result set. Additionally, you will need to include one or more INSERT statements for copying values from one or more record sources into the return set.

The preceding sample returns all the columns from the *Orders* table. One of these rows includes a *Shipvia* column, which is a numeric field that indicates the shipper. However, many users prefer a result set that lists the company name of a shipper instead of a numeric index that references the shipper. The following ALTER FUNCTION statement illustrates the syntax for a multistatement function that accomplishes this task. You also can accomplished this task by using an in-line function that includes a join. The sample for the multistatement function is extraordinarily simple so that you can focus on its main syntax issues.

This sample doesn't nest the function to compute the overall average. For example, it can return records based on a measure other than the average, such as the geometric mean or median. In addition, you can compute this value in T-SQL or elsewhere, because the criterion for including records passes to the function as an argument value. Notice that the return statement includes a table name before its TABLE specification for the function's return type. Following the table declaration are declarations for the table's individual columns. In this example, these declarations include a column name and data type.

The AS keywork marks the transition from the function's declaration area to its T-SQL code area. All T-SQL code must exist within a BEGIN...END block. At a minimum, this T-SQL code must include one INSERT statement that specifies to which columns you will add data as well as the source for those columns. The source in this case is the joined *Shippers* and *Orders* tables. By joining the two tables, the function gains the ability to replace the numeric *Shipvia* column values with string values denoting the company names for the shippers.

Because you can include T-SQL statements for computations, references to more than one record source, and branching logic, it's possible to construct much more elaborate result sets. No matter how many additional statements you include in your multistatement table-valued user-defined functions, you must always include the basic structural components denoted here:

```
ALTER FUNCTION dbo.AboveAverageOrdersJoinedToShippers
    (@averageorder money)
RETURNS @AboveAverageOrdersByShipper TABLE
    (
    CompanyName varchar(24),
    OrderID int,
    OrderDate datetime,
    Freight money
    )
AS
BEGIN
    INSERT INTO @AboveAverageOrdersByShipper
        SELECT TOP 100 Percent S.CompanyName, O.OrderID,
            O.OrderDate, O.Freight
        FROM Shippers AS S INNER JOIN Orders AS O
        ON (S.ShipperID = O.Shipvia)
        WHERE O.FREIGHT > @averageorder
        ORDER BY Freight
    RETURN
END
```

You can readily run multistatement functions such as the preceding one from VBA modules. In fact, the preceding sample actually calls for some kind of programmatic execution because it requests a parameter that reflects the average. A program is ideally suited to create the average for the function's input as an argument.

The following procedure illustrates one approach to displaying a subset of the result set from the multistatement function. It starts by invoking the *AVG_Freight_overall* function. This scalar user-defined function returns the average value that you want as input to the multistatement user-defined function. The VBA procedure calls both functions with a string variable that specifies the source argument for the *Open* method of a *Recordset* object. This approach eliminates the need for parameters for a *Command* object and then passes the result set from the *Command* object to a *Recordset* object. However, it forfeits the ability to perform strong data typing on the arguments for functions. After opening the second recordset, the VBA procedure simply lists the five records in the result set. As mentioned previously, you can revise the size of the result set.

```
Sub ReturnResultsSetFromMultistatementTableFunction()
Dim rst1 As ADODB.Recordset
Dim str1 As String
Dim str2 As String
Dim byt1 As Byte

'Compute overall average freight with user-defined function
Set rst1 = New ADODB.Recordset
rst1.Open "Select dbo.AVG_Freight_overall()", CurrentProject.Connection
str1 = rst1(0)

'Invoke multistatement function for table, and
'pass overall average freight
rst1.Close
rst1.MaxRecords = 5
str2 = "SELECT * FROM dbo.AboveAverageOrdersJoinedToShippers(" & _
    str1 & ")"
rst1.Open str2, CurrentProject.Connection

'Print a subset of results set record from the in-line function
Do Until rst1.EOF
    Debug.Print "Results for record " & (byt1 + 1)
    For Each fld1 In rst1.Fields
        Debug.Print "   " & fld1.Name & " = " & rst1.Fields(fld1.Name)
    Next fld1
    rst1.MoveNext
    byt1 = byt1 + 1
    Debug.Print
Loop

End Sub
```

15

Using Access to Build
SQL Server Solutions: Part II

Microsoft Access projects are powerful development tools for at least two key reasons. First, they expose many of the most powerful features of Microsoft SQL Server. Also, Access projects facilitate the application of many of the most powerful Access development capabilities to SQL Server databases. Chapter 14, "Using Access to Build SQL Server Solutions: Part I," focused on user interface (UI) and programmatic coverage of tables, views, stored procedures, and user-defined functions. These topics are all server-side objects in a client/server solution supported by Access projects.

This chapter continues the saga of how to build client/server solutions with Access projects. However, this chapter switches the focus, at least partially, to the client-side tools. Several early sections in the chapter examine how to use forms with SQL Server record sources. These are followed by another section on building solutions with reports. Do not feel that you are limited to the form and report techniques covered in this chapter. In fact, most techniques for applying forms and reports in Access database files also apply in Access projects; this chapter describes selected differences. This capability to use forms and reports means that you can refer back to the coverage of these topics in earlier chapters for more ways to create SQL Server solutions with Access.

Another focus of this chapter is how to program SQL Server solutions with Microsoft Visual Basic for Applications (VBA) procedures in modules within Access projects. This chapter pays particular attention to programming SQL-DMO, the SQL Server Distributed Management Objects model. With this model, you can control any aspect of SQL Server administration and data definition. After introducing the basics of SQL-DMO programming, the chapter presents several samples of how to apply SQL-DMO.

The last focus of the chapter is programming SQL Server security. Programming SQL Server security is substantially more important with Access 2002 than with Access 2000 because the graphical UI for SQL Server security from Access 2000 is dropped in Access 2002. This chapter's presentation of the topic builds on the SQL-DMO programming skills developed earlier in the chapter. Use the samples in this chapter as a foundation for learning even more about programmatically specifying security for your multiuser Access project solutions.

Creating a Form Based on a Table with One Click

One of the most remarkable features of Access projects is the ease and power that they bring to developing form-based solutions for SQL Server databases. For example, the AutoForm Wizard enables you to create a form based on a table with just a single click. When working with the AutoForm Wizard, remember that you do not select Forms in the Objects bar. Instead, you select a class, such as Tables. Then you highlight the database object to serve as the source for the form and click the AutoForm control on the toolbar.

A single click of the AutoForm Wizard creates a form that's bound to the table. If the table has a parent-child relationship with another table, the wizard automatically creates a form that has a main form control for the parent record and a subform control for its child records. If the table for the subform also has a parent-child relationship with a third table, the wizard automatically creates subdatasheets for the rows to represent the child records of the subform's parent records.

The automatic capturing of subform and subdatasheet relationships in Access 2002 is an improvement upon Access 2000. The earlier version of Access allowed you to manually construct subforms, but it did not construct them automatically. In addition, Access 2000 did not manage subdatasheet relationships. However, Access 2002 manages subdatasheets for tables and uses that information when constructing forms.

Using the AutoForm Wizard with an Unrelated Table

The main sample database for this chapter includes the database objects from the NorthwindCS database. One of these objects is the *Order Details* table. This table contains a row with five columns of information. The *OrderID* column value repeats for as many rows as there are line items in the order denoted by the order ID.

Figure 15-1 shows a form based on the *Order Details* table. You can generate a form like this by selecting the *Order Details* table in the Database window and clicking the AutoForm tool. The form permits users to browse, update, add, and delete records from the underlying table. You can save that form by clicking File-Save. Then type a name for the form (such as *frmOrderDetails*) in the Save As dialog box and click OK.

Figure 15-1 A form created with one click for the *Order Details* table in a SQL Server database.

The form depicted in Figure 15-1 is available in the sample Access project for this chapter as *frmOrderDetails*. This form resides with the Access project, Chapter 15.adp. The project references its own custom database, which is Chapter 15SQL on my local server. Both the Access project file and the database files are available on the book's companion CD. See the "Attaching and Detaching Database Files" section later in this chapter for sample code illustrating how to attach the database files to your local SQL Server.

Creating a Main/Subform with a Bound Image

Creating a main form with a subform control using the AutoForm Wizard is no more complicated than generating a form with one click, as just described. In fact, your main form can even display bound graphic images if they're saved as bitmap (.bmp) files in the database. Figure 15-2 shows a main/subform based on the *Categories* table in the sample database for this chapter. The form is available in the Access project for this file as *frmCategories*. Notice that *frmCategories* includes a bound graphic image depicting the products in a category. The image that appears on each record originates from the *Picture* column of the *Categories* table. A Bound Object Frame control renders the image on the form. The AutoForm Wizard automatically selects the control based on the *Picture* column's data type and contents.

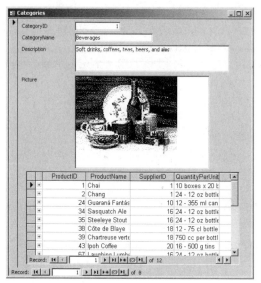

Figure 15-2 A main/subform generated by the AutoForm Wizard for the *Categories* table.

The *Categories* table in the Chapter 15SQL database has a subdatasheet based on the *Products* table. This subdatasheet allows users to view the products within a category. The *Products* subdatasheet for the *Categories* table, in turn, has its own subdatasheet that shows rows in the *Order Details* table that reference the *ProductID* column value in the *Products* table. The form depicted in Figure 15-2 accurately reflects the relationship between the *Categories* and *Products* tables. The subform in the figure presents the products within the current category on the main form. The subform navigator control is on Chai, the first of 12 products in the Beverages category. Clicking the expand indicator (the plus sign) on the row containing Chai displays a subdatasheet of rows from the *Order Details* table that reference the product ID for Chai.

All the functionality of *frmCategories* was obtained by a single click of the AutoForm Wizard. Remember to highlight the *Categories* table before clicking the AutoForm Wizard. After the wizard generates the form, choose File-Save and assign a name to the form, such as *frmCategories*.

Another Main/Subform Example

The AutoForm Wizard is a great tool, but it has its limitations. The next main/subform example we'll discuss illustrates two of these drawbacks. Figure 15-3 displays the output from the AutoForm Wizard for the *Employees* table. This form is available in the chapter's project as *frmEmployees*. The *Employees* table, which is the record source for the main form in *frmEmployees*, has a subdatasheet that points at the *Orders* table. Users can open this subdatasheet to examine the orders made by any employee. The *Orders* table, in turn, has a subdatasheet that points at the *Order Details* table.

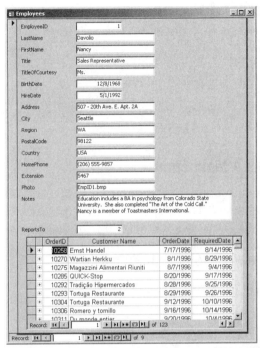

Figure 15-3 A main/subform generated by the AutoForm Wizard for the *Employees* table.

The *frmEmployees* form reflects the data relationships for the *Employees* table. The main form shows all the fields in the *Employees* table. The subform shows all the orders made by the current employee on the main form. The expand indicator allows a user to expand the view to include the line items for a particular order.

Figure 15-3 highlights two limitations of the AutoForm Wizard. Fortunately, a little programming can easily resolve both of these problems. The first limitation is that the Photo row shows an image address rather than an image. Notice that the contents of the Photo cell reads EmpID1.bmp. This is the filename for the bitmap file depicting an employee named Nancy Davolio. When working with large collections of graphic images, a popular development option is to leave the images as files and store their filenames in a database. This speeds up performance, but it requires an extra step when displaying the graphic image. Happily, that extra step is quick and easy. The second limitation is that the AutoForm Wizard includes no prompts for automatically selecting or aggregating subform values on the main form. However, selecting or aggregating subform values is a common requirement for main/subform designs.

Extending AutoForm-Generated Forms

This section tackles two issues. First, it shows how to reference items on a subform programmatically from the code behind a main form. This enables you to compute values based on subform fields or just extract a particular subform field value (which can eliminate the need to scroll a subform). Second, this section explains how to show pictures in a form when the table serving as the form's record source contains image file addresses instead of bound images.

Referencing Subform Fields from a Main Form

Figure 15-4 shows an adaptation of the form depicted in Figure 15-3. The new form has the name *frmEmployees1*. The adaptation drops the Notes text box and adds two others in its place. The Notes text box in *frmEmployees* is bound to the *Notes* column in the *Employees* table. The two new text boxes are both unbound. Their captions are Total Freight and Last OrderDate.

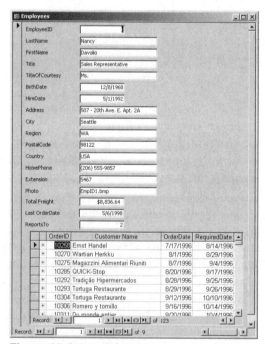

Figure 15-4 A main/subform based on the *Employees* table with two unbound text boxes that display subform content on the main form.

It's easy to edit the AutoForm-generated form in Figure 15-3 so that it adopts the design of the form in Figure 15-4. You use the same techniques as you would with standard Access database files. First, select the Notes text box in Design view. Then click the Delete key on the keyboard to remove the form and its corresponding label, which is a caption for the Notes text box. Second, open the Toolbox. Third, drag a couple of text boxes to the form from the Toolbox. Assign *txtTotalFreight* as the name for the first new text box and *txtLastOrderDate* as the name for the second new text box. Then select the label for each text box and assign its *Caption* property a name similar to the one in Figure 15-4. Finally, align and size the labels and text boxes with the other controls already on the form.

After these steps, you will have two text boxes that appear blank in Form view. In Design view, the forms contain the word *Unbound*. You can insert values into the unbound text boxes using any of the standard form development techniques. For example, you can programmatically assign values to the text boxes. One of the most common places to insert code that programmatically modifies a form is in the event procedures behind a form and its controls.

This following sample uses two form events: *Current* and *Open*. The *Current* event fires whenever a form access a new record. The form can access a new record when a user opens the form, navigates from one record to the next, or requeries the form. The sample code populates the *txtTotalFreight* and *txtLastOrderDate* controls with the current event procedure for the form. After a form event procedure populates a text box, it will have the default formatting unless you explicitly program another format. The sample uses an *Open* event procedure to assign formats to the two unbound controls that match the content developed by the *Current* event procedure. The *Open* event fires whenever a form opens. This can happen when a user opens a closed form or a developer switches from Design view to Form view.

You can open a template for a form event procedure in an Access project just as you would for an Access database file. Select the form in Design view. (See Chapter 6, "Forms, Controls, and Data," if you need to review how to do this.) Then open its Properties dialog box. Select the Event tab on the dialog box. Then click the Build button next to the *Event* property that matches the event procedure you want to program. For example, click the Build button for the *On Current* event property to open a template for the *Current* event. Choose Code Builder in the Choose Builder dialog box, and then choose OK to open the template.

The next two VBA scripts show the *Form_Current* and *Form_Open* event procedures for the *frmEmployees1* form. The *Form_Current* event procedure uses the *ctl1* object reference to point at the *sbfOrders* control on the *frmEmployees1* form. This control contains the subform. The procedure uses the *Form* property of the *sbfOrders* control to reference individual control values on the subform. For example, the event procedure points *ctl2* at the *Freight* control on the subform.

Next the event procedure opens a loop on the recordset behind the subform. The syntax for pointing at the recordset behind a subform is *ctl1.Form.Recordset*. In this instance, *ctl1* points at the subform control. *Form* displays the collection of form properties behind the subform control, and *Recordset* specifies the particular property of interest. The loop travels through the records behind the subform until it encounters an *EOF* (end of file) flag. During each pass through the loop, the code accumulates the value of the *Freight* control in the *cur1* local variable. The code within the loop also saves the current value of the *OrderDate* control in the *dat1* local memory variable. During the last pass through the loop, *dat1* receives the value of the last *OrderDate* value for the current employee. After exiting the loop, the procedure saves the values of *cur1* and *dat1* in the *txtTotalFreight* and *txtLastOrderDate* text boxes on the main form. This way, the procedure reflects subform control values on the main form.

The procedure makes the subform invisible during its operation. Setting the subform control's visibility property to False hides updates to the control at the procedure's start, and a closing property setting of True restores the visibility of the subform at the end of the procedure. In between, the procedure moves from one record to the next on the subform. Setting the subform control's *Visible* property to False hides this movement between records on the subform. Just before restoring the subform's visibility, the procedure moves the current record in the subform back to the first record in the recordset.

```
Private Sub Form_Current()
Dim ctl1 As Control
Dim ctl2 As Control
Dim cur1 As Currency
Dim dat1 As Date

'Set reference for subform control
Set ctl1 = Me.sbfOrders
ctl1.Visible = False

'Set reference to Freight control on subform
Set ctl2 = Me.sbfOrders.Form("Freight")

'Loop through subform rows in subform recordset.
'Accumulate total freight.
'Save OrderDate values for last subform row.
Do Until ctl1.Form.Recordset.EOF
    cur1 = cur1 + ctl2.Value
    dat1 = Me.sbfOrders.Form("OrderDate")
    ctl1.Form.Recordset.MoveNext
```

```
Loop
Me.txtTotalFreight = cur1
Me.txtLastOrderDate = dat1

'Reposition current record at top of recordset
ctl1.Form.Recordset.MoveFirst

ctl1.Visible = True

End Sub
```

The following *Form_Open* event procedure formats the two unbound controls added to *frmEmployees1*. The assignment of *"Currency"* to the *Format* property of the *txtTotalFreight* control represents its quantity as a currency. This assignment adds a leading currency sign, and it aligns the total value so that it appears on the box's right-hand side. The second assignment right-justifies the date in the *txtLastOrderDate* control. Access does not have enum members to represent the *TextAlign* formatting settings. Therefore, the procedure assigns a constant naming the correct value for right alignment. This makes the code easier to read and maintain. Without the *TextAlign* property assignment, the date value in *txtLastOrderDate* appears as a left-justified label.

```
Private Sub Form_Open(Cancel As Integer)

'Set the Format and TextAlign properties for the
'two unbound text boxes
Const conRightAlign = 3

Me.txtTotalFreight.Format = "Currency"
Me.txtLastOrderDate.TextAlign = conRightAlign

End Sub
```

Showing Images Based on Image Addresses

One problem with the form shown in Figure 15-3 is that it displays the address of the photo image, but not the image itself. The AutoForm Wizard didn't assign the address to a control and didn't put code behind the form to display the image that corresponds to an address on each record. (It's fixing little things like this that helps you justify getting paid the big bucks.) This section takes two approaches to the task. First, it shows how to work with the addresses in the *Employees* table. These point at bitmap images. While this image format is acceptable for many purposes, Web applications often use different image formats, such as files with a .gif or .jpg extension. The second sample in this section demonstrates the use of images with a .jpg format.

To use image files from the *Employees* table, I build a simple query statement in a view. The view's name is *Employee_Pic_addresses*. This view contains three fields: *EmployeeID*, *EmployeeName*, and *Photo*. The *Photo* column contains the image filenames. The *EmployeeName* field is computed as the *FirstName* field, plus a space, plus the *LastName* field. Notice from the following T-SQL statement that SQL Server syntax uses a plus sign (+) to concatenate strings:

```
SELECT EmployeeID, FirstName + ' ' + LastName AS EmployeeName, Photo
FROM dbo.Employees
```

To create a form that displays the three column values in the *Employee_Pic_addresses* view and the images corresponding to the filenames in the *Photo* column, you can create a form based on the view. Use the AutoForm Wizard to get off to a quick start. Then, in Design view, click the Image control in the Toolbox and select the location where you want the control in the form's top-left corner. When the Insert Image dialog box appears, choose EmpID1.bmp. This file will reside in the folder where you store the image files. For example, Microsoft Office XP installs the image files for the *Employees* table by default at c:\program files\microsoft office\office10\samples\. When the form initially opens, it will automatically show this image. Any code you run from event procedures can substitute a new image. Assign *pic_image* to the Image control's *Name* property by using the Properties dialog box for the control.

Insert the following script for the form's current event procedure. This procedure starts by assigning a value to a path, which represents the path to the image files. You can use any path you have for the image files. If the *Photo* column value is not Null, the procedure assigns the concatenation of the path and filename to the image control's *Picture* property. This branch of the *If…Then…Else… End If* statement also assigns a value of True to the image control's *Visible* property. This property is True by default, but the procedure assigns False to the property when the filename for the image is Null. Therefore, setting the *Visible* property to True when an image exists ensures that the employee's picture appears on the form.

```
Private Sub Form_Current()
'Assign a path for the image filename files
Const path _
    = "c:\program files\microsoft office\office10\samples\"

'If the image exists, assign the path and photo address
'to the pic_image's Picture property. Otherwise, make
'pic_image invisible.
If IsNull(Me.Photo) Then
    Me.pic_image.Visible = False
```

```
Else
    Me.pic_image.Picture = path & Me.Photo
    Me.pic_image.Visible = True
End If

End Sub
```

Figure 15-5 shows the *frmEmployee_Pic_addresses* form with the image of the first employee. Users can move through the records with the normal navigation controls at the bottom of the form. With each new record, the image changes. The table contains only nine records. As a developer, you can add new employees and photo addresses to the table to enable the form to show additional employee pictures. With a very modest amount of code, you can enable end users to add images for display on the form.

Figure 15-5 A form containing employee photo images that correspond to the photo filenames in the *Employees* table.

The next sample uses a very similar design. But instead of showing the employee photos from the Northwind database, this sample shows the photos for the *Pic_Addresses* table initially developed in Chapter 14. Recall that the table has three columns: *PictureID*, *Pic_description*, and *Pic_address*. These columns roughly correspond to those in the *Employees* table, with two important exceptions. First, the addresses in the *Pic_address* column include both the path and filename. Second, the addresses in *Pic_Addresses* point at .jpg files. This file type is popular for Web applications that show photo images. Therefore, bitmap files tend to have a larger file size for comparable images and resolutions. Using the Image control, you can display bitmap as well as JPEG files (those with a .jpg extension).

Because the *Pic_address* column includes both a path and filename for an image file, the *Form_Current* event procedure doesn't need a path specification for the image filenames. Aside from this minor distinction (based on the *Pic_address* column values and the name of the column containing image filenames), the *Form_Current* event for the *Employees* photos and the *Pic_Addresses* table are identical. The script for the form showing images from the *Pic_Addresses* table appears next:

```
Private Sub Form_Current()

'If the image exists, assign the Pic_address value
'to the pic_image's Picture property. Otherwise, make
'pic_image invisible.
If IsNull(Me.Pic_address) Then
    Me.pic_image.Visible = False
Else
    Me.pic_image.Picture = Me.Pic_address
    Me.pic_image.Visible = True
End If

End Sub
```

Figure 15-6 shows the *frmPic_Addresses* form during the transition from the first to the second record. This dialog box alerts you to the fact that the .jpg file is being imported. The *PictureID* value points at the second record. However, the image is still importing, and the navigator control at the bottom of the screen hasn't updated for the second record yet. Notice that it still points at the first record. While the dialog box appears for just an instant, you do notice it.

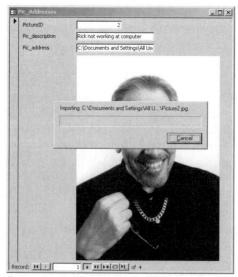

Figure 15-6 Importing a .jpg file into an Image control on a form.

> **Note**   The Image control prompts an importing dialog box when it loads a .jpg file. I've never discovered a way to present .jpg image files that suppresses this dialog box. In any event, this dialog box appears very briefly, so it's not a major distraction. Moreover, it doesn't appear for bitmap images.

Creating Unbound Combo Boxes on Forms

Creating an unbound combo box on a form is a very popular technique for controlling the flow of an application. Users make a selection from a combo box to launch a second form. When the list of values for a combo box is very large, your application can use multiple combo boxes so that users pick from two or more combo boxes to control the flow of an application. Replacing a single combo box with two combo boxes can speed the operation of an application by avoiding a long wait for a single combo box to display a list.

This section illustrates several different approaches to working with unbound combo boxes. An unbound combo box shows the values from a field in a record source, but it doesn't enter values into that field when users make selections from the control. The section initially revisits using the Combo Box Wizard with SQL Server. Being able to use such a lowly tool with a database as advanced as SQL Server is a major breakthrough. This capability minimizes the complexity of building solutions based on an advanced database manager such as SQL Server. This section also illustrates multiple ways to build combo box solutions with code, including writing a procedure that actually creates an event procedure.

Using the Combo Box Wizard with SQL Server

You can invoke the Combo Box Wizard from a blank form in Design view. Open the Toolbox, and select the Control Wizards button. Recall that you can show the name for a control in the Toolbox, on toolbars, and elsewhere by holding the cursor over the control. Next click the Combo Box control in the Toolbox, and then click on a central area on the blank form. The Combo Box Wizard dialog box opens. The features of this dialog box are mostly identical to those in the dialog box for Access database files. Make the selections for a combo box that shows the *CategoryName* but saves the *CategoryID* column values from the *Categories* table. Instead of having a check box to hide the first column with *CategoryID*, you must drag the column width to an extent of zero to hide the column. See Figure 15-7 for an illustration of this process.

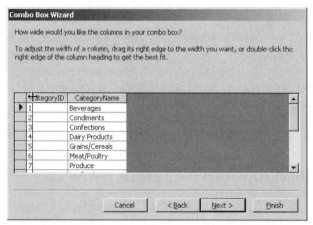

Figure 15-7 Collapsing the first column to hide it with a combo box list, even while the combo box binds to the column value after a selection.

After using the Combo Box Wizard as just described, you'll have a form that resembles Form1, contained in the Access project for this chapter. Figure 15-8 shows the sample combo box created by this process. While the combo box allows you to select items from a list, nothing happens after you do so. To enable some action based on a selection from the combo box, you need an *AfterUpdate* event procedure. In this section, I'll describe a couple of approaches to building this type of event procedure, and I'll show the event procedure performing a couple of different tasks.

Figure 15-8 A combo box created with the Combo Box Wizard against a SQL Server database that shows *CategoryNames* but saves the corresponding *CategoryID*.

Programming a Combo Box with an Event Procedure

Programming a combo box with an event procedure on a form involves three steps. First, you create the form. Second, you add the combo box control to the form. Third, you program the addition of an event procedure for the combo box.

The next VBA sample contains three procedures for programmatically creating a blank form with a designated name. The main routine, *CreatefrmForCbo*, calls the other two procedures. The first called procedure drops a prior version of the form, if it exists. The second called procedure creates the new form and assigns it a specific name. Before calling either of the other procedures, the main routine assigns a string variable the name *frmName*, which will be the name of the new form.

The *Drop_a_form* procedure loops through the *AllForms* collection. If the procedure finds a form that has the name created by the sample, it attempts to delete the form from the Access Database window by using the *DeleteObject* method for the *DoCmd* object. Before invoking the method, the procedure closes the form. This step is necessary because Access cannot delete an open form. If the form is already closed, Access ignores the request to close it.

The *Create_a_form* procedure adds a form to the application based on the default template. The *CreateForm* method accomplishes this task but doesn't offer a way to assign a name to the form. Therefore, the procedure saves the default name and closes the form to save it. Next the procedure selects the form with the default name in the Database window and renames the form with the value of the string saved in *frmName*. In this instance, the new form assumes the name *frmForCbo*.

```
Sub CreatefrmForCbo()
Dim frmName As String

'Create a form for programmatically specified
'combo box
frmName = "frmForCbo"
Drop_a_form frmName
Create_a_form frmName

End Sub



Sub Drop_a_form(frmName As String)
Dim obj1 As AccessObject

'If form exists, close it and delete it
For Each obj1 In CurrentProject.AllForms
    If obj1.Name = frmName Then
        DoCmd.Close acForm, obj1.Name
        DoCmd.DeleteObject acForm, obj1.Name
    End If
Next obj1

End Sub
```

(continued)

```
Sub Create_a_form(frmName As String)
Dim frm1 As Form
Dim str1 As String

'Create form and close it with a default name
Set frm1 = CreateForm
str1 = frm1.Name
DoCmd.Close acForm, str1, acSaveYes

'Change from default (str1) to custom name (frmName)
DoCmd.SelectObject acForm, str1, True
DoCmd.Rename frmName, acForm, str1

End Sub
```

The next step is to add a combo box to the programmatically created form. The two procedures in the next sample illustrate this. The first procedure simply passes a name to the second procedure. Then the second procedure uses the name to open a form to which it will add a combo box. If the code is passed the name of a form with controls that already exist, the procedure removes each control on the form by invoking the *DeleteControl* method.

When the procedure finishes looping through any existing controls on the form, it invokes the *CreateControl* method to add a new combo box to the form named by the value *frmName*. After adding the combo box control, the procedure makes two types of settings for the combo box. The first pair of settings positions the combo box on the form. The settings for the control's *Left* and *Top* properties are offsets in twips from the form's left and top borders. The next five settings for the combo box control specify a combo box that shows *CategoryName* but saves *CategoryID* from the *Categories* table. Once the combo box settings are complete, the procedure saves the changes to the form. Just before closing, the procedure asks whether the user wants to show the form. Because the procedure can add a control to a form in Design view only, this final prompt gives Access an opportunity to reopen the form in Normal view if the user wants to preview the form with its new combo box control.

```
Sub CallAddUnboundCboToForm()
Dim frmName As String

'Call a procedure to add a combo box to form
frmName = "frmForCbo"
AddUnboundCboToForm frmName

End Sub
```

```
Sub AddUnboundCboToForm(frmName As String)
Dim frm1 As Form
Dim ctl1 As Control
Dim cbo1 As ComboBox

'Open the form in Design view
DoCmd.OpenForm frmName, acDesign
Set frm1 = Forms(frmName)

'Remove all controls from the form
For Each ctl1 In Forms(frmName).Controls
    DeleteControl frmName, ctl1.Name
Next ctl1

'Add a new combo box
Set cbo1 = CreateControl(frmName, acComboBox)
cbo1.Left = 2880
cbo1.Top = 720

'Assign combo box settings
cbo1.RowSourceType = "Table/View/StoredProc"
cbo1.RowSource = _
    "SELECT CategoryID, CategoryName FROM Categories"
cbo1.ColumnCount = 2
cbo1.ColumnWidths = "0,2"
cbo1.BoundColumn = 1

'Save settings
DoCmd.Close acForm, frm1.Name, acSaveYes

If MsgBox("Do you want to show form?", _
    vbYesNo, _
    "Programming Microsoft Access Version 2002") = vbYes Then
    DoCmd.OpenForm frmName
End If

End Sub
```

The last step is to add an event procedure to the combo box programmatically. The next sample illustrates one direct way to accomplish this. Again, the first procedure just passes a form name to the second procedure, which programs the event procedure for a combo box on the form.

The second procedure in this sample starts by opening the form with the name passed to it. Next the procedure clears any lines of code in the module behind the form. Then it searches through the controls on the form for a combo box. Actually, it searches for all the combo boxes on the form, but because the form has just one combo box, the set of all combo boxes contains just that one combo box. When the procedure finds the combo box, it invokes the *CreateEvent-Proc* method to add an *AfterUpdate* event procedure to the combo box. This method takes two arguments. One is a string that names the type of event procedure. The second argument is another string that represents the name of the control to which you'll add the event procedure. The *InsertLines* method for a module object writes the code to the module behind the control's form. The procedure's first line creates a string that denotes a filter for opening a form based on the selected item in the combo box. The procedure's second line specifies the opening of the *frmProducts* form and references the filter from the first line. This event procedure programs the *frmProducts* form to display only products from the category selected in the combo box.

The second procedure concludes by opening the form with the combo box so that you can try out the application. Switch from the Code window to the Access application environment so that you can use the combo box to open the *frmProducts* table for a single category of products. Here's the syntax for the procedures just described:

```
Sub CallAddAfterUpdateEvent()
Dim frmName As String

'Call a procedure to add an AfterUpdate event procedure
'to a combo box
frmName = "frmForCbo"
AddAfterUpdateEventToCbo frmName

End Sub


Sub AddAfterUpdateEventToCbo(frmName As String)
Dim frm1 As Form
Dim cbo1 As ComboBox
Dim ctl1 As Control
Dim mdl1 As Module
Dim str1 As String

'Open the form in Design view
DoCmd.OpenForm frmName, acDesign
Set frm1 = Forms(frmName)

'Set reference to module for form, and delete
'all previously existing procedures
Set mdl1 = frm1.Module
mdl1.DeleteLines 1, mdl1.CountOfLines
```

```
'Add event procedure to open frmProducts for the
'category selected in the combo box; loop through form
'controls to find combo box
For Each ctl1 In frm1.Controls
    If TypeOf ctl1 Is ComboBox Then
        lngReturn = mdl1.CreateEventProc("AfterUpdate", ctl1.Name)
        mdl1.InsertLines lngReturn + 2, _
        "str1 = " & _
        """CategoryID = """ & " & Cstr(" & ctl1.Name & ".Value)"
        mdl1.InsertLines lngReturn + 3, _
         "DoCmd.OpenForm ""frmProducts"", , , str1" & vbCr
    End If
Next ctl1

'Save settings and reopen form in Normal view
DoCmd.Close acForm, frm1.Name, acSaveYes
DoCmd.OpenForm frmName

End Sub
```

This sample writes the *AfterUpdate* event procedure listed next for the combo box named Combo3. The procedure that writes the event procedure never actually searches for a control with this specific name. It merely searches for combo boxes. If you want to update a specific combo box, you can reference its name as well as the type of the control inside the loop within the procedure that writes the event procedure. Notice that the completed event procedure has two lines. Compare their construction with that of the sample that writes them, to see the string syntax rules for constructing event procedures programmatically.

```
Private Sub Combo3_AfterUpdate()

str1 = "CategoryID = " & CStr(Combo3.Value)
DoCmd.OpenForm "frmProducts", , , str1

End Sub
```

Programming Conditional Combo Boxes

Instead of opening a form based directly on a combo box selection, you sometimes will want to base a form (either directly or indirectly) on two or more combo box selections. The sample in this section shows how to generate the list for a second combo box depending upon the selection made in an initial combo box. Only the selection from the second combo box is directly used to open the form.

The *frmTwoCboOpenForm* form in the sample Access project for this chapter contains a couple of combo boxes. The first combo box lets a user pick from a list of category names. The list for the second combo box shows products just

867

for the category selected in first combo box. After a user selects a product from the second combo box, *frmTwoCboOpenForm* opens *frmProducts* for the specific product selected. Figure 15-9 shows how the combo boxes and forms work together. In the figure, the user initially picks the Confections category from the first combo box. This sets the source for the second combo box to show only products in the Confections category. If a user chooses Chocolade in the second combo box on *frmTwoCboOpenForm*, *frmProducts* will open and display detailed product data for Chocolade. The caption for *frmProducts* is Products.

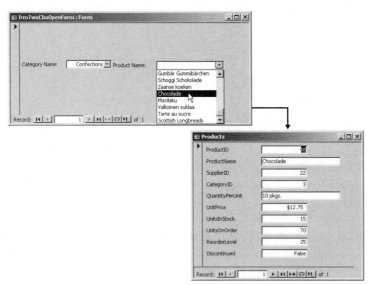

Figure 15-9 A combo box that's conditional upon another and opens a second form.

To make the *frmProducts* form show another product, close the form by clicking its top right Close control. Then make new selections from first and second combo boxes on *frmTwoCboOpenForm*. Making a selection from the first combo box is optional. If you do make a new selection in the first combo box, it will alter the selection list for the second combo box. After making a selection from the second combo box, *frmProducts* will reopen to the new product selection for the second box.

I created this sample by adding two combo boxes to a form (without using the Combo Box Wizard). In fact, the second combo box is just a duplicate of the first one. You can create such a copy with the Edit-Duplicate command from the form Design view menu bar. Figure 15-10 shows the combo boxes in Design view. Because you're just creating one combo box and then duplicating it, this design is quick to set up manually. The code behind the form does all the formatting and makes all the data assignments for the combo boxes.

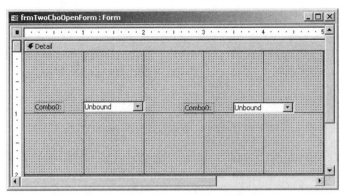

Figure 15-10 Design view of the *frmTwoCboOpenForm* form.

Aside from adding the combo boxes and positioning them in the style of those shown in Figure 15-10, the sample depicted in Figure 15-9 requires one more manual setup step: assigning names to the combo boxes and their labels. Use the Name property setting on a control's Properties dialog box to assign the control a name. The names for the first label and combo box are *lblCategoryName* and *cboCategoryName*, respectively. The names for the second label and its combo box are *lblProductName* and *cboProductName*.

The following three event procedures drive the application. The *Form_Open* event procedure formats the two combo boxes and makes the data assignments for the first combo box, which displays the list of categories. Recall that this combo box displays values from the *CategoryName* column in the *Categories* table but saves values from the *CategoryID* column. The code for this in the *Form_Open* event procedure relieves a developer from having to use the Combo Box Wizard to add the control. It also eliminates the need to manually make assignments in the combo box's Properties dialog box to control its selection list.

Formatting the combo boxes might be the most novel feature of the *Form_ Open* event procedure. This is because of the way the code positions controls in relation to one another. In addition, this event procedure uses an assortment of combo box and label control properties. The procedure positions the label control for the first combo box 60 twips from the form's left border. It also assigns a width and caption for the label. Next the procedure arranges the first combo box so that its left border begins where its label ends. After setting the selection for the first combo box, the procedure positions the label for the second combo box. This label starts 40 twips to the right of where the first combo box ends. The label control width for the second combo box matches that of the first combo box. The second combo box itself has a wider width than any of the other three controls, but it begins where its label ends. After setting the position of the second combo box, the procedure concludes by clearing the combo box.

```
Private Sub Form_Open(Cancel As Integer)
Dim ctl1 As Control
Dim cbo1 As ComboBox

'Position CategoryName label 60 twips from form's
'left border and 1 inch (1440 twips) wide
Set ctl1 = Me.lblCategoryName
ctl1.Left = 60
ctl1.Width = 1440
ctl1.Caption = "Category Name:"

'Set CategoryName combo box to start where text box ends,
'and set combo box's width to 1 inch (1440 twips)
Set ctl1 = Me.cboCategoryName
ctl1.Left = 60 + Me.lblCategoryName.Left + _
    ctl1.Width

'Assign data/display settings for CategoryName combo box
ctl1.RowSourceType = "Table/View/StoredProc"
ctl1.RowSource = _
    "SELECT CategoryID, CategoryName FROM Categories"
ctl1.ColumnCount = 2
ctl1.ColumnWidths = "0,2"
ctl1.BoundColumn = 1

'Position ProductName label 40 twips from right edge of
'cboCategoryName and make 1 inch (1440 twips) wide
Set ctl1 = Me.lblProductName
ctl1.Left = Me.cboCategoryName.Left + _
    Me.cboCategoryName.Width + 40
ctl1.Width = Me.lblCategoryName.Width
ctl1.Caption = "Product Name:"

'Set ProductName combo box to start where text box ends,
'and lengthen combo box to 1.5 inches (2160 twips)
Set ctl1 = Me.cboProductName
ctl1.Width = 2160
ctl1.Left = Me.lblProductName.Left + Me.lblProductName.Width
ctl1.Value = ""

End Sub
```

While the *Form_Open* event procedure configures the layout of controls and the contents of the selection list for the first combo box, the two *AfterUpdate* event procedures make the form responsive to user input. Making a selection from the *cboCategoryName* combo box assigns an SQL string as the *RowSource* property to the *cboProductName* combo box. The *cboCateoryName_AfterUpdate* event procedure enables this as well as other actions. The SQL string for the *cboProduct-*

Name RowSource property relies on the value in the *cboCateogoryName* combo box to filter the product names that appear in the *cboProductName* combo box. Other assignments in the *cboCategoryName_AfterUpdate* event procedure enable the *cboProductName* control to show *ProductName* column values but save *ProductID* column values.

```
Private Sub cboCategoryName_AfterUpdate()
Dim ctl1 As Control

'Assign data/display settings for ProductName combo box
'based on CategoryName combo box selection
Set ctl1 = Me.cboProductName
ctl1.RowSourceType = "Table/View/StoredProc"
ctl1.RowSource = _
    "SELECT ProductID, ProductName FROM Products " & _
    "WHERE CategoryID = " & Me.cboCategoryName
ctl1.ColumnCount = 2
ctl1.ColumnWidths = "0,2"
ctl1.BoundColumn = 1

End Sub
```

The *cboProductName_AfterUpdate* event procedure is very simple. It creates a string for identifying a single product that appears in the *frmProducts* form. This string depends on the value a user selects from the *cboProductName* list. The event procedure uses that string as an argument for the *OpenForm* method to show the *frmProducts* form with the selected item from the *cboProductName* list.

```
Private Sub cboProductName_AfterUpdate()
Dim str1 As String

'Open frmProducts based on cboProductName selection
str1 = "ProductID = " & Me.cboProductName
DoCmd.OpenForm "frmProducts", , , str1

End Sub
```

SQL Server Form Issues

As noted earlier, one of the great strengths of Access projects is that you can program them in a way that's very similar to programming Access database files. Therefore, many of the topics covered in Chapter 6 apply to the use of forms in Access projects. However, some issues are unique to Access projects. (This section considers two of these issues—see the first two subsection titles.) In addition, while not solely applicable to Access projects, some other topics are more salient for them. Server filters, which we'll discuss in this section, is such a subject.

Specifying a Form's *RecordsetType* Property in Access Projects

Forms have a *RecordsetType* property in both Access projects and Access database files, but the settings for this property—along with the capabilities they provide—differ between the two kinds of files. Access projects offer two settings for a form's *RecordsetType* property. The default setting is an updatable snapshot. This setting allows a user to edit all fields bound to any table. You can programmatically assign this setting with a value of *4*. A form's *RecordsetType* property settings do not belong to an enum class. Therefore, you have to use a numeric constant. When your applications call for read-only access to data, you can use the snapshot setting, which has a numeric value of *3*. With this setting, users can use a form to browse data, but they cannot edit it. In addition, they cannot add or delete records from the record source for a form.

The following procedure illustrates the syntax for working with a form's *RecordsetType* property. Although you can run the procedure automatically and have it provide feedback, I urge you to step through the code. This will give you a better feel for the performance of the *RecordsetType* settings.

The procedure has a compiler flag that simplifies working with the *frmOrder-Details* form in two ways. When you run the *ReadWriteOrReadOnly* procedure using a value of True for the *ReadOnly* compiler constant, as in the following code listing, the procedure assigns a snapshot setting to the form. This makes it impossible to update the *Order Details* table through the form. If you change the *ReadOnly* compiler constant to False, the form opens with an updatable snapshot setting for its *RecordsetType* property. This enables users to manually modify the *Orders Details* table through the *frmOrderDetails* form.

The procedure simulates a manual update of the data through the form by attempting to modify the *Quantity* field on the form's first record. If the form has an updatable snapshot setting, the update succeeds. Otherwise, the initial attempt to update the form fails. However, the procedure asks the user whether she is sure she wants to edit the quantity. When the user responds yes, the procedure resets the *RecordsetType* property so that the form provides read-write access to its data. Then the procedure tries again.

The following procedure begins by opening the *frmOrderDetails* form. Then it sets the form's *RecordsetType* property to *conReadOnly*. A *Const* declaration assigns a value of *3* to *conReadOnly*. This is the *RecordsetType* setting for a snapshot that does not permit updates, additions, or deletions from a form's record source. Then the sample multiplies the value of the *Quantity* field by 100 and stores the result in the text box. Next the code invokes the form's *Refresh* method, updating the database on the server with the value in the form's *Quantity* text box. After updating the server, the procedure ends with an *Exit Sub* statement.

If you run the sample with the code listing's value for the *ReadOnly* compiler constant, it won't take the main path through the program. Instead, when the procedure attempts to write over the *Quantity* value in the text box, it will generate error number −2147352567. The procedure traps this error and prompts the user, asking whether he's sure about wanting to edit the value. If the user responds yes, the procedure resets the form's *RecordsetType* property to *conReadWrite*, which has a numeric value of *4*. This setting permits the procedure to succeed at updating the record source behind the form.

If you run this procedure a second time without restoring the *Quantity* field for the first record to its initial value (or some other relatively small value), you can generate an overflow. This is easy to do because *Quantity* has a Smallint data type with a maximum value of 32,767 and the expression for revising the value of *Quantity* multiplies it by 100. The procedure traps this overflow error and prints a message to remind the user that one common cause of this error is failing to reset the value of *Quantity* for the first record to its initial value of *12*. The procedure leaves the reset process to the user. However, it does offer another procedure for accomplishing this process automatically.

```
'Step through this procedure to see the flow and understand
'its logic
Sub ReadWriteOrReadOnly()
On Error GoTo ReadWrite_Trap

Dim frm1 As Form
Dim int1 As Integer
Const conReadOnly = 3
Const conReadWrite = 4
#Const ReadOnly = True

'Open frmOrderDetails, set reference to it, and
'assign ReadOnly setting to RecordsetType property
DoCmd.OpenForm "frmOrderDetails"
Set frm1 = Forms("frmOrderDetails")
#If ReadOnly = True Then
    frm1.RecordsetType = conReadOnly
#Else
    frm1.RecordsetType = conReadWrite
#End If

'Multiply the value of Quantity for the first record by 100,
'and refresh value on server
int1 = frm1.Quantity
frm1.Quantity = 100 * int1
frm1.Refresh
```

(continued)

```
'Close form and exit sub
ReadWrite_Exit:
DoCmd.Close acForm, frm1.Name
Exit Sub

ReadWrite_Trap:
If Err.Number = -2147352567 And frm1.RecordsetType = conReadOnly Then
'If data is not updatable and RecordsetType is ReadOnly,
'offer option to change setting
    If MsgBox("Are you sure you want to edit quantity?", _
        vbYesNo, _
        "Programming Microsoft Access Version 2002") = vbYes Then
        frm1.RecordsetType = conReadWrite
        Resume
    Else
        Resume ReadWrite_Exit
    End If
ElseIf Err.Number = 6 Then
'If it is an overflow error, you might be able to recover
'by restoring Quantity to its initial value
    MsgBox "Quantity may exceed its limit; " & _
        "its current value is " & frm1.Quantity & ".  " & _
        "Consider running RestoreFirstQuantityTo12", _
        vbInformation, _
        "Programming Microsoft Access Version 2002"
Else
    Debug.Print Err.Number; Err.Description
End If

End Sub
```

If a user runs this procedure with a *ReadOnly* compiler constant of True but doesn't accept the option to revise the value of the *Quantity* field, the sample leaves the *RecordsetType* property equal to *conReadOnly*. This complicates working with the form because you cannot update its data manually without first resetting the *RecordsetType* property to an updatable snapshot. This is especially important when your application requires you to update form field values, such as when you want to restore the value of *Quantity* in the first record. The following code sample illustrates this process of attempting to restore the *Quantity* field in the first record to its initial value of *12*.

If the *ReadWriteOrReadOnly* procedure leaves the form in a read-write state, the procedure simply restores the form's *Quantity* field and writes the value back to the server. However, if the previous procedure or another technique leaves the value of the form's *RecordsetType* property equal to a snapshot, the procedure prevents the resulting error from trying to revise the value of *Quantity* for the first record. Then the procedure resets the *RecordsetType* property to an updatable snapshot before resuming the attempt to revise field's value to *12*.

```
Sub RestoreFirstQuantityTo12()
On Error GoTo RestoreFirstQuantity_Trap
Dim frm1 As Form
Const conReadOnly = 3
Const conReadWrite = 4

'Open frmOrderDetails, set reference to it, and
'assign ReadOnly setting to RecordsetType property
DoCmd.OpenForm "frmOrderDetails"
Set frm1 = Forms("frmOrderDetails")

'Restore Quantity with saved value
frm1.Quantity = 12
frm1.Refresh

'Close form
DoCmd.Close acForm, frm1.Name

RestoreFirstQuantity_Exit:
Exit Sub

RestoreFirstQuantity_Trap:
If Err.Number = -2147352567 And frm1.RecordsetType = conReadOnly Then
'If data is not updatable and RecordsetType is ReadOnly,
'offer option to change setting
    If MsgBox("Are you sure you want to restore quantity to 12?", _
        vbYesNo, _
        "Programming Microsoft Access Version 2002") = vbYes Then
        frm1.RecordsetType = conReadWrite
        Resume
    End If
Else
    Debug.Print Err.Number, Err.Description
End If

End Sub
```

Processing Hyperlinks in an Access Project Form

Access database files permit a Hyperlink data type that embraces and extends the standard hyperlinks found on Web pages. Recall from Chapter 6 that the Hyperlink data type permits you to navigate from Access to Web pages on a local intranet or the Internet. Additionally, applications can use hyperlinks to let users navigate between database objects in the current database file, another Access database file, or any Office document file. A hyperlink data value can also open the e-mail package on a workstation with a specified recipient and subject.

Access projects do not offer a Hyperlink data type. This is because SQL Server does not directly support such a data type. However, Access projects do permit the setting of an *IsHyperlink* property for form fields in text box and combo box controls. When the value of this property is True, Access interprets the value in a control as though it were a hyperlink. When the *IsHyperlink* property is False, the control's contents appear as a normal text field.

Recall that a Hyperlink data type can have up to four segments. The pound sign (#) delimits the segments (or elements) from one another within a field. The first segment is the text that a hyperlink displays. By default, a hyperlink field displays the combination of its second and third segments, but you can override this setting with a text label for the first segment. The second and third elements of a hyperlink value designate the destination to which the link navigates. These two elements can take on different meanings depending on the type of destination. The links that appear in the next sample illustrate the broad range of possibilities. The final hyperlink segment represents the text that appears when the cursor hovers over a link. (Search Access Help for "About Hyperlinks" for more in-depth coverage of hyperlink parts, and see Chapter 6 for a couple of practical uses for hyperlinks within Access applications.)

Before you can use hyperlinks in an Access project, you need a table of hyperlink values. The following code sample demonstrates one approach to creating such a table. The sample also includes the *Drop_a_table* procedure. This short procedure initially appeared in Chapter 14. The following sample repeats the listing so that you have it readily available as you move through the other samples in this chapter. This sample starts by referencing the current project with a *Connection* object and then drops any prior version of the *Links* table.

This *Links* table stores the hyperlinks that the sample creates. After dropping an earlier version of the table, the code creates a new table that has four columns. The first of these is an *autonumber* field that serves as the table's primary key. The second column holds a descriptive name for the field. This serves the same purpose as the first hyperlink element, but it's not a physical part of the hyperlink. The third column contains the actual hyperlink data value. This field is 128 characters long, which is sufficient for the sample data. Keep in mind, however, that each hyperlink segment can contain up to 2000 characters. The fourth column designates the purposes of the hyperlink—for example, to open a Web page, an e-mail message, or a database object. This column is limited to six characters.

The sample procedure concludes by exercising the INSERT INTO statement five times. Each instance of the INSERT INTO statement adds another link to the

Links table. The first link in the table illustrates the format for specifying a hyper-link to a Web page. This link assigns ProgrammingMSAccess.com as the display text that appears when a user navigates to www.programmingmsaccess.com. The second link starts the e-mail package on a workstation. This link specifies my e-mail address and a subject line of "Your book is great!" (Feel free to use this link to send me messages with feedback about the book or suggestions for ways that I can improve it in future editions.) The third link indicates the format of a hyperlink that points at the *Links* table in the current project. The fourth link points at the *Employees* table in the Northwind.mdb file. This link specifies the default location for the file. The final hyperlink navigates to a bookmark on a Web page. A bookmark is a reference location on a page. In this instance, the bookmark points to descriptive materials for the prior edition of this book.

```
Sub CreateLinksTable()
Dim str1 As String
Dim cnn1 As ADODB.Connection
Dim TableName As String

'Point a Connection object at the current project
Set cnn1 = CurrentProject.Connection

'Delete the table if it exists already
TableName = "Links"
Drop_a_table cnn1, TableName

'Create the table
str1 = "CREATE TABLE " & TableName & " " & _
    "( " & _
    "LinkID int IDENTITY (1, 1) NOT NULL PRIMARY KEY CLUSTERED, " & _
    "LinkName varchar(96) NULL , " & _
    "LinkURL varchar(128) NOT NULL , " & _
    "LinkType varchar(6) NULL " & _
    ")"
cnn1.Execute str1

str1 = "INSERT INTO " & TableName & " " & _
    "VALUES('Link to Page', " & _
        "'ProgrammingMSAccess.com#" & _
        "http://www.programmingmsaccess.com', " & _
        "'page') " & _
    "INSERT INTO " & TableName & " " & _
    "VALUES('Start email for praise', " & _
        "'Link for email#mailto:rickd@cabinc.net" & _
        "?subject=Your book is great!#', " & _
        "'email') " & _
```

(continued)

```
            "INSERT INTO " & TableName & " " & _
            "VALUES('Link for table in current project', " & _
                "'Links##Table Links', " & _
                "'object') " & _
            "INSERT INTO " & TableName & " " & _
            "VALUES('Link to table in a database file', " & _
                "'Link to Access database file table#" & _
                "../../../../Program Files/Microsoft Office/" & _
                "Office10/Samples/Northwind.mdb#Table Employees', " & _
                "'object') " & _
            "INSERT INTO " & TableName & " " & _
            "VALUES('Link for bookmark on web page', " & _
                "'Bookmark link" & _
                "#http://www.programmingmsaccess.com/thebook/" & _
                "#PMA2K', 'page') "
    cnn1.Execute str1

    'Refresh Database window to show new table
    RefreshDatabaseWindow

End Sub


Sub Drop_a_table(cnn1 As ADODB.Connection, TableName As String)

    'Delete the table if it exists already
    str1 = "IF EXISTS (SELECT TABLE_NAME " & _
        "FROM INFORMATION_SCHEMA.TABLES " & _
        "WHERE TABLE_NAME = '" & TableName & "') " & _
        "DROP TABLE " & TableName
    cnn1.Execute str1

End Sub
```

Figure 15-11 shows an excerpt from the *Links* table that contains the five column values in the third column. Recall that this column holds the actual hyperlink data values. Use these sample hyperlinks to gain an appreciation of the various formatting options offered by the Access Hyperlink data type. Also, notice that the links in this table are not active. This is because SQL Server has no Hyperlink data type. SQL Server tables can hold hyperlink data, but they can't interpret its segments. Therefore, Access displays the values in the third column of the *Links* table as text values.

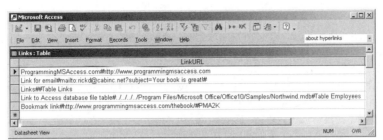

Figure 15-11 Column values containing hyperlink data from the *CreateLinksTable* procedure.

Figure 15-12 shows the *frmLinks* table that you can create with the AutoForm Wizard for the *Links* table. The most obvious feature is that the *LinkURL* field appears as a hyperlink. Unlike the third column in the *Links* table, the *LinkURL* field on the form is an active hyperlink (meaning users can activate the link by clicking it). To activate the table's links, you can set the LinkURL control's *IsHyperlink* property to True in VBA, or you can select Yes from the control's Properties dialog box for its Is Hyperlink property. If you don't perform either of these steps, the form displays the *LinkURL* column values as ordinary text rather than as functioning links.

Figure 15-12 The *frmLinks* form that displays values from the *Links* table.

Programming Form Server Filters

Server filters operate at the database server, independently of the traditional form *Filter* property and the ActiveX Data Objects (ADO) recordset *Filter* property. In addition, the programming interface is different for all three of these filtering techniques. A server filter also operates differently than the WHERE clause syntax for the *OpenForm* method. Recall that the WHERE clause syntax for the *Open-Form* method lets you determine the records available to a form when it loads. The other filter methods allow an application to dynamically change the filtered records after the form loads.

Unlike a traditional filter, which operates on a form's local data cache, a server filter operates at the server. With a server filter, your applications can speed up performance by downloading smaller record sources for a form. When users finish working with a subset of a larger record source, they can filter for a new subset from the larger source. Server filters for forms apply to bound forms. This makes a server filter easier to use than the ADO *Filter* property, which applies to an ADO recordset rather than a form. Unlike the ADO *Filter* property, a server filter can accept SQL strings that reference multiple fields.

Figure 15-13 presents a sample form that we'll use to examine programming techniques for the form's server filter property. One good way to familiarize yourself with the flexibility provided by the server filter is to use this form. The name of the sample form is *frmvwEmployeesOrderDetails*, and you'll find it in the Access project for this chapter. The record source for this sample form is the vwEmployeesOrderDetails view. The view merely links the *Employees* table to the *Order Details* table and then selects a subset of the columns from both tables. The form always opens without any filters. The sample in Figure 15-13 shows a total of 2155 records in the record source for the form. You can elect to filter by the employee last name, the discount for an order, or both. Any filtering reduces the form record count to those records that satisfy the filter.

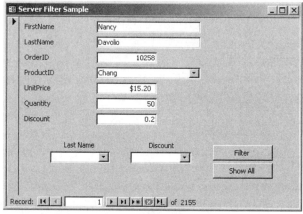

Figure 15-13 A sample form in the chapter's Access project that demonstrates how to program the *ServerFilter* property.

You can launch filtering by making selections from one or both combo boxes at the bottom of the form and clicking the command button with the caption Filter. When the form opens, the combo boxes show all employees and all discount percents. After a user selects an employee from the Last Name combo box, the other combo box shows just the discount percents for that employee. This prevents you from specifying a filter that returns no records. Clicking the command button labeled Show All clears any existing filters. The Show All button also clears both combo boxes and resets the combo box for discount percents so that it shows the discounts for all employees.

A server filter setting doesn't take effect until you refresh a form against the server. Recall that the filter operates at the server level. The invocation of the *Refresh* method makes a filter property operate. When you load a form that was closed with a filter in place, the filter setting persists. The sample form in Figure 15-13 addresses this behavior by clearing the server filter property setting when the form opens. This is a simple way to keep the filter setting controls synchronized with the server filter setting for the form.

The following set of event procedures shows the code controlling the form that appears in Figure 15-13. The *Form_Open* event procedure prepares the form for filtering. After setting the caption, the code clears any existing filter from a prior session by setting the form's *ServerFilter* property to a zero-length string and refreshing the form against the server. Next the procedure sets the *RowSource* property for the two combo boxes. These settings display all employees and all distinct discount percents. To maintain the integrity of the filter criteria settings, the procedure limits the combo boxes to the items in their row source specification. The *Form_Open* event concludes by clearing the two filter combo boxes. This brings the display in line with the *ServerFilter* property setting made at the top of the procedure.

```
Private Sub Form_Open(Cancel As Integer)
Dim str1 As String

'Assign form's caption
Me.Caption = "Server Filter Sample"

'Clear any filter from a prior session
Me.ServerFilter = ""
Me.Refresh

'Develop row source string for cboLastNames
'and assign it
str1 = "SELECT LastName " & _
    "FROM Employees "
Me.cboLastNames.RowSource = str1

'Develop row source string for cboDiscounts
'independent of cboLastNames and assign it
str1 = "SELECT DISTINCT Discount " & _
    "FROM vwEmployeesOrderDetails "
Me.cboDiscounts.RowSource = str1
```

(continued)

```
'Restrict combo boxes to list and clear them
Me.cboDiscounts.LimitToList = True
Me.cboLastNames.LimitToList = True
Me.cboDiscounts = Null
Me.cboLastNames = Null

End Sub
```

The *cboLastNames_AfterUpdate* event procedure revises the *RowSource* property setting for the combo box that shows discount percents. After a user selects an employee's last name, this event procedure restricts the selection list from the second combo box to just those discount percents that the selected employee offered on one or more occasions. The procedure also clears the combo box for showing discounts. This setting was relevant when the user previously filtered by discount percent.

```
Private Sub cboLastNames_AfterUpdate()
Dim str1

'Develop row source string for cboDiscounts
'and assign it
str1 = "SELECT DISTINCT Discount " & _
    "FROM vwEmployeesOrderDetails " & _
    "WHERE LastName = '" & cboLastNames & "'"
Me.cboDiscounts.RowSource = str1

'Clear prior setting from cboDiscounts
Me.cboDiscounts = ""

End Sub
```

The heart of the application is the *cmdFilter_Click* event procedure. This procedure reads the two combo box settings and assigns a value to the form's *ServerFilter* property based on the combo box values. The procedure closes by refreshing the form against the server to apply the *ServerFilter* property for the form. The procedure offers four possible paths for setting the *ServerFilter* property. The first applies to cases in which the Discount combo box has a selection but the Last Name combo box is blank. The second path is for the reverse scenario: a user selects an employee name but does not specify a discount amount. The third path uses both an employee last name and a discount percent to designate a filter. The final path clears the filter when both combo boxes are Null. This situation can occur when a user manually clears both boxes of their previous filter selections and clicks the Filter command button.

```
Private Sub cmdFilter_Click()
Dim str1 As String

'Set filter based on combo box settings
If IsNull(Me.cboLastNames) And _
    IsNull(Me.cboDiscounts) = False Then
    Me.ServerFilter = "Discount = " & cboDiscounts
ElseIf IsNull(Me.cboLastNames) = False And _
    IsNull(Me.cboDiscounts) Then
    Me.ServerFilter = "LastName = '" & cboLastNames & "'"
ElseIf IsNull(Me.cboLastNames) = False And _
    IsNull(Me.cboDiscounts) = False Then
    str1 = "LastName = '" & cboLastNames & "'"
    str1 = str1 & " AND Discount = " & cboDiscounts
    Me.ServerFilter = str1
ElseIf IsNull(Me.cboLastNames) And _
    IsNull(Me.cboDiscounts) Then
    Me.ServerFilter = ""
End If

'Apply the filter
Me.Refresh

End Sub
```

The *cmdRemoveFilter_Click* event procedure removes all existing filters. It also clears the combo boxes to synchronize them with the filter setting and resets the *RowSource* property setting for the combo box showing discount percents. The new setting shows discounts offered by any employee.

```
Private Sub cmdRemoveFilter_Click()

'Clear filter and combo boxes
Me.ServerFilter = ""
Me.Refresh

'Clear both combo boxes
Me.cboLastNames = Null
Me.cboDiscounts = Null

'Restore initial row source for cboDiscounts
str1 = "SELECT DISTINCT Discount " & _
    "FROM vwEmployeesOrderDetails "
Me.cboDiscounts.RowSource = str1

End Sub
```

Programming Reports in Access Projects

You can program reports in Access projects similarly to the way that you program reports in Access database files. In addition, nearly all the same wizards you know about from Access database files are available for building reports based on SQL Server database objects. While you aren't likely to find these reports suitable for creating a final, professional report, they're definitely a useful starting point for creating a custom report. Due to the extreme similarity between Access reports in Access database files and Access projects, I recommend you revisit Chapter 7, "Reports, Controls, and Data." That chapter demonstrates many useful techniques for generating reports for Access projects.

Both samples in this section cover interesting report topics. The first sample illustrates how to create a report that lets a user specify the sort key and sort direction at run time. The ability to set report features at run time is a topic that has wide appeal. The key to setting report features at run time is knowing the structure of reports and report objects. This sort sample demonstrates the use of two report properties. The second sample reveals how to set and restore input parameters for the record source behind a report. This sample fires a procedure to restore an *InputParameters* report property after a report closes. Firing a procedure after closing a report is necessary because you cannot modify a report's *InputParameters* property while it's open in Preview or Print modes. This solution comes in handy for any report application in which you need to restore report properties after a report finishes printing.

Sorting on Any Field in Any Direction

One of the many uses for reports in SQL Server applications is to sort the result set from views (and other database objects) at run time. Unless you specify a TOP clause in the SELECT statement for a SQL Server view, the view's statement will not support an ORDER BY clause. Even if you do anticipate this need and include the TOP clause, views from other developers might not be sorted. In other cases, views might be sorted, but not on the sort key or in the direction that you prefer.

The following sample shows how to dynamically control the sort order of a result set from a view when you show that result set in a report. Start with a tabular report for the view. If your view's columns fit nicely on one page, you can use the AutoReport: Tabular Wizard to create the report's layout. You can access this wizard by selecting Reports in the Objects bar on the Database window and clicking New. Then highlight AutoReport: Tabular, and select a view from the drop-down list below the report types in the New Report dialog box. Launch the creation of the report by clicking OK. This technique applies equally well to tables, row-returning stored procedures, and user-defined functions that can also serve as record sources for reports.

If the report's columns do not fit on a single page, choose the Report Wizard in the New Report dialog box. Choose as many columns as you need from the wizard's first screen, and then accept the defaults for the second and third screens by choosing Next. On the Report Wizard's fourth screen, clear the check box with the label that reads Adjust The Width So All Fields Fit On A Page. Then click Finish to create a tabular report that spreads the report's columns across multiple pages.

I created and saved a tabular report named rptvwEmployeesOrderDetails based on the vwEmployeesOrderDetails view. This view served as the source for the form sample in the preceding section and is available in the Access project for this chapter. The custom view displays columns from the *Employees* and *Order Details* tables. The column name qualifiers denote the table owners and table names. To merge fields from the *Employees* and *Order Details* tables, the SQL statement for the view requires the *Orders* table. The following T-SQL statement represents the view that serves as the source for the report:

```
SELECT dbo.Employees.FirstName, dbo.Employees.LastName,
dbo.[Order Details].OrderID, dbo.[Order Details].ProductID,
dbo.[Order Details].UnitPrice, dbo.[Order Details].Quantity,
dbo.[Order Details].Discount
FROM dbo.Employees INNER JOIN
dbo.Orders ON dbo.Employees.EmployeeID =
dbo.Orders.EmployeeID INNER JOIN
dbo.[Order Details] ON dbo.Orders.OrderID =
dbo.[Order Details].OrderID
```

The report sorts rows natively first by *EmployeeID*, second by *OrderID*, and third by *ProductID*. (See Figure 15-14.) This arrangement of records reflects the primary keys for the *Employees* and *Order Details* tables. However, sometimes you might prefer to show the output in another order.

The next sample, which is based on a pair of procedures, implements the core logic for dynamically assigning a sort on any field in a report's record source. In addition, the sample lets you sort in either ascending or descending order on any key. Before analyzing the code, you might find it useful to review how a report handles sorting programmatically. A *Report* object has two properties to facilitate sorting: *OrderBy* and *OrderByOn*. The *OrderBy* property is a string that represents the ORDER BY clause of an SQL statement without the ORDER BY keyword. Therefore, the *OrderBy* property should contain a string of field names, followed by an optional keyword designating the sort order on each key field. If you have more than one sort key, separate them by commas. By itself, setting a report's *OrderBy* property does not establish a sort order based. You must also set the *OrderByOn* property to True.

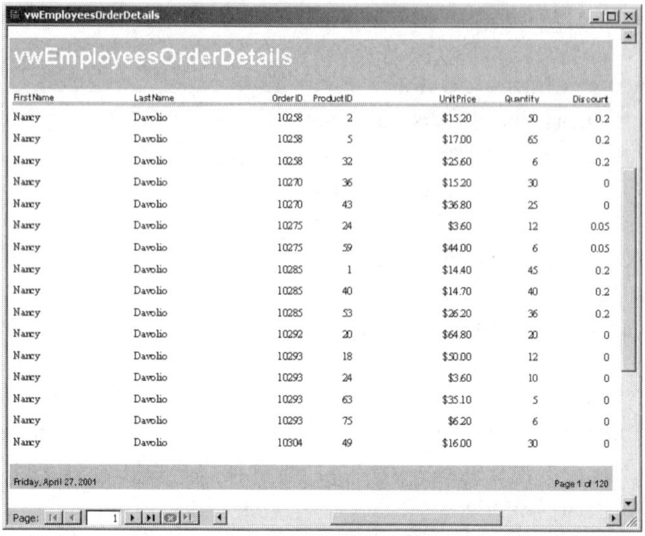
vwEmployeesOrderDetails

vwEmployeesOrderDetails

FirstName	LastName	Order ID	ProductID	UnitPrice	Quantity	Discount
Nancy	Davolio	10258	2	$15.20	50	0.2
Nancy	Davolio	10258	5	$17.00	65	0.2
Nancy	Davolio	10258	32	$25.60	6	0.2
Nancy	Davolio	10270	36	$15.20	30	0
Nancy	Davolio	10270	43	$36.80	25	0
Nancy	Davolio	10275	24	$3.60	12	0.05
Nancy	Davolio	10275	59	$44.00	6	0.05
Nancy	Davolio	10285	1	$14.40	45	0.2
Nancy	Davolio	10285	40	$14.70	40	0.2
Nancy	Davolio	10285	53	$26.20	36	0.2
Nancy	Davolio	10292	20	$64.80	20	0
Nancy	Davolio	10293	18	$50.00	12	0
Nancy	Davolio	10293	24	$3.60	10	0
Nancy	Davolio	10293	63	$35.10	5	0
Nancy	Davolio	10293	75	$6.20	6	0
Nancy	Davolio	10304	49	$16.00	30	0

Friday, April 27, 2001 Page 1 of 120

Page: 1

Figure 15-14 An excerpt from the rptvwEmployeesOrderDetails report. It shows the sort of *OrderID* and *ProductID* within *EmployeeID*.

Access permits you to set both the *OrderBy* and *OrderByOn* properties in Preview mode after a report is open. Settings made this way do not persist until the next time the report opens. This feature makes the properties ideal for dynamically assigning sort keys. Your property settings apply exclusively to the current Preview session for a report.

The following code listing represents one combination of settings for this sample's functionality. The first procedure allows a user to specify the report name and the field name on which to perform a sort. As an option, you can specify a third argument in the first procedure that designates either an ascending or a descending sort order. If you do specify a sort order argument, the application sorts in ascending order by default. This default assignment takes place in the second procedure. After setting the argument values, the first procedure passes them to the second procedure.

The second procedure accepts three arguments, but the last of these is preceded by the *Optional* keyword. This keyword applies to the *Asc* argument. This argument is a Boolean value for designating an ascending sort order. Its default value is True in its declarations for the second procedure. The sample listing doesn't designate a third argument, so the default value for *Asc* applies. You can designate a descending sort order by specifying a value of False for the third argument in the first procedure, which passes the arguments to the second procedure.

The second procedure begins by opening a report. The first argument passed to the second procedure names the report. After creating a reference to the report, the procedure starts an *If...Then...Else...End If* statement. The *Then* clause assigns the second argument as the value of the report's *OrderBy* property. This argument is the field name on which to perform the sort. Because the default order is ascending and there isn't any order specification, the *Then* clause assigns an ascending sort. The *Else* clause designates a descending sort order. Before closing, the procedure sets the report's *OrderByOn* property to True. This assignment activates the *OrderBy* property setting.

```
Sub CallSortReport()
Dim rptName As String
Dim fldName As String
Dim bolAsc As Boolean

'Specify sort name and sort field
rptName = "rptvwEmployeesOrderDetails"
fldName = "Discount"

'Pass arguments to procedure to
'prepare sorted report
SortReport rptName, fldName

End Sub


Sub SortReport(rptName As String, SortKey As String, _
    Optional Asc As Boolean = True)
Dim rpt1 As Report
Dim str1 As String

'Open the report
DoCmd.OpenReport rptName, acViewPreview
Set rpt1 = Reports(rptName)

'Sort in ascending or descending order on sort
'key according to optional argument value
If Asc = True Then
    rpt1.OrderBy = SortKey
Else
    str1 = SortKey & " DESC"
    rpt1.OrderBy = str1
End If

rpt1.OrderByOn = True

End Sub
```

Figure 15-15 shows an excerpt from the report. Notice that this excerpt sorts rows on the *Discount* value before the primary key settings for the view's source tables. Contrast this with the report excerpt in Figure 15-14 to see the effects of the sort. The primary key settings for the source still apply, but only after the sort specification in the sample code. By resetting the *Fieldname* argument, users can sort the report on any column containing numeric or string values in the view.

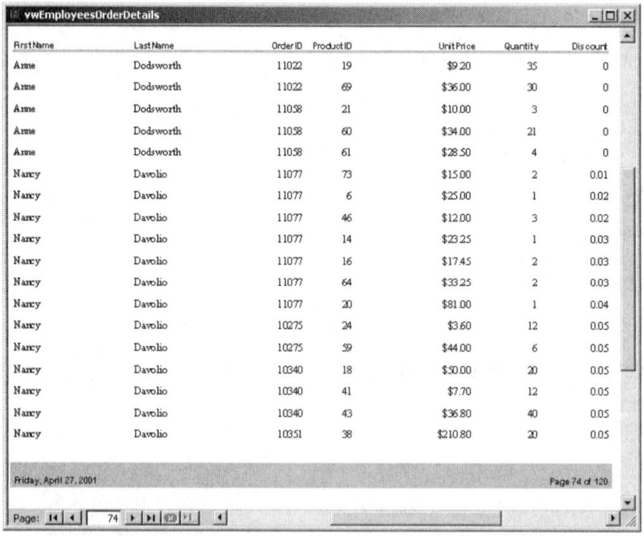

First Name	Last Name	Order ID	Product ID	Unit Price	Quantity	Discount
Anne	Dodsworth	11022	19	$9.20	35	0
Anne	Dodsworth	11022	69	$36.00	30	0
Anne	Dodsworth	11058	21	$10.00	3	0
Anne	Dodsworth	11058	60	$34.00	21	0
Anne	Dodsworth	11058	61	$28.50	4	0
Nancy	Davolio	11077	73	$15.00	2	0.01
Nancy	Davolio	11077	6	$25.00	1	0.02
Nancy	Davolio	11077	46	$12.00	3	0.02
Nancy	Davolio	11077	14	$23.25	1	0.03
Nancy	Davolio	11077	16	$17.45	2	0.03
Nancy	Davolio	11077	64	$33.25	2	0.03
Nancy	Davolio	11077	20	$81.00	1	0.04
Nancy	Davolio	10275	24	$3.60	12	0.05
Nancy	Davolio	10275	59	$44.00	6	0.05
Nancy	Davolio	10340	18	$50.00	20	0.05
Nancy	Davolio	10340	41	$7.70	12	0.05
Nancy	Davolio	10340	43	$36.80	40	0.05
Nancy	Davolio	10351	38	$210.80	20	0.05

Friday, April 27, 2001 — Page 74 of 120

Page: 74

Figure 15-15 An excerpt from the rptvwEmployeesOrderDetails report after sorting by the preceding code sample.

Setting and Restoring the *InputParameters* Property

Another typical run-time request is to make the record source for a report dynamic. Instead of just re-sorting the same records on different criteria, users might need to specify different subsets from a record source at run time. One way to do this is to define a stored procedure with parameters. For example, a user might want to view specifications for all cars in a given price range—for example, $20,000 to $30,000. Another user might want to examine the same specifications report but might need to see cars priced over $50,000. Database consultants often have to make the same report available to different users with different needs. This section shows you how to do this for your clients.

The sample in this section relies on a stored procedure named *Employee Sales by Country*. This procedure ships with the NorthwindCS database. It returns the sales amount for each order by employee and by the customer's country. Users can specify a start date and an end date that indicate the period for which the procedure should return this data.

The *Employee Sales by Country* stored procedure is available on the Access project for this chapter along with the view and tables that it references. The T-SQL script from an Access template for the stored procedure appears next. Note that it contains two parameters: *@Beginning_Date* and *@Ending_Date*. By setting these parameters just before calling the procedure, users can restrict the range of dates indicating when the stored procedure returns data. If you have a report based on the stored procedure, that report will display only data for the range specified by the *@Beginning_Date* and *@Ending_Date* parameters.

```
ALTER PROCEDURE dbo.[Employee Sales by Country]
@Beginning_Date datetime,
@Ending_Date datetime)
AS
SELECT dbo.Employees.Country, dbo.Employees.LastName,
dbo.Employees.FirstName, dbo.Orders.ShippedDate,
dbo.Orders.OrderID, dbo.[Order Subtotals].Subtotal AS SaleAmount
FROM dbo.Employees INNER JOIN
dbo.Orders INNER JOIN
dbo.[Order Subtotals] ON dbo.Orders.OrderID =
dbo.[Order Subtotals].OrderID ON dbo.Employees.EmployeeID =
dbo.Orders.EmployeeID
WHERE (dbo.Orders.ShippedDate BETWEEN @Beginning_Date AND @Ending_Date)
```

The sample Access project for this chapter includes an Access report named rptEmployeeSalesbyCountry that's based on the previous stored procedure. You can create a tabular report such as rptEmployeeSalesbyCountry with steps similar to those used for the preceding report example. However, Access will prompt you for a starting and ending date as you build the report. If you save the report as is, every time a user runs it he or she will have to respond to prompts for the beginning and ending dates for the report data.

You might need to specify some default starting and ending dates so that these prompts do not appear when a user is willing to accept a default range of dates. More importantly, you will definitely want the ability to specify the starting and ending dates for a report without requiring the user to respond to the report prompts. For example, you might want end users to select values from a custom form in your application. When a user specifies parameter values that differ from the default ones, you will want their selections to override the default values. In any event, you'll probably want your application to restore the default parameter settings after the report closes. The sample application in this section illustrates how to manage these processes.

There are several elements to the application. First, it needs to specify default values for the stored procedure through the report. By specifying the default values through the report, you preserve the integrity of the stored procedure's design for other applications. Second, the sample needs to override the default specification for the starting and ending dates. Third, the sample needs to restore the default parameter settings after the report closes. This is trickier than it might seem at first because you cannot modify the input parameters for a report other than in Design view. However, the report will open and close in Print or Preview mode. Therefore, the solution needs to reopen the report after it closes and then reset its parameter settings in Design view.

Use the Input Parameters setting on the Data tab of a report's Properties dialog box to set default parameters for a stored procedure that serves as the record source for a report. Developers can devise programs that override these default parameters. However, a user opening a report through the Database window will always have the default parameters assigned to the stored procedure. Figure 15-16 shows some settings for the sample application that cause the report to return data for all of 1998. The format for a parameter assignment is *parametername datatype = value*. If the stored procedure for a report has more than one parameter, you must delimit the setting for each parameter with a comma. Recall from Chapter 14 that SQL Server permits you to set a date parameter with a string. Figure 15-16 demonstrates this syntax.

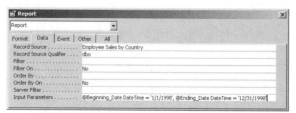

Figure 15-16 The Data tab for a report's Properties dialog box reveals the syntax for assigning parameter values to the *Employee Sales by Country* stored procedure.

While it can be useful to have default settings for the parameters, programmatically setting the parameters at run time is more interesting. The following two procedures demonstrate such an approach. Notice that I include the specification of two public variables. You must declare public variables at the top of a module, before declaring any procedures. These public variable declarations aren't absolutely necessary for setting the parameters at run time, but they're very useful for restoring the original default parameters. I'll discuss restoring the default parameters immediately after I explain how to set parameters programmatically.

The first procedure starts by assigning the report name to one of the public variables, *pubrepName*. Next the code assigns values to two string variables, denoting the start and end dates for which you want to the report to display data. These are local variables. The first procedure uses two different mechanisms for passing its variable assignments to the second procedure. The local variables, *strStart* and *strEnd*, travel between procedures as passed arguments. Notice that the public variable, *pubrepName*, does not appear in the argument list. This is because public variables are within the scope of all procedures in all modules and even all projects (if you're concurrently working with more than one project). Therefore, the second procedure can detect the value of *pubrepName* even though the first procedure assigned the variable a value.

The second procedure opens in Design view the report whose name is in *pubrepName* and sets a reference (*rpt1*) to the report. You must use Design view because Access doesn't permit the specification of the *InputParameters* property from Print mode or Preview mode. Next the procedure saves the setting for the report's *InputParameters* property in *initialparams*. (Notice from the declarations before the procedures that *intialparams* is the name of the second public variable.) After saving the initial *InputParameters* property value, the procedure makes a new assignment for the property based on the start and end dates passed from the first to the second procedure. The procedure next saves the report with the new *InputParameters* setting. This step prevents Access from prompting users about whether they want to commit the report changes when the second procedure's last line opens the report in Preview mode.

The last line leaves the report open so that you can examine the values in the report. These values will all be for 1997. Recall from Figure 15-16 that the default parameter settings specify values for 1998. The assignment of arguments passed to the second procedure overrides the default parameter settings.

```
Public pubrepName As String
Public initialparams As String

Sub CallPreviewrptEmployeeSalesbyCountry()
Dim strStart As String
Dim strEnd As String

'Set report name as public variable
pubrepName = "rptEmployeeSalesByCountry"

'Set start and end dates for report
strStart = "1/1/1997"
strEnd = "12/31/1997"

'Pass arguments to procedure for opening report
PreviewrptEmployeeSalesbyCountry pubrepName, strStart, strEnd

End Sub
```

(continued)

```
Sub PreviewrptEmployeeSalesbyCountry _
    (repName As String, strStart As String, _
    strEnd As String)
Dim rpt1 As Report
Dim str1 As String

'Set the InputParameters property in Design view
DoCmd.OpenReport repName, acViewDesign
Set rpt1 = Reports(repName)
initialparams = rpt1.InputParameters
rpt1.InputParameters = "@Beginning_Date DateTime = '" & _
    strStart & "', @Ending_Date DateTime = '" & strEnd & "'"
DoCmd.Close acReport, rpt1.Name, acSaveYes

'Then examine the output based on the parameters
'in Print Preview
DoCmd.OpenReport repName, acViewPreview

End Sub
```

When you're done examining the results from the parameter assignment, close the report. Closing the report starts a process that restores the default parameter settings. This process starts with the report's *Close* event. The report's *Close* event procedure opens a form named *frmToResetReportParameters*. This form has a timer event that concludes after the report closes. The *Close* event is the last to execute before physically closing the report. The following script shows the event procedure:

```
Private Sub Report_Close()

'Start timer that concludes after report closes
DoCmd.OpenForm "frmToResetReportParameters"

End Sub
```

The *frmToResetReportParameters* form has two event procedures and a label on it. The label explains the purpose of the form: to reset the parameters. The first event procedure handles the *Load* event. The procedure sets the form's *TimerInterval* property to *5000*. This schedules a timer event 5 seconds after the form loads. Because the *Close* event procedure for the rptEmployeeSalesby-Country report opens the form, the form's timer event occurs 5 seconds after the report closes. You can shorten this interval if you find it excessive. In turn, the timer event invokes the *RestoreReportParameters* procedure in Module1. As an option, you can add code to make sure the rptEmployeeSalesbyCountry report closed successfully. Recall that the *AllReports* collection supports this function. The two form event procedures appear next.

> **Note**   The *Module1* qualifier for the *RestoreReportParameters* proce-
> dure is optional, unless you have a procedure with the same name in a
> different module.

```
Private Sub Form_Load()

'Set timer interval to delay after deactivation
'of report before resetting parameters
Me.TimerInterval = 5000

End Sub


Private Sub Form_Timer()

'Invoke procedure to restore parameters
'in a report
Module1.RestoreReportParameters

End Sub
```

The final and crucial step for restoring the default parameters occurs in the
RestoreReportParameters procedure, whose listing appears next. This procedure
reopens the rptEmployeeSalesbyCountry report in Design view. Next it assigns
the saved default parameter settings in *initialparams* to the report's *InputParameters*
property. Then it closes the report and saves the changes. The last step is to close
the *frmToResetReportParameters* form. This step concludes the application.

```
Sub RestoreReportParameters()
Dim rpt1 As Report
Dim repName As String

'Assign public repName variable as report for
'which to restore parameters
repName = pubrepName

'Open report and make reference to it
DoCmd.OpenReport repName, _
    acViewDesign
Set rpt1 = Reports(repName)

'Restore initial parameters and save changes
rpt1.InputParameters = initialparams
DoCmd.Close acReport, rpt1.Name, acSaveYes
```

(continued)

```
'Close form that resets parameters
DoCmd.Close acForm, "frmToResetReportParameters", _
    acSaveNo

End Sub
```

SQL-DMO Programming

As mentioned in Chapter 14, SQL-DMO, or SQL Distributed Management Objects, is a hierarchical programming model for SQL Server administration and data definition tasks. You can use SQL-DMO to enumerate databases and their objects on a server. With this capability, you can perform such tasks as referencing all the databases on a server or all the stored procedures within a database. You can also view and edit the contents of databases and the objects they contain, as well as create new objects. With SQL-DMO, developers can view and edit the design of tables, triggers, views, and stored procedures within databases. In addition, you can create new instances of SQL-DMO objects. For example, you can create a new table within a database. You can even copy the script for a table from one database to create a duplicate table within another database. In fact, you use SQL-DMO programming to copy the contents between different instances of SQL Server on different computers. For example, you can detach a database from one server, copy its files to another server, and then attach those database files for use on a second server.

There are three main reasons for Access developers (and other developers using Microsoft SQL Server 2000 Desktop Engine) to become familiar with SQL-DMO:

■   Administration is much more important for SQL Server databases than Access databases. By programmatically performing database administration chores, you improve your ability to manage SQL Server databases.

■   Microsoft SQL Server 2000 Desktop Engine (MSDE 2000)—and Microsoft Data Engine (MSDE)—do not ship with Enterprise Manager, a graphical client management tool that offers many more database administration features than the Access project UI. This tool is available to users of all other SQL Server editions. Because Microsoft programmed Enterprise Manager with SQL-DMO, you can incorporate selective subsets of Enterprise Manager functionality into your custom applications.

■   SQL-DMO is a hierarchical model for SQL Server components. Office developers who have a history of working with hierarchical models will feel comfortable adapting to its programming conventions as opposed to the more procedurally oriented T-SQL programming environment.

SQL-DMO installs with either MSDE 2000 or any other version of SQL Server 2000. Installing either MSDE 2000 or SQL Server 2000 adds sqldmo.dll and sqldmo.rll to a workstation. The .dll file implements SQL-DMO, and the .rll file is a localized resource file. Except for MSDE 2000, all versions of SQL Server 2000 ship with sqldmo80.hlp, the file that provides context-sensitive help. However, MSDE 2000 developers can get support for SQL-DMO from the downloadable or online versions of Books Online for SQL Server 7. To reference the SQL-DMO object model, your project must have a reference to the SQLDMO Object Library in the References dialog box that the Tools-References command opens.

SQL-DMO files also ship with SQL Server 7 and MSDE. SQL-DMO scripts developed with the SQL Server 7 version will run in SQL Server 2000 and MSDE 2000. Because of new features and an incompatible type library file, SQL-DMO scripts developed for SQL Server 2000 do not run in SQL Server 7. On the other hand, the SQL Server 2000 version of SQL-DMO provides new capabilities and features not available with SQL Server 7. For example, SQL-DMO for SQL Server 2000 supports user-defined functions. To tap the features associated with the latest version of SQL-DMO, you must use new object class names. One of this chapter's SQL-DMO samples demonstrates an approach to this task.

Figure 15-17 presents an excerpt from the SQL-DMO object model for SQL Server 2000. Your SQL-DMO applications will frequently start by connecting to a *SQLServer* object. The *SQLServer* object represents your application's connection to a SQL Server database server. SQL-DMO doesn't share this connection with ADO or other SQL Server client software. This is because the objects from the ADODB and SQLDMO libraries are not compatible. After specifying a connection to a server, your application can "walk the model" to return information about individual databases on a server and the objects within them. For example, SQL-DMO makes it easy to enumerate the databases on a server or the views within those databases. You can easily list and update the T-SQL script for a view.

Note   SQL-DMO for SQL Server 2000 readily supports multiple instances of SQL Server running on a single computer. This feature is only available with the version of SQL-DMO that comes with SQL Server 2000. (However, you can install a SQL Server 2000 instance alongside a SQL Server 7 installation.) The topic of installing and managing multiple instances of SQL Server on a single computer is beyond the scope of this book. See Books Online for more coverage of this topic.

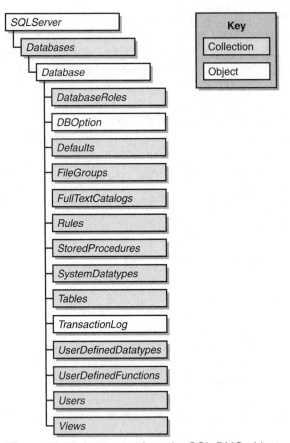

Figure 15-17 An excerpt from the SQL-DMO object model.

Chapter 14 offered detailed coverage of many objects and collections portrayed in Figure 15-17. In fact, SQL Server databases, tables, views, stored procedures, and user-defined functions all received extensive coverage in that chapter. The *Users* collection and *DatabaseRoles* collection support SQL Server security. We'll consider these topics later in this chapter in "Programming SQL Server Security." The remaining collections and individual objects from Figure 15-17 pertain to SQL Server database administration and data definition features. See Books Online for coverage of these topics.

Ensuring Secure Login and Enumerating Databases

When you connect to a server, you can use either of two types of authentication: Microsoft Windows authentication or SQL Server authentication. Authentication is the process by which a client application verifies its credentials to connect to a SQL server. There are three general classes of authentication:

- Microsoft Windows NT or Windows 2000 can authenticate a user and then pass along this authentication to SQL Server. In this Windows style of authentication, SQL Server accepts the Windows verification of the user's status. Users can specify a single login account for accessing Windows and SQL Server.

- SQL Server can maintain its own list of login accounts that it uses in place of those in Windows. When SQL Server 2000 or MSDE 2000 runs on a Windows 98 or Windows Millennium Edition computer, this is the only form of authentication. In addition, you might find SQL Server authentication especially useful when you run a Windows 2000 or Windows NT computer disconnected from a network. This is because you aren't likely to have the same login identity for your corporate network server as for your own workstation. One major downside of SQL Server authentication is that users might have to authenticate themselves twice—once to the Windows server, and a second time to the SQL server.

- You can also use a mix of both Windows and SQL Server authentication. This authentication option enables users to connect to a SQL server with either their Windows credentials or special SQL Server credentials. We'll discuss this option in more detail momentarily.

In general, Windows authentication is the best choice. However, you might find situations in which SQL Server authentication makes more sense. For example, if tight local control of a database is essential, you might require SQL Server authentication. Or, if Windows support staff aren't available to interact with a database administrator (DBA) on a timely basis, this might warrant SQL Server authentication.

When an SQL-DMO application connects to a SQL server with the Windows login account of a user, it must specify a secure login. The following sample illustrates the syntax for doing this as well as enumerating the databases on a server. The first procedure merely specifies the name of a SQL server and passes the information along to the second procedure as an argument. The name for a SQL server is typically the name of the computer on which the program runs. This sample designates the SQL server named cab2000.

If you move the application from one computer to another, you'll have to specify a new server name when you reference the local server on the second computer. Alternatively, you can designate the server name as the string *"(local)"*. This second approach ensures that you always reference the local SQL server. But what if you want to connect to a specific server regardless of the workstation your application runs from? To do so, you must name the specific server to which your application needs to connect. There are advantages to both ways of designating a computer. Use the one that best suits your needs.

The second procedure in the next sample begins by instantiating an instance of the *SQLServer* object as *srv1*. Then the sample sets the *LoginSecure* property of *srv1* to True. This property sets the authentication method that a login attempt uses to Windows authentication. The next line invokes the *Connect* method for the *srv1* object instance. This method attempts to connect to a server. The method can take up to three arguments. The sample uses a single argument to represent the name of the SQL server. If you don't use any arguments for the *Connect* method, the code attempts to point the *SQLServer* object at the main instance of SQL Server running on the local computer. A subsequent sample demonstrates the use of the second and third arguments.

After making a connection to the cab2000 server, the sample prints the number of databases on the server by referencing the *Count* property of the *Databases* collection for *srv1*. Then the second procedure uses a *For...Next* loop to enumerate the members of the *Databases* collection.

```
Sub CallLoginSecureAndListDBs()
Dim srvName As String

'Assign name to server
srvName = "cab2000"

'Pass server name to login routine
LoginSecureAndListDBs srvName

End Sub


Sub LoginSecureAndListDBs(srvName As String)
Dim srv1 As SQLDMO.SQLServer
Dim dbs1 As SQLDMO.Database

'Instantiate a SQLServer object, and connect
'using integrated security
Set srv1 = New SQLDMO.SQLServer
srv1.LoginSecure = True
srv1.Connect srvName

'Report the count of the databases on a server
Debug.Print "Server " & srv1.Name & " has " & _
    srv1.Databases.Count & " on it." & vbCr & _
    "There names are:" & vbCr

'Enumerate the names of databases
For Each dbs1 In srv1.Databases
    Debug.Print vbTab & dbs1.Name
Next dbs1
```

```
'Clean up objects
srv1.DisConnect
set srv1 = Nothing

End Sub
```

Setting Mixed Authentication

When an organization's IT structure or resources make using mixed authentication desirable, you might need to change from a Windows-only authentication mode to a mixed mode that lets users connect to a SQL server with login accounts managed by SQL Server and Windows. The next sample shows how to create and manage this transition. If you install MSDE 2000 on a Windows NT or Windows 2000 computer, your installation automatically starts with Windows-only authentication. If you prefer to use mixed authentication, you can use the following sample to set up the sa account and your server for mixed authentication. Recall that the sa account has broad control within a SQL server and is impossible to delete.

This sample uses four procedures. The first one designates the server's name and demonstrates the syntax for explicitly referencing a computer's local SQL server. The first procedure passes the name of the server to the second procedure.

The second procedure attempts to log in to the server with SQL Server credentials. In other words, the *Connect* method specifies a login account and password for SQL Server. There are at least two ways that the attempt to log in can fail. First, the authentication mode can be set to Windows-only authentication. You can fix this by changing the server's authentication style. Second, the password for the sa account might be incorrect. You can remedy this problem by assigning a new password to the account and then using it. The second procedure uses error traps to detect either of these conditions. If the attempt to log in fails because the login request designates SQL Server credentials, the second procedure calls the *WindowsToMixedAuthentication* procedure. This procedure changes the security mode from Windows-only to mixed security, permitting SQL Server and Windows authentication. If the attempt to log in fails because of a faulty password, the second procedure calls *AssignNewPassword*. This procedure assigns a known password to the sa login. For both error conditions, the second procedure tries to log in again after fixing the detected error.

The second procedure starts by assigning a string to *NewPassword*. The value of the string in the listing is *password*. You can change this to any more secure string that your needs dictate. This string contains the new password that the procedure will assign to the sa login account. The second procedure then instantiates an instance of the *SQLServer* object and attempts to log in with SQL Server credentials. Notice that the procedure doesn't set the *LoginSecure* property of *srv1* to True. The property's default value is False when designating SQL Server authentication. The *Connect* method specifies sa as the login account, and it references the value of *NewPassword* for sa's password. If the attempt succeeds, the procedure exits normally. This happens when the server permits mixed mode security and the sa password equals the value set for *NewPassword*.

When the authentication mode for the server is Windows-only, you have to alter the security mode to accommodate SQL Server authentication. The second procedure detects the need for this alteration when the *Connect* method generates an error number of −2147203052. The second procedure calls *Windows-ToMixedAuthentication* and passes the server name. The called procedure requires the name of the server to change the security mode for. After the control returns to the second procedure, the second procedure attempts to log in again with SQL Server authentication by invoking the *Resume* method. If this second attempt fails, it can generate an error number of −2147203048. This number is consistent with the error generated by a bad password. Therefore, the procedure updates the password for the sa account by calling the *AssignNewPassword* procedure. Then the second procedure passes the server name and the string value for the new password. When control returns from the called procedure, the second procedure tries to connect again to the local server. If this attempt succeeds, the procedure exits normally. Otherwise, you get another error, and the procedure writes a message to the Immediate window. (For example, the *Connect* method can fail because of a faulty physical connection.)

```
Sub CalAddSQLServerAuthentication()
Dim srvName As String

'Specify server name
srvName = "(local)"

'Pass server name
AddSQLServerAuthentication srvName

End Sub



Sub AddSQLServerAuthentication(srvName As String)
On Error GoTo SQLAuth_Trap
Dim srv1 As SQLDMO.SQLServer
Dim NewPassword As String

'Override assigned password, if you prefer
NewPassword = "password"

'Attempt to log in with sa and assigned password
Set srv1 = New SQLDMO.SQLServer
srv1.Connect srvName, "sa", NewPassword
```

```
SQLAuth_Exit:
srv1.DisConnect
Set srv1 = Nothing
Exit Sub

SQLAuth_Trap:
Select Case Err.Number
    Case -2147203052
'If no trusted connection, enable
'SQL Server authentication
        WindowsToMixedAuthentication srvName
        Resume
    Case -2147203048
'If sa login fails, set password for sa to password
        AssignNewPassword srvName, NewPassword
        Resume
    Case Else
        Debug.Print Err.Number, Err.Description
End Select

'Clean up objects
srv1.DisConnect
Set srv1 = Nothing

End Sub
```

The *WindowsToMixedAuthentication* procedure opens a connection using Windows authentication to the server named in the argument passed to it. This permits the *Connection* method to succeed even when SQL Server authentication is not in place. Next the procedure sets the *SecurityMode* property to *SQLDMO Security_Mixed*. This property assignment applies to the *IntegratedSecurity* object instead of the *SQLServer* object. This assignment denotes mixed security using either Windows or SQL Server authentication. Two other possible *SecurityMode* property settings include *SQLDMOSecurity_Integrated* for Windows authentication and *SQLDMOSecurity_Normal* for SQL Server authentication.

Making the property assignment does not enforce the setting. You must first stop and restart the server. This involves several steps, which the balance of the procedure manages. The trickiest of these steps is the loop after the invocation of the *Stop* method. When your code issues the *Stop* method, the SQL server does not instantly stop. Therefore, trying to restart the computer can result in a situation where your code attempts to restart a server that's still running, which causes a run-time error. The *Status* property of the *SQLServer* object can detect when a server stops. After issuing the *Stop* method, the procedure loops until the server's *Status* property indicates that the procedure responded completely to the invocation of the method. Next the procedure restarts the server. This is essential if you plan to use the server any further because SQL-DMO cannot use the *Connect* method to connect to a stopped server.

```
Sub WindowsToMixedAuthentication(srvName As String)
Dim srv1 As SQLDMO.SQLServer

'Instantiate a SQLServer object and connect
'using integrated security
Set srv1 = New SQLDMO.SQLServer
srv1.LoginSecure = True
srv1.Connect srvName

'Set security mode to mixed Windows/SQL Server
'authentication
srv1.IntegratedSecurity.SecurityMode = _
    SQLDMOSecurity_Mixed
srv1.DisConnect

'Invoke command to stop server and wait
'until it stops
srv1.Stop
Do Until srv1.Status = SQLDMOSvc_Stopped
Loop

'Restart server with SecurityMode setting
srv1.Start True, srvName

'Clean up objects
srv1.DisConnect
Set srv1 = Nothing

End Sub
```

The *AssignNewPassword* procedure takes as many as three arguments, but it only requires two: the server name and the string for the new password. The third password is the login account name. This is an optional argument with a default value of *sa*. This value will automatically change the password for the sa login unless the calling procedure explicitly specifies another login. Because the *AddSQLServerAuthentication* procedure does not change the password, the *AssignNewPassword* procedure sets the sa password to *password*.

```
Sub AssignNewPassword(srvName As String, _
    NewPassword As String, _
    Optional lgnName As String = "sa")
Dim srv1 As SQLDMO.SQLServer

'Instantiate a SQLServer object, and connect
'using integrated security
```

```
Set srv1 = New SQLDMO.SQLServer
srv1.LoginSecure = True
srv1.Connect srvName

'Assign new password to login
srv1.Logins(lgnName).SetPassword "", NewPassword

'Clean up objects
srv1.DisConnect
Set srv1 = Nothing

End Sub
```

Without much comment, I give you two other utility procedures for managing security mode and password. I found these utilities useful while developing the preceding sample, and you might find them useful for other purposes. The first utility procedure has the name *MixedToWindowsAuthentication*. It does what its name implies. The second procedure, *BlankPasswordForsa*, assigns a blank password to the sa login for the local SQL server. Although you definitely should not run a production system with a blank password for sa, some developers find it convenient to build an application with at least one account that has no password.

```
Sub MixedToWindowsAuthentication()
Dim srv1 As SQLDMO.SQLServer

'Assign whatever server name you like;
'default is cab2000
srvName = "cab2000"

'Instantiate a SQLServer object, and connect
'using integrated security
Set srv1 = New SQLDMO.SQLServer
srv1.LoginSecure = True
srv1.Connect srvName

'Set security mode to mixed Windows/SQL Server
'authentication
srv1.IntegratedSecurity.SecurityMode = SQLDMOSecurity_Integrated
srv1.DisConnect

'Invoke command to stop server and wait
'until it stops
srv1.Stop
Do Until srv1.Status = SQLDMOSvc_Stopped
Loop
```

(continued)

```
'Restart server with mixed security
srv1.Start True, srvName

'Clean up objects
srv1.DisConnect
Set srv1 = Nothing

End Sub


Sub BlankPasswordForsa()
Dim NewPassword As String
Dim lgnName As String

NewPassword = ""

AssignNewPassword "(local)", NewPassword

End Sub
```

Building a SQL Server Object Navigator

Because of its hierarchical design, SQL-DMO is particularly convenient for enumerating the objects within a database. An earlier sample showed how to enumerate the databases on a server to the Immediate window. This is easy to do with SQL-DMO because the *Databases* collection is hierarchically dependent on the server. You also can enumerate the tables, views, stored procedures, and user-defined functions within a database easily because collections for these objects are hierarchically dependent on a database. The next sample shows how to do this with a custom Access form.

Figure 15-18 shows an Access form that illustrates one approach to browsing the database objects on the local server. When the form opens, it automatically displays the names of the databases on the local SQL server in its first list box. Users can display the names of tables, views, stored procedures, and user-defined functions on the local SQL server in the last list box by following three steps. First select a database name from the first list box. Second click an option button to select a type of object from the option group control. Third click the button on the last list box. The second step is optional because the form automatically selects Tables as the default database object type. However, users must select a database name for the browser to return the names of an object type in a database.

The form's layout has three critical input controls and one critical output control. I added the first and last list boxes without using the Controls Wizard. The only customization I performed was the sizing and positioning of the list boxes. Event procedures behind the form set the sources for both list boxes. The first list box, lstDBs, is an input control because a user must make a selection from it. The last box, lstDBObjects, is an output control that displays the objects on the local server when a user clicks the button above it. The opgDBObjectTypes option group control always displays the same four objects, so I used the Controls Wizard for its design. However, I chose not to select a default value when building the control. This is because the sample application uses an event procedure behind the form to assign a default value to the control. By making the assignment in the event procedure, your application can adjust the default setting for the option group control along with any other required settings. The last critical control is the command button above lstDBObjects. A click to the cmdRefreshList command button updates the display in lstDBObjects according to the values of lstDBs and opgDBObjectTypes.

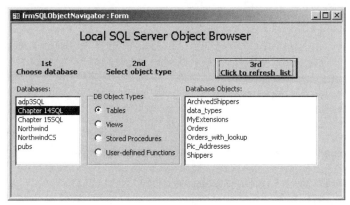

Figure 15-18 An Access form that lets a user browse selected database objects on the local SQL server.

With just two short event procedures, you can manage the contents of the controls. However, the event procedures rely on two function procedures in Module1 of the VBA project for this chapter. Recall that a function procedure returns a value.

The *Form_Open* event procedure (shown next) performs three main tasks. First it populates the *lstDBs* control by setting its *RowSourceType* and *RowSource* properties. Notice that the *RowSourceType* property is set to *"Value List"*. The procedures makes this assignment because it sets the *RowSource* property for *lstDBs* to the return value for the *LoginSecureandListDBs2* function. This function takes a single argument, the name of a server. It returns a semicolon-delimited list of names for the databases on the server specified in its argument. This is a valid format for a *RowSourceType* property setting of Value List. Second the

Form_Open event procedure assigns a value of *1* to the *opgDBObjectTypes* control. You can change this value to *2*, *3*, or *4*, which respectively designate views, stored procedures, and user-defined functions. This last option is only appropriate for SQL Server 2000 and MSDE 2000 databases because SQL Server 7 and MSDE do not recognize user-defined functions. Finally the *Form_Open* event procedure performs some minor formatting to remove form display elements for data selection and record navigation—functions that do not apply to this form.

> **Note**   The assignment for *srvName* in the *Form_Open* event is at the module level. Therefore, it doesn't appear in the following *Form_Open* event procedure listing. The module-level declaration of *srvName* makes the assignment in the *Form_Open* event procedure available to the form's second event procedure.

```
Private Sub Form_Open(Cancel As Integer)

'Populate database object list box with
'names of databases on local server
Me.lstDBs.RowSourceType = "Value List"
srvName = "(local)"
Me.lstDBs.RowSource = LoginSecureAndListDBs2(srvName)

'Set Tables as the default database type
opgDBObjectTypes = 1

'Perform selected minor formatting
Me.NavigationButtons = False
Me.RecordSelectors = False
Me.DividingLines = False

End Sub
```

The click event procedure for the *cmdRefreshList* command button performs just two tasks. First it checks the value of *lstDBs*. The sample requires the user to make a selection from the first list box. If the user does not make this selection, the attempt to develop a list of objects within a database can generate a run-time error. When the event procedure doesn't detect a selection, it prints a message reminding the user to make this selection and exits before the command generates the error. Second the procedure uses the *DBObjectsList* function in Module1 to populate the *RowSource* property for the *lstDBObjects* control. The function procedure returns a semicolon-delimited list of objects based on the selections for database name and object type from the local server.

```
Private Sub cmdRefreshList_Click()

'Abort if user did not select a database
If IsNull(Me.lstDBs) Then
    MsgBox "Please select a database before " & _
        "attempting to list the objects within it.", _
        vbInformation, _
        "Programming Microsoft Access Version 2002"
    Exit Sub
End If

'Populate database object list box based on
'server name, database name, and object type
Me.lstDBObjects.RowSourceType = _
    "Value List"
Me.lstDBObjects.RowSource = _
    DBObjectList(srvName, lstDBs, opgDBObjectTypes)

End Sub
```

LoginSecureAndListDBs2 is an adaptation of a procedure described earlier in this section that had the same name except for the trailing *2*. The adaptation uses a function procedure format instead of the sub procedure format of the earlier version. There are two additional distinctions between the two procedures. This version of the procedure uses the *SystemObject* property to exclude system databases. This prevents users from browsing the objects in system databases such as the master database. Also, the function procedure constructs its return value in a format suitable for the *RowSource* property to a list box with a Value List *RowSourceType* setting. This simply involves appending a trailing semicolon and a space to each database name. After passing through the list of databases on the a server, the procedure clips off the last semicolon and space by using the *Left* function.

```
Function LoginSecureAndListDBs2(srvName As String) As String
Dim srv1 As SQLDMO.SQLServer
Dim dbs1 As SQLDMO.Database

'Instantiate a SQLServer object, and connect
'using integrated security
Set srv1 = New SQLDMO.SQLServer
srv1.LoginSecure = True
srv1.Connect srvName
```

(continued)

```
'Store delimited names of databases in function
For Each dbs1 In srv1.Databases
    If dbs1.SystemObject = False Then
        LoginSecureAndListDBs2 = _
            LoginSecureAndListDBs2 & dbs1.Name & "; "
    End If
Next dbs1

'Strip trailing delimiter
LoginSecureAndListDBs2 = _
    Left(LoginSecureAndListDBs2, _
        Len(LoginSecureAndListDBs2) - 2)

'Clean up objects
srv1.DisConnect
Set srv1 = Nothing

End Function
```

The *DBObjectList* function procedure appears next. This procedure returns a semicolon-delimited list of database objects based on the database name and object type selected in the *frmSQLObjectNavigator* form shown in Figure 15-18. The argument list accepts the value of the *opgDBObjectTypes* control as *bytObjectType*, which has a Byte data type declaration. This procedure begins by making a selection to the server name passed to it. The sample's *Form_Open* event procedure designates the local server, but you can change the code to reference another server. When you change the assignment in the *Form_Open* event procedure, it automatically affects the *DBObjectList* and *LoginSecureAndListDBs2* function procedures.

The heart of the *DBObjectList* procedure is a *Select Case* statement that has a separate case for each of the four values that the *opgDBObjectTypes* control can return. When I created the opgDBObjectTypes control, I set these values to 1 through 4. If you change the Option button control settings within the option group control so that they return other values, be sure to update the *Case* values accordingly.

When the *opgDBObjectTypes* control equals *1* in the sample, the procedure enumerates the user-defined *Tables* collection within the database name selected on the form. If the *opgDBObjectTypes* control value is either *2* or *3*, the procedure enumerates user-defined views or stored procedures, respectively. The code for enumerating views and stored procedures must exclude some object names that begin with ~TMPCLP. Although SQL Server generates objects with this prefix for its own internal use, it considers such objects user defined.

An *opgDBObjectTypes* control value of *4* causes the code to enumerate user-defined functions. SQL Server 2000 is the first version of SQL Server to introduce this object class. Therefore, SQL-DMO must use the *Database2* object as opposed to the default *Database* object used for the other object collections. The declaration for *dbs2* at the beginning of the procedure illustrates the syntax for an object reference to the new *Database2* object class. The code for the clause when the *Case bytObjectType* value equals *4* illustrates how to use this object to enumerate the user-defined functions in a database.

```
Function DBObjectList(srvName As String, _
    DBname As String, _
    bytObjectType As Byte) As String
Dim tbl1 As SQLDMO.Table
Dim vew1 As SQLDMO.View
Dim spr1 As SQLDMO.StoredProcedure
Dim dbs2 As SQLDMO.Database2
Dim udf1 As SQLDMO.UserDefinedFunction

'Instantiate a SQLServer object, and connect
'using integrated security
Set srv1 = New SQLDMO.SQLServer
srv1.LoginSecure = True
srv1.Connect srvName

'Pass back from function--delimited object names function.
'All objects used are available with Databases collection
'(default of SQL Server 7), except for UserDefinedFunctions,
'which require a Database2 object.
Select Case bytObjectType
    Case 1
        For Each tbl1 In srv1.Databases(DBname).Tables
            If tbl1.SystemObject = False Then
                DBObjectList = _
                    DBObjectList & tbl1.Name & "; "
            End If
        Next tbl1
    Case 2
        For Each vew1 In srv1.Databases(DBname).Views
            If vew1.SystemObject = _
                False And Left(vew1.Name, 7) <> "~TMPCLP" Then
                DBObjectList = _
                    DBObjectList & vew1.Name & "; "
            End If
        Next vew1
```

(continued)

909

```
      Case 3
          For Each spr1 In srv1.Databases(DBname).StoredProcedures
              If spr1.SystemObject = _
                  False And Left(spr1.Name, 7) <> "~TMPCLP" Then
                  DBObjectList = _
                      DBObjectList & spr1.Name & "; "
              End If
          Next spr1
      Case 4
          Set dbs2 = srv1.Databases(DBname)
          For Each udf1 In dbs2.UserDefinedFunctions
              If udf1.SystemObject = False Then
                  DBObjectList = _
                      DBObjectList & udf1.Name & "; "
              End If
          Next udf1
  End Select

  'Strip trailing delimiter
  If DBObjectList <> "" Then
      DBObjectList = _
          Left(DBObjectList, _
          Len(DBObjectList) - 2)
  Else
          DBObjectList = "None"
          Exit Function
  End If

  'Clean up objects
  srv1.DisConnect
  Set srv1 = Nothing

  End Function
```

Copying a Table's Design from One Database to Another

If you become even moderately handy with SQL-DMO, you can get it to do your T-SQL programming for you. The following sample demonstrates how to use SQL-DMO to copy a table's design from one database to another. In this particular instance, the code copies the *Pic_Addresses* table initially created in Chapter 14. The sample re-creates the table in the database for this chapter's Access project by copying the T-SQL for the table from the Chapter 14SQL database, editing it slightly, and then running the altered code in the current database. After the code generates a new table, the procedure next copies the data from the table in the other database.

The sample first opens a connection to the server with the database containing the table we plan to copy. In my environment, this is the cab2000 server. You can use any server that maintains the database for Chapter 14. (The database's name is Chapter 14SQL.) If you haven't attached the database files for Chapter 14 to your server, now would be a great time to do so. The code uses SQL Server authentication with the sa login and a password string of *password*. You can change the login style, login name, and password string to match the setup of your database server and the password for the sa login.

The trick to getting SQL-DMO to write the T-SQL syntax for a database object is to use the *Script* method. This method returns the T-SQL batch to re-create an object. *Script* automatically creates the T-SQL batch for any object to which you apply it. Unfortunately, the T-SQL batch ends with a GO command for Query Analyzer, a SQL Server client management tool we discussed in Chapter 14. To use the batch in a VBA module, we need to strip the trailing GO command, which appears in the last eight characters of the script. The following sample demonstrates the use of this technique for the *Pic_Addresses* table in the Chapter 14SQL database. After editing the script, this sample removes any prior version of the *Pic_Addresses* table from the current database. Then it runs the edited T-SQL statement for creating a new copy of the *Pic_Addresses* table. Notice that the procedure uses an ADO *Connection* object to execute the T-SQL strip. Chapter 14 initially demonstrated and described this technique.

After creating the table based on the script, you're left with an empty table. The next step is to populate the table with data from the original table in the other database, Chapter 14SQL. An INSERT INTO statement can facilitate this. Use a SELECT statement instead of a VALUES list as the source for the data to insert. In the FROM clause of the SELECT statement, specify the table in the source database. After constructing the string, the sample invokes the statement with an ADO *Connection* object.

```
Sub CreatePic_Addresses()
Dim srv1 As SQLDMO.SQLServer
Dim str1 As String
Dim cnn1 As ADODB.Connection
Dim int1 As Integer
#Const PrintScript = True

'Assign server name
srvName = "cab2000"

'Make connection to remote server
Set srv1 = New SQLDMO.SQLServer
srv1.Connect srvName, "sa", "password"
```

(continued)

```
'Copy, optionally print, and edit script for table
str1 = srv1.Databases("Chapter 14SQL"). _
    Tables("Pic_Addresses").Script
#If PrintScript Then
    Debug.Print str1
#End If
int1 = Len(str1) - 8
str1 = Left(str1, int1)

'Execute edited script for table;
'drop prior version of table, if necessary
Set cnn1 = CurrentProject.Connection
Drop_a_table cnn1, "Pic_Addresses"
cnn1.Execute str1

'Insert descriptions and addresses from Pic_addresses
'in Chapter 14SQL database on cab2000 server
str1 = "INSERT INTO Pic_Addresses " & _
    "SELECT Pic_description, Pic_address " & _
    "FROM [Chapter 14SQL].dbo.Pic_Addresses"
cnn1.Execute str1

'Refresh Database window to show new table
RefreshDatabaseWindow

'Clean up objects
srv1.DisConnect
Set srv1 = Nothing

End Sub
```

If you want to populate the table with new data, you'll need a slightly different version of the VBA procedure to create *Pic_Addresses*. This alternate version will still use the *Script* method to derive the T-SQL for the *Pic_Addresses* table. However, the alternate procedure uses a simple VALUES list, as in the samples shown in Chapter 14. The alternate procedure appears in the Access project for this chapter on the book's companion CD and has the name *CreatePic_Addresses2*.

When I was developing this sample, it was useful to scan the end of the T-SQL batch statement generated by the *Script* method. In particular, I needed to examine the characters towards the end of the method's return value. The following pair of procedures demonstrates one approach to printing an index number and a string value for each of the last 50 characters in the string returned from the *Script* method. You can use this code sample to verify the number of characters to cut from the end of the *Script* method's return value. You can easily adapt this code sample to examine any number of characters at the end of any string.

```
Sub CallTrailingCharactersInString()
Dim srv1 As SQLDMO.SQLServer
Dim str1 As String

'Assign server name
srvName = "cab2000"

'Make connection to remote server with sa login
Set srv1 = New SQLDMO.SQLServer
srv1.Connect srvName, "sa", "password"

'Copy script for table to str1
str1 = srv1.Databases("Chapter 14SQL"). _
    Tables("Pic_Addresses").Script

'Print trailing 50 characters in table script
TrailingCharactersInString str1, 50

'Clean up objects
srv1.DisConnect
Set srv1 = Nothing

End Sub


Sub TrailingCharactersInString(str1 As String, _
    bytCharacters As Byte)
Dim int1 As Integer
Dim int2 As Integer

int1 = Len(str1)

'Print bytCharacter trailing characters in str1
For int2 = 1 To int1
    If (int1 - int2) <= bytCharacters Then _
        Debug.Print int2, Mid(str1, int2, 1)
Next int2

Debug.Print "Total number of characters in str1: " & int1

End Sub
```

Attaching and Detaching Database Files

Attaching and detaching and database files is a flexible way to transfer databases between different SQL servers. Chapter 14 demonstrated how to attach a database file with T-SQL. Because this is an administrative function, SQL-DMO also offers good support for this kind of activity. In fact, you can easily automate working with sets of files. This section starts with a pair of samples for attaching and detaching individual files. Then it moves on to manipulate a set of database files all at once.

The following pair of procedures shows how to attach a single SQL Server database file with an .mdf extension to the local server. Access developers are used to thinking of an .mdb file as a database. However, with SQL Server, the database file is not visible until you attach it to a server. Once you do, users interact with the database by addressing the server. They never have direct access to the file as is common with Access file-server applications.

The sample's first procedure specifies the database name and the .mdf file name. Then it passes this information to the *AttachADB* procedure. This second procedure starts by making a connection to the local server. Then it invokes the *SQLServer* object's *AttachDB* method. This method requires a function specification in which you set the function's return value to a string.

```
Sub CallAttachADB()
Dim DBName As String
Dim MdfFilePath As String

'Specify database name and filepath to .mdf
DBName = "adp4SQL"
MdfFilePath = "c:\mssql7\data\adp4sql.mdf"
AttachADB DBName, MdfFilePath

End Sub



Sub AttachADB(DBName As String, MdfFilePath)
Dim srv1 As New SQLDMO.SQLServer
Dim str1 As String

'Connect to local server
srv1.LoginSecure = True
srv1.Connect "(local)"

'Attach database with with passed arguments
str1 = srv1.AttachDB(DBName, MdfFilePath)

End Sub
```

The *AttachDB* method is very flexible. For example, its argument list can optionally include a log file with an .ldf extension. If the database spans multiple operating system files, you can specify up to 16 files for it. You can also use this method to attach database files to a server other than the one on your workstation. When using a remote server, do not specify the path to the database file with Uniform Naming Convention (UNC) notation. Instead, specify a local drive and path. For example, if your remote server has the name MyRemote-Server and the .mdf file is on its C share (that points to the remote server's c: drive), do not specify the path to the file as \\MyRemoteServer\C\mydbfile.mdf. Instead, specify c:\mydbfile.mdf.

Detaching a database file is even easier than attaching one. First use the *DetachDB* method for a server. Then specify the name of the databases on the server. The following code shows a sample that detaches adp4SQL from the local server:

```
Sub CallDetachADB()
Dim DBName As String

'Specify database name
DBName = "adp4SQL"
DetachADB DBName

End Sub


Sub DetachADB(DBName As String)
Dim srv1 As New SQLDMO.SQLServer

srv1.LoginSecure = True
srv1.Connect "(local)"

srv1.DetachDB (DBName)
End Sub
```

If you're attaching a file to another database, it's common to derive the file by detaching it from another server. You cannot copy or move a database file until you first detach it from a server. After processing a database file for use on another server (for example, to make a copy of it), you can reattach the original .mdf file to the server from which you detached it.

Recovering MSDE Database Files After Installing MSDE 2000

The *AttachDB* method can be particularly handy when you want to transfer a set of database files after upgrading from MSDE to MSDE 2000. If you follow the instructions in Access Help for installing MSDE 2000—see "Install and Configure SQL Server 2000 Desktop Engine"—your first step will be to uninstall MSDE. This orphans any existing database files you developed for MSDE. Happily, you can use the following sample to make your old database files available with your new server.

This sample consists of two procedures. The first requires a reference to the Microsoft Scripting Runtime library. This procedure uses the library to facilitate looping through the files in the c:\mssql7\data path. This is the default location where MSDE and SQL Server 7 store database files. If you use another location or you've deployed your MSDE/SQL Server 7 database files in multiple paths, you need to update the procedure accordingly. For each .mdf file that the procedure discovers in the target folder, the sample creates a database name (DBName) based on the filename (less the extension). In addition, the procedure assigns a value to the *MdfFilePath* variable that consists of the path for your MSDE or SQL Server 7 database files and the filename for the .mdf database file (including the extension). Before attempting to attach the old database file to the new server, the procedure prints the path and filename for the .mdf file to the Immediate window.

The second procedure takes *DBName* and *MdfFilePath* as arguments. After connecting to the local server, this procedure invokes the *AttachDB* method to attempt to attach the database file to the server. If no run-time error occurs, the method succeeds and transfers control back to the loop in the first procedure. If a run-time error occurs (for example, if you already have a database with the same name), the procedure prints the *Err* object's *Number* and *Description* properties to the Immediate window. When combined with the output from the first procedure, the output from this routine creates a log that highlights the errors resulting from the attempt to attach database files. The path and filename for the database files precede the log's error description.

```
'Requires Microsoft Scripting Runtime reference
Sub AttachOldDataFiles()
Dim fso1 As Scripting.FileSystemObject
Dim str1 As String
Dim fil1 As Scripting.File
Dim DBName As String
Dim MdfFilePath As String

'Set reference to FileSystemObject
Set fso1 = New Scripting.FileSystemObject

'Loop through files in target folder;
'attempt to attach .mdf files to local
'database server
str1 = "c:\mssql7\data\"
For Each fil1 In fso1.GetFolder(str1).Files
    If fil1.Type = "MDF File" Then
        Debug.Print str1 & fil1.Name
        DBName = Left(fil1.Name, Len(fil1.Name) - 4)
```

```
            MdfFilePath = str1 & fill.Name
            AttachMyDB DBName, MdfFilePath
        End If
Next fill

End Sub


Sub AttachMyDB(DBName As String, MdfFilePath As String)
On Error GoTo Attach_Trap
Dim srv1 As New SQLDMO.SQLServer
Dim str1 As String

'Set reference to local database server,
'and attach MdfFilePath as DBName
srv1.LoginSecure = True
srv1.Connect "(local)"
str1 = srv1.AttachDB(DBName, MdfFilePath)

Attach_Exit:
srv1.DisConnect
Set srv1 = Nothing
Exit Sub

Attach_Trap:
'Print error log
Debug.Print Err.Number, Err.Description

End Sub
```

Programming SQL Server Security

SQL Server has a different security model than the one covered for Jet databases in Chapter 12, "Working with Multiuser Databases." In addition, the Access project UI changed from Access 2000 to Access 2002 to remove some screens for manually controlling SQL Server security. As a consequence, the programmatic solutions for managing SQL Server security are more important than ever.

There are at least two programmatic interfaces for managing SQL Server security. The first of these is T-SQL. Using T-SQL to administer SQL Server security can often be straightforward because T-SQL includes many commands tailored for managing security. In addition, Books Online offers numerous detailed samples that illustrate the use of T-SQL for programming database security. SQL-DMO, a hierarchical programming language for SQL Server, is another programmatic interface you can use to manage SQL Server security. Your experience with the Office hierarchical models transfers readily to SQL-DMO programming of SQL Server security. This section emphasizes SQL-DMO programming, but it includes some examples of T-SQL programming as well.

SQL Server security is a huge topic. The goal of this section is to acquaint you with selected SQL Server security issues. Once you have this foundation, you can advance your knowledge of the topic as much as your circumstances warrant.

SQL Server Security Issues

Before starting with programming, I briefly summarize the core SQL Server security concepts. You can think of SQL Server security as having two main locks. The first lock is authentication. If SQL Server authenticates a user, the user can log into the server. In fact, the credentials a user presents for entry into a SQL server are referred to as a login account. As noted previously in this chapter, SQL Server or Windows can authenticate a login account for entry into a SQL server. Even if a user takes advantage of Windows authentication, her login credentials must still correspond to a valid login account on a SQL server.

Once inside a SQL server, a user typically has to unlock a second lock to gain access to a database on the server. A user's level of authority to perform SQL Server administrative tasks and work with databases will depend on the membership of his login account in fixed server roles. There are eight fixed server roles. (This number increased by one since the release of SQL Server 7, which is the version that Access 2000 was compatible with when it was released. As you'll recall, Access 2002 is compatible with SQL Server 2000.)

A login account can belong to no, one, or more fixed server roles. The sa login is a member of the sysadmin role. Members of this role can do anything in SQL Server, including performing all administrative and database functions. In addition, sysadmin members can add and drop other members from any fixed server role. Earlier in the chapter, you saw how to programmatically shut down and restart SQL Server. To run this program, you must connect to a SQL server with a login that's a member of either the sysadmin or serveradmin fixed server roles. Chapter 14 showed some code for programmatically creating a database. For that sample to run, a user needs a login account that belongs to either the dbCreator or sysadmin fixed server roles.

To access a database, a user must typically have a user account. Just as login accounts provide access to SQL Server, user accounts permit access to the databases within a server. In addition, SQL Server has a collection of fixed database roles with associated database permissions. There are nine fixed database roles, but you can also create your own user-defined roles. The db_datareader fixed database role enables SELECT permission for any object within a database. The db_datawriter fixed database role conveys UPDATE, INSERT, and DELETE permission for any object in a database. With user-defined roles, you can explicitly grant, deny, and revoke database permissions against individual database objects. You can add and drop user-defined roles but not fixed database roles.

> **Note**   *Grant*, *deny*, and *revoke* are technical SQL Server security terms. To grant a permission means to allow a user to work with data or execute T-SQL statements. Denying a permission explicitly disallows a user from working with data or executing T-SQL statements. In addition, a user account that's denied a permission cannot inherit the permission from its membership in a role that has the permission. To revoke a permission means to remove a prior granting or denial of a permission. You can grant, deny, and revoke permissions to individual user accounts or database roles. You lower your security management overhead by managing permissions for roles and then adding and dropping members from those roles.

A public role complements the nine fixed database roles and user-defined roles within each database. All users automatically belong to the public role. You can neither remove the public role nor remove users from it. However, you can grant, deny, and revoke database permissions for the role. Remove all permissions from this role if you want your other roles to uniquely define database object permissions. By default, the public role has no permissions for user-defined database objects, but it does have some permissions for system-defined objects within a database.

A login account can have no, one, or more user accounts associated with it. With the exception of login accounts in the sysadmin role and the guest user account, a login account gains database access through its user accounts. You can programmatically assign user accounts to login accounts to grant database access. By adding the user accounts to database roles, you grant permissions in a database. These roles include the fixed database roles as well as user-defined roles. The members of the sysadmin role can perform any function in any database even without a database user account. Login accounts without a user account for a database can still gain access to a database, if the database has a guest user account. You can add or remove permissions from a guest user account, just as you can add and remove the guest account from a database. By default, new databases do not have a guest user account.

T-SQL Help for Roles

Two special system stored procedures remind you about the different kinds of fixed server roles and their capabilities. The *sp_helpsrvrole* system stored procedure returns a list of the fixed server roles along with a brief description of each role. The *sp_srvrolepermission* stored procedure can return the server permissions associated with all the fixed server roles or with a specific one. You can run either stored procedure from the Create Text Stored Procedure template in an Access project or from a VBA procedure. When you use a VBA procedure, you can run these two stored procedures from the *Command* object and then pass the result set to a *Recordset* object for display in the Immediate window or elsewhere in an Access application.

The following sample demonstrates the syntax for running both the *sp_helpsrvrole* and *sp_srvrolepermission* system stored procedures in a single VBA procedure. The output from this procedure is a convenient, top-level, detailed report documenting the functionality provided by each fixed server role. The procedure instantiates a command and then uses it to run a T-SQL statement that invokes the *sp_helpsrvrole* system stored procedure. After transferring the result to a recordset, the procedure loops through the recordset's rows to enumerate the fixed server names and descriptions. Next the VBA procedure reuses the command and recordset to enumerate detailed permissions for the fixed server roles.

```
Sub SummarizeFixedServerRoles()
Dim cmd1 As ADODB.Command
Dim rst1 As ADODB.Recordset

'Instantiate a Command object and let it use
'the connection for the current project
Set cmd1 = New ADODB.Command
cmd1.ActiveConnection = CurrentProject.Connection

'Summarize fixed server roles
cmd1.CommandText = "Exec sp_helpsrvrole"
Set rst1 = New ADODB.Recordset
Set rst1 = cmd1.Execute
Debug.Print "Print Fixed Server Roles and Descriptions"
Do Until rst1.EOF
    Debug.Print rst1(0), rst1(1)
    rst1.MoveNext
Loop
Debug.Print String(2, vbCr)

'Provide detailed permissions
cmd1.CommandText = "EXEC sp_srvrolepermission"
Set rst1 = cmd1.Execute
Debug.Print "Print Fixed Server Roles and Permissions"
Do Until rst1.EOF
    Debug.Print rst1(0), rst1(1)
    rst1.MoveNext
Loop
```

```
'Clean up objects
rst1.Close
Set rst1 = Nothing
Set cmd1 = Nothing

End Sub
```

The next sample shows the application of the same basic logic to documenting the fixed database roles. In this case, the *sp_helpdbfixedrole* system stored procedure enumerates the individual fixed database roles along with brief descriptions. The *sp_dbfixedrolepermission* system stored procedure lists the individual permission descriptions for each fixed database role. Because the names for the fixed database roles vary more in length than they do for fixed server roles, you must pad the end of the names with spaces so that the second column of descriptions aligns evenly across all fixed database role names.

```
Sub SummarizeFixedDBRoles()
Dim cmd1 As ADODB.Command
Dim rst1 As ADODB.Recordset

'Instantiate a Command object and let it use
'the connection for the current project
Set cmd1 = New ADODB.Command
cmd1.ActiveConnection = CurrentProject.Connection

'Summarize fixed database roles
cmd1.CommandText = "Exec sp_helpdbfixedrole"
Set rst1 = New ADODB.Recordset
Set rst1 = cmd1.Execute
Debug.Print "Print Fixed Database Roles and Descriptions"
Do Until rst1.EOF
    Debug.Print rst1(0) & _
        String(18 - Len(rst1(0)), " ") & rst1(1)
    rst1.MoveNext
Loop
Debug.Print String(2, vbCr)

'Provide detailed permissions
cmd1.CommandText = "EXEC sp_dbfixedrolepermission"
Set rst1 = cmd1.Execute
Debug.Print "Print Fixed Database Roles and Permissions"
Do Until rst1.EOF
    Debug.Print rst1(0) & _
        String(18 - Len(rst1(0)), " ") & rst1(1)
    rst1.MoveNext
Loop

End Sub
```

> **Note**   For your convenience, the book's companion CD includes the SecurityDemo1 database files. If you prefer, you can just attach them to your server instead of running the sample procedures to create the sample security database with its tables.

Creating Login and User Accounts

Creating a new SQL Server user for a database requires several steps. First you have to add a login account. The user can log on to the server with the database using this account. SQL-DMO represents a login account with a *Login* object.

Setting Up the SQL Server Security Demonstrations

My presentation of SQL Server security programming techniques relies on a new database, SecurityDemo1, which has a pair of tables, *Pic_Addresses* and *Employees*. This simple database design will help you understand the basics of security programming. The security code samples all operate from the Access project for this chapter. These samples demonstrate how to programmatically control the security for one database from an Access project connected to a second database. Chapter 12 showed the same kind of programming technique for Jet security.

Several heavily commented procedures in the Access project for this chapter create the SecurityDemo1 database and its two tables. The main procedure names are *CallCreateDBOnFilePath*, *CreatePic_Addresses3*, and *CreateEmployees*. These procedures borrow from and sometimes extend the programming methods presented in Chapter 14 and earlier in this chapter. Run *CallCreateDBOnFilePath* before either of the other two main procedures. *CallCreateDBOnFilePath* calls two others: one that drops a prior version of the SecurityDemo1 database if it exists, and another to create a new copy of the SecurityDemo1 database. When you run *CallCreateDBOnFilePath*, make sure there are no active users for the SecurityDemo1 database, such as another Access project connected to the database. You can run the other two procedures in either order. They create the *Pic_Addresses* and *Employees* tables in the SecurityDemo1 database. The *CreatePic_Addresses3* procedure relies on the prior installation of the Chapter 14SQL database on your server, and the *CreateEmployees* procedure requires that you have the Chapter 15SQL database attached to your server.

This object is a member of the *Logins* collection that belongs to a *SQLServer* object. Second, you can create a user account for the database. This user account should reference the login account that you just created. SQL-DMO represents a user account with a *User* object. This object is a member of the *Users* collection that belongs to the *Database* object. Third, you can assign the user account to a database role. This lets the user account inherit the permissions assigned to the role. SQL-DMO represents a database role with a *DatabaseRole* object. This object is a member of the *DatabaseRoles* collection that belongs to a *Database* object.

The following sample shows a general procedure for creating a new login and a user account in a database. The procedure also makes the user a member in a database role. You must supply five arguments to target the procedure's behavior. The *srvName* argument designates the server for the login account. The *dbsName* argument specifies the database name for the user account. The *lgnName* and *usrName* arguments designate the names for the login and user accounts. The *dbrName* argument is the name of a database role. The procedure makes the user account a member of this role.

The procedure has a main flow and an error trap flow. After creating a *SQLServer* object that points at the server named *srvName*, the procedure's main flow immediately attempts to remove a prior user account with the name of *usrName* and a prior login account. The error flow accounts for various run-time errors that can occur when you attempt to remove a *Login* or a *User* object. (For example, the object might not exist.)

The procedure starts to create a new login account by instantiating a login object (*lgn1*). Then it assigns a name to the object. Unless you explicitly specify otherwise, all logins have a SQL Server standard type by default. This type property is for SQL Server authentication. Two other login *Type* property settings can designate a login for Windows NT authentication. The sample invokes the *SetPassword* method to assign the login a password equal to the string password. You can override this default password in the procedure. Regardless of whether you change this password, users can change it once you make the login account available to them. For example, users can invoke the Tools-Security-Set Login Password command in an Access project to change their password. After designating the login properties, the code adds the new *Login* object to the *Logins* collection for the server instantiated at the start of the procedure.

> **Note**   If you change the password setting for the login in this procedure, you should revise it in the other procedures (discussed next) that reference it.

Next the procedure moves on to creating a new user account. The procedure begins this process by instantiating a new *User* object. The next two lines of code assign a name property to the user and associate the user with a login, which is the login just created. After specifying these core user properties, the procedure appends the *User* object to the *Users* collection for the database named in dbsname.

The procedure's final step before exiting is to add the new user to a database role. This step lets the user inherit the permissions that belong to the role. The *AddMember* method of the *DatabaseRole* object enables the assignment of a user to a role. The argument takes a string with the name of the user that it adds to a role.

```
Sub AddLoginAndUserToDBRole(srvName As String, _
    dbsName As String, _
    lgnName As String, _
    usrName As String, _
    dbrName As String)
On Error GoTo AddLogin_Trap
Dim srv1 As SQLDMO.SQLServer
Dim lgn1 As SQLDMO.Login
Dim usr1 As SQLDMO.User
Dim cnn1 As ADODB.Connection

'Instantiate a SQLServer object, and connect
'using integrated security
Set srv1 = New SQLDMO.SQLServer
srv1.LoginSecure = True
srv1.Connect srvName

'Remove prior user and login accounts, if they exist,
'by first removing user object and then removing
'login object
srv1.Databases(dbsName).Users(usrName).Remove
srv1.Logins(lgnName).Remove

'Add login by instantiating a login object, giving it a
'name, assigning it a default database, setting its
'password, and adding it to a server's Logins collection
Set lgn1 = New SQLDMO.Login
lgn1.Name = lgnName
lgn1.SetPassword "", "password"
srv1.Logins.Add lgn1

'Add a user by instantiating it, giving it a name,
'assigning a corresponding login, and adding it to
'a database's Users collection
```

```
Set usr1 = New SQLDMO.User
usr1.Name = usrName
usr1.Login = lgn1.Name
srv1.Databases(dbsName).Users.Add usr1

'Assign database permissions to user by adding
'the user to fixed database role
srv1.Databases(dbsName). _
    DatabaseRoles(dbrName).AddMember usr1.Name

AddLogin_Exit:
Set usr1 = Nothing
Set lgn1 = Nothing
srv1.DisConnect
Set srv1 = Nothing
Exit Sub

AddLogin_Trap:
If Err.Number = -2147199728 Then
'User does not exist
    Resume Next
ElseIf Err.Number = -2147206330 Then
'lngCanSelectOnly still logged on
    Set cnn1 = New ADODB.Connection
    cnn1.Open "Provider=sqloledb;Data Source=(local);" & _
        "Initial Catalog=SecurityDemo1; " & _
        "User Id=lgnCanSelectOnly;" & _
        "Password=password;"
    cnn1.Close
    Set cnn1 = Nothing
    Resume Next
ElseIf Err.Number = -2147200496 Then
'Login does not exist
    Resume Next
Else
    Debug.Print Err.Number, Err.Description
End If

End Sub
```

Testing User Accounts

The preceding sample, which was based on the *AssignLoginAndUserToDBRole* procedure, needs another procedure to call it. At a minimum, this second procedure must supply values for the sample that creates the login and user accounts. The following sample accomplishes this, and it verifies the operation of a user account with membership in the db_datareader role. This role authorizes the ability to use a SELECT statement with any object in a database.

The sample procedure for this section, *TestSelectPermissionLogin*, performs several tasks. First, it invokes the *AssignLoginAndUserToDBRole* procedure. Using the arguments passed to the procedure in the preceding sample, the code creates a login named *lgnCanSelectOnly* and a user named *usrCanSelectOnly*. The user belongs to the SecurityDemo1 database and is a member of the db_datareader fixed database role.

After creating the login and user, the code starts to use them. It begins by making a connection to the SecurityDemo1 database on the local server. Notice that you use the value of *lgnName* (rather than *usrName*) for the user ID in the connection string. Next the code opens a recordset with a T-SQL SELECT statement for the *Pic_Addresses* table. This is one of the two tables in the Security-Demo1 database. To confirm the selection, the procedure prints the number of records in the *Pic_Addresses* table to the Immediate window. Then the procedure closes the recordset and connection before removing both of them from memory.

The success of the attempt to select from the *Pic_Addresses* table depends on the status of the *usrCanSelectOnly* user as a member of the db_datareader role. By dropping the *User* object from the role, you can invalidate an attempt by the *usrCanSelectOnly* user to select from the *Pic_Addresses* table. The next segment of code in *TextSelectPermissionLogin* drops the user from the db_datareader role and then tries to execute the T-SQL statement that previously succeeded. An in-line error trap catches the error from the attempt to open the recordset. If the error is the one that points to a missing SELECT permission, the procedure opens a message box informing the user and suggesting she contact the DBA.

```
Sub TestSelectPermissionLogin()
Dim cnn1 As ADODB.Connection
Dim rst1 As ADODB.Recordset
Dim srv1 As SQLDMO.SQLServer
Dim srvName As String
Dim dbsName As String
Dim lgnName As String
Dim usrName As String
Dim dbrName As String

'Create lgnName on srvName and usrName in dbsName
'with dbrName database role
srvName = "(local)"
dbsName = "SecurityDemo1"
lgnName = "lgnCanSelectOnly"
usrName = "usrCanSelectOnly"
dbrName = "db_datareader"
AddLoginAndUserToDBRole srvName, dbsName, _
    lgnName, usrName, dbrName
```

```
'Connect using lgnName login to dbsName database with
'password equal to password
Set cnn1 = New ADODB.Connection
cnn1.Open "Provider=sqloledb;Data Source=" & srvName & ";" & _
    "Initial Catalog=" & dbsName & "; " & _
    "User Id=" & lgnName & ";" & _
    "Password=password;"

'Open Pic_Addresses table and return record count
Set rst1 = New ADODB.Recordset
rst1.Open "SELECT * FROM Pic_Addresses", cnn1, _
    adOpenKeyset, adLockOptimistic, adCmdText
Debug.Print "Count of records is: " & rst1.RecordCount & _
    ".  Attempt to open succeeds when user belongs to " & _
    "db_datareader role."

'Close and remove from memory recordset and connection
rst1.Close
Set rst1 = Nothing
cnn1.Close
Set cnn1 = Nothing

'Instantiate a SQLServer object, and connect
'using integrated security; drop usrCanSelectOnly from
'db_datareader role for SecurityDemo1
srvName = "(local)"
Set srv1 = New SQLDMO.SQLServer
srv1.LoginSecure = True
srv1.Connect srvName
srv1.Databases(dbsName). _
    DatabaseRoles(dbrName).DropMember usrName
srv1.DisConnect
Set srv1 = Nothing

'Connect using lgnName login to dbsName database with
'password equal to password
Set cnn1 = New ADODB.Connection
cnn1.Open "Provider=sqloledb;Data Source=" & srvName & ";" & _
    "Initial Catalog=" & dbsName & "; " & _
    "User Id=" & lgnName & ";" & _
    "Password=password;"

'See if usrCanSelectOnly can select after it is removed
'from db_datareader role
Set rst1 = New ADODB.Recordset
On Error Resume Next
rst1.Open "SELECT * FROM Pic_Addresses", cnn1, _
    adOpenKeyset, adLockOptimistic, adCmdText
```

(continued)

```
'Simple trap for no SELECT permission error
If Err.Number = -2147217911 Then
    MsgBox "No SELECT permission for Pic_Addresses " & _
    "table.  See DBA for assignment of SELECT permission " & _
    "to user account: usrCanSelectOnly.", vbCritical, _
    "Programming Microsoft Access Version 2002"
    Exit Sub
End If

End Sub
```

Dynamically Adding Permissions to a User Account

Instead of sending a user to the DBA to get permission, you can dynamically add permissions to a user account when your application discovers that the account has insufficient permissions to perform some task. The next sample offers one approach to handling the dynamic assignment of a permission.

This sample starts out like the preceding one—it sets up the login and user accounts for *lgnName* and *usrName*. These accounts are endowed with the same SELECT permission for the tables in the SecurityDemo1 database. The select query statement that serves as the source of the recordset is also identical to the one in the preceding sample. The two procedures start to diverge after the invocation of the *Open* method for the recordset. This sample's code assigns a new value to the recordset value with the statement *rst1(1) = "foo"*. At this point in the procedure, the change is still local. However, the *rst1.Update* statement alerts the server to the client application's desire to modify a value on the server.

The attempt to invoke the *Update* method generates a run-time error. This run-time error occurs because the *usrCanSelectOnly* user belongs to just one fixed database role, db_datareader. This role conveys SELECT permission for any object. However, the role does not authorize its members to update any record source. On the other hand, the db_datawriter role does grant the ability the modify any updatable record source tied to a SQL Server database. The remainder of the procedure lets the user know about the problem, and it provides the user with a way to dynamically add the *usrCanSelectOnly* user to the db_datawriter role.

This approach to dynamically adding a *User* object to a new database role starts just before the line of code that triggers the run-time error *rst1.Update*. Notice that the preceding line opens an in-line error trap with an *On Error Resume Next* statement. The line after the attempt to update the record source is merely an *If...Then...Else...End If* statement. This statement permits the execution of the code within the block when the *Number* property value for the *Err* object matches the value of a run-time error resulting from an attempt to update a value without UPDATE permission. The code within the *Then* clause of the *If...Then... Else...End If* statement first presents an error message briefly explaining the problem in a message box. Then the code uses an *InputBox* function to ask for the secret word that will upgrade the user account to include the UPDATE permission. Users responding with the secret word *update* have the *usrCanSelectOnly User* object upgraded to include membership in the db_datawriter role. After this upgrade occurs, the procedure executes the *Update* method a second time just before printing a message about the success of the update. If a user does not reply to the prompt from the *InputBox* function with the correct secret word, the procedure tells him to get help from the DBA.

```
Sub DynamicallyAddUpdatePermission()
Dim cnn1 As ADODB.Connection
Dim rst1 As ADODB.Recordset
Dim str1 As String
Dim srv1 As SQLDMO.SQLServer
Dim srvName As String
Dim dbsName As String
Dim lgnName As String
Dim usrName As String
Dim dbrName As String
Dim str2 As String

'Create lgnName on srvName and usrName in dbsName
'with dbrName database role
srvName = "(local)"
dbsName = "SecurityDemo1"
lgnName = "lgnCanSelectOnly"
usrName = "usrCanSelectOnly"
dbrName = "db_datareader"
AddLoginAndUserToDBRole srvName, dbsName, _
    lgnName, usrName, dbrName

'Connect using lgnName login to dbsName database with
'password equal to password
Set cnn1 = New ADODB.Connection
cnn1.Open "Provider=sqloledb;Data Source=" & srvName & ";" & _
    "Initial Catalog=" & dbsName & "; " & _
    "User Id=" & lgnName & ";" & _
    "Password=password;"

'Attempt to update a table with a user account that has
'only SELECT permission
Set rst1 = New ADODB.Recordset
rst1.Open "SELECT * FROM Pic_Addresses", cnn1, _
    adOpenKeyset, adLockOptimistic, adCmdText
str1 = rst1(1)
Debug.Print rst1(1)
rst1(1) = "foo"
```

(continued)

```
'Setup to process error from attempt to update a table
'with a user account that has only SELECT permission
On Error Resume Next
rst1.Update
If Err.Number = -2147217911 Then
    MsgBox "No UPDATE permission for Pic_Addresses " & _
    "table.", vbCritical, _
    "Programming Microsoft Access Version 2002"
    str2 = InputBox("Do you know the secret word for UPDATE " & _
    "permission?", _
    "Programming Microsoft Access Version 2002", _
    "I don't know.")
    If str2 = "update" Then
'If user knows secret word, add permission to user account
'immediately and perform update
        srvName = "(local)"
        Set srv1 = New SQLDMO.SQLServer
        srv1.LoginSecure = True
        srv1.Connect srvName
        srv1.Databases("SecurityDemo1"). _
            DatabaseRoles("db_datawriter").AddMember _
            "usrCanSelectOnly"
        srv1.DisConnect
        Set srv1 = Nothing
        rst1.Update
        str2 = "Update from " & """" & str1 & """" & " to " & _
            """" & rst1(1) & """" & " succeeded."
        MsgBox str2, vbInformation, _
            "Programming Microsoft Access Version 2002"
    Else
'If user does not know the secret word, refer to DBA
        str2 = "Wrong secret word; see your DBA for " & _
            "UPDATE permission."
        MsgBox str2, vbCritical, _
            "Programming Microsoft Access Version 2002"
    End If
End If

End Sub
```

Selectively Applying Object Permissions

The db_datareader and db_datawriter roles, along with the other fixed database roles, apply permissions indiscriminately to all database objects. However, it's common for security needs to selectively apply to database objects. For example, a typical require-ment is for users to be able to select from all tables—except those containing salary and other sensitive information. To accommodate this need, you must create user-defined roles with custom permissions for individual database objects.

The code in the next sample demonstrates how to set up a user-defined role and then add a user to it. This may or may not be sufficient for your security requirements. This is because user accounts can belong to multiple database roles. Therefore, if a user cannot accomplish a task with the permissions for one database role membership, she might be able to succeed with her membership in another database role. I will drill down on the syntax for creating a user-defined database role and assigning a new user as I walk you through the sample code. You will also learn how to drop a user from a database role. The sample concludes by conditionally executing one of two select query statements for a recordset. When the user takes the path associated with a value of True for the *UseWrongSelect* compiler constant, the program generates a run-time error but the other path leads to a normal exit. Because this sample demonstrates the behavior of user accounts based on roles, it doesn't build an error trap for taking the wrong path.

The procedure starts by setting a *SQLServer* object at the local server. Then the code instantiates a *DatabaseRole* object, gives it a name, and assigns the object to the *DatabaseRoles* collection for the database at which the *dbsName* string points. The new role's name is SelectEmployeesNotPics. After adding the *Database-Role* object, the procedure invokes the *Grant* method for the *Employees* table. With this method, the procedure adds a SELECT permission for the table to the SelectEmployeesNotPics database role. The sample references this role with dbr1. Next the sample adds the *usrCanSelectOnly* user, represented by *usrName*, to the SelectEmployeesNotPics user-defined role. Notice that the dbr1 role has no permission for the *Pic_Addresses* table.

Now the procedure is ready to start testing the security of the database. First it opens a connection to the SecurityDemo1 database for the *usrCanSelectOnly* user. Then it uses the *Connection* object to open a recordset based on a select query for the *Pic_Addresses* table. Although the SelectEmployeesNotPics database role grants SELECT permission for just the *Employees* table, the recordset for the *Pic_Addresses* table still opens. This is because the *usrCanSelectOnly* user belongs to the db_datareader role, which grants SELECT permission for all database objects.

After successfully executing the select query, the sample performs one more database definition. The next statement drops the *usrCanSelectOnly* user from the db_datareader role. This completes the steps necessary to restrict *usrCan-SelectOnly* SELECT privileges to the *Employees* table. The final statement in the sample is a *#If... Then... #Else...#End If* statement that runs one of two recordset *Open* method statements based on the value of the *UseWrongSelect* compiler constant. When the constant's value is False, as in this next sample, the procedure ends normally.

When you change constant's value to True, the procedure can fail in a couple of ways that do not illustrate the impact of the compiler constant setting. For this reason, run the *DropSelectEmployeesNotPics* procedure after each execution of the following procedure. The *DropSelectEmployeesNotPics* procedure—the last sample procedure in the chapter—removes the SelectEmployeesNotPics role and restores the membership of the *usrCanSelectOnly* user in the db_datareader role. With these two fixes, the following procedure is ready to run again and show the effects of a changed compiler constant setting. When you run the procedure with a compiler constant of True, the procedure fails in the *Then* clause of the *#If...Then...#Else...#End If* statement because the code tries to run a select query against the *Pic_Addresses* table.

```
'Run after DynamicallyAddUpdatePermission procedure so that
'usrCanSelectOnly has db_datareader and db_datawriter
'role memberships
Sub CreateDBRoleAndGrantSelectPermission()
Dim srvName As String
Dim dbsName As String
Dim lgnName As String
Dim usrName As String
Dim srv1 As SQLDMO.SQLServer
Dim dbr1 As SQLDMO.DatabaseRole
#Const UseWrongSelect = False

'Assign selected string names
srvName = "(local)"
dbsName = "SecurityDemo1"
lgnName = "lgnCanSelectOnly"
usrName = "usrCanSelectOnly"

'Connect to server
Set srv1 = New SQLDMO.SQLServer
srv1.LoginSecure = True
srv1.Connect srvName

'Instantiate, name, and add new custom database role
Set dbr1 = New SQLDMO.DatabaseRole
dbr1.Name = "SelectEmployeesNotPics"
srv1.Databases(dbsName).DatabaseRoles.Add dbr1

'Grant SELECT permission to the Employees table but not
'the Pic_Addresses table to dbr1 role, and add user
'account with usrName to dbr1 database role
srv1.Databases(dbsName).Tables("Employees"). _
    Grant SQLDMOPriv_Select, dbr1.Name
```

```
srv1.Databases(dbsName). _
    DatabaseRoles("SelectEmployeesNotPics"). _
    AddMember usrName

'Connect using lgnName login to dbsName database with
'password equal to password
Set cnn1 = New ADODB.Connection
cnn1.Open "Provider=sqloledb;Data Source=" & srvName & ";" & _
    "Initial Catalog=" & dbsName & "; " & _
    "User Id=" & lgnName & ";" & _
    "Password=password;"

'Attempt to select a table with a user account that belongs
'to the the db_datareader and db_datawrite roles
Set rst1 = New ADODB.Recordset
rst1.Open "SELECT * FROM Pic_Addresses", cnn1, _
    adOpenKeyset, adLockOptimistic, adCmdText

'Drop usrName user account from db_datareader role
srv1.Databases(dbsName). _
    DatabaseRoles("db_datareader"). _
    DropMember usrName

'If UseWrongSelect is True, click End on error message dialog box
#If UseWrongSelect = True Then
    Set rst1 = New ADODB.Recordset
    rst1.Open "SELECT * FROM Pic_Addresses", cnn1, _
        adOpenKeyset, adLockOptimistic, adCmdText
#Else
    Set rst1 = New ADODB.Recordset
    rst1.Open "SELECT * FROM Employees", cnn1, _
        adOpenKeyset, adLockOptimistic, adCmdText
#End If

End Sub


'Utility to restore security after running
'the CreateDBRoleAndGrantSelectPermission procedure
Sub DropSelectEmployeesNotPics()
Dim srv1 As SQLDMO.SQLServer

'Connect to server
Set srv1 = New SQLDMO.SQLServer
srv1.LoginSecure = True
srv1.Connect "(local)"
```

(continued)

```
'Remove member, and then drop role
srv1.Databases("SecurityDemo1"). _
    DatabaseRoles("SelectEmployeesNotPics"). _
    DropMember "usrCanSelectOnly"
srv1.Databases("SecurityDemo1"). _
    DatabaseRoles("SelectEmployeesNotPics").Remove

srv1.Databases("SecurityDemo1"). _
    DatabaseRoles("db_datareader"). _
    AddMember "usrCanSelectOnly"

End Sub
```

16

Access Does the Web: Part I

For many businesses, Web services are the way of the future. However, Web development techniques are often novel and unintuitive to typical Microsoft Access developers. Access 2002 addresses the need of programmers to deliver powerful, full-featured Web applications in an easy and familiar development environment. Access 2002 offers rapid application development (RAD) techniques for the Web based on enhanced data access pages and the Microsoft Office XP Web Components. In addition, Access 2002 enables you to work with XML data. This chapter shows you how to tap into all these capabilities to write innovative Web solutions for your clients.

After providing a Web development overview targeting the special needs of Access developers, this chapter gives a quick introduction to Microsoft FrontPage 2002. Because FrontPage 2002 ships with Office XP, it's a natural tool for managing the Web sites that make your solutions available to users. The chapter next presents some step-by-step examples of creating forms and reports on Web pages using graphical design techniques. These forms and reports bind directly to the Access database files and Microsoft SQL Server databases described throughout this book. I'll show you how to make these forms and reports dynamic and interactive by reviewing the new (since Access 2000) integrated development environment (IDE) behind them. You'll also see several samples in the chapter that illustrate how to build event procedures. Furthermore, you'll learn some easy ways to tackle advanced topics, such as programmatically creating Web-based forms and reports. Access 2002 enables you to create new Web-based forms and reports on the Access forms and reports you previously created.

Overview of Web Technologies

Access developers building Web solutions will typically use FrontPage and at least one of these four technologies: data access pages, Office Web Components, Active Server Pages (ASP), or XML data formats. All four technologies let you share data with other users on a web. Each has characteristics that make it best suited for particular scenarios. This section provides brief summaries of each of these technologies to help you evaluate which tools best meet the needs of your clients.

When building Web solutions with any of the technologies just mentioned, you will typically deploy files to a Web site where others can access them. FrontPage is a Web site management tool that ships with several versions of Office. In addition, FrontPage has a look and feel that resembles other Office components. Therefore, FrontPage enables the typical Office user to contribute content to a Web site readily and enables a developer with limited Web experience to serve as a Web site administrator.

Data Access Pages

A data access page is a Web page with special ties to Access 2002, which allow Access to make available graphical tools for building Web solutions that resemble Access forms and reports. A Web solution can consist of one or more data access pages, or it can contain a mix of data access pages, other kinds of Web pages, and additional files, such as those with graphic images. In addition, you can publish some Access reports and forms as data access pages. This makes it possible to build a form or report in Access and then publish it as a data access page. Access also offers a programming environment that complements and extends the graphical development tools that make data access pages so easy to create solutions with.

You need to understand that, unlike Access forms and reports residing within Access database files and Access projects, a data access page is a standalone file. The Access Database window includes a Pages collection just like the Forms and Reports collections. However, the items in the Database window representing pages are links that point at external files.

Like forms, data access pages have two key views. Page view shows the data, if any, on the page. For example, if a page represents a form tied to a table, you can use the form to navigate the table records. You can also open a data access page in a browser by pointing the browser at the URL of the standalone file for the data access page. Design view reveals the objects within a data access page. These objects are controls, many of which are similar to those for forms. However, some of these controls are especially tailored for the Web environment. Both the Page view and Design view are available directly from the Database window. Just select the page name in the Database window, and click Open for the Page view or Design for the Design view. A third view, named Web Page Preview, is available from either of the first two views. Selecting this third view opens a browser session as a container for the data access page. This view shows a Web page designer exactly how the page looks in a browser. You can access the Web Page Preview from the standard View control on the toolbar.

Office Web Components

There are four Office Web Components: the Data Source Control object, the Chart control, the PivotTable list control, and the Spreadsheet control. The Data Source Control object is the data engine behind data access pages. A separate ActiveX control implements each of the Office Web Components. You can use these components in isolation on Web pages or in combination. For example, one Web page can use the Data Source Control object to include a form based on data in a table. You can also use the Spreadsheet control to build a spreadsheet on the Web page that can create projections based on the data that displays in the form. And you can use the Chart control to create a chart on the page that can graph the projections in the spreadsheet.

The PivotTable list control mainly targets solutions for business decision analysts. Many business analysts are already familiar with PivotTables because they use them in Microsoft Excel. The PivotTable list control enables developers to publish subsets of data from a database. Developers can enable end users to manipulate the data by publishing subsets of it on Web pages containing PivotTable list controls. By publishing the data in a PivotTable, developers save end users from having to write queries whenever they want to process data. Developers can also precisely specify the scope of data to which end users have access by restricting the record sources that contribute to a PivotTable list. In addition to supporting security, this capability can improve performance by avoiding poorly constructed and overly broad queries.

Office Web Components is distributed through the installation of Office XP. Two .dll files, MSOWC.DLL and OCW10.DLL, implement the components. You can get programming help for Office Web Components from OWCVBA10.CHM, which is installed by default in a subfolder of the C:\Program Files\Common Files\Microsoft Shared\Web Components folder.

XML Data Formats

XML offers an application-independent way of sharing data via the Internet and e-mail. You can use XML to represent data, such as the column values in a table, the result set from a query, or the datasheet behind an Access form or report. Leading software firms, including Microsoft, are working with the World Wide Web Consortium to iron out XML standards for all products offering data access and processing capabilities. As these standards continue to evolve, it will become easier to exchange data between applications from the same manufacturer and even between those from different manufacturers.

XML is a markup language like HTML. Three related but independent XML-based languages deal with representing data values, schemas for describing data, and ways of transforming and displaying data. XML is the language for representing data values. XSD (XML Schema Definition) is the language for describing the structure of a dataset. XSLT (XML Stylesheet Language Transformation) helps you transform documents into different formats (such as transforming an HTML document to a Rich Text Format, or RTF, one).

New Access *Application* object methods facilitate the importing and exporting of data in an XML format. These methods permit you to explicitly reference XML, XSD, and XSLT files for any dataset. You can easily export Access data for tables, queries, views, datasheets, forms, and reports with the *Export* method. A new *Import* method lets you import data that was exported with the *Export* method. With these commands, you can share data among multiple Access database files or Access projects over the Internet.

Access 2002 introduces a new ReportML language for describing Access forms, reports, and data access pages, along with their events and properties. ReportML is a markup language similar to HTML and XML. Saving a form or a report as XML saves the structure of the form or report in ReportML. The ReportML representation of the report or form creates a data access page for the datasheet behind the form or report that's suitable for display on the Web. You can also save selected Access forms and reports directly as data access pages. Due to the ease and power of representing Access forms and reports as data access pages, this chapter drills down on tools that accomplish this.

Active Server Pages

Active Server Pages (ASP) is a Microsoft Internet Information Services (IIS) technology that lets you script pages on a server for client browsers. One very popular use for ASP files is the presentation of dynamic Web pages, including those that reflect ongoing data updates. You can also use ASP files to process forms in a Web environment. We'll drill down on ASP files in Chapter 17, "Access Does the Web: Part II."

While data access pages offer a rich graphical environment from Access, ASP files aren't primarily considered a strong graphical development tool. You can populate ASP files with HTML and a scripting language, such as Microsoft Visual Basic, Scripting Edition (VBScript). The script and HTML run on the Web server to create a file for the server to send to a browser. The page for the browser doesn't contain any server-side script and can include pure HTML.

The client environment you use is one of the main distinctions between data access pages and ASP files. Because ASP files can write pure HTML, their output can be appropriate for any browser that reads HTML (which is essentially all browsers). In contrast, data access pages work exclusively in Microsoft Internet Explorer 5 or higher. In fact, the data access page format is different in Access 2000 and Access 2002. Therefore, you must upgrade your Access 2000 workstation if you want to open in Page view data access pages created with Access 2002.

> **Note**   The Microsoft documentation explains that you must install Office Web Components for Office XP if you want to view data access pages created with Access 2002 from Access 2000 workstations. However, this upgrade does not permit you to open Access 2002 data access pages in Design view on an Access 2000 workstation. To gain that additional level of functionality, you must install Access 2002 as a part of Office XP. You can have Access 2000 and Access 2002 running simultaneously on the same workstation.

ASP files make their connection to a database through script running on IIS. All connection with a database takes place in the script running on the Web server. The browser never has access to security information for linking to the database. Data access pages nearly always make a connection with a data source through their Web page. The data access page has a built-in connection to a database, either directly or through an intermediate tier. In other words, ASP files always use at least a three-tier model (browser, Web server, and database). Data access pages can use either a two-tier model (browser and database) or a three-tier model (browser, middle tier—such as RDS.Data Factory, and database). When a data access page uses a three-tier model, the middle tier between the browser and the database can be the Remote Data Service of ActiveX Data Objects (ADO). Microsoft recommends using only two-tier data access pages for behind firewalls because of security reasons.

> **Note**   This book discusses using data access pages behind a firewall on a local intranet. See the Microsoft white paper titled, "Creating Secure Data Access Pages," at msdn.microsoft.com/library/techart/securedap.htm for more in-depth coverage on securing data access pages.

FrontPage 2002

FrontPage 2002 ships with Office XP Professional Special Edition and Office XP Developer Edition. FrontPage 2002 integrates tightly with IIS, Microsoft's Web server, and it's a graceful extension of the core functionality of FrontPage 2000.

FrontPage enables you to create a Web site and manage its Web pages. For example, you can save your data access pages, XML, ASP, and other Web files at a FrontPage Web site. Users can connect to these files using http from a browser. This conveniently lets your Web-based solutions from a FrontPage Web site serve large communities of users.

FrontPage includes a variety of tools for creating and editing Web pages. For example, the graphical Database wizard, which simplifies Web page creation and editing, will be of special interest to those of you who build solutions with ASP. In addition, FrontPage features tools for simplifying the creation of Web-based forms that connect to Access database files and SQL Server databases via ASP.

Using FrontPage 2002

If you plan to manage a Web site, you need a Web server and a Web site management tool. For the writing of this book, I ran IIS 5 on a computer equipped with Microsoft Windows 2000 Server. IIS is the Web server for Windows 2000 Server and Windows 2000 Professional. Microsoft also makes available Personal Web Manager, a free Web server that ships with Windows 98. You can install Personal Web Manager by choosing Programs-Accessories-Internet Tools-Personal Web Server from the Start button. You can also access a Web server from an Internet host provider, a firm that runs a Web server shared by many Web sites. The host provider manages the Web server, the setup of Web sites, and the installation of a Web site manager. Additional details on the installation and management of a Web server are beyond the scope of this book. Check with your system administrator regarding the proper installation of operating system and Web server software. Microsoft maintains a list of registered providers of Web hosting services; see www.microsoftwpp.com/wppsearch/ for further details.

FrontPage 2002 is a Web site manager and Web authoring tool that installs as part of certain Office XP editions. If you are managing a Web site on a Web server with FrontPage 2002, you typically will want to install the FrontPage 2002 Server Extensions on the computer running your Web server. These server extensions let you perform select advanced features, such as creating a Web site and using the Database wizard to create ASP files. These extensions aren't installed as part of the typical installation. However, you can use the standard Office XP setup program to select the server extensions for installation, or you can run a complete install of all of Office XP to install the FrontPage 2002 Server Extensions.

> **Note**   The FrontPage 2002 Server Extensions run on Windows NT and Windows 2000 computers only. Windows NT computers require the installation of Service Pack 5. You cannot install the FrontPage 2002 Server Extensions on Windows 98 computers. Therefore, you cannot create new Web sites with FrontPage 2002 on the Personal Web Server for Windows 98. This is a departure from FrontPage 2000, which did support the installation of its server extensions on Windows 98 computers.

Creating a Web Site

A Web site serves as a folder within the computer running your Web server; it acts as a file collector and an administration point. This folder typically resides under the wwwroot directory of the Inetpub folder for a computer's root directory. Although the files for a Web site reside in a standard Windows folder, you do not create or administer the files from Windows Explorer.

You can use FrontPage 2002 to create a new Web site and manage an existing one. To create a new Web site with FrontPage 2002, choose File-New-Page Or Web. This opens the Task Pane found in all Office XP applications. See Chapter 10, "Microsoft Office Objects," for a discussion of the Task Pane in Access 2002. Click the Empty Web link in the New group. This opens the Web Site Templates dialog box. From this dialog box, you must specify a URL for your new Web site. You can also designate a type of Web site, as shown in Figure 16-1.

When you work with a Web server on your intranet, you can type *http:// yourservername/yoursitename* in the Web Site Templates dialog box to specify the location of the new Web site. For example, the Web server I used in my office while writing this book has the name cab2000. The Web site for this book has the name pma10. Therefore, I typed *http:/cab2000/pma10* when creating the Web site for the book. If your Web site exists on the Internet, you can specify your new site name with a syntax such as http://www.*yourcompany*.com/ *yoursitename*. The first part, www.*yourcompany*.com, designates the main portal into your company from the Web. The *yoursitename* trailer denotes a Web site available from the portal.

> **Note**   If you work with a host provider firm, the firm designates the URL for a site. Then you simply use FrontPage to connect to the site to populate it with content.

Before clicking OK to create your site, consider selecting the Web site template that you prefer. When following the instructions for opening the Web Sites Templates dialog box, FrontPage 2002 automatically selects Empty Web. This is suitable for the book's site. Figure 16-1 shows the dialog box for the book's site. Of course, you will need to replace cab2000 with the name of your Web server or an appropriate Internet URL. Clicking OK creates the new empty Web site.

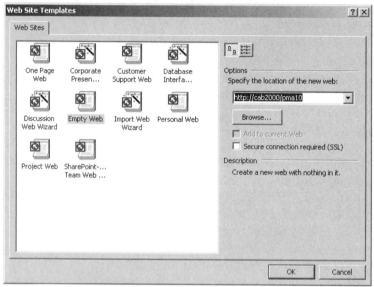

Figure 16-1 The Web Site Templates dialog box for creating a new Web site with FrontPage 2002.

Choose View-Folders to present a split pane view that shows folders on the left, and files and folders on the right. When you initially create a Web site with the instructions just outlined, your site will include two default folders and no pages. The _private folder is used for confidential files that you don't want visitors browsing through. The images folder can contain images that your site uses. Note that you can place images anywhere else within your Web site.

Click the toolbar control for creating a new normal page. When you perform this task immediately after creating a Web site, FrontPage names the page Default.htm by default. When users navigate to your site with their browser, this is the first page they encounter; it is your home page.

After adding a home page, add some content to it and close FrontPage. Start by double-clicking Default.htm in the right-hand pane. This opens the page. You'll notice a tab at the top of the page labeled Default.htm. Include any content on this page that you want visitors to see when they initially arrive at your site. For example, you could type *This is the home page for the pma10 Web site.* Save the page by clicking the Save control on the toolbar. If the Folder List does not already appear to the left of page, click the right edge of the Toggle Pane control and select Folder List. This opens a split-pane view. The left pane reveals the folders for the Web site and the files in the root folder. The current open page, Default.htm, appears in the right pane. Choose File-Exit to close FrontPage.

Opening an Existing Web Site

The next time you open FrontPage, it automatically resumes with the last Web site on which you worked. You can manage multiple Web sites with a single version of FrontPage. If you need to open another Web site besides the one with which you worked most recently, you can choose it from the File-Recent Webs menu. To open a Web site that doesn't appear in the menu, choose File-Open Web. Then type the URL for the Web site, such as *http://cab2000/pma10*, and click Open in the Open Web dialog box. Opening a Web site in any of these ways does so with the window arrangement from the last time that you were on the Web site.

Editing a Web Page

One of the most popular ways to edit a Web page is to add hyperlinks. FrontPage offers an Insert Hyperlink control on its toolbar that resembles the one in Access. To add a hyperlink, select some text or an image to which you want to apply a link. Then click the Insert Hyperlink tool to open the dialog box with the same name. At this point, you can choose to link to an existing file or Web page, a bookmark inside the current Web page, or a new Web page. You can also specify an e-mail address with which the e-mail package opens in the To field.

Figure 16-2 shows the pma10 site after multiple pages have been added to it. The figure shows the construction of a link to another page (dapEmployeePics.htm) on the site. The new link will add to the existing ones on the site's home page, whose name (Default.htm) appears on the tab at its top. You can also view the dialog box for setting the screen tip when the cursor is positioned over the link. Click the Screen Tip button on the Insert Hyperlink dialog box to open the Set Hyperlink Screen Tip dialog box. Figure 16-2 shows an entry in this dialog box just before it's closed by a user clicking OK.

Note   An asterisk (*) appears after the page name on which the example denotes the construction of hyperlinks. You can have multiple pages open for viewing and can navigate among them by selecting their tabs. The tabs for dirty pages have an asterisk. The asterisk serves as a reminder to save the pages to commit your changes.

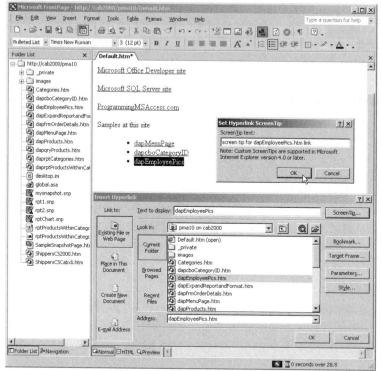

Figure 16-2 Creating a hyperlink on a page by using FrontPage.

The home page also includes links to sites other than the current one. You can click on the Browse The Web control in the Insert Hyperlink dialog box, or you can type a URL in the Address text box within the dialog box to add a link to another Web site.

If you select an existing hyperlink and click the Insert Hyperlink control, FrontPage opens the Edit Hyperlink dialog box with all settings for the selected link. You can edit those settings as your needs dictate. For example, if the URL for a link changes, you can type in the new URL.

Just below the Insert Hyperlink dialog box in Figure 16-2 you'll notice three tab controls. FrontPage names these tabs Normal, HTML, and Preview. Normal shows the currently selected Web page. This tab is a text and graphical representation of a page on which you can work, in many ways, just as you do in Microsoft Word. The HTML tab represents the layout of the currently selected Web page in HTML. If you are unfamiliar with HTML, you can teach yourself this language by designing pages in Normal view and then viewing the outcome on the HTML tab. The Preview tab shows many Web pages as they appear in a browser. For example, you can change the page appearing on the Preview tab by clicking a link. In addition, the Preview tab offers a right-click menu with a selection of commands available in a browser, such as Back and Forward.

The following HTML block shows the complete script for the page in Figure 16-2. Notice the pattern of symmetric tags. The page starts with an <html> tag and ends with an </html> tag. This is characteristic of HTML syntax, although not all tag types require—or even allow—opening and closing tags. The image in Figure 16-2 clips a title, My Favorites List, which appears at the top of the page. The page's HTML script shows the title. Since the title appears between paragraph tags, it rests on a line by itself.

The following script shows a couple of different ways to represent hyperlinks in HTML. The URLs shown include the full address of the Internet location as the argument for an href attribute of the <a> tag. The <a> tag is an anchor tag that specifies a link. The href attribute setting designates the destination for the link. After the first anchor tag completes, some normal text outside the tag indicates how the link displays on a page. The trailing anchor tag (</a>) completes the hyperlink specification. Since each hyperlink appears within paragraph tags (<p> and </p>), it appears on a separate line within the page.

Two of the three sample links for the pma10 site use the same general format that's used for links to Internet locations, except that the href attribute merely specifies a page's filename. Recall that the third tag has a screen tip. HTML uses a title attribute for the anchor tag to denote a screen tip. As with the URL specification for links, the screen tip appears in quotes. Using quote marks to delimit field assignment values is common for many arguments in HTML—even when dealing with numeric values. When a tag such as the anchor tag for dapEmployee-Pics has more than one attribute, you use one or more spaces to delimit these attributes. The three links for the current site appear as bulleted text. The <ul> tag marks a block of text as bulleted, and the <li> tags denote the insertion of individual bullets. The <blockquote> tag marks text and sets it apart from the regular text on a page.

```
<html>

<head>
<meta http-equiv="Content-Type" content="text/html;
  charset=windows-1252">
<meta http-equiv="Content-Language" content="en-us">
<title>Home Page</title>
<meta name="GENERATOR" content="Microsoft FrontPage 5.0">
<meta name="ProgId" content="FrontPage.Editor.Document">
</head>
```

(continued)

```
<body>
This is the home page for the pma10 site.
<p>My Favorites List</p>
<p><a href="http://msdn.microsoft.com/office/">
Microsoft Office Developer site</a></p>
<p><a href="http://www.microsoft.com/sql/default.asp">
Microsoft SQL Server site</a></p>
<p><a href="http://www.programmingmsaccess.com">
ProgrammingMSAccess.com</a></p>
<p>Samples at this site</p>
<blockquote>
  <ul>
    <li><a href="dapMenuPage.htm">dapMenuPage</a></li>
    <li><a href="dapcboCategoryID.htm">dapcboCategoryID</a></li>
    <li>
    <a title="screen tip for dapEmployeePics.htm link"
      href="dapEmployeePics.htm">dapEmployeePics</a></li>
  </ul>
</blockquote>
</body>

</html>
```

Getting Started with Forms on Data Access Pages

Data access pages can exhibit behavior similar to traditional Access forms and reports, except that they work across a web. When all clients use Internet Explorer 5 or later and you can install the Office XP Web Components on all workstation clients, data access pages offer a quick and easy route to developing forms that work across the Web.

In many ways, building solutions with forms for data access pages is very similar to building a solution for forms within Access. This similarity makes data access pages an attractive technology for Access developers who want to begin building Web solutions. Despite the fact that building data access pages is similar to creating forms, data access pages are Web pages. This means that the appropriate browsers can open them just as they would any other Web page. Of course, Access forms and reports do not have this characteristic.

The sample application for this section creates a form on a data access page that displays selected fields from the *Products* table. Then it creates another form on another data access page that allows users to filter the products that the first data access page shows.

Creating a Product Tracking Form

The sample database file for this chapter, Chapter 16.mdb, has links to the Northwind database. This means you can readily exhibit data from the *Products* table, which includes inventory information about products. One common way to view data, especially if users might need to update it, is with a form. You can build a data access page that lets Web users browse and update the contents of the *Products* table.

There are at least two graphical ways you can build a form for the *Products* table. One relies on a wizard similar to the Form wizard. You can launch the Page wizard by selecting Pages on the Objects bar in the Database window and then double-clicking Create Data Access Page By Using A Wizard. This way of building pages targets end users and beginning developers. The second approach lets you construct a form in an environment that is similar but not identical to the Design view for Access forms. This approach shows more basic functionality than using the Page wizard does. This section and much of the remaining discussion about data access pages highlight managing data access pages in Design view.

Begin creating a form on a data access page for the *Products* table by highlighting Pages in the Objects bar on the Database window and double-clicking Create Data Access Page In Design View. When you get to the Design view, you will see a grid for positioning controls on your form (unless you changed the default setting) as well as a title area above the grid. You can optionally click in the title area and type text for the page's title. Otherwise, the area appears blank. Since our task is to build a form for the *Products* table, we need to bind the form to this table.

> **Note**   The visibility of the grid that denotes the area for positioning controls is optional. You can control the visibility of the grid by using the View-Grid command.

The grid area is the area that you bind to a record source for your form. If you click anywhere inside the grid, handle controls appear around the grid to indicate that you've selected it. Display the properties for the grid by clicking the Properties tool on the Design view toolbar. Notice that the grid is a *Section* object with an assigned name of *SectionUnbound*; this name changes as you specify the design of your page. Select the Data tab on the Properties dialog box, and observe the *RecordSource* property setting control. Clicking the down arrow lets you specify any table or row-returning query as a record source for the grid.

After selecting the *Products* table as a record source, Access divides the original grid into two sections. A navigation control appears below a blank grid. If you select each section and examine their Properties dialog boxes, you will discover that they have section names: *HeaderProducts* for the top grid area, and *NavigationProducts* for the bottom grid area. These names appear in the title bar for the Properties dialog box. Captions appear in bars at the top of each similarly named section on the data access page. These bars and captions appear only in Design view. Each section has a *RecordSource* property. The setting for both sections is Recordset: Products. If the Field List isn't already visible from a previous page design session, a Field List control opens to the right of the data access page when you specify a *RecordSource* property for the grid.

You can add individual controls to the grid to help design a form. There are at least two approaches to this. First, you can open the Toolbox and then position controls from it to the grid to specify a form's layout. This works similarly to the Design view of an Access form, except that some different controls are available. When you take this first approach, you must individually specify a *ControlSource* property for all bound text box controls that you add. The *ControlSource* setting binds the text box to a field in the *RecordSource* property for the section. The second approach is to move items from the Field List to the top area of the grid. One easy way to do this is to successively double-click the fields in the Field List that you want to add to your form. This technique automatically creates bound controls.

> **Note**   Before double-clicking fields in the Field List to add them to a data access page, be sure to select the section to which you want to add the fields as controls.

If you click the *ProductID, ProductName, UnitsInStock, ReorderLevel,* and *Discontinued* fields, your top section will contain four text boxes and a check box for the *Discontinued* field. Each bound data control on the form has a matching label control as well. However, the text boxes appear in a default width that is too small for several product names. You can update the *Width* property of the ProductName text box by selecting it and then dragging its right edge to make it wider. Alternatively, you can type a number followed by a unit of measurement in the Width setting on the Format tab of the Properties dialog box for the ProductName text box. For example, type *2in* to designate a width of 2 inches.

There are two possible metrics for specifying the width: inch and pixel. However, pixel is the default. If you type a number without designating a unit of measurement, Access assumes that the number represents the width of the text box in pixels. Similarly, when you drag the width of the text box, Access converts the setting from its default value of 1 inch to some other width specified in pixels.

You can resize the other text box controls to match the width of the Product-Name text box. However, it's not necessary to manually reset the width for each of the other three text boxes to match that of ProductName. Instead, you can use the Alignment And Sizing toolbar. Open this toolbar by choosing View-Toolbars-Alignment And Sizing. Next select the ProductName text box if it isn't already selected. Then double-click the Size Width control on the Alignment And Sizing toolbar. This double-click causes the cursor to include a representation of the Size Width control. Next click each of the remaining three text boxes in the top section. Then move the cursor back to the Size Width control and click it once to unlatch the control, returning the cursor to its normal function. It's faster to latch the control when making several other controls match the position or size of one particular control. The alternative is to reselect the standard control and an item on the Alignment And Sizing toolbar before clicking each additional control that you want to match the standard control you've selected. Figure 16-3 shows the data access page just before the widening of the ReorderLevel text box.

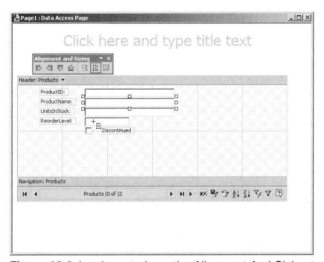

Figure 16-3 Latch controls on the Alignment And Sizing toolbar speed up the process of making new settings to controls.

As in Design view for Access forms, you can preview your layout by leaving Design view. There are two alternatives to Design view: Page view and Web Page Preview. You are restricted to using Page view until you commit your design by saving the data access page. However, switching to Page view opens the page within Access. It also lets you examine the form's layout and manipulate the data on the page with the help of the controls and the navigation bar.

Figure 16-4 shows the page from Figure 16-3 open in Page view. Notice that the form is on record 1 of 77 from the *Products* table. Besides controlling the flow from one record to the next and adding or deleting records, the navigation bar performs multiple functions. Figure 16-4 depicts an edit to the contents of the ProductName text box. (Notice the three trailing x characters.) After making a change to the contents of a cell, you can undo that change by clicking the Undo control on the navigation bar. The control to the immediate left of the Undo control commits a change on the current record. Moving off the current record also commits any pending change to the contents of a control. Users can additionally sort the records behind a form in ascending or descending order on the field behind any control. The records return to their native order the next time the form opens, and one user's sort does not affect the order of the records for another simultaneous user. Another pair of navigation bar controls let users filter by form and clear an active filter. Finally, a Help control on the navigation bar opens a file that explains how users can take advantage of data access pages as well as Office Web Components.

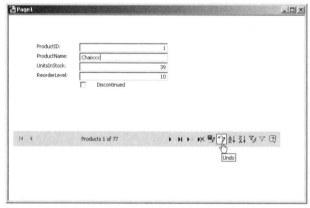

Figure 16-4 By using the navigation bar, end users can navigate, update, add, and delete records as well as sort and filter the data behind a form.

Saving a Data Access Page

Once you design a data access page the way you like, you need to save it so that others can use it. This is where a Web site comes in handy, although it's not essential to have one. This is because data access pages open over a local area network (LAN) even with a browser. In addition, you can open pages with a link in the *Pages* collection of a Database window. Any Access project with a link to the standalone file can open the page. However, a Web location makes your data access pages conveniently available with the other Web pages for a project. No matter where you store your data access pages, users with a browser can open them as long as they have a license for Office XP and Office XP Web Components installed on a workstation. In order to edit data access pages, a workstation must have Access 2002 installed. This is the only environment in which a data access page opens in Design view. One especially easy way to enjoy the full functionality of data access pages is to install any version of Office XP with Access 2002 on a workstation. Remember, you can install both Access 2002 and Access 2000 on the same computer.

Note   While you can start editing the design of a data access page from a browser, the browser actually opens Access 2002.

Before saving the file for a data access page, you need to remember two things. First, you must revise the path to the Access database file to Uniform Naming Convention (UNC) notation. By default, Access references a local path using drive letters to specify that path to the data source behind a data access page. However, users from other workstations aren't likely to use the same drive letters to map the drives on your workstation. Using UNC notation enables other users to reference the data source for a data access page independent from how they map physical drives to drive letters. Second, when you save a data access page, you store a standalone file. A convenient but not a mandatory location for this file is at a Web site, such as the pma10 Web site created earlier in this chapter. However, if you save only this file, there is no immediate way for the current Access project to reference the data access page. Therefore, Access also saves a shortcut for the page in the Database window.

I recommend a two-step approach to saving the file for a data access page that references an Access database on the local computer. First save the data access page file with the default local drive letter designation. (This is how Access automatically creates a specification for the database file with the record source for the page.) This initial step enables Access to reliably create a shortcut in the Access database file for the standalone data access page file. Then use the shortcut to reopen the page. Edit the connection path to reflect the UNC path, and resave the file.

> **Note**   When you create a data access page for a database file on a different workstation, Access specifies the path to the database with UNC notation automatically. You can save the page with that designation, and Access reliably creates a link to the page in the Database window of the Access database file.

To change the path designation for a data access page, you can start by opening its Field List in Design view. Then click the Page Connection Properties control on the upper left edge of the Field List. (Recall that you can also discover the name for a control by moving your cursor over the control until its Tooltip appears.) This opens a Data Link Properties dialog box. From the Select Or Enter A Database Name text box on the dialog box, revise the path designation to UNC notation. For example, if the database name is

```
C:\path1\databasename.mdb
```

you should change it to

```
\\workstationname\sharenamefordriveC\path1\databasename.mdb
```

> **Note**   When it's time to delete a data access page from the Database window, Access asks whether you want to delete the link only or the link and the file. The link refers to the shortcut to a data access page in a Database window. Choosing to remove the link only enables you to delete a link to a data access page within a database; you retain the data access page for use with other databases.

Opening and Filtering Forms with Links

When saving the preceding sample, I assigned it the name dapProducts in the root folder of the pma10 Web site. Since Access automatically assigns an .htm extension and the pma10 Web site is on the cab2000 Web server in my office, the URL for the page in my office environment is cab2000/pma10/dapProducts.htm. Typing this address into an Address box in Internet Explorer 5 or later opens the form in a browser with the full set of functionality presented in Figure 16-4. Any user who can connect to the pma10 server and has the Office XP Web Components running on their workstation can open the page.

Web applications normally don't require users to type URLs into a browser's Address box. Instead, developers typically create pages with links. By clicking a link, users automatically navigate from one page to another.

The example in the "Editing a Web Page" section demonstrated how to create links with FrontPage for a collection of URLs. You can also create links directly in data access pages. The tool for creating hyperlinks in data access pages has a special feature to facilitate filtering the records that appear on a form. This makes it easy to create links that display different records from the same form. In the current example, a hyperlink can optionally filter the records in the form on the dapProducts page by *CategoryID* value. Although *CategoryID* does not appear on the form, it's available for filtering because the form references the whole *Products* table as its record source. *CategoryID* is a column in the *Products* table. The trick is the setting of the *ServerFilter* property for the record source. Access database files do not support this property, except for data access pages. Recall that this property is always available for use with Access projects for SQL Server databases.

You add a hyperlink to a data access page in Design view with the Hyperlink tool in the Toolbox. A hyperlink on a data access page has *Href* and *ServerFilter* properties. You can assign settings to these properties from the Anchor tab of the Properties dialog box for the hyperlink. Because a hyperlink is essentially a label with some special settings for page navigation, you can also set properties that control its appearance on a data access page, such as its *FontSize* property. This property appears on the Format tab. Two other property settings on the Other tab of a hyperlink Properties dialog box are critical for mastering the use of hyperlinks on data access pages. The *InnerText* property designates the display text for a hyperlink. By default, this is the same as the *Href* property, but you will typically want to override this default setting to provide a friendlier title. The *Id* property denotes a name for the hyperlink. This name appears in the title for a hyperlink's Properties dialog box. When your application programmatically references hyperlinks on a page, it uses the *Id* property setting as the name for the link.

Figure 16-5 shows a collection of hyperlinks on a data access page. This page, which exists in this chapter's sample files as dapMenuPage.htm, has nine hyperlinks. All the hyperlinks open the same page, dapProducts.htm, but they show different records. Since all the hyperlinks open the same page, their *Href* property settings are identical (http://cab2000/pma10/dapProducts.htm). The center hyperlink (All Products) has the largest font. This hyperlink opens the form on the dapProducts.htm page for all the records in the *Products* table. Therefore, this hyperlink has no *ServerFilter* property setting associated with it. The links on either side of the center link all have a *ServerFilter* property setting that points at a single *CategoryID* value. For example, the hyperlink with an *InnerText* property setting of Beverages has a *ServerFilter* property value of *CategoryID=1*. Figure 16-5 shows the syntax for this assignment. The other seven links on the page, which appear to either side of the center link, have a different *CategoryID* assignments that range from 2 through 8.

Figure 16-5 Use the *ServerFilter* property of a hyperlink to control the data that a form displays.

Figure 16-6 shows the link and filter operation in action as the application transfers control from the dapMenuPage.htm file to the dapProducts.htm file. In dapMenuPage.htm, the user clicks the Seafood hyperlink, which has a *ServerFilter* property of *CategoryID=8*. When the link executes, it filters the data on the form for dapProducts.htm so that only seafood products appear. Notice that the *ServerFilter* setting transfers as a parameter that follows the URL in the Address box. A question mark (?) signifies the end of the URL and the start of the passed parameter. Built-in software on the data access page properly interprets the parameter assignment. In Chapter 17, you'll learn how to write your own application software to accept parameters. Keep in mind that the beauty of data access pages is that they let you save your programming efforts for other application requirements when their built-in capabilities are sufficient.

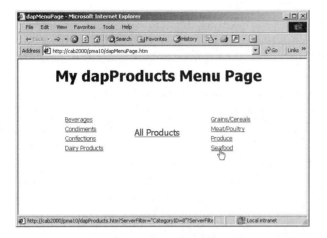

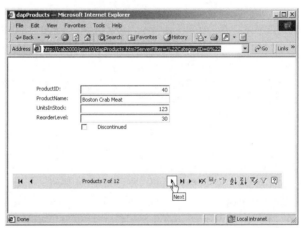

Figure 16-6 Hyperlinks can transmit a *ServerFilter* property assignment after the URL as a parameter.

Programming Events on Data Access Pages

Programming events involves two steps. First you place objects on a page. Then you design code that runs when events fire for those objects or for the page itself. Access developers have experience with both of these requirements for Access forms. However, implementing these requirements is a little different for data access pages than for Access forms. The sample in this section describes the implementation of a typical event procedure for a data access page. You'll also see an event procedure sample in this chapter's "Creating Interactive Reports with Computed Fields" section.

Adding a Drop-Down List Control

While links are a common tool in Web-based solutions, unbound drop-down list controls offer several attractive advantages as well. First, you can base a drop-down list on a record source. Therefore, you can alter the items in the list without having to redesign the form; instead, you just update the SQL for the record source. Second, developers are used to creating drop-down list controls in Access solutions. The wizard for creating drop-down list controls further invites Access developers to try this approach. Third, the ability to create event procedures for these controls is another motivator for using them. Access developers have substantial familiarity with these powerful and often compact pieces of code.

There are two main tasks for using unbound drop-down list controls on a data access page. First you must physically add the control to the page and specify what it shows and what it saves. Happily, the Toolbox and its Control wizards simplify this. By the way, the Toolbox calls a drop-down list control a Dropdown List. Second you must create an event procedure that reads the value a user selects with the control and performs some action based on it, such as opening a form with a filter.

The easiest way to add an unbound drop-down list control to a data access page is to invoke the Control wizards. Click and engage the Control Wizards button within the Toolbox before clicking the Dropdown List button. Then click on the grid within the data access page where you want the control to appear. The similarities between the drop-down list and the more familiar Access combo box will be apparent immediately. This is because the wizard's first screen has the caption Combo Box wizard in its title bar. Make your selections for the instance of the drop-down list on the page as you normally would for a combo box on an Access form.

After responding to the Combo Box wizard dialog boxes, you'll have a drop-down list control that displays some items from a record source. Users will be able to select items from the control, but nothing will happen as a result. Use an event procedure to cause an action based on a user choice.

For this example, I added a drop-down list control to a page. The record source for the control was the *Categories* table. The control displays category names, but it saves the corresponding *CategoryID* value for the name a user selects. I assigned an *Id* setting of cboCategoryID to the control. Although I created all these settings (except for the *Id* property value) with the Combo Box wizard, you can set them easily on your own. Merely add the drop-down list control with the Control wizards turned off. Then open the Properties dialog box for the control, and select the Data tab. Type *CategoryID* for *ListBoundField*, *CategoryName* for *ListDisplayField*, and select Table: Categories for *ListRowSource*. Access automatically converts the last selection to Recordset: Categories. Specify *cboCategoryID*, or whatever name you choose for your control, to the *Id* property setting box on the Other tab. Any event procedures you create for the control will reference the control by its *Id* setting.

Figure 16-7 shows the Design view for the drop-down list control on the data access page. The display shows the cboCategoryID control selected. Below the grid for the page, the Toolbox appears with the Control Wizards button selected. To the right of the cboCategoryID control is the Properties dialog box for the control. You also can see all four settings discussed in the preceding paragraph.

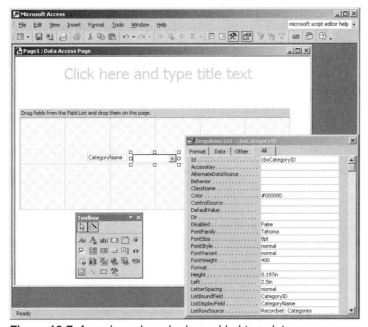

Figure 16-7 An unbound combo box added to a data access page.

Before ending this section, I'd like to note that there's more to data access pages than their drop-down list controls and labels with a caption for the control. For example, the control sits on a grid. The grid is a *Section* object from the Office Web Component model that can represent a hierarchical element within a data access page. The *Section* object in Figure 16-7 contains the drop-down list control and its label, but the section resides within the body of the page. The caption on top of the grid that starts with the words *Drag fields* resides in a banner for the section sitting below it. The large, gray text above the banner for the section is the page's heading text. The caption in the page's title bar indicates that Page1 is the top-level object in the data access page.

Using the Microsoft Script Editor

There's good news and bad news about using event procedures for controls on data access pages. The good news is that you can create event procedures using a language much like the one you already know in an environment that bears some similarity to the integrated development environment (IDE) that you're already accustomed to. The bad news is that the language is not exactly Visual Basic for Applications (VBA) and the IDE is not the Visual Basic Editor (VBE) window. Of the two popular languages for scripting data access pages, the one you're likely to find easiest is VBScript. The IDE for the code behind a data access page is the Microsoft Script Editor. If you programmed data access pages much in Access 2000 or you used Microsoft Visual InterDev 6 or later, you probably have some familiarity with the layout and operation of the IDE for data access pages.

To open the Script Editor, click the Microsoft Script Editor tool on the toolbar for the Design view of a data access page. The Script Editor displays the data access page in HTML and scripts. Not only can a page have multiple scripts to make it dynamic and interactive, each script can be programmed in a different language. The two scripting languages that are readily available for this are VBScript and JScript.

> **Note**   There's plenty of help for learning about the Script Editor and the tools to use it properly. From the Script Editor, you can open the Help system by choosing Help-Microsoft Script Editor Help. Then type *Microsoft Script Editor Help* in the Assistant, and select the item with the same name. This takes you to a Help system with information about the Script Editor, HTML, VBScript, and JScript. This Help system also provides detailed explanations of the *FileSystemObject* object, which we've used in several samples throughout the book (and will use in this chapter's final sample). Help for *FileSystemObject* is available under the VBScript Help menu.

After you initially open the Script Editor for a data access page, a control on the Windows status bar permits you to toggle between Design view in Access and the Script Editor, provided you're working with just these two windows. If the toggle control doesn't work, use another technique for navigating between windows, such as selecting a window with the Alt+Tab key combination. Making a change in one representation knocks that representation out of sync with the other one. You need to switch between these two views because doing so resynchronizes the two representations of the data access page.

Figure 16-8 presents a collection of three windows within the Script Editor for the data access page shown in Figure 16-7. These are the Document Outline, Properties, and Document windows. The Document Outline window offers two representations of a data access page. The view appearing in Figure 16-8 is for the HTML Outline. It depicts the hierarchical relationship among the objects that comprise a page. At the top level is Page1, the name for the data access page. Within Page1 are three objects: the Data Source Control (MSODSC), a *Script* object representing a script for the page, and a *Body* object that contains all the other HTML tags defining the data access page. MSODSC contains the specification of the data source for the drop-down list control. The *Script* object contains two built-in scripts that check for the availability of an appropriate browser and a version of Office Web Components.

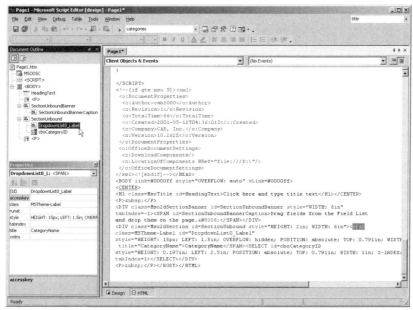

Figure 16-8 A Script Editor view that contrasts with the Design view of the data access page shown in Figure 16-7.

The items within the *Body* object show the HTML tags that lay out content on the data access page. The Document Outline window denotes these tags by their ID setting, when one exists. Otherwise, the window just references the tags. In order of appearance, the items within the *Body* object are a *HeadingText* object, a paragraph tag (<p>), a banner for an unbound section, the unbound section, and the closing paragraph tag (</p>). Additional hierarchical elements, such as the drop-down list control (cboCategoryID) and its label, reside within the unbound section banner and objects.

The highlighted object in the Document Outline window also controls the focus in the Properties and Document windows. The Properties window appears directly below the Document Outline window. Since the Document Outline window depicts the *DropdownList0_Label* element selected, the Properties window indicates properties for that element. This selection is convenient for changing the ID value from its default setting to one that more precisely defines its purpose, such as *cboCategoryID_Label*. The Document window appears to the right of both the Document Outline and Properties windows. You can use this window to improve the appearance of the label so that it reads Category Name instead of CategoryName. Just insert a space between the words *Category* and *Name*, which appear between the <span> and </span> tags. These tags can denote a label, and the text between the tags comprises the *InnerText* property value for the label control.

The suggested updates in the Document window will cause the *Id* and *InnerText* property values for the label to revise in Design view when you synchronize the two data access page representations. Click the Page1 Script Editor control on the Windows status bar to toggle control back to Design view for the data access page. After a while, Access updates the view with the changes made in the Script Editor.

Adding an Event Procedure to a Control

Recall that cboCategoryID, the drop-down list control on the data access page we're building, lets a user choose a category name and stores the corresponding *CategoryID* value for the selected category name. However, nothing happens after that. With the help of an event procedure attached to the control, you can open the dapProducts data access page filtered by the *CategoryID* value in cboCategoryID. This section shows how to build an event procedure that accomplishes this.

You build event procedures for the objects on a data access page from the Document Outline window. This window offers two views. You saw the first of these, the HTML Outline view, in Figure 16-8. An alternative view is the Script Outline view, which can display all the client objects with their events and any existing client scripts in a data access page. Two controls just below the title bar for the Document Outline window allow you to switch between the two views.

Figure 16-9 shows the Document Outline window in its Script Outline view after you click the *onchange* event for the *cboCategoryID* object. You can expose the events for other objects by clicking the plus sign (+) next to them. Each client object has a set of events appropriate to it. The *onchange* event for drop-down list controls on data access pages works like an *afterupdate* event for combo boxes on Access forms. Therefore, the *onchange* event fires right after the user changes the value saved in the cboCategoryID control by making a selection from it.

Figure 16-9 A Document Outline window with the *onchange* event for the cboCategoryID control selected.

Double-click Onchange in the Document Outline window to make the Script Editor insert the shell for an *onchange* event procedure for the *cboCategoryID* object in the Document window. The shell appears as shown below. Notice that the *for* and *event* attributes denote the purpose of the *Script* object. The language attribute is the default one, vbscript. The <!-- and --> markers denote comments. These comment markers cause the text for the event procedure to disappear from a page when the browser reading the page cannot interpret VBScript. If the browser can interpret VBScript, the code executes.

```
<script language=vbscript for=cboCategoryID event=onchange>
<!--


-->
</script>
```

The following script shows the code for the event procedure. Insert the code between the comment markers shown in the preceding shell. The code checks the value of the *cboCategoryID* control. If the control has a value of 1 through 8, it transfers control to the dapProducts data access page with a server filter setting for the control's current value. If the control returns a different value because the *Categories* table has changed, the procedure presents a message reminding the user to update the filter code and to make another selection in the meantime.

The expression *window.location.href* transfers control to a URL. The value of the expression determines the location and any filters that apply to the transferred location. Notice that the URL specifications start with a protocol (http) followed by a Web address, namely the dapProducts.htm file on the pma10 Web site at the cab2000 Web server. A question mark (?) follows the address, and the filter specification begins. The general form for a filter expression is *ServerFilter="filter string"*. In this instance, the expression cannot use quote marks (") because the whole URL appears in quotes. Therefore, the expression uses the HTML code for quote marks (%22) to avoid a run-time error caused by embedding quote marks within quote marks.

```
If cboCategoryID.value=1 Then
    window.location.href= _
    "http://cab2000/pma10/dapProducts.htm?ServerFilter=" _
    "%22CategoryID=1%22"
ElseIf cboCategoryID.value=2 Then
    window.location.href= _
    "http://cab2000/pma10/dapProducts.htm?ServerFilter=" _
    "%22CategoryID=2%22"
ElseIf cboCategoryID.value=3 Then
    window.location.href= _
    "http://cab2000/pma10/dapProducts.htm?ServerFilter=" _
    "%22CategoryID=3%22"
ElseIf cboCategoryID.value=4 Then
    window.location.href= _
    "http://cab2000/pma10/
dapProducts.htm?ServerFilter=%22CategoryID=4%22"
ElseIf cboCategoryID.value=5 Then
    window.location.href= _
    "http://cab2000/pma10/dapProducts.htm?ServerFilter=" _
    "%22CategoryID=5%22"
ElseIf cboCategoryID.value=6 Then
    window.location.href= _
    "http://cab2000/pma10/dapProducts.htm?ServerFilter=" _
    "%22CategoryID=6%22"
ElseIf cboCategoryID.value=7 Then
    window.location.href= _
    "http://cab2000/pma10/dapProducts.htm?ServerFilter=" _
    "%22CategoryID=7%22"
ElseIf cboCategoryID.value=8 Then
    window.location.href= _
    "http://cab2000/pma10/dapProducts.htm?ServerFilter=" _
    "%22CategoryID=8%22"
Else
    MsgBox "Requires update to filter code." & _
    "Make another selection.",, _
        "Programming Microsoft Access Version 2002"
End If
```

After inserting the code into the event procedure shell, you can return to Design view for the data access page under construction. This gives the environment a chance to update with any changes made to the page in the Script Editor.

In this chapter's sample page (dapcboCategoryID.htm) on the book's companion CD, I added some instructions on how to use the page in the <headingtext> tag. You can make the instructions in either the Design view or the Script Editor representations of the data access page. When using Design view, click in the gray text at the top of the page and type your replacement text. In the Script Editor, replace the text between the <h1> and </h1> tags with the *Id* setting of *Heading-Text*. In addition, clear the value for the assignment to the class attribute—that is, change it from "MsoTitle" to "". The initial setting references a style that causes the text between the tags with an *Id* of HeadingText to disappear.

Managing Images on a Data Access Page

Displaying images on data access pages has several commonalities with displaying images on forms in Access, with some qualifying distinctions. Happily, you can use an image control to display your image on a data access page. But instead of directing the control at the filename and path for an image, you're likely to use the URL for an image that specifies a protocol, path, and filename.

And just as with a LAN-based solution for an Access form, you're likely to maintain your image addresses in a separate table with a primary key that matches the primary key for the rest of the data about your entities (items that the pictures represent). However, when using data access pages, you join the two tables directly behind the page instead of in a separate query. This is because using a standalone query as the record source for a form on a data access page makes the form read-only. This is not necessarily the case for Access forms on LANs.

A third distinction between presenting images on data access pages and presenting them on Access forms is that data access pages save you from having to rely on event procedures to manage the display of images. You can merely designate a field with a URL as the *ControlSource* property for the Image control. The navigation bar controls on data access pages are smart enough to eliminate the need for any custom coding. With Access forms, to avoid an error, event procedures typically must detect whether a user is moving beyond the first or last record.

Creating Your Image Files for the Web

The sample described in this section works with a variation of the employee pictures that ship with the Access database file for the Northwind sample. Although the picture images ship with the sample, they are standalone files. As you'll recall, these files have a bitmap image format, which is uncommon in Web applications. Alternative graphic formats, such as those with a .jpg file type, represent images with fewer bytes than bitmap files. I used the Microsoft PhotoDraw package (from Office 2000) to create another set of employee image files based on the original images that ship with the Northwind database. PhotoDraw permits you to open a bitmap (.bmp) file and save the image in another file type, such as .jpg. With this approach, I was able to cut the image sizes in half from around 40 KB per image to around 20 KB per image.

> **Note**   If you do not have PhotoDraw available, you can use the .jpg images on the book's CD. You can also use your favorite graphics package instead of PhotoDraw to convert image file types. When applying the techniques just discussed to image files other than those in the example, request an appropriate format from the supplier of the images if you don't have a package for performing the conversion.

After you save your new image files in a format appropriate for the Web, copy them to a Web site. You do this differently for an intranet to which you have LAN access than you do for a remote Web site that you must connect to over the Internet. If you're working with an intranet to which you also have a LAN connection, just use Windows Explorer to copy the files to the appropriate folder on the Web site. If you don't have a LAN connection to your Web site, you can use FrontPage 2002 to copy the files. Open FrontPage to the Web site to which you want to import the image files (or any other kind of file). From the Folder List, select a location where you want to import the image files. Then choose File-Import. Use the Add File button to successively select as many files as you want to import to the Web site from your local workstation or LAN. If all the files that you want to import reside in one folder, use the Add Folder button to specify the whole folder in one step. When you finish specifying the location of the files to import to the Web site, click OK. When the import completes, click Close to remove the Import dialog box.

After copying the image files to this book's sample Web site, the images folder of the pma10 Web site has nine image files. Their names range from EMPID1.jpg to EMPID9.jpg. Figure 16-10 shows the Folder List window from FrontPage containing the image files (along with other selected files on the Web site).

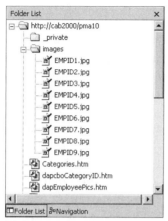

Figure 16-10 A collection of .jpg files in the Images folder of a Web site for use as images on a data access page.

Creating a Record Source with Picture Addresses

The sample application for displaying images on a data access page shows selected column values from the *Employees* table, along with the image for each employee. There are several ways to organize this data for use as the record source for a data access page. This presentation opts for simplicity and read/write functionality for the bound fields.

Create a table with a name such as *EmployeePic_Addresses* that contains EmployeeID and URL fields for the image of each employee. For example, the URL for the first employee in the current sample is cab2000/pma10/images/empid1.jpg. Name the column of URL values for images *Pic_Address*. You will need an application for adding, deleting, and possibly updating records in the table. Review Chapter 5, "Jet SQL, the ADOX Library, and Queries," for sample code that describes how to create and maintain the table with Jet SQL statements.

> **Note**   A complete version of the *EmployeePic_Addresses* table is in this chapter's sample Access database file on the companion CD. It's imperative that the table have a primary key that's a foreign key for the *Employees* table with all the remaining fields for individual employees. If this condition is not True, you won't be able to update field values in the *Employees* table through the form on the data access page.

Creating a Page to Display Images

There are several different approaches to developing data access pages on record sources. This example illustrates some variations on the preceding example for the dapProducts page. Start by generating a blank data access page for editing in Design view. To do this, select Pages in the Objects bar of the Database window. Then click New on the Database window, and click OK in the New Data Access Page dialog box. If the Field List does not show, click its control on the toolbar to make it appear. This completes the generation of a blank data access page and prepares it for editing.

Next populate the page with fields from the *Employees* table. Open the Tables folder, and click the expand control for the *Employees* table in that folder. Successively double-click the fields to add to the form. These are *EmployeeID*, *FirstName*, *LastName*, *Country*, *HomePhone*, and *Extension*. These steps add a subset of fields from the *Employees* table for display on the data access page.

It will be helpful to show the URL for the image that the form will ultimately display. You can do this with a text box bound to the *Pic_Address* column in the *EmployeePic_Addresses* table. To add this text box to the page, select the text box with a *ControlSource* property setting of Extension. Selecting this text box enables Access to add a new text box below it. Then click the plus sign (+) to expand the *EmployeePic_Addresses* table in the Field List. Finally double-click the *Pic_Address* column name. Access automatically opens a Relationship Wizard dialog box to link the *EmployeePic_Addresses* table to the *Employees* table. (See Figure 16-11.) Accepting the default setting is important for preserving the updatability of *Employee* table fields through the form on the page. The wizard specifies that the *EmployeePic_Addresses* table is in a one-to-many relationship with the *Employees* table and that the *EmployeePic_Addresses* table is on the many side of the relationship.

The steps in the preceding paragraph complete the specification of a form with a set of text boxes similar in design to the dapProducts page. However, this example demonstrates how to make a couple of changes to this basic form. First, the example replaces the text box for the *Country* field with a bound drop-down list control. This makes it easy for users to change the *Country* field to another legitimate value. Second, the example illustrates how to add an image control to a form and base its display on a field in the current row on the record source for the data access page.

The drop-down list control for this data access page is different from the one in the preceding sample. The preceding data access page illustrated how to create an unbound control, but the drop-down list control for this data access page is bound to the *Country* column. Therefore, the control always shows the value of the column for the current row in the data access page's record source. In addition, you can use the drop-down list to update that value.

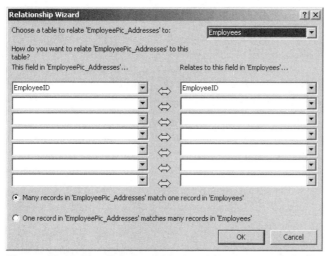

Figure 16-11 The Relationship wizard for dynamically building relationships for the tables behind a form on a data access page.

To add a bound drop-down list control for the *Country* field, delete the text box for the *Country* field so that the drop-down list control can take its place. Remove the text box by selecting it and then pressing the Delete key on the keyboard. Next open the Toolbox and clear the Control Wizards button if it's selected. Then add a drop-down list control from the Toolbox to the data access page. Select *Country* as the ControlSource setting on the Data tab of the drop-down list control's Properties dialog box. This binds the control to the *Country* column in the record source for the page. Next type *SELECT DISTINCT Country FROM Employees* into the ListRowSource property setting. This statement, along with two other settings, enables the drop-down list to show each country in the *Employees* table without duplicating any country. Then select *Country* as the ListBoundField and the ListDisplayField property values. This completes the control property settings that determines whether the control displays values and permits updates.

There are some additional settings that the control needs. Change the Id setting on the Other tab from DropdownList0 to *cboCountry*. Next select the label for the drop-down list control. Make two changes on the Other tab of its Properties dialog box. First type *cboCountry_Label* as the Id setting. Second type *Country:* as the InnerText property setting. Finish the insertion of the bound drop-down list control into the form on the page by moving its label and control so that they take the empty slot left by the deleted text box for the *Country* field.

The form is now ready for the addition of an image control. Click the image control in the Toolbox, and then click the upper left corner where you want your image to appear. At this point, a dialog box prompts you to insert a picture. It's not mandatory that you designate a picture, but choosing a file that contains an image with the right dimensions sizes the image control for you automatically. This is convenient when you don't want the image control to clip or distort the dimensions of your images. You can type the address of the image for the first employee, such as *http://cab2000/pma10/empid1.jpg*. This creates a static image for the control no matter which record shows, but the control does have the right size for the image file. Next open the Properties dialog box for the image control. Then highlight Pic_Address from the drop-down list for the ControlSource property on the Data tab. This assignment allows the image control to reflect the image for the current employee.

Complete the layout of the data access page by dragging the lower edge of the section above the navigation bar so that there is sufficient space to move the Pic_Address text box below the image control. Then drag the text box below the image control, and resize the text box so that it's wide enough to show the URLs for images. Complete the example by saving the page.

Creating Interactive Reports with Computed Fields

Data access pages support another use for controls: using interactive reports. An interactive report lets you represent a parent-child relationship. Interactive reports have a section-based architecture that resembles the sections in Access reports. These Web-based reports are considered interactive because they feature controls that let users expand a parent record and see the child records associated with it. In Design view, you can promote a field so that it becomes a parent. This capability is particularly appropriate for foreign key fields that repeat across many rows in a record source. The parent fields group the repetitions as child records. Just as with forms on data access pages, you can base interactive reports on multiple record sources. The first version of data access pages in Access 2000 didn't let you edit values in interactive reports. However, the Access 2002 version supports the editing of field values within a report.

This section gives step-by-step instructions on building two-level reports and three-level reports. You will also learn techniques for improving the appearance of data access pages by using calculated fields. The section closes with a code sample for an event procedure that illustrates how to implement conditional formatting for the data values on a data access page.

Building a Two-Level Report

You populate a data access page with controls the same way whether you're building an interactive report or a form. When adding fields to an interactive report, it's important to have one field serve as a parent for the other fields on the report. For example, most of the fields in the *Products* table relate to individual products; however, the *CategoryID* field in the *Products* table is a parent field that can have one or more products below it.

When you build multilevel reports, you initially add all fields to a report at the same level. All fields are siblings of one another. Then you promote at least one field above the others. In the case of the *Products* table, promoting *CategoryID* will lead to a grouping of product records with the same *CategoryID* field value. If users interactively expand a *CategoryID* value, they will see the products with that *CategoryID* value.

You can start to build a two-level report with fields from the *Products* table by adding *CategoryID*, *ProductName*, *UnitsInStock*, and *ReorderLevel* to a blank data access page. This creates a form on a page similar to several of the preceding examples in this chapter—namely, it contains what looks like a form. Next select the *CategoryID* field and choose Promote on the toolbar. This creates a new section on the page with the banner Header: Products-CategoryID. Clicking Promote also moves the *CategoryID* field into the new section, and the label for the field changes to Group Of CategoryID. The new label aptly describes the section, since it groups products with the same category ID value.

Figure 16-12 shows a Page view for the data access page after some rearrangement of the fields to make the report layout more compact. The *CategoryID* groups for 1–5 and 7–8 are collapsed so that you cannot see the detail records below them. However, the detail records for products with a category ID value of *6* show on the report. This is because I expanded this group. You can see the cursor on the control. Clicking the collapse control (the minus sign [–]) will hide the detail records for products with a category ID value of *6*.

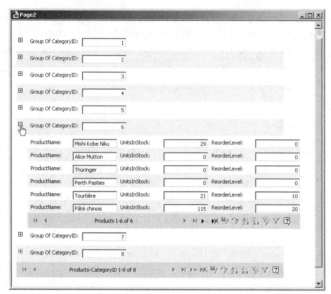

Figure 16-12 A two-level interactive report with an expanded group for the category ID of 6.

Notice that the report contains two navigation bars. The one with the label of Products 1–6 Of 6 is the inner navigation bar. This bar does not appear unless a user expands at least one *CategoryID* group. By default, the maximum number of records that the bar shows at one time is 10. You can increase or decrease this amount by using the Properties dialog box for the navigation bar. The outer navigation bar appears whenever the data access page opens. Again, all 8 category ID values show at one time since there are less than 10.

Building a Three-Level Report

You can build multilevel reports from multiple record sources. Figure 16-13 shows a three-level report with *CustomerID* on the outer level, *OrderID* on the middle level, and fields from the *Order Details* table on the inner level. The complete report is available in this chapter's files on the companion CD. The standalone file is for the report dapThreeLevelReport.htm, which appears as dapThreeLevel-Report in the Database window for the chapter's database file. This report design lets a user open the order details for any customer order. This interactive report depicted in Figure 16-13 shows the three line items for *OrderID* 10643 for the customer whose *CustomerID* is ALFKI. The figure displays the two inner navigation bars. The outer navigation bar isn't visible in the figure. However, the outer navigation bar shows that there are 89 customers. This is two customers less than the number of rows in the *Customers* table since two customers have no orders.

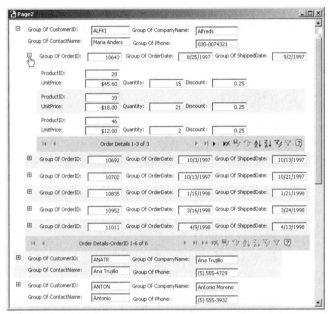

Figure 16-13 A three-level interactive report with an expanded group showing line items within *OrderID* groups, within *CustomerID* groups.

You can build a report like this one with three basic steps. A fourth step performs any report layout editing needed. These steps are as follows:

1. Add all the fields that you need in your report. Use the Relationship Wizard dialog box to define relationships between tables when you add the first field from a new record source. Don't try to add a table as a record source unless it already has a relationship to an existing record source for the report.

2. Select a field that you want to serve as the top-level field, and click the Promote tool. This creates a new section in the report and inserts the selected field into it. In the report shown in Figure 16-13, the top-level field is *CustomerID*. Move fields related to the top-level field—such as *CompanyName*, *ContactName*, and *Phone*—into the new section

3. Select a field that you want to serve as the key field for the report's second tier. In this example, that field is *OrderID*. Then click Promote. This adds another new section to the report containing the selected field. Again, add related fields to the new section.

4. Perform whatever rearrangement and editing of control labels your application requires. For example, the sample report in Figure 16-13 aligned controls horizontally to conserve space so that you could see as much information as possible in a single screen.

Adding Calculated Fields to a Report

Including calculated fields in a report can improve the report's usefulness by providing summary information before a user expands a control or by deriving conclusions based on the available data. This section demonstrates how to use calculated fields in interactive reports to benefit from these advantages. In addition, this section shows how to replace numeric fields used for grouping with string values that are easier to read and interpret.

The starting point for this section is the dapTwoLevelReport we developed earlier. The example saves the report under a new name, dapCalculatedFields. It then makes three main edits to the report before resaving it. If you're authoring the report from the same workstation that stores the data access page for the interactive report, you'll have to revert from UNC notation for specifying the connection to a local drive designation. To achieve this, save the dapTwo-LevelReport with a local drive designation. Next you can reopen the dapTwoLevel-Report, and then invoke the File-Save As command to save a new copy of the report as dapCalculated fields. Before editing dapCalculatedFields to make the improvements, resave dapTwoLevelReport with a UNC specification for connection.

The preceding manipulations are only necessary if you're editing a data access page from the same workstation that stores it and your data source is an Access data file. (This is a relatively common scenario for processing data access pages, but it's not the only one.) If you're copying the dapTwoLevelReport from a workstation other than the one storing the file for the page, you can just open dapTwoLevelReport with its UNC notation and resave it with the inherited UNC notation. This method is clearly simpler, but it requires you to perform your editing from a workstation different than the one storing the file for a page.

Once you have your copy of dapTwoLevelReport saved as dapCalculated-Fields, you can start editing it. Begin by replacing the text box that displays a different category ID value with the actual name of the category. This will make it easier for users unfamiliar with the category ID codes to interact with the report. Since the *Products* table does not include a *CategoryName* field, it's necessary to add a new record source to the data source control that manages data for the report.

Using a SQL Server Database for the Data Source of a Data Access Page

Data access pages can have only two kinds of data sources: Access database files and SQL Server databases. This chapter focuses on the use of Access database files. However, you can also have a SQL Server database act as the data source for a page. It's possible to designate a SQL Server database as the source for a page even when you're authoring the page from an Access database file.

When you create a blank data access page, Access automatically assigns the local database as the source. If you're working from an Access database file and you want a SQL Server database to serve as the page's data source, click the Page connection properties control on the Field List. This opens a Data Link Properties dialog box. On the dialog box's Provider tab, select Microsoft OLE DB Provider For SQL Server. Complete the Connection tab as described in Chapter 14, "Using Access to Build SQL Server Solutions: Part I," (in the section "Creating and Opening Access Projects") for an Access project's Data Link Properties dialog box. Figure 16-14 shows the two tabs that designate the NorthwindCS database on the CAB2000 SQL server as the data source for a data access page.

When working with SQL Server data sources, you don't need to set the path to a database with UNC notation. This is because a SQL Server database specifies the connection to a data source in terms of the server name and the database's name on the server.

 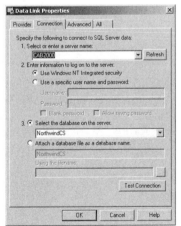

Figure 16-14 A pair of Data Link Properties tabs for setting the data source of a data access page to the NorthwindCS database.

Before adding a new record source, remove the text box and its label in the Products-CategoryID report section. Next click the expand control for the *Categories* table in the Field List, and drag the *CategoryName* field just to the right of the expand control in the Products-CategoryID section. Then drag the edges of the bound span control for *CategoryName* and its label so that you can easily select either control. A bound span control displays the contents of a text or memo field, but it doesn't enable editing. This limitation is acceptable for a field that acts as a label. Select the bound span control, and change its TotalType setting on the Data tab of its Properties dialog box to dscNone. Use the drop-down list for the ControlSource property to select *CategoryName*. Update the ID setting on the Other tab of the Properties dialog box to bspCategoryName. Next select the label for the bound span control. On its Other tab, type *bspCategoryName_Label* as its ID setting and *Category Name:* as its InnerText setting. Finish the editing for the bound span control and its label by positioning and sizing them the way you want on the report.

Next add another bound span control to the Products_CategoryID section that counts the number of product records within a category. You initially get this control from the Toolbox. Next select the new bound span control, and open its Properties dialog box to the Data tab. Use the drop-down list for the ControlSource setting to designate *ProductID*. Then select dscCount from the TotalType setting. These two settings cause the bound span control to count the number of unique *ProductID* values within each category. On the Other tab, update the ID setting to *bspCountOfProductID*. Then select the label for the new bound span control. Change its InnerText value on the Other tab of its Properties dialog box to *Count of Products* and its ID setting to *bspCountOfProductID_Label*. In the Products-CategoryID section, adjust the size and position of the bound span control and its label until you get the results you want. In doing so, you might find it useful to set the *TextAlign* property of the bound span control to *Left*. The setting is available on the Format tab of the control's Properties dialog box.

The last task is to add a computed field that tells the report user whether it's time to reorder a product. The report uses an expression that returns *Yes* whenever *UnitsInStock* is less than *ReorderLevel*. Otherwise, the expression returns *No*.

Before adding the new bound span control in the Products section of the report, rearrange the text box controls so that those for *ProductName* and *UnitsInStock* appear on the first row and the text box for *ReorderLevel* appears in the second row along with the new bound span control. Type the following expression into the *ControlSource* property for the bound span control. Notice that it relies on a familiar *Immediate If* statement.

```
ReorderNow: IIf(UnitsInStock<ReorderLevel,"Yes","No")
```

Next change the InnerText setting for the bound span control's label to *Reorder?*. This label cryptically asks the question, "Is it time to reorder?" The expression on the bound span control's *ControlSource* property answers this question. Also, assign *bspReorderNow* to the control's ID setting. This ID setting will demonstrate its usefulness shortly.

Complete the application with the normal resizing and repositioning. You might also want to assign a title for the page. In HTML, you set this property to determine the contents of the browser's title bar when it opens a page. You will also notice the property when you examine a data access page in Page view. To assign a value to the page's *Title* property, click the page's title bar in Design view. Then open the Properties dialog box. On the Other tab, type a name that reflects the page's purpose or role, such as *dapCalculatedFields*. Finally save the page with UNC notation that designates its connection to the database file. A completed version of the report is available on the book's CD in the dapCalculatedFields.htm file.

The report in Figure 16-15 illustrates the outcome of the enhancements to the dapTwoLevelReport data access page presented in Figure 16-12. Notice that the labels describing the products within a category show the name of the category rather than a *CategoryID* code number. In addition, users can tell how many products are in a category without opening that category to get the information from the inner navigation bar. Finally, the report computes whether it's time to reorder a product and displays the results with a Yes or No.

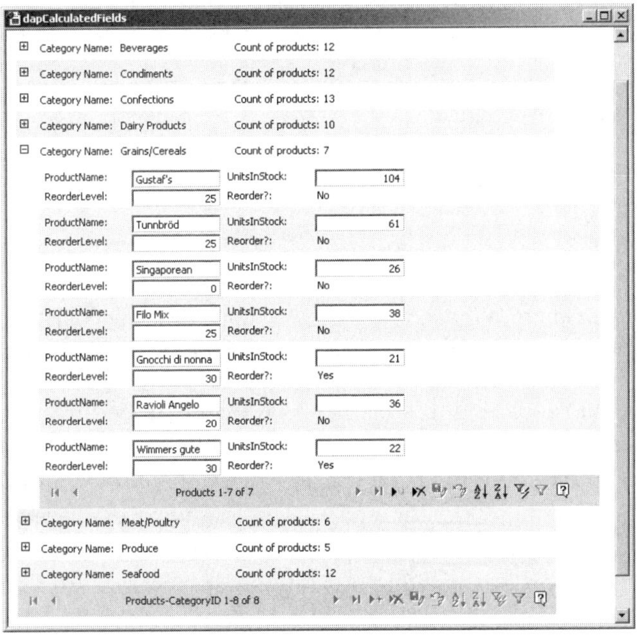

Figure 16-15 With calculated fields, you can dramatically improve the ease of interpreting an interactive report.

Applying Conditional Formatting to a Report

As improved as the report in Figure 16-15 is over the one in Figure 16-12, if there was a long list of products within a category, it might be difficult to see which products need a new order. One way to resolve this is to apply a bold font selectively to the computed value for reordering. The event procedure in this section applies a bold font to those products with a value of *Yes*, which serves as an answer to the question about whether it's time to reorder. Figure 16-16 shows another version of the report with conditional formatting of bold for products with a *bspReorderNow* value of *Yes*. See how much easier it is now to tell which products need a new order?

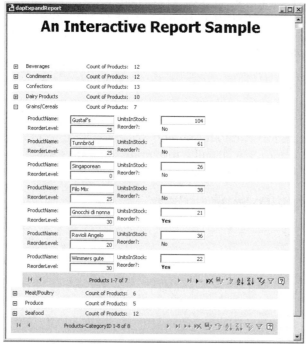

Figure 16-16 You can improve readability by implementing conditional formatting with an event procedure for the data source control in a data access page.

This improved readability results from an event procedure for the page's data source control. Each time a user opens a child section of a report, the data source control on the page reloads the page. The data source control is the top-level container in the data model for a page. The following event procedure fires when the data source control for the report page finishes reloading in response to a user opening the products within a category. The procedure loops through the sections on a page. The *NextSibling* property allows the procedure to advance from one section of a report to the next. When any HTML controls fall within in a section that has a value of *RecordLevel* greater than *UnitsInStock*, the procedure assigns a bold font to the *bspReorderNow* control.

```
<SCRIPT event=DataPageComplete(dscei) for=MSODSC language=vbscript>
<!--
'Highlight items that are almost out of stock
dim sect
dim dscconst
dim bandHTML

'Check that event fired for DataPage in the Products GroupLevel
if (dscei.DataPage.GroupLevel.RecordSource = "Products") then
    set dscconst = MSODSC.Constants
    set sect = dscei.DataPage.FirstSection

    'Go through the sections of the event's DataPage object
    do
        'Want to ignore the caption section
        if (sect.Type = dscconst.sectTypeHeader) then
            set bandHTML = sect.HTMLContainer

            'Conditional formatting on the bspReorderNow control.
            'Change the text to bold if the ReorderLevel is
            'greater than UnitsInStock.
            if (CInt(bandHTML.children("ReorderLevel").innerText) > _
                CInt(bandHTML.children("UnitsInStock").innerText)) _
                Then
                bandHTML.children("bspReorderNow").style.fontweight _
                    = "bold"
            end if
        end if
        set sect = sect.NextSibling
    loop until (sect is nothing)
end if
-->
</SCRIPT>
```

You type the script similarly to the way described earlier in this chapter for the *onchange* event procedure. Open the Script Editor. Select the Script Outline view of the Document Outline window. Then expand the events for MSODSC, which represents the data source control object on a page. Double-click the *DataPageComplete* event. This opens the shell for the event procedure. Finally copy the body of the event procedure into the shell.

Programming Data Access Pages with VBA

You can program solutions with data access pages at several different levels. This section explores solutions based on VBA, the *AllDataAccessPages* collection, the *DataAccessPage* object, and selected methods of the *DoCmd* object. Programmatic manipulation of data access pages by using VBA can serve multiple administrative needs.

Enumerating Data Access Pages and Their Properties

The *AllDataAccessPages* collection works like the *AllForms* and *AllReports* collections. Its members are not database objects, but rather *AccessObject* objects. These objects are available whether or not a data access page is open. The *AllDataAccessPages* collection lets you track the full set of all data access pages associated with a database. The following short VBA procedure inventories all the data access pages associated with the *CurrentProject* object of an Access database file or an Access project, and the procedure notes whether the pages are open.

The *FullName* property of an *AccessObject* object in the *AllDataAccessPages* collection has a special meaning. Recall that pages are not stored as objects in the database file; they are separate HTML files. The location of the pages can be anywhere on a LAN. The *FullName* property indicates the path and filename for a data access page. The next procedure lists all the pages in a project and itemizes them by their *Name* and *FullName* properties. The *Name* property value is the shortcut for the data access page that appears in the database window.

```
Sub ListMyPages()
Dim obj1 As AccessObject

'Iterate through the members of the AllDataPages collection.
'Print link name, whether its page is loaded, and
'the address at which the link points.
For Each obj1 In CurrentProject.AllDataAccessPages
    Debug.Print "Link name: " & obj1.Name
    Debug.Print String(5, " ") & "Is loaded: " & obj1.IsLoaded
    Debug.Print String(5, " ") & "Link address: " & obj1.FullName
    Debug.Print
Next obj1

End Sub
```

Because the *AllDataAccessPages* collection has a limited number of properties, you are likely to need the *DataAccessPages* collection to get more information about the data access pages associated with a database. While the *AllDataAccessPages* collection belongs to the *CurrentProject* object shown in the preceding sample, the *DataAccessPages* collection belongs to the *Application* object. In addition to this distinction, data access pages belong to the *DataAccessPages* collection only when they are open. Therefore, you must open a data access page before you can reference it as a member of the *DataAccessPages* collection. Since proper applications restore settings to the way they were before their operation, you should close any data access pages that you opened to make them members of the *DataAccessPages* collection.

The following procedure prints the links, the path and filename for the page links, and the data source specification for selected data access pages. The first two items are available from the *AllDataAccessPages* collection. However, the last item requires an excerpt from the connection string for a member of the *DataAccessPages* collection. The data source specification within the *Connection-String* property for a *DataAccessPages* member starts with the string *"Data Source"* and ends with the first semicolon after *"Data Source"*. If you create a new copy of a database with the most recent data, it's possible that some of your data access pages will reference an incorrect, older version of that database. You can put the called procedure in the following sample within a loop and go through the data access pages in the *CurrentProject* object. The previous sample illustrates this type of design. When you have just a few objects to report on, you can speed up your application by referencing just a subset of items with indexes, as the following code illustrates.

> **Note**   If you change the target files in the first procedure, save it to avoid a file-locking error. The sample needs an exclusive lock on the current database, and it cannot make the lock if uncommitted changes exist.

```
'Save module after updating dapName settings
Sub CallPrintDAPConnectionString()
Dim dapName As String

'Pass the name of two data access page links
'for lookup of target properties
dapName = "dapMenuPage"
PrintDAPConnectionString dapName
dapName = "dapProducts"
PrintDAPConnectionString dapName

End Sub
```

(continued)

```
Sub PrintDAPConnectionString(dapName As String)
Dim bol1 As Boolean
Dim str1 As String
Dim int1 As Integer
Dim int2 As Integer

bol1 = True

'If file is not loaded, set bol1 to False
If CurrentProject.AllDataAccessPages(dapName).IsLoaded = False Then
    DoCmd.OpenDataAccessPage dapName, acDataAccessPageBrowse
    bol1 = False
End If

'Print target for page link and data source for page at
'which the link points
str1 = DataAccessPages(dapName).ConnectionString
int1 = InStr(str1, "Data Source")
int2 = InStr(int1, str1, ";")
Debug.Print CurrentProject.AllDataAccessPages(dapName).Name
Debug.Print String(5, " ") & "Link points at " & _
    CurrentProject.AllDataAccessPages(dapName).FullName
Debug.Print String(5, " ") & "Data file for page points at " & _
    Mid(str1, int1, int2 - int1)

'If file was initially closed, close it again
If bol1 = False Then
    DoCmd.Close acDataAccessPage, dapName, acSaveNo
End If

End Sub
```

Revising Data Access Page Properties

In addition to viewing settings made manually, you can revise them. One of the features we haven't discussed yet improves the appearance of your data access pages: the application of themes. Access offers more than 60 preformatted themes. You can apply any of these themes in Design view. You can also perform the same task with the *ApplyTheme* method. This section illustrates how.

We did describe how to assign titles to your data access pages earlier. Recall that these titles appear in the top title bar of a browser when users view your data access pages. By default, Access names a page Page*n*, where *n* is a sequential number. In case you forget your title or aren't sure what title you want for a page, you can programmatically revise a title after it's initially created. A second sample in this section illustrates how to loop through all the page links in the *Current-Project* object and update the page titles.

Applying a Theme to a Page

It's very simple to beautify your data access pages with the *ApplyTheme* method. The hardest part is learning the names of the more than 60 themes so that you know which one to apply to your data access page. You can start learning the names with the Theme dialog box, which opens with the Format-Theme command in Design view. This dialog box lets you preview the design effects of the different themes on a general page. You can see the effect a theme has on a specific data access page only after applying that theme. For example, you might discover that a theme makes a font too large for the text controls on a page. If this happens, you can redesign the controls or text or remove the theme.

The following pair of procedures illustrates how to apply a theme programmatically to any data access page in the current project. The first procedure names a link to the data access page with its *dapName* setting. This requires a link to an existing data access page. Next the first procedure calls the second procedure by passing it a theme name and the name of the link for the data access page. I recommend using either the Blends or Artsy theme. Not all themes load with a typical installation; however, these two themes typically do. You can load additional themes with the standard Office XP setup program.

The second procedure in the application for applying a theme contains a couple of noteworthy steps. First the procedure opens the page in Design view. You cannot apply a theme to a page in any other view. After invoking the *Apply-Theme* method, the procedure both saves and closes the page. By itself, the standard process of closing and saving changes doesn't capture design changes to a page from the *ApplyTheme* method. Figure 16-17 shows the impact of the Blends theme on the dapProducts page created earlier in this chapter. You can restore the original look of the page by following the instructions given in the comments at the top of this listing:

```
Sub CallSetTheme()
Dim dapName As String

'Test with Artsy or Blends, and
'clear with Format > Theme > (No Theme) or
'apply the Blank theme

dapName = "dapProducts"
setTheme "Blends", dapName

End Sub


Sub setTheme(ThemeName As String, dapName As String)
Dim dap1 As DataAccessPage
```

(continued)

```
'Open target page in Design view
DoCmd.OpenDataAccessPage dapName, acDataAccessPageDesign

'Apply theme; then save and close the page
DataAccessPages(dapName).ApplyTheme ThemeName
DoCmd.Save acDataAccessPage, dapName
DoCmd.Close acDataAccessPage, dapName, acSaveNo

End Sub
```

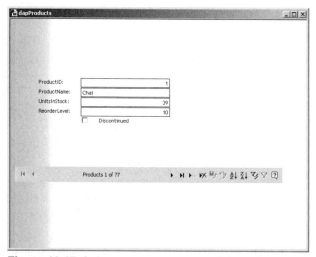

Figure 16-17 A data access page containing a form with the Blends theme.

Changing a Page Title

The procedure for changing a page title relies on the *Document* property of a data access page. This property returns the document for a page so that you can access the document's properties, including the *Title* property. You can set a page's *Title* property with a string value.

The sample procedure loops through all the page links that are members of the *AllDataAccessPages* collections of the *CurrentProject* object. This includes every page link that appears in the Database window for a project. Any pages with titles that begin with *Page* are offered a new title. Understand that the page link in the Access project points at a page and that this page has a title. The page link name, page name, and title can all be different. The procedure computes a new prospective page title based on the filename for the data access page at which the page link points. A message box identifies the page being examined with the new prospective page title. If the user says yes to the prompt from the message box, the procedure assigns the new title to the page. Regardless of whether the procedure updates a page's title property, the procedure closes the page and saves any changes. In this case, you do not have to explicitly invoke the *Save* method.

One nice feature of this sample application is that it shows how to save the loaded status and view for a data access page and restore them before an application closes. In addition, the sample asks users after processing each page whether they want to continue looping through pages. This permits a user to start an edit and then resume later when he or she has more time to complete the task or has an opportunity to gather information needed to complete the task.

```
Sub ChangePageTitles()
Dim bol1 As Boolean
Dim obj1 As AccessObject
Dim dap1 As DataAccessPage
Dim str1 As String
Dim str2 As String
Dim str3 As String
Dim str4 As String
Dim str5 As String
Dim int1 As Integer
Dim int2 As Integer
Const conPageView = 2


'Iterate through the members of the AllDataPages collection
For Each obj1 In CurrentProject.AllDataAccessPages

'This assignment is just for clarity because Boolean
'variables are False by default
    bol1 = False

'If file is loaded, save its loaded status and current
'view setting before closing it
    If CurrentProject.AllDataAccessPages(obj1.Name).IsLoaded _
        = True Then
        int1 = CurrentProject. _
            AllDataAccessPages(obj1.Name).CurrentView
        bol1 = True
        DoCmd.Close acDataAccessPage, obj1.Name, acSaveYes
    End If

'Open data access page in Design view and set a reference to it
    DoCmd.OpenDataAccessPage obj1.Name, acDataAccessPageDesign
    Set dap1 = DataAccessPages(obj1.Name)

'Compute candidate title based on filename (link name
'does not have to point to filename), and save selected
'string values for message box prompt
    str1 = obj1.Name
    str2 = Left(obj1.FullName, Len(obj1.FullName) - 4)
    str3 = dap1.Document.Title
```

(continued)

```
        int2 = InStrRev(str2, "\")
        str4 = Mid(str2, int2 + 1, Len(str2))

    'If page Title property starts with Page, ask if user
    'wants to change title to filename
        If Left(str3, 4) = "Page" Then
            str5 = "Link " & str1 & ", which points at " & str2 & _
                ".htm has a page title of " & str3 & ".  Do " & _
                "want to change the title to " & str4 & "."
    'Make Title property assignment if user says to
            If MsgBox(str5, vbYesNo, _
                "Programming Microsoft Access 2002") = vbYes Then
                dap1.Document.Title = str4
            End If

        End If

    'Save any changes to page
        DoCmd.Close acDataAccessPage, obj1.Name, acSaveYes

    'Restore page loaded status and view
        If bol1 = True And int1 <> conPageView Then
            DoCmd.OpenDataAccessPage obj1.Name, acDataAccessPageDesign
        ElseIf bol1 = True And int1 = conPageView Then
            DoCmd.OpenDataAccessPage obj1.Name, acDataAccessPageBrowse
        End If

    'Exit loop if user says to
        If MsgBox("Do you want to continue?", vbYesNo) = vbNo Then
            Exit For
        End If

Next obj1

End Sub
```

One of the most involved portions of the procedure is the code that computes the prompt for the message box. The code works with several different field values, including the page link, the data access page path and filename, and the current page title. The prompt additionally shows the new prospective title. Figure 16-18 shows a prompt for the dapThreeLevelReport link. In this case, the link has the same name as the filename for the data access page. However, the title is Page2. The prompt gives the user a chance to revise the title to the link name. You can use different code if your application requires a different algorithm for revising page titles.

Figure 16-18 A prompt from a custom application that lets a user change a page title.

Creating, Deleting, and Relinking Data Access Pages

If you programmed data access pages much with Access 2000, you might have noticed the *CreateDataAccessPage* method. This method belonged to the *Application* object, and it enabled the creation of new, blank data access pages as well as new links to existing data access pages. If you look up help for this method in Access 2002, you'll get this message: "This keyword is not implemented. It is reserved for future use." Actually, the method still exists, but it generates a run-time error. Happily, it's relatively easy to program around the run-time error. Access 2002 retained the *acDataAccessPage* argument for the *DeleteObject* method. This method is handy for discarding page links that you no longer need as well as relinking existing pages with new data access pages.

The following pair of VBA procedures shows the new technique for using the *CreateDataAccessPage* method for making a new data access page file and linking to it in the current project. Recall that a data access page for an Access project has three important characteristics. First, it is a standalone Web page. Second, it must have a data source control that specifies a relationship to a data source. Third, it's the target of a link inside an Access database file or Access project that points at the standalone Web page.

The *CreateDataAccessPage* method takes two arguments. The first of these is for the path and filename of the standalone Web page. Your specification for this first argument doesn't require an extension. Therefore, you should not end it with .htm. The method automatically appends the correct extension to the file for the data access page. The second argument takes a Boolean variable assignment. An assignment value of True causes the method to create a new data access page file. A value of False is appropriate when you're creating a new link for an existing standalone page. When you invoke the method, it opens a blank data access page in memory. You must provide a memory variable for the return value from the method. Failing to do so generates a compile-time error. You can give the variable an *AccessObject* data type.

After invoking the *CreateDataAccessPage* method as described, you will generate a run-time error. In my tests of the method, the most common result was error 13, with a description of Type Mismatch. If I ran the procedure successively without erasing the previously created data access page, I also generated error 2023. This error can occur when your application tries to create a data access page file that already exists.

The sample application that follows includes traps and fixes for both of the errors that I encountered. Other errors are logged to the Immediate window before a normal exit. The sample application sets the filename and path for the data access page in the first procedure. The second procedure combines these arguments for the *CreateDataAccessPage* method and invokes the method. This procedure also includes error traps. One of these traps is for the case in which the application tries to write over a previously existing data access page. When the application detects this error, it invokes a third procedure to delete the old file and then retries the *CreateDataAccessPage* method. Notice that the called procedure removes both the page link with the *DeleteObject* method and the file to which it links with the *Kill* statement. The other error trap is for the type mismatch error. This is the normal result of trying to create a new data access page with the method. While the method generates a run-time error, it successfully creates a new page with a data source control set to the database for the current project. The page resides in memory. Therefore, when the second procedure traps this error, it saves the page in memory and closes the page. This completes the task.

```
Sub CallNewDataAccessPageForNewPage()
Dim dapName As String
Dim dapPath As String

dapName = "dapfoo3"
dapPath = "\\cab2000\c\inetpub\wwwroot\pma10\"

NewDataAccessPage dapName, dapPath

End Sub


Sub NewDataAccessPage(dapName As String, dapPath As String)
On Error GoTo NewPageTrap
Dim dapPathFile
Dim dap1 As AccessObject

'Concatenate path and file for CreateDataAccessPage method
dapPathFile = dapPath + dapName

'Create new data access page and wipe old copy
'if it exists
Set dap1 = CreateDataAccessPage(dapPathFile, True)

NewPageExit:
'This normal exit path is not strictly necessary because
'procedure does not end normally
Exit Sub
```

```
NewPageTrap:
If Err.Number = 2023 Then
'Delete old version of page, if it already exists
    DeleteDap dapName, dapPath
    Resume
ElseIf Err.Number = 13 Then
'Save page and close page, to finish method
    DoCmd.RunCommand acCmdSave
    DoCmd.Close
Else
'Print out error number and description otherwise
    Debug.Print Err.Number, Err.Description
End If

End Sub



Sub DeleteDap(dapName As String, dapPath As String)
Dim dapPathFile
Dim dap As AccessObject

'Specify file to delete with extension
dapPathFile = dapPath + dapName + ".htm"

'First delete link in Database window
DoCmd.DeleteObject acDataAccessPage, dapName

'Next kill file for data access page
Kill dapPathFile

End Sub
```

Just as data access pages designate data sources, page links point at files. The standalone file for a data access page points at a data source. When the source is an Access database, this source is a file. The data source can also be a SQL Server database. In any event, the link inside a Database window points at a Web page. As long as you run the page links on the same computer you used to create them, they will operate successfully whether you use local drives or UNC naming conventions to specify the path to a data access page. However, if you try to invoke a link that specifies its target file with local drives on another computer, Access will ask the user to update the link. This requires the user to know the correct address for the data access page. If you use UNC notation, a user on another computer can open the file for the page just by clicking the link.

A previous sample enumerated page links and showed the files at which they point. The output from that sample shows either a local drive or a UNC specification for the file at which the link points. You can use the following sample to change the specification for any page link appearing in a Database window. The link changes the file at which the dapfoo link in the current project points. This file has a small form on it. Changing the link specification for the data access page does not affect that page. It only affects how you access the page.

The sample relies on two procedures. In the first procedure, the code designates the name of the link and the path to the file. The second procedure relies on the fact that the link name and the filename for the data access page are the same. If the link name and filename are different, you need to modify the sample so that users can separately designate the filename. Before preparing to invoke the *CreateDataAccessPage* method, the procedure deletes a previous version of the link. If the link does not exist, a run-time error occurs. You can modify the procedure in any number of ways to handle this error, including using an error trap. After setting an inline error trap for the *CreateDataAccessPage* method, the procedure invokes the method. This use of the method sets its second argument to False. With this specification, the method does not attempt to create a data access page file. It creates only a link that points at an existing file. After invoking the method, the procedure cleans up after the normal run-time error by saving the link and closing the open data access page.

> **Note** Programmatically manipulating a page in VBA has the same restriction against authoring on the same computer from which you publish your pages as creating a page manually does. Revert back to a local drive specification for the data source of pages you're editing on a local machine. After you finish editing, convert back to a UNC format for designating the page's link to a data source page. When editing a data access page from a different computer than the one you're using to publish your page, you can complete the whole task in UNC format.

```
Sub CallChangeLink()
Dim dapName As String
Dim dapPath As String

dapName = "dapfoo"
dapPath = "\\cab2000\c\inetpub\wwwroot\pma10\"

'You can toggle the path for a link specification
'by exchanging on alternate runs the following
'assignment with the preceding dapPath assignment
'dapPath = "C:\inetpub\wwwroot\pma10\"
```

```
ChangePageLink dapName, dapPath

End Sub


Sub ChangePageLink(dapName, dapPath)
Dim dap As AccessObject

'Delete former link to dapName page at dapPath
DoCmd.DeleteObject acDataAccessPage, dapName

'Concatenate path and file for CreateDataAccessPage method
dapPathFile = dapPath + dapName

'Make a new link to the existing dapName page
'at dapPath
On Error Resume Next
Set dap = CreateDataAccessPage(dapPathFile, False)
If Err.Number = 13 Then
'Save page and close page
    DoCmd.RunCommand acCmdSave
    DoCmd.Close
End If

End Sub
```

Basing Data Access Pages on Access Forms and Reports

Data access pages were a very popular new feature back when I was explaining the benefits of Access 2000 in the seminars I gave throughout the United States. The attendees told me they liked data access pages because they had the look and feel of Access forms and reports. Data access pages were viewed as relatively familiar and easy to develop. Perhaps the most common question asked by seminar registrants was, "Is there any automatic way to base a data access page on an existing Access form or report?" At the time, when only Access 2000 was available, the answer was No—however, it changed to Yes when Access 2002 was introduced. While the conversion process is not perfect in every case, it's always automatic.

The process for automatically creating a data access page works for both Access forms and reports. In addition, you can do so both manually and programmatically. To perform the process manually, select either an Access form or report in the Database window and choose File-Save As. Access responds by opening a Save As dialog box. In the drop-down list control on the dialog box, select Data Access Page. In the New Data Access Page dialog box, designate a folder and name for the new data access page based on the form or report. Then click OK to save the data access page in memory to disk.

You can achieve results comparable to the File-Save As command by using the *DoCmd* object's *OutputTo* method. Using the programmatic solution to base data access pages on forms and reports has a couple of advantages over the manual technique. First, the programmatic approach makes it easy to process sets of forms and reports to data access pages in one step. Second, by learning to use the programmatic solution, you can offer this capability to users of your custom solutions.

When outputting a data access page based on a form or a report, you will typically specify as many as four arguments for the *OutputTo* method. The first argument is an intrinsic constant for either a form (*acForm*) or a report (*acReport*), depending on the type of Access object on which you base your data access page. The second argument is a string denoting the name of the Access form or report that serves as the basis for the new data access page. The third argument is another intrinsic constant (*acFormatDAP*) to specify that the method will generate a data access page. This is necessary because the *OutputTo* method can generate many different types of output, including text files, Excel workbooks, ASP, XML files, and more. The fourth argument represents the name of the path and file that will store the new data access page.

When you create a data access page with the *OutputTo* method, you're responsible for archiving any existing files that have the same name as your new data access page. If you specify a name for your new page that's identical to one that already exists in the same path, Access silently copies over the old file. You're also responsible for creating a link in the project that points at the file for the new data access page. An excerpt from the prior sample for pointing a link at a new page supports this function. If you already have a link pointing at the new data access page based on the page's filename, Access creates another link with the same name, except it appends an underscore and a sequential number to the link's name. You can ensure that the new link is correct with operational procedures or with programming. For example, you can delete the old link if it exists.

To demonstrate automating the creation of a data access page on an Access form, I used the AutoForm wizard to generate an Access form named *frmOrder-Details* based on the *Order Details* table. This form is available in the Access database file for this chapter. Next I ran the following procedure to create a data access page based on the form and a link to the new page. The procedure has two parts. The first part creates the new page with the *OutputTo* method. The second part creates a link for the page in the Database window for the Access database file.

```
Sub dapfrmOrderDetails()
Dim dap As AccessObject
Dim dapPath As String

'Create a new data access page in dapPath based on
'the frmOrderDetails form
dapPath = _
    "\\cab2000\c\inetpub\wwwroot\pma10\dapfrmOrderDetails.htm"
DoCmd.OutputTo acForm, _
    "frmOrderDetails", _
    acFormatDAP, _
    dapPath

'This code creates a link in the current project to the
'data access page at dapPath
On Error Resume Next
Set dap = _
    CreateDataAccessPage(dapPath, False)
If Err.Number = 13 Then
    DoCmd.RunCommand acCmdSave
    DoCmd.Close
End If

End Sub
```

Figure 16-19 shows the original Access form and its data access page representation inside an Access window. The original form in the upper left portion of the screen translates perfectly into a data access page. There are even some extra touches in the lower right corner. For example, both the original form and its representation on a data access page have a record selector with the same kind of functionality. You can also view the total number of records in both forms and move among them with navigator controls. The data access page offers enhanced functionality, such as filtering and sorting. However, you can programmatically or manually restrict the availability of these capabilities to the form on the data access page.

While this approach is very promising, it has a couple of limitations. First, a subform in a main/subform combination doesn't get translated; the *OutputTo* method generates just the main form. Second, bound graphic images do not translate from Access forms to their data access page counterparts. You can use the technique discussed in the "Managing Images on a Data Access Page" section earlier in this chapter to display images tied to data values for forms generated automatically by the *OutputTo* method.

Figure 16-19 Automatically generated data access pages can have the same look and feel as Access forms.

As mentioned in Chapter 7, "Reports, Controls, and Data," you can represent parent-child data relationships with nested sections in Access reports. This lets you display the same kind of information found in a main/subform. Figure 16-20 shows an excerpt from the report rptProductsWithinCategories. As you can see, the report lists products within categories. For each category, the report shows the *UnitsInStock* and *ReorderLevel* field values.

The following VBA procedure shows how to convert the report shown in Figure 16-20 into an interactive report on a data access page. As you can see, the changes are very minor in relation to the earlier sample for converting a form to a data access page. The code still must perform two main functions. Access automatically recognizes the source object as a form and the nesting in the original report. With the same basic syntax, Access adjusts to the input changes and creates a new output in the style of an interactive report.

```
Sub daprptProductsWithinCategories()
Dim dap As AccessObject
Dim dapPath As String

'Create a new data access page in dapPath based on
'the rptProductsWithinCategories report
dapPath = _
    "\\cab2000\c\inetpub\wwwroot\pma10\" & _
    "daprptProductsWithinCategories.htm"
```

```
DoCmd.OutputTo acReport, _
    "rptProductsWithinCategories", _
    acFormatDAP, _
    dapPath

'This code creates a link in the current project to the
'data access page at dapPath
On Error Resume Next
Set dap = _
    CreateDataAccessPage(dapPath, False)
If Err.Number = 13 Then
    DoCmd.RunCommand acCmdSave
    DoCmd.Close
End If

End Sub
```

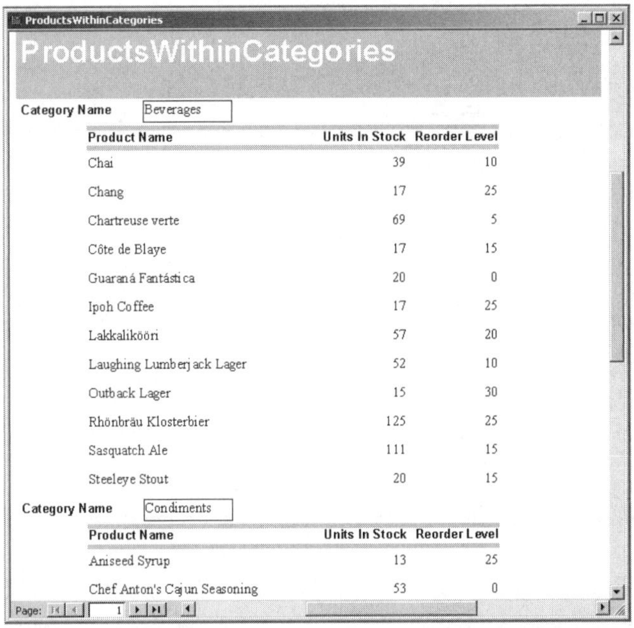

Figure 16-20 An Access report with a nested relationship showing how the *OutputTo* method generates an interactive report for this kind of data relationship.

Figure 16-21 shows a slightly edited version of the automatically created interactive report based on the report in Figure 16-20. Notice that the report uses a caption area above the data values to label the values for products within a category. This caption area is a special kind of header section, just like those discussed in the "Getting Started with Forms on Data Access Pages" section and elsewhere throughout this chapter. As attractive and efficient as this report is, it could benefit from some of the techniques demonstrated for computed fields earlier. I moved the category name legend in Design view so that it does not overlap with the expand control (the plus sign [+]) on the interactive report. I also added meaningful labels to the two navigator bars. You can do this by selecting the descriptor in each bar and then updating its RecordsetLabel property on the Data tab. It takes at least two clicks to select the label for a navigator bar. First you select the bar. Then you select the label on the bar. After making these and any other changes you want, you can save the interactive report just like any other data access page.

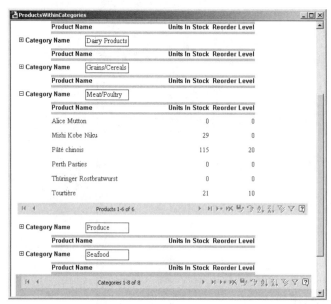

Figure 16-21 A very slightly edited interactive report based on the Access report in Figure 16-20.

Office XP Web Components

Three Office XP Web Components ship with Office XP: the Spreadsheet, Chart, and PivotTable list components. You can use them on data access pages to enhance their functionality. The data access page is actually driven by a fourth Office XP Component called a Data Source Component. You apply this component by managing data access pages as we have discussed throughout this chapter. If a site has a license that permits intranet distribution, the site administrator can configure browsers under the license to automatically download and configure Office XP Web Components the first time they load a page using a component. For more information on configuring Office XP Web Components, see the Microsoft Office XP Resource Kit at www.microsoft.com/Office/ORK/xp/WELCOME/depf05.htm.

Office Spreadsheet Sample

Figure 16-22 shows one use of a spreadsheet component (or control) on a data access page. Controls on the page show the *CategoryName*, *ProductName*, and *ProductSales* fields for the *Sales By Category* query in the sample database. The query is excerpted from the Northwind database sample. This query computes sales by product in 1997 for each product. The query lists the category ID and name of each product along with its sales.

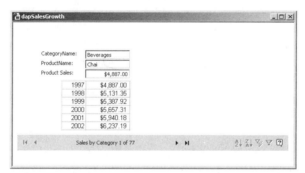

Figure 16-22 The spreadsheet component on this data access page uses sales from the database for 1997 to project sales through 2002.

The sample in Figure 16-22 extends the basic query by projecting sales from 1997 through 2002. First an event procedure copies the current value of the *ProductSales* control from the page to a spreadsheet cell. Then formulas in the component apply a progressive series of growth rates to sales starting with 1998. These rates increase sales from one year to the next. While the growth rates are the same for all products, the actual sales levels vary between products because the 1997 sales are different for each product. Finally, to protect the formulas in the current session from damage, you can lock selected spreadsheets to block users from inadvertently changing them. This is a minor issue since the correct values reappear on the next load of the page. (Clicking Refresh on the browser does not restore the original values.)

You can add a spreadsheet component to the data access page based on the *Sales by Category* query in the same way that you add any other control from the

Toolbox. Access sequentially numbers controls of each type as it adds them to a page. Therefore, the first spreadsheet added in a session has the name spreadsheet0. You can override this setting by opening a spreadsheet component's Properties dialog box and making an assignment to the Id property for the component.

In addition to a Properties dialog box, Office Web Components have a Commands And Options dialog box. You can cause the dialog box to appear by right-clicking the spreadsheet in Design view and selecting Commands And Options from the menu. This dialog box lets you set and examine specialized properties for a component. For example, you can choose to remove the row and column headers to make the spreadsheet component's appearance integrate more tightly with the rest of the page. The sample in Figure 16-22 made these and other adjustments to the spreadsheet through its Commands And Options dialog box.

The following script shows the event procedure that transfers the current value of the contents in the productsales text box to the spreadsheet—in particular, cell B1. The code is for the *onrowenter* event of the document. The document is an object that denotes the page, and the *onrowenter* event fires when new values are available on the object. This is similar to the current event for Access forms because it signals that new data is ready for an object. This event fires when a user first loads a page or moves between the records behind form controls. Each time the event fires, the procedure copies the current value of the productsales text box to the cell in row 1 and column 2 of the Sheet1 worksheet. By default, a spreadsheet component initially has three worksheets. You can add extra ones and add and remove the tab control for showing the active worksheet within a spreadsheet component.

```
<SCRIPT event=onrowenter for=document language=vbscript>
<!--

spreadsheet0.Worksheets("Sheet1").cells(1,2) = productsales.value

-->
</SCRIPT>
```

Figure 16-23 shows the Design view of the data access page in Figure 16-22. In the current figure, cell B2 is selected on Sheet1. This is one row below the row automatically populated by the preceding event procedure. In addition, the Commands And Options dialog box for the spreadsheet component appears. The Formula tab on this dialog box displays any formula for the currently selected cell. In this instance, the formula computes the value in cell B2 so that it is 5 percent greater than the value in cell B1. Cells B3 through B6 contain formulas that yield progressively larger values than those from the preceding years. As you can see from the values in column A, these rows represent successive years.

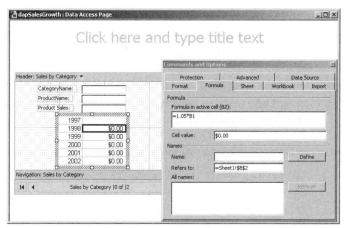

Figure 16-23 The Design view of the data access page from Figure 16-22 with the Commands And Options dialog box for its spreadsheet component.

Office Chart Sample

The sample in this section builds on the preceding one by adding an Office XP Chart component that charts the values in the spreadsheet. The chart shows a graphical depiction of how sales grow over time for each product. Figure 16-24 shows a product with its spreadsheet projections. In addition, a graphical depiction of the projections appears on the right side of the page. The 3D line chart dynamically updates each time the values in the spreadsheet change. Recall that these values change whenever the user navigates to a new product.

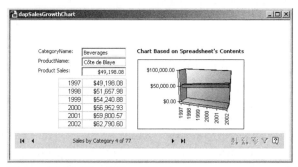

Figure 16-24 The Office XP Chart component on a data access page accepts values from a Spreadsheet component that changes its sales projections when a user moves off the current record.

To add a Chart component to your data access pages, select it from the Toolbox and then drag it to the area on your page where you want the chart. Click inside the Microsoft Office Web Component placeholder to launch the

Commands and Options Builder. This builder lets you specify a data source for the chart and designate ranges in the data source for the chart to display. Figure 16-25 depicts a data access page after the addition of a chart and the selection of Spreadsheet0 as the data source for the chart. As you can see from the Data Source tab, the next step is to designate the specific ranges for the chart. In the chart shown in Figure 16-24, this includes a Category Labels range that runs along the horizontal axis and a Values range that plots against the vertical axis.

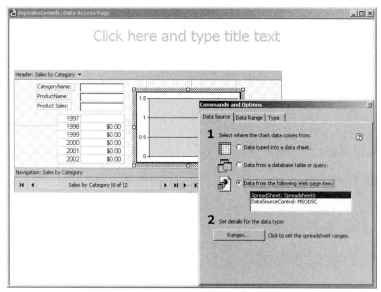

Figure 16-25 The initial Commands And Options dialog box for specifying the data source for a Chart component.

The Data Range tab opens after you click the Ranges button on the Data Source tab. Click the Add button on the Data Range tab. This creates a new data series for the chart. In this example, the builder types *Series1* as the Series name. Specify the Category Labels range with this string: *"Sheet1!$A$1:$A:$6"*. The cell values in the Category Labels range appear along the horizontal axis of your chart. Next designate the Values range with *"Sheet1!$B$1:$B:$6"*. The cells in the Values range plot against the chart's vertical axis. Finish specifying the chart by selecting the Type tab. Click Line to display the different types of line charts from which you can choose. Then highlight the 3D Line option. Since this completes the specification, close the builder dialog box.

After making these selections for your chart, the line will appear flat. This is because you are in Design view. Therefore, there are no values to plot. Switch into Page view to see your chart with data. Notice how the values in the 3D line chart change when you move to a new record. This happens because the spreadsheet values revise and the spreadsheet is, in turn, dependent on the productsales text box.

Creating and Using Office PivotTable Lists

The PivotTable list control lets users sort, group, filter, outline, and manipulate data. It can also work with data from more providers than a normal data access page or other Office XP Web Components can. For example, you can apply a PivotTable list control to Jet and SQL Server databases. You can also apply it to any ODBC data source, multidimensional data cubes, and nontraditional data sources, such as Outlook Search results. A particularly powerful feature of the PivotTable list control is that when you base a Chart control on a PivotTable list control, the chart behaves like a PivotChart. This enables filtering and analytical capabilities, including summing, adding, and averaging numeric quantities. Developers can set up a PivotTable list and let users work within the confines of a data environment without forcing them to know a data structure and a query language to extract results.

You add a PivotTable list control to a data access page from the Toolbox. By default, the control connects to the data source for the page on which it resides. You can override this default connection by right-clicking the control and choosing Commands And Options. On the Data Source tab of the Commands And Options dialog box, click Edit. In the Select Data Source dialog box, double-click Connect To New Data Source.odc, highlight Other/Advanced for the kind of data source to which you want to connect, and click Next. This presents the Provider tab of a Data Link Properties dialog box with the full list of OLE DB providers to which you can connect your PivotTable list control. Since one of these is the OLE DB Provider For ODBC Drivers, the list of data source types to which you can connect includes any source with an ODBC driver. Complete the other tabs to specify your connection to a data source besides the one for the data access page.

You can build a PivotTable list control with the same general techniques that you use within Access to do so. (See Chapter 8, "Designing and Using Pivot-Tables and PivotCharts.") Figure 16-26 shows a PivotTable list control under construction within a data access page. The figure illustrates adding the *Product-Name* field to the row drop area. By subsequently dragging the *ProductSales* field to the detail drop area, the resulting pivot table will display total sales by product within the category.

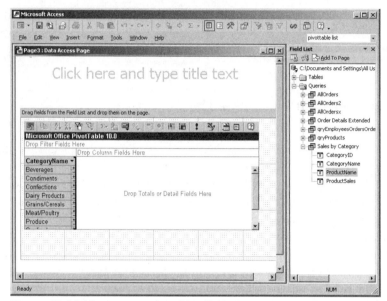

Figure 16-26 You can populate PivotTable list controls on data access pages as you would within normal Access applications.

Users can browse data access pages with PivotTable list controls and perform any desired analysis that you enable. For example, Figure 16-27 shows two different analyses in a browser window for the same basic PivotTable list control with the *CategoryName*, *ProductName*, and *ProductSales* fields on a data access page. The top browser window shows *ProductSales* aggregated by *CategoryName*. The bottom browser window presents a list of *ProductSales* by *ProductName* filtered by the Meat/Poultry category. The bottom browser does not aggregate the *ProductSales* field from the *Sales by Category* query that serves as the source for the PivotTable list control behind both browser windows.

You can add a Chart control to a data access page and designate a PivotTable list control as its source. This process is easier for developers and more flexible for users who are comfortable with analysis using pivot tables and pivot charts. Pivot charts are easier to design because you don't have to type in spreadsheet cell ranges as you do when basing a Chart component on a Spreadsheet component. You simply designate the PivotTable list control as a source and then graphically lay out any fields in the chart. It hardly matters what fields you put where because the point of a pivot chart is that users can modify these fields.

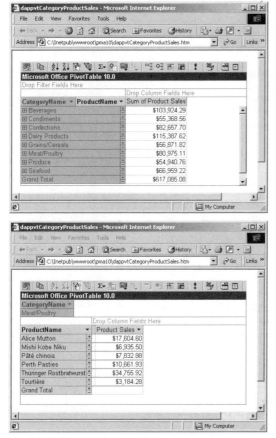

Figure 16-27 A pair of different browser windows illustrates some of the variety that users can generate from the same PivotTable list control.

Figure 16-28 shows a pivot chart on the same Web page as the PivotTable list from the preceding sample. Notice there is a filter for products in the Meat/Poultry category. When you add an item to the detail drop area in a pivot chart, the control automatically aggregates it. You cannot plot an unaggregated field with a pivot chart. The control does not allow it. Notice also that the PivotTable list and PivotChart controls are in sync. When Access created the aggregate to plot product sales, it also updated the PivotTable list and added total and grand total values.

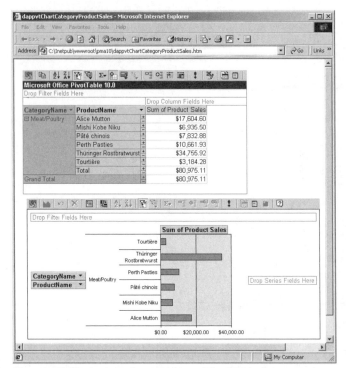

Figure 16-28 A pivot chart tied to a PivotTable list control.

Working with XML Data Representations

As I write this, XML is skyrocketing in popularity among developers. Like HTML, XML is a markup language. HTML uses tags to mark up text. These tags format the text that they mark—for example, by specifying a font size and italics for a text string. HTML has gained wide acceptance as a markup language for formatting text, graphics, and other content for display in a Web browser. In a data context, an HTML tag can mark the beginning or end of a record or a field.

XML proponents are still identifying the main application areas for this markup language, but representing data—especially for Web transport—is clearly a leading function of the "killer XML app." XML files are relatively compact. This means they travel over communication lines quickly. In addition, XML files do not necessarily involve scripts for execution. Therefore, they cannot serve as a virus delivery device as typical Office files that enable VBA macros do.

Access 2002 is the first version of Access to have integrated support for processing XML files. While Access 2000 can save and open XML files, this capability derives from ADO and is not a native Access feature. With Access 2002, the *ExportXML* and *ImportXML* methods belong to the Access *Application* object. In addition, the Access 2002 XML file processing capabilities are consistent with the more popular element-centric approach for representing data (as opposed to ADO's attribute-centric format).

This section introduces you to XML by presenting the Access 2002 capabilities for XML file processing. It will also show you different methods for displaying Access content in a browser by exporting data to XML files. You will also see a simple way of processing XML files for later reuse.

Exporting XML Files from Access 2002

The *ExportXML* method exports up to three different kinds of XML file types. This method writes out the contents of an Access record source. The record source can be any Access database object that contains data, including objects in Access database files and objects to which Access projects connect—namely, SQL Server database objects. This method can write up to three XML files, and it can even generate an .htm file to view in a browser. The .htm file requires all three XML files and generates a standard HTML table based on the contents of the record source.

The three XML files that the *ExportXML* method can write provide complementary information about a record source. Each file has its own file extension. The most fundamental file that the *ExportXML* method creates has an .xml extension. This file represents the data in a record source. However, it has no schema information. For example, it does not convey which field or fields serve as the primary key, and it provides no information about the data types for the columns in a record source. However, the .xml file is simply a text file that's easy to read. Although this file type does display by itself in a browser, it does not appear as an HTML table. Even Internet Explorer 4 can render the file in a friendly format. You can use the .xml file to make Access data available over the Web to others who do not have Access on their workstation.

> **Note**   I tested the .xml file generated by the *ExportXML* method with Netscape Navigator 4. While the browser did not render the .xml file, it did download the file for viewing with Notepad or any other program that views text files.

The .xsd file is an XML file containing schema information about the data in an .xml file. It describes the schema for a dataset. You need the .xsd file to learn about the structure of a database. The .xsd file contains schema information for the overall record source as well as its individual column values. The .xsd file can answer many questions about the structure of record source values represented in an .xml file. For example: Is a sequentially numbered field an AutoNumber or just a Long Integer data type? What's the maximum length of a string field? Is a column with numbers a numeric field or a field of strings that displays numbers? The contents of the .xml file don't answer any of these questions. However, the .xsd file delivers this valuable information about a record source.

The .xsl file is the third file written out by the *ExportXML* method. An .xsl file can serve two purposes for XML data. First, it can serve as a stylesheet for representing the data in an .xml file. Second, you can use .xsl files to transform data. For example, you can use XSLT, the programming language for .xsl files, to apply bolding to fields based on their values. (XSLT stands for Extensible Stylesheet Language Transformations.) With XSLT, you can transform an .xml file to a .pdf file or an .rtf file. Although beyond the scope of this book, these topics convey the potential uses of XSLT as a programming language. At this point, it's sufficient for you to grasp that the *ExportXML* method uses the .xsl file to specify the transformation that determines how the data in the .xml file appears in a browser.

The following script exports the *Shippers* table in one of two ways to the pma10 Web site on the cab2000 server. If the *XMLOnly* compiler constant is True, the procedure writes just the ShippersExport.xml file to a single XML file that represents the data values from the *Shippers* table. If the *XMLOnly* compiler constant is False, the procedure writes all three XML files plus the .htm file.

Since a value of False for *XMLOnly* generates the .htm file, let me point out that the .htm file does not contain HTML. Instead, the .htm file actually contains JavaScript that generates an HTML table, and it references an ActiveX object. This means that browsers unable to render ActiveX objects and workstations without the specific ActiveX object referenced by the .htm file can't view the page. The required ActiveX object is the Microsoft XML Document Object Model, which implements a set of standards for accessing and manipulating the contents of XML files.

This sample demonstrates the syntax for writing the contents of the *Shippers* table to a local intranet server. However, a slight modification of the syntax lets you write the XML files to an Internet Web site. The sample includes as a comment an example of this syntax, which you can adapt for your Internet server and Web site.

```
Sub ExportDataOrScript()
#Const XMLOnly = True

'Write the .xml data file or all three .xml files
#If XMLOnly = True Then
    Application.ExportXML acExportTable, "Shippers", _
        "http://cab2000/pma10/ShippersExport.xml"
#Else
    Application.ExportXML acExportTable, "Shippers", _
        "http://cab2000/pma10/ShippersExport.xml", _
        "http://cab2000/pma10/ShippersExport.xsd", _
        "http://cab2000/pma10/ShippersExport.xsl"
#End If

'Works for the Internet too!
'Application.ExportXML acExportTable, "Shippers", _
    "http://www.yourserver.com/yoursite/ShippersExport.xml", _
    "http://www.yourserver.com/yoursite/ShippersExport.xsd", _
    "http://www.yourserver.com/yoursite/ShippersExport.xsl"

End Sub
```

Figure 16-29 illustrates how an Internet Explorer 5 browser renders the ShippersExport.xml file. Notice that you can read the values in the table. However, the values do not appear in a tabular format. Instead, they appear within XML tags that signify their role. The <Shippers> and </Shippers> tags mark the beginning and end of each record. Similarly, each field within a record has beginning and ending tags. The overall document starts with an <?xml> tag that specifies the document as an XML document. This line is really a declaration. The <?xml> tag is the only one in the document that does not require a trailing tag to signify the end of the block. The <dataroot> and </dataroot> tags mark the beginning and end of data within the document. Both the <?xml> and <dataroot> tags have attribute settings. For example, the <?xml> tag has version and encoding attributes. The version attribute designates a version number. The value 1.0 is mandatory for this attribute. This ensures compatibility with future versions of XML. The encoding attribute specifies the computer format for representing characters within a document. The document in Figure 16-29 uses the UTF-8 format. This representation scheme uses a single byte to handle ASCII characters, and it can handle other character sets in 2 to 5 bytes. The UTF stands for Unicode Transformation Format.

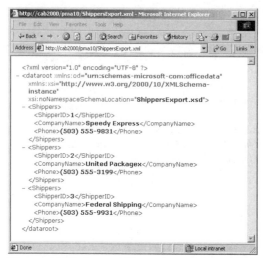

Figure 16-29 An .xml file generated by the *ExportXML* method in a browser window.

Figure16-30 shows an excerpt from the ShippersExport.xsd file in a browser. As you can see, the file's first line starts with an <?xml> tag that declares the document type. The excerpt shows the schema settings for the *ShipperID* and *CompanyName* columns in the *Shippers* table. The shipper ID specification declares *ShipperID* as the primary key, and the index for the primary key even has a clustered setting for SQL Server databases. Since this *Shippers* table is from an Access database file, the clustered attribute setting is *no*. The specification for the *CompanyName* column indicates that it has a text data type with a maximum length of 40 characters.

The settings in this .xsd file are vital to importing the data from an .xml file into an Access database file or the SQL Server database to which an Access project connects. Recall that the .xml file contains data but no information about the structure of the data. Likewise, the .xsd file contains structure information, but no data.

I do not show the .xsl file because it's long and difficult to read. You can find the full listing on the book's companion CD for your reference. Just like the .xml and .xsd files, the .xsl file has a text format, and its first line contains an <?xml> tag. The .xsl file also contains a mix of tags, including HTML tags and procedures with variable declarations, variable assignments, and conditional logic.

When you choose to generate .xml, .xsd, and .xsl files, Access also creates an .htm file. However, this file does not contain HTML. When a user renders the page with an Internet Explorer 5 browser, it runs the JavaScript code that appears as follows. As you can see, this script explicitly references both the .xml and .xsl files. The last two lines write the data from the .xml file in the style specified by the .xsl file over the script in the .htm file. For this reason, when a user chooses View-Source from the menu in a browser that renders ShippersExport.htm, the browser opens a page with data and HTML tags instead of this next script.

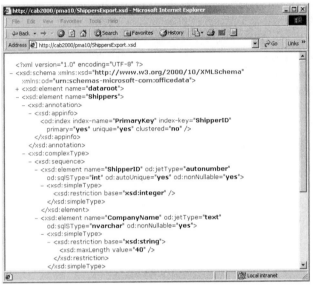

Figure 16-30 An excerpt from the .xsd file generated by the preceding code sample.

```
<HTML xmlns:signature="urn:schemas-microsoft-com:office:access">
<HEAD>
<META HTTP-EQUIV="Content-Type" CONTENT="text/html;charset=UTF-8"/>
</HEAD>

<SCRIPT event=onload for=window>
  objData = new ActiveXObject("MSXML.DOMDocument");
  objData.async = false;
  objData.load("ShippersExport.xml");
  if (objData.parseError.errorCode != 0)
    alert(objData.parseError.reason);

  objStyle = new ActiveXObject("MSXML.DOMDocument");
  objStyle.async = false;
  objStyle.load("ShippersExport.xsl");
  if (objStyle.parseError.errorCode != 0)
    alert(objStyle.parseError.reason);

  document.open("text/html","replace");
  document.write(objData.transformNode(objStyle));
</SCRIPT>

</HTML>
```

ADO-Generated vs. Access-Generated XML Files

Since ADO can generate XML files with its *Save* method for the *Recordset* object, you might think that this generates files consistent with the *ExportXML* method. However, this is not so. The following script recalls the syntax for persisting a recordset in XML format with the recordset's *Save* method:

```
Sub ForShippersSave()
Dim rst1 As ADODB.Recordset
Dim varLocalAddress As Variant
Dim int1 As Integer

'Open a recordset on the Shippers table in
'the current project
Set rst1 = New ADODB.Recordset
rst1.Open "Shippers", CurrentProject.Connection, _
    adOpenKeyset, adLockOptimistic, adCmdTable

'Make a new .xml file based on the table
varLocalAddress = "c:\Inetpub\wwwroot\pma10\" & _
    "ShippersSave.xml"
Kill varLocalAddress
rst1.Save varLocalAddress, adPersistXML

'Clean up objects
rst1.Close
Set rst1 = Nothing

End Sub
```

Figure 16-31 shows the ShippersSave.xml file generated by the preceding script, as displayed in a browser. Notice that the layout of this document differs in a couple of ways from the ShippersExport.xml file shown in Figure 16-29. First, the document in Figure 16-31 contains schema information in the same file with the data. Second, the data values appear as attribute settings toward the end of the document. Recall that the .xml file generated by the *ExportXML* method represents data values between tags (or *elements* in XML speak). For this reason, it's common to describe ADO-generated XML files as attribute-centric and Access-generated XML files as element-centric.

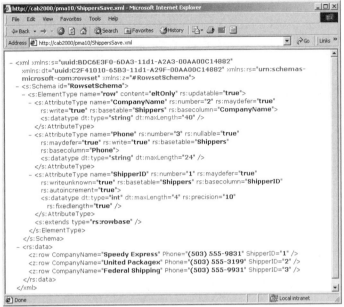

Figure 16-31 An .xml file generated by the ADO *Save* method as displayed in a browser window.

Note There are a couple of approaches to making ADO-generated XML files compatible with Access-generated ones, but both require more experience with XML programming than this book assumes. First, Access Help references a technique to use the *Save* method that generates a result compatible with the *ExportXML* method. (See the "Save Method" topic in Microsoft Visual Basic Help for more information.) This technique inserts the XML document from the *Save* method directly into an XML document tree. This book's CD includes a code sample for writing *Save* method results to an XML document tree. Second, Knowledge Base article Q285329 includes an XSLT file and a VBA procedure for transforming ADO-generated XML files into Access-generated XML files. To view the code, go to search.support.microsoft.com/kb/. Select Access 2002 in the My Search Is About box, and type *Q285329* into the My Question Is box. Then click Go.

The following script consists of three procedures. The first sets parameters and passes values to the two other procedures. The second procedure loops through the records and columns of a recordset based on an ADO-generated XML file. The third procedure illustrates the use of the ADO *Stream* object to print the XML document generated by the *Save* method. This alternative representation of the file shows all the XML tags and their attribute settings with the actual data values.

```
Sub CallShowStreamForFile()
Dim varLocalAddress As Variant
Dim fName As String

'Print the data in the .xml file
varLocalAddress = "c:\Inetpub\wwwroot\pma10\ShippersSave.xml"
AccessXMLFile varLocalAddress

'Print the XML code for the file
fName = "ShippersSave.xml"
ShowStreamForFile fName

End Sub


Sub AccessXMLFile(varLocalAddress As Variant)
Dim rst1 As ADODB.Recordset
Dim int1 As Integer

'Open the saved .xml file
Set rst1 = New ADODB.Recordset
rst1.Open varLocalAddress, "Provider=MSPersist;", _
    , , adCmdFile

'Loop through all rows; with each row, loop through all columns
Do Until rst1.EOF
    For int1 = 0 To rst1.Fields.Count - 1
        Debug.Print rst1.Fields(int1).Name, rst1(int1)
    Next int1
    rst1.MoveNext
Loop

'Clean up objects
rst1.Close
Set rst1 = Nothing

End Sub
```

```
Sub ShowStreamForFile(fName As String)
Dim rec1 As ADODB.Record
Dim stm1 As ADODB.Stream
Dim str1 As String

'Instantiate Record and Stream objects
Set rec1 = New ADODB.Record
Set stm1 = New ADODB.Stream

'Open a record for an HTML file
rec1.Open fName, "URL=http://cab2000/pma10"

'Set selected stream properties for printing with an
'ASCII character set, and open the stream on the file
'to which the record points
stm1.Type = adTypeText
stm1.Charset = "ascii"
stm1.Open rec1, adModeRead, adOpenStreamFromRecord

'Read all the lines from the stream to a string variable,
'and print the string variable
str1 = stm1.ReadText
Debug.Print str1

End Sub
```

You cannot run the *AccessXMLFile* procedure from this code sample against an XML file generated by the *ExportXML* method. On the other hand, the *ShowStreamforFile* procedure in the sample works with the XML file generated by either the *Save* method or the *ExportXML* method. This second procedure treats the XML files in a neutral way that reflects its text-based nature and doesn't depend on any special schema for the data.

Importing XML Files into Access

The *ImportXML* method lets you create Access tables based on the content of XML files in the format of those generated by the *ExportXML* method. Like the *ExportXML* method, the *ImportXML* method belongs to the Access *Application* object. The *ImportXML* method relies on the availability of the .xml and .xsd files. The Access Help topic for *ImportXML* does not properly describe the syntax for the method. Use the documentation given here instead.

This is the format for the *ImportXML* method:

```
ImportXML <PathAndFilename>, <intrinsicconstant>
```

The *ImportXML* method takes two arguments. The first argument is for the data source. It is the path and filename for an XML file. The second argument has three intrinsic constants. Table 16-1 lists these constants and describes their capabilities.

Table 16-1   ImportXML Argument Values

Constant	Description
acStructureAndData	Creates a table and populates it with data from an .xml file
acStructureOnly	Creates the structure for a table without populating the table with data
acAppendData	Appends the data in an .xml file to an existing table

> **Note**   Although you cannot use the *ImportXML* method to import XML files created by the ADO recordset *Save* method, the sample shown on pages 1010–1011 demonstrates how to use the ADO *Open* method and the ADO *Stream* object to examine the contents of files generated by the *Save* method.

The next sample demonstrates how to use two of the *ImportXML* intrinsic constants. It relies on two procedures. The first procedure shows the syntax for using the two intrinsic constants. The first constant creates a new table. The second constant adds records to the table created by the first use of the *ImportXML* method. In between the first and second invocation of *ImportXML*, the procedure modifies the XML file so that the second application of *ImportXML* will have new rows to add to the table. A call to the second procedure updates the original ShippersExport.xml file created by the *ExportXML* method.

The sample commences by renaming the *Shippers* table originally used to generate the ShippersExport set of XML files. This is necessary because the *ImportXML* method (used with the *acStructureAndData* constant) attempts to restore the table from which the initial XML files were created. There is no way to specify an alternative table name. After renaming the original version of the *Shippers* table, the procedure generates a new copy of the table based on the ShippersExport set of XML files. When using the *acStructureAndData* constant, the *ImportXML* method generates a run-time error unless you have the .xml and .xsd files that the *ExportXML* method created available. Next the code calls the *CreateShippersExport2* procedure to create a new .xml file with updated *ShipperID* column values that are unique from the initial values. Then the program invokes *ImportXML* a second time. In this case, the procedure specifies the updated .xml file whose name is ShippersExport2.xml. This adds three new rows to the *Shippers* table, yielding a total of six rows in the table. The procedure concludes by printing to the Immediate window the column values for each row in the table. Figure 16-32 shows this output.

```
Sub CreateAccessTableBasedOnXMLFile()
Dim rst1 As ADODB.Recordset
Dim int1 As Integer

'Rename linked Shippers table to Shipper2
DoCmd.Rename "Shipper2", acTable, "Shippers"

'Invoke the ImportXML method against the
'ShippersExport.xml file
Application.ImportXML _
    "C:\Inetpub\wwwroot\pma10\ShippersExport.xml", _
    acStructureAndData

'Update the XML document to avoid writing over the intial data or
'rejecting the new data because it duplicates the existing data
CreateShippersExport2 "ShippersExport.xml"

'Invoke the ImportXML method against the modified XML document
Application.ImportXML _
    "C:\Inetpub\wwwroot\pma10\ShippersExport2.xml", _
    acAppendData

'Open the saved .xml file
Set rst1 = New ADODB.Recordset
rst1.Open "Shippers", CurrentProject.Connection, , , cmdTable

'Loop through all rows; with each row, loop through all columns
Do Until rst1.EOF
    For int1 = 0 To rst1.Fields.Count - 1
        Debug.Print rst1.Fields(int1).Name, rst1(int1)
    Next int1
    rst1.MoveNext
Loop

'Clean up objects
rst1.Close
Set rst1 = Nothing

End Sub
```

Figure 16-32 The output from the *CreateAccessTableBasedOnXMLFile* procedure.

The second procedure illustrates a simple approach for updating the data values in an .xml file. Recall that the .xml file is element-centric. Therefore, data values appear between tags. Because the sample updates the shipper ID values, it can change the string *"<ShipperID>1"* to *"<ShipperID>4"*. The sample illustrates how to achieve this kind of transformation with the VBA *Replace* function. The function revises the *ShipperID* values of *1*, *2*, and *3* to *4*, *5*, and *6*, respectively. To further reinforce your grasp of XML files and build on the skills presented earlier in this book, the procedure demonstrates one approach for reading the .xml file and a second technique for rewriting the new .xml file. The procedure uses the ADO *Record* and *Stream* objects for opening the file and accessing its contents. After updating the *ShipperID* values, the procedure writes the new .xml file with these values using the *FileSystemObject* object. I could have used the *FileSystemObject* object to both read and write the .xml files. You might find it a useful exercise to revise the sample as suggested.

> **Note**   If you want to rerun this sample, you need to remove the *Shippers* table and rename the *Shipper2* table to *Shippers*. When you rerun the sample, it will automatically preserve your original data in the *Shippers* table by renaming it (to *Shipper2*).

```
Sub CreateShippersExport2(fName As String)
Dim rec1 As ADODB.Record
Dim stm1 As ADODB.Stream
Dim str1 As String

'Instantiate Record and Stream objects
Set rec1 = New ADODB.Record
Set stm1 = New ADODB.Stream

'Open a record for an HTML file
rec1.Open fName, "URL=http://cab2000/pma10"

'Set selected stream properties for printing with an
'ASCII character set, and open the stream on the file
'to which the record points
stm1.Type = adTypeText
stm1.Charset = "ascii"
stm1.Open rec1, adModeRead, adOpenStreamFromRecord

'Read all the lines from the stream to a string variable
str1 = stm1.ReadText

'Replace original values with new ones
str1 = Replace(str1, "<ShipperID>1", "<ShipperID>4")
str1 = Replace(str1, "<ShipperID>2", "<ShipperID>5")
str1 = Replace(str1, "<ShipperID>3", "<ShipperID>6")

'Use FileSystemObject to create a new file
Set fs = CreateObject("Scripting.FileSystemObject")
Set f = fs.CreateTextFile( _
    "c:\inetpub\wwwroot\pma10\ShippersExport2.xml", True)
f.Write str1
f.Close

'Clean up objects
stm1.Close
Set stm1 = Nothing
rec1.Close
Set rec1 = Nothing
Set f = Nothing
Set fs = Nothing

End Sub
```

17

Access Does the Web: Part II

This chapter continues the discussion of making Microsoft Access database contents available to users over webs, including intranets, extranets, and the Internet. We'll examine Web-based techniques that integrate less tightly with Access 2002 and Microsoft Office XP than the tools covered in Chapter 16, "Access Does the Web: Part I." The tight integration of the tools covered in the preceding chapter dramatically simplifies the process of sharing the contents of Microsoft Access and Microsoft SQL Server databases over webs. However, nearly all the techniques mentioned in Chapter 16 require clients running Office XP for you to review documents created with those techniques. When you cannot rely on your client workstations to have Office XP (or at least elements of it) installed, the techniques discussed in this chapter offer viable alternatives for sharing database content over the Web.

This chapter is divided into three major sections. The first section explores Access-based techniques for publishing datasheets over webs, both statically and dynamically. Despite being Access based, these techniques permit you to share any data source to which Access can connect. Furthermore, these techniques enable users to view datasheets published with them from any browser that reads HTML. The second section in the chapter explores Microsoft FrontPage–based techniques for publishing datasheets. The carefully constructed examples and instructions in this section show the flexibility and ease of using the FrontPage Database Wizard. This section also discusses how to create forms for searching a database, including a datasheet to display search results. The chapter's third section introduces programmatic techniques for creating forms that dynamically display the contents of a database and permit users to interact with that database in ways not possible with a standard Web-based datasheet.

Publishing Datasheets

Webs are great mechanisms for sharing data—especially with widespread audiences. However, webs are not organized for efficiently storing, retrieving, and manipulating data. While database managers such as Access offer many tools for performing these tasks, they have limited publication capabilities—especially for large audiences who might not be well connected to a server. Developers and database administrators can increase the value of resources they manage by sharing their database content over webs. This heightened value stems from making their data accessible to more people in more circumstances—for example, regardless of whether users have a permanent, physical connection to a server.

This section first focuses on sharing datasheets via webs. Typical datasheets might contain product prices, stock unit inventory levels, and customer or employee contact data. Sharing a datasheet enables an application to display a whole table, the data behind a form or a report, or the rows returned by a query. This section dwells specifically on sharing datasheets based on tables, but the same techniques apply to other database objects.

Your applications can share data either statically or dynamically. Both approaches produce snapshots of the contents of a database. A statically shared datasheet will not change until a new datasheet replaces it. The database snapshot is always based on the last time an application or database manager published the datasheet. A dynamically shared datasheet refreshes itself whenever a browser opens it over the Web. Whenever a dynamic datasheet is opened this way, it shows the most recent data. The user, instead of the application or database manager, controls the updates of the database snapshot.

We'll also discuss techniques for presenting datasheets over webs in this section. You'll learn about the manual and programmatic ways to share both static and dynamic datasheets on line.

Manually Publishing Access Tables as HTML Tables

Publishing a table is the process of capturing the data in an Access table and making it available from a Web site or other location. The act of publishing a table or other database object from an Access database file or project creates a new file with an .html extension. Before you publish an Access table as an HTML table, you must pick a destination. Access gives you a lot of flexibility in this regard. This is because, like data access pages, Access tables don't require you to store an .html file on a Web site. Instead, you can store an .html file just about anywhere, either on a Web site or anywhere on your local area network (LAN). No matter where your file is located, you can open it with your browser. Just point the browser at the URL or LAN path and filename, and the table will appear.

> **Note**   When you use Access to publish a table, the published HTML always has an .html extension. Data access pages and ordinary HTML pages in FrontPage, however, have an .htm extension. When searching for files by file extension, it's helpful to keep this distinction in mind.

Like an Access table, an HTML table is static. In addition, HTML tables can be likened to snapshots of Access tables and other Access database objects. If you update the Access table after saving an HTML table that's based on it, the HTML table doesn't change in a corresponding way. The only way to update an HTML table when an Access database object changes is to republish the HTML table. This restriction is convenient when you publish reports at regular intervals for record sources that can change between intervals. You to freely change the original source for the publication without impacting your published Web report. The datasheet report does not update until the next time you publish it.

Use the File-Export command to publish reports manually. However, start by selecting the table that you want to publish in the Database window. If the table does not belong to the current Access database file, link it. After choosing File-Export, update the Save In box so that it points at a LAN location, such as your intranet Web site or a folder that you will transmit to your remote Web site. See "Creating Your Image Files for the Web" in Chapter 16 for instructions on using FrontPage to transmit files to a remote Web site from a local workstation. Next select HTML Documents (*.html;*.htm) from the Save As Type box. Before clicking Export, you can optionally change the default filename assignment for the Web page with the HTML table. The default name is the same as the table name. Clicking Export saves the Access table in an .html file as an HTML table.

There are several options you can select when publishing an Access table. One of the most crucial options is the ability to change the file's name from its default one. Therefore, if you are saving the *Shippers* table, the process generates a new file named Shippers.html. If you are saving different versions of a table, say by month, you can include a version number indicating the month in the file's name. Without this step, Access silently copies over the prior version of the .html file whenever you republish a table.

At least four additional features allow you to customize the publication of Access tables as HTML tables. First, you can click the Save Formatted check box on the Export Table dialog box. Doing so formats the HTML table so that it looks like a standard table in Access, as opposed to a traditional HTML table. Second, you can click the Autostart check box on the Export Table dialog box. This opens the published HTML table in the default browser immediately after Access publishes it. Once you've selected the Save Formatted check box, clicking Export prompts an HTML Output Options dialog box to appear. This lets you select a page at the destination Web site with formatting that can apply to your published HTML table. For example, the Web page can contain a theme that adds to the impact of the data in the HTML table. You can also specify format encoding for the data in the .html file. Unless you specifically need to work with extended character sets for international applications, accept the default encoding.

Figure 17-1 presents two published versions of the *Shippers* table from this chapter's database file on the companion CD. The top browser window shows the *Shippers* table published with the default settings. While the table has a title, it does not contain column headers. The bottom browser window uses the Save Formatted check box and a template page that applies the Blends theme. Many viewers will prefer the formatted look shown in the bottom of Figure 17-1.

Figure 17-1 Two published versions of the *Shippers* table: one the default, the other formatted.

The File-Export command generates HTML code to mark up the text for the tables that appear in Figure 17-1. The browser reads the HTML and renders the text according to the instructions encoded with the HTML. The following script shows the code for the top window in Figure 17-1. If you plan to do Web work on anything but a very infrequent basis, a working knowledge of HTML will prove very useful.

Recall from the Document Outline view discussed in Chapter 16 that HTML organizes documents hierarchically. HTML tags include several sets that denote different parts of the document, including the <body> and </body> tags, which mark the beginning and end of the Web page's display area. The document's <body> tags contain another pair of tags, <table> and </table>, which mark the beginning and end of the table. Within the <table> tags, the <tr> and </tr> tags designate the beginning and end of each row within the table. The row tags contain tag sets that mark the beginning and end of each cell within a row; these are <td> and </td>.

Selected HTML tags have attribute settings that guide the browser in interpreting a tag. For example, the align attribute for the *ShipperID* field has a setting of "right", but the align attribute is set to "left" for both the *Company Name* and *Phone* fields. Finally, within the cell tags, the HTML document contains text for display in the table. Let's take a look at the script now:

```
<HTML DIR=LTR>
<HEAD>
<META HTTP-EQUIV="Content-Type" CONTENT="text/html;
  charset=Windows-1252">
<TITLE>Shippers</TITLE>
</HEAD>
<BODY>
<TABLE DIR=LTR BORDER>
<CAPTION>Shippers</CAPTION>
<TR>
<TD DIR=LTR ALIGN=RIGHT>1</TD>
<TD DIR=LTR ALIGN=LEFT>Speedy Express</TD>
<TD DIR=LTR ALIGN=LEFT>(503) 555-9831</TD>
</TR>
<TR>
<TD DIR=LTR ALIGN=RIGHT>2</TD>
<TD DIR=LTR ALIGN=LEFT>United Package</TD>
<TD DIR=LTR ALIGN=LEFT>(503) 555-3199</TD>
</TR>
<TR>
<TD DIR=LTR ALIGN=RIGHT>3</TD>
<TD DIR=LTR ALIGN=LEFT>Federal Shipping</TD>
<TD DIR=LTR ALIGN=LEFT>(503) 555-9931</TD>
</TR>
</TABLE>
</BODY>
</HTML>
```

Programmatically Exporting and Importing HTML Tables

You can publish Access tables programmatically as HTML tables by using the *OutputTo* method for the *DoCmd* object. Unlike the *ExportXML* method, *OutputTo* restricts you to publishing results to a LAN location. If you need to publish pages to a remote Web server, you must complement Access with another package that supports transporting HTML files across a Web connection (for example, FrontPage).

The *OutputTo* method takes a relatively long list of arguments, but programming it is actually straightforward. This paragraph describes the arguments for the following code sample. When publishing a table, the method's first argument will be *acOutputTable*. With this first argument, you can specify a broad mix of database objects that lets you publish the result set from Access query statements, SQL Server stored procedures, views, and user-defined functions, as well as the data behind Access forms and reports. The second argument, *Shippers*, is a string that denotes the name of the object containing the data for publication. The third argument in the script denotes an HTML format. (The *OutputTo* method can save database objects in many different formats.) The fourth argument specifies the location to which you want to save your HTML file. If you are publishing to an intranet site, you can designate the path and filename for the HTML file. Otherwise, store the file in a staging area such a folder for subsequent transport to a remote Web server. The fifth argument is a Boolean. When this argument is true, Access automatically opens a browser session to display the page with the HTML table. The sixth argument designates a Web page with format settings that apply to the published Web page with the HTML table. In this case, the Chapter_17_Template.htm page has a Blends theme. You can make this assignment to a page with the Format-Themes command in the page's Normal view. Several other page format settings carry over as well. Experiment with them on a template page to see which ones transfer to a published page.

```
Sub PublishShippersInHTML()

'Export the Shippers table in HTML format to the pma10
'Web site on local server.
'Base page for table on Chapter_17_Template.htm.
'Open after exported.
DoCmd.OutputTo _
    acOutputTable, _
    "Shippers", _
    acFormatHTML, _
    "c:\inetpub\wwwroot\pma10\htmlShippers.html", _
    True, _
    "c:\inetpub\wwwroot\pma10\Chapter_17_Template.htm"

End Sub
```

Because it's so easy to publish a page manually, you're not likely to find much use for *OutputTo* method when publishing a single page for your own needs. However, several situations do merit its use. First, you might want to enable users of your custom applications to automatically publish an Access table in HTML format. Second, if you need to publish a number of tables, it might be easier to write a short program that does this rather than repeat the manual steps for each table. Third, you might want to automatically republish, based on a form's *Timer* event, a database object, such as a table, or an application object, such as a form. This technique enables a statically published HTML table to display fresh results on a regular basis. All you need is an open Access database or project file to let the *Timer* event republish the HTML every several minutes, hours, or days.

The following sample publishes all the user-defined tables in an Access database file. It uses a *For...Each* loop to pass through the members of the *AllTables* collection and a filter to exclude system tables. When using this type of automated publishing scheme, you typically won't want to open an individual browser session for each published table. Therefore, the code sample sets the *OutputTo* method's fifth argument to False.

```
Sub PublishAllTablesInHTML()
Dim tbl1 As AccessObject

Set dbs = Application.CurrentData

'Export all user-defined tables in HTML format
For Each tbl1 In dbs.AllTables
    If Left(tbl1.Name, 4) <> "MSys" Then
        DoCmd.OutputTo _
            acOutputTable, _
            tbl1.Name, _
            acFormatHTML, _
            "c:\inetpub\wwwroot\pma10\html" & tbl1.Name & ".html", _
            False, _
            "c:\inetpub\wwwroot\pma10\Chapter_17_Template.htm"
    End If
Next tbl1

End Sub
```

In some situations, an application requires you to create an Access table based on a HTML table (instead of the other way around). Before the emergence of XML, this was one of the leading ways to transport data between applications over a web. If you have colleagues still using legacy versions of Access or another package that does not export XML in a format suitable for the *ImportXML* method covered in Chapter 16, using HTML tables might be an easy way for you to share data. Use the *TransferText* method for the *DoCmd* object to import an

HTML table. Unlike the *OutputTo* method, *TransferText* receives data from a remote Web server via HTTP as well as over a LAN. You can use the *TransferText* method to link or import an HTML table. As with linking text files, linking HTML files allows your local workstation to view updates to the record source without letting users update the source.

> **Note**   As in any Web-based application, to show the most recent data in a table, the *TransferText* method for importing HTML tables requires a refreshed link when linking a file. The link refreshes whenever you open an Access database file or Access project.

The following procedure shows two approaches for using the *TransferText* method to retrieve an HTML table to the current database. The uncommented version shows the syntax for importing the HTML table in the htmlShippers.html file into the current database with a table name of *htmlShippers*. (The preceding code sample automatically generates htmlShippers.html.) The method imports the file. Swapping *acImportHTML* for *acLinkHTML* will cause a live link that automatically displays any updates to the HTML table whenever the Access project or Access database file opens. The commented version illustrates the syntax for referencing the *TableForBook.htm* table in the pma10 folder of the www.programmingmsaccess.com Web site. Because this demonstration has no column headers, its fifth argument is set to False to indicate that it is a typical HTML table but one without column headers.

```
Sub ImporthtmlShippers()

'Import htmlShippers.html from pma10 Web site on
'local server
DoCmd.TransferText _
    acImportHTML, _

    , _
    "htmlShippers", _
    "c:\inetpub\wwwroot\pma10\htmlShippers.html", _
    True

'This shows the syntax for importing foo2.htm to the
'local Access database or project as htmlfoo2. Notice
'that the target file is on the Web.
'DoCmd.TransferText _
    acImportHTML, _

    , _
```

```
    "htmlTableForBook", _
    "http://www.programmingmsaccess.com/pma10/TableForBook.htm", _
    False

End Sub
```

Manually Publishing Access Tables with Active Server Pages

Many applications call for the publication of dynamic (instead of static) datasheets based on database objects. Dynamic datasheets allow users to see updates to the data behind a database object whenever they refresh their link to a page based on that object. When you publish an Access table or other database object as an ASP file, the Web-based datasheet is dynamic.

To publish a dynamic datasheet, Access and your Web server need to co-operate in two ways. First, there must be a dynamic link between the Web page and the database. A data source name (DSN), which embodies an ODBC connection, offers one way to satisfy this requirement. Second, the Web server needs to construct a version of the page whenever a user surfs to it. When a Web server reconstructs a page in response to a user browsing it, the page delivers the most recent data available from a record source.

> **Note**   ODBC (open database connectivity) is a low-level data access programming interface. All modern database products come with ODBC drivers, and this standard has the support of the American National Standards Institute (ANSI) and the International Organization for Standards (ISO).

Microsoft invented Active Server Pages (ASP), which are embodied in ASP files, to permit dynamic Web behavior, including live links to data. ASP technology is a part of Microsoft Internet Information Server (IIS). If you use IIS version 3 or later as your Web server, you can use ASP files to connect with data sources, including Access database files, SQL Server databases, and any ODBC data source. Access provides manual and programmatic means for publishing database objects as .asp files via ASP technology. These capabilities enable developers to publish dynamic datasheets that always show the most recent data in the database object, such as a table, behind a datasheet.

Creating a DSN

Before you can publish an Access table or other object in a database file or Access project with the built-in Access features, you need a DSN that points at the database. When your ASP file runs, it will use a DSN on the server. Therefore, your Web server or Web site administrator is likely to create a DSN for you and tell you its name. If you fill this role because you manage your own server, you'll have to create the DSN yourself, an easy task. Locate the ODBC Data Source Administrator. On a Microsoft Windows 2000 computer, you'll find this within the Administrative Tools group on the Control Panel. The name for the tool is Data Sources (ODBC). On a Microsoft Windows NT or Windows 98 computer, you can open the ODBC Data Source Administrator directly from the Control Panel. The tool is named Data Sources (ODBC) or ODBC Data Sources (32bit), depending on the operating system.

When creating a DSN for an ASP file that you will create with Access, you should always create a System DSN. To do so, begin creating a DSN for an .mdb file by selecting the System DSN tab. Click Add, select Microsoft Access Driver (*.mdb), and click Finish to open an empty DSN for an Access database file. On the ODBC Microsoft Access Setup dialog box, type a name in the Data Source Name text box, such as *Northwindmdb*. This is the name by which you will refer to the DSN. Next click Select in the Database group. This opens the Select Database dialog box that lets you navigate to the Access database file to which you want the DSN to point. After navigating to the Access database file, you can click OK to complete the creation of an unsecured DSN.

> **Note**   Your Web work will almost always involve unsecured Access database files. DSNs do allow you to designate a system database file so that you can work with secured database files.

The preceding steps explain how to build a DSN for an Access database file. However, the steps for specifying a DSN vary for different database types. Work with a database administrator to ensure that you make the proper selection for the database you're using.

Dynamically Publishing the *Shippers* Table

The first steps you take to publish a table as an ASP file are the same ones you would take when publishing a table as an .html file. Highlight a table that you want to publish, such as *Shippers*. After Access opens the Export Table dialog box in response to the File-Export command, use the Save In drop-down control to select a path on your LAN. This path can be a location in the directory for a Web site on your intranet. For example, the path in my office is c:\inetpub\wwwroot\pma10. You can also designate an ordinary folder from which to subsequently transport the file to a remote Web site. Next in the Save As Type drop-down control, select Microsoft Active Server Pages (*.asp). Access always saves ASP files as formatted. Therefore, Access automatically selects the Save Formatted check box and grays it so that you cannot change the setting. Clicking Export opens the Microsoft Active Server Pages Output Options dialog box. This dialog box contains one entry that you must complete for an Access database file: you must type the DSN. Again, recall that this is the name of a DSN on the Web server that you defined previously. You can, optionally, designate a template for your dynamic datasheet. Use the path and filename for a template file on the Web site to which you're publishing the ASP file. Finally, click OK to publish the page.

After publishing an Access table as an ASP file, you can open the table with your browser. For example, I adapted the instructions from the preceding paragraph to create an ASP file named aspShippers.asp. This file is based on the *Shippers* table in this chapter's sample Access database file. I saved the ASP file in the root directory of the pma10 Web site on the cab2000 server.

> **Note**   The *Shippers* table in this chapter's Access database file links to the Northwind database for the *Shippers* table. Therefore, the DSN used for creating aspShippers.asp points at the Northwind database file.

Figure 17-2 shows the interaction between the contents of the *Shippers* table and the aspShippers.asp file. The top two windows show the *Shippers* table with its default entries and the browser opened to the aspShippers.asp file. The bottom two windows show an update to the *CompanyName* field in the second row. Clicking the Refresh button on the browser toolbar updates the link and gets the new field value for *CompanyName* in the second row. This behavior confirms the dynamic nature of ASP files. Depending on your browser's buffer settings, you might need to close the page and reopen it.

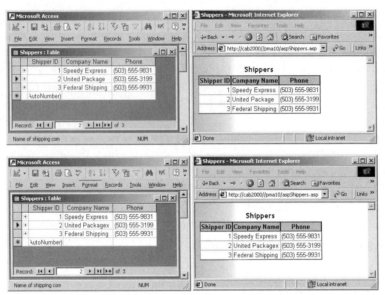

Figure 17-2 ASP files change when you refresh them if their underlying data changes.

The following script shows a short excerpt from the HTML that a user views if she chooses View-Source from her browser's menu. Notice that there is no Microsoft Visual Basic Scripting Edition (VBScript) or JScript code. In fact, there isn't any in the entire file. Although the Web server runs script when it creates the page, that script creates HTML that the browser passes to the client browser. This totally secures the database and its connection information. Yet as Figure 17-2 demonstrates, by refreshing the page in the browser, users can view any changes to the database as they occur.

The page excerpt starts with the <body> tag. This page is much more highly formatted than the preceding .html file, beginning on page 1024. Tag attribute settings implement the formatting. These attribute settings make the page's HTML code and text more difficult to read than those of the preceding example. Nevertheless, pages like this one can teach the beginning HTML author many valuable lessons. Design the page with different themes, and watch for the changes in the HTML. Revise selected attribute settings, such as color and font-size, to discern their impact on the page's layout.

In addition to the attribute settings, also notice the types and arrangement of tags. Notice that a <table> tag opens within the <body> tag. Then a <thead> tag opens within the <table> tag that contains other tags. Eventually, bound header information appears within <font> tags. Below the closing <thead> tag, a <tbody> tag opens, marking the beginning of the table's body. Then a <tr> tag opens with <td> tags nested within it, bounding the values for the first row.

```
<body background="_themes/blends/blegtext.gif" bgcolor="#CCCCCC"
text="#000000" link="#993300" vlink="#0000FF" alink="#FF9900">
<!--mstheme--><font face="Trebuchet MS, Arial, Helvetica">
<!--mstheme--></font>
<TABLE BORDER=1 BGCOLOR=#ffffff CELLSPACING=0
bordercolordark="#000000" bordercolorlight="#999999">
<FONT FACE="Arial" COLOR=#000000><!--mstheme--></font>
<CAPTION><!--mstheme--><font face="Trebuchet MS, Arial,
Helvetica"><B>Shippers</B><!--mstheme--></font>
</CAPTION><!--mstheme--><font face="Trebuchet MS, Arial,
Helvetica"></FONT>

<THEAD>
<TR>
<TH BGCOLOR=#c0c0c0 BORDERCOLOR=#000000 ><!--mstheme-->
<font face="Trebuchet MS, Arial, Helvetica">
<FONT style=FONT-SIZE:10pt FACE="Arial" COLOR=#000000>
Shipper ID</FONT></TH>
<TH BGCOLOR=#c0c0c0 BORDERCOLOR=#000000 ><!--mstheme-->
<font face="Trebuchet MS, Arial, Helvetica">
<FONT style=FONT-SIZE:10pt FACE="Arial" COLOR=#000000>
Company Name</FONT></TH>
<TH BGCOLOR=#c0c0c0 BORDERCOLOR=#000000 ><!--mstheme-->
<font face="Trebuchet MS, Arial, Helvetica">
<FONT style=FONT-SIZE:10pt FACE="Arial" COLOR=#000000>
Phone</FONT></TH>

</TR>
</THEAD>
<TBODY>

<TR VALIGN=TOP>
<TD BORDERCOLOR=#c0c0c0  ALIGN=RIGHT><!--mstheme-->
<font face="Trebuchet MS, Arial, Helvetica">
<FONT style=FONT-SIZE:10pt FACE="Arial" COLOR=#000000>
1<BR></FONT><!--mstheme--></font></TD>
<TD BORDERCOLOR=#c0c0c0 ><!--mstheme-->
<font face="Trebuchet MS, Arial, Helvetica">
<FONT style=FONT-SIZE:10pt FACE="Arial" COLOR=#000000>
Speedy Express<BR></FONT><!--mstheme--></font></TD>
<TD BORDERCOLOR=#c0c0c0 ><!--mstheme-->
<font face="Trebuchet MS, Arial, Helvetica">
<FONT style=FONT-SIZE:10pt FACE="Arial" COLOR=#000000>
(503) 555-9831<BR></FONT><!--mstheme--></font></TD>

</TR>
```

The more important code for the aspShippers.asp file is available from the HTML tab of the ASP file in FrontPage. That script appears next in its entirety, offering a good starting point for understanding ASP script. When the script in the file on the server runs, it generates the HTML for the page that the server passes to the browser.

Notice that the page's script contains two different kinds of code. VBScript appears with the <% and %> delimiters. Outside these delimiters you'll see HTML, with one exception that I will describe in a moment. After the <body> tag, the first two blocks of VBScript manage the connection to the Northwind database and the recordset based on the *Shippers* table in that database. Some of this code is basic ActiveX Data Objects (ADO) code that you should recognize from Chapter 2, "Data Access Models: Part I." Other elements in the code, such as the *Session* object references, follow from the ASP object model. As you can see, the *Session("Shippers_rs")* object supports the caching and reusing of the recordset based on the *Shippers* table. This caching and reusing of the recordset improves the page's performance by reducing the load on the database server and on network traffic. The block of code for the *Connection* object has the same general structure to denote caching and reusing the object. However, it caches its new connection with one *Session("??Northwindmdb_conn")* object but then checks whether there's an existing connection with a different session object, *Session("Northwindmdb_conn")*. Consequently, the page's code creates a new connection every time the page reopens within a Web server session. The subsequent sample on page 1031 shows how to diagnose the problem and fix the code to reuse the *Connection* object.

Notice that the script contains only two HTML rows. One of these is for the column header text. The other row resides within a *Do* loop that iterates through the recordset created earlier for as many rows as the record source contains. On successive passes through the loop, the VBScript code creates a new row of HTML for the page that the server passes to the browser. Instead of containing text in the innermost tags within the loop, the HTML references recordset fields. Access uses an *HTMLEncode* function to translate special HTML tag delimiters (< and >) to their HTML escape sequence (< and > respectively). Then the code uses the <%= and %> delimiters to pass the encoded field values to the server for insertion on the page. You can use <%= and %> generally to convey the output from VBScript to an HTML page.

```
<html>

<head>
<meta http-equiv="Content-Language" content="en-us">
<meta name="GENERATOR" content="Microsoft FrontPage 5.0">
<meta name="ProgId" content="FrontPage.Editor.Document">
```

```
<meta http-equiv="Content-Type" content="text/html;
  charset=windows-1252">
<title>Shippers</title>
<meta name="Microsoft Theme" content="blends 011">
</head>

<body><%
If IsObject(Session("Northwindmdb_conn")) Then
    Set conn = Session("Northwindmdb_conn")
Else
    Set conn = Server.CreateObject("ADODB.Connection")
    conn.open "Northwindmdb","",""
    Set Session("??Northwindmdb_conn") = conn
End If
%>
<%
If IsObject(Session("Shippers_rs")) Then
    Set rs = Session("Shippers_rs")
Else
    sql = "SELECT * FROM [Shippers]"
    Set rs = Server.CreateObject("ADODB.Recordset")
    rs.Open sql, conn, 3, 3
    If rs.eof Then
        rs.AddNew
    End If
    Set Session("Shippers_rs") = rs
End If
%> <TABLE BORDER=1 BGCOLOR=#ffffff CELLSPACING=0>
<CAPTION><B>Shippers</B></CAPTION>

<THEAD>
<TR>
<TH BGCOLOR=#c0c0c0 BORDERCOLOR=#000000 >
<FONT style=FONT-SIZE:10pt FACE="Arial" COLOR=#000000>
Shipper ID</FONT></TH>
<TH BGCOLOR=#c0c0c0 BORDERCOLOR=#000000 >
<FONT style=FONT-SIZE:10pt FACE="Arial" COLOR=#000000>
Company Name</FONT></TH>
<TH BGCOLOR=#c0c0c0 BORDERCOLOR=#000000 >
<FONT style=FONT-SIZE:10pt FACE="Arial" COLOR=#000000>
Phone</FONT></TH>

</TR>
</THEAD>
<TBODY>
<%
On Error Resume Next
rs.MoveFirst
```

(continued)

```
do while Not rs.eof
 %>
<TR VALIGN=TOP>
<TD BORDERCOLOR=#c0c0c0  ALIGN=RIGHT>
<FONT style=FONT-SIZE:10pt FACE="Arial"
COLOR=#000000><%=Server.HTMLEncode(rs.Fields("ShipperID").Value)%>
<BR></FONT></TD>
<TD BORDERCOLOR=#c0c0c0 >
<FONT style=FONT-SIZE:10pt FACE="Arial"
COLOR=#000000><%=Server.HTMLEncode(rs.Fields("CompanyName").Value)%>
<BR></FONT></TD>
<TD BORDERCOLOR=#c0c0c0 >
<FONT style=FONT-SIZE:10pt FACE="Arial"
COLOR=#000000><%=Server.HTMLEncode(rs.Fields("Phone").Value)%>
<BR></FONT></TD>

</TR>
<%
rs.MoveNext
loop%>
</TBODY>
<TFOOT></TFOOT>
</TABLE></body>

</h(continued)tml>
```

Editing Published Pages

Because ASP script is a mix of VBScript, ADO, and HTML, it's easy to edit. In fact, revising an existing ASP file is an excellent way to begin learning ASP scripting techniques. As it turns out, the automatically generated code does not reuse the *Connection* object. This is because the code saves a new ADO *Connection* object in a *Session* variable named *??Northwindmdb_conn*. However, the code sample looks for a previously cached *Connection* object with a *Session* variable named *Northwindmdb_conn*. *Northwindmdb_conn* does not match *??Northwindmdb_conn*, so the code does not discover the previously cached *Connection* object.

Diagnosing the problem is straightforward. Start by making a copy of aspShippers.asp in FrontPage. Select the page in the Folder list of a Page view. Right-click the page, and choose Copy. Then right-click the copied file whose name is aspShippers_Copy(1).asp, and rename the copied file aspShippers_2.asp.

To determine whether the page ever reuses an existing connection, assign different values to the same string variable in each path of the *If* statement that checks whether a *Session* object named *Northwindmdb_conn* exists. When this statement detects a previously defined *Session* object named *Northwindmdb_conn*, it assigns that object to the *conn* object reference that specifies the connection for the page. The following script uses *str1* as the string variable to monitor the flow through the *If* statement. It prints the value of *str1* by embedding it within the <%= and %> delimiters. This excerpt illustrates the syntax for the edits I've just described:

```
<body><%
If IsObject(Session("Northwindmdb_conn")) Then
    Set conn = Session("Northwindmdb_conn")
    str1 = "Re-used existing connection for this page."
Else
    Set conn = Server.CreateObject("ADODB.Connection")
    conn.open "Northwindmdb","",""
    Set Session("??Northwindmdb_conn") = conn
    str1 = "Created new connection for this page."
End If
%>
<%= str1 %>
```

Figure 17-3 shows the result of opening aspShippers_2.asp. Notice that the page includes a message above the table that says the page was completed with a new connection. No matter how many times you click the Refresh button, the message stays the same. This is because the *If* statement never checks the *Session* object named *??Northwindmdb_conn* used to save the connection. Because the statement doesn't find a saved connection, it always creates a new connection for the page. In a heavily trafficked Web site, caching can have a material effect on the performance of a page.

Figure 17-3 A message prints above the table for the aspShippers_2.asp file.

To allow the page to reuse a previously created *Connection* object, you just need to look for the *Connection* object with the same name you save it with. The built-in code generator doesn't follow this convention; it's a simple oversight. The following code excerpt from an ASP file named aspShippers_3.asp fixes the problem by removing the leading *??* from the name of the *Session* object used to store a connection:

```
<body><%
If IsObject(Session("Northwindmdb_conn")) Then
    Set conn = Session("Northwindmdb_conn")
    str1 = "Re-used existing connection for this page."
Else
    Set conn = Server.CreateObject("ADODB.Connection")
    conn.open "Northwindmdb","",""
    Set Session("Northwindmdb_conn") = conn
    str1 = "Created new connection for this page."
End If
%>
<%= str1 %>
```

The top panel of Figure 17-4 shows the look of aspShippers_3.asp when the page opens for the first time. The page looks the same as the browser image shown in Figure 17-3, except this browser shows the aspShippers_3.asp file instead of aspShippers_2.asp. Clicking the Refresh button shows the table with the same values, but the message changes to say that the page reuses an existing connection. This simple example proves that even a basic understanding of ASP files combined with your knowledge of Visual Basic for Applications (VBA) and ADO enables you to improve the performance of ASP files created with the File-Export command.

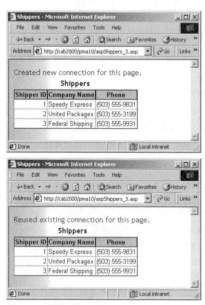

Figure 17-4 The aspShippers_3.asp file creates a connection the first time you use it and reuses that connection all subsequent times in the same Web session.

Creating an ASP File Without a DSN

You have numerous options to customize a page generated by the File-Export command. There's so much repetition in HTML code that it's often wise to use an auto-generated page as a starting point. As a database programmer who is just starting with Web development or who doesn't require the Web for most applications, you will likely want to spend more of your time adapting VBScript.

One way to use VBScript is to specify a custom connection string that does not depend on a DSN. This frees you from having to rely on the graphical technique described earlier for specifying a connection to your database file. Even if you like graphical approaches, there will be times when the graphical approach isn't readily available—for example, when working with a remote Web site.

Wouldn't it be great if you could tap your knowledge of writing ADO connection strings (discussed in Chapter 2) for your Web development projects? As it turns out, you can! The following sample offers several variations of this technique. In addition, the sample uses more familiar abbreviations for the *Connection* and *Recordset* objects and simplifies the code for creating these objects. Although caching is cool for exceptionally busy Web sites, it doesn't yield a noticeable performance savings for sites with 5 to 10 database hits at a time. Five visitors per minute might not sound like much, but running at this rate 24/7 will generate more than 7,000 visitors per day or 200,000 visitor sessions per month. Therefore, if the site you're programming has a lower visitor volume than this, using a simpler approach to caching should be fine.

The sample we'll look at momentarily has several sections and illustrates some secondary issues I have not mentioned yet. The first section shows three approaches to developing a connection string. The next section uses the connection string as one of the arguments for the recordset *Open* method. After that, the sample repeats the same basic flow as the code auto-generated from the File-Export command you saw on page 1029. However, it substitutes a more familiar reference name, *rst1*, for the *Recordset* object. If you like to name your objects after their sources, you might replace *rst1* with *rstShippers*. However, this is strictly arbitrary. The point is that you aren't locked into the reference names that the File-Export command produces.

A connection string argument for a Jet database file can contain as few as two elements. One element names the provider. The second denotes the path and file for the Access database file. The sample uses the variable *filepath* to designate the second element.

The specification for the *filepath* variable dictates that the three approaches for specifying the connection string differ. The first approach uses the *MapPath* method of the ASP *Server* object to reference the drive and root directory of the server. The expression in the first approach appends a string to this return value with the path within a Web site on the database file's server. The database file is fpnwind.mdb, which is a sample file that ships with FrontPage 2002. The pma10 Web site's root folder is pma10, and the fpnwind.mdb file resides in a subfolder named fpdb. The *cnn1.Open* statement shows the syntax for concatenating the *filepath* argument to the end of the connection string for *cnn1*.

The second and third approaches to developing a connection string begin with comment markers. Both approaches demonstrate interesting syntax variations that you might find useful in some situations. When the database file is in the root folder of a Web site, as in the second approach, you can simplify the expression for the *filepath* string by including the database filename in quotes as the argument for the *MapPath* method. In this case, the database name references a database with a single table—the *Shippers* table. The third approach gives an example of the syntax for specifying the path to a folder that isn't necessarily located at the Web site. The path leads to the database file for this chapter. The file resides in a folder outside the \inetpub directory for the Web server but on the same computer as the Web server.

> **Note**   Attempting to reference a file on a remote computer can generate an error when working with Jet database files and ASP.

After specifying the connection, the procedure writes a diagnostic message to the page that the server returns to the browser. This message identifies the drive, path, and filename for the Access database file to which the page connects. The message appears on two lines. One line is ordinary text explaining the meaning of the second line. This second line is the value of the *filepath* variable. Because your code specifies this variable's value in VBScript, you can use the <%= and %> delimiters to include this value on the page. Just before the two lines specifying the source for the table, the listing shows the syntax for designating a comment. Although this line does not appear on the Web page, you can view it from the listing. By moving the three trailing characters (→) to the end of the second line, you can make the message about the page's source invisible but retain the code for subsequent use.

The next block of code shows the syntax for specifying a recordset for the page. All three potential data sources include a *Shippers* table, and the *Open* statement simply designates this table name as its source. Also, notice that the code uses intrinsic constants. ASP does not natively define these constants. You can use an ASP *#include* directive to reference a file with the constants, or you can just define some constants and use them in your code. The sample demonstrates the latter approach.

The remainder of the procedure is a direct copy of the code auto-generated by the File-Export command, with one exception. It uses a new name for the recordset reference. Obviously, if you change the recordset reference name when instantiating the recordset, your code needs to use that name when writing rows of data to the HTML table for the browser. Developers switching to ASP code must keep such details in mind as they begin their migration.

```
<HTML>
<TITLE>Shippers With ADO Path Spec</TITLE>
</HEAD>
<BODY>
<%
'Alternative specifications for a database filepath
'Using Server.MapPath("\") returns string with drive letter and
'Web server root directory
'filePath = Server.MapPath("\") & "\pma10\fpdb\fpnwind.mdb"

'Using Server.MapPath("filename") returns string with drive letter,
'root folder for current Web site, and filename
filePath = Server.MapPath("ShippersTable.mdb")

'You can also directly specify the path with a drive,
'path, and filename
'filePath = _
'    "c:\PMA Samples\Chapter 17.mdb"

'Use the filepath in an ADO connection string argument
Set cnn1 = Server.CreateObject("ADODB.Connection")
cnn1.Open "Provider=Microsoft.Jet.OLEDB.4.0;Data Source=" & _
    filePath
%>

<!-- Remove the next two lines from the product version -->
The filepath for the following table appears on the next line.<BR>
<%= filePath %></p>

<%
Const acOpenStatic = 3
Const adLockOptimistic = 3
Const adCmdTable

Set rst1 = Server.CreateObject("ADODB.Recordset")
rst1.Open "Shippers", cnn1, acOpenStatic, adLockOptimistic, _
    adCmdTable
%>
```

(continued)

```
<TABLE BORDER=1 BGCOLOR=#ffffff CELLSPACING=0>
<FONT FACE="Arial" COLOR=#000000><CAPTION><B>Shippers</B>
</CAPTION></FONT>

<THEAD>
<TR>
<TH BGCOLOR=#c0c0c0 BORDERCOLOR=#000000 >
<FONT style=FONT-SIZE:10pt FACE="Arial" COLOR=#000000>
Shipper ID</FONT></TH>
<TH BGCOLOR=#c0c0c0 BORDERCOLOR=#000000 >
<FONT style=FONT-SIZE:10pt FACE="Arial" COLOR=#000000>
Company Name</FONT></TH>
<TH BGCOLOR=#c0c0c0 BORDERCOLOR=#000000 >
<FONT style=FONT-SIZE:10pt FACE="Arial" COLOR=#000000>
Phone</FONT></TH>

</TR>
</THEAD>
<TBODY>
<%
On Error Resume Next
rst1.MoveFirst
do while Not rst1.eof
 %>
<TR VALIGN=TOP>
<TD BORDERCOLOR=#c0c0c0  ALIGN=RIGHT>
<FONT style=FONT-SIZE:10pt FACE="Arial" COLOR=#000000>
<%=Server.HTMLEncode(rst1.Fields("ShipperID").Value)%>
<BR></FONT></TD>
<TD BORDERCOLOR=#c0c0c0 >
<FONT style=FONT-SIZE:10pt FACE="Arial" COLOR=#000000>
<%=Server.HTMLEncode(rst1.Fields("CompanyName").Value)%>
<BR></FONT></TD>
<TD BORDERCOLOR=#c0c0c0 >
<FONT style=FONT-SIZE:10pt FACE="Arial" COLOR=#000000>
<%=Server.HTMLEncode(rst1.Fields("Phone").Value)%>
<BR></FONT></TD>

</TR>
<%
rst1.MoveNext
loop%>
</TBODY>
<TFOOT></TFOOT>
</TABLE>
</BODY>
</HTML>
```

Using the FrontPage Database Wizard

The Insert-Database command in FrontPage lets you graphically add ASP files to a Web site via the Database Wizard. This graphical tool offers more options than those available with the Table Export dialog box from the File-Export command in Access. On the other hand, the Database Wizard doesn't produce files that you can edit by changing the code. This is because the wizard collects input from its dialog boxes and passes the responses to Web bots that perform the processing outside the page, where it isn't accessible to a developer.

> **Note**   Using the FrontPage Database Wizard requires you to install the FrontPage 2002 Server Extensions. This, in turn, requires a computer running Windows 2000 or Windows NT.

The Database Wizard offers five main dialog boxes and several optional dialog boxes that page designers can open from the main ones. If you're building a simple to slightly complex Web site, you can bypass two to three of the main dialog boxes. The first dialog box requires you to specify a connection to a data source for the Web page. Typically, you will specify a data source such as a database file in the current Web site, a database denoted by a system DSN, or a network connection to a database residing on a server. FrontPage also ships with fpnwind.mdb, a sample database that you can load from the wizard's first dialog box. The fpnwind.mdb database contains the tables from the Northwind database but not its other database objects. The second dialog box requires you to specify a record source within the data source for the page. For example, if you're referencing the fpnwind.mdb database, you can designate the *Employees* table. Alternatively, you can specify an SQL string to represent a record source.

The third through the fifth dialog boxes allow you to specify the layout and formatting for data on a Web page. The third dialog box lets you select a subset of fields and the order in which they appear on a page. This dialog box also allows you to create search forms for a record source. The fourth dialog box lets you specify how to display the result set from a record source. Many developers will routinely accept the default table format, but this dialog box also offers a columnar display, which it describes as List—One Field Per Item, and a drop-down list box. The final dialog box lets you specify how many records to group on a page within a table. This feature appeals to many database users. It lets them browse through records in a table by groups of records. Page designers can specify any number for the group size. The default is five records per page.

After completing all five of the main dialog boxes, you must save the resulting page before you can view it in a browser. Be sure to save the page with an .asp extension.

Publishing a Datasheet with the Database Wizard

One useful exercise is to publish a telephone directory of the employees in the fpnwind.mdb database. This example will show you how to install the fpnwind.mdb database. It will also demonstrate how to select a subset of the fields from a record source for inclusion in a table on a Web page.

To use the Database Wizard, you must always have a Web page open. This is because the sole function of the wizard is to create a database region on a Web page with an .asp file type. To keep the focus on the Database Wizard, the example starts with a blank page. Click the Create A New Normal Page control on the FrontPage toolbar. Position the cursor on the page where you want your table. Then invoke the wizard by choosing Insert-Database-Results. This command is available only from the page's Normal view.

To use the fpnwind.mdb database for the first time, choose the Use A Sample Database Connection (Northwind) radio, or option, button. Clicking Next advances you to the second dialog box. Highlight Employees from the Record Source drop-down list. This selects the *Employees* table as the record source for the table on the Web page. Click Next. In the third dialog box, click the Edit List button to select a subset of fields to include in the table on the Web page. Figure 17-5 shows Displayed Fields dialog box after the selection of the *FirstName*, *LastName*, *Country*, *HomePhone*, and *Extension* fields. Initially, all fields appear in the Displayed Fields list box. Use the Remove button to transfer selected items to the Available Fields list box. If desired, use the Move Up or Move Down buttons to control the order of the fields in the Displayed Fields list box. Click OK, and then click Next to advance to the fourth dialog box. Accept the remaining defaults by clicking Next and Finish on the last two dialog boxes.

After completing the specification, you must save the page. Choose File-Save As. Verify the destination folder (for example, use the root folder on your site), and choose Active Server Pages (*.asp;*aspx) as the file type. After designating a filename, click Save to save your file. You can now view it with a browser. In the address box, type *serververname/websitename/filename.asp* for a page on the intranet or *www.websitename.com/path/filename.asp* for a page published to the Internet.

Figure 17-5 The Displayed Fields dialog box lets you select a subset of fields to appear in a table on a Web page.

Figure 17-6 shows the first page of the table created with these instructions for the pma10 Web site. The filename is fpEmployeesDirectory.asp. Notice the navigator buttons in the bottom row of the table. The first two buttons have dashes, which signifies that they aren't currently functioning. The third button has a right-pointing arrow that you can use to shift the focus to the next page. The fourth button has a page indicator that informs you that the display is of the first of two pages. Clicking either the third or fourth buttons moves the display to the second (and last) page in the table. The navigator buttons change automatically to reflect that you can move backward but not forward.

FirstName	LastName	Country	HomePhone	Extension
Nancy	Davolio	USA	(206) 555-9857	5467
Andrew	Fuller	USA	(206) 555-9482	3457
Janet	Leverling	USA	(206) 555-3412	3355
Margaret	Peacock	USA	(206) 555-8122	5176
Steven	Buchanan	UK	(71) 555-4848	3453

[1/2]

Figure 17-6 The FrontPage Database Wizard automatically paginates a table and includes buttons for navigating between pages.

Specifying a Sorted Table Based on a DSN

The FrontPage Database Wizard is a natural tool for working with a DSN that specifies a database. This is because both the wizard and the ODBC Administrator dialog box let developers create a solution graphically. The example in this section creates a page for the Northwind database based on the Northwindmdb DSN used earlier in the chapter. This example will also show you how easy it is to specify a sort order for the records in a table.

Starting with a blank page, choose InsertDatabase-Results. In the drop-down list control for referencing an existing database connection, select Northwindmdb. This list entry is available because an earlier sample used this system DSN that points at the Northwind database. Click Next to advance to the second dialog box. Then select Shippers from the Record Source drop-down list box to specify the *Shippers* table as the source for the table on the Web page. Click Next to advance to the wizard's third dialog box. You specify a nonstandard sort order from this dialog box. Click the More Options button, and then click the Ordering button. Highlight *CompanyName* in the Available Fields list box, and click Add to move this field to the Sort Order list box. This causes the records to sort on *CompanyName* in ascending order. You can use the Change Sort button to reverse the sort's direction. Click OK twice and then Next to exit the third dialog box. Click Next on the fourth dialog box and Finish on the fifth dialog box. Save the page as fpShippersTable.asp.

Figure 17-7 shows the outcome of these instructions. Notice that the address box points at the saved file. In addition, observe that the URL includes an HTTP protocol specification. While you can sometimes open data access pages based on their file location, you must always refer to ASP files by their URL address on a Web server. The Web server must run the code to compile the page for the browser. In addition, notice that the table does not show rows ordered by *ShipperID*. Instead, records appear in ascending order based on the *CompanyName* field. The company name for United Package still includes a trailing *x*, which demonstrates the ability of ASP files to reflect updates.

Figure 17-7 It's easy to specify a custom sort order with the FrontPage Database Wizard.

Specifying a Network Connection to a SQL Server Database

The FrontPage Database Wizard works with databases flexibly. This gives you several options for specifying a data source. The first time you specify a connection to a SQL Server database for which you do not have a system DSN previously defined, you can use the instructions demonstrated in this example. This example also shows how to use a custom query as a record source for a table on a Web page.

> **Note**   After initially creating any database connection, you can select it for reuse on another page from the Use An Existing Database Connection drop-down list box on the Database Wizard's first dialog box.

In the first Database Wizard dialog box, select the Use A New Database Connection radio button and click Create. In the Web Settings dialog box on the Database tab, click Add. The New Database Connection dialog box allows you to name your connection specification for future reference and pick one of four ways to specify the source. This example uses the network connection to the database server route to denote a connection to the NorthwindCS database. (See Chapter 14, "Using Access to Build SQL Server Solutions: Part I," for a discussion of this sample database.) After specifying a name for the database and selecting the radio button for a network connection specification, click Browse. (See Figure 17-8.)

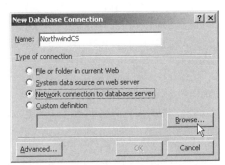

Figure 17-8 You can make a direct network connection to a SQL Server database instead of referencing a DSN.

This opens the Network Database Connection dialog box. You can use this dialog box to specify connections to either SQL Server or Oracle databases. Other databases require you to use one of the other three alternatives for specifying the relationship. Specify the server name and database name. For example, in my office, my SQL Server machine has the name cab2000, and the name of the database is NorthwindCS. The dialog box in Figure 17-9 shows these entries. Notice the drop-down list at the top of the form for selecting a type of database. After completing the entries for the Network Database Connection dialog box, click OK.

Figure 17-9 Use the Network Database Connection dialog box to denote a connection to a database on a SQL server or an Oracle database server.

When working with a SQL Server database, you have the option to designate a username and password. These correspond to a SQL Server login account name and its password. It's a good idea to take advantage of this feature because it enables you to precisely define an identity for any user accessing the database through the Web page. By using SQL Server security settings (discussed in Chapter 15, "Using Access to Build SQL Server Solutions: Part II"), you can assign permissions for your Web page's users. Click Advanced on the New Database Connection dialog box to open the Advanced Connection Properties dialog box. Type a username and password appropriate for your application. Figure 17-10 shows an entry with a username of *FrontPageDBUser* and a password that happens to be *password*. For the page to work, you have to create the corresponding login and user accounts on SQL Server and the NorthwindCS database.

After specifying a username and password, click OK three times to return to the first wizard dialog box. Then click Next. Now you can complete the dialog boxes using any of the previous examples.

This particular example demonstrates how to create a custom query. When you use a custom query, you aren't limited to using previously saved database objects. To create a custom query, select the Custom Query radio button on the second dialog box and click Edit. Next type or copy an SQL string for your custom query into the Custom Query dialog box. Figure 17-11 shows this entry. You might want to develop the query statement graphically using any of the graphical designers available with Access and then paste that statement into the dialog box. Figure 17-11 shows a statement created this way.

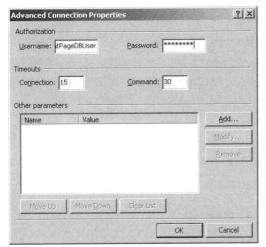

Figure 17-10 Reference a specific username and password on a SQL Server machine for your Web pages that connect to SQL Server data sources.

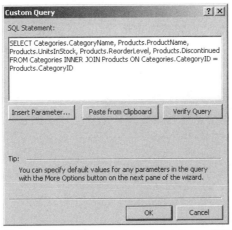

Figure 17-11 You can type or paste an SQL statement into the Custom Query dialog box.

After specifying your query, generating a Web page with a table based on the query it is easy. Click OK to return to the second dialog box. Then click Next three times and Finish once. You must save your page before you can view it. The page for the SQL statement in Figure 17-11 is available as fpProdsWithinCats.asp.

You can either re-create this page in your computing environment or re-use the one provided for you on the companion CD, which was created from the preceding instructions. If you decide to re-create the page, adapt the instructions to your computing environment. If you opt to reuse the existing page, you'll need to create a database connection on your Web server by using the database settings in this example. When you do so, change the SQL Server name to the name of the server that's using the NorthwindCS database. In addition, you might want to change the username and password. You can modify an existing connection or add a new one without using the Database Wizard. Choose Tools-Web Settings, and then select the Database tab on the Web Settings dialog box. This same tab also permits you to modify an existing connection. Because adapting the connections is such a large part of deploying the page on a Web server, you should consider re-creating the page. For your convenience, the database file for this chapter includes a query (qryProdsWithinCats) with the SQL string pasted into the Custom Query dialog box shown in Figure 17-11.

Creating a Search Form

One of the greatest strengths of the FrontPage Database Wizard is that it simplifies constructing a basic search form. This next example is a lookup form for employees. When the user specifies a country, the search form displays a list of contact information for the employees in that country. Figure 17-12 shows a text box into which users can type a country, such as UK or USA. Clicking Submit Query returns a table with information about the employees from that country. In this example, users must type an exact match for the country they want. However, you can set alternative rules that permit users to input part of a country name and still retrieve the correct data.

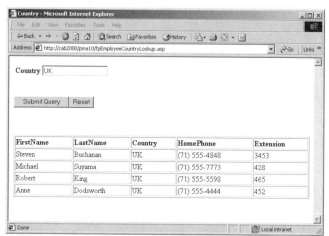

Figure 17-12 The Database Wizard can automatically generate a search form such as this one.

Specify a data source for the search form in the wizard's first dialog box. This example uses the fpnwind.mdb database. If you create a reference to this database as described in the first example in the Database Wizard discussion (on page 1040), you can select the Use An Existing Database Connection radio button and then pick Sample from the drop-down list box below the button. Click Next to transition from the wizard's first dialog box to its second one. In the second dialog box, highlight Employees as the record source. Click Next. This completes the specification of the record source (the *Employees* table) within a data source (the fpnwind.mdb database).

The wizard's third dialog box is where you make the specifications for the search form. Start by clicking More Options. Next click Criteria on the More Options dialog box. Then on the Criteria dialog box, click Add. In the Add Criteria dialog box, use the drop-down list to select Country as the Field Name entry. Users of the Web page will base their search on the field you select for the Field Name. Accept the default comparison of Equals. Clicking the drop-down list displays a long list of alternative comparisons, such as Not Equal, Begins With, Not Begin With, Ends With, Not End With, and Contains. Several of these options enable users to input part of a criterion—for example, the Contains option allows users to type in a partial country name and still have their entry recognized. Do not edit the default entry in the Value box. In addition, leave the check box for Use This Search Form Field selected. Click OK to specify Country as a criterion for selecting employees. (See Figure 17-13.)

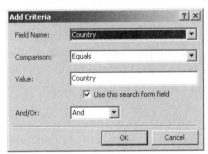

Figure 17-13 Use the Add Criteria dialog box to designate criterion fields for search forms.

If your application requires additional search criteria, you can specify them by adding another criterion field in the Criteria dialog box. Make sure that the preceding criterion has an And/Or operator that satisfies your requirement for combining multiple criterion fields. When you are finished specifying criteria, click OK on the Criteria dialog box. Then click OK on the More Options dialog box to return to the wizard's third dialog box.

After specifying your search criteria, you can click Edit List to modify the fields on the form so that they match the display in Figure 17-12. Once you return to the wizard's third dialog box, you can click Next twice to move to the wizard's fifth dialog box. Click Finish on this last dialog box and save the page so that you can view it.

Programmatically Designing Forms with ASP

Instead of relying on the File-Export command or the FrontPage Database Wizard, you can write your own ASP files. This approach is particularly useful when building a form-based system for displaying or processing data with a Web page. Because ASP files write HTML, any browser that can read them will be ready to process the output from an ASP file. Users of systems constructed with ASP do not require Office XP or a license to use Office XP on each workstation. Your application files execute on the Web server, so your code is secure from client browsers that might accidentally or intentionally corrupt or borrow the intellectual property in your custom applications. ASP files send HTML to browsers, not server-side code. As an option, you can create ASP files that execute on the server but also pass client-side scripts to browser clients.

As you begin processing HTML forms with ASP files, it might help to think of ASP form processing as a call-and-response game between a browser and a Web server. The browser user fills in the fields and clicks the Submit button for the form. When the browser sends the form to the server, it transmits the form's field values to the server-side program that knows what to do with them. This is the *call* part of the game. The server-side program can echo the input values, check them for validity, append them to a record source, look up data from a record source, and more. It typically prepares some kind of return page for the browser. This is the *response*. ASP files can serve as both the initial form that accepts the call and the response program that replies to the call. However, you will often just collect data in the first call file and process it in a second response file. In this scenario, the first file will have an .htm extension, and the second file will have an .asp extension.

ASP files do not have to perform data access over the Web, but they can serve that purpose. As database developers, you probably will turn most of your attention to this subset of ASP functionality. When coding database solutions with Access, you likely will use either Access or SQL Server files. This book has emphasized ADO techniques while presenting data processing techniques. One reason for learning about this approach instead of Data Access Objects (DAO) is that ADO works perfectly well in ASP files that perform data access and management, as well as Access database files and Access projects. Therefore, your knowledge of ADO connections, recordsets, commands, and parameters can serve you well as you build ASP solutions for your Web-based programs. If you find that the ADO coverage in this section does not offer sufficient explanation, review the introductory material presented in Chapters 2 and 3, "Data Access Models" (Parts I and II).

Creating a Telephone Lookup Application

Figure 17-14 shows a pair of HTML forms that illustrate the call-and-response character of HTML form processing. The top form includes a drop-down list box with the names of employees in the fpnwind.mdb database. A user can select a name, such as Buchanan, and click Get Extension to submit the form to the server. This is the call action. The Web server takes the input form and passes it to telereturn.asp, which reads the entry in the drop-down list box, looks up the telephone number for the employee, and writes a page with the information for the browser. The Web server sends the page back to the browser. This is the response action. Because both the call and response files in this application require data access, both files are ASP files. When the call program is just collecting data, it can have an .htm extension.

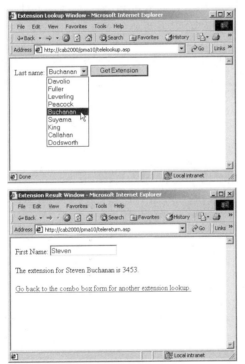

Figure 17-14 The HTML form on the top calls the Web server and invokes the reply page on the bottom.

Access 2002 does not include built-in wizards for building pages with HTML forms, but the process is straightforward. The sidebar discusses design issues for laying out form controls and specifying essential properties in FrontPage 2002. From a programming perspective, the main challenge is to learn the syntax for a few HTML form controls as well as how to intermix HTML and script, such as VBScript, in an ASP file. The syntax beginning on page 1051 is all the code required by the top page in Figure 17-14. The filename for this code is telelookup.asp. Its name appears in the Address list box on the top page.

Building an HTML Form for ASP Processing with FrontPage

When creating an HTML form for ASP processing, start with a blank page. Although unnecessary, you might find this simplifies your page design—especially when you're first beginning to do Web work. Position the cursor where you want the form, and choose Insert-Form. Select the control you initially want to add to your form, such as a drop-down list control. FrontPage uses the term *drop-down box* to designate such a control.

FrontPage does some extra work the first time that you add a control to a Web page. In addition to the control, you get a form container for the control and two additional controls, a Submit button and a Reset button. By default, FrontPage represents all controls—including text boxes, drop-down list controls, check boxes, and radio buttons—within forms. Although you can remove both the Submit and Reset buttons, you are likely to find these buttons—especially Submit—very useful in many contexts. The Submit button passes all the form field values from the browser to a Web server. The Reset button clears the controls on a form and restores any default settings for them.

Repeatedly use the Insert-Form command to add as many controls as your application requires. Option buttons automatically serve as radio buttons on HTML forms. When you click one button, it clears any other selections in the group. Check boxes do not serve this role. You can add text next to the form controls just as you would use labels on Access forms and reports. In FrontPage, it's common to label controls with text added to the form. The label control has more limited applicability than in Access, and it's not necessary to use the label control in form design. Many page designers add a table inside the form. Then they position their controls and their text strings serving as labels in different columns within the table. This practice can simplify the task of aligning controls and making controls contiguous with their labels.

Building an HTML Form for ASP Processing with FrontPage *(continued)*

By default, HTML forms created with FrontPage write to a file in the _private folder of a FrontPage Web site. However, when you plan to process a form with ASP files, you should change this by making a new form property setting. Click anywhere inside the form, and choose Form Properties. Then click the Send To Other radio button and leave the drop-down control next to it at its default setting of Custom ISAPI, NSAPI, CGI, Or ASP Script. After laying out the form, you will need to transition from the Normal tab to the HTML tab. The form tag should have at least one attribute setting, which sets method attribute to "*Post*". Add another attribute whose name is action. Set this attribute to the name of the ASP file that will process your form.

```
<%

filePath = Server.MapPath("\") & "\pma10\fpdb\fpnwind.mdb"
Set cnn1 = Server.CreateObject("ADODB.Connection")
cnn1.Open "Provider=Microsoft.Jet.OLEDB.4.0;Data Source=" & _
    filePath

set rst1 = Server.CreateObject("ADODB.Recordset")
rst1.open "SELECT * FROM employees", cnn1
%>

<html>
<head><title>Extension Lookup Window</title>
</head>
<body>

<form name=MyForm method=Post action="telereturn.asp">

Last name: <select name=DCombo>

<%
do while not rst1.eof
%>
    <option value=<%=rst1.fields("EmployeeID")%>>
      <%=rst1.Fields("LastName")%>
```

(continued)

```
<%
rst1.MoveNext
Loop
%>
</select>

<input type="Submit" value="Get Extension"><br><br>

</form>

</body>
</html>
```

Notice that the script is delimited by <% and %>. The first script segment opens a connection to the fpnwind.mdb database through OLE DB drivers that do not require a DSN. The first segment also creates a recordset with the information that populates the drop-down list control. Next some HTML code starts a page and a form on it. In the form declaration, the code assigns telereturn.asp as the program that processes the form. Just before starting a *Do* loop, the program declares a drop-down list box with the HTML select keyword. It names the control dcombo. (Names in HTML are not case sensitive.) The *Do* loop populates the list box with values from the recordset created by the first script segment. The list box shows employee last names, but it stores the *EmployeeID* column value corresponding to the selected employee. The form closes with a Submit button that has the label Get Extension.

The telereturn.asp file also starts by opening a connection and creating a recordset, as shown in the next code segment. However, this open action has an important difference from the one in telelookup.asp. The code reads the value of dcombo and uses it to form the SQL statement for the query that looks up an employee's telephone number. As stated in the preceding paragraph, dcombo contains a numeric value corresponding to the selected employee's *EmployeeID* value. This fits its role in the SQL statement.

After creating a recordset with information for the employee selected in telelookup.asp, telereturn.asp formats a page. The page contains the employee's first name in an HTML text box, a simple HTML string with the name and extension, and a hyperlink for returning control to telelookup.asp. The href attribute setting for the anchor (<a>) tag sending control back to the telelookup.asp page will change depending on where you store this file at your Web site. When the Web server passes this page back to the browser, the call-and-response cycle ends.

```
<%
filePath = Server.MapPath("\") & "\pma10\fpdb\fpnwind.mdb"
Set cnn1 = Server.CreateObject("ADODB.Connection")
cnn1.Open "Provider=Microsoft.Jet.OLEDB.4.0;Data Source=" & filePath
```

```
set rst1= Server.CreateObject("ADODB.Recordset")
sql = "select * from employees"
sql = sql & " where employees.employeeid = "
sql = sql & Request.Form("dcombo")
rst1.open sql,cnn1
%>

<html>
<head><title>Extension Result Window</title>
</head>
<body>

<form>
First Name: <input TYPE="TEXT"
VALUE="<%=rst1.fields("FirstName")%>" size="10">
</form>

The extension for
<%=rst1.fields("FirstName")%> <%=rst1.fields("LastName")%>
 is <%=rst1.fields("Extension")%>.<p>
 <a href="../pma10/telelookup.asp">Go back to the combo box form for
 another extension lookup.</a>

</body>
</html>
```

Viewing, Adding, and Deleting Items from a Table

One of the most common uses for database applications is to maintain a database—in other words, to add and delete records. Typically when you build an application to add and delete records to a record source, you need to provide a capability for displaying the current items in the list. This section presents an application that performs these three basic functions: adding, deleting, and displaying records. As you will see, the code is very easy to follow, and it works in just about any browser. In addition, the code does not depend on Office being installed on a workstation. This combination of core functionality, broad compatibility, and easy development makes this section one of the most important in the book. The ProgrammingMSAccess.com Web site includes a variation of this sample that you can try for yourself; you'll find it at www.programmingmsaccess.com/iwla99/.

The sample application discussed in this section consists of five files: two .htm files and three .asp files. You can access this sample application on the book's companion CD at Shippersdefault.htm. This file contains a menu of hyperlinks, as shown in Figure 17-15. By clicking a hyperlink, users can access one of the three functions that the application offers. Each link opens another file that either offers a link back to the main menu or transfers control to a second file that links to the main menu. See the section "Editing a Web Page" in Chapter 16 for detailed instructions on how to build a menu with hyperlinks in FrontPage.

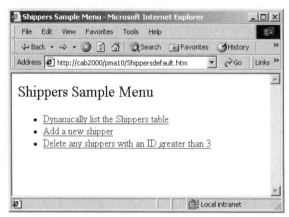

Figure 17-15 Create a main menu for your applications built with ASP files by using a list of links.

Viewing the Records in a Table

The first link in Figure 17-15 leads to the dynamicshipperslist.asp file. This file constructs a simple table for showing all the records in the *Shippers* table. Its ASP script, which follows, integrates tightly with the other files in this sample application. Even though I gave this subject ample coverage earlier in the chapter, I think it's important for you to see how this capability rounds out the application. This listing serves that purpose. It applies the *MapPath* method of the ASP *Server* object to reference the path to the root directory for the server. The script in the file appends the rest of the path to the fpnwind.mdb file. The presentation on the FrontPage Database Wizard explains how to install this Access database file. Its default location is at the path and filename computed in the *filepath* variable.

The *Open* method for the recordset accepts the defaults for most parameters, but it explicitly specifies an *Options* parameter using an intrinsic constant (*adCmdTable*). Recall that intrinsic constants are not available by default in ASP files. Therefore, the script declares a constant to represent the value. Declaring a constant improves the maintainability of the code by using a meaningful string to replace a number (the constant's value). Search the ADODB library with the Object Browser in Access for the values of intrinsic constants that you want to use in your programs. The rest of the file performs a loop to capture all the rows from the *Shippers* table.

> **Note**   Microsoft ships a file (adovbs.inc) with Windows that you can
> include in your ASP applications to automatically recognize all intrinsic
> constants. The file resides in different locations on different versions of
> Windows; you can perform a search to uncover its location on your sys-
> tem. To use this file, you must properly specify a *#include* directive. See
> the IIS help file for guidance on the syntax for a *#include* directive. If IIS
> runs on your local workstation, you can open it from localhost/iishelp/.
> Refer to msdn.microsoft.com/library/psdk/iisref/serv24bp.htm for online
> guidance about the *#include* directive.

```
<html>

<head>
<title>List Updatable Shippers</title>
</head>

<body>

<%

'Connect to the fpnwind.mdb database
filePath = Server.MapPath("\") & "\pma10\fpdb\fpnwind.mdb"
Set cnn1 = Server.CreateObject("ADODB.Connection")
cnn1.Open "Provider=Microsoft.Jet.OLEDB.4.0;Data Source=" & filePath

Const adCmdText = 1
'Select all columns from all rows
set rst1 = Server.CreateObject("ADODB.Recordset")
rst1.open "SELECT * FROM Shippers", cnn1,,,adCmdText

%>

<TABLE BORDER=1 BGCOLOR=#ffffff CELLSPACING=0>
<CAPTION><B>Shippers</B></CAPTION>

<THEAD>
<TR>
<TH BGCOLOR=#c0c0c0 BORDERCOLOR=#000000 >
<FONT style=FONT-SIZE:10pt FACE="Arial" COLOR=#000000>
Shipper ID</FONT></TH>
<TH BGCOLOR=#c0c0c0 BORDERCOLOR=#000000 >
<FONT style=FONT-SIZE:10pt FACE="Arial" COLOR=#000000>
Company Name</FONT></TH>
```

(continued)

```
<TH BGCOLOR=#c0c0c0 BORDERCOLOR=#000000 >
<FONT style=FONT-SIZE:10pt FACE="Arial" COLOR=#000000>
Phone</FONT></TH>

</TR>
</THEAD>
<TBODY>
<%
'Start looping through records in the Shippers table
On Error Resume Next
rst1.MoveFirst
do while Not rst1.eof
 %>
<TR VALIGN=TOP>
<TD BORDERCOLOR=#c0c0c0  ALIGN=RIGHT>
<FONT style=FONT-SIZE:10pt FACE="Arial" COLOR=#000000>
<%=Server.HTMLEncode(rst1.Fields("ShipperID").Value)%>
<BR></FONT></TD>
<TD BORDERCOLOR=#c0c0c0 >
<FONT style=FONT-SIZE:10pt FACE="Arial" COLOR=#000000>
<%=Server.HTMLEncode(rst1.Fields("CompanyName").Value)%>
<BR></FONT></TD>
<TD BORDERCOLOR=#c0c0c0 >
<FONT style=FONT-SIZE:10pt FACE="Arial" COLOR=#000000>
<%=Server.HTMLEncode(rst1.Fields("Phone").Value)%>
<BR></FONT></TD>

</TR>
<%
'Move to the next record and complete looping through
'the Shippers table
rst1.MoveNext
loop%>
</TBODY>
</TABLE>

<p><a href="Shippersdefault.htm">Shippers's Sample Menu</a></p>

</body>
</html>
```

Adding a Record to a Table

The second link on the main menu points to the NewShipperForm.htm file. This file contains a form that lets a user specify the *CompanyName* and *Phone* fields for a new shipper. The form references the addFromHandler.asp file on the Web server. This form handler adds the record specified in the NewShipperForm.htm file to the *Shippers* table in the fpnwind.mdb database and prints a confirmation of the task. (In Web applications, it's often useful to give users confirmation of an action.) The form handler page also includes a link back to the main menu.

The following listing shows the HTML code for the NewShipperForm.htm file. There are three key points to note. First, the .htm file references its form handler, addFormHandler.asp, with the action attribute of the form variable. Second, the text boxes for the *CompanyName* and *Phone* fields specify default values with a value attribute setting. These default value assignments are not meant to represent a value to use in the application. Instead, the Enter Company Name value for the CompanyName text box reminds users what the text box is for. (This use for default values is common in Web applications.) Third, all the form's controls and labels appear in a table within the <form> and </form> tags. The table cells containing the text strings labeling the CompanyName and Phone text boxes have an align attribute setting of *"right"*. This makes the label flush with the values in the text box, which align left by default. Figure 17-16 shows the form that the HTML script represents.

```
<html>

<head>
<title>Form to add a shipper</title>
</head>

<body>

<p><font size="5"><b>Shipper Input Form</b></font></p>
<form method="Post" action="addFormHandler.asp">
    <table border="0" width="358">
      <tr>
        <td align="right" width="152">Company Name:</td>
        <td width="192"><input type="text" name="CompanyName"
          size="26" value="Enter Company Name"></td>
      </tr>
      <tr>
        <td align="right" width="152">Phone:</td>
        <td width="192"><input type="text" name="Phone"
          size="26" value="(xxx) xxx-xxxx"></td>
      </tr>
      <tr>
        <td width="152">
          <p align="right"><input type="submit"
            value="Submit" name="B1"></p>
        </td>
```

(continued)

```
    <td width="192"><input type="reset"
        value="Reset" name="B2"></td>
    </tr>
  </table>
</form>

</body>
</html>
```

Figure 17-16 A data entry form for the *Shippers* table.

The handler for the form shown in Figure 17-16 has three main segments. First, it retrieves data passed to it by the form. It uses the *Form* collection of the ASP *Request* object to accomplish this task. The second form in the telephone lookup sample discussed earlier used this technique without explicit comment. Whenever a form uses a method setting of *"Post"* as this sample application does, you can retrieve values with the *Form* collection. You can use an index value that is the name of the control for which you want the value. Therefore, in this sample, the indexes are *CompanyName* and *Phone*. The sample uses the VBScript *Replace* function to replace a single occurrence of a quote mark (') with two contiguous single quote marks ("). This replacement allows the SQL statement with the INSERT keyword to successfully process company names, such as O'Henry's Movers.

The second segment of the form handler makes the connection to the fpnwind.mdb database and instantiates a command that inserts into the *Shippers* table the record values passed to the handler by the NewShipperForm.htm file. The command uses a *CommandText* property setting that is an SQL statement. This is one of three techniques for performing an action query in ASP files.

> **Note**   Another technique for performing an action query relies on an ADO *Connection* object. The next ASP file in our example illustrates the syntax for this approach. The third technique for implementing an action query relies on a saved query. This last approach improves performance by using a saved query, but its syntax can get more complicated when you have parameters, as is common with action queries. The last sample in this chapter demonstrates the saved query approach.

The third segment of the form handler starts with an HTML comment describing its purpose, which is to provide feedback and offer a link to the main menu. The feedback mixes straight text with an embedded reference to the *CompanyName* form field value passed to the form handler. The <%= and %> delimiters mark the embedded reference.

```
<html>

<head>
<title>Insert confirmation</title>
</head>
<%

'Get CompanyName field and convert ' mark for
'embedding in string with ' marks
comName = Request.Form("CompanyName")
comName = Replace(comName,"'","''")

'Get Phone field
comPhone = Request.Form("Phone")

%>
<body>

<%

'Make connection to fpnwind.mdb database
filePath = Server.MapPath("\") & "\pma10\fpdb\fpnwind.mdb"
Set cnn1 = Server.CreateObject("ADODB.Connection")
cnn1.Open "Provider=Microsoft.Jet.OLEDB.4.0;Data Source=" & filePath

'Execute command to insert new shipper into Shippers table
Const adCmdText=1
set cmd1 = Server.CreateObject("ADODB.Command")
cmd1.ActiveConnection = cnn1
```

(continued)

```
cmd1.CommandText = "INSERT Into Shippers " & _
    "(CompanyName, Phone) VALUES (" &_
    "'" & comName & "'" & ",'" & comPhone & "')"
cmd1.CommandType = adCmdText
cmd1.Execute

%>

<!--Provide confirmation feedback and link to main menu -->
<p>Thank you for your data entry.</p>
<p>Shipper's Name: <%= Request.Form("CompanyName") %></p>
<p><a href="Shippersdefault.htm">Shippers's Sample Menu</a></p>

</body>
</html>
```

Deleting Records from a Table

The third link points at an ASP file (DeleteShipper.asp) that removes all records from the *Shippers* table that have a *ShipperID* value greater than 3. This gives the application a chance to restore the table's entries to the initial three shippers. Because the SQL code for this delete statement (shown next) is so simple, its ASP file is very short and you don't need a form to specify which records to delete. You can adapt the samples presented earlier in this book to specify WHERE clauses that selectively limit the records that a DELETE statement removes from a table. (As an example, see "Deleting Records" in Chapter 3.) In this case, you will likely use a form to let users interact with the application by specifying parameters for the WHERE clause of a DELETE statement.

```
<html>

<head>
<title>Delete records and confirm</title>
</head>
<%

'Connect to the fpnwind.mdb database
filePath = Server.MapPath("\") & "\pma10\fpdb\fpnwind.mdb"
Set cnn1 = Server.CreateObject("ADODB.Connection")
cnn1.Open "Provider=Microsoft.Jet.OLEDB.4.0;Data Source=" & filePath

'Delete all records from the Shippers table with a
'ShipperID value greater than 3
cnn1.Execute ("DELETE * FROM Shippers WHERE ShipperID>3")

%>
```

```
<body>
Records with an ID greater than 3 are deleted.
<p><a href="Shippersdefault.htm">Shippers's Sample Menu</a></p>

</body>
</html>
```

Registering Seminar Participants

The closing sample in this chapter presents a basic seminar registration form. This form has five fields. One of these is an option group comprised of a set of eight radio, or option, buttons. The SeminarSignup.htm file that holds the form references echoreg.asp as its handler. The ASP file performs just two major functions, but each of them requires more code and is more sophisticated in its approach than the functions presented in earlier samples in this chapter.

The first function of the form handler is to confirm the registration. Actually, the appearance of a confirmation is optional. If a user fails to input a valid entry for Number Of Days, the form handler returns a directive to remedy the condition. The confirmation message provides precise information about who registered for what. The application uses the current date to determine whether a registration qualifies for the early-bird discount rate. If the registration is after the cutoff date, the form handler uses the standard price schedule. After confirming the registration, the file appends the new registrant's information to the table holding registrations. The code uses a saved query. This sample passes parameters to the saved query based on the form field values and the date.

> **Note**   Although the page creates the confirmation message before appending the new record, the file aborts with an error if the application cannot add the new registration. Therefore, users do not receive confirmation messages for failed registration attempts.

Figure 17-17 shows the registration form in a browser. It contains four text box controls and an option group. The box around the eight option buttons does not strictly force the controls to act as a group. For example, if the controls inside the option group were check boxes instead of option buttons, users could select multiple check boxes. On the other hand, option buttons act as a set by default. In addition, if you include two option group controls on a form and then populate each with option buttons, the two sets of option buttons operate independently of one another.

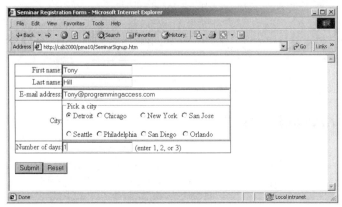

Figure 17-17 A seminar registration form.

The following HTML script shows the code behind the form in Figure 17-17. Notice the size and maxlength attribute settings for the first, second, and fourth text box controls. All these settings are 20. The third text box has size and maxlength settings of 50. The size attribute setting specifies the width of an Input control, but it does not designate how many characters can fit in the control. In contrast, the maxlength attribute value designates the maximum number of characters a user can type into a text box. Consider setting these attributes so that they make sense in your application. In the sample application, the first name and last name form fields get stored in table fields that each have a maximum number of 20 characters. While the value in the text box for the number of days gets stored in a numeric field, making the size 20 characters gives this last text box the same width as the first two text boxes. Because the last text box holds a numeric value with some code that checks its validity, a maxlength setting is not important. You can omit the maxlength attribute for this control without any consequence for the application.

The text box for the e-mail address has size and maxlength attribute settings of 50. This gives registrants more space to accommodate lengthy e-mail addresses. The table field that holds this form field value has a maximum width of 50 characters. In actual practice, you might have to determine through trial and error how wide to make fields. In my experience, it's common to require more than 50 characters for e-mail addresses. Our sample demonstrates that e-mail addresses can easily be longer than other fields.

Notice that all the option button controls have a type setting of *"radio"*. In addition, all the radio type controls share the same name attribute setting, *"City"*. Option buttons with the same name act as a set. For example, clicking one option button clears any previously selected option buttons or default settings with the same name. Using the keyword checked before the name attribute for one radio control signifies that FrontPage selects that control by default. The value attribute settings for option groups specifies which value the radio button set returns when a user selects that button. Notice that the buttons have values ranging from 1 through 8. The set of radio buttons populates a field in a table that has a lookup property. This field can look up city names that correspond to the numbers 1 through 8. (See the Design view for the *SeminarRegistrations* and *SeminarCities* tables in the chapter's sample .mdb file to confirm the details of how this works.)

```
<html>

<head>
<title>Seminar Registration Form</title>
</head>

<body>

<form method="Post" action="echoreg.asp">
  <table border="1" cellpadding="0" cellspacing="0"
    style="border-collapse: collapse" bordercolor="#111111"
    width="64%" id="AutoNumber1">
    <tr>
      <td width="22%" align="right">First name:</td>
      <td width="78%"><input type="text" name="FirstName"
        size="20" maxlength="20"></td>
    </tr>
    <tr>
      <td width="22%" align="right">Last name:</td>
      <td width="78%"><input type="text" name="LastName"
        size="20" maxlength="20"></td>
    </tr>
    <tr>
      <td width="22%" align="right">E-mail address:</td>
      <td width="78%">
      <input type="text" name="eAddress" size="50"
        maxlength="50">
      </td>
    </tr>
    <tr>
      <td width="22%" align="right">City:</td>
      <td width="78%"><fieldset style="padding: 2">
      <legend>Pick a city</legend>
      <input type="radio" value="1" checked name="City">Detroit 
      <input type="radio" name="City" value="2">Chicago 
            
```

(continued)

```
          <input type="radio" name="City" value="3">New York 
          <input type="radio" name="City" value="4">San Jose<p>
          <input type="radio" name="City" value="5">Seattle
          <input type="radio" name="City" value="6">Philadelphia
          <input type="radio" name="City" value="7">San Diego 
          <input type="radio" name="City" value="8">Orlando</p>
          </fieldset></td>
      </tr>
      <tr>
        <td width="22%" align="right">Number of days:</td>
        <td width="78%"><input type="text" name="NumberOfDays"
          size="20"> (enter 1, 2, or 3)</td>
      </tr>
      </table>
    <p><input type="submit" value="Submit" name="B1">
      <input type="reset" value="Reset" name="B2"></p>
  </form>

  </body>
  </html>
```

The next and final block of script in this chapter shows the form handler
for the preceding form. The code starts by transferring the field values to local
variables. These assignments eliminate the need to open the *Form* collection
members whenever the form handler needs one of its values. Instead, the handler refers to a memory variable. After transferring the form field values, the
handler checks the value of the *NumberOfDays* field that it represents as days.
The only legitimate values for this field are 1, 2, or 3. Therefore, if the form field
has any other value, the code instructs the user to return to the form and enter
a valid number.

If the number of days value falls within the range of 1 through 3, the handler starts to confirm the registration. If the days value is valid, the user will see
a confirmation message appear. Figure 17-18 shows the confirmation for the form
entry from Figure 17-17. Notice how the message echoes the name of the registrant as it thanks the person. Also notice how the application determines a price
without asking the user to enter a price. The price for a seminar registrant depends on two factors: how many days the registrant attends, and whether the
registration occurs before the early-bird discount deadline.

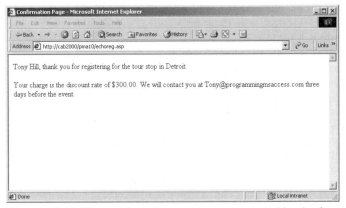

Figure 17-18 The confirmation message generated by the form handler for the form shown in Figure 17-17.

The following code sample makes heavy use of the *Write* method for the *Response* object. While the *Request* object can help to get values into a form handler, the *Response* object can help to get values from a form handler to a Web page. The *Write* method can print to Web page string constants, HTML tags, and memory variables, either individually or concatenated together. Actually, HTML tags simply embed in ASCII character streams, but memory variable values append to them. The confirmation message, which is a compilation of multiple *Response.Write* statements, demonstrates all of these features. The first instance of *Response.Write* after the *Else* statement concatenates memory variables and string constants. The name of the city for which a registrant schedules attendance results from a *Response.Write* statement in a *Select Case* statement. The period marking the end of the first sentence with a trailing paragraph tag (</p>) results from yet another *Response.Write* statement. Another combination of *If...Then...Else*, *Select Case*, and *Response.Write* statements confirms to users the price of the registration that they scheduled. Finally, the confirmation message concludes with a note about an e-mail follow-up three days before the seminar.

```
<html>

<head>
<title>Confirmation Page</title>
</head>

<body>
<%
```

(continued)

```
'Create references for form field values
days = Request.Form("NumberOfDays")
fname = Request.Form("FirstName")
lname = Request.Form("LastName")
semCity = Request.Form("City")
email = Request.Form("eAddress")

'Send the user back to registration form to correctly complete
'it or process the input on the form
if Not(days=1 Or days=2 Or days=3) Then
'If wrong days, send user back to form
    Response.Write "Wrong number of days entered."  & _
        "  Click Back and enter a number from 1 " & _
        " through 3."
Else
'Create confirmation message
'Include the name of the person
    Response.Write fname & " " & _
        lname & ", thank you for " & _
        "registering for the tour stop in "
'In addition, include the city for which user registers
    Select Case semCity
        Case 1
            Response.Write "Detroit"
        Case 2
            Response.Write "Chicago"
        Case 3
            Response.Write "New York"
        Case 4
            Response.Write "San Jose"
        Case 5
            Response.Write "Seattle"
        Case 6
            Response.Write "Philadelphia"
        Case 7
            Response.Write "San Diego"
        Case 8
            Response.Write "Orlando"
    End Select
    Response.Write ". <P>"

'Assign the registrant the early-bird discount or standard rate
    DiscountCutoff = #8/1/2001#
    If Now() <= DiscountCutOff Then
        Response.Write "  Your charge is the discount rate of "
```

```
        Select Case days
            Case 1
                Response.Write "$300.00"
                amt = 300
            Case 2
                Response.Write "$550.00"
                amt = 550
            Case 3
                Response.Write "$750.00"
                amt = 750
        End Select
    Else
        Response.Write "  Your charge is the standard rate of "
        Select Case days
            Case 1
                Response.Write "$300.00"
                amt = 300
            Case 2
                Response.Write "$600.00"
                amt = 600
            Case 3
                Response.Write "$850.00"
                amt = 850
        End Select
    End If

'Notify user that you will contact him before the seminar
    Response.Write ".  We will contact you at " & _
        email & _
        " three days before the event."

'Then append new registration to SeminarRegistrations table
'through the InsertReg parameter query
    Set cnn1 = Server.CreateObject("ADODB.Connection")
    cnn1.open "DSN=Chapter_17"

    Const adCmdStoredProc = 4
    Const adVarChar = 200
    Const adInteger = 3
    Const adDate = 7
    Const adCurrency = 6
    Const adParamInput = 1

    set cmd1 = Server.CreateObject("ADODB.Command")
    cmd1.ActiveConnection = cnn1
    cmd1.CommandType = adCmdStoredProc
    cmd1.CommandText = "InsertReg"
```

(continued)

```
        cmd1.Parameters.Append
          cmd1.CreateParameter("[fname]",adVarChar,adParamInput, 50)
        cmd1.Parameters("[fname]") = fname
        cmd1.Parameters.Append
          cmd1.CreateParameter("[lname]",adVarChar,adParamInput, 50)
        cmd1.Parameters("[lname]") = lname
        cmd1.Parameters.Append
          cmd1.CreateParameter("[email]",adVarChar,adParamInput, 50)
        cmd1.Parameters("[email]") = email
        cmd1.Parameters.Append cmd1.CreateParameter("[semCity]",
          adInteger, adParamInput)
        cmd1.Parameters("[semCity]") = semCity
        cmd1.Parameters.Append cmd1.CreateParameter("[days]",
          adInteger, adParamInput)
        cmd1.Parameters("[days]") = days
        cmd1.Parameters.Append cmd1.CreateParameter("[regDate]",
          adDate, adParamInput)
        cmd1.Parameters("[regDate]") = Now()
        cmd1.Parameters.Append cmd1.CreateParameter("[amt]",
          adCurrency, adParamInput)
        cmd1.Parameters("[amt]") = amt

        cmd1.Execute
End If
%>

</body>
</html>
```

The last block of code in the form handler updates the seminar registration table by invoking a saved query, InsertReg. The query resides in the database file for this chapter, Chapter 17.mdb. The SQL statement for the query appears next. Notice that the query uses the INSERT INTO statement to add a new record to a table. The field values appear in parentheses after the table name (namely, *SeminarRegistrations*) into which the query appends a record. All the table field values appear without brackets, except for *Date*, which is an Access reserved word. The addition of brackets permits the use of this term as a table field name. The SELECT list denotes the parameter values to insert into the *SeminarRegistration* table.

```
INSERT INTO SeminarRegistrations ( FirstName, LastName, eAddress,
City, NumberOfDays, [Date], Amount )
SELECT [fname], [lname], [email], [semCity], [days], [regDate], [amt]
```

The code to assign values to the parameters must set four different data types: *Text, Long Integer, Date/Time*, and *Currency*. These Access data type names correspond to the following ADO data type names: *adVarChar, adInteger, adDate*, and *adCurrency*. The code sample defines constants for each of the ADO data type names, such as *adVarChar*. The form handler references the saved query by denoting it as a stored procedure. For each parameter, the ASP file uses two lines. The first line appends the parameter to the *Parameters* collection of the *Command* object. The second line assigns a value to the appended parameter. The assignments derive from three sources: registration form fields, computed values, and the current date and time (*Now()*). After assigning values to all seven parameters, the ASP file invokes the *Execute* method for the command. This final step appends the parameter values as fields to a new record in the *SeminarRegistration* table.

Appendix

Microsoft Office XP Developer

Microsoft Access 2002 is available to Office developers in three regular Office XP editions: Office XP Professional, Office XP Professional Special Edition, and Office XP Developer (MOD XP). Access developers should avoid the Office XP Standard edition because it doesn't include Access 2002. If you want Microsoft FrontPage 2002 to use with Access 2002, you must choose an Office XP version that includes FrontPage as well. Check www.microsoft.com/office/howtobuy/ choosing.htm to verify the latest information about version component contents.

The MOD XP version of Office is a significant upgrade that offers exceptional value for professional or aspiring Access developers. This appendix provides an overview of MOD XP, paying special attention to how it serves the needs of Access developers.

Reasons for Using Office XP Developer

There are at least three database-related reasons Access developers should acquire MOD XP instead of the other editions of Office XP. The first reason is that MOD XP makes it easy to deploy solutions built on a developer's workstation to one or more client workstations. The second reason is that this edition offers special resources for building workflow solutions. The third reason is its graphical tool for facilitating the management of Jet-based replica sets. In addition, some excellent developer productivity add-ins ship with MOD XP, further enhancing the value of the package for Access programmers.

One of the main requirements for developers is the ability to create solutions that run on computers other than their own. MOD XP offers several tools to assist with this. First, developers building solutions with Jet databases gain the right to distribute their solutions with a run-time version of Access. This permits client workstations that don't have Access 2002 installed to run a Jet-based solution. Second, ownership of MOD XP conveys the right to redistribute solutions that you build with the Microsoft SQL Server 2000 Desktop Engine (abbreviated as MSDE 2000 in this book). MSDE 2000 is inherently redistributable, but a license to redistribute it is available only with the MOD XP edition of Office XP. Third, the Packaging Wizard that ships with MOD XP guides you through the process of packaging your Access solutions to run on other computers. The Packaging Wizard bundles your Access files (with .mdb or .adp extensions), either the run-time version of Access or the redistributable MSDE 2000, and any other files necessary for your solution to run on another computer (such as the SQL Server database files).

> **Note**   Although the Packaging Wizard bundles MSDE 2000 with your Access solution file, it doesn't complete the task of installing MSDE on another computer. It also doesn't attach your database files to the server. Scott Smith from Microsoft authored a helpful white paper that provides code samples to assist in performing these tasks; you can find it at msdn.microsoft.com/library/techart/odc_modmsde.htm.

Another exciting part of MOD XP is its tools for building solutions that manage workflow processes. When you install MOD XP, you have the option to add Workflow Developer Tools. Two of the options in this area enable Access developers to tap graphical and programmatic tools for building workflow solutions with SQL Server.

Workflow modeling enables you to build systems that track business entities—such as repair requests or stock-keeping unit introductions—in terms of their states, events, and transitions. The available states depend on the process for handling an entity. A repair request might have the states of submitted, scheduled, visited, fixed, billed, paid, and closed. Events are often associated with states. However, you can have additional events as well, such as an archive event that occurs after a repair request enters the closed state. Transitions move entities between states. For example, a payment event can move a repair request from a billed state to a paid state.

MOD XP workflow solutions target small workgroups, such as branch offices. You can run them with either MSDE 2000 or SQL Server in either the SQL Server 7 or SQL Server 2000 versions. Although MOD XP workflow solutions are not meant for enterprise solutions, you can readily transfer workflow solutions between servers. This capability makes it possible to build a solution at your company headquarters or a consultant's office and then distribute it to multiple branch offices.

Replication Manager is a graphical tool that ships with MOD XP and lets you manage multiple replica sets. It permits indirect synchronization between replica members, allows the scheduling of automatic synchronizations, and facilitates replication over the Internet. Replication Manager uses synchronizers to manage the exchange of information between the members of a replica set. Any one replica can be managed by just one synchronizer, but a single synchronizer can manage multiple replicas. With indirect synchronization, a replica member can launch a synchronization cycle with another replica, even when that other replica is off line. When a replica member is off line, the messages that normally go to the other member transfer to a dropbox folder instead. Later, when the other member logs on to a local area network (LAN), its synchronizer recovers its messages from the dropbox folder.

Scheduling with Replication Manager lets you automatically arrange for replica members to synchronize with one another. This relieves the manager of an overall replica set from depending on the managers of individual replicas to launch synchronization. You can schedule synchronization in one of three ways:

- For two or more existing replicas managed by a single synchronizer

- Between two synchronizers that, in turn, propagate updates to members they manage

- As a default synchronization when you initiate the creation of a new replica

Before ending this discussion, it's worth noting that there are many other excellent reasons for Access developers to adopt MOD XP. I'll mention some of these in the next section. However, the next section does not cover the Add-Ins menu item that MOD XP adds to the menu bar in the Microsoft Visual Basic Editor (VBE). This item permits you to load and invoke as many as 11 of the special add-ins available when you install MOD XP. The Packaging Wizard we just discussed is one of these add-ins. Another add-in that deserves special mention is the Code Librarian. The Code Librarian offers a user interface for archiving, storing, displaying and retrieving code samples (either snippets or full procedures). A team of developers can use the Code Librarian along with another add-in, the VBA

Source Code Control, to manage source code control, code sharing, and the reuse of code samples. In order to use the VBA Source Code Control add-in, developers must install Microsoft Visual SourceSafe on their workstations. The Visual SourceSafe application is available on one of the CDs that ships with MOD XP.

What's in the Box

MOD XP ships with seven CDs in its box. These CDs are labeled as follows:

- Microsoft Office XP Developer
- Microsoft Windows Component Update
- Microsoft Visual SourceSafe
- Microsoft Exchange 2000 Server Developer Edition
- Microsoft SQL Server 2000 for Office XP Developer
- Microsoft Office XP Professional with FrontPage
- Microsoft Office XP Media Content

These CDs deliver much more than the core Office XP functionality. For example, the Windows Component Update CD updates your Windows operating system as needed. It installs Service Pack 1 for Windows 2000 systems, and it adds Service Pack 6A to Microsoft Windows NT systems. These Windows enhancements are necessary for running selected Office XP or Office XP Developer features. The Office XP installation program in MOD XP automatically detects the operating system and installs the appropriate service pack, as well as the FrontPage 2002 Server Extensions.

As a database developer, you're likely to value the Microsoft SQL Server 2000 for Office XP Developer CD. With this CD, you can install a developer edition of SQL Server 2000 on your system. If you plan to use SQL Server to build solutions, installing this edition can yield important benefits. With it, you gain the Enterprise Manager and Query Analyzer tools, Books Online for SQL Server 2000, the pubs database, and the Help file for SQL-DMO. None of these elements ship with MSDE 2000, the SQL Server 2000 technology that ships as part of any version of Office XP that includes Access 2002.

The extra resources you gain with the Microsoft SQL Server 2000 for Office XP Developer CD will help you get up to speed with SQL Server. In addition, they can expedite your efforts to create new solutions with SQL Server that match the caliber of the solutions you're already creating for Jet databases.

Enterprise Manager is the primary graphical, administrative tool for managing SQL Server. Its many offerings include the ability to select SQL Server authentication styles and define SQL Server logins and database users. Enterprise Manager also features an explorer for examining database objects such as tables, views, stored procedures, user-defined functions, and database diagrams.

Query Analyzer allows you to run T-SQL statements, system stored procedures, and script files. Unlike the stored procedure template in Access projects, Query Analyzer readily returns multiple databases. All the T-SQL code samples provided in Books Online work in Query Analyzer without requiring any editing. Because you will also have the pubs database, you can use Query Analyzer to follow and examine the many T-SQL code samples in Books Online that refer to this database.

While MSDE 2000 includes the dynamic-link library (DLL) for SQL-DMO, which is named sqldmo.dll, it doesn't include the Help file that ships with the Microsoft SQL Server 2000 for Office XP Developer CD, called sqldmo80.hlp. This help file is a valuable resource that integrates tightly with the VBE window for identifying and describing the objects, methods, properties, and events in the SQL-DMO object model.

Many developers will be delighted to find high-quality printed documentation in the MOD XP box. The *Microsoft Office XP Developer's Guide* is the new book that replaces the former *Microsoft Office 2000/Visual Basic Programmer's Guide*. This new resource totals nearly 750 pages. The book includes extensive coverage of several features introduced since the release of Office 2000—in particular, building workflow applications with SQL Server and Exchange 2000 Server, developing digital dashboards, and using the new XML functionality. This book provides authoritative commentary and code samples for many advanced Office developer topics, such as VBA debugging and error handling, creating add-ins, and using methods to create custom classes. You'll also find a number of examples showing how to use objects based on those classes. The book concludes with a series of diagrams for the various Office object models. These diagrams can help you quickly understand how the objects in a model relate to one another.

> **Note**   A digital dashboard is an Active Server Page that references one or more Web Parts. Web Parts are components that display content from sources such as XML code, HTML pages, or Visual Basic Scripting Edition (VBScript). Office XP developers will need to install the developer edition of Exchange 2000 Server in order to build digital dashboard solutions.

Finally, I want to mention that Microsoft has created a new interface for Office XP Developer Help that is modeled in many ways after Books Online for SQL Server. You can access it from the Windows Start menu by choosing Microsoft Office XP Developer and then Microsoft Office XP Developer Online Documentation. This resource offers in machine-readable format all the content from the *Microsoft Office XP Developer's Guide*, plus material not available in the book. Although the physical book has a detailed table of contents, it doesn't have an index. Office XP Developer Help, on the other hand, offers a table of contents, an index, and a keyword search capability. The user interface for MOD XP Help enables you to jump to the Web to explore topics not covered completely in the Office XP Developer Help system.

Index

Note: Italicized page references indicate figures, tables, or code listings.

Numbers and Symbols

3-D charts
  updating bar charts to 3-D, 488–89
  updating line charts to 3-D, 492–94, *494*
asterisk (*), as wildcard, *245*, 248
caret (^), as wildcard, 249
exclamation point (!), as wildcard, *245*, 247,
    248–49
percent symbol (%), as wildcard, *245*, 246
pound sign (#), 253
square brackets ([ ]), and wildcards, *245*, 246
underscore (_), as wildcard, *245*, 246

A

AccessObject objects
  and *Allxxx* collections, 531–36
  collection members as, 438–39
  DateCreated property, 198
  DateModified property, 198
  determining when tables are open, 199
  enumerating *Allxxx* collection members, 533–34
  enumerating forms, 374
  enumerating in any *Allxxx* collection, 439,
    531–32
  enumerating members of *AllTables* collection,
    197–99
  enumerating reports, 439–41
  enumerating tables, 190–96
  FullName property, 978
  IsLoaded property, 374, 531, 535
  Name property, 374, 531, 978
  Type property, 531, 534
AccessObjectProperty variable, 546, 549
Access projects
  adapting Books online code for SQL pane
    viewing, 765–68
  architecture overview, 747–50
  AutoForm Wizard, 850–54
  building custom startup forms, 554–56
  as client side of client/server applications, 747

Access projects, *continued*
  copying table design between databases, 910–13
  creating and opening, 754–64
  creating desktop shortcuts, 755
  creating forms based on tables, 850–54
  creating new databases programmatically,
    760–64
  creating new databases using wizard, 759
  file type (.adp), 4, 533, 534, 746, 754
  and NorthwindCS database, 748, *748*, *755*,
    755–56
  opening existing files, 754–56
  opening new files for existing databases, 757–58
  opening new files for new databases, 758–59
  overview, 746–47
  processing hyperlinks in forms, 875–79
  programming reports, 884–94
  Query Designer, 796–97, *797*
  and SQL Server versions, 746, 747, 750–51
  unique form issues, 871–83
ACCESS TABLE *Type* property value, *186*
action queries, 297–306
Activate event, 425
ActiveConnection property
  Catalog object, 185–86, 190, 191, 194, 200, 216,
    483, 685
  Recordset object, 97, 103, 104
  Replica object, 723, 724
Active Directory Service, OLE DB data
    provider, *78*
Active Server Pages (ASP)
  adding to Web sites using Database Wizard,
    1039–47
  creating files without DSNs, 1035–38
  vs. data access pages, 938–39
  editing scripts, 1032–34
  form handler for seminar registration form,
    1064–69
  vs. HTML tables, 1028–32
  overview, 938–39

Index

Active Server Pages (ASP), *continued*
  programmatically designing forms, 1048–69
  publishing Access tables with, 1025–32
  reading with *Stream* objects, 171–73
ActiveView property, 473
ActiveX control, Office Web Component, 937
AddCbrBtns procedure, 605–7
AddContacts procedure, 639–40
AddFromFile method, 523, 527
AddGroupToUser procedure, 686, 687–88
AddItem method, 564, 565
AddItemsToPMAContacts procedure, 645–46
AddLoginAndUserToDBRole procedure, 924–25
Add method
  Controls collection, 603
  NewFileTaskPane object, 575
  PropertyTests collection, 569
AddNew method, 102, 110–11, 225, 621
AddNorthwindReference procedure, 40
AddReference procedure, 526, 527
AddShowAssistantsAndRocky procedure, 604, 605
ADD statement, 696
AddTotal method, 473–77
ADO (ActiveX Data Objects). *See also* Microsoft
  ActiveX Data Objects Library (ADODB)
  vs. DAO, 73, 74, 77
  event model, 77
  event programming example, 175–81
  generating XML files, 1008–11
  and Jet SQL, 696
  mapping SQL Server to data types, 780–85
  and Microsoft Access, 73
  overview, 74–80
  programming events, 173–81
  reference models, 74
  ReportBasedOnADORecordset procedure, 436–38
  using recordset as record source for forms,
    330–33
  using recordset as record source for reports,
    435–38
  wildcards, *245*, 245–49
ADODB library. *See* Microsoft ActiveX Data
  Objects Library (ADODB)
ADODB object library
  object model, *80*
ADOX. *See also* Microsoft ADO Ext. 2.5 for DDL
  and Security (ADOX)
  vs. Access data types, 201, 205–8
  column property settings, 205–8

ADOX, *continued*
  vs. Jet SQL and ADO, 696
  managing row-returning queries, 281–97
  object model, 184–85, *185,* 681, *682*
  and user-level security, 681–95
.adp files, 4, 533, 534, 746, 754. *See also*
  Access projects
AfterUpdate event, 369, 866, 867, 870–71, 883
aggregated fields, 255–58
AllDataAccessPages collection, 438, 532, 978–79
AllDatabaseDiagrams collection, 438, 532–33
AllForms collection, 6, 438, 440, 484, 540, 541
  AccessObject object, 531–32
  EnumerateAllForms procedure, 533–34
  enumerating forms and controls, 374–76
  procedure for listing modules, 534–36
AllMacros collection, 438, 532
AllModules collection, 438, 537
  AccessObject object, 531–32
  procedure for listing modules, 534–36
AllowDetails property, 479–80
AllowFiltering property, 479
AllQueries collection, 438, 532
AllReports collection, 388, 438–39, 440, 532
AllStoredProcedures collection, 438, 532–33
AllTables collection, 435, 438, 532
  EnumerateAllTables procedure, 533–34
  printing table details, 197–99
AllViews collection, 438, 532
Allxxx collections
  enumerating *AccessObject* objects, 531–32
  enumerating members, 533–34
  object model, 531–33, *532*
  overview, 438, 531
ALTER COLUMN statement, SQL, 309
ALTER DATABASE PASSWORD keyword, 676
ALTER PROCEDURE statement, 770
ALTER statement, 696
ALTER TABLE statement, SQL, 24, 309, 310
Animation property, 578
animations
  adding to Assistants, 577–79
  displaying in searches, 580–81
  previewing Assistant characters, 583–86
  selecting types, 581, *582*
  using in searching, 580–81
anonymous database replicas, 716, 717
AnswerHelp procedure, 592–93
AnswerWizard object, *545*

Index

Index

Index

Index

Index

Index

Notepad, 445
Ntext SQL Server data type, *777*
Number property, 158
NumericScale property, 187
Nvarchar SQL Server data type, *777*

O

Object Browser
  browsing in, 16
  illustrated, *141*
  opening, 15
  overview, 12, 14–16
  searching in, 15–16
object classes
  client-side vs. server-side, 749
  Database Diagrams object class, 749, *750*
  Forms object class, 749, *750*
  Macros object class, 749, *750*
  Modules object class, 749, *750*
  on Objects bar, 749–50, *750*
  Pages object class, 749, *750*
  Queries object class, 749, *750*
  Reports object class, 749, *750*
  Tables object class, 749, *750*
Object data type, *26*
object libraries
  adding references to VBA projects, 15
  creating references to, 76
  Office Object Library, 579–80
  overview, 14–15
  searching, 15–16
  version issues, 77
  viewing in Object Browser, 14–16
object models
  ADODB object library, 80, *80*
  ADOX, 184–85, *185,* 681, *682*
  Allxxx collections, 531–33, *532*
  Assistant object, 577, *577*
  CommandBar object, 594, *594*
  FileSearch object, 556, *557*
  JRO, 708–9, *709*
  Microsoft Outlook, 642, *643*
  SQLDMO, 896, *896*
object permissions, 930–34

objects
  in ADODB object model, *80*
  assigning to classes, 509–12
  closing and setting to *Nothing,* 82, 104
  as containers, 5
  enumerating within local server databases,
    904–10
  methods overview, 5, 8
  overview, 5
  property overview, 5, 7
  syntax, 7
Objects bar, 5, *6*
ODBC. *See* Open Database Connectivity (ODBC)
ODBC Data Source Administrator, 1026
ODBC Data Sources (32bit), 1026
ODBCDirect, 77
Office. *See* Microsoft Office
Office Assistant, 577. *See also Assistant* object
OfficeDataSourceObject object, *545*
Office Object Library, 579–80
Office Web Components
  ActiveX control, 937
  Chart control, 937, 994, 997–99
  Data Source Control object, 937, 994–95
  overview, 937
  as part of Office XP, 994–1002
  PivotTable list control, 937, 994, 999–1002
  Spreadsheet control, 937, 994, 995–97
OLE DB connections, as link between SQL Server
    and Access projects, 747, 748–49
OLE DB data providers
  lists of Microsoft-supplied providers, 77, *78*
  overview, 77–78
OLE DB Provider for Microsoft Jet, *78,* 92
OLE DB service providers, 78–79, *79*
OLE objects for charting data, 397, 399
On Click event setting, *326,* 327
On Error statement, 86–87, 210, 510
OpenARecordsetReadOnly procedure, 508
OpenConnection method, 761–62
OpenCurrentDatabase method, 441
Open Database Connectivity (ODBC), *78,* 1025
OpenDataSource method, 615–16, 654, 655, 657
OpenDBConnection procedure, 664
Open event, 424–25, 429, 855

Index

Index

Index

Index

tables
- adding columns, 200–202
- adding from database diagrams, 789–91
- adding records, 225–36
- in *AllTables* collection, 198–99
- archiving updated and deleted records, 834–37
- ASP script for adding records, 1056–60
- ASP script for deleting records, 1060–61
- ASP script for viewing records, 1054–56
- changing with triggers, 831–32
- column data types, 775, *776–78, 778–79*
- converting raw HTML-formatted data, 447–51
- copying design between databases, 910–13
- creating, 200–202
- creating based on Excel worksheets, 622–25
- creating forms using AutoForm Wizard, 850–54
- creating using CREATE TABLE statement, 785–89, 794–96
- deleting, 203
- detecting when open, 199
- enumerating, 190–96
- filtering types, 192–94
- importing FrontPage guestbook data into, 445–46
- inner joins, 258–60
- Jet SQL syntax for select queries, 240–49
- joining for lookups, 799–803
- linking in database diagrams, 791–93
- linking sources using *Connection* object, 229–31
- linking sources using *DoCmd* object, 231–36
- list of types, 186, *186*
- manually publishing with Active Server Pages, 1025–32
- outer joins, 260–63
- programmatically exporting as HTML tables, 1022–23
- publishing as ASP files, 1026–32
- publishing as HTML tables, 1018–21
- replacing, 204–5
- in replication applications, 712–14, 737–39
- self joins, 263–64
- setting group permissions, 692–94
- standard vs. linked, 186, 198
- and subdatasheets, 342–43
- system, 186, *186*, 198
- using stored procedures to delete records, 827–29

tables, *continued*
- using stored procedures to insert records, 821–25
- using stored procedures to update records, 826–27
- *WebBasedListBadData* table, 453–54, *455*
- *WebBasedList* table, 447, *447*, 452, 453–54, *455*
- working with Word from Access, 649–52

Tables collection
- *Append* method, 201, 204
- *Delete* method, 203, 235
- list of table types, 186, *186*
- overview, 186
- using to enumerate tables, 190–96

Tables object class, 749, *750*

TABLE *Type* property value, *186*

tabular reports, 884–88

Tag property, 443

Task Pane
- adding links, 574–75, 576
- opening existing Access project files, 755, 757
- opening new Access project files, 758
- opening recent Access project files, 755
- overview, 574
- removing links, 575–76

telephone lookup application, 1049–53

Terminate event, 496, 498, 510

testing user accounts, 925–28

TestRowLock.mdb file, 671, 673

TestSelectPermissionLogin procedure, 926–28

text boxes
- for lookup forms, 366–67
- Running Sum property, 430

text files
- importing data from, 236–38
- reading with *Stream* objects, 171–73

Text/HTML ISAM, 25

TextOrProperty property, 562

Text property, 586, 587

Text SQL Server data type, 777

themes, applying to data access pages, 981–82

tiling images, 319

time-based line charts, 489–92, *492*

Timer event
- overview, 318
- role in refreshing forms, 322–23
- role in splash screens, 320–21

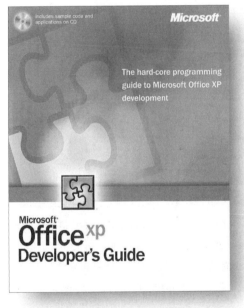

The
definitive guide
to programming the
Windows CE API

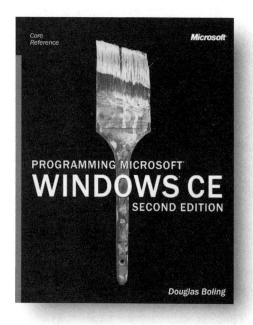

U.S.A. **$59.99**
Canada $86.99
ISBN: 0-7356-1443-1

Design sleek, high-performance applications for the newest generation of smart devices with this practical, authoritative reference. It fully explains how to extend your Microsoft® Windows® or embedded programming skills to the Windows CE handheld and Pocket PC environments. You'll review the basics of event-driven development and then tackle the intricacies of this modular, compact architecture. Investigate platform-specific programming considerations, and use specialized techniques for handling memory, storage, and power constraints. Dive into serial, network, and RAPI communications. Advance your skill with modules, processes, and threads, and build or modify code to meet the requirements of new devices such as the Pocket PC.

Microsoft®

mspress.microsoft.com

Use XML and SQL Server
to turn business data into
powerfully integrated
solutions
for employees, customers, and partners.

U.S.A. **$59.99**
Canada $86.99
ISBN: 0-7356-1369-9

Discover how to transform your organization's relational databases into potent business-to-business, e-commerce, and Web applications with this core reference for solution developers. The rich XML support in Microsoft® SQL Server™ 2000 makes it easy to map XML and relational data with familiar standards such as XPath, XDR schemas, XSL Transformation, HTTP, and OLE DB, as well as newer tools. You'll learn how to retrieve XML data from the database, insert XML data into the database, and manipulate it in extensible database solutions. And you'll examine real-world solutions—including knowledge-management systems and high-volume electronic retail databases—that demonstrate how to use SQL Server and XML to move your critical business processes to the Web. An appendix discusses XML specifics for SQL Server developers.

Microsoft Press® products are available worldwide wherever quality computer books are sold. For more information, contact your book or computer retailer, software reseller, or local Microsoft Sales Office, or visit our Web site at mspress.microsoft.com. To locate your nearest source for Microsoft Press products, or to order directly, call 1-800-MSPRESS in the United States (in Canada, call 1-800-268-2222).

Prices and availability dates are subject to change.

Microsoft®

mspress.microsoft.com

Tap into the *built-in* programmatic power

of Visio Version 2002!

U.S.A.   **$59.99**
Canada $87.99
ISBN: 0-7356-1353-2

This is the comprehensive guide for any software developer, system analyst, architect, engineer, CAD program user, or advanced computer user who wants to tap directly into the programming power of Microsoft® Visio® Version 2002. It provides all the practical programming information you need to extend the power of this latest version of Visio as a development platform. This guide comes direct from the source—the Microsoft Visio development team—to give you complete details about how to create customized shapes and solutions, program Visio with Microsoft Visual Basic®, Visual Basic for Applications (VBA), and C++, and incorporate Visio as a powerful graphical component in other applications.

Microsoft®

mspress.microsoft.com

Rick Dobson

Rick Dobson, Ph.D., is an author and trainer specializing in Microsoft Access, Microsoft SQL Server, and Web technologies. He is a big fan of programmatic solutions, particularly those that involve VBA, ADO, Jet SQL, T-SQL, or SQL-DMO.

Rick is the author of two other books on Access and SQL Server. This book thoroughly examines ADO as well as how to build SQL Server and Web solutions. It also provides in-depth coverage of Access fundamentals, such as form and report design, Access security, and how to build queries and program custom menus. While *Programming Microsoft Access Version 2002* targets intermediate and advanced developers, Rick's first book, *Programming Microsoft Access 2000* (Microsoft Press, 1999), serves the needs of beginning and intermediate developers and includes numerous easy-to-understand program samples. His second book, *Professional SQL Server Development with Access 2000* (Wrox Press, 2000), addresses both Access and SQL Server developers.

Rick and his wife, Virginia, jointly run their practice, CAB, Inc. *(www.cabinc. net)*. Rick aims his content production at intermediate and advanced Access, SQL Server, and Web developers. Rick also writes for leading computer resources, such as *SQL Server Magazine*, MSDN *(www.msdn.microsoft.com)*, *Microsoft OfficePro*, and *Visual Basic Programmer's Journal*. Virginia targets Access power users and beginning developers. She writes a monthly column for *www.smartcomputing.com* and is a regular contributor to *Microsoft OfficePro* and other publications.

CAB sponsors *www.programmingmsaccess.com* and its developer seminars. This Web site features code samples, live demonstrations, tutorials, FAQs, and links to online resources for Access and SQL Server developers. CAB is sponsoring the Access 2002 and SQL Server Development Seminar that will tour eight North American cities in fall 2001. Earlier tours attracted a broad range of database developers and administrators from large and mid-sized organizations, such as Ford, EDS at GM, Prudential, the U.S. Navy, and Panasonic. You can get in touch with Rick at rickd@cabinc.net.

Gear Puller

The gear puller is a versatile tool that comes in many strengths and sizes. Typically, the gear puller comes with either two or three "jaws" to securely grasp the item to be pulled. In the middle of the jaws is a screw that allows gears to be removed with relative ease. Smaller gear pullers (two jaws) are designed to remove magneto and generator bearing gears. They are ideal for electric motors and refrigeration applications. Gear pullers with three jaws add additional stability to the job at hand and are typically used on large motors, such as those found in cars, boats, and airplanes.

Tools are central to the progress of the human race. People are adept at building and using tools to accomplish important (and unimportant) tasks. Software is among the most powerful of tools moving us forward, and Microsoft is proud to create tools used by millions worldwide and to contribute to continuing innovation.

The manuscript for this book was prepared and galleyed using Microsoft Word 98. Pages were composed by Microsoft Press using Adobe PageMaker 6.52 for Windows, with text in Garamond and display type in Helvetica Condensed. Composed pages were delivered to the printer as electronic prepress files.

Cover Designer: Methodologie, Inc.
Interior Graphic Designer: James D. Kramer
Principal Compositor: Barbara Levy
Interior Artist: Joel Panchot
Principal Copy Editors: Lisa Pawlewicz, Cheryl Penner
Indexer: Julie Kawabata

Get a **Free**
e-mail newsletter, updates,
special offers, links to related books,
and more when you

register on line!

Register your Microsoft Press® title on our Web site and you'll get a FREE subscription to our e-mail newsletter, *Microsoft Press Book Connections.* You'll find out about newly released and upcoming books and learning tools, online events, software downloads, special offers and coupons for Microsoft Press customers, and information about major Microsoft® product releases. You can also read useful additional information about all the titles we publish, such as detailed book descriptions, tables of contents and indexes, sample chapters, links to related books and book series, author biographies, and reviews by other customers.

Registration is easy. Just visit this Web page and fill in your information:

http://mspress.microsoft.com/register

Microsoft®

Proof of Purchase

Use this page as proof of purchase if participating in a promotion or rebate offer on this title. Proof of purchase must be used in conjunction with other proof(s) of payment such as your dated sales receipt—see offer details.

Programming Microsoft® Access Version 2002 (Core Reference)
ISBN 0-7356-1405-9

CUSTOMER NAME

Microsoft Press, PO Box 97017, Redmond, WA 98073-9830

MICROSOFT LICENSE AGREEMENT

Book Companion CD

IMPORTANT—READ CAREFULLY: This Microsoft End-User License Agreement ("EULA") is a legal agreement between you (either an individual or an entity) and Microsoft Corporation for the Microsoft product identified above, which includes computer software and may include associated media, printed materials, and "online" or electronic documentation ("SOFTWARE PRODUCT"). Any component included within the SOFTWARE PRODUCT that is accompanied by a separate End-User License Agreement shall be governed by such agreement and not the terms set forth below. By installing, copying, or otherwise using the SOFTWARE PRODUCT, you agree to be bound by the terms of this EULA. If you do not agree to the terms of this EULA, you are not authorized to install, copy, or otherwise use the SOFTWARE PRODUCT; you may, however, return the SOFTWARE PRODUCT, along with all printed materials and other items that form a part of the Microsoft product that includes the SOFTWARE PRODUCT, to the place you obtained them for a full refund.

SOFTWARE PRODUCT LICENSE

The SOFTWARE PRODUCT is protected by United States copyright laws and international copyright treaties, as well as other intellectual property laws and treaties. The SOFTWARE PRODUCT is licensed, not sold.

1. **GRANT OF LICENSE.** This EULA grants you the following rights:

   a. **Software Product.** You may install and use one copy of the SOFTWARE PRODUCT on a single computer. The primary user of the computer on which the SOFTWARE PRODUCT is installed may make a second copy for his or her exclusive use on a portable computer.

   b. **Storage/Network Use.** You may also store or install a copy of the SOFTWARE PRODUCT on a storage device, such as a network server, used only to install or run the SOFTWARE PRODUCT on your other computers over an internal network; however, you must acquire and dedicate a license for each separate computer on which the SOFTWARE PRODUCT is installed or run from the storage device. A license for the SOFTWARE PRODUCT may not be shared or used concurrently on different computers.

   c. **License Pak.** If you have acquired this EULA in a Microsoft License Pak, you may make the number of additional copies of the computer software portion of the SOFTWARE PRODUCT authorized on the printed copy of this EULA, and you may use each copy in the manner specified above. You are also entitled to make a corresponding number of secondary copies for portable computer use as specified above.

   d. **Sample Code.** Solely with respect to portions, if any, of the SOFTWARE PRODUCT that are identified within the SOFTWARE PRODUCT as sample code (the "SAMPLE CODE"):

      i. **Use and Modification.** Microsoft grants you the right to use and modify the source code version of the SAMPLE CODE, *provided* you comply with subsection (d)(iii) below. You may not distribute the SAMPLE CODE, or any modified version of the SAMPLE CODE, in source code form.

      ii. **Redistributable Files.** Provided you comply with subsection (d)(iii) below, Microsoft grants you a nonexclusive, royalty-free right to reproduce and distribute the object code version of the SAMPLE CODE and of any modified SAMPLE CODE, other than SAMPLE CODE, or any modified version thereof, designated as not redistributable in the Readme file that forms a part of the SOFTWARE PRODUCT (the "Non-Redistributable Sample Code"). All SAMPLE CODE other than the Non-Redistributable Sample Code is collectively referred to as the "REDISTRIBUTABLES."

      iii. **Redistribution Requirements.** If you redistribute the REDISTRIBUTABLES, you agree to: (i) distribute the REDISTRIBUTABLES in object code form only in conjunction with and as a part of your software application product; (ii) not use Microsoft's name, logo, or trademarks to market your software application product; (iii) include a valid copyright notice on your software application product; (iv) indemnify, hold harmless, and defend Microsoft from and against any claims or lawsuits, including attorney's fees, that arise or result from the use or distribution of your software application product; and (v) not permit further distribution of the REDISTRIBUTABLES by your end user. Contact Microsoft for the applicable royalties due and other licensing terms for all other uses and/or distribution of the REDISTRIBUTABLES.

2. **DESCRIPTION OF OTHER RIGHTS AND LIMITATIONS.**

   - **Limitations on Reverse Engineering, Decompilation, and Disassembly.** You may not reverse engineer, decompile, or disassemble the SOFTWARE PRODUCT, except and only to the extent that such activity is expressly permitted by applicable law notwithstanding this limitation.

   - **Separation of Components.** The SOFTWARE PRODUCT is licensed as a single product. Its component parts may not be separated for use on more than one computer.

   - **Rental.** You may not rent, lease, or lend the SOFTWARE PRODUCT.

   - **Support Services.** Microsoft may, but is not obligated to, provide you with support services related to the SOFTWARE PRODUCT ("Support Services"). Use of Support Services is governed by the Microsoft policies and programs described in the user manual, in "online" documentation, and/or in other Microsoft-provided materials. Any supplemental software code provided to you as part of the Support Services shall be considered part of the SOFTWARE PRODUCT and subject to the terms and conditions of this EULA. With respect to technical information you provide to Microsoft as part of the Support Services, Microsoft may use such information for its business purposes, including for product support and development. Microsoft will not utilize such technical information in a form that personally identifies you.

- **Software Transfer.** You may permanently transfer all of your rights under this EULA, provided you retain no copies, you transfer all of the SOFTWARE PRODUCT (including all component parts, the media and printed materials, any upgrades, this EULA, and, if applicable, the Certificate of Authenticity), **and** the recipient agrees to the terms of this EULA.

- **Termination.** Without prejudice to any other rights, Microsoft may terminate this EULA if you fail to comply with the terms and conditions of this EULA. In such event, you must destroy all copies of the SOFTWARE PRODUCT and all of its component parts.

3. **COPYRIGHT.** All title and copyrights in and to the SOFTWARE PRODUCT (including but not limited to any images, photographs, animations, video, audio, music, text, SAMPLE CODE, REDISTRIBUTABLES, and "applets" incorporated into the SOFTWARE PRODUCT) and any copies of the SOFTWARE PRODUCT are owned by Microsoft or its suppliers. The SOFTWARE PRODUCT is protected by copyright laws and international treaty provisions. Therefore, you must treat the SOFTWARE PRODUCT like any other copyrighted material **except** that you may install the SOFTWARE PRODUCT on a single computer provided you keep the original solely for backup or archival purposes. You may not copy the printed materials accompanying the SOFTWARE PRODUCT.

4. **U.S. GOVERNMENT RESTRICTED RIGHTS.** The SOFTWARE PRODUCT and documentation are provided with RESTRICTED RIGHTS. Use, duplication, or disclosure by the Government is subject to restrictions as set forth in subparagraph (c)(1)(ii) of the Rights in Technical Data and Computer Software clause at DFARS 252.227-7013 or subparagraphs (c)(1) and (2) of the Commercial Computer Software—Restricted Rights at 48 CFR 52.227-19, as applicable. Manufacturer is Microsoft Corporation/One Microsoft Way/Redmond, WA 98052-6399.

5. **EXPORT RESTRICTIONS.** You agree that you will not export or re-export the SOFTWARE PRODUCT, any part thereof, or any process or service that is the direct product of the SOFTWARE PRODUCT (the foregoing collectively referred to as the "Restricted Components"), to any country, person, entity, or end user subject to U.S. export restrictions. You specifically agree not to export or re-export any of the Restricted Components (i) to any country to which the U.S. has embargoed or restricted the export of goods or services, which currently include, but are not necessarily limited to, Cuba, Iran, Iraq, Libya, North Korea, Sudan, and Syria, or to any national of any such country, wherever located, who intends to transmit or transport the Restricted Components back to such country; (ii) to any end user who you know or have reason to know will utilize the Restricted Components in the design, development, or production of nuclear, chemical, or biological weapons; or (iii) to any end user who has been prohibited from participating in U.S. export transactions by any federal agency of the U.S. government. You warrant and represent that neither the BXA nor any other U.S. federal agency has suspended, revoked, or denied your export privileges.

DISCLAIMER OF WARRANTY

NO WARRANTIES OR CONDITIONS. MICROSOFT EXPRESSLY DISCLAIMS ANY WARRANTY OR CONDITION FOR THE SOFTWARE PRODUCT. THE SOFTWARE PRODUCT AND ANY RELATED DOCUMENTATION ARE PROVIDED "AS IS" WITHOUT WARRANTY OR CONDITION OF ANY KIND, EITHER EXPRESS OR IMPLIED, INCLUDING, WITHOUT LIMITATION, THE IMPLIED WARRANTIES OF MERCHANTABILITY, FITNESS FOR A PARTICULAR PURPOSE, OR NONINFRINGEMENT. THE ENTIRE RISK ARISING OUT OF USE OR PERFORMANCE OF THE SOFTWARE PRODUCT REMAINS WITH YOU.

LIMITATION OF LIABILITY. TO THE MAXIMUM EXTENT PERMITTED BY APPLICABLE LAW, IN NO EVENT SHALL MICROSOFT OR ITS SUPPLIERS BE LIABLE FOR ANY SPECIAL, INCIDENTAL, INDIRECT, OR CONSEQUENTIAL DAMAGES WHATSOEVER (INCLUDING, WITHOUT LIMITATION, DAMAGES FOR LOSS OF BUSINESS PROFITS, BUSINESS INTERRUPTION, LOSS OF BUSINESS INFORMATION, OR ANY OTHER PECUNIARY LOSS) ARISING OUT OF THE USE OF OR INABILITY TO USE THE SOFTWARE PRODUCT OR THE PROVISION OF OR FAILURE TO PROVIDE SUPPORT SERVICES, EVEN IF MICROSOFT HAS BEEN ADVISED OF THE POSSIBILITY OF SUCH DAMAGES. IN ANY CASE, MICROSOFT'S ENTIRE LIABILITY UNDER ANY PROVISION OF THIS EULA SHALL BE LIMITED TO THE GREATER OF THE AMOUNT ACTUALLY PAID BY YOU FOR THE SOFTWARE PRODUCT OR US$5.00; PROVIDED, HOWEVER, IF YOU HAVE ENTERED INTO A MICROSOFT SUPPORT SERVICES AGREEMENT, MICROSOFT'S ENTIRE LIABILITY REGARDING SUPPORT SERVICES SHALL BE GOVERNED BY THE TERMS OF THAT AGREEMENT. BECAUSE SOME STATES AND JURISDICTIONS DO NOT ALLOW THE EXCLUSION OR LIMITATION OF LIABILITY, THE ABOVE LIMITATION MAY NOT APPLY TO YOU.

MISCELLANEOUS

This EULA is governed by the laws of the State of Washington USA, except and only to the extent that applicable law mandates governing law of a different jurisdiction.

Should you have any questions concerning this EULA, or if you desire to contact Microsoft for any reason, please contact the Microsoft subsidiary serving your country, or write: Microsoft Sales Information Center/One Microsoft Way/Redmond, WA 98052-6399.

PN 097-0002296